Supersite

There's more to this program than meets the page.

Get course tools and resources any time you need with the **Panorama** Supersite.

Why Supersite means better learning:

- Engages and focuses students
- Improves student performance
- Saves you time with auto-grading, quick setup, and reporting tools
- Provides flexibility to personalize your course
- Offers cost-saving digital options

Visit vistahigherlearning.com/new-supersite to learn more.

5th EDITION

INSTRUCTOR'S ANNOTATED EDITION

PANORAMA

INTRODUCCIÓN A LA LENGUA ESPAÑOLA

JOSÉ A. BLANCO

PHILIP REDWINE DONLEY, LATE
Austin Community College

VISTA®
HIGHER LEARNING
Boston, Massachusetts

Publisher: José A. Blanco
Editorial Development: Judith Bach, Jo Hanna Kurth, Gonzalo Montoya
Project Management: Kayli Brownstein, Sharon Inglis
Rights Management: Liliana Bobadilla, Ashley Dos Santos, Annie Pickert Fuller, Caitlin O'Brien
Technology Production: Fabián Montoya, Paola Ríos Schaaf
Design: Gabriel Noreña, Andrés Vanegas
Production: Manuela Arango, Oscar Díez

Student Text (Casebound) ISBN: 978-1-68004-329-7
Instructor's Annotated Edition ISBN: 978-1-68004-331-0

Library of Congress Control Number: 2015948647

1 2 3 4 5 6 7 8 9 TC 20 19 18 17 16 15

Printed in Canada

Instructor's Annotated Edition

Table of Contents

THE VISTA HIGHER LEARNING STORY

Your Specialized Foreign Language Publisher

Independent, specialized, and privately owned, Vista Higher Learning was founded in 2000 with one mission: to raise the teaching and learning of world languages to a higher level. This mission is based on the following beliefs:

- It is essential to prepare students for a world in which learning another language is a necessity, not a luxury.
- Language learning should be fun and rewarding, and all students should have the tools necessary for achieving success.
- Students who experience success learning a language will be more likely to continue their language studies both inside and outside the classroom.

With this in mind, we decided to take a fresh look at all aspects of language instructional materials. Because we are specialized, we dedicate 100 percent of our resources to this goal and base every decision on how well it supports language learning.

That is where you come in. Since our founding in 2000, we have relied on the continuous and invaluable feedback from language instructors and students nationwide. This partnership has proved to be the cornerstone of our success by allowing us to constantly improve our programs to meet your instructional needs.

The result? Programs that make language learning exciting, relevant, and effective through:

- an unprecedented access to resources
- a wide variety of contemporary, authentic materials
- the integration of text, technology, and media, and
- a bold and engaging textbook design

By focusing on our singular passion, we let you focus on yours.

The Vista Higher Learning Team

VISTA® HIGHER LEARNING

500 Boylston Street, Suite 620, Boston, MA 02116-3736 TOLL-FREE: 800-618-7375
TELEPHONE: 617-426-4910 FAX: 617-426-5209 www.vistahigherlearning.com

Getting to Know PANORAMA

Now in its Fifth Edition, **PANORAMA** is better than ever. Its fresh, student-friendly approach to introductory Spanish makes both teaching and learning easier, more enjoyable, and more successful. The pedagogical approach of **PANORAMA** continues to be communicative. It presents vocabulary and grammar as tools for effective personalized communication as it develops students' listening, reading, writing, and speaking skills. Moreover, because cultural knowledge is an integral part of both language learning and successful communication, **PANORAMA** introduces students to all of the countries in the Spanish-speaking world and the everyday lives of Spanish speakers.

PANORAMA offers features that make it truly different from other textbooks based on these same principles. Here are a few of our distinguishing features:

- **PANORAMA** and its parent textbook, **VISTAS**, were the first textbooks to cohesively integrate a dramatic video into the student text to model target structures. The goal of the **Fotonovela** is to motivate and inspire the next generation of Spanish students.
- **PANORAMA** and **VISTAS** were also the first introductory college Spanish textbooks to incorporate graphic design—page layout, use of colors, typefaces, and other graphic elements—as an integral part of the learning process. To enhance learning and make navigation easy, lesson sections are color-coded and appear either completely on one page or on spreads of two facing pages. The textbook pages themselves are also visually dramatic.
- **PANORAMA** offers student sidebars with on-the-spot linguistic, cultural, and language-learning information, as well as **recursos** boxes with on-page correlations of student supplements, increasing students' comfort level and saving them time.
- **PANORAMA** provides a unique four-part practice sequence for virtually every grammar point. It moves from form-focused **¡Inténtalo!** exercises to directed, yet meaningful, **Práctica** exercises to communicative, interactive **Comunicación** activities, and lastly to cumulative, open-ended **Síntesis** activities.
- **PANORAMA** also offers two cultural videos, **Flash cultura** and **Panorama cultural**, as well as authentic TV clips and short films in **En pantalla**.
- vText—the interactive, online text—perfect for hybrid courses. Now, in an iPad®-friendly* format!

NEW! to the Fifth Edition

- New, animated grammar tutorials—now with interactive questions that check understanding
- Online chat activities for synchronous communication and oral practice
- Online practice tests with diagnostics
- Task-based activities—for use in class or for assessment
- 4 new **En pantalla** videos: 2 TV clips and 2 short films
- Customizable study lists for vocabulary words
- Illustration bank for use with instructor-created activities
- Enhanced Supersite—groundbreaking technology with powerful course management, and options for customization, now with iPad®-friendly* access

*Students must use a computer for audio recording and select presentations and tools that require Flash or Shockwave.

table of contents

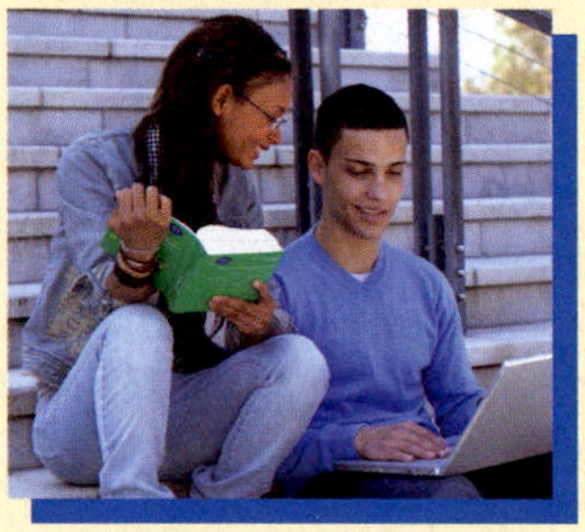

cultura	estructura	adelante
En detalle: Saludos y besos en los países hispanos ...... 10 **Perfil:** La plaza principal 11	**1.1** Nouns and articles ...... 12 **1.2** Numbers 0–30 .... 16 **1.3** Present tense of **ser** ..... 19 **1.4** Telling time .... 24 **Recapitulación** 28	**Lectura:** Tira cómica de Quino . . 30 **Panorama:** Estados Unidos y Canadá 32
En detalle: La elección de una carrera universitaria .... 44 **Perfil:** La Universidad de Salamanca 45	**2.1** Present tense of **-ar** verbs .... 46 **2.2** Forming questions in Spanish .... 51 **2.3** Present tense of **estar**.... 55 **2.4** Numbers 31 and higher . . . 59 **Recapitulación** 62	**Lectura:** *¡Español en Madrid!* . . 64 **Panorama:** España 66
En detalle: ¿Cómo te llamas? . . . 78 **Perfil:** La familia real española 79	**3.1** Descriptive adjectives.... 80 **3.2** Possessive adjectives .... 85 **3.3** Present tense of **-er** and **-ir** verbs .... 88 **3.4** Present tense of **tener** and **venir** .... 92 **Recapitulación** 96	**Lectura:** *Gente... Las familias*. . . 98 **Escritura** .... 100 **Escuchar** ....101 **En pantalla:** Anuncio........ 102 **En pantalla:** Cortometraje.... 103 **Panorama:** Ecuador 104
En detalle: Real Madrid y Barça: rivalidad total ...... 116 **Perfiles:** Miguel Cabrera y Paola Espinosa 117	**4.1** Present tense of **ir** ....118 **4.2** Stem-changing verbs: **e→ie, o→ue** .... 121 **4.3** Stem-changing verbs: **e→i** .... 125 **4.4** Verbs with irregular **yo** forms .... 128 **Recapitulación** 132	**Lectura:** *No sólo el fútbol* .... 134 **Panorama:** México 136

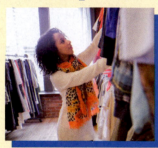

cultura	estructura	adelante

cultura	estructura	adelante

ICONS AND *RECURSOS* BOXES

Icons

Familiarize yourself with these icons that appear throughout **PANORAMA, Fifth Edition**.

Icons legend	
Listening activity/section	Hoja de actividades
Pair activity	Textbook activity available online
Group activity	Content on the Supersite available for this section
Information Gap activity	

- The Information Gap activities and those involving **Hojas de actividades** (*activity sheets*) require handouts from the instructor.
- You will see the listening icon in **Contextos**, **Pronunciación**, **Escuchar,** and **Vocabulario** sections.
- A note next to the Supersite icon will let you know exactly what type of content is available online.
- Additional practice on the Supersite, not included in the textbook, is indicated with this icon:

Practice more at **vhlcentral.com.**

Recursos

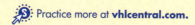

Recursos boxes let you know exactly what print and technology ancillaries you can use to reinforce and expand on every section of the lessons in your textbook. They even include page numbers when applicable.

Recursos boxes legend			
WB pp. 37–38	Workbook	VM pp. 219–220	Video Manual
LM p. 19	Lab Manual		PANORAMA Supersite

vText: Virtual, Interactive Student Edition

- Browser-based electronic text for online viewing
- Links on the vText page to all mouse-icon textbook activities*, audio, and video
- Access to all Supersite resources
- Highlighting and note taking
- Easy navigation with searchable table of contents and page number browsing
- iPad®-friendly*
- Single- and double-page view*, zooming
- Automatically adds auto-graded activities in teacher gradebook

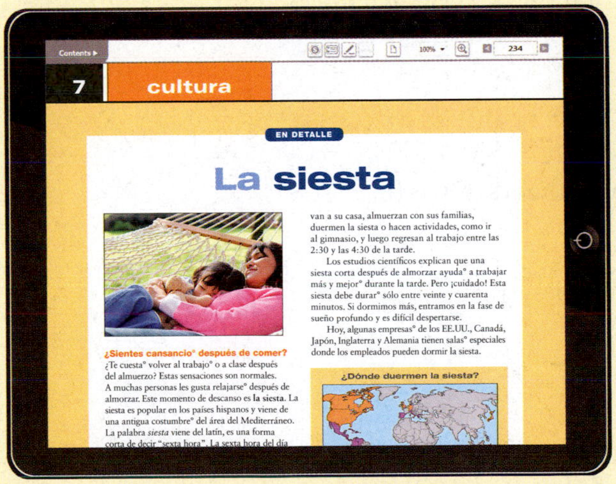

*iPad®-friendly: vText has single-page view only. Students must use a computer for audio recording and select presentations and tools that require Flash or Shockwave.

The PANORAMA, Fifth Edition, Supersite

The **PANORAMA** Supersite is a learning environment designed especially for world language instruction, based on feedback from language educators. Its simplified interface, innovative new tools, and seamless textbook-technology integration will help you reach students and build their love of language.

For students:

- engaging media
- motivating user experience
- improved performance
- helpful resources

For educators:

- freedom to teach
- powerful course management
- time-saving tools
- enhanced support

Resources

Specialized resources ensure successful implementation.

- Online assessments and Testing Program files in editable formats
- Audio- and videoscripts with English translations
- Grammar presentation slides
- Sample syllabus
- Sample lesson plan
- Activity Pack
- Textbook Images and Illustration Bank
- Answer keys
- Additional vocabulary

Content

Meaningful, integrated content means less prep time and a more powerful student experience.
(See page IAE-18 for details.)

Educator tools

Enhanced online tools facilitate instruction and save time.

Easy course management

A powerful setup wizard lets you customize your course settings, copy previous courses to save time, and create your all-in-one gradebook. Grades for teacher-created assignments (pop quizzes, class participation, etc.) can be incorporated for a true, up-to-date cumulative grade.

Customized content

Tailor the Supersite to fit your needs. Create your own open-ended or video Partner Chat activities, add video or outside resources, and modify existing content with your own personalized notes.

Grading tools

Grade efficiently via spot-checking, student-by-student, and question-by-question options. Use in-line editing tools to give targeted feedback and voice comments—it's the perfect tool for busy language educators!

Assessment solutions

Administer online quizzes and tests from the Testing Program or develop your own—such as open-ended writing prompts or chat activities for an oral assessment portfolio. Adapt premade online assessments by reordering or removing content as needed. Plus, new tools allow for time limits and password protection.

Plus!

- Single sign-on for easy integration with your school's LMS
- Live Chat for video chat, audio chat, and instant messaging with students
- A communication center for announcements, notifications, and help requests
- An option for hiding content from a course
- Voiceboards for oral assignments, group discussions, homework, and more
- Reporting tools for summarizing student data

Partner Chat

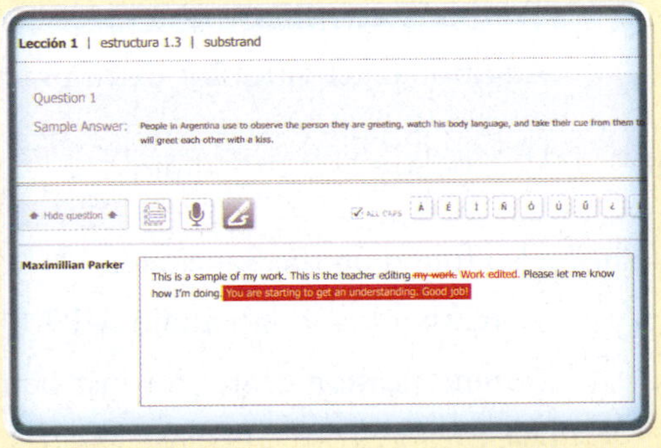

In-line editing

Supersite

Each section of your textbook comes with activities on the **PANORAMA** Supersite, many of which are auto-graded for immediate feedback. Plus, the Supersite is iPad®-friendly*, so it can be accessed on the go! Visit **vhlcentral.com** to explore this wealth of exciting resources.

CONTEXTOS

- Vocabulary tutorials
- Image-based vocabulary activity with audio
- Audio activities
- Textbook activities
- Additional activities for extra practice
- Chat activities for conversational skill-building and oral practice

FOTONOVELA

- Streaming video of **Fotonovela**, with instructor-managed options for subtitles and transcripts in Spanish and English
- Textbook activities
- Additional activities for extra practice
- Audio files for **Pronunciación**
- Record-compare practice

CULTURA

- Reading available online
- Keywords and support for **Conexión Internet**
- Textbook activities
- Additional activities for extra practice
- Additional reading
- Streaming video of **Flash cultura** series, with instructor-managed options for subtitles and transcripts in Spanish and English

ESTRUCTURA

- Interactive grammar tutorials
- Grammar presentations available online
- Textbook activities
- Additional activities for extra practice
- Chat activities for conversational skill-building and oral practice
- Diagnostics in **Recapitulación** section

ADELANTE

- Audio-sync reading in **Lectura**
- Additional reading
- Writing activity in **Escritura** with composition engine
- Audio files for listening activity in **Escuchar**
- Textbook activities and additional activities for extra practice
- Streaming **En pantalla** TV clips or short films, with instructor-managed options for subtitles and transcripts in Spanish and English

PANORAMA

- Interactive map
- Textbook activities
- Additional activities for extra practice
- Streaming video of **Panorama cultural** series, with instructor-managed options for subtitles and transcripts in Spanish and English

VOCABULARIO

- Vocabulary list with audio
- Customizable study lists

Plus! Also found on the Supersite:

- All textbook and lab audio MP3 files
- Communication center for instructor notifications and feedback
- Live Chat tool for video chat, audio chat, and instant messaging without leaving your browser
- A single gradebook for all Supersite activities
- WebSAM online Workbook/Video Manual/Lab Manual
- vText online interactive student edition with access to Supersite activities, audio, and video

Supersite features vary by access level. Visit **vistahigherleaning.com** to explore which Supersite level is right for you.

*Students must use a computer for audio recording and select presentations and tools that require Flash or Shockwave.

INTERACTIVE GRAMMAR TUTORIALS

Research shows that a little humor is engaging, stimulates the brain, and helps with memory retention. Interactive grammar tutorials, **NEW!** for **PANORAMA**, **Fifth Edition**, feature the Professor, an amusing character who grabs your attention with his humorous gags and lighthearted approach to grammar. The tutorials entertain and inform by pairing grammar rules with fun explanations and examples. The Professor always uses the new grammar in a humorous way at the end of each tutorial.

There are five learning scenarios: the classroom, the library, the theater, the café, and the Professor's living room. These settings offer opportunities for humor and for cultural references.

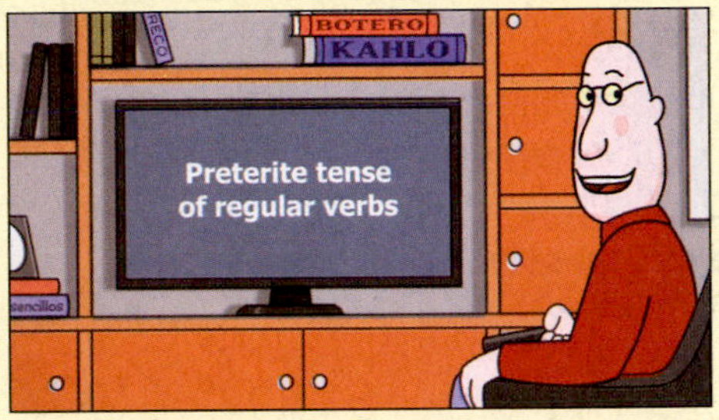

The Professor explains the grammar in an informal, conversational way. The Narrator pronounces words in charts and reads example sentences. Animation features such as color and pulsing emphasize the grammar being taught. The examples often appear with pictures that illustrate their meaning.

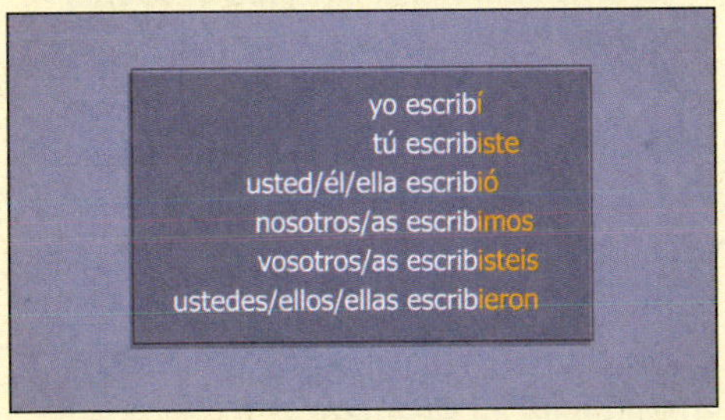

Each tutorial has one or two Quick Checks, which are pauses in the instruction to give you a chance to react to what has just been presented. It's a way to make sure you understand one concept before tackling the next one. It's also a way to make the tutorial interactive and keep you interested and engaged throughout the tutorial. Formats include multiple choice, sorting, fill in the blank, and ordering sentence elements. The Professor may also guide the Quick Check by having you listen and repeat, listen to cues and give the answers orally, or read cues and give the answers aloud.

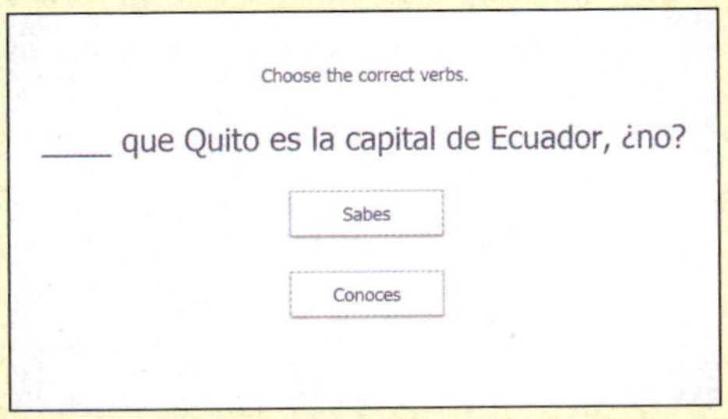

Each tutorial features a **Repaso** section at the end that summarizes what you have learned.

These interactive grammar tutorials are a handy reference tool and support independent study.

Program Components

Students

Print

- **Student Edition**
  Available in hardcover or loose-leaf format
- **Student Activities Manual (Workbook/Video Manual/Lab Manual) (SAM)**
  The Workbook contains the workbook activities for each textbook lesson.

  The Video Manual contains activities for the **Fotonovela** Video, and pre-, while-, and post-viewing activities for the **Flash cultura** and **Panorama cultural** Videos.

  The Lab Manual contains lab activities for each textbook lesson for use with the Lab Audio Program.

Online

- **Supersite**
  Student access to the Supersite (vhlcentral.com) is provided with the purchase of a new student edition. See page IAE-18 for all Supersite resources available to students.
- **vText**
  This virtual, interactive student edition provides students with a digital text, plus interactive links to all Supersite activities and media.
- **WebSAM**
  Online version of the Student Activities Manual (Workbook/Video Manual/Lab Manual)

Instructors

Print

- **Instructor's Annotated Edition (IAE)**
  The IAE contains a wealth of teaching information. The expanded trim size and enhanced design make the annotations easy to reference.
- **Activity Pack**
  The **PANORAMA** Activity Pack offers discrete and communicative practice for individuals, pairs, and groups. Formats include multiple-choice questions, information gap activities, board games, **NEW!** task-based activities, and more. (*Also available on Supersite as PDFs*)

Online

- **Instructor Supersite**
  The password-protected Instructor Supersite offers the resources, tools, and content necessary to facilitate language instruction, and allows instructors to assign activities and track student progress through its course management system. See pages IAE-16 and IAE-17 for details.
- **Video Programs**
  Fotonovela, Flash cultura, Panorama cultural, and **En pantalla** video programs are available on the Supersite. *For a physical DVD (from the Panorama 4e program), contact your Modern Language Specialist.*
- **Testing Program**
  The Testing Program is provided in RTF format.
  - Vocabulary **minipruebas** (2 versions for each lesson)
  - Grammar **minipruebas** per lesson (2 versions for each grammar point)
  - Lesson Tests – 6 versions for each lesson
  - Multi-lesson exams – 2 versions for each exam

Lesson Openers
outline the content and features of each lesson.

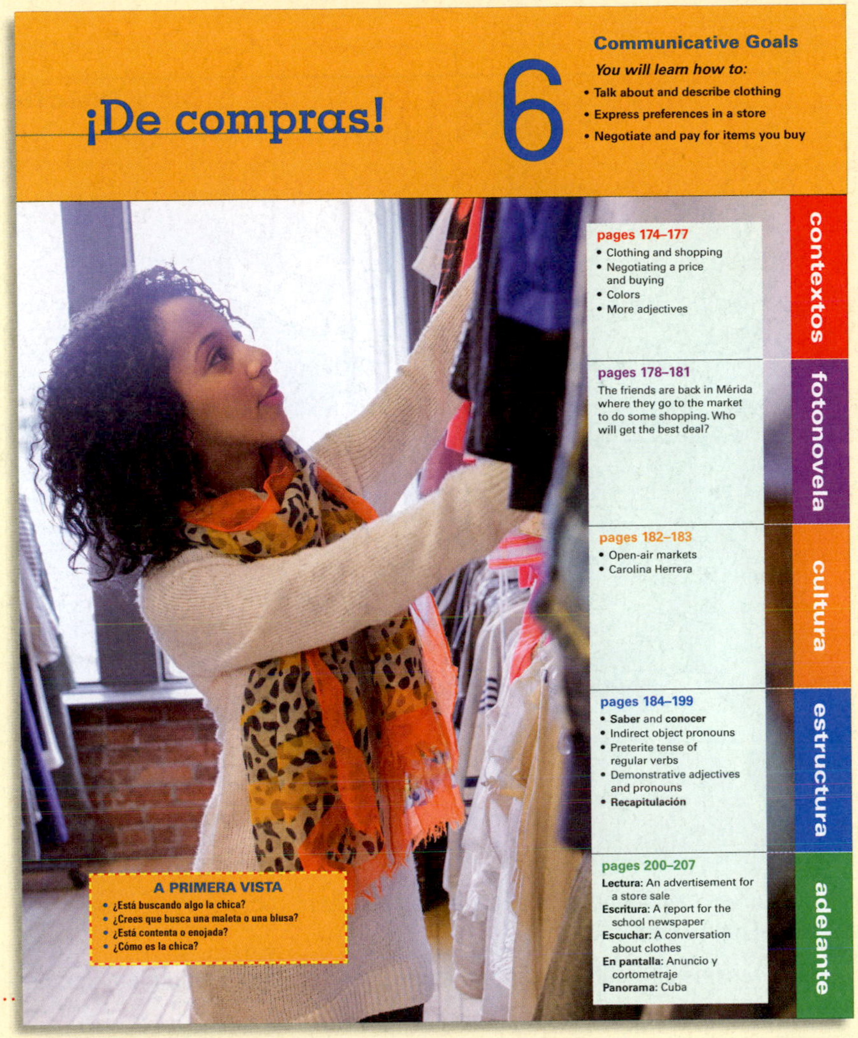

¡De compras!
6
Communicative Goals
You will learn how to:
• Talk about and describe clothing
• Express preferences in a store
• Negotiate and pay for items you buy
pages 174–177
• Clothing and shopping
• Negotiating a price and buying
• Colors
• More adjectives
contextos
pages 178–181
The friends are back in Mérida where they go to the market to do some shopping. Who will get the best deal?
fotonovela
pages 182–183
• Open-air markets
• Carolina Herrera
cultura
pages 184–199
• Saber and conocer
• Indirect object pronouns
• Preterite tense of regular verbs
• Demonstrative adjectives and pronouns
• Recapitulación
estructura
pages 200–207
Lectura: An advertisement for a store sale
Escritura: A report for the school newspaper
Escuchar: A conversation about clothes
En pantalla: Anuncio y cortometraje
Panorama: Cuba
adelante
A PRIMERA VISTA
• ¿Está buscando algo la chica?
• ¿Crees que busca una maleta o una blusa?
• ¿Está contenta o enojada?
• ¿Cómo es la chica?

A primera vista activities jump-start the lessons, allowing you to use the Spanish you know to talk about the photos.

Communicative goals highlight the real-life tasks you will be able to carry out in Spanish by the end of each lesson.

Supersite

Supersite resources are available for every section of the lesson at **vhlcentral.com**. Icons show you which textbook activities are also available online, and where additional practice activities are available. The description next to the Ⓢ icon indicates what additional resources are available for each section: videos, recordings, tutorials, presentations, and more!

Contextos

presents vocabulary in meaningful contexts.

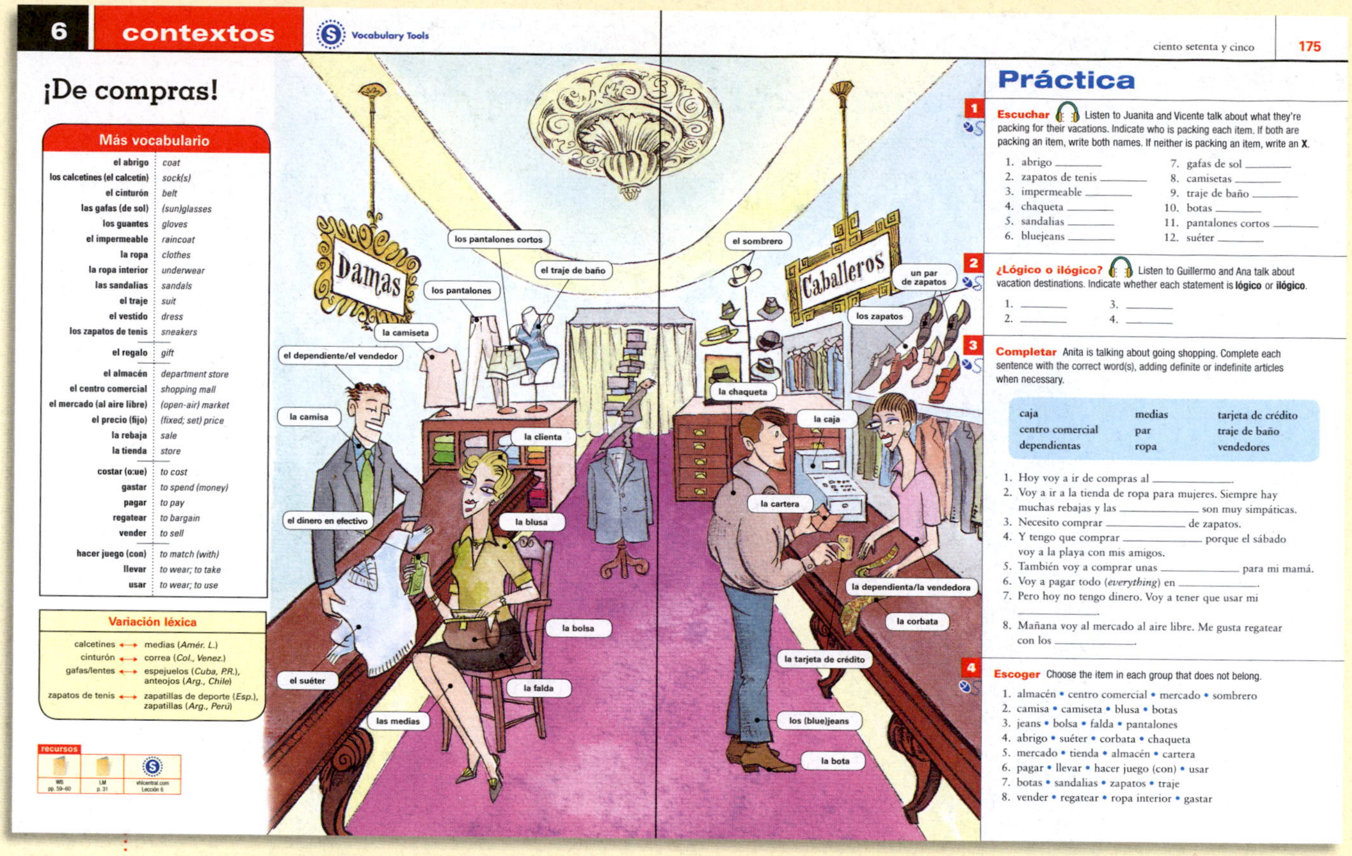

6 **contextos** Vocabulary Tools

¡De compras!

Más vocabulario

el abrigo	*coat*
los calcetines (el calcetín)	*sock(s)*
el cinturón	*belt*
las gafas (de sol)	*(sun)glasses*
los guantes	*gloves*
el impermeable	*raincoat*
la ropa	*clothes*
la ropa interior	*underwear*
las sandalias	*sandals*
el traje	*suit*
el vestido	*dress*
los zapatos de tenis	*sneakers*
el regalo	*gift*
el almacén	*department store*
el centro comercial	*shopping mall*
el mercado (al aire libre)	*(open-air) market*
el precio (fijo)	*(fixed; set) price*
la rebaja	*sale*
la tienda	*store*
costar (o:ue)	*to cost*
gastar	*to spend (money)*
pagar	*to pay*
regatear	*to bargain*
vender	*to sell*
hacer juego (con)	*to match (with)*
llevar	*to wear; to take*
usar	*to wear; to use*

Variación léxica

calcetines ⟷ medias (*Amér. L.*)
cinturón ⟷ correa (*Col., Venez.*)
gafas/lentes ⟷ espejuelos (*Cuba, P.R.*), anteojos (*Arg., Chile*)
zapatos de tenis ⟷ zapatillas de deporte (*Esp.*), zapatillas (*Arg., Perú*)

recursos
WB pp. 59–60 | LM p. 31 | vhlcentral.com Lección 6

ciento setenta y cinco 175

Práctica

1 Escuchar Listen to Juanita and Vicente talk about what they're packing for their vacations. Indicate who is packing each item. If both are packing an item, write both names. If neither is packing an item, write an **X**.

1. abrigo ______
2. zapatos de tenis ______
3. impermeable ______
4. chaqueta ______
5. sandalias ______
6. bluejeans ______
7. gafas de sol ______
8. camisetas ______
9. traje de baño ______
10. botas ______
11. pantalones cortos ______
12. suéter ______

2 ¿Lógico o ilógico? Listen to Guillermo and Ana talk about vacation destinations. Indicate whether each statement is **lógico** or **ilógico**.

1. ______
2. ______
3. ______
4. ______

3 Completar Anita is talking about going shopping. Complete each sentence with the correct word(s), adding definite or indefinite articles when necessary.

caja	medias	tarjeta de crédito
centro comercial	par	traje de baño
dependientas	ropa	vendedores

1. Hoy voy a ir de compras al ______.
2. Voy a ir a la tienda de ropa para mujeres. Siempre hay muchas rebajas y las ______ son muy simpáticas.
3. Necesito comprar ______ de zapatos.
4. Y tengo que comprar ______ porque el sábado voy a la playa con mis amigos.
5. También voy a comprar unas ______ para mi mamá.
6. Voy a pagar todo (*everything*) en ______.
7. Pero hoy no tengo dinero. Voy a tener que usar mi ______.
8. Mañana voy al mercado al aire libre. Me gusta regatear con los ______.

4 Escoger Choose the item in each group that does not belong.

1. almacén • centro comercial • mercado • sombrero
2. camisa • camiseta • blusa • botas
3. jeans • bolsa • falda • pantalones
4. abrigo • suéter • corbata • chaqueta
5. mercado • tienda • almacén • cartera
6. pagar • llevar • hacer juego (con) • usar
7. botas • sandalias • zapatos • traje
8. vender • regatear • ropa interior • gastar

Más vocabulario boxes call out other important theme-related vocabulary in easy-to-reference Spanish-English lists.

Variación léxica presents alternate words and expressions used throughout the Spanish-speaking world.

Illustrations High-frequency vocabulary is introduced through expansive, full-color illustrations.

Recursos The icons in the **Recursos** boxes let you know exactly which print and technology ancillaries you can use to reinforce and expand on every section of every lesson.

Práctica This section always begins with two listening exercises and continues with activities that practice the new vocabulary in meaningful contexts.

Comunicación activities allow you to use the vocabulary creatively in interactions with a partner, a small group, or the entire class.

Supersite

- Vocabulary tutorials
- Audio support for vocabulary presentation
- Textbook activities
- Additional online-only practice activities
- Chat activities for conversational skill-building and oral practice
- Vocabulary activities in Activity Pack

Fotonovela

follows the adventures of a group of students living and traveling in Mexico.

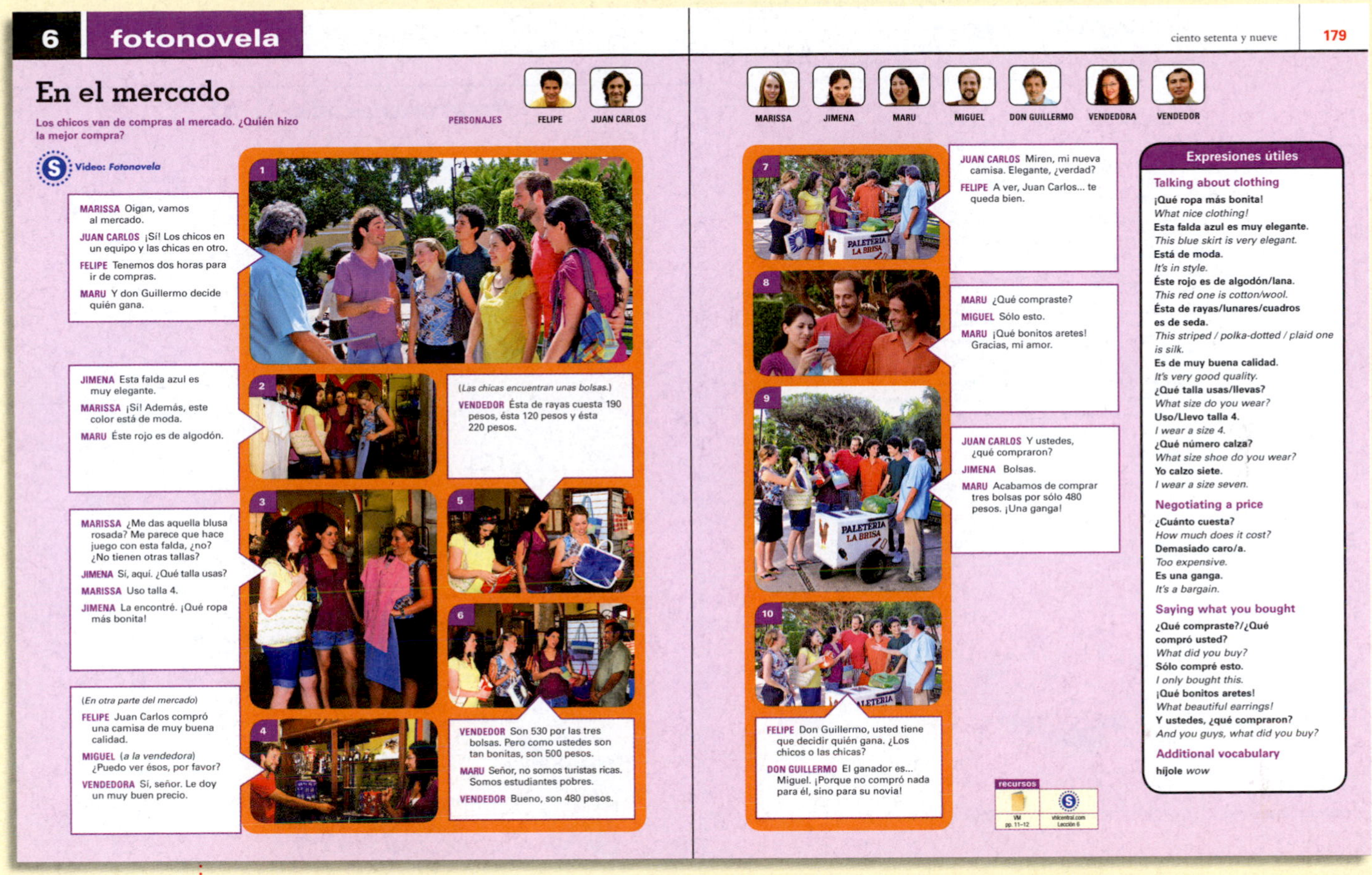

6 fotonovela

ciento setenta y nueve 179

En el mercado

PERSONAJES FELIPE JUAN CARLOS MARISSA JIMENA MARU MIGUEL DON GUILLERMO VENDEDORA VENDEDOR

Los chicos van de compras al mercado. ¿Quién hizo la mejor compra?

Video: *Fotonovela*

1
MARISSA Oigan, vamos al mercado.
JUAN CARLOS ¡Sí! Los chicos en un equipo y las chicas en otro.
FELIPE Tenemos dos horas para ir de compras.
MARU Y don Guillermo decide quién gana.

2
JIMENA Esta falda azul es muy elegante.
MARISSA ¡Sí! Además, este color está de moda.
MARU Éste rojo es de algodón.

3
MARISSA ¿Me das aquella blusa rosada? Me parece que hace juego con esta falda, ¿no? ¿No tienen otras tallas?
JIMENA Sí, aquí. ¿Qué talla usas?
MARISSA Uso talla 4.
JIMENA La encontré. ¡Qué ropa más bonita!

4
(*En otra parte del mercado*)
FELIPE Juan Carlos compró una camisa de muy buena calidad.
MIGUEL (*a la vendedora*) ¿Puedo ver ésos, por favor?
VENDEDORA Sí, señor. Le doy un muy buen precio.

5
(*Las chicas encuentran unas bolsas.*)
VENDEDOR Ésta de rayas cuesta 190 pesos, ésta 120 pesos y ésta 220 pesos.

6
VENDEDOR Son 530 por las tres bolsas. Pero como ustedes son tan bonitas, son 500 pesos.
MARU Señor, no somos turistas ricas. Somos estudiantes pobres.
VENDEDOR Bueno, son 480 pesos.

7
JUAN CARLOS Miren, mi nueva camisa. Elegante, ¿verdad?
FELIPE A ver, Juan Carlos... te queda bien.

8
MARU ¿Qué compraste?
MIGUEL Sólo esto.
MARU ¡Qué bonitos aretes! Gracias, mi amor.

9
JUAN CARLOS Y ustedes, ¿qué compraron?
JIMENA Bolsas.
MARU Acabamos de comprar tres bolsas por sólo 480 pesos. ¡Una ganga!

10
FELIPE Don Guillermo, usted tiene que decidir quién gana. ¿Los chicos o las chicas?
DON GUILLERMO El ganador es... Miguel. ¡Porque no compró nada para él, sino para su novia!

Expresiones útiles

Talking about clothing
¡Qué ropa más bonita!
What nice clothing!
Esta falda azul es muy elegante.
This blue skirt is very elegant.
Está de moda.
It's in style.
Éste rojo es de algodón/lana.
This red one is cotton/wool.
Ésta de rayas/lunares/cuadros es de seda.
This striped / polka-dotted / plaid one is silk.
Es de muy buena calidad.
It's very good quality.
¿Qué talla usas/llevas?
What size do you wear?
Uso/Llevo talla 4.
I wear a size 4.
¿Qué número calza?
What size shoe do you wear?
Yo calzo siete.
I wear a size seven.

Negotiating a price
¿Cuánto cuesta?
How much does it cost?
Demasiado caro/a.
Too expensive.
Es una ganga.
It's a bargain.

Saying what you bought
¿Qué compraste?/¿Qué compró usted?
What did you buy?
Sólo compré esto.
I only bought this.
¡Qué bonitos aretes!
What beautiful earrings!
Y ustedes, ¿qué compraron?
And you guys, what did you buy?

Additional vocabulary
híjole *wow*

recursos
VM pp. 11–12
vhlcentral.com Lección 6

Personajes The photo-based conversations take place among a cast of recurring characters—a Mexican family with two college-age children, and their group of friends.

Icons signal activities by type (pair, group, audio, info gap) and let you know which activities can be completed online.

Fotonovela Video The video episodes that correspond to this section are available for viewing online.

Expresiones útiles These expressions organize new, active structures by language function so you can focus on using them for real-life, practical purposes.

Conversations Taken from the **Fotonovela** Video, the conversations reinforce vocabulary from **Contextos**. They also preview structures from the upcoming **Estructura** section in context and in a comprehensible way.

Supersite

- Streaming video of the **Fotonovela** episode
- Textbook activities
- Additional online-only practice activities

Pronunciación & Ortografía
present the rules of Spanish pronunciation and spelling.

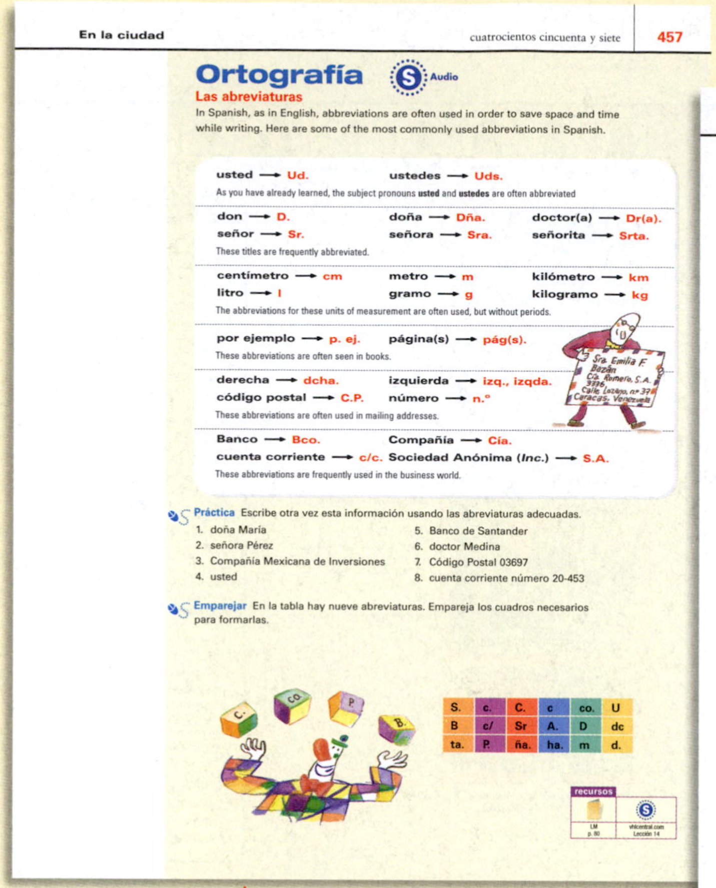

En la ciudad — cuatrocientos cincuenta y siete — 457

Ortografía
Audio

Las abreviaturas

In Spanish, as in English, abbreviations are often used in order to save space and time while writing. Here are some of the most commonly used abbreviations in Spanish.

usted → Ud. **ustedes** → Uds.

As you have already learned, the subject pronouns **usted** and **ustedes** are often abbreviated

don → D. **doña** → Dña. **doctor(a)** → Dr(a).
señor → Sr. **señora** → Sra. **señorita** → Srta.

These titles are frequently abbreviated.

centímetro → cm **metro** → m **kilómetro** → km
litro → l **gramo** → g **kilogramo** → kg

The abbreviations for these units of measurement are often used, but without periods.

por ejemplo → p. ej. **página(s)** → pág(s).

These abbreviations are often seen in books.

derecha → dcha. **izquierda** → izq., izqda.
código postal → C.P. **número** → n.º

These abbreviations are often used in mailing addresses.

Banco → Bco. **Compañía** → Cía.
cuenta corriente → c/c. **Sociedad Anónima (*Inc.*)** → S.A.

These abbreviations are frequently used in the business world.

Práctica Escribe otra vez esta información usando las abreviaturas adecuadas.

1. doña María
2. señora Pérez
3. Compañía Mexicana de Inversiones
4. usted
5. Banco de Santander
6. doctor Medina
7. Código Postal 03697
8. cuenta corriente número 20-453

Emparejar En la tabla hay nueve abreviaturas. Empareja los cuadros necesarios para formarlas.

S.	c.	C.	c	co.	U
B	c/	Sr	A.	D	dc
ta.	P.	ña.	ha.	m	d.

recursos
LM p. 80
vhlcentral.com Lección 14

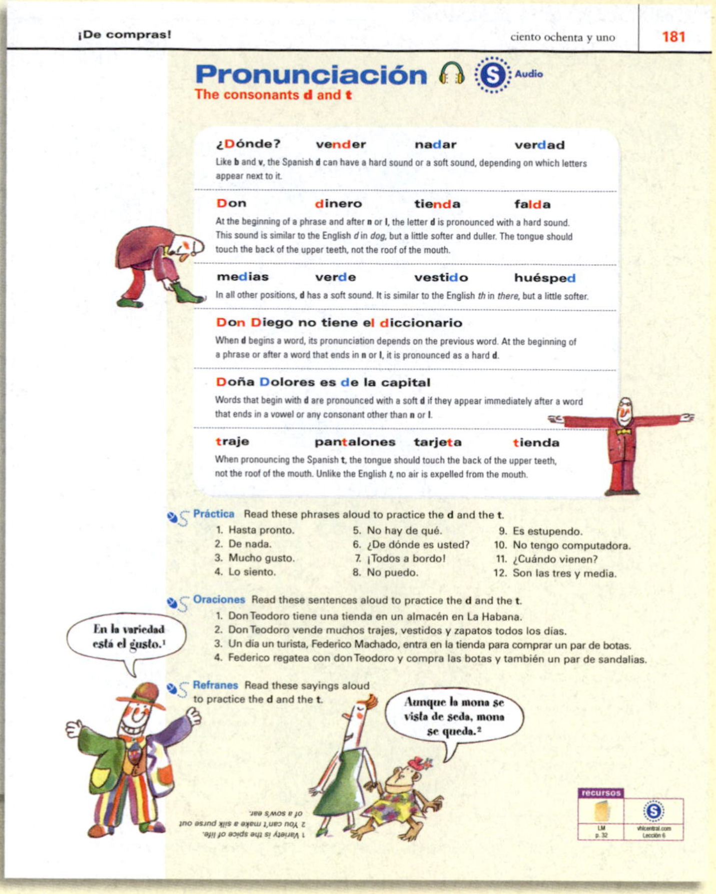

¡De compras! — ciento ochenta y uno — 181

Pronunciación
Audio

The consonants d and t

¿Dónde? **vender** **nadar** **verdad**

Like **b** and **v**, the Spanish **d** can have a hard sound or a soft sound, depending on which letters appear next to it.

Don **dinero** **tienda** **falda**

At the beginning of a phrase and after **n** or **l**, the letter **d** is pronounced with a hard sound. This sound is similar to the English *d* in *dog*, but a little softer and duller. The tongue should touch the back of the upper teeth, not the roof of the mouth.

medias **verde** **vestido** **huésped**

In all other positions, **d** has a soft sound. It is similar to the English *th* in *there*, but a little softer.

Don Diego no tiene el diccionario

When **d** begins a word, its pronunciation depends on the previous word. At the beginning of a phrase or after a word that ends in **n** or **l**, it is pronounced as a hard **d**.

Doña Dolores es de la capital

Words that begin with **d** are pronounced with a soft **d** if they appear immediately after a word that ends in a vowel or any consonant other than **n** or **l**.

traje **pantalones** **tarjeta** **tienda**

When pronouncing the Spanish **t**, the tongue should touch the back of the upper teeth, not the roof of the mouth. Unlike the English *t*, no air is expelled from the mouth.

Práctica Read these phrases aloud to practice the **d** and the **t**.

1. Hasta pronto.
2. De nada.
3. Mucho gusto.
4. Lo siento.
5. No hay de qué.
6. ¿De dónde es usted?
7. ¡Todos a bordo!
8. No puedo.
9. Es estupendo.
10. No tengo computadora.
11. ¿Cuándo vienen?
12. Son las tres y media.

Oraciones Read these sentences aloud to practice the **d** and the **t**.

1. Don Teodoro tiene una tienda en un almacén en La Habana.
2. Don Teodoro vende muchos trajes, vestidos y zapatos todos los días.
3. Un día un turista, Federico Machado, entra en la tienda para comprar un par de botas.
4. Federico regatea con don Teodoro y compra las botas y también un par de sandalias.

Refranes Read these sayings aloud to practice the **d** and the **t**.

En la variedad está el gusto.[1]
Aunque la mona se vista de seda, mona se queda.[2]

1 Variety is the spice of life.
2 You can't make a silk purse out of a sow's ear.

recursos
LM p. 32
vhlcentral.com Lección 6

Pronunciación explains the sounds and pronunciation of Spanish in Lessons 1–9.

Ortografía focuses on topics related to Spanish spelling in Lessons 10–15.

Supersite

- Audio for pronunciation explanation
- Record-compare textbook activities

Cultura

exposes you to different aspects of Hispanic culture tied to the lesson theme.

Flash CULTURA

EN DETALLE

Video: *Flash cultura*

Los mercados al aire libre

Mercados al aire libre are an integral part of commerce and culture in the Spanish-speaking world. Whether they take place daily or weekly, these markets are an important forum where tourists, locals, and vendors interact. People come to the marketplace to shop, socialize, taste local foods, and watch street performers. Wandering from one **puesto** (*stand*) to the next, one can browse for fresh fruits and vegetables, clothing, CDs and DVDs, and **artesanías** (*crafts*). Some markets offer a mix of products, while others specialize in food, fashion, or used merchandise, such as antiques and books.

When shoppers see an item they like, they can bargain with the vendor. Friendly bargaining is an expected ritual and may result in a significantly lower price. When selling food, vendors may give the customer a little extra of what they purchase; this free addition is known as **la ñapa**.

Many open-air markets are also tourist attractions. The market in Otavalo, Ecuador, is world-famous and has taken place every Saturday since pre-Incan times. This market is well-known for the colorful textiles woven by the **otavaleños**, the indigenous people of the area. One can also find leather goods and wood carvings from nearby towns. Another popular market is **El Rastro**, held every Sunday in Madrid, Spain. Sellers set up **puestos** along the streets to display their wares, which range from local artwork and antiques to inexpensive clothing and electronics.

Mercado de Otavalo

mariscos *seafood* **pescado** *fish* **verduras** *vegetables* **flores** *flowers*

Otros mercados famosos

Mercado	Lugar	Productos
Feria Artesanal de Recoleta	Buenos Aires, Argentina	artesanías
Mercado Central	Santiago, Chile	mariscos°, pescado°, frutas, verduras°
Tianguis Cultural del Chopo	Ciudad de México, México	ropa, música, revistas, libros, arte, artesanías
El mercado de Chichicastenango	Chichicastenango, Guatemala	frutas y verduras, flores°, cerámica, textiles

ACTIVIDADES

1 ¿Cierto o falso? Indicate whether these statements are **cierto** or **falso**. Correct the false statements.

1. Generally, open-air markets specialize in one type of goods.
2. Bargaining is commonplace at outdoor markets.
3. Only new goods can be found at open-air markets.
4. A Spaniard in search of antiques could search at **El Rastro**.
5. If you are in Guatemala and want to buy ceramics, you can go to Chichicastenango.
6. A **ñapa** is a tax on open-air market goods.
7. The **otavaleños** weave colorful textiles to sell on Saturdays.
8. Santiago's **Mercado Central** is known for books and music.

ASÍ SE DICE

La ropa

la chamarra (Méx.)	la chaqueta
de manga corta/larga	*short/long-sleeved*
los mahones (P. Rico); el pantalón de mezclilla (Méx.); los tejanos (Esp.); los vaqueros (Arg., Cuba, Esp., Uru.)	los bluejeans
la marca	*brand*
la playera (Méx.); la remera (Arg.)	la camiseta

EL MUNDO HISPANO

Diseñadores de moda

- **Adolfo Domínguez** (España) Su ropa tiene un estilo minimalista y práctico. Usa telas° naturales y cómodas en sus diseños.
- **Silvia Tcherassi** (Colombia) Los colores vivos y las líneas asimétricas de sus vestidos y trajes muestran influencias tropicales.

- **Óscar de la Renta** (República Dominicana) Diseñó ropa opulenta para la mujer clásica.
- **Narciso Rodríguez** (EE.UU.) En sus diseños delicados y finos predominan los colores blanco y negro. Hizo° el vestido de boda° de Carolyn Bessette Kennedy. También diseñó varios vestidos para Michelle Obama.

telas *fabrics* **Hizo** *He made* **de boda** *wedding*

PERFIL

Carolina Herrera

In 1980, at the urging of some friends, **Carolina Herrera** created a fashion collection as a "test." The Venezuelan designer received such a favorable response that within one year she moved her family from Caracas to New York City and created her own label, Carolina Herrera, Ltd.

"I love elegance and intricacy, but whether it is in a piece of clothing or a fragrance, the intricacy must appear as simplicity," Herrera once stated. She quickly found that many sophisticated women agreed; from the start, her sleek and glamorous designs have been in constant demand. Over the years, Herrera has grown her brand into a veritable fashion empire that encompasses her fashion and bridal collections, cosmetics, perfume, and accessories that are sold around the globe.

Conexión Internet

¿Qué marcas de ropa son populares en el mundo hispano?

Go to **vhlcentral.com** to find more cultural information related to this **Cultura** section.

ACTIVIDADES

2 Comprensión Complete these sentences.

1. Adolfo Domínguez usa telas ________ y ________ en su ropa.
2. Si hace fresco en el D.F., puedes llevar una ________.
3. La diseñadora ________ hace ropa, perfumes y más.
4. La ropa de ________ muestra influencias tropicales.
5. Los ________ son una ropa casual en Puerto Rico.

3 Mi ropa favorita Write a brief description of your favorite article of clothing. Mention what store it is from, the brand, colors, fabric, style, and any other information. Then get together with a small group, collect the descriptions, and take turns reading them aloud at random. Can the rest of the group guess whose favorite piece of clothing is being described?

Practice more at **vhlcentral.com**.

recursos: VM pp. 83–84; vhlcentral.com Lección 6

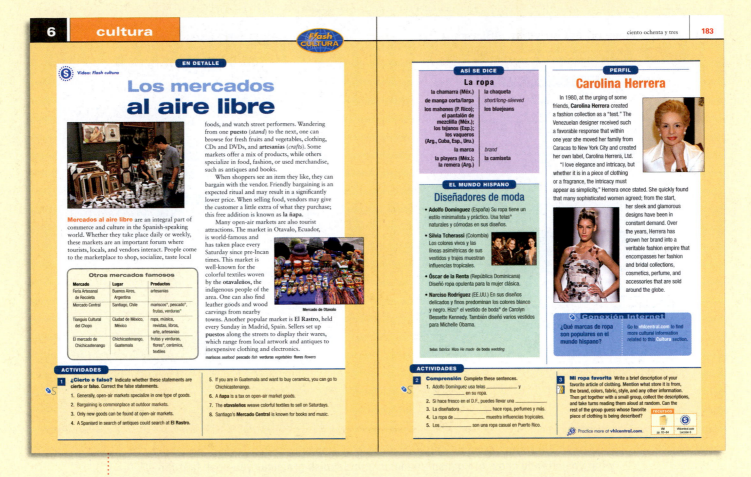

En detalle & Perfil(es) Two articles on the lesson theme focus on a specific place, custom, person, group, or tradition in the Spanish-speaking world. In Spanish starting in Lesson 7, these features also provide reading practice.

Coverage While the **Panorama** section takes a regional approach to cultural coverage, **Cultura** is theme-driven, covering several Spanish-speaking regions in every lesson.

Así se dice & El mundo hispano Lexical and comparative features expand cultural coverage to people, traditions, customs, trends, and vocabulary throughout the Spanish-speaking world.

Flash cultura An icon lets you know that the enormously successful **Flash cultura** Video offers specially shot content tied to the lesson theme.

Supersite

- **Cultura** article
- Textbook activities
- Additional online-only practice activities
- **Conexión Internet** activity with questions and keywords related to lesson theme
- Additional cultural reading
- Streaming video of **Flash cultura**

Estructura

presents Spanish grammar in a graphic-intensive format.

6.3 Preterite tense of regular verbs

Tutorial

ANTE TODO In order to talk about events in the past, Spanish uses two simple tenses: the preterite and the imperfect. In this lesson, you will learn how to form the preterite tense, which is used to express actions or states completed in the past.

Preterite of regular -ar, -er, and -ir verbs

		-ar verbs **comprar**	-er verbs **vender**	-ir verbs **escribir**
SINGULAR FORMS	yo	compr**é** *I bought*	vend**í** *I sold*	escrib**í** *I wrote*
	tú	compr**aste**	vend**iste**	escrib**iste**
	Ud./él/ella	compr**ó**	vend**ió**	escrib**ió**
PLURAL FORMS	nosotros/as	compr**amos**	vend**imos**	escrib**imos**
	vosotros/as	compr**asteis**	vend**isteis**	escrib**isteis**
	Uds./ellos/ellas	compr**aron**	vend**ieron**	escrib**ieron**

- **¡Atención!** The **yo** and **Ud./él/ella** forms of all three conjugations have written accents on the last syllable to show that it is stressed.
- As the chart shows, the endings for regular **-er** and **-ir** verbs are identical in the preterite.

- Note that the **nosotros/as** forms of regular **-ar** and **-ir** verbs in the preterite are identical to the present tense forms. Context will help you determine which tense is being used.

En invierno **compramos** ropa.
In the winter, we buy clothes.

Anoche **compramos** unos zapatos.
Last night we bought some shoes.

- **-Ar** and **-er** verbs that have a stem change in the present tense are regular in the preterite. They do *not* have a stem change.

	PRESENT	PRETERITE
cerrar (e:ie)	La tienda **cierra** a las seis.	La tienda **cerró** a las seis.
volver (o:ue)	Carlitos **vuelve** tarde.	Carlitos **volvió** tarde.
jugar (u:ue)	Él **juega** al fútbol.	Él **jugó** al fútbol.

- **¡Atención!** **-Ir** verbs that have a stem change in the present tense also have a stem change in the preterite.

CONSULTA
There are a few high-frequency irregular verbs in the preterite. You will learn more about them in **Estructura 9.1**, p. 286.

CONSULTA
You will learn about the preterite of **-ir** stem-changing verbs in **Estructura 8.1**, p. 254.

- Verbs that end in **-car**, **-gar**, and **-zar** have a spelling change in the first person singular (**yo** form) in the preterite.

busc**ar** ▶ busc**-** ▶ **qu-** ▶ yo bus**qué**
lleg**ar** ▶ lle**g-** ▶ **gu-** ▶ yo lle**gué**
empe**zar** ▶ empe**z-** ▶ **c-** ▶ yo empe**cé**

- Except for the **yo** form, all other forms of **-car**, **-gar**, and **-zar** verbs are regular in the preterite.
- Three other verbs—**creer**, **leer**, and **oír**—have spelling changes in the preterite. The **i** of the verb endings of **creer**, **leer**, and **oír** carries an accent in the **yo**, **tú**, **nosotros/as**, and **vosotros/as** forms, and changes to **y** in the **Ud./él/ella** and **Uds./ellos/ellas** forms.

creer ▶ cre- ▶ creí, creíste, creyó, creímos, creísteis, creyeron
leer ▶ le- ▶ leí, leíste, leyó, leímos, leísteis, leyeron
oír ▶ o- ▶ oí, oíste, oyó, oímos, oísteis, oyeron

- **Ver** is regular in the preterite, but none of its forms has an accent.

ver → vi, viste, vio, vimos, visteis, vieron

Words commonly used with the preterite

anoche	*last night*	**pasado/a** (*adj.*)	*last; past*
anteayer	*the day before yesterday*	**el año pasado**	*last year*
ayer	*yesterday*	**la semana pasada**	*last week*
de repente	*suddenly*	**una vez**	*once*
desde... hasta...	*from... until...*	**dos veces**	*twice*
		ya	*already*

Ayer llegué a Santiago de Cuba.
Yesterday I arrived in Santiago de Cuba.

Anoche oí un ruido extraño.
Last night I heard a strange noise.

- **Acabar de** + [*infinitive*] is used to say that something has just occurred. Note that **acabar** is in the present tense in this construction.

Acabo de comprar una falda.
I just bought a skirt.

Acabas de ir de compras.
You just went shopping.

recursos
WB pp. 64–65
LM p. 35
vhlcentral.com Lección 6

¡INTÉNTALO! Provide the appropriate preterite forms of the verbs.

	comer	salir	comenzar	leer
1. ellas	comieron	salieron	comenzaron	leyeron
2. tú	______	______	______	______
3. usted	______	______	______	______
4. nosotros	______	______	______	______
5. yo	______	______	______	______

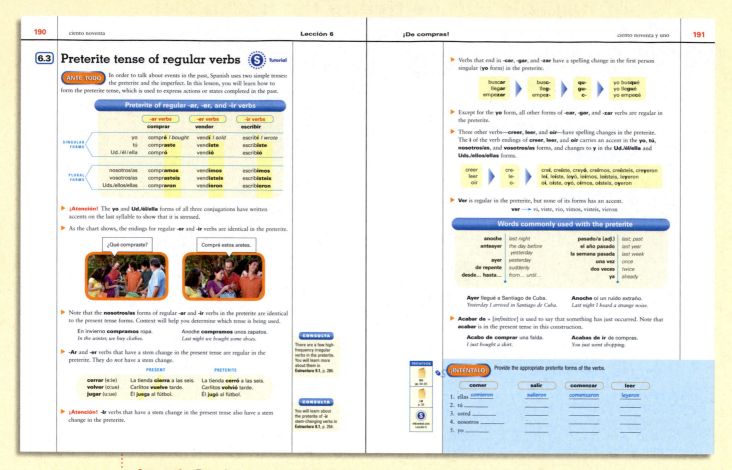

Ante todo Ease into grammar with definitions of grammatical terms, reminders about what you already know of English grammar, and Spanish grammar you have learned in earlier lessons.

Charts To help you learn, colorful, easy-to-use charts call out key grammatical structures and forms, as well as important related vocabulary.

Compare & Contrast This feature focuses on aspects of grammar that native speakers of English may find difficult, clarifying similarities and differences between Spanish and English.

Student sidebars provide you with on-the-spot linguistic, cultural, or language-learning information directly related to the materials in front of you.

Diagrams Clear and easy-to-grasp grammar explanations are reinforced by colorful diagrams that present sample words, phrases, and sentences.

¡Inténtalo! offers an easy first step into each grammar point.

Supersite

- Interactive, animated grammar tutorials with quick checks
- Textbook activities

Estructura

provides directed and communicative practice.

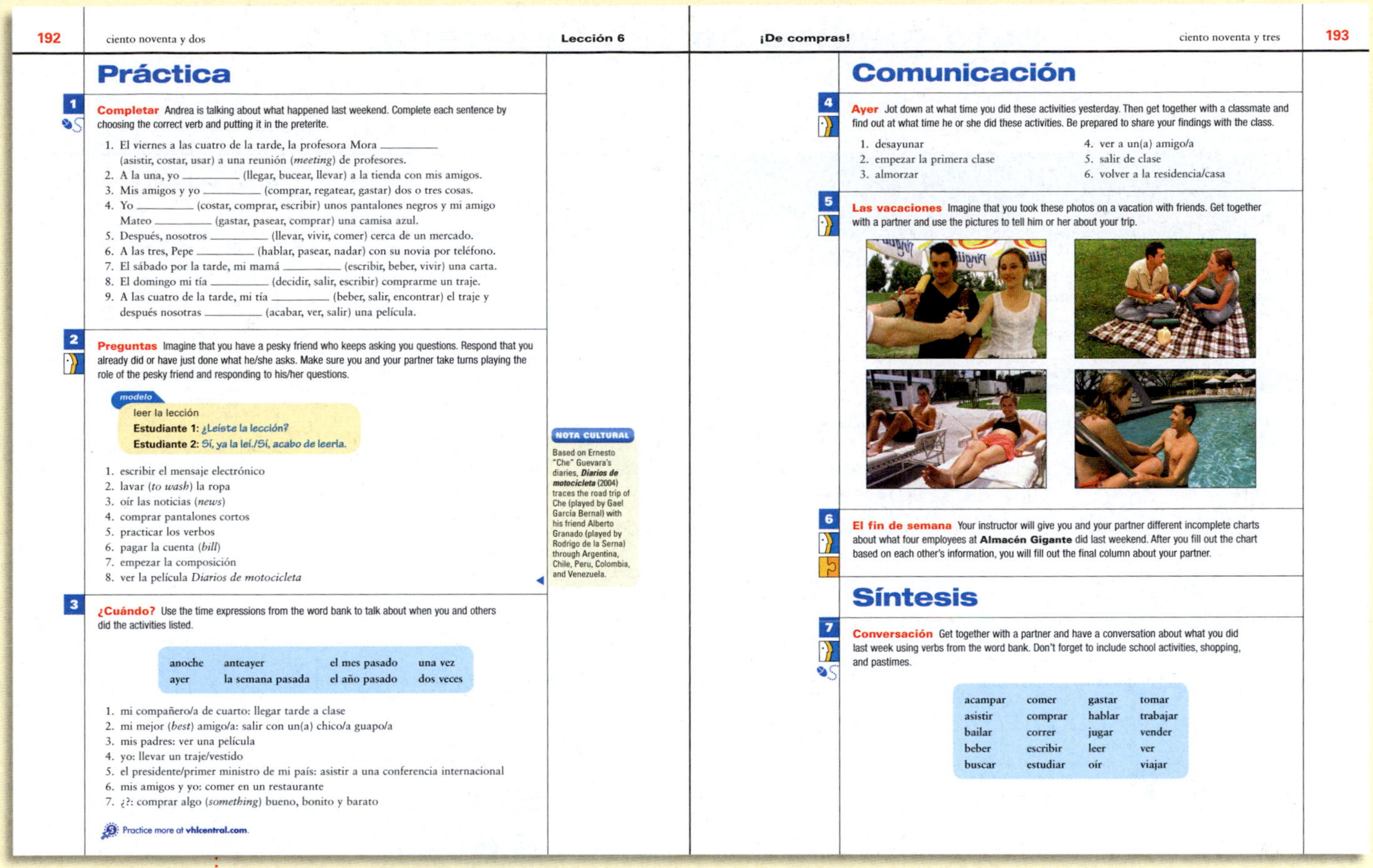

192 ciento noventa y dos — Lección 6

Práctica

1 **Completar** Andrea is talking about what happened last weekend. Complete each sentence by choosing the correct verb and putting it in the preterite.

1. El viernes a las cuatro de la tarde, la profesora Mora ________ (asistir, costar, usar) a una reunión (*meeting*) de profesores.
2. A la una, yo ________ (llegar, bucear, llevar) a la tienda con mis amigos.
3. Mis amigos y yo ________ (comprar, regatear, gastar) dos o tres cosas.
4. Yo ________ (costar, comprar, escribir) unos pantalones negros y mi amigo Mateo ________ (gastar, pasear, comprar) una camisa azul.
5. Después, nosotros ________ (llevar, vivir, comer) cerca de un mercado.
6. A las tres, Pepe ________ (hablar, pasear, nadar) con su novia por teléfono.
7. El sábado por la tarde, mi mamá ________ (escribir, beber, vivir) una carta.
8. El domingo mi tía ________ (decidir, salir, escribir) comprarme un traje.
9. A las cuatro de la tarde, mi tía ________ (beber, salir, encontrar) el traje y después nosotras ________ (acabar, ver, salir) una película.

2 **Preguntas** Imagine that you have a pesky friend who keeps asking you questions. Respond that you already did or have just done what he/she asks. Make sure you and your partner take turns playing the role of the pesky friend and responding to his/her questions.

modelo
leer la lección
Estudiante 1: ¿Leíste la lección?
Estudiante 2: Sí, ya la leí./Sí, acabo de leerla.

1. escribir el mensaje electrónico
2. lavar (*to wash*) la ropa
3. oír las noticias (*news*)
4. comprar pantalones cortos
5. practicar los verbos
6. pagar la cuenta (*bill*)
7. empezar la composición
8. ver la película *Diarios de motocicleta*

NOTA CULTURAL
Based on Ernesto "Che" Guevara's diaries, ***Diarios de motocicleta*** (2004) traces the road trip of Che (played by Gael García Bernal) with his friend Alberto Granado (played by Rodrigo de la Serna) through Argentina, Chile, Peru, Colombia, and Venezuela.

3 **¿Cuándo?** Use the time expressions from the word bank to talk about when you and others did the activities listed.

anoche	anteayer	el mes pasado	una vez
ayer	la semana pasada	el año pasado	dos veces

1. mi compañero/a de cuarto: llegar tarde a clase
2. mi mejor (*best*) amigo/a: salir con un(a) chico/a guapo/a
3. mis padres: ver una película
4. yo: llevar un traje/vestido
5. el presidente/primer ministro de mi país: asistir a una conferencia internacional
6. mis amigos y yo: comer en un restaurante
7. ¿?: comprar algo (*something*) bueno, bonito y barato

Practice more at **vhlcentral.com**.

¡De compras! — ciento noventa y tres 193

Comunicación

4 **Ayer** Jot down at what time you did these activities yesterday. Then get together with a classmate and find out at what time he or she did these activities. Be prepared to share your findings with the class.

1. desayunar
2. empezar la primera clase
3. almorzar
4. ver a un(a) amigo/a
5. salir de clase
6. volver a la residencia/casa

5 **Las vacaciones** Imagine that you took these photos on a vacation with friends. Get together with a partner and use the pictures to tell him or her about your trip.

6 **El fin de semana** Your instructor will give you and your partner different incomplete charts about what four employees at **Almacén Gigante** did last weekend. After you fill out the chart based on each other's information, you will fill out the final column about your partner.

Síntesis

7 **Conversación** Get together with a partner and have a conversation about what you did last week using verbs from the word bank. Don't forget to include school activities, shopping, and pastimes.

acampar	comer	gastar	tomar
asistir	comprar	hablar	trabajar
bailar	correr	jugar	vender
beber	escribir	leer	ver
buscar	estudiar	oír	viajar

Práctica Guided, yet meaningful exercises weave current and previously learned vocabulary together with the current grammar point.

Information Gap activities You and your partner each have only half of the information you need, so you must work together to accomplish the task at hand.

Comunicación Opportunities for creative expression use the lesson's grammar and vocabulary.

Sidebars The **Notas culturales** expand coverage of the cultures of Spanish-speaking peoples and countries, while the other sidebars provide on-the-spot language support.

Síntesis activities integrate the current grammar point with previously learned points, providing built-in, consistent review.

Supersite

- Textbook activities
- Additional online-only practice activities
- Chat activities for conversational skill-building and oral practice
- Grammar activities in Activity Pack

Estructura

Recapitulación reviews the grammar of each lesson and provides a short quiz, available with auto-grading on the Supersite.

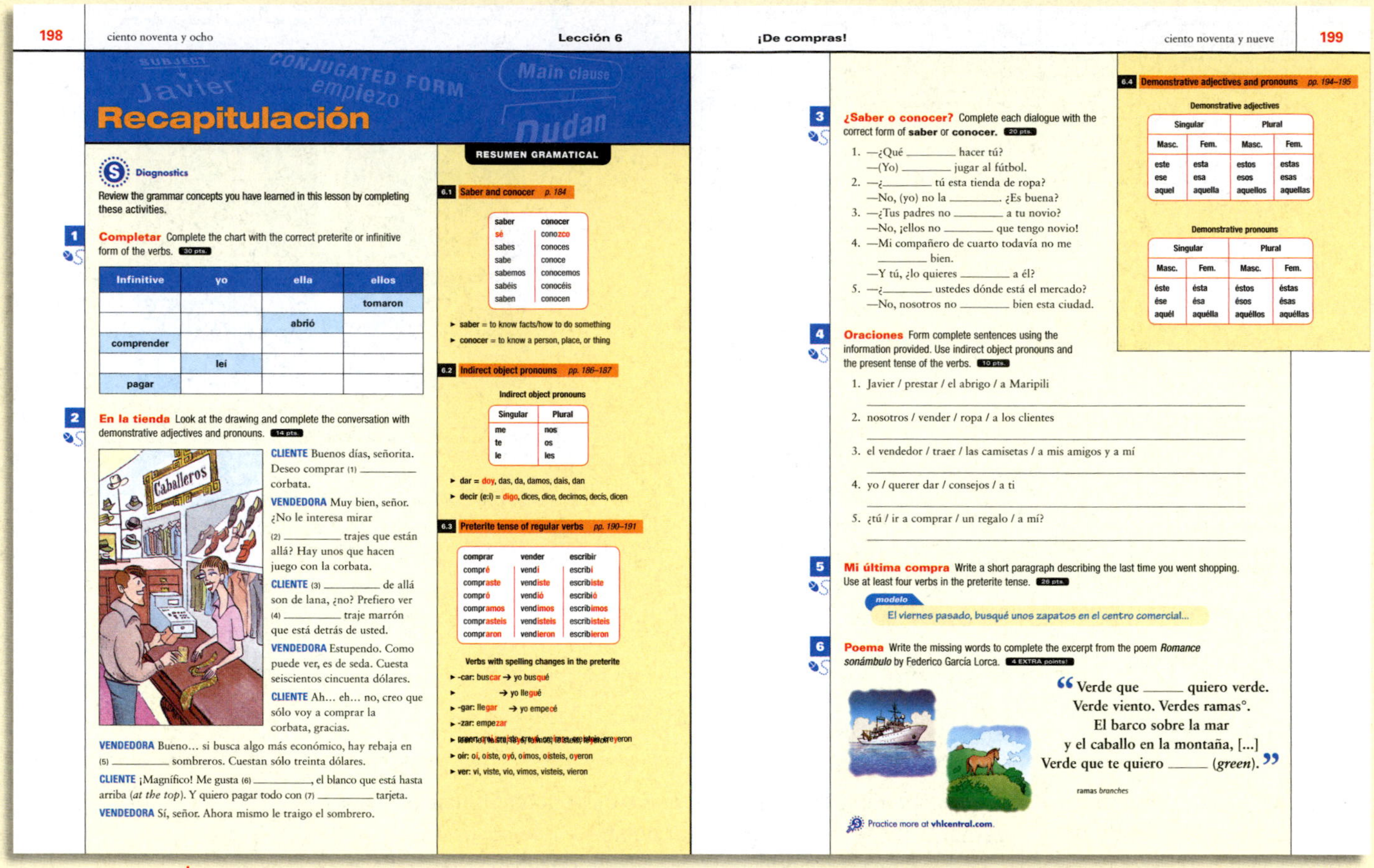

198 ciento noventa y ocho Lección 6

Recapitulación

Diagnostics

Review the grammar concepts you have learned in this lesson by completing these activities.

1 **Completar** Complete the chart with the correct preterite or infinitive form of the verbs. 30 pts.

Infinitive	yo	ella	ellos
			tomaron
		abrió	
comprender			
	leí		
pagar			

2 **En la tienda** Look at the drawing and complete the conversation with demonstrative adjectives and pronouns. 14 pts.

CLIENTE Buenos días, señorita. Deseo comprar (1) ________ corbata.

VENDEDORA Muy bien, señor. ¿No le interesa mirar (2) ________ trajes que están allá? Hay unos que hacen juego con la corbata.

CLIENTE (3) ________ de allá son de lana, ¿no? Prefiero ver (4) ________ traje marrón que está detrás de usted.

VENDEDORA Estupendo. Como puede ver, es de seda. Cuesta seiscientos cincuenta dólares.

CLIENTE Ah… eh… no, creo que sólo voy a comprar la corbata, gracias.

VENDEDORA Bueno… si busca algo más económico, hay rebaja en (5) ________ sombreros. Cuestan sólo treinta dólares.

CLIENTE ¡Magnífico! Me gusta (6) ________, el blanco que está hasta arriba (*at the top*). Y quiero pagar todo con (7) ________ tarjeta.

VENDEDORA Sí, señor. Ahora mismo le traigo el sombrero.

RESUMEN GRAMATICAL

6.1 Saber and conocer p. 184

saber	conocer
sé	conozco
sabes	conoces
sabe	conoce
sabemos	conocemos
sabéis	conocéis
saben	conocen

- saber = to know facts/how to do something
- conocer = to know a person, place, or thing

6.2 Indirect object pronouns pp. 186–187

Indirect object pronouns

Singular	Plural
me	nos
te	os
le	les

- dar = doy, das, da, damos, dais, dan
- decir (e:i) = digo, dices, dice, decimos, decís, dicen

6.3 Preterite tense of regular verbs pp. 190–191

comprar	vender	escribir
compré	vendí	escribí
compraste	vendiste	escribiste
compró	vendió	escribió
compramos	vendimos	escribimos
comprasteis	vendisteis	escribisteis
compraron	vendieron	escribieron

Verbs with spelling changes in the preterite

- -car: buscar → yo busqué
- → yo llegué
- -gar: llegar → yo empecé
- -zar: empezar
- [illegible]
- oír: oí, oíste, oyó, oímos, oísteis, oyeron
- ver: vi, viste, vio, vimos, visteis, vieron

¡De compras! ciento noventa y nueve 199

3 **¿Saber o conocer?** Complete each dialogue with the correct form of **saber** or **conocer.** 20 pts.

1. —¿Qué ________ hacer tú?
   —(Yo) ________ jugar al fútbol.
2. —¿________ tú esta tienda de ropa?
   —No, (yo) no la ________. ¿Es buena?
3. —¿Tus padres no ________ a tu novio?
   —No, ¡ellos no ________ que tengo novio!
4. —Mi compañero de cuarto todavía no me ________ bien.
   —Y tú, ¿lo quieres ________ a él?
5. —¿________ ustedes dónde está el mercado?
   —No, nosotros no ________ bien esta ciudad.

4 **Oraciones** Form complete sentences using the information provided. Use indirect object pronouns and the present tense of the verbs. 10 pts.

1. Javier / prestar / el abrigo / a Maripili
2. nosotros / vender / ropa / a los clientes
3. el vendedor / traer / las camisetas / a mis amigos y a mí
4. yo / querer dar / consejos / a ti
5. ¿tú / ir a comprar / un regalo / a mí?

5 **Mi última compra** Write a short paragraph describing the last time you went shopping. Use at least four verbs in the preterite tense. 26 pts.

modelo

El viernes pasado, busqué unos zapatos en el centro comercial...

6 **Poema** Write the missing words to complete the excerpt from the poem *Romance sonámbulo* by Federico García Lorca. 4 EXTRA points!

"Verde que ______ quiero verde.
Verde viento. Verdes ramas°.
El barco sobre la mar
y el caballo en la montaña, […]
Verde que te quiero ______ (*green*)."

ramas *branches*

Practice more at **vhlcentral.com.**

6.4 Demonstrative adjectives and pronouns pp. 194–195

Demonstrative adjectives

Singular		Plural	
Masc.	Fem.	Masc.	Fem.
este	esta	estos	estas
ese	esa	esos	esas
aquel	aquella	aquellos	aquellas

Demonstrative pronouns

Singular		Plural	
Masc.	Fem.	Masc.	Fem.
éste	ésta	éstos	éstas
ése	ésa	ésos	ésas
aquél	aquélla	aquéllos	aquéllas

Resumen gramatical This review panel provides you with an easy-to-study summary of the basic concepts of the lesson's grammar, with page references to the full explanations.

Points Each activity is assigned a point value to help you track your progress. All **Recapitulación** sections add up to one hundred points, plus four additional points for successfully completing the bonus activity.

Activities A series of activities, moving from directed to open-ended, systematically test your mastery of the lesson's grammar. The section ends with a riddle or puzzle using the grammar from the lesson.

Supersite

- Textbook activities with follow-up support and practice
- Additional online-only review activities
- Review activities in Activity Pack
- Practice quiz with diagnostics

Adelante

Lectura develops reading skills in the context of the lesson theme.

Audio: Reading
Additional Reading

Lectura

Antes de leer

Estrategia
Skimming

Skimming involves quickly reading through a document to absorb its general meaning. This allows you to understand the main ideas without having to read word for word. When you skim a text, you might want to look at its title and subtitles. You might also want to read the first sentence of each paragraph.

Examinar el texto

Look at the format of the reading selection. How is it organized? What does the organization of the document tell you about its content?

Buscar cognados

Scan the reading selection to locate at least five cognates. Based on the cognates, what do you think the reading selection is about?

1. ___________ 4. ___________
2. ___________ 5. ___________
3. ___________

The reading selection is about ___________.

Impresiones generales

Now skim the reading selection to understand its general meaning. Jot down your impressions. What new information did you learn about the document by skimming it? Based on all the information you now have, answer these questions in Spanish.

1. Who created this document?
2. What is its purpose?
3. Who is its intended audience?

Practice more at **vhlcentral.com**.

Corona
http://corona.cl
Corona
¡Corona tiene las ofertas más locas del verano!
La tienda más elegante de la ciudad con precios increíbles
niños mujeres casa baño equipaje
Faldas largas
ROPA BONITA
Algodón. De distintos colores
Talla mediana
Precio especial: 8.000 pesos
Blusas de seda
BAMBÚ
De cuadros y de lunares
Ahora: 21.000 pesos
40% de rebaja
Vestido de algodón
PANAMÁ
Colores blanco, azul y verde
Ahora: 18.000 pesos
30% de rebaja
Accesorios
BELLEZA
Cinturones, gafas de sol, sombreros, medias
Diversos estilos
Todos con un 40% de rebaja
Carteras
ELEGANCIA
Colores anaranjado, blanco, rosado y amarillo
Ahora: 15.000 pesos
50% de rebaja
Sandalias de playa
GINO
Números del 35 al 38
A sólo 12.000 pesos
50% de descuento
Lunes a sábado de 9 a 21 horas.
Domingo de 10 a 14 horas.
Real° Liquidación°
¡La rebaja está de moda en Corona!
¡Grandes rebajas!
y con la tarjeta de crédito más conveniente del mercado.
bebé hombres jardín joyas electrónica
Chaquetas
CASINO
Microfibra. Colores negro, café y gris
Tallas: P, M, G, XG
Ahora: 22.500 pesos
Traje inglés
GALES
Modelos originales
Ahora: 105.000 pesos
30% de rebaja
Pantalones
OCÉANO
Colores negro, gris y café
Ahora: 11.500 pesos
30% de rebaja
Accesorios
GUAPO
Gafas de sol, corbatas, cinturones, calcetines
Diversos estilos
Todos con un 40% de rebaja
Zapatos
COLOR
Italianos y franceses
Números del 40 al 45
A sólo 20.000 pesos
Ropa interior
ATLÁNTICO
Tallas: P, M, G
Colores blanco, negro y gris
40% de rebaja
Real Royal Liquidación Clearance sale
Por la compra de 40.000 pesos, puede llevar un regalo gratis.
• Un hermoso cinturón de mujer
• Un par de calcetines
• Una corbata de seda
• Una bolsa para la playa
• Una mochila
• Unas medias

Después de leer

Completar

Complete this paragraph about the reading selection with the correct forms of the words from the word bank.

almacén	hacer juego	tarjeta de crédito
caro	increíble	tienda
dinero	pantalones	verano
falda	rebaja	zapato

En este anuncio, el ___________ Corona anuncia la liquidación de ___________ con grandes ___________. Con muy poco ___________ usted puede conseguir ropa fina y elegante. Si no tiene dinero en efectivo, puede utilizar su ___________ y pagar luego. Para el caballero con gustos refinados, hay ___________ importados de París y Roma. La señora elegante puede encontrar blusas de seda que ___________ con todo tipo de ___________ o ___________. Los precios de esta liquidación son realmente ___________.

¿Cierto o falso?

Indicate whether each statement is **cierto** or **falso**. Correct the false statements.

1. Hay sandalias de playa.
2. Las corbatas tienen una rebaja del 30%.
3. El almacén Corona tiene un departamento de zapatos.
4. Normalmente las sandalias cuestan 22.000 pesos.
5. Cuando gastas 30.000 pesos en la tienda, llevas. un regalo gratis.
6. Tienen carteras amarillas.

Preguntas

In pairs, take turns asking and answering these questions.

1. Imagina que vas a ir a la tienda Corona. ¿Qué departamentos vas a visitar? ¿El departamento de ropa para señoras, el departamento de ropa para caballeros…?
2. ¿Qué vas a buscar en Corona?
3. ¿Hay tiendas similares a la tienda Corona en tu pueblo o ciudad? ¿Cómo se llaman? ¿Tienen muchas gangas?

Antes de leer Valuable reading strategies and pre-reading activities strengthen your reading abilities in Spanish.

Readings Selections related to the lesson theme recycle vocabulary and grammar you have learned. The selections in Lessons 1–12 are cultural texts, while those in Lessons 13–15 are literary pieces.

Después de leer Activities include post-reading exercises that review and check your comprehension of the reading as well as expansion activities.

Supersite

- Audio-sync reading that highlights text as it is being read
- Textbook activities
- Additional reading

Adelante

In Lessons 3, 6, 9, 12, and 15, *Escritura* develops writing skills while *Escuchar* practices listening skills.

Escritura

Estrategia
How to report an interview

There are several ways to prepare a written report about an interview. For example, you can transcribe the interview verbatim, you can simply summarize it, or you can summarize it but quote the speakers occasionally. In any event, the report should begin with an interesting title and a brief introduction, which may include the five Ws (*what, where, when, who, why*) and the H (*how*) of the interview. The report should end with an interesting conclusion. Note that when you transcribe dialogue in Spanish, you should pay careful attention to format and punctuation.

Writing dialogue in Spanish

- If you need to transcribe an interview verbatim, you can use speakers' names to indicate a change of speaker.

CARMELA ¿Qué compraste? ¿Encontraste muchas gangas?
ROBERTO Sí, muchas. Compré un suéter, una camisa y dos corbatas. Y tú, ¿qué compraste?
CARMELA Una blusa y una falda muy bonitas. ¿Cuánto costó tu camisa?
ROBERTO Sólo diez dólares. ¿Cuánto costó tu blusa?
CARMELA Veinte dólares.

- You can also use a dash (*raya*) to mark the beginning of each speaker's words.

—¿Qué compraste?
—Un suéter y una camisa muy bonitos. Y tú, ¿encontraste muchas gangas?
—Sí... compré dos blusas, tres camisetas y un par de zapatos.
—¡A ver!

Tema
Escribe un informe

Write a report for the school newspaper about an interview you conducted with a student about his or her shopping habits and clothing preferences. First, brainstorm a list of interview questions. Then conduct the interview using the questions below as a guide, but feel free to ask other questions as they occur to you.

Examples of questions:

- ¿Cuándo vas de compras?
- ¿Adónde vas de compras?
- ¿Con quién vas de compras?
- ¿Qué tiendas, almacenes o centros comerciales prefieres?
- ¿Compras ropa de catálogos o por Internet?
- ¿Prefieres comprar ropa cara o barata? ¿Por qué? ¿Te gusta buscar gangas?
- ¿Qué ropa llevas cuando vas a clase?
- ¿Qué ropa llevas cuando sales a bailar?
- ¿Qué ropa llevas cuando practicas un deporte?
- ¿Cuáles son tus colores favoritos? ¿Compras mucha ropa de esos colores?
- ¿Les das ropa a tu familia o a tus amigos/as?

Escuchar
Audio

Estrategia
Listening for linguistic cues

You can enhance your listening comprehension by listening for specific linguistic cues. For example, if you listen for the endings of conjugated verbs, or for familiar constructions, such as **acabar de** + [*infinitive*] or **ir a** + [*infinitive*], you can find out whether an event already took place, is taking place now, or will take place in the future. Verb endings also give clues about who is participating in the action.

To practice listening for linguistic cues, you will now listen to four sentences. As you listen, note whether each sentence refers to a past, present, or future action. Also jot down the subject of each sentence.

Preparación

Based on the photograph, what do you think Marisol has recently done? What do you think Marisol and Alicia are talking about? What else can you guess about their conversation from the visual clues in the photograph?

Ahora escucha

Now you are going to hear Marisol and Alicia's conversation. Make a list of the clothing items that each person mentions. Then put a check mark after the item if the person actually purchased it.

Marisol	Alicia
1. ________	1. ________
2. ________	2. ________
3. ________	3. ________
4. ________	4. ________

Practice more at **vhlcentral.com**.

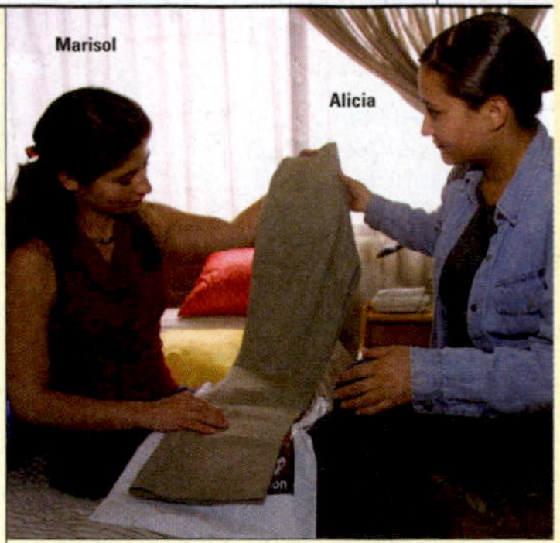

Comprensión
¿Cierto o falso?

Indicate whether each statement is **cierto** or **falso.** Then correct the false statements.

1. Marisol y Alicia acaban de ir de compras juntas (*together*).
2. Marisol va a comprar unos pantalones y una blusa mañana.
3. Marisol compró una blusa de cuadros.
4. Alicia compró unos zapatos nuevos hoy.
5. Alicia y Marisol van a ir al café.
6. Marisol gastó todo el dinero de la semana en ropa nueva.

Preguntas

Discuss the following questions with a classmate. Be sure to explain your answers.

1. ¿Crees que Alicia y Marisol son buenas amigas? ¿Por qué?
2. ¿Cuál de las dos estudiantes es más ahorradora (*frugal*)? ¿Por qué?
3. ¿Crees que a Alicia le gusta la ropa que Marisol compró?
4. ¿Crees que la moda es importante para Alicia? ¿Para Marisol? ¿Por qué?
5. ¿Es importante para ti estar a la moda? ¿Por qué?

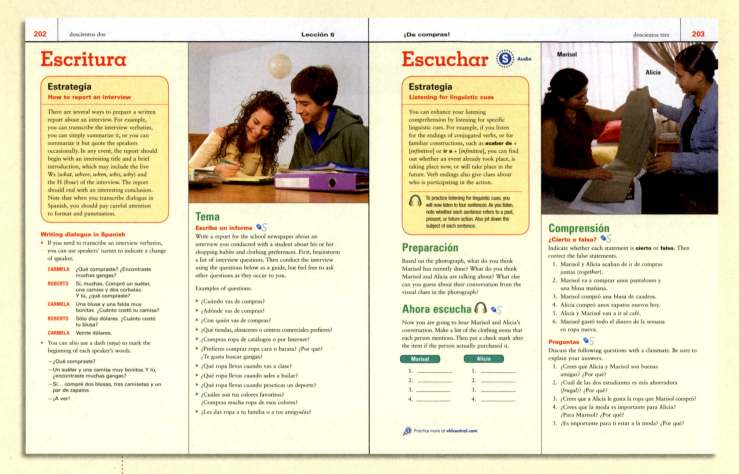

Estrategia Strategies help you prepare for the writing and listening tasks to come.

Escritura The **Tema** describes the writing topic and includes suggestions for approaching it.

Escuchar A recorded conversation or narration develops your listening skills in Spanish. **Preparación** prepares you for listening to the recorded passage.

Ahora escucha walks you through the passage, and **Comprensión** checks your listening comprehension.

Supersite

- Composition engine for writing activity in **Escritura**
- Audio for listening activity in **Escuchar**
- Textbook activities
- Additional online-only practice activities

Adelante

In Lessons 3, 6, 9, 12, and 15, *En pantalla* presents authentic TV clips and short films.

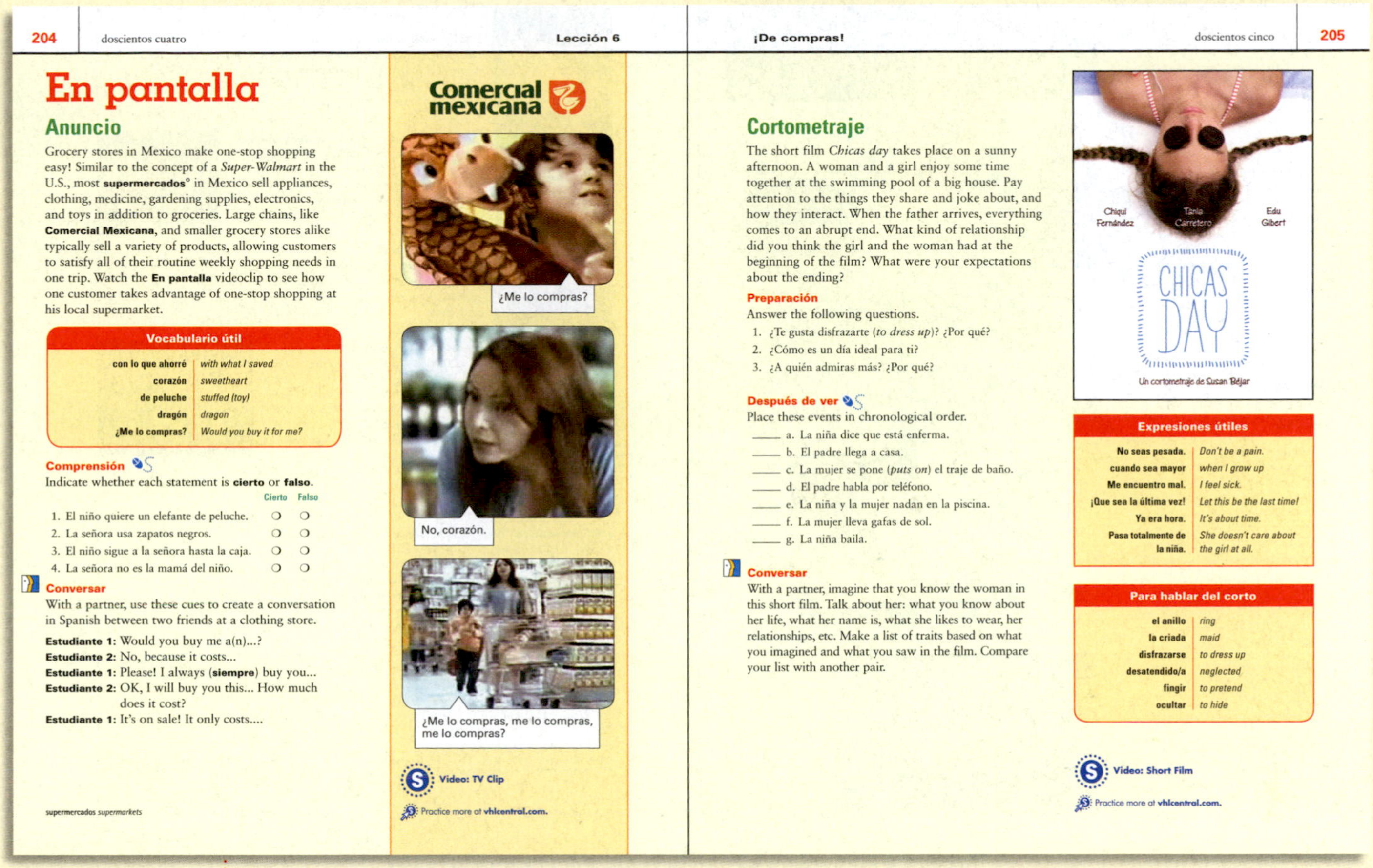

En pantalla

Anuncio

Grocery stores in Mexico make one-stop shopping easy! Similar to the concept of a *Super-Walmart* in the U.S., most **supermercados**° in Mexico sell appliances, clothing, medicine, gardening supplies, electronics, and toys in addition to groceries. Large chains, like **Comercial Mexicana**, and smaller grocery stores alike typically sell a variety of products, allowing customers to satisfy all of their routine weekly shopping needs in one trip. Watch the **En pantalla** videoclip to see how one customer takes advantage of one-stop shopping at his local supermarket.

Vocabulario útil

con lo que ahorré	*with what I saved*
corazón	*sweetheart*
de peluche	*stuffed (toy)*
dragón	*dragon*
¿Me lo compras?	*Would you buy it for me?*

Comprensión

Indicate whether each statement is **cierto** or **falso**.

	Cierto	Falso
1. El niño quiere un elefante de peluche.	❍	❍
2. La señora usa zapatos negros.	❍	❍
3. El niño sigue a la señora hasta la caja.	❍	❍
4. La señora no es la mamá del niño.	❍	❍

Conversar

With a partner, use these cues to create a conversation in Spanish between two friends at a clothing store.

Estudiante 1: Would you buy me a(n)...?
Estudiante 2: No, because it costs...
Estudiante 1: Please! I always (**siempre**) buy you...
Estudiante 2: OK, I will buy you this... How much does it cost?
Estudiante 1: It's on sale! It only costs....

supermercados *supermarkets*

Comercial mexicana

¿Me lo compras?

No, corazón.

¿Me lo compras, me lo compras, me lo compras?

Video: TV Clip

Practice more at **vhlcentral.com.**

Cortometraje

The short film *Chicas day* takes place on a sunny afternoon. A woman and a girl enjoy some time together at the swimming pool of a big house. Pay attention to the things they share and joke about, and how they interact. When the father arrives, everything comes to an abrupt end. What kind of relationship did you think the girl and the woman had at the beginning of the film? What were your expectations about the ending?

Preparación

Answer the following questions.

1. ¿Te gusta disfrazarte (*to dress up*)? ¿Por qué?
2. ¿Cómo es un día ideal para ti?
3. ¿A quién admiras más? ¿Por qué?

Después de ver

Place these events in chronological order.

_____ a. La niña dice que está enferma.
_____ b. El padre llega a casa.
_____ c. La mujer se pone (*puts on*) el traje de baño.
_____ d. El padre habla por teléfono.
_____ e. La niña y la mujer nadan en la piscina.
_____ f. La mujer lleva gafas de sol.
_____ g. La niña baila.

Conversar

With a partner, imagine that you know the woman in this short film. Talk about her: what you know about her life, what her name is, what she likes to wear, her relationships, etc. Make a list of traits based on what you imagined and what you saw in the film. Compare your list with another pair.

Chiqui Fernández
Tania Carretero
Edu Gilbert
CHICAS DAY
Un cortometraje de Susan Béjar

Expresiones útiles

No seas pesada.	*Don't be a pain.*
cuando sea mayor	*when I grow up*
Me encuentro mal.	*I feel sick.*
¡Que sea la última vez!	*Let this be the last time!*
Ya era hora.	*It's about time.*
Pasa totalmente de la niña.	*She doesn't care about the girl at all.*

Para hablar del corto

el anillo	*ring*
la criada	*maid*
disfrazarse	*to dress up*
desatendido/a	*neglected*
fingir	*to pretend*
ocultar	*to hide*

Video: Short Film

Practice more at **vhlcentral.com.**

En pantalla: Anuncio TV clips, two **NEW!** to this edition, give you additional exposure to authentic language. The clips are all commercials.

Presentation Cultural notes, video stills with captions, and vocabulary support all prepare you to view the clips and short films. Activities check your comprehension and expand on the ideas presented.

En pantalla: Cortometraje This page features authentic short films from Mexico and Spain, including pre- and post-viewing support.

Supersite

- Streaming video of **En pantalla**
- Textbook activities
- Additional online-only practice activities

Panorama

presents the nations of the Spanish-speaking world.

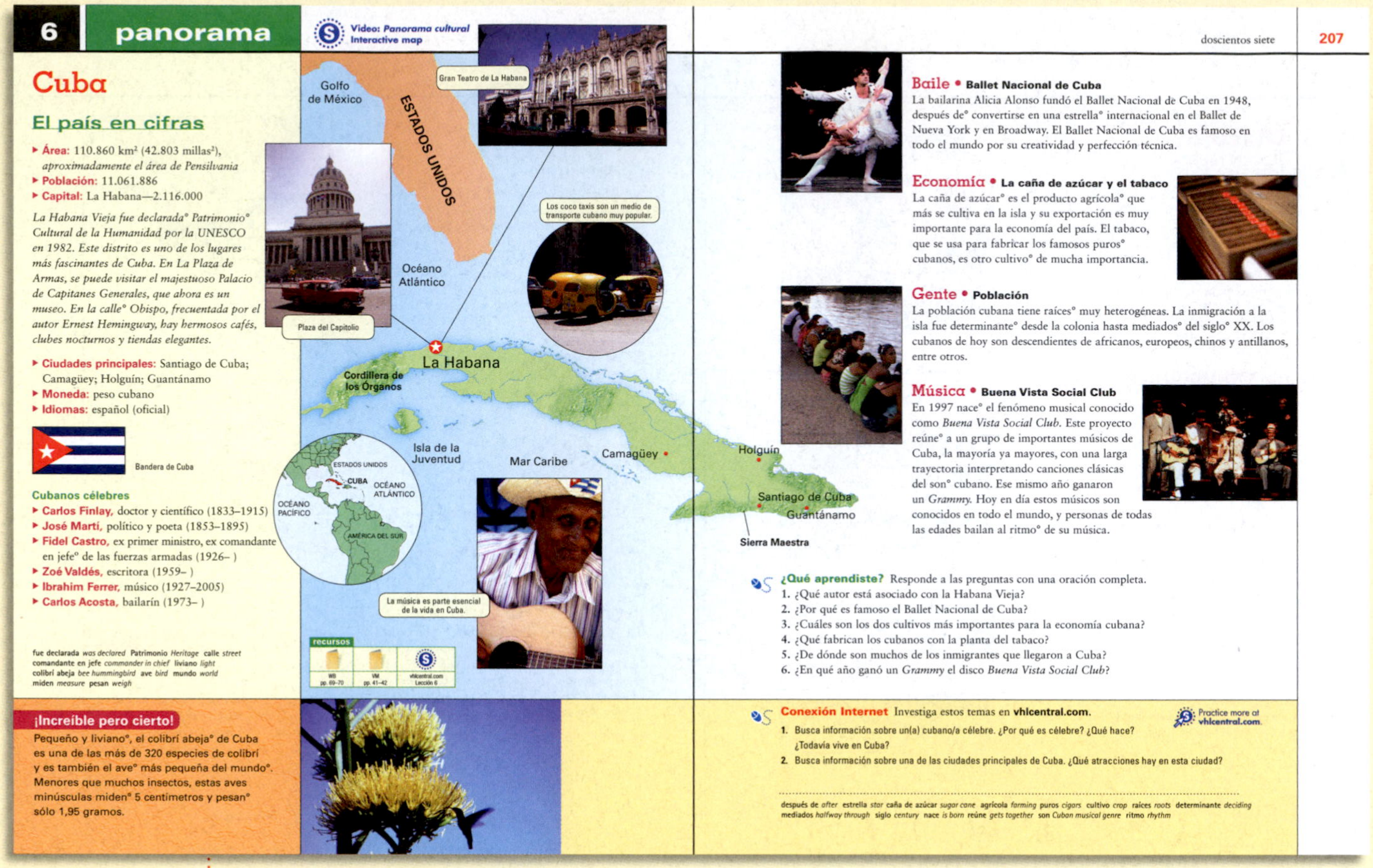

6 panorama

Video: Panorama cultural
Interactive map

Cuba

El país en cifras

- Área: 110.860 km² (42.803 millas²), *aproximadamente el área de Pensilvania*
- Población: 11.061.886
- Capital: La Habana—2.116.000

La Habana Vieja fue declarada° Patrimonio° Cultural de la Humanidad por la UNESCO en 1982. Este distrito es uno de los lugares más fascinantes de Cuba. En La Plaza de Armas, se puede visitar el majestuoso Palacio de Capitanes Generales, que ahora es un museo. En la calle° Obispo, frecuentada por el autor Ernest Hemingway, hay hermosos cafés, clubes nocturnos y tiendas elegantes.

- Ciudades principales: Santiago de Cuba; Camagüey; Holguín; Guantánamo
- Moneda: peso cubano
- Idiomas: español (oficial)

Bandera de Cuba

Cubanos célebres

- Carlos Finlay, doctor y científico (1833–1915)
- José Martí, político y poeta (1853–1895)
- Fidel Castro, ex primer ministro, ex comandante en jefe° de las fuerzas armadas (1926–)
- Zoé Valdés, escritora (1959–)
- Ibrahim Ferrer, músico (1927–2005)
- Carlos Acosta, bailarín (1973–)

fue declarada *was declared* Patrimonio *Heritage* calle *street* comandante en jefe *commander in chief* liviano *light* colibrí abeja *bee hummingbird* ave *bird* mundo *world* miden *measure* pesan *weigh*

¡Increíble pero cierto!

Pequeño y liviano°, el colibrí abeja° de Cuba es una de las más de 320 especies de colibrí y es también el ave° más pequeña del mundo°. Menores que muchos insectos, estas aves minúsculas miden° 5 centímetros y pesan° sólo 1,95 gramos.

doscientos siete 207

Baile • Ballet Nacional de Cuba

La bailarina Alicia Alonso fundó el Ballet Nacional de Cuba en 1948, después de° convertirse en una estrella° internacional en el Ballet de Nueva York y en Broadway. El Ballet Nacional de Cuba es famoso en todo el mundo por su creatividad y perfección técnica.

Economía • La caña de azúcar y el tabaco

La caña de azúcar° es el producto agrícola° que más se cultiva en la isla y su exportación es muy importante para la economía del país. El tabaco, que se usa para fabricar los famosos puros° cubanos, es otro cultivo° de mucha importancia.

Gente • Población

La población cubana tiene raíces° muy heterogéneas. La inmigración a la isla fue determinante° desde la colonia hasta mediados° del siglo° XX. Los cubanos de hoy son descendientes de africanos, europeos, chinos y antillanos, entre otros.

Música • Buena Vista Social Club

En 1997 nace° el fenómeno musical conocido como *Buena Vista Social Club*. Este proyecto reúne° a un grupo de importantes músicos de Cuba, la mayoría ya mayores, con una larga trayectoria interpretando canciones clásicas del son° cubano. Ese mismo año ganaron un *Grammy*. Hoy en día estos músicos son conocidos en todo el mundo, y personas de todas las edades bailan al ritmo° de su música.

¿Qué aprendiste? Responde a las preguntas con una oración completa.

1. ¿Qué autor está asociado con la Habana Vieja?
2. ¿Por qué es famoso el Ballet Nacional de Cuba?
3. ¿Cuáles son los dos cultivos más importantes para la economía cubana?
4. ¿Qué fabrican los cubanos con la planta del tabaco?
5. ¿De dónde son muchos de los inmigrantes que llegaron a Cuba?
6. ¿En qué año ganó un *Grammy* el disco *Buena Vista Social Club*?

Conexión Internet Investiga estos temas en **vhlcentral.com**.

Practice more at vhlcentral.com.

1. Busca información sobre un(a) cubano/a célebre. ¿Por qué es célebre? ¿Qué hace? ¿Todavía vive en Cuba?
2. Busca información sobre una de las ciudades principales de Cuba. ¿Qué atracciones hay en esta ciudad?

después de *after* estrella *star* caña de azúcar *sugar cane* agrícola *farming* puros *cigars* cultivo *crop* raíces *roots* determinante *deciding* mediados *halfway through* siglo *century* nace *is born* reúne *gets together* son *Cuban musical genre* ritmo *rhythm*

El país en cifras presents interesting key facts about the featured country.

¡Increíble pero cierto! highlights an intriguing fact about the country or its people.

Maps point out major cities, rivers, and geographical features and situate the country in the context of its immediate surroundings and the world.

Readings A series of brief paragraphs explores facets of the country's culture such as history, places, fine arts, literature, and aspects of everyday life.

***Panorama cultural* Video** This video's authentic footage takes you to the featured Spanish-speaking country, letting you experience the sights and sounds of an aspect of its culture.

Supersite

- Interactive map
- Streaming video of the **Panorama cultural** program
- Textbook activities
- Additional online-only practice activities
- **Conexión Internet** activity with questions and keywords related to lesson theme

Vocabulario
summarizes all the active vocabulary of the lesson.

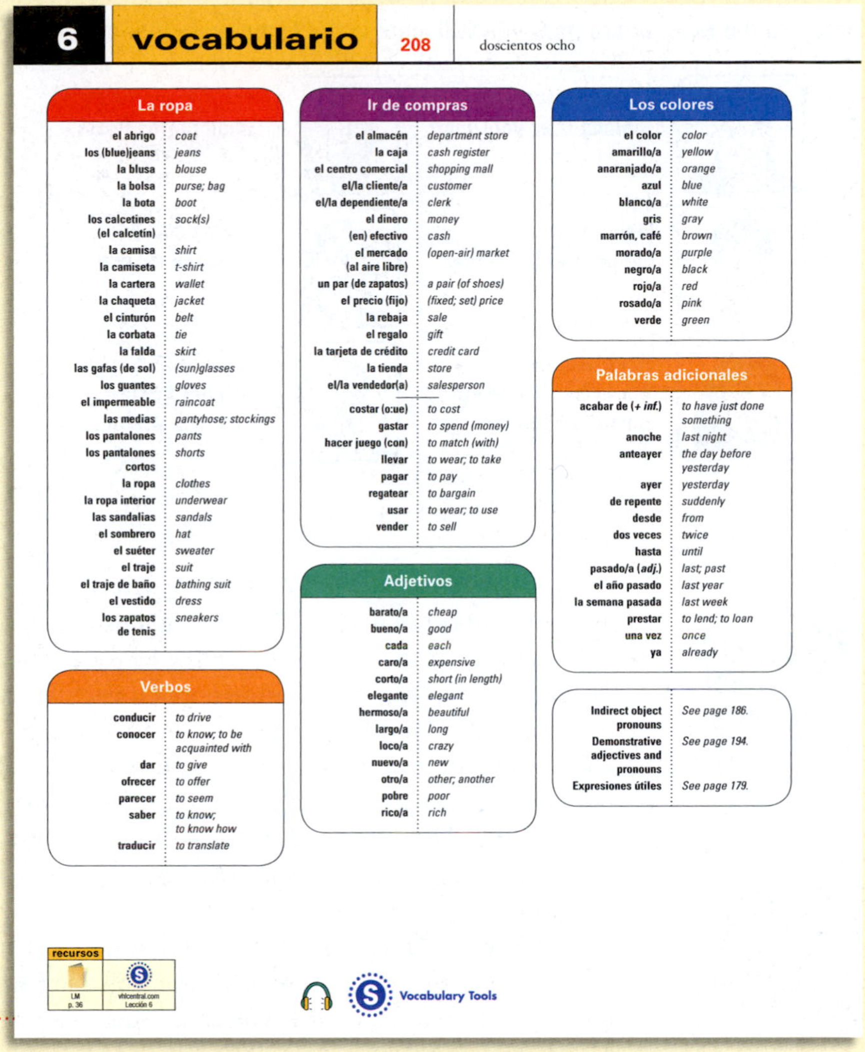

6 **vocabulario** 208 doscientos ocho

La ropa

el abrigo	coat
los (blue)jeans	jeans
la blusa	blouse
la bolsa	purse; bag
la bota	boot
los calcetines (el calcetín)	sock(s)
la camisa	shirt
la camiseta	t-shirt
la cartera	wallet
la chaqueta	jacket
el cinturón	belt
la corbata	tie
la falda	skirt
las gafas (de sol)	(sun)glasses
los guantes	gloves
el impermeable	raincoat
las medias	pantyhose; stockings
los pantalones	pants
los pantalones cortos	shorts
la ropa	clothes
la ropa interior	underwear
las sandalias	sandals
el sombrero	hat
el suéter	sweater
el traje	suit
el traje de baño	bathing suit
el vestido	dress
los zapatos de tenis	sneakers

Verbos

conducir	to drive
conocer	to know; to be acquainted with
dar	to give
ofrecer	to offer
parecer	to seem
saber	to know; to know how
traducir	to translate

Ir de compras

el almacén	department store
la caja	cash register
el centro comercial	shopping mall
el/la cliente/a	customer
el/la dependiente/a	clerk
el dinero	money
(en) efectivo	cash
el mercado (al aire libre)	(open-air) market
un par (de zapatos)	a pair (of shoes)
el precio (fijo)	(fixed; set) price
la rebaja	sale
el regalo	gift
la tarjeta de crédito	credit card
la tienda	store
el/la vendedor(a)	salesperson
costar (o:ue)	to cost
gastar	to spend (money)
hacer juego (con)	to match (with)
llevar	to wear; to take
pagar	to pay
regatear	to bargain
usar	to wear; to use
vender	to sell

Adjetivos

barato/a	cheap
bueno/a	good
cada	each
caro/a	expensive
corto/a	short (in length)
elegante	elegant
hermoso/a	beautiful
largo/a	long
loco/a	crazy
nuevo/a	new
otro/a	other; another
pobre	poor
rico/a	rich

Los colores

el color	color
amarillo/a	yellow
anaranjado/a	orange
azul	blue
blanco/a	white
gris	gray
marrón, café	brown
morado/a	purple
negro/a	black
rojo/a	red
rosado/a	pink
verde	green

Palabras adicionales

acabar de (+ *inf.*)	to have just done something
anoche	last night
anteayer	the day before yesterday
ayer	yesterday
de repente	suddenly
desde	from
dos veces	twice
hasta	until
pasado/a (*adj.*)	last; past
el año pasado	last year
la semana pasada	last week
prestar	to lend; to loan
una vez	once
ya	already

Indirect object pronouns	See page 186.
Demonstrative adjectives and pronouns	See page 194.
Expresiones útiles	See page 179.

recursos LM p. 36 · vhlcentral.com Lección 6

Vocabulary Tools

Vocabulario The end-of-lesson page lists the active vocabulary from each lesson. This is the vocabulary that may appear on quizzes or tests.

Supersite

- Audio for all vocabulary items
- Customizable study lists

Fotonovela Video Program

The cast

Here are the main characters you will meet in the **Fotonovela** Video:

From Mexico,
Jimena Díaz Velázquez

From Argentina,
Juan Carlos Rossi

From Mexico,
Felipe Díaz Velázquez

From the U.S.,
Marissa Wagner

From Mexico,
María Eugenia (Maru) Castaño Ricaurte

From Spain,
Miguel Ángel Lagasca Martínez

The **PANORAMA 5/e Fotonovela** Video is a dynamic and contemporary window into the Spanish language. The video centers around the Díaz family, whose household includes two college-aged children and a visiting student from the U.S. Over the course of an academic year, Jimena, Felipe, Marissa, and their friends explore **el D.F.** and other parts of Mexico as they make plans for their futures. Their adventures take them through some of the greatest natural and cultural treasures of the Spanish-speaking world, as well as the highs and lows of everyday life.

The **Fotonovela** section in each textbook lesson is actually an abbreviated version of the dramatic episode featured in the video. Therefore, each **Fotonovela** section can be done before you see the corresponding video episode, after it, or as a section that stands alone.

In each dramatic segment, the characters interact using the vocabulary and grammar you are studying. As the storyline unfolds, the episodes combine new vocabulary and grammar with previously taught language, exposing you to a variety of authentic accents along the way. At the end of each episode, the **Resumen** section highlights the grammar and vocabulary you are studying.

We hope you find the **Fotonovela** Video to be an engaging and useful tool for learning Spanish!

En pantalla Video Program

The **PANORAMA** Supersite features an authentic TV clip and short film for Lessons 3, 6, 9, 12, and 15. These TV clips and short films, four of which are **NEW!** to the Fifth Edition, have been carefully chosen to be comprehensible for students learning Spanish, and are accompanied by activities and vocabulary lists to facilitate understanding. More importantly, though, these clips and short films are a fun and motivating way to improve your Spanish!

Here are the countries represented in **En pantalla**:

Lesson 3 Chile and Mexico

Lesson 6 Mexico and Spain

Lesson 9 Chile and Mexico

Lesson 12 Spain

Lesson 15 Spain

Carolina Bang
036
un corto de Juan Fernando Andrés Parrilla y Esteban Roel García Vázquez

Flash cultura Video Program

In the dynamic **Flash cultura** Video, young people from all over the Spanish-speaking world share aspects of life in their countries with you. The similarities and differences among Spanish-speaking countries that come up through their adventures will challenge you to think about your own cultural practices and values. The segments provide valuable cultural insights as well as linguistic input; the episodes will introduce you to a variety of accents and vocabulary as they gradually move into Spanish.

Panorama cultural Video Program

The **Panorama cultural** Video is integrated with the **Panorama** section in each lesson. Each segment is 2–3 minutes long and consists of documentary footage from each of the countries featured. The images were specially chosen for interest level and visual appeal, while the all-Spanish narrations were carefully written to reflect the vocabulary and grammar covered in the textbook.

PANORAMA and the *Standards for Foreign Language Learning*

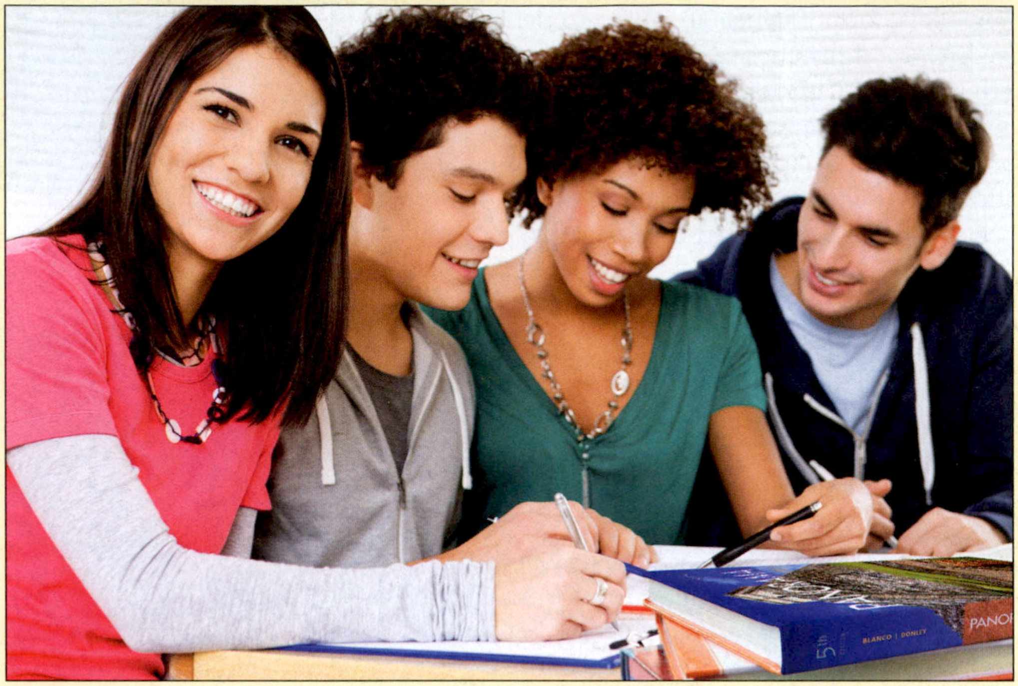

Since 1982, when the *ACTFL Proficiency Guidelines* were first published, that seminal document and its subsequent revisions have influenced the teaching of modern languages in the United States. **PANORAMA** and its parent book, **VISTAS**, were written with the concerns and philosophy of the *ACTFL Proficiency Guidelines* in mind, incorporating a proficiency-oriented approach from its planning stages.

The pedagogy of **PANORAMA** and **VISTAS** was also informed from its inception by the *Standards for Foreign Language Learning in the 21st Century*. First published in 1996 under the auspices of the National Standards in Foreign Language Education Project, the Standards are organized into five goal areas, often called the Five Cs: Communication, Cultures, Connections, Comparisons, and Communities.

Since **PANORAMA** takes a communicative approach to the teaching and learning of Spanish, the Communication goal is central to the student text. For example, the diverse formats used in **Comunicación** and **Síntesis** activities—pair work, small group work, class circulation, information gap, task-based, and so forth—engage students in communicative exchanges, providing and obtaining information, and expressing feelings and emotions.

The Cultures goal is most evident in the lessons' **Cultura** sections, **Nota cultural** student sidebars, and **En pantalla, Flash cultura,** and **Panorama** sections, but **PANORAMA** also weaves culture into virtually every page, exposing students to the multiple facets of practices, products, and perspectives of the Spanish-speaking world. In keeping with the Connections goal, students can connect with other disciplines such as geography, history, fine arts, and science in the **Panorama** section; they can acquire information and recognize distinctive cultural viewpoints in the non-literary and literary texts of the **Lectura** sections.

The **Estructura** sections, with their clear explanations and special *Compare & Contrast* features, reflect the Comparisons goal. Students can work toward the Connections and Communities goal when they do the **Cultura** and **Panorama** sections' **Conexión Internet** activities, as well as the activities and information on the **PANORAMA** Supersite. In addition, special Standards icons appear on the student text pages of your IAE to call out sections that have a particularly strong relationship with the Standards. These are a few examples of how **PANORAMA** was written with the Standards firmly in mind, but you will find many more as you use the textbook and its ancillaries.

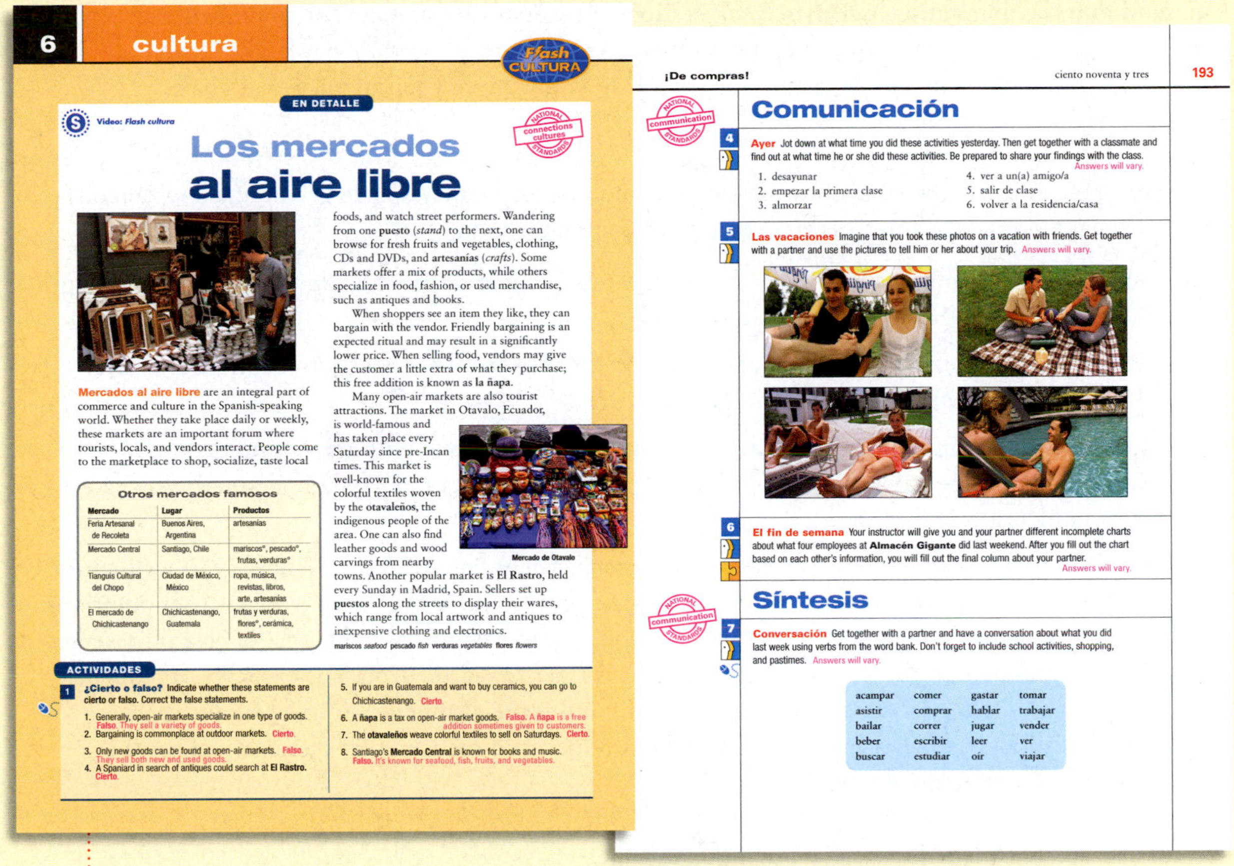

6 cultura

Flash CULTURA

EN DETALLE

Video: *Flash cultura*

NATIONAL connections cultures STANDARDS

Los mercados al aire libre

Mercados al aire libre are an integral part of commerce and culture in the Spanish-speaking world. Whether they take place daily or weekly, these markets are an important forum where tourists, locals, and vendors interact. People come to the marketplace to shop, socialize, taste local foods, and watch street performers. Wandering from one **puesto** (*stand*) to the next, one can browse for fresh fruits and vegetables, clothing, CDs and DVDs, and **artesanías** (*crafts*). Some markets offer a mix of products, while others specialize in food, fashion, or used merchandise, such as antiques and books.

When shoppers see an item they like, they can bargain with the vendor. Friendly bargaining is an expected ritual and may result in a significantly lower price. When selling food, vendors may give the customer a little extra of what they purchase; this free addition is known as **la ñapa**.

Many open-air markets are also tourist attractions. The market in Otavalo, Ecuador, is world-famous and has taken place every Saturday since pre-Incan times. This market is well-known for the colorful textiles woven by the **otavaleños**, the indigenous people of the area. One can also find leather goods and wood carvings from nearby towns. Another popular market is **El Rastro**, held every Sunday in Madrid, Spain. Sellers set up **puestos** along the streets to display their wares, which range from local artwork and antiques to inexpensive clothing and electronics.

Mercado de Otavalo

Otros mercados famosos

Mercado	Lugar	Productos
Feria Artesanal de Recoleta	Buenos Aires, Argentina	artesanías
Mercado Central	Santiago, Chile	mariscos°, pescado°, frutas, verduras°
Tianguis Cultural del Chopo	Ciudad de México, México	ropa, música, revistas, libros, arte, artesanías
El mercado de Chichicastenango	Chichicastenango, Guatemala	frutas y verduras, flores°, cerámica, textiles

mariscos *seafood* **pescado** *fish* **verduras** *vegetables* **flores** *flowers*

ACTIVIDADES

1 **¿Cierto o falso?** Indicate whether these statements are **cierto** or **falso**. Correct the false statements.

1. Generally, open-air markets specialize in one type of goods. Falso. They sell a variety of goods.
2. Bargaining is commonplace at outdoor markets. Cierto.
3. Only new goods can be found at open-air markets. Falso. They sell both new and used goods.
4. A Spaniard in search of antiques could search at **El Rastro.** Cierto.
5. If you are in Guatemala and want to buy ceramics, you can go to Chichicastenango. Cierto.
6. A **ñapa** is a tax on open-air market goods. Falso. A **ñapa** is a free addition sometimes given to customers.
7. The **otavaleños** weave colorful textiles to sell on Saturdays. Cierto.
8. Santiago's **Mercado Central** is known for books and music. Falso. It's known for seafood, fish, fruits, and vegetables.

¡De compras! ciento noventa y tres 193

NATIONAL communication STANDARDS

Comunicación

4 **Ayer** Jot down at what time you did these activities yesterday. Then get together with a classmate and find out at what time he or she did these activities. Be prepared to share your findings with the class. Answers will vary.

1. desayunar
2. empezar la primera clase
3. almorzar
4. ver a un(a) amigo/a
5. salir de clase
6. volver a la residencia/casa

5 **Las vacaciones** Imagine that you took these photos on a vacation with friends. Get together with a partner and use the pictures to tell him or her about your trip. Answers will vary.

6 **El fin de semana** Your instructor will give you and your partner different incomplete charts about what four employees at **Almacén Gigante** did last weekend. After you fill out the chart based on each other's information, you will fill out the final column about your partner. Answers will vary.

Síntesis

NATIONAL communication STANDARDS

7 **Conversación** Get together with a partner and have a conversation about what you did last week using verbs from the word bank. Don't forget to include school activities, shopping, and pastimes. Answers will vary.

acampar	comer	gastar	tomar
asistir	comprar	hablar	trabajar
bailar	correr	jugar	vender
beber	escribir	leer	ver
buscar	estudiar	oír	viajar

Communication Understand and be understood: read and listen to understand the Spanish-speaking world, converse with others, and share your thoughts clearly through speaking and writing.

Cultures Experience Spanish-speaking cultures through their own viewpoints, in the places, objects, behaviors, and beliefs important to the people who live them.

Connections Apply what you learn in your Spanish course to your other studies; apply what you know from other courses to your Spanish studies.

Comparisons Discover in which ways the Spanish language and Spanish-speaking cultures are like your own—and how they differ.

Communities Engage with Spanish-speaking communities locally, nationally, and internationally both in your courses and beyond—for life.

Your Instructor's Annotated Edition

PANORAMA, Fifth Edition, offers you the most thoroughly developed Instructor's Annotated Edition ever written for introductory college Spanish. The IAE features reduced student text pages, overprinted with answers, and a wealth of teaching resources in the side and bottom panels. The annotations complement and support varied teaching styles, extending the already rich content of the student textbook and saving you time in class preparation and course management.

This section is designed as a quick orientation to the principal types of instructor annotations you will find in the **PANORAMA 5/e** IAE. As you familiarize yourself with them, it is important to keep in mind that the annotations are merely suggestions. Any Spanish questions, or simulated instructor-student exchanges are not meant to be prescriptive. You are encouraged to view these suggested "scripts" as flexible points of departure that will help you achieve your instructional goals.

Icons

For your convenience, the suggestions in the side and bottom channels have been tagged with icons if they engage one of the three different modes of communication.

Interpretive communication Suggestions for exercises that target students' reading or listening skills and assess their comprehension

Presentational communication Ideas and contexts that require students to produce a written or verbal presentation in the target language

Interpersonal communication Activities that provide students with opportunities to carry out language functions in simulated real-life contexts or engage in personalized communication with others

For an annotation to merit one of these icons, it must use the target language at a discourse level in a sustained context. As with the activities in the student text, many of these annotations employ more than one mode of communication; in these cases the mode that is best represented in the "product" of the activity is the one that is reflected in the icon. For example, if students are asked to talk to a classmate (interpersonal) and write a summary of the conversation (presentational), the written summary is the product, and the icon will therefore reflect the presentational mode of communication.

On the Lesson Opener Pages

- **Lesson Goals** A list of the lexical, grammatical, and socio-cultural goals of the lesson, including language-learning strategies and skill-building techniques
- **A primera vista** Questions related to the photograph for jump-starting the lesson
- **Instructional Resources** A correlation to all student and instructor supplements available to reinforce the lesson

The **PANORAMA** Supersite provides additional instructor materials for each lesson. Visit **vhlcentral.com** for extra activities, supplemental vocabulary, assessment materials, and more!

In the Side Panels

- **Section Goals** A list of the goals of the corresponding section
- **Instructional Resources** A correlation to student and instructor ancillaries
- **Teaching Tips** Suggestions for recycling language, leading into the corresponding section, working with materials, and carrying out specific activities
- **Expansion** Expansions and variations for the activities in the student textbook
- **Script** Transcripts of the audio and video recordings
- **Possible Conversation** Answers based on known vocabulary, grammar, and language functions that students might produce
- **Video Recap** Questions to help students recall the events of the previous lesson's **Fotonovela** episode
- **Video Synopsis** A summary of each lesson's **Fotonovela** episode
- **Expresiones útiles** Suggestions for introducing upcoming **Estructura** grammar points incorporated into the **Fotonovela** episode
- **Estrategia** Suggestions for working with the reading, writing, and listening strategies presented in the **Lectura**, **Escritura**, and **Escuchar** sections, respectively
- **Tema** Ideas for presenting and expanding the writing assignment topic in **Escritura**
- **El país en cifras** Additional information expanding on the data presented for each Spanish-speaking country featured in the **Panorama** sections
- **¡Increíble pero cierto!** Curious facts about a lesser-known aspect of the country featured in the **Panorama** sections
- **Section-specific Annotations** Suggestions for presenting, expanding, varying, and reinforcing individual instructional elements, including the sidebars in the student text (**¡Atención!**, **Ayuda**, **Nota cultural**, etc.)
- **Successful Language Learning** Strategies to enhance students' language-learning experience
- **The Affective Dimension** Suggestions for reducing students' language-learning anxieties

In the *Teaching Options* Boxes

- **Extra Practice, Pairs, Small Groups,** and **Large Groups** Additional activities intended to supplement those in the student textbook
- **Game** Games that practice the language of the section and/or recycle previously learned language
- **TPR** Total Physical Response activities that engage students physically in learning Spanish
- **Variación léxica** Extra information related to the **Variación léxica** boxes in **Contextos**, terms that come up in **Lectura**, and terms from the Spanish-speaking countries featured in **Panorama**
- **Worth Noting** More detailed information about an interesting aspect of the history, geography, culture, or people of the Spanish-speaking countries in **Panorama**
- **Heritage Speakers** Suggestions and activities tailored to heritage speakers, who in many colleges and universities are enrolled in the same introductory courses as non-heritage speakers
- **Video** Techniques and activities for using the **PANORAMA** video program with **Fotonovela** and other lesson sections
- **Evaluation** Rubrics for grading students' work in **Escritura**

General Teaching Considerations

Orienting Students to the Student Textbook

Because **PANORAMA 5/e** treats graphic design as an integral part of students' language-learning experience, you may want to take a few minutes to orient students to the student textbook. Have them flip through one lesson, and point out that all lessons are organized the same way. Also point out how the major sections of each lesson are color-coded for easy navigation: red for **Contextos**, purple for **Fotonovela**, orange for **Cultura**, blue for **Estructura**, green for **Adelante**, and gold for **Vocabulario**. Let them know that, because of these design elements, they can be confident that they will always know "where they are" in their textbook.

Emphasize that sections are self-contained, occupying either a full page or a spread of two facing pages, thereby eliminating "bad breaks" and the need to flip back and forth to do activities or to work with explanatory material. Finally, call students' attention to the use of color to highlight key information in elements such as charts, diagrams, word lists, and activity **modelos**, titles, and sidebars.

Flexible Lesson Organization

PANORAMA 5/e uses a flexible lesson organization designed to accommodate diverse teaching styles, institutions, and instructional goals. For example, you can begin with the lesson opener page and progress sequentially through a lesson. If you do not want to devote class time to grammar, you can assign the **Estructura** explanations for outside study, freeing up class time for other purposes like developing oral communication skills; building listening, reading, or writing skills; learning more about the Spanish-speaking world; or working with the video program. You might decide to work extensively with the **Cultura** and **Adelante** sections in order to focus on students' reading, writing, and listening skills and their knowledge of the Spanish-speaking world. Or, you might prefer to use these sections periodically in response to your students' interests as the opportunity arises. If you plan on using the **PANORAMA** Testing Program, however, be aware that the quizzes, tests, and exams check language presented in **Contextos**, **Estructura**, and the **Expresiones útiles** boxes of **Fotonovela**.

Identifying Active Vocabulary

All words and expressions taught in the illustrations and **Más vocabulario** lists in **Contextos** are considered active, testable vocabulary. Any items in the **Variación léxica** or **Así se dice** boxes, however, are intended for receptive learning and are presented for enrichment only. The words and expressions in the **Expresiones útiles** boxes in **Fotonovela**, as well as words in charts, word lists, **¡Atención!** sidebars, and sample sentences in **Estructura** are also part of the active vocabulary load. At the end of each lesson, **Vocabulario** provides a convenient one-page summary of the items students should know and that may appear on tests and exams. Point this out to students and tell them that an easy way to study from **Vocabulario** is to cover up the Spanish half of each section, leaving only the English equivalents exposed. They can then quiz themselves on the Spanish items. To focus on the English equivalents of the Spanish entries, they simply reverse this process.

Taking into Account the Affective Dimension

While many factors contribute to the quality and success rate of learning experiences, two factors are particularly germane to language learning. One is students' beliefs about how language is learned; the other is language-learning anxiety.

As studies show and experienced instructors know, students often come to modern language courses either with a lack of knowledge about how to approach language learning or with mistaken notions about how to do so. For example, many students believe that making mistakes when speaking the target language must be avoided because doing so will lead to permanent errors. Others are convinced that learning another language is like learning any other academic subject. In other words, they believe that success is guaranteed, provided they attend class regularly, learn the assigned vocabulary words and grammar rules, and study for exams. In fact, in a study of college-level beginning language learners in the United States, over one-third of the participants thought that they could become fluent if they studied the language for only one hour a day for two years or less. Mistaken and unrealistic beliefs such as these can cause frustration and ultimately demotivation, thereby significantly undermining students' ability to achieve a successful language-learning experience.

Another factor that can negatively impact students' language-learning experience is language-learning anxiety. As Professor Elaine K. Horwitz of The University of Texas at Austin and Senior Consulting Editor of **PANORAMA 1/e** wrote, "Surveys indicate that up to one-third of American foreign language students feel moderately to highly anxious about studying another language. Physical symptoms of foreign language anxiety can include heart-pounding or palpitations, sweating, trembling, fast breathing, and general feelings of unease." The late Dr. Philip Redwine Donley, **PANORAMA** co-author and author of articles on language-learning anxiety, spoke with many students who reported feeling nervous or apprehensive in their classes. They mentioned freezing when called on by their instructors or going inexplicably blank when taking tests. Some so dreaded their classes that they skipped them or dropped the course.

PANORAMA contains several features aimed at reducing students' language anxiety and supporting successful language-learning. Its highly structured, visually dramatic design was conceived as a learning tool to make students feel comfortable with the content and confident about navigating the lessons. The Instructor's Annotated Edition includes *Affective Dimension* annotations with suggestions for managing and/or reducing language-learning anxieties, as well as *Successful Language Learning* annotations with learning strategies for enhancing students' learning experiences. In addition, the student text provides a wealth of helpful sidebars that assist students by making relevant connections with new information or reminding them of previously learned concepts.

Student Sidebars

¡Atención!	Provides active, testable information about the vocabulary or grammar point
Ayuda	Offers specific grammar and vocabulary reminders related to a particular activity or suggests pertinent language-learning strategies
Consulta	References related material introduced in previous or upcoming lessons
¡Lengua viva!	Presents relevant information on everyday language use
Nota cultural	Provides a wide range of cultural information relevant to the topic of an activity or section

General Suggestions for Using the PANORAMA *Fotonovela* Video

The **Fotonovela** section in each lesson of the student textbook and the **PANORAMA Fotonovela** Video were created as interlocking pieces. All photos in this section are images from the corresponding video module, while the printed conversations are abbreviated versions of the video module's dramatic segment. Both the **Fotonovela** conversations and their expanded video versions represent comprehensible input at the discourse level; they were purposely written to use language from the corresponding lesson's **Contextos** and **Estructura** sections. Thus, as of **Lección 2**, they recycle known language, preview grammar points students will study later in the lesson, and, in keeping with the concept of "i + 1," contain a small amount of unknown language.

You can use the **Fotonovela** Video and corresponding textbook section in many ways. For instance, you can use the **Fotonovela** spread as an advance organizer, presenting it before showing the video module. You can also show the video module first. You can even use Fotonovela as a stand-alone, video-independent section. You might decide to show all video modules in class or to assign them solely for viewing outside of the classroom. You could begin by showing the first one or two episodes in class to gain familiarity with the characters, storyline, style, and **Resumen** sections. After that, you could work in class only with

Fotonovela pages and have students view the remaining episodes outside of class. For each episode, there are **¿Qué pasó?** activities in the **Fotonovela** section of the corresponding textbook lesson and video activities in the Video Manual section of the **PANORAMA 5/e** Student Activities Manual and on the Supersite.

You might also want to use the **Fotonovela** Video in class when working with Estructura. You could play parts of the dramatic episode that demonstrate the grammar point you are teaching or show selected scenes that review old grammar points and ask students to identify them. In class, you could play the parts of the **Resumen** section that exemplify individual grammar points as you progress through each **Estructura** section. You could also wait until you complete an **Estructura** section and review it by showing the corresponding **Resumen** section in its entirety.

No matter which approach you choose, students have ample materials to support viewing the video independently and processing it in a meaningful way. We hope you and your students will continue to find the **Fotonovela** Video and corresponding materials to be an engaging and effective tool for language-learning.

General Suggestions for Using the *Panorama cultural* and *Flash cultura* Videos

The **Panorama cultural** Video contains documentary and travelogue footage of each country featured in the lesson's **Panorama** section. The **Flash cultura** Video expands on an aspect of the lesson theme in the format of a news broadcast. Like the conversations in the **Fotonovela** Video, these video segments deliver comprehensible input. Each was written to make the most of the vocabulary and grammar students learned in the corresponding and previous lessons, while still providing a controlled amount of unknown language.

Activities for the **Flash cultura** and **Panorama cultural** Videos are located in the Video Manual section of the **PANORAMA 5/e** Student Activities Manual and on the Supersite. They follow a process approach of pre-viewing, while-viewing, and post-viewing and use a variety of formats to prepare students for watching the video segments, to focus them while watching, and to check comprehension after they have watched the footage.

When showing the **videos** in class, you might also want to implement a process approach. You could start with an activity that prepares students for the video segment by taking advantage of what they learned in previous lessons. This could be followed by an activity that students do while you play certain parts or all of the video segment. The final activity, done in the same class period or in the next one as warm-up, could recap what students saw and heard and expand on the video segment's topic. The following suggestions for working with the **Flash cultura** Video in class can be carried out as described or expanded upon in any number of ways.

Before viewing

- After students have practiced the lesson's vocabulary and grammar and worked through the **Cultura** section of the student textbook, mention the video segment's title and ask them to guess what the segment might be about.
- Have pairs make a list of the lesson vocabulary they expect to hear in the video segment.
- Read the class a list of true/false or multiple-choice questions about the video. Students must use what they learned in the **Cultura** section to guess the answers. Confirm their guesses after watching the segment.

While viewing

- Show the video segment with the audio turned off and ask students to use lesson vocabulary and structures to describe what is happening. Have them confirm their guesses by showing the segment again with the audio on.
- Have students refer to the list of words they brainstormed before viewing the video and put a check mark in front of any words they actually see in the segment.
- First, have students simply watch the video. Then, show it again and ask students to take notes on what they see and hear. Finally, have them compare their notes in pairs or groups for confirmation.
- Photocopy the segment's Videoscript from the Supersite and white out words and expressions related to the lesson theme, in order to create cloze paragraphs. Distribute the scripts for pairs or groups to complete the sentences.

After viewing

- Have students say what aspects of the cultural information presented in their textbook appear in the video segment.
- Ask groups to write a brief summary of the content of the video segment. Have them exchange papers with another group for peer editing.
- Ask students to discuss any aspects of the featured country and topic of which they were unaware before watching. Encourage them to explain why they did not expect those aspects to be true of the country in question.
- Have students pick one characteristic about the country and topic that they learned from watching the video segment. Have them research additional information about that topic and write a brief composition that expands on it.

acknowledgments

On behalf of its authors and editors, Vista Higher Learning expresses its sincere appreciation to the many instructors and college professors across the U.S. and Canada who contributed their ideas and suggestions.

PANORAMA, Fifth Edition, is the direct result of extensive reviews and ongoing input from both students and instructors using the Fourth Edition. Accordingly, we gratefully acknowledge those who shared their suggestions, recommendations, and ideas as we prepared this Fifth Edition.

We express our sincere appreciation to the instructors who completed our online review.

Reviewers

Osiris Albrecht
St. Petersburg College, FL

Salvador Alvarez
Victor Valley College, CA

Carlos Arazi
Borough of Manhattan Community College, NY

Rafael Arias
Los Angeles Valley College, CA

Kenneth Atwood
Webb School of Knoxville, TN

Sharon Baker Bucklin
University of Wisconsin-Rock County, WI

Tamra Bassett
Idaho State University, ID

Carmen Beaty
Fort Valley State University, GA

Sarah Bentley
Portland Community College, OR

Melanie Bloom
University of Nebraska Omaha, NE

Jeanne Boettcher
Madison Area Technical College, WI

Alan Bruflat
Wayne State College, NE

Silvia Campazzo
University of Wisconsin Oshkosh, WI

Ines Carrera-Junco
Borough of Manhattan Community College, NY

Tulio Cedillo
Lynchburg College, VA

Margarita Chavez
Harold Washington College, IL

Arsenio Cicero
Madison Area Technical College, WI

Alicia Class
El Camino College, CA

Magdalena Coll
Madison Area Technical College, WI

Andrea Colvin
Ohio Wesleyan University, OH

Alphonse Dattolo
Bergen Community College, NJ

Cindy Davis
Central Michigan University, MI

Richard DCamp
University of Wisconsin Oshkosh, WI

William O. Deaver, Jr.
Armstrong State University, GA

Carmen Del Castillo-Zerbe
York College of Pennsylvania, PA

Aurea Diab
Dillard University, LA

Conxita Domenech
University of Wyoming, WY

Margaret Donghia
Appomattox High School, VA

Dorian Dorado
Louisiana State University, LA

Cindy Doutrich
York College of Pennsylvania, PA

Ana Eire
Stetson University, FL

Georgina Elortegui
Montgomery County Community College, PA

Belkis M. Farris
Emmanuel College, GA

Giti Farudi
Xavier University of Louisiana, LA

Ileana Feistritzer
York College of Pennsylvania, PA

Ronna Feit
Nassau Community College, NY

Arlene F. Fuentes
Southern Virginia University, VA

John Gant
University of North Carolina at Asheville, NC

José M. García-Sánchez
Eastern Washington University, WA

Don Goetz
Northwestern Connecticut Community College, CT

Jill Gomez
Miami University, OH

Karen Hall Zetrouer
Santa Fe College, FL

Helen Haselnuss
Pace University, NY

Jason Herbeck
Boise State University, ID

Lorena Hernandez Ramirez
Lehman College, NY

Marvin Huber
Mount Marty College, SD

Harriet Hutchinson
Bunker Hill Community College, MA

Tamise Ironstrack
Miami University, OH

Isabel Izquierdo
Diablo Valley College, CA

Tammy Jandrey Hertel
Lynchburg College, VA

Herman Johnson
Xavier University of Louisiana, LA

Randy Johnson
College of the Redwoods, CA

Karen Jones
Santa Fe College, TX

Anne Kelly-Glasoe
South Puget Sound Community College, WA

Maria Lee-Lopez
Portland Community College, OR

Nilda Lowe
Concord University, WV

Kenneth V. Luna
California State University, Northridge, CA

Anne-Marie Martin
Portland Community College, OR

Kristin McDonald
Northwestern College, IA

Megan McDonald
Lewis & Clark College, OR

Leslie Meeder
Lycoming College, PA

Jacqueline Mitchell
Point Loma Nazarene University, CA

Libardo Mitchell
Portland Community College, OR

Lorena Molina
Citrus College, CA

Julia Morton
Bridgewater College, VA

Pablo M. Oliva
Monterey Institute of International Studies, CA

Raquel Olivera
Moorpark College, CA

Jamilet Ortiz
Purchase College, NY

Kristin-Ann Osowski
Diablo Valley College, CA

Ruth Owens
Arkansas State University, AR

Nancy Pastrana
Victor Valley College, CA

Keith Phillips
Lansing Community College, MI

Marcela Pineda-Volk
Shippensburg University, PA

Thomas R. Porter
Southern Virginia University, VA

Marcie Pratt
University of Wisconsin-Baraboo/Sauk County, WI

Julie Raich
College of the Redwoods, CA

Carmen Ramos-Castro
Cabrillo College, CA

Francis Bernie Rang
El Camino College, CA

Jose Ricardo-Osorio
Shippensburg University, PA

Nilsa Rodríguez-Jaca
Culinary Institute of America, NY

Nicole Roger-Hogan
Purdue University, IN

Eunice Rojas
Lynchburg College, VA

Juan Armando Rojas
Ohio Wesleyan University, OH

Gracia Roldán
Armstrong State University, GA

Aldo M. Romero
University of Northern Colorado, CO

Clinia Saffi
Presbyterian College, SC

David A. Salomon
Russell Sage College, NY

Bethany Sanio
University of Nebraska-Lincoln, NE

Ana Ligia Scott
Purdue University, IN

Gabriela Segal
Arcadia University, PA

Amy Sellin
Fort Lewis College, CO

Nila Serrano
Victor Valley College, CA

Irena Stefanova
Contra Costa College, CA

Victoria Stewart
Globe University/Minnesota School of Business, MN

Luz I. Strohfeldt
Cincinnati State Technical and Community College, OH

Nancy Stucker
Cabrillo College, CA

Rosa Tapia
Lawrence University, WI

Robert Taylor
Cincinnati State Technical and Community College, OH

Georgina Tenny
Washburn University, KS

Silvina Trica-Flores
Nassau Community College, NY

Nicholas J. Uliano
Cabrini College, PA

Jan Underwood
Portland Community College, OR

Freddy Vilches
Lewis & Clark College, OR

Genevieve Watson
Darton State College, GA

Rebecca White
Indiana University Southeast, IN

Amy Williamson
Mississippi College, MS

Elizabeth Willingham
Calhoun Community College, AL

James R. Wilson
Madison Area Technical College, WI

Helga Winkler
Moorpark College, CA

Sheri Woodworth
Southern Vermont College, VT

Joy Woolf
Westminster College, UT

Laly Yahyawi-Valenzuela
University of Wisconsin Oshkosh, WI

Jean Zenor
Springfield Technical Community College, MA

Hola, ¿qué tal?

1

Communicative Goals

You will learn how to:

- **Greet people in Spanish**
- **Say goodbye**
- **Identify yourself and others**
- **Talk about the time of day**

A PRIMERA VISTA

- **Guess what the people on the photo are saying:**
  a. Adiós. b. Hola. c. salsa
- **Most likely they would also say:**
  a. Gracias. b. fiesta c. Buenos días.
- **The women are:**
  a. amigas b. chicos c. señores

Lesson Goals

In **Lección 1**, students will be introduced to the following:

- terms for greetings and goodbyes
- identifying where one is from
- courtesy expressions
- greetings in the Spanish-speaking world
- the **plaza principal**
- nouns and articles (definite and indefinite)
- numbers 0–30
- present tense of **ser**
- telling time
- recognizing cognates
- reading a comic strip
- a video about **plazas** and greetings
- demographic and cultural information about Hispanics in the United States and Canada

A primera vista Have students look at the photo and ask them what they think the young people are doing. Explain that it is common in Hispanic cultures for friends to greet each other with one or two kisses on the cheek. As a class, discuss how friends typically greet each other in North America.

Teaching Tip You will see a series of icons pointing out communicative expansions, activities, and teaching tips in the instructor annotations. Follow this key:

→•←	**Interpretive communication**
←•→	**Presentational communication**
•↔•	**Interpersonal communication**

INSTRUCTIONAL RESOURCES

Supersite (vhlcentral.com)
Video: ***Fotonovela, Flash cultura, Panorama cultural***
Audio: Textbook and Lab MP3 Files
Activity Pack: Information Gap Activities, games, additional activity handouts
Resources: SAM Answer Key, Scripts, Translations, **Vocabulario adicional**, sample lesson plan, Grammar Presentation Slides, Digital Image Bank
Testing Program: Quizzes, Tests, Exams, MP3s
Student Activities Manual: Workbook/Video Manual/Lab Manual
WebSAM (online Student Activities Manual)

Section Goals

In **Contextos**, students will learn and practice:

- basic greetings
- introductions
- courtesy expressions

Instructional Resources

Supersite: Audio (Textbook and Lab MP3 Files); Resources (Digital Image Bank, **Vocabulario adicional**, Activity Pack, Scripts, Answer Keys); Testing Program (Quizzes)
WebSAM
Workbook, pp. 1–2
Lab Manual, p. 1

Teaching Tips

- To familiarize students with lesson headings and vocabulary for classroom interactions, hand out ***Vocabulario adicional: Más vocabulario para la clase de español*** from the Supersite.
- For a sample lesson plan, go to **vhlcentral.com** to access the instructor's part of the **PANORAMA** Supersite.
- Use the **Lección 1 Contextos** digital images to assist with this presentation.
- Write a few greetings, farewells, and courtesy expressions on the board, explain their meaning, and model their pronunciation. Circulate around the class, greeting students, making introductions, and encouraging responses. Then have students open to pages 2–3, and ask them to identify which conversations seem to be exchanges between friends and which seem more formal. Draw attention to the use of **usted** vs. **tú** in these conversations. Explain situations in which each form is appropriate.

Hola, ¿qué tal?

Más vocabulario

Buenos días.	*Good morning.*
Buenas noches.	*Good evening; Good night.*
Hasta la vista.	*See you later.*
Hasta pronto.	*See you soon.*
¿Cómo se llama usted?	*What's your name? (form.)*
Le presento a...	*I would like to introduce you to (name). (form.)*
Te presento a...	*I would like to introduce you to (name). (fam.)*
el nombre	*name*
¿Cómo estás?	*How are you? (fam.)*
No muy bien.	*Not very well.*
¿Qué pasa?	*What's happening?; What's going on?*
por favor	*please*
De nada.	*You're welcome.*
No hay de qué.	*You're welcome.*
Lo siento.	*I'm sorry.*
Gracias.	*Thank you; Thanks.*
Muchas gracias.	*Thank you very much; Thanks a lot.*

Variación léxica

Items are presented for recognition purposes only.

Buenos días. ⟷ Buenas.
De nada. ⟷ A la orden.
Lo siento. ⟷ Perdón.
¿Qué tal? ⟷ ¿Qué hubo? (*Col.*)
Chau ⟷ Ciao; Chao

recursos

WB pp. 1–2	LM p. 1	vhlcentral.com Lección 1

1

ELENA Patricia, le presento a Jorge Perales.
PATRICIA Encantada.
SEÑOR PERALES Igualmente. ¿De dónde es usted, señorita?
PATRICIA Soy de México. ¿Y usted?
SEÑOR PERALES De Puerto Rico.

2

TOMÁS ¿Qué tal, Alberto?
ALBERTO Regular. ¿Y tú?
TOMÁS Bien. ¿Qué hay de nuevo?
ALBERTO Nada.

3

SEÑOR VARGAS Buenas tardes, señora Wong. ¿Cómo está usted?
SEÑORA WONG Muy bien, gracias. ¿Y usted, señor Vargas?
SEÑOR VARGAS Bien, gracias.
SEÑORA WONG Hasta mañana, señor Vargas. Saludos a la señora Vargas.
SEÑOR VARGAS Adiós.

TEACHING OPTIONS

Extra Practice Bring in photos or magazine images of people greeting each other or saying goodbye. Ask pairs to write dialogue captions for each photo. Remind students to use formal and informal expressions as appropriate.

Groups Write questions and possible answers from the new set of expressions in **Contextos** on separate note cards. Give each student one note card and have them find the student with the matching card that completes their question/answer. Then have students work with other pairs to see if they can create a longer dialogue with their expressions.

Extra Practice Prepare name tags with a variety of different names, titles, and ages. Ex: **señora Lopez, 63; Carlos de la Vega, 22,** etc. Each student should wear a name tag and greet their peers according to the information on their tags.

AYUDA

In Spanish, people can be addressed either formally or informally. Dialogues 1 and 3 are formal exchanges and use **usted** (*you*) forms. Dialogues 2, 4, and 5 are informal and use the familiar **tú** (*you*) form or other informal expressions. You will learn more about this in **Estructura 1.3**.

4

BERTA Hasta luego, Tere.
TERESA Chau, Berta. Nos vemos mañana.

5

CARMEN Buenas tardes. Me llamo Carmen. ¿Cómo te llamas tú?
ANTONIO Buenas tardes. Me llamo Antonio. Mucho gusto.
CARMEN El gusto es mío. ¿De dónde eres?
ANTONIO Soy de los Estados Unidos, de California.

Práctica

1 Escuchar Listen to each question or statement, then choose the correct response.

1. a. Muy bien, gracias. b. Me llamo Graciela. b
2. a. Lo siento. b. Mucho gusto. b
3. a. Soy de Puerto Rico. b. No muy bien. a
4. a. No hay de qué. b. Regular. a
5. a. Mucho gusto. b. Hasta pronto. b
6. a. Nada. b. Igualmente. a
7. a. Me llamo Guillermo Montero. b. Muy bien, gracias. b
8. a. Buenas tardes. ¿Cómo estás? b. El gusto es mío. a
9. a. Saludos a la Sra. Ramírez. b. Encantada. b
10. a. Adiós. b. Regular. b

2 Identificar You will hear a series of expressions. Identify the expression (**a**, **b**, **c**, or **d**) that does not belong in each series.

1. c
2. a
3. b
4. c

3 Escoger For each expression, write another word or phrase that expresses a similar idea.

modelo
¿Cómo estás? *¿Qué tal?*

1. De nada. No hay de qué.
2. Encantado. Mucho gusto.
3. Adiós. Chau o Hasta luego/mañana/pronto.
4. Hasta la vista. Hasta luego.
5. Mucho gusto. El gusto es mío.

4 Ordenar Work with a partner to put this scrambled conversation in order. Then act it out.

—Muy bien, gracias. Soy Rosabel.
—Soy de México. ¿Y tú?
—Mucho gusto, Rosabel.
—Hola. Me llamo Carlos. ¿Cómo estás?
—Soy de Argentina.
—Igualmente. ¿De dónde eres, Carlos?

CARLOS Hola. Me llamo Carlos. ¿Cómo estás?
ROSABEL Muy bien, gracias. Soy Rosabel.
CARLOS Mucho gusto, Rosabel.
ROSABEL Igualmente. ¿De dónde eres, Carlos?
CARLOS Soy de México. ¿Y tú?
ROSABEL Soy de Argentina.

TEACHING OPTIONS

Game Divide the class into two teams. Point to a team member and call out an original statement or question based on **Contextos**. If the student responds appropriately, his or her team earns one point. The team with the most points at the end wins.

Pairs Write several times on the board. Ex: **9:00 a.m., 4:00 p.m., 10:30 p.m.** Have students work in pairs to greet each other according to the time of day.

Heritage Speakers Ask heritage speakers to mention other greetings and courtesy expressions that are used in their families' countries of origin. Have them indicate if the expressions are used in formal or informal situations, and write the phrases on the board in these categories. Then ask volunteers to state who in the **Contextos** illustration would use each expression.

1 Teaching Tip Before students listen, ask them to read through the items and write down the questions or statements they think would elicit those responses.

1 Script 1. a. ¿Cómo te llamas? 2. Te presento a Juan Pablo. 3. ¿De dónde es usted? 4. Muchas gracias. 5. Nos vemos. 6. ¿Qué pasa? 7. ¿Cómo está usted? 8. Buenas tardes, señor Fernández. 9. Susana, te presento al señor Ramírez. 10. ¿Qué tal?
Textbook MP3s

2 Teaching Tip To simplify, provide two categories for each item. Ex: 1. a. asking how you are; b. asking where you are from. Then, as students listen to the audio, have them write the letter of the appropriate category.

2 Script 1. a. ¿Qué tal? b. ¿Cómo estás? c. ¿De dónde eres? d. ¿Qué hay de nuevo? 2. a. De nada. b. Adiós. c. Hasta luego. d. Nos vemos mañana. 3. a. Mucho gusto. b. Lo siento. c. Encantada. d. El gusto es mío. 4. a. Buenos días. b. Hola. c. Bien, gracias. d. Buenas tardes.
Textbook MP3s

3 Expansion To challenge students, have them provide the question or statement that would elicit each item. Ex: **1. —Gracias. —De nada.**

4 Teaching Tip Have volunteers role-play the finished conversations for the class. Encourage students to add to the conversations by ad-libbing additional phrases they've learned in **Contextos**.

4 Expansion In small groups, ask students to write a new conversation and then to scramble the order of the dialogue. Have groups exchange papers and put the conversations in order.

5 Teaching Tip Have pairs share their responses with the class.

5 Expansion Have pairs or small groups create conversations that include the expressions used in **Actividad 5**. Ask volunteers to present their conversations to the class.

6 Teaching Tips
- Discuss the **modelo** before assigning the activity to pairs.
- After students have completed the activity, have pairs role-play the corrected mini-conversations. Ask them to substitute their own names and personal information where possible.
- Have volunteers write each mini-conversation on the board. Work as a class to identify and explain any errors.

¡Lengua viva! Have students locate examples of the titles in **Actividad 6**. Then ask them to create short sentences in which they use the titles with people they know.

5 **Completar** Work with a partner to complete these dialogues. Some answers will vary. Suggested answers:

modelo
Estudiante 1: ¿Cómo estás?
Estudiante 2: Muy bien, gracias.

1. **Estudiante 1:** Buenos días.
   Estudiante 2: Buenos días. ¿Qué tal?
2. **Estudiante 1:** ¿Cómo te llamas?
   Estudiante 2: Me llamo Carmen Sánchez.
3. **Estudiante 1:** ¿De dónde eres?
   Estudiante 2: De Canadá.
4. **Estudiante 1:** Te presento a Marisol.
   Estudiante 2: Encantado/a.
5. **Estudiante 1:** Gracias.
   Estudiante 2: De nada.
6. **Estudiante 1:** ¿Qué tal?
   Estudiante 2: Regular.
7. **Estudiante 1:** ¿Qué pasa?
   Estudiante 2: Nada.
8. **Estudiante 1:** ¡Hasta la vista!
   Estudiante 2: Answers will vary.

6 **Cambiar** Work with a partner and correct the second part of each conversation to make it logical. Answers will vary.

modelo
Estudiante 1: ¿Qué tal?
Estudiante 2: ~~No hay de qué.~~ Bien. ¿Y tú?

1. **Estudiante 1:** Hasta mañana, señora Ramírez. Saludos al señor Ramírez.
   Estudiante 2: *Muy bien, gracias.*
2. **Estudiante 1:** ¿Qué hay de nuevo, Alberto?
   Estudiante 2: *Sí, me llamo Alberto. ¿Cómo te llamas tú?*
3. **Estudiante 1:** Gracias, Tomás.
   Estudiante 2: *Regular. ¿Y tú?*
4. **Estudiante 1:** Miguel, te presento a la señorita Perales.
   Estudiante 2: *No hay de qué, señorita.*
5. **Estudiante 1:** ¿De dónde eres, Antonio?
   Estudiante 2: *Muy bien, gracias. ¿Y tú?*
6. **Estudiante 1:** ¿Cómo se llama usted?
   Estudiante 2: *El gusto es mío.*
7. **Estudiante 1:** ¿Qué pasa?
   Estudiante 2: *Hasta luego, Alicia.*
8. **Estudiante 1:** Buenas tardes, señor. ¿Cómo está usted?
   Estudiante 2: *Soy de Puerto Rico.*

¡LENGUA VIVA!

The titles **señor, señora**, and **señorita** are abbreviated **Sr., Sra.**, and **Srta.** Note that these abbreviations are capitalized, while the titles themselves are not.

•••

There is no Spanish equivalent for the English title *Ms.*; women are addressed as **señora** or **señorita.**

Practice more at **vhlcentral.com**.

TEACHING OPTIONS

Extra Practice Add an auditory exercise to this vocabulary practice. Read some phrases aloud and ask if students would use them with a person of the same age or someone older. Ex: **1. Te presento a Luis.** (same age) **2. ¿Cómo estás?** (same age) **3. Buenos días, doctor Soto.** (older) **4. ¿De dónde es usted, señora?** (older) **5. Chau, Teresa.** (same age) **6. No hay de qué, señor Perales.** (older)

Game Prepare a series of response statements using language in **Contextos**. Divide the class into two teams and invite students to guess the question or statement that would have elicited each of your responses. Read one statement at a time. The first team to correctly guess the question or statement earns a point. Ex: **Me llamo Lupe Torres Garza. (¿Cómo se llama usted? / ¿Cómo te llamas?)** The team with the most points at the end wins.

NATIONAL communication STANDARDS

Comunicación

7 **Diálogos** With a partner, complete and act out these conversations. Answers will vary.

Conversación 1

—Hola. Me llamo Teresa. ¿Cómo te llamas tú?

—______________________________

—Soy de Puerto Rico. ¿Y tú?

—______________________________

Conversación 2

—______________________________

—Muy bien, gracias. ¿Y usted, señora López?

—______________________________

—Hasta luego, señora. Saludos al señor López.

—______________________________

Conversación 3

—______________________________

—Regular. ¿Y tú?

—______________________________

—Nada.

8 **Conversaciones** This is the first day of class. Write four short conversations based on what the people in this scene would say. Answers will vary.

9 **Situaciones** In groups of three, write and act out these situations. Answers will vary.

1. On your way out of class on the first day of school, you strike up a conversation with the two students who were sitting next to you. You find out each student's name and where he or she is from before you say goodbye and go to your next class.
2. At the next class you meet up with a friend and find out how he or she is doing. As you are talking, your friend Elena enters. Introduce her to your friend.
3. As you're leaving the bookstore, you meet your parents' friends Mrs. Sánchez and Mr. Rodríguez. You greet them and ask how each person is. As you say goodbye, you send greetings to Mrs. Rodríguez.
4. Make up and act out a real-life situation that you and your classmates can role-play with the language you've learned.

7 Expansion

- Have students work in small groups to write a few mini-conversations modeled on this activity. Then ask them to copy the dialogues, omitting a few words or phrases. Have groups exchange papers and fill in the blanks.
- Have students rewrite **Conversaciones 1** and **3** in the formal register and **Conversación 2** in the informal register.

8 Teaching Tip To simplify, have students brainstorm who the people in the illustration are and what they are talking about. Ask students which groups would be speaking to each other in the **usted** form, and which would be using the **tú** form.

8 Expansion
In pairs, have students take turns selecting a person from the drawing and providing 2-3 statements that he or she might be saying. The partner will try to guess who it is.

9 Teaching Tip
To challenge students, have each group pick a situation to write and perform. Tell groups not to memorize every word of the conversation, but rather to re-create it.

The Affective Dimension
Have students rehearse the situations a few times, so that they will feel more comfortable with the material and less anxious when presenting it before the class.

TEACHING OPTIONS

Extra Practice Have students circulate around the classroom and conduct unrehearsed mini-conversations in Spanish with other students, using the words and expressions that they learned on pages 2–3. Monitor students' work and offer assistance if requested.

Heritage Speakers Ask heritage speakers to role-play some of the conversations and situations in these **Comunicación** activities, modeling correct pronunciation and intonation for the class. Remind students that, just as in English, there are regional differences in the way Spanish is pronounced. Help clarify unfamiliar vocabulary as necessary.

Section Goals

In **Fotonovela**, students will:

- receive comprehensible input from free-flowing discourse
- learn functional phrases that preview lesson grammatical structures

Instructional Resources
Supersite: Video (***Fotonovela***); Resources (Scripts, Translations, Answer Keys)
WebSAM
Video Manual, pp. 1–2

Video Synopsis **Marissa,** an American college student, arrives in Mexico City for a year abroad. She meets her Mexican hosts, **Carolina** and **Roberto Díaz**, and their doorman, **Don Diego**. As **Marissa** unpacks, the **Díaz** children, **Felipe** and **Jimena**, take away her English-Spanish dictionary as a joke. **Marissa** accepts the challenge and leaves the dictionary with **Carolina**.

Teaching Tips

- In small groups, have students cover the captions and guess the plot based on the video stills. Write their predictions on the board. After students have watched the video, compare their predictions to what actually happened in the episode.
- Point out that **don** is a title of respect and neither equivalent nor related to the English name *Don*. Ask if students think **Diego** is the doorman's first or last name. (It is his first name.) Students will learn more about the titles **don** and **doña** on page 8.
- Tell students that all items in **Expresiones útiles** on page 7 are active vocabulary. Model the pronunciation of each item and have the class repeat.
- You can also practice the **Expresiones útiles** by using them in short conversations with individual students.

Bienvenida, Marissa

NATIONAL STANDARDS communication cultures

Marissa llega a México para pasar un año con la familia Díaz.

PERSONAJES

MARISSA

SRA. DÍAZ

Video: *Fotonovela*

MARISSA ¿Usted es de Cuba?
SRA. DÍAZ Sí, de La Habana. Y Roberto es de Mérida. Tú eres de Wisconsin, ¿verdad?
MARISSA Sí, de Appleton, Wisconsin.

MARISSA ¿Quiénes son los dos chicos de las fotos? ¿Jimena y Felipe?
SRA. DÍAZ Sí. Ellos son estudiantes.

DON DIEGO Buenas tardes, señora. Señorita, bienvenida a la Ciudad de México.
MARISSA ¡Muchas gracias!

MARISSA ¿Cómo se llama usted?
DON DIEGO Yo soy Diego. Mucho gusto.
MARISSA El gusto es mío, don Diego.

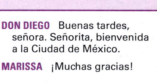

DON DIEGO ¿Cómo está usted hoy, señora Carolina?
SRA. DÍAZ Muy bien, gracias. ¿Y usted?
DON DIEGO Bien, gracias.

SRA. DÍAZ Ahí hay dos maletas. Son de Marissa.
DON DIEGO Con permiso.

TEACHING OPTIONS

Video Tips General suggestions for using video clips in the classroom can be found in the front matter of this Instructor's Annotated Edition.

Bienvenida, Marissa Have students make a three-column chart with these headings: *Greetings, Self-Identification,* and *Courtesy Expressions.* Have students suggest two or three possible phrases for each category. Then play the **Bienvenida, Marissa** episode once and ask students to fill in the first column with the basic greetings that they hear. Repeat this process for the second column, where they should list the expressions the characters use to identify themselves. Play the video a third time for students to jot down courtesy expressions, such as ways to say "pleased to meet you" and "pardon me."

DON DIEGO

SR. DÍAZ

FELIPE

JIMENA

7

SR. DÍAZ ¿Qué hora es?

FELIPE Son las cuatro y veinticinco.

8

SRA. DÍAZ Marissa, te presento a Roberto, mi esposo.

SR. DÍAZ Bienvenida, Marissa.

MARISSA Gracias, señor Díaz.

9

JIMENA ¿Qué hay en esta cosa?

MARISSA Bueno, a ver, hay tres cuadernos, un mapa... ¡Y un diccionario!

JIMENA ¿Cómo se dice mediodía en inglés?

FELIPE *"Noon".*

10

FELIPE Estás en México, ¿verdad?

MARISSA ¿Sí?

FELIPE Nosotros somos tu diccionario.

recursos

VM pp. 1-2

vhlcentral.com Lección 1

Expresiones útiles

Identifying yourself and others

¿Cómo se llama usted?
What's your name?
Yo soy Diego, el portero. Mucho gusto.
I'm Diego, the doorman. Nice to meet you.
¿Cómo te llamas?
What's your name?
Me llamo Marissa.
My name is Marissa.
¿Quién es...? / ¿Quiénes son...?
Who is...? / Who are...?
Es mi esposo.
He's my husband.
Tú eres..., ¿verdad?/¿cierto?/¿no?
You are..., right?

Identifying objects

¿Qué hay en esta cosa?
What's in this thing?
Bueno, a ver, aquí hay tres cuadernos...
Well, let's see, here are three notebooks...
Oye/Oiga, ¿cómo se dice *suitcase* en español?
Hey, how do you say suitcase *in Spanish?*
Se dice *maleta*.
You say maleta.

Saying what time it is

¿Qué hora es?
What time is it?
Es la una. / Son las dos.
It's one o'clock. / It's two o'clock.
Son las cuatro y veinticinco.
It's four twenty-five.

Polite expressions

Con permiso.
Pardon me; Excuse me. (to request permission)
Perdón.
Pardon me; Excuse me. (to get someone's attention or excuse yourself)
¡Bienvenido/a! *Welcome!*

Expresiones útiles Identify forms of the verb **ser** and point out some subject pronouns. Identify time-telling expressions. Point out the verb form **hay** and explain that it means *there is/are*. Tell students that they will learn more about these concepts in **Estructura.**

Teaching Tip Have volunteers read individual parts of the **Fotonovela** captions aloud. Then have students work in groups of six to role-play the episode, ad-libbing when possible. Have one or two groups present the episode to the class.

Successful Language Learning Tell students that their conversational skills will grow more quickly as they learn each lesson's **Expresiones útiles.** This feature is designed to teach phrases that will be useful in conversation, and it will also help students understand key phrases in each **Fotonovela**.

Nota cultural Mexico City's metropolitan area is the largest in the hemisphere, with about 21 million people. This number is still only a fraction of Mexico's total population of 118 million. It is the most highly populated Spanish-speaking country in the world.

TEACHING OPTIONS

Extra Practice Photocopy pages 6–7 or the **Fotonovela** Videoscript (Supersite) and white out some key words. Play the episode once, and then distribute the photocopied scripts. Play the video a second time and ask students to fill in the missing words. Go over the answers as a class.

Extra Practice Write questions and phrases from **Expresiones útiles** on the board. Ex: **Es la una. Con permiso. ¿Cómo te llamas?** With their books closed, have students describe a context in which each question or phrase could be used.

Pairs In pairs, have students predict whom **Marissa** will get along with better: **Felipe** or **Jimena**. Have them support their opinions with specific scenes from the episode.

1 Expansion Give students these true/false statements as items 8–10: **8. En la mochila de Marissa hay una foto de Jimena y Felipe. (Cierto.) 9. No hay cuadernos en la mochila de Marissa. (Falso.) 10. Hay cuatro personas en la familia Díaz. (Cierto.)**

2 Expansion Ask volunteers to call out additional statements that were made in the **Fotonovela**. The class should guess which character made each statement.

¡Lengua viva! Ask students how they might address **Sr. Díaz (don Roberto).**

Nota cultural **Señor(a)** and **señorita** may also be used with a person's first name as a sign of respect. Using these titles with a first name also shows a greater level of intimacy or warmth; **señor Díaz** sounds more formal than **señor Roberto.**

3 Teaching Tip Go over the activity by asking volunteers to take the roles of **don Diego** and **Marissa.**

4 Teaching Tip To simplify, ask students to read through the cues and jot down possible phrases for each one.

4 Possible Conversation
E1: Buenas tardes. ¿Cómo te llamas?
E2: Hola. Me llamo Felipe. Y tú, ¿cómo te llamas?
E1: Me llamo Luisa. Mucho gusto.
E2: El gusto es mío.
E1: ¿Cómo estás?
E2: Bien, gracias.
E1: ¿De dónde eres?
E2: Soy de Venezuela.
E2: ¡Uf! Es la una. ¡Adiós!
E2: Chau.

The Affective Dimension
Point out that many people feel nervous when speaking in front of a group. Encourage students to think of anxious feelings as extra energy that will help them accomplish their goals.

¿Qué pasó?

1 **¿Cierto o falso?** Indicate if each statement is **cierto** or **falso**. Then correct the false statements.

	Cierto	Falso	
1. La Sra. Díaz es de Caracas.	❍	✔	La Sra. Díaz es de La Habana.
2. El Sr. Díaz es de Mérida.	✔	❍	
3. Marissa es de Los Ángeles, California.	❍	✔	Marissa es de Appleton, Wisconsin.
4. Jimena y Felipe son profesores.	❍	✔	Jimena y Felipe son estudiantes.
5. Las dos maletas son de Jimena.	❍	✔	Las dos maletas son de Marissa.
6. El Sr. Díaz pregunta "¿qué hora es?".	✔	❍	
7. Hay un diccionario en la mochila (*backpack*) de Marissa.	✔	❍	

2 **Identificar** Indicate which person would make each statement. One name will be used twice.

1. Son las cuatro y veinticinco, papá. Felipe
2. Roberto es mi esposo. Sra. Díaz
3. Yo soy de Wisconsin, ¿de dónde es usted? Marissa
4. ¿Qué hay de nuevo, doña Carolina? don Diego
5. Yo soy de Cuba. Sra. Díaz
6. ¿Qué hay en la mochila, Marissa? Jimena

MARISSA

FELIPE

SRA. DÍAZ

DON DIEGO

JIMENA

¡LENGUA VIVA!
In Spanish-speaking countries, **don** and **doña** are used with first names to show respect: **don Diego, doña Carolina**. Note that these titles, like **señor** and **señora**, are not capitalized.

3 **Completar** Complete the conversation between Don Diego and Marissa.

DON DIEGO Hola, (1) señorita.
MARISSA Hola, señor. ¿Cómo se (2) llama usted?
DON DIEGO Yo me llamo Diego, ¿y (3) usted?
MARISSA Yo me llamo Marissa. (4) Encantada.
DON DIEGO (5) Igualmente, señorita Marissa.
MARISSA Nos (6) vemos, don Diego.
DON DIEGO Hasta (7) luego/pronto/la vista, señorita Marissa.

4 **Conversar** Imagine that you are chatting with a traveler you just met at the airport. With a partner, prepare a conversation using these cues. Some answers will vary.

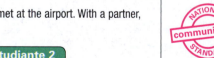

NATIONAL communication STANDARDS

Estudiante 1	Estudiante 2
Say "good afternoon" to your partner and ask for his or her name.	Say hello and what your name is. Then ask what your partner's name is.
Say what your name is and that you are glad to meet your partner.	Say that the pleasure is yours.
Ask how your partner is.	Say that you're doing well, thank you.
Ask where your partner is from.	Say where you're from.
Say it's one o'clock and say goodbye.	Say goodbye.

Practice more at **vhlcentral.com.**

TEACHING OPTIONS

Small Groups Ask students to work in small groups to ad-lib the exchanges between **Marissa** and **Sra. Díaz, Marissa** and **don Diego,** and **Marissa, Felipe,** and **Jimena.** Tell them to convey the general meaning using vocabulary and expressions they know, and assure them that they do not have to stick to the original dialogues word for word. Then, ask volunteers to present their exchanges to the class.

Extra Practice Choose four or five lines of the **Fotonovela** to use as a dictation. Read the lines twice slowly to give students sufficient time to write. Then read them again at normal speed to allow students to correct any errors or fill in any gaps. You may have students correct their own work by checking it against the **Fotonovela** text and ask follow-up questions to test comprehension.

Pronunciación

Audio

The Spanish alphabet

The Spanish and English alphabets are almost identical, with a few exceptions. For example, the Spanish letter **ñ (eñe)** doesn't occur in the English alphabet. Furthermore, the letters **k (ka)** and **w (doble ve)** are used only in words of foreign origin. Examine the chart below to find other differences.

Letra	Nombre(s)	Ejemplos	Letra	Nombre(s)	Ejemplos
a	a	adiós	m	eme	mapa
b	be	bien, problema	n	ene	nacionalidad
c	ce	cosa, cero	ñ	eñe	mañana
ch	che	chico	o	o	once
d	de	diario, nada	p	pe	profesor
e	e	estudiante	q	cu	qué
f	efe	foto	r	ere	regular, señora
g	ge	gracias, Gerardo, regular	s	ese	señor
h	hache	hola	t	te	tú
i	i	igualmente	u	u	usted
j	jota	Javier	v	ve	vista, nuevo
k	ka, ca	kilómetro	w	doble ve	*walkman*
l	ele	lápiz	x	equis	existir, México
ll	elle	llave	y	i griega, ye	yo
			z	zeta, ceta	zona

El alfabeto Repeat the Spanish alphabet and example words after your instructor.

Práctica Spell these words aloud in Spanish.

1. nada
2. maleta
3. quince
4. muy
5. hombre
6. por favor
7. San Fernando
8. Estados Unidos
9. Puerto Rico
10. España
11. Javier
12. Ecuador
13. Maite
14. gracias
15. Nueva York

Refranes Read these sayings aloud

Ver es creer.[1]
En boca cerrada no entran moscas.[2]

[1] Seeing is believing.
[2] Silence is golden.

recursos
LM p. 2
vhlcentral.com Lección 1

NATIONAL comparisons STANDARDS

¡LENGUA VIVA!

Note that **ch** and **ll** are digraphs, or two letters that together produce one sound. Conventionally they have been considered part of the alphabet, but **ch** and **ll** do not have their own entries when placing words in alphabetical order, as in a glossary.

AYUDA

The letter combination **rr** produces a strong trilled sound which does not have an English equivalent. English speakers commonly make this sound when imitating the sound of a motor. This sound occurs with the **rr** between vowels and with the **r** at the beginning of a word: **puertorriqueño, terrible, Roberto,** etc. See **Lección 7**, p. 217, for more information.

Section Goals

In **Pronunciación**, students will be introduced to:
- the Spanish alphabet
- the names of the letters

Instructional Resources
Supersite: Audio (Textbook and Lab MP3 Files); Resources (Scripts, Answer Keys)
WebSAM
Lab Manual, p. 2

Teaching Tip Point out that the **Real Academia Española** has decided that **ch** and **ll** are no longer letters. In 2010 the **Real Academia** recommended the use of a unified naming convention for the alphabet. The suggested names for **r, v, w,** and **y** are **erre, uve, doble uve,** and **ye.** However, most Spanish speakers tend to use the traditional naming conventions followed in their countries.

TEACHING OPTIONS

Extra Practice Do a dictation activity in which you spell aloud Spanish words (e.g., world capitals and countries). Spell each word twice to allow students sufficient time to write. After you have finished, write your list on the board or project it on a transparency and have students check their work. You can also have students spell their names in Spanish.

Extra Practice Here are four additional **refranes** to practice the alphabet: **De tal palo, tal astilla** (*A chip off the old block*); **Los ojos son el espejo del alma** (*Eyes are the window to the soul*); **El rayo nunca cae dos veces en el mismo lugar** (*Lightning never strikes twice in the same place*); **No dejes para mañana lo que puedas hacer hoy** (*Don't put off until tomorrow what you can do today*).

Flash CULTURA

Section Goals

In **Cultura**, students will:
- read about greetings in Spanish-speaking countries
- learn informal greetings and leave-takings
- read about the **plaza principal**
- read about famous friends and couples

Instructional Resources
Supersite: Video (***Flash cultura***); Resources (Scripts, Translations, Answer Keys)
WebSAM
Video Manual, pp. 73–74

En detalle

Antes de leer Ask students to share how they would normally greet a friend or family member.

Lectura
- Linguists have determined that, in the U.S., friends generally remain at least eighteen inches apart while chatting. Hispanic friends would probably deem eighteen inches to be excessive.
- Show students the locations mentioned here by referring them to the maps in their textbooks. Explain that there may be regional variations within each country.
- Explain that an "air kiss" is limited to a grazing of cheeks.

Después de leer Call on two volunteers to stand in front of the class. Point out the natural distance between them. Then demonstrate reduced personal space in Hispanic cultures by having the volunteers face each other with their toes touching and start a conversation. Tell the rest of the class to do the same. Ask students to share their feelings on this change in personal space.

1 Expansion Ask students to write three more true/false statements for a classmate to complete.

EN DETALLE

Video: *Flash cultura*

NATIONAL STANDARDS connections cultures

Saludos y besos en los países hispanos

In Spanish-speaking countries, kissing on the cheek is a customary way to greet friends and family members. Even when people are introduced for the first time, it is common for them to kiss, particularly in non-business settings. Whereas North Americans maintain considerable personal space when greeting, Spaniards and Latin Americans tend to decrease their personal space and give one or two kisses (**besos**) on the cheek, sometimes accompanied by a handshake or a hug. In formal business settings, where associates do not know one another on a personal level, a simple handshake is appropriate.

Greeting someone with a **beso** varies according to gender and region. Men generally greet each other with a hug or warm handshake, with the exception of Argentina, where male friends and relatives lightly kiss on the cheek. Greetings between men and women, and between women, generally include kissing, but can differ depending on the country and context. In Spain, it is customary to give **dos besos**, starting with the right cheek first. In Latin American countries, including Mexico, Costa Rica, Colombia, and Chile, a greeting consists of a single "air kiss" on the right cheek. Peruvians also "air kiss," but strangers will simply shake hands. In Colombia, female acquaintances tend to simply pat each other on the right forearm or shoulder.

Tendencias

País	Beso	País	Beso
Argentina	💋	España	💋💋
Bolivia	💋	México	💋
Chile	💋	Paraguay	💋💋
Colombia	💋	Puerto Rico	💋
El Salvador	💋	Venezuela	💋/💋💋

ACTIVIDADES

1 **¿Cierto o falso?** Indicate whether these statements are true (**cierto**) or false (**falso**). Correct the false statements.

1. Hispanic people use less personal space when greeting than in the U.S. Cierto.
2. Men never greet with a kiss in Spanish-speaking countries. Falso. Argentine men can greet with a light kiss
3. Shaking hands is not appropriate for a business setting in Latin America. Falso. In most business settings, people greet one another by shaking hands.
4. Spaniards greet with one kiss on the right cheek. Falso. They greet with one kiss on each cheek.
5. In Mexico, people greet with an "air kiss." Cierto.
6. Gender can play a role in the type of greeting given. Cierto.
7. If two women acquaintances meet in Colombia, they should exchange two kisses on the cheek. Falso. They pat one another on the right forearm or shoulder.
8. In Peru, a man and a woman meeting for the fi rst time would probably greet each other with an "air kiss." Falso. They would probably shake hands.

TEACHING OPTIONS

Game Divide the class into two teams. Give situations in which people greet one another, and have one member from each team identify the appropriate way to greet. Ex: Two male friends in Argentina. (light kiss on the cheek) Give one point for each correct answer. The team with the most points at the end wins.

Un beso Kisses are not only a form of greeting in Hispanic cultures. It is also common to end phone conversations and close letters or e-mails with the words **un beso** or **besos**. Additionally, friends may use **un abrazo** to end a written message. In a more formal e-mail, one can write **un saludo (cordial)** or **saludos**.

ASÍ SE DICE

Saludos y despedidas

¿Cómo te/le va?	*How are things going (for you)?*
¡Cuánto tiempo!	*It's been a long time!*
Hasta ahora.	*See you soon.*
¿Qué hay?	*What's new?*
¿Qué onda? (Méx., Arg., Chi.); ¿Qué más? (Ven., Col.)	*What's going on?*

EL MUNDO HISPANO

Parejas y amigos famosos

Here are some famous couples and friends from the Spanish-speaking world.

- **Penélope Cruz** (España) y **Javier Bardem** (España) Both Oscar-winning actors, the couple married in 2010. They starred together in ***Vicky Cristina Barcelona*** (2008).
- **Gael García Bernal** (México) y **Diego Luna** (México) These lifelong friends became famous when they starred in the 2001 Mexican film ***Y tu mamá también***. They continue to work together on projects, such as the 2012 film ***Casa de mi padre***.
- **Salma Hayek** (México) y **Penélope Cruz** (España) These two close friends developed their acting skills in their home countries before meeting in Hollywood.

PERFIL

La plaza principal

In the Spanish-speaking world, public space is treasured. Small city and town life revolves around the **plaza principal**. Often surrounded by cathedrals or municipal buildings like the **ayuntamiento** (*city hall*), the pedestrian **plaza** is designated as a central meeting place for family and friends. During warmer months, when outdoor cafés usually line the **plaza**, it is a popular spot to have a leisurely cup of coffee, chat, and people watch. Many town festivals, or **ferias**, also take place in this space. One of the most famous town squares is the **Plaza Mayor** in the university town of Salamanca, Spain. Students gather underneath its famous clock tower to meet up with friends or simply take a coffee break.

La Plaza Mayor de Salamanca

La Plaza de Armas, Lima, Perú

Conexión Internet

What are the plazas principales in large cities such as Mexico City and Caracas?

Go to vhlcentral.com to find more cultural information related to this Cultura section.

ACTIVIDADES

2 Comprensión Answer these questions. Some answers may vary. Suggested answers:

1. What are two types of buildings found on the **plaza principal?** municipal buildings and cathedrals
2. What two types of events or activities are common at a **plaza principal?** meeting with friends and festivals
3. How would Diego Luna greet his friends? ¿Qué onda?
4. Would Salma Hayek and Gael García Bernal greet each other with one kiss or two? one

3 Saludos Role-play these greetings with a partner. Include a verbal greeting as well as a kiss or handshake, as appropriate. Role-plays will vary according to student gender.

1. friends in Mexico
2. business associates at a conference in Chile
3. friends meeting in Madrid's Plaza Mayor
4. Peruvians meeting for the first time
5. relatives in Argentina

Practice more at **vhlcentral.com**.

recursos: VM pp. 73–74; vhlcentral.com Lección 1

Así se dice
- Ask students to identify situations in which these expressions can be used.
- To challenge students, add these phrases to the list: **Hasta siempre** (*Farewell*), **Que te/le vaya bien** (*Have a nice day/time*).
- Explain that greetings frequently are pronounced in a shortened way. Ex: **Hasta ahora** → **Stahora**.

Perfil
- Construction on Salamanca's **Plaza Mayor** began in 1729, led by **Alberto Churriguera**. Silhouettes of prominent Spaniards are carved between the stone arches that border the square. City Hall is situated at the north end of the plaza.
- Lima's **Plaza de Armas** is flanked on three sides by three-story arcades. On the east end of the square lies the massive **Catedral**, begun in 1535.

El mundo hispano
Have pairs choose any two people from **El mundo hispano**. Ask them to write a brief dialogue in which they meet for the first time. Encourage them to use phrases from **Así se dice**. Have volunteers role-play their dialogues for the class.

2 Expansion Ask students to write two additional questions for a classmate to answer.

3 Teaching Tip Before beginning this activity, ask students if they would use **tú** or **usted** in each situation.

TEACHING OPTIONS

Cultural Activity For homework, have students use the Internet to research a famous **plaza principal** in a Spanish-speaking city or town. They should find out the **plaza**'s location in the city, when it was built, current uses, and other significant information. Encourage them to bring in a photo. Then have the students present their findings to the class.

Heritage Speakers Ask heritage speakers to describe cities and towns from their families' countries of origin. Is there a **plaza principal**? How is it used? Ask the class to think of analogous public spaces in the U.S. (Ex: a common or "town green" in small New England towns)

Section Goals

In **Estructura 1.1**, students will be introduced to:

- gender of nouns
- definite and indefinite articles

Instructional Resources
Supersite: Audio (Lab MP3 Files); Resources (Grammar Presentation Slides, Activity Pack, Scripts, Answer Keys); Testing Program (Quizzes)
WebSAM
Workbook, p. 3
Lab Manual, p. 3

Teaching Tips

- Write these nouns from the **Fotonovela** on the board: **chicos, diccionario, estudiantes, maleta.** Ask volunteers what each means. Point out the different endings and introduce grammatical gender in Spanish. Explain what a noun is and give examples of people (**chicos**), places (**universidad**), things (**documentos**), and ideas (**nacionalidad**). Ask volunteers to point out which of these nouns are singular or plural and why.
- Point out that while nouns for male beings are generally masculine and those for female beings are generally feminine, grammatical gender does not necessarily correspond to the actual gender of the being.
- Point out patterns of noun endings **–o, –a; –or, –ora.** Stress that **–ista** can refer to males or females, and give additional examples: **el/la artista, el/la dentista.**

1.1 Nouns and articles

Tutorial

NATIONAL STANDARDS comparisons

Spanish nouns

ANTE TODO A noun is a word used to identify people, animals, places, things, or ideas. Unlike English, all Spanish nouns, even those that refer to non-living things, have gender; that is, they are considered either masculine or feminine. As in English, nouns in Spanish also have number, meaning that they are either singular or plural.

Nouns that refer to living things

Masculine nouns		Feminine nouns	
el hombre	*the man*	**la mujer**	*the woman*
ending in *–o*		ending in *–a*	
el chico	*the boy*	**la chica**	*the girl*
el pasajero	*the (male) passenger*	**la pasajera**	*the (female) passenger*
ending in *–or*		ending in *–ora*	
el conductor	*the (male) driver*	**la conductora**	*the (female) driver*
el profesor	*the (male) teacher*	**la profesora**	*the (female) teacher*
ending in *–ista*		ending in *–ista*	
el turista	*the (male) tourist*	**la turista**	*the (female) tourist*

- Generally, nouns that refer to males, like **el hombre**, are masculine, while nouns that refer to females, like **la mujer**, are feminine.
- Many nouns that refer to male beings end in **–o** or **–or**. Their corresponding feminine forms end in **–a** and **–ora**, respectively.

el conductor

la profesora

- The masculine and feminine forms of nouns that end in **–ista**, like **turista**, are the same, so gender is indicated by the article **el** (masculine) or **la** (feminine). Some other nouns have identical masculine and feminine forms.

el joven
the young man

la joven
the young woman

el estudiante
the (male) student

la estudiante
the (female) student

¡LENGUA VIVA!

Profesor(a) and **turista** are *cognates*— words that share similar spellings and meanings in Spanish and English. Recognizing cognates will help you determine the meaning of many Spanish words. Here are some other cognates: **la administración, el animal, el apartamento, el cálculo, el color, la decisión, la historia, la música, el restaurante, el/la secretario/a.**

AYUDA

Cognates can certainly be very helpful in your study of Spanish. Beware, however, of "false" cognates, those that have similar spellings in Spanish and English, but different meanings:

la carpeta *folder*
el/la conductor(a) *driver*
el éxito *success*
la fábrica *factory*

TEACHING OPTIONS

Extra Practice Write ten singular nouns on the board. Make sure the nouns represent a mix of the different types of noun endings. In a rapid-response drill, call on students to give the appropriate gender. For **–ista** words, accept either masculine or feminine, but clarify that both are used. You may also do this as a completely oral drill by not writing the words on the board.

Game Divide the class into teams of three or four. Bring in photos or magazine pictures showing objects or people. Hold up each photo and say the Spanish noun without the article. Call on teams to indicate the noun's gender. Give one point for each correct answer. Deduct one point for each incorrect answer. The team with the most points at the end wins.

Nouns that refer to non-living things

Masculine nouns		Feminine nouns	
ending in –o		**ending in –a**	
el cuaderno	*the notebook*	**la computadora**	*the computer*
el diario	*the diary*	**la cosa**	*the thing*
el diccionario	*the dictionary*	**la escuela**	*the school*
el número	*the number*	**la maleta**	*the suitcase*
el video	*the video*	**la palabra**	*the word*
ending in –ma		**ending in –ción**	
el problema	*the problem*	**la lección**	*the lesson*
el programa	*the program*	**la conversación**	*the conversation*
ending in –s		**ending in –dad**	
el autobús	*the bus*	**la nacionalidad**	*the nationality*
el país	*the country*	**la comunidad**	*the community*

¡LENGUA VIVA!
The Spanish word for *video* can be pronounced with the stress on the **i** or the **e**. For that reason, you might see the word written with or without an accent: **video** or **vídeo**.

- As shown above, certain noun endings are strongly associated with a specific gender, so you can use them to determine if a noun is masculine or feminine.
- Because the gender of nouns that refer to non-living things cannot be determined by foolproof rules, you should memorize the gender of each noun you learn. It is helpful to learn each noun with its corresponding article, **el** for masculine and **la** for feminine.
- Another reason to memorize the gender of every noun is that there are common exceptions to the rules of gender. For example, **el mapa** (*map*) and **el día** (*day*) end in **–a**, but are masculine. **La mano** (*hand*) ends in **–o**, but is feminine.

Plural of nouns

- To form the plural, add **–s** to nouns that end in a vowel. For nouns that end in a consonant, add **–es**. For nouns that end in **z**, change the **z** to **c**, then add **–es**.

el chic**o** → los chic**os**
el diari**o** → los diari**os**
el problem**a** → los problem**as**
la nacionalida**d** → las nacionalida**des**
el paí**s** → los paí**ses**
el lápi**z** (*pencil*) → los lápi**ces**

CONSULTA
You will learn more about accent marks in **Lección 4, Pronunciación**, p. 115.

- In general, when a singular noun has an accent mark on the last syllable, the accent is dropped from the plural form.

la lecci**ón** → las lecci**ones**
el autob**ús** → los autob**uses**

- Use the masculine plural form to refer to a group that includes both males and females.

1 pasajer**o** + 2 pasajer**as** = 3 pasajer**os**
2 chic**os** + 2 chic**as** = 4 chic**os**

Teaching Tips

- Work through the list of nouns, modeling their pronunciation. Point out patterns of gender, including word endings **–ma**, **–ción**, and **–dad**. Give cognate nouns with these endings and ask students to indicate the gender. Ex: **diagrama, acción, personalidad**. Point out common exceptions to gender agreement rules for **el mapa**, **el día**, and **la mano**.
- Stress the addition of **–s** to nouns that end in vowels and **–es** to nouns that end in consonants. Write ten nouns on the board and ask volunteers to give the plural forms, along with the appropriate articles.
- Point to three male students and ask if the group is **los** or **las estudiantes** (**los**). Next, point to three female students and ask the same question (**las**). Then indicate a group of males and females and ask for the correct term to refer to them (**los estudiantes**). Stress that even if a group contains 100 women and one man, the masculine plural form and article are used.
- Point out that words like **lección** and **autobús** lose the written accent in the plural form in order to keep the stress on the same syllable as in the singular noun.

The Affective Dimension

Tell students that many people feel anxious when learning grammar. Tell them that grammar will seem less intimidating if they think of it as a description of how the language works instead of a list of strict rules.

TEACHING OPTIONS

TPR Give four students each a card with a different definite article. Give the other students each a card with a noun (include a mix of masculine, feminine, singular, and plural). Have students form a circle; each student's card should be visible to others. Call out one of the nouns; that student must step forward. The student with the corresponding article has five seconds to join the noun student.

Game Divide the class into two teams, A and B. Point to a member of team A and say a singular noun. The student repeats the noun with the definite article, and then spells it. Then point to a team B member, who will supply the plural form and spell it. Award one point per correct answer and deduct one point for each wrong answer. Make sure to give each team a variety of both plural and singular nouns. The team with the most points wins.

Teaching Tips

- Write **¿El, la, los o las?** on the board and ask students to identify the correct definite article for these words: **1. hombre (el) 2. computadora (la) 3. profesor (el) 4. universidades (las) 5. turistas (los/las) 6. diccionario (el) 7. problema (el) 8. mujeres (las)**
- Write **¿Un, una, unos o unas?** on the board and ask students to identify the correct indefinite article for these words. **1. pasajeros (unos) 2. chico (un) 3. escuela (una) 4. lecciones (unas) 5. autobuses (unos) 6. maleta (una) 7. programas (unos) 8. cosa (una)**
- Do a pair of conversion activities. Students respond with the article and the noun: **Definido → Indefinido 1. los turistas (unos turistas) 2. la computadora (una computadora) 3. el hombre (un hombre) 4. las mujeres (unas mujeres) 5. el programa (un programa) Indefinido → Definido 1. unas lecciones (las lecciones) 2. una maleta (la maleta) 3. unos lápices (los lápices) 4. unas pasajeras (las pasajeras) 5. un diario (el diario)**

Spanish articles

ANTE TODO As you know, English often uses definite articles (*the*) and indefinite articles (*a, an*) before nouns. Spanish also has definite and indefinite articles. Unlike English, Spanish articles vary in form because they agree in gender and number with the nouns they modify.

Definite articles

▶ Spanish has four forms that are equivalent to the English definite article *the*. Use definite articles to refer to specific nouns.

Masculine

SINGULAR

el diccionario
the dictionary

PLURAL

los diccionarios
the dictionaries

Feminine

SINGULAR

la computadora
the computer

PLURAL

las computadoras
the computers

Indefinite articles

▶ Spanish has four forms that are equivalent to the English indefinite article, which according to context may mean *a*, *an*, or *some*. Use indefinite articles to refer to unspecified persons or things.

Masculine

SINGULAR

un pasajero
a (one) passenger

PLURAL

unos pasajeros
some passengers

Feminine

SINGULAR

una fotografía
a (one) photograph

PLURAL

unas fotografías
some photographs

¡LENGUA VIVA!

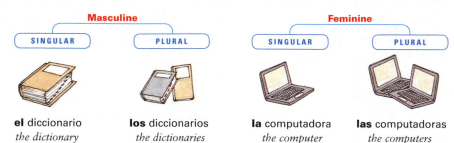

Feminine singular nouns that begin with a stressed **a-** or **ha-** require the masculine articles **el** and **un**. This is done in order to avoid repetition of the **a** sound. The plural forms still use the feminine articles.

el agua *water*
las aguas *waters*
un hacha *ax*
unas hachas *axes*

¡LENGUA VIVA!

Since **la fotografía** is feminine, so is its shortened form, **la foto**, even though it ends in **–o**.

¡INTÉNTALO! Provide a definite article for each noun in the first column and an indefinite article for each noun in the second column.

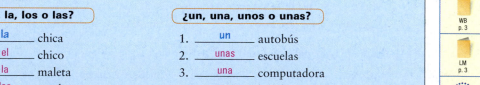

¿el, la, los o las?	¿un, una, unos o unas?
1. __la__ chica	1. __un__ autobús
2. __el__ chico	2. __unas__ escuelas
3. __la__ maleta	3. __una__ computadora
4. __los__ cuadernos	4. __unos__ hombres
5. __el__ lápiz	5. __una__ señora
6. __las__ mujeres	6. __unos__ lápices

recursos
WB p. 3
LM p. 3
vhlcentral.com Lección 1

TEACHING OPTIONS

Extra Practice Add a visual aspect to this grammar practice. Hold up or point to objects whose names students are familiar with (Ex: **diccionario, lápiz, computadora, foto[grafía]**). Ask students to indicate the appropriate definite article and the noun. Include a mix of singular and plural nouns. Repeat the exercise with indefinite articles.

Pairs Have pairs jot down a mix of ten singular and plural nouns, without their articles. Have them exchange their lists with another pair. Each pair then has to write down the appropriate definite and indefinite articles for each item. After pairs have finished, have them exchange lists and correct them.

Práctica

1 **¿Singular o plural?** If the word is singular, make it plural. If it is plural, make it singular.

1. el número los números
2. un diario unos diarios
3. la estudiante las estudiantes
4. el conductor los conductores
5. el país los países
6. las cosas la cosa
7. unos turistas un turista
8. las nacionalidades la nacionalidad
9. unas computadoras una computadora
10. los problemas el problema
11. una fotografía unas fotografías
12. los profesores el profesor
13. unas señoritas una señorita
14. el hombre los hombres
15. la maleta las maletas
16. la señora las señoras

2 **Identificar** For each drawing, provide the noun with its corresponding definite and indefinite articles.

modelo
las maletas, unas maletas

1. la computadora, una computadora

2. los cuadernos, unos cuadernos

3. las mujeres, unas mujeres

4. el chico, un chico

5. la escuela, una escuela

6. las fotos, unas fotos

7. los autobuses, unos autobuses

8. el diario, un diario

NATIONAL communication STANDARDS

Comunicación

3 **Charadas** In groups, play a game of charades. Individually, think of two nouns for each charade, for example, a boy using a computer (**un chico**; **una computadora**). The first person to guess correctly acts out the next charade. Answers will vary.

Practice more at **vhlcentral.com**.

1 Expansion Reverse the activity by reading the on-page answers and having students convert the singular to plural and vice versa. Make sure they close their books. Give the nouns in random order.

2 Expansion As an additional visual exercise, bring in photos or magazine pictures that illustrate items whose names students know. Ask students to indicate the definite article and the noun. Include a mix of singular and plural nouns. Repeat the exercise with indefinite articles.

3 Teaching Tip Model the game of charades by writing some new cognates on the board (Ex: **la guitarra, el teléfono, la televisión**). Act out sitting on a couch and flipping channels on a remote and invite students to guess. Emphasize that the student acting out the charade must not speak and that he or she may show the number of syllables by using fingers.

3 Expansion Split the class into two teams, with volunteers from each team acting out the charades. Give a point to each team for correctly guessing the charade. The team with the most points wins.

TEACHING OPTIONS

Video Show the **Fotonovela** episode again to offer more input on singular and plural nouns and articles. With their books closed, have students write down every noun and article that they hear. After viewing the video, ask volunteers to list the nouns and articles they heard. Explain that the **las** used when telling time refers to **las horas** (Ex: **Son las cinco = Son las cinco horas**).

Extra Practice To challenge students, slowly read aloud a short passage from a novel, story, poem, or newspaper article written in Spanish, preferably one with a great number of nouns and articles. As a listening exercise, have students write down every noun and article they hear, even unfamiliar ones (the articles may cue when nouns appear).

Section Goals

In **Estructura 1.2**, students will be introduced to:
- numbers 0–30
- the verb form **hay**

Instructional Resources
Supersite: Audio (Lab MP3 Files); Resources (Grammar Presentation Slides, Activity Pack, Scripts, Answer Keys); Testing Program (Quizzes)
WebSAM
Workbook, p. 4
Lab Manual, p. 4

Teaching Tips

- Introduce numbers by asking students if they can count to ten in Spanish. Model the pronunciation of each number. Write individual numbers on the board and call on students at random to say the number.
- Say numbers aloud at random and have students hold up the appropriate number of fingers. Then reverse the drill; hold up varying numbers of fingers at random and ask students to shout out the corresponding number in Spanish.
- Emphasize the variable forms of **uno** and **veintiuno**, giving examples of each. Ex: **veintiún profesores, veintiuna profesoras.**
- Ask questions like these: **¿Cuántos estudiantes hay en la clase? (Hay ____ estudiantes en la clase.)**

1.2 Numbers 0–30

Tutorial

NATIONAL STANDARDS comparisons

Los números 0 a 30

0	cero				
1	uno	**11**	once	**21**	veintiuno
2	dos	**12**	doce	**22**	veintidós
3	tres	**13**	trece	**23**	veintitrés
4	cuatro	**14**	catorce	**24**	veinticuatro
5	cinco	**15**	quince	**25**	veinticinco
6	seis	**16**	dieciséis	**26**	veintiséis
7	siete	**17**	diecisiete	**27**	veintisiete
8	ocho	**18**	dieciocho	**28**	veintiocho
9	nueve	**19**	diecinueve	**29**	veintinueve
10	diez	**20**	veinte	**30**	treinta

AYUDA

Though it is less common, the numbers 16 through 29 (except 20) can also be written as three words: **diez y seis, diez y siete...**

- The number **uno** (*one*) and numbers ending in **-uno**, such as **veintiuno**, have more than one form. Before masculine nouns, **uno** shortens to **un**. Before feminine nouns, **uno** changes to **una**.

  un hombre → veinti**ún** hombres   **una** mujer → veinti**una** mujeres

- **¡Atención!** The forms **uno** and **veintiuno** are used when counting (**uno, dos, tres... veinte, veintiuno, veintidós...**). They are also used when the number *follows* a noun, even if the noun is feminine: **la lección uno**.

- To ask *how many people* or *things* there are, use **cuántos** before masculine nouns and **cuántas** before feminine nouns.

- The Spanish equivalent of both *there is* and *there are* is **hay**. Use **¿Hay...?** to ask *Is there...?* or *Are there...?* Use **no hay** to express *there is not* or *there are not*.

—¿**Cuántos** estudiantes **hay**?
How many students are there?

—**Hay** seis estudiantes en la foto.
There are six students in the photo.

—¿**Hay** chicos en la fotografía?
Are there guys in the picture?

—**Hay** tres chicas y **no hay** chicos.
There are three girls, and there are no guys.

¡INTÉNTALO!

Provide the Spanish words for these numbers.

1. **7** siete
2. **16** dieciséis
3. **29** veintinueve
4. **1** uno
5. **0** cero
6. **15** quince
7. **21** veintiuno
8. **9** nueve
9. **23** veintitrés
10. **11** once
11. **30** treinta
12. **4** cuatro
13. **12** doce
14. **28** veintiocho
15. **14** catorce
16. **10** diez

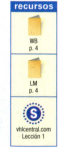

recursos
WB p. 4
LM p. 4
vhlcentral.com Lección 1

TEACHING OPTIONS

TPR Assign ten students a number from 0–30 and line them up in front of the class. Call out one of the numbers at random, and have the student assigned that number step forward. When two students have stepped forward, ask them to repeat their numbers. Then ask individuals to add (Say: **Suma**) or subtract (Say: **Resta**) the two numbers, giving the result in Spanish.

Game Ask students to write B-I-N-G-O across the top of a blank piece of paper. Have them draw five squares vertically under each letter and randomly fill in the squares with numbers from 0–30, without repeating any numbers. Draw numbers from a hat and call them out in Spanish. The first student to mark five in a row (horizontally, vertically, or diagonally) yells **¡Bingo!** and wins. Have the winner confirm the numbers for you in Spanish.

Práctica

1 **Contar** Following the pattern, write out the missing numbers in Spanish.

1. 1, 3, 5, ..., 29 7, 9, 11, 13, 15, 17, 19, 21, 23, 25, 27
2. 2, 4, 6, ..., 30 8, 10, 12, 14, 16, 18, 20, 22, 24, 26, 28
3. 3, 6, 9, ..., 30 12, 15, 18, 21, 24, 27
4. 30, 28, 26, ..., 0 24, 22, 20, 18, 16, 14, 12, 10, 8, 6, 4, 2
5. 30, 25, 20, ..., 0 15, 10, 5
6. 28, 24, 20, ..., 0 16, 12, 8, 4

2 **Resolver** Solve these math problems with a partner.

AYUDA

+ → más
– → menos
= → son

modelo

5 + 3 =
Estudiante 1: *cinco más tres son...*
Estudiante 2: *ocho*

1. **2 + 15 =** Dos más quince son diecisiete.
2. **20 – 1 =** Veinte menos uno son diecinueve.
3. **5 + 7 =** Cinco más siete son doce.
4. **18 + 12 =** Dieciocho más doce son treinta.
5. **3 + 22 =** Tres más veintidós son veinticinco.
6. **6 – 3 =** Seis menos tres son tres.
7. **11 + 12 =** Once más doce son veintitrés.
8. **7 – 2 =** Siete menos dos son cinco.
9. **8 + 5 =** Ocho más cinco son trece.
10. **23 – 14 =** Veintitrés menos catorce son nueve.

3 **¿Cuántos hay?** How many persons or things are there in these drawings?

modelo

Hay tres maletas.

1. Hay veinte lápices.

2. Hay un hombre.

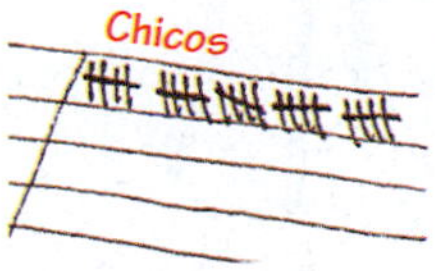

3. Hay veinticinco chicos.

4. Hay una conductora.

5. Hay cuatro fotos.

6. Hay treinta cuadernos.

7. Hay seis turistas.

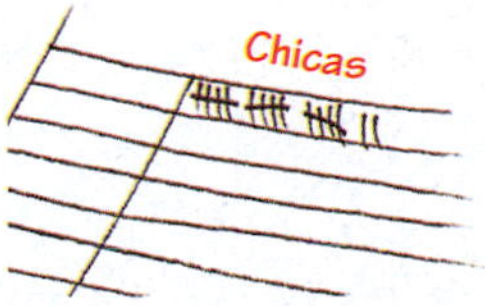

8. Hay diecisiete chicas.

1 Teaching Tips
- Before beginning the activity, make sure students know each pattern: odds (**los números impares**), evens (**los números pares**), count by threes (**contar de tres en tres**).
- To simplify, write complete patterns out on the board.

1 Expansion Explain that a prime number (**un número primo**) is any number that can only be divided by itself and 1. To challenge students, ask the class to list the prime numbers up to 30. (They are: 1, 2, 3, 5, 7, 11, 13, 17, 19, 23, 29.)

2 Expansion Do simple multiplication problems. Introduce the phrases **multiplicado por** and **dividido por**. Ex: **Cinco multiplicado por cinco son... (veinticinco). Veinte dividido por cuatro son... (cinco).**

3 Teaching Tip Have students read the directions and the model. Cue student responses by asking questions related to the drawings. Ex: **¿Cuántos lápices hay? (Hay veinte lápices.)**

3 Expansion Add an additional visual aspect to this activity. Hold up or point to classroom objects and ask how many there are. Since students will not know the names of many items, a simple number or **hay** + the number will suffice to signal comprehension. Ex:
—¿Cuántas plumas hay aquí?
—(Hay) Dos.

TEACHING OPTIONS

TPR Give ten students each a card that contains a different number from 0–30. The cards should be visible to the other students. Then call out simple math problems (addition or subtraction) involving the assigned numbers. When the first two numbers are called, each student steps forward. The student whose assigned number completes the math problem then has five seconds to join them.

Extra Practice Ask questions about your university and the town or city in which it is located. Ex: **¿Cuántos profesores hay en el departamento de español? ¿Cuántas universidades hay en ____? ¿Cuántas pizzerías hay en ____?** Encourage students to guess the number. If a number exceeds 30, write that number on the board and model its pronunciation.

4 Teaching Tip For items 3, 4, 7, and 9, ask students: **¿Cuántos/as hay?** If there are no examples of the item listed, students should say: **No hay ___.**

4 Expansion After completing the activity, call on individuals to give rapid responses for the same items. To challenge students, mix up the order of items.

5 Teaching Tip Remind students that they will be forming sentences with **hay** and a number. Give them four minutes to do the activity. You might also have students write out their answers.

5 Expansion After pairs have finished analyzing the drawing, call on individuals to respond. Convert the statements into questions in Spanish. Ask: **¿Cuántos chicos hay? ¿Cuántas mujeres hay?**

5 Expansion Have students work in pairs to role-play conversations between one of the family members in the drawing and an exchange student that has come to live with them. Encourage students to use phrases they learned in **Contextos**, as well as simple questions about the host family, such as **¿Cuántas personas hay en la casa?**

Comunicación

4 **En la clase** With a partner, take turns asking and answering these questions about your classroom. Answers will vary.

1. ¿Cuántos estudiantes hay?
2. ¿Cuántos profesores hay?
3. ¿Hay una computadora?
4. ¿Hay una maleta?
5. ¿Cuántos mapas hay?
6. ¿Cuántos lápices hay?
7. ¿Hay cuadernos?
8. ¿Cuántos diccionarios hay?
9. ¿Hay hombres?
10. ¿Cuántas mujeres hay?

5 **Preguntas** With a partner, take turns asking and answering questions about the drawing. Talk about: Answers will vary.

1. how many children there are
2. how many women there are
3. if there are some photographs
4. if there is a boy
5. how many notebooks there are
6. if there is a bus
7. if there are tourists
8. how many pencils there are
9. if there is a man
10. how many computers there are

Practice more at **vhlcentral.com**.

TEACHING OPTIONS

Pairs Have each student draw a scene similar to the one on this page. Of course, stick figures are perfectly acceptable! Give them three minutes to draw the scene. Encourage students to include multiple numbers of particular items (**cuadernos, maletas, lápices**). Then have pairs take turns describing what is in their partner's picture. The student who created the drawing should ask questions to verify the accuracy of the description.

Pairs Divide the class into pairs. Give half of the pairs magazine pictures that contain images of familiar words or cognates. Give the other half written descriptions of the pictures, using **hay**. Ex: **En la foto hay dos mujeres, un chico y una chica.** Have pairs circulate around the room to match the descriptions with the corresponding pictures.

1.3 Present tense of ser

Tutorial

NATIONAL STANDARDS comparisons

Subject pronouns

ANTE TODO In order to use verbs, you will need to learn about subject pronouns. A subject pronoun replaces the name or title of a person or thing and acts as the subject of a verb.

Subject pronouns

SINGULAR		PLURAL	
yo	*I*	**nosotros**	*we* (masculine)
		nosotras	*we* (feminine)
tú	*you* (familiar)	**vosotros**	*you* (masc., fam.)
usted (Ud.)	*you* (formal)	**vosotras**	*you* (fem., fam.)
		ustedes (Uds.)	*you*
él	*he*	**ellos**	*they* (masc.)
ella	*she*	**ellas**	*they* (fem.)

¡LENGUA VIVA!

In Latin America, **ustedes** is used as the plural for both **tú** and **usted**. In Spain, however, **vosotros** and **vosotras** are used as the plural of **tú**, and **ustedes** is used only as the plural of **usted**.

• • •

Usted and **ustedes** are abbreviated as **Ud.** and **Uds.**, or occasionally as **Vd.** and **Vds.**

- Spanish has two subject pronouns that mean *you* (singular). Use **tú** when addressing a friend, a family member, or a child you know well. Use **usted** to address a person with whom you have a formal or more distant relationship, such as a superior at work, a professor, or an older person.

Tú eres de Canadá, ¿verdad, David?	¿**Usted** es la profesora de español?
You are from Canada, right, David?	*Are you the Spanish professor?*

- The masculine plural forms **nosotros**, **vosotros**, and **ellos** refer to a group of males or to a group of males and females. The feminine plural forms **nosotras**, **vosotras**, and **ellas** can refer only to groups made up exclusively of females.

nosotros, vosotros, ellos

nosotros, vosotros, ellos

nosotras, vosotras, ellas

- There is no Spanish equivalent of the English subject pronoun *it*. Generally *it* is not expressed in Spanish.

Es un problema.	Es una computadora.
It's a problem.	*It's a computer.*

Section Goals

In **Estructura 1.3**, students will be introduced to:
- subject pronouns
- the present tense of the verb **ser**
- the uses of **ser** (to identify, to indicate possession, to describe origin, and to talk about professions or occupations)

Instructional Resources
Supersite: Audio (Lab MP3 Files); Resources (Grammar Presentation Slides, Activity Pack, Scripts, Answer Keys); Testing Program (Quizzes)
WebSAM
Workbook, pp. 5–6
Lab Manual, p. 5

Teaching Tips

- Point to yourself and say: **Yo soy profesor(a)**. Then point to a student and ask: **¿Tú eres profesor(a) o estudiante?** (**estudiante**) Say: **Sí, tú eres estudiante**. Indicate the whole class and tell them: **Ustedes son estudiantes**. Once the pattern has been established, include other subject pronouns and forms of **ser** while indicating other students. Ex: **Él es…**, **Ella es…**, **Ellos son…**
- Review familiar and formal forms of address students learned in **Contextos**.
- You may want to point out that while **usted** and **ustedes** are second person forms of address equivalent to the English *you*, they take third person verb forms.

Note: While the **vosotros/as** forms are listed in verb paradigms in **PANORAMA**, they will not be actively practiced.

TEACHING OPTIONS

Extra Practice Indicate people in the classroom and have students give subject pronouns based on their point of view. Ex: Point to yourself (**usted**), a female student (**ella**), everyone in the class (**nosotros**).
Extra Practice Ask students to indicate whether certain people would be addressed as **tú** or **usted**. Ex: A roommate, a friend's grandfather, a doctor, a neighbor's child.

Heritage Speakers Ask heritage speakers how they address elder members of their family, such as parents, grandparents, aunts, and uncles—whether they use **tú** or **usted**. Also ask them if they use **vosotros/as** (they typically will not unless they or their family are from Spain) or **voseo**. Explain that **voseo** is the use of the second-person subject pronoun **vos** instead of **tú**. It is used extensively in much of Latin America, including Argentina, Uruguay, and Costa Rica.

Teaching Tips

- Work through the explanation and the forms of **ser** in the chart. Emphasize that **es** is used for **usted, él,** and **ella**, and that **son** is used for **ustedes, ellos,** and **ellas**. Context, subject pronouns, or names will determine who is being addressed or talked about.
- Explain that **ser** is used to identify people and things. At this point there is no need to explain that **estar** also means *to be*; it will be introduced in **Lección 2**.
- Explain the meaning of **¿quién?** and ask questions about students. Ex: ____, **¿quién es ella? Sí, es** ____. **¿Quién soy yo? Sí, soy el/la profesor(a)** ____. Introduce **¿qué?** and ask questions about items in the class. Ex: (*Pointing to a map*) **¿Qué es? Sí, es un mapa**.
- Point out the construction of **ser** + **de** to indicate possession. Stress that the construction [*apostrophe* + *s*] does not exist in Spanish. Pick up objects belonging to students and ask questions. Ex: **¿De quién es el cuaderno? (Es de** ____.**) ¿De quién son los libros? (Son de** ____.**)** Then hold up items from two different students and ask: **¿De quiénes son las plumas? Son de** ____ **y** ____.
- Introduce the contraction **de + el = del**. Emphasize that **de** does not make contractions with other definite articles, and provide examples. Ex: **Soy del estado de** ____. **El diccionario no es de la profesora de** ____. Also use examples of possession to illustrate the contraction. Ex: **¿Es el mapa del profesor?**

The present tense of ser

ANTE TODO In **Contextos** and **Fotonovela**, you have already used several present-tense forms of **ser** (*to be*) to identify yourself and others, and to talk about where you and others are from. **Ser** is an irregular verb; its forms do not follow the regular patterns that most verbs follow. You need to memorize the forms, which appear in this chart.

The verb ser (*to be*)

SINGULAR FORMS	yo	**soy**	*I am*
	tú	**eres**	*you are* (fam.)
	Ud./él/ella	**es**	*you are* (form.)*; he/she is*
PLURAL FORMS	nosotros/as	**somos**	*we are*
	vosotros/as	**sois**	*you are* (fam.)
	Uds./ellos/ellas	**son**	*you are; they are*

Uses of *ser*

▶ Use **ser** to identify people and things.

—¿Quién **es** él?
Who is he?

—**Es** Felipe Díaz Velázquez.
He's Felipe Díaz Velázquez.

—¿Qué **es**?
What is it?

—**Es** un mapa de España.
It's a map of Spain.

Es Marissa.

Es una maleta.

▶ **Ser** also expresses possession, with the preposition **de**. There is no Spanish equivalent of the English construction [*noun*] + 's (*Maru's*). In its place, Spanish uses [*noun*] + **de** + [*owner*].

—¿**De** quién **es**?
Whose is it?

—**Es** el diario **de** Maru.
It's Maru's diary.

—¿**De** quién **son**?
Whose are they?

—**Son** los lápices **de** la chica.
They are the girl's pencils.

▶ When **de** is followed by the article **el**, the two combine to form the contraction **del**. **De** does *not* contract with **la**, **las**, or **los**.

—**Es** la computadora **del** conductor.
It's the driver's computer.

—**Son** las maletas **del** chico.
They are the boy's suitcases.

TEACHING OPTIONS

Extra Practice As a rapid-response drill, call out subject pronouns and have students answer with the correct form of **ser**. Ex: **tú (eres)**, **ustedes (son)**. Reverse the drill by starting with forms of **ser**. Students must give the subject pronouns. Accept multiple answers for **es** and **son**.

TPR Have students form a circle. Toss a ball to individual students. When a student catches it, call on another to state whose ball it is. Ex: **Es de** ____. Take two balls and toss them to different students to elicit **Son de** ____ **y** ____.

▶ **Ser** also uses the preposition **de** to express origin.

¿De dónde eres?
Yo soy de Wisconsin.

¿De dónde es usted?
Yo soy de Cuba.

—¿**De** dónde **es** Juan Carlos?
Where is Juan Carlos from?

—Es **de** Argentina.
He's from Argentina.

—¿**De** dónde **es** Maru?
Where is Maru from?

—**Es de** Costa Rica.
She's from Costa Rica.

▶ Use **ser** to express profession or occupation.

Don Francisco **es conductor**.
Don Francisco is a driver.

Yo **soy estudiante**.
I am a student.

▶ Unlike English, Spanish does not use the indefinite article (**un**, **una**) after **ser** when referring to professions, unless accompanied by an adjective or other description.

Marta **es** profesora.
Marta is a teacher.

Marta **es una** profesora excelente.
Marta is an excellent teacher.

Somos
Perú
LanPerú

¡INTÉNTALO! Provide the correct subject pronouns and the present forms of **ser**.

1. Gabriel ___él___ ___es___
2. Juan y yo ___nosotros___ ___somos___
3. Óscar y Flora ___ellos___ ___son___
4. Adriana ___ella___ ___es___
5. las turistas ___ellas___ ___son___
6. el chico ___él___ ___es___
7. los conductores ___ellos___ ___son___
8. los señores Ruiz ___ellos___ ___son___

¡LENGUA VIVA!

Some geographic locations can be referred to either with or without a definite article:

Soy de Estados Unidos./Soy de los Estados Unidos.

•••

Sometimes a definite article is a part of a proper name, as in **El Salvador, El Paso,** and **Los Ángeles**. In these cases, **de** and **el** do not contract:

Soy de El Salvador.

CONSULTA

You will learn more about adjectives in **Estructura 3.1**, pp. 80–82.

NOTA CULTURAL

Created in 1998, LAN Perú is an affiliate of the Chilean-based LAN Airlines, one of the largest carriers in South America. LAN Perú operates out of Lima, offering domestic flights and international service to select major cities in the Americas and Spain.

recursos

WB pp. 5–6

LM p. 5

vhlcentral.com Lección 1

Teaching Tips

- Explain **ser** + **de** to express origin. Start practicing this construction by indicating where you are from. Ex: **Soy de** ____. You may also want to further practice and contrast the contraction **del**. Ex: **Soy del estado de** ____ **/de la región (de)** ____. Introduce **¿de dónde?** and ask students where they are from. Ex: ____, **¿de dónde eres?** After a student answers, ask another student: **¿De dónde es** ____**? (Es de** ____**.)**
- Explain the use of **ser** to describe professions or occupations. Say: **Yo soy profesor(a) de español**. **¿Qué eres tú?** Response: **Soy estudiante**. Say: **Sí, eres estudiante**. To challenge students, or if they want to name occupations or professions, give them additional vocabulary from the ***Vocabulario adicional*** for **Lección 16** (Supersite). Ex: ____ **es científico.**
- Emphasize that the indefinite articles **un** and **una** are not used with **ser** and professions or occupations. Ex: **Él es arquitecto. Somos estudiantes.** However, stress that **un** and **una** are required if there is a descriptor present. Ex: **Él es un arquitecto importante. Somos unos estudiantes inteligentes.**
- At this point you may want to present ***Vocabulario adicional: Más vocabulario para los países*** from the Supersite.

TEACHING OPTIONS

Extra Practice Write cognates on the board and ask students to identify the professions of famous people. Ex: **actor/actriz, presidente, artista, pianista.** Ask: **¿Qué es Brad Pitt? (Es actor.) ¿Quién es presidente?** (____ **es presidente.**)

Pairs Have pairs interview each other. Write sample questions on the board. Have students report about their partners. Students should begin by saying **Él/Ella es...**

TPR Say what state you are from. Then ask individuals: **¿De dónde eres?** As students answer, have them stand in groups according to state, town, neighborhood, or street. Then point to individuals, pairs, and groups at random, and ask where people are from. Alternate direct questions (**¿De dónde son ustedes?**) with questions for the whole class to answer (**¿De dónde es ella?**). Encourage students to link arms when answering with **nosotros/as**.

1 Teaching Tip Review **tú** and **usted**, asking students which pronoun they would use in a formal situation and which they would use in an informal situation.

1 Expansion Once students have identified the correct subject pronouns, ask them to give the form of **ser** they would use when *addressing* each person and when *talking about* each person.

2 Expansion Give additional names of well-known Spanish speakers and ask students to tell where they are from. Have students give the country names in English if they do not know the Spanish equivalent. Ex: **¿De dónde es Javier Bardem? (Es de España.)**

3 Teaching Tips
- To simplify, before beginning the activity, guide students in identifying the objects.
- You might tell students to answer the second part of the question (**¿De quién es?**) with any answer they wish. Have students take turns asking and answering questions.

Práctica

1 **Pronombres** What subject pronouns would you use to (a) talk *to* these people directly and (b) talk *about* them to others?

modelo
un joven *tú, él*

1. una chica *tú, ella*
2. el presidente de México *Ud., él*
3. tres chicas y un chico *Uds., ellos*
4. un estudiante *tú, él*
5. la señora Ochoa *Ud., ella*
6. dos profesoras *Uds., ellas*

2 **Identidad y origen** With a partner, take turns asking and answering these questions about the people indicated: **¿Quién es?/¿Quiénes son?** and **¿De dónde es?/¿De dónde son?**

modelo
Selena Gomez (Estados Unidos)
Estudiante 1: *¿Quién es?*
Estudiante 2: *Es Selena Gomez.*
Estudiante 1: *¿De dónde es?*
Estudiante 2: *Es de los Estados Unidos.*

1. Enrique Iglesias (España)
   E1: ¿Quién es? E2: Es Enrique Iglesias. E1: ¿De dónde es? E2: Es de España.
2. Robinson Canó (República Dominicana)
   E2: ¿Quién es? E1: Es Robinson Canó. E2: ¿De dónde es? E1: Es de (la) República Dominicana.
3. Eva Mendes y Marc Anthony (Estados Unidos) E1: ¿Quiénes son? E2: Son Eva Mendes y Marc Anthony. E1: ¿De dónde son? E2: Son de (los) Estados Unidos.
4. Carlos Santana y Salma Hayek (México) E2: ¿Quiénes son? E1: Son Carlos Santana y Salma Hayek. E2: ¿De dónde son? E1: Son de México.
5. Shakira (Colombia)
   E1: ¿Quién es? E2: Es Shakira. E1: ¿De dónde es? E2: Es de Colombia.
6. Antonio Banderas y Penélope Cruz (España) E2: ¿Quiénes son? E1: Son Antonio Banderas y Penélope Cruz. E2: ¿De dónde son? E1: Son de España.
7. Taylor Swift y Demi Lovato (Estados Unidos) E1: ¿Quiénes son? E2: Son Taylor Swift y Demi Lovato. E1: ¿De dónde son? E2: Son de (los) Estados Unidos.
8. Daisy Fuentes (Cuba) E2: ¿Quién es? E1: Es Daisy Fuentes. E2: ¿De dónde es? E1: Es de Cuba.

3 **¿Qué es?** Ask your partner what each object is and to whom it belongs.

modelo
Estudiante 1: *¿Qué es?*
Estudiante 2: *Es un diccionario.*
Estudiante 1: *¿De quién es?*
Estudiante 2: *Es del profesor Núñez.*

1. 

2. 

3. 

4. 

1. E1: ¿Qué es?
   E2: Es una maleta.
   E1: ¿De quién es?
   E2: Es de la Sra. Valdés.
2. E1: ¿Qué es?
   E2: Es un cuaderno.
   E1: ¿De quién es?
   E2: Es de Gregorio.
3. E1: ¿Qué es?
   E2: Es una computadora.
   E1: ¿De quién es?
   E2: Es de Rafael.
4. E1: ¿Qué es?
   E2: Es un diario.
   E1: ¿De quién es?
   E2: Es de Marisa.

TEACHING OPTIONS

Video Replay the **Fotonovela**, having students focus on subject pronouns and the verb **ser**. Ask them to copy down as many examples of sentences that use forms of **ser** as they can. Stop the video where appropriate to ask comprehension questions on what the characters said.

Heritage Speakers Encourage heritage speakers to describe themselves and their family briefly. Make sure they use the cognates **familia, mamá,** and **papá**. Call on students to report the information given. Ex: **Francisco es de la Florida. La mamá de Francisco es de España. Ella es profesora. El papá de Francisco es de Cuba. Él es dentista.**

Comunicación

4

Preguntas Using the items in the word bank, ask your partner questions about the ad. Be imaginative in your responses. Answers will vary.

¿Cuántas?	¿De dónde?	¿Qué?
¿Cuántos?	¿De quién?	¿Quién?

SOMOS ECOTURISTA, S.A.

Los autobuses oficiales de la Ruta Maya

- 25 autobuses en total
- 30 conductores del área
- pasajeros internacionales
- mapas de la región

¡Todos a bordo!

5

¿Quién es? In small groups, take turns pretending to be a famous person from a Spanish-speaking country (such as Spain, Mexico, Puerto Rico, Cuba, or the United States). Use the list of professions to think of people from a variety of backgrounds. Your partners will ask you questions and try to guess who you are. Answers will vary.

actor *actor*	cantante *singer*	escritor(a) *writer*
actriz *actress*	deportista *athlete*	músico/a *musician*

modelo

Estudiante 3: ¿Eres de Puerto Rico?
Estudiante 1: No. Soy de Colombia.
Estudiante 2: ¿Eres hombre?
Estudiante 1: Sí. Soy hombre.
Estudiante 3: ¿Eres escritor?
Estudiante 1: No. Soy actor.
Estudiante 2: ¿Eres John Leguizamo?
Estudiante 1: ¡Sí! ¡Sí!

Practice more at **vhlcentral.com**.

NOTA CULTURAL

John Leguizamo was born in Bogotá, Colombia. John is best known for his work as an actor and comedian. He has appeared in movies such as *Moulin Rouge* and *The Happening*. Here are some other Hispanic celebrities: Laura Esquivel (writer from Mexico), Andy García (actor from Cuba), and Don Omar (singer from Puerto Rico).

4 Teaching Tip If students ask, explain that the abbreviation **S.A.** in the ad stands for **Sociedad Anónima** and is equivalent to the English abbreviation *Inc.* (*Incorporated*).

4 Expansion Ask pairs to write four true/false statements about the ad. Call on volunteers to read their sentences. The class will indicate whether the statements are true (**cierto**) or false (**falso**) and correct the false statements.

5 Teaching Tips

- To simplify, have students brainstorm a list of names in the categories suggested.
- Have three students read the **modelo** aloud.

5 Expansion Have each group select a famous person that was mentioned during the activity and write a description of him or her. Before they begin writing, brainstorm some useful cognate adjectives that students can use, and tell them to be sure not to use the person's name in their description.
Then have groups take turns reading their descriptions aloud for the class to guess the person's identity. If this guessing proves too difficult, allow the class to ask for a hint (**una pista**), such as a song or movie title.

TEACHING OPTIONS

Small Groups Bring in personal photos or magazine pictures that show people. In small groups, have students invent stories about the people: who they are, where they are from, and what they do. Circulate around the room and assist with unfamiliar vocabulary as necessary, but encourage students to use terms they already know.

Game Hand out individual strips of paper with names of famous people on them. There should be several duplicates of each name. Then give descriptions of one of the famous people (**Es de ____. Es** [*profession*].), including cognate adjectives if you wish (**inteligente, pesimista**). The first person to stand and indicate that the name they have is the one you are describing (**¡Yo lo tengo!**) wins that round.

1.4 Telling time

Tutorial

ANTE TODO In both English and Spanish, the verb *to be* (**ser**) and numbers are used to tell time.

▶ To ask what time it is, use **¿Qué hora es?** When telling time, use **es + la** with **una** and **son + las** with all other hours.

Es la una.

Son las dos.

Son las seis.

▶ As in English, you express time in Spanish from the hour to the half hour by adding minutes.

Son las cuatro **y cinco.**

Son las once **y veinte.**

▶ You may use either **y cuarto** or **y quince** to express fifteen minutes or quarter past the hour. For thirty minutes or half past the hour, you may use either **y media** or **y treinta**.

Es la una **y cuarto.**

Son las nueve **y quince.**

Son las doce **y media.**

Son las siete **y treinta.**

▶ You express time from the half hour to the hour in Spanish by subtracting minutes or a portion of an hour from the next hour.

Es la una **menos cuarto.**

Son las tres **menos quince.**

Son las ocho **menos veinte.**

Son las tres **menos diez.**

Section Goals

In **Estructura 1.4**, students will be introduced to:
- asking and telling time
- times of day

Instructional Resources

Supersite: Audio (Lab MP3 Files); Resources (Grammar Presentation Slides, Digital Image Bank, Activity Pack, Scripts, Answer Keys); Testing Program (Quizzes)
WebSAM
Workbook, pp. 7–8
Lab Manual, p. 6

Teaching Tips

- To prepare students for telling time, review **es** and **son** and numbers 0–30.
- Use the **Lección 1** digital images to assist with this presentation.
- Introduce **es la una** and **son las dos** (**tres, cuatro…**). Remind students that **las** in time constructions refers to **las horas**. Introduce **y cinco** (**diez, veinte…**), **y quince/cuarto**, and **y treinta/media**.
- Draw three clocks on the board, each displaying a different time. Ask the class: **¿Qué hora es?** and have students correctly identify the time for each one. Concentrate on this until students are relatively comfortable with expressing the time in Spanish.
- Introduce **menos diez** (**cuarto, veinte…**) and explain this method of telling time in Spanish. It typically takes students longer to master this aspect of telling time. Spend about five minutes with your moveable-hands clock and ask students to state the times shown.

TEACHING OPTIONS

Extra Practice Draw a large clock face on the board with numbers but without hands. Say a time and ask a volunteer to come up to the board and draw the hands to indicate that time. The rest of the class verifies that their classmate has written the correct time. Continue until several volunteers have participated.

Pairs Tell the class **tengo** means *I have*. Have pairs take turns telling each other what time their classes are this semester/quarter. (Ex: **Tengo una clase a las…**) For each time given, the other student draws a clock face with the corresponding time. The first student verifies the time. To challenge students, give a list of course names (**las matemáticas, la biología**, etc.)

▶ To ask at what time a particular event takes place, use the phrase **¿A qué hora (...)?** To state at what time something takes place, use the construction **a la(s)** + *time*.

¿**A qué hora** es la clase de biología? *(At) what time is biology class?*	La clase es **a las dos**. *The class is at two o'clock.*
¿**A qué hora** es la fiesta? *(At) what time is the party?*	**A las ocho**. *At eight.*

¡LENGUA VIVA!

Other useful expressions for telling time:
Son las doce (del día). It is twelve o'clock (p.m.).
Son las doce (de la noche). It is twelve o'clock (a.m.).

▶ Here are some useful words and phrases associated with telling time.

Son las ocho **en punto**. *It's 8 o'clock on the dot/sharp.*	Son las nueve **de la mañana**. *It's 9 a.m./in the morning.*
Es **el mediodía**. *It's noon.*	Son las cuatro y cuarto **de la tarde**. *It's 4:15 p.m./in the afternoon.*
Es **la medianoche**. *It's midnight.*	Son las diez y media **de la noche**. *It's 10:30 p.m./at night.*

¿Qué hora es?
Son las cuatro menos diez.

¿Qué hora es?
Son las cuatro y veinticinco.

recursos
WB pp. 7–8
LM p. 6
vhlcentral.com Lección 1

¡INTÉNTALO! Practice telling time by completing these sentences.

1. (1:00 a.m.) Es la ___una___ de la mañana.
2. (2:50 a.m.) Son las tres ___menos___ diez de la mañana.
3. (4:15 p.m.) Son las cuatro y ___cuarto/quince___ de la tarde.
4. (8:30 p.m.) Son las ocho y ___media/treinta___ de la noche.
5. (9:15 a.m.) Son las nueve y quince de la ___mañana___.
6. (12:00 p.m.) Es el ___mediodía___.
7. (6:00 a.m.) Son las seis de la ___mañana___.
8. (4:05 p.m.) Son las cuatro y cinco de la ___tarde___.
9. (12:00 a.m.) Es la ___medianoche___.
10. (3:45 a.m.) Son las cuatro menos ___cuarto/quince___ de la mañana.
11. (2:15 a.m.) Son las ___dos___ y cuarto de la mañana.
12. (1:25 p.m.) Es la una y ___veinticinco___ de la tarde.
13. (6:50 a.m.) Son las ___siete___ menos diez de la mañana.
14. (10:40 p.m.) Son las once menos veinte de la ___noche___.

Teaching Tips

- Review **¿Qué hora es?** and introduce **¿A qué hora?** and make sure students know the difference between them. Ask a few questions to contrast the constructions. Ex: **¿Qué hora es? ¿A qué hora es la clase de español?** Emphasize the difference between the questions by looking at your watch as you ask **¿Qué hora es?** and shrugging your shoulders with a quizzical look when asking **¿A qué hora es?**
- Go over **en punto**, **mediodía**, and **medianoche**. Explain that **medio/a** means *half*.
- Go over **de la mañana/tarde/noche**. Ask students what time it is now.
- You may wish to explain that Spanish speakers tend to view times of day differently than English speakers do. In many countries, only after someone has eaten lunch does one say **Buenas tardes**. Similarly, with the evening, Spanish speakers tend to view 6:00 and even 7:00 as **de la tarde**, not **de la noche**.

¡Lengua viva! Introduce the Spanish equivalents for noon (**las doce del día**) and midnight (**las doce de la noche**).

TEACHING OPTIONS

Extra Practice Give half of the class slips of paper with clock faces depicting certain times. Give the corresponding times written out in Spanish to the other half of the class. Have students circulate around the room to match their times. To increase difficulty, include duplicates of each time with **de la mañana** or **de la tarde/noche** on the written-out times and a sun or a moon on the clock faces.

Heritage Speakers Ask heritage speakers if they generally tell time as presented in the text. If they use different constructions, ask them to share these with the class. Some ways Hispanics use time constructions include (1) stating the hour and the minute (**Son las diez cuarenta**) rather than using **menos**, and (2) asking the question **¿Qué horas son?** Stress, however, that the constructions presented in the text are the ones students should focus on.

1 Teaching Tip To add a visual aspect to this activity, have students draw clock faces showing the times presented in the activity. Have them compare drawings with a partner to verify accuracy.

2 Teaching Tip Read aloud the two ways of saying *4:15* in the model sentence. Point out that the clocks and watches indicate the part of day (morning, afternoon, or evening) as well as the hour. Have students include this information in their responses.

2 Expansion At random, say aloud times shown in the activity. Students must give the number of the clock or watch you describe.
Ex: **Es la una de la mañana. (Es el número 2.)**

3 Teaching Tips
- To simplify, go over new vocabulary introduced in this activity and model pronunciation. Have students repeat the items after you to build confidence.
- Have partners switch roles and ask and answer the questions again.

3 Expansion Have students come up with three additional items to ask their partner, who should respond with actual times. Ex: **—¿A qué hora es el programa *Modern Family*? —Es a las nueve de la noche.**

Práctica

1 Ordenar Put these times in order, from the earliest to the latest.

a. Son las dos de la tarde. 4
b. Son las once de la mañana. 2
c. Son las siete y media de la noche. 6
d. Son las seis menos cuarto de la tarde. 5
e. Son las dos menos diez de la tarde. 3
f. Son las ocho y veintidós de la mañana. 1

2 ¿Qué hora es? Give the times shown on each clock or watch.

modelo
Son las cuatro y cuarto/quince de la tarde.

1. p.m. Son las doce y media/treinta de la tarde.
2. Es la una de la mañana.
3. p.m. Son las cinco y cuarto/quince de la tarde.
4. p.m. Son las ocho y diez de la noche.
5. a.m. Son las cinco y media/treinta de la mañana.

6. a.m. Son las once menos cuarto/quince de la mañana.
7. Son las dos y doce de la tarde.
8. a.m. Son las siete y cinco de la mañana.
9. p.m. Son las cuatro menos cinco de la tarde.
10. Son las doce menos veinticinco de la noche.

NOTA CULTURAL
Many Spanish-speaking countries use both the 12-hour clock and the 24-hour clock (that is, military time). The 24-hour clock is commonly used in written form on signs and schedules. For example, 1 p.m. is **13h**, 2 p.m. is **14h** and so on.

3 ¿A qué hora? Ask your partner at what time these events take place. Your partner will answer according to the cues provided.

modelo
la clase de matemáticas (2:30 p.m.)
Estudiante 1: *¿A qué hora es la clase de matemáticas?*
Estudiante 2: *Es a las dos y media de la tarde.*

1. el programa *Las cuatro amigas* (*11:30 a.m.*)
2. el drama *La casa de Bernarda Alba* (*7:00 p.m.*)
3. el programa *Las computadoras* (*8:30 a.m.*)
4. la clase de español (*10:30 a.m.*)
5. la clase de biología (*9:40 a.m.*)
6. la clase de historia (*10:50 a.m.*)
7. el partido (*game*) de béisbol (*5:15 p.m.*)
8. el partido de tenis (*12:45 p.m.*)
9. el partido de baloncesto (*basketball*) (*7:45 p.m.*)

1. E1: ¿A qué hora es el programa *Las cuatro amigas*? E2: Es a las once y media/treinta de la mañana.
2. E1: ¿A qué hora es el drama *La casa de Bernarda Alba*? E2: Es a las siete de la noche.
3. E1: ¿A qué hora es el programa *Las computadoras*? E2: Es a las ocho y media/treinta de la mañana.
4. E1: ¿A qué hora es la clase de español? E2: Es a las diez y media/treinta de la mañana.
5. E1: ¿A qué hora es la clase de biología? E2: Es a las diez menos veinte de la mañana.
6. E1: ¿A qué hora es la clase de historia? E2: Es a las once menos diez de la mañana.
7. E1: ¿A qué hora es el partido de béisbol? E2: Es a las cinco y cuarto/quince de la tarde.
8. E1: ¿A qué hora es el partido de tenis? E2: Es a la una menos cuarto/quince de la tarde.
9. E1: ¿A qué hora es el partido de baloncesto? E2: Es a las ocho menos cuarto/quince de la noche.

NOTA CULTURAL
La casa de Bernarda Alba is a famous play by Spanish poet and playwright **Federico García Lorca** (1898–1936). Lorca was one of the most famous writers of the 20th century and a close friend of Spain's most talented artists, including the painter Salvador Dalí and the filmmaker Luis Buñuel.

Practice more at **vhlcentral.com**.

TEACHING OPTIONS

Pairs Have students work with a partner to create an original conversation in which they: (1) greet each other appropriately, (2) ask for the time, (3) ask what time a particular class is, and (4) say goodbye. Have pairs role-play their conversations for the class.

Game Divide the class into two teams and have each team form a line. Write two city names on the board. (Ex: **Los Ángeles** and **Miami**) Check that students know the time difference and then list a time underneath the first city. (Ex: **10:30 a.m.**) Point to the first member of each team and ask: **En Los Ángeles son las diez y media de la mañana. ¿Qué hora es en Miami?** The first student to write the correct time in Spanish under the second column earns a point for their team. Vary the game with different times and cities. The team with the most points wins.

Comunicación

NATIONAL communication STANDARDS

4 **En la televisión** With a partner, take turns asking questions about these television listings. Answers will vary.

modelo

Estudiante 1: ¿A qué hora es el documental *Las computadoras*?
Estudiante 2: Es a las nueve en punto de la noche.

NOTA CULTURAL

Telenovelas are the Latin American version of soap operas, but they differ from North American soaps in many ways. Many **telenovelas** are prime-time shows enjoyed by a large segment of the population. They seldom run for more than one season and they are sometimes based on famous novels.

TV Hoy – Programación

11:00 am	Telenovela: *La casa de la familia Díaz*
12:00 pm	Película: *El cóndor* (drama)
2:00 pm	Telenovela: *Dos mujeres y dos hombres*
3:00 pm	Programa juvenil: *Fiesta*
3:30 pm	Telenovela: *¡Sí, sí, sí!*
4:00 pm	Telenovela: *El diario de la Sra. González*
5:00 pm	Telenovela: *Tres mujeres*
6:00 pm	Noticias
7:00 pm	Especial musical: *Música folklórica de México*
7:30 pm	La naturaleza: *Jardín secreto*
8:00 pm	Noticiero: *Veinticuatro horas*
9:00 pm	Documental: *Las computadoras*

5 **Preguntas** With a partner, answer these questions based on your own knowledge. Some answers will vary.

1. Son las tres de la tarde en Nueva York. ¿Qué hora es en Los Ángeles? Es el mediodía./ Son las doce.
2. Son las ocho y media en Chicago. ¿Qué hora es en Miami? Son las nueve y media/treinta.
3. Son las dos menos cinco en San Francisco. ¿Qué hora es en San Antonio? Son las cuatro menos cinco.
4. ¿A qué hora es el programa *Saturday Night Live*? Es a las once y media/treinta de la noche.

6 **Más preguntas** Using the questions in the previous activity as a model, make up four questions of your own. Then get together with a classmate and take turns asking and answering each other's questions. Answers will vary.

Síntesis

NATIONAL communication STANDARDS

7 **Situación** With a partner, play the roles of a journalism student interviewing a visiting literature professor (**profesor(a) de literatura**) from Venezuela. Be prepared to act out the conversation for your classmates. Answers will vary.

Estudiante	Profesor(a) de literatura
Ask the professor his/her name.	→ Ask the student his/her name.
Ask the professor what time his/her literature class is.	→ Ask the student where he/she is from.
Ask how many students are in his/her class.	→ Ask to whom the notebook belongs.
Say thank you and goodbye.	→ Say thank you and you are pleased to meet him/her.

4 Teaching Tip Before beginning the activity, have students scan the schedule for cognates and predict their meanings. Guide them in understanding the meanings of other programming categories: **película, programa juvenil, noticias/noticiero**.

4 Expansion Ask students what time popular TV programs are shown.

5 Teaching Tip Remind students that there are four time zones in the continental United States, and that when it is noon in the Eastern Time zone, it is three hours earlier in the Pacific Time zone.

6 Expansion Have pairs give their two most challenging questions to another pair to see if they can stump them.

7 Teaching Tip Point out that this activity synthesizes everything students have learned in this lesson: greetings and leave-takings, nouns and articles, numbers 0–30 and **hay**, the verb **ser**, and telling time. Spend a few moments reviewing these topics.

TEACHING OPTIONS

Small Groups Have small groups prepare skits. Students can choose any situation they wish, provided that they use material presented in the **Contextos** and **Estructura** sections. Possible situations include: meeting to go on an excursion, meeting between classes, and introducing friends to professors.

Heritage Speakers Ask heritage speakers to describe popular shows that are currently featured on Spanish-language television, noting the type of show (**telenovela, reality,** etc.), the channel (**canal**), and time when they are shown. As a class, try to think of English-language versions or similar programs. Examples may include *American Idol, Big Brother, Dancing with the Stars,* and their respective Latin American counterparts.

Section Goal

In **Recapitulación**, students will review the grammar concepts from this lesson.

Instructional Resource
Supersite

1 Teaching Tips

- Before beginning the activity, remind students that nouns ending in **-ma** tend to be masculine, despite ending in an **-a**.
- To add an auditory aspect to this activity, read aloud a masculine or feminine noun, then call on individuals to supply the other form. Do the same for plural and singular nouns. Keep a brisk pace.

1 Expansion Have students identify the corresponding definite and indefinite articles in both singular and plural forms for all of the nouns.

2 Teaching Tips

- Have students explain why they chose their answers. Ex: 1. **Cuántas** is feminine and modifies **chicas**.
- Ask students to explain the difference between **¿Tienes un diccionario?** and **¿Tienes el diccionario?** (general versus specific).

2 Expansion

- Ask students to rewrite the dialogue with information from one of their own classes.
- Have volunteers ask classmates questions using possessives with **ser**. Ex:
  —**¿De quién es esta mochila?**
  —**Es de ella.**

Recapitulación

Diagnostics

Review the grammar concepts you have learned in this lesson by completing these activities.

1 **Completar** Complete the charts according to the models. **28 pts.**

Masculino	Femenino
el chico	*la chica*
el profesor	**la profesora**
el amigo	**la amiga**
el señor	la señora
el pasajero	**la pasajera**
el estudiante	la estudiante
el turista	**la turista**
el joven	la joven

Singular	Plural
una cosa	*unas cosas*
un libro	unos libros
una clase	**unas clases**
una lección	unas lecciones
un conductor	unos conductores
un país	**unos países**
un lápiz	**unos lápices**
un problema	unos problemas

2 **En la clase** Complete each conversation with the correct word. **22 pts.**

César   **Beatriz**

CÉSAR ¿(1) Cuántas (Cuántos/Cuántas) chicas hay en la (2) clase (maleta/clase)?
BEATRIZ Hay (3) catorce (catorce/cuatro) [*14*] chicas.
CÉSAR Y, ¿(4) cuántos (cuántos/cuántas) chicos hay?
BEATRIZ Hay (5) trece (tres/trece) [*13*] chicos.
CÉSAR Entonces (*Then*), en total hay (6) veintisiete (veintiséis/veintisiete) (7) estudiantes (estudiantes/chicas) en la clase.

Ariana   **Daniel**

ARIANA ¿Tienes (*Do you have*) (8) un (un/una) diccionario?
DANIEL No, pero (*but*) aquí (9) hay (es/hay) uno.
ARIANA ¿De quién (10) es (son/es)?
DANIEL (11) Es (Son/Es) de Carlos.

RESUMEN GRAMATICAL

1.1 Nouns and articles *pp. 12–14*

Gender of nouns

Nouns that refer to living things

	Masculine		Feminine
-o	el chico	-a	la chica
-or	el profesor	-ora	la profesora
-ista	el turista	-ista	la turista

Nouns that refer to non-living things

	Masculine		Feminine
-o	el libro	-a	la cosa
-ma	el programa	-ción	la lección
-s	el autobús	-dad	la nacionalidad

Plural of nouns

- ending in vowel + *-s* la chica → las chicas
- ending in consonant + *-es* el señor → los señores
  (-z → -ces un lápiz → unos lápices)
- Definite articles: el, la, los, las
- Indefinite articles: un, una, unos, unas

1.2 Numbers 0–30 *p. 16*

0	cero	8	ocho	16	dieciséis
1	uno	9	nueve	17	diecisiete
2	dos	10	diez	18	dieciocho
3	tres	11	once	19	diecinueve
4	cuatro	12	doce	20	veinte
5	cinco	13	trece	21	veintiuno
6	seis	14	catorce	22	veintidós
7	siete	15	quince	30	treinta

1.3 Present tense of *ser* *pp. 19–21*

yo	soy	nosotros/as	somos
tú	eres	vosotros/as	sois
Ud./él/ella	es	Uds./ellos/ellas	son

TEACHING OPTIONS

Extra Practice To add a visual aspect to this grammar review, bring in pictures from newspapers, magazines, or the Internet of nouns that students have learned. Ask them to identify the people or objects using **ser**. As a variation, ask students questions about the photos, using **hay**. Ex: **¿Cuántos/as ____ hay en la foto?**

TPR Give certain times of day and night and ask students to identify who would be awake: **vigilante** (*night watchman*), **estudiante**, or **los dos**. Have students raise their left hand for the **vigilante**, right hand for the **estudiante**, and both hands for **los dos**. Ex: **Son las cinco menos veinte de la mañana.** (left hand) **Es la medianoche.** (both hands)

1.4 Telling time pp. 24–25

Es la una.	*It's 1:00.*
Son las dos.	*It's 2:00.*
Son las tres y diez.	*It's 3:10.*
Es la una **y cuarto/quince.**	*It's 1:15.*
Son las siete **y media/treinta.**	*It's 7:30.*
Es la una **menos cuarto/quince.**	*It's 12:45.*
Son las once **menos veinte.**	*It's 10:40.*
Es **el mediodía.**	*It's noon.*
Es **la medianoche.**	*It's midnight.*

3 **Presentaciones** Complete this conversation with the correct form of the verb **ser**. 12 pts.

JUAN ¡Hola! Me llamo Juan. (1) Soy estudiante en la clase de español.

DANIELA ¡Hola! Mucho gusto. Yo (2) soy Daniela y ella (3) es Mónica. ¿De dónde (4) eres (tú), Juan?

JUAN De California. Y ustedes, ¿de dónde (5) son ?

MÓNICA Nosotras (6) somos de Florida.

4 **¿Qué hora es?** Write out in words the following times, indicating whether it's morning, noon, afternoon, or night. 10 pts.

1. It's 12:00 p.m.
Es el mediodía./Son las doce del día.
2. It's 7:05 a.m.
Son las siete y cinco de la mañana.
3. It's 9:35 p.m.
Son las diez menos veinticinco de la noche.
4. It's 5:15 p.m.
Son las cinco y cuarto/quince de la tarde.
5. It's 1:30 p.m.
Es la una y media/treinta de la tarde.

5 **¡Hola!** Write five sentences introducing yourself and talking about your classes. You may want to include your name, where you are from, who your Spanish teacher is, the time of your Spanish class, how many students are in the class, etc. 28 pts. Answers will vary.

6 **Canción** Use the two appropriate words from the list to complete this children's song. 4 EXTRA points!

cinco	cuántas	cuatro	media	quiénes

"Cuántas patas°
tiene un gato°?
Una, dos, tres y
cuatro ."

patas *legs* tiene un gato *does a cat have*

Practice more at **vhlcentral.com**.

3 Teaching Tip Before beginning the activity, orally review the conjugation of **ser**.

3 Expansion Ask questions about the characters in the dialogue. Ex: **¿Quién es Juan? (Juan es un estudiante en la clase de español.) ¿De dónde es? (Es de California.)**

4 Teaching Tip Go over the answers with the class and point out that items 1, 4, and 5 may be written two ways.

4 Expansion To challenge students, give them these times as items 6–10: **6. It's 3:13 p.m., 7. It's 4:29 a.m., 8. It's 1:04 a.m., 9. It's 10:09 a.m., 10. It's 12:16 a.m.**

4 Expansion Have students write down five additional times in Spanish. Then have them get together with a partner and take turns reading the times aloud. The partner will draw a clock showing the appropriate time, plus a sun or moon to indicate a.m. or p.m. Students should check each other's drawings to verify accuracy.

5 Expansion For further practice with **ser** and **hay**, ask students to share the time and size of their other classes. Be certain to list necessary vocabulary on the board, such as **matemáticas, ciencias, literatura,** and **historia**.

6 Teaching Tip Point out the word **Una** in line 3 of the song. To challenge students, have them work in pairs to come up with an explanation for why **Una** is used. (It refers to **pata** [**una pata, dos patas…**]).

TEACHING OPTIONS

Game Have students make a five-column, five-row chart with B-I-N-G-O written across the top of the columns. Tell them to fill in the squares at random with different times of day. (Remind them to use only full, quarter, or half hours.) Draw times from a hat and call them out in Spanish. The first student to mark five in a row (horizontally, vertically, or diagonally) yells **¡Bingo!** and wins.

Extra Practice Have students imagine they have a new pen pal in a Spanish-speaking country. Ask them to write a short e-mail in which they introduce themselves, state where they are from, and give information about their class schedule. (You may want to give students the verb form **tengo** and class subjects vocabulary.) Encourage them to finish the message with questions about their pen pal.

Audio: Reading
Additional Reading

Section Goals

In **Lectura**, students will:

- learn to recognize cognates
- use prefixes and suffixes to recognize cognates
- read a biography on **Joaquín Salvador Lavado (Quino)**
- read a comic strip

Instructional Resource
Supersite

Estrategia Have students look at the cognates in the **Estrategia** box. Write some of the common suffix correspondences between Spanish and English on the board: **–ción/–sión** = *–tion/–sion* (**nación, decisión**); **–ante/–ente** = *–ant/–ent* (**importante, inteligente, elegante**); **–ia/–ía** = *–y* (**farmacia, sociología, historia**); **–dad** = *–ty* (**oportunidad, universidad**).

The Affective Dimension Tell students that reading in Spanish will be less anxiety-provoking if they follow the advice in the **Estrategia** sections, which are designed to reinforce and improve reading comprehension skills.

Examinar el texto Ask students to tell you what type of text this is and how they can tell. *(It is a comic strip and it consists of a series of drawings with speech bubbles.)*

Cognados Ask students to mention any cognates that they see in the author's biography or the comic strip. Discuss the cognates and ask students to look for other examples of words with suffixes that have correspondence to English. Ex: **protagonista; -ista** = *-ist*

Lectura

NATIONAL STANDARDS communication cultures

Antes de leer

Estrategia

Recognizing cognates

As you learned earlier in this lesson, cognates are words that share similar meanings and spellings in two or more languages. When reading in Spanish, it's helpful to look for cognates and use them to guess the meaning of what you're reading. But watch out for false cognates. For example, **librería** means *bookstore*, not *library*, and **embarazada** means *pregnant*, not *embarrassed*. Look at this list of Spanish words, paying special attention to prefixes and suffixes. Can you guess the meaning of each word?

importante	oportunidad
farmacia	cultura
inteligente	activo
dentista	sociología
decisión	espectacular
televisión	restaurante
médico	policía

Examinar el texto

Glance quickly at the reading selection and guess what type of document it is. Explain your answer.

Cognados

Read the document and make a list of the cognates you find. Guess their English equivalents, then compare your answers with those of a partner.

Practice more at **vhlcentral.com**.

Joaquín Salvador Lavado nació (*was born*) en Argentina en 1932 (mil novecientos treinta y dos). Su nombre profesional es **Quino**. Es muy popular en Latinoamérica, Europa y Canadá por sus tiras cómicas (*comic strips*). *Mafalda* es su serie más famosa. La protagonista, Mafalda, es una chica muy inteligente de seis años (*years*). La tira cómica ilustra las aventuras de ella y su grupo de amigos. Las anécdotas de Mafalda y los chicos también presentan temas (*themes*) importantes como la paz (*peace*) y los derechos humanos (*human rights*).

Después de leer

Preguntas

Answer these questions. Some answers may vary. Suggested answers:

1. What is Joaquín Salvador Lavado's pen name?
   Quino
2. What is Mafalda like?
   She is a precocious six-year-old.
3. Where is Mafalda in panel 1? What is she doing?
   She is in bed, counting sheep in order to fall asleep.
4. What happens to the sheep in panel 3? Why?
   It is left balancing on the hurdle because Mafalda falls asleep.
5. Why does Mafalda wake up?
   The sheep says *¡Béeee!*
6. What number corresponds to the sheep in panel 5?
   veintiséis
7. In panel 6, what is Mafalda doing? How do you know?
   She is sleeping; the Zs indicate this.

TEACHING OPTIONS

Extra Practice If time and resources permit, bring in a few more ***Mafalda*** comics for students to read. If possible, bring in examples of another Spanish-language comic, such as ***Baldo***, which deals with topics particular to the experience of growing up as a Latino in the U.S. Have students compare and contrast the comic strips.

Extra Practice Write some Spanish words on the board and have students name the English cognate: **democracia, actor, eficiente, nacionalidad, diferencia, guitarrista, artista, doctora, dificultad, exploración**.

Preguntas Have students work in pairs to answer the questions. Then check the answers as a class.

Los animales

This comic strip uses a device called onomatopoeia: a word that represents the sound that it stands for. Did you know that many common instances of onomatopoeia are different from language to language? The noise a sheep makes is *baaaah* in English, but in Mafalda's language it is **béeeee.** Do you think you can match these animals with their Spanish sounds? First, practice saying aloud each animal sound in group B. Then, match each animal with its sound in Spanish. If you need help remembering the sounds the alphabet makes in Spanish, see p. 9.

A

1. f gato

2. d perro

3. b vacas

4. a gallo

5. c rana

6. e pato

7. g cerdo

B

a. kikirikí b. muuu c. croac d. guau

e. cuac cuac f. miau g. oinc

Los animales

- Have a volunteer read aloud the animal names in group A.
- Model the animal sounds in group B and have students repeat them so that they become comfortable making these sounds.
- Review the answers as a class. Then, ask students if any of the animal/sound combinations were surprising to them and why.
- Write the names of a few more animals (Ex: **pollito, búho, pavo**) accompanied by simple drawings on the board and have students try to guess what the sound would be in Spanish (**pío pío, uu uu, gluglú**).

TEACHING OPTIONS

Small Groups In small groups, have students create an alternate ending for the ***Mafalda*** comic above. Ask them to create new content for panels 3 through 6. When they are finished, have groups share their comic strips, and have the class vote for the funniest or most creative.

Heritage Speakers Ask heritage speakers if they are familiar with any other classic Spanish-language comic strips, such as ***Condorito***. Have them describe the general characteristics of the main character. As a class, compare this character to ***Mafalda***.

Video: *Panorama cultural*
Interactive map

Section Goal

In **Panorama**, students will read demographic and cultural information about Hispanics in the United States and Canada.

Instructional Resources
Supersite: Video (***Panorama cultural***); Resources (Scripts, Translations, Digital Image Bank, Answer Keys)
WebSAM
Workbook, pp. 9–10
Video Manual, pp. 31–32

Teaching Tips

- Use **Lección 1 Panorama** digital images to assist with this presentation.
- Have students look at the map. Have volunteers read aloud the labeled cities and geographic features. Model Spanish pronunciation of names as necessary. Have students jot down as many names of places and geographic features with Spanish origins as they can.

El país en cifras Have volunteers read the bulleted headings in **El país en cifras**. Point out cognates and clarify unfamiliar words. Explain that numerals in Spanish have a comma where English would use a decimal point (**3,5%**) and have a period where English would use a comma (**14.013.719**). Explain that **EE.UU.** is the abbreviation of **Estados Unidos**, and the doubling of the initial letters indicates plural. Model the pronunciation of **Florida** (accent on the second syllable) and point out that it is often used with an article (**la Florida**) by Spanish speakers. For perspective, give the total populations for the five states: California, 37,253,956; Texas, 25,145,561; Florida, 18,801,310; New York, 19,378,102; Illinois, 12,830,632.

¡Increíble pero cierto! Assure students that they are not expected to produce numbers greater than 30 at this point.

Estados Unidos

NATIONAL STANDARDS: connections, cultures

El país en cifras°

- **Población° de los EE.UU.:** 317 millones
- **Población de origen hispano:** 50 millones
- **País de origen de hispanos en los EE.UU.:**

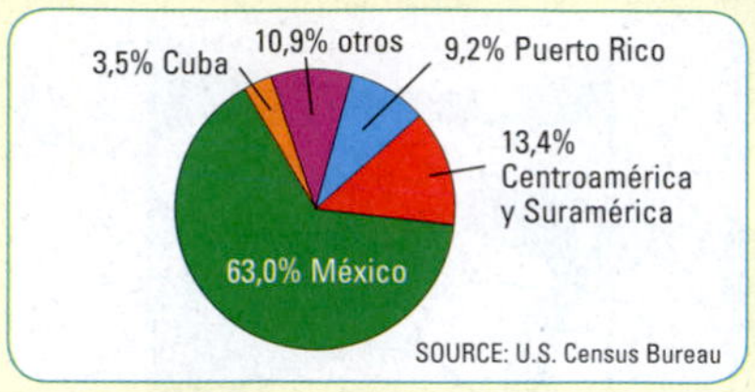

- **Estados con la mayor° población hispana:**

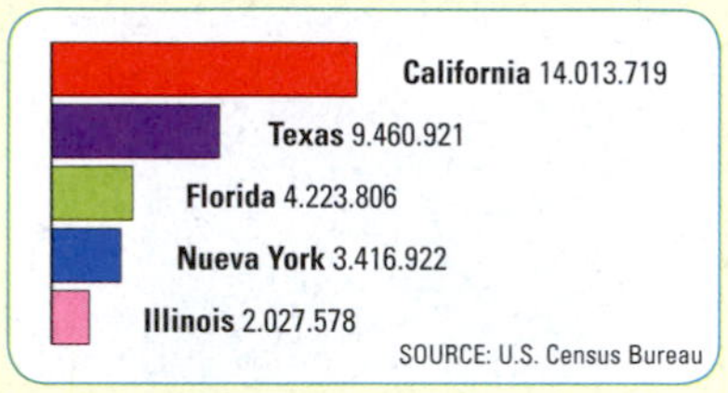

Canadá

El país en cifras

- **Población de Canadá:** 35 millones
- **Población de origen hispano:** 700.000
- **País de origen de hispanos en Canadá:**

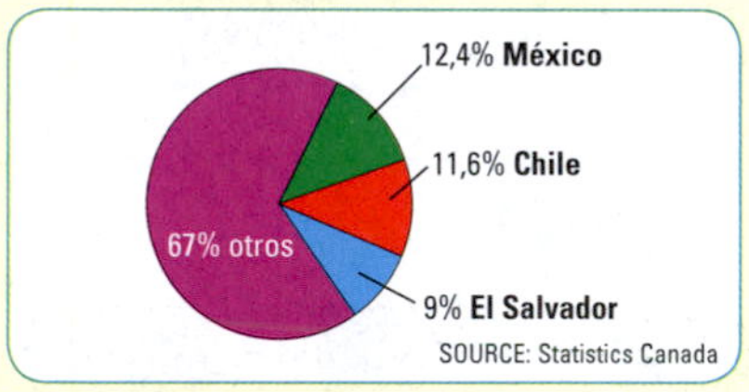

- **Ciudades° con la mayor población hispana:** Montreal, Toronto, Vancouver

en cifras *by the numbers* Población *Population* mayor *largest* Ciudades *Cities* creció *grew* más *more* cada *every* niños *children* Se estima *It is estimated* va a ser *it is going to be*

Mission District, en San Francisco

El Álamo, en San Antonio, Texas

recursos
WB pp. 9–10 | VM pp. 31–32 | vhlcentral.com Lección 1

¡Increíble pero cierto!

La población hispana en los EE.UU. creció° un 48% entre los años 2000 (dos mil) y 2011 (dos mil once) (16,7 millones de personas más°). Hoy, uno de cada° cinco niños° en los EE.UU. es de origen hispano. Se estima° que en el año 2034 va a ser° uno de cada tres.

TEACHING OPTIONS

Heritage Speakers Ask heritage speakers to describe the celebrations that are held in their families' countries of origin. Ask them to tell the date when the celebration takes place, the event it commemorates, and some of the particulars of the celebration. Possible celebrations: **Cinco de Mayo, Día de la Raza, Día de los Muertos, Fiesta de San Juan, Carnaval**.

Game Divide the class into teams of five. Give teams five minutes to brainstorm place names (cities, states, lakes, rivers, mountain ranges) in the United States that have Spanish origins. One team member should jot down the names in a numbered list. After five minutes, go over the names with the class, confirming the accuracy of each name. The team with the greatest number wins.

Comida • La comida mexicana

La comida° mexicana es muy popular en los Estados Unidos. Los tacos, las enchiladas, las quesadillas y los frijoles frecuentemente forman parte de las comidas de muchos norteamericanos. También° son populares las variaciones de la comida mexicana en los Estados Unidos: el tex-mex y el cali-mex.

Lugares • La Pequeña Habana

La Pequeña Habana° es un barrio° de Miami, Florida, donde viven° muchos cubanoamericanos. Es un lugar° donde se encuentran° las costumbres° de la cultura cubana, los aromas y sabores° de su comida y la música salsa. La Pequeña Habana es una parte de Cuba en los Estados Unidos.

Costumbres • Desfile puertorriqueño

Cada junio, desde° 1958 (mil novecientos cincuenta y ocho), los puertorriqueños celebran su cultura con un desfile° en Nueva York. Es un gran espectáculo con carrozas° y música salsa, merengue y hip-hop. Muchos espectadores llevan° la bandera° de Puerto Rico en su ropa° o pintada en la cara°.

Comunidad • Hispanos en Canadá

En Canadá viven° muchos hispanos. Toronto y Montreal son las ciudades° con mayor° población hispana. Muchos de ellos tienen estudios universitarios° y hablan° una de las lenguas° oficiales: inglés o francés°. Los hispanos participan activamente en la vida cotidiana° y profesional de Canadá.

¿Qué aprendiste? Completa las oraciones con la información adecuada (*appropriate*).

1. Hay __50 millones__ de personas de origen hispano en los Estados Unidos.
2. Los cuatro estados con las poblaciones hispanas más grandes son (en orden) __California__, Texas, Florida y __Nueva York__.
3. Toronto, Montreal y __Vancouver__ son las ciudades con más población hispana de Canadá.
4. Las quesadillas y las enchiladas son platos (*dishes*) __mexicanos__.
5. La Pequeña __Habana__ es un barrio de Miami.
6. En Miami hay muchas personas de origen __cubano__.
7. Cada junio se celebra en Nueva York un gran desfile para personas de origen __puertorriqueño__.
8. Muchos hispanos en Canadá hablan __inglés__ o francés.

Conexión Internet Investiga estos temas en **vhlcentral.com**.

Practice more at **vhlcentral.com**.

1. Haz (*Make*) una lista de seis hispanos célebres de los EE.UU. o Canadá. Explica (*Explain*) por qué (*why*) son célebres.
2. Escoge (*Choose*) seis lugares en los Estados Unidos con nombres hispanos e investiga sobre el origen y el significado (*meaning*) de cada nombre.

comida *food* También *Also* La Pequeña Habana *Little Havana* barrio *neighborhood* viven *live* lugar *place* se encuentran *are found* costumbres *customs* sabores *flavors* Cada junio desde *Each June since* desfile *parade* con carrozas *with floats* llevan *wear* bandera *flag* ropa *clothing* cara *face* viven *live* ciudades *cities* mayor *most* tienen estudios universitarios *have a degree* hablan *speak* lenguas *languages* inglés o francés *English or French* vida cotidiana *daily life*

Teaching Tip Ask volunteers to read sentences from **¡Increíble pero cierto!**, **Comida**, **Lugares**, **Costumbres**, and **Comunidad**. As necessary, model pronunciation, pause to point out cognates, and clarify unfamiliar words.

La comida mexicana Ask students if they have tried these dishes. Have students look at illustrated cookbooks or recipes to identify the ingredients and variations of the dishes mentioned in the paragraph.

La Pequeña Habana Many large cities in the United States have neighborhoods where people of Hispanic origin predominate. Encourage students to talk about the neighborhoods they know.

Desfile puertorriqueño The Puerto Rican Day Parade takes place on the weekend nearest the feast day of St. John the Baptist (**San Juan Bautista**), the patron saint of San Juan, capital of Puerto Rico.

Hispanos en Canadá The Canadian Hispanic Business Association holds a national awards program every year that honors the ten most influential Hispanic Canadians. Nominees represent countries from all over the Spanish-speaking world. Past winners have included researchers, corporate executives, judges, lawyers, entrepreneurs, musicians, artists, and politicians.

Conexión Internet Students will find supporting Internet activities and links at **vhlcentral.com**.

Teaching Tip You may want to wrap up this section by playing the ***Panorama cultural*** video footage for this lesson.

TEACHING OPTIONS

Variación léxica Hispanic groups in the United States refer to themselves with various names. The most common of these terms, **hispano** and **latino**, refer to all people who come from Hispanic backgrounds, regardless of the country of origin of their ancestors. **Puertorriqueño**, **cubanoamericano**, and **mexicoamericano** refer to Hispanics whose ancestors came from Puerto Rico, Cuba, and Mexico, respectively.

Many Mexican Americans also refer to themselves as **chicanos**. This word has stronger socio-political connotations than **mexicoamericano**. Use of the word **chicano** implies identification with Mexican Americans' struggle for civil rights and equal opportunity in the United States. It also suggests an appreciation of the indigenous aspects of Mexican and Mexican-American culture.

Instructional Resources
Supersite: Audio (Textbook & Lab MP3s); Testing Program (Tests, MP3s)
WebSAM
Lab Manual, p. 6

Teaching Tip Tell students that this is active vocabulary for which they are responsible and that it will appear on tests and exams.

Saludos

Hola.	*Hello; Hi.*
Buenos días.	*Good morning.*
Buenas tardes.	*Good afternoon.*
Buenas noches.	*Good evening; Good night.*

Despedidas

Adiós.	*Goodbye.*
Nos vemos.	*See you.*
Hasta luego.	*See you later.*
Hasta la vista.	*See you later.*
Hasta pronto.	*See you soon.*
Hasta mañana.	*See you tomorrow.*
Saludos a...	*Greetings to…*
Chau.	*Bye.*

¿Cómo está?

¿Cómo está usted?	*How are you?* (form.)
¿Cómo estás?	*How are you?* (fam.)
¿Qué hay de nuevo?	*What's new?*
¿Qué pasa?	*What's happening?; What's going on?*
¿Qué tal?	*How are you?; How is it going?*
(Muy) bien, gracias.	*(Very) well, thanks.*
Nada.	*Nothing.*
No muy bien.	*Not very well.*
Regular.	*So-so; OK.*

Expresiones de cortesía

Con permiso.	*Pardon me; Excuse me.*
De nada.	*You're welcome.*
Lo siento.	*I'm sorry.*
(Muchas) gracias.	*Thank you (very much); Thanks (a lot).*
No hay de qué.	*You're welcome.*
Perdón.	*Pardon me; Excuse me.*
por favor	*please*

Títulos

señor (Sr.); don	*Mr.; sir*
señora (Sra.); doña	*Mrs.; ma'am*
señorita (Srta.)	*Miss*

Presentaciones

¿Cómo se llama usted?	*What's your name?* (form.)
¿Cómo te llamas?	*What's your name?* (fam.)
Me llamo...	*My name is…*
¿Y usted?	*And you?* (form.)
¿Y tú?	*And you?* (fam.)
Mucho gusto.	*Pleased to meet you.*
El gusto es mío.	*The pleasure is mine.*
Encantado/a.	*Delighted; Pleased to meet you.*
Igualmente.	*Likewise.*
Le presento a...	*I would like to introduce you to* (name). (form.)
Te presento a...	*I would like to introduce you to* (name). (fam.)
el nombre	*name*

¿De dónde es?

¿De dónde es usted?	*Where are you from?* (form.)
¿De dónde eres?	*Where are you from?* (fam.)
Soy de...	*I'm from…*

Palabras adicionales

¿cuánto(s)/a(s)?	*how much/many?*
¿de quién...?	*whose…?* (sing.)
¿de quiénes...?	*whose…?* (plural)
(no) hay	*there is (not); there are (not)*

Sustantivos

el autobús	*bus*
el chico	*boy*
la chica	*girl*
la computadora	*computer*
la comunidad	*community*
el/la conductor(a)	*driver*
la conversación	*conversation*
la cosa	*thing*
el cuaderno	*notebook*
el día	*day*
el diario	*diary*
el diccionario	*dictionary*
la escuela	*school*
el/la estudiante	*student*
la foto(grafía)	*photograph*
el hombre	*man*
el/la joven	*young person*
el lápiz	*pencil*
la lección	*lesson*
la maleta	*suitcase*
la mano	*hand*
el mapa	*map*
la mujer	*woman*
la nacionalidad	*nationality*
el número	*number*
el país	*country*
la palabra	*word*
el/la pasajero/a	*passenger*
el problema	*problem*
el/la profesor(a)	*teacher*
el programa	*program*
el/la turista	*tourist*
el video	*video*

Verbo

ser	*to be*

Numbers 0–30	*See page 16.*
Telling time	*See pages 24–25.*
Expresiones útiles	*See page 7.*

Vocabulary Tools

recursos
LM p. 6
vhlcentral.com Lección 1

En la universidad 2

Communicative Goals

You will learn how to:

- **Talk about your classes and school life**
- **Discuss everyday activities**
- **Ask questions in Spanish**
- **Describe the location of people and things**

A PRIMERA VISTA

- ¿Hay un chico y una chica en la foto?
- ¿Hay una computadora o dos?
- ¿Son turistas o estudiantes?
- ¿Qué hora es, la una de la mañana o de la tarde?

Lesson Goals

In **Lección 2**, students will be introduced to the following:

- classroom- and university-related words
- names of academic courses and fields of study
- class schedules
- days of the week
- universities and majors in the Spanish-speaking world
- the **Universidad de Salamanca**
- present tense of regular **–ar** verbs
- forming negative sentences
- the verb **gustar**
- forming questions
- the present tense of **estar**
- prepositions of location
- numbers 31 and higher
- using text formats to predict content
- brainstorming and organizing ideas for writing
- a video about the **Universidad Nacional Autónoma de México (UNAM)**
- cultural, geographic, and economic information about Spain

A primera vista Have students look at the photo. Say: **Es una foto de dos jóvenes en la universidad.** Then ask: **¿Qué son los jóvenes? (Son estudiantes.) ¿Qué hay en la mano del chico? (Hay una computadora.)**

Teaching Tip Look for these icons for additional communicative practice:

→•←	**Interpretive communication**
←•→	**Presentational communication**
•↔•	**Interpersonal communication**

INSTRUCTIONAL RESOURCES

Supersite (vhlcentral.com)
Video: ***Fotonovela, Flash cultura, Panorama cultural***
Audio: Textbook and Lab MP3 Files
Activity Pack: Information Gap Activities, games, additional activity handouts
Resources: SAM Answer Key, Scripts, Translations, **Vocabulario adicional**, sample lesson plan, Grammar Presentation Slides, Digital Image Bank
Testing Program: Quizzes, Tests, Exams, MP3s
Student Activities Manual: Workbook/Video Manual/Lab Manual
WebSAM (online Student Activities Manual)

Vocabulary Tools

Section Goals

In **Contextos**, students will learn and practice:

- names for people, places, and things at the university
- names of academic courses

Instructional Resources
Supersite: Audio (Textbook and Lab MP3 Files); Resources (Digital Image Bank, **Vocabulario adicional**, Activity Pack, Scripts, Answer Keys); Testing Program (Quizzes)
WebSAM
Workbook, pp. 11–12
Lab Manual, p. 7

Teaching Tips

- Introduce vocabulary for classroom objects such as **mesa, libro, pluma, lápiz, papel**. Hold up or point to an object and say: **Es un lápiz.** Ask questions that include **¿Hay/No hay...?** and **¿Cuántos/as...?**
- Use the **Lección 2 Contextos** digital images to assist with this presentation.
- Point to objects in the classroom and ask questions such as: **¿Qué es? ¿Es una mesa? ¿Es un reloj?** Vary by asking: **¿Qué hay en el escritorio? ¿Qué hay en la mesa? ¿Cuántas tizas hay en la pizarra? ¿Hay una pluma en el escritorio de ____?**

Successful Language Learning Encourage students to make flash cards to help them memorize new vocabulary words.

Note: At this point you may want to present ***Vocabulario adicional: Más vocabulario para las clases*** from the Supersite.

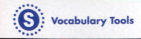

En la universidad

Más vocabulario

la biblioteca	*library*
la cafetería	*cafeteria*
la casa	*house; home*
el estadio	*stadium*
el laboratorio	*laboratory*
la librería	*bookstore*
la residencia estudiantil	*dormitory*
la universidad	*university; college*
el/la compañero/a de clase	*classmate*
el/la compañero/a de cuarto	*roommate*
la clase	*class*
el curso	*course*
la especialización	*major*
el examen	*test; exam*
el horario	*schedule*
la prueba	*test; quiz*
el semestre	*semester*
la tarea	*homework*
el trimestre	*trimester; quarter*
la administración de empresas	*business administration*
el arte	*art*
la biología	*biology*
las ciencias	*sciences*
la computación	*computer science*
la contabilidad	*accounting*
la economía	*economics*
el español	*Spanish*
la física	*physics*
la geografía	*geography*
la música	*music*

Variación léxica

pluma ⟷ bolígrafo
pizarra ⟷ tablero (*Col.*)

recursos

WB pp. 11–12	LM p. 7	vhlcentral.com Lección 2

TEACHING OPTIONS

Heritage Speakers Ask heritage speakers to tell the class any other terms they or their families use to talk about people, places, or things at school. Ask them to tell where these terms are used. Possible responses: **el boli, la ciudad universitaria, el profe, el catedrático, la facultad, el profesorado, la asignatura, el gimnasio, el pizarrón, el salón de clases, el aula, el pupitre, el gis, el alumno.**

Game Divide the class into two teams. Then, in English, name an academic course and ask one of the teams to provide the Spanish equivalent. If the team provides the correct term, it gets a point. If not, the second team gets a chance at the same item. Alternate between teams until you have read all the course names. The team with the most points at the end wins.

Práctica

1 Escuchar Listen to Professor Morales talk about her Spanish classroom, then check the items she mentions.

puerta	✓	tiza	✓	plumas	✓
ventanas	✓	escritorios	✓	mochilas	○
pizarra	✓	sillas	○	papel	✓
borrador	○	libros	✓	reloj	✓

2 Identificar You will hear a series of words. Write each one in the appropriate category.

Personas	Lugares	Materias
el estudiante	el estadio	la química
la profesora	la biblioteca	las lenguas extranjeras
el compañero de clase	la residencia estudiantil	el inglés

3 Emparejar Match each question with its most logical response. **¡Ojo!** (*Careful!*) One response will not be used.

1. ¿Qué clase es? d
2. ¿Quiénes son? g
3. ¿Quién es? e
4. ¿De dónde es? c
5. ¿A qué hora es la clase de inglés? f
6. ¿Cuántos estudiantes hay? a

a. Hay veinticinco.
b. Es un reloj.
c. Es de Perú.
d. Es la clase de química.
e. Es el señor Bastos.
f. Es a las nueve en punto.
g. Son los profesores.

4 Identificar Identify the word that does not belong in each group.

1. examen • casa • tarea • prueba casa
2. economía • matemáticas • biblioteca • contabilidad biblioteca
3. pizarra • tiza • borrador • librería librería
4. lápiz • cafetería • papel • cuaderno cafetería
5. veinte • diez • pluma • treinta pluma
6. conductor • laboratorio • autobús • pasajero laboratorio

5 ¿Qué clase es? Name the class associated with the subject matter.

modelo
los elementos, los átomos *Es la clase de química.*

1. Abraham Lincoln, Winston Churchill Es la clase de historia.
2. Picasso, Leonardo da Vinci Es la clase de arte.
3. Freud, Jung Es la clase de psicología.
4. África, el océano Pacífico Es la clase de geografía.
5. la cultura de España, verbos Es la clase de español.
6. Hemingway, Shakespeare Es la clase de literatura.
7. geometría, calculadora Es la clase de matemáticas.

1 Expansion Have students circle the items that they see in their own classroom.

1 Script ¿Qué hay en mi clase de español? ¡Muchas cosas! Hay una puerta y cinco ventanas. Hay una pizarra con tiza. Hay muchos escritorios para los estudiantes. En los escritorios de los estudiantes hay libros y plumas. En la mesa de la profesora hay papel. Hay un mapa y un reloj en la clase también.
Textbook MP3s

2 Teaching Tip To simplify, have students prepare for listening by predicting a few words for each category.

2 Script el estudiante, la química, el estadio, las lenguas extranjeras, la profesora, la biblioteca, el inglés, el compañero de clase, la residencia estudiantil
Textbook MP3s

3 Expansion Have student pairs ask each other the questions and answer truthfully, based on your class. Ex: **1. ¿Qué clase es? (Es la clase de español.)** For items 2–4, the questioner should indicate specific people in the classroom.

4 Expansion Have students write four additional items for a partner to complete.

5 Expansion Have the class associate famous people with these fields: **periodismo, computación, humanidades**. Then have them guess the fields associated with these people: Albert Einstein (**física**), Charles Darwin (**biología**).

TEACHING OPTIONS

Extra Practice Ask students what phrases or vocabulary words they associate with these items: **1. la pizarra** (Ex: **la tiza, el borrador**), **2. la residencia estudiantil** (Ex: **el/la compañero(a) de cuarto, el/la estudiante**), **3. el reloj** (Ex: **¿Qué hora es?, Son las…, Es la…**), **4. la biblioteca** (Ex: **los libros, los exámenes, las materias**).

Extra Practice On the board, write **¿Qué clases tomas?** and **Tomo…** Explain the meaning of these phrases and ask students to circulate around the classroom and imagine that they are meeting their classmates for the first time. Tell them to introduce themselves, find out where each person is from, and ask what classes they are taking. Follow up by asking individual students what their classmates are taking.

Teaching Tips
- Write these questions and answers on the board, explaining their meaning as you do so:
  —**¿Qué día es hoy?**
  —**Hoy es ____.**
  —**¿Qué día es mañana?** (Students learned **mañana** in **Lección 1**.)
  —**Mañana es ____.**
  —**¿Cuándo es la prueba?**
  —**Es el ____.**
  Then ask students the questions on the board.
- Explain that Monday is considered the first day of the week in the Spanish-speaking world and usually appears as such on calendars.

Los días de la semana

septiembre

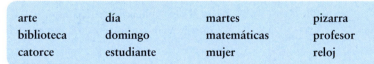

lunes	martes	miércoles	jueves	viernes	sábado	domingo
	1	2	3	4	5	6
7	8	9	10			

¡LENGUA VIVA!

The days of the week are never capitalized in Spanish.

•••

Monday is considered the first day of the week in Spanish-speaking countries.

CONSULTA

Note that September in Spanish is **septiembre**. For all of the months of the year, go to **Contextos, Lección 5**, p. 142.

6 **¿Qué día es hoy?** Complete each statement with the correct day of the week.

1. Hoy es martes. Mañana es miércoles. Ayer fue (*Yesterday was*) lunes.
2. Ayer fue sábado. Mañana es lunes. Hoy es domingo.
3. Mañana es viernes. Hoy es jueves. Ayer fue miércoles.
4. Ayer fue domingo. Hoy es lunes. Mañana es martes.
5. Hoy es jueves. Ayer fue miércoles. Mañana es viernes.
6. Mañana es lunes. Hoy es domingo. Ayer fue sábado.

6 Expansion To challenge students, ask them questions such as: **Mañana es viernes... ¿qué día fue ayer? (miércoles); Ayer fue domingo... ¿qué día es mañana? (martes)**

7 **Analogías** Use these words to complete the analogies. Some words will not be used.

arte	día	martes	pizarra
biblioteca	domingo	matemáticas	profesor
catorce	estudiante	mujer	reloj

1. maleta ⟷ pasajero ⊜ mochila ⟷ estudiante
2. chico ⟷ chica ⊜ hombre ⟷ mujer
3. pluma ⟷ papel ⊜ tiza ⟷ pizarra
4. inglés ⟷ lengua ⊜ miércoles ⟷ día
5. papel ⟷ cuaderno ⊜ libro ⟷ biblioteca
6. quince ⟷ dieciséis ⊜ lunes ⟷ martes
7. Cervantes ⟷ literatura ⊜ Dalí ⟷ arte
8. autobús ⟷ conductor ⊜ clase ⟷ profesor
9. los EE.UU. ⟷ mapa ⊜ hora ⟷ reloj
10. veinte ⟷ veintitrés ⊜ jueves ⟷ domingo

Practice more at **vhlcentral.com**.

7 Teaching Tip To simplify, before doing this activity, have students review the list of **sustantivos** on page 34 and numbers 0–30 on page 16.

TEACHING OPTIONS

Extra Practice Have students prepare a day-planner for the upcoming week. Tell them to list each day of the week and the things they expect to do each day, including classes, homework, tests, appointments, and social events. Provide unfamiliar vocabulary as needed. Tell them to include the time each activity takes place. Have them exchange their day-planners with a partner and check each other's work for accuracy.

Game Have groups of five or six play a "word-chain" game in which the first group member says a word in Spanish (e.g., **estudiante**). The next student has to say a word that begins with the last letter of the first person's word (e.g., **español**). If a student cannot think of a word, he or she is eliminated and it is the next student's turn. The last student left in the game is the winner.

NATIONAL communication STANDARDS

Comunicación

8 **Horario** Choose three courses from the chart to create your own class schedule, then discuss it with a classmate. Answers will vary.

materia	horas	días	profesor(a)
historia	9–10	lunes, miércoles	Prof. Ordóñez
biología	12–1	lunes, jueves	Profa. Dávila
periodismo	2–3	martes, jueves	Profa. Quiñones
matemáticas	2–3	miércoles, jueves	Prof. Jiménez
arte	12–1:30	lunes, miércoles	Prof. Molina

modelo

Estudiante 1: *Tomo (I take) biología los lunes y jueves, de 12 a 1, con (with) la profesora Dávila.*

Estudiante 2: *¿Sí? Yo no tomo biología. Yo tomo arte los lunes y miércoles, de 12 a 1:30, con el profesor Molina.*

¡ATENCIÓN!

Use **el** + [*day of the week*] when an activity occurs on a specific day and **los** + [*day of the week*] when an activity occurs regularly.

El lunes tengo un examen.
***On Monday** I have an exam.*

Los lunes y miércoles tomo biología.
***On Mondays and Wednesdays** I take biology.*

•••

Except for **sábados** and **domingos**, the singular and plural forms for days of the week are the same.

9 **Memoria** How well do you know your Spanish classroom? Take a good look around and then close your eyes. Your partner will ask you questions about the classroom, using these words and other vocabulary. Each person should answer six questions and switch roles every three questions. Answers will vary.

escritorio	mapa	pizarra	reloj
estudiante	mesa	profesor(a)	ventana
libro	mochila	puerta	silla

modelo

Estudiante 1: *¿Cuántas ventanas hay?*

Estudiante 2: *Hay cuatro ventanas.*

10 **Nuevos amigos** During the first week of class, you meet a new student in the cafeteria. With a partner, prepare a conversation using these cues. Then act it out for the class. Answers will vary.

Estudiante 1		Estudiante 2
Greet your new acquaintance.	→	Introduce yourself.
Find out about him or her.	→	Tell him or her about yourself.
Ask about your partner's class schedule.	→	Compare your schedule to your partner's.
Say nice to meet you and goodbye.	→	Say nice to meet you and goodbye.

8 Teaching Tip Point out the professors' names in the chart and the use of the abbreviations **Prof.** and **Profa.**

8 Expansion Tell students to write their name at the top of their schedules, and have pairs exchange papers with another pair. Then have them repeat the activity with the new schedules, asking and answering questions in the third person. Ex: **—¿Qué clases toma ____? —Los lunes y jueves ____ toma biología con la profesora Dávila.**

9 Expansion Repeat the activity with campus-related vocabulary.

Successful Language Learning Remind the class that errors are a natural part of language learning. Point out that it is impossible to speak "perfectly" in any language. Emphasize that their spoken and written Spanish will improve if they make the effort to practice.

10 Teaching Tip To simplify, quickly review the basic greetings, courtesy expressions, and introductions taught in **Lección 1, Contextos,** pages 2–3.

10 Expansion Ask volunteers to introduce their new acquaintances to the class and present any new information they learned about their partners.

TEACHING OPTIONS

Groups Have students do **Actividad 10** in groups, imagining that they meet several new students in the cafeteria. Have the groups present this activity as a skit for the class. Give the groups time to prepare and rehearse, and tell them that they will be presenting it without a script or any other kind of notes.

Game Point out the **modelo** in **Actividad 8**. Have students write a few simple sentences that describe their own course schedules. Ex: **Tomo dos clases. Los lunes, miércoles y viernes, de 10 a 11, tomo español con la profesora Morales. Los martes y jueves, de 2:30 a 4, tomo arte con el profesor Casas.** Then collect the descriptions, shuffle them, and read them aloud. The class should guess who wrote each description.

Section Goals

In **Fotonovela**, students will:

- receive comprehensible input from free-flowing discourse
- learn functional phrases that preview lesson grammatical structures

Instructional Resources
Supersite: Video (***Fotonovela***); Resources (Scripts, Translations, Answer Keys)
WebSAM
Video Manual, pp. 3–4

Video Recap: Lección 1
Before doing this **Fotonovela** section, review the previous episode with these questions:
1. En la familia Díaz, ¿quiénes son estudiantes? (Felipe y Jimena son estudiantes.) 2. ¿Quién es Roberto? (Es el esposo de Carolina.) 3. ¿De dónde es Marissa? (Es de Wisconsin.) 4. ¿De dónde es la señora Díaz? (Es de Cuba.) 5. ¿Es de Felipe el diccionario? (No, es de Marissa.)

Video Synopsis **Felipe** takes **Marissa** around Mexico City. Along the way, they meet some friends, **Juan Carlos** and **Miguel**. **Felipe, Marissa,** and **Juan Carlos** compare schedules for the upcoming semester, while **Miguel** rushes off to meet **Maru**.

Teaching Tips

- Have students cover up the **Expresiones útiles**. Have them scan the **Fotonovela** captions to find phrases about classes and then phrases that express what people like.
- Ask a few basic questions that use the **Expresiones útiles**. Ex: **¿Cuántas clases tomas? ¿Te gusta la clase de _____?**

¿Qué estudias?

NATIONAL STANDARDS communication cultures

Felipe, Marissa, Juan Carlos y Miguel visitan Chapultepec y hablan de las clases.

PERSONAJES

MARISSA

FELIPE

Video: *Fotonovela*

1

FELIPE Dos boletos, por favor.

2

EMPLEADO Dos boletos son 64 pesos.
FELIPE Aquí están 100 pesos.
EMPLEADO 100 menos 64 son 36 pesos de cambio.

3

FELIPE Ésta es la Ciudad de México.

4

FELIPE Oye, Marissa, ¿cuántas clases tomas?
MARISSA Tomo cuatro clases: español, historia, literatura y también geografía. Me gusta mucho la cultura mexicana.

5

MIGUEL Marissa, hablas muy bien el español... ¿Y dónde está tu diccionario?
MARISSA En casa de los Díaz. Felipe necesita practicar inglés.
MIGUEL ¡Ay, Maru! Chicos, nos vemos más tarde.

6

FELIPE Juan Carlos, ¿quién enseña la clase de química este semestre?
JUAN CARLOS El profesor Morales. Ah, ¿por qué tomo química y computación?
FELIPE Porque te gusta la tarea.

TEACHING OPTIONS

Video Tips General suggestions for using video clips in the classroom can be found in the front matter of this Instructor's Annotated Edition.

¿Qué estudias? Play the **¿Qué estudias?** episode of the **Fotonovela** and have students give you a "play-by-play" description of the action. Write their descriptions on the board. Give the class a moment to read the descriptions you have written and then play the episode a second time so that students can add more details to the descriptions or consolidate information. Finally, discuss the material on the board with the class and call attention to any incorrect information. Help students prepare a brief plot summary.

JUAN CARLOS

MIGUEL

EMPLEADO

MARU

7

FELIPE Los lunes y los miércoles, economía a las 2:30. Tú tomas computación los martes en la tarde, y química, a ver... Los lunes, los miércoles y los viernes ¿a las 10? ¡Uf!

8

FELIPE Y Miguel, ¿cuándo regresa?

JUAN CARLOS Hoy estudia con Maru.

MARISSA ¿Quién es Maru?

9

MIGUEL ¿Hablas con tu mamá?

MARU Mamá habla. Yo escucho. Es la 1:30.

MIGUEL Ay, lo siento. Juan Carlos y Felipe...

MARU Ay, Felipe.

10

MARU Y ahora, ¿adónde? ¿A la biblioteca?

MIGUEL Sí, pero primero a la librería. Necesito comprar unos libros.

recursos

VM pp. 3–4

vhlcentral.com Lección 2

Expresiones útiles

Talking about classes

¿Cuántas clases tomas?
How many classes are you taking?
Tomo cuatro clases.
I'm taking four classes.
Mi especialización es en arqueología.
My major is archeology.
Este año, espero sacar buenas notas y, por supuesto, viajar por el país.
This year, I hope / I'm hoping to get good grades. And, of course, travel through the country.

Talking about likes/dislikes

Me gusta mucho la cultura mexicana.
I like Mexican culture a lot.
Me gustan las ciencias ambientales.
I like environmental science.
Me gusta dibujar.
I like to draw.
¿Te gusta este lugar?
Do you like this place?

Paying for tickets

Dos boletos, por favor.
Two tickets, please.
Dos boletos son sesenta y cuatro pesos.
Two tickets are sixty-four pesos.
Aquí están cien pesos.
Here's a hundred pesos.
Son treinta y seis pesos de cambio.
That's thirty-six pesos change.

Talking about location and direction

¿Dónde está tu diccionario?
Where is your dictionary?
Está en casa de los Díaz.
It's at the Díaz house.
Y ahora, ¿adónde? ¿A la biblioteca?
And now, where to? To the library?
Sí, pero primero a la librería.
Está al lado.
Yes, but first to the bookstore.
It's next door.

Expresiones útiles Identify forms of **tomar** and **estar**. Point out the questions and interrogative words. Tell students that they will learn more about these concepts in **Estructura**. Point out that **gusta** is used when what is liked is singular, and **gustan** when what is liked is plural. A detailed discussion of the **gustar** construction (see **Estructura 2.1**, page 48) is unnecessary here. Emphasize the **me/te gusta(n)** forms, as these are the only ones that will appear on tests until **Lección 7**.

Teaching Tip Have the class read through the entire **Fotonovela**, with volunteers playing the parts of **Felipe**, **Marissa**, **Juan Carlos**, **Miguel**, **Maru**, and the **empleado**.

TEACHING OPTIONS

Pairs Have students scan the captions and **Expresiones útiles**. They should then underline the **gustar** contructions and jot down the phrases that best describe themselves. Repeat the exercise with the verb **tomar**. Then, in pairs, have students guess which phrases their partners used to describe themselves.
Ex: **—Te gusta la tarea, ¿no?**

Extra Practice Ask pairs to write five true/false statements based on the **¿Qué estudias?** captions. Then have them exchange papers with another pair, who will complete the activity and correct the false statements. Ask volunteers to read a few statements for the class, and have students answer and point out the caption that contains the information.

¿Qué pasó?

1 Escoger Choose the answer that best completes each sentence.

1. Marissa toma (*is taking*) ___c___ en la universidad.
   a. español, psicología, economía y música b. historia, inglés, sociología y periodismo
   c. español, historia, literatura y geografía
2. El profesor Morales enseña (*teaches*) ___a___.
   a. química b. matemáticas c. historia
3. Juan Carlos toma química ___b___.
   a. los miércoles, jueves y viernes b. los lunes, miércoles y viernes
   c. los lunes, martes y jueves
4. Miguel necesita ir a (*needs to go to*) ___c___.
   a. la biblioteca b. la residencia estudiantil c. la librería

2 Identificar Indicate which person would make each statement. The names may be used more than once.

1. ¿Maru es compañera de ustedes? ___Marissa___
2. Mi mamá habla mucho. ___Maru___
3. El profesor Morales enseña la clase de química este semestre. ___Juan Carlos___
4. Mi diccionario está en casa de Felipe y Jimena. ___Marissa___
5. Necesito estudiar con Maru. ___Miguel___
6. Yo tomo clase de computación los martes por la tarde. ___Juan Carlos___

3 Completar These sentences are similar to things said in the **Fotonovela**. Complete each sentence with the correct word(s).

Castillo de Chapultepec	estudiar	miércoles
clase	inglés	tarea

1. Marissa, éste es el ___Castillo de Chapultepec___.
2. Felipe tiene (*has*) el diccionario porque (*because*) necesita practicar ___inglés___.
3. A Juan Carlos le gusta mucho la ___tarea___.
4. Hay clase de economía los lunes y ___miércoles___.
5. Miguel está con Maru para ___estudiar___.

4 Preguntas personales Interview a partner about his/her university life. Answers will vary.

1. ¿Qué clases tomas en la universidad?
2. ¿Qué clases tomas los martes?
3. ¿Qué clases tomas los viernes?
4. ¿En qué clase hay más chicos?
5. ¿En qué clase hay más chicas?
6. ¿Te gusta la clase de español?

Practice more at **vhlcentral.com**.

NOTA CULTURAL

Maru is a shortened version of the name **María Eugenia.** Other popular "combination names" in Spanish are **Juanjo (Juan José)** and **Maite (María Teresa).**

NOTA CULTURAL

The **Castillo de Chapultepec** is one of Mexico City's most historic landmarks. Constructed in 1785, it was the residence of emperors and presidents. It has been open to the public since 1944 and now houses the National Museum of History.

1 Teaching Tips
- Before doing this activity, review the names of courses, pages 36–37, and the days of the week, page 38.
- Alternatively, reformat this activity as a matching exercise in which students match the name of the character with the corresponding information.

2 Expansion Give these statements to the class as items 7–10: **7. La cultura mexicana es interesante. (Marissa) 8. Mi diccionario está en la casa de Felipe. (Marissa) 9. Yo compro los boletos. (Felipe) 10. Necesito comprar unas cosas en la librería. (Miguel)**

3 Expansion Point out that one of the answers in the word bank will not be used. After students complete this activity, have them write a sentence that includes the unused item **(clase).**

Nota cultural The name **Chapultepec** derives from *Chapoltepēc*, which means "at the grasshopper hill" in Nahuatl. Covering 1,700 acres, **El Bosque de Chapultepec** consists of forest, lakes, and landscaped areas. It also houses a zoo, an amusement park, and **Los Pinos,** the official residence of the President of Mexico.

4 Expansion
Ask volunteers to reenact their conversation for the class.

The Affective Dimension
If students appear anxious about speaking, reassure them that perfect pronunciation is not necessary for communication and that their pronunciation will improve with practice.

TEACHING OPTIONS

Small Groups Have students work in small groups to create a skit in which a radio reporter asks local university students where they are from, which classes they are taking, and which classes they like. Encourage students to use the phrases in **Expresiones útiles** as much as possible. Have one or two groups role-play their skit for the class.

Extra Practice Have students close their books and complete these statements with information from the **Fotonovela**. You may slowly read aloud the sentences or write them on the board. Ex: **1. Tomo cuatro ____: español, historia, literatura y geografía. (clases) 2. Y Miguel, ¿cuándo ____? (regresa) 3. Dos ____ son 64 pesos. (boletos) 4. ¿Dónde ____ tu diccionario? (está)**

NATIONAL STANDARDS comparisons

Pronunciación Audio

Spanish vowels

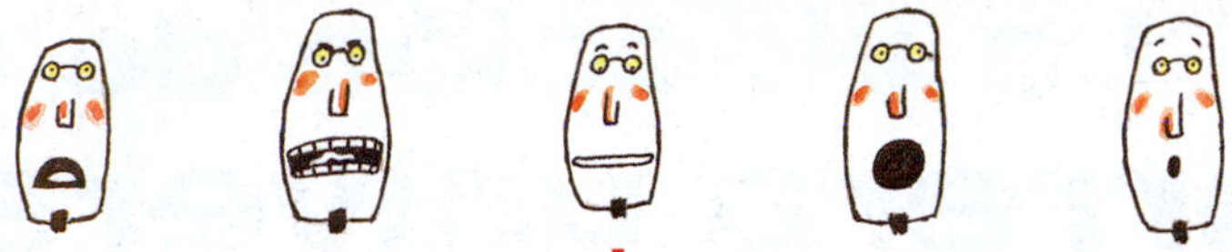

a **e** **i** **o** **u**

Spanish vowels are never silent; they are always pronounced in a short, crisp way without the glide sounds used in English.

Álex **clase** **nada** **encantada**

The letter **a** is pronounced like the *a* in *father*, but shorter.

el **ene** **mesa** **elefante**

The letter **e** is pronounced like the *e* in *they*, but shorter.

Inés **chica** **tiza** **señorita**

The letter **i** sounds like the *ee* in *beet*, but shorter.

hola **con** **libro** **don Francisco**

The letter **o** is pronounced like the *o* in *tone*, but shorter.

uno **regular** **saludos** **gusto**

The letter **u** sounds like the *oo* in *room*, but shorter.

Práctica Practice the vowels by saying the names of these places in Spain.

1. Madrid
2. Alicante
3. Tenerife
4. Toledo
5. Barcelona
6. Granada
7. Burgos
8. La Coruña

Oraciones Read the sentences aloud, focusing on the vowels.

1. Hola. Me llamo Ramiro Morgado.
2. Estudio arte en la Universidad de Salamanca.
3. Tomo también literatura y contabilidad.
4. Ay, tengo clase en cinco minutos. ¡Nos vemos!

Refranes Practice the vowels by reading these sayings aloud.

Del dicho al hecho hay un gran trecho.[1]

1 Easier said than done.
2 To each his own.

recursos
LM p. 8
vhlcentral.com Lección 2

AYUDA

Although **hay** and **ay** are pronounced identically, they do not have the same meaning. As you learned in **Lección 1**, **hay** is a verb form that means *there is/are*. **Hay veinte libros**. (*There are twenty books*.) **¡Ay!** is an exclamation expressing pain, shock, or affliction: *Oh!; Oh, dear!*

Section Goal

In **Pronunciación**, students will be introduced to Spanish vowels and how they are pronounced.

Instructional Resources

Supersite: Audio (Textbook and Lab MP3 Files); Resources (Scripts, Answer Keys)
WebSAM
Lab Manual, p. 8

Teaching Tips

- Point out that the drawings above the vowels on this page indicate the approximate position of the mouth as the vowels are pronounced.
- Model the pronunciation of each vowel and have students pay attention to the shape of your mouth. Have them repeat the vowel after you. Then go through the example words.
- To practice pure vowel sounds, teach students this chant: **A-E-I-O-U, ¡el burro sabe más que tú!**
- Pronounce a few of the example words and have the students write them on the board with their books closed.

Práctica/Oraciones/Refranes

These exercises are recorded on the *Textbook MP3s*. You may want to play the audio so that students practice listening to Spanish spoken by speakers other than yourself.

TEACHING OPTIONS

Extra Practice Provide additional names of places in Spain. Have students spell each name aloud in Spanish, then ask them to pronounce each one. Avoid names that contain diphthongs. Ex: **Sevilla, Salamanca, Santander, Albacete, Gerona, Lugo, Badajoz, Tarragona, Logroño, Valladolid, Orense, Pamplona, Ibiza.**

Small Groups Have the class turn to the **Fotonovela,** pages 40–41, and work in groups of four to read all or part of the **Fotonovela** aloud, focusing on the correct pronunciation of the vowels. Circulate among the groups and, as needed, model the correct pronunciation and intonation of words and phrases.

Section Goals

In **Cultura**, students will:

- learn how students choose their majors and enter the university
- learn academic-related terms
- read about the **Universidad de Salamanca**
- read about university enrollment

Instructional Resources
Supersite: Video (***Flash cultura***); Resources (Scripts, Translations, Answer Keys)
WebSAM
Video Manual, pp. 75–76

En detalle

Antes de leer Ask students about their experiences entering the university. What were important factors in their decision of where to study? Have they chosen their majors yet? If so, how did they decide?

Lectura

- Many students tend to live at home. If they do live on campus, they usually live in a **residencia estudiantil** or a **colegio mayor**. The **colegio mayor** tends to offer more student life, similar to that of a sorority or fraternity.
- Because enrollments are high, campuses are scattered, with buildings in different areas of the city or town. Unlike a U.S. university, where one might find a quadrangle where students gather, student life in Hispanic universities might take place in individual **facultades**.

Después de leer Ask students which university system they prefer.

1 Expansion Give students these sentences as items 11–12: 11. An undergraduate degree is often called a **licenciatura**. (**Cierto.**) 12. The majority of Hispanics that study in the U.S. are Colombian. (**Falso**. There are more Mexican than Colombian students in the U.S.)

Flash CULTURA

EN DETALLE

Video: *Flash cultura*

NATIONAL STANDARDS connections cultures

La elección de una carrera universitaria

Since higher education in the Spanish-speaking world is heavily state-subsidized, tuition is almost free. As a result, public universities see large enrollments. Spanish and Latin American students generally choose their **carrera universitaria** (major) when they're eighteen—which is either the year they enter the university or the year before. In order to enroll, all students must complete a high school degree, known as the **bachillerato.** In countries like Bolivia, Mexico, and Peru, the last year of high school (**colegio***) tends to be specialized in an area of study, such as the arts or natural sciences.

Students then choose their major according to their area of specialization. Similarly, university-bound students in Argentina focus their studies on specific fields, such as the humanities and social sciences, natural sciences, communication, art and design, and economics and business, during their five years of high school. Based on this coursework, Argentine students choose their **carrera**. Finally, in Spain, students choose their major according to the score they receive on the **prueba de aptitud** (skills test or entrance exam).

University graduates receive a **licenciatura**, or bachelor's degree. In Argentina and Chile, a **licenciatura** takes four to six years to complete, and may be considered equivalent to a master's degree. In Peru and Venezuela, a bachelor's degree is a five-year process. Spanish and Colombian **licenciaturas** take four to five years, although some fields, such as medicine, require six or more.

Universidad Central de Venezuela en Caracas

Estudiantes hispanos en los EE.UU.

In the 2013–14 academic year, over 14,500 Mexican students (1.7% of all international students) studied at U.S. universities. Colombians were the second-largest Spanish-speaking group, with over 7,000 students.

*¡Ojo! **El colegio** is a false cognate. In most countries, it means *high school*, but in some regions it refers to an elementary school. All undergraduate study takes place at **la universidad**.

ACTIVIDADES

1 **¿Cierto o falso?** Indicate whether these statements are cierto or falso. Correct the false statements.

1. Students in Spanish-speaking countries must pay large amounts of money toward their college tuition. Falso. At public universities tuition is almost free.
2. **Carrera** refers to any undergraduate or graduate program that students enroll in to obtain a professional degree. Cierto.
3. After studying at a **colegio**, students receive their **bachillerato**. Cierto.
4. Undergraduates study at a **colegio** or an **universidad**. Falso. An undergraduate student takes classes at an **universidad**.
5. In Latin America and Spain, students usually choose their majors in their second year at the university. Falso. They choose their majors either upon entering the university or the year before.
6. In Argentina, students focus their studies in their high school years. Cierto.
7. In Mexico, the **bachillerato** involves specialized study. Cierto.
8. In Spain, majors depend on entrance exam scores. Cierto.
9. Venezuelans complete a **licenciatura** in five years. Cierto.
10. According to statistics, Colombians constitute the third-largest Latin American group studying at U.S. universities. Falso. Colombians are the second-largest group.

TEACHING OPTIONS

Small Groups In groups of three, have students describe the photos on this page. Ask them to write as much as they can in Spanish about the university and students pictured. Then have volunteers read their descriptions to the class.

Cultural Activity Ask student pairs to create a list of comparisons between U.S. universities and universities in Spanish-speaking countries. Encourage them to consider enrollment, student life, majors, tuition, and other significant aspects. Then survey the class and summarize the results on the board.

ASÍ SE DICE

Clases y exámenes

aprobar	*to pass*
la asignatura (Esp.)	la clase, la materia
la clase anual	*year-long course*
el examen parcial	*midterm exam*
la facultad	*department, school*
la investigación	*research*
el profesorado	*faculty*
reprobar; suspender (Esp.)	*to fail*
sacar buenas/ malas notas	*to get good/ bad grades*
tomar apuntes	*to take notes*

EL MUNDO HISPANO

Las universidades hispanas

It is not uncommon for universities in Spain and Latin America to have extremely large student body populations.

- **Universidad de Buenos Aires** (Argentina) 308.700 estudiantes
- **Universidad Autónoma de Santo Domingo** (República Dominicana) 170.500 estudiantes
- **Universidad Complutense de Madrid** (España) 84.900 estudiantes
- **Universidad Central de Venezuela** (Venezuela) 62.600 estudiantes

PERFIL

La Universidad de Salamanca

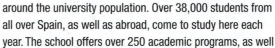

The University of Salamanca, established in 1218, is the oldest university in Spain. It is located in Salamanca, one of the most spectacular Renaissance cities in Europe. Salamanca is nicknamed **La Ciudad Dorada** (*The Golden City*) for the golden glow of its famous sandstone buildings, and it was declared a UNESCO World Heritage Site in 1988.

Salamanca is a true college town, as its prosperity and city life depend on and revolve around the university population. Over 38,000 students from all over Spain, as well as abroad, come to study here each year. The school offers over 250 academic programs, as well as renowned Spanish courses for foreign students. To walk through the university's historic grounds is to follow the footsteps of immortal writers like Miguel de Cervantes and Miguel de Unamuno.

Conexión Internet

To which **facultad** does your major belong in Spain or Latin America?

Go to **vhlcentral.com** to find more cultural information related to this **Cultura** section.

ACTIVIDADES

2 Comprensión Complete these sentences.

1. The University of Salamanca was established in the year __1218__.
2. A __clase anual__ is a year-long course.
3. Salamanca is called __La Ciudad Dorada__
4. Over 300,000 students attend the __Universidad de Buenos Aires__
5. An __examen parcial__ occurs about halfway through a course.

3 La universidad en cifras With a partner, research a Spanish or Latin American university online and find five statistics about that institution (for instance, the total enrollment, majors offered, year it was founded, etc.). Using the information you found, create a dialogue between a prospective student and a university representative. Present your dialogue to the class. Answers will vary.

Practice more at **vhlcentral.com**.

recursos: VM pp. 75–76; vhlcentral.com Lección 2

Así se dice
- Model the pronunciation of each term and have students repeat it.
- To challenge students, add these words to the list: **la beca** (*scholarship*); **el préstamo educativo** (*student loan*); **el/la profe** (*professor, colloquial*).
- Ask simple questions using the terms. Ex: **¿Hay un examen parcial en esta clase?**

Perfil Perhaps the most iconic of the **Universidad de Salamanca's** buildings is the **Escuelas Mayores**, which was completed in 1533. Hidden among the hundreds of items on its ornately carved façade is the figure of a small frog. According to tradition, being able to find the frog brings success.

El mundo hispano Have students read the enrollment numbers. Ask a volunteer to state your university's enrollment. Then have students discuss the advantages and disadvantages of studying at a large university.

2 Expansion Give students these sentences as items 6–8:
6. About ____ students take classes at the **Universidad de Salamanca**. (38,000)
7. A ____ is a university department or school. (**facultad**)
8. The ____ is located in the Dominican Republic. (**Universidad Autónoma de Santo Domingo**)

3 Expansion To add a visual aspect to this exercise, have the same pairs design a university brochure to attract prospective students. Encourage students to highlight the university's strengths and unique traits.

TEACHING OPTIONS

Extra Practice Tell students to imagine they have the opportunity to study abroad at one of the universities listed in **El mundo hispano** or **Perfil**. Have them choose a location and explain why they would like to attend that particular school. You may want to assign this as homework, and ask students to research the universities on the Internet in order to reach their decision.

Game Play a Pictionary-style game. Divide the class into two teams, A and B. Have one member from each team go to the board, and hand each one an index card with a university-related vocabulary word. The member from team A has one minute to draw a representation of that word, while the rest of team A guesses what the word is. Alternate between teams and award one point for each correct answer. The team with the most points wins.

Section Goals

In **Estructura 2.1**, students will learn:

- the present tense of regular **–ar** verbs
- the formation of negative sentences
- the verb **gustar**

Instructional Resources

Supersite: Audio (Lab MP3 Files); Resources (Grammar Presentation Slides, Activity Pack, Scripts, Answer Keys); Testing Program (Quizzes)
WebSAM
Workbook, pp. 13–14
Lab Manual, p. 9

Teaching Tips

- Check students' progress through comprehensible input. Point out that students have been using verbs and verb constructions from the start: **¿Cómo te llamas?, hay, ser,** and so forth. Ask a student: **¿Qué clases tomas?** Model student answer as **Yo tomo...** Then ask another student: **¿Qué clases toma ____? (Toma ____.)**
- Explain that, since the verb endings indicate the person speaking or spoken about, subject pronouns are usually optional in Spanish.
- To drill verb conjugation, divide the class into groups of three. Hand each group a small bag in which you have placed strips of paper containing subject pronouns or names. Assign each group member one of the following verbs: **bailar, estudiar,** or **trabajar**. Students should take turns drawing out a strip of paper and reading aloud the subject pronoun or name(s). Each group member then writes on a separate sheet of paper the correct conjugation for their assigned verb. As a follow-up, you may want students that were assigned the same infinitive to form new groups and compare their lists.

2.1 Present tense of -ar verbs

Tutorial

NATIONAL STANDARDS comparisons

ANTE TODO In order to talk about activities, you need to use verbs. Verbs express actions or states of being. In English and Spanish, the infinitive is the base form of the verb. In English, the infinitive is preceded by the word *to*: *to study*, *to be*. The infinitive in Spanish is a one-word form and can be recognized by its endings: **-ar**, **-er**, or **-ir**.

-ar verb		*-er* verb		*-ir* verb	
estudiar	*to study*	**comer**	*to eat*	**escribir**	*to write*

▶ In this lesson, you will learn the forms of regular **-ar** verbs.

The verb estudiar (*to study*)

SINGULAR FORMS	yo	estudi**o**	*I study*
	tú	estudi**as**	*you* (fam.) *study*
	Ud./él/ella	estudi**a**	*you* (form.) *study; he/she studies*
PLURAL FORMS	nosotros/as	estudi**amos**	*we study*
	vosotros/as	estudi**áis**	*you* (fam.) *study*
	Uds./ellos/ellas	estudi**an**	*you study; they study*

Juan Carlos estudia ciencias ambientales.

Y tú, ¿qué estudias, Miguel?

▶ To create the forms of most regular verbs in Spanish, drop the infinitive endings (**-ar**, **-er**, **-ir**). You then add to the stem the endings that correspond to the different subject pronouns. This diagram will help you visualize verb conjugation.

Conjugation of *-ar* verbs

INFINITIVE	VERB STEM	CONJUGATED FORM
estudi**ar**	estudi-	yo estudi**o**
bail**ar**	bail-	tú bail**as**
trabaj**ar**	trabaj-	nosotros trabaj**amos**

TEACHING OPTIONS

Extra Practice Do a pattern practice drill. Write an infinitive from the list of common **–ar** verbs on page 47 on the board and ask individual students to provide conjugations for the subject pronouns and names you suggest. Reverse the activity by saying a conjugated form and asking students to give the corresponding subject pronoun. Allow multiple answers for the third-person singular and plural.

Extra Practice Ask questions using **estudiar, bailar,** and **trabajar**. Students should answer in complete sentences. Ask additional questions to get more information. Ex: —____, **¿trabajas? —Sí, trabajo. —¿Dónde trabajas? —Trabajo en ____.** • **—¿Quién baila los sábados? —Yo bailo los sábados. —¿Bailas merengue?** • **—¿Estudian mucho ustedes? —¿Quién estudia más? —¿Cuántas horas estudias los lunes? ¿Y los sábados?**

Common *-ar* verbs

bailar	*to dance*	**estudiar**	*to study*
buscar	*to look for*	**explicar**	*to explain*
caminar	*to walk*	**hablar**	*to talk; to speak*
cantar	*to sing*	**llegar**	*to arrive*
cenar	*to have dinner*	**llevar**	*to carry*
comprar	*to buy*	**mirar**	*to look (at); to watch*
contestar	*to answer*	**necesitar (+ *inf.*)**	*to need*
conversar	*to converse, to chat*	**practicar**	*to practice*
desayunar	*to have breakfast*	**preguntar**	*to ask (a question)*
descansar	*to rest*	**preparar**	*to prepare*
desear (+ *inf.*)	*to desire; to wish*	**regresar**	*to return*
dibujar	*to draw*	**terminar**	*to end; to finish*
enseñar	*to teach*	**tomar**	*to take; to drink*
escuchar	*to listen (to)*	**trabajar**	*to work*
esperar (+ *inf.*)	*to wait (for); to hope*	**viajar**	*to travel*

▶ **¡Atención!** Unless referring to a person, the Spanish verbs **buscar**, **escuchar**, **esperar**, and **mirar** do not need to be followed by prepositions as they do in English.

Busco la tarea.
I'm looking for the homework.

Escucho la música.
I'm listening to the music.

Espero el autobús.
I'm waiting for the bus.

Miro la pizarra.
I'm looking at the blackboard.

COMPARE & CONTRAST

English uses three sets of forms to talk about the present: (1) the simple present (*Paco works*), (2) the present progressive (*Paco is working*), and (3) the emphatic present (*Paco does work*). In Spanish, the simple present can be used in all three cases.

Paco **trabaja** en la cafetería.
1. *Paco works in the cafeteria.*
2. *Paco is working in the cafeteria.*
3. *Paco does work in the cafeteria.*

In Spanish and English, the present tense is also sometimes used to express future action.

Marina **viaja** a Madrid mañana.
1. *Marina travels to Madrid tomorrow.*
2. *Marina will travel to Madrid tomorrow.*
3. *Marina is traveling to Madrid tomorrow.*

▶ When two verbs are used together with no change of subject, the second verb is generally in the infinitive. To make a sentence negative in Spanish, the word **no** is placed before the conjugated verb. In this case, **no** means *not*.

Deseo hablar con el señor Díaz.
I want to speak with Mr. Díaz.

Alicia **no** desea bailar ahora.
Alicia doesn't want to dance now.

Teaching Tips

- Remind students that **vosotros/as** forms will not be practiced actively in **PANORAMA**.
- Model the pronunciation of each infinitive and have students repeat it after you.
- Model the **yo** form of several verbs, creating simple sentences about yourself (Ex: **Bailo con mis amigos.**) and asking students if they do the same activities (Ex: **¿Bailas mucho con los amigos?**). Restate students' answers using the **él/ella** forms of the **–ar** verbs and then ask them to verify their classmates' answers. Ex: **¿____ baila mucho? No, ____ no baila.**
- To personalize the information presented here, have students ask each other about the activities they do on a typical day of the week (e.g., Friday). Write on the board **¿A qué hora...?** and underneath list **desayunar, terminar las clases,** and **cenar**. Model question and answer formation with your own information. Have students interview each other in pairs and then report back to the class.
- Explain that the simple present tense in Spanish is the equivalent of the three present tense forms of English. Model sentences and give a few additional examples.
- Write additional examples of a conjugated verb followed by an infinitive on the board.
- Explain that, when answering questions negatively, **no** must be used twice. To practice this construction, ask questions of students that will most likely result in negative answers. Ex: —____, **¿bailas tango?** —**No, no bailo tango.**

TEACHING OPTIONS

Heritage Speakers Have heritage speakers talk about their current semester/quarter: what they study, if/where they work, which television programs they watch, etc. Ask the rest of the class comprehension questions.

Extra Practice Ask students to create a two-column chart with the heads **Necesito...** and **Espero...**, and have them complete it with six things they need to do this week, and six things they hope to do after the semester is over. Ex: **Necesito estudiar. Espero viajar.** Then have them interview a classmate and report back to the class.

Pairs Ask student pairs to write ten sentences using the verbs presented in this section. Point out that students can use vocabulary words from **Contextos** with these verbs. Have pairs share their sentences with the class.

- Spanish speakers often omit subject pronouns because the verb endings indicate who the subject is. In Spanish, subject pronouns are used for emphasis, clarification, or contrast.

—¿Qué enseñan? *What do they teach?*	—**Ella** enseña arte y **él** enseña física. *She teaches art, and he teaches physics.*
—¿Quién desea trabajar hoy? *Who wants to work today?*	—**Yo** no deseo trabajar hoy. *I don't want to work today.*

The verb gustar

- **Gustar** is different from other **-ar** verbs. To express your likes and dislikes, use the expression **(no) me gusta** + **el/la** + [*singular noun*] or **(no) me gustan** + **los/las** + [*plural noun*]. Note: You may use the phrase **a mí** for emphasis, but never the subject pronoun **yo**.

Me gusta la música clásica. *I like classical music.*	**Me gustan las clases** de español y biología. *I like Spanish and biology classes.*
A mí me gustan las artes. *I like the arts.*	**A mí no me gusta el programa.** *I don't like the program.*

- To talk about what you like and don't like to do, use **(no) me gusta** + [*infinitive(s)*]. Note that the singular **gusta** is always used, even with more than one infinitive.

No me gusta viajar en autobús. *I don't like to travel by bus.*	**Me gusta cantar** y **bailar**. *I like to sing and dance.*

- To ask a friend about likes and dislikes, use the pronoun **te** instead of **me**. Note: You may use **a ti** for emphasis, but never the subject pronoun **tú**.

—¿Te gusta la geografía? *Do you like geography?*	**—Sí, me gusta. Y a ti, ¿te gusta el inglés?** *Yes, I like it. And you, do you like English?*

- You can use this same structure to talk about other people by using the pronouns **nos**, **le**, and **les**. Unless your instructor tells you otherwise, only the **me** and **te** forms will appear on test materials until **Lección 7**.

Nos gusta dibujar. (nosotros) *We like to draw.*	**Nos gustan las clases de español e inglés. (nosotros)** *We like Spanish class and English class.*
No le gusta trabajar. (usted, él, ella) *You don't like to work. He/She doesn't like to work.*	**Les gusta el arte. (ustedes, ellos, ellas)** *You like art. They like art.*

¡ATENCIÓN!

Note that **gustar** does not behave like other **-ar** verbs. You must study its use carefully and pay attention to prepositions, pronouns, and agreement.

AYUDA

Use the construction **a** + [*name/pronoun*] to clarify to whom you are referring. This construction is not always necessary.

A Gabriela le gusta bailar.

A Sara y a él les gustan los animales.

A mí me gusta viajar.

¿**A ti** te gustan las clases?

CONSULTA

For more on **gustar** and other verbs like it, see **Estructura 7.4**, pp. 230–231.

¡INTÉNTALO! Provide the present tense forms of these verbs. The first items have been done for you.

hablar	gustar
1. Yo ___hablo___ español.	1. ___Me gusta___ el café. (a mí)
2. Ellos ___hablan___ español.	2. ¿___Te gustan___ las clases? (a ti)
3. Inés ___habla___ español.	3. No ___te gusta___ el café. (a ti)
4. Nosotras ___hablamos___ español.	4. No ___me gustan___ las clases. (a mí)
5. Tú ___hablas___ español.	5. No ___me gusta___ el café. (a mí)

recursos

WB pp. 13–14

LM p. 9

vhlcentral.com Lección 2

Teaching Tips

- Model clarification/contrast sentences. Ask several students: **¿Dónde desayunas?** Then, pointing to two students who answered differently, ask the class: **¿Dónde desayunan? (Él desayuna en la cafetería y ella desayuna en la residencia estudiantil.)** Then show how to use subject pronouns to give emphasis. Ex: —____, **¿te gusta bailar? —No, no me gusta bailar. —____ no baila. Yo bailo.**
- Point out the position of subjects and subject pronouns with regard to the verbs in affirmative and negative sentences.
- Stress that subject pronouns are never used with **gustar**. They appear in the grammar explanation only for guidance.
- Point out that, just as subject pronouns can be used for clarification or emphasis, students should use the prepositional phrases **a mí**, **a ti**, etc., with the verb **gustar** to clarify or give emphasis. Also point out the written accent on **mí** and the lack of an accent on **ti**.
- Point out that, even when two or more infinitives are used, the form remains singular: **gusta**.
- Divide the board into two columns. On the left side, list the indirect object pronouns (**me**, **te**). On the right side, provide a mix of infinitives and plural and singular nouns, and have students supply **gusta** or **gustan** for each one. Then call on volunteers to combine elements from each column to form sentences.
- If you wish to practice the third person, write the headings **Gustos** and **Disgustos** on the board. Have the class brainstorm likes and dislikes among the students at your school, including classes, pastimes, music, and movies. Use the lists to form statements and questions.

TEACHING OPTIONS

Video Show the **Fotonovela** again and stop the video where appropriate to discuss how certain verbs were used and to ask questions.

Pairs Write five word pairs (mix of infinitives and plural and singular nouns) on the board. Ex: **la *Coca-Cola*/la *Pepsi*** Have student pairs take turns asking each other what they like better: **¿Qué te gusta más…?** Then have them write a summary of what each of them likes to share with the class.

Game Divide the class into two teams. Call on one team member at a time, alternating between teams. Give an **-ar** verb in its infinitive form and name a subject pronoun. The team member should say the corresponding present tense verb form. Give one point per correct answer. Deduct one point for each wrong answer. The team with the most points at the end wins.

Práctica

1

Completar Complete the conversation with the appropriate forms of the verbs in parentheses.

JUAN ¡Hola, Linda! ¿Qué tal las clases?

LINDA Bien. (1) Tomo (Tomar) tres clases... química, biología y computación. Y tú, ¿cuántas clases (2) tomas (tomar)?

JUAN (3) Tomo (Tomar) tres también... biología, arte y literatura. El doctor Cárdenas (4) enseña (enseñar) la clase de biología.

LINDA ¿Ah, sí? Lily, Alberto y yo (5) tomamos (tomar) biología a las diez con la profesora Garza.

JUAN ¿(6) Estudian (Estudiar) mucho ustedes?

LINDA Sí, porque hay muchos exámenes. Alberto y yo (7) necesitamos (necesitar) estudiar dos horas todos los días (*every day*).

2

Oraciones Form sentences using the words provided. Remember to conjugate the verbs and add any other necessary words.

1. ustedes / practicar / vocabulario Ustedes practican el vocabulario.
2. ¿preparar (tú) / tarea? ¿Preparas la tarea?
3. clase de español / terminar / once La clase de español termina a las once.
4. ¿qué / buscar / ustedes? ¿Qué buscan ustedes?
5. (nosotros) buscar / pluma Buscamos una pluma.
6. (yo) comprar / calculadora Compro una calculadora.

3

Gustos Read what these people do. Then use the information in parentheses to tell what they like.

modelo

Yo enseño en la universidad. (las clases) *Me gustan las clases.*

1. Tú deseas mirar cuadros (*paintings*) de Picasso. (el arte) Te gusta el arte.
2. Soy estudiante de economía. (estudiar) Me gusta estudiar.
3. Tú estudias italiano y español. (las lenguas extranjeras) Te gustan las lenguas extranjeras.
4. No descansas los sábados. (cantar y bailar) Te gusta cantar y bailar.
5. Busco una computadora. (la computación) Me gusta la computación.

4

Actividades Get together with a partner and take turns asking each other if you do these activities. Which activities does your partner like? Which do you both like? Answers will vary.

modelo

tomar el autobús

Estudiante 1: *¿Tomas el autobús?*

Estudiante 2: *Sí, tomo el autobús, pero (but) no me gusta./ No, no tomo el autobús.*

bailar merengue	escuchar música rock	practicar el español
cantar bien	estudiar física	trabajar en la universidad
dibujar en clase	mirar la televisión	viajar a Europa

AYUDA

The Spanish **no** translates to both *no* and *not* in English. In negative answers to questions, you will need to use **no** twice: **¿Estudias geografía? No, no estudio geografía.**

TEACHING OPTIONS

Pairs Have individual students write five dehydrated sentences and exchange them with a partner, who will complete them. After pairs have completed their sentences, ask volunteers to share some of their dehydrated sentences. Write them on the board and have the class "hydrate" them.

Game Divide the class into two teams. Prepare brief descriptions of easily recognizable people, using **–ar** verbs. Write each name on a card, and give each team a set of names. Then read the descriptions aloud. The first team to hold up the correct name earns a point. Ex: **Ella canta, baila y viaja a muchos países. (Jennifer López)**

1 Teaching Tip To simplify, guide the class to first identify the subject and verb ending for each item.

1 Expansion Go over the answers quickly as a class. Then ask volunteers to role-play the dialogue.

2 Teaching Tip Point out that students will need to conjugate the verbs and add missing articles and other words to complete these dehydrated sentences. Tell them that subject pronouns in parentheses are not necessary in the completed sentences. Model completion of the first sentence for the class.

2 Expansion Give these dehydrated sentences to the class as items 7–10: **7. (yo) desear / practicar / verbos / hoy (Deseo practicar los verbos hoy.) 8. mi compañero de cuarto / regresar / lunes (Mi compañero de cuarto regresa el lunes.) 9. ella / cantar / y / bailar / muy bien (Ella canta y baila muy bien.) 10. jóvenes / necesitar / descansar / ahora (Los jóvenes necesitan descansar ahora.)**

3 Teaching Tip To simplify, start by reading the model aloud. Then ask students why **me** is used in the answer (the first-person singular is used in the example sentence) and why **gustan** is needed (**las clases** is plural). Have students identify the indirect object pronoun and choose **gusta** or **gustan** for each item, then complete the activity.

3 Expansion If you wish to practice the third-person forms, repeat the activity, providing different subjects for each item. Ex: **1. Deseamos mirar cuadros de Picasso. (Nos gusta el arte.)**

4 Teaching Tip Before beginning the activity, give a two- to three-minute oral rapid-response drill. Provide infinitives and subjects, and call on students to give the conjugated form.

Comunicación

5

Describir With a partner, describe what you see in the pictures using the given verbs. Also ask your partner whether or not he/she likes one of the activities. Answers will vary.

modelo

enseñar

La profesora enseña química. ¿Te gusta la química?

1. caminar, hablar, llevar

2. buscar, descansar, estudiar

3. dibujar, cantar, escuchar

4. llevar, tomar, viajar

6

Charadas In groups of three, play a game of charades using the verbs in the word bank. For example, if someone is studying, you say "**Estudias.**" The first person to guess correctly acts out the next charade. Answers will vary.

bailar	cantar	descansar	enseñar	mirar
caminar	conversar	dibujar	escuchar	preguntar

Síntesis

7

Conversación Get together with a classmate and pretend that you are friends who have not seen each other on campus for a few days. Have a conversation in which you catch up on things. Mention how you're feeling, what classes you're taking, what days and times you have classes, and which classes you like and don't like. Answers will vary.

Practice more at **vhlcentral.com**.

5 Teaching Tip To challenge students, make copies of this activity with the text removed so that students can only see the illustrations. Pass out the copies and have students close their books. Write all the verbs of the activity in one list on the board. Tell students to complete the activity using three of the verbs from the board for each drawing.

5 Expansion Ask students to write additional descriptions of the drawings. Ex: **La profesora habla en clase. Hay números y letras en la pizarra. Ella explica la tarea.** Have volunteers share their descriptions with the class.

6 Teaching Tip You may want to split the class into two teams with volunteers from each team acting out the charades. Give points for correct guesses. The team with the most points at the end wins.

7 Teaching Tip Point out that, in addition to practicing –**ar** verbs, this activity recycles and reviews material from **Lección 1**: greetings, leave-takings, and telling time. Allow students several minutes to plan their conversation before they begin speaking.

TEACHING OPTIONS

Extra Practice Have students write a description of themselves made up of activities they like or do not like to do, using sentences containing **(no) me gusta...** Collect the descriptions and read them aloud. Have the class guess who wrote each description.

Game To add a visual aspect to this grammar practice, play **Concentración**. Choose eight infinitives taught in this section, and write each one on a separate card. On another eight cards, draw or paste a picture that illustrates the action of each infinitive. Randomly place the cards facedown in four rows of four. Play with even-numbered groups of students. In pairs, students select two cards. If the two cards match, the pair keeps them. If the cards do not match, students return them to their original position. The pair that finishes with the most cards wins.

2.2 Forming questions in Spanish

Tutorial

ANTE TODO There are three basic ways to ask questions in Spanish. Can you guess what they are by looking at the photos and photo captions on this page?

Te gusta mucho la tarea, ¿no?
¿Hablas con tu mamá?
¿Estudia Maru?

AYUDA

With a partner, take turns saying out loud the example statements and questions on this page. Your pitch indicates whether you are making a statement or asking a question. Then take turns making up statements of your own and turning them into questions, using all three methods.

▶ One way to form a question is to raise the pitch of your voice at the end of a declarative sentence. When writing any question in Spanish, be sure to use an upside-down question mark (**¿**) at the beginning and a regular question mark (**?**) at the end of the sentence.

Statement	Question
Ustedes trabajan los sábados. *You work on Saturdays.*	¿Ustedes trabajan los sábados? *Do you work on Saturdays?*
Carlota busca un mapa. *Carlota is looking for a map.*	¿Carlota busca un mapa? *Is Carlota looking for a map?*

▶ You can also form a question by inverting the order of the subject and the verb of a declarative statement. The subject may even be placed at the end of the sentence.

Statement	Question
SUBJECT VERB **Ustedes trabajan** los sábados. *You work on Saturdays.*	VERB SUBJECT ¿**Trabajan ustedes** los sábados? *Do you work on Saturdays?*
SUBJECT VERB **Carlota regresa** a las seis. *Carlota returns at six.*	VERB SUBJECT ¿**Regresa** a las seis **Carlota**? *Does Carlota return at six?*

▶ Questions can also be formed by adding the tags **¿no?** or **¿verdad?** at the end of a statement.

Statement	Question
Ustedes trabajan los sábados. *You work on Saturdays.*	Ustedes trabajan los sábados, **¿no?** *You work on Saturdays, don't you?*
Carlota regresa a las seis. *Carlota returns at six.*	Carlota regresa a las seis, **¿verdad?** *Carlota returns at six, right?*

Section Goals

In **Estructura 2.2**, students will be introduced to:

- forming questions in Spanish
- rising and falling intonation in questions and statements
- tag questions
- interrogative words

Instructional Resources

Supersite: Audio (Lab MP3 Files); Resources (Grammar Presentation Slides, Activity Pack, Scripts, Answer Keys); Testing Program (Quizzes)
WebSAM
Workbook, pp. 15–16
Lab Manual, p. 10

Teaching Tips

- Review questions such as: **¿Cómo te llamas? ¿Qué clases tomas?** Ask volunteers to suggest others.
- Model the pronunciation and intonation of the various types of questions in the photo captions and example statements and questions. Point out that these types of questions signal a yes/no response.
- Explain that a more common way to form questions in Spanish is to invert the subject and verb.
- Point out that the inverted question mark does not necessarily appear at the beginning of the sentence.

TEACHING OPTIONS

TPR To add a listening aspect to this grammar presentation, read aloud a series of statements and questions, including tag questions. Have students raise their right hand when they hear a statement and their left hand when they hear a question.

Extra Practice Write ten statements on the board. Ask students to convert the statements into questions by inverting the subject and the verb. Students can work in pairs to write their questions. When they have finished, ask volunteers to write the questions on the board. Model rising intonation and inverting subject/verb order in the questions. Have the class repeat the questions after you.

Extra Practice Using the same ten statements on the board from the previous activity, ask students to say them aloud using tag questions.

Teaching Tips

- Model pronunciation by asking questions. Ex: **¿Cómo estás? ¿Cuál es tu clase favorita?**
- Point out written accent marks on interrogative words.
- Explain that **¿qué?** and **¿cuál?** are not used interchangeably. The word **¿qué?** precedes nouns while **¿cuál?** is used with verbs. Compare and contrast the following: **¿Qué clase te gusta? ¿Cuál es tu clase favorita?** Write similar questions on the board but leave out the interrogative word. Ask students whether **¿qué?** or **¿cuál?** should be used for each.
- Point out **¿cuáles?** and **¿quiénes?** and give examples for each.
- Clarify singular/plural and masculine/feminine variants for **¿cuánto/a?** and **¿cuántos/as?** Ex: **¿Cuánta tarea hay? ¿Cuántos libros hay?**
- Model the pronunciation of example sentences, asking similar questions of students. Ex: ___, **¿dónde trabajas?** Ask other students to verify their classmates' answers. Ex: ____ **trabaja en** ____.
- Explain that the answer to the question **¿por qué?** is **porque**.

Question words

Interrogative words

¿Adónde?	*Where (to)?*	**¿De dónde?**	*From where?*
¿Cómo?	*How?*	**¿Dónde?**	*Where?*
¿Cuál?, ¿Cuáles?	*Which?; Which one(s)?*	**¿Por qué?**	*Why?*
¿Cuándo?	*When?*	**¿Qué?**	*What?; Which?*
¿Cuánto/a?	*How much?*	**¿Quién?**	*Who?*
¿Cuántos/as?	*How many?*	**¿Quiénes?**	*Who* (plural)?

▶ To ask a question that requires more than a *yes* or *no* answer, use an interrogative word.

¿Cuál de ellos estudia en la biblioteca?
Which of them studies in the library?

¿Adónde caminamos?
Where are we walking (to)?

¿Cuántos estudiantes hablan español?
How many students speak Spanish?

¿Por qué necesitas hablar con ella?
Why do you need to talk to her?

¿Dónde trabaja Ricardo?
Where does Ricardo work?

¿Quién enseña la clase de arte?
Who teaches the art class?

¿Qué clases tomas?
What classes are you taking?

¿Cuánta tarea hay?
How much homework is there?

CONSULTA

You will learn more about the difference between **qué** and **cuál** in **Estructura 9.3**, p. 292.

▶ When pronouncing this type of question, the pitch of your voice falls at the end of the sentence.

¿Cómo llegas a clase?
How do you get to class?

¿Por qué necesitas estudiar?
Why do you need to study?

▶ Notice the difference between **¿por qué?**, which is written as two words and has an accent, and **porque**, which is written as one word without an accent.

¿Por qué estudias español?
Why do you study Spanish?

¡**Porque** es divertido!
Because it's fun!

▶ In Spanish **no** can mean both *no* and *not*. Therefore, when answering a yes/no question in the negative, you need to use **no** twice.

¿Caminan a la universidad?
Do you walk to the university?

No, no caminamos a la universidad.
No, we do not walk to the university.

¡INTÉNTALO! Make questions out of these statements. Use the intonation method in column 1 and the tag **¿no?** method in column 2.

Statement	Intonation	Tag questions
1. Hablas inglés.	¿Hablas inglés?	Hablas inglés, ¿no?
2. Trabajamos mañana.	¿Trabajamos mañana?	Trabajamos mañana, ¿no?
3. Ustedes desean bailar.	¿Ustedes desean bailar?	Ustedes desean bailar, ¿no?
4. Raúl estudia mucho.	¿Raúl estudia mucho?	Raúl estudia mucho, ¿no?
5. Enseño a las nueve.	¿Enseño a las nueve?	Enseño a las nueve, ¿no?
6. Luz mira la televisión.	¿Luz mira la televisión?	Luz mira la televisión, ¿no?

recursos

WB pp. 15–16

LM p. 10

vhlcentral.com Lección 2

TEACHING OPTIONS

Video Show the **Fotonovela** again to give students more input on forming questions. Stop the video where appropriate to discuss how certain questions, including tag questions, are formed. Have students focus on characters' rising and falling intonation in questions and statements.

Heritage Speakers Ask heritage speakers to give original statements and questions at random. Have the rest of the class determine whether each sentence is a statement or a question.

Pairs Give pairs of students five minutes to write original questions using as many interrogative words as they can. Can any pair come up with questions using all interrogative words?

Práctica

1 **Preguntas** Change these sentences into questions by inverting the word order.

modelo

Ernesto habla con su compañero de clase.
¿Habla Ernesto con su compañero de clase? / ¿Habla con su compañero de clase Ernesto?

1. La profesora Cruz prepara la prueba. ¿Prepara la profesora Cruz la prueba? / ¿Prepara la prueba la profesora Cruz?
2. Sandra y yo necesitamos estudiar. ¿Necesitamos Sandra y yo estudiar? / ¿Necesitamos estudiar Sandra y yo?
3. Los chicos practican el vocabulario. ¿Practican los chicos el vocabulario? / ¿Practican el vocabulario los chicos?
4. Jaime termina la tarea. ¿Termina Jaime la tarea? / ¿Termina la tarea Jaime?
5. Tú trabajas en la biblioteca. ¿Trabajas tú en la biblioteca? / ¿Trabajas en la biblioteca tú?

2 **Completar** Irene and Manolo are chatting in the library. Complete their conversation with the appropriate questions. Answers will vary.

IRENE Hola, Manolo. (1) ¿Cómo estás?/¿Qué tal?
MANOLO Bien, gracias. (2) ¿Y tú?
IRENE Muy bien. (3) ¿Qué hora es?
MANOLO Son las nueve.
IRENE (4) ¿Qué estudias?
MANOLO Estudio historia.
IRENE (5) ¿Por qué?
MANOLO Porque hay un examen mañana.
IRENE (6) ¿Te gusta la clase?
MANOLO Sí, me gusta mucho la clase.
IRENE (7) ¿Quién enseña la clase?
MANOLO El profesor Padilla enseña la clase.
IRENE (8) ¿Tomas psicología este semestre?
MANOLO No, no tomo psicología este (*this*) semestre.
IRENE (9) ¿A qué hora regresas a la residencia?
MANOLO Regreso a la residencia a las once.
IRENE (10) ¿Deseas tomar una soda?
MANOLO No, no deseo tomar una soda. ¡Deseo estudiar!

3 **Dos profesores** In pairs, create a dialogue, similar to the one in **Actividad 2**, between Professor Padilla and his colleague Professor Martínez. Use question words. Answers will vary.

modelo

Prof. Padilla: ¿Qué enseñas este semestre?
Prof. Martínez: Enseño dos cursos de sociología.

Practice more at **vhlcentral.com**.

1 Teaching Tip Ask students to give both ways of forming questions for each item. Then have student pairs take turns making the statements and converting them into questions.

1 Expansion Make the even statements negative. Then have students add tag questions to the statements.

2 Expansion Have pairs of students create a similar conversation, replacing Manolo's answers with information that is true for them. Then ask volunteers to role-play their conversations for the class.

3 Teaching Tip To prepare students for the activity, have them brainstorm possible topics of conversation.

TEACHING OPTIONS

Heritage Speakers Ask students to interview heritage speakers, whether in the class or outside. Students should prepare questions about who the person is, if he or she works and when/where, what he or she studies and why, and so forth. Have students use the information they gather in the interviews to write a brief profile of the person.

Large Groups Divide the class into two groups, A and B. To each member of group A give a strip of paper with a question on it. Ex: **¿Cuántos estudiantes hay en la clase?** Give an answer to each member of group B. Ex: **Hay treinta estudiantes en la clase.** Have students find their partners. Be sure that each question has only one possible answer.

4 Teaching Tips

- If this is the first time students are completing an activity from the Activity Pack, explain that they need a handout.
- Distribute the ***Hojas de actividades*** (Activity Pack/ Supersite) and explain that students must actively approach their classmates with their ***Hoja*** in hand. When they find someone who answers affirmatively, that student signs his or her name.
- For survey-type activities, encourage students to ask one question per person and move on. This will promote circulation throughout the room and prevent students from remaining in clusters.

4 Expansion Ask students to say the name of someone who signed their ***Hoja***. Then ask that student for more information. Ex: **¿Quién estudia computación? Ah, ¿sí? ____ estudia computación. ¿Dónde estudias computación, ____? ¿Quién es el/la profesor(a)?**

5 Expansion Play this game with the entire class. Select a few students to play the contestants and to "buzz in" their answers.

6 Teaching Tip Write **la clase, los compañeros de clase,** and **la universidad** on the board. Guide students in brainstorming questions and write each one in the appropriate column.

7 Teaching Tip Brainstorm ideas for interview questions and write them on the board, or have students prepare their questions as homework for an in-class interview session.

Comunicación

NATIONAL communication STANDARDS

4 **Encuesta** Your instructor will give you a worksheet. Change the categories in the first column into questions, then use them to survey your classmates. Find at least one person for each category. Be prepared to report the results of your survey to the class. Answers will vary.

5 **Un juego** In groups of four or five, play a game (**un juego**) of Jeopardy®. Each person has to write two clues. Then take turns reading the clues and guessing the questions. The person who guesses correctly reads the next clue. Answers will vary.

Es algo que...	**Es un lugar donde...**	**Es una persona que...**
It's something that...	*It's a place where...*	*It's a person that...*

modelo

Estudiante 1: Es un lugar donde estudiamos.
Estudiante 2: ¿Qué es la biblioteca?

Estudiante 1: Es algo que escuchamos.
Estudiante 2: ¿Qué es la música?

Estudiante 1: Es un director de España.
Estudiante 2: ¿Quién es Pedro Almodóvar?

NOTA CULTURAL

Pedro Almodóvar is an award-winning film director from Spain. His films are full of both humor and melodrama, and their controversial subject matter has often sparked great debate. His film ***Hable con ella*** won the Oscar for Best Original Screenplay in 2002. His 2006 hit ***Volver*** was nominated for numerous awards, and won the Best Screenplay and Best Actress award for the entire female cast at the Cannes Film Festival.

6 **El nuevo estudiante** Imagine you are a transfer student and today is your first day of Spanish class. Ask your partner questions to find out all you can about the class, your classmates, and the university. Then switch roles. Answers will vary.

modelo

Estudiante 1: Hola, me llamo Samuel. ¿Cómo te llamas?
Estudiante 2: Me llamo Laura.
Estudiante 1: ¿Quiénes son ellos?
Estudiante 2: Son Melanie y Lucas.
Estudiante 1: Y él, ¿de dónde es?
Estudiante 2: Es de California.
Estudiante 1: En la universidad hay cursos de ciencias, ¿verdad?
Estudiante 2: Sí, hay clases de biología, química y física.
Estudiante 1: ¿Cuántos exámenes hay en esta clase?
Estudiante 2: Hay dos.

Síntesis

NATIONAL communication STANDARDS

7 **Entrevista** Imagine that you are a reporter for the school newspaper. Write five questions about student life at your school and use them to interview two classmates. Be prepared to report your findings to the class. Answers will vary.

TEACHING OPTIONS

Extra Practice Have students go back to the **Fotonovela** on pages 40–41 and write as many questions as they can about what they see in the photos. Ask volunteers to share their questions as you write them on the board. Then call on individual students to answer them.

Extra Practice Prepare eight questions and answers. Write only the answers on the board in random order. Then read the questions aloud and have students identify the appropriate answer. Ex: **¿Cuándo es la clase de español? (Es los lunes, miércoles y viernes.)**

CONSULTA

To review the forms of **ser**, see **Estructura 1.3**, pp. 19–21.

2.3 Present tense of estar

Tutorial

NATIONAL STANDARDS comparisons

ANTE TODO In **Lección 1**, you learned how to conjugate and use the verb **ser** (*to be*). You will now learn a second verb which means *to be*, the verb **estar**. Although **estar** ends in **-ar**, it does not follow the pattern of regular **-ar** verbs. The **yo** form (**estoy**) is irregular. Also, all forms have an accented **á** except the **yo** and **nosotros/as** forms.

The verb estar (*to be*)

SINGULAR FORMS	yo	est**oy**	*I am*
	tú	est**ás**	*you* (fam.) *are*
	Ud./él/ella	est**á**	*you* (form.) *are; he/she is*
PLURAL FORMS	nosotros/as	est**amos**	*we are*
	vosotros/as	est**áis**	*you* (fam.) *are*
	Uds./ellos/ellas	est**án**	*you are; they are*

¡Estamos en Perú!

María está en la biblioteca.

COMPARE & CONTRAST

Compare the uses of the verb **estar** to those of the verb **ser**.

Uses of *estar*

Location
Estoy en casa.
I am at home.
Marissa **está** al lado de Felipe.
Marissa is next to Felipe.

Health
Juan Carlos **está** enfermo hoy.
Juan Carlos is sick today.

Well-being
—¿Cómo **estás**, Jimena?
How are you, Jimena?
—**Estoy** muy bien, gracias.
I'm very well, thank you.

Uses of *ser*

Identity
Hola, **soy** Maru.
Hello, I'm Maru.

Occupation
Soy estudiante.
I'm a student.

Origin
—¿**Eres** de México?
Are you from Mexico?
—Sí, **soy** de México.
Yes, I'm from Mexico.

Telling time
Son las cuatro.
It's four o'clock.

AYUDA

Use **la casa** to express *the house*, but **en casa** to express *at home*.

CONSULTA

To learn more about the difference between **ser** and **estar**, see **Estructura 5.3**, pp. 158–159.

Section Goals

In **Estructura 2.3**, students will be introduced to:
- the present tense of **estar**
- contrasts between **ser** and **estar**
- prepositions of location used with **estar**

Instructional Resources
Supersite: Audio (Lab MP3 Files); Resources (Grammar Presentation Slides, Digital Image Bank, Activity Pack, Scripts, Answer Keys); Testing Program (Quizzes)
WebSAM
Workbook, pp. 17–18
Lab Manual, p. 11

Teaching Tips

- Point out that only the **yo** and **nosotros/as** forms do not have a written accent.
- Emphasize that the principal distinction between **estar** and **ser** is that **estar** is generally used to express temporary conditions (**Juan Carlos está enfermo hoy**) and **ser** is generally used to express inherent qualities (**Juan Carlos es inteligente**).
- On the board, make a chart similar to the one in **Compare & Contrast**, but create sample sentences using the names of your students and information about them.
- Students will learn to compare **ser** and **estar** formally in **Estructura 5.3**.

TEACHING OPTIONS

TPR Have students write **ser** and **estar** on separate sheets of paper. Give statements in English and have students indicate if they would use **ser** or **estar** in each by holding up the appropriate paper. Ex: *I'm at home.* (**estar**) *I'm a student.* (**ser**) *I'm tired.* (**estar**) *I'm glad.* (**estar**) *I'm generous.* (**ser**)

Extra Practice Ask students to tell where certain people are or probably are at this moment. Ex: **¿Dónde estás? (Estoy en la clase.) ¿Dónde está el presidente? (Está en Washington, D.C.)**

Heritage Speakers Ask heritage speakers to name instances where either **ser** or **estar** may be used. They may point out more advanced uses, such as with certain adjectives: **Es aburrido** vs. **Está aburrido**. This may help to compare and contrast inherent qualities and temporary conditions.

Teaching Tips

- Explain that prepositions typically indicate where one thing or person is in relation to another thing or person: *near, far, on, between, below.*
- Point out that **estar** is used in the model sentences to indicate presence or existence in a place.
- Take a book or other object and place it in various locations in relation to your desk or a student's. Ask individual students about its location. Ex: **¿Dónde está el libro? ¿Está cerca o lejos del escritorio de ____? ¿Qué objeto está al lado del libro?** Work through various locations, eliciting all of the prepositions of location.
- Ask where students are in relation to one another. Ex: ____, **¿dónde está ____? Está al lado (a la derecha/izquierda, delante, detrás) de ____.**
- Describe students' locations in relation to each other. Ex: **Esta persona está lejos de ____. Está delante de ____. Está al lado de ____...** Have the class call out the student you identify. Ex: **Es ____.** Then have students describe other students' locations for a partner to guess.

▶ **Estar** is often used with certain prepositions and adverbs to describe the location of a person or an object.

Prepositions and adverbs often used with estar

al lado de	*next to*	**delante de**	*in front of*
a la derecha de	*to the right of*	**detrás de**	*behind*
a la izquierda de	*to the left of*	**en**	*in; on*
allá	*over there*	**encima de**	*on top of*
allí	*there*	**entre**	*between*
cerca de	*near*	**lejos de**	*far from*
con	*with*	**sin**	*without*
debajo de	*below*	**sobre**	*on; over*

La tiza **está al lado de** la pluma.
The chalk is next to the pen.

Los libros **están encima del** escritorio.
The books are on top of the desk.

El laboratorio **está cerca de** la clase.
The lab is near the classroom.

Maribel **está delante de** José.
Maribel is in front of José.

La maleta **está allí**.
The suitcase is there.

El estadio no **está lejos de** la librería.
The stadium isn't far from the bookstore.

El mapa **está entre** la pizarra y la puerta.
The map is between the blackboard and the door.

Los estudiantes **están en** la clase.
The students are in class.

La calculadora **está sobre** la mesa.
The calculator is on the table.

Los turistas **están allá**.
The tourists are over there.

Estamos lejos de casa.

La biblioteca está al lado de la librería.

¡INTÉNTALO! Provide the present tense forms of **estar**.

1. Ustedes ___están___ en la clase.
2. José ___está___ en la biblioteca.
3. Yo ___estoy___ bien, gracias.
4. Nosotras ___estamos___ en la cafetería.
5. Tú ___estás___ en el laboratorio.
6. Elena ___está___ en la librería.
7. Ellas ___están___ en la clase.
8. Ana y yo ___estamos___ en la clase.
9. ¿Cómo ___está___ usted?
10. Javier y Maribel ___están___ en el estadio.
11. Nosotros ___estamos___ en la cafetería.
12. Yo ___estoy___ en el laboratorio.
13. Carmen y María ___están___ enfermas.
14. Tú ___estás___ en la clase.

recursos
WB pp. 17–18
LM p. 11
vhlcentral.com Lección 2

TEACHING OPTIONS

Extra Practice Name well-known campus buildings and ask students to describe their location in relation to other buildings. Model sample sentences so students will know how to answer. You may wish to write **la Facultad de...** on the board and explain its meaning. Ex: **—¿Dónde está la biblioteca? —Está al lado de la Facultad de Química y detrás de la librería.**

TPR Have students remain seated. One student starts with a ball. Identify another student by his or her location with reference to other students. Ex: **Es la persona a la derecha de ____.** The student with the ball has to throw it to the student you described. The latter student must then toss the ball to the next person you identify.

Práctica

1

Completar Daniela has just returned home from the library. Complete this conversation with the appropriate forms of **ser** or **estar**.

MAMÁ Hola, Daniela. ¿Cómo (1) estás ?
DANIELA Hola, mamá. (2) Estoy bien. ¿Dónde (3) está papá? ¡Ya (*Already*) (4) son las ocho de la noche!
MAMÁ No (5) está aquí. (6) Está en la oficina.
DANIELA Y Andrés y Margarita, ¿dónde (7) están ellos?
MAMÁ (8) Están en el restaurante La Palma con Martín.
DANIELA ¿Quién (9) es Martín?
MAMÁ (10) Es un compañero de clase. (11) Es de México.
DANIELA Ah. Y el restaurante La Palma, ¿dónde (12) está ?
MAMÁ (13) Está cerca de la Plaza Mayor, en San Modesto.
DANIELA Gracias, mamá. Voy (*I'm going*) al restaurante. ¡Hasta pronto!

NOTA CULTURAL

In many Spanish-speaking countries, students attend college in their home city. Many tend to live at home instead of in a college dormitory. However, students from small towns without universities typically study away from home.

2

Escoger Choose the preposition that best completes each sentence.

1. La pluma está (encima de / detrás de) la mesa. encima de
2. La ventana está (a la izquierda de / debajo de) la puerta. a la izquierda de
3. La pizarra está (debajo de / delante de) los estudiantes. delante de
4. Las sillas están (encima de / detrás de) los escritorios. detrás de
5. Los estudiantes llevan los libros (en / sobre) la mochila. en
6. La biblioteca está (sobre / al lado de) la residencia estudiantil. al lado de
7. España está (cerca de / lejos de) Puerto Rico. lejos de
8. México está (cerca de / lejos de) los Estados Unidos. cerca de
9. Felipe trabaja (con / en) Ricardo en la cafetería. con

3

La librería Imagine that you are in the school bookstore and can't find various items. Ask the clerk (your partner) the location of five items in the drawing. Then switch roles. Answers will vary.

modelo

Estudiante 1: *¿Dónde están los diccionarios?*
Estudiante 2: *Los diccionarios están debajo de los libros de literatura.*

Practice more at **vhlcentral.com**.

NOTA CULTURAL

Many universities in the Spanish-speaking world do not have a central campus bookstore. Students generally purchase their texts at designated commercial bookstores.

1 Teaching Tips
- To simplify, guide students in choosing **ser** or **estar** for each item.
- Ask students to explain why they chose **ser** or **estar** in each case.

1 Expansion Ask two volunteers to role-play the conversation for the class.

2 Expansion
- To challenge students, rework items 1 through 6, asking questions about items in the classroom or places at the university. Ex: **¿Qué objeto está encima de la mesa? ¿Dónde está la ventana?**
- To add a visual aspect to this exercise, ask students to create simple illustrations that show the relationship of location in items 1–8.

3 Teaching Tip Use the **Lección 2** digital images to assist with the presentation of this activity.

3 Expansion Assign one student the role of **vendedor(a)** and another the role of **cliente/a**. Then name several of the items in the drawing and ask the participants to create mini-conversations as in the activity.

TEACHING OPTIONS

Extra Practice Add a visual aspect to this grammar practice. Use a large world map (one with Spanish labels is best), and/or the maps at the back of this textbook. Ask students where countries and cities are in relation to each other on the map(s). Ex: **¿Uruguay está más cerca de Chile o de Ecuador? ¿Qué país está entre Colombia y Costa Rica?**

Small Groups Have each group member think of a country or campus location and describe it with progressively more specific statements. After each statement, the other group members guess what country/location it is; the student presenting clarifies by reacting to their guesses. Ex: **—Es un país. Está en Europa. —¿Es Italia? —No, pero está a la izquierda de Italia y Suiza en el mapa. Está cerca de España. —¿Es Francia? —¡Sí, es Francia!**

Comunicación

4 **¿Dónde estás...?** Get together with a partner and take turns asking each other where you normally are at these times. Answers will vary.

modelo

lunes / 10:00 a.m.
Estudiante 1: *¿Dónde estás los lunes a las diez de la mañana?*
Estudiante 2: *Estoy en la clase de español.*

1. sábados / 6:00 a.m.
2. miércoles / 9:15 a.m.
3. lunes / 11:10 a.m.
4. jueves / 12:30 a.m.
5. viernes / 2:25 p.m.
6. martes / 3:50 p.m.
7. jueves / 5:45 p.m.
8. miércoles / 8:20 p.m.

5 **La ciudad universitaria** You are an exchange student at a Spanish university. Tell a classmate which buildings you are looking for and ask for their location relative to where you are. Answers will vary.

modelo

Estudiante 1: *¿Está lejos la Facultad de Medicina?*
Estudiante 2: *No, está cerca. Está a la izquierda de la Facultad de Administración de Empresas.*

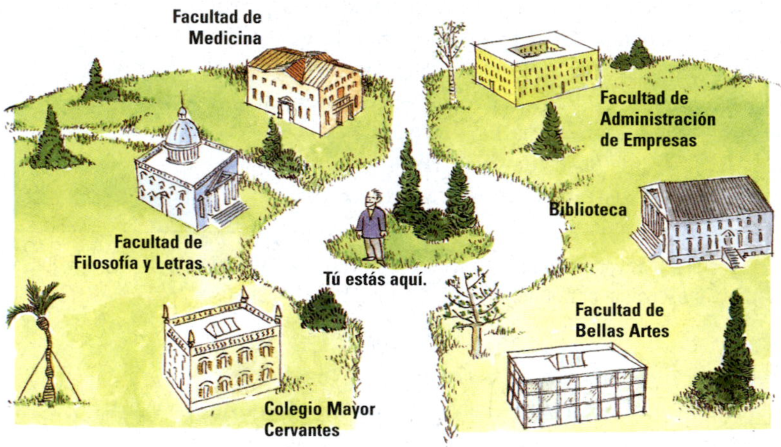

Síntesis

6 **Entrevista** In groups of three, ask each other these questions. Answers will vary.

1. ¿Cómo estás?
2. ¿Dónde tomas la clase de inglés/periodismo/física/computación?
3. ¿Dónde está tu (*your*) compañero/a de cuarto ahora?
4. ¿Cuántos estudiantes hay en tu clase de historia/literatura/química/matemáticas?
5. ¿Quién(es) no está(n) en la clase hoy?
6. ¿A qué hora terminan tus clases los lunes?
7. ¿Estudias mucho?
8. ¿Cuántas horas estudias para (*for*) una prueba?

4 Teaching Tips
- Ask two volunteers to read the model aloud.
- Have students scan the days and times and ask you for any additional vocabulary.

4 Expansion After students have completed the activity, ask the same questions of selected individuals. Then expand on their answers by asking additional questions. Ex: **—¿Dónde estás los sábados a las seis de la mañana? —Estoy en la residencia estudiantil. —¿Dónde está la residencia?**

5 Expansion
- Have students choose a new location in the drawing and repeat the activity.
- Make copies of your campus map and distribute them to the class. Ask questions about where particular buildings are. Give yourself a starting point so that you can ask questions with as many prepositions as possible. Ex: **Estoy en la biblioteca. ¿Está lejos la librería?**
- Have students form groups of three and take turns describing the location of different places on your campus. Ex: **—Está lejos de la cafetería y la biblioteca. Está al lado de la librería. —¿Es el estadio?**

6 Expansion Call on students to share the information they obtained with the class.

¡LENGUA VIVA!

La Facultad (*School*) **de Filosofía y Letras** includes departments such as language, literature, philosophy, history, and linguistics. Fine arts can be studied in **la Facultad de Bellas Artes**. In Spain, the business school is sometimes called **la Facultad de Administración de Empresas. Residencias estudiantiles** are referred to as **colegios mayores**.

TEACHING OPTIONS

Video Show the **Fotonovela** again to give students more input. Stop the video where appropriate to discuss how **estar** and prepositions were used and to ask comprehension questions.

Pairs Write a list of well-known monuments, places, and people on the board. Ex: **el Space Needle, Bill Gates, las Cataratas del Niágara, Jessica Alba.** Have student pairs take turns asking each other the location of each item. Ex: **—¿Dónde está el Space Needle? —Está en Seattle, Washington.**

Game Divide the class into two teams. Select a student from team A to think of an item in the classroom. Team B can ask five questions about where this item is. The first student can respond only with **sí, no, caliente** (*hot*), or **frío** (*cold*). If a team guesses the item within five tries, award it a point. If not, give the other team a point. The team with the most points wins.

2.4 Numbers 31 and higher

Tutorial

ANTE TODO You have already learned numbers 0–30. Now you will learn the rest of the numbers.

Numbers 31–100

▶ Numbers 31–99 follow the same basic pattern as 21–29.

Numbers 31–100

31	treinta y uno	**40**	cuarenta	**50**	cincuenta
32	treinta y dos	**41**	cuarenta y uno	**51**	cincuenta y uno
33	treinta y tres	**42**	cuarenta y dos	**52**	cincuenta y dos
34	treinta y cuatro	**43**	cuarenta y tres	**60**	sesenta
35	treinta y cinco	**44**	cuarenta y cuatro	**63**	sesenta y tres
36	treinta y seis	**45**	cuarenta y cinco	**64**	sesenta y cuatro
37	treinta y siete	**46**	cuarenta y seis	**70**	setenta
38	treinta y ocho	**47**	cuarenta y siete	**80**	ochenta
39	treinta y nueve	**48**	cuarenta y ocho	**90**	noventa
		49	cuarenta y nueve	**100**	cien, ciento

▶ **Y** is used in most numbers from **31** through **99**. Unlike numbers 21–29, these numbers must be written as three separate words.

Hay **noventa y dos** exámenes.
There are ninety-two exams.

Hay **cuarenta y dos** estudiantes.
There are forty-two students.

Hay cuarenta y siete estudiantes en la clase de geografía.

Cien menos sesenta y cuatro son treinta y seis pesos de cambio.

▶ With numbers that end in **uno** (31, 41, etc.), **uno** becomes **un** before a masculine noun and **una** before a feminine noun.

Hay **treinta y un** chicos.
There are thirty-one guys.

Hay **treinta y una** chicas.
There are thirty-one girls.

▶ **Cien** is used before nouns and in counting. The words **un**, **una**, and **uno** are never used before **cien** in Spanish. Use **cientos** to say *hundreds.*

Hay **cien** libros y **cien** sillas.
There are one hundred books and one hundred chairs.

¿Cuántos libros hay? **Cientos.**
How many books are there? Hundreds.

Section Goal

In **Estructura 2.4**, students will be introduced to numbers 31 and higher.

Instructional Resources
Supersite: Audio (Lab MP3 Files); Resources (Grammar Presentation Slides, Activity Pack, Scripts, Answer Keys); Testing Program (Quizzes)
WebSAM
Workbook, pp. 19–20
Lab Manual, p. 12

Teaching Tips

- Review 0–30 by having the class count with you. When you reach 30, ask individual students to count through 39. Count 40 yourself and have students continue counting through 100.
- Write on the board numbers not included in the chart: 56, 68, 72, and so forth. Ask students to say the number in Spanish.
- Drill numbers 31–100 counting in sequences of twos and threes. Point to individuals at random and have them supply the next number in the series. Keep a brisk pace.
- Emphasize that from 31 to 99, numbers that don't end in 0 are written as three words (**treinta y nueve**).
- Remind students that **uno** changes to **un** and **una**, as in **veintiún** and **veintiuna**.
- Bring in a newspaper or magazine ad that shows phone numbers and prices. Call on volunteers to read the numbers aloud.

TEACHING OPTIONS

Extra Practice Give simple math problems (addition and subtraction) with numbers 31 and higher. Include the numbers 0–30 as well, for a balanced review. Remind students that **más** = *plus*, **menos** = *minus*, and **es/son** = *equals*.
Extra Practice Write the beginning of a series of numbers on the board and have students continue the sequence.
Ex: **45, 50, 55...** or **77, 80, 83, 86...**

Heritage Speakers Add an auditory aspect to this grammar presentation. Ask heritage speakers to give the house or apartment number where they live (they do not have to give the street name). Ask them to give the addresses in tens (**1471 = catorce setenta y uno**). Have volunteers write the numbers they say on the board.

Teaching Tips

- Write these phrases on the board: **cuatrocientos estudiantes, novecientas personas, dos mil libros, once millones de viajeros.** Help students deduce the meanings of the numbers.
- Write numbers on the board and call on volunteers to read them aloud.
- To practice agreement, write numbers from 101 to 999 followed by various nouns and have students read them aloud.
- To make sure that students do not say **un mil** for *one thousand*, list **1.000, 2.000, 3.000,** and **4.000** on the board. Have the class call out the numbers as you point to them randomly in rapid succession. Repeat this process for **cien mil**. Then emphasize that **un** is used with **millón**.
- Point out that **de** is used between **millón/millones** and a noun.
- Slowly dictate pairs of large numbers for students to write on separate pieces of paper. When finished writing, students should hold up the larger number. Ex: You say **seiscientos cincuenta y ocho mil, ciento catorce; quinientos setenta y siete mil, novecientos treinta y seis**; students hold up **658.114; 577.936**.
- Point out how dates are expressed in Spanish and have volunteers read aloud the examples on this page. Then provide word groups that describe famous historical events. Ex: **Cristóbal Colón, las Américas; Neil Armstrong, la luna.** Have students state the year that they associate with each one. Ex: **Mil cuatrocientos noventa y dos.**

Numbers 101 and higher

NATIONAL STANDARDS comparisons

▶ As shown in the chart, Spanish uses a period to indicate thousands and millions, rather than a comma, as is used in English.

Numbers 101 and higher

101	ciento uno	**1.000**	mil
200	doscientos/as	**1.100**	mil cien
300	trescientos/as	**2.000**	dos mil
400	cuatrocientos/as	**5.000**	cinco mil
500	quinientos/as	**100.000**	cien mil
600	seiscientos/as	**200.000**	doscientos/as mil
700	setecientos/as	**550.000**	quinientos/as cincuenta mil
800	ochocientos/as	**1.000.000**	un millón (de)
900	novecientos/as	**8.000.000**	ocho millones (de)

▶ Notice that you should use **ciento**, not **cien**, to count numbers over 100.

110 = **ciento diez** 118 = **ciento dieciocho** 150 = **ciento cincuenta**

▶ The numbers 200 through 999 agree in gender with the nouns they modify.

324 plum**as**
trescient**as** veinticuatro plum**as**

3.505 libr**os**
tres mil quinient**os** cinco libr**os**

▶ The word **mil**, which can mean *a thousand* and *one thousand*, is not usually used in the plural form to refer to an exact number, but it can be used to express the idea of *a lot*, *many*, or *thousands*. **Cientos** can also be used to express *hundreds* in this manner.

¡Hay **miles** de personas en el estadio!
There are thousands of people in the stadium!

Hay **cientos** de libros en la biblioteca.
There are hundreds of books in the library.

▶ To express a complex number (including years), string together all of its components.

55.422 cincuenta y cinco mil cuatrocientos veintidós

¡LENGUA VIVA!

In Spanish, years are not expressed as pairs of two-digit numbers as they are in English (1979, *nineteen seventy-nine*): **1776, mil setecientos setenta y seis; 1945, mil novecientos cuarenta y cinco; 2016, dos mil dieciséis.**

¡ATENCIÓN!

When **millón** or **millones** is used before a noun, the word **de** is placed between the two:
1.000.000 hombres = un millón de hombres
12.000.000 casas = doce millones de casas.

¡INTÉNTALO! Write out the Spanish equivalent of each number.

1. **102** ciento dos
2. **5.000.000** cinco millones
3. **201** doscientos uno
4. **76** setenta y seis
5. **92** noventa y dos
6. **550.300** quinientos cincuenta mil trescientos
7. **235** doscientos treinta y cinco
8. **79** setenta y nueve
9. **113** ciento trece
10. **88** ochenta y ocho
11. **17.123** diecisiete mil ciento veintitrés
12. **497** cuatrocientos noventa y siete

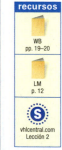

recursos
WB pp. 19–20
LM p. 12
vhlcentral.com Lección 2

TEACHING OPTIONS

TPR Write number patterns on cards (one number per card) and distribute them among the class. Begin a number chain by calling out the first two numbers in the pattern. Ex: **veinticinco, cincuenta**. The students holding these cards have five seconds to get up and stand in front of the class. The rest of the class continues by calling out the numbers in the pattern for the students to join the chain. Continue until the chain is broken or complete; then begin a new pattern.

Pairs Ask students to create a list of nine items containing three numerals in the hundreds, three in the thousands, and three in the millions; each numeral should be followed by a masculine or feminine noun. Have students exchange lists with a classmate, who will read the items aloud. Partners should listen for the correct number and gender agreement. Ex: **204 personas (doscientas cuatro personas)**

Práctica y Comunicación

NATIONAL communication STANDARDS

1 **Baloncesto** Provide these basketball scores in Spanish.

1. Ohio State 76, Michigan 65
2. Florida 92, Florida State 104
3. Stanford 83, UCLA 89
4. Purdue 81, Indiana 78
5. Princeton 67, Harvard 55
6. Duke 115, Virginia 121

1. setenta y seis, sesenta y cinco 2. noventa y dos, ciento cuatro 3. ochenta y tres, ochenta y nueve 4. ochenta y uno, setenta y ocho 5. sesenta y siete, cincuenta y cinco 6. ciento quince, ciento veintiuno

2 **Completar** Following the pattern, write out the missing numbers in Spanish.

1. 50, 150, 250 ... 1.050 trescientos cincuenta, cuatrocientos cincuenta, quinientos cincuenta, seiscientos cincuenta, setecientos cincuenta, ochocientos cincuenta, novecientos cincuenta
2. 5.000, 20.000, 35.000 ... 95.000 cincuenta mil, sesenta y cinco mil, ochenta mil
3. 100.000, 200.000, 300.000 ... 1.000.000 cuatrocientos mil, quinientos mil, seiscientos mil, setecientos mil, ochocientos mil, novecientos mil
4. 100.000.000, 90.000.000, 80.000.000 ... 0 setenta millones, sesenta millones, cincuenta millones, cuarenta millones, treinta millones, veinte millones, diez millones

3 **Resolver** In pairs, take turns reading the math problems aloud for your partner to solve.

AYUDA
\+ → **más**
– → **menos**
= → **son**

modelo
200 + 300 =
Estudiante 1: Doscientos más trescientos son...
Estudiante 2: ...quinientos.

1. 1.000 + 753 = Mil más setecientos cincuenta y tres son mil setecientos cincuenta y tres.
2. 1.000.000 – 30.000 = Un millón menos treinta mil son novecientos setenta mil.
3. 10.000 + 555 = Diez mil más quinientos cincuenta y cinco son diez mil quinientos cincuenta y cinco.
4. 15 + 150 = Quince más ciento cincuenta son ciento sesenta y cinco.
5. 100.000 + 205.000 = Cien mil más doscientos cinco mil son trescientos cinco mil.
6. 29.000 – 10.000 = Veintinueve mil menos diez mil son diecinueve mil.

4 **Entrevista** Find out the telephone numbers and e-mail addresses of four classmates. Answers will vary.

AYUDA
arroba *at* (@)
punto *dot* (.)

modelo
Estudiante 1: ¿Cuál es tu (*your*) número de teléfono?
Estudiante 2: Es el 635-19-51.
Estudiante 1: ¿Y tu dirección de correo electrónico?
Estudiante 2: Es a-Smith-arroba-pe-ele-punto-e-de-u. (asmith@pl.edu)

NATIONAL communication STANDARDS

Síntesis

5 **¿A qué distancia...?** Your instructor will give you and a partner incomplete charts that indicate the distances between Madrid and various locations. Fill in the missing information on your chart by asking your partner questions. Answers will vary.

modelo
Estudiante 1: ¿A qué distancia está Arganda del Rey?
Estudiante 2: Está a veintisiete kilómetros de Madrid.

Practice more at **vhlcentral.com**.

1 Expansion In pairs, have each student write three additional basketball scores and dictate them to his or her partner, who writes them down.

2 Teaching Tip To simplify, have students identify the pattern of each sequence. Ex: 1. Add one hundred.

3 Expansion To challenge students, have them create four additional math problems for a partner to solve.

4 Teaching Tips
- Write your own e-mail address on the board as you pronounce it.
- Point out that **el correo electrónico** means *e-mail*.
- Reassure students that, if they are uncomfortable revealing their personal information, they can invent a number and address.
- Ask volunteers to share their phone numbers and e-mail addresses. Other students write them on the board.

5 Teaching Tips
- If this is the first time students are completing an activity from the Activity Pack, explain that they will need a handout.
- Divide the class into pairs and distribute the handouts associated with this Information Gap activity (Activity Pack/Supersite). Explain that in this type of exercise, each partner has information that the other needs, and the only way to get this information is by asking the partner questions.
- Point out and model **está a ____ de...** to express distance.
- Give students ten minutes to complete this activity.

TEACHING OPTIONS

Small Groups In groups of three or four, ask students to think of a city or town within a 100-mile radius of the university. Have them find out the distance in miles (**Está a ____ millas de la universidad.**) and what other cities or towns are nearby (**Está cerca de...**). Then have groups read their descriptions for the class to guess.

Game Ask for two volunteers and station them at opposite ends of the board so neither one can see what the other is writing. Say a number for them to write on the board. If both students are correct, continue to give numbers until one writes an incorrect number. The winner continues on to play against another student.

Section Goal

In **Recapitulación**, students will review the grammar concepts from this lesson.

Instructional Resource
Supersite

1 Teaching Tips

- To simplify, ask students to identify the infinitive of the verb in each row.
- Complete this activity orally as a class. Write each form on the board as students call them out.

1 Expansion Ask students to provide the third-person singular (**Ud./él/ella**) conjugations.

2 Expansion

- Ask students to write five more numbers above 31. Have them read the numbers to a partner, who will jot them down. Remind students to check each other's answers.
- To challenge students, have them complete the activity and then say what they can buy with that amount of money. Model the first item for the class. Ex: **Con 49 dólares, compro una mochila.**

3 Teaching Tips

- Remind students that all question words should carry accent marks.
- Remind students that verbs in Spanish do not require subject pronouns; they are used for emphasis or clarification.

Recapitulación

Diagnostics

Review the grammar concepts you have learned in this lesson by completing these activities.

1 Completar Complete the chart with the correct verb forms. 24 pts.

yo	tú	nosotros	ellas
compro	compras	compramos	compran
deseo	**deseas**	deseamos	desean
miro	miras	**miramos**	miran
pregunto	preguntas	preguntamos	**preguntan**

2 Números Write these numbers in Spanish. 16 pts.

modelo
645: seiscientos cuarenta y cinco

1. **49:** cuarenta y nueve
2. **97:** noventa y siete
3. **113:** ciento trece
4. **632:** seiscientos treinta y dos
5. **1.781:** mil setecientos ochenta y uno
6. **3.558:** tres mil quinientos cincuenta y ocho
7. **1.006.015:** un millón seis mil quince
8. **67.224.370:** sesenta y siete millones doscientos veinticuatro mil trescientos setenta

3 Preguntas Write questions for these answers. 12 pts.

1. —¿De dónde es Patricia?
   —Patricia es de Colombia.
2. —¿Quién es él?
   —Él es mi amigo (*friend*).
3. —¿Cuántos idiomas hablas (tú)?
   —Hablo dos idiomas (*languages*).
4. —¿Qué desean (tomar) (ustedes)?
   —Deseamos tomar café.
5. —¿Por qué tomas biología?
   —Tomo biología porque me gustan las ciencias.
6. —¿Cuándo descansa Camilo?
   —Camilo descansa por las mañanas.

RESUMEN GRAMATICAL

2.1 Present tense of -*ar* verbs pp. 46–48

estudiar	
estudio	estudiamos
estudias	estudiáis
estudia	estudian

The verb gustar

(no) me gusta + el/la + [*singular noun*]

(no) me gustan + los/las + [*plural noun*]

(no) me gusta + [*infinitive(s)*]

Note: You may use **a mí** for emphasis, but never **yo**.

To ask a friend about likes and dislikes, use **te** instead of **me**, but never **tú**.

¿Te gusta la historia?

2.2 Forming questions in Spanish pp. 51–52

- ¿Ustedes trabajan los sábados?
- ¿Trabajan ustedes los sábados?
- Ustedes trabajan los sábados, ¿verdad?/¿no?

Interrogative words

¿Adónde?	¿Cuánto/a?	¿Por qué?
¿Cómo?	¿Cuántos/as?	¿Qué?
¿Cuál(es)?	¿De dónde?	¿Quién(es)?
¿Cuándo?	¿Dónde?	

2.3 Present tense of *estar* pp. 55–56

- estar: estoy, estás, está, estamos, estáis, están

2.4 Numbers 31 and higher pp. 59–60

31	treinta y uno	101	ciento uno
32	treinta y dos (*and so on*)	200	doscientos/as
		500	quinientos/as
40	cuarenta	700	setecientos/as
50	cincuenta	900	novecientos/as
60	sesenta	1.000	mil
70	setenta	2.000	dos mil
80	ochenta	5.100	cinco mil cien
90	noventa	100.000	cien mil
100	cien, ciento	1.000.000	un millón (de)

TEACHING OPTIONS

Pairs Have students write ten questions using the interrogative words from **Estructura 2.2** to ask their partner about his/her family, house, friends, etc. Remind students that **¿Cuánto/a?** and **¿Cuántos/as?** should agree with their corresponding nouns. Then have students exchange papers with a classmate and answer the questions. Finally, have pairs work together to review the answers. Have them write sentences using **nosotros/as** about any items they have in common.

Extra Practice On the board, write a list of landmarks (libraries, parks, churches, restaurants, hotels, and so forth) in the community. Have students choose a landmark and write a short paragraph describing its location. Ex: **El Hotel Plaza está al lado de la biblioteca. Está cerca de la catedral y delante de Sebastian's Café. Está lejos de mi casa.**

4 **Al teléfono** Complete this telephone conversation with the correct forms of the verb **estar**. 16 pts.

MARÍA TERESA Hola, señora López. (1) ¿ ___Está___ Elisa en casa?

SRA. LÓPEZ Hola, ¿quién es?

MARÍA TERESA Soy María Teresa. Elisa y yo (2) ___estamos___ en la misma (*same*) clase de literatura.

SRA. LÓPEZ ¡Ah, María Teresa! ¿Cómo (3) ___estás___ ?

MARÍA TERESA (4) ___Estoy___ muy bien, gracias. Y usted, ¿cómo (5) ___está___ ?

SRA. LÓPEZ Bien, gracias. Pues, no, Elisa no (6) ___está___ en casa. Ella y su hermano (*her brother*) (7) ___están___ en la Biblioteca Cervantes.

MARÍA TERESA ¿Cervantes?

SRA. LÓPEZ Es la biblioteca que (8) ___está___ al lado del café Bambú.

MARÍA TERESA ¡Ah, sí! Gracias, señora López.

SRA. LÓPEZ Hasta luego, María Teresa.

5 **¿Qué te gusta?** Write a paragraph of at least five sentences stating what you like and don't like about your university. If possible, explain your likes and dislikes. 32 pts. Answers will vary.

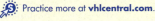

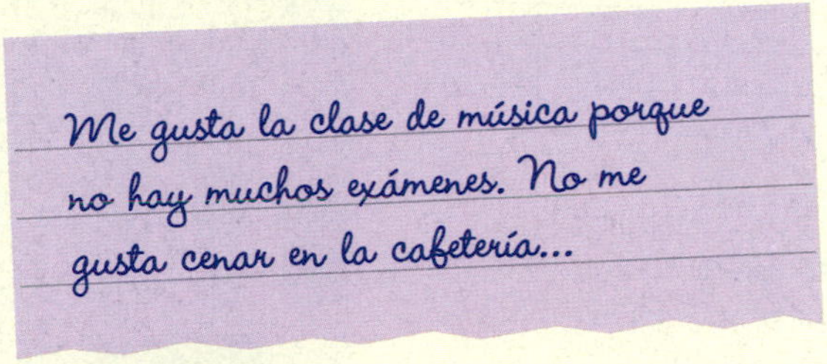

Me gusta la clase de música porque
no hay muchos exámenes. No me
gusta cenar en la cafetería...

6 **Canción** Use the appropriate forms of the verb **gustar** to complete the beginning of a popular song by Manu Chao. 4 EXTRA points!

"Me ___gustan___ los aviones°,
me gustas tú,
me ___gusta___ viajar,
me gustas tú,
me gusta la mañana,
me gustas tú."

aviones *airplanes*

Practice more at **vhlcentral.com**.

TEACHING OPTIONS

Pairs Write **más, menos, multiplicado por,** and **dividido por** on the board. Model a few simple problems using numbers 31 and higher. Ex: **Cien mil trescientos menos diez mil son noventa mil trescientos. Mil dividido por veinte son cincuenta.** Then ask students to write two math problems of each type for a classmate to solve. Have partners verify each other's work.

Small Groups Tell students to think of a famous person and write five statements about their likes and dislikes from that person's point of view. Tell them to progressively give more clues to the person's identity and to end with **¿Quién soy?** Then, in small groups, have students read their statements aloud for their partners to guess. Have them respond to the guesses with more information as necessary.

4 Expansion Ask student pairs to write a brief phone conversation based on the one in **Actividad 4**. Have volunteers role-play their dialogues for the class.

5 Teaching Tips
- Before writing their paragraphs, have students brainstorm a list of words or phrases related to universities.
- Remind students of when to use **gusta** versus **gustan.** Write a few example sentences on the board.
- Have students exchange papers with a partner to peer-edit each other's paragraphs.

6 Teaching Tip Point out the form **gustas** in lines 2, 4, and 6, and ask students to guess the translation of the phrase **me gustas tú** (*I like you*, literally, *you are pleasing to me*). Tell students that **me gustas** and **le gustas** are not used as much as their English counterparts. Most often they are used in romantic situations.

6 Canción **Manu Chao** (born 1961) is a French singer of Spanish origin. In the 80's he and his brother started the band **Mano Negra**. Since the band's breakup in 1995, he has led a successful solo career. His music, which draws on diverse influences such as punk, ska, reggae, salsa, and Algerian raï, is popular throughout Europe and Latin America. **Chao** often mixes several languages in one song.

Audio: Reading
Additional Reading

Section Goals

In **Lectura**, students will:

- learn to use text formats to predict content
- read documents in Spanish

Instructional Resource
Supersite

Estrategia Introduce the strategy. Point out that many documents have easily identifiable formats that can help readers predict content. Have students look at the document in the **Estrategia** box, and ask them to name the recognizable elements (days of the week, time, classes). Ask what kind of document it is (a student's weekly schedule).

Cognados Have pairs of students scan **¡Español en Madrid!** and identify cognates and guess their meanings.

Examinar el texto Ask students what type of information is contained in **¡Español en Madrid!** (It is a brochure for an intensive Spanish-language summer program.) Discuss elements of the recognizable format that helped them predict the content, such as the headings, the lists of courses, and the course schedule with dates.

Lectura

NATIONAL STANDARDS communication cultures

Antes de leer

Estrategia

Predicting content through formats

Recognizing the format of a document can help you to predict its content. For instance, invitations, greeting cards, and classified ads follow an easily identifiable format, which usually gives you a general idea of the information they contain. Look at the text and identify it based on its format.

	lunes	martes	miércoles	jueves	viernes
8:30	biología		biología		biología
9:00		historia		historia	
9:30	inglés		inglés		inglés
10:00					
10:30					
11:00					
12:00					
12:30					
1:00					
2:00	arte		arte		arte

If you guessed that this is a page from a student's schedule, you are correct. You can now infer that the document contains information about a student's weekly schedule, including days, times, and activities.

Cognados

With a partner, make a list of the cognates in the text and guess their English meanings. What do cognates reveal about the content of the document?

Examinar el texto

Look at the format of the document entitled ***¡Español en Madrid!*** What type of text is it? What information do you expect to find in this type of document?

Practice more at **vhlcentral.com**.

¡ESPAÑOL EN MADRID!
UAE
Programa de Cursos Intensivos de Español
Universidad Autónoma de España

Después de leer

Correspondencias

Provide the letter of each item in Column B that matches the words in Column A. Two items will not be used.

A

1. profesores f
2. vivienda h
3. Madrid d
4. número de teléfono a
5. Español 2B c
6. número de fax g

B

a. (34) 91 523 4500
b. (34) 91 524 0210
c. 23 junio–30 julio
d. capital cultural de Europa
e. 16 junio–22 julio
f. especializados en enseñar español como lengua extranjera
g. (34) 91 523 4623
h. familias españolas

TEACHING OPTIONS

Extra Practice For homework, ask students to write a weekly schedule (**horario semanal**) of a friend or family member. Ask them to label the days of the week in Spanish and add notes for that person's appointments and activities as well. In class, ask students questions about the schedules they wrote.
Ex: **¿Qué clase toma _____ hoy? ¿Trabaja _____ manaña? ¿Cuántos días trabaja _____ esta semana?**

Heritage Speakers Ask heritage speakers who have attended a school in the Spanish-speaking world to describe their schedule there, comparing and contrasting it with their schedule now. Invite them to make other comparisons between U.S. or Canadian institutions and those in the Spanish-speaking world.

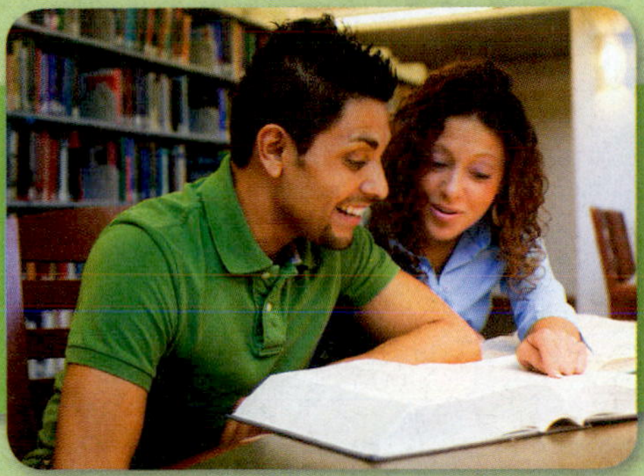

Universidad Autónoma de España

Madrid, la capital cultural de Europa, y la UAE te ofrecen cursos intensivos de verano° para aprender° español como nunca antes°.

¿Dónde?
En el campus de la UAE, edificio° de la Facultad de Filosofía y Letras.

¿Quiénes son los profesores?
Son todos hablantes nativos del español y catedráticos° de la UAE especializados en enseñar el español como lengua extranjera.

¿Qué niveles se ofrecen?
Se ofrecen tres niveles° básicos:

1. Español Elemental, A, B y C
2. Español Intermedio, A y B
3. Español Avanzado, A y B

Viviendas
Para estudiantes extranjeros se ofrece vivienda° con familias españolas.

¿Cuándo?
Este verano desde° el 16 de junio hasta el 10 de agosto. Los cursos tienen una duración de 6 semanas.

Cursos	Empieza°	Termina
Español 1A	16 junio	22 julio
Español 1B	23 junio	30 julio
Español 1C	30 junio	10 agosto
Español 2A	16 junio	22 julio
Español 2B	23 junio	30 julio
Español 3A	16 junio	22 julio
Español 3B	23 junio	30 julio

Información
Para mayor información, sirvan comunicarse con la siguiente° oficina:

Universidad Autónoma de España
Programa de Español como Lengua Extranjera
Calle del Valle de Mena 95, 28039 Madrid, España
Tel. (34) 91 523 4500, **Fax** (34) 91 523 4623
www.uae.es

verano *summer* aprender *to learn* nunca antes *never before* edificio *building* catedráticos *professors* niveles *levels* vivienda *housing* desde *from* Empieza *Begins* siguiente *following*

¿Cierto o falso?

Indicate whether each statement is **cierto** or **falso**. Then correct the false statements.

	Cierto	Falso
1. La Universidad Autónoma de España ofrece (*offers*) cursos intensivos de italiano. *Ofrece cursos intensivos de español.*	❍	✓
2. La lengua nativa de los profesores del programa es el inglés. *La lengua nativa de los profesores es el español.*	❍	✓
3. Los cursos de español son en la Facultad de Ciencias. *Son en el edificio de la Facultad de Filosofía y Letras.*	❍	✓
4. Los estudiantes pueden vivir (*can live*) con familias españolas.	✓	❍
5. La universidad que ofrece los cursos intensivos está en Salamanca. *Está en Madrid.*	❍	✓
6. Español 3B termina en agosto. *Termina en julio.*	❍	✓
7. Si deseas información sobre (*about*) los cursos intensivos de español, es posible llamar al (34) 91 523 4500.	✓	❍
8. Español 1A empieza en julio. *Empieza en junio.*	❍	✓

Correspondencias Go over the answers as a class or assign pairs of students to work together to check each other's answers.

¿Cierto o falso? Give students these true-false statements as items 9–16: **9. El campus de la UAE está en la Ciudad de México. (Falso; está en Madrid.) 10. Los cursos terminan en junio. (Falso; terminan en julio y agosto.) 11. Hay un curso de español intermedio. (Falso; hay dos cursos.) 12. Los cursos se ofrecen en el verano. (Cierto) 13. Hay una residencia estudiantil para los estudiantes extranjeros en el campus. (Falso; hay vivienda con familias españolas para estudiantes extranjeros.) 14. Hay un número de teléfono en la universidad para más información. (Cierto) 15. Todos los profesores son hablantes nativos. (Cierto) 16. Los cursos tienen una duración de doce semanas. (Falso; tienen una duración de seis semanas.)**

Expansion Divide the class into pairs. Instruct one student to research a Spanish-language summer program in Spain and the other student a program in Mexico. Tell them to compile information on the program's dates, fees, housing options, professors, and courses offered. Then, have pairs compare their findings and decide which program they prefer. Have volunteers describe to the class the program they chose.

TEACHING OPTIONS

Language Notes Explain that in Spanish dates are usually written in the order of day/month/year rather than month/day/year, as they are in the United States and Canada. Someone from Mexico with a birthdate of July 5, 1998, would write his or her birthdate as 5/7/98.

Pairs Provide pairs of students with Spanish-language magazines and newspapers. Ask them to look for documents with easily recognizable formats, such as classified ads or advertisements. Ask them to use cognates and other context clues to predict the content. Then have partners present their examples and findings to the class.

Section Goal

In **Panorama**, students will read about the geography, culture, and economy of Spain.

Instructional Resources
Supersite: Video (***Panorama cultural***); Resources (Scripts, Translations, Digital Image Bank, Answer Keys)
WebSAM
Workbook, pp. 21–22
Video Manual, pp. 33–34

Teaching Tips

- Have students use the map in their books to find the places mentioned. Explain that the Canary Islands are located in the Atlantic Ocean, off the northwestern coast of Africa. Point out the photos that accompany the map on this page.
- Use the **Lección 2** digital images to assist with this presentation.

El país en cifras After students have read **Idiomas**, associate the regional languages with the larger map by asking questions such as: **¿Hablan catalán en Barcelona? ¿Qué idioma hablan en Madrid?** Point out that the names of languages may be capitalized as map labels, but are not capitalized when they appear in running text.

¡Increíble pero cierto! In addition to festivals related to economic and agricultural resources, Spain has many festivals rooted in Catholic tradition. Among the most famous is **Semana Santa** (*Holy Week*), which is celebrated annually in Seville, and many other towns and cities, with great reverence and pageantry.

Video: *Panorama cultural*
Interactive map

España

NATIONAL STANDARDS connections cultures

El país en cifras

- **Área:** 505.370 km² (kilómetros cuadrados) o 195.124 millas cuadradas°, incluyendo las islas Baleares y las islas Canarias
- **Población:** 47.043.000
- **Capital:** Madrid—5.762.000
- **Ciudades° principales:** Barcelona—5.029.000, Valencia—812.000, Sevilla, Zaragoza
- **Moneda°:** euro
- **Idiomas°:** español o castellano, catalán, gallego, valenciano, euskera

Bandera de España

Españoles célebres

- **Miguel de Cervantes,** escritor° (1547–1616)
- **Pedro Almodóvar,** director de cine° (1949–)
- **Rosa Montero,** escritora y periodista° (1951–)
- **Fernando Alonso,** corredor de autos° (1981–)
- **Paz Vega,** actriz° (1976–)
- **Severo Ochoa,** Premio Nobel de Medicina, 1959; doctor y científico (1905–1993)

millas cuadradas *square miles* Ciudades *Cities* Moneda *Currency* Idiomas *Languages* escritor *writer* cine *film* periodista *reporter* corredor de autos *race car driver* actriz *actress* pueblo *town* Cada año *Every year* Durante todo un día *All day long* se tiran *throw at each other* varias toneladas *many tons*

La Sagrada Familia en Barcelona

Plaza Mayor en Madrid

El baile flamenco

recursos

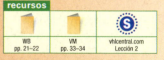

WB pp. 21–22	VM pp. 33–34	vhlcentral.com Lección 2

¡Increíble pero cierto!

En Buñol, un pueblo° de Valencia, la producción de tomates es un recurso económico muy importante. Cada año° se celebra el festival de *La Tomatina*. Durante todo un día°, miles de personas se tiran° tomates. Llegan turistas de todo el país, y se usan varias toneladas° de tomates.

TEACHING OPTIONS

Heritage Speakers **Paella,** the national dish of Spain, is the ancestor of the popular Latin American dish **arroz con pollo**. Ask heritage speakers if they know of any traditional dishes in their families that have their roots in Spanish cuisine. Invite them to describe the dish(es) to the class.

Variación léxica Tell students that they may also see the word **euskera** spelled **euskara** and **eusquera.** The letter **k** is used in Spanish only in words of foreign origin. **Euskara** is the Basque name of the Basque language, which linguists believe is unrelated to any other known language. The Spanish name for *Basque* is **vascuence** or **vasco.**

Gastronomía • José Andrés

José Andrés es un chef español famoso internacionalmente°. Le gusta combinar platos° tradicionales de España con las técnicas de cocina más innovadoras°. Andrés vive° en Washington, DC, es dueño° de varios restaurantes en los EE.UU. y presenta° un programa en PBS (foto, izquierda). También° ha estado° en *Late Show with David Letterman* y *Top Chef*.

Cultura • La diversidad

La riqueza° cultural y lingüística de España refleja la combinación de las diversas culturas que han habitado° en su territorio durante siglos°. El español es la lengua oficial del país, pero también son oficiales el catalán, el gallego, el euskera y el valenciano.

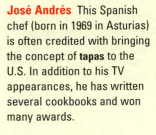

Sóc molt fan de la pàgina 335.
Ajuntament de Barcelona

Póster en catalán

Las meninas, Diego Velázquez, 1656

Artes • Velázquez y el Prado

El Prado, en Madrid, es uno de los museos más famosos del mundo°. En el Prado hay pinturas° importantes de Botticelli, de El Greco y de los españoles Goya y Velázquez. *Las meninas* es la obra° más conocida° de Diego Velázquez, pintor° oficial de la corte real° durante el siglo° XVII.

Comida • La paella

La paella es uno de los platos más típicos de España. Siempre se prepara° con arroz° y azafrán°, pero hay diferentes recetas°. La paella valenciana, por ejemplo, es de pollo° y conejo°, y la paella marinera es de mariscos°.

La costa de Ibiza

¿Qué aprendiste? Completa las oraciones con la información adecuada.

1. El chef español <u>José Andrés</u> es muy famoso.
2. El arroz y el azafrán son ingredientes básicos de la <u>paella</u>.
3. El Prado está en <u>Madrid</u>.
4. José Andrés vive en <u>Washington, DC/EE.UU.</u>.
5. El chef José Andrés tiene un <u>programa</u> de televisión en PBS.
6. El gallego es una de las lenguas oficiales de <u>España</u>.

Conexión Internet Investiga estos temas en **vhlcentral.com**.

Practice more at **vhlcentral.com**.

1. Busca información sobre la Universidad de Salamanca u otra universidad española. ¿Qué cursos ofrece (*does it offer*)? ¿Ofrece tu universidad cursos similares?
2. Busca información sobre un español o una española célebre (por ejemplo, un[a] político/a, un actor, una actriz, un[a] artista). ¿De qué parte de España es y por qué es célebre?

internacionalmente *internationally* platos *dishes* más innovadoras *most innovative* vive *lives* dueño *owner* presenta *hosts* También *Also* ha estado *has been* riqueza *richness* han habitado *have lived* durante siglos *for centuries* mundo *world* pinturas *paintings* obra *work* más conocida *best-known* pintor *painter* corte real *royal court* siglo *century* Siempre se prepara *It is always prepared* arroz *rice* azafrán *saffron* recetas *recipes* pollo *chicken* conejo *rabbit* mariscos *seafood*

José Andrés This Spanish chef (born in 1969 in Asturias) is often credited with bringing the concept of **tapas** to the U.S. In addition to his TV appearances, he has written several cookbooks and won many awards.

La diversidad Have students consult the map of Spain at the back of the textbook. As you name each language (Ex: **catalán**), have students search for the corresponding region name (**Cataluña**).

Velázquez y el Prado Point out **la infanta Margarita**, the royal princess, with her attendants. The name **Las meninas** comes from the Portuguese word for "girls," used to refer to royal attendants. Reflected in the mirror are **Margarita's** parents, **los reyes Felipe IV y Mariana de Asturias**. Have students find **Velázquez** himself, standing paintbrush in hand, before an enormous canvas. You may wish to ask students to research the identity of the man in the doorway.

La paella Pairs can role-play a restaurant scene: the customer asks the waiter/waitress about the ingredients in the paella, then chooses **paella valenciana** or **paella marinera**.

Conexión Internet Students will find supporting Internet activities and links at **vhlcentral.com**.

Teaching Tip You may want to wrap up this section by playing the ***Panorama cultural*** video footage for this lesson.

TEACHING OPTIONS

Variación léxica Regional cultures and languages have remained strong in Spain, despite efforts made in the past to suppress them in the name of national unity. The language that has come to be called *Spanish*, **español,** is the language of the region of north central Spain called **Castilla**. Because Spain was unified under the Kingdom of Castile at the end of the Middle Ages, the language of Castile, **castellano**, became the principal language of government, business, and literature. Even today one is likely to hear Spanish speakers refer to Spanish as **castellano** or **español**. Efforts to suppress the regional languages, though often harsh, were ineffective, and after the death of the dictator **Francisco Franco** and the return of power to regional governing bodies, the regional languages of Spain were given co-official status.

Instructional Resources
Supersite: Audio (Textbook & Lab MP3s); Testing Program (Tests, MP3s)
WebSAM
Lab Manual, p. 12

La clase y la universidad

el/la compañero/a de clase	*classmate*
el/la compañero/a de cuarto	*roommate*
el/la estudiante	*student*
el/la profesor(a)	*teacher*
el borrador	*eraser*
la calculadora	*calculator*
el escritorio	*desk*
el libro	*book*
el mapa	*map*
la mesa	*table*
la mochila	*backpack*
el papel	*paper*
la papelera	*wastebasket*
la pizarra	*blackboard*
la pluma	*pen*
la puerta	*door*
el reloj	*clock; watch*
la silla	*seat*
la tiza	*chalk*
la ventana	*window*
la biblioteca	*library*
la cafetería	*cafeteria*
la casa	*house; home*
el estadio	*stadium*
el laboratorio	*laboratory*
la librería	*bookstore*
la residencia estudiantil	*dormitory*
la universidad	*university; college*
la clase	*class*
el curso, la materia	*course*
la especialización	*major*
el examen	*test; exam*
el horario	*schedule*
la prueba	*test; quiz*
el semestre	*semester*
la tarea	*homework*
el trimestre	*trimester; quarter*

Vocabulary Tools

recursos

LM p. 12 | vhlcentral.com Lección 2

Las materias

la administración de empresas	*business administration*
la arqueología	*archeology*
el arte	*art*
la biología	*biology*
las ciencias	*sciences*
la computación	*computer science*
la contabilidad	*accounting*
la economía	*economics*
el español	*Spanish*
la física	*physics*
la geografía	*geography*
la historia	*history*
las humanidades	*humanities*
el inglés	*English*
las lenguas extranjeras	*foreign languages*
la literatura	*literature*
las matemáticas	*mathematics*
la música	*music*
el periodismo	*journalism*
la psicología	*psychology*
la química	*chemistry*
la sociología	*sociology*

Preposiciones y adverbios

al lado de	*next to*
a la derecha de	*to the right of*
a la izquierda de	*to the left of*
allá	*over there*
allí	*there*
cerca de	*near*
con	*with*
debajo de	*below*
delante de	*in front of*
detrás de	*behind*
en	*in; on*
encima de	*on top of*
entre	*between*
lejos de	*far from*
sin	*without*
sobre	*on; over*

Palabras adicionales

¿Adónde?	*Where (to)?*
ahora	*now*
¿Cuál?, ¿Cuáles?	*Which?; Which one(s)?*
¿Por qué?	*Why?*
porque	*because*

Verbos

bailar	*to dance*
buscar	*to look for*
caminar	*to walk*
cantar	*to sing*
cenar	*to have dinner*
comprar	*to buy*
contestar	*to answer*
conversar	*to converse, to chat*
desayunar	*to have breakfast*
descansar	*to rest*
desear	*to wish; to desire*
dibujar	*to draw*
enseñar	*to teach*
escuchar la radio/música	*to listen (to) the radio/music*
esperar (+ *inf.*)	*to wait (for); to hope*
estar	*to be*
estudiar	*to study*
explicar	*to explain*
gustar	*to like*
hablar	*to talk; to speak*
llegar	*to arrive*
llevar	*to carry*
mirar	*to look (at); to watch*
necesitar (+ *inf.*)	*to need*
practicar	*to practice*
preguntar	*to ask (a question)*
preparar	*to prepare*
regresar	*to return*
terminar	*to end; to finish*
tomar	*to take; to drink*
trabajar	*to work*
viajar	*to travel*

Los días de la semana

¿Cuándo?	*When?*
¿Qué día es hoy?	*What day is it?*
Hoy es...	*Today is...*
la semana	*week*
lunes	*Monday*
martes	*Tuesday*
miércoles	*Wednesday*
jueves	*Thursday*
viernes	*Friday*
sábado	*Saturday*
domingo	*Sunday*

Numbers 31 and higher	*See pages 59–60.*
Expresiones útiles	*See page 41.*

La familia

3

Communicative Goals

You will learn how to:

- **Talk about your family and friends**
- **Describe people and things**
- **Express possession**

A PRIMERA VISTA

- ¿Cuántos chicos hay en la foto?
- ¿Hay una mujer detrás de la chica? ¿Y a la izquierda?
- ¿Hay una cosa en la mano del chico?
- ¿Conversan ellos? ¿Trabajan? ¿Descansan?
- ¿Están en su casa?

contextos

pages 70–73

- The family
- Identifying people
- Professions and occupations

fotonovela

pages 74–77

The Díaz family spends Sunday afternoon in Xochimilco. Marissa meets the extended family and answers questions about her own family. The group has a picnic and takes a boat ride through the canals.

cultura

pages 78–79

- Surnames and families in the Spanish-speaking world
- Spain's Royal Family

estructura

pages 80–97

- Descriptive adjectives
- Possessive adjectives
- Present tense of **-er** and **-ir** verbs
- Present tense of **tener** and **venir**
- **Recapitulación**

adelante

pages 98–105

Lectura: A brief article about families
Escritura: A letter to a friend
Escuchar: A conversation between friends
En pantalla: Anuncio y cortometraje
Panorama: Ecuador

Lesson Goals

In **Lección 3**, students will be introduced to the following:

- terms for family relationships
- names of various professions
- surnames and families in the Spanish-speaking world
- Spain's Royal Family
- descriptive adjectives
- possessive adjectives
- the present tense of common regular **–er** and **–ir** verbs
- the present tense of **tener** and **venir**
- context clues to unlock meaning of unfamiliar words
- using idea maps when writing
- how to write a friendly letter
- strategies for asking clarification in oral communication
- a television commercial for **Jumbo**, a Chilean superstore chain
- the short film ***La despedida***
- a video about two Ecuadorian families
- geographical and cultural information about Ecuador

A primera vista Here are some additional questions you can ask to personalize the photo: **¿Cuántas personas hay en tu familia? ¿De qué conversas con ellos? ¿Estudias lejos o cerca de la casa de tu familia? ¿Viajas mucho con ellos?**

Teaching Tip Look for these icons for additional communicative practice:

	Interpretive communication
	Presentational communication
	Interpersonal communication

INSTRUCTIONAL RESOURCES

Supersite (vhlcentral.com)
Video: ***Fotonovela, Flash cultura, Anuncio, Cortometraje, Panorama cultural***
Audio: Textbook and Lab MP3 Files
Activity Pack: Information Gap Activities, games, additional activity handouts
Resources: SAM Answer Key, Scripts, Translations, **Vocabulario adicional**, sample lesson plan, Grammar Presentation Slides, Digital Image Bank
Testing Program: Quizzes, Tests, Exams, MP3s
Student Activities Manual: Workbook/Video Manual/Lab Manual
WebSAM (online Student Activities Manual)

Section Goals

In **Contextos**, students will learn and practice:

- terms for family relationships
- names of professions

Instructional Resources

Supersite: Audio (Textbook and Lab MP3 Files); Resources (Digital Image Bank, **Vocabulario adicional**, Activity Pack, Scripts, Answer Keys); Testing Program (Quizzes)
WebSAM
Workbook, pp. 23–24
Lab Manual, p. 13

Teaching Tips

- Use the **Lección 3 Contextos** digital images to assist with this presentation.
- Point out the meanings of plural family terms and explain that the masculine plural forms can refer to mixed groups of males and females:
  los hermanos *brothers; siblings; brothers and sisters*
  los primos *male cousins; male and female cousins*
  los sobrinos *nephews; nieces and nephews*
  los tíos *uncles; aunts and uncles*
- Introduce active lesson vocabulary. Ask: **¿Cómo se llama tu hermano?** Ask another student: **¿Cómo se llama el hermano de ____?** Work your way through various family relationships.
- Point out that the family tree is drawn from the point of view of **José Miguel Pérez Santoro.** Have students refer to the family tree to answer your questions about it. Ex: **¿Cómo se llama la madre de Víctor?**
- If students request vocabulary on pets, use ***Vocabulario adicional: Más vocabulario relacionado con las nacionalidades y las mascotas*** from the Supersite.

La familia

Más vocabulario

los abuelos	*grandparents*
el/la bisabuelo/a	*great-grandfather/ great-grandmother*
el/la gemelo/a	*twin*
el/la hermanastro/a	*stepbrother/stepsister*
el/la hijastro/a	*stepson/stepdaughter*
la madrastra	*stepmother*
el medio hermano/ la media hermana	*half-brother/ half-sister*
el padrastro	*stepfather*
los padres	*parents*
los parientes	*relatives*
el/la cuñado/a	*brother-in-law/ sister-in-law*
la nuera	*daughter-in-law*
el/la suegro/a	*father-in-law/ mother-in-law*
el yerno	*son-in-law*
el/la amigo/a	*friend*
el apellido	*last name*
la gente	*people*
el/la muchacho/a	*boy/girl*
el/la niño/a	*child*
el/la novio/a	*boyfriend/girlfriend*
la persona	*person*
el/la artista	*artist*
el/la ingeniero/a	*engineer*
el/la doctor(a), el/la médico/a	*doctor; physician*
el/la periodista	*journalist*
el/la programador(a)	*computer programmer*

Variación léxica

madre ↔ mamá, mami (*colloquial*)
padre ↔ papá, papi (*colloquial*)
muchacho/a ↔ chico/a

recursos

WB pp. 23–24	LM p. 13	vhlcentral.com Lección 3

La familia de José Miguel Pérez Santoro

¡LENGUA VIVA!

In Spanish-speaking countries, it is common for people to go by both their first name and middle name, such as **José Miguel** or **Juan Carlos.** You will learn more about names and naming conventions on p. 78.

TEACHING OPTIONS

Extra Practice Draw your own family tree on the board. Ask students questions about it. Ex: **¿Es ____ mi tío o mi abuelo? ¿Cómo se llama mi madre? ____ es el primo de ____, ¿verdad? ¿____ es el sobrino o el hermano de ____? ¿Quién es el cuñado de ____?** Help students identify the relationships between members. Encourage them to ask you questions.

Heritage Speakers Ask heritage speakers to tell the class any other terms they use to refer to members of their families. These may include terms of endearment. Ask them to tell where these terms are used. Possible responses: **nene/a, guagua, m'hijo/a, chamaco/a, chaval(a), cuñis, tata, viejo/a, cielo, cariño, corazón.**

Práctica

1 **Escuchar** Listen to each statement made by José Miguel Pérez Santoro, then indicate whether it is **cierto** or **falso**, based on his family tree.

	Cierto	Falso		Cierto	Falso
1.	✓	○	6.	✓	○
2.	✓	○	7.	✓	○
3.	○	✓	8.	○	✓
4.	✓	○	9.	○	✓
5.	○	✓	10.	✓	○

2 **Personas** Indicate each word that you hear mentioned in the narration.

1. _____ cuñado
2. __✓__ tía
3. __✓__ periodista
4. __✓__ niño
5. __✓__ esposo
6. __✓__ abuelos
7. _____ ingeniera
8. __✓__ primo

3 **Emparejar** Provide the letter of the phrase that matches each description. Two items will not be used.

1. Mi hermano programa las computadoras. c
2. Son los padres de mi esposo. e
3. Son los hijos de mis (*my*) tíos. h
4. Mi tía trabaja en un hospital. a
5. Es el hijo de mi madrastra y el hijastro de mi padre. b
6. Es el esposo de mi hija. l
7. Es el hijo de mi hermana. k
8. Mi primo dibuja y pinta mucho. i
9. Mi hermanastra enseña en la universidad. j
10. Mi padre trabaja con planos (*blueprints*). d

a. Es médica.
b. Es mi hermanastro.
c. Es programador.
d. Es ingeniero.
e. Son mis suegros.
f. Es mi novio.
g. Es mi padrastro.
h. Son mis primos.
i. Es artista.
j. Es profesora.
k. Es mi sobrino.
l. Es mi yerno.

4 **Definiciones** Define these family terms in Spanish. Some answers may vary.

modelo

hijastro *Es el hijo de mi esposo/a, pero no es mi hijo.*

1. abuela
2. bisabuelo
3. tío
4. primas
5. suegra
6. cuñado
7. nietos
8. medio hermano

1. la madre de mi madre/padre
2. el abuelo de mi madre/padre
3. el hermano de mi madre/padre
4. las hijas de mis tíos/as
5. la madre de mi esposo/a
6. el esposo de mi hermana
7. los hijos de mis hijos
8. el hijo de mi padre pero no de mi madre

1 Expansion To challenge students, write the false statements on the board and have students correct them by referring to the family tree.

1 Script 1. Beatriz Alicia es mi hermana. 2. Rubén es el abuelo de Víctor Miguel. 3. Silvia es mi sobrina. 4. Mirta y Rubén son los tíos de Héctor Manuel. 5. Anita es mi prima. 6. Ernesto es el hermano de mi madre. 7. Soy el tío de Anita. 8. Víctor Miguel es mi nieto. 9. Carmen, Beatriz Alicia y Marina son los nietos de Juan y Socorro. 10. El hijo de Juan y Socorro es el tío de Beatriz Alicia.
Textbook MP3s

2 Teaching Tips
- To simplify, read through the list as a class before playing the audio. Remind students to focus only on these words as they listen.
- Tell students that the words, if they appear in the narration, will not follow the sequence in the list.

2 Script Julia y Daniel son mis abuelos. Ellos viven en Montreal con mi tía Leti, que es periodista, y con mi primo César. César es un niño muy bueno y dibuja muy bien. Hoy voy a hablar por teléfono con todos ellos y con el esposo de Leti. Él es de Canadá.
Textbook MP3s

3 Expansion After students finish, ask volunteers to provide complete sentences combining elements from the numbered and lettered lists. Ex: **Los padres de mi esposo son mis suegros. Mis primos son los hijos de mis tíos.**

4 Expansion Have student pairs write five additional definitions following the pattern of those in the activity.

TEACHING OPTIONS

TPR Make a "living" family tree. Assign students different roles as family members and have students write down the term assigned to them on a sheet of paper. Arrange students as in a family tree and ask questions about relationships. Ex: **¿Quién es la madre de ____? ¿Cómo se llama el tío de ____?**

Game Have students state the relationship between people on **José Miguel's** family tree; have their classmates guess which person they are describing. Ex: **Es la hermana de Ernesto y su padre es Juan. (Mirta) Héctor Manuel es su hermano y Beatriz Alicia es su prima. (Carmen o Silvia)** Take turns until each member of the class or group has stated a relationship.

5 Teaching Tips

- To challenge students, ask them to provide other possible responses for items 2, 4, 5, and 8. Ex: **2. esposos 4. tío/sobrino, hijastro/padrastro 5. niños, muchachos, amigos, primos, chicos, hermanastros, medios hermanos 8. bisabuelo, tío, padre, cuñado, padrastro**
- Ask the class questions about the photos and captions in the textbook. Ex: **¿Quién es artista? (Elena Vargas Soto es artista.) ¿Trabaja Irene? (Sí, es ingeniera.)**

5 Expansion

- Have pairs of students create an additional sentence for each of the photos on this page. Ask one student to write sentences for the first four photos and the other student to write sentences for the remainder. Then have them exchange papers and check each other's work.
- Bring to class family-related photos. Prepare a fill-in-the-blank sentence for each. Talk about the photos, and ask volunteers to complete the sentences.

5 **Escoger** Complete the description of each photo using words you have learned in **Contextos**.
Some answers will vary. Possible answers:

1. La familia de Sara es grande.

2. Héctor y Lupita son novios.

3. Maira Díaz es periodista.

4. Rubén habla con su hijo/padre.

5. Los dos hermanos están en el parque.

6. Irene es ingeniera.

7. Elena Vargas Soto es artista.

8. Don Manuel es el abuelo de Martín.

Practice more at **vhlcentral.com**.

TEACHING OPTIONS

Extra Practice Add an additional visual aspect to this vocabulary practice. Ask students to bring in a family-related photo of their own or a photo from the Internet or a magazine. Have them write a fill-in-the-blank sentence to go with it. Working in pairs, have them guess what is happening in each other's photo and complete the sentence.

Pairs In pairs, have students take turns assuming the identity of a person pictured in **Actividad 5** and making statements using **gustar** and **-ar** verbs. Encourage them to be creative. (Ex: **Me gusta cenar con mi novio.**) Their partner will try to guess the person's identity (**Eres Lupita.**).

Comunicación

6

Una familia With a classmate, identify the members in the family tree by asking questions about how each family member is related to Graciela Vargas García.

modelo

Estudiante 1: *¿Quién es Beatriz Pardo de Vargas?*
Estudiante 2: *Es la abuela de Graciela.*

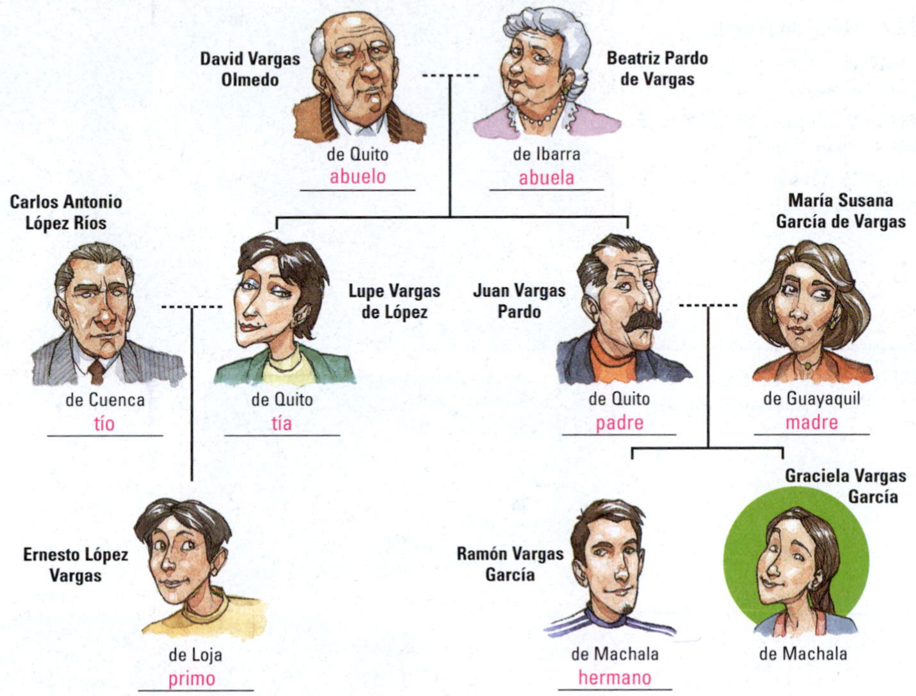

CONSULTA

To see the cities where these family members live, look at the map in **Panorama** on p. 104.

Now take turns asking each other these questions. Then invent three original questions.

1. ¿Cómo se llama el primo de Graciela? Se llama Ernesto López Vargas.
2. ¿Cómo se llama la hija de David y de Beatriz? Se llama Lupe Vargas de López.
3. ¿De dónde es María Susana? Es de Guayaquil.
4. ¿De dónde son Ramón y Graciela? Son de Machala.
5. ¿Cómo se llama el yerno de David y de Beatriz? Se llama Carlos Antonio López Ríos.
6. ¿De dónde es Carlos Antonio? Es de Cuenca.
7. ¿De dónde es Ernesto? Es de Loja.
8. ¿Cuáles son los apellidos del sobrino de Lupe? Son Vargas García.

7

Preguntas personales With a classmate, take turns asking each other these questions. Answers will vary.

1. ¿Cuántas personas hay en tu familia?
2. ¿Cómo se llaman tus padres? ¿De dónde son? ¿Dónde trabajan?
3. ¿Cuántos hermanos tienes? ¿Cómo se llaman? ¿Dónde estudian o trabajan?
4. ¿Cuántos primos tienes? ¿Cuáles son los apellidos de ellos? ¿Cuántos son niños y cuántos son adultos? ¿Hay más chicos o más chicas en tu familia?
5. ¿Eres tío/a? ¿Cómo se llaman tus sobrinos/as? ¿Dónde estudian o trabajan?
6. ¿Quién es tu pariente favorito?
7. ¿Tienes novio/a? ¿Tienes esposo/a? ¿Cómo se llama?

AYUDA

tu, tus *your* (sing., pl.)
mi, mis *my* (sing., pl.)
tienes *you have*
tengo *I have*

TEACHING OPTIONS

Extra Practice For homework, ask students to draw their own family tree or that of a fictional family. Have them label each position on the tree with the appropriate family term and the name of their family member. In class, ask students questions about their families. Ex: **¿Cómo se llama tu prima? ¿Cómo es ella? ¿Ella es estudiante? ¿Cómo se llama tu madre? ¿Quién es tu cuñado?**

Pairs Tell students to imagine that they have the opportunity to interview a famous person from a Spanish-speaking country. In pairs, using the questions in **Actividad 7** as a guide, have one student play the role of the famous person and the other student conduct the interview. Have volunteers perform their dialogues for the class to guess the famous person's identity.

6 Teaching Tip Remind students that it is common for Spanish speakers to go by two names (like **Carlos Antonio** in this chart). Students will learn about surnames on page 78; however, you may want to preview that information by pointing out how **Graciela** and her brother got their last names.

6 Expansion

- Ask students to write five statements about people in the chart (Ex: **Es la prima de Ernesto; Es una mujer de Quito.**). Then, in pairs, have them take turns reading their statements aloud. The other student should identify the person (**Es Graciela; Es Lupe**).
- Model the pronunciation of the Ecuadorian cities mentioned. Ask students to locate each on the map of Ecuador, page 104. Ask students to talk about each city based on the map. Ex: **Guayaquil y Machala son ciudades de la costa del Pacífico. Quito, Loja y Cuenca son ciudades de la cordillera de los Andes. Quito es la capital de Ecuador.**

7 Teaching Tips

- Tell students to take notes on their partner's responses. When they are finished, ask students questions about their partner's answers.
- As an alternative, first read through the questions as a class. Tell students to select a partner that they have not worked with before. Individually, have them jot down guesses to their partner's responses for a few of the questions. Students can write down any other predictions they may have about their partner's family. Then have pairs get together and complete the activity. Survey the class to find out the accuracy of the predictions.

Section Goals

In **Fotonovela**, students will:

- receive comprehensible input from free-flowing discourse
- learn functional phrases for talking about their families

Instructional Resources
Supersite: Video (***Fotonovela***); Resources (Scripts, Translations, Answer Keys)
WebSAM
Video Manual, pp. 5–6

Video Recap: Lección 2
Before doing this **Fotonovela** section, review the previous episode with these questions:
1. ¿Quién estudia historia del arte? (Miguel estudia historia del arte.) 2. ¿Quién toma cuatro clases? (Marissa toma cuatro clases.) 3. ¿Qué necesita comprar Miguel? (Necesita comprar unos libros.) 4. ¿Qué enseña el profesor Morales? (Enseña la clase de química.)

Video Synopsis The **Díaz** family spends Sunday afternoon in **Xochimilco. Marissa** meets some of the extended family and answers questions about her own family. The group has a picnic and the women take a boat ride through the canals. **Carolina** makes arrangements for **Marissa** and her friends to travel to **Mérida.**

Teaching Tips

- Ask students to read the title, glance at the video stills, and predict what they think the episode will be about.
- Work through the **Expresiones útiles** by asking students about their families. React to their responses and ask other students questions about their classmates' answers. Ex: **¿Tienes hermanos? (Sí, tengo una hermana menor.)** Ask another student: **¿Tiene hermanos ____? (Sí, tiene una hermana menor.)**

Un domingo en familia

NATIONAL STANDARDS communication cultures

Marissa pasa el día en Xochimilco con la familia Díaz.

PERSONAJES

FELIPE

TÍA NAYELI

Video: *Fotonovela*

JIMENA Hola, tía Nayeli.
TÍA NAYELI ¡Hola, Jimena! ¿Cómo estás?
JIMENA Bien, gracias. Y, ¿dónde están mis primas?
TÍA NAYELI No sé. ¿Dónde están mis hijas? ¡Ah!

MARISSA ¡Qué bonitas son tus hijas! Y ¡qué simpáticas!

FELIPE Soy guapo y delgado.
JIMENA Ay, ¡por favor! Eres gordo, antipático y muy feo.

TÍO RAMÓN ¿Tienes una familia grande, Marissa?
MARISSA Tengo dos hermanos mayores, Zack y Jennifer, y un hermano menor, Adam.

MARISSA La verdad, mi familia es pequeña.
SRA. DÍAZ ¿Pequeña? Yo soy hija única. Bueno, y ¿qué más? ¿Tienes novio?
MARISSA No. Tengo mala suerte con los novios.

MARISSA Tía Nayeli, ¿cuántos años tienen tus hijas?
TÍA NAYELI Marta tiene ocho años y Valentina doce.

TEACHING OPTIONS

Video Tips General suggestions for using video clips in the classroom can be found in the front matter of this Instructor's Annotated Edition.
Un domingo en familia Before viewing the **Un domingo en familia** episode of the **Fotonovela**, ask students to brainstorm a list of what they might see and hear in an episode in which the characters find out about each other's families. Then play the video once without sound and have the class create a plot summary based on visual clues. Next, show the episode with sound and have the class correct any mistaken guesses and fill in any gaps in the plot summary. Ask comprehension questions as a follow-up.

JIMENA MARTA VALENTINA SRA. DÍAZ TÍO RAMÓN SR. DÍAZ MARISSA

7

SRA. DÍAZ Chicas, ¿compartimos una trajinera?

MARISSA ¡Claro que sí! ¡Qué bonitas son!

SRA. DÍAZ ¿Vienes, Jimena?

JIMENA No, gracias. Tengo que leer.

8

MARISSA Me gusta mucho este sitio. Tengo ganas de visitar otros lugares en México.

SRA. DÍAZ ¡Debes viajar a Mérida!

TÍA NAYELI ¡Sí, con tus amigos! Debes visitar a Ana María, la hermana de Roberto y de Ramón.

9

(*La Sra. Díaz habla por teléfono con la tía Ana María.*)

SRA. DÍAZ ¡Qué bien! Excelente. Sí, la próxima semana. Muchísimas gracias.

10

MARISSA ¡Gracias, Sra. Díaz!

SRA. DÍAZ Tía Ana María.

MARISSA Tía Ana María.

SRA. DÍAZ ¡Un beso, chau!

MARISSA *Bye!*

recursos

VM pp. 5–6 | vhlcentral.com Lección 3

Expresiones útiles

Talking about your family

¿Tienes una familia grande?
Do you have a big family?
Tengo dos hermanos mayores y un hermano menor.
I have two older siblings and a younger brother.
La verdad, mi familia es pequeña.
The truth is, my family is small.
¿Pequeña? Yo soy hija única.
Small? I'm an only child.

Describing people

¡Qué bonitas son tus hijas! Y ¡qué simpáticas!
Your daughters are so pretty! And so nice!
Soy guapo y delgado.
I'm handsome and slim.
¡Por favor! Eres gordo, antipático y muy feo.
Please! You're fat, unpleasant, and very ugly.

Talking about plans

¿Compartimos una trajinera?
Shall we share a trajinera*?*
¡Claro que sí! ¡Qué bonitas son!
Of course! They're so pretty!
¿Vienes, Jimena?
Are you coming, Jimena?
No, gracias. Tengo que leer.
No, thanks. I have to read.

Saying how old people are

¿Cuántos años tienen tus hijas?
How old are your daughters?
Marta tiene ocho años y Valentina doce.
Marta is eight and Valentina twelve.

Additional vocabulary

ensayo *essay*
pobrecito/a *poor thing*
próxima *next*
sitio *place*
todavía *still*
trajinera *type of barge*

Expresiones útiles Draw attention to the descriptive and possessive adjectives and the present tense forms of **tener** in the **Fotonovela** captions, **Expresiones útiles**, and as they occur in your conversation with the students. Point out that this material will be formally presented in **Estructura**. If students make errors of noun-adjective agreement or with verb conjugations, provide correct forms as needed, but do not expect them to be able to produce the forms accurately at this time.

Teaching Tip Ask students to read aloud the **Fotonovela** captions in groups of six, with one person assigned to each character. Then ask one or two groups to role-play the conversation for the class. Encourage students to ad-lib as they go.

Nota cultural The **Xochimilcas** arrived in the Valley of Mexico around 900 A.D. and settled on the hill of **Cuahilama**, southeast of present-day Mexico City. From the 14th century the **Xochimilcas** were in conflict with the Aztecs, and were finally conquered by them in the mid-15th century.

TEACHING OPTIONS

TPR As you play the **Fotonovela** episode, have students raise their right hand when they hear family-related vocabulary and their left hand when they hear a word or phrase related to professions.

Extra Practice As a preview to **Estructura 3.1**, have students scan pages 74–75, and guide them in identifying the descriptive adjectives. Then ask students to rephrase the sentences to reflect their own families. Ex: **Mi papá es hijo único.**

Pairs Have students create a two-column chart with the heads ***Marissa*** and ***Roberto***. Play the **Fotonovela** episode and have students jot down the names and family-related words they hear in the appropriate column. Then have them use the chart to create simple family trees for **Marissa** and **Roberto.** Finally, in pairs, have students examine the trees for accuracy and make statements describing the familial relationships.

1 Expansion Give these true/false statements to the class as items 7–10: **7. Jimena dice que Felipe es feo. (Cierto.) 8. Marissa tiene un novio. (Falso. Tiene mala suerte con los novios.) 9. Valentina tiene una hermana menor. (Cierto.) 10. Jimena no comparte la trajinera porque tiene que asistir a clase. (Falso. Tiene que leer.)**

2 Expansion **Sra. Díaz** is the only person not associated with a statement. Ask students to look at the **Fotonovela** captions and **Expresiones útiles** on pages 74–75 and invent a statement for her. Remind them not to use her exact words. Ex: **Hablo por teléfono con mi cuñada.**

Nota cultural In the 19th century, the **chinampas** fulfilled agricultural purposes. At that time, **trajineras** were used to transport crops from the islands of **Xochimilco** to markets in Mexico City.

3 Expansion Have pairs who wrote about the same family exchange papers and compare their descriptions. Ask them to share the differences with the class.

4 Teaching Tip Model the activity by providing answers based on your own family.

4 Expansion Ask volunteers to share their partners' answers with the rest of the class.

¿Qué pasó?

1 **¿Cierto o falso?** Indicate whether each sentence is **cierto** or **falso**. Correct the false statements.

	Cierto	Falso	
1. Marissa dice que (*says that*) tiene una familia grande.	○	✓	Marissa dice que tiene una familia pequeña.
2. La Sra. Díaz tiene dos hermanos.	○	✓	La señora Díaz es hija única.
3. Marissa no tiene novio.	✓	○	
4. Valentina tiene veinte años.	○	✓	Valentina tiene doce años.
5. Marissa comparte una trajinera con la Sra. Díaz y la tía Nayeli.	✓	○	
6. A Marissa le gusta mucho Xochimilco.	✓	○	

NOTA CULTURAL

Xochimilco is famous for its system of canals and **chinampas**, or artificial islands, which have been used for agricultural purposes since Pre-Hispanic times. In 1987, UNESCO declared **Xochimilco** a World Heritage Site.

2 **Identificar** Indicate which person would make each statement. The names may be used more than once. **¡Ojo!** One name will not be used.

1. Felipe es antipático y feo. Jimena
2. Mis hermanos se llaman Jennifer, Adam y Zack. Marissa
3. ¡Soy un joven muy guapo! Felipe
4. Mis hijas tienen ocho y doce años. tía Nayeli
5. ¡Qué bonitas son las trajineras! Marissa
6. Ana María es la hermana de Ramón y Roberto. tía Nayeli
7. No puedo (*I can't*) compartir una trajinera porque tengo que leer. Jimena
8. Tus hijas son bonitas y simpáticas, tía Nayeli. Marissa

SRA. DÍAZ

JIMENA

MARISSA

FELIPE

TÍA NAYELI

NOTA CULTURAL

Trajineras are large passenger barges that you can rent in **Xochimilco**. Each boat is named and decorated and has a table and chairs so passengers can picnic while they ride.

3 **Escribir** In pairs, choose Marissa, Sra. Díaz, or tía Nayeli and write a brief description of her family. Be creative! Answers will vary.

MARISSA

Marissa es de los EE.UU. ¿Cómo es su familia?

SRA. DÍAZ

La Sra. Díaz es de Cuba. ¿Cómo es su familia?

TÍA NAYELI

La tía Nayeli es de México. ¿Cómo es su familia?

4 **Conversar** With a partner, use these questions to talk about your families. Answers will vary.

1. ¿Cuántos años tienes?
2. ¿Tienes una familia grande?
3. ¿Tienes hermanos o hermanas?
4. ¿Cuántos años tiene tu abuelo (tu hermana, tu primo, etc.)?
5. ¿De dónde son tus padres?

AYUDA

Here are some expressions to help you talk about age.

Yo tengo... años.
I am... years old.

Mi abuelo tiene... años.
My grandfather is... years old.

Practice more at **vhlcentral.com**.

TEACHING OPTIONS

Extra Practice Ask volunteers to ad-lib the **Fotonovela** episode for the class. Assure them that it is not necessary to memorize the script or stick strictly to its content. They should try to get the general meaning across with the vocabulary and expressions they know, and they also should feel free to be creative. Give students time to prepare.

Small Groups Have groups of three interview each other about their families. Assign one person as the interviewer, one the interviewee, and the third person as the note taker. At three-minute intervals, have students switch roles. When everyone has been interviewed, have students report back to the class.

Pronunciación
Diphthongs and linking

Audio

hermano	**niña**	**cuñado**

In Spanish, **a**, **e**, and **o** are considered strong vowels. The weak vowels are **i** and **u**.

ruido	**parientes**	**periodista**

A diphthong is a combination of two weak vowels or of a strong vowel and a weak vowel. Diphthongs are pronounced as a single syllable.

mi hijo **una clase excelente**

Two identical vowel sounds that appear together are pronounced like one long vowel.

la abuela

con Natalia	**sus sobrinos**	**las sillas**

Two identical consonants together sound like a single consonant.

es ingeniera	**mis abuelos**	**sus hijos**

A consonant at the end of a word is linked with the vowel sound at the beginning of the next word.

mi hermano	**su esposa**	**nuestro amigo**

A vowel at the end of a word is linked with the vowel sound at the beginning of the next word.

Práctica Say these words aloud, focusing on the diphthongs.

1. historia
2. nieto
3. parientes
4. novia
5. residencia
6. prueba
7. puerta
8. ciencias
9. lenguas
10. estudiar
11. izquierda
12. ecuatoriano

Oraciones Read these sentences aloud to practice diphthongs and linking words.

1. Hola. Me llamo Anita Amaral. Soy del Ecuador.
2. Somos seis en mi familia.
3. Tengo dos hermanos y una hermana.
4. Mi papá es del Ecuador y mi mamá es de España.

Refranes Read these sayings aloud to practice diphthongs and linking sounds.

Cuando una puerta se cierra, otra se abre.[1]

Hablando del rey de Roma, por la puerta se asoma.[2]

recursos: LM p. 14 | vhlcentral.com Lección 3

1 When one door closes, another opens.
2 Speak of the devil and he will appear.

Section Goals

In **Pronunciación**, students will be introduced to:

- the strong and weak vowels
- common diphthongs
- linking in pronunciation

Instructional Resources
Supersite: Audio (Textbook and Lab MP3 Files); Resources (Scripts, Answer Keys)
WebSAM
Lab Manual, p. 14

Teaching Tips

- Write **hermano, niña**, and **cuñado** on the board. Ask students to identify the strong and weak vowels.
- Pronounce **ruido, parientes,** and **periodista**, and have students identify the diphthong in each word. Point out that the strong vowels (**a, e, o**) do not combine with each other to form diphthongs. When two strong vowels come together, they are in different syllables.
- Pronounce **mi hermano** and **su esposa** and ask volunteers to write them on the board. Point out that the linked vowels form a diphthong and are pronounced as one syllable.
- Follow the same procedure with **es ingeniera** and **mis abuelos**. You may want to introduce linking involving the other final consonants (**l, n, r, z**). Ex: **Son hermanos. El hermano mayor está aquí. ¿Cuál es tu hermana?**
- Ask students to provide words they learned in **Lecciones 1** and **2** and **Contextos** and **Fotonovela** of this lesson that exemplify each point.

Práctica/Oraciones/Refranes

These exercises are recorded on the *Textbook MP3s*. Play the audio so that students practice listening to Spanish spoken by speakers other than yourself.

TEACHING OPTIONS

Heritage Speakers Ask heritage speakers if they know of other **refranes**. Write each **refrán** on the board and have the student who volunteered it explain what it means. Ex: **A quien Dios no le dio hijos, el diablo le da sobrinos. Más sabe el diablo por viejo que por diablo.**

Video Add an additional auditory aspect to this **Pronunciación** presentation. Play the **Fotonovela** segment and have students identify diphthongs and linking words.

Extra Practice Here are additional sentences for extra practice with diphthongs and linking: **Los estudiantes extranjeros hablan inglés. Mi abuela Ana tiene ochenta años. Juan y Enrique son hermanos. ¿Tu esposa aprende una lengua extranjera? Tengo un examen en la clase de español hoy.** Read them aloud and have students identify diphthongs and linking words.

Flash CULTURA

Section Goals

In **Cultura**, students will:

- read about surnames and families in the Spanish-speaking world
- learn terms related to family and friends
- read about Spain's Royal Family
- read about average household size

Instructional Resources
Supersite: Video (***Flash cultura***); Resources (Scripts, Translations, Answer Keys)
WebSAM
Video Manual, pp. 77–78

En detalle

Antes de leer Have students brainstorm a list of famous Spanish speakers with two last names (Ex: **Gael García Bernal**).

Lectura

- **Gabriel García Márquez** was a Nobel Prize–winning writer from Colombia. He and his wife also had another son (not pictured), **Gonzalo García Barcha**, an artist and graphic designer for film. **Rodrigo García Barcha** is a TV and film director (*Six Feet Under, Big Love, In Treatment, Albert Nobbs*).
- Point out that **de** may also appear as an indicator of ancestral origin (Ex: **Ramón del Valle**). In the case of **Juan Carlos de Borbón** (page 79), **de** refers to the House of Bourbon, a European royal dynasty.
- Explain that it is common to drop the second last name in informal settings.
- Point out that it is possible to have the same maternal and paternal surnames. Ex: **María Sánchez Sánchez**

Después de leer Have students tell the class what their name would be following this naming convention.

1 Teaching Tip For each item, have students cite an example from the article or one from real life.

EN DETALLE

Video: *Flash cultura*

NATIONAL STANDARDS connections cultures

¿Cómo te llamas?

In the Spanish-speaking world, it is common to have two last names: one paternal and one maternal. In some cases, the conjunctions **de** or **y** are used to connect the two. For example, in the name **Juan Martínez de Velasco**, *Martínez* is the paternal surname (**el apellido paterno**), and *Velasco* is the maternal surname (**el apellido materno**); **de** simply links the two. This convention of using two last names (**doble apellido**) is a European tradition that Spaniards brought to the Americas. It continues to be practiced in many countries, including Chile, Colombia, Mexico, Peru, and Venezuela. There are exceptions, however. In Argentina, the prevailing custom is for children to inherit only the father's last name.

When a woman marries in a country where two last names are used, legally she retains her two maiden surnames. However, socially she may take her husband's paternal surname in place of her inherited maternal surname. For example, **Mercedes Barcha Pardo**, widow of Colombian writer **Gabriel García Márquez**, might use the names **Mercedes Barcha García** or **Mercedes Barcha de García** in social situations (although officially her name remains **Mercedes Barcha Pardo**). Adopting a husband's last name for social purposes, though widespread, is only legally recognized in Ecuador and Peru.

Most parents do not break tradition upon naming their children; regardless of the surnames the mother uses, they use the father's first surname followed by the mother's first surname, as in the name **Rodrigo García Barcha.** However, one should note that both surnames come from the grandfathers, and therefore all **apellidos** are effectively paternal.

Gabriel García Márquez — Mercedes Barcha Pardo — Rodrigo García Barcha

Hijos en la casa

In Spanish-speaking countries, family and society place very little pressure on young adults to live on their own (**independizarse**), and children often live with their parents well into their thirties. For example, about 60% of Spaniards under 34 years of age live at home with their parents. This delay in moving out is both cultural and economic—lack of job security or low wages coupled with a high cost of living may make it impractical for young adults to live independently before they marry.

ACTIVIDADES

1 ¿Cierto o falso? Indicate whether these statements are **cierto** or **falso**. Correct the false statements.

1. Most Spanish-speaking people have three last names. Falso. Most people have two last names.
2. Hispanic last names generally consist of the paternal last name followed by the maternal last name. Cierto.
3. It is common to see **de** or **y** used in a Hispanic last name. Cierto.
4. Someone from Argentina would most likely have two last names. Falso. They would use only the father's last name.
5. Generally, married women legally retain two maiden surnames. Cierto.
6. In social situations, a married woman often uses her husband's last name in place of her inherited paternal surname. Falso. She often uses it in place of her inherited maternal surname.
7. Adopting a husband's surname is only legally recognized in Peru and Ecuador. Cierto.
8. Hispanic last names are effectively a combination of the maternal surnames from the previous generation. Falso. They are a combination of the paternal surnames from the previous generation.

TEACHING OPTIONS

Los apellidos Explain that surnames began to be widely used in Europe in the Middle Ages, and that many refer to the person's profession, title, or place of origin. Using common American last names, brainstorm examples of each type. Ex: Baker, Miller (professions); Carlson (son of Carl). Explain that Hispanic surnames have similar roots. Ex: **Sastre, Zapatero, Herrero** (professions); **Fernández, Rodríguez** (**-ez** denotes "son of"); **Hidalgo, Conde** (titles); **Aragón, Castillo** (places).

Large Group Write examples of Hispanic first and last names on the board. Then have students circulate around the room and introduce themselves to their classmates using a Hispanic last name. The other student must guess their mother's and father's last names. Ex: **Soy Roberto Domínguez Trujillo. (Tu padre es el señor Domínguez y tu madre es la señora Trujillo.)**

ASÍ SE DICE

Familia y amigos

el/la bisnieto/a	*great-grandson/daughter*
el/la chamaco/a (Méx.); el/la chamo/a (Ven.); el/la chaval(a) (Esp.); el/la pibe/a (Arg.)	el/la muchacho/a
mi colega (Esp.); mi cuate (Méx.); mi parcero/a (Col.); mi pana (Ven., P. Rico, Rep. Dom.)	*my pal; my buddy*
la madrina	*godmother*
el padrino	*godfather*
el/la tatarabuelo/a	*great-great-grandfather/ great-great-grandmother*

EL MUNDO HISPANO

Las familias

Although worldwide population trends show a decrease in average family size, households in many Spanish-speaking countries are still larger than their U.S. counterparts.

- **México** 4,0 personas
- **Colombia** 3,9 personas
- **Argentina** 3,6 personas
- **Uruguay** 3,0 personas
- **España** 2,9 personas
- **Estados Unidos** 2,6 personas

PERFIL

La familia real española

Undoubtedly, Spain's most famous family is **la familia real** (*Royal*). In 1962, the then prince **Juan Carlos de Borbón** married Princess **Sofía** of Greece. In the 1970s, **el Rey** (*King*) **Juan Carlos** and **la Reina** (*Queen*) **Sofía** helped transition Spain to democracy after a forty-year dictatorship. The royal couple has three children: las **infantas** (*Princesses*) **Elena** and **Cristina**, and a son, **el príncipe** (*Prince*) **Felipe**, whose official title was **el Príncipe de Asturias**. In 2004, Felipe married **Letizia Ortiz Rocasolano,** a journalist and TV presenter. They have two daughters, **las infantas Leonor** (born in 2005) and **Sofía** (born in 2007). In 2014, Juan Carlos decided to abdicate the throne in favor of his son.

Conexión Internet

What role do padrinos and madrinas have in today's Hispanic family?

Go to **vhlcentral.com** to find more cultural information related to this **Cultura** section.

ACTIVIDADES

2 Comprensión Complete these sentences.

1. Spain's royals were responsible for guiding in __democracy__.
2. In Spanish, your godmother is called __la madrina__.
3. Princess Leonor is the __granddaughter__ of Queen Sofía.
4. Uruguay's average household has __3.0__ people.
5. If a Venezuelan calls you **mi pana**, you are that person's __friend__.

3 Una familia famosa Create a genealogical tree of a famous family, using photos or drawings labeled with names and ages. Present the family tree to a classmate and explain who the people are and their relationships to each other.

Answers will vary.

Practice more at **vhlcentral.com.**

recursos: VM pp. 77–78 | vhlcentral.com Lección 3

Así se dice
- To challenge students, add these words to the list: **el/la enamorado/a (Ecu., Perú), el/la pololo/a (Chi.)** (*boyfriend/girlfriend*); **el/la novio/a, el/la comprometido/a (Méx.), el/la prometido/a (Amér. L.)** (*fiancé/fiancée*); **el/la tutor(a)** (*[legal] guardian*).
- Ask simple questions using the terms. Ex: **¿Cómo se llama tu tatarabuelo?**

Perfil In addition to **Leonor** and **Sofía,** Spain's royal couple has six other grandchildren. Their daughter **Elena** has a son and a daughter, **don Felipe** and **doña Victoria**. Their other daughter, **Cristina,** has three sons and a daughter: **don Juan, don Pablo, don Miguel,** and **doña Irene**. However, it is **Leonor** who is next in the succession of the Spanish throne.

El mundo hispano
- Remind students that in Spanish a comma is often used instead of a period to indicate a decimal. In spite of this, it is possible to use **punto** or **coma** when saying these numbers (Ex: **México, cuatro coma cero** or **cuatro punto cero**).
- If time permits, find the average family size of other Spanish-speaking countries. Ask students if any of the statistics are surprising to them.

2 Expansion Ask students to write two additional fill-in-the-blank statements. Then have them exchange papers with a partner and complete the sentences.

3 Teaching Tip To challenge students, have them prepare a list of questions in Spanish about their partner's genealogical tree.

TEACHING OPTIONS

Cultural Comparison Have student pairs research a famous English-speaking family (such as the Kennedys) and write a brief comparison with the Spanish Royal Family. Ask students to include information about their prominence in the media, involvement in politics, and general popularity. This activity may have to be done using English.

La familia hispana Explain to students that the concept **la familia** in Spanish-speaking countries is somewhat more inclusive than it is in English. When people say **la familia**, the majority of them are referring to their extended family. Extended families, if they do not live in the same dwelling, tend to live in closer geographical proximity in Latin America than they do in the U.S. and Canada.

Section Goals

In **Estructura 3.1**, students will learn:

- forms, agreement, and position of adjectives ending in **–o/–a**, **–e**, or a consonant
- high-frequency descriptive adjectives and some adjectives of nationality

Instructional Resources
Supersite: Audio (Lab MP3 Files); Resources (Grammar Presentation Slides, Activity Pack, Scripts, Answer Keys); Testing Program (Quizzes)
WebSAM
Workbook, pp. 25–26
Lab Manual, p. 15

Teaching Tips

- Write these adjectives on the board: **ecuatoriana, alto, bonito, viejo, trabajador**. Ask what each means and whether it is masculine or feminine. Model one of the adjectives in a sentence and ask volunteers to use the others in sentences.
- Work through the discussion of adjective forms point by point, writing examples on the board. Test comprehension as you proceed by asking volunteers to supply the correct form of adjectives for nouns you suggest. Remind students that grammatical gender does not necessarily reflect actual gender.
- Drill gender by pointing to individuals and asking the class to supply the correct form. Ex: (Pointing to male student) **¿Guapo o guapa?** (Pointing to female) **¿Simpático o simpática?** Then use adjectives ending in **–e**. Point to a male and say **inteligente**, then point to a female and have students provide the correct form. Continue with plurals. Keep a brisk pace.

3.1 Descriptive adjectives

Tutorial

NATIONAL comparisons STANDARDS

ANTE TODO Adjectives are words that describe people, places, and things. In Spanish, descriptive adjectives are used with the verb **ser** to point out characteristics such as nationality, size, color, shape, personality, and appearance.

Forms and agreement of adjectives

COMPARE & CONTRAST

In English, the forms of descriptive adjectives do not change to reflect the gender (masculine/feminine) and number (singular/plural) of the noun or pronoun they describe.

*Juan is **nice**.* *Elena is **nice**.* *They are **nice**.*

In Spanish, the forms of descriptive adjectives agree in gender and/or number with the nouns or pronouns they describe.

Juan es simpátic**o**. Elena es simpátic**a**. Ellos son simpátic**os**.

▶ Adjectives that end in **-o** have four different forms. The feminine singular is formed by changing the **-o** to **-a**. The plural is formed by adding **-s** to the singular forms.

Masculine SINGULAR	Masculine PLURAL	Feminine SINGULAR	Feminine PLURAL
el mucha**o** alt**o**	los mucha**os** alt**os**	la mucha**a** alt**a**	las mucha**as** alt**as**

¡Qué bonitas son tus hijas, tía Nayeli!

Felipe es gordo, antipático y muy feo.

▶ Adjectives that end in **-e** or a consonant have the same masculine and feminine forms.

Masculine SINGULAR	Masculine PLURAL	Feminine SINGULAR	Feminine PLURAL
el chico inteligent**e**	los chicos inteligent**es**	la chica inteligent**e**	las chicas inteligent**es**
el examen difíci**l**	los exámenes difíci**les**	la clase difíci**l**	las clases difíci**les**

▶ Adjectives that end in **-or** are variable in both gender and number.

Masculine SINGULAR	Masculine PLURAL	Feminine SINGULAR	Feminine PLURAL
el hombre trabajad**or**	los hombres trabajad**ores**	la mujer trabajad**ora**	las mujeres trabajad**oras**

TEACHING OPTIONS

Extra Practice Have pairs of students write sentences using adjectives such as **inteligente, alto, joven**. When they have finished, ask volunteers to dictate their sentences to you to write on the board. After you have written a sentence and corrected any errors, ask volunteers to suggest a sentence that uses the antonym of the adjective.

Variación léxica Clarify that the adjective **americano/a** applies to all inhabitants of North and South America, not just citizens of the United States. Residents of the United States usually are referred to with the adjective **norteamericano/a**. In more formal contexts, such as official documents, the adjective **estadounidense** is used.

AYUDA

Many adjectives are cognates, that is, words that share similar spellings and meanings in Spanish and English.

A cognate can be a noun like **profesor** or a descriptive adjective like **interesante**.

¡ATENCIÓN!

Note that **joven** takes an accent in its plural form. **Los jóvenes estudian mucho**.

▶ Use the masculine plural form to refer to groups that include males and females.

Manuel es alt**o**. Lola es alt**a**. Manuel y Lola son alt**os**.

Common adjectives

alto/a	*tall*	**gordo/a**	*fat*	**mucho/a**	*much; many; a lot of*
antipático/a	*unpleasant*	**grande**	*big*	**pelirrojo/a**	*red-haired*
bajo/a	*short (in height)*	**guapo/a**	*good-looking*	**pequeño/a**	*small*
		importante	*important*		
bonito/a	*pretty*	**inteligente**	*intelligent*	**rubio/a**	*blond(e)*
bueno/a	*good*	**interesante**	*interesting*	**simpático/a**	*nice; likeable*
delgado/a	*thin*	**joven**	*young*	**tonto/a**	*foolish*
difícil	*difficult*	**malo/a**	*bad*	**trabajador(a)**	*hard-working*
fácil	*easy*	**mismo/a**	*same*	**viejo/a**	*old*
feo/a	*ugly*	**moreno/a**	*brunet(te)*		

Adjectives of nationality

▶ Unlike in English, Spanish adjectives of nationality are **not** capitalized. Proper names of countries, however, are capitalized.

Some adjectives of nationality

alemán, alemana	*German*	**francés, francesa**	*French*
argentino/a	*Argentine*	**inglés, inglesa**	*English*
canadiense	*Canadian*	**italiano/a**	*Italian*
chino/a	*Chinese*	**japonés, japonesa**	*Japanese*
costarricense	*Costa Rican*	**mexicano/a**	*Mexican*
cubano/a	*Cuban*	**norteamericano/a**	*(North) American*
ecuatoriano/a	*Ecuadorian*	**puertorriqueño/a**	*Puerto Rican*
español(a)	*Spanish*	**ruso/a**	*Russian*
estadounidense	*from the U.S.*		

▶ Adjectives of nationality are formed like other descriptive adjectives. Those that end in **-o** change to **-a** when forming the feminine.

chin**o** → chin**a** mexican**o** → mexican**a**

The plural is formed by adding an **-s** to the masculine or feminine form.

argentin**o** → argentin**os** cuban**a** → cuban**as**

▶ Adjectives of nationality that end in **-e** have only two forms, singular and plural.

canadiens**e** → canadiens**es** estadounidens**e** → estadounidens**es**

▶ To form the feminine of adjectives of nationality that end in a consonant, add **–a**.

alemá**n** → aleman**a**
japoné**s** → japones**a**

españo**l** → españo**la**
inglé**s** → ingle**sa**

¡ATENCIÓN!

Note that adjectives with an accent on the last syllable drop the accent in the feminine and plural forms.

inglés → inglesa
alemán → alemanes

Teaching Tips

- Point out that when referring to people, **bonito/a** can only be used for females, but **guapo/a** can be used for both males and females. Some heritage speakers may use **moreno/a** to refer to someone with dark skin, and **rubio/a** for someone with light brown hair.
- Use pictures or names of celebrities to teach descriptive adjectives in semantic pairs. Ex: **¿Marc Gasol es alto o bajo? (Es alto.) ¿Salma Hayek es fea? (No, es bonita.)**
- Use names of celebrities to practice adjectives of nationality. Ex: **Daniel Craig, ¿es canadiense? (No, es inglés.) Hillary Clinton, ¿es francesa? (No, es norteamericana.)**
- Point out that adjectives with an accent mark on the last syllable drop the accent mark in the feminine and plural forms. Ex: **inglés, inglesa, ingleses, inglesas**
- Point out that adjectives of nationality also can be used as nouns. Ex: **La chica rusa es guapa. La rusa es guapa.** Like adjectives, nouns of nationality are not capitalized.
- At this point you may want to present ***Vocabulario adicional: Más adjetivos*** and ***Más vocabulario relacionado con las nacionalidades y las mascotas*** from the Supersite.
- You may want to add to the list of nationalities. Ex: **¿Kylie Minogue es australiana? (Sí, es australiana.) ¿Cuáles son las formas plurales de *australiano*? (australianos/australianas)**

TEACHING OPTIONS

Pairs If the majority of your students are **norteamericanos**, have pairs ask each other their family's origin. Write **¿Cuál es el origen de tu familia?** and **Mi familia es de origen...** on the board. Brainstorm other adjectives of nationality as necessary (Ex: **galés, indígena, nigeriano, polaco**). Point out that since **el origen** is masculine and singular, any adjectives they use will be as well.

TPR Create two sets of note cards with a city and a corresponding adjective of nationality. Shuffle the cards and distribute them. Have students circulate around the room to find the person who shares their nationality. Ex: **¿De dónde eres? Soy de Toronto. Soy canadiense.** Then students should arrange themselves in a "map," finding their place by asking other pairs' nationality (**¿De dónde son ustedes? Somos cubanos.**).

Teaching Tips

- Introduce the position of descriptive adjectives and adjectives of nationality. Ask simple questions, such as: **¿Tienes amigos inteligentes? ¿Tomas clases difíciles? ¿Tienes profesores simpáticos o antipáticos?**
- To practice position of descriptive adjectives, write simple sentences (similar to the example sentences on this page) on paper and cut them into strips, one word per strip. In pairs, have students arrange the words in the correct order.
- Practice adjectives of quantity by saying: **Hay mucha tarea en esta clase, ¿verdad?** You may want to introduce **poco/a** for contrast. Survey the class: **¿En qué clases hay mucha tarea? ¿En qué clases hay poca tarea?**
- Introduce **bueno/a, malo/a,** and **grande,** and explain the process by which they get shortened. Clarify that **bueno** and **malo** are shortened only before masculine singular nouns and their meaning does not change. However, **grande** is shortened before any singular noun, regardless of gender, and there is a change in meaning.
- To practice **bueno/a, malo/a,** and **grande,** write a series of cloze sentences on the board. In pairs, have students fill in the blanks.

Position of adjectives

▶ Descriptive adjectives and adjectives of nationality generally follow the nouns they modify.

El niño **rubio** es de España.
The blond boy is from Spain.

La mujer **española** habla inglés.
The Spanish woman speaks English.

▶ Unlike descriptive adjectives, adjectives of quantity precede the modified noun.

Hay **muchos** libros en la biblioteca.
There are many books in the library.

Hablo con **dos** turistas puertorriqueños.
I am talking with two Puerto Rican tourists.

▶ **Bueno/a** and **malo/a** can appear before or after a noun. When placed before a masculine singular noun, the forms are shortened: **bueno → buen; malo → mal.**

Joaquín es un **buen** amigo.
Joaquín es un amigo **bueno**. → *Joaquín is a good friend.*

Hoy es un **mal** día.
Hoy es un día **malo**. → *Today is a bad day.*

▶ When **grande** appears before a singular noun, it is shortened to **gran**, and the meaning of the word changes: **gran** = *great* and **grande** = *big, large*.

Don Francisco es un **gran** hombre.
Don Francisco is a great man.

La familia de Inés es **grande**.
Inés' family is large.

¡LENGUA VIVA!

Like **bueno** and **grande, santo** (*saint*) is also shortened before masculine nouns (unless they begin with **To-** or **Do-**): **San Francisco, San José** (but: **Santo Tomás, Santo Domingo**). **Santa** is used with names of female saints: **Santa Bárbara, Santa Clara**.

¡INTÉNTALO! Provide the appropriate forms of the adjectives.

simpático
1. Mi hermano es simpático.
2. La profesora Martínez es simpática.
3. Rosa y Teresa son simpáticas.
4. Nosotros somos simpáticos.

alemán
1. Hans es alemán.
2. Mis primas son alemanas.
3. Marcus y yo somos alemanes.
4. Mi tía es alemana.

difícil
1. La química es difícil.
2. El curso es difícil.
3. Las pruebas son difíciles.
4. Los libros son difíciles.

guapo
1. Su esposo es guapo.
2. Mis sobrinas son guapas.
3. Los padres de ella son guapos.
4. Marta es guapa.

recursos
WB pp. 25–26
LM p. 15
vhlcentral.com Lección 3

TEACHING OPTIONS

Video Show the **Fotonovela** episode again, stopping where appropriate to discuss how certain adjectives were used.
TPR Divide the class into two teams and have them line up. Point to a member from each team and give a certain form of an adjective (Ex: **rubios**). Then name another form that you want students to provide (Ex: feminine singular) and have them race to the board. The first student who writes the correct form earns one point for his or her team. Deduct one point for each wrong answer. The team with the most points at the end wins.
Extra Practice Create sentences similar to those in **¡Inténtalo!** Say the sentence, have students repeat it, then say a different subject. Have students say the sentence with the new subject, changing adjectives and verbs as necessary.

Práctica

1 **Emparejar** Find the words in column B that are the opposite of the words in column A. One word in B will not be used.

A		B
1. guapo	d	a. delgado
2. moreno	f	b. pequeño
3. alto	h	c. malo
4. gordo	a	d. feo
5. joven	e	e. viejo
6. grande	b	f. rubio
7. simpático	g	g. antipático
		h. bajo

2 **Completar** Indicate the nationalities of these people by selecting the correct adjectives and changing their forms when necessary.

1. Penélope Cruz es española.
2. Alfonso Cuarón es un gran director de cine de México; es mexicano.
3. Ellen Page y Avril Lavigne son canadienses.
4. Giorgio Armani es un diseñador de modas (*fashion designer*) italiano.
5. Daisy Fuentes es de La Habana, Cuba; ella es cubana.
6. Emma Watson y Daniel Radcliffe son actores ingleses.
7. Heidi Klum y Michael Fassbender son alemanes.
8. Serena Williams y Michael Phelps son estadounidenses.

NOTA CULTURAL

Alfonso Cuarón (1961–) became the first Mexican winner of the Best Director Academy Award for his film *Gravity* (2013).

3 **Describir** Look at the drawing and describe each family member using as many adjectives as possible. Some answers will vary. Possible answers:

1. Susana Romero Barcos es delgada, rubia, alta.
2. Tomás Romero Barcos es pelirrojo, inteligente, gordo.
3. Los dos hermanos son jóvenes.
4. Josefina Barcos de Romero es alta, bonita, rubia.
5. Carlos Romero Sandoval es bajo, gordo, pelirrojo.
6. Alberto Romero Pereda es viejo, bajo, gordo.
7. Tomás y su (*his*) padre son pelirrojos, gordos.
8. Susana y su (*her*) madre son altas, delgadas, rubias.

Practice more at **vhlcentral.com**.

1 Expansion
- Ask volunteers to create sentences describing famous people, using an adjective from column A and its opposite from B. Ex: **Barack Obama no es gordo; es delgado. Jennifer Lawrence no es morena; es rubia.**
- Have students describe **Jorge** and **Marcos** using as many of the antonyms as they can. Ex: **Jorge es muy simpático, pero Marcos es antipático.**

2 Teaching Tip To simplify, guide students in first identifying the gender and number of the subject for each sentence.

2 Expansion Ask pairs of students to write four original statements modeled on the activity. Have them leave a blank where the adjectives of nationality should go. Ask each pair to exchange its sentences with another pair, who will fill in the adjectives.

3 Teaching Tip To challenge students, ask them to provide all possible answers for each item. Ex: **1. joven, bonita, guapa**

3 Expansion
- Have students say what each person in the drawing is not. Ex: **Susana no es vieja. Tomás no es moreno.**
- Have students ask each other questions about the family relationships shown in the illustration. Ex: —**Tomás Romero Barcos es el hijo de Alberto Romero Pereda, ¿verdad?** —**No, Tomás es el hijo de Carlos Romero Sandoval.**

TEACHING OPTIONS

Extra Practice Have students write brief descriptions of themselves. Ask them to mention where they are from and what they study, as well as describe their personalities and what they look like. Collect the descriptions, shuffle them, and read a few of them to the class. Have the class guess who wrote each description.

Heritage Speakers Ask heritage speakers to use adjectives of nationality to describe their family's origin.

Extra Practice Add an auditory aspect to this grammar practice. Prepare descriptions of easily recognizable people. Write their names on the board in random order. Then read your descriptions and have students match each one to the appropriate name. Ex: **Son hermanas. Son jóvenes, morenas y atléticas. Practican el tenis todos los días. (Venus & Serena Williams)**

4 Expansion Have student pairs brainstorm a list of additional famous people, places, and things. Ask them to include some plural items. Then ask students to exchange papers with another pair and discuss the people, places, and things on the lists they receive.

5 Teaching Tip Have students divide a sheet of paper into two columns, labeling one **Yo** and the other **Mi novio/a ideal** or **Mi esposo/a ideal**. Have them brainstorm Spanish adjectives for each column. Ask them to rank each adjective in the second column in terms of its importance to them.

5 Expansion Ask small groups to write a personal ad describing a fictional person and his or her ideal mate. Have groups exchange and respond to each other's ads.

6 Teaching Tips
- Divide the class into pairs and distribute the handouts from the Activity Pack that correspond to this Information Gap Activity (Activity Pack/Supersite). Give students ten minutes to complete this activity.
- To simplify, have students brainstorm a list of adjectives for each person in their drawing, then have them proceed with the activity.

6 Expansion
- Ask questions based on the artwork. Ex: **¿Es alto el abuelo? ¿Es delgado el hijo menor?**
- Have volunteers take turns stating the differences. Then have them invent stories based on these families.

Comunicación

4 **¿Cómo es?** With a partner, take turns describing each item on the list. Tell your partner whether you agree (**Estoy de acuerdo**) or disagree (**No estoy de acuerdo**) with their descriptions. Answers will vary.

modelo

San Francisco
Estudiante 1: *San Francisco es una ciudad (city) muy bonita.*
Estudiante 2: *No estoy de acuerdo. Es muy fea.*

1. Nueva York
2. Steve Carell
3. las canciones (*songs*) de Taylor Swift
4. el presidente de los Estados Unidos
5. Steven Spielberg
6. la primera dama (*first lady*) de los Estados Unidos
7. el/la profesor(a) de español
8. las personas de Los Ángeles
9. las residencias de mi universidad
10. mi clase de español

AYUDA
Here are some tips to help you complete the descriptions:
- **Steve Carell es actor de cine y de televisión.**
- **Taylor Swift es cantante.**
- **Steven Spielberg es director de cine.**

5 **Anuncio personal** Write a personal ad that describes yourself and your ideal boyfriend, girlfriend, or mate. Then compare your ad with a classmate's. How are you similar and how are you different? Are you looking for the same things in a romantic partner? Answers will vary.

SOY ALTA, morena y bonita. Soy cubana, de Holguín. Estudio arte en la universidad. Busco un chico similar. Mi novio ideal es alto, moreno, inteligente y muy simpático.

AYUDA
casado/a *married*
divorciado/a *divorced*
soltero/a *single; unmarried*
These words and others like them are presented in **Contextos, Lección 9**, p. 278.

Síntesis

6 **Diferencias** Your instructor will give you and a partner each a drawing of a family. Describe your version of the drawing to your partner in order to find at least five differences between your picture and your partner's. Answers will vary.

modelo

Estudiante 1: *Susana, la madre, es rubia.*
Estudiante 2: *No, la madre es morena.*

TEACHING OPTIONS

Heritage Speakers Ask heritage speakers to describe members of their extended families. Ask the rest of the class comprehension questions.

Extra Practice Research zodiac signs on the Internet and prepare a simple personality description for each sign, using cognates and adjectives from this lesson. Divide the class into pairs and distribute the descriptions. Have students guess their partners' sign. Ex: **—Eres Aries, ¿verdad? —No, no soy Aries. No soy impulsiva y no soy aventurera.**

Extra Practice Encourage students to collect pictures of people from the Internet, magazines, or newspapers. Have them prepare a description of one of the pictures. Invite students to display their pictures and give their descriptions orally. The class should guess which picture is being described.

3.2 Possessive adjectives

Tutorial

NATIONAL STANDARDS comparisons

ANTE TODO Possessive adjectives, like descriptive adjectives, are words that are used to qualify people, places, or things. Possessive adjectives express the quality of ownership or possession.

Forms of possessive adjectives

SINGULAR FORMS	PLURAL FORMS	
mi	**mis**	*my*
tu	**tus**	*your* (fam.)
su	**sus**	*his, her, its, your* (form.)
nuestro/a	**nuestros/as**	*our*
vuestro/a	**vuestros/as**	*your* (fam.)
su	**sus**	*their, your*

COMPARE & CONTRAST

In English, possessive adjectives are invariable; that is, they do not agree in gender and number with the nouns they modify. Spanish possessive adjectives, however, do agree in number with the nouns they modify.

my cousin	*my cousins*	*my aunt*	*my aunts*
mi primo	**mis** primos	**mi** tía	**mis** tías

The forms **nuestro** and **vuestro** agree in both gender and number with the nouns they modify.

nuestr**o** prim**o** — nuestr**os** prim**os** — nuestr**a** tí**a** — nuestr**as** tí**as**

- Possessive adjectives are always placed before the nouns they modify.

—¿Está **tu novio** aquí?
Is your boyfriend here?

—No, **mi novio** está en la biblioteca.
No, my boyfriend is in the library.

- Because **su** and **sus** have multiple meanings (*your, his, her, their, its*), you can avoid confusion by using this construction instead: [*article*] + [*noun*] + **de** + [*subject pronoun*].

sus parientes →
- los parientes **de él/ella** — *his/her relatives*
- los parientes **de Ud./Uds.** — *your relatives*
- los parientes **de ellos/ellas** — *their relatives*

AYUDA

Look at the context, focusing on nouns and pronouns, to help you determine the meaning of **su(s)**.

¡INTÉNTALO! Provide the appropriate form of each possessive adjective.

1. Es __mi__ (*my*) libro.
2. __Mi__ (*My*) familia es ecuatoriana.
3. __Tu__ (*Your*, fam.) esposo es italiano.
4. __Nuestro__ (*Our*) profesor es español.
5. Es __su__ (*her*) reloj.
6. Es __tu__ (*your*, fam.) mochila.
7. Es __su__ (*your*, form.) maleta.
8. __Su__ (*Their*) sobrina es alemana.

1. __Sus__ (*Her*) primos son franceses.
2. __Nuestros__ (*Our*) primos son canadienses.
3. Son __sus__ (*their*) lápices.
4. __Sus__ (*Their*) nietos son japoneses.
5. Son __nuestras__ (*our*) plumas.
6. Son __mis__ (*my*) papeles.
7. __Mis__ (*My*) amigas son inglesas.
8. Son __sus__ (*his*) cuadernos.

recursos
WB pp. 27–28
LM p. 16
vhlcentral.com Lección 3

Section Goals

In **Estructura 3.2**, students will be introduced to:
- possessive adjectives
- ways of clarifying **su(s)** when the referent is ambiguous

Instructional Resources
Supersite: Audio (Lab MP3 Files); Resources (Grammar Presentation Slides, Activity Pack, Scripts, Answer Keys); Testing Program (Quizzes)
WebSAM
Workbook, pp. 27–28
Lab Manual, p. 16

Teaching Tips

- Introduce the concept of possessive adjectives. Hold up your book, jacket, or other personal possession and ask individuals: **¿Es *tu* libro? (No.)** Then, as you point to one student, ask the class: **¿Es el libro de ____? ¿Es *su* libro?** Link arms with another student and ask the class: **¿Es *nuestro* libro?** Indicate the whole class and ask: **¿Es el libro de ustedes? ¿Es *su* libro?** Finally, hug the object dramatically and say: **No. Es *mi* libro.** Then ask volunteers personalized questions. Ex: **¿Es simpática tu madre?**
- Use each possessive adjective with a noun to illustrate agreement. Point out that all agree in number with the noun they modify but that only **nuestro/a** and **vuestro/a** show gender. Point out that **tú** (subject) has an accent mark; **tu** (possessive) does not.
- Ask students to give plural or singular possessive adjectives with nouns. Say: **Da el plural: nuestra clase. (nuestras clases)** Say: **Da el singular: mis manos. (mi mano)**
- Write **su familia** and **sus amigos** on the board and ask volunteers to supply all possible equivalent phrases using **de**.

TEACHING OPTIONS

Pairs In pairs, have students take turns making true/false statements about the locations of objects in the classroom, using possessive adjectives or the construction [*article*] + [*noun*] + **de** + [*subject pronoun*]. The other student should respond with **Cierto** or **Falso** and correct any false statements. Ex: **El reloj del profesor está en la silla. Falso; Su reloj está encima de los papeles.**

Small Groups Give small groups a few minutes to brainstorm as many words as they can associated with the phrases **nuestro país, nuestro estado, nuestra universidad,** and **en nuestra clase de español**. Have them model their responses to **En nuestra clase hay ____** and **Nuestro país es ____**. Have the groups share their associations with the rest of the class.

1 Teaching Tip Point out the **Ayuda** sidebar and guide students in applying this information to item 1. (**Manolo** is the possessor and **hermano/Federico** is what is possessed.)

1 Expansion
- Have students change the number and gender of the nouns in items 1–7. Then have them say each new sentence, changing the possessives as necessary.
- Have students respond to the question in item 8.

2 Expansion
- Change the subject pronouns in parentheses and have the class provide new answers. Then have groups of students provide new nouns and the corresponding answers.
- Give the class sentences such as **Es su libro** and have volunteers rephrase them with a clarifying prepositional phrase.

3 Teaching Tips
- Before doing the activity, quickly review **estar** by writing the present-tense forms on the board.
- Remind students that **estar** is used to indicate location.

3 Expansion Ask questions about objects that are in the classroom. Ex: **¿Dónde está mi escritorio? ¿Dónde está el libro de ____? ¿Dónde están las plumas de ____? ¿Dónde están tus lápices?**

Práctica

1 **La familia de Manolo** Complete each sentence with the correct possessive adjective from the options in parentheses. Use the subject of each sentence as a guide.

1. Me llamo Manolo, y ___mi___ (nuestro, mi, sus) hermano es Federico.
2. ___Nuestra___ (Nuestra, Sus, Mis) madre Silvia es profesora y enseña química.
3. Ella admira a ___sus___ (tu, nuestro, sus) estudiantes porque trabajan mucho.
4. Yo estudio en la misma universidad, pero no tomo clases con ___mi___ (mi, nuestras, tus) madre.
5. Federico trabaja en una oficina con ___nuestro___ (mis, tu, nuestro) padre.
6. ___Su___ (Mi, Su, Tu) oficina está en el centro de la Ciudad de México.
7. Javier y Óscar son ___mis___ (mis, mi, sus) tíos de Oaxaca.
8. ¿Y tú? ¿Cómo es ___tu___ (mi, su, tu) familia?

2 **Clarificar** Clarify each sentence with a prepositional phrase. Follow the model.

modelo
Su hermana es muy bonita. (ella)
La hermana de ella es muy bonita.

1. Su casa es muy grande. (ellos) La casa de ellos es muy grande.
2. ¿Cómo se llama su hermano? (ellas) ¿Cómo se llama el hermano de ellas?
3. Sus padres trabajan en el centro. (ella) Los padres de ella trabajan en el centro.
4. Sus abuelos son muy simpáticos. (él) Los abuelos de él son muy simpáticos.
5. Maribel es su prima. (ella) Maribel es la prima de ella.
6. Su primo lee los libros. (ellos) El primo de ellos lee los libros.

3 **¿Dónde está?** With a partner, imagine that you can't remember where you put some of the belongings you see in the pictures. Your partner will help you by reminding you where your things are. Take turns playing each role. Answers will vary.

modelo
Estudiante 1: *¿Dónde está mi mochila?*
Estudiante 2: *Tu mochila está encima del escritorio.*

1.

2.

3.

4.

5.

6.

Practice more at **vhlcentral.com**.

AYUDA
Remember that possessive adjectives don't agree in number or gender with the owner of an item; they always agree with the item(s) being possessed.

CONSULTA
For a list of useful prepositions, refer to the table *Prepositions often used with **estar***, in **Estructura 2.3**, p. 56.

TEACHING OPTIONS

Extra Practice Ask students a few questions about the members of their immediate and extended families. Ex: **¿Cómo son tus padres? ¿Cómo se llama tu tío favorito? ¿Es el hermano de tu madre o de tu padre? ¿Tienes muchos primos? ¿Cómo se llaman tus primos? ¿De dónde son tus abuelos? ¿Hablas mucho con tus abuelos?**

Heritage Speakers Ask heritage speakers to talk briefly about a favorite relative. Have them include the characteristics that make that relative their favorite. Ask the rest of the class comprehension questions.

Comunicación

4 **Describir** With a partner, describe the people and places listed below. Make note of any similarities and be prepared to share them with the class. Answers will vary.

modelo

la biblioteca de su universidad

La biblioteca de nuestra universidad es muy grande. Hay muchos libros en la biblioteca. Mis amigos y yo estudiamos en la biblioteca.

1. tu profesor favorito
2. tu profesora favorita
3. su clase de español
4. la librería de su universidad
5. tus padres
6. tus abuelos
7. tu mejor (*best*) amigo
8. tu mejor amiga
9. su universidad
10. tu país de origen

5 **Una familia famosa** Assume the identity of a member of a famous family, real or fictional (the Obamas, Clintons, Bushes, Kardashians, Simpsons, etc.), and write a description of "your" family. Be sure not to use any names! Then, in small groups, take turns reading the descriptions aloud. The other group members may ask follow-up questions to help them identify the famous person. Answers will vary.

modelo

Estudiante 1: *Soy periodista. Mi esposo se llama Felipe. Tengo dos hijas.*
Estudiante 2: *¿Eres española?*
Estudiante 1: *Sí.*
Estudiante 3: *¿Eres Letizia Ortiz Rocasolano?*
Estudiante 1: *Sí.*

Síntesis

6 **Describe a tu familia** Get together with two classmates and describe your family to them in several sentences (**Mi padre es alto y moreno. Mi madre es delgada y muy bonita. Mis hermanos son...**). They will work together to try to repeat your description (**Su padre es alto y moreno. Su madre...**). If they forget any details, they can ask you questions (**¿Es alto tu hermano?**). Alternate roles until all of you have described your families. Answers will vary.

TEACHING OPTIONS

Extra Practice Have students work in small groups to prepare a description of a famous person, such as a politician, a movie star, or a sports figure, and his or her extended family. Tell them to feel free to invent family members as necessary. Have groups present their descriptions to the class.

Heritage Speakers Ask heritage speakers to describe their families' home countries (**países de origen**) to the class. As they are giving their descriptions, ask them questions that elicit more information. Clarify for the class any unfamiliar words and expressions they may use.

4 Teaching Tips
- Ask students to suggest a few more details to add to the **modelo**.
- Remind students to use **nuestro/a** and **nuestros/as** when reporting on the similarities they found.

5 Teaching Tips
- Quickly review the descriptive adjectives on page 81. You can do this by saying an adjective and having a volunteer give its antonym (**antónimo**).
- Before dividing the class into groups, have students edit their paragraphs for subject-verb and noun-adjective agreement. First, have them underline each subject, circle its corresponding verb, and then verify the correct conjugation. Then have students draw an arrow from each adjective to the word it modifies and make sure that they agree in gender and/or number.

5 Expansion Have each group choose their favorite description and share it with the class.

6 Teaching Tips
- Review the family vocabulary on pages 70–71.
- Explain that the class will be divided into groups of three. One student will describe his or her own family (using **mi**), and then the other two will describe the first student's family to one another (using **su**) and ask for clarification as necessary (using **tu**).
- You may want to model this for the class. Before beginning, ask students to list the family members they plan to describe.

3.3 Present tense of -er and -ir verbs

Tutorial

ANTE TODO In **Lección 2,** you learned how to form the present tense of regular **-ar** verbs. You also learned about the importance of verb forms, which change to show who is performing the action. The chart below shows the forms from two other important groups, **-er** verbs and **-ir** verbs.

Present tense of -er and -ir verbs

		comer (to eat)	escribir (to write)
SINGULAR FORMS	yo	com**o**	escrib**o**
	tú	com**es**	escrib**es**
	Ud./él/ella	com**e**	escrib**e**
PLURAL FORMS	nosotros/as	com**emos**	escrib**imos**
	vosotros/as	com**éis**	escrib**ís**
	Uds./ellos/ellas	com**en**	escrib**en**

▶ **-Er** and **-ir** verbs have very similar endings. Study the preceding chart to detect the patterns that make it easier for you to use them to communicate in Spanish.

Felipe y su tío comen.

Jimena lee.

▶ Like **-ar** verbs, the **yo** forms of **-er** and **-ir** verbs end in **-o.**

Yo com**o**. Yo escrib**o**.

▶ Except for the **yo** form, all of the verb endings for **-er** verbs begin with **-e.**

-es	**-emos**	**-en**
-e	**-éis**	

▶ **-Er** and **-ir** verbs have the exact same endings, except in the **nosotros/as** and **vosotros/as** forms.

nosotros: com**emos**, escrib**imos**

vosotros: com**éis**, escrib**ís**

NATIONAL STANDARDS comparisons

CONSULTA

To review the conjugation of **-ar** verbs, see **Estructura 2.1**, p. 46.

AYUDA

Here are some tips on learning Spanish verbs:

1) Learn to identify the verb's stem, to which all endings attach.

2) Memorize the endings that go with each verb and verb tense.

3) As often as possible, practice using different forms of each verb in speech and writing.

4) Devote extra time to learning irregular verbs, such as **ser** and **estar**.

Section Goals

In **Estructura 3.3**, students will learn:

- the present-tense forms of regular –**er** and –**ir** verbs
- some high-frequency regular –**er** and –**ir** verbs

Instructional Resources

Supersite: Audio (Lab MP3 Files); Resources (Grammar Presentation Slides, Activity Pack, Scripts, Answer Keys); Testing Program (Quizzes)

WebSAM

Workbook, pp. 29–30

Lab Manual, p. 17

Teaching Tips

- Review the present tense of –**ar** verbs. Write **trabajo** on the board and ask for the corresponding subject pronoun. (**yo**) Continue until you have the entire paradigm. Underline the endings, pointing out the characteristic vowel (–**a**–) where it appears and the personal endings.
- Ask questions and make statements that use the verb **comer** to elicit all the present-tense forms. Ex: **¿Comes en la cafetería o en un restaurante? Yo no como en la cafetería. ¿Come ____ en casa o en un bar?** As you elicit responses, write just the verbs on the board until you have the complete conjugation. Repeat the process with **escribir**. Ex: **¿Quién escribe muchas cartas? ¿A quién escribes?** When you have a complete paradigm of both verbs, contrast it with the paradigm of **trabajar**. Help students identify the ending that is the same in all three conjugations. **yo** = (–**o**)

TEACHING OPTIONS

Heritage Speakers Have heritage speakers make statements about themselves or their family members, using different verbs from the chart on page 89. Some statements should be true and others should be false. Have the class guess which statements they think are true, and encourage them to ask any follow-up questions.

Game Divide the class into two teams. Name an infinitive and a subject pronoun (Ex: **creer/yo**) and have a member of team A give the appropriate conjugation. If the student answers correctly, team A gets one point. If he or she is incorrect, give a member of team B the same items. If that student doesn't know the answer, say the correct form and start over with a new infinitive and subject pronoun. The team with the most points at the end wins.

Common -er and -ir verbs

-er verbs		-ir verbs	
aprender (a + *inf.*)	*to learn*	**abrir**	*to open*
beber	*to drink*	**asistir (a)**	*to attend*
comer	*to eat*	**compartir**	*to share*
comprender	*to understand*	**decidir (+ *inf.*)**	*to decide*
correr	*to run*	**describir**	*to describe*
creer (en)	*to believe (in)*	**escribir**	*to write*
deber (+ *inf.*)	*should*	**recibir**	*to receive*
leer	*to read*	**vivir**	*to live*

Ellos **corren** en el parque.

Él **escribe** una carta.

¡INTÉNTALO! Provide the appropriate present tense forms of these verbs.

correr
1. Graciela corre.
2. Tú corres.
3. Yo corro.
4. Sara y Ana corren.
5. Usted corre.
6. Ustedes corren.
7. La gente corre.
8. Marcos y yo corremos.

abrir
1. Ellos abren la puerta.
2. Carolina abre la maleta.
3. Yo abro las ventanas.
4. Nosotras abrimos los libros.
5. Usted abre el cuaderno.
6. Tú abres la ventana.
7. Ustedes abren las maletas.
8. Los muchachos abren los cuadernos.

aprender
1. Él aprende español.
2. Maribel y yo aprendemos inglés.
3. Tú aprendes japonés.
4. Tú y tu hermanastra aprenden francés.
5. Mi hijo aprende chino.
6. Yo aprendo alemán.
7. Usted aprende inglés.
8. Nosotros aprendemos italiano.

recursos
WB pp. 29–30
LM p. 17
vhlcentral.com Lección 3

Teaching Tips

- Point out the characteristic vowel (**–e–**) of **–er** verbs. Help students see that all the present-tense endings of regular **–er/–ir** verbs are the same except for the **nosotros/as** and **vosotros/as** forms.
- Reinforce **–er/–ir** endings and introduce the verbs by asking the class questions. First, ask a series of questions with a single verb until you have elicited all of its present-tense forms. Have students answer with complete sentences. Ex: **¿Aprenden ustedes historia en nuestra clase? ¿Aprendes álgebra en tu clase de matemáticas? ¿Qué aprenden ____ y ____ en la clase de computación? Aprendo mucho cuando leo, ¿verdad?** Then, ask questions using all the verbs at random.
- Prepare a series of sentences about students and professors using the verbs on this page, but do not include the subjects. Have students write **estudiante** and **profesor** on separate sheets of paper. Read each sentence aloud and have students hold up **estudiante** if it refers to a student, **profesor** if it refers to a professor, or both pieces of paper if it can relate to either person. Ex: **No vive en una residencia estudiantil.** (students hold up **profesor**) **Aprende los verbos.** (students hold up **estudiante**) **Hoy decide comer en la cafetería.** (students hold up both papers)
- Ask questions based on the photos. Ex: **¿Quiénes corren en el parque en la foto? ¿Ustedes corren? ¿Dónde corren? ¿A quién creen que escribe el chico? ¿Escribe a su novia? ¿A quién escriben ustedes?**
- Ask students to write a description of things they routinely do in Spanish class or in any of their other classes. Encourage them to use as many of the **–er/–ir** verbs that they can.

TEACHING OPTIONS

Video Replay the **Fotonovela**. Have students listen for **–er/–ir** verbs and write down those they hear. Afterward, write the verbs on the board and ask their meanings. Have students write original sentences using each verb.

Extra Practice Have students answer questions about their Spanish class. Have them answer in complete sentences. Ex: **¿Ustedes estudian mucho para la clase de español o deben estudiar más? ¿Leen las lecciones? Escriben mucho en clase, ¿verdad? ¿Abren los libros? Asisten al laboratorio de lenguas, ¿verdad? ¿Comen sándwiches en la clase? ¿Beben café? Comprenden el libro, ¿no?** Pairs may ask each other these questions by changing the verbs to the **tú** form.

Práctica

1 Expansion
- As a class, come up with the questions that would elicit the statements in this activity. Ex: **¿Dónde viven tú y tu familia? ¿Cuántos libros tienes? ¿Por qué tienes muchos libros? ¿Cómo es tu hermano Alfredo? ¿Cuándo asiste Alfredo a sus clases? ¿Cuándo corren ustedes? ¿Qué comen tus padres los domingos? ¿Cuánto deben comer tus padres?**
- Have small groups describe the family pictured here. Ask the groups to invent each person's name, using Hispanic naming conventions, and include a physical description, place of origin, and the family relationship to the other people in the photo.

2 Teaching Tip To simplify, guide students in classifying the infinitives as **–er** or **–ir**. Then help them identify the subject for each verb and the appropriate verb ending. Finally, aid students in identifying any missing words.

2 Expansion Have pairs create two additional dehydrated sentences for another pair to write out.

3 Teaching Tip To challenge students, add these words to the list: **aprender historia japonesa, comer más *sushi*, escribir más cartas, describir sus experiencias.**

3 Expansion Have students imagine that they are studying abroad in a Spanish-speaking country. Using the verbs in the word bank as a guide, have them write an e-mail to a friend back home. Tell students to state four things they are doing, three things they and their classmates are doing, and two things that they should be doing.

1 Completar Complete Susana's sentences about her family with the correct forms of the verbs in parentheses. One of the verbs will remain in the infinitive.

1. Mi familia y yo _vivimos_ (vivir) en Mérida, Yucatán.
2. Tengo muchos libros. Me gusta _leer_ (leer).
3. Mi hermano Alfredo es muy inteligente. Alfredo _asiste_ (asistir) a clases los lunes, miércoles y viernes.
4. Los martes y jueves Alfredo y yo _corremos_ (correr) en el Parque del Centenario.
5. Mis padres _comen_ (comer) mucha lasaña los domingos y se quedan dormidos (*they fall asleep*).
6. Yo _creo_ (creer) que (*that*) mis padres deben comer menos (*less*).

2 Oraciones Juan is talking about what he and his friends do after school. Form complete sentences by adding any other necessary elements.

modelo
yo / correr / amigos / lunes y miércoles
Yo corro con mis amigos los lunes y miércoles.

1. Manuela / asistir / clase / yoga Manuela asiste a la clase de yoga.
2. Eugenio / abrir / correo electrónico (*e-mail*) Eugenio abre su correo electrónico.
3. Isabel y yo / leer / biblioteca Isabel y yo leemos en la biblioteca.
4. Sofía y Roberto / aprender / hablar / inglés Sofía y Roberto aprenden a hablar inglés.
5. tú / comer / cafetería / universidad Tú comes en la cafetería de la universidad.
6. mi novia y yo / compartir / libro de historia Mi novia y yo compartimos el libro de historia.

3 Consejos Mario and his family are spending a year abroad to learn Japanese. In pairs, use the words below to say what he and/or his family members are doing or should do to adjust to life in Japan. Then, create one more sentence using a verb not on the list. Answers will vary.

modelo
recibir libros / deber practicar japonés
Estudiante 1: *Mario y su esposa reciben muchos libros en japonés.*
Estudiante 2: *Los hijos deben practicar japonés.*

aprender japonés	decidir explorar el país
asistir a clases	escribir listas de palabras en japonés
beber sake	leer novelas japonesas
deber comer cosas nuevas	vivir con una familia japonesa
¿?	¿?

Practice more at **vhlcentral.com**.

TEACHING OPTIONS

Pairs Have pairs of students role-play an interview with a movie star. Allow sufficient time to plan and practice; they can review previous lesson vocabulary if needed. After completing the activity ask a few of them to introduce their characters and perform the interview for the class.

TPR Create a list of phrases similar to those in **Actividad 3**, but change the context to a Spanish-speaking country. In groups of three, have students act out the activities for their classmates to guess.

Heritage Speakers Have heritage speakers brainstorm a list of things that a study-abroad student in a Spanish-speaking country might want to do. Have them base their list on **Actividad 3** using as many **–er/–ir** verbs as they can. Then have the rest of the class write complete sentences based on the list.

Comunicación

4 **Entrevista** In pairs, use these questions to interview each other. Be prepared to report the results of your interviews to the class. Answers will vary.

1. ¿Dónde comes al mediodía? ¿Comes mucho?
2. ¿Cuándo asistes a tus clases?
3. ¿Cuál es tu clase favorita? ¿Por qué?
4. ¿Dónde vives?
5. ¿Con quién vives?
6. ¿Qué cursos debes tomar el próximo (*next*) semestre?
7. ¿Lees el periódico (*newspaper*)? ¿Qué periódico lees y cuándo?
8. ¿Recibes muchos mensajes de texto (*text messages*)? ¿De quién(es)?
9. ¿Escribes poemas?
10. ¿Crees en fantasmas (*ghosts*)?

5 **¿Acción o descripción?** In small groups, take turns choosing a verb from the list. Then choose to act out the verb or give a description. The other members of the group will say what you are doing. Be creative! Answers will vary.

abrir (un libro, una puerta, una mochila)
aprender (a bailar, a hablar francés, a dibujar)
asistir (a una clase de yoga, a un concierto de rock, a una clase interesante)
beber (agua, Coca-Cola)
comer (pasta, un sándwich, pizza)
compartir (un libro, un sándwich)
correr (en el parque, en un maratón)
escribir (una composición, un mensaje de texto [*text message*], con lápiz)
leer (una carta [*letter*] de amor, un mensaje electrónico [*e-mail message*], un periódico [*newspaper*])
recibir un regalo (*gift*)
¿?

modelo

Estudiante 1: (*pantomimes typing a keyboard*)
Estudiante 2: ¿Escribes un mensaje electrónico?
Estudiante 1: Sí.

modelo

Estudiante 1: Soy estudiante y tomo muchas clases. Vivo en Roma.
Estudiante 2: ¿Comes pasta?
Estudiante 1: No, no como pasta.
Estudiante 3: ¿Aprendes a hablar italiano?
Estudiante 1: ¡Sí!

Síntesis

6 **Horario** Your instructor will give you and a partner incomplete versions of Alicia's schedule. Fill in the missing information on the schedule by talking to your partner. Be prepared to reconstruct Alicia's complete schedule with the class. Answers will vary.

TEACHING OPTIONS

Small Groups Have small groups talk about their favorite classes and teachers. They should describe the classes and the teachers and indicate why they like them. They should also mention what days and times they attend each class. Ask a few volunteers to present a summary of their conversations.

Extra Practice Add an auditory aspect to this grammar practice. Use these sentences as a dictation. Read each twice, pausing after each time for students to write. **1. Mi hermana Juana y yo asistimos a la Universidad de Quito. 2. Ella vive en la casa de mis padres y yo vivo en una residencia. 3. Juana es estudiante de literatura y lee mucho. 4. Yo estudio computación y aprendo a programar computadoras.**

4 Teaching Tips
- Tell students that one of them should complete their interview before switching roles.
- This activity is also suited to a group of three students, one of whom acts as note taker. They should switch roles at the end of each interview until each student has played all three roles.

5 Teaching Tip Make sure that students understand that they have the option of acting out an activity or describing it in a creative way. Write a verb phrase on the board and model both methods. Ex: Write on the board **beber té** (*tea*). First, act out sitting primly in a chair, serving tea from a teapot, stirring in sugar, and holding the cup daintily while taking small sips. Then give a description: **Estoy en Londres. Son las cuatro de la tarde. Deseo tomar algo** (*something*).

5 Expansion Write **asociación** on the board. Have students repeat the activity, but this time they must make associations with the verbs instead of acting them out or describing them. Ex: **Santa Claus/Papá Noel (recibir un regalo); clases de tango (aprender a bailar)**

6 Teaching Tip Divide the class into pairs and distribute the handouts from the Activity Pack that correspond to this Information Gap Activity (Activity Pack/Supersite). Give students ten minutes to complete this activity.

6 Expansion
- Ask questions based on **Alicia's** schedule. Ex: **¿Qué hace Alicia a las nueve? (Ella desayuna.)**
- Have volunteers take turns reading aloud **Alicia's** schedule. Then have them write their own schedules using as many **–er/–ir** verbs as they can.

Section Goals

In **Estructura 3.4**, students will:

- learn the present tense forms of **tener** and **venir**
- learn several common expressions with **tener**

Instructional Resources

Supersite: Audio (Lab MP3 Files); Resources (Grammar Presentation Slides, Activity Pack, Scripts, Answer Keys); Testing Program (Quizzes)
WebSAM
Workbook, pp. 31–32
Lab Manual, p. 18

Teaching Tips

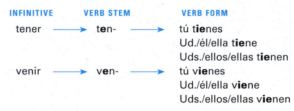

- Model **tener** by asking volunteers questions. Ex: **¿Tienes una familia grande? ¿Tienes hermanos? ¿Cuántos tíos tiene ____? ¿Tienes muchos primos?** Point out that students have been using forms of **tener** since the beginning of the lesson.
- Point out that the **yo** form of **tener** is irregular and ends in **–go**. Begin a paradigm for **tener** by writing **tengo** on the board. Ask volunteers questions that elicit **tengo** such as: **Tengo una pluma, ¿quién tiene un lápiz?**
- Write **tienes, tiene, tienen** in the paradigm. Point out that in the **tú, usted,** and **ustedes** forms, the **–e–** of the verb stem changes to **–ie–**.
- Write **tenemos** in the paradigm and point out that this form is regular.
- Follow the same procedure to present **venir**. Have students give you the **nosotros** forms of **beber** and **escribir** for comparison.

3.4 Present tense of tener and venir

Tutorial

NATIONAL comparisons STANDARDS

ANTE TODO The verbs **tener** (*to have*) and **venir** (*to come*) are among the most frequently used in Spanish. Because most of their forms are irregular, you will have to learn each one individually.

The verbs tener and venir

		tener	venir
SINGULAR FORMS	yo	ten**go**	ven**go**
	tú	tien**es**	vien**es**
	Ud./él/ella	tien**e**	vien**e**
PLURAL FORMS	nosotros/as	ten**emos**	ven**imos**
	vosotros/as	ten**éis**	ven**ís**
	Uds./ellos/ellas	tien**en**	vien**en**

▶ The endings are the same as those of regular **-er** and **-ir** verbs, except for the **yo** forms, which are irregular: **tengo, vengo.**

▶ In the **tú, Ud.,** and **Uds.** forms, the **e** of the stem changes to **ie,** as shown below.

INFINITIVE	VERB STEM	VERB FORM
tener →	ten- →	tú **tie**nes
		Ud./él/ella **tie**ne
		Uds./ellos/ellas **tie**nen
venir →	ven- →	tú **vie**nes
		Ud./él/ella **vie**ne
		Uds./ellos/ellas **vie**nen

¿Tienes una familia grande, Marissa?

No, tengo una familia pequeña.

▶ Only the **nosotros** and **vosotros** forms are regular. Compare them to the forms of **comer** and **escribir** that you learned on page 88.

	tener	comer	venir	escribir
nosotros/as	ten**emos**	com**emos**	ven**imos**	escrib**imos**
vosotros/as	ten**éis**	com**éis**	ven**ís**	escrib**ís**

AYUDA

Use what you already know about regular **-er** and **-ir** verbs to identify the irregularities in **tener** and **venir**.

1) Which verb forms use a regular stem? Which use an irregular stem?

2) Which verb forms use the regular endings? Which use irregular endings?

TEACHING OPTIONS

Pairs Have students work in pairs to write a short conversation in which they use forms of **tener, venir,** and other **-er/-ir** verbs they know. Tell them their conversations should involve the family and should include some descriptions of family members. Have pairs role-play their conversations for the class.

Extra Practice For further practice with the conjugation of **tener** and **venir**, first write a sentence on the board and have students say it. Then say a new subject and have students repeat the sentence, substituting the new subject and making all necessary changes. Ex: **Yo tengo una familia grande. (Ernesto y yo, usted, tú, ellos) Claudia y Pilar vienen a la clase de historia. (nosotras, Ernesto, ustedes, tú)**

▶ In certain idiomatic or set expressions in Spanish, you use the construction **tener** + [*noun*] to express *to be* + [*adjective*]. This chart contains a list of the most common expressions with **tener**.

Expressions with tener

tener... años	*to be... years old*	**tener (mucha) prisa**	*to be in a (big) hurry*
tener (mucho) calor	*to be (very) hot*	**tener razón**	*to be right*
tener (mucho) cuidado	*to be (very) careful*	**no tener razón**	*to be wrong*
tener (mucho) frío	*to be (very) cold*	**tener (mucha) sed**	*to be (very) thirsty*
tener (mucha) hambre	*to be (very) hungry*	**tener (mucho) sueño**	*to be (very) sleepy*
tener (mucho) miedo (de)	*to be (very) afraid/ scared (of)*	**tener (mucha) suerte**	*to be (very) lucky*

—¿**Tienen** hambre ustedes?
Are you hungry?

—Sí, y **tenemos** sed también.
Yes, and we're thirsty, too.

▶ To express an obligation, use **tener que** (*to have to*) + [*infinitive*].

—¿Qué **tienes que** estudiar hoy?
What do you have to study today?

—**Tengo que** estudiar biología.
I have to study biology.

▶ To ask people if they feel like doing something, use **tener ganas de** (*to feel like*) + [*infinitive*].

—¿**Tienes ganas de** comer?
Do you feel like eating?

—No, **tengo ganas de** dormir.
No, I feel like sleeping.

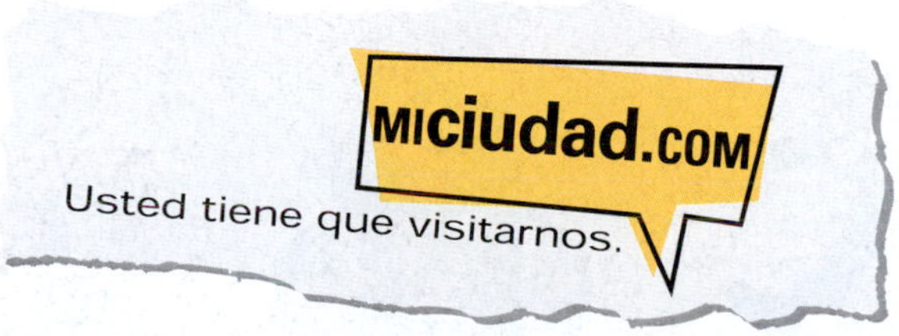
MIciudad.COM
Usted tiene que visitarnos.

¡INTÉNTALO! Provide the appropriate forms of **tener** and **venir**.

tener

1. Ellos tienen dos hermanos.
2. Yo tengo una hermana.
3. El artista tiene tres primos.
4. Nosotros tenemos diez tíos.
5. Eva y Diana tienen un sobrino.
6. Usted tiene cinco nietos.
7. Tú tienes dos hermanastras.
8. Ustedes tienen cuatro hijos.
9. Ella tiene una hija.

venir

1. Mis padres vienen de México.
2. Tú vienes de España.
3. Nosotras venimos de Cuba.
4. Pepe viene de Italia.
5. Yo vengo de Francia.
6. Ustedes vienen de Canadá.
7. Alfonso y yo venimos de Portugal.
8. Ellos vienen de Alemania.
9. Usted viene de Venezuela.

recursos
WB pp. 31–32
LM p. 18
vhlcentral.com Lección 3

Teaching Tips

- Remind the class that Spanish uses **tener** + [*noun*] in many cases where English uses *to be* + [*adjective*].
- Model the use of the expressions by talking about yourself and asking students questions about themselves. Ex: **Tengo ____ años. Y tú, ¿cuántos años tienes? Esta mañana tengo frío. ¿Tienen frío ustedes? Y tú, ____, ¿tienes frío también o tienes calor? Yo no tengo sueño esta mañana. Me gusta enseñar por la mañana.**
- Present **tener que** + [*infinitive*] and **tener ganas de** + [*infinitive*] together. Go around the class asking questions that use the expressions, having students answer in complete sentences. Ex: ____, **¿tienes que estudiar más para la clase de español? ¿Tienes ganas de ir a la biblioteca ahora?**
- Give locations and have students name the **tener** expressions that they associate with those places. Accept all possible responses. Ex: **el desierto del Sahara (tener calor, tener sed); un debate político en Washington D.C. (tener razón, no tener razón)**

TEACHING OPTIONS

TPR Assign gestures to each expression with **tener**. Ex: **tener calor:** *wipe brow*; **tener cuidado:** *look around suspiciously*; **tener frío:** *wrap arms around oneself and shiver*; **tener miedo:** *hold hand over mouth in fear.* Have students stand. Say an expression at random (Ex: **Tienes sueño**) and point at a student, who should perform the appropriate gesture. Vary by pointing to more than one student (Ex: **Ustedes tienen hambre**).

Variación léxica Point out that **tener que** + [*infinitive*] not only expresses obligation, but also need. **Tengo que estudiar más** can mean either *I have to (am obligated to) study more* or *I need to study more.* Another way of expressing need is with the regular **–ar** verb **necesitar** + [*infinitive*]. Ex: **Necesito estudiar más.** This can also be said with **deber** + [*infinitive*]. Ex: **Debo estudiar más.**

Práctica

1 **Emparejar** Find the expression in column B that best matches an item in column A. Then, come up with a new item that corresponds with the leftover expression in column B.

A		B
1. el Polo Norte	c	a. tener calor
2. una sauna	a	b. tener sed
3. la comida salada (*salty food*)	b	c. tener frío
4. una persona muy inteligente	d	d. tener razón
5. un abuelo	g	e. tener ganas de
6. una dieta	f	f. tener hambre
		g. tener 75 años

2 **Completar** Complete the sentences with the correct forms of **tener** or **venir**.

1. Hoy nosotros __tenemos__ una reunión familiar (*family reunion*).
2. Yo __vengo__ en autobús de la Universidad de Quito.
3. Todos mis parientes __vienen__, excepto mi tío Manolo y su esposa.
4. Ellos no __tienen__ ganas de venir porque viven en Portoviejo.
5. Mi prima Susana y su novio no __vienen__ hasta las ocho porque ella __tiene__ que trabajar.
6. En las fiestas, mi hermana siempre (*always*) __viene__ muy tarde (*late*).
7. Nosotros __tenemos__ mucha suerte porque las reuniones son divertidas (*fun*).
8. Mi madre cree que mis sobrinos son muy simpáticos. Creo que ella __tiene__ razón.

3 **Describir** Describe what these people are doing or feeling using an expression with **tener**.

1. Tiene (mucha) prisa.

2. Tiene (mucho) calor.

3. Tiene veintiún años.

4. Tienen (mucha) hambre.

5. Tienen (mucho) frío.

6. Tiene (mucha) sed.

Practice more at **vhlcentral.com**.

1 Teaching Tip Go over the activity with the class, reading a statement in column A and having volunteers give the corresponding phrase in column B. Note that option **e (tener ganas de)** does not match any items in column A. Help students think of a word or phrase that would match it. Ex: **comer una pizza, asistir a un concierto**

1 Expansion Have pairs of students write sentences by combining elements from the two columns. Ex: **Sonia está en el Polo Norte y tiene mucho frío. José es una persona muy inteligente pero no tiene razón.**

2 Expansion Have students write the questions that would elicit the sentences in this activity. Ex: **¿Qué tienen ellos hoy? ¿Cómo viene el narrador a la reunión? ¿Quién no viene?**

3 Teaching Tip Before doing this activity as a class, have students identify which picture is referred to in each of these questions. Have them answer: **La(s) persona(s) del dibujo número ____.** Ask: **¿Quién bebe Coca-Cola? (6), ¿Quién asiste a una fiesta? (3), ¿Quiénes comen pizza? (4), ¿Quiénes esperan el autobús? (5), ¿Quién corre a la oficina? (1), ¿Quién hace ejercicio en una bicicleta? (2)**

3 Expansion Describe different situations and have students respond using **tener** expressions. Ex: **Pedro come mucho. ¿Por qué? (Porque tiene hambre.)**

TEACHING OPTIONS

Extra Practice Have students complete sentences with **tener** and **venir**. Ex: **1. Paula y Luis no tienen hambre, pero yo sí ____ mucha hambre. (tengo) 2. Mis padres vienen del laboratorio, pero mis hermanos y yo ____ de la escuela. (venimos) 3. ¿Tienes frío, Marta? Pues, Carlos y yo ____ calor. (tenemos) 4. Enrique viene de la residencia. ¿De dónde ____ tú, Angélica? (vienes) 5. ¿Ustedes tienen que trabajar hoy? Ellos no ____ que trabajar. (tienen)**

Small Groups In groups of three, ask students to write nine sentences, each of which uses a different expression with **tener**, including **tener que** + [*infinitive*] and **tener ganas de** + [*infinitive*]. Ask volunteers to write some of their group's best sentences on the board. Work with the class to read the sentences and check for accuracy.

Comunicación

4

¿Sí o no? Indicate whether these statements apply to you by checking either **Sí** or **No**.
Answers will vary.

	Sí	No
1. Mi padre tiene 50 años.	❍	❍
2. Mis amigos vienen a mi casa todos los días (*every day*).	❍	❍
3. Vengo a la universidad los martes.	❍	❍
4. Tengo hambre.	❍	❍
5. Tengo dos computadoras.	❍	❍
6. Tengo sed.	❍	❍
7. Tengo que estudiar los domingos.	❍	❍
8. Tengo una familia grande.	❍	❍

Now interview a classmate by transforming each statement into a question. Be prepared to report the results of your interview to the class. Answers will vary.

modelo

Estudiante 1: ¿Tiene tu padre 50 años?
Estudiante 2: No, no tiene 50 años. Tiene 65.

5

Preguntas Get together with a classmate and ask each other these questions. Answers will vary.

1. ¿Tienes que estudiar hoy?
2. ¿Cuántos años tienes? ¿Y tus hermanos/as?
3. ¿Cuándo vienes a la clase de español?
4. ¿Cuándo vienen tus amigos a tu casa, apartamento o residencia estudiantil?
5. ¿De qué tienes miedo? ¿Por qué?
6. ¿Qué tienes ganas de hacer esta noche (*tonight*)?

6

Conversación Use an expression with **tener** to hint at what's on your mind. Your partner will ask questions to find out why you feel that way. If your partner cannot guess what's on your mind after three attempts, tell him/her. Then switch roles. Answers will vary.

modelo

Estudiante 1: Tengo miedo.
Estudiante 2: ¿Tienes que hablar en público?
Estudiante 1: No.
Estudiante 2: ¿Tienes un examen hoy?
Estudiante 1: Sí, y no tengo tiempo para estudiar.

Síntesis

7

Minidrama Act out this situation with a partner: you are introducing your boyfriend/girlfriend to your extended family. To avoid any surprises before you go, talk about who is coming and what each family member is like. Switch roles. Answers will vary.

4 Teaching Tip Give students two minutes to read the statements and mark their answers. Then form pairs and model question formation. Encourage students to answer with complete sentences.

5 Teaching Tips
- You may want to provide additional vocabulary for item 5.
- Ask volunteers to summarize the responses. Record these responses on the board as a survey about the class's characteristics.

6 Teaching Tip Model the activity by giving an expression with **tener**. Ex: **Tengo mucha prisa.** Encourage students to guess the reason, using **tener** and **venir**. If they guess incorrectly, give them more specific clues. Ex: **Tengo mucho que hacer hoy. Es un día especial. (Viene un amigo a la casa.)**

7 Teaching Tip Before doing **Síntesis**, have students quickly review this material: family vocabulary on pages 70–71; descriptive adjectives on pages 80–82; possessive adjectives on page 85; and the forms of **tener** and **venir** on pages 92–93.

TEACHING OPTIONS

Small Groups Have small groups prepare skits in which one person takes a few friends to a family reunion. The introducer should make polite introductions and tell the people he or she is introducing a few facts about each other. All the people involved should attempt to make small talk.

Pairs Give pairs of students five minutes to write a conversation in which they use as many **tener** expressions as they can in a logical manner. Have the top three pairs perform their conversations for the class.

Section Goal

In **Recapitulación**, students will review the grammar concepts from this lesson.

Instructional Resource
Supersite

1 Teaching Tips
- To add an auditory aspect to the activity, have students read their answers aloud, emphasizing the adjective ending sounds **–a(s)** and **–o(s)**.
- Remind students that some adjectives have the same masculine and feminine forms.

1 Expansion Ask students to rewrite the sentences to convey an opposite or different meaning. Ex: **1. Mi tía es francesa. Vive en París. 2. Mi primo no es moreno, es rubio.**

2 Teaching Tip Remind students that possessive adjectives agree in number (and in gender for **nuestro/a** and **vuestro/a**) with the nouns they modify, not with the subject. Therefore, in item 1, even though **Esteban y Julio** is a plural subject, **su** is singular to agree with **tía**.

2 Expansion Have students rewrite the sentences using different subjects. Encourage them to add additional sentences to each item using any of the **-er/-ir** verbs they have learned in this chapter. Ex: **Yo tengo una tía. Es mi tía. Ella vive en Nueva York.**

3 Teaching Tip To simplify, have students circle the subject and underline the verb before forming the sentences.

3 Expansion Have pairs create two additional dehydrated sentences for another pair to write out.

Recapitulación

Diagnostics

Review the grammar concepts you have learned in this lesson by completing these activities.

1 Adjetivos Complete each phrase with the appropriate adjective from the list. Make all necessary changes. 12 pts.

antipático	interesante	mexicano
difícil	joven	moreno

1. Mi tía es mexicana. Vive en Guadalajara.
2. Mi primo no es rubio, es moreno.
3. Mi novio cree que la clase no es fácil; es difícil.
4. Los libros son interesantes; me gustan mucho.
5. Mis hermanos son antipáticos; no tienen muchos amigos.
6. Las gemelas tienen quince años. Son jóvenes.

2 Completar For each set of sentences, provide the appropriate form of the verb **tener** and the possessive adjective. Follow the model. 24 pts.

modelo
Él tiene un libro. Es su libro.

1. Esteban y Julio tienen una tía. Es su tía.
2. Yo tengo muchos amigos. Son mis amigos.
3. Tú tienes tres primas. Son tus primas.
4. María y tú tienen un hermano. Es su hermano.
5. Nosotras tenemos unas mochilas. Son nuestras mochilas.
6. Usted tiene dos sobrinos. Son sus sobrinos.

3 Oraciones Arrange the words in the correct order to form complete logical sentences. **¡Ojo!** Don't forget to conjugate the verbs. 10 pts.

1. libros / unos / tener / interesantes / tú / muy
   Tú tienes unos libros muy interesantes.
2. dos / leer / fáciles / compañera / tu / lecciones
   Tu compañera lee dos lecciones fáciles.
3. mi / francés / ser / amigo / buen / Hugo
   Hugo es mi buen amigo francés./Mi buen amigo francés es Hugo.
4. ser / simpáticas / dos / personas / nosotras
   Nosotras somos dos personas simpáticas.
5. a / clases / menores / mismas / sus / asistir / hermanos / las
   Sus hermanos menores asisten a las mismas clases.

RESUMEN GRAMATICAL

3.1 Descriptive adjectives *pp. 80–82*

Forms and agreement of adjectives

Masculine		Feminine	
Singular	Plural	Singular	Plural
alto	altos	alta	altas
inteligente	inteligentes	inteligente	inteligentes
trabajador	trabajadores	trabajadora	trabajadoras

- Descriptive adjectives follow the noun: **el chico rubio**
- Adjectives of nationality also follow the noun: **la mujer española**
- Adjectives of quantity precede the noun: **muchos libros, dos turistas**
- When placed before a singular masculine noun, these adjectives are shortened.

  bueno → buen malo → mal
- When placed before a singular noun, **grande** is shortened to **gran**.

3.2 Possessive adjectives *p. 85*

Singular		Plural	
mi	nuestro/a	mis	nuestros/as
tu	vuestro/a	tus	vuestros/as
su	su	sus	sus

3.3 Present tense of -er and -ir verbs *pp. 88–89*

comer		escribir	
como	comemos	escribo	escribimos
comes	coméis	escribes	escribís
come	comen	escribe	escriben

3.4 Present tense of tener and venir *pp. 92–93*

tener		venir	
tengo	tenemos	vengo	venimos
tienes	tenéis	vienes	venís
tiene	tienen	viene	vienen

TEACHING OPTIONS

TPR Make sets of cards containing **–er** and **–ir** infinitives that are easy to act out. Divide the class into groups of five. Have students take turns drawing a card and acting out the verb for the group. Once someone has correctly guessed the verb, the group members must take turns providing the conjugated forms.

Extra Practice To add a visual aspect to this grammar review, bring in magazine or newspaper photos of people and places. Have students describe the people and places using descriptive adjectives.

4 **Carta** Complete this letter with the appropriate forms of the verbs in the word list. Not all verbs will be used. 20 pts.

abrir	correr	recibir
asistir	creer	tener
compartir	escribir	venir
comprender	leer	vivir

Hola, Ángel:
¿Qué tal? (Yo) (1) Escribo esta carta (*this letter*) en la biblioteca. Todos los días (2) vengo aquí y (3) leo un buen libro. Yo (4) creo que es importante leer por diversión. Mi compañero de apartamento no (5) comprende por qué me gusta leer. Él sólo (6) abre/lee los libros de texto. Pero nosotros (7) compartimos unos intereses. Por ejemplo, los dos somos atléticos; por las mañanas nosotros (8) corremos. También nos gustan las ciencias; por las tardes (9) asistimos a nuestra clase de biología. Y tú, ¿cómo estás? ¿(Tú) (10) Tienes mucho trabajo (*work*)?

5 **Su familia** Write a brief description of a friend's family. Describe the family members using vocabulary and structures from this lesson. Write at least five sentences. 34 pts.
Answers will vary.

modelo
La familia de mi amiga Gabriela es grande. Ella tiene tres hermanos y una hermana. Su hermana mayor es periodista...

6 **Proverbio** Complete this proverb with the correct forms of the verbs in parentheses. 4 EXTRA points!

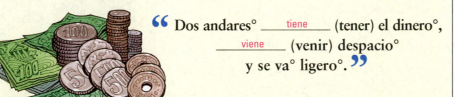

"Dos andares° tiene (tener) el dinero°,
viene (venir) despacio°
y se va° ligero°."

andares *speeds* dinero *money* despacio *slowly*
se va *it leaves* ligero *quickly*

Practice more at **vhlcentral.com**.

4 Expansion
- Ask students to create sentences with the verbs not used (**recibir** and **vivir**).
- Ask students questions using vocabulary and sentence structures from the letter. Ex: **¿Compartes muchos intereses con tus amigos? ¿Lees en la biblioteca todos los días? ¿Crees que es importante leer aparte de las clases?**
- To challenge students, ask them to write a response from **Ángel**. Encourage them to use lesson vocabulary.

5 Teaching Tip
You may want to have students interview a classmate about his or her family.

5 Expansion
- Ask students questions about their friends' families. **¿Tu amigo/a tiene una familia pequeña o grande? ¿Cuántos hermanos/as tiene tu amigo/a?**
- Have students choose one of their friend's family members and write a more detailed description.

6 Teaching Tips
- Have a volunteer read the proverb aloud. Help students understand the inverted word order in the first line. Explain that this is a common literary technique. Have a volunteer restate the first line in a colloquial manner (**El dinero tiene dos andares**).
- Have students discuss their interpretation of the proverb. Ask heritage speakers if they have heard this proverb or if they know of similar ones.

TEACHING OPTIONS

Game Create two *Mad-Libs*-style paragraphs that have blanks where the nouns and descriptive adjectives should be. Underneath each blank, indicate the type of word needed. Ex: ____ (*singular, feminine adjective*) Give each pair a set of paragraphs and have them take turns asking their partner to supply the missing words. Tell them they can use any nouns or adjectives that they have learned up to this point. When students have finished, ask them to read their paragraphs aloud. Have the class vote for the funniest one.

Extra Practice Name **tener** expressions and have students say what they or their family members do in that situation. Ex: **tener hambre (Cuando tengo hambre, como pizza. Cuando mis hermanos tienen hambre, comen en McDonald's.); tener prisa (Cuando mi padre tiene prisa, toma el autobús.)**

Audio: Reading
Additional Reading

Section Goals

In **Lectura**, students will:
- learn to use context clues in reading
- read context-rich selections about Hispanic families

Instructional Resource
Supersite

Estrategia Tell students that they can often infer the meaning of an unfamiliar Spanish word by looking at the word's context and by using common sense. Five types of context clues are:
- synonyms
- antonyms
- clarifications
- definitions
- additional details

Have students read the sentence **Ayer fui a ver a mi tía abuela, la hermana de mi abuela** from the letter. Point out that the meaning of **tía abuela** can be inferred from its similarity to the known word **abuela** and from the clarification that follows (**la hermana de mi abuela**).

Examinar el texto Have students read Paragraph 1 silently, without looking up the glossed words. Point out the phrase **salgo a pasear** and ask a volunteer to explain how the context might give clues to the meaning. Afterward, point out that **salgo** is the first-person singular form of **salir** (*to go out*). Tell students they will learn all the forms of **salir** in **Lección 4**.

Examinar el formato Guide students to see that the photos and captions reveal that the paragraphs are about several different families.

Lectura

Antes de leer

Estrategia

Guessing meaning from context

As you read in Spanish, you'll often come across words you haven't learned. You can guess what they mean by looking at the surrounding words and sentences. Look at the following text and guess what **tía abuela** means, based on the context.

¡Hola, Claudia!
¿Qué hay de nuevo?
¿Sabes qué? Ayer fui a ver a mi tía abuela, la hermana de mi abuela. Tiene 85 años, pero es muy independiente. Vive en un apartamento en Quito con su prima Lorena, quien también tiene 85 años.

If you guessed *great-aunt*, you are correct, and you can conclude from this word and the format clues that this is a letter about someone's visit with his or her great-aunt.

Examinar el texto

Quickly read through the paragraphs and find two or three words you don't know. Using the context as your guide, guess what these words mean. Then glance at the paragraphs where these words appear and try to predict what the paragraphs are about.

Examinar el formato

Look at the format of the reading. What clues do the captions, photos, and layout give you about its content?

Practice more at **vhlcentral.com**.

Gente . . . Las familias

1. Me llamo Armando y tengo setenta años, pero no me considero viejo. Tengo seis nietas y un nieto. Vivo con mi hija y tengo la oportunidad de pasar mucho tiempo con ella y con mi nieto. Por las tardes salgo a pasear° por el parque con él y por la noche le leo cuentos°.

Armando. Tiene seis nietas y un nieto.

2. Mi prima Victoria y yo nos llevamos muy bien. Estudiamos juntas° en la universidad y compartimos un apartamento. Ella es muy inteligente y me ayuda° con los estudios. Además°, es muy simpática y generosa. Si necesito cualquier° cosa, ¡ella me la compra!

Diana. Vive con su prima.

3. Me llamo Ramona y soy paraguaya, aunque° ahora vivo en los Estados Unidos. Tengo tres hijos, uno de nueve años, uno de doce y el mayor de quince. Es difícil a veces, pero mi esposo y yo tratamos° de ayudarlos y comprenderlos siempre°.

Ramona. Sus hijos son muy importantes para ella.

TEACHING OPTIONS

Extra Practice Ask students to use the paragraphs in **Gente… Las familias** as models for writing paragraphs about their families, but from the perspective of another family member (e.g., their mother). Have volunteers read their paragraphs aloud.

Extra Practice Use these items, each of which contains an unfamiliar word or phrase, to practice using context clues. **1. Mi tío Daniel es maestro en una escuela secundaria; enseña ciencias. 2. No, Daniel no es antipático, ¡es un cariño! 3. Por favor, ¿tienes un boli o un lápiz? Te escribo su número de teléfono.**

4. Tengo mucha suerte. Aunque mis padres están divorciados, tengo una familia muy unida. Tengo dos hermanos y dos hermanas. Me gusta hablar y salir a fiestas con ellos. Ahora tengo novio en la universidad y él no conoce a mis hermanos. ¡Espero que se lleven bien!

Ana María. Su familia es muy unida.

5. Antes quería° tener hermanos, pero ya no° es tan importante. Ser hijo único tiene muchas ventajas°: no tengo que compartir mis cosas con hermanos, no hay discusiones° y, como soy nieto único también, ¡mis abuelos piensan° que soy perfecto!

Fernando. Es hijo único.

6. Como soy joven todavía°, no tengo ni esposa ni hijos. Pero tengo un sobrino, el hijo de mi hermano, que es muy especial para mí. Se llama Benjamín y tiene diez años. Es un muchacho muy simpático. Siempre tiene hambre y por lo tanto vamos° frecuentemente a comer hamburguesas. Nos gusta también ir al cine° a ver películas de acción. Hablamos de todo. ¡Creo que ser tío es mejor que ser padre!

Santiago. Cree que ser tío es divertido.

salgo a pasear *I go take a walk* cuentos *stories* juntas *together* me ayuda *she helps me* Además *Besides* cualquier *any* aunque *although* tratamos *we try* siempre *always* quería *I wanted* ya no *no longer* ventajas *advantages* discusiones *arguments* piensan *think* todavía *still* vamos *we go* ir al cine *to go to the movies*

Después de leer

Emparejar

Glance at the paragraphs and see how the words and phrases in column A are used in context. Then find their definitions in column B.

A		B
1. me la compra	d	a. the oldest
2. nos llevamos bien	h	b. movies
3. no conoce	g	c. the youngest
4. películas	b	d. buys it for me
5. mejor que	j	e. borrows it from me
6. el mayor	a	f. we see each other
		g. doesn't know
		h. we get along
		i. portraits
		j. better than

Seleccionar

Choose the sentence that best summarizes each paragraph.

1. Párrafo 1 a
   a. Me gusta mucho ser abuelo.
   b. No hablo mucho con mi nieto.
   c. No tengo nietos.
2. Párrafo 2 c
   a. Mi prima es antipática.
   b. Mi prima no es muy trabajadora.
   c. Mi prima y yo somos muy buenas amigas.
3. Párrafo 3 a
   a. Tener hijos es un gran sacrificio, pero es muy bonito también.
   b. No comprendo a mis hijos.
   c. Mi esposo y yo no tenemos hijos.
4. Párrafo 4 c
   a. No hablo mucho con mis hermanos.
   b. Comparto mis cosas con mis hermanos.
   c. Mis hermanos y yo somos como (*like*) amigos.
5. Párrafo 5 a
   a. Me gusta ser hijo único.
   b. Tengo hermanos y hermanas.
   c. Vivo con mis abuelos.
6. Párrafo 6 b
   a. Mi sobrino tiene diez años.
   b. Me gusta mucho ser tío.
   c. Mi esposa y yo no tenemos hijos.

Emparejar If students have trouble inferring the meaning of any item, help them identify the corresponding context clues. **1. me la compra (si necesito cualquier cosa) 2. nos llevamos bien (compartimos un apartamento) 3. no conoce (ahora tengo novio en la universidad) 4. películas (cine) 5. mejor que (ser tío, ser padre) 6. el mayor (uno de nueve años, uno de doce; de quince)**

Seleccionar You might wish to ask students these listening comprehension questions: **1. ¿Cuántos años tiene Armando? (setenta) 2. ¿Con quién vive Armando? (con su hija) 3. ¿Con quién comparte un apartamento Diana? (con su prima, Victoria) 4. ¿Cómo es Victoria? (inteligente, simpática y generosa) 5. ¿De dónde es Ramona? (Es de Paraguay.) 6. ¿En qué país vive Ramona ahora? (en los Estados Unidos) 7. ¿Cómo es la familia de Ana María? (muy unida) 8. ¿Ana María tiene novio? (Sí, tiene novio.) 9. ¿Qué tiene muchas ventajas para Fernando? (ser hijo único) 10. ¿Qué piensan los abuelos de Fernando? (que él es perfecto) 11. ¿Cómo se llama el sobrino de Santiago? (Benjamín) 12. ¿Por qué comen hamburguesas con frecuencia? (porque Benjamín siempre tiene hambre)**

Teaching Tip Encourage students to record unfamiliar words and phrases that they learn in **Lectura** in their portfolios (**carpetas**).

TEACHING OPTIONS

Pairs Have pairs of students work together to read aloud several paragraphs and write a question about each. When they have finished, ask them to exchange their questions with another pair, who can work together to answer them.

Extra Practice Give students true/false statements about the paragraphs in **Lectura**. For the false statements, have them provide the correct information. Ex: **Armando es muy joven. (Falso. Tiene setenta años.)**

Section Goals

In **Escritura**, students will:
- learn to write a friendly letter in Spanish
- integrate vocabulary and structures taught in **Lección 3** and before

Instructional Resource
Supersite

Estrategia Have students create their idea maps in Spanish. Some students may find it helpful to create their idea maps with note cards. They can write each detail that would be contained in a circle on a separate card to facilitate rearrangement.

Tema
- Introduce students to the common salutations (**saludos**) and closings (**despedidas**) used in friendly letters in Spanish. Point out that the salutation **Estimado/a** is more formal than **Querido/a**, which is rather familiar. Also point out that **Un abrazo** is less familiar in Spanish than its translation *A hug* would be in English.
- Point out that **Estimado/a** and **Querido/a** are adjectives and therefore agree in gender and number with the nouns they modify. Write these salutations on the board and have students supply the correct form:
  ____ **Señora Martínez: (Estimada)**
  ____ **Allison: (Querida)**
  ____ **padres: (Queridos)**
- Point out the use of the colon (**dos puntos**). Tell students that a colon is used instead of a comma in letter salutations.

Escritura

Estrategia

Using idea maps

How do you organize ideas for a first draft? Often, the organization of ideas represents the most challenging part of the process. Idea maps are useful for organizing pertinent information. Here is an example of an idea map you can use:

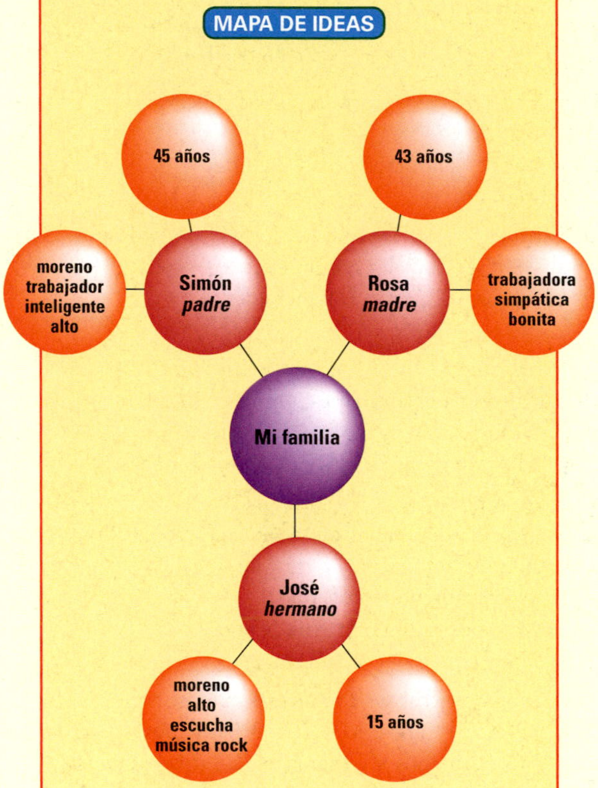

Tema

Escribir un mensaje electrónico

A friend you met in a chat room for Spanish speakers wants to know about your family. Using some of the verbs and adjectives you have learned in this lesson, write a brief e-mail describing your family or an imaginary family, including:

- Names and relationships
- Physical characteristics
- Hobbies and interests

Here are some useful expressions for writing an e-mail or letter in Spanish:

Salutations

Estimado/a Julio/Julia:	*Dear Julio/Julia,*
Querido/a Miguel/Ana María:	*Dear Miguel/Ana María,*

Closings

Un abrazo,	*A hug,*
Abrazos,	*Hugs,*
Cariños,	*Much love,*
¡Hasta pronto!	*See you soon!*
¡Hasta la próxima semana!	*See you next week!*

EVALUATION: Mensaje electrónico

Criteria	Scale
Appropriate salutations/closings	1 2 3 4 5
Appropriate details	1 2 3 4 5
Organization	1 2 3 4 5
Accuracy	1 2 3 4 5

Scoring	
Excellent	18–20 points
Good	14–17 points
Satisfactory	10–13 points
Unsatisfactory	< 10 points

Escuchar

Audio

Estrategia

Asking for repetition/ Replaying the recording

Sometimes it is difficult to understand what people say, especially in a noisy environment. During a conversation, you can ask someone to repeat by saying **¿Cómo?** (*What?*) or **¿Perdón?** (*Pardon me?*). In class, you can ask your teacher to repeat by saying **Repita, por favor** (*Repeat, please*). If you don't understand a recorded activity, you can simply replay it.

To help you practice this strategy, you will listen to a short paragraph. Ask your professor to repeat it or replay the recording, and then summarize what you heard.

Preparación

Based on the photograph, where do you think Cristina and Laura are? What do you think Laura is saying to Cristina?

Ahora escucha

Now you are going to hear Laura and Cristina's conversation. Use **R** to indicate which adjectives describe Cristina's boyfriend, Rafael. Use **E** for adjectives that describe Laura's boyfriend, Esteban. Some adjectives will not be used.

___ **rubio**	E **interesante**
___ **feo**	___ **antipático**
R **alto**	R **inteligente**
E **trabajador**	R **moreno**
E **un poco gordo**	___ **viejo**

Practice more at **vhlcentral.com**.

Comprensión

Identificar

Which person would make each statement: Cristina or Laura?

	Cristina	Laura
1. Mi novio habla sólo de fútbol y de béisbol.	✓	○
2. Tengo un novio muy interesante y simpático.	○	✓
3. Mi novio es alto y moreno.	✓	○
4. Mi novio trabaja mucho.	○	✓
5. Mi amiga no tiene buena suerte con los muchachos.	○	✓
6. El novio de mi amiga es un poco gordo, pero guapo.	✓	○

¿Cierto o falso?

Indicate whether each sentence is **cierto** or **falso**, then correct the false statements.

	Cierto	Falso
1. Esteban es un chico interesante y simpático.	✓	○
2. Laura tiene mala suerte con los chicos. Cristina tiene mala suerte con los chicos.	○	✓
3. Rafael es muy interesante. Esteban es muy interesante.	○	✓
4. Laura y su novio hablan de muchas cosas.	✓	○

Section Goals

In **Escuchar**, students will:
- listen to and summarize a short paragraph
- learn strategies for asking for clarification in oral communication
- answer questions based on the content of a recorded conversation

Instructional Resources
Supersite: Audio (Textbook MP3s); Resources (Scripts)

Estrategia
Script La familia de María Dolores es muy grande. Tiene dos hermanos y tres hermanas. Su familia vive en España. Pero la familia de Alberto es muy pequeña. No tiene hermanos ni hermanas. Alberto y sus padres viven en el Ecuador.

Ahora escucha
Script LAURA: ¿Qué hay de nuevo, Cristina?
CRISTINA: No mucho… sólo problemas con mi novio.
L: ¿Perdón?
C: No hay mucho de nuevo… sólo problemas con mi novio, Rafael.
L: ¿Qué les pasa?
C: Bueno, Rafael es alto y moreno… es muy guapo. Y es buena gente. Es inteligente también… pero es que no lo encuentro muy interesante.
L: ¿Cómo?
C: No es muy interesante. Sólo habla del fútbol y del béisbol. No me gusta hablar del fútbol las veinticuatro horas al día. No comprendo a los muchachos. ¿Cómo es tu novio, Laura?
L: Esteban es muy simpático. Es un poco gordo, pero creo que es muy guapo. También es muy trabajador.
C: ¿Es interesante?
L: Sí. Hablamos dos o tres horas cada día. Hablamos de muchas cosas… las clases, los amigos… de todo.
C: ¡Qué bien! Siempre tengo mala suerte con los novios.

Section Goals

In **En pantalla**, students will:
- read about the seasons in Chile
- watch a television commercial for **Jumbo**, a Chilean superstore chain
- read about farewells
- watch the short film ***La despedida***

Instructional Resources
Supersite: Video (***En pantalla***); Resources (Scripts, Translations)

Introduction To check comprehension, ask these questions. 1. What is the season in the southern hemisphere during the cold-weather months in North America? (summer) 2. In what months does summer start and end in Chile? (December to March) 3. What months are included in Chile's academic calendar? (March to December)

Antes de ver
- Have students look at the video stills, read the captions, and discuss when the scene takes place and how the characters are related.
- Read through the **Vocabulario útil** as a class. Point out that students already know how to conjugate **ahorrar**, **aprovechar**, and **preocupar**.
- Before showing the video, explain to students that they do not need to understand every word they hear. Tell them to rely on visual cues and to listen for cognates and words from **Vocabulario útil**.

¿Qué hay? To challenge students, have them write a list in Spanish of objects they see as they watch the ad.

¿Qué quieres?
This activity can also be done in pairs. Have a student ask a partner what he or she wants and where to buy it. Ex: **¿Qué quieres? ¿Por qué? ¿Dónde compro ____?**

En pantalla

NATIONAL STANDARDS communication cultures

Anuncio

Christmas is not celebrated in winter everywhere. During the cold-weather months in North America, it's summer in the Southern Hemisphere. In Chile, for example, summer starts in December and lasts until March. Summer vacation coincides with these months, since almost all academic calendars run from early March to late December.

Vocabulario útil

quería	*I wanted*	**aprovecha**	*take advantage of*
pedirte	*to ask you*	**nuestras**	*our*
te preocupa	*it worries you*	**ofertas**	*deals, sales*
ahorrar	*to save (money)*	**calidad**	*quality*
Navidad	*Christmas*	**no cuesta**	*doesn't cost*

¿Qué hay?

For each item, write **sí** if it appears in the TV clip or **no** if it does not.

no 1. papelera
sí 2. lápiz
sí 3. mesa
no 4. computadora
no 5. diccionario
sí 6. cuaderno
no 7. tiza
sí 8. ventana

¿Qué quieres?

Write a list of things that you want for your next birthday. Then read it to the class so they know what to get you. Use as much Spanish as you can.
Answers will vary.

Lista de cumpleaños°

Quiero°...

cumpleaños *birthday* Quiero *I want* Viejito Pascuero *Santa Claus (Chile)*

JUMBO

Viejito Pascuero°...

¿Cómo se escribe *mountain bike*?

M... O...

Video: TV Clip

Practice more at **vhlcentral.com**.

TEACHING OPTIONS

Jumbo Latin American supermarkets differ from those in the U.S.; they are similar to a Wal-Mart superstore. **Jumbo** is an **hipermercado** that sells groceries, televisions, clothing, and school supplies.

Viejito Pascuero The idea of Santa Claus differs throughout t he Spanish-speaking world. In Chile, he is referred to as **Viejito Pascuero** or **Viejo Pascuero.** In other countries, such as Colombia, young people expect gifts from **El Niño Jesús**. In Spain and Argentina, **Los Reyes Magos** deliver gifts on January 6.

TPR Have students stand in a circle. As you toss a ball to a student, ask him or her to spell a word from this lesson. Ex: **¿Cómo se escribe *tiza?*** If the student spells the word correctly, he or she tosses the ball to another student and asks a question. If a student misspells a word, he or she sits down. The last person standing wins.

Cortometraje

In the words of Shakespeare's Juliet, "Parting is such sweet sorrow." Farewells can be some of the most painful and heartbreaking experiences human beings go through, but what happens when there is nobody to say goodbye to? In the short film *La despedida* by Mexican director Yanet Pantoja Neri, a man and a woman are saying goodbye at the train station, but there's a chance that they aren't experiencing the same emotions.

Preparación

What has been the hardest farewell you ever had to go through? Where was it? Who else was involved? What did you say?

Después de ver

Indicate whether each statement is **cierto** or **falso**. Then correct the false statements.

	Cierto	Falso
1. La mujer tiene que tomar un tren. El hombre tiene que tomar un tren.	❍	✓
2. El hombre es rubio. El hombre es moreno.	❍	✓
3. Ellos tienen prisa.	✓	❍
4. Son las ocho. Son las cinco.	❍	✓
5. Hay sillas, mesas y un reloj grande en la estación de tren.	✓	❍

Una despedida

With a partner, imagine a farewell between two people. Be creative!

a. Write down the following information about the people.

- ¿Cómo se llaman?
- ¿Dónde están?
- ¿Cómo son?
- ¿Qué relación tienen?
- ¿Por qué tienen que despedirse (*to say goodbye*)?

b. Now write the conversation between the two people. Then perform it for the class. Answers will vary.

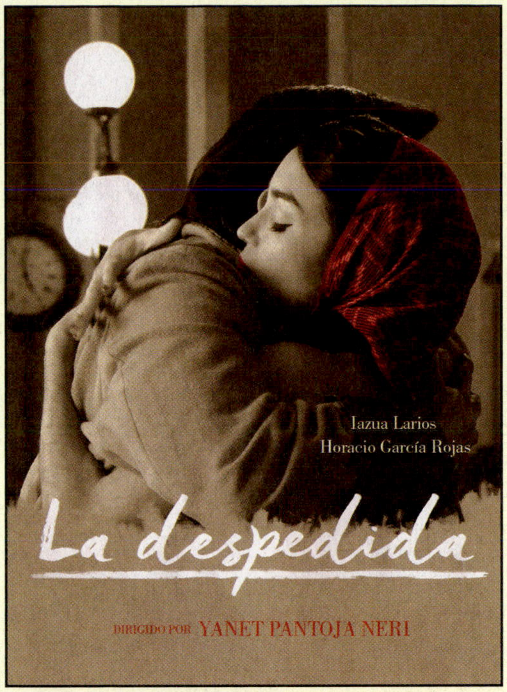

Expresiones útiles

el abrazo	*hug*
la despedida	*farewell*
las lágrimas	*tears*
nadie	*no one, nobody*
No sé qué decir.	*I don't know what to say.*
Te amo.	*I love you.*
Ya es hora.	*It's time.*

Para hablar del corto

la estación de tren	*train station*
llorar	*to cry*
solo/a	*alone; lonely*
triste	*sad*

Video: Short Film

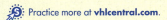

Practice more at **vhlcentral.com**.

Antes de ver
- Have students guess what the film is about, based on the poster.
- Read through the **Expresiones útiles** and **Para hablar del corto** vocabulary with students to model pronunciation and practice using the terms.
- Reassure students that they do not need to understand every word they hear in the short film. Tell them to rely on visual cues and listen for cognates and words from **Expresiones útiles.**

Preparación Have students share their farewell experiences with a partner.

Después de ver Have students create a backstory for the man in the film by answering questions like these: **¿Dónde vive? ¿Adónde viaja? ¿Cómo es? ¿Por qué está solo?**

Una despedida Have students share the information in part a with the class before performing their farewell. The class will vote for the best one.

TEACHING OPTIONS

El cine latinoamericano In recent decades, there has been a boom of Latin American filmmaking. **Yanet Pantoja Neri**, whose film is presented here, is just one of many talented independent filmmakers whose works are largely shown at film festivals. ***La despedida*** (2014) is her directorial debut.

Pairs In pairs, have students continue the film by writing the second farewell. Encourage them to be creative. Then have them act it out for the class.

Video: *Panorama cultural*
Interactive map

Section Goal

In **Panorama**, students will receive comprehensible input by reading about the geography and culture of Ecuador.

Instructional Resources
Supersite: Video (***Panorama cultural***); Resources (Scripts, Translations, Digital Image Bank, Answer Keys)
WebSAM
Workbook, pp. 33–34
Video Manual, pp. 35–36

Teaching Tip
- Have students examine the map of Ecuador and look at the call-out photos and read the captions. Encourage students to mention anything they may know about Ecuador.
- Use the **Lección 3 Panorama** digital images to assist with this presentation.

El país en cifras
- Ask students to glance at the headings. Establish the kind of information contained in each and clarify unfamiliar words. Point out that most words in the headings have an English cognate.
- Point out that in September 2000, the U.S. dollar became the official currency of Ecuador.

¡Increíble pero cierto!
Mt. St. Helens in Washington and **Cotopaxi** in Ecuador are just two of a chain of volcanoes that stretches along the entire Pacific coast of North and South America, from Mt. McKinley in Alaska to **Monte Sarmiento** in the **Tierra del Fuego** of southern Chile.

Ecuador

NATIONAL STANDARDS connections cultures

El país en cifras

- **Área:** 283.560 km² (109.483 millas²), *incluyendo las islas Galápagos, aproximadamente el área de Colorado*
- **Población:** 15.439.000
- **Capital:** Quito — 1.622.000
- **Ciudades° principales:** Guayaquil — 2.634.000, Cuenca, Machala, Portoviejo
- **Moneda:** dólar estadounidense
- **Idiomas:** español (oficial), quichua

La lengua oficial de Ecuador es el español, pero también se hablan° otras° lenguas en el país. Aproximadamente 4.000.000 de ecuatorianos hablan lenguas indígenas; la mayoría° de ellos habla quichua. El quichua es el dialecto ecuatoriano del quechua, la lengua de los incas.

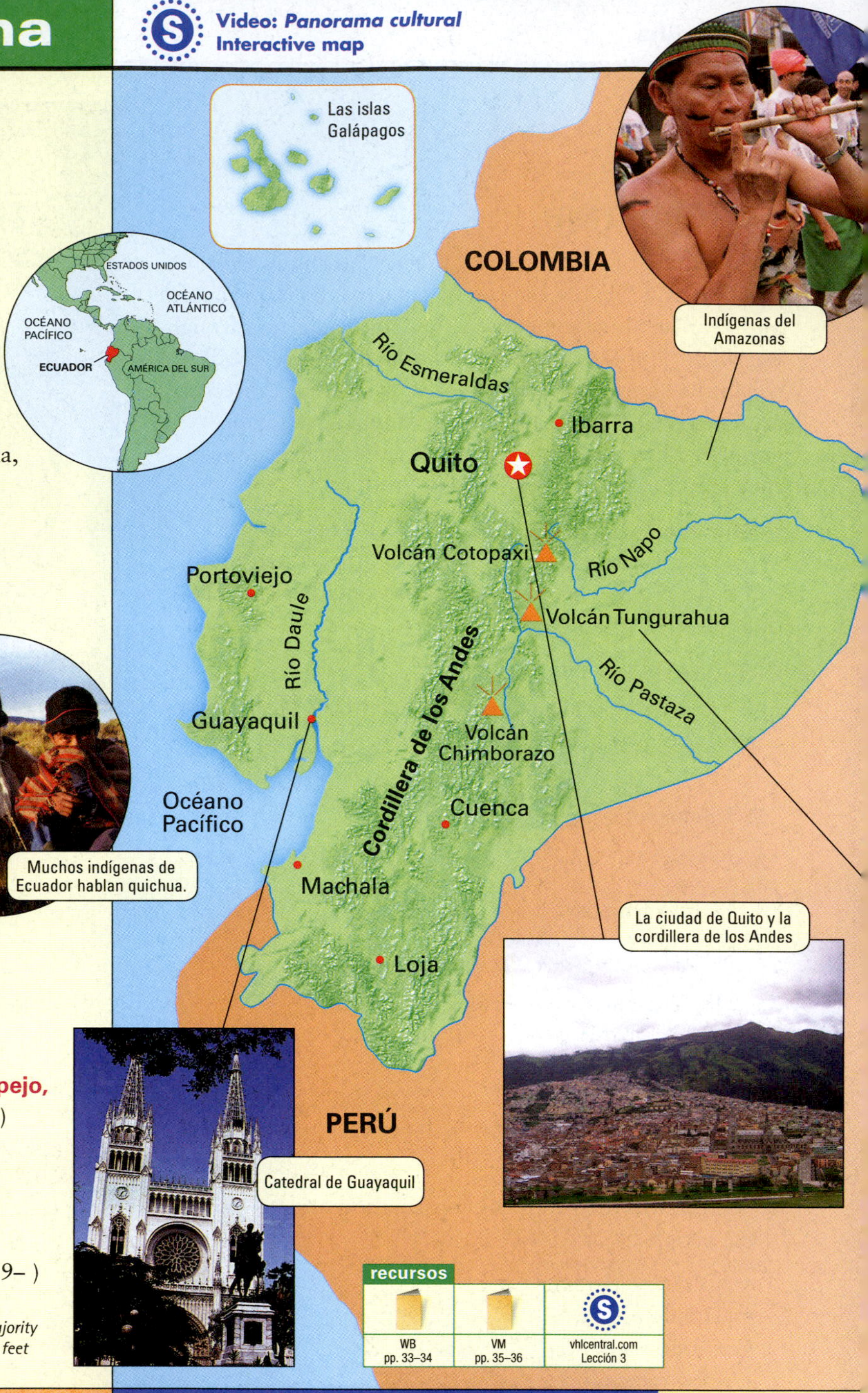

Indígenas del Amazonas

La ciudad de Quito y la cordillera de los Andes

Catedral de Guayaquil

Muchos indígenas de Ecuador hablan quichua.

Bandera de Ecuador

Ecuatorianos célebres

- **Francisco Eugenio de Santa Cruz y Espejo,** médico, periodista y patriota (1747–1795)
- **Juan León Mera,** novelista (1832–1894)
- **Eduardo Kingman,** pintor° (1913–1997)
- **Rosalía Arteaga,** abogada°, política y ex vicepresidenta (1956–)
- **Iván Vallejo Ricafuerte,** montañista (1959–)

recursos

WB pp. 33–34	VM pp. 35–36	vhlcentral.com Lección 3

Ciudades *cities* se hablan *are spoken* otras *other* mayoría *majority* pintor *painter* abogada *lawyer* sur *south* mundo *world* pies *feet* dos veces más alto que *twice as tall as*

¡Increíble pero cierto!

El volcán Cotopaxi, situado a unos 60 kilómetros al sur° de Quito, es considerado el volcán activo más alto del mundo°. Tiene una altura de 5.897 metros (19.340 pies°). Es dos veces más alto que° el monte Santa Elena (2.550 metros o 9.215 pies) en el estado de Washington.

TEACHING OPTIONS

Heritage Speakers If a heritage speaker is of Ecuadorian origin or has visited Ecuador, ask him or her to share some of his or her favorite experiences there. Encourage the rest of the class to ask follow-up questions, and if a particular topic piques their interest, to find out more online.

Language Notes Remind students that **km²** is the abbreviation for **kilómetros cuadrados** and that **millas²** is the abbreviation for **millas cuadradas**. Ask a volunteer to explain why **kilómetros** takes **cuadrados** and **millas** takes **cuadradas**.

Lugares • Las islas Galápagos

Muchas personas vienen de lejos a visitar las islas Galápagos porque son un verdadero tesoro° ecológico. Aquí Charles Darwin estudió° las especies que inspiraron° sus ideas sobre la evolución. Como las Galápagos están lejos del continente, sus plantas y animales son únicos. Las islas son famosas por sus tortugas° gigantes.

Artes • Oswaldo Guayasamín

Oswaldo Guayasamín fue° uno de los artistas latinoamericanos más famosos del mundo. Fue escultor° y muralista. Su expresivo estilo viene del cubismo y sus temas preferidos son la injusticia y la pobreza° sufridas° por los indígenas de su país.

Deportes • El *trekking*

El sistema montañoso de los Andes cruza° y divide Ecuador en varias regiones. La Sierra, que tiene volcanes, grandes valles y una variedad increíble de plantas y animales, es perfecta para el *trekking*. Muchos turistas visitan Ecuador cada° año para hacer° *trekking* y escalar montañas°.

Lugares • Latitud 0

Hay un monumento en Ecuador, a unos 22 kilómetros (14 millas) de Quito, donde los visitantes están en el hemisferio norte y el hemisferio sur a la vez°. Este monumento se llama la Mitad del Mundo° y es un destino turístico muy popular.

Explosión del volcán Tungurahua

¿Qué aprendiste? Completa las oraciones con la información correcta.

1. La ciudad más grande (*biggest*) de Ecuador es Guayaquil.
2. La capital de Ecuador es Quito.
3. Unos 4.000.000 de ecuatorianos hablan lenguas indígenas
4. Darwin estudió el proceso de la evolución en las islas Galápagos.
5. Dos temas del arte de Guayasamín son la pobreza y la injusticia.
6. Un monumento muy popular es la Mitad del Mundo.
7. La Sierra es un lugar perfecto para el *trekking*.
8. El volcán Cotopaxi es el volcán activo más alto del mundo.

Conexión Internet Investiga estos temas en **vhlcentral.com**.

Practice more at **vhlcentral.com**.

1. Busca información sobre una ciudad de Ecuador. ¿Te gustaría (*Would you like*) visitar la ciudad? ¿Por qué?
2. Haz una lista de tres animales o plantas que viven sólo en las islas Galápagos. ¿Dónde hay animales o plantas similares?

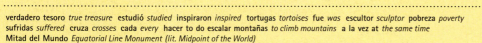

verdadero tesoro *true treasure* **estudió** *studied* **inspiraron** *inspired* **tortugas** *tortoises* **fue** *was* **escultor** *sculptor* **pobreza** *poverty* **sufridas** *suffered* **cruza** *crosses* **cada** *every* **hacer** *to do* **escalar montañas** *to climb mountains* **a la vez** *at the same time* **Mitad del Mundo** *Equatorial Line Monument (lit. Midpoint of the World)*

Las islas Galápagos Bring in books, magazines, or Internet articles about the Galapagos Islands for students to read. For more information about **las islas Galápagos**, you may want to play the ***Panorama cultural*** video footage for this lesson.

Oswaldo Guayasamín The name **Guayasamín** means *white bird* in Quichua. The artist took this name out of solidarity with his Incan ancestors. If possible, bring reproductions of some of **Guayasamín's** work to class. Show a variety of his paintings and encourage students to talk about what the artist's social and political stance might be.

El *trekking* Although the word **senderismo** is widely used, *trekking* is one of many English words that have been incorporated into Spanish. Generally, these are words for phenomena whose popularity originated in the English-speaking world. Some words enter Spanish without much change: **camping**, **marketing**. Others are modified to match Spanish spelling patterns, as **líder** (*leader*) or **mitin** (*meeting*).

Latitud 0 Bring in a globe and have students find Ecuador and point out its location on the equator.

Conexión Internet Students will find supporting Internet activities and links at **vhlcentral.com.**

TEACHING OPTIONS

Variación léxica A word that the Quichua language has contributed to English is *jerky* (salted, dried meat), which comes from the Quichua word **charqui**. The Quichua-speaking peoples of the Andean highlands had perfected techniques for "freeze-drying" both vegetable tubers and meat before the first Spaniards arrived in the region. (Freeze-dried potatoes, called **chuño**, are a staple in the diet of the inhabitants of the Andes.)

In Ecuador and throughout the rest of South America, **charqui** is the word used to name meat preserved by drying. **Charqui** is an important component in the national cuisines of South America, and in Argentina, Uruguay, and Brazil, its production is a major industry. In other parts of the Spanish-speaking world, you may hear the terms **tasajo** or **carne seca** used instead of **charqui**.

Instructional Resources
Supersite: Audio (Textbook & Lab MP3s); Testing Program (Tests, MP3s)
WebSAM
Lab Manual, p. 18

La familia

el/la abuelo/a	*grandfather/ grandmother*
los abuelos	*grandparents*
el apellido	*last name*
el/la bisabuelo/a	*great-grandfather/ great-grandmother*
el/la cuñado/a	*brother-in-law/ sister-in-law*
el/la esposo/a	*husband/wife; spouse*
la familia	*family*
el/la gemelo/a	*twin*
el/la hermanastro/a	*stepbrother/ stepsister*
el/la hermano/a	*brother/sister*
el/la hijastro/a	*stepson/ stepdaughter*
el/la hijo/a	*son/daughter*
los hijos	*children*
la madrastra	*stepmother*
la madre	*mother*
el/la medio/a hermano/a	*half-brother/ half-sister*
el/la nieto/a	*grandson/ granddaughter*
la nuera	*daughter-in-law*
el padrastro	*stepfather*
el padre	*father*
los padres	*parents*
los parientes	*relatives*
el/la primo/a	*cousin*
el/la sobrino/a	*nephew/niece*
el/la suegro/a	*father-in-law/ mother-in-law*
el/la tío/a	*uncle/aunt*
el yerno	*son-in-law*

Otras personas

el/la amigo/a	*friend*
la gente	*people*
el/la muchacho/a	*boy/girl*
el/la niño/a	*child*
el/la novio/a	*boyfriend/girlfriend*
la persona	*person*

Profesiones

el/la artista	*artist*
el/la doctor(a), el/la médico/a	*doctor; physician*
el/la ingeniero/a	*engineer*
el/la periodista	*journalist*
el/la programador(a)	*computer programmer*

Nacionalidades

alemán, alemana	*German*
argentino/a	*Argentine*
canadiense	*Canadian*
chino/a	*Chinese*
costarricense	*Costa Rican*
cubano/a	*Cuban*
ecuatoriano/a	*Ecuadorian*
español(a)	*Spanish*
estadounidense	*from the U.S.*
francés, francesa	*French*
inglés, inglesa	*English*
italiano/a	*Italian*
japonés, japonesa	*Japanese*
mexicano/a	*Mexican*
norteamericano/a	*(North) American*
puertorriqueño/a	*Puerto Rican*
ruso/a	*Russian*

Adjetivos

alto/a	*tall*
antipático/a	*unpleasant*
bajo/a	*short (in height)*
bonito/a	*pretty*
buen, bueno/a	*good*
delgado/a	*thin*
difícil	*difficult*
fácil	*easy*
feo/a	*ugly*
gordo/a	*fat*
grande	*big*
guapo/a	*good-looking*
importante	*important*
inteligente	*intelligent*
interesante	*interesting*
joven (sing.), jóvenes (pl.)	*young*
mal, malo/a	*bad*
mismo/a	*same*
moreno/a	*brunet(te)*
mucho/a	*much; many; a lot of*
pelirrojo/a	*red-haired*
pequeño/a	*small*
rubio/a	*blond(e)*
simpático/a	*nice; likeable*
tonto/a	*foolish*
trabajador(a)	*hard-working*
viejo/a	*old*

Verbos

abrir	*to open*
aprender (a + *inf.*)	*to learn*
asistir (a)	*to attend*
beber	*to drink*
comer	*to eat*
compartir	*to share*
comprender	*to understand*
correr	*to run*
creer (en)	*to believe (in)*
deber (+ *inf.*)	*should*
decidir (+ *inf.*)	*to decide*
describir	*to describe*
escribir	*to write*
leer	*to read*
recibir	*to receive*
tener	*to have*
venir	*to come*
vivir	*to live*

Possessive adjectives	*See page 85.*
Expressions with *tener*	*See page 93.*
Expresiones útiles	*See page 75.*

Vocabulary Tools

recursos
LM p. 18
vhlcentral.com Lección 3

Los pasatiempos 4

Communicative Goals

You will learn how to:

- Talk about pastimes, weekend activities, and sports
- Make plans and invitations

A PRIMERA VISTA

- **¿Es esta persona un atleta o un artista?**
- **¿En qué tiene interés, en el ciclismo o en el tenis?**
- **¿Es viejo? ¿Es delgado?**
- **¿Tiene frío o calor?**

contextos

fotonovela

The friends spend the day exploring Mérida and the surrounding area. Maru, Jimena, and Miguel take Marissa to a **cenote**; Felipe and Juan Carlos join Felipe's cousins for soccer and lunch.

cultura

estructura

adelante

Lesson Goals

In **Lección 4**, students will be introduced to the following:

- names of sports and other pastimes
- names of places in a city
- soccer rivalries
- Mexican diver **Paola Espinosa** and Venezuelan baseball player **Miguel Cabrera**
- present tense of **ir**
- the contraction **al**
- **ir a** + [*infinitive*]
- present tense of common stem-changing verbs
- verbs with irregular **yo** forms
- predicting content from visual elements
- a video about soccer in Spain
- cultural, historical, economic, and geographic information about Mexico

A primera vista Ask these additional questions to personalize the photo: **¿Te gusta practicar los deportes? ¿Crees que son importantes los pasatiempos? ¿Estudias mucho los sábados y domingos? ¿Bailas? ¿Lees? ¿Escuchas música?**

Teaching Tip Look for these icons for additional communicative practice:

→👤←	Interpretive communication
←👤→	Presentational communication
👤↔👤	Interpersonal communication

INSTRUCTIONAL RESOURCES

Supersite (vhlcentral.com)
Video: ***Fotonovela, Flash cultura, Panorama cultural***
Audio: Textbook and Lab MP3 Files
Activity Pack: Information Gap Activities, games, additional activity handouts
Resources: SAM Answer Key, Scripts, Translations, **Vocabulario adicional**, sample lesson plan, Grammar Presentation Slides, Digital Image Bank
Testing Program: Quizzes, Tests, Exams, MP3s
Student Activities Manual: Workbook/Video Manual/Lab Manual
WebSAM (online Student Activities Manual)

Section Goals

In **Contextos**, students will learn and practice:

- names of sports and other pastimes
- names of places in a city

Instructional Resources

Supersite: Audio (Textbook and Lab MP3 Files); Resources (Digital Image Bank, **Vocabulario adicional**, Activity Pack, Scripts, Answer Keys); Testing Program (Quizzes)
WebSAM
Workbook, pp. 37–38
Lab Manual, p. 19

Teaching Tips

- Write **practicar un deporte** on the board and explain what it means. Ask: **¿Qué deportes practicas?** Offer some cognates as suggestions: **¿Practicas el béisbol? ¿El vóleibol? ¿El tenis? ¿El golf?** After the student answers, ask another student: **¿Qué deporte practica ____?**
- Use the **Lección 4 Contextos** digital images to assist with this presentation.
- Ask true/false questions about the illustration. Ex: **¿Cierto o falso? Una chica nada en la piscina. (Falso. Es un chico.)** Next, name famous athletes and have students give the sports they play. Ex: **¿Qué deporte practica Roger Federer?**
- Point out that, except for the **nosotros/as** and **vosotros/as** forms, all present tense forms of **esquiar** carry an accent over the **i**: **esquío, esquías, esquía, esquían.**

Note: At this point you may want to present ***Vocabulario adicional: Más vocabulario para el fin de semana*** from the Supersite.

Los pasatiempos

Más vocabulario

el béisbol	*baseball*
el ciclismo	*cycling*
el esquí (acuático)	*(water) skiing*
el fútbol americano	*football*
el golf	*golf*
el hockey	*hockey*
la natación	*swimming*
el tenis	*tennis*
el vóleibol	*volleyball*
el equipo	*team*
el parque	*park*
el partido	*game; match*
la plaza	*city or town square*
andar en patineta	*to skateboard*
bucear	*to scuba dive*
escalar montañas (*f., pl.*)	*to climb mountains*
esquiar	*to ski*
ganar	*to win*
ir de excursión	*to go on a hike*
practicar deportes (*m., pl.*)	*to play sports*
escribir una carta/ un mensaje electrónico	*to write a letter/ an e-mail*
leer el correo electrónico	*to read e-mail*
leer una revista	*to read a magazine*
deportivo/a	*sports-related*

Variación léxica

piscina ⟷ pileta (*Arg.*); alberca (*Méx.*)
baloncesto ⟷ básquetbol (*Amér. L.*)
béisbol ⟷ pelota (*P. Rico, Rep. Dom.*)

recursos

WB pp. 37–38	LM p. 19	vhlcentral.com Lección 4

TEACHING OPTIONS

Pairs Ask students to write down in Spanish their three favorite sports or leisure activities. Have students pair up and share the information using complete sentences. Ex: **Me gusta practicar la natación. Es un deporte divertido. Nado en mi piscina. ¿Qué deportes practicas?** As a class, call on individuals to report their partners' favorite pastimes. Partners will confirm or correct the information.

Variación léxica Point out that many sports in Spanish are referred to by names derived from English (**básquetbol, béisbol, fútbol**), including many in **Más vocabulario**: **el golf, el hockey, el vóleibol**. Ask students to guess the meaning of these activities (be sure to use Spanish pronunciation): **el footing** (*jogging*), **el camping, el surf(ing), el windsurf**.

Práctica

1 Escuchar Indicate the letter of the activity in Column B that best corresponds to each statement you hear. Two items in Column B will not be used.

A	B
1. b	a. leer el correo electrónico
2. d	b. tomar el sol
3. f	c. pasear en bicicleta
4. c	d. ir a un partido de fútbol americano
5. g	e. escribir una carta
6. h	f. practicar muchos deportes
	g. nadar
	h. ir de excursión

2 Ordenar Order these activities according to what you hear in the narration.

5 a. pasear en bicicleta
1 b. nadar
4 c. leer una revista
3 d. tomar el sol
6 e. practicar deportes
2 f. patinar en línea

3 ¿Cierto o falso? Indicate whether each statement is **cierto** or **falso** based on the illustration.

	Cierto	Falso
1. Un hombre nada en la piscina.	✓	
2. Un hombre lee una revista.		✓
3. Un chico pasea en bicicleta.	✓	
4. Dos muchachos esquían.		✓
5. Una mujer y dos niños visitan un monumento.	✓	
6. Un hombre bucea.		✓
7. Hay un equipo de hockey.		✓
8. Una mujer toma el sol.	✓	

4 Clasificar Fill in the chart below with as many terms from **Contextos** as you can. Answers will vary.

Actividades	Deportes	Personas

1 Teaching Tip Have students check their answers with a partner before going over **Actividad 1** with the class.

1 Script 1. No me gusta nadar pero paso mucho tiempo al lado de la piscina. 2. Alicia y yo vamos al estadio a las cuatro. Creemos que nuestro equipo va a ganar. 3. Me gusta patinar en línea, esquiar y practicar el tenis. 4. El ciclismo es mi deporte favorito. 5. Me gusta mucho la natación. Paso mucho tiempo en la piscina. 6. Mi hermana es una gran excursionista.
Textbook MP3s

2 Teaching Tips
- To simplify, prepare the class for listening by having students read the list aloud.
- Ask students if the verbs in the list are conjugated or if they are infinitives. Tell them that the verbs they hear in the audio recording may be in the infinitive or conjugated form.

2 Script Hoy es sábado y mis amigos y yo estamos en el parque. Todos tenemos pasatiempos diferentes. Clara y Daniel nadan en la piscina. Luis patina en línea. Sergio y Paco toman el sol. Dalia lee una revista. Rosa y yo paseamos en bicicleta. Y tú, ¿practicas deportes?
Textbook MP3s

3 Expansion Ask students to write three additional true/false sentences based on the illustration. Have volunteers read sentences aloud for the rest of the class to answer.

4 Expansion Ask students to write three sentences using the words they listed in each category. You can cue students to elicit more responses. Ex: **¿Qué es la natación? (La natación es un deporte.)**

TEACHING OPTIONS

Extra Practice Add an auditory aspect to this vocabulary practice. Prepare short descriptions of different places you need to visit using the vocabulary from the chapter. Read each description aloud and have students name an appropriate location. Ex: **Necesito estudiar en un lugar tranquilo. También deseo leer una revista y unos periódicos. Aquí la gente no debe comer ni beber ni hablar por teléfono. (la biblioteca)**

Game Play a modified version of **20 Preguntas**. Ask a volunteer to choose an activity, person, or place from the illustration or **Más vocabulario** that other students will take turns guessing by asking yes/no questions. Limit the attempts to ten questions, after which the volunteer will reveal the item. You may need to provide some phrases on the board.

Teaching Tip Ask brief yes/no questions to review vocabulary in **En el centro** and **Más vocabulario**. Ex: **¿Hay muchas diversiones en el centro? No tienen ratos libres los fines de semana, ¿verdad? ¿Pasan ustedes los ratos libres en el museo?**

5 Expansion
- Have students read each item aloud, and ask individuals to respond. After each answer is given, ask a different student to verify whether the answer is correct, using a complete sentence. Do the first verification yourself to model possible student responses. Ex: **—Tomamos una limonada. —Es un café/restaurante. —Sí. En un café/restaurante tomamos una limonada.**
- To challenge students, ask them to convert items into yes/no questions. Ex: **¿Tomamos una limonada en el café? (Sí.) ¿Vemos una película en el restaurante? (No.)** Have pairs take turns answering questions.

6 Teaching Tip Quickly review the verbs in the list. Make sure that students understand the meaning of **¿Qué haces...?** Tell them that they will use this phrase throughout the activity.

6 Expansion
- Ask additional questions and have volunteers answer. Ex: **¿Qué haces en la residencia estudiantil?** Suggested places: **un apartamento, la casa de un amigo/una amiga, el centro, un gimnasio**
- Write a new list of places on the board. Then, in pairs, have students perform the activity again, this time including information specific to a Spanish-speaking country. Their partner will guess where they are. Ex: **—¿Qué haces cuando estás en un restaurante? —Como paella. —¿Estás en España? —Sí.**

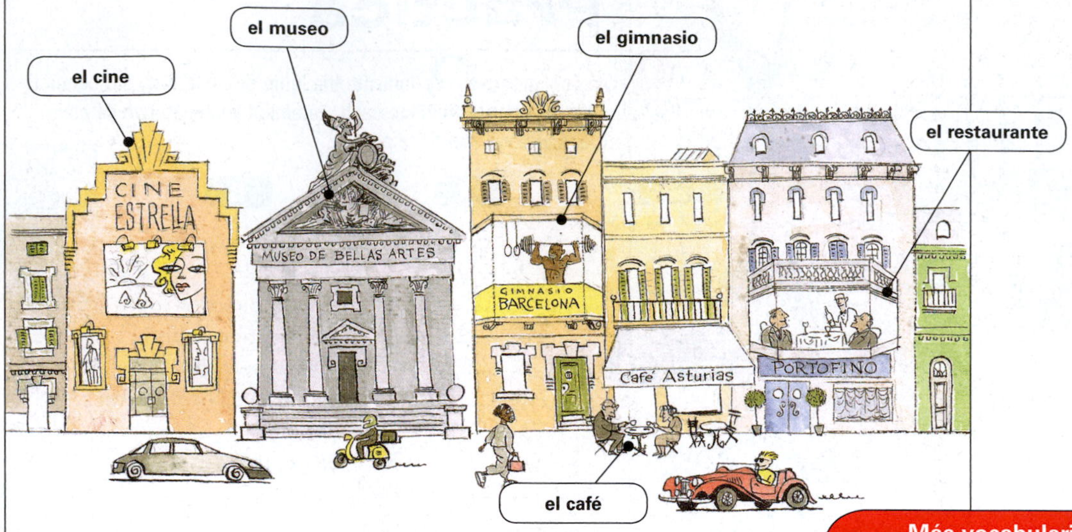

En el centro

Más vocabulario

la diversión	fun activity; entertainment; recreation
el fin de semana	weekend
el pasatiempo	pastime; hobby
los ratos libres	spare (free) time
el videojuego	video game
la iglesia	church
el lugar	place
ver películas (*f., pl.*)	to watch movies
favorito/a	favorite

5 **Identificar** Identify the place where these activities would take place.

modelo
Esquiamos. *Es una montaña.*

1. Tomamos una limonada. Es un café./Es un restaurante.
2. Vemos una película. Es un cine.
3. Nadamos y tomamos el sol. Es una piscina./Es un parque.
4. Hay muchos monumentos. Es un parque./Es una plaza.
5. Comemos tacos y fajitas. Es un restaurante.
6. Miramos pinturas (*paintings*) de Diego Rivera y Frida Kahlo. Es un museo.
7. Hay mucho tráfico. Es el centro.
8. Practicamos deportes. Es un gimnasio./Es un parque.

6 **Preguntar** Ask a classmate what he or she does in the places mentioned below. Your classmate will respond using verbs from the word bank. Answers will vary.

modelo
una plaza
Estudiante 1: *¿Qué haces (do you do) cuando estás en una plaza?*
Estudiante 2: *Camino por la plaza y miro a las personas.*

beber	escalar	mirar	practicar
caminar	escribir	nadar	tomar
correr	leer	patinar	visitar

1. una biblioteca
2. un estadio
3. una plaza
4. una piscina
5. las montañas
6. un parque
7. un café
8. un museo

Practice more at **vhlcentral.com**.

TEACHING OPTIONS

Extra Practice Give students five minutes to write a short description of three to five sentences about a typical weekend: what they do and where, and with whom they spend time. Circulate through the class and help with unfamiliar vocabulary. Have volunteers share their paragraphs with the class. Then have the class discuss what a "typical weekend" consists of; compose a description on the board.

Game Have students tell a chain story. For example, one student begins with: **Es el sábado por la mañana y voy [al café].** The next student continues with: **Estoy en el café y tomo una *Coca-Cola*.** You may need to provide some phrases on the board: **voy a/al/a la..., luego, después.** The story may change location; set a time limit for each response. The game ends after ten minutes or when all students have participated.

NATIONAL communication STANDARDS

Comunicación

7

Crucigrama Your instructor will give you and your partner an incomplete crossword puzzle. Yours has the words your partner needs and vice versa. In order to complete the puzzle, take turns giving each other clues, using definitions, examples, and phrases. Answers will vary.

modelo

2 horizontal: *Es un deporte que practicamos en la piscina.*
6 vertical: *Es un mensaje que escribimos con lápiz o con pluma.*

8

Entrevista In pairs, take turns asking and answering these questions. Answers will vary.

1. ¿Hay un café cerca de la universidad? ¿Dónde está?
2. ¿Cuál es tu restaurante favorito?
3. ¿Te gusta viajar y visitar monumentos? ¿Por qué?
4. ¿Te gusta ir al cine los fines de semana?
5. ¿Cuáles son tus películas favoritas?
6. ¿Te gusta practicar deportes?
7. ¿Cuáles son tus deportes favoritos? ¿Por qué?
8. ¿Cuáles son tus pasatiempos favoritos?

CONSULTA

To review expressions with **gustar**, see **Estructura 2.1**, p. 48.

9

Conversación Using the words and expressions provided, work with a partner to prepare a short conversation about pastimes. Answers will vary.

¿a qué hora?	¿con quién(es)?	¿dónde?
¿cómo?	¿cuándo?	¿qué?

modelo

Estudiante 1: *¿Cuándo patinas en línea?*
Estudiante 2: *Patino en línea los domingos. Y tú, ¿patinas en línea?*
Estudiante 1: *No, no me gusta patinar en línea. Me gusta practicar el béisbol.*

10

Pasatiempos In pairs, tell each other what pastimes three of your friends and family members enjoy. Be prepared to share with the class any pastimes you noticed they have in common. Answers will vary.

modelo

Estudiante 1: *Mi hermana pasea mucho en bicicleta, pero mis padres practican la natación. Mi hermano no nada, pero visita muchos museos.*
Estudiante 2: *Mi primo lee muchas revistas, pero no practica muchos deportes. Mis tíos esquían y practican el golf...*

7 Teaching Tip Model the different ways that students can give clues. Write **el gimnasio** on the board. Then write: **Es un lugar donde la gente corre. (definición) / En nuestra universidad se llama The Plex. (ejemplo) / un lugar para practicar deportes (frase)** Explain that while the definition and phrase could apply to other places, the person receiving the clue should use the empty letter spaces to figure out the answer.

7 Expansion In pairs, have students create another type of word puzzle, such as a word search. Tell them to use vocabulary related to sports and pastimes.

8 Teaching Tip Before beginning the activity, review the verb **gustar**.

8 Expansion Have the same pairs ask each other additional questions. Then ask volunteers to share their mini-conversations with the class.

9 Teaching Tip After students have asked and answered questions, ask volunteers to report their partners' activities back to the class. The partners should verify the information and provide at least one additional detail.

10 Expansion
- Ask volunteers to share any pastimes they and their partners, friends, and families have in common.
- In pairs, have students write sentences about the pastimes of a famous person without using their name. Encourage them to also recycle the descriptive adjectives and adjectives of nationality they learned in Lesson 3. Then have them work with another pair, asking questions as necessary, to guess the identity of the person being described.

TEACHING OPTIONS

Large Group Have students write down six activities they enjoy and then circulate around the room to collect signatures from others who enjoy the same activities (**¿Te gusta...? Firma aquí, por favor.**). Ask volunteers to report back to the class.

Game Ask students to take out a piece of paper and write anonymously a set of activities that best corresponds to them. Collect and shuffle the slips of paper. Divide the class into two teams. Pull out and read aloud each slip of paper, and have the teams take turns guessing the student's identity.

4 fotonovela

Section Goals

In **Fotonovela**, students will:
- receive comprehensible input from free-flowing discourse
- learn functional phrases that preview lesson grammatical structures

Instructional Resources
Supersite: Video (***Fotonovela***); Resources (Scripts, Translations, Answer Keys)
WebSAM
Video Manual, pp. 7–8

Video Recap: Lección 3
Before doing this **Fotonovela** section, review the previous episode with these fill-in-the-blank sentences:
1. Marta y Valentina son las ____ de Jimena y Felipe. (primas) 2. Marissa tiene ____ hermanos y una hermana. (dos) 3. ____ es hija única. (la Sra. Díaz) 4. Las mujeres comparten una ____. (trajinera) 5. Marissa tiene planes para visitar a ____. (tía Ana María)

Video Synopsis The friends have arrived at **tía Ana María's** house in **Mérida. Juan Carlos** and **Felipe** head off to play soccer with **Felipe's** cousins, **Eduardo** and **Pablo.** Meanwhile, **Maru, Miguel,** and **Jimena** take **Marissa** to explore a **cenote**.

Teaching Tips
- Have students quickly glance over the **Fotonovela** captions and make a list of the cognates they find. Then, ask them to predict what this episode is about.
- Have students look for a few expressions used to talk about pastimes. Then ask a few questions. Ex: **¿Qué te gusta hacer en tus ratos libres? ¿Te gusta el fútbol?**

Fútbol, cenotes y mole

Maru, Miguel, Jimena y Marissa visitan un cenote, mientras Felipe y Juan Carlos van a un partido de fútbol.

PERSONAJES

MIGUEL

PABLO

Video: *Fotonovela*

MIGUEL Buenos días a todos.
TÍA ANA MARÍA Hola, Miguel. Maru, ¿qué van a hacer hoy?
MARU Miguel y yo vamos a llevar a Marissa a un cenote.

MARISSA ¿No vamos a nadar? ¿Qué es un cenote?
MIGUEL Sí, sí vamos a nadar. Un cenote... difícil de explicar. Es una piscina natural en un hueco profundo.
MARU ¡Ya vas a ver! Seguro que te va a gustar.

ANA MARÍA Marissa, ¿qué te gusta hacer? ¿Escalar montañas? ¿Ir de excursión?
MARISSA Sí, me gusta ir de excursión y practicar el esquí acuático. Y usted, ¿qué prefiere hacer en sus ratos libres?

PABLO Mi mamá tiene muchos pasatiempos y actividades.
EDUARDO Sí. Ella nada y juega al tenis y al golf.
PABLO Va al cine y a los museos.
ANA MARÍA Sí, salgo mucho los fines de semana

(unos minutos después)
EDUARDO Hay un partido de fútbol en el parque. ¿Quieren ir conmigo?
PABLO Y conmigo. Si no consigo más jugadores, nuestro equipo va a perder.

FELIPE ¿Recuerdas el restaurante del mole?
EDUARDO ¿Qué restaurante?
JIMENA El mole de mi tía Ana María es mi favorito.
MARU Chicos, ya es hora. ¡Vamos!

TEACHING OPTIONS

Video Tips General suggestions for using video clips in the classroom can be found in the front matter of this Instructor's Annotated Edition.
Fútbol, cenotes y mole Play the last half of the **Fútbol, cenotes y mole** episode and have the class give you a description of what they saw. Write their observations on the board, pointing out any incorrect information. Repeat this process to allow the class to pick up more details of the plot. Then ask students to use the information they have accumulated to guess what happened at the beginning of the episode. Write their guesses on the board. Then play the entire episode and, through discussion, help the class summarize the plot.

ANA MARÍA | MARU | MARISSA | EDUARDO | FELIPE | JUAN CARLOS | JIMENA | DON GUILLERMO

7

(*más tarde, en el parque*)

PABLO No puede ser. ¡Cinco a uno!

FELIPE ¡Vamos a jugar! Si perdemos, compramos el almuerzo. Y si ganamos...

EDUARDO ¡Empezamos!

8

(*mientras tanto, en el cenote*)

MARISSA ¿Hay muchos cenotes en México?

MIGUEL Sólo en la península de Yucatán.

MARISSA ¡Vamos a nadar!

9

(*Los chicos visitan a don Guillermo, un vendedor de paletas heladas.*)

JUAN CARLOS Don Guillermo, ¿dónde podemos conseguir un buen mole?

FELIPE Eduardo y Pablo van a pagar el almuerzo. Y yo voy a pedir un montón de comida.

10

FELIPE Sí, éste es el restaurante. Recuerdo la comida.

EDUARDO Oye, Pablo... No tengo...

PABLO No te preocupes, hermanito.

FELIPE ¿Qué buscas? (*muestra la cartera de Pablo*) ¿Esto?

Expresiones útiles

Making invitations

Hay un partido de fútbol en el parque. ¿Quieren ir conmigo?
There's a soccer game in the park. Do you want to come with me?
¡Yo puedo jugar!
I can play!
Mmm... no quiero.
Hmm... I don't want to.
Lo siento, pero no puedo.
I'm sorry, but I can't.
¡Vamos a nadar!
Let's go swimming!
Sí, vamos.
Yes, let's go.

Making plans

¿Qué van a hacer hoy?
What are you going to do today?
Vamos a llevar a Marissa a un cenote.
We are taking Marissa to a cenote.
Vamos a comprar unas paletas heladas.
We're going to buy some popsicles.
Vamos a jugar. Si perdemos, compramos el almuerzo.
Let's play. If we lose, we'll buy lunch.

Talking about pastimes

¿Qué te gusta hacer? ¿Escalar montañas? ¿Ir de excursión?
What do you like to do? Mountain climbing? Hiking?
Sí, me gusta ir de excursión y practicar esquí acuático.
Yes, I like hiking and water skiing.
Y usted, ¿qué prefiere hacer en sus ratos libres?
And you, what do you like to do in your free time?
Salgo mucho los fines de semana.
I go out a lot on the weekends.
Voy al cine y a los museos.
I go to the movies and to museums.

Additional vocabulary

el/la aficionado/a *fan*
la cartera *wallet*
el hueco *hole*
un montón de *a lot of*

recursos
VM pp. 7–8 | vhlcentral.com Lección 4

Expresiones útiles

- Point out the written accents in the words **fútbol, sí, ¿Qué?,** and **excursión.** Explain that accents indicate a stressed syllable in a word. Remind students that all question words have accent marks. Tell students that they will learn more about word stress and accent marks in **Pronunciación.**
- Mention that **Vamos, van,** and **Voy** are present-tense forms of the verb **ir.** Point out that **ir a** is used with an infinitive to tell what is going to happen. Ask: **¿Qué vas a hacer esta noche? ¿Por qué no vamos al parque?** Explain that **Quieren, quiero,** and **siento** are forms of **querer** and **sentir,** which undergo a stem change from **e** to **ie** in certain forms. Tell students that they will learn more about these concepts in **Estructura.**

Teaching Tip Have the class read through the entire **Fotonovela,** with volunteers playing various parts. Have students take turns playing the roles so that more students participate.

Nota cultural Traditionally, **mole** ingredients are ground on a flat slab of volcanic stone known as a **metate**, using a **mano**, or rounded grinding stone. The **metate** has been used for grinding grains (especially corn) and spices since pre-Columbian times, and although electric blenders and grinders have replaced many **metates** in Mexican homes, this utensil has experienced a resurgence. Many claim that using the **metate**, although time-consuming, gives dishes better flavor.

TEACHING OPTIONS

Extra Practice Ask students to write six true/false statements about the **Fotonovela** episode. Have them exchange papers with a classmate, who will complete the activity, correcting any false information.

Large Groups Go through the **Expresiones útiles** as a class. Then have students stand and form a circle. Call out a question or statement from **Expresiones útiles** and toss a ball to a student. He or she must respond appropriately and toss the ball back to you.

1 Teaching Tip Read the activity items to the class as true/false sentences. Ask students to correct the false statements. Ex: **Marissa, Maru y Miguel desean correr por el parque. (Falso. Desean nadar.)**

2 Expansion Tell the class to add **Jimena** to the list of possible answers. Then give students these statements as items 6–8: **6. Recuerdo un restaurante donde sirven mole. (Felipe) 7. Mi hermano no encuentra su cartera. (Pablo) 8. Prefiero el mole de la tía Ana María. (Jimena)**

Nota cultural Since the **Yucatán** peninsula does not have any rivers, **cenotes** were an important source of potable water for the pre-Hispanic Maya. One of the peninsula's most famous **cenotes** is the **Cenote Sagrado**, located near **Chichén Itzá**. It was used by Mayans in pre-Hispanic times for worship of the rain god **Chaac**.

3 Expansion Give these questions to the class as items 5–6: **5. ¿Qué le pregunta Juan Carlos a don Guillermo? (Le pregunta dónde pueden conseguir un buen mole.) 6. ¿Quiénes pierden dos partidos? (Eduardo y Pablo pierden dos partidos.)**

4 Possible Conversation
E1: ¿Qué prefieres hacer en tus ratos libres?
E2: Me gustan los deportes.
E1: ¿Te gusta el fútbol?
E2: Sí, mucho. Me gusta también nadar y correr. Oye, ¿qué vas a hacer esta noche?
E1: No tengo planes.
E2: ¿Quieres ir a correr conmigo?
E1: Lo siento, pero no me gusta correr. ¿Te gusta patinar en línea? ¿Por qué no vamos al parque a patinar?
E2: Sí, vamos.

¿Qué pasó?

1 Escoger Choose the answer that best completes each sentence.

1. Marissa, Maru y Miguel desean __a__.
   a. nadar b. correr por el parque c. leer el periódico
2. A Marissa le gusta __c__.
   a. el tenis b. el vóleibol c. ir de excursión y practicar esquí acuático
3. A la tía Ana María le gusta __b__.
   a. jugar al hockey b. nadar y jugar al tenis y al golf c. hacer ciclismo
4. Pablo y Eduardo pierden el partido de __a__.
   a. fútbol b. béisbol c. baloncesto
5. Juan Carlos y Felipe desean __c__.
   a. patinar b. esquiar c. comer mole

NOTA CULTURAL
Mole is a typical sauce in Mexican cuisine. It is made from pumpkin seeds, chile, and chocolate, and it is usually served with chicken, beef, or pork. To learn more about **mole**, go to page 252.

2 Identificar Identify the person who would make each statement.

1. A mí me gusta nadar, pero no sé qué es un cenote. __Marissa__
2. Mamá va al cine y al museo en sus ratos libres. __Pablo/Eduardo__
3. Yo voy a pedir mucha comida. __Felipe__
4. ¿Quieren ir a jugar al fútbol con nosotros en el parque? __Pablo/Eduardo__
5. Me gusta salir los fines de semana. __tía Ana María__

NOTA CULTURAL
Cenotes are deep, freshwater sinkholes found in caves throughout the Yucatán peninsula. They were formed in prehistoric times by the erosion and collapse of cave walls. The Mayan civilization considered the **cenotes** sacred, and performed rituals there. Today, they are popular destinations for swimming and diving.

3 Preguntas Answer the questions using the information from the **Fotonovela.**

1. ¿Qué van a hacer Miguel y Maru?
   Miguel y Maru van a llevar a Marissa a un cenote.
2. ¿Adónde van Felipe y Juan Carlos mientras sus amigos van al cenote?
   Felipe y Juan Carlos van a jugar al fútbol con Pablo y Eduardo.
3. ¿Quién gana el partido de fútbol?
   Felipe y Juan Carlos ganan el partido de fútbol.
4. ¿Quiénes van al cenote con Maru y Miguel?
   Marissa y Jimena van al cenote con Maru y Miguel.

4 Conversación With a partner, prepare a conversation in which you talk about pastimes and invite each other to do some activity together. Use these expressions and also look at **Expresiones útiles** on the previous page. Answers will vary.

¿A qué hora? *(At) What time?*	¿Dónde? *Where?*	Nos vemos a las siete. *See you at seven.*
contigo *with you*	No puedo porque... *I can't because...*	

- ¿Eres aficionado/a a...?
- ¿Te gusta...?
- ¿Por qué no...?
- ¿Quieres... conmigo?
- ¿Qué vas a hacer esta noche?

Practice more at **vhlcentral.com**.

TEACHING OPTIONS

Small Groups Have the class quickly glance at frames 7, 8, and 10 of the **Fotonovela**. Then have students work in groups of three to ad-lib what transpires between the friends. Assure them that it is not necessary to follow the **Fotonovela** word for word. Students should be creative while getting the general meaning across with the vocabulary and expressions they know.

Extra Practice Have students close their books and complete these statements with words from the **Fotonovela**. **1. ¿Qué prefiere _____ usted en sus ratos libres? (hacer) 2. ¿Dónde _____ conseguir un buen mole? (podemos) 3. ¿Nosotros _____ a nadar? (vamos) 4. Eduardo y Pablo _____ a pagar el almuerzo. (van) 5. ¿Ustedes _____ ir conmigo al partido de fútbol? (quieren)**

Pronunciación

Audio

Word stress and accent marks

pe-lí-cu-la **e-di-fi-cio** **ver** **yo**

Every Spanish syllable contains at least one vowel. When two vowels are joined in the same syllable they form a **diphthong***. A **monosyllable** is a word formed by a single syllable.

bi-blio-te-ca **vi-si-tar** **par-que** **fút-bol**

The syllable of a Spanish word that is pronounced most emphatically is the "stressed" syllable.

pe-lo-ta **pis-ci-na** **ra-tos** **ha-blan**

Words that end in **n, s,** or a **vowel** are usually stressed on the next-to-last syllable.

na-ta-ción **pa-pá** **in-glés** **Jo-sé**

If words that end in **n, s,** or a **vowel** are stressed on the last syllable, they must carry an accent mark on the stressed syllable.

bai-lar **es-pa-ñol** **u-ni-ver-si-dad** **tra-ba-ja-dor**

Words that do not end in **n, s,** or a **vowel** are usually stressed on the last syllable.

béis-bol **lá-piz** **ár-bol** **Gó-mez**

If words that do not end in **n, s,** or a **vowel** are stressed on the next-to-last syllable, they must carry an accent mark on the stressed syllable.

**The two vowels that form a diphthong are either both weak or one is weak and the other is strong.*

En la unión está la fuerza.²

Práctica Pronounce each word, stressing the correct syllable. Then give the word stress rule for each word.

1. profesor
2. Puebla
3. ¿Cuántos?
4. Mazatlán
5. examen
6. ¿Cómo?
7. niños
8. Guadalajara
9. programador
10. México
11. están
12. geografía

Oraciones Read the conversation aloud to practice word stress.

MARINA Hola, Carlos. ¿Qué tal?
CARLOS Bien. Oye, ¿a qué hora es el partido de fútbol?
MARINA Creo que es a las siete.
CARLOS ¿Quieres ir?
MARINA Lo siento, pero no puedo. Tengo que estudiar biología.

Refranes Read these sayings aloud to practice word stress.

Quien ríe de último, ríe mejor.¹

recursos
LM p. 20
vhlcentral.com Lección 4

1 He who laughs last, laughs best.
2 United we stand.

Section Goals

In **Pronunciación**, students will be introduced to:
- the concept of word stress
- diphthongs and monosyllables
- accent marks

Instructional Resources
Supersite: Audio (Textbook and Lab MP3 Files); Resources (Scripts, Answer Keys)
WebSAM
Lab Manual, p. 20

Teaching Tips

- Write **película, edificio, ver,** and **yo** on the board. Model their pronunciation. Ask the class to identify the diphthongs and the monosyllables.
- Remind students of the strong and weak vowels that they learned about in **Lección 3**. Strong: **a, e, o**; Weak: **i, u**
- Write **biblioteca, visitar,** and **parque** on the board. Model their pronunciation, then ask which syllables are stressed.
- As you go through each point in the explanation, write the example words on the board, pronounce them, and have students repeat. Then, ask students to provide words they learned in **Lecciones 1–3** and **Contextos** and **Fotonovela** of this lesson that exemplify each point.

Práctica/Oraciones/Refranes

These exercises are recorded on the *Textbook MP3s*. You may want to play the audio so that students practice listening to Spanish spoken by speakers other than yourself.

TEACHING OPTIONS

Extra Practice Write on the board a list of Mexican place names. Have the class pronounce each name, paying particular attention to word stress. Ex: **Campeche, Durango, Culiacán, Tepic, Chichén Itzá, Zacatecas, Colima, Nayarit, San Luis Potosí, Sonora, Puebla, Morelos, Veracruz, Toluca, Guanajuato, Pachuca, El Tajín, Chetumal.** Model pronunciation as necessary.

Small Groups On the board, write a list of words that students already know. Then have the class work in small groups to come up with the word stress rule that applies to each word. Ex: **lápiz, equipo, pluma, Felipe, chicas, comer, mujer, tenis, hombre, libros, papel, parque, béisbol, excursión, deportes, fútbol, pasear, esquí.**

Flash CULTURA

Section Goals

In **Cultura**, students will:
- read about soccer rivalries
- learn sports-related terms
- read about **Miguel Cabrera** and **Paola Espinosa**
- read about renowned athletes

Instructional Resources
Supersite: Video (***Flash cultura***); Resources (Scripts, Translations, Answer Keys)
WebSAM
Video Manual, pp. 79–80

En detalle

Antes de leer Ask students to predict the content of this reading based on the title and photos. Have them share what they know about these teams or about other sports rivalries.

Lectura
- Use the map on page 66 to point out the locations of Barcelona and Madrid. Briefly explain that Spain's regional cultures (Basque, Catalan, Galician, etc.) were at odds with the authoritarian, centralized approach of **Franco's** regime, which banned the public use of regional languages. Point out that the nickname **Barça** is Catalan, which is why it has a cedilla to indicate a soft **c**.
- Describe the stadiums: **Camp Nou** (Catalan for *new field*) holds about 100,000 spectators and is the largest soccer stadium in Europe. Madrid's **Estadio Santiago Bernabéu**, named after an ex-player and club president, can seat about 80,000.
- Remind students that **el fútbol** is *soccer* and **el fútbol americano** is *football*.

Después de leer Ask students what facts in this reading are new or surprising to them.

1 Expansion To challenge students, ask them to write two additional items. Then have them exchange papers with a classmate and complete the activity.

EN DETALLE

Video: *Flash cultura*

Real Madrid y Barça: rivalidad total

NATIONAL STANDARDS connections cultures

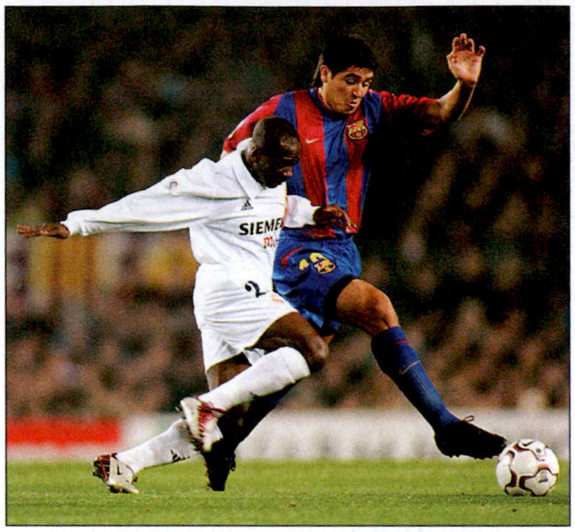

Soccer in Spain is a force to be reckoned with, and no two teams draw more attention than **Real Madrid** and the **Fútbol Club Barcelona.** Whether the venue is Madrid's **Santiago Bernabéu** or Barcelona's **Camp Nou,** the two cities shut down for the showdown, paralyzed by **fútbol** fever. A ticket to the actual game is always the hottest ticket in town.

The rivalry between **Real Madrid** and **Barça** is about more than soccer. As the two biggest, most powerful cities in Spain, Barcelona and Madrid are constantly compared to one another and have a natural rivalry. There is also a political component to the dynamic. Barcelona, with its distinct language and culture, has long struggled for increased autonomy from Madrid's centralized government. Under Francisco Franco's rule (1939–1975), when repression of the Catalan identity was at its height, a game between **Real Madrid** and **FC Barcelona** was wrapped up with all the symbolism of the regime versus the resistance, even though both teams suffered casualties in Spain's civil war and the subsequent Franco dictatorship.

Although the dictatorship is long over, the momentum of all those decades of competition still transforms both cities into a frenzied, tense panic leading up to the game. Once the final score is announced, one of those cities is transformed again, this time into the best party in the country.

Rivalidades del fútbol

Argentina:	Boca Juniors vs. River Plate
México:	Águilas del América vs. Chivas del Guadalajara
Chile:	Colo Colo vs. Universidad de Chile
Guatemala:	Comunicaciones vs. Municipal
Uruguay:	Peñarol vs. Nacional
Colombia:	Millonarios vs. Independiente Santa Fe

ACTIVIDADES

1 **¿Cierto o falso?** Indicate whether each statement is cierto or falso. Correct the false statements.

1. People from Spain don't like soccer. Falso. People from Spain like soccer very much.
2. Madrid and Barcelona are the most important cities in Spain. Cierto.
3. Santiago Bernabéu is a stadium in Barcelona. Falso. It is a stadium in Madrid.
4. The rivalry between Real Madrid and FC Barcelona is not only in soccer. Cierto.
5. Barcelona has resisted Madrid's centralized government. Cierto.
6. Only the FC Barcelona team was affected by the civil war. Falso. Both teams were affected by the civil war.
7. During Franco's regime, the Catalan culture thrived. Falso. Catalan culture was repressed during Franco's regime.
8. There are many famous rivalries between soccer teams in the Spanish-speaking world. Cierto.
9. River Plate is a popular team from Argentina. Cierto.
10. Comunicaciones and Peñarol are famous rivals in Guatemala. Falso. Comunicaciones and Municipal are important rivals in Guatemala.

TEACHING OPTIONS

Project Have small groups choose famous soccer rivalries, then split up to research and create a web page for each of the rival teams. The pages should feature each team's colors, players, home stadium, official song, and other significant or interesting information. Have the groups present their rivals' web pages to the class.

¡Gooooooool! Explain that sportscasters in the Spanish-speaking world are famous for their theatrical commentaries. One example is **Andrés Cantor**, who provides commentary for soccer matches on Spanish-language stations in the U.S. Each time a goal is scored, fans know they can hear a drawn-out bellow of **¡Gooooooool! Cantor's** call, which can last for nearly thirty seconds, was made into a ringtone for cell phones in the U.S.

ASÍ SE DICE

Los deportes

el/la árbitro/a	*referee*
el/la atleta	*athlete*
la bola; el balón	**la pelota**
el campeón/ la campeona	*champion*
la carrera	*race*
competir	*to compete*
empatar	*to tie*
la medalla	*medal*
el/la mejor	*the best*
mundial	*worldwide*
el torneo	*tournament*

EL MUNDO HISPANO

Atletas importantes

World-renowned Hispanic athletes:

- **Rafael Nadal** (España) has won 14 Grand Slam singles titles and the 2008 Olympic gold medal in singles tennis.
- **Lionel Andrés Messi** (Argentina) is one of the world's top soccer players. He plays for **FC Barcelona** and for the Argentine national team.
- **Mireia Belmonte García** (España) won two silver medals in swimming at the 2012 Olympics.
- **Lorena Ochoa** (México) was the top-ranked female golfer in the world when she retired in 2010 at the age of 28. She still hosts an LPGA golf tournament, the Lorena Ochoa Invitational, every year.

PERFILES

Miguel Cabrera y Paola Espinosa

Miguel Cabrera, considered one of the best hitters in baseball, now plays first base for the Detroit Tigers. Born in Venezuela in 1983, he made his Major League debut at the age of 20. Cabrera has been selected for both the National League and American League All-Star Teams. In 2012, he became the first player since 1967 to win the Triple Crown.

Mexican diver **Paola Milagros Espinosa Sánchez**, born in 1986, has competed in three Olympics (2004, 2008, and 2012). She and her partner Tatiana Ortiz took home a bronze medal in 2008. In 2012, she won a silver medal with partner Alejandra Orozco. She won three gold medals at the Pan American Games in 2007 and again in 2011.

Conexión Internet

¿Qué deportes son populares en los países hispanos?

Go to **vhlcentral.com** to find more cultural information related to this **Cultura** section.

ACTIVIDADES

2 Comprensión Write the name of the athlete described in each sentence.

1. Es un jugador de fútbol de Argentina. Lionel Messi
2. Es una mujer que practica el golf. Lorena Ochoa
3. Es un jugador de béisbol de Venezuela. Miguel Cabrera
4. Es una mujer mexicana que practica un deporte en la piscina. Paola Milagros Espinosa Sánchez

3 ¿Quién es? Write a short paragraph describing an athlete that you like, but do not mention his/her name. What does he/she look like? What sport does he/she play? Where does he/she live? Read your description to the class to see if they can guess who it is. Answers will vary.

recursos: VM pp. 79–80; vhlcentral.com Lección 4

Practice more at **vhlcentral.com**.

TEACHING OPTIONS

Los campeones For homework, ask students to research one of the athletes from **El mundo hispano**. They should write five Spanish sentences about the athlete's life and career, and bring in a photo from the Internet. Have students who researched the same person work as a group to present that athlete to the class.

Heritage Speakers Ask heritage speakers to describe sports preferences in their families' countries of origin, especially ones that are not widely known in the United States, such as **jai-alai**. What well-known athletes in the U.S. are from their families' countries of origin?

Así se dice

- Model the pronunciation of each term and have students repeat it.
- To challenge students, add these words to the list: **el atletismo** (*track and field*); **el/la golfista** (*golfer*); **marcar un gol** (*to score a goal*); **el palo de golf** (*golf club*); **el/la portero/a** (*goalie*).

Perfiles

- Miguel Cabrera has played left field, right field, third base, and first base. In 2012, he led the American League with a .330 batting average, 44 home runs, and 139 runs batted in. Cabrera was named the American League's Most Valuable Player in 2012 and 2013.
- **Paola Espinosa**'s Olympic medals are in the 10m platform synchronized diving event. She won gold medals at the Pan American Games for individual and synchronized events.

El mundo hispano Have students write three true/false sentences about this section. Then have them get together with a classmate and take turns reading and correcting their statements.

2 Expansion Give students these sentences as items 5–6:
5. ____ es una mujer española que practica la natación. (Mireia Belmonte García)
6. El ____ es el deporte favorito de Rafael Nadal. (tenis)

3 Teaching Tip Have students get together with a classmate and peer edit each other's paragraphs, paying close attention to gender agreement.

Section Goals

In **Estructura 4.1**, students will learn:
- the present tense of **ir**
- the contraction **al**
- **ir a** + [*infinitive*] to express future events
- **vamos a** to express *let's*…

Instructional Resources
Supersite: Audio (Lab MP3 Files); Resources (Grammar Presentation Slides, Activity Pack, Scripts, Answer Keys); Testing Program (Quizzes)
WebSAM
Workbook, pp. 39–40
Lab Manual, p. 21

Teaching Tips
- Write your next day's schedule on the board. Ex: **8:00—la biblioteca; 12:00—comer**. Explain where you are going or what you are going to do, using the verb **ir**. Ask volunteers about their schedules, using forms of **ir**.
- Add a visual aspect to this grammar presentation. Write names of Spanish-speaking countries on construction paper, and pin up the papers at different points around the classroom in order to make a "map." Point to your destination "country," and as you pantomime flying there, ask students: **¿Adónde voy? (Vas a Chile.)** Once there, act out an activity, asking: **¿Qué voy a hacer? (Vas a esquiar.)**
- Practice **vamos a** to express the idea of *let's* by asking volunteers to suggest things to do. Ex: **Tengo hambre. (Vamos a la cafetería.)**

Ayuda Point out the difference in usage between **dónde** and **adónde**. Ask: **¿Adónde va el presidente de los Estados Unidos para descansar? (Va a Camp David.) ¿Dónde está Camp David? (Está en Maryland.)**

4.1 Present tense of ir

Tutorial

ANTE TODO The verb **ir** (*to go*) is irregular in the present tense. Note that, except for the **yo** form (**voy**) and the lack of a written accent on the **vosotros** form (**vais**), the endings are the same as those for regular present tense **-ar** verbs.

The verb ir (*to go*)

Singular forms		Plural forms	
yo	**voy**	nosotros/as	**vamos**
tú	**vas**	vosotros/as	**vais**
Ud./él/ella	**va**	Uds./ellos/ellas	**van**

▶ **Ir** is often used with the preposition **a** (*to*). If **a** is followed by the definite article **el**, they combine to form the contraction **al**. If **a** is followed by the other definite articles (**la, las, los**), there is no contraction.

a + el = al

Voy **al** parque con Juan.
I'm going to the park with Juan.

Mis amigos van **a las** montañas.
My friends are going to the mountains.

▶ The construction **ir a** + [*infinitive*] is used to talk about actions that are going to happen in the future. It is equivalent to the English *to be going* + [*infinitive*].

Va a leer el periódico.
He is going to read the newspaper.

Van a pasear por el pueblo.
They are going to walk around town.

¡Voy a ir con ellos!

Ella va al cine y a los museos.

▶ **Vamos a** + [*infinitive*] can also express the idea of let's (*do something*).

Vamos a pasear.
Let's take a walk.

¡**Vamos a** comer!
Let's eat!

NATIONAL STANDARDS comparisons

CONSULTA
To review the contraction **de + el**, see **Estructura 1.3**, pp. 20–21.

AYUDA
When asking a question that contains a form of the verb **ir**, remember to use **adónde**:
¿Adónde vas?
(To) Where are you going?

recursos
WB pp. 39–40
LM p. 21
vhlcentral.com Lección 4

¡INTÉNTALO! Provide the present tense forms of **ir**.

1. Ellos __van__.
2. Yo __voy__.
3. Tu novio __va__.
4. Adela __va__.
5. Mi prima y yo __vamos__.
6. Tú __vas__.
7. Ustedes __van__.
8. Nosotros __vamos__.
9. Usted __va__.
10. Nosotras __vamos__.
11. Miguel __va__.
12. Ellas __van__.

TEACHING OPTIONS

TPR Invent gestures to act out the activities mentioned in **Lección 4**. Ex: **leer el periódico** (act out reading and holding a newspaper), **patinar** (skate), **nadar** (move arms as if swimming). Signal individuals to gesture appropriately as you cue activities with **Vamos a**. Keep a brisk pace.

Pairs Have students form pairs, and tell them they are going somewhere with a friend. On paper strips, write varying dollar amounts, ranging from three dollars to five thousand. Have each pair draw out a dollar amount at random and tell the class where they will go and what they will do with the money they've drawn. Encourage creativity. Ex: **Tenemos seis dólares. Vamos a McDonald's para comer. Ella va a cenar, pero yo voy a beber agua porque no tenemos más dinero./Tenemos cinco mil dólares. Vamos a cenar en París…**

Práctica

Practice more at **vhlcentral.com.**

1 **¿Adónde van?** Everyone in your neighborhood is dashing off to various places. Say where they are going.

1. la señora Castillo / el centro La señora Castillo va al centro.
2. las hermanas Gómez / la piscina Las hermanas Gómez van a la piscina.
3. tu tío y tu papá / el partido de fútbol Tu tío y tu papá van al partido de fútbol.
4. yo / el Museo de Arte Moderno (Yo) Voy al Museo de Arte Moderno.
5. nosotros / el restaurante Miramar (Nosotros) Vamos al restaurante Miramar.

2 **¿Qué van a hacer?** These sentences describe what several students in a college hiking club are doing today. Use **ir a** + [*infinitive*] to say that they are also going to do the same activities tomorrow.

modelo

Martín y Rodolfo nadan en la piscina.
Van a nadar en la piscina mañana también.

1. Sara lee una revista. Va a leer una revista mañana también.
2. Yo practico deportes. Voy a practicar deportes mañana también.
3. Ustedes van de excursión. Van a ir de excursión mañana también.
4. El presidente del club patina. Va a patinar mañana también.
5. Tú tomas el sol. Vas a tomar el sol mañana también.
6. Paseamos con nuestros amigos. Vamos a pasear con nuestros amigos mañana también.

3 **Preguntas** With a partner, take turns asking and answering questions about where the people are going and what they are going to do there. Some answers will vary.

modelo

Estudiante 1: *¿Adónde va Estela?*
Estudiante 2: *Va a la Librería Sol.*
Estudiante 1: *Va a comprar un libro.*

Estela

1. Álex y Miguel ¿Adónde van Álex y Miguel? Van al parque. Van a...

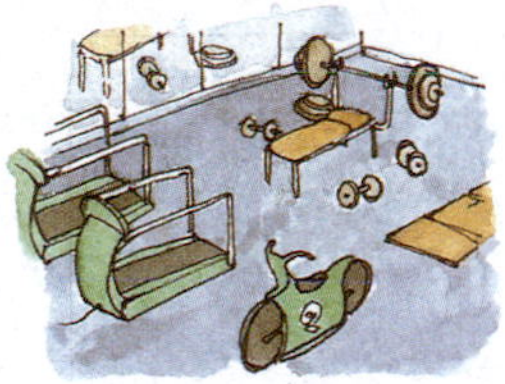

2. mi amigo ¿Adónde va mi amigo? Va al gimnasio. Va a...

3. tú ¿Adónde vas? Voy al restaurante. Voy a...

4. los estudiantes ¿Adónde van los estudiantes? Van al estadio. Van a...

5. la profesora Torres ¿Adónde va la profesora Torres? Va a la Biblioteca Nacional. Va a...

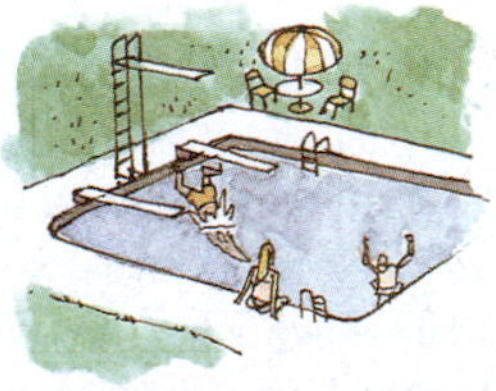

6. ustedes ¿Adónde van ustedes? Vamos a la piscina. Vamos a...

1 Teaching Tip To add a visual aspect to this exercise, bring in photos of people dressed for a particular activity. As you hold up each photo, have the class say where they are going, using the verb **ir**. Ex: Show a photo of a basketball player. **(Va al gimnasio./Va a un partido.)**

1 Expansion After completing the activity, extend each answer with **pero** and a different name or pronoun, and have students complete the sentence. Ex: **La señora Castillo va al centro, pero el señor Castillo... (va al trabajo).**

2 Expansion

- Show the same photos you used for **Actividad 1** and ask students to describe what the people are going to do. Ex: **Va a jugar al baloncesto.**
- Ask students about tomorrow's activities. Ex: **¿Qué van a hacer tus amigos mañana? ¿Qué va a hacer tu compañero/a mañana?**

3 Expansion

Ask pairs to write a riddle using **ir a** + [*infinitive*]. Ex: **Ángela, Laura, Tomás y Manuel van a hacer cosas diferentes. Tomás va a nadar y Laura va a comer, pero no en casa. Uno de los chicos y una de las chicas van a ver una película. ¿Adónde van todos?** Then have pairs exchange papers to solve the riddles.

TEACHING OPTIONS

Heritage Speakers Ask heritage speakers to write six sentences with the verb **ir** indicating places they go on weekends either by themselves or with friends and family. Ex: **Mi familia y yo vamos a visitar a mi abuela los domingos...** Share the descriptions with the class and ask comprehension questions.

Game Have students work in teams to write a brief description of a well-known fictional character's activities for tomorrow, using the verb **ir**. Ex: **Mañana va a dormir de día. Va a caminar de noche. Va a buscar una muchacha bonita. La muchacha va a tener mucho miedo.** Have each team read their description aloud without naming the character. Teams can ask for and share more details about the person as needed. The first team to correctly identify the person **(Es Drácula.)** receives a point. The team with the most points at the end wins.

4 Expansion Have students make the phrases negative and then provide a new appropriate ending. Ex: **Cuando no deseo descansar, voy al gimnasio.**

5 Teaching Tip Model question formation. Ex: **1. ¿Vas a comer en un restaurante chino hoy?** Then distribute the ***Hojas de actividades*** (Activity Pack/Supersite) that correspond to this activity. Allow students five minutes to fill out the surveys.

5 Expansion After collecting the surveys, ask individuals about their plans. Ex: If someone's name appears by **ver una película de terror**, ask him or her: **¿Qué película vas a ver hoy?**

6 Teaching Tip Add a visual aspect to this activity. Ask students to use an idea map to brainstorm a trip they would like to take. Have them write **lugar** in the central circle, and in the surrounding ones: **visitar, deportes, otras actividades, comida, compañeros/as**.

7 Teaching Tips
- To simplify, have students make two columns on a sheet of paper. The first one should be headed **El fin de semana tengo que…** and the other **El fin de semana tengo ganas de…** Give students a few minutes to brainstorm about their activities for the weekend.
- Before students begin the last step, brainstorm a list of expressions as a class. Ex: **—¿Quieres jugar al tenis conmigo? —Lo siento, pero no puedo./Sí, vamos.**

Comunicación

NATIONAL communication STANDARDS

4 **Situaciones** Work with a partner and say where you and your friends go in these situations. Answers will vary.

1. Cuando deseo descansar…
2. Cuando mi novio/a tiene que estudiar…
3. Si mis compañeros de clase necesitan practicar el español…
4. Si deseo hablar con mis amigos…
5. Cuando tengo dinero (*money*)…
6. Cuando mis amigos y yo tenemos hambre…
7. En mis ratos libres…
8. Cuando mis amigos desean esquiar…
9. Si estoy de vacaciones…
10. Si tengo ganas de leer…

5 **Encuesta** Your instructor will give you a worksheet. Walk around the class and ask your classmates if they are going to do these activities today. Find one person to answer **Sí** and one to answer **No** for each item and note their names on the worksheet in the appropriate column. Be prepared to report your findings to the class. Answers will vary.

modelo

Tú: ¿Vas a leer el periódico hoy?
Ana: Sí, voy a leer el periódico hoy.
Luis: No, no voy a leer el periódico hoy.

Actividades	Sí	No
1. comer en un restaurante chino		
2. leer el periódico	Ana	Luis
3. escribir un mensaje electrónico		
4. correr 20 kilómetros		
5. ver una película de terror		
6. pasear en bicicleta		

6 **Entrevista** Talk to two classmates in order to find out where they are going and what they are going to do on their next vacation. Answers will vary.

modelo

Estudiante 1: ¿Adónde vas de vacaciones (*on vacation*)?
Estudiante 2: Voy a Guadalajara con mis amigos.
Estudiante 3: ¿Y qué van a hacer (*to do*) ustedes en Guadalajara?
Estudiante 2: Vamos a visitar unos monumentos y museos. ¿Y tú?

Síntesis

NATIONAL communication STANDARDS

7 **Planes** Make a schedule of your activities for the weekend. Then, share with a partner. Answers will vary.

- For each day, list at least three things you have to do.
- For each day, list at least two things you will do for fun.
- Tell a classmate what your weekend schedule is like. He or she will write down what you say.
- Switch roles to see if you have any plans in common.
- Take turns asking each other to participate in some of the activities you listed.

TEACHING OPTIONS

Pairs Write these times on the board: **8:00 a.m., 12:00 p.m., 12:45 p.m., 4:00 p.m., 6:00 p.m., 10:00 p.m.** Have student pairs take turns reading a time and suggesting an appropriate activity or place. Ex: **E1: Son las ocho de la mañana. E2: Vamos a correr./Vamos al gimnasio.**

Game Divide the class into teams. Name a category (Ex: **lugares públicos**) and set a time limit of two minutes. The first team member will write down one answer on a piece of paper and pass it to the next person. The paper will continue to be passed from student to student until the two minutes are up. The team with the most words wins.

Video Show the **Fotonovela** episode again to give students more input containing the verb **ir**. Stop the video where appropriate to discuss how **ir** is used to express different ideas.

4.2 Stem-changing verbs: e→ie, o→ue

Tutorial

NATIONAL STANDARDS comparisons

ANTE TODO Stem-changing verbs deviate from the normal pattern of regular verbs. When stem-changing verbs are conjugated, they have a vowel change in the last syllable of the stem.

INFINITIVE	VERB STEM	STEM CHANGE	CONJUGATED FORM
empezar	empez-	empiez-	empi**e**zo
volver	volv-	vuelv-	vu**e**lvo

CONSULTA

To review the present tense of regular **-ar** verbs, see **Estructura 2.1**, p. 46.

To review the present tense of regular **-er** and **-ir** verbs, see **Estructura 3.3**, p. 88.

▶ In many verbs, such as **empezar** (*to begin*), the stem vowel changes from **e** to **ie**. Note that the **nosotros/as** and **vosotros/as** forms don't have a stem change.

The verb empezar (e:ie) (*to begin*)

Singular forms		Plural forms	
yo	emp**ie**zo	nosotros/as	empezamos
tú	emp**ie**zas	vosotros/as	empezáis
Ud./él/ella	emp**ie**za	Uds./ellos/ellas	emp**ie**zan

Los chicos empiezan a hablar de su visita al cenote.

Ellos vuelven a comer en el restaurante.

▶ In many other verbs, such as **volver** (*to return*), the stem vowel changes from **o** to **ue**. The **nosotros/as** and **vosotros/as** forms have no stem change.

The verb volver (o:ue) (*to return*)

Singular forms		Plural forms	
yo	v**ue**lvo	nosotros/as	volvemos
tú	v**ue**lves	vosotros/as	volvéis
Ud./él/ella	v**ue**lve	Uds./ellos/ellas	v**ue**lven

▶ To help you identify stem-changing verbs, they will appear as follows throughout the text:

empezar (e:ie), volver (o:ue)

Section Goals

In **Estructura 4.2**, students will be introduced to:
- present tense of stem-changing verbs: **e → ie**; **o → ue**
- common stem-changing verbs

Instructional Resources

Supersite: Audio (Lab MP3 Files); Resources (Grammar Presentation Slides, Activity Pack, Scripts, Answer Keys); Testing Program (Quizzes)
WebSAM
Workbook, pp. 41–42
Lab Manual, p. 22

Teaching Tips

- Take a survey of students' habits. Ask: **¿Quiénes empiezan las clases a las ocho?** Make a chart with students' names on the board. Ask: **¿Quiénes vuelven a casa a las seis?** Then create sentences based on the chart. Ex: **Tú vuelves a casa a las siete, pero Amanda vuelve a las seis. Daniel y yo volvemos a las cinco.**
- Copy the forms of **empezar** and **volver** on the board. Reiterate that the personal endings for the present tense of all the verbs listed in **Estructura 4.2** are the same as those for the present tense of regular **–ar**, **–er**, and **–ir** verbs.
- Explain that an easy way to remember which forms of these verbs have stem changes is to think of them as boot verbs. Draw a line around the stem-changing forms in each paradigm to show the boot-like shape.

TEACHING OPTIONS

Extra Practice Write a pattern sentence on the board. Ex: **Ella empieza una carta**. Have students write down the model, and then dictate a list of subjects (Ex: **Carmen, nosotras, don Miguel**), pausing after each one to allow students to write a complete sentence using the model verb. Ask volunteers to read their sentences aloud.

Heritage Speakers Ask heritage speakers to work in pairs to write a mock interview with a Spanish-speaking celebrity such as **Lorena Ochoa, Salma Hayek, Manu Ginóbili,** or **Benicio del Toro,** in which they use the verbs **empezar, volver, querer,** and **recordar**. Ask them to role-play their interview for the class, who will write down the forms of **empezar, volver, querer,** and **recordar** that they hear.

Teaching Tips

- Write **e:ie** and **o:ue** on the board and explain that some very common verbs have these types of stem changes. Point out that all the verbs listed are conjugated like **empezar** or **volver**. Model the pronunciation of the verbs and ask students a few questions using verbs of each type. Have them answer in complete sentences. Ex: **¿A qué hora cierra la biblioteca? ¿Duermen los estudiantes hasta tarde, por lo general? ¿Qué piensan hacer este fin de semana? ¿Quién quiere comer en un restaurante esta noche?**
- Point out the structure **jugar al** used with sports. Practice it by asking students about the sports they play. Have them answer in complete sentences. Ex: ____, **¿te gusta jugar al fútbol? Y tú,** ____, **¿juegas al fútbol? ¿Prefieres jugar al fútbol o ver un partido en el estadio? ¿Cuántos juegan al tenis? ¿Qué prefieres,** ____, **jugar al tenis o jugar al fútbol?**
- Prepare a few dehydrated sentences. Ex: **Raúl / empezar / la lección; ustedes / mostrar / los trabajos; nosotros / jugar / al fútbol** Write them on the board one at a time, and ask students to form complete sentences based on the cues.

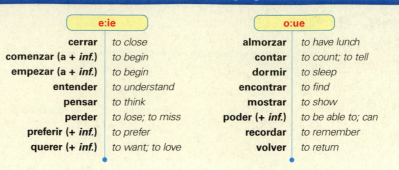

Common stem-changing verbs

e:ie		o:ue	
cerrar	*to close*	**almorzar**	*to have lunch*
comenzar (a + *inf.*)	*to begin*	**contar**	*to count; to tell*
empezar (a + *inf.*)	*to begin*	**dormir**	*to sleep*
entender	*to understand*	**encontrar**	*to find*
pensar	*to think*	**mostrar**	*to show*
perder	*to lose; to miss*	**poder (+ *inf.*)**	*to be able to; can*
preferir (+ *inf.*)	*to prefer*	**recordar**	*to remember*
querer (+ *inf.*)	*to want; to love*	**volver**	*to return*

¡LENGUA VIVA!

The verb **perder** can mean *to lose* or *to miss*, in the sense of "to miss a train."

Siempre pierdo mis llaves.
I always lose my keys.

Es importante no perder el autobús.
It's important not to miss the bus.

▶ **Jugar** (*to play a sport or a game*) is the only Spanish verb that has a **u:ue** stem change. **Jugar** is followed by **a** + [*definite article*] when the name of a sport or game is mentioned.

Ella juega al tenis y al golf.

Los chicos juegan al fútbol.

▶ **Comenzar** and **empezar** require the preposition **a** when they are followed by an infinitive.

Comienzan a jugar a las siete.
They begin playing at seven.

Ana **empieza a** escribir una postal.
Ana is starting to write a postcard.

▶ **Pensar** + [*infinitive*] means *to plan* or *to intend to do something*. **Pensar en** means *to think about someone* or *something*.

¿**Piensan** ir al gimnasio?
Are you planning to go to the gym?

¿**En** qué **piensas**?
What are you thinking about?

¡INTÉNTALO!

Provide the present tense forms of these verbs.

cerrar (e:ie)

1. Ustedes cierran.
2. Tú cierras.
3. Nosotras cerramos.
4. Mi hermano cierra.
5. Yo cierro.
6. Usted cierra.
7. Los chicos cierran.
8. Ella cierra.

dormir (o:ue)

1. Mi abuela no duerme.
2. Yo no duermo.
3. Tú no duermes.
4. Mis hijos no duermen.
5. Usted no duerme.
6. Nosotros no dormimos.
7. Él no duerme.
8. Ustedes no duermen.

recursos
WB pp. 41–42
LM p. 22
vhlcentral.com Lección 4

TEACHING OPTIONS

TPR Add an auditory aspect to this grammar presentation. At random, call out infinitives of regular and **e:ie** stem-changing verbs. Have students raise their hands if the verb has a stem change. Repeat for **o:ue** stem-changing verbs.

Extra Practice For additional drills of stem-changing verbs, do the **¡Inténtalo!** activity orally using infinitives other than **cerrar** and **dormir**. Keep a brisk pace.

TPR Have the class stand in a circle. As you toss a ball to a student, call out the infinitive of a stem-changing verb, followed by a pronoun. (Ex: **querer, tú**) The student should say the appropriate verb form (**quieres**), then name a different pronoun (Ex: **usted**) and throw the ball to another student. When all subject pronouns have been covered, start over with another infinitive.

Práctica

1

Completar Complete this conversation with the appropriate forms of the verbs. Then act it out with a partner.

PABLO Óscar, voy al centro ahora.
ÓSCAR ¿A qué hora (1) piensas (pensar) volver? El partido de fútbol (2) empieza (empezar) a las dos.
PABLO (3) Vuelvo (Volver) a la una. (4) Quiero (Querer) ver el partido.
ÓSCAR (5)¿ Recuerdas (Recordar) que (*that*) nuestro equipo es muy bueno? (6)¡ Puede (Poder) ganar!
PABLO No, (7) pienso (pensar) que va a (8) perder (perder). Los jugadores de Guadalajara son salvajes (*wild*) cuando (9) juegan (jugar).

2

Preferencias With a partner, take turns asking and answering questions about what these people want to do, using the cues provided.

modelo
Guillermo: estudiar / pasear en bicicleta
Estudiante 1: *¿Quiere estudiar Guillermo?*
Estudiante 2: *No, prefiere pasear en bicicleta.*

1. tú: trabajar / dormir
   ¿Quieres trabajar? No, prefiero dormir.
2. ustedes: mirar la televisión / jugar al dominó
   ¿Quieren ustedes mirar la televisión? No, preferimos jugar al dominó.
3. tus amigos: ir de excursión / descansar
   ¿Quieren ir de excursión tus amigos? No, mis amigos prefieren descansar.
4. tú: comer en la cafetería / ir a un restaurante
   ¿Quieres comer en la cafetería? No, prefiero ir a un restaurante.
5. Elisa: ver una película / leer una revista
   ¿Quiere ver una película Elisa? No, prefiere leer una revista.
6. María y su hermana: tomar el sol / practicar el esquí acuático
   ¿Quieren tomar el sol María y su hermana? No, prefieren practicar el esquí acuático.

NOTA CULTURAL

Dominó (*Dominoes*) is a popular pastime throughout Colombia, Venezuela, Central America, and the Spanish-speaking countries of the Caribbean. It's played both socially and competitively by people of all ages.

3

Describir Use a verb from the list to describe what these people are doing.

almorzar cerrar contar dormir encontrar mostrar

1. las niñas Las niñas duermen.

2. yo (Yo) Cierro la ventana.

3. nosotros (Nosotros) Almorzamos.

4. tú (Tú) Encuentras una maleta.

5. Pedro Pedro muestra una foto.

6. Teresa Teresa cuenta.

Practice more at **vhlcentral.com**.

1 Teaching Tip Divide the class into pairs and give them three minutes to role-play the conversation. Then have partners switch roles. Encourage students to ad-lib as they go.

1 Expansion
- To challenge students, supply them with short-answer prompts based on the conversation. They should provide questions that would elicit the answers. Ex: **A las dos. (¿A qué hora empieza el partido de fútbol?) Porque quiere ver el partido. (¿Por qué vuelve Pablo a la una?)**
- Ask questions using **pensar** + [*infinitive*], **pensar en,** and **perder** (in both senses). Ex: **¿Qué piensas hacer mañana? ¿En qué piensas ahora? ¿Cuándo pierdes las cosas?**

2 Teaching Tip To challenge students, have **Estudiante 2** be creative and use other stem-changing verbs in their responses. For example, in the model, **Estudiante 2** could also respond: **No, no puede porque va a pasear en bicicleta** or **No, porque piensa pasear en bicicleta.**

2 Expansion Have students ask each other questions of their own using the same pattern. Ex: **—¿Quieres jugar al baloncesto? —No, prefiero jugar al tenis. —¿Por qué? —¡Porque no puedo encontrar la pelota de baloncesto!**

3 Expansion Bring in photos or magazine pictures to extend this activity. Choose images that are easy to describe with common stem-changing verbs.

TEACHING OPTIONS

TPR Brainstorm gestures for stem-changing verbs. Have students act out the activity you mention. Tell them that only male students should respond to **él/ellos** and only females to **ella/ellas**. Everyone should respond to **nosotros**.

Game Arrange students in rows of five (or six if you use **vosotros**). Give the first person in each row a piece of paper and tell the class they should be silent while they are completing this activity. Call out the infinitive of a stem-changing verb. The first person writes down the **yo** form and gives the paper to the next student, who writes the **tú** form and passes the paper on. The last person in the row holds up the paper and says, **¡Terminamos!** The first team to finish the conjugation correctly gets a point. Have students rotate positions in their row before calling out another infinitive.

4 Teaching Tip Model the activity by asking questions about famous people. Ex: **¿Con qué frecuencia juega al fútbol americano Tom Brady?** Write the answers on the board.

4 Expansion After tallying results on the board, have students work in pairs to graph them. Have them refer to **Lectura,** pages 134–135, for models.

5 Teaching Tips
- Model the activity by stating two programs from the listing that you want to watch and asking the class to react.
- Remind students that the 24-hour clock is often used for schedules. Model a few of the program times. Then ask: **Quiero ver *Héroes* y mi amigo prefiere ver *Elsa y Fred*. ¿Hay un conflicto? (No.) ¿Por qué? (Porque *Héroes* es a las 15:00 y *Elsa y Fred* es a las 22:00.)** Give students the option of answering with the 12-hour clock.

5 Expansion First, guide students in identifying the shows and movies that have versions in English: **Yo soy Betty, la fea; Héroes; Hermanos y hermanas; El padrastro; 60 Minutos**. Then, have students personalize the activity by choosing their favorite programs from the list. Divide the class into pairs and have them compare and contrast their reasons for their choices.

6 Teaching Tip Divide the class into pairs and distribute the handouts from the Activity Pack (Activity Pack/Supersite) that correspond to this Information Gap Activity.

6 Expansion Have volunteers take turns completing the information in the puzzle. Then have students invent their own stories, using stem-changing verbs, about what happens to the same group of tourists.

Comunicación

National communication Standards

4 **Frecuencia** In pairs, take turns using the verbs from the list and other stem-changing verbs you know to tell your partner which activities you do daily (**todos los días**), which you do once a month (**una vez al mes**), and which you do once a year (**una vez al año**). Record your partner's responses in the chart so that you can report back to the class. Answers will vary.

modelo

Estudiante 1: *Yo recuerdo a mi familia todos los días.*
Estudiante 2: *Yo pierdo uno de mis libros una vez al año.*

cerrar	perder
dormir	poder
empezar	preferir
encontrar	querer
jugar	recordar
¿?	¿?

todos los días	una vez al mes	una vez al año

5 **En la televisión** Read the television listings for Saturday. In pairs, write a conversation between two siblings arguing about what to watch. Be creative and be prepared to act out your conversation for the class. Answers will vary.

modelo

Hermano: *Podemos ver la Copa Mundial.*
Hermana: *¡No, no quiero ver la Copa Mundial! Prefiero ver...*

	13:00	14:00	15:00	16:00	17:00	18:00	19:00	20:00	21:00	22:00	23:00
7	Copa Mundial (*World Cup*) de fútbol			República Deportiva		Campeonato (*Championship*) Mundial de Vóleibol: México-Argentina				Torneo de Natación	
8	Abierto (*Open*) Mexicano de Tenis: Santiago González (México) vs. Nicolás Almagro (España). Semifinales			Campeonato de baloncesto: Los Correcaminos de Tampico vs. los Santos de San Luis				Aficionados al buceo		Cozumel: Aventuras	
12	Yo soy Betty, la fea		Héroes	Hermanos y hermanas			Película: **Sin nombre**		Película: **El coronel no tiene quien le escriba**		
13	El padrastro		60 Minutos				El esquí acuático			Patinaje artístico	
17	Biografías: La artista Frida Kahlo			Música de la semana			Entrevista del día: Iker Casillas y su pasión por el fútbol			Cine de la noche: **Elsa y Fred**	

NOTA CULTURAL

Iker Casillas Fernández is a famous goalkeeper for **Real Madrid**. A native of Madrid, he is among the best goalkeepers of his generation.

Síntesis

National communication Standards

6 **Situación** Your instructor will give you and your partner each a partially illustrated itinerary of a city tour. Complete the itineraries by asking each other questions using the verbs in the captions and vocabulary you have learned. Answers will vary.

modelo

Estudiante 1: *Por la mañana, empiezan en el café.*
Estudiante 2: *Y luego...*

TEACHING OPTIONS

Small Groups Have students choose their favorite pastime and work in small groups with other students who have chosen that same activity. Have each group write six sentences about the activity, using a different stem-changing verb in each.

Pairs Ask students to write incomplete dehydrated sentences (only subjects and infinitives) about people and groups at the university. Ex: **el equipo de béisbol / perder / ¿?** Then have them exchange papers with a classmate, who will form a complete sentence by conjugating the verb and inventing an appropriate ending. Ask volunteers to write sentences on the board.

4.3 Stem-changing verbs: e→i

Tutorial

NATIONAL STANDARDS comparisons

ANTE TODO You've already seen that many verbs in Spanish change their stem vowel when conjugated. There is a third kind of stem-vowel change in some verbs, such as **pedir** (*to ask for; to request*). In these verbs, the stressed vowel in the stem changes from **e** to **i**, as shown in the diagram.

INFINITIVE	VERB STEM	STEM CHANGE	CONJUGATED FORM
pedir	ped-	pid-	pido

▶ As with other stem-changing verbs you have learned, there is no stem change in the **nosotros/as** or **vosotros/as** forms in the present tense.

The verb pedir (e:i) (*to ask for; to request*)

Singular forms		Plural forms	
yo	pido	nosotros/as	pedimos
tú	pides	vosotros/as	pedís
Ud./él/ella	pide	Uds./ellos/ellas	piden

▶ To help you identify verbs with the **e:i** stem change, they will appear as follows throughout the text:

pedir (e:i)

▶ These are the most common **e:i** stem-changing verbs:

conseguir	**decir**	**repetir**	**seguir**
to get; to obtain	*to say; to tell*	*to repeat*	*to follow; to continue; to keep (doing something)*

Pido favores cuando es necesario.
I ask for favors when it's necessary.

Javier **dice** la verdad.
Javier is telling the truth.

Sigue con su tarea.
He continues with his homework.

Consiguen ver buenas películas.
They get to see good movies.

▶ **¡Atención!** The verb **decir** is irregular in its **yo** form: **yo digo**.

▶ The **yo** forms of **seguir** and **conseguir** have a spelling change in addition to the stem change **e:i**.

Sigo su plan.
I'm following their plan.

Consigo novelas en la librería.
I get novels at the bookstore.

¡LENGUA VIVA!

As you learned in **Lección 2, preguntar** means *to ask a question.* **Pedir,** however, means *to ask for something:*

Ella me pregunta cuántos años tengo.
She asks me how old I am.

Él me pide ayuda.
He asks me for help.

recursos

WB pp. 43–44

LM p. 23

vhlcentral.com Lección 4

¡INTÉNTALO! Provide the correct forms of the verbs.

repetir (e:i)

1. Arturo y Eva ___repiten___.
2. Yo ___repito___.
3. Nosotros ___repetimos___.
4. Julia ___repite___.
5. Sofía y yo ___repetimos___.

decir (e:i)

1. Yo ___digo___.
2. Él ___dice___.
3. Tú ___dices___.
4. Usted ___dice___.
5. Ellas ___dicen___.

seguir (e:i)

1. Yo ___sigo___.
2. Nosotros ___seguimos___.
3. Tú ___sigues___.
4. Los chicos ___siguen___.
5. Usted ___sigue___.

Section Goal

In **Estructura 4.3**, students will learn the present tense of stem-changing verbs: **e → i**.

Instructional Resources

Supersite: Audio (Lab MP3 Files); Resources (Grammar Presentation Slides, Activity Pack, Scripts, Answer Keys); Testing Program (Quizzes)
WebSAM
Workbook, pp. 43–44
Lab Manual, p. 23

Teaching Tips

- Take a survey of students' habits. Ask questions like: **¿Quiénes piden *Coca-Cola*?** Make a chart on the board. Then form sentences based on the chart.
- Ask volunteers to answer questions using **conseguir**, **decir**, **pedir**, **repetir**, and **seguir**.
- Reiterate that the personal endings for the present tense of all the verbs listed are the same as those for the present tense of regular **–ir** verbs.
- Point out the spelling changes in the **yo** forms of **seguir** and **conseguir**.
- Prepare dehydrated sentences and write them on the board one at a time. Ex: **1. tú / pedir / café 2. usted / repetir / la pregunta 3. nosotros / decir / la verdad** Have students form complete sentences based on the cues.
- For additional drills with stem-changing verbs, do the **¡Inténtalo!** activity orally using other infinitives, such as **conseguir**, **impedir**, **pedir**, and **servir**. Keep a brisk pace.

Note: Students will learn more about **decir** with indirect object pronouns in **Estructura 6.2**.

TEACHING OPTIONS

Game Divide the class into two teams. Name an infinitive and a subject pronoun (Ex: **decir / yo**). Have the first member of team A give the appropriate conjugated form of the verb. If the team member answers correctly, team A gets one point. If not, give the first member of team B the same example. If he or she does not know the answer, give the correct verb form and move on. The team with the most points at the end wins.

Extra Practice Add a visual aspect to this grammar presentation. Bring in magazine pictures or photos of parks and city centers where people are doing fun activities. In small groups, have students describe the photos using as many stem-changing verbs from **Estructura 4.2** and **4.3** as they can. Give points to the groups who use the most stem-changing verbs.

1 Expansion Have students use **conseguir, decir, pedir, repetir,** and **seguir** to write sentences about their own family members. Then have them exchange papers with a partner for peer editing.

Nota cultural Have students read about **El Bosque de Chapultepec** in Spanish in either the library or on the Internet and bring a photo of the park to class. Ask them to share one new fact they learned about the park.

2 Teaching Tips

- Before beginning the activity, point out that not all verbs in column B have an **e:i** stem change. Have students identify those that do not (**poder, dormir, perder**).
- In pairs, have students decide which activities in column B are characteristic of a good student. Ex: **Un buen estudiante repite el vocabulario.**

2 Expansion In pairs, have students read their sentences aloud. Their partner must decide if they are true or false.

3 Teaching Tip Remind students that their partners may guess information that is true, but not necessarily what they wrote for **Actividad 2**.

4 Teaching Tip As you check answers, ask follow-up questions so that students provide more details.

Práctica

1 Completar Complete these sentences with the correct form of the verb provided.

1. Cuando mi familia pasea por la ciudad, mi madre siempre (*always*) va a un café y ___pide___ (pedir) una soda.
2. Pero mi padre ___dice___ (decir) que perdemos mucho tiempo. Tiene prisa por llegar al Bosque de Chapultepec.
3. Mi padre tiene suerte, porque él siempre ___consigue___ (conseguir) lo que (*that which*) desea.
4. Cuando llegamos al parque, mis hermanos y yo ___seguimos___ (seguir) conversando (*talking*) con nuestros padres.
5. Mis padres siempre ___repiten___ (repetir) la misma cosa: "Nosotros tomamos el sol aquí sin ustedes".
6. Yo siempre ___pido___ (pedir) permiso para volver a casa un poco más tarde porque me gusta mucho el parque.

NOTA CULTURAL

A popular weekend destination for residents and tourists, **el Bosque de Chapultepec** is a beautiful park located in Mexico City. It occupies over 2.5 square miles and includes lakes, several wooded areas, several museums, and a botanical garden. You may recognize this park from **Fotonovela, Lección 2.**

2 Combinar Combine words from the two columns to create sentences about yourself and people you know. Answers will vary.

A	B
yo	(no) pedir muchos favores
mi compañero/a de cuarto	nunca (*never*) pedir perdón
mi mejor (*best*) amigo/a	nunca seguir las instrucciones
mi familia	siempre seguir las instrucciones
mis amigos/as	conseguir libros en Internet
mis amigos/as y yo	repetir el vocabulario
mis padres	poder hablar dos lenguas
mi hermano/a	dormir hasta el mediodía
mi profesor(a) de español	siempre perder sus libros

3 Opiniones In pairs, take turns guessing how your partner completed the sentences from **Actividad 2**. If you guess incorrectly, your partner must supply the correct answer. Answers will vary.

modelo

Estudiante 1: Creo que tus padres consiguen libros en Internet.
Estudiante 2: ¡No! Mi hermana consigue libros en Internet.

CONSULTA

To review possessive adjectives, see **Estructura 3.2**, p. 85.

4 ¿Quién? Your instructor will give you a worksheet. Talk to your classmates until you find one person who does each of the activities. Use **e:ie**, **o:ue**, and **e:i** stem-changing verbs.

modelo

Tú: ¿Pides consejos con frecuencia?
Maira: No, no pido consejos con frecuencia.
Tú: ¿Pides consejos con frecuencia?
Lucas: Sí, pido consejos con frecuencia.

Practice more at **vhlcentral.com**.

TEACHING OPTIONS

Pairs Ask students to write four simple statements using **e:i** verbs. Then have them read their sentences to a partner, who will guess where the situation takes place. Ex: **Consigo libros para las clases. (Estás en la biblioteca.)** Then reverse the activity, allowing them to answer with verbs from **Estructura 4.2**.

Small Groups Explain to students that movie titles for English-language films are frequently not directly translated into Spanish and that titles may vary from country to country. Bring in a list of movie titles in Spanish. Ex: ***La guerra de las galaxias*** (*Star Wars*); ***Lo que el viento se llevó*** (*Gone with the Wind*). In groups, have students guess the movies based on the Spanish titles. Then ask them to state which movies they'd prefer to watch.

Comunicación

5 **Las películas** Use these questions to interview a classmate. Answers will vary.

1. ¿Prefieres las películas románticas, las películas de acción o las películas de terror? ¿Por qué?
2. ¿Dónde consigues información sobre (*about*) cine y televisión?
3. ¿Dónde consigues las entradas (*tickets*) para ver una película?
4. Para decidir qué películas vas a ver, ¿sigues las recomendaciones de los críticos de cine? ¿Qué dicen los críticos en general?
5. ¿Qué cines en tu comunidad muestran las mejores (*best*) películas?
6. ¿Vas a ver una película esta semana? ¿A qué hora empieza la película?

Síntesis

6 **El cine** In pairs, first scan the ad and jot down all the stem-changing verbs. Then answer the questions. Be prepared to share your answers with the class. Answers will vary.

1. ¿Qué palabras indican que *Gravity* es una película dramática?
2. ¿Cómo está el personaje (*character*) del póster? ¿Qué quiere hacer?
3. ¿Te gustan las películas como ésta (*this one*)? ¿Por qué?
4. Describe tu película favorita con los verbos de la **Lección 4**. Answers will vary.

★★★★★

Ganadora de siete premios Óscar

Cuando todo comienza a fallar, ellos no pierden la esperanza.

Del director de Hijos de los hombres y Harry Potter y el prisionero de Azkaban

Un accidente espacial deja a Ryan Stone y Matt Kowalski atrapados en el espacio. Sólo quieren una cosa: seguir vivos.

¿Consiguen sobrevivir? ¿Vuelven finalmente a la Tierra?

5 Teaching Tips
- Have students report to the class what their partner said. After the presentation, encourage them to ask each other questions.
- Take a class poll to find out students' film genre and local movie theater preferences.

5 Expansion To challenge students, write some key movie-related words on the board, such as **actor, actriz, argumento,** and **efectos especiales.** Explain how to use **mejor** and **peor** as adjectives. Have student pairs say which movies this year they think should win Oscars. Model by telling them: **Pienso que____ es la mejor película del año. Debe ganar porque...** Then ask students to nominate the year's worst. Have them share their opinions with the class.

6 Teaching Tips
- Write the stem-changing verbs from the ad on the board. Have students conjugate the verbs using different subjects.
- Go over student responses to item 4.

6 Expansion In pairs, have students use the verbs from the ad to write a dramatic dialogue. Have volunteers role-play their dialogues for the class.

TEACHING OPTIONS

Small Groups Select a few scenes from different Spanish-language films or plays that contain stem-changing verbs. White out the verbs and have students work in small groups to complete each dialogue. Ask them to try to identify the genre and, if possible, the title of each work. Then have volunteers act out each scene for the class, ad-libbing as appropriate.

Heritage Speakers Ask heritage speakers to start a discussion with the rest of the class about popular Spanish-language films. Brainstorm with the class a list of questions about the films, using stem-changing verbs from **Estructura 4.2** and **4.3**. Have students ask the heritage speakers the questions. Ex: **¿Dónde podemos conseguir la película aquí? ¿Dices que es tu película favorita? ¿Prefieres las películas en inglés?**

Section Goal

In **Estructura 4.4**, students will learn verbs with irregular **yo** forms.

Instructional Resources
Supersite: Audio (Lab MP3 Files); Resources (Grammar Presentation Slides, Activity Pack, Scripts, Answer Keys); Testing Program (Quizzes)
WebSAM
Workbook, pp. 45–46
Lab Manual, p. 24

Teaching Tips
- Quickly review the present tense of **decir, tener,** and **venir,** pointing out the **–go** ending of the **yo** forms.
- Ask specific students questions to elicit the **yo** forms of the verbs. Ex: **María, ¿haces la tarea en casa o en la biblioteca? (Hago la tarea en la biblioteca.) ¿Traes un diccionario a clase? (Sí, traigo un diccionario a clase.)** As students respond, write the verbs on the board until you have listed all the irregular **yo** forms.
- Go over the uses of **salir.** Model an additional example of each use.
- You may want to tell students that in many Latin American countries (e.g., Mexico, Venezuela, Colombia, and Peru), the verb **prender** is used to express *to turn on an electrical device or appliance.*

NATIONAL STANDARDS comparisons

4.4 Verbs with irregular yo forms

S Tutorial

ANTE TODO In Spanish, several verbs have irregular **yo** forms in the present tense. You have already seen three verbs with the **-go** ending in the **yo** form: **decir → digo, tener → tengo,** and **venir → vengo.**

▶ Here are some common expressions with **decir.**

decir la verdad *to tell the truth*	**decir mentiras** *to tell lies*
decir que *to say that*	**decir la respuesta** *to say the answer*

▶ The verb **hacer** is often used to ask questions about what someone does. Note that when answering, **hacer** is frequently replaced with another, more specific action verb.

Verbs with irregular yo forms

	hacer (to do; to make)	**poner** (to put; to place)	**salir** (to leave)	**suponer** (to suppose)	**traer** (to bring)
SINGULAR FORMS	**hago**	**pongo**	**salgo**	**supongo**	**traigo**
	haces	pones	sales	supones	traes
	hace	pone	sale	supone	trae
PLURAL FORMS	hacemos	ponemos	salimos	suponemos	traemos
	hacéis	ponéis	salís	suponéis	traéis
	hacen	ponen	salen	suponen	traen

Salgo mucho los fines de semana.

Yo no salgo, yo hago la tarea y veo películas en la televisión.

▶ **Poner** can also mean to *turn on* a household appliance.

Carlos **pone** la radio. *Carlos turns on the radio.*	María **pone** la televisión. *María turns on the television.*

▶ **Salir de** is used to indicate that someone is leaving a particular place.

Hoy **salgo del** hospital. *Today I leave the hospital.*	**Sale de** la clase a las cuatro. *He leaves class at four.*

TEACHING OPTIONS

TPR Have students act out actions as you make statements with irregular **yo** forms. Ex: **Hago la tarea.** (Students imitate writing their homework.) **Pongo la radio.** (They imitate turning on a radio.)

Game Divide the class into teams of three. Each team has a piece of paper. Call out an infinitive and a person. Ex: **traer / primera persona plural.** Each team has to compose a sentence, with each member writing one part. The first team member thinks of an appropriate subject or proper name and writes it down (Ex: **nosotras**). The second writes the correct form of the verb (Ex: **traemos**). The third completes the sentence in a logical way (Ex: **el libro**). The first team to write a logical and correct sentence wins. Team members should rotate positions each time a new verb is given.

▶ **Salir para** is used to indicate someone's destination.

Mañana **salgo para** México. *Tomorrow I leave for Mexico.*	Hoy **salen para** España. *Today they leave for Spain.*

▶ **Salir con** means *to leave with someone* or *something*, or *to date someone*.

Alberto **sale con** su mochila. *Alberto is leaving with his backpack.*	Margarita **sale con** Guillermo. *Margarita is going out with Guillermo.*

The verbs ver and oír

▶ The verb **ver** (*to see*) has an irregular **yo** form. The other forms of **ver** are regular.

The verb ver (*to see*)

Singular forms		Plural forms	
yo	**veo**	nosotros/as	vemos
tú	ves	vosotros/as	veis
Ud./él/ella	ve	Uds./ellos/ellas	ven

▶ The verb **oír** (*to hear*) has an irregular **yo** form and the spelling change **i:y** in the **tú**, **usted/él/ella**, and **ustedes/ellos/ellas** forms. The **nosotros/as** and **vosotros/as** forms have an accent mark.

The verb oír (*to hear*)

Singular forms		Plural forms	
yo	**oigo**	nosotros/as	o**í**mos
tú	o**y**es	vosotros/as	o**í**s
Ud./él/ella	o**y**e	Uds./ellos/ellas	o**y**en

▶ While most commonly translated as *to hear*, **oír** is also used in contexts where the verb *to listen* would be used in English.

Oigo a unas personas en la otra sala. *I hear some people in the other room.*	¿**Oyes** la radio por la mañana? *Do you listen to the radio in the morning?*

recursos
WB pp. 45–46
LM p. 24
vhlcentral.com Lección 4

¡INTÉNTALO! Provide the appropriate forms of these verbs.

1. salir	Isabel sale.	Nosotros salimos.	Yo salgo.
2. ver	Yo veo.	Uds. ven.	Tú ves.
3. poner	Rita y yo ponemos.	Yo pongo.	Los niños ponen.
4. hacer	Yo hago.	Tú haces.	Ud. hace.
5. oír	Él oye.	Nosotros oímos.	Yo oigo.
6. traer	Ellas traen.	Yo traigo.	Tú traes.
7. suponer	Yo supongo.	Mi amigo supone.	Nosotras suponemos.

TEACHING OPTIONS

Extra Practice Add an auditory aspect to this grammar presentation. Call out subject pronouns and titles of songs or movies (Ex: **ustedes, *Gravedad***). Have students respond with a complete sentence, using **ver** or **oír**. (Ex: **Ustedes ven *Gravedad*.**)

Pairs Have pairs create questions using the vocabulary of the chapter to ask each other about their habits. Ex: **¿Sales a comer a restaurantes con tus amigos? ¿Ves la televisión en español? ¿Supones que una clase de matemáticas es muy difícil?** Have students record their partner's answers and be prepared to share the information with the class.

Teaching Tips

- Point out that **oír** is irregular in all forms. Write a model sentence on the board. Ex: **Ustedes oyen el programa de radio todos los viernes.** Then change the subject, and have students give the new sentence. Ex: **tú (Tú oyes el programa de radio todos los viernes.)**
- Call out different forms of the verbs in **Estructura 4.4** and have volunteers say the infinitive. Ex: **oyen (oír)**. Keep a brisk pace.
- Do a chain drill. Start by writing **¿Qué haces los sábados?** on the board. Model an appropriate answer, such as **Salgo con mis amigos**. Ask one student to respond (Ex: **Veo una película.**). The next student you call on should repeat what the first said and add on (Ex: **Cindy ve una película y yo salgo con...**). Continue until the chain becomes too long; then start with a new question. Keep a brisk pace.
- Write these phrases on the board: **ver la tele, traer un sándwich a la universidad, salir con amigos**, and **hacer yoga**. Model the question and possible answers for each phrase. Then elicit follow-up questions (Ex: **¿Dónde ves la tele?**). Have student pairs take turns asking and answering the questions. They should be prepared to report to the class about their partners' habits.
- Explain to students that the **i → y** spelling change strengthens the **i** sound between vowels, which clarifies to the ear that the verb is **oír**.
- Explain the difference between **escuchar** (*to listen*) and **oír** (*to hear*). Ex: **Escucho la radio. No oigo el perro.**

1 Teaching Tip Quickly review the new verbs with irregular **yo** forms. Then, ask pairs to complete and role-play the conversation, encouraging them to ad-lib as they go.

1 Expansion In pairs, have students write a conversation between **David** and **Luisa** as they are waiting for the movie to start. Have volunteers act out their conversations for the class.

2 Teaching Tip To simplify, lead the class to identify key words in each sentence. Then have students choose the infinitive that best fits with the key words and name any missing words for each item. After students complete the activity individually, have volunteers write the sentences on the board.

2 Expansion
- Change the subjects of the dehydrated sentences in the activity and have students write or say aloud the new sentences.
- Ask students to form questions that would elicit the statements in **Actividad 2**. Ex: **¿Qué hago antes de salir?**
- Have students write three sentences, each using a verb from **Estructura 4.4**. Then ask them to copy their sentences onto a sheet of paper in dehydrated form, following the model of **Actividad 2**. Students should exchange papers with a partner, who writes the complete sentences. Finally, have partners check each other's work.

3 Expansion Use magazine pictures which elicit the target verbs to extend the activity. Encourage students to add further descriptions if they can.

Práctica

1 **Completar** Complete this conversation with the appropriate forms of the verbs. Then act it out with a partner.

ERNESTO David, ¿qué (1) haces (hacer) hoy?
DAVID Ahora estudio biología, pero esta noche (2) salgo (salir) con Luisa. Vamos al cine. Los críticos (3) dicen (decir) que la nueva (*new*) película de Almodóvar es buena.
ERNESTO ¿Y Diana? ¿Qué (4) hace (hacer) ella?
DAVID (5) Sale (Salir) a comer con sus padres.
ERNESTO ¿Qué (6) hacen (hacer) Andrés y Javier?
DAVID Tienen que (7) hacer (hacer) las maletas. (8) Salen (Salir) para Monterrey mañana.
ERNESTO Pues, ¿qué (9) hago (hacer) yo?
DAVID Yo (10) supongo (suponer) que puedes estudiar o (11) ver (ver) la televisión.
ERNESTO No quiero estudiar. Mejor (12) pongo (poner) la televisión. Mi programa favorito empieza en unos minutos.

2 **Oraciones** Form sentences using the cues provided and verbs from **Estructura 4.4**.

modelo
tú / ________ / cosas / en / su lugar / antes de (*before*) / salir
Tú pones las cosas en su lugar antes de salir.

1. mis amigos / ________ / conmigo / centro Mis amigos salen conmigo al centro.
2. tú / ________ / mentiras / pero / yo ________ / verdad Tú dices mentiras, pero yo digo la verdad.
3. Alberto / ________ / música del café Pasatiempos Alberto oye la música del café Pasatiempos.
4. yo / no / ________ / muchas películas Yo no veo muchas películas.
5. domingo / nosotros / ________ / mucha / tarea El domingo nosotros hacemos mucha tarea.
6. si / yo / ________ / que / yo / querer / ir / cine / mis amigos / ir / también Si yo digo que quiero ir al cine, mis amigos van también.

3 **Describir** Use the verbs from **Estructura 4.4** to describe what these people are doing.

1. Fernán Fernán pone la mochila en el escritorio/trae una mochila.

2. los aficionados Los aficionados salen del estadio/para sus casas.

3. yo Yo traigo/salgo con una cámara.

4. nosotros Nosotros vemos el monumento.

5. la señora Vargas La señora Vargas no oye bien.

6. el estudiante El estudiante hace su tarea.

Practice more at **vhlcentral.com**.

TEACHING OPTIONS

Game Ask students to write three sentences about themselves: two should be true and one should be false. Then, in groups of four, have students share their sentences with the group, who must decide whether that person **dice la verdad** or **dice una mentira**. Survey the class to uncover the most convincing liars.

Extra Practice Have students use five of the target verbs from **Estructura 4.4** to write sentences about their habits that others may find somewhat unusual. Ex: **Traigo doce plumas en la mochila. Hago la tarea en un café en el centro. No pongo la televisión hasta las diez de la noche.**

NATIONAL communication STANDARDS

Comunicación

4 **Tu rutina** In pairs, take turns asking each other these questions. Answers will vary.

1. ¿Qué traes a clase?
2. ¿Quiénes traen un diccionario a clase? ¿Por qué traen un diccionario?
3. ¿A qué hora sales de tu residencia estudiantil o de tu casa por la mañana? ¿A qué hora sale tu compañero/a de cuarto?
4. ¿Dónde pones tus libros cuando regresas de clase? ¿Siempre (*Always*) pones tus cosas en su lugar?
5. ¿Qué prefieres hacer, oír la radio o ver la televisión?
6. ¿Oyes música cuando estudias?
7. ¿Ves películas en casa o prefieres ir al cine?
8. ¿Haces mucha tarea los fines de semana?
9. ¿Sales con tus amigos los fines de semana? ¿A qué hora? ¿Qué hacen?
10. ¿Te gusta ver deportes en la televisión o prefieres ver otros programas? ¿Cuáles?

5 **Charadas** In groups, play a game of charades. Each person should think of two phrases containing the verbs **hacer, oír, poner, salir, traer,** or **ver**. The first person to guess correctly acts out the next charade. Answers will vary.

6 **Entrevista** You are doing a market research report on lifestyles. Interview a classmate to find out when he or she goes out with these people and what they do for entertainment. Answers will vary.

- los/las amigos/as
- el/la novio/a
- el/la esposo/a
- la familia

NATIONAL communication STANDARDS

Síntesis

7 **Situación** Imagine that you are speaking with your roommate. With a partner, prepare a conversation using these cues. Answers will vary.

Estudiante 1	Estudiante 2
Ask your partner what he or she is doing.	→ Tell your partner that you are watching TV.
Say what you suppose he or she is watching.	→ Say that you like the show ______. Ask if he or she wants to watch.
Say no, because you are going out with friends, and tell where you are going.	→ Say you think it's a good idea, and ask what your partner and his or her friends are doing there.
Say what you are going to do, and ask your partner whether he or she wants to come along.	→ Say no and tell your partner what you prefer to do.

TEACHING OPTIONS

Pairs Have pairs of students role-play an awful first date. Students should write their script first, then present it to the class. Encourage students to use descriptive adjectives as well as the new verbs learned in **Estructura 4.4**.

Heritage Speakers Ask heritage speakers to talk about a social custom in their cultural community. Remind them to use familiar vocabulary and simple sentences.

4 Teaching Tip Model the activity by having volunteers answer the first two items.

4 Expansion
Ask volunteers to call out some of their answers. The class should speculate about the reason behind each answer and offer more information. Have the volunteer confirm or deny the speculation.
Ex: —**Traigo mi tarea a clase.**
—**Eres un(a) buen(a) estudiante.**
—**Sí, soy un(a) buen(a) estudiante porque hago mi tarea.**

5 Teaching Tips
- Model the activity by doing a charade for the class to guess. Ex: **Pongo un lápiz en la mesa.** Then divide the class into small groups.
- Ask each group to choose the best **charada**. Then have students present them to the class, who will guess the activities.

6 Teaching Tip Model the activity by giving a report on your lifestyle. Ex: **Salgo al cine con mis amigas. Me gusta comer en restaurantes con mi esposo. En familia vemos deportes en la televisión.** Remind students that a market researcher and the interviewee would address each other with the **usted** form of verbs.

7 Possible Conversation
E1: ¿Qué haces?
E2: Veo la tele.
E1: Supongo que ves *Los Simpson*.
E2: Sí. Me gusta el programa. ¿Quieres ver la tele conmigo?
E1: No puedo. Salgo con mis amigos a la plaza.
E2: Buena idea. ¿Qué hacen en la plaza?
E1: Vamos a escuchar música y a pasear. ¿Quieres venir?
E2: No. Prefiero descansar.

Section Goal

In **Recapitulación**, students will review the grammar concepts from this lesson.

Instructional Resource
Supersite

1 Teaching Tips

- To simplify, before students begin the activity, have them identify the stem change (if any) in each row.
- Complete this activity orally as a class.

1 Expansion Ask students to provide the remaining forms of the verbs.

2 Teaching Tip To challenge students, ask them to provide alternative verbs for the blanks. Ex: **1. vemos/miramos** Then ask: Why can't **ir** be used for item 4? (needs **a**)

2 Expansion

- Ask questions about **Cecilia's** typical day. Have students answer with complete sentences. **¿Qué hace Cecilia a las siete y media? ¿Por qué le gusta llegar temprano?**
- Write on the board the verb phrases about **Cecilia's** day. (Ex: **ver la televisión por la mañana, almorzar a las 12:30, jugar al vóleibol por la tarde**) Brainstorm a few more entries. (Ex: **hacer la tarea por la noche**) Ask students to make a two-column chart, labeled **yo** and **compañero/a**. They should initial each activity they perform. Then have them interview a partner and report back to the class.

Recapitulación

Diagnostics

Review the grammar concepts you have learned in this lesson by completing these activities.

1 **Completar** Complete the chart with the correct verb forms. **30 pts.**

Infinitive	yo	nosotros/as	ellos/as
volver	**vuelvo**	volvemos	vuelven
comenzar	comienzo	**comenzamos**	comienzan
hacer	hago	**hacemos**	**hacen**
ir	voy	vamos	van
jugar	**juego**	jugamos	juegan
repetir	repito	repetimos	**repiten**

2 **Un día típico** Complete the paragraph with the appropriate forms of the verbs in the word list. Not all verbs will be used. Some may be used more than once. **20 pts.**

almorzar	ir	salir
cerrar	jugar	seguir
empezar	mostrar	ver
hacer	querer	volver

¡Hola! Me llamo Cecilia y vivo en Puerto Vallarta, México. ¿Cómo es un día típico en mi vida (*life*)? Por la mañana bebo café con mis padres y juntos (*together*) (1) __vemos__ las noticias (*news*) en la televisión. A las siete y media, (*yo*) (2) __salgo__ de mi casa y tomo el autobús. Me gusta llegar temprano (*early*) a la universidad porque siempre (*always*) (3) __veo__ a mis amigos en la cafetería. Tomamos café y planeamos lo que (4) __queremos__ hacer cada (*each*) día. A las ocho y cuarto, mi amiga Sandra y yo (5) __vamos__ al laboratorio de lenguas. La clase de francés (6) __empieza__ a las ocho y media. ¡Es mi clase favorita! A las doce y media (*yo*) (7) __almuerzo__ en la cafetería con mis amigos. Después (*Afterwards*), yo (8) __sigo__ con mis clases. Por las tardes, mis amigos (9) __vuelven__ a sus casas, pero yo (10) __juego__ al vóleibol con mi amigo Tomás.

RESUMEN GRAMATICAL

4.1 Present tense of ir *p. 118*

yo	voy	nos.	vamos
tú	vas	vos.	vais
él	va	ellas	van

- ir a + [*infinitive*] = *to be going* + [*infinitive*]
- a + el = al
- vamos a + [*infinitive*] = *let's* (*do something*)

4.2 Stem-changing verbs e:ie, o:ue, u:ue *pp. 121–122*

	empezar	volver	jugar
yo	empiezo	vuelvo	juego
tú	empiezas	vuelves	juegas
él	empieza	vuelve	juega
nos.	empezamos	volvemos	jugamos
vos.	empezáis	volvéis	jugáis
ellas	empiezan	vuelven	juegan

- Other e:ie verbs: **cerrar, comenzar, entender, pensar, perder, preferir, querer**
- Other o:ue verbs: **almorzar, contar, dormir, encontrar, mostrar, poder, recordar**

4.3 Stem-changing verbs e:i *p. 125*

pedir

yo	pido	nos.	pedimos
tú	pides	vos.	pedís
él	pide	ellas	piden

- Other e:i verbs: **conseguir, decir, repetir, seguir**

4.4 Verbs with irregular yo forms *pp. 128–129*

hacer	poner	salir	suponer	traer
hago	pongo	salgo	supongo	traigo

- **ver:** veo, ves, ve, vemos, veis, ven
- **oír:** oigo, oyes, oye, oímos, oís, oyen

TEACHING OPTIONS

Pairs Pair weaker students with more advanced students. Give each pair a numbered list of the target verbs from **Resumen gramatical** and a small plastic bag containing subject pronouns written on strips of paper. Model the first verb for students by drawing out a subject pronoun at random and conjugating the verb on the board. Ask: **¿Correcto o incorrecto?** Have students take turns and correct each other's work. Keep a brisk pace.

Extra Practice Introduce the word **nunca** and have students write a short description about things they never do. Have them use as many target verbs from this lesson as possible. Ex: **Nunca veo películas románticas. Nunca pongo la televisión cuando estudio...** Collect the descriptions, shuffle them, and read them aloud. Have the class guess the person that is being described.

3 **Oraciones** Arrange the cues provided in the correct order to form complete sentences. Make all necessary changes. 14 pts.

1. tarea / los / hacer / sábados / nosotros / la
   Los sábados nosotros hacemos la tarea./Nosotros hacemos la tarea los sábados.
2. en / pizza / Andrés / una / restaurante / el / pedir
   Andrés pide una pizza en el restaurante.
3. a / ? / museo / ir / ¿ / el / (tú)
   ¿(Tú) Vas al museo?
4. de / oír / amigos / bien / los / no / Elena
   Los amigos de Elena no oyen bien.
5. libros / traer / yo / clase / mis / a
   Yo traigo mis libros a clase.
6. película / ver / en / Jorge y Carlos / pensar / cine / una / el
   Jorge y Carlos piensan ver una película en el cine.
7. unos / escribir / Mariana / electrónicos / querer / mensajes
   Mariana quiere escribir unos mensajes electrónicos.

4 **Escribir** Write a short paragraph about what you do on a typical day. Use at least six of the verbs you have learned in this lesson. You can use the paragraph on the opposite page (**Actividad 2**) as a model. 36 pts. Answers will vary.

Un día típico

Hola, me llamo Julia y vivo en Vancouver, Canadá. Por la mañana, yo...

5 **Rima** Complete the rhyme with the appropriate forms of the correct verbs from the list. 4 EXTRA points!

contar	poder
oír	suponer

"Si no __puedes__ dormir
y el sueño deseas,
lo vas a conseguir
si __cuentas__ ovejas°."

ovejas *sheep*

Practice more at **vhlcentral.com**.

3 Teaching Tip To simplify, provide the first word for each sentence.

3 Expansion Give students these sentences as items 8–11: **8. la / ? / ustedes / cerrar / ventana / ¿ / poder (¿Pueden ustedes cerrar la ventana?) 9. cine / del / tú / las / salir / once / a (Tú sales del cine a las once.) 10. el / conmigo / a / en / ellos / tenis / el / jugar / parque (Ellos juegan al tenis conmigo en el parque.) 11. que / partido / mañana / un / decir / hay / Javier (Javier dice que hay un partido mañana.)**

4 Teaching Tips
- To simplify, ask students to make a three-column chart with the headings **Por la mañana, Por la tarde,** and **Por la noche**. Have them brainstorm at least three verbs or verb phrases for each column and circle any stem-changing or irregular **yo** verbs.
- Have students exchange paragraphs with a classmate for peer editing. Ask them to underline grammatical and spelling errors.

5 Teaching Tip Point out the inverted word order in line 2 of the rhyme and ask students what the phrase would be in everyday Spanish (**y deseas el sueño**).

5 Expansion Come up with similar rhymes and have students complete them. Ex: **Si no ____ descansar y diversión deseas, lo vas a encontrar si ____ con ellas. (quieres, juegas)**

TEACHING OPTIONS

Game Make a *Bingo* card of places at school or around town, such as dorm names, libraries, cafeterias, movie theaters, and cafés. Give each student a card and model possible questions (Ex: for a cafeteria, **¿Almuerzas en ____?/¿Dónde almuerzas?**). Encourage them to circulate around the room, asking only one question per person; if they get an affirmative answer, they should write that person's name in the square. The first student to complete a horizontal, vertical, or diagonal row and yell **¡Bingo!** is the winner.

Heritage Speakers Ask heritage speakers if counting sheep is common advice for sleeplessness in their families. Have them describe other insomnia remedies they have heard of or practiced.

Audio: Reading
Additional Reading

Lectura

NATIONAL STANDARDS communication cultures

Antes de leer

Estrategia

Predicting content from visuals

When you are reading in Spanish, be sure to look for visual clues that will orient you as to the content and purpose of what you are reading. Photos and illustrations, for example, will often give you a good idea of the main points that the reading covers. You may also encounter very helpful visuals that are used to summarize large amounts of data in a way that is easy to comprehend; these include bar graphs, pie charts, flow charts, lists of percentages, and other sorts of diagrams.

Examinar el texto

Take a quick look at the visual elements of the magazine article in order to generate a list of ideas about its content. Then compare your list with a classmate's. Are they the same or are they different? Discuss your lists and make any changes needed to produce a final list of ideas.

Contestar

Read the list of ideas you wrote in **Examinar el texto**, and look again at the visual elements of the magazine article. Then answer these questions:

1. Who is the woman in the photo, and what is her role? María Úrsula Echevarría is the author of this article.
2. What is the article about? The article is about sports in the Hispanic world.
3. What is the subject of the pie chart? The most popular sports among college students.
4. What is the subject of the bar graph? Hispanic countries in world soccer championships.

por María Úrsula Echevarría

El fútbol es el deporte más popular en el mundo° hispano, según° una encuesta° reciente realizada entre jóvenes universitarios. Mucha gente practica este deporte y tiene un equipo de fútbol favorito. Cada cuatro años se realiza la Copa Mundial°. Argentina y Uruguay han ganado° este campeonato° más de una vez°. Los aficionados siguen los partidos de fútbol en casa por tele y en muchos otros lugares como bares, restaurantes, estadios y clubes deportivos. Los jóvenes juegan al fútbol con sus amigos en parques y gimnasios.

Países hispanos en campeonatos mundiales de fútbol (1930–2014)

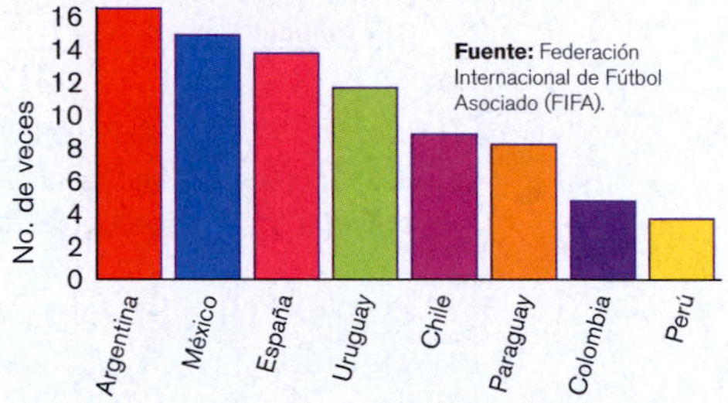

Pero, por supuesto°, en los países de habla hispana también hay otros deportes populares. ¿Qué deporte sigue al fútbol en estos países? Bueno, ¡depende del país y de otros factores!

Después de leer

Evaluación y predicción

Which of the following sporting events would be most popular among the college students surveyed? Rate them from one (most popular) to five (least popular). Which would be the most popular at your college or university? Answers will vary.

_______ 1. la Copa Mundial de Fútbol
_______ 2. los Juegos Olímpicos
_______ 3. el Campeonato de Wimbledon
_______ 4. la Serie Mundial de Béisbol
_______ 5. el Tour de Francia

Practice more at **vhlcentral.com**.

Section Goals

In **Lectura**, students will:
- learn the strategy of predicting content by surveying the graphic elements in reading matter
- read a magazine article containing graphs and charts

Instructional Resource
Supersite

Estrategia Tell students that they can infer a great deal of information about the content of an article by surveying the graphic elements included in it. When students survey an article for its graphic elements, they should look for such things as:
- headlines or headings
- bylines
- photos
- photo captions
- graphs and tables

Examinar el texto Give students two minutes to take a look at the visual clues in the article and write down all the ideas the clues suggest.

Contestar After going over students' responses, ask them how accurate their predictions were from **Examinar el texto**.

Evaluación y predicción Write two headings on the board: **Entre los jóvenes del mundo hispano** and **Entre los jóvenes de nuestra universidad**. Ask for a show of hands to respond to your questions about the ranking of each sporting event. Tally the responses as you proceed. Ask: **¿Quiénes creen que entre los jóvenes hispanos la Copa Mundial de Fútbol es el evento más popular? ¿Quiénes creen que los Juegos Olímpicos son el evento más popular?** Then ask: **Entre los jóvenes de nuestra universidad, ¿quiénes de ustedes creen que la Copa Mundial de Fútbol es el evento más popular?** Briefly discuss the differences indicated by student responses.

TEACHING OPTIONS

Variación léxica Remind students that the term **fútbol** in the Hispanic world refers to soccer, and that in the English-speaking world outside of the United States and Canada, soccer is called *football*. The game that English speakers call *football* is **fútbol americano** in the Spanish-speaking world.

Extra Practice Ask questions that require students to refer to the article. Model the use of the definite article with percentages. **¿Qué porcentaje prefiere el fútbol? (el 69 por ciento) ¿Qué porcentaje prefiere el vóleibol? (el 2 por ciento)**

No sólo el fútbol

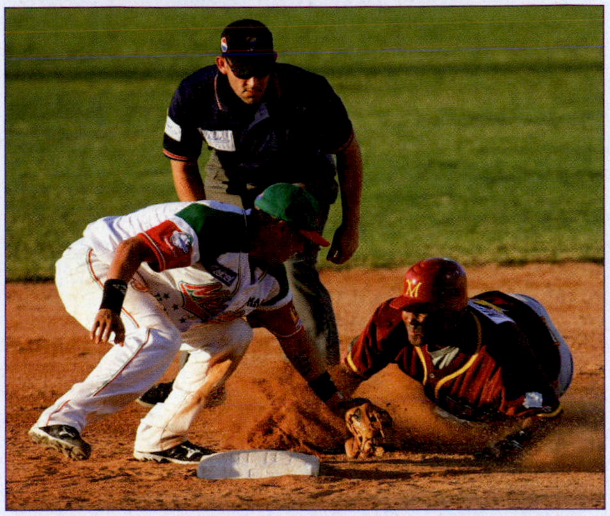

En Colombia, el béisbol también es muy popular después del fútbol, aunque° esto varía según la región del país. En la costa del norte de Colombia, el béisbol es una pasión. Y el ciclismo también es un deporte que los colombianos siguen con mucho interés.

Donde el béisbol es más popular

En los países del Caribe, el béisbol es el deporte predominante. Éste es el caso en Puerto Rico, Cuba y la República Dominicana. Los niños empiezan a jugar cuando son muy pequeños. En Puerto Rico y la República Dominicana, la gente también quiere participar en otros deportes, como el baloncesto, o ver los partidos en la tele. Y para los espectadores aficionados del Caribe, el boxeo es número dos.

Deportes más populares

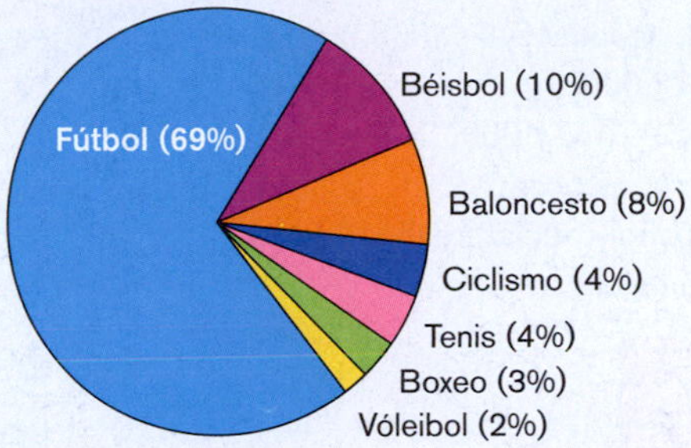

Donde el fútbol es más popular

En México, el béisbol es el segundo° deporte más popular después° del fútbol. Pero en Argentina, después del fútbol, el rugby tiene mucha importancia. En Perú a la gente le gusta mucho ver partidos de vóleibol. ¿Y en España? Muchas personas prefieren el baloncesto, el tenis y el ciclismo.

mundo *world* según *according to* encuesta *survey* se realiza la Copa Mundial *the World Cup is held* han ganado *have won* campeonato *championship* más de una vez *more than once* por supuesto *of course* segundo *second* después *after* aunque *although*

¿Cierto o falso?

Indicate whether each sentence is **cierto** or **falso**, then correct the false statements.

	Cierto	Falso
1. El vóleibol es el segundo deporte más popular en México. Es el béisbol.	❍	✓
2. En España a la gente le gustan varios deportes como el baloncesto y el ciclismo.	✓	❍
3. En la costa del norte de Colombia, el tenis es una pasión. El béisbol es una pasión.	❍	✓
4. En el Caribe, el deporte más popular es el béisbol.	✓	❍

Preguntas

Answer these questions in Spanish. Answers will vary.

1. ¿Dónde ven el fútbol los aficionados? Y tú, ¿cómo ves tus deportes favoritos?
2. ¿Te gusta el fútbol? ¿Por qué?
3. ¿Miras la Copa Mundial en la televisión?
4. ¿Qué deportes miras en la televisión?
5. En tu opinión, ¿cuáles son los tres deportes más populares en tu universidad? ¿En tu comunidad? ¿En tu país?
6. ¿Practicas deportes en tus ratos libres?

TEACHING OPTIONS

Pairs In pairs, have students read the article aloud and write three questions about it. Then, ask students to exchange their questions with another pair. Alternatively, you can ask pairs to read their questions to the class.

Heritage Speakers Ask heritage speakers to prepare a short presentation about soccer in their families' home countries. Encourage them to include how popular the sport is, what the principal teams are, and whether their country has participated in a World Cup. Ask the class comprehension questions.

¿Cierto o falso? After completing the activity, ask students to write an additional sentence about sports in each country or region mentioned. Ex: **El fútbol es el deporte más popular en México.**

Preguntas Give students these questions as items 7–10: **7. ¿Cuál es el deporte más popular en el mundo hispano? (el fútbol) 8. ¿En qué países es el béisbol el deporte más popular? (en los países del Caribe) 9. ¿Pueden nombrar algunos jugadores de béisbol hispanos en los Estados Unidos?** (Answers will vary.) **10. ¿Participan muchos países hispanos en campeonatos mundiales de fútbol? (sí)**

Video: *Panorama cultural*
Interactive map

Section Goals

In **Panorama**, students will read about:

- the geography, history, economy, and culture of Mexico
- Mexico's relationship with the United States

Instructional Resources
Supersite: Video (***Panorama cultural***); Resources (Scripts, Translations, Digital Image Bank, Answer Keys)
WebSAM
Workbook, pp. 47–48
Video Manual, pp. 37–38

Teaching Tips

- Use the **Lección 4 Panorama** digital images to assist with this presentation.
- Have students look at the map of Mexico. Ask them questions about the locations of cities and natural features of Mexico. Ex: **¿Dónde está la capital? (en el centro del país)**

El país en cifras Ask questions related to section content. Ex: After looking at the map, ask: **¿Qué ciudad mexicana está en la frontera con El Paso, Texas? (Ciudad Juárez)** Ask students if they can name other sister cities (**ciudades hermanas**) on the Mexico-U.S. border. (Tijuana/San Diego, Calexico/Mexicali, Laredo/Nuevo Laredo, etc.)

¡Increíble pero cierto! Mexico's **Día de Muertos**, like many holidays in Latin America, blends indigenous and Catholic practices. The date coincides with the Catholic All Saints' Day; however, the holiday's indigenous origins are evident in the gravesite offerings, **el pan de muertos**, and the belief that on this day the deceased can communicate with the living. Students will see a **Día de Muertos** celebration in the **Lección 9 Fotonovela**.

México

NATIONAL STANDARDS connections cultures

El país en cifras

Cabo San Lucas

- **Área:** 1.972.550 km² (761.603 millas²), *casi° tres veces° el área de Texas*

La situación geográfica de México, al sur° de los Estados Unidos, ha influido en° la economía y la sociedad de los dos países. Una de las consecuencias es la emigración de la población mexicana al país vecino°. Hoy día, más de 33 millones de personas de ascendencia mexicana viven en los Estados Unidos.

- **Población:** 118.818.000
- **Capital:** México, D.F. (y su área metropolitana)—19.319.000
- **Ciudades principales:** Guadalajara—4.338.000, Monterrey—3.838.000, Puebla—2.278.000, Ciudad Juárez—1.321.000
- **Moneda:** peso mexicano
- **Idiomas:** español (oficial), náhuatl, otras lenguas indígenas

Bandera de México

Mexicanos célebres

- **Benito Juárez,** héroe nacional (1806–1872)
- **Octavio Paz,** poeta (1914–1998)
- **Elena Poniatowska,** periodista y escritora (1932–)
- **Mario Molina,** Premio Nobel de Química, 1995; químico (1943–)
- **Paulina Rubio,** cantante (1971–)

casi *almost* veces *times* sur *south* ha influido en *has influenced* vecino *neighboring* se llenan de luz *get filled with light* flores *flowers* Muertos *Dead* se ríen *laugh* muerte *death* lo cual se refleja *which is reflected* calaveras de azúcar *sugar skulls* pan *bread* huesos *bones*

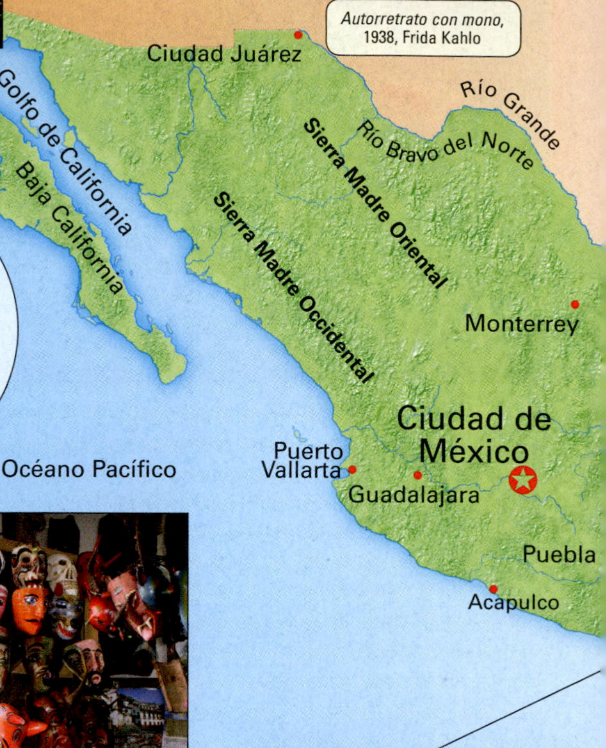

Autorretrato con mono, 1938, Frida Kahlo

Artesanías en Taxco, Guerrero

Pirámide de Kukulcán en Chichén Itzá

recursos
WB pp. 47-48 | VM pp. 37–38 | vhlcentral.com Lección 4

¡Increíble pero cierto!

Cada dos de noviembre los cementerios de México se llenan de luz°, música y flores°. El Día de Muertos° no es un evento triste; es una fiesta en honor a las personas muertas. En ese día, los mexicanos se ríen° de la muerte°, lo cual se refleja° en detalles como las calaveras de azúcar° y el pan° de muerto —pan en forma de huesos°.

TEACHING OPTIONS

Extra Practice Mexico is a large and diverse nation, with many regions and regional cultures. Have students select a region that interests them, research it, and present a short oral report to the class. Encourage them to include information about the cities, art, history, geography, customs, and cuisine of the region.

Small Groups Many of the dishes that distinguish Mexican cuisine have pre-Hispanic origins. To these native dishes have been added elements of Spanish and French cuisines, making Mexican food, like Mexican civilization, a dynamic mix of ingredients. Have groups of students research recipes that exemplify this fusion of cultures. Have each group describe one recipe's origins to the class.

Ciudades • México, D.F.

La Ciudad de México, fundada° en 1525, también se llama el D.F. o Distrito Federal. Muchos turistas e inmigrantes vienen a la ciudad porque es el centro cultural y económico del país. El crecimiento° de la población es de los más altos° del mundo. El D.F. tiene una población mayor que las de Nueva York, Madrid o París.

Artes • Diego Rivera y Frida Kahlo

Frida Kahlo y Diego Rivera eran° artistas mexicanos muy famosos. Se casaron° en 1929. Los dos se interesaron° en las condiciones sociales de la gente indígena de su país. Puedes ver algunas° de sus obras° en el Museo de Arte Moderno de la Ciudad de México.

Historia • Los aztecas

Los aztecas dominaron° en México del siglo° XIV al siglo XVI. Sus canales, puentes° y pirámides con templos religiosos eran muy importantes.
El fin del imperio azteca comenzó° con la llegada° de los españoles en 1519, pero la presencia azteca sigue hoy. La Ciudad de México está situada en la capital azteca de Tenochtitlán, y muchos turistas van a visitar sus ruinas.

Economía • La plata

México es el mayor productor de plata° del mundo°. Estados como Zacatecas y Durango tienen ciudades fundadas cerca de los más grandes yacimientos° de plata del país. Estas ciudades fueron° en la época colonial unas de las más ricas e importantes. Hoy en día, aún° conservan mucho de su encanto° y esplendor.

¿Qué aprendiste? Responde a cada pregunta con una oración completa.

1. ¿Qué lenguas hablan los mexicanos? *Los mexicanos hablan español y lenguas indígenas.*
2. ¿Cómo es la población del D.F. en comparación con la de otras ciudades? *La población del D.F. es mayor.*
3. ¿En qué se interesaron Frida Kahlo y Diego Rivera? *Se interesaron en las condiciones sociales de la gente indígena de su país.*
4. Nombra algunas de las estructuras de la arquitectura azteca. *Hay canales, puentes y pirámides con templos religiosos.*
5. ¿Dónde está situada la capital de México? *Está situada en la capital azteca de Tenochtitlán.*
6. ¿Qué estados de México tienen los mayores yacimientos de plata? *Zacatecas y Durango tienen los mayores yacimientos de plata.*

Conexión Internet Investiga estos temas en **vhlcentral.com**.

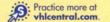

Practice more at **vhlcentral.com**.

1. Busca información sobre dos lugares de México. ¿Te gustaría (*Would you like*) vivir allí? ¿Por qué?
2. Busca información sobre dos artistas mexicanos. ¿Cómo se llaman sus obras más famosas?

fundada *founded* crecimiento *growth* más altos *highest* eran *were* Se casaron *They got married* se interesaron *were interested* algunas *some* obras *works* dominaron *dominated* siglo *century* puentes *bridges* comenzó *started* llegada *arrival* plata *silver* mundo *world* yacimientos *deposits* fueron *were* aún *still* encanto *charm*

México, D.F. Mexicans usually refer to their capital as **México** or **el D.F.** The monument pictured here is **El Ángel de la Independencia,** located on the **Paseo de la Reforma** in **el D.F.**

Diego Rivera y Frida Kahlo Show students paintings by **Rivera** and **Kahlo**, and discuss the indigenous Mexican themes that dominate their works: **Rivera's** murals have largely proletarian and political messages, while **Kahlo** incorporated indigenous motifs in her portrayals of suffering.

Los aztecas Explain that the coat of arms on the Mexican flag represents an Aztec prophecy. Legend states that nomadic Aztecs wandered present-day Mexico in search of a place to establish a city. According to their gods, the precise location would be indicated by an eagle devouring a snake while perched atop a nopal cactus. The Aztecs saw this sign on an island in Lake Texcoco, where they founded Tenochtitlán.

La plata Taxco, in the state of Guerrero, is the home to the annual **Feria Nacional de la Plata**. Although Taxco has exploited its silver mines since pre-Columbian days, the city did not have a native silvermaking industry until American William Spratling founded his workshop there in the 1930s. Spratling, known as the father of contemporary Mexican silver, incorporated indigenous Mexican motifs in his innovative silver designs.

Conexión Internet Students will find supporting Internet activities and links at **vhlcentral.com**.

Teaching Tip You may want to wrap up this section by playing the ***Panorama cultural*** video footage for this lesson.

TEACHING OPTIONS

Variación léxica Over 52 languages are spoken by indigenous communities in Mexico today; of these, Mayan languages are the most prevalent. Also, **náhuatl,** the language of the Aztecs, is spoken by a significant part of the population. Some **náhuatl** words have entered Mexican Spanish, such as **aguacate** (*avocado*), **guajolote** (*turkey*), **cacahuate** (*peanut*), **ejote** (*green bean*), **chile** (*chili pepper*), and **elote** (*corn*). Two food names of **náhuatl** origin that are now used in world languages are *tomato* and *chocolate*, as these foods are native to Mexico and were brought to Europe in the sixteenth century.

Instructional Resources
Supersite: Audio (Textbook & Lab MP3s); Testing Program (Tests, MP3s)
WebSAM
Lab Manual, p. 24

Pasatiempos

andar en patineta	*to skateboard*
bucear	*to scuba dive*
escalar montañas (*f., pl.*)	*to climb mountains*
escribir una carta	*to write a letter*
escribir un mensaje electrónico	*to write an e-mail*
esquiar	*to ski*
ganar	*to win*
ir de excursión	*to go on a hike*
leer el correo electrónico	*to read e-mail*
leer un periódico	*to read a newspaper*
leer una revista	*to read a magazine*
nadar	*to swim*
pasear	*to take a walk*
pasear en bicicleta	*to ride a bicycle*
patinar (en línea)	*to (inline) skate*
practicar deportes (*m., pl.*)	*to play sports*
tomar el sol	*to sunbathe*
ver películas (*f., pl.*)	*to watch movies*
visitar monumentos (*m., pl.*)	*to visit monuments*
la diversión	*fun activity; entertainment; recreation*
el fin de semana	*weekend*
el pasatiempo	*pastime; hobby*
los ratos libres	*spare (free) time*
el videojuego	*video game*

Deportes

el baloncesto	*basketball*
el béisbol	*baseball*
el ciclismo	*cycling*
el equipo	*team*
el esquí (acuático)	*(water) skiing*
el fútbol	*soccer*
el fútbol americano	*football*
el golf	*golf*
el hockey	*hockey*
el/la jugador(a)	*player*
la natación	*swimming*
el partido	*game; match*
la pelota	*ball*
el tenis	*tennis*
el vóleibol	*volleyball*

Adjetivos

deportivo/a	*sports-related*
favorito/a	*favorite*

Lugares

el café	*café*
el centro	*downtown*
el cine	*movie theater*
el gimnasio	*gymnasium*
la iglesia	*church*
el lugar	*place*
el museo	*museum*
el parque	*park*
la piscina	*swimming pool*
la plaza	*city or town square*
el restaurante	*restaurant*

Verbos

almorzar (o:ue)	*to have lunch*
cerrar (e:ie)	*to close*
comenzar (e:ie)	*to begin*
conseguir (e:i)	*to get; to obtain*
contar (o:ue)	*to count; to tell*
decir (e:i)	*to say; to tell*
dormir (o:ue)	*to sleep*
empezar (e:ie)	*to begin*
encontrar (o:ue)	*to find*
entender (e:ie)	*to understand*
hacer	*to do; to make*
ir	*to go*
jugar (u:ue)	*to play (a sport or a game)*
mostrar (o:ue)	*to show*
oír	*to hear*
pedir (e:i)	*to ask for; to request*
pensar (e:ie)	*to think*
pensar (+ *inf.*)	*to intend*
pensar en	*to think about*
perder (e:ie)	*to lose; to miss*
poder (o:ue)	*to be able to; can*
poner	*to put; to place*
preferir (e:ie)	*to prefer*
querer (e:ie)	*to want; to love*
recordar (o:ue)	*to remember*
repetir (e:i)	*to repeat*
salir	*to leave*
seguir (e:i)	*to follow; to continue*
suponer	*to suppose*
traer	*to bring*
ver	*to see*
volver (o:ue)	*to return*

***Decir* expressions**	*See page 128.*
Expresiones útiles	*See page 113.*

recursos
LM p. 24 | vhlcentral.com Lección 4

Vocabulary Tools

Las vacaciones

5

Communicative Goals

You will learn how to:

- **Discuss and plan a vacation**
- **Describe a hotel**
- **Talk about how you feel**
- **Talk about the seasons and the weather**

pages 140–145
- Travel and vacation
- Months of the year
- Seasons and weather
- Ordinal numbers

contextos

pages 146–149
Felipe plays a practical joke on Miguel, and the friends take a trip to the coast. They check in to their hotel and go to the beach, where Miguel gets his revenge.

fotonovela

pages 150–151
- **Las cataratas del Iguazú**
- **Punta del Este**

cultura

pages 152–167
- **Estar** with conditions and emotions
- The present progressive
- **Ser** and **estar**
- Direct object nouns and pronouns
- **Recapitulación**

estructura

pages 168–171
Lectura: A hotel brochure from Puerto Rico
Panorama: Puerto Rico

adelante

A PRIMERA VISTA

- **¿Están ellos en una montaña o en un museo?**
- **¿Son viejos o jóvenes?**
- **¿Pasean o ven una película? ¿Andan en patineta o van de excursión?**
- **¿Es posible esquiar en este lugar?**

Lesson Goals

In **Lección 5**, students will be introduced to the following:

- terms for traveling and vacations
- seasons and months
- weather expressions
- ordinal numbers (1st–10th)
- **Las cataratas del Iguazú**
- **Punta del Este**, Uruguay
- **estar** with conditions and emotions
- adjectives for conditions and emotions
- present progressive of regular and irregular verbs
- comparison of the uses of **ser** and **estar**
- direct object nouns and pronouns
- personal **a**
- scanning to find specific information
- a video about **Machu Picchu**
- cultural, geographic, and historical information about Puerto Rico

A primera vista Here are some additional questions you can ask to personalize the photo: **¿Dónde te gusta pasar tus ratos libres? ¿Qué haces en tus ratos libres? ¿Te gusta explorar otras culturas? ¿Te gusta viajar a otros países? ¿Adónde quieres ir en las próximas vacaciones?**

Teaching Tip Look for these icons for additional communicative practice:

	Interpretive communication
	Presentational communication
	Interpersonal communication

INSTRUCTIONAL RESOURCES

Supersite (vhlcentral.com)
Video: ***Fotonovela, Flash cultura, Panorama cultural***
Audio: Textbook and Lab MP3 Files
Activity Pack: Information Gap Activities, games, additional activity handouts
Resources: SAM Answer Key, Scripts, Translations, **Vocabulario adicional**, sample lesson plan, Grammar Presentation Slides, Digital Image Bank
Testing Program: Quizzes, Tests, Exams, MP3s
Student Activities Manual: Workbook/Video Manual/Lab Manual
WebSAM (online Student Activities Manual)

Vocabulary Tools

Section Goals

In **Contextos**, students will learn and practice:

- travel- and vacation-related vocabulary
- seasons and months of the year
- weather expressions
- ordinal numbers

Instructional Resources

Supersite: Audio (Textbook and Lab MP3 Files); Resources (Digital Image Bank, **Vocabulario adicional,** Activity Pack, Scripts, Answer Keys); Testing Program (Quizzes)
WebSAM
Workbook, pp. 49–50
Lab Manual, p. 25

Teaching Tips

- Ask: **¿A quién le gusta mucho viajar? ¿Cómo prefieres viajar?** Introduce cognates as suggestions: **¿Te gusta viajar en auto?** Write each term on the board as you say it. Ask: **¿Adónde te gusta viajar? ¿A México?** Ask students about their classmates' statements: **¿Adónde le gusta viajar a ____? ¿Cómo puede viajar?**
- Ask questions about transportation in your community. Ex: **Si quiero ir de la universidad al aeropuerto, ¿cómo puedo ir?** Ask what type of transportation students use to go home on school break.
- Use the **Lección 5 Contextos** digital images to assist with this presentation.
- Give students two minutes to review the four scenes, and then ask questions. Ex: **¿Quién trabaja en una agencia de viajes? (el/la agente de viajes)**

Note: At this point you may want to present ***Vocabulario adicional: Más vocabulario para las vacaciones*** from the Supersite.

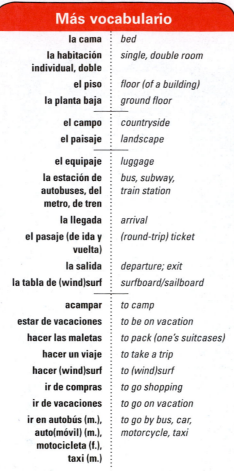

Las vacaciones

Más vocabulario

la cama	*bed*
la habitación individual, doble	*single, double room*
el piso	*floor (of a building)*
la planta baja	*ground floor*
el campo	*countryside*
el paisaje	*landscape*
el equipaje	*luggage*
la estación de autobuses, del metro, de tren	*bus, subway, train station*
la llegada	*arrival*
el pasaje (de ida y vuelta)	*(round-trip) ticket*
la salida	*departure; exit*
la tabla de (wind)surf	*surfboard/sailboard*
acampar	*to camp*
estar de vacaciones	*to be on vacation*
hacer las maletas	*to pack (one's suitcases)*
hacer un viaje	*to take a trip*
hacer (wind)surf	*to (wind)surf*
ir de compras	*to go shopping*
ir de vacaciones	*to go on vacation*
ir en autobús (m.), auto(móvil) (m.), motocicleta (f.), taxi (m.)	*to go by bus, car, motorcycle, taxi*

Variación léxica

automóvil ⟷ coche (*Esp.*), carro (*Amér. L.*)
autobús ⟷ camión (*Méx.*), guagua (*Caribe*)
motocicleta ⟷ moto (*coloquial*)

recursos

WB	LM	vhlcentral.com
pp. 49–50	p. 25	Lección 5

En la agencia de viajes

En el hotel

TEACHING OPTIONS

Extra Practice Ask questions about the people, places, and activities in **Contextos**. Ex: **¿Qué actividades pueden hacer los turistas en una playa? ¿Pueden nadar? ¿Tomar el sol? ¿Sacar fotos?** Then expand questions to ask students what they specifically do at these places. _____, **¿qué haces tú cuando vas a la playa?** Students should respond in complete sentences.

Variación léxica Point out that these are just some of the different Spanish names for vehicles. Ask heritage speakers if they are familiar with other terms. While some of these terms are mutually understood in different regions (**el coche, el carro, el auto, el automóvil**), others are specific to a region and may not be understood by others (**la guagua, el camión**). Stress that the feminine article **la** is used with the abbreviation **moto**.

En el aeropuerto

En la playa

Práctica

1 Escuchar Indicate who would probably make each statement you hear. Each answer is used twice.

a. el agente de viajes
b. el inspector de aduanas
c. un empleado del hotel

1. a
2. a
3. c
4. b
5. c
6. b

2 ¿Cierto o falso? Mario and his wife, Natalia, are planning their next vacation with a travel agent. Indicate whether each statement is **cierto** or **falso** according to what you hear in the conversation.

	Cierto	Falso
1. Mario y Natalia están en Puerto Rico.	❍	✓
2. Ellos quieren hacer un viaje a Puerto Rico.	✓	❍
3. Natalia prefiere ir a la montaña.	❍	✓
4. Mario quiere pescar en Puerto Rico.	✓	❍
5. La agente de viajes va a confirmar la reservación.	✓	❍

3 Escoger Choose the best answer for each sentence.

1. Un huésped es una persona que _b_.
   a. toma fotos b. está en un hotel c. pesca en el mar
2. Abrimos la puerta con _a_.
   a. una llave b. un caballo c. una llegada
3. Enrique tiene _a_ porque va a viajar a otro (*another*) país.
   a. un pasaporte b. una foto c. una llegada
4. Antes de (*Before*) ir de vacaciones, hay que _c_.
   a. pescar b. ir en tren c. hacer las maletas
5. Nosotros vamos en _a_ al aeropuerto.
   a. autobús b. pasaje c. viajero
6. Me gusta mucho ir al campo. El _a_ es increíble.
   a. paisaje b. pasaje c. equipaje

4 Analogías Complete the analogies using the words below. Two words will not be used.

auto	huésped	mar	sacar
empleado	llegada	pasaporte	tren

1. acampar → campo ⊜ pescar → mar
2. agencia de viajes → agente ⊜ hotel → empleado
3. llave → habitación ⊜ pasaje → tren
4. estudiante → libro ⊜ turista → pasaporte
5. aeropuerto → viajero ⊜ hotel → huésped
6. maleta → hacer ⊜ foto → sacar

1 Expansion In pairs, have students select one of the statements they hear and then write a conversation based on it.

1 Script 1. ¡Deben ir a Puerto Rico! Allí hay unas playas muy hermosas y pueden acampar. 2. Deben llamarme el lunes para confirmar la reservación. *Script continues on page 142.*

2 Expansion To challenge students, give them these true/false statements as items 6–9: **6. Mario prefiere una habitación doble. (Cierto.) 7. Natalia no quiere ir a la playa. (Falso.) 8. El hotel está en la playa. (Cierto.) 9. Mario va a montar a caballo. (Falso.)**

2 Script MARIO: Queremos ir de vacaciones a Puerto Rico. AGENTE: ¿Desean hacer un viaje al campo? NATALIA: Yo quiero ir a la playa. M: Pues, yo prefiero una habitación doble en un hotel con un buen paisaje. A: Puedo reservar para ustedes una habitación en el hotel San Juan que está en la playa. M: Es una buena idea, así yo voy a pescar y tú vas a montar a caballo. N: Muy bien, ¿puede confirmar la reservación? A: Claro que sí. *Textbook MP3s*

3 Expansion Ask a volunteer to help you model making statements similar to item 1. Say: **Un turista es una persona que… (va de vacaciones).** Then ask volunteers to do the same with **una agente de viajes, una inspectora de aduanas, un empleado de hotel.**

4 Teaching Tip Present these items using the following formula: ***Acampar* tiene la misma relación con *campo* que *pescar* tiene con… (*mar*).**

TEACHING OPTIONS

Small Groups Have students work in groups of three to write a riddle about one of the people or objects in the **Contextos** illustrations. The group must come up with at least three descriptions of their subject. Then one of the group members reads the description to the class and asks **¿Qué soy?** Ex: **Soy un pequeño libro. Tengo una foto de una persona. Soy necesario si un viajero quiere viajar a otro país. ¿Qué soy? (Soy un pasaporte.)**

Large Groups Split the class into two evenly-numbered groups. Hand out cards at random to the members of each group. One type of card should contain a verb or verb phrase (Ex: **confirmar una reservación**). The other will contain a related noun (Ex: **el agente de viajes**). The people within the groups must find their partners.

1 Script (continued) 3. Muy bien, señor… aquí tiene la llave de su habitación. 4. Lo siento, pero tengo que abrir sus maletas. 5. Su habitación está en el piso once, señora. 6. Necesito ver su pasaporte y sus maletas, por favor. *Textbook MP3s*

Teaching Tips

- Use the **Lección 5 Contextos** digital images to assist with this presentation.
- Point out that the names of months are not capitalized.
- Have students look over the seasons and months of the year. Call out the names of holidays or campus events and ask students to say when they occur.
- Use magazine pictures to cover as many weather conditions as possible from this page. Begin describing one of the pictures. Then, ask volunteers questions to elicit other weather expressions. Point out the use of **mucho/a** before nouns and **muy** before adjectives.
- Drill months by calling out a month and having students name the two that follow. Ex: **abril** (**mayo, junio**).
- Point out the use of **primero** for the first day of the month.
- Ask volunteers to associate seasons (or months) and general weather patterns. Ex: **En invierno, hace frío/ nieva. En marzo, hace viento.**
- Review the shortened forms **buen** and **mal** before **tiempo**.
- Point out that **Llueve** and **Nieva** can also mean *It rains* and *It snows*. **Está lloviendo** and **Está nevando** emphasize *at this moment*. Students will learn more about this concept in **Estructura 5.2**.

Las estaciones y los meses del año

el invierno: diciembre, enero, febrero

la primavera: marzo, abril, mayo

el verano: junio, julio, agosto

el otoño: septiembre, octubre, noviembre

—¿Cuál es la fecha de hoy?	*What is today's date?*
—Es el primero de octubre.	*It's the first of October.*
—Es el dos de marzo.	*It's March 2nd.*
—Es el diez de noviembre.	*It's November 10th.*

El tiempo

—¿Qué tiempo hace?	*How's the weather?*
—Hace buen/mal tiempo.	*The weather is good/bad.*

Hace (mucho) calor.
It's (very) hot.

Hace (mucho) frío.
It's (very) cold.

Llueve. (llover o:ue)
It's raining.

Está lloviendo.
It's raining.

Nieva. (nevar e:ie)
It's snowing.

Está nevando.
It's snowing.

Más vocabulario

Está (muy) nublado.	*It's (very) cloudy.*
Hace fresco.	*It's cool.*
Hace (mucho) sol.	*It's (very) sunny.*
Hace (mucho) viento.	*It's (very) windy.*

TEACHING OPTIONS

Pairs Have pairs of students write descriptions for each of the drawings on this page. Ask one student to write sentences for the first four drawings and the other to write sentences for the the next four. When finished, ask them to check their partner's work.

TPR Introduce the question **¿Cuándo es tu cumpleaños?** and the phrase **Mi cumpleaños es…** Allow students five minutes to ask questions and line up according to their birthdays.

Extra Practice Create a series of cloze sentences about the weather in a certain place. Ex: **En Puerto Rico ____ mucho calor. (hace) No ____ muy nublado cuando ____ sol. (está; hace) No ____ frío pero a veces ____ fresco. (hace; hace) Cuando ____ mal tiempo, ____ y ____ viento pero nunca ____. (hace; llueve; hace; nieva)**

5 **El Hotel Regis** Label the floors of the hotel.

Números ordinales

primer *(before a masculine singular noun)*, **primero/a**	*first*
segundo/a	*second*
tercer *(before a masculine singular noun)*, **tercero/a**	*third*
cuarto/a	*fourth*
quinto/a	*fifth*
sexto/a	*sixth*
séptimo/a	*seventh*
octavo/a	*eighth*
noveno/a	*ninth*
décimo/a	*tenth*

a. séptimo piso
b. sexto piso
c. quinto piso
d. cuarto piso
e. tercer piso
f. segundo piso
g. primer piso
h. planta baja

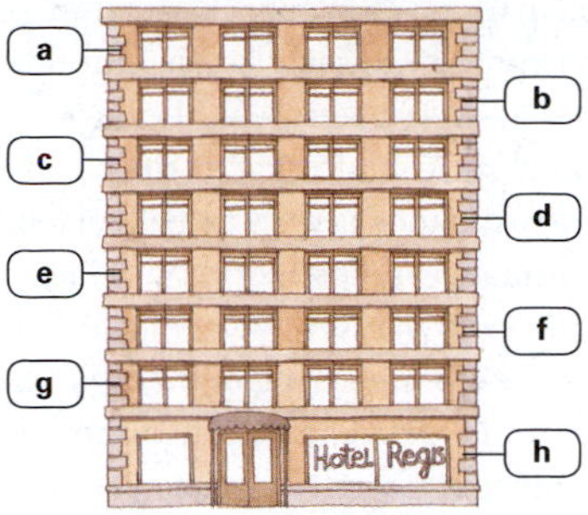

6 **Contestar** Look at the illustrations of the months and seasons on the previous page. In pairs, take turns asking each other these questions.

modelo
Estudiante 1: ¿Cuál es el primer mes de la primavera?
Estudiante 2: marzo

1. ¿Cuál es el primer mes del invierno? diciembre
2. ¿Cuál es el segundo mes de la primavera? abril
3. ¿Cuál es el tercer mes del otoño? noviembre
4. ¿Cuál es el primer mes del año? enero
5. ¿Cuál es el quinto mes del año? mayo
6. ¿Cuál es el octavo mes del año? agosto
7. ¿Cuál es el décimo mes del año? octubre
8. ¿Cuál es el segundo mes del verano? julio
9. ¿Cuál es el tercer mes del invierno? febrero
10. ¿Cuál es el sexto mes del año? junio

7 **Las estaciones** Name the season that applies to the description. Some answers may vary.

1. Las clases terminan. la primavera
2. Vamos a la playa. el verano
3. Acampamos. el verano
4. Nieva mucho. el invierno
5. Las clases empiezan. el otoño
6. Hace mucho calor. el verano
7. Llueve mucho. la primavera
8. Esquiamos. el invierno
9. el entrenamiento (*training*) de béisbol la primavera
10. el Día de Acción de Gracias (*Thanksgiving*) el otoño

8 **¿Cuál es la fecha?** Give the dates for these holidays.

modelo
el día de San Valentín 14 de febrero

1. el día de San Patricio 17 de marzo
2. el día de Halloween 31 de octubre
3. el primer día de verano 20–23 de junio
4. el Año Nuevo primero de enero
5. mi cumpleaños (*birthday*) Answers will vary.
6. mi día de fiesta favorito Answers will vary.

5 Teaching Tips
- Point out that for numbers greater than ten, Spanish speakers tend to use cardinal numbers instead: **Está en el piso veintiuno.**
- Add a visual aspect to this vocabulary presentation. Write out each ordinal number on a separate sheet of paper and distribute them at random among ten students. Ask them to go to the front of the class, hold up their signs, and stand in the correct order.

5 Expansion Ask students questions about their lives, using ordinal numbers. Ex: **¿En qué piso vives? ¿En qué piso está mi oficina?**

6 Teaching Tip Before beginning this activity, have students close their books. Review seasons and months of the year by asking questions. Ex: **¿Qué estación tiene los meses de junio, julio y agosto?**

6 Expansion Ask a student which month his or her birthday is in. Ask another student to give the season the first student's birthday falls in.

7 Expansion
Ask volunteers to describe events, situations, or holidays that are important to them or their families. Have the class guess the event and name the season that applies.

8 Teaching Tip Bring in a Spanish-language calendar. Ask students to name the important events and their scheduled dates.

8 Expansion
- Give these holidays to students as items 7–10: **7. Independencia de los EE.UU. (4 de julio) 8. Navidad (25 de diciembre) 9. Día de Acción de Gracias (cuarto jueves de noviembre) 10. Día de los Inocentes (primero de abril)**
- Ask heritage speakers to provide other important holidays, such as saints' days.

TEACHING OPTIONS

TPR Ask ten volunteers to line up facing the class. Make sure students know the starting point and what number in line they are. At random, call out ordinal numbers. The student to which each ordinal number corresponds has three seconds to step forward. If the student does not, he or she sits down and the order changes for the rest of the students further down the line. Who will be the last student(s) standing?

Game Ask four or five volunteers to come to the front of the room and hold races. (Make it difficult to reach the finish line; for example, have students hop on one foot or recite the ordinal numbers backwards.) Teach the words **llegó** and **fue** and, after each race, ask the class to summarize the results. Ex: ____ **llegó en quinto lugar.** ____ **fue la tercera persona (en llegar).**

9 Teaching Tip Review weather expressions by asking students about current weather conditions around the world. Ex: **¿Hace calor en Alaska hoy? ¿Nieva en Puerto Rico?**

9 Expansion Use the alternate choices in the exercise to ask students weather-related questions. Ex: **No nieva en Yucatán. ¿Dónde nieva?**

10 Teaching Tip Point out the words **soleado, lluvia,** and **nieve** in the key. Have students guess the meaning of these words based on the context. Finally, explain that **soleado** is an adjective and **lluvia** and **nieve** are nouns related to **llover** and **nevar**.

10 Expansion

- Ask students questions that compare and contrast the weather conditions presented in the activity or on the weather page of a Spanish-language newspaper. Ex: **Cuando la temperatura está a 85 grados en Buenos Aires, ¿a cuánto está en Tokio?**
- To challenge students, ask them to predict tomorrow's weather for these cities, based on the same cues. Have them use **ir a** + [*infinitive*]. Ex: **En Montreal, mañana va a nevar y va a hacer mucho frío.**

11 Teaching Tip Model the activity by completing the first two sentences about yourself.

11 Expansion Tell students to imagine that they are six years old again. Then have them write a short paragraph repeating the activity.

9 Seleccionar

Paco is talking about his family and friends. Choose the word or phrase that best completes each sentence.

1. A mis padres les gusta ir a Yucatán porque (hace sol, nieva). hace sol
2. Mi primo de Kansas dice que durante (*during*) un tornado, hace mucho (sol, viento). viento
3. Mis amigos van a esquiar si (nieva, está nublado). nieva
4. Tomo el sol cuando (hace calor, llueve). hace calor
5. Nosotros vamos a ver una película si hace (buen, mal) tiempo. mal
6. Mi hermana prefiere correr cuando (hace mucho calor, hace fresco). hace fresco
7. Mis tíos van de excursión si hace (buen, mal) tiempo. buen
8. Mi padre no quiere jugar al golf si (hace fresco, llueve). llueve
9. Cuando hace mucho (sol, frío) no salgo de casa y tomo chocolate caliente (*hot*). frío
10. Hoy mi sobrino va al parque porque (está lloviendo, hace buen tiempo). hace buen tiempo

10 El clima

With a partner, take turns asking and answering questions about the weather and temperatures in these cities. Use the model as a guide. Answers will vary.

modelo

Estudiante 1: ¿Qué tiempo hace hoy en Nueva York?
Estudiante 2: Hace frío y hace viento.
Estudiante 1: ¿Cuál es la temperatura máxima?
Estudiante 2: Treinta y un grados (*degrees*).
Estudiante 1: ¿Y la temperatura mínima?
Estudiante 2: Diez grados.

soleado *lluvia* *nieve* *nublado* *viento*

Nueva York	Miami	Chicago	París	Madrid	Tokio
Máx. 31°	Máx. 84°	Máx. 23°	Máx. 38°	Máx. 42°	Máx. 49°
Mín. 10°	Mín. 62°	Mín. 5°	Mín. 26°	Mín. 27°	Mín. 34°

Montreal	México D.F.	Cozumel	Caracas	Quito	Buenos Aires
Máx. 18°	Máx. 76°	Máx. 91°	Máx. 80°	Máx. 60°	Máx. 85°
Mín. 2°	Mín. 41°	Mín. 73°	Mín. 72°	Mín. 51°	Mín. 59°

NOTA CULTURAL

In most Spanish-speaking countries, temperatures are given in degrees Celsius. Use these formulas to convert between **grados centígrados** and **grados Fahrenheit**.

degrees C × 9 ÷ 5 + 32 = degrees F

degrees F - 32 × 5 ÷ 9 = degrees C

11 Completar

Complete these sentences with your own ideas. Answers will vary.

1. Cuando hace sol, yo...
2. Cuando llueve, mis amigos y yo...
3. Cuando hace calor, mi familia...
4. Cuando hace viento, la gente...
5. Cuando hace frío, yo...
6. Cuando hace mal tiempo, mis amigos...
7. Cuando nieva, muchas personas...
8. Cuando está nublado, mis amigos y yo...
9. Cuando hace fresco, mis padres...
10. Cuando hace buen tiempo, mis amigos...

Practice more at **vhlcentral.com**.

CONSULTA

Calor and **frío** can apply to both weather and people. Use **hacer** to describe weather conditions or climate.

(**Hace frío en Santiago.** *It's cold in Santiago.*)

Use **tener** to refer to people.

(**El viajero tiene frío.** *The traveler is cold.*)

See **Estructura 3.4**, p. 93.

TEACHING OPTIONS

TPR Have volunteers mime situations that elicit weather-related vocabulary from the class. Ex: A shiver might elicit **hace frío**.

Heritage Speakers Ask heritage speakers to talk about typical weather-dependent activities in their families' countries of origin. Refer them to **Actividad 11** as a model. Ex: **En México, cuando hace frío, la gente bebe ponche de frutas (una bebida caliente).**

Small Groups Have students form groups of two to four. Hand out cards that contain the name of a holiday or other annual event. The group must come up with at least three sentences to describe the holiday or occasion without mentioning its name. They can, however, mention the season of the year. After discussing, other groups must first guess the month and day on which the event takes place, then name the holiday or event itself.

Comunicación

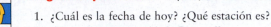

12 **Preguntas personales** In pairs, ask each other these questions. Answers will vary.

1. ¿Cuál es la fecha de hoy? ¿Qué estación es?
2. ¿Te gusta esta estación? ¿Por qué?
3. ¿Qué estación prefieres? ¿Por qué?
4. ¿Prefieres el mar o las montañas? ¿La playa o el campo? ¿Por qué?
5. Cuando haces un viaje, ¿qué te gusta hacer y ver?
6. ¿Piensas ir de vacaciones este verano? ¿Adónde quieres ir? ¿Por qué?
7. ¿Qué deseas ver y qué lugares quieres visitar?
8. ¿Cómo te gusta viajar? ¿En avión? ¿En motocicleta...?

13 **Encuesta** Your instructor will give you a worksheet. How does the weather affect what you do? Walk around the class and ask your classmates what they prefer or like to do in the weather conditions given. Note their responses on your worksheet. Make sure to personalize your survey by adding a few original questions to the list. Be prepared to report your findings to the class. Answers will vary.

14 **La reservación** In pairs, imagine that one of you is a receptionist at a hotel and the other is a tourist calling to make a reservation. Read only the information that pertains to you. Then role-play the situation.

Turista

Vas a viajar a Yucatán con un amigo. Llegan a Cancún el 23 de febrero y necesitan una habitación con baño privado para cuatro noches. Ustedes quieren descansar y prefieren una habitación con vista (*view*) al mar. Averigua (*Find out*) toda la información que necesitas (el costo, cuántas camas, etc.) y decide si quieres hacer la reservación o no.

Empleado/a

Trabajas en la recepción del Hotel Oceanía en Cancún. Para el mes de febrero, sólo quedan (*remain*) dos habitaciones: una individual ($168/noche) en el primer piso y una doble ($134/noche) en el quinto piso que tiene descuento porque no hay ascensor. Todas las habitaciones tienen baño privado y vista (*view*) a la piscina.

15 **Minidrama** With two or three classmates, prepare a skit about people who are on vacation or are planning a vacation. The skit should take place in one of these locations. Answers will vary.

- una agencia de viajes
- una casa
- un aeropuerto, una estación de tren/autobuses
- un hotel
- el campo o la playa

Síntesis

16 **Un viaje** You are planning a trip to Mexico and have many questions about your itinerary on which your partner, a travel agent, will advise you. Your instructor will give you and your partner each a sheet with different instructions for acting out the roles. Answers will vary.

12 Expansion Have pairs imagine that one of them is a journalist and the other is a celebrity. Then have them conduct the interview using questions 3–8.

13 Teaching Tip Model the activity by asking volunteers what they enjoy doing in hot weather. Ex: **Cuando hace calor, ¿qué haces? (Nado.)** Then distribute the ***Hojas de actividades*** (Activity Pack/Supersite).

14 Teaching Tips
- Have students sit back-to-back to better simulate a telephone conversation.
- Survey the class to see which room was the most popular. Have volunteers explain why.

15 Teaching Tip To simplify, ask the class to brainstorm a list of people and topics that may be encountered in each situation. Write the lists on the board.

15 Expansion Have students rate the skits as most original, funniest, most realistic, etc.

16 Teaching Tip Divide the class into pairs and distribute the handouts from the Activity Pack (Activity Pack/Supersite) that correspond to this Information Gap Activity. Give students ten minutes to complete the activity.

16 Expansion Have pairs put together an ideal itinerary for someone else traveling to Mexico, like a classmate, a relative, someone famous, or **el/la profesor(a)**.

TEACHING OPTIONS

Pairs Tell students they are part of a scientific expedition to Antarctica (**la Antártida**). Have them write a letter back home about the weather conditions and their activities there. Begin the letter for them by writing **Queridos amigos** on the board.

Game Have each student create a *Bingo* card with 25 squares (five rows of five). Tell them to write **GRATIS** (*FREE*) in the center square and the name of a different city in each of the other squares. Have them exchange cards. Call out different weather expressions. Ex: **Hace viento.** Students who think this description fits a city or cities on their card should mark the square with the weather condition. In order to win, a student must have marked five squares in a row and be able to give the weather condition for each one. Ex: **Hace mucho viento en Chicago.**

Section Goals

In **Fotonovela**, students will:

- receive comprehensible input from free-flowing discourse
- learn functional phrases that preview lesson grammatical structures

Instructional Resources
Supersite: Video (***Fotonovela***); Resources (Scripts, Translations, Answer Keys)
WebSAM
Video Manual, pp. 9–10

Video Recap: Lección 4
Before doing this **Fotonovela** section, review the previous episode with these questions:
1. ¿Qué prefiere hacer tía Ana María en sus ratos libres? (Ella nada, juega al tenis y al golf y va al cine y a los museos.) 2. ¿Adónde van Miguel, Maru, Marissa y Jimena? (Van a un cenote.) 3. ¿Qué van a hacer Felipe y Juan Carlos? (Van a jugar al fútbol con Eduardo y Pablo.) 4. ¿Qué quieren comer los chicos después de jugar al fútbol? (Quieren comer mole.)

Video Synopsis The friends watch the weather report on TV and discuss weather and seasons in their hometowns. **Felipe** rouses **Miguel** so they don't miss the bus to the beach. The group checks in to their hotel. At the beach, **Maru** and **Miguel** windsurf. **Miguel** gets back at **Felipe**.

Teaching Tips

- Have the class glance over the **Fotonovela** captions and list words and phrases related to tourism.
- Ask individuals how they are today, using **cansado/a** and **aburrido/a**.
- Ask the class to describe the perfect hotel. Ex: **¿Cómo es el hotel ideal? ¿Cómo es la habitación de hotel perfecta?**

¡Vamos a la playa!

Los seis amigos hacen un viaje a la playa.

PERSONAJES

FELIPE

JUAN CARLOS

Video: *Fotonovela*

TÍA ANA MARÍA ¿Están listos para su viaje a la playa?
TODOS Sí.
TÍA ANA MARÍA Excelente... ¡A la estación de autobuses!
MARU ¿Dónde está Miguel?
FELIPE Yo lo traigo.

(*se escucha un grito de Miguel*)
FELIPE Ya está listo. Y tal vez enojado. Ahorita vamos.

EMPLEADO Bienvenidas. ¿En qué puedo servirles?
MARU Hola. Tenemos una reservación para seis personas para esta noche.
EMPLEADO ¿A nombre de quién?
JIMENA ¿Díaz? ¿López? No estoy segura.

EMPLEADO No encuentro su nombre. Ah, no, ahora sí lo veo, aquí está. Díaz. Dos habitaciones en el primer piso para seis huéspedes.

FELIPE No está nada mal el hotel, ¿verdad? Limpio, cómodo... ¡Oye, Miguel! ¿Todavía estás enojado conmigo? (*a Juan Carlos*) Miguel está de mal humor. No me habla.
JUAN CARLOS ¿Todavía?

EMPLEADO Aquí están las llaves de sus habitaciones.
MARU Gracias. Una cosa más. Mi novio y yo queremos hacer windsurf, pero no tenemos tablas.
EMPLEADO El botones las puede conseguir para ustedes.

TEACHING OPTIONS

Video Tips General suggestions for using video clips in the classroom can be found in the front matter of this Instructor's Annotated Edition.

¡Vamos a la playa! Before viewing the **¡Vamos a la playa!** episode of the **Fotonovela**, ask students to brainstorm a list of things that might happen in an episode in which the characters check in to a hotel and go to the beach. Then play the **¡Vamos a la playa!** episode once without sound and have the class create a plot summary based on visual clues. Finally, show the video segment with sound and have the class correct any mistaken guesses and fill in any gaps. Ask comprehension questions as a follow-up.

MARISSA JIMENA MARU MIGUEL MAITE FUENTES ANA MARÍA EMPLEADO

7

JUAN CARLOS ¿Qué hace este libro aquí? ¿Estás estudiando en la playa?

JIMENA Sí, es que tengo un examen la próxima semana.

8

JUAN CARLOS Ay, Jimena. ¡No! ¿Vamos a nadar?

JIMENA Bueno, como estudiar es tan aburrido y el tiempo está tan bonito...

9

MARISSA Yo estoy un poco cansada. ¿Y tú? ¿Por qué no estás nadando?

FELIPE Es por causa de Miguel.

10

MARISSA Hmm, estoy confundida.

FELIPE Esta mañana. ¡Sigue enojado conmigo!

MARISSA No puede seguir enojado tanto tiempo.

Expresiones útiles

Talking with hotel personnel

¿En qué puedo servirles?
How can I help you?
Tenemos una reservación.
We have a reservation.
¿A nombre de quién?
In whose name?
¿Quizás López? ¿Tal vez Díaz?
Maybe López? Maybe Díaz?
Ahora lo veo, aquí está. Díaz.
Now I see it. Here it is. Díaz.
Dos habitaciones en el primer piso para seis huéspedes.
Two rooms on the first floor for six guests.
Aquí están las llaves.
Here are the keys.

Describing a hotel

No está nada mal el hotel.
The hotel isn't bad at all.
Todo está tan limpio y cómodo.
Everything is so clean and comfortable.
Es excelente/estupendo/fabuloso/fenomenal/increíble/magnífico/maravilloso/perfecto.
It's excellent/stupendous/fabulous/phenomenal/incredible/magnificent/marvelous/perfect.

Talking about how you feel

Yo estoy un poco cansado/a.
I am a little tired.
Estoy confundido/a. *I'm confused.*
Todavía estoy/Sigo enojado/a contigo.
I'm still angry with you.

Additional vocabulary

afuera *outside*
amable *nice; friendly*
el balde *bucket*
el/la botones *bellhop*
la crema de afeitar *shaving cream*
el frente (frío) *(cold) front*
el grito *scream*
la temporada *period of time*
entonces *so, then*
es igual *it's the same*

recursos
VM pp. 9–10 | vhlcentral.com Lección 5

Expresiones útiles Remind students that **está, están**, and **estoy** are present-tense forms of the verb **estar**, which is often used with adjectives that describe conditions and emotions. Remind students that **Es** is a present-tense form of the verb **ser**, which is often used to describe characteristics of people and things and to make generalizations. Draw students' attention to video stills 7 and 9. Point out that **Estás estudiando** and **estás nadando** are examples of the present progressive, which is used to emphasize an action in progress. Finally, point out the captions for video stills 1, 4, and 6 and explain that **lo** and **las** are examples of direct object pronouns. Explain that these are words that replace direct object nouns in order to avoid repetition. Tell students that they will learn more about these concepts in **Estructura**.

Teaching Tip Have students work in groups of six to read the **Fotonovela** captions aloud (have one student read the role of both **tía Ana María** and the **empleado**). Then have one group come to the front of the class and role-play the scenes. Encourage them to use props and gestures.

Nota cultural The **Yucatán** peninsula is warm year-round, but there are rainy and dry seasons. Generally, the dry season lasts from November to April and the wet season runs from May through October. Hurricanes occur in the late summer and fall. The **Yucatán's** average temperature is 25°C to 27°C (77°F to 81°F), rarely dropping below 16°C (61°F) or rising above 49°C (120°F).

TEACHING OPTIONS

Pairs Ask pairs to write five true/false statements based on the **¡Vamos a la playa!** captions. Then have them exchange papers with another pair, who will complete the activity and correct the false statements. Ask volunteers to read a few statements for the class, who will answer and point out the caption that contains the information.

Large Groups Ask students to work in groups to rewrite the **¡Vamos a la playa!** episode using a different ending or location. Suggest new locations such as a ski resort, a big city, or a campground. Allow groups time to prepare, and ask them to ad-lib their new versions for the class. You may want to assign this activity as homework and have students present it in the next class period for review.

1 Teaching Tip To challenge students, ask them to create sentences with the unused items from the word bank.

1 Expansion Have students create a follow-up question for each item, based on the **Fotonovela.** Then, in pairs, have them take turns reading the completed statements and asking their questions.

2 Expansion Tell the class to add **Marissa** and **Jimena** to the list of possible answers. Then, give these statements to the class as items 6–7: **6. No estoy segura del nombre. (Jimena) 7. Yo estoy confundida. (Marissa)**

Nota cultural Buses in Mexico provide an excellent alternative to rental cars. Mexican buses are generally efficient, comfortable, and inexpensive. A second-class ticket usually offers less leg room, a cheaper fare, and more stops than first-class. One major first-class bus company is **Autobuses del Oriente.**

3 Expansion After students have determined the correct order, have pairs write sentences that describe what happens chronologically between items.

4 Teaching Tip To simplify, have students prepare individually for their roles by brainstorming some phrases.

4 Possible Conversation
E1: Buenas tardes, señor. Tengo una reservación.
E2: Perdón, señorita, pero no encuentro su reservación.
E1: Está en mi nombre... Meg Adams.
E2: Ah, sí... aquí está. Tiene una habitación doble.
E1: Este hotel está muy limpio y cómodo.
E2: Sí. Bienvenida. Aquí están las llaves.
E1: ¿Puede llamar al botones para llevar mi equipaje, por favor?
E2: Claro. Don Raúl...

¿Qué pasó?

1 Completar Complete these sentences with the correct term from the word bank.

aburrido	botones	la llave
el aeropuerto	la estación de autobuses	montar a caballo
amable	habitaciones	reservación

1. Los amigos van a __la estación de autobuses__ para ir a la playa.
2. La __reservación__ del hotel está a nombre de los Díaz.
3. Los amigos tienen dos __habitaciones__ para seis personas.
4. El __botones__ puede conseguir tablas de windsurf para Maru.
5. Jimena dice que estudiar en vacaciones es muy __aburrido__.

CONSULTA The meaning of some adjectives, such as **aburrido**, changes depending on whether they are used with **ser** or **estar**. See **Estructura 5.3**, pp. 158–159.

2 Identificar Identify the person who would make each statement.

EMPLEADO MARU TÍA ANA MARÍA FELIPE JUAN CARLOS

1. No lo encuentro, ¿a nombre de quién está su reservación? empleado
2. ¿Por qué estás estudiando en la playa? ¡Mejor vamos a nadar! Juan Carlos
3. Nuestra reservación es para seis personas en dos habitaciones. Maru
4. El hotel es limpio y cómodo, pero estoy triste porque Miguel no me habla. Felipe
5. Suban al autobús y ¡buen viaje a la playa! Ana María

3 Ordenar Place these events in the correct order.

__3__ a. El empleado busca la reservación.
__5__ b. Marissa dice que está confundida.
__1__ c. Los amigos están listos para ir a la playa.
__4__ d. El empleado da (*gives*) las llaves de las habitaciones a las chicas.
__2__ e. Miguel grita (*screams*).

4 Conversar With a partner, use these cues to create a conversation between a hotel employee and a guest in Mexico. Answers will vary.

Huésped	Empleado/a
Say hi to the employee and ask for your reservation.	Tell the guest that you can't find his/her reservation.
Tell the employee that the reservation is in your name.	Tell him/her that you found the reservation and that it's for a double room.
Tell the employee that the hotel is very clean and comfortable.	Say that you agree with the guest, welcome him/her, and give him/her the keys.
Ask the employee to call the bellhop to help you with your luggage.	Call the bellhop to help the guest with his/her luggage.

NATIONAL communication STANDARDS

Practice more at **vhlcentral.com.**

TEACHING OPTIONS

Extra Practice Give students some true/false statements about the **Fotonovela**. Have them correct the false items. Ex: **1. Felipe todavía está enojado. (Falso. Miguel todavía está enojado.) 2. El botones puede llevar el equipaje a las habitaciones. (Cierto.) 3. La reservación es para siete huéspedes. (Falso. Es para seis huéspedes.) 4. Felipe no está nadando porque tiene que estudiar. (Falso. Es por causa de Miguel.)**

Small Groups Have students work in groups of four to prepare a skit to present to the class. In the skit, two friends check in to a hotel, have a bellhop carry their suitcases to their rooms, and decide what to do for the rest of the day. Students should specify what city they are visiting, describe the hotel and their rooms, and explain what activities they want to do while they are visiting the city.

Pronunciación

Audio

Spanish b and v

bueno **vóleibol** **biblioteca** **vivir**

There is no difference in pronunciation between the Spanish letters **b** and **v**. However, each letter can be pronounced two different ways, depending on which letters appear next to them.

bonito **viajar** **también** **investigar**

B and **v** are pronounced like the English hard *b* when they appear either as the first letter of a word, at the beginning of a phrase, or after **m** or **n**.

deber **novio** **abril** **cerveza**

In all other positions, **b** and **v** have a softer pronunciation, which has no equivalent in English. Unlike the hard **b**, which is produced by tightly closing the lips and stopping the flow of air, the soft **b** is produced by keeping the lips slightly open.

bola **vela** **Caribe** **declive**

In both pronunciations, there is no difference in sound between **b** and **v**. The English *v* sound, produced by friction between the upper teeth and lower lip, does not exist in Spanish. Instead, the soft **b** comes from friction between the two lips.

Verónica y su esposo cantan boleros.

When **b** or **v** begins a word, its pronunciation depends on the previous word. At the beginning of a phrase or after a word that ends in **m** or **n**, it is pronounced as a hard **b**.

Benito es de Boquerón pero vive en Victoria.

Words that begin with **b** or **v** are pronounced with a soft **b** if they appear immediately after a word that ends in a vowel or any consonant other than **m** or **n**.

Práctica Read these words aloud to practice the **b** and the **v**.

1. hablamos
2. trabajar
3. botones
4. van
5. contabilidad
6. bien
7. doble
8. novia
9. béisbol
10. nublado
11. llave
12. invierno

No hay mal que por bien no venga.[1]

Oraciones Read these sentences aloud to practice the **b** and the **v**.

1. Vamos a Guaynabo en autobús.
2. Voy de vacaciones a la Isla Culebra.
3. Tengo una habitación individual en el octavo piso.
4. Víctor y Eva van en avión al Caribe.
5. La planta baja es bonita también.
6. ¿Qué vamos a ver en Bayamón?
7. Beatriz, la novia de Víctor, es de Arecibo, Puerto Rico.

Hombre prevenido vale por dos.[2]

Refranes Read these sayings aloud to practice the **b** and the **v**.

recursos

LM p. 26 | vhlcentral.com Lección 5

1 Every cloud has a silver lining.
2 An ounce of prevention equals a pound of cure.

Section Goal

In **Pronunciación**, students will be introduced to the pronunciation of **b** and **v**.

Instructional Resources

Supersite: Audio (Textbook and Lab MP3 Files); Resources (Scripts, Answer Keys)

WebSAM

Lab Manual, p. 26

Teaching Tips

- Emphasize that **b (alta/grande)** and **v (baja/chica)** are pronounced identically in Spanish, but depending on the letter's position in a word, each can be pronounced two ways. Pronounce **vóleibol** and **vivir** and have students listen for the difference between the initial and medial sounds represented by **b** and **v**.
- Explain the cases in which **b** and **v** are pronounced like English *b* in *boy* and model the pronunciation of **bonito**, **viajar**, **también**, and **investigar**.
- Point out that before **b** or **v**, **n** is usually pronounced **m**.
- Explain that in all other positions, **b** and **v** are fricatives. Pronounce **deber**, **novio**, **abril**, and **cerveza** and stress that the friction is between the two lips.
- Remind the class that Spanish has no sound like the English **v**. Pronounce **vida**, **vacaciones**, **avión**, and **automóvil**.
- Explain that the same rules apply in connected speech. Practice with phrases like **de vacaciones** and **de ida y vuelta**.

Práctica/Oraciones/Refranes

These exercises are recorded on the *Textbook MP3s*. You may want to play the audio so that students practice listening to Spanish spoken by speakers other than yourself.

TEACHING OPTIONS

Extra Practice Write some additional proverbs on the board and have the class practice saying each one. Ex: **Más vale que sobre y no que falte.** (*Better too much than too little.*) **No sólo de pan vive el hombre.** (*Man doesn't live by bread alone.*) **A caballo regalado no se le ve el colmillo.** (*Don't look a gift horse in the mouth.*) **Más vale dar que recibir.** (*It's better to give than to receive.*)

Small Groups Have students work in small groups and take turns reading aloud sentences from the **Fotonovela** on pages 146–147, focusing on the correct pronunciation of **b** and **v**. If a group member has trouble pronouncing a word that contains **b** or **v**, the rest of the group should supply the rule that explains how it should be pronounced.

Flash CULTURA

Section Goals

In **Cultura**, students will:
- read about **Las cataratas del Iguazú**
- learn travel-related terms
- read about **Punta del Este**, Uruguay
- read about popular vacation destinations in the Spanish-speaking world

Instructional Resources
Supersite: Video (*Flash cultura*); Resources (Scripts, Translations, Answer Keys)
WebSAM
Video Manual, pp. 81–82

En detalle

Antes de leer Ask students what kind of travel interests them. Ex: **¿Te gusta acampar o dormir en un hotel? ¿Adónde prefieres ir: a la ciudad, a las montañas…? Cuando estás de vacaciones, ¿te gusta descansar o vivir una aventura? ¿Visitar museos o observar paisajes?** Then ask students to predict what a tourist would see and do near a waterfall.

Lectura
- Explain that the **Guaraní** are an indigenous group who traditionally inhabit areas of Paraguay, northern Argentina, southern Brazil, and parts of Uruguay and Bolivia. The **Guaraní** language is one of the two official languages of Paraguay.
- The first European to find **Iguazú** was the Spaniard **Álvar Núñez Cabeza de Vaca** in 1541.
- The **Iguazú** Falls have been featured in many movies, most notably in *The Mission* (1986), starring Robert DeNiro and Jeremy Irons.

Después de leer Ask students through which country they would prefer to visit **Iguazú** and why.

1 Expansion Give students these true/false statements as items 11–12: 11. The **Tren Ecológico de la Selva** takes tourists to San Martín Island. (**Falso.** It takes them to the walkways.) 12. **Piedra Volada** is the tallest waterfall in Mexico. (**Cierto.**)

EN DETALLE

Video: *Flash cultura*

NATIONAL STANDARDS connections cultures

Las cataratas del Iguazú

Imagine the impressive and majestic Niagara Falls, the most powerful waterfall in North America. Now, if you can, imagine a waterfall four times as wide and almost twice as tall that caused Eleanor Roosevelt to exclaim "Poor Niagara!" upon seeing it for the first time. Welcome to **las cataratas del Iguazú!**

Iguazú is located in Iguazú National Park, an area of subtropical jungle where Argentina meets Brazil. Its name comes from the indigenous Guaraní word for "great water." A UNESCO World Heritage Site, **las cataratas del Iguazú** span three kilometers and comprise 275 cascades split into two main sections by San Martín Island. Most of the falls are about 82 meters (270 feet) high. The horseshoe-shaped cataract **Garganta del Diablo** (Devil's Throat) has the greatest water flow and is considered to be the most impressive; it also marks the border between Argentina and Brazil.

Each country offers different views and tourist options. Most visitors opt to use the numerous catwalks that are available on both sides; however, from the Argentinean side, tourists can get very close to the falls, whereas Brazil provides more panoramic views. If you don't mind getting wet, a jet boat tour is a good choice; those looking for wildlife—such as toucans, ocelots, butterflies, and jaguars—should head for San Martín Island. Brazil boasts less conventional ways to view the falls, such as helicopter rides and rappelling, while Argentina focuses on sustainability with its **Tren Ecológico de la Selva** (*Ecological Jungle Train*), an environmentally friendly way to reach the walkways.

No matter which way you choose to enjoy the falls, you are certain to be captivated.

Más cascadas° en Latinoamérica

Nombre	País	Altura°	Datos
Salto Ángel	Venezuela	979 metros	la más alta° del mundo°
Catarata del Gocta	Perú	771 metros	descubierta° en 2006
Piedra Volada	México	453 metros	la más alta de México

cascadas *waterfalls* Altura *Height* más alta *tallest* mundo *world* descubierta *discovered*

ACTIVIDADES

1 **¿Cierto o falso?** Indicate whether these statements are cierto or falso. Correct the false statements.

1. Iguazú Falls is located on the border of Argentina and Brazil. **Cierto.**
2. Niagara Falls is four times as wide as Iguazú Falls. **Falso.** Iguazú is four times as wide as Niagara Falls.
3. Iguazú Falls has a few cascades, each about 82 meters. **Falso.** Iguazú is composed of 275 cascades about 82 meters tall.
4. Tourists visiting Iguazú can see exotic wildlife. **Cierto.**
5. *Iguazú* is the Guaraní word for "blue water." **Falso.** *Iguazú* is the Guaraní word for "great water."
6. You can access the walkways by taking the **Garganta del Diablo**. **Falso.** One way of accessing the walkways is taking the **Tren Ecológico de la Selva.**
7. It is possible for tourists to visit Iguazú Falls by air. **Cierto.**
8. **Salto Ángel** is the tallest waterfall in the world. **Cierto.**
9. There are no waterfalls in Mexico. **Falso.** The **Piedra Volada** is in Mexico.
10. For the best views of Iguazú Falls, tourists should visit the Brazilian side. **Cierto.**

TEACHING OPTIONS

La leyenda Share this legend of the **Iguazú** Falls with students: Many ages ago, in the **Iguazú** River there lived a god-serpent, **Mboí**, to whom the **Guaraní** tribes sacrificed a young woman during their annual gathering. At one such gathering, a young man named **Tarobá** instantly fell in love with **Naipí**, who was to be sacrificed. After pleading in vain to have her spared, one night **Tarobá** took **Naipí** and tried to flee with her in his canoe. The furious **Mboí** awoke and split the river in two, forming the waterfall and trapping the pair. He transformed **Naipí** into a rock at the base of the falls and **Tarobá** into a tree perched at the edge of the abyss. Lest the lovers try to reunite, the watchful **Mboí** keeps an eternal vigil from deep under the waters of the **Garganta del Diablo**. Now ask them to think of other creation legends they know (Ex: Paul Bunyan and the Great Lakes).

ASÍ SE DICE

Viajes y turismo

el asiento del medio, del pasillo, de la ventanilla	*center, aisle, window seat*
el itinerario	*itinerary*
media pensión	*breakfast and one meal included*
el ómnibus (Perú)	el autobús
pensión completa	*all meals included*
el puente	*long weekend (lit., bridge)*

EL MUNDO HISPANO

Destinos populares

- **Las playas del Parque Nacional Manuel Antonio** (Costa Rica) ofrecen° la oportunidad de nadar y luego caminar por el bosque tropical°.
- **Teotihuacán** (México) Desde antes de la época° de los aztecas, aquí se celebra el equinoccio de primavera en la Pirámide del Sol.
- **Puerto Chicama** (Perú), con sus olas° de cuatro kilómetros de largo°, es un destino para surfistas expertos.
- **Tikal** (Guatemala) Aquí puedes ver las maravillas de la selva° y ruinas de la civilización maya.
- **Las playas de Rincón** (Puerto Rico) Son ideales para descansar y observar ballenas°.

ofrecen *offer* bosque tropical *rainforest*
Desde antes de la época *Since before the time* olas *waves*
de largo *in length* selva *jungle* ballenas *whales*

PERFIL

Punta del Este

One of South America's largest and most fashionable beach resort towns is Uruguay's **Punta del Este**, a narrow strip of land containing twenty miles of pristine beaches. Its peninsular shape gives it two very different seascapes. **La Playa Mansa**, facing the bay and therefore the more protected side, has calm waters. Here, people practice water sports like swimming, water skiing, windsurfing, and diving. **La Playa Brava**, facing the east, receives the Atlantic Ocean's powerful, wave-producing winds, making it popular for surfing, body boarding, and kite surfing. Besides the beaches, posh shopping, and world-famous nightlife, **Punta** offers its 600,000 yearly visitors yacht and fishing clubs, golf courses, and excursions to observe sea lions at the **Isla de Lobos** nature reserve.

Conexión Internet

¿Cuáles son los sitios más populares para el turismo en Puerto Rico?

Go to **vhlcentral.com** to find more cultural information related to this **Cultura** section.

ACTIVIDADES

2 Comprensión Complete the sentences.

1. En las playas de Rincón puedes ver ___ballenas___.
2. Cerca de 600.000 turistas visitan ___Punta del Este___ cada año.
3. En el avión pides un ___asiento de la ventanilla___ si te gusta ver el paisaje.
4. En Punta del Este, la gente prefiere nadar en la Playa ___Mansa___.
5. El ___ómnibus___ es un medio de transporte en Perú.

3 De vacaciones Spring break is coming up, and you want to go on a short vacation with some friends. Working in a small group, decide which of the locations featured on these pages best suits the group's likes and interests. Come to an agreement about how you will get there, where you prefer to stay and for how long, and what each of you will do during free time. Present your trip to the class. Answers will vary.

Practice more at **vhlcentral.com**.

recursos: VM pp. 81–82; vhlcentral.com Lección 5

Así se dice
- To challenge students, add these airport-related words to the list: **el/la auxiliar de vuelo** (*flight attendant*), **aterrizar** (*to land*), **el bolso de mano** (*carry-on bag*), **despegar** (*to take off*), **facturar** (*to check*), **hacer escala** (*to stop over*), **el retraso** (*delay*), **la tarjeta de embarque** (*boarding pass*).
- To practice vocabulary from the list, survey the class about their travel habits. Ex: **¿Prefieres el asiento de la ventanilla, del medio o del pasillo? ¿Por qué?**

Perfil **Punta del Este** is located 80 miles east of Uruguay's capital, Montevideo, on a small peninsula that separates the Atlantic Ocean and the **Río de la Plata** estuary. At the beginning of the nineteenth century, **Punta** was nearly deserted and only visited by fishermen and sailors. Its glamorous hotels, dining, nightlife, and beaches have earned it the nickname "the St. Tropez of South America."

El mundo hispano
- Add a visual aspect to this list by using a map to point out the locations of the different **destinos populares**.
- Ask students which destination interests them the most and why.

2 Expansion Ask students to write two additional cloze statements about the information on this page. Then have them exchange papers with a partner and complete the sentences.

3 Teaching Tip To simplify, make a list on the board of the vacation destinations mentioned on this spread. As a class, brainstorm tourist activities in Spanish for each location.

TEACHING OPTIONS

Cultural Comparison For homework, ask student pairs to use the Internet to research a famous beach in the U.S. or Canada and one in the Spanish-speaking world. Ask them to make a list of **similitudes** and **diferencias** about the beaches, including the types of activities available, visitors, the high and low season, and local accommodations. Have pairs present their comparisons to the class.

Heritage Speakers Ask heritage speakers to describe some popular beaches, ruins, or historical sites in their families' countries of origin. If possible, ask them to bring in a map or pictures of the locations. Have the class ask follow-up questions and compare and contrast the locations with those described on these pages.

Tutorial

5.1 Estar with conditions and emotions

ANTE TODO As you learned in **Lecciones 1** and **2**, the verb **estar** is used to talk about how you feel and to say where people, places, and things are located. **Estar** is also used with adjectives to talk about certain emotional and physical conditions.

▶ Use **estar** with adjectives to describe the physical condition of places and things.

La habitación **está** sucia.
The room is dirty.

La puerta **está** cerrada.
The door is closed.

▶ Use **estar** with adjectives to describe how people feel, both mentally and physically.

Yo estoy cansada.

¿Están listos para su viaje?

▶ **¡Atención!** Two important expressions with **estar** that you can use to talk about conditions and emotions are **estar de buen humor** (*to be in a good mood*) and **estar de mal humor** (*to be in a bad mood*).

Adjectives that describe emotions and conditions

abierto/a	*open*	**contento/a**	*content*	**listo/a**	*ready*
aburrido/a	*bored*	**desordenado/a**	*disorderly*	**nervioso/a**	*nervous*
alegre	*happy*	**enamorado/a (de)**	*in love (with)*	**ocupado/a**	*busy*
avergonzado/a	*embarrassed*	**enojado/a**	*angry*	**ordenado/a**	*orderly*
cansado/a	*tired*	**equivocado/a**	*wrong*	**preocupado/a (por)**	*worried (about)*
cerrado/a	*closed*	**feliz**	*happy*	**seguro/a**	*sure*
cómodo/a	*comfortable*	**limpio/a**	*clean*	**sucio/a**	*dirty*
confundido/a	*confused*			**triste**	*sad*

¡INTÉNTALO! Provide the present tense forms of **estar**, and choose which adjective best completes the sentence.

1. La biblioteca ___*está*___ (cerrada / nerviosa) los domingos por la noche. *cerrada*
2. Nosotros ___estamos___ muy (ocupados / equivocados) todos los lunes. ocupados
3. Ellas ___están___ (alegres / confundidas) porque tienen vacaciones. alegres
4. Javier ___está___ (enamorado / ordenado) de Maribel. enamorado
5. Diana ___está___ (enojada / limpia) con su novio. enojada
6. Yo ___estoy___ (nerviosa / abierta) por el viaje. nerviosa
7. La habitación siempre ___está___ (ordenada / segura) cuando vienen sus padres. ordenada
8. Ustedes no comprenden; ___están___ (equivocados / tristes). equivocados

NATIONAL STANDARDS comparisons

CONSULTA

To review the present tense of **estar**, see **Estructura 2.3**, p. 55.

•••

To review the present tense of **ser**, see **Estructura 1.3**, p. 20.

recursos

WB pp. 51–52

LM p. 27

vhlcentral.com Lección 5

Section Goals

In **Estructura 5.1**, students will learn:
- to use **estar** to describe conditions and emotions
- adjectives that describe conditions and emotions

Instructional Resources
Supersite: Audio (Lab MP3 Files); Resources (Grammar Presentation Slides, Activity Pack, Scripts, Answer Keys); Testing Program (Quizzes)
WebSAM
Workbook, pp. 51–52
Lab Manual, p. 27

Teaching Tips

- Ask students to find examples of **estar** used with adjectives in the **Fotonovela**. Have volunteers explain why **estar** instead of **ser** is used in each example.
- Remind students that adjectives agree in number and gender with the nouns they modify.
- Add a visual aspect to this grammar presentation. Bring in personal or magazine photos of people with varying facial expressions. Hold up each one and state the person's emotion. Ex: **Mi esposa y yo estamos contentos.**
- Point to objects and people and have volunteers supply the correct form of **estar** + [*adjective*]. Ex: Point to windows. (**Están abiertas.**)
- Use TPR to practice the adjectives. Have the class stand, and signal a student. Say: ____, **estás enojado/a.** (Student will make an angry face.) Vary by indicating more than one student.
- Point out the use of **de** with **enamorado/a** and **por** with **preocupado/a**. Write cloze sentences on the board and have students complete them. Ex: **Michelle Obama está ____ Barack Obama. (enamorada de)**

TEACHING OPTIONS

TPR Call out a sentence using an adjective and have students mime the emotion or show the condition. Ex: **Sus libros están abiertos.** (Students show their open books.) **Ustedes están alegres.** (Students act happy.) Next, call on volunteers to act out an emotion or condition, and have the class tell what is going on. Ex: A student pretends to cry. (**Carlos está triste.**)

Video Replay the **Fotonovela** episode and ask comprehension questions using **estar** and adjectives expressing emotions or conditions. Ex: **¿Cómo está el hotel? (Está limpio y cómodo.) ¿Está de mal humor Miguel? (Sí, está de mal humor.) ¿Quién está cansado? (Marissa está cansada.)**

Práctica y Comunicación

1 ¿Cómo están? Complete Martín's statements about how he and other people are feeling. In the first blank, fill in the correct form of **estar**. In the second blank, fill in the adjective that best fits the context. Some answers may vary.

AYUDA
Make sure that there is agreement between:
• Subjects and verbs in person and number
• Nouns and adjectives in gender and number
Ell**os** no est**án** enferm**os**.
They are not sick.

1. Yo ___estoy___ un poco ___nervioso___ porque tengo un examen mañana.
2. Mi hermana Patricia ___está___ muy ___contenta___ porque mañana va a hacer una excursión al campo.
3. Mis hermanos Juan y José salen de la casa a las cinco de la mañana. Por la noche, siempre ___están___ muy ___cansados___.
4. Mi amigo Ramiro ___está___ ___enamorado___; su novia se llama Adela.
5. Mi papá y sus colegas ___están___ muy ___ocupados___ hoy. ¡Hay mucho trabajo!
6. Patricia y yo ___estamos___ un poco ___preocupados___ por ellos porque trabajan mucho.
7. Mi amiga Mónica ___está___ un poco ___triste/enojada___ porque su novio no puede salir esta noche.
8. Esta clase no es muy interesante. ¿Tú ___estás___ ___aburrido/a___ también?

2 Describir Describe these people and places. Answers will vary. Sample answers:

1. Anabela
Está contenta/alegre/feliz.

2. Juan y Luisa
Están enojados.

3. la habitación de Teresa
Está ordenada/limpia.

4. la habitación de César
Está desordenada/sucia.

3 Situaciones With a partner, use **estar** to talk about how you feel in these situations. Answers will vary.

1. Cuando hace sol…
2. Cuando tomas un examen…
3. Cuando viajas en avión…
4. Cuando estás en la clase de español…
5. Cuando ves una película con tu actor/actriz favorito/a…

4 En la tele In small groups, imagine that you are a family that stars on a reality TV show. You are vacationing together, but the trip isn't going well for everyone. Write the script of a scene from the show and then act it out. Use at least six adjectives from the previous page and be creative!

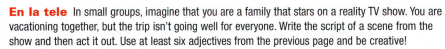

modelo
Papá: *¿Por qué estás enojada, María Rosa? El hotel es muy bonito y las habitaciones están limpias.*
Mamá: *¡Pero mira, Roberto! Las maletas de Elisa están abiertas y, como siempre, sus cosas están muy desordenadas.*

Practice more at **vhlcentral.com**.

1 Teaching Tip Have a volunteer model the first sentence by supplying the correct form of **estar** and an appropriate adjective. Ask the student to explain his or her choices.

1 Expansion Have students write five additional sentences missing **estar** and an adjective. Then have them exchange papers and complete the sentences.

2 Expansion
- Have students write a few sentences about the illustrations explaining why the people feel the way they do and why the rooms look this way.
- Have students pretend they are **Anabela, Juan,** or **Luisa** and give a short oral description of who they are and how they feel today.

3 Teaching Tip Have partners alternate completing the sentences until each has answered all items.

3 Expansion Ask students to keep a record of their partners' responses. Take a classroom poll to see what percentage of students felt a particular way for each situation.

4 Teaching Tip As an alternative, have students imagine that they are a family that is currently appearing on a reality show.

TEACHING OPTIONS

Pairs Have students write a list of four questions using different conjugations of **estar** and four adjectives that have an antonym from the list on page 152. Students ask partners their questions. They respond negatively, then use the opposite adjective in an affirmative statement. Ex: **¿Está abierta la biblioteca? (No, no está abierta. Está cerrada.)**

Extra Practice For homework, have students pick eight adjectives of emotion from the list on page 152, and write sentences about what they do when they feel that way. Ex: **Cuando estoy preocupado, hablo por teléfono con mi madre…** In class, have students form small groups and share their sentences. Survey the class to see if there are any common activities.

Section Goals

In **Estructura 5.2**, students will learn:
- the present progressive of regular and irregular verbs
- the present progressive versus the simple present tense in Spanish

Instructional Resources
Supersite: Audio (Lab MP3 Files); Resources (Grammar Presentation Slides, Digital Image Bank, Activity Pack, Scripts, Answer Keys); Testing Program (Quizzes)
WebSAM
Workbook, p. 53
Lab Manual, p. 28

Teaching Tips

- Use regular verbs to ask questions about things students are not doing. Ex: **¿Estás comiendo pizza? (No, no estoy comiendo pizza.)**
- Explain the formation of the present progressive, writing examples on the board.
- Add a visual aspect to this grammar presentation. Use photos to elicit sentences with the present progressive. Ex: **¿Qué está haciendo el hombre alto? (Está sacando fotos.)** Include present participles ending in **–yendo** as well as those with stem changes.
- Point out that the present progressive is rarely used with the verbs **ir**, **poder**, and **venir** since they already imply an action in progress.

5.2 The present progressive

Tutorial

NATIONAL STANDARDS comparisons

ANTE TODO Both Spanish and English use the present progressive, which consists of the present tense of the verb *to be* and the present participle of another verb (the *-ing* form in English).

Las chicas están hablando con el empleado del hotel.

¿Estás estudiando en la playa?

- Form the present progressive with the present tense of **estar** and a present participle.

FORM OF ESTAR	+ PRESENT PARTICIPLE	FORM OF ESTAR	+ PRESENT PARTICIPLE
Estoy	**pescando.**	**Estamos**	**comiendo.**
I am	*fishing.*	*We are*	*eating.*

- The present participle of regular **-ar**, **-er**, and **-ir** verbs is formed as follows:

INFINITIVE	STEM	ENDING	PRESENT PARTICIPLE
hablar	habl-	**-ando**	habl**ando**
comer	com-	**-iendo**	com**iendo**
escribir	escrib-	**-iendo**	escrib**iendo**

- **¡Atención!** When the stem of an **-er** or **-ir** verb ends in a vowel, the present participle ends in **-yendo**.

INFINITIVE	STEM	ENDING	PRESENT PARTICIPLE
leer	le-	**-yendo**	le**yendo**
oír	o-	**-yendo**	o**yendo**
traer	tra-	**-yendo**	tra**yendo**

- **Ir**, **poder**, and **venir** have irregular present participles (**yendo**, **pudiendo**, **viniendo**). Several other verbs have irregular present participles that you will need to learn.

- **-Ir** stem-changing verbs have a stem change in the present participle.

-ir stem-changing verbs

e:ie in the present tense	**e → i** in the present participle
preferir →	pref**i**riendo
e:i in the present tense	**e → i** in the present participle
conseguir →	cons**i**guiendo
o:ue in the present tense	**o → u** in the present participle
dormir →	d**u**rmiendo

TEACHING OPTIONS

TPR Divide the class into three groups. Appoint leaders and give them a list of verbs. Leaders call out a verb and a subject (Ex: **seguir/yo**), then toss a ball to someone in the group. That student says the appropriate present progressive form of the verb (Ex: **estoy siguiendo**) and tosses the ball back. Leaders should use all the verbs on the list and be sure to toss the ball to each member of the group.

TPR Play charades. In groups of four, have students take turns miming actions for the rest of the group to guess. Ex: Student pretends to read a newspaper. (**Estás leyendo el periódico.**) For incorrect guesses, the student should respond negatively. Ex: **No, no estoy estudiando.**

COMPARE & CONTRAST

The use of the present progressive is much more restricted in Spanish than in English. In Spanish, the present progressive is mainly used to emphasize that an action is in progress at the time of speaking.

Maru **está escuchando** música latina **ahora mismo**.
Maru is listening to Latin music right now.

Felipe y su amigo **todavía están jugando** al fútbol.
Felipe and his friend are still playing soccer.

In English, the present progressive is often used to talk about situations and actions that occur over an extended period of time or in the future. In Spanish, the simple present tense is often used instead.

Xavier **estudia** computación este semestre.
Xavier is studying computer science this semester.

Marissa **sale** mañana para los Estados Unidos.
Marissa is leaving tomorrow for the United States.

¿Está pensando en su futuro?
Nosotros, sí.
BANCO
CONGRESO
Preparándolo para el mañana

¡INTÉNTALO! Create complete sentences by putting the verbs in the present progressive.

1. mis amigos / descansar en la playa *Mis amigos están descansando en la playa.*
2. nosotros / practicar deportes Estamos practicando deportes.
3. Carmen / comer en casa Carmen está comiendo en casa.
4. nuestro equipo / ganar el partido Nuestro equipo está ganando el partido.
5. yo / leer el periódico Estoy leyendo el periódico.
6. él / pensar comprar una bicicleta Está pensando comprar una bicicleta.
7. ustedes / jugar a las cartas Ustedes están jugando a las cartas.
8. José y Francisco / dormir José y Francisco están durmiendo.
9. Marisa / leer el correo electrónico Marisa está leyendo el correo electrónico.
10. yo / preparar sándwiches Estoy preparando sándwiches.
11. Carlos / tomar fotos Carlos está tomando fotos.
12. ¿dormir / tú? ¿Estás durmiendo?

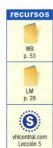

recursos
WB p. 53
LM p. 28
vhlcentral.com Lección 5

Teaching Tips

- Discuss each point in the **Compare & Contrast** box.
- Write these statements on the board and ask students if they would use the present or the present progressive in Spanish for each item. 1. I'm going on vacation tomorrow. 2. She's packing her suitcase right now. 3. They are fishing in Puerto Rico this week. 4. Roberto is still working. Then ask students to translate the items. **(1. Voy de vacaciones mañana. 2. Está haciendo la maleta ahora mismo. 3. Pescan en Puerto Rico esta semana. 4. Roberto todavía está trabajando.)**
- In this lesson, students learn **todavía** to mean *still* in the present progressive tense. You may want to point out that **todavía** also means *yet*. They will be able to use that meaning in later lessons as they learn the past tenses.
- Have students rewrite the sentences in the **¡Inténtalo!** activity using the simple present. Ask volunteers to explain how the sentences change depending on whether the verb is in the present progressive or the simple present.

TEACHING OPTIONS

Pairs Have students write eight sentences in Spanish modeled after the examples in the **Compare & Contrast** box. There should be two sentences modeled after each example. Ask students to replace the verbs with blanks. Then, have students exchange papers with a partner and complete the sentences.

Extra Practice For homework, ask students to find five photos from a magazine or create five simple drawings of people performing different activities. For each image, have them write one sentence telling where the people are, one explaining what they are doing, and one describing how they feel. Ex: **Juan está en la biblioteca. Está estudiando. Está cansado.**

1 Expansion Ask students comprehension questions that elicit the present progressive. Ex: **¿Quién está buscando información? (Marta y José Luis están buscando información.) ¿Qué información están buscando? (Están buscando información sobre San Juan.)**

2 Teaching Tips
- Use the **Lección 5 Estructura** digital images to assist with the presentation of this activity.
- Before starting the activity, ask students questions about each drawing to elicit a description of what they see. Ex: **¿Quién está en el dibujo número 5? (Samuel está en el dibujo.) ¿Dónde está Samuel? (Está en la playa.) ¿Qué más ven en el dibujo? (Vemos una silla y el mar.)**

3 Teaching Tip To simplify, first read through the names in column A as a class. Point out the profession clues in the **Ayuda** box, then guide students in matching each name with an infinitive. Finally, have students form sentences.

3 Expansion Have students choose five more celebrities and write descriptions of what they are doing at this moment.

Práctica

1

Completar Alfredo's Spanish class is preparing to travel to Puerto Rico. Use the present progressive of the verb in parentheses to complete Alfredo's description of what everyone is doing.

1. Yo __estoy investigando__ (investigar) la situación política de la isla (*island*).
2. La esposa del profesor __está haciendo__ (hacer) las maletas.
3. Marta y José Luis __están buscando__ (buscar) información sobre San Juan en Internet.
4. Enrique y yo __estamos leyendo__ (leer) un correo electrónico de nuestro amigo puertorriqueño.
5. Javier __está aprendiendo__ (aprender) mucho sobre la cultura puertorriqueña.
6. Y tú __estás practicando__ (practicar) el español, ¿verdad?

2

¿Qué están haciendo? María and her friends are vacationing at a resort in San Juan, Puerto Rico. Complete her description of what everyone is doing right now.

CONSULTA
For more information about Puerto Rico, see **Panorama**, pp. 170–171.

1. Yo
estoy escribiendo una carta.

2. Javier
está buceando en el mar.

3. Alejandro y Rebeca
están jugando a las cartas.

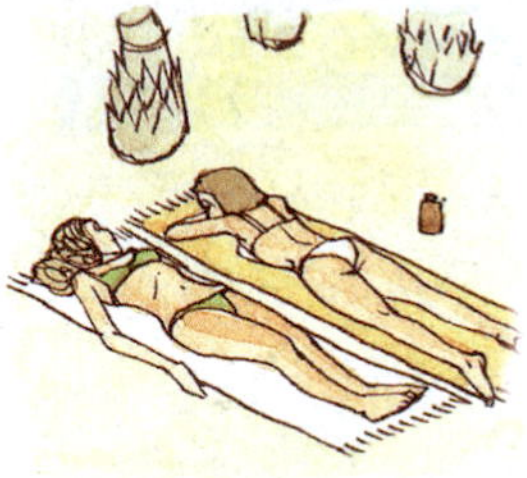
4. Celia y yo
estamos tomando el sol.

5. Samuel
está escuchando música.

6. Lorenzo
está durmiendo.

3

Personajes famosos Say what these celebrities are doing right now, using the cues provided.
Answers will vary.

modelo
Shakira
Shakira está cantando una canción ahora mismo.

A		B	
Isabel Allende	Nelly Furtado	bailar	hacer
Rachael Ray	Dwight Howard	cantar	jugar
James Cameron	Las Rockettes de Nueva York	correr	preparar
Venus y Serena Williams	¿?	escribir	¿?
Joey Votto	¿?	hablar	¿?

AYUDA
Isabel Allende: **novelas**
Rachael Ray: **televisión, negocios** (*business*)
James Cameron: **cine**
Venus y Serena Williams: **tenis**
Joey Votto: **béisbol**
Nelly Furtado: **canciones**
Dwight Howard: **baloncesto**
Las Rockettes de Nueva York: **baile**

Practice more at **vhlcentral.com**.

TEACHING OPTIONS

Pairs Have students bring in photos from a vacation. Ask them to describe the photos to a partner. Students should explain what the weather is like, who is in the photo, and what they are doing. The partner should try to guess the location the student is describing. Students can ask additional questions until they guess correctly.

Game Have the class form a circle. Appoint one student to be the starter, who will mime an action (Ex: eating) and say what he or she is doing (Ex: **Estoy comiendo.**). The next student mimes the same action, says what that person is doing (____ **está comiendo.**), and then mimes and states a different action (Ex: sleeping/**Estoy durmiendo.**). Have students continue until the chain breaks. Have students see how long the chain can get in three minutes.

Comunicación

4

Preguntar With a partner, take turns asking each other what you are doing at these times. Answers will vary.

modelo

8:00 a.m.
Estudiante 1: *¡Hola, Andrés! Son las ocho de la mañana. ¿Qué estás haciendo?*
Estudiante 2: *Estoy desayunando.*

1. 5:00 a.m.
2. 9:30 a.m.
3. 11:00 a.m.
4. 12:00 p.m.
5. 2:00 p.m.
6. 5:00 p.m.
7. 9:00 p.m.
8. 11:30 p.m.

5

Describir Work with a partner and use the present progressive to describe what is going on in this Spanish beach scene. Answers will vary.

NOTA CULTURAL

More than 60 million tourists travel to Spain every year, many of them drawn by the warm climate and beautiful coasts. Tourists wanting a beach vacation go mostly to the **Costa del Sol** or the Balearic Islands, in the Mediterranean.

6

Conversar Imagine that you and a classmate are each babysitting a group of children. With a partner, prepare a telephone conversation using these cues. Be creative and add further comments. Answers will vary.

Estudiante 1	Estudiante 2
Say hello and ask what the kids are doing.	→ Say hello and tell your partner that two of your kids are doing their homework. Then ask what the kids at his/her house are doing.
Tell your partner that two of your kids are running and dancing in the house.	→ Tell your partner that one of the kids is reading.
Tell your partner that you are tired and that two of your kids are watching TV and eating pizza.	→ Tell your partner that one of the kids is sleeping.
Tell your partner you have to go; the kids are playing soccer in the house.	→ Say goodbye and good luck (**¡Buena suerte!**).

Síntesis

7

¿Qué están haciendo? A group of classmates is traveling to San Juan, Puerto Rico, for a week-long Spanish immersion program. In order for the participants to be on time for their flight, you and your partner must locate them. Your instructor will give you each a handout to help you complete this task. Answers will vary.

TEACHING OPTIONS

Video Show the **Fotonovela** episode again, pausing after each exchange. Ask students to describe what each person in the shot is doing at that moment.
TPR Write sentences with the present progressive on strips of paper. Call on volunteers to draw papers out of a hat to act out. The class should guess what the sentences are. Ex: **Yo estoy durmiendo en la cama.**

Pairs Add an auditory aspect to this grammar practice. Ask students to write a short paragraph using the present progressive. Students should try to make their sentences as complex as possible. Have students dictate their sentences to a partner. After pairs have finished dictating their sentences, have them exchange papers to check for accuracy. Circulate around the room and look over students' work.

4 Teaching Tip To simplify, first have students outline their daily activities and at what time they do them. Remind students to use **a la(s)** when expressing time.

4 Expansion Reverse the activity by having students state what they are doing. Their partner should guess the time of day. Alternatively, students could say that they are doing season-specific activities (Ex: **Estoy tomando el sol.**) and their partner will guess the month.

5 Teaching Tip Use the **Lección 5 Estructura** digital images to assist with the presentation of this activity.

5 Expansion In pairs, have students write a conversation between two or more of the people in the drawing. Conversations should consist of at least three exchanges.

6 Teaching Tip To simplify, before beginning their conversation, have students prepare for their roles by brainstorming two lists: one with verbs that describe what the children are doing at home and the other with adjectives that describe how the babysitter feels.

6 Expansion Ask pairs to tell each other what the parents of the two sets of children are doing. Ex: **Los padres de los niños buenos están visitando el museo. Los padres de los niños malos están en una fiesta.**

7 Teaching Tip Divide the class into pairs and distribute the handouts from the Activity Pack (Activity Pack/Supersite) that correspond to this Information Gap Activity.

7 Expansion Have pairs discuss what each program participant is doing in flight. Ex: **Pedro está leyendo una novela.**

Section Goal

In **Estructura 5.3**, students will review and compare the uses of **ser** and **estar**.

Instructional Resources
Supersite: Audio (Lab MP3 Files); Resources (Grammar Presentation Slides, Digital Image Bank, Activity Pack, Scripts, Answer Keys); Testing Program (Quizzes)
WebSAM
Workbook, pp. 54–55
Lab Manual, p. 29

Teaching Tips

- Use the **Lección 5** Grammar Presentation Slides to assist with this presentation.
- Have pairs brainstorm as many uses of **ser** with examples as they can. Compile a list on the board, and repeat for **estar**.
- Divide the board into two columns. In column one, write sentences using **ser** and **estar** in random order (Ex: **Miguel es de España.**). In column two, write the uses of **ser** and **estar** taught so far, also in random order (Ex: place of origin). Ask volunteers to match the sentence with its corresponding use.
- Write cloze sentences on the board. Ask students to supply the correct form of **ser** or **estar**. Ex: **Mi casa ____ lejos de aquí. (estar, location; está)** If either **ser** or **estar** could be used, ask students to explain how the meaning of the sentence would change.
- Contrast the uses of **ser** and **estar** by talking about celebrities. Ex: **Shakira es colombiana y su familia es de origen libanés. Es bonita y delgada. Es cantante. Ella está en los Estados Unidos ahora. Está haciendo una gira de conciertos. Tiene un concierto hoy; es a las ocho. El concierto es en un estadio. El estadio está en Miami.** Pause after each sentence and have students identify the use(s).

5.3 Ser and estar

Tutorial

NATIONAL comparisons STANDARDS

ANTE TODO You have already learned that **ser** and **estar** both mean *to be* but are used for different purposes. These charts summarize the key differences in usage between **ser** and **estar**.

¡ATENCIÓN!
Ser de expresses not only origin (**Es de Buenos Aires.**) and possession (**Es la pluma de Maru.**), but also what material something is made of (**La bicicleta es de metal.**).

Uses of ser

1. **Nationality and place of origin**	Juan Carlos **es** argentino. **Es** de Buenos Aires.
2. **Profession or occupation**	Adela **es** agente de viajes. Francisco **es** médico.
3. **Characteristics of people and things**	José y Clara **son** simpáticos. El clima de Puerto Rico **es** agradable.
4. **Generalizations**	¡**Es** fabuloso viajar! **Es** difícil estudiar a la una de la mañana.
5. **Possession**	**Es** la pluma de Jimena. **Son** las llaves del señor Díaz.
6. **What something is made of**	La bicicleta **es** de metal. Los pasajes **son** de papel.
7. **Time and date**	Hoy **es** martes. **Son** las dos. Hoy **es** el primero de julio.
8. **Where or when an event takes place**	El partido **es** en el estadio Santa Fe. La conferencia **es** a las siete.

Ellos son mis amigos.

Miguel está enojado conmigo.

Uses of estar

1. **Location or spatial relationships**	El aeropuerto **está** lejos de la ciudad. Tu habitación **está** en el tercer piso.
2. **Health**	¿Cómo **estás**? **Estoy** bien, gracias.
3. **Physical states and conditions**	El profesor **está** ocupado. Las ventanas **están** abiertas.
4. **Emotional states**	Marissa **está** feliz hoy. **Estoy** muy enojado con Maru.
5. **Certain weather expressions**	**Está** lloviendo. **Está** nublado.
6. **Ongoing actions (progressive tenses)**	**Estamos** estudiando para un examen. Ana **está** leyendo una novela.

TEACHING OPTIONS

Extra Practice Add an auditory aspect to this grammar presentation. Call out sentences containing forms of **ser** or **estar**. Ask students to identify the use of the verb.

Extra Practice Ask students to write a postcard to a friend or family member about a vacation in Puerto Rico, incorporating as many of the uses of **ser** and **estar** as they can.

Game Divide the class into two teams. Call out a use of **ser** or **estar**. The first member of each team runs to the board and writes a sample sentence. The first student to finish a sentence correctly earns a point for his or her team. Practice all uses of each verb and make sure each team member has at least two turns. Then tally the points to see which team wins.

Ser and estar with adjectives

- With many descriptive adjectives, **ser** and **estar** can both be used, but the meaning will change.

Juan **es** delgado. *Juan is thin.*	Ana **es** nerviosa. *Ana is a nervous person.*
Juan **está** más delgado hoy. *Juan looks thinner today.*	Ana **está** nerviosa por el examen. *Ana is nervous because of the exam.*

- In the examples above, the statements with **ser** are general observations about the inherent qualities of Juan and Ana. The statements with **estar** describe conditions that are variable.
- Here are some adjectives that change in meaning when used with **ser** and **estar**.

With ser	With estar
El chico **es listo**. *The boy is **smart**.*	El chico **está listo**. *The boy is **ready**.*
La profesora **es mala**. *The professor is **bad**.*	La profesora **está mala**. *The professor is **sick**.*
Jaime **es aburrido**. *Jaime is **boring**.*	Jaime **está aburrido**. *Jaime is **bored**.*
Las peras **son verdes**. *Pears are **green**.*	Las peras **están verdes**. *The pears are **not ripe**.*
El gato **es muy vivo**. *The cat is very **clever**.*	El gato **está vivo**. *The cat is **alive**.*
Iván **es un hombre seguro**. *Iván is a **confident** man.*	Iván no **está seguro**. *Iván is **not sure**.*

¡ATENCIÓN!

When referring to objects, **ser seguro/a** means *to be safe*.

El puente es seguro.
The bridge is safe.

¡INTÉNTALO! Form complete sentences by using the correct form of **ser** or **estar** and making any other necessary changes.

1. Alejandra / cansado — Alejandra está cansada.
2. ellos / pelirrojo — Ellos son pelirrojos.
3. Carmen / alto — Carmen es alta.
4. yo / la clase de español — Estoy en la clase de español.
5. película / a las once — La película es a las once.
6. hoy / viernes — Hoy es viernes.
7. nosotras / enojado — Nosotras estamos enojadas.
8. Antonio / médico — Antonio es médico.
9. Romeo y Julieta / enamorado — Romeo y Julieta están enamorados.
10. libros / de Ana — Los libros son de Ana.
11. Marisa y Juan / estudiando — Marisa y Juan están estudiando.
12. partido de baloncesto / gimnasio — El partido de baloncesto es en el gimnasio.

recursos
WB pp. 54–55
LM p. 29
vhlcentral.com Lección 5

Teaching Tips

- Ask students if they notice any context clues in the examples that would help them choose between **ser** and **estar**.
- Write sentences like these on the board: 1. Pilar is worried because she has a quiz tomorrow. **(Pilar está preocupada porque tiene una prueba mañana.)** 2. The employee is very busy right now. **(El empleado está muy ocupado ahora.)** 3. The beach is pretty. **(La playa es bonita.)** 4. **Juan** is/looks very handsome today. **(Juan está muy guapo hoy.)** Have students translate the sentences into Spanish and ask them why they chose either **ser** or **estar** for their translation.
- Ask students questions to practice the different meanings of adjectives, depending on whether they are used with **ser** or **estar**. Ex: **1. Manuel es un muchacho muy inteligente. ¿Está listo o es listo? 2. No me gusta la clase de física. ¿Está aburrida o es aburrida? 3. No sé si Carlos tiene 50 ó 51 años. ¿No estoy seguro/a o no soy seguro/a? 4. ¿El color del taxi es verde o está verde? 5. El profesor no enseña muy bien. ¿Está malo o es malo?**

The Affective Dimension

If students feel anxious that Spanish has two verbs that mean *to be*, reassure them that they will soon feel more comfortable with this concept as they read more examples and have more practice. Point out that **ser** and **estar** express rich shades of meaning.

TEACHING OPTIONS

Extra Practice Ask students to write sentences illustrating the contrasting meanings of adjectives used with **ser** or **estar**. Have students exchange papers for peer editing before going over them with the class.

Video Show the **Fotonovela** episode again. Have students jot down the forms of **ser** or **estar** that they hear. Discuss each use of **ser** and **estar**.

Pairs Tell students to imagine that they are going to interview a celebrity visiting their hometown. Ask them to write questions with at least ten different uses of **ser** and **estar**. Next, have them interview a partner and record the answers. Have students write a summary of their interviews.

1 Teaching Tip Have students identify the use(s) of **ser** or **estar** for each item.

1 Expansion To challenge students, ask them to use each adjective in a sentence. If the adjective can take both verbs, have them provide two sentences.

2 Teaching Tip To simplify, ask students to point out context clues that will help them determine whether to use **ser** or **estar**. Ex: The word **hoy** in line 2 suggests that **guapo** is a variable physical state.

2 Expansion Have pairs write a continuation of the conversation and then present it to the class.

3 Teaching Tip Use the **Lección 5 Estructura** digital images to assist with the presentation of this activity.

3 Expansion Add another visual aspect to this grammar practice. Bring in photos or magazine pictures that show many different people performing a variety of activities. Have students use **ser** and **estar** to write short descriptions of the scenes.

Práctica

1 **¿Ser o estar?** Indicate whether each adjective takes **ser** or **estar**. **¡Ojo!** Three of them can take both verbs.

	ser	estar		ser	estar
1. delgada	✓	✓	5. seguro	✓	✓
2. canadiense	✓	○	6. enojada	○	✓
3. enamorado	○	✓	7. importante	✓	○
4. lista	✓	✓	8. avergonzada	○	✓

2 **Completar** Complete this conversation with the appropriate forms of **ser** and **estar**.

EDUARDO ¡Hola, Ceci! ¿Cómo (1) estás?
CECILIA Hola, Eduardo. Bien, gracias. ¡Qué guapo (2) estás hoy!
EDUARDO Gracias. (3) Eres muy amable. Oye, ¿qué (4) estás haciendo? (5) ¿Estás ocupada?
CECILIA No, sólo le (6) estoy escribiendo una carta a mi prima Pilar.
EDUARDO ¿De dónde (7) es ella?
CECILIA Pilar (8) es de Ecuador. Su papá (9) es médico en Quito. Pero ahora Pilar y su familia (10) están de vacaciones en Ponce, Puerto Rico.
EDUARDO Y... ¿cómo (11) es Pilar?
CECILIA (12) Es muy lista. Y también (13) es alta, rubia y muy bonita.

3 **En el parque** With a partner, take turns describing the people in the drawing. Your descriptions should answer the questions provided. Answers will vary.

1. ¿Quiénes son?
2. ¿Dónde están?
3. ¿Cómo son?
4. ¿Cómo están?
5. ¿Qué están haciendo?
6. ¿Qué estación es?
7. ¿Qué tiempo hace?
8. ¿Quiénes están de vacaciones?

Practice more at **vhlcentral.com**.

TEACHING OPTIONS

Extra Practice Have students write a paragraph about a close friend, including the person's physical appearance, general disposition, place of birth, birthday, profession, and where the friend is now. Ask volunteers to share their descriptions with the class.

Pairs Ask pairs to role-play this scenario: Student A is at the beach with some friends while Student B is at home. Student A calls Student B, trying to convince him or her to come to the beach. Students should try to employ as many uses of **ser** and **estar** in their scenario as possible. After acting out the scene once, have students switch roles.

NATIONAL communication STANDARDS

Comunicación

4

Describir With a classmate, take turns describing these people. Mention where they are from, what they are like, how they are feeling, and what they are doing right now. Answers will vary.

modelo

tu compañero/a de cuarto
Mi compañera de cuarto es de San Juan, Puerto Rico. Es muy inteligente. Está cansada pero está estudiando porque tiene un examen.

1. tu mejor (*best*) amigo/a
2. tu actor/actriz favorito/a
3. tu profesor(a) favorito/a
4. tu novio/a o esposo/a
5. tus abuelos
6. tus padres

5

Adivinar Get together with a partner and take turns describing a celebrity using these items as a guide. Don't mention the celebrity's name. Can your partner guess who you are describing? Answers will vary.

- descripción física
- cómo está ahora
- origen
- dónde está ahora
- qué está haciendo ahora
- profesión u ocupación

6

En el aeropuerto In groups of three, take turns assuming the identity of a character from this drawing. Your partners will ask you questions using **ser** and **estar** until they figure out who you are. Answers will vary.

modelo

Estudiante 3: *¿Dónde estás?*
Estudiante 1: *Estoy cerca de la puerta.*
Estudiante 2: *¿Qué estás haciendo?*
Estudiante 1: *Estoy escuchando a otra persona.*
Estudiante 3: *¿Eres uno de los pasajeros?*
Estudiante 1: *No, soy empleado del aeropuerto.*
Estudiante 2: *¿Eres Camilo?*

NATIONAL communication STANDARDS

Síntesis

7

Conversación In pairs, imagine that you and your partner are two of the characters in the drawing in **Actividad 6**. After boarding, you are seated next to each other and strike up a conversation. Act out what you would say to your fellow passenger. Answers will vary.

4 Expansion Have pairs select two descriptions to present to the class.

5 Teaching Tip Model the activity for the class. You may want to tell students to use **una persona** to create ambiguity in their descriptions. Ex: **Es una persona alta…**

6 Teaching Tip Use the **Lección 5 Estructura** digital images to assist with the presentation of this activity.

6 Expansion
Have students pick one of the individuals pictured and write a one-paragraph description, employing as many different uses of **ser** and **estar** as possible.

7 Teaching Tips
- To simplify, first have students write a character description for the person they will be playing. Then, as a class, brainstorm topics of conversation.
- Make sure that students use **ser** and **estar**, the present progressive, and stem-changing verbs in their conversations, as well as vacation-, pastime-, and family-related vocabulary.

The Affective Dimension
Encourage students to consider pair and group activities as a cooperative venture in which group members support and motivate each other.

TEACHING OPTIONS

Small Groups Have students work in small groups to write a television commercial for a vacation resort in the Spanish-speaking world. Ask them to employ as many uses of **ser** and **estar** as they can. If possible, after they have written the commercial, have them tape it to show to the class.

TPR Call on a volunteer and whisper the name of a celebrity in his or her ear. The volunteer acts out verbs and characteristics and uses props to elicit descriptions from the class. Ex: The volunteer points to the U.S. on a map. (**Es de los Estados Unidos.**) He or she then indicates a tall, thin man. (**Es un hombre atlético y delgado.**) He or she acts out swimming. (**Está nadando. ¿Es Michael Phelps?**)

Section Goals

In **Estructura 5.4**, students will study:
- direct object nouns
- the personal **a**
- direct object pronouns

Instructional Resources
Supersite: Audio (Lab MP3 Files); Resources (Grammar Presentation Slides, Activity Pack, Scripts, Answer Keys); Testing Program (Quizzes)
WebSAM
Workbook, p. 56
Lab Manual, p. 30

Teaching Tips

- Write these sentences on the board: **—¿Quién tiene el pasaporte? —Juan lo tiene.** Underline **pasaporte** and explain that it is a direct object noun. Then underline **lo** and explain that it is the masculine singular direct object pronoun. Translate both sentences. Continue with: **—¿Quién saca fotos? —Simón las saca. —¿Quién tiene la llave? —Pilar la tiene.**
- Read this exchange aloud: **—¿Haces las maletas? —No, no hago las maletas. —¿Por qué no haces las maletas? —No hago las maletas porque las maletas no están aquí.** Ask students if the exchange sounds natural to them. Then write it on the board and ask students to use direct object pronouns to avoid repetition. If students try to say **no las están** in the last sentence, point out that direct object pronouns cannot replace the subject of a verb. The only option is to eliminate the subject: **no están.**
- Ask individuals questions to elicit the personal **a: ¿Visitas a tu abuela los fines de semana? ¿Llamas a tu padre los sábados?**
- Ask questions to elicit third-person direct object pronouns. Ex: **¿Quién ve el lápiz de Marcos? ¿Quién quiere estos diccionarios?**

5.4 Direct object nouns and pronouns

Tutorial

NATIONAL STANDARDS comparisons

SUBJECT	VERB	DIRECT OBJECT NOUN
Juan Carlos y Jimena	están tomando	fotos.
Juan Carlos and Jimena	*are taking*	*photos.*

- A direct object noun receives the action of the verb directly and generally follows the verb. In the example above, the direct object noun answers the question *What are Juan Carlos and Jimena taking?*

- When a direct object noun in Spanish is a person or a pet, it is preceded by the word **a**. This is called the personal **a**; there is no English equivalent for this construction.

Mariela mira **a** Carlos.
Mariela is watching Carlos.

Mariela mira televisión.
Mariela is watching TV.

- In the first sentence above, the personal **a** is required because the direct object is a person. In the second sentence, the personal **a** is not required because the direct object is a thing, not a person.

Miguel no me perdona.

No tenemos tablas de windsurf.

El botones las puede conseguir para ustedes.

- Direct object pronouns are words that replace direct object nouns. Like English, Spanish uses a direct object pronoun to avoid repeating a noun already mentioned.

	DIRECT OBJECT		DIRECT OBJECT PRONOUN	
Maribel hace	las maletas.	Maribel	las	hace.
Felipe compra	el sombrero.	Felipe	lo	compra.
Vicky tiene	la llave.	Vicky	la	tiene.

Direct object pronouns

SINGULAR		PLURAL	
me	*me*	**nos**	*us*
te	*you* (fam.)	**os**	*you* (fam.)
lo	*you* (m., form.)	**los**	*you* (m.)
	him; it (m.)		*them* (m.)
la	*you* (f., form.)	**las**	*you* (f.)
	her; it (f.)		*them* (f.)

TEACHING OPTIONS

TPR Call out a series of sentences with direct object nouns, some of which require the personal **a** and some of which do not. Ex: **Visito muchos museos. Visito a mis tíos.** Have students raise their hands if the personal **a** is used.

Extra Practice Write six sentences on the board that have direct object nouns. Use two verbs in the simple present tense, two in the present progressive, and two using **ir a** + [*infinitive*]. Draw a line through the direct objects as students call them out. Have students state which pronouns to write to replace them. Then, draw an arrow from each pronoun to where it goes in the sentence, as indicated by students.

▶ In affirmative sentences, direct object pronouns generally appear before the conjugated verb. In negative sentences, the pronoun is placed between the word **no** and the verb.

Adela practica **el tenis.**
Adela **lo** practica.

Gabriela no tiene **las llaves.**
Gabriela **no las** tiene.

Carmen compra **los pasajes.**
Carmen **los** compra.

Diego no hace **las maletas.**
Diego **no las** hace.

▶ When the verb is an infinitive construction, such as **ir a** + [*infinitive*], the direct object pronoun can be placed before the conjugated form or attached to the infinitive.

Ellos van a escribir **unas postales.** → Ellos **las** van a escribir. / Ellos van a escribir**las.**

Lidia quiere ver **una película.** → Lidia **la** quiere ver. / Lidia quiere ver**la.**

▶ When the verb is in the present progressive, the direct object pronoun can be placed before the conjugated form or attached to the present participle. **¡Atención!** When a direct object pronoun is attached to the present participle, an accent mark is added to maintain the proper stress.

Gerardo está leyendo **la lección.** → Gerardo **la** está leyendo. / Gerardo está leyéndo**la.**

Toni está mirando **el partido.** → Toni **lo** está mirando. / Toni está mirándo**lo.**

CONSULTA

To learn more about accents, see **Lección 4, Pronunciación**, p. 115, **Lección 10, Ortografía**, p. 315, and **Lección 11, Ortografía**, p. 349.

¡INTÉNTALO! Choose the correct direct object pronoun for each sentence.

1. Tienes el libro de español. *c*
   a. La tienes. b. Los tienes. c. Lo tienes.
2. Voy a ver el partido de baloncesto. a
   a. Voy a verlo. b. Voy a verte. c. Voy a vernos.
3. El artista quiere dibujar a Luisa y a su mamá. c
   a. Quiere dibujarme. b. Quiere dibujarla. c. Quiere dibujarlas.
4. Marcos busca la llave. b
   a. Me busca. b. La busca. c. Las busca.
5. Rita me lleva al aeropuerto y también lleva a Tomás. a
   a. Nos lleva. b. Las lleva. c. Te lleva.
6. Puedo oír a Gerardo y a Miguel. b
   a. Puedo oírte. b. Puedo oírlos. c. Puedo oírlo.
7. Quieren estudiar la gramática. c
   a. Quieren estudiarnos. b. Quieren estudiarlo. c. Quieren estudiarla.
8. ¿Practicas los verbos irregulares? a
   a. ¿Los practicas? b. ¿Las practicas? c. ¿Lo practicas?
9. Ignacio ve la película. a
   a. La ve. b. Lo ve. c. Las ve.
10. Sandra va a invitar a Mario a la excursión. También me va a invitar a mí. c
    a. Los va a invitar. b. Lo va a invitar. c. Nos va a invitar.

recursos

WB p. 56
LM p. 30
vhlcentral.com Lección 5

Teaching Tips

- Play a memory game. In view of the class, quickly distribute various items in quantities of either one or two to many different students, then tell them to hide the objects in their bag or backpack. Ask the class who has what. Ex: **¿Quién tiene las plumas? (David las tiene.) ¿Quién tiene el *iPod*? (Jessica lo tiene.)**
- Elicit first- and second-person direct object pronouns by asking questions first of individual students and then groups of students. Ex: **¿Quién te invita a bailar con frecuencia? (Mi novio me invita a bailar con frecuencia.) ¿Quién te comprende? (Mi amigo me comprende.)**
- Ask questions directed at the class as a whole to elicit first-person plural direct object pronouns. Ex: **¿Quiénes los llaman los fines de semana? (Nuestros padres nos llaman.) ¿Quiénes los esperan después de la clase? (Los amigos nos esperan.)**
- Add a visual aspect to this grammar presentation. Use magazine pictures to practice the third-person direct object pronouns with infinitives and the present progressive. Ex: **¿Quién está practicando el tenis? (Rafael Nadal lo está practicando./Rafael Nadal está practicándolo.) ¿Quién va a mirar la televisión? (El hombre pelirrojo la va a mirar./El hombre pelirrojo va a mirarla.)**
- Point out that the direct object pronoun **los** refers to both masculine and mixed groups. **Las** refers only to feminine groups.

TEACHING OPTIONS

Large Group Make a list of 20 questions requiring direct object pronouns in the answer. Arrange students in two concentric circles. Students in the center circle ask questions from the list to those in the outer circle until you say stop (**¡Paren!**). The outer circle moves one person to the right and the questions begin again. Continue for five minutes, then have the students in the outer circle ask the questions.

Pairs Have students write ten sentences about a vacation they want to take using direct object nouns. Their sentences should also include a mixture of verbs in the present progressive, simple present, and **ir a** + [*infinitive*]. Ask students to exchange their sentences with a partner, who will rewrite them using direct object pronouns. Students should check their partner's work.

1 Teaching Tip To simplify, ask individual students to identify the direct object in each sentence before beginning the activity.

2 Expansion Ask questions (using direct objects) about the people in the activity to elicit **Sí/No** answers. Ex: **¿Tiene Ramón reservaciones en el hotel? (Sí, las tiene.) ¿Tiene su mochila? (No, no la tiene.)**

3 Expansion
- Ask students questions about who does what in the activity. Ex: **¿La señora Garza busca la cámara? (No, María la busca.)**
- Ask additional questions about the family's preparations, allowing students to decide who does what. Ex: **¿Quién compra una revista para leer en el avión? ¿Quién llama al taxi? ¿Quién practica el español?**

Práctica

1 **Simplificar** Professor Vega's class is planning a trip to Costa Rica. Describe their preparations by changing the direct object nouns into direct object pronouns.

modelo
La profesora Vega tiene su pasaporte.
La profesora Vega lo tiene.

1. Gustavo y Héctor confirman las reservaciones. Gustavo y Héctor las confirman.
2. Nosotros leemos los folletos (*brochures*). Nosotros los leemos.
3. Ana María estudia el mapa. Ana María lo estudia.
4. Yo aprendo los nombres de los monumentos de San José. Yo los aprendo.
5. Alicia escucha a la profesora. Alicia la escucha.
6. Miguel escribe las instrucciones para ir al hotel. Miguel las escribe.
7. Esteban busca el pasaje. Esteban lo busca.
8. Nosotros planeamos una excursión. Nosotros la planeamos.

¡LENGUA VIVA!
There are many Spanish words that correspond to *ticket*. **Billete** and **pasaje** usually refer to a ticket for travel, such as an airplane ticket. **Entrada** refers to a ticket to an event, such as a concert or a movie. **Boleto** can be used in either case.

2 **Vacaciones** Ramón is going to San Juan, Puerto Rico, with his friends, Javier and Marcos. Express his thoughts more succinctly using direct object pronouns.

modelo
Quiero hacer una excursión.
Quiero hacerla./La quiero hacer.

1. Voy a hacer mi maleta. Voy a hacerla./La voy a hacer.
2. Necesitamos llevar los pasaportes. Necesitamos llevarlos./Los necesitamos llevar.
3. Marcos está pidiendo el folleto turístico. Marcos está pidiéndolo./Marcos lo está pidiendo.
4. Javier debe llamar a sus padres. Javier debe llamarlos./Javier los debe llamar.
5. Ellos desean visitar el Viejo San Juan. Ellos desean visitarlo./Ellos lo desean visitar.
6. Puedo llamar a Javier por la mañana. Puedo llamarlo./Lo puedo llamar.
7. Prefiero llevar mi cámara. Prefiero llevarla./La prefiero llevar.
8. No queremos perder nuestras reservaciones de hotel. No queremos perderlas./No las queremos perder.

NOTA CULTURAL
Puerto Rico is a U.S. territory, so people do not need travel documents when traveling to and from Puerto Rico from the U.S. mainland. However, everyone must meet all requirements for entering the U.S. when traveling directly to Puerto Rico from abroad.

3 **¿Quién?** The Garza family is preparing to go on a vacation to Puerto Rico. Based on the clues, answer the questions. Use direct object pronouns in your answers.

modelo
¿Quién hace las reservaciones para el hotel? (el Sr. Garza)
El Sr. Garza las hace.

1. ¿Quién compra los pasajes para el vuelo (*flight*)? (la Sra. Garza)
La Sra. Garza los compra.
2. ¿Quién tiene que hacer las maletas de los niños? (María)
María tiene que hacerlas./María las tiene que hacer.
3. ¿Quiénes buscan los pasaportes? (Antonio y María)
Antonio y María los buscan.
4. ¿Quién va a confirmar las reservaciones de hotel? (la Sra. Garza)
La Sra. Garza va a confirmarlas./La Sra. Garza las va a confirmar.
5. ¿Quién busca la cámara? (María)
María la busca.
6. ¿Quién compra un mapa de Puerto Rico? (Antonio) Antonio lo compra.

Practice more at **vhlcentral.com**.

TEACHING OPTIONS

Small Groups Split the class into small groups. Have students take turns asking the group who does these activities: **leer revistas, practicar el ciclismo, ganar todos los partidos, visitar a sus padres durante las vacaciones, leer el periódico, escribir cartas, escuchar a sus profesores, practicar la natación.** Ex: **—¿Quién lee revistas? —Yo las leo.**

Heritage Speakers Pair heritage speakers with other students. Ask the pairs to create a dialogue between a travel agent and client. Assign the role of traveler to the heritage speaker, who would like to visit his or her family's home country. Encourage both students to draw on their experiences from past vacations and trips to Spanish-speaking countries. Have students role-play their dialogues for the class.

Comunicación

4

Entrevista Take turns asking and answering these questions with a classmate. Be sure to use direct object pronouns in your responses. Answers will vary.

1. ¿Ves mucho la televisión?
2. ¿Cuándo vas a ver tu programa favorito?
3. ¿Quién prepara la comida (*food*) en tu casa?
4. ¿Te visita mucho tu familia?
5. ¿Visitas mucho a tus abuelos?
6. ¿Nos entienden nuestros padres a nosotros?
7. ¿Cuándo ves a tus amigos/as?
8. ¿Cuándo te llaman tus amigos/as?

5

Los pasajeros Get together with a partner and take turns asking each other questions about the drawing. Use the word bank and direct object pronouns. Answers will vary.

AYUDA
For travel-related vocabulary, see **Contextos**, pp. 140–141.

modelo

Estudiante 1: *¿Quién está leyendo el libro?*
Estudiante 2: *Susana lo está leyendo./Susana está leyéndolo.*

buscar	confirmar	escribir	leer	tener	vender
comprar	encontrar	escuchar	llevar	traer	¿?

Síntesis

6

Adivinanzas In pairs, take turns describing a person, place, or thing for your partner to guess. Each of you should give at least five descriptions. Answers will vary.

modelo

Estudiante 1: *Lo uso para (I use it to) escribir en mi cuaderno. No es muy grande y tiene borrador. ¿Qué es?*
Estudiante 2: *¿Es un lápiz?*
Estudiante 1: *¡Sí!*

4 Teaching Tip Ask students to record their partner's answers. After the interviews, have students review answers in groups and report the most common responses to the class.

4 Expansion Have students write five additional questions, then continue their interviews. Encourage students to comment on their partner's answers.

5 Teaching Tip Before assigning the activity, ask individual students to identify different objects in the picture that might be used as direct objects in questions and answers.

5 Expansion
- Reverse the activity by having students say what the people are doing. Their partner will guess who it is. Ex: **Está escribiendo en su cuaderno. (Es Miguelito.)**
- Have students use **ser** and **estar** to write descriptions of the people in the drawing.

6 Teaching Tip To simplify this activity, have students first write out their descriptions.

6 Expansion Have pairs write out five additional riddles. Have volunteers read them aloud for the class to answer.

TEACHING OPTIONS

Game Play a game of **20 Preguntas**. Divide the class into two teams. Think of an object in the room and alternate calling on teams to ask questions. Once a team knows the answer, the team captain should raise his or her hand. If right, the team gets a point. If wrong, the team loses a point. Play until one team has earned five points.

Pairs Have students create five questions that include the direct object pronouns **me**, **te**, and **nos**. Then have them ask their partners the questions on their list. Ex: **—¿Quién te llama mucho? —Mi novia me llama mucho. —¿Quién nos escucha cuando hacemos preguntas en español? —El/La profesor(a) y los estudiantes nos escuchan.**

Section Goal

In **Recapitulación**, students will review the grammar concepts from this lesson.

Instructional Resource
Supersite

1 Expansion Create a list of present participles and have students supply the infinitive. Ex: **durmiendo (dormir)**

2 Teaching Tip Ask students to explain why they chose **ser** or **estar** for each item.

2 Expansion Have students use **ser** and **estar** to write a brief paragraph describing **Julia's** first few days in Paris.

3 Teaching Tip To simplify, have students begin by underlining the direct object nouns and identifying the corresponding direct object pronouns.

Recapitulación

Diagnostics

Review the grammar concepts you have learned in this lesson by completing these activities.

1 Completar Complete the chart with the correct present participle of these verbs. 16 pts.

Infinitive	Present participle	Infinitive	Present participle
hacer	haciendo	estar	estando
acampar	acampando	ser	siendo
tener	teniendo	vivir	viviendo
venir	viniendo	estudiar	estudiando

2 Vacaciones en París Complete this paragraph about Julia's trip to Paris with the correct form of **ser** or **estar**. 24 pts.

Hoy (1) es (es/está) el 3 de julio y voy a París por tres semanas. (Yo) (2) Estoy (Soy/Estoy) muy feliz porque voy a ver a mi mejor amiga. Ella (3) es (es/está) de Puerto Rico, pero ahora (4) está (es/está) viviendo en París. También (yo) (5) estoy (soy/estoy) un poco nerviosa porque (6) es (es/está) mi primer viaje a Francia. El vuelo (*flight*) (7) es (es/está) hoy por la tarde, pero ahora (8) está (es/está) lloviendo. Por eso (9) estamos (somos/estamos) preocupadas, porque probablemente el avión va a salir tarde. Mi equipaje ya (10) está (es/está) listo. (11) Es (Es/Está) tarde y me tengo que ir. ¡Va a (12) ser (ser/estar) un viaje fenomenal!

3 ¿Qué hacen? Respond to these questions by indicating what people do with the items mentioned. Use direct object pronouns. 10 pts.

modelo
¿Qué hacen ellos con la película? (ver)
La ven.

1. ¿Qué haces tú con el libro de viajes? (leer) Lo leo.
2. ¿Qué hacen los turistas en la ciudad? (explorar) La exploran.
3. ¿Qué hace el botones con el equipaje? (llevar) Lo lleva (a la habitación).
4. ¿Qué hace la agente con las reservaciones? (confirmar) Las confirma.
5. ¿Qué hacen ustedes con los pasaportes? (mostrar) Los mostramos.

RESUMEN GRAMATICAL

5.1 Estar with conditions and emotions *p. 152*

- Yo estoy aburrido/a, feliz, nervioso/a.
- El cuarto está desordenado, limpio, ordenado.
- Estos libros están abiertos, cerrados, sucios.

5.2 The present progressive *pp. 154–155*

- The present progressive is formed with the present tense of **estar** plus the present participle.

Forming the present participle

infinitive	stem	ending	present participle
hablar	habl-	-ando	hablando
comer	com-	-iendo	comiendo
escribir	escrib-	-iendo	escribiendo

-ir stem-changing verbs

	infinitive	present participle
e:ie	preferir	prefiriendo
e:i	conseguir	consiguiendo
o:ue	dormir	durmiendo

- Irregular present participles: **yendo (ir), pudiendo (poder), viniendo (venir)**

5.3 Ser and estar *pp. 158–159*

- Uses of **ser**: nationality, origin, profession or occupation, characteristics, generalizations, possession, what something is made of, time and date, time and place of events
- Uses of **estar**: location, health, physical states and conditions, emotional states, weather expressions, ongoing actions
- Many adjectives can be used with both **ser** and **estar**, but the meaning of the adjectives will change.

Juan **es** delgado. *Juan is thin.*	Juan **está** más delgado hoy. *Juan looks thinner today.*

TEACHING OPTIONS

Extra Practice Add an auditory aspect to this grammar review. Go around the room and read a sentence with a direct object. Each student must repeat the sentence using a direct object pronoun. Ex: **María y Jennifer están comprando sus libros para la clase. (María y Jennifer los están comprando./María y Jennifer están comprándolos.)**

TPR Divide the board into two columns, with the heads **ser** and **estar**. Ask a volunteer to stand in front of each verb. The rest of the class should take turns calling out a use of **ser** or **estar**. The volunteer standing in front of the correct verb should step forward and give an example sentence. Ex: nationality or origin (**Soy norteamericano/a.**) After each volunteer has given two sentences, call on different students to take their places. Continue this way until everyone has had a turn.

5.4 Direct object nouns and pronouns *pp. 162–163*

Direct object pronouns

Singular		Plural	
me	lo	nos	los
te	la	os	las

In affirmative sentences:
Adela practica el tenis. → Adela lo practica.

In negative sentences: Adela no lo practica.

With an infinitive:
Adela lo va a practicar./Adela va a practicarlo.

With the present progressive:
Adela lo está practicando./Adela está practicándolo.

4 **Opuestos** Complete these sentences with the appropriate form of the verb **estar** and an antonym for the underlined adjective. 10 pts.

modelo
Mis respuestas están bien, pero las de Susana *están mal*.

1. Las tiendas están abiertas, pero la agencia de viajes está cerrada.
2. No me gustan las habitaciones desordenadas. Incluso (*Even*) mi habitación de hotel está ordenada.
3. Nosotras estamos tristes cuando trabajamos. Hoy comienzan las vacaciones y estamos contentas/alegres/felices
4. En esta ciudad los autobuses están sucios, pero los taxis están limpios.
5. —El avión sale a las 5:30, ¿verdad? —No, estás confundida. Yo estoy seguro/a de que el avión sale a las 5:00.

5 **En la playa** Describe what these people are doing. Complete the sentences using the present progressive tense. 8 pts.

1. El Sr. Camacho está pescando.
2. Felicia está paseando en barco.
3. Leo está montando a caballo.
4. Nosotros estamos jugando a las cartas.

6 **Antes del viaje** Write a paragraph of at least six sentences describing the time right before you go on a trip. Say how you feel and what you are doing. You can use **Actividad 2** as a model. 32 pts. Answers will vary.

modelo
Hoy es viernes, 27 de octubre. Estoy en mi habitación...

7 **Refrán** Complete this Spanish saying by filling in the missing present participles. Refer to the translation and the drawing. 4 EXTRA points!

"Se consigue más haciendo que diciendo."

(*You can accomplish more by doing than by saying.*)

Practice more at **vhlcentral.com.**

4 Expansion Have students create three sentences about their own lives, using antonyms. Ex: **Mi hermano es desordenado, pero yo soy muy ordenado.** Tell them to make one of the sentences false. Then, in pairs, have students read their sentences aloud. Their partner should try to guess which statement is false.

5 Expansion To challenge students, have them imagine that the people in the illustration are now in a hotel. Ask students to say what they are doing. Ex: **Leo está mirando un programa sobre caballos.**

6 Teaching Tips

- Have students exchange papers with a partner for peer editing.
- To make this activity more challenging, require students to include at least two examples of **ser**, **estar**, and direct object pronouns.

7 Teaching Tip Explain the use of the impersonal **se** and explain that **Se consigue** means *You can accomplish* (as in the translation) or *One can accomplish*. Students will learn the impersonal **se** in **Estructura 10.3**.

7 Expansion To challenge students, have them work in pairs to create a short dialogue that ends with this saying. Encourage them to be creative.

TEACHING OPTIONS

TPR Prepare five anonymous descriptions of easily recognizable people, using **ser** and **estar**. Write each name on a separate card and give each student a set of cards. Read the descriptions aloud and have students hold up the corresponding name. Ex: **Es cantante y compositora. Es rubia. No es delgada. Es inglesa. Está muy ocupada. (Adele)**

Extra Practice Give students these items to make sentences with the present progressive. **1. con / madre / hablar / yo / mi / estar (Yo estoy hablando con mi madre.) 2. nuestro / equipaje / buscar / nosotros / estar (Nosotros estamos buscando nuestro equipaje.) 3. ¿ / llover / playa / la / estar / en / ? (¿Está lloviendo en la playa?) 4. el / Nueva York / pasaje / ella / para / comprar / estar (Ella está comprando el pasaje para Nueva York.)**

Audio: Reading
Additional Reading

Section Goals

In **Lectura**, students will:

- learn the strategy of scanning to find specific information in reading matter
- read a brochure about ecotourism in Puerto Rico

Instructional Resource
Supersite

Estrategia Explain to students that a good way to get an idea of what an article or other text is about is to scan it before reading. Scanning means running one's eyes over a text in search of specific information that can be used to infer the content of the text. Explain that scanning a text before reading it is a good way to improve Spanish reading comprehension.

The Affective Dimension Point out to students that becoming familiar with cognates will help them feel less overwhelmed when they encounter new Spanish texts.

Examinar el texto Do the activity orally as a class. Some cognates that give a clue to the content of the text are: **turismo ecológico, teléfono, TV por cable, Internet, hotel, aire acondicionado, perfecto, Parque Nacional Foresta, Museo de Arte Nativo, Reserva, Biosfera, Santuario**. These clues should tell a reader scanning the text that it is about a hotel promoting ecotourism.

Preguntas Ask the questions orally of the class. Possible responses: 1. travel brochure 2. Puerto Rico 3. photos of beautiful tropical beaches, bays, and forests; The document is trying to attract the reader. 4. **Hotel Vistahermosa** in Lajas, Puerto Rico; attract guests

Lectura

NATIONAL STANDARDS communication cultures

Antes de leer

Estrategia
Scanning

Scanning involves glancing over a document in search of specific information. For example, you can scan a document to identify its format, to find cognates, to locate visual clues about the document's content, or to find specific facts. Scanning allows you to learn a great deal about a text without having to read it word for word.

Examinar el texto

Scan the reading selection for cognates and write down a few of them. Answers will vary.

1. ____________ 4. ____________
2. ____________ 5. ____________
3. ____________ 6. ____________

Based on the cognates you found, what do you think this document is about?

____

Preguntas

Read these questions. Then scan the document again to look for answers. Answers will vary.

1. What is the format of the reading selection?
____
2. Which place is the document about?
____
3. What are some of the visual cues this document provides? What do they tell you about the content of the document?
____
4. Who produced the document, and what do you think it is for?
____

Practice more at **vhlcentral.com**.

Turismo ecológico en Puerto Rico

Hotel Vistahermosa

~ Lajas, Puerto Rico ~

- 40 habitaciones individuales
- 15 habitaciones dobles
- Teléfono/TV por cable/Internet
- Aire acondicionado
- Restaurante (Bar)
- Piscina
- Área de juegos
- Cajero automático°

El hotel está situado en Playa Grande, un pequeño pueblo de pescadores del mar Caribe. Es el lugar perfecto para el viajero que viene de vacaciones. Las playas son seguras y limpias, ideales para tomar el sol, descansar, tomar fotografías y nadar. Está abierto los 365 días del año. Hay una rebaja° especial para estudiantes universitarios.

DIRECCIÓN: Playa Grande 406, Lajas, PR 00667, cerca del Parque Nacional Foresta.

Cajero automático *ATM* rebaja *discount*

TEACHING OPTIONS

Heritage Speakers Ask heritage speakers of Puerto Rican descent who have lived on or visited the island to talk briefly about any experiences they have had with the beaches, nature preserves, or wildlife of Puerto Rico.

Small Groups Have students work in small groups to research and prepare a short presentation about the climate, geography, or people of Puerto Rico. If possible, ask them to illustrate their presentations with photos or illustrations.

Small Groups Lead a discussion about vacations. Have students work in groups to brainstorm what are important aspects of an "ideal" vacation. Each student should contribute at least one idea. When each group has its list, ask for volunteers to share the information with the rest of the class. How do the groups differ? How are they similar?

Atracciones cercanas

Playa Grande ¿Busca la playa perfecta? Playa Grande es la playa que está buscando. Usted puede pescar, sacar fotos, nadar y pasear en bicicleta. Playa Grande es un paraíso para el turista que quiere practicar deportes acuáticos. El lugar es bonito e interesante y usted va a tener muchas oportunidades para descansar y disfrutar en familia.

Valle Niebla Ir de excursión, tomar café, montar a caballo, caminar, hacer picnics. Más de cien lugares para acampar.

Bahía Fosforescente Sacar fotos, salidas de noche, excursión en barco. Una maravillosa experiencia llena de luz°.

Arrecifes de Coral Sacar fotos, bucear, explorar. Es un lugar único en el Caribe.

Playa Vieja Tomar el sol, pasear en bicicleta, jugar a las cartas, escuchar música. Ideal para la familia.

Parque Nacional Foresta Sacar fotos, visitar el Museo de Arte Nativo. Reserva Mundial de la Biosfera.

Santuario de las Aves Sacar fotos, observar aves°, seguir rutas de excursión.

llena de luz *full of light* aves *birds*

Después de leer

Listas

Which amenities of Hotel Vistahermosa would most interest these potential guests? Explain your choices. Answers will vary.

1. dos padres con un hijo de seis años y una hija de ocho años
____
2. un hombre y una mujer en su luna de miel (*honeymoon*)
____
3. una persona en un viaje de negocios (*business trip*)
____

Conversaciones

With a partner, take turns asking each other these questions. Answers will vary.

1. ¿Quieres visitar el Hotel Vistahermosa? ¿Por qué?
2. Tienes tiempo de visitar sólo tres de las atracciones turísticas que están cerca del hotel. ¿Cuáles vas a visitar? ¿Por qué?
3. ¿Qué prefieres hacer en Valle Niebla? ¿En Playa Vieja? ¿En el Parque Nacional Foresta?

Situaciones

You have just arrived at Hotel Vistahermosa. Your partner is the concierge. Use the phrases below to express your interests and ask for suggestions about where to go. Answers will vary.

1. montar a caballo
2. bucear
3. pasear en bicicleta
4. pescar
5. observar aves

Contestar

Answer these questions. Answers will vary.

1. ¿Quieres visitar Puerto Rico? Explica tu respuesta.
____
2. ¿Adónde quieres ir de vacaciones el verano que viene? Explica tu respuesta.
____

Listas
- Ask these comprehension questions. **1. ¿El Hotel Vistahermosa está situado cerca de qué mar? (el mar Caribe) 2. ¿Qué playa es un paraíso para el turista? (la Playa Grande) 3. ¿Dónde puedes montar a caballo? (en el Valle Niebla)**
- Encourage discussion of each of the items by asking questions such as: **En tu opinión, ¿qué tipo de atracciones buscan los padres con hijos de seis y ocho años? ¿Qué esperan de un hotel? Y una pareja en su luna de miel, ¿qué tipo de atracciones espera encontrar en un hotel? En tu opinión, ¿qué busca una persona en un viaje de negocios?**

Conversaciones Ask individuals about what their partners said. Ex: **¿Por qué (no) quiere ____ visitar el Hotel Vistahermosa? ¿Qué atracciones quiere ver?** Ask other students: **Y tú, ¿quieres visitar el Parque Nacional Foresta o prefieres visitar otro lugar?**

Situaciones
- Give students a couple of minutes to review **Más vocabulario** on page 140, and **Expresiones útiles** on page 147.
- To challenge students, add to the list activities such as **sacar fotos, correr, nadar,** and **ir de excursión.**

Contestar Have volunteers explain how the reading selection might influence their choice of a vacation destination for next summer.

TEACHING OPTIONS

Pairs Have pairs of students work together to read the brochure aloud and write three questions about it. After they have finished, ask pairs to exchange papers with another pair, who will work together to answer them. Alternatively, you might pick pairs to read their questions to the class. Ask volunteers to answer them.

Small Groups To practice scanning written material to infer its content, bring in short, simple Spanish-language magazine or newspaper articles you have read. Have small groups scan the articles to determine what they are about. Have them write down all the clues that help them. When each group has come to a decision, ask it to present its findings to the class. Confirm the accuracy of the inferences.

Video: ***Panorama cultural***
Interactive map

Section Goal

In **Panorama**, students will read about the geography, history, and culture of Puerto Rico.

Instructional Resources
Supersite: Video (***Panorama cultural***); Resources (Scripts, Translations, Digital Image Bank, Answer Keys)
WebSAM
Workbook, pp. 57–58
Video Manual, pp. 39–40

Teaching Tips

- Use the **Lección 5 Panorama** digital images to assist with this presentation.
- Have students look at the map of Puerto Rico. Discuss Puerto Rico's location in relation to the U.S. mainland and the other Caribbean islands. Encourage students to describe what they see in the photos on this page.

El país en cifras After reading **Puertorriqueños célebres**, ask volunteers who are familiar with these individuals to tell a little more about each one. For example, **José Rivera** is a playwright and screenwriter who was nominated for an Academy Award for his screenplay of *Diarios de motocicleta* (2004). You might also mention **Rita Moreno**, the only Hispanic female performer to have won an Oscar, a Tony, an Emmy, and a Grammy, and novelist **Rosario Ferré**, whose *House on the Lagoon* ***(La casa de la laguna)*** gives a fictional portrait of a large part of Puerto Rican history.

¡Increíble pero cierto! The **río Camuy** caves are actually a series of karstic sinkholes, formed by water sinking into and eroding limestone. Another significant cave in this system is **Cueva Clara**, located in the **Parque de las Cavernas del Río Camuy**. The entrance of the 170-foot-high cave resembles the façade of a cathedral.

Puerto Rico

NATIONAL STANDARDS connections cultures

El país en cifras

- **Área:** 8.959 km² (3.459 millas²) *menor° que el área de Connecticut*
- **Población:** 3.667.084

Puerto Rico es una de las islas más densamente pobladas° del mundo. Más de la mitad de la población vive en San Juan, la capital.

- **Capital:** San Juan—2.730.000
- **Ciudades principales:** Arecibo, Bayamón, Fajardo, Mayagüez, Ponce
- **Moneda:** dólar estadounidense
- **Idiomas:** español (oficial); inglés (oficial)

Aproximadamente la cuarta parte de la población puertorriqueña habla inglés, pero en las zonas turísticas este porcentaje es mucho más alto. El uso del inglés es obligatorio para documentos federales.

Bandera de Puerto Rico

Puertorriqueños célebres

- **Raúl Juliá,** actor (1940–1994)
- **Roberto Clemente,** beisbolista (1934–1972)
- **Julia de Burgos,** escritora (1914–1953)
- **Benicio del Toro,** actor y productor (1967–)
- **Rosie Pérez,** actriz y bailarina (1964–)
- **José Rivera,** dramaturgo y guionista (1955–)

menor *less* pobladas *populated* río subterráneo *underground river* más largo *longest* cuevas *caves* bóveda *vault* fortaleza *fort* caber *fit*

Faro en Arecibo

Playa en San Juan

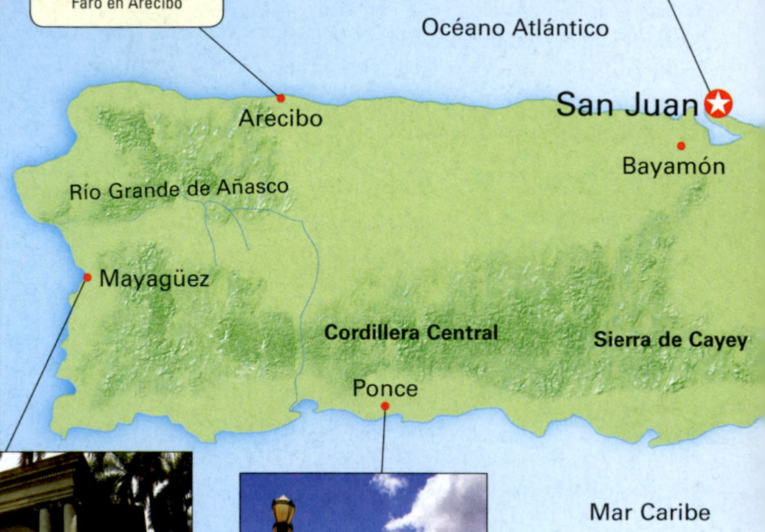

Universidad de Puerto Rico en Mayagüez

Iglesia en Ponce

recursos

WB pp. 57–58	VM pp. 39–40	vhlcentral.com Lección 5

¡Increíble pero cierto!

El río Camuy es el tercer río subterráneo° más largo° del mundo y tiene el sistema de cuevas° más grande del hemisferio occidental. La Cueva de los Tres Pueblos es una gigantesca bóveda°, tan grande que toda la fortaleza° del Morro puede caber° en su interior.

TEACHING OPTIONS

Heritage Speakers Encourage heritage speakers of Puerto Rican descent who have visited or lived on the island to share their impressions of it with the class. Ask them to describe people they knew or met, places they saw, and experiences they had. Have the class ask follow-up questions.

El béisbol Baseball is a popular sport in Puerto Rico, home of the Winter League. **Roberto Clemente**, a player with the Pittsburgh Pirates who died tragically in a plane crash, was the first Latino to be inducted into the Baseball Hall of Fame. He is venerated all over the island with buildings and monuments. There are numerous Major League Baseball players that were born in Puerto Rico, such as **Carlos Beltrán, Iván Rodríguez, Jorge Posada, Carlos Delgado,** and **Yadier Molina.**

Lugares • El Morro

El Morro es una fortaleza que se construyó para proteger° la bahía° de San Juan desde principios del siglo° XVI hasta principios del siglo XX. Hoy día muchos turistas visitan este lugar, convertido en un museo. Es el sitio más fotografiado de Puerto Rico. La arquitectura de la fortaleza es impresionante. Tiene misteriosos túneles, oscuras mazmorras° y vistas fabulosas de la bahía.

Artes • Salsa

La salsa, un estilo musical de origen puertorriqueño y cubano, nació° en el barrio latino de la ciudad de Nueva York. Dos de los músicos de salsa más famosos son Tito Puente y Willie Colón, los dos de Nueva York. Las estrellas° de la salsa en Puerto Rico son Felipe Rodríguez y Héctor Lavoe. Hoy en día, Puerto Rico es el centro internacional de este estilo musical. El Gran Combo de Puerto Rico es una de las orquestas de salsa más famosas del mundo°.

Ciencias • El Observatorio de Arecibo

El Observatorio de Arecibo tiene uno de los radiotelescopios más grandes del mundo. Gracias a este telescopio, los científicos° pueden estudiar las propiedades de la Tierra°, la Luna° y otros cuerpos celestes. También pueden analizar fenómenos celestiales como los quasares y pulsares, y detectar emisiones de radio de otras galaxias, en busca de inteligencia extraterrestre.

Historia • Relación con los Estados Unidos

Puerto Rico pasó a ser° parte de los Estados Unidos después de° la guerra° de 1898 y se hizo° un estado libre asociado en 1952. Los puertorriqueños, ciudadanos° estadounidenses desde° 1917, tienen representación política en el Congreso, pero no votan en las elecciones presidenciales y no pagan impuestos° federales. Hay un debate entre los puertorriqueños: ¿debe la isla seguir como estado libre asociado, hacerse un estado como los otros° o volverse° independiente?

¿Qué aprendiste? Responde a las preguntas con una oración completa.

1. ¿Cuál es la moneda de Puerto Rico? La moneda de Puerto Rico es el dólar estadounidense.
2. ¿Qué idiomas se hablan (*are spoken*) en Puerto Rico? Se hablan español e inglés en Puerto Rico.
3. ¿Cuál es el sitio más fotografiado de Puerto Rico? El Morro es el sitio más fotografiado de Puerto Rico.
4. ¿Qué es el Gran Combo? Es una orquesta de Puerto Rico.
5. ¿Qué hacen los científicos en el Observatorio de Arecibo? Los científicos estudian las propiedades de la Tierra y la Luna y detectan emisiones de otras galaxias.

Conexión Internet Investiga estos temas en **vhlcentral.com**.

Practice more at **vhlcentral.com**.

1. Describe a dos puertorriqueños famosos. ¿Cómo son? ¿Qué hacen? ¿Dónde viven? ¿Por qué son célebres?
2. Busca información sobre lugares en los que se puede hacer ecoturismo en Puerto Rico. Luego presenta un informe a la clase.

proteger *protect* **bahía** *bay* **siglo** *century* **mazmorras** *dungeons* **nació** *was born* **estrellas** *stars* **mundo** *world* **científicos** *scientists* **Tierra** *Earth* **Luna** *Moon* **pasó a ser** *became* **después de** *after* **guerra** *war* **se hizo** *became* **ciudadanos** *citizens* **desde** *since* **pagan impuestos** *pay taxes* **otros** *others* **volverse** *to become*

El Morro

- Remind students that at the time **El Morro** was built, piracy was a major concern for Spain and its Caribbean colonies. If possible, show other photos of **El Morro**, San Juan Bay, and **Viejo San Juan**.
- For additional information about **El Morro** and **Viejo San Juan**, you may want to play the ***Panorama cultural*** video footage for this lesson.

Salsa With students, listen to **salsa** or **merengue** from the Dominican Republic, and **rumba** or **mambo** from Cuba. Encourage them to identify common elements in the music (strong percussion patterns rooted in African traditions, alternating structure of soloist and ensemble, incorporation of Western instruments and musical vocabulary). Then, have them point out contrasts.

El Observatorio de Arecibo The Arecibo Ionospheric Observatory has the world's most sensitive radio telescope. It can detect objects up to 13 billion light years away. The telescope dish is 1,000 feet in diameter and covers 20 acres. The dish is made of about 40,000 aluminum mesh panels. The Arecibo Observatory celebrated its 50th anniversary in 2013.

Relación con los Estados Unidos Point out that only Puerto Ricans living on the island vote in plebiscites (or referenda) on the question of the island's political relationship with the United States.

Conexión Internet Students will find supporting Internet activities and links at **vhlcentral.com**.

TEACHING OPTIONS

Variación léxica When the first Spanish colonists arrived on the island they were to name Puerto Rico, they found it inhabited by the Taínos, who called the island **Boriquen**. Puerto Ricans still use **Borinquen** to refer to the island, and they frequently call themselves **boricuas**. The Puerto Rican national anthem is ***La borinqueña***. Some other Taíno words that have entered Spanish (and English) are **huracán**, **hamaca**, **canoa**, and **iguana**. **Juracán** was the name of the Taíno god of the winds whose anger stirred up the great storms that periodically devastated the island. The hammock, of course, was the device the Taínos slept in, and canoes were the boats made of great hollowed-out logs with which they paddled between islands. The Taíno language also survives in many Puerto Rican place names: **Arecibo, Bayamón, Guayama, Sierra de Cayey, Yauco,** and **Coamo**.

Instructional Resources
Supersite: Audio (Textbook & Lab MP3s); Testing Program (Tests, MP3s)
WebSAM
Lab Manual, p. 30

Los viajes y las vacaciones

acampar	*to camp*
confirmar una reservación	*to confirm a reservation*
estar de vacaciones (*f. pl.*)	*to be on vacation*
hacer las maletas	*to pack (one's suitcases)*
hacer un viaje	*to take a trip*
hacer (wind)surf	*to (wind)surf*
ir de compras (*f. pl.*)	*to go shopping*
ir de vacaciones	*to go on vacation*
ir en autobús (*m.*), auto(móvil) (*m.*), avión (*m.*), barco (*m.*), moto(cicleta) (*f.*), taxi (*m.*)	*to go by bus, car, plane, boat, motorcycle, taxi*
jugar a las cartas	*to play cards*
montar a caballo (*m.*)	*to ride a horse*
pescar	*to fish*
sacar/tomar fotos (*f. pl.*)	*to take photos*
el/la agente de viajes	*travel agent*
el/la inspector(a) de aduanas	*customs inspector*
el/la viajero/a	*traveler*
el aeropuerto	*airport*
la agencia de viajes	*travel agency*
el campo	*countryside*
el equipaje	*luggage*
la estación de autobuses, del metro, de tren	*bus, subway, train station*
la llegada	*arrival*
el mar	*sea*
el paisaje	*landscape*
el pasaje (de ida y vuelta)	*(round-trip) ticket*
el pasaporte	*passport*
la playa	*beach*
la salida	*departure; exit*
la tabla de (wind)surf	*surfboard/sailboard*

El hotel

el ascensor	*elevator*
la cama	*bed*
el/la empleado/a	*employee*
la habitación individual, doble	*single, double room*
el hotel	*hotel*
el/la huésped	*guest*
la llave	*key*
el piso	*floor (of a building)*
la planta baja	*ground floor*

Adjetivos

abierto/a	*open*
aburrido/a	*bored; boring*
alegre	*happy*
amable	*nice; friendly*
avergonzado/a	*embarrassed*
cansado/a	*tired*
cerrado/a	*closed*
cómodo/a	*comfortable*
confundido/a	*confused*
contento/a	*content*
desordenado/a	*disorderly*
enamorado/a (de)	*in love (with)*
enojado/a	*angry*
equivocado/a	*wrong*
feliz	*happy*
limpio/a	*clean*
listo/a	*ready; smart*
nervioso/a	*nervous*
ocupado/a	*busy*
ordenado/a	*orderly*
preocupado/a (por)	*worried (about)*
seguro/a	*sure; safe; confident*
sucio/a	*dirty*
triste	*sad*

Los números ordinales

primer, primero/a	*first*
segundo/a	*second*
tercer, tercero/a	*third*
cuarto/a	*fourth*
quinto/a	*fifth*
sexto/a	*sixth*
séptimo/a	*seventh*
octavo/a	*eighth*
noveno/a	*ninth*
décimo/a	*tenth*

Palabras adicionales

ahora mismo	*right now*
el año	*year*
¿Cuál es la fecha (de hoy)?	*What is the date (today)?*
de buen/mal humor	*in a good/bad mood*
la estación	*season*
el mes	*month*
todavía	*yet; still*

Seasons, months, and dates	*See page 142.*
Weather expressions	*See page 142.*
Direct object pronouns	*See page 162.*
Expresiones útiles	*See page 147.*

recursos

LM p. 30	vhlcentral.com Lección 5

Vocabulary Tools

¡De compras!

6

Communicative Goals

You will learn how to:

- **Talk about and describe clothing**
- **Express preferences in a store**
- **Negotiate and pay for items you buy**

A PRIMERA VISTA

- **¿Está buscando algo la chica?**
- **¿Crees que busca una maleta o una blusa?**
- **¿Está contenta o enojada?**
- **¿Cómo es la chica?**

Lesson Goals

In **Lección 6**, students will be introduced to the following:

- terms for clothing and shopping
- colors
- open-air markets
- Venezuelan clothing designer **Carolina Herrera**
- the verbs **saber** and **conocer**
- indirect object pronouns
- preterite tense of regular verbs
- demonstrative adjectives and pronouns
- skimming a document
- how to report an interview
- writing a report
- listening for linguistic cues
- a television commercial for the Mexican supermarket **Comercial Mexicana**
- the short film ***Chicas day***
- a video about open-air markets
- cultural, geographic, economic, and historical information about Cuba

A primera vista Here are some additional questions you can ask to personalize the photo: **¿Te gusta ir de compras? ¿Por qué? ¿Estás de buen humor cuando vas de compras? ¿Piensas ir de compras este fin de semana? ¿Adónde? ¿Qué compras cuando estás de vacaciones?**

Teaching Tip Look for these icons for additional communicative practice:

→●←	Interpretive communication
←●→	Presentational communication
●↔●	Interpersonal communication

INSTRUCTIONAL RESOURCES

Supersite (vhlcentral.com)
Video: ***Fotonovela, Flash cultura, Anuncio, Cortometraje, Panorama cultural***
Audio: Textbook and Lab MP3 Files
Activity Pack: Information Gap Activities, games, additional activity handouts
Resources: SAM Answer Key, Scripts, Translations, **Vocabulario adicional**, sample lesson plan, Grammar Presentation Slides, Digital Image Bank
Testing Program: Quizzes, Tests, Exams, MP3s
Student Activities Manual: Workbook/Video Manual/Lab Manual
WebSAM (online Student Activities Manual)

Vocabulary Tools

Section Goals

In **Contextos**, students will learn and practice:

- clothing vocabulary
- vocabulary to use while shopping
- colors

Instructional Resources
Supersite: Audio (Textbook and Lab MP3 Files); Resources (Digital Image Bank, **Vocabulario adicional**, Activity Pack, Scripts, Answer Keys); Testing Program (Quizzes)
WebSAM
Workbook, pp. 59–60
Lab Manual, p. 31

Teaching Tips

- Use the **Lección 6 Contextos** digital images to assist with this presentation.
- Ask volunteers about shopping preferences and habits. Ex: **¿Qué te gusta comprar? ¿Música? ¿Libros? ¿Ropa?** (Point to your own clothing.) **¿Adónde vas para comprar esas cosas? ¿Las compras en una tienda o en Internet?** (Pretend to reach in your pocket and pay for something.) **¿Cuánto dinero gastas normalmente?** Ask another student: **¿Adónde va de compras ____? (Va a ____.) ¿Y qué compra allí? (Compra ____.)**
- Have students guess the meanings of **damas** and **caballeros.** As they refer to the scene, make true/false statements. Ex: **El hombre paga con tarjeta de crédito. (Cierto.) No venden zapatos en la tienda. (Falso.) Se puede regatear en el almacén. (Falso.)** Use as many clothing items and verbs from **Más vocabulario** as you can.

Note: At this point you may want to present ***Vocabulario adicional: Más vocabulario para ir de compras*** from the Supersite.

¡De compras!

Más vocabulario

el abrigo	*coat*
los calcetines (el calcetín)	*sock(s)*
el cinturón	*belt*
las gafas (de sol)	*(sun)glasses*
los guantes	*gloves*
el impermeable	*raincoat*
la ropa	*clothes*
la ropa interior	*underwear*
las sandalias	*sandals*
el traje	*suit*
el vestido	*dress*
los zapatos de tenis	*sneakers*
el regalo	*gift*
el almacén	*department store*
el centro comercial	*shopping mall*
el mercado (al aire libre)	*(open-air) market*
el precio (fijo)	*(fixed; set) price*
la rebaja	*sale*
la tienda	*store*
costar (o:ue)	*to cost*
gastar	*to spend (money)*
pagar	*to pay*
regatear	*to bargain*
vender	*to sell*
hacer juego (con)	*to match (with)*
llevar	*to wear; to take*
usar	*to wear; to use*

Variación léxica

calcetines ⟷	medias (*Amér. L.*)
cinturón ⟷	correa (*Col., Venez.*)
gafas/lentes ⟷	espejuelos (*Cuba, P.R.*), anteojos (*Arg., Chile*)
zapatos de tenis ⟷	zapatillas de deporte (*Esp.*), zapatillas (*Arg., Perú*)

recursos

WB pp. 59–60	LM p. 31	vhlcentral.com Lección 6

TEACHING OPTIONS

TPR Call out a list of clothing items at random. Have students raise their right hand if they hear an item they associate with summer (Ex: **los pantalones cortos**), their left hand if they associate the item with winter (Ex: **el abrigo**), or both hands if the item can be worn in both seasons (Ex: **el cinturón**).

Variación léxica Point out that, although terms for clothing vary widely throughout the Spanish-speaking world, speakers in different regions can mutually understand each other.

TPR Have students stand in a circle. Name a sport, place, or activity and toss a ball to a student, who has three seconds to name a clothing item that goes with it. That student then names another sport, place, or activity and tosses the ball to another student. If a student cannot think of an item in time, he or she is eliminated. The last person standing wins.

Práctica

1 Escuchar Listen to Juanita and Vicente talk about what they're packing for their vacations. Indicate who is packing each item. If both are packing an item, write both names. If neither is packing an item, write an **X**.

1. abrigo Vicente
2. zapatos de tenis Juanita, Vicente
3. impermeable X
4. chaqueta Vicente
5. sandalias Juanita
6. bluejeans Juanita, Vicente
7. gafas de sol Vicente
8. camisetas Juanita, Vicente
9. traje de baño Juanita
10. botas Vicente
11. pantalones cortos Juanita
12. suéter Vicente

2 ¿Lógico o ilógico? Listen to Guillermo and Ana talk about vacation destinations. Indicate whether each statement is **lógico** or **ilógico**.

1. ilógico
2. lógico
3. ilógico
4. lógico

3 Completar Anita is talking about going shopping. Complete each sentence with the correct word(s), adding definite or indefinite articles when necessary.

caja	medias	tarjeta de crédito
centro comercial	par	traje de baño
dependientas	ropa	vendedores

1. Hoy voy a ir de compras al centro comercial.
2. Voy a ir a la tienda de ropa para mujeres. Siempre hay muchas rebajas y las dependientas son muy simpáticas.
3. Necesito comprar un par de zapatos.
4. Y tengo que comprar un traje de baño porque el sábado voy a la playa con mis amigos.
5. También voy a comprar unas medias para mi mamá.
6. Voy a pagar todo (*everything*) en la caja.
7. Pero hoy no tengo dinero. Voy a tener que usar mi tarjeta de crédito.
8. Mañana voy al mercado al aire libre. Me gusta regatear con los vendedores.

4 Escoger Choose the item in each group that does not belong.

1. almacén • centro comercial • mercado • (sombrero)
2. camisa • camiseta • blusa • (botas)
3. jeans • (bolsa) • falda • pantalones
4. abrigo • suéter • (corbata) • chaqueta
5. mercado • tienda • almacén • (cartera)
6. (pagar) • llevar • hacer juego (con) • usar
7. botas • sandalias • zapatos • (traje)
8. vender • regatear • (ropa interior) • gastar

1 Expansion Have students form pairs and discuss what the weather will be like at each destination. Then have them name three more articles that each person should pack.

1 Script JUANITA: Hola. Me llamo Juanita. Mi familia y yo salimos de vacaciones mañana y estoy haciendo mis maletas. Para nuestra excursión al campo ya tengo bluejeans, camisetas y zapatos de tenis. También vamos a la playa… ¡no puedo esperar! *Script continues on page 176.*

2 Teaching Tip You may want to do this activity as a TPR exercise. Have students raise their right hands if they hear a logical statement and their left hands if they hear an illogical statement.

2 Script 1. Este verano quiero ir de vacaciones a un lugar caliente, con playas y mucho, mucho sol; por eso, necesito comprar un abrigo y botas. 2. A mí me gustaría visitar Costa Rica en la estación de lluvias. Hace mucho calor, pero llueve muchísimo. Voy a necesitar mi impermeable todo el tiempo. 3. Mi lugar favorito para ir de vacaciones es Argentina en invierno. Me gusta esquiar en las montañas. No puedo ir sin mis sandalias ni mi traje de baño. 4. En mi opinión, el lugar ideal para ir de vacaciones es mi club. Allí juego mi deporte favorito, el tenis, y también asisto a fiestas elegantes. Por eso siempre llevo mis zapatos de tenis y a veces traje y corbata. *Textbook MP3s*

3 Expansion Ask students to write three additional fill-in-the-blank sentences for a partner to complete.

4 Expansion Go over the answers quickly in class. After each answer, have volunteers indicate why a particular item does not belong. Ex: **1. Un sombrero no es un lugar donde compras cosas.**

TEACHING OPTIONS

Extra Practice Suggest a vacation spot and then ask students at random what clothing they need to take. Make it a continuing narration whereby the next student must say all of the items of clothing that came before and add one. Ex: **Vas a la playa. ¿Qué vas a llevar? (E1: Voy a llevar un traje de baño. E2: Voy a llevar un traje de baño y gafas de sol. E3: Voy a llevar un traje de baño, gafas de sol y…)**

TPR Play a game of *Simon Says* (**Simón dice…**). Write on the board **levántense** and **siéntense** and explain that they mean *stand up* and *sit down*, respectively. Then start by saying: **Simón dice… los que llevan jeans, levántense.** Students wearing jeans should stand up and remain standing until further instruction. Work through various articles of clothing. Be sure to give some instructions without saying **Simón dice**.

1 Script (continued)
Para ir a la playa necesito un traje de baño, pantalones cortos y sandalias. ¿Qué más necesito? Creo que es todo. VICENTE: Buenos días. Soy Vicente. Estoy haciendo mis maletas porque mi familia y yo vamos a las montañas a esquiar. Los primeros dos días vamos a hacer una excursión por las montañas. Necesito zapatos de tenis, camisetas, una chaqueta y bluejeans. El tercer día vamos a esquiar. Necesito un abrigo, un suéter y botas… y gafas de sol.
Textbook MP3s

Teaching Tips
- Read the color words aloud, slowly, one at a time. Point to each drawing and ask: **¿De qué color es esta camiseta?** Ask about combinations. Ex: **Si combino rojo y azul, ¿qué color resulta? (morado)**
- Point to objects in the classroom and clothes you and students are wearing to elicit color words.
- Give dates and have students name the colors that they associate with each one. Ex: **el 14 de febrero (rojo, rosado); el 31 de octubre (negro, anaranjado)** You may want to repeat the process with brand names. Ex: FedEx **(anaranjado, morado, blanco)**
- Point out that color words are adjectives and agree in number and gender with the nouns they modify.

5 Expansion Add a visual aspect to this activity. Show magazine pictures of various products (cars, computers, etc.) and ask questions. Ex: **¿Es cara o barata esta computadora? (Es barata.)**

6 Expansion Point to individuals and ask other students what color of clothing each is wearing. Ex: ____, **¿de qué color es la falda de ____? (Es ____.)**

Los colores

Adjetivos

barato/a	*cheap*
bueno/a	*good*
cada	*each*
caro/a	*expensive*
corto/a	*short (in length)*
elegante	*elegant*
hermoso/a	*beautiful*
largo/a	*long*
loco/a	*crazy*
nuevo/a	*new*
otro/a	*other; another*
pobre	*poor*
rico/a	*rich*

5 Contrastes Complete each phrase with the opposite of the underlined word.

1. una corbata barata • unas camisas… caras
2. unas vendedoras malas • unos dependientes… buenos
3. un vestido corto • una falda… larga
4. un hombre muy pobre • una mujer muy… rica
5. una cartera nueva • un cinturón… viejo
6. unos trajes hermosos • unos jeans… feos
7. un impermeable caro • unos suéteres… baratos
8. unos calcetines blancos • unas medias… negras

6 Preguntas Answer these questions with a classmate.

1. ¿De qué color es la rosa de Texas? Es amarilla.
2. ¿De qué color es la bandera (*flag*) de Canadá? Es roja y blanca.
3. ¿De qué color es la casa donde vive el presidente de los EE.UU.? Es blanca.
4. ¿De qué color es el océano Atlántico? Es azul.
5. ¿De qué color es la nieve? Es blanca.
6. ¿De qué color es el café? Es marrón./Es café.
7. ¿De qué color es el dólar de los EE.UU.? Es verde y blanco.
8. ¿De qué color es la cebra (*zebra*)? Es negra y blanca.

Practice more at **vhlcentral.com**.

¡LENGUA VIVA!
The names of colors vary throughout the Spanish-speaking world. For example, in some countries, **anaranjado/a** may be referred to as **naranja, morado/a** as **púrpura**, and **rojo/a** as **colorado/a.**
Other terms that will prove helpful include **claro** (*light*) and **oscuro** (*dark*): **azul claro, azul oscuro**.

CONSULTA
Like other adjectives you have seen, colors must agree in gender and number with the nouns they modify.
Ex: **las camisas verdes, el vestido amarillo.**
For a review of descriptive adjectives, see **Estructura 3.1**, pp. 80–81.

TEACHING OPTIONS

Pairs Ask student pairs to write a physical description of a well-known TV or cartoon character. Then have them read their descriptions for the rest of the class to guess. Ex: **Soy bajo y un poco gordo. Llevo pantalones cortos azules y una camiseta roja. Tengo el pelo amarillo. También soy amarillo. ¿Quién soy? (Bart Simpson)**
Game Add a visual aspect to this vocabulary practice by playing

Concentración. On eight cards, write descriptions of clothing, including colors. Ex: **unos pantalones negros** On another eight cards, draw pictures that match the descriptions. Shuffle the cards and place them face-down in four rows of four. In pairs, students select two cards. If the cards match, the pair keeps them. If the cards do not match, students replace them in their original position. The pair with the most cards at the end wins.

Comunicación

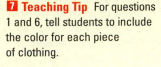

7

Las maletas With a classmate, answer these questions about the drawings.

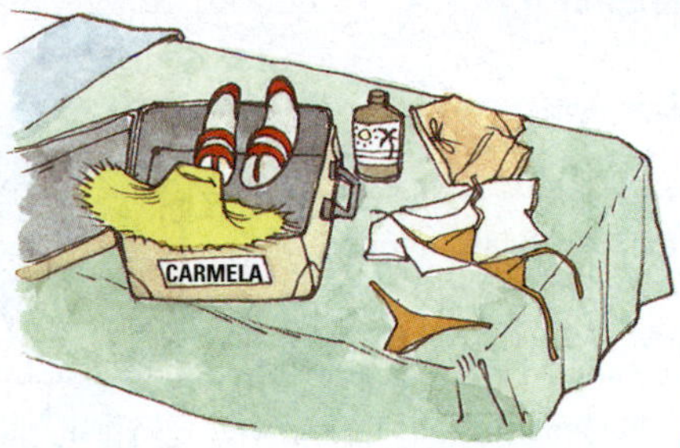

1. ¿Qué ropa hay al lado de la maleta de Carmela?
   Hay una camiseta, unos pantalones cortos y un traje de baño.
2. ¿Qué hay en la maleta?
   Hay un sombrero y un par de sandalias.
3. ¿De qué color son las sandalias?
   Las sandalias son rojas.
4. ¿Adónde va Carmela?
   Va a la playa.
5. ¿Qué tiempo va a hacer?
   Va a hacer sol./ Va a hacer calor.
6. ¿Qué hay al lado de la maleta de Pepe?
   Hay un par de calcetines, un par de guantes, un suéter y un abrigo.
7. ¿Qué hay en la maleta?
   Hay dos pantalones.
8. ¿De qué color es el suéter?
   El suéter es rosado.
9. ¿Qué va a hacer Pepe en Bariloche?
   Va a esquiar.
10. ¿Qué tiempo va a hacer?
    Va a hacer frío./ Va a nevar.

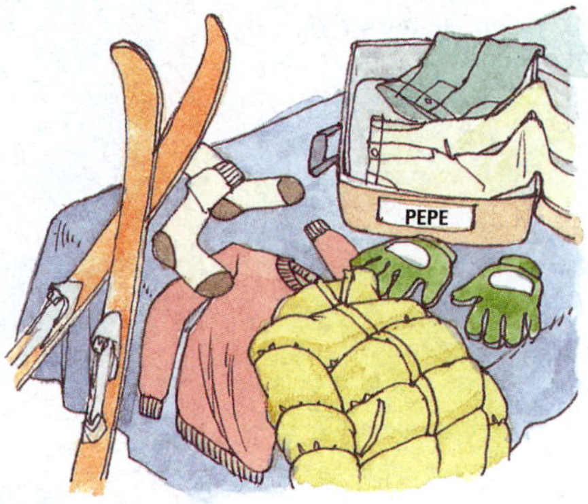

CONSULTA

To review weather, see **Lección 5, Contextos**, p. 142.

NOTA CULTURAL

Bariloche is a popular resort for skiing in South America. Located in Argentina's Patagonia region, the town is also known for its chocolate factories and its beautiful lakes, mountains, and forests.

8

El viaje Get together with two classmates and imagine that the three of you are going on vacation. Pick a destination and then draw three suitcases. Write in each one what clothing each person is taking. Present your drawings to the rest of the class, answering these questions. Answers will vary.

- ¿Adónde van?
- ¿Qué tiempo va a hacer allí?
- ¿Qué van a hacer allí?
- ¿Qué hay en sus maletas?
- ¿De qué color es la ropa que llevan?

9

Preferencias Take turns asking and answering these questions with a classmate. Answers will vary.

1. ¿Adónde vas a comprar ropa? ¿Por qué?
2. ¿Qué tipo de ropa prefieres? ¿Por qué?
3. ¿Cuáles son tus colores favoritos?
4. En tu opinión, ¿es importante comprar ropa nueva frecuentemente? ¿Por qué?
5. ¿Gastas mucho dinero en ropa cada mes? ¿Buscas rebajas?
6. ¿Regateas cuando compras ropa? ¿Usas tarjetas de crédito?

7 Teaching Tip For questions 1 and 6, tell students to include the color for each piece of clothing.

7 Expansion

- In pairs, have students discuss what essential items might be missing from the suitcases. Students may agree or disagree with their partner's suggestions. Ex: —**Pepe debe llevar unas botas y unas gafas de sol.** —**Sí, Pepe necesita unas botas para esquiar.**
- Ask volunteers what kind of clothing they would take with them to these destinations: **Seattle en la primavera, la Florida en el verano, Toronto en el invierno, San Francisco en el otoño.**

8 Teaching Tip One class period before doing this activity, assign groups and have them discuss where they are going.

8 Expansion Have students guess where the groups are going, based on the content of the suitcases. Facilitate guessing by asking items 2–5 from the list.

9 Expansion

- Ask students to report the findings of their interviews to the class. Ex: _____ **va a H&M para comprar ropa porque allí la ropa no es cara. Prefiere ropa informal...**
- Have students work with different partners. Tell students to assume the identity of a famous person and explain their clothing preferences, using questions similar to those in **Actividad 9**.

TEACHING OPTIONS

Pairs Have students form pairs, and tell them they are going on a shopping spree. On paper strips, write varying dollar amounts, from ten dollars to three thousand, and distribute them. Have pairs discuss what they will buy. Encourage creativity. Ex: **Tenemos quince dólares y vamos a *Old Navy*. Ella va a comprar medias amarillas. Yo voy a comprar un sombrero en rebaja.**

Extra Practice Add an auditory aspect to this vocabulary practice. Ask students to write an anonymous description of the article of clothing or outfit that best defines them. Collect the papers, shuffle them, and read the descriptions aloud for the class to guess.

Pairs Have pairs take turns describing classmates' clothing and guessing the person. Ex: **Esta persona lleva jeans y una blusa marrón. Lleva sandalias blancas. (Es _____.)**

Section Goals

In **Fotonovela**, students will:

- receive comprehensible input from free-flowing discourse
- learn functional phrases involving clothing and how much things cost

Instructional Resources

Supersite: Video (***Fotonovela***); Resources (Scripts, Translations, Answer Keys)
WebSAM
Video Manual, pp. 11–12

Video Recap: Lección 5
Before doing this **Fotonovela** section, review the previous episode with these questions:
1. ¿Qué problema hay cuando hablan con el empleado? (El empleado no encuentra la reservación.)
2. ¿Qué piensa Felipe del hotel? (Piensa que no está nada mal; es limpio y cómodo.)
3. ¿Qué deporte quieren hacer Miguel y Maru en la playa? (Quieren hacer windsurf.)
4. ¿Quién consigue las tablas de windsurf para Maru y Miguel? (El botones las consigue.)
5. ¿Quiénes nadan? (Juan Carlos y Jimena nadan.)

Video Synopsis The friends are back in **Mérida** where they go to the market to do some shopping. They split into two teams, the boys versus the girls, to see who is better at bargaining. Who will get the best deal?

Teaching Tips

- Have students scan the **Fotonovela** captions for vocabulary related to clothing or colors.
- Point out the clothing that a few individual students are wearing and ask them some questions about it.
  Ex: **Me gusta esa camisa azul. ¿Es de algodón? ¿Dónde la compraste?**

En el mercado

National Standards: communication, cultures

Los chicos van de compras al mercado. ¿Quién hizo la mejor compra?

PERSONAJES

FELIPE

JUAN CARLOS

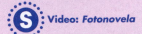

Video: *Fotonovela*

1

MARISSA Oigan, vamos al mercado.
JUAN CARLOS ¡Sí! Los chicos en un equipo y las chicas en otro.
FELIPE Tenemos dos horas para ir de compras.
MARU Y don Guillermo decide quién gana.

2

JIMENA Esta falda azul es muy elegante.
MARISSA ¡Sí! Además, este color está de moda.
MARU Éste rojo es de algodón.

3

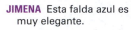

MARISSA ¿Me das aquella blusa rosada? Me parece que hace juego con esta falda, ¿no? ¿No tienen otras tallas?
JIMENA Sí, aquí. ¿Qué talla usas?
MARISSA Uso talla 4.
JIMENA La encontré. ¡Qué ropa más bonita!

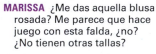

4

(En otra parte del mercado)
FELIPE Juan Carlos compró una camisa de muy buena calidad.
MIGUEL *(a la vendedora)* ¿Puedo ver ésos, por favor?
VENDEDORA Sí, señor. Le doy un muy buen precio.

5

(Las chicas encuentran unas bolsas.)
VENDEDOR Ésta de rayas cuesta 190 pesos, ésta 120 pesos y ésta 220 pesos.

6

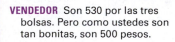

VENDEDOR Son 530 por las tres bolsas. Pero como ustedes son tan bonitas, son 500 pesos.
MARU Señor, no somos turistas ricas. Somos estudiantes pobres.
VENDEDOR Bueno, son 480 pesos.

TEACHING OPTIONS

Video Tips General suggestions for using video clips in the classroom can be found in the front matter of this Instructor's Annotated Edition.

En el mercado Photocopy the **Fotonovela** Videoscript (Supersite) and white out 7–10 words in order to create a master for a cloze activity. Distribute photocopies of the master and have students fill in the missing words as they watch the **En el mercado** episode. You may want students to work in small groups and help each other fill in any gaps.

MARISSA

JIMENA

MARU

MIGUEL

DON GUILLERMO

VENDEDORA

VENDEDOR

7

JUAN CARLOS Miren, mi nueva camisa. Elegante, ¿verdad?

FELIPE A ver, Juan Carlos... te queda bien.

8

MARU ¿Qué compraste?

MIGUEL Sólo esto.

MARU ¡Qué bonitos aretes! Gracias, mi amor.

9

JUAN CARLOS Y ustedes, ¿qué compraron?

JIMENA Bolsas.

MARU Acabamos de comprar tres bolsas por sólo 480 pesos. ¡Una ganga!

10

FELIPE Don Guillermo, usted tiene que decidir quién gana. ¿Los chicos o las chicas?

DON GUILLERMO El ganador es... Miguel. ¡Porque no compró nada para él, sino para su novia!

Expresiones útiles

Talking about clothing

¡Qué ropa más bonita!
What nice clothing!
Esta falda azul es muy elegante.
This blue skirt is very elegant.
Está de moda.
It's in style.
Éste rojo es de algodón/lana.
This red one is cotton/wool.
Ésta de rayas/lunares/cuadros es de seda.
This striped / polka-dotted / plaid one is silk.
Es de muy buena calidad.
It's very good quality.
¿Qué talla usas/llevas?
What size do you wear?
Uso/Llevo talla 4.
I wear a size 4.
¿Qué número calza?
What size shoe do you wear?
Yo calzo siete.
I wear a size seven.

Negotiating a price

¿Cuánto cuesta?
How much does it cost?
Demasiado caro/a.
Too expensive.
Es una ganga.
It's a bargain.

Saying what you bought

¿Qué compraste?/¿Qué compró usted?
What did you buy?
Sólo compré esto.
I only bought this.
¡Qué bonitos aretes!
What beautiful earrings!
Y ustedes, ¿qué compraron?
And you guys, what did you buy?

Additional vocabulary

híjole *wow*

recursos

VM pp. 11–12 | vhlcentral.com Lección 6

Expresiones útiles

- Point out the verb forms **compraste, compró, compré,** and **compraron.** Tell the class that these are forms of the verb **comprar** in the preterite tense, which is used to talk about events in the past. Tell them that **Esta** is an example of a demonstrative adjective, which is used to single out particular nouns; explain that the accented forms, **Éste** and **Ésta**, are pronouns. Tell students that **esto** is one of three neuter demonstrative pronouns. Have students scan the **Fotonovela** captions for other demonstratives. Also point out the captions for stills 3 and 4 and explain that **Me** and **Le** are examples of indirect object pronouns, which show *to whom* or *for whom* an action is done. Tell students that they will learn more about these concepts in **Estructura.**
- Help students with adjective placement and agreement when talking about clothing. Ask them to translate these phrases: 1. a white tie with gray and brown stripes (**una corbata blanca con rayas grises y marrones**) 2. black wool pants (**unos pantalones negros de lana**) 3. a yellow cotton shirt with purple polka dots (**una camisa amarilla de algodón con lunares morados**) 4. a red silk dress (**un vestido rojo de seda**) Discuss different possibilities for adjective placement and how it affects agreement. Ex: **Un vestido rojo de seda** versus **Un vestido de seda roja.**

Nota cultural When bargaining in open-air markets, one can typically expect to arrive at an agreed price of about 10 to 20% lower than the original. Bargaining is usually a friendly, pleasant experience and an expected and welcome ritual.

TEACHING OPTIONS

TPR Ask students to write **clientes** and **vendedores** on separate sheets on paper. Read aloud phrases from **Expresiones útiles** and have them hold up the paper(s) that correspond(s) to the people that would say that expression. Ex: **¿Qué número calza usted? (vendedores)**

Small Groups Have the class work in small groups to write statements about the **Fotonovela**. Then ask groups to exchange papers and write out a question that would have elicited each statement. Ex: **Miguel compra unos aretes para su novia. (¿Qué compra Miguel para su novia?)**

¿Qué pasó?

1 **¿Cierto o falso?** Indicate whether each sentence is **cierto** or **falso**. Correct the false statements.

	Cierto	Falso	
1. Jimena dice que la falda azul no es elegante.	❍	✔	Jimena dice que la falda azul es muy elegante.
2. Juan Carlos compra una camisa.	✔	❍	
3. Marissa dice que el azul es un color que está de moda.	✔	❍	
4. Miguel compra unas sandalias para Maru.	❍	✔	Miguel compra unos aretes para Maru.

2 **Identificar** Provide the first initial of the person who would make each statement.

M 1. ¿Te gusta cómo se me ven mis nuevos aretes?
F 2. Juan Carlos compró una camisa de muy buena calidad.
M 3. No podemos pagar 500, señor, eso es muy caro.
J 4. Aquí tienen ropa de muchas tallas.
J 5. Esta falda me gusta mucho, el color azul es muy elegante.
F 6. Hay que darnos prisa, sólo tenemos dos horas para ir de compras.

MARU

FELIPE

JIMENA

3 **Completar** Answer the questions using the information in the **Fotonovela**.

1. ¿Qué talla es Marissa? Marissa usa talla 4.
2. ¿Cuánto les pide el vendedor por las tres bolsas? Las bolsas cuestan 500 pesos.
3. ¿Cuál es el precio que pagan las tres amigas por las bolsas? El precio que pagan es 480 pesos.
4. ¿Qué dice Juan Carlos sobre su nueva camisa? Juan Carlos dice que su nueva camisa es elegante.
5. ¿Quién ganó al hacer las compras? ¿Por qué? Ganó Miguel porque le compró unos aretes a su novia.

4 **Conversar** With a partner, role-play a conversation between a customer and a salesperson in an open-air market. Use these expressions and also look at **Expresiones útiles** on the previous page.
Answers will vary.

¿Qué desea?	Estoy buscando...	Prefiero el/la rojo/a.
What would you like?	*I'm looking for...*	*I prefer the red one.*

Cliente/a		Vendedor(a)
Say good afternoon.	→	Greet the customer and ask what he/she would like.
Explain that you are looking for a particular item of clothing.	→	Show him/her some items and ask what he/she prefers.
Discuss colors and sizes.	→	Discuss colors and sizes.
Ask for the price and begin bargaining.	→	Tell him/her a price. Negotiate a price.
Settle on a price and purchase the item.	→	Accept a price and say thank you.

Practice more at **vhlcentral.com**.

NOTA CULTURAL

Las guayaberas are a popular men's shirt worn in hot climates. They are usually made of cotton, linen, or silk and decorated with pleats, pockets, and sometimes embroidery. They can be worn instead of a jacket to formal occasions or as everyday clothing.

AYUDA

When discussing prices, it's important to keep in mind singular and plural forms of verbs.

La **camisa cuesta** diez dólares.

Las **botas cuestan** sesenta dólares.

El **precio** de las botas **es** sesenta dólares.

Los **precios** de la ropa **son** altos.

1 Expansion Once statements have been corrected, ask pairs to find the places in the episode that support their answers. Have pairs role-play the scenes for the class. Ask comprehension questions as a follow-up.

2 Expansion Give students these statements as items 7–9: **7. Somos estudiantes y por eso no tenemos mucho dinero. (M) 8. La ropa que compró Juan Carlos le queda muy bien. (F) 9. Don Guillermo debe decidir el ganador. (M)**

3 Expansion Ask pairs to write two additional questions. Then have pairs exchange papers and answer each other's questions.

Nota cultural Shoe sizes in Mexico are different from the U.S. and Canada. Men's sizes in Mexico are 2 numbers smaller, and women's, 3 sizes smaller. For example, a man's size 11 shoe in the U.S. and Canada would be a size 9 in Mexico, and a woman's size 7.5 would be a 4.5.

4 Possible Conversation
E1: Buenas tardes.
E2: Buenas tardes. ¿Qué desea?
E1: Estoy buscando una camisa.
E2: Pues, tengo estas camisas de algodón y estas camisas de seda. ¿Cuál prefiere usted?
E1: Busco una camisa blanca o azul de algodón. Uso talla mediana.
E2: Las camisas de algodón son de talla mediana. Tengo esta camisa azul de algodón.
E1: Quiero comprarla, pero no soy rico/a. ¿Cuánto cuesta?
E2: Veinte dólares. Pero para usted... sólo diecisiete dólares.
E1: Muy bien. La compro, pero sólo tengo quince dólares.
E2: Está bien. Muchas gracias.

TEACHING OPTIONS

Extra Practice Have the class answer questions about the **Fotonovela**. Ex: **1. ¿Quién piensa que el color azul está de moda? (Marissa) 2. ¿Quiénes regatean por tres bolsas? (Maru, Jimena y Marissa) 3. ¿Qué acaba de comprar Miguel? (Acaba de comprar unos aretes para Maru.)**

Pairs Divide the class into pairs. Tell them to imagine that they are awards show commentators on the red carpet (**la alfombra roja**). Ask each pair to choose six celebrities and write a description of their outfits. Encourage creativity, and provide additional vocabulary if needed. Then have pairs read their descriptions for the class. Ex: **Aquí estamos en la alfombra roja de los *Video Music Awards*. Ahora viene Beyoncé con Jay-Z. Ella lleva un vestido azul de seda y sandalias grises. ¡Qué ropa tan bonita! Jay-Z usa jeans y...**

NATIONAL STANDARDS comparisons

Pronunciación

Audio

The consonants d and t

¿Dónde? **vender** **nadar** **verdad**

Like **b** and **v**, the Spanish **d** can have a hard sound or a soft sound, depending on which letters appear next to it.

Don **dinero** **tienda** **falda**

At the beginning of a phrase and after **n** or **l**, the letter **d** is pronounced with a hard sound. This sound is similar to the English *d* in *dog*, but a little softer and duller. The tongue should touch the back of the upper teeth, not the roof of the mouth.

medias **verde** **vestido** **huésped**

In all other positions, **d** has a soft sound. It is similar to the English *th* in *there*, but a little softer.

Don Diego no tiene el diccionario

When **d** begins a word, its pronunciation depends on the previous word. At the beginning of a phrase or after a word that ends in **n** or **l**, it is pronounced as a hard **d**.

Doña Dolores es de la capital

Words that begin with **d** are pronounced with a soft **d** if they appear immediately after a word that ends in a vowel or any consonant other than **n** or **l**.

traje **pantalones** **tarjeta** **tienda**

When pronouncing the Spanish **t**, the tongue should touch the back of the upper teeth, not the roof of the mouth. Unlike the English *t*, no air is expelled from the mouth.

Práctica Read these phrases aloud to practice the **d** and the **t**.

1. Hasta pronto.
2. De nada.
3. Mucho gusto.
4. Lo siento.
5. No hay de qué.
6. ¿De dónde es usted?
7. ¡Todos a bordo!
8. No puedo.
9. Es estupendo.
10. No tengo computadora.
11. ¿Cuándo vienen?
12. Son las tres y media.

Oraciones Read these sentences aloud to practice the **d** and the **t**.

1. Don Teodoro tiene una tienda en un almacén en La Habana.
2. Don Teodoro vende muchos trajes, vestidos y zapatos todos los días.
3. Un día un turista, Federico Machado, entra en la tienda para comprar un par de botas.
4. Federico regatea con don Teodoro y compra las botas y también un par de sandalias.

Refranes Read these sayings aloud to practice the **d** and the **t**.

Aunque la mona se vista de seda, mona se queda.[2]

1 Variety is the spice of life.
2 You can't make a silk purse out of a sow's ear.

recursos
LM p. 32
vhlcentral.com Lección 6

Section Goal

In **Pronunciación**, students will be introduced to the pronunciation of the letters **d** and **t**.

Instructional Resources
Supersite: Audio (Textbook and Lab MP3 Files); Resources (Scripts, Answer Keys)
WebSAM
Lab Manual, p. 32

Teaching Tips

- Explain that **d** has a hard sound at the beginning of a phrase or after **n** or **l**. Write **don, dinero, tienda,** and **falda** on the board and have the class pronounce them.
- Explain that **d** has a soft sound in all other positions. Pronounce **medias, verde, vestido,** and **huésped** and have the class repeat.
- Point out that within phrases, **d** at the beginning of a word has a hard or soft sound depending on the last sound of the preceding word. Read the examples aloud and have the class repeat.
- Explain that **t** is pronounced with the tongue at the back of the upper teeth and that, unlike English, no air is expelled from the mouth. Pronounce **traje, pantalones, tarjeta,** and **tienda** and have the class repeat. Then pronounce pairs of similar-sounding Spanish and English words, having students focus on the difference between the **t** sounds: **ti/*tea*; tal/*tall*; todo/*toad*; tema/*tame*; tela/*tell*.**

Práctica/Oraciones/Refranes These exercises are recorded on the *Textbook MP3s*. You may want to play the audio so that students practice listening to Spanish spoken by speakers other than yourself.

TEACHING OPTIONS

Extra Practice Write some additional proverbs on the board and have the class practice saying each one. Ex: **De tal padre, tal hijo.** (*Like father, like son.*) **El que tiene tejado de cristal no tira piedras al vecino.** (*People who live in glass houses shouldn't throw stones.*) **Cuatro ojos ven más que dos.** (*Two heads are better than one.*) **Donde come uno, comen dos, y donde comen dos, comen todos.** (*There's always room for one more at the table.*)

Extra Practice Write on the board the names of these famous Cuban literary figures: **José Martí, Julián del Casal, Gertrudis Gómez de Avellaneda,** and **Dulce María Loynaz**. Say the names aloud and have the class repeat. Then ask volunteers to explain the pronunciation of each **d** and **t** in these names.

Flash CULTURA

Section Goals

In **Cultura**, students will:
- read about open-air markets
- learn clothing-related terms
- read about Venezuelan clothing designer **Carolina Herrera**
- read about the fashions of Hispanic designers

Instructional Resources
Supersite: Video (***Flash cultura***); Resources (Scripts, Translations, Answer Keys)
WebSAM
Video Manual, pp. 83–84

En detalle

Antes de leer
Lead a discussion about open-air markets, such as a flea market. Have students share their experiences, including the market's location, goods sold there, and prices. Ask them to predict what might be sold at a market in a Spanish-speaking country.

Lectura
- Explain that open-air markets that specialize in second-hand or low-priced goods are often referred to as **mercados de pulgas** (*flea markets*).
- Point out that many local artists take advantage of open-air markets to sell their pieces or display new works.
- Explain that **la ñapa** can be considered similar to the Anglo tradition of a baker's dozen.

Después de leer Ask students what facts are new or surprising to them.

1 Expansion Give students these statements as items 9–11: 9. The **Tianguis Cultural del Chopo** is not a good place to go if you are interested in Mexican crafts and art. (**Falso.** The **Tianguis Cultural del Chopo** has crafts and art.) 10. Market stands are referred to as **puestos.** (**Cierto.**) 11. Bargaining often raises the price of an item significantly. (**Falso.** It usually lowers the price significantly.)

EN DETALLE

Video: *Flash cultura*

NATIONAL STANDARDS connections cultures

Los mercados al aire libre

Mercados al aire libre are an integral part of commerce and culture in the Spanish-speaking world. Whether they take place daily or weekly, these markets are an important forum where tourists, locals, and vendors interact. People come to the marketplace to shop, socialize, taste local foods, and watch street performers. Wandering from one **puesto** (*stand*) to the next, one can browse for fresh fruits and vegetables, clothing, CDs and DVDs, and **artesanías** (*crafts*). Some markets offer a mix of products, while others specialize in food, fashion, or used merchandise, such as antiques and books.

When shoppers see an item they like, they can bargain with the vendor. Friendly bargaining is an expected ritual and may result in a significantly lower price. When selling food, vendors may give the customer a little extra of what they purchase; this free addition is known as **la ñapa**.

Many open-air markets are also tourist attractions. The market in Otavalo, Ecuador, is world-famous and has taken place every Saturday since pre-Incan times. This market is well-known for the colorful textiles woven by the **otavaleños**, the indigenous people of the area. One can also find leather goods and wood carvings from nearby towns. Another popular market is **El Rastro**, held every Sunday in Madrid, Spain. Sellers set up **puestos** along the streets to display their wares, which range from local artwork and antiques to inexpensive clothing and electronics.

Mercado de Otavalo

Otros mercados famosos

Mercado	Lugar	Productos
Feria Artesanal de Recoleta	Buenos Aires, Argentina	artesanías
Mercado Central	Santiago, Chile	mariscos°, pescado°, frutas, verduras°
Tianguis Cultural del Chopo	Ciudad de México, México	ropa, música, revistas, libros, arte, artesanías
El mercado de Chichicastenango	Chichicastenango, Guatemala	frutas y verduras, flores°, cerámica, textiles

mariscos *seafood* **pescado** *fish* **verduras** *vegetables* **flores** *flowers*

ACTIVIDADES

1 ¿Cierto o falso? Indicate whether these statements are **cierto** or **falso**. Correct the false statements.

1. Generally, open-air markets specialize in one type of goods. **Falso.** They sell a variety of goods.
2. Bargaining is commonplace at outdoor markets. **Cierto.**
3. Only new goods can be found at open-air markets. **Falso.** They sell both new and used goods.
4. A Spaniard in search of antiques could search at **El Rastro.** **Cierto.**
5. If you are in Guatemala and want to buy ceramics, you can go to Chichicastenango. **Cierto.**
6. A **ñapa** is a tax on open-air market goods. **Falso.** A **ñapa** is a free addition sometimes given to customers.
7. The **otavaleños** weave colorful textiles to sell on Saturdays. **Cierto.**
8. Santiago's **Mercado Central** is known for books and music. **Falso.** It's known for seafood, fish, fruits, and vegetables.

TEACHING OPTIONS

TPR Create a series of true/false statements about goods one can purchase at the open-air markets mentioned in **En detalle**. Tell students to raise their right hand if a statement is true or their left hand if it is false. Ex: **Compro mariscos en El Rastro.** (left hand) **Compro flores en el mercado de Chichicastenango.** (right hand)

Small Groups Have students work in groups of three. For homework, have them research another famous open-air market in the Spanish-speaking world. Ex: **Pisac** (Peru), **La Romana** (Dominican Republic), **La Cancha** (Bolivia). In class, have each group present the location of the market, how often it takes place, what is sold, and any other significant information. Encourage students to bring in photos.

ASÍ SE DICE

La ropa

la chamarra (Méx.)	la chaqueta
de manga corta/larga	*short/long-sleeved*
los mahones (P. Rico); el pantalón de mezclilla (Méx.); los tejanos (Esp.); los vaqueros (Arg., Cuba, Esp., Uru.)	los bluejeans
la marca	*brand*
la playera (Méx.); la remera (Arg.)	la camiseta

EL MUNDO HISPANO

Diseñadores de moda

- **Adolfo Domínguez** (España) Su ropa tiene un estilo minimalista y práctico. Usa telas° naturales y cómodas en sus diseños.
- **Silvia Tcherassi** (Colombia) Los colores vivos y las líneas asimétricas de sus vestidos y trajes muestran influencias tropicales.

- **Óscar de la Renta** (República Dominicana) Diseñó ropa opulenta para la mujer clásica.
- **Narciso Rodríguez** (EE.UU.) En sus diseños delicados y finos predominan los colores blanco y negro. Hizo° el vestido de boda° de Carolyn Bessette Kennedy. También diseñó varios vestidos para Michelle Obama.

telas *fabrics* Hizo *He made* de boda *wedding*

PERFIL

Carolina Herrera

In 1980, at the urging of some friends, **Carolina Herrera** created a fashion collection as a "test." The Venezuelan designer received such a favorable response that within one year she moved her family from Caracas to New York City and created her own label, Carolina Herrera, Ltd.

"I love elegance and intricacy, but whether it is in a piece of clothing or a fragrance, the intricacy must appear as simplicity," Herrera once stated. She quickly found that many sophisticated women agreed; from the start, her sleek and glamorous designs have been in constant demand. Over the years, Herrera has grown her brand into a veritable fashion empire that encompasses her fashion and bridal collections, cosmetics, perfume, and accessories that are sold around the globe.

Conexión Internet

¿Qué marcas de ropa son populares en el mundo hispano?

Go to **vhlcentral.com** to find more cultural information related to this **Cultura** section.

ACTIVIDADES

2 Comprensión Complete these sentences.

1. Adolfo Domínguez usa telas __naturales__ y __cómodas__ en su ropa.
2. Si hace fresco en el D.F., puedes llevar una __chamarra__.
3. La diseñadora __Carolina Herrera__ hace ropa, perfumes y más.
4. La ropa de __Silvia Tcherassi__ muestra influencias tropicales.
5. Los __mahones__ son una ropa casual en Puerto Rico.

3 Mi ropa favorita Write a brief description of your favorite article of clothing. Mention what store it is from, the brand, colors, fabric, style, and any other information. Then get together with a small group, collect the descriptions, and take turns reading them aloud at random. Can the rest of the group guess whose favorite piece of clothing is being described?
Answers will vary.

Practice more at **vhlcentral.com**.

recursos: VM pp. 83–84 | vhlcentral.com Lección 6

Así se dice
- Model the pronunciation of each term and have students repeat it.
- To challenge students, add these words to this list: **la americana (Esp.), el saco (Amér. L.)** (*suit jacket, sport coat*); **las bermudas** (*knee-length shorts*); **las chanclas, las chancletas** (*sandals, flip-flops*); **el cuero** (*leather*); **de tacón alto** (*high-heeled*); **la gabardina** (*raincoat*); **la polera (Chi.)** (*t-shirt*); **el pulóver, el jersey** (*sweater*).

Perfil
- **Carolina Herrera** worked as a personal designer for Jacqueline Kennedy Onassis during the last twelve years of the former First Lady's life. Her designs have also been worn by another First Lady, Michelle Obama. **Herrera's** designs make regular appearances at red carpet events worldwide.
- Bring in photos of some of **Herrera's** clothing. Have students look at the photos and write descriptions.

El mundo hispano Ask comprehension questions such as these: **¿De qué estilo es la ropa de Adolfo Domínguez? ¿Quién hizo el vestido de boda de Carolyn Bessette Kennedy?**

2 Expansion Ask students to create three additional cloze sentences for a partner to complete.

3 Teaching Tip To simplify, create a word bank of clothing-related vocabulary on the board for students to use in their paragraphs.

TEACHING OPTIONS

Heritage Speakers Ask heritage speakers to talk about clothing and fashion in their families' home countries. Have them describe where most people shop, how young people dress, and what brands or designers are popular there.

Pairs Have pairs choose a celebrity and give him or her a style makeover. Have them discuss the person's current overall style and make suggestions for a new look, using **deber, necesitar,** and **tener que.** Have a few pairs present their makeovers to the class.

Las marcas Have students research one of the brands from the **Conexión Internet** activity and write a short paragraph about the brand, including the type(s) of clothing, where it is sold, who wears it, and any other significant information.

Section Goals

In **Estructura 6.1**, students will learn:
- the uses of **saber** and **conocer**
- more uses of the personal **a**
- other verbs conjugated like **conocer**

Instructional Resources
Supersite: Audio (Lab MP3 Files); Resources (Grammar Presentation Slides, Activity Pack, Scripts, Answer Keys); Testing Program (Quizzes)
WebSAM
Workbook, p. 61
Lab Manual, p. 33

Teaching Tips

- Use the **Lección 6** Grammar Presentation Slides to assist with this presentation.
- Point out the irregular **yo** forms of **saber** and **conocer**.
- Divide the board into two columns with the headings **saber** and **conocer**. In the first column, write the uses of **saber** and model them by asking individuals what they know how to do and what factual information they know. Ex: ____, **¿sabes bailar salsa? ¿Sabes mi número de teléfono?** In the second column, write the uses of **conocer** and model them by asking individuals about people and places they know. Ex: ____, **¿conoces Cuba? ¿Conoces a Yasiel Puig?**
- Further distinguish the uses of **saber** and **conocer** by making statements such as: **Sé quién es el presidente de este país, pero no lo conozco.**
- Point out the first **¡Atención!** bullet. Ask volunteers to write the full conjugation of these verbs on the board.
- Point out the similar **yo** form for **conocer, parecer, ofrecer, conducir,** and **traducir.**
- Ask questions using the new verbs. Ex: **¿Quiénes conducen? ¿Qué carro conduces?**

6.1 Saber and conocer

Tutorial

NATIONAL STANDARDS comparisons

ANTE TODO Spanish has two verbs that mean *to know*: **saber** and **conocer**. They cannot be used interchangeably. Note the irregular **yo** forms.

The verbs saber and conocer

		saber (*to know*)	**conocer** (*to know*)
SINGULAR FORMS	yo	**sé**	**conozco**
	tú	**sabes**	**conoces**
	Ud./él/ella	**sabe**	**conoce**
PLURAL FORMS	nosotros/as	**sabemos**	**conocemos**
	vosotros/as	**sabéis**	**conocéis**
	Uds./ellos/ellas	**saben**	**conocen**

▶ **Saber** means *to know a fact or piece(s) of information* or *to know how to do something.*

No **sé** tu número de teléfono.
I don't know your telephone number.

Mi hermana **sabe** hablar francés.
My sister knows how to speak French.

▶ **Conocer** means *to know* or *be familiar/acquainted* with a person, place, or thing.

¿**Conoces** la ciudad de Nueva York?
Do you know New York City?

No **conozco** a tu amigo Esteban.
I don't know your friend Esteban.

▶ When the direct object of **conocer** is a person or pet, the personal **a** is used.

¿Conoces La Habana?
Do you know Havana?

but

¿Conoces **a** Celia Cruz?
Do you know Celia Cruz?

▶ **¡Atención! Parecer** (*to seem*) and **ofrecer** (*to offer*) are conjugated like **conocer**.

▶ **¡Atención! Conducir** (*to drive*) and **traducir** (*to translate*) also have an irregular **yo** form, but since they are **-ir** verbs, they are conjugated differently from **conocer**.

conducir	**conduzco, conduces, conduce, conducimos, conducís, conducen**
traducir	**traduzco, traduces, traduce, traducimos, traducís, traducen**

NOTA CULTURAL
Cuban singer **Celia Cruz** (1925–2003), known as the "Queen of Salsa," recorded many albums over her long career. Adored by her fans, she was famous for her colorful and lively on-stage performances.

¡INTÉNTALO! Provide the appropriate forms of these verbs.

saber
1. José no sabe la hora.
2. Sara y yo sabemos jugar al tenis.
3. ¿Por qué no sabes tú estos verbos?
4. Mis padres saben hablar japonés.
5. Yo sé a qué hora es la clase.
6. Usted no sabe dónde vivo.
7. Mi hermano no sabe nadar.
8. Nosotros sabemos muchas cosas.

conocer
1. Usted y yo conocemos bien Miami.
2. ¿Tú conoces a mi amigo Manuel?
3. Sergio y Taydé conocen mi pueblo.
4. Emiliano conoce a mis padres.
5. Yo conozco muy bien el centro.
6. ¿Ustedes conocen la tienda Gigante?
7. Nosotras conocemos una playa hermosa.
8. ¿Usted conoce a mi profesora?

recursos
WB p. 61
LM p. 33
vhlcentral.com Lección 6

TEACHING OPTIONS

TPR Divide the class into two teams, **saber** and **conocer**, and have them line up. Indicate the first member of each team and call out a sentence in English that uses *to know.* (Ex: We know the answer.) The team member whose verb corresponds to the English sentence has to step forward and provide the Spanish translation.

Extra Practice Ask students to jot down three things they know how to do well (**saber** + [*infinitive*] + **bien**). Collect the papers, shuffle them, and read the sentences aloud. Have the rest of the class guess who wrote the sentences.

Práctica y Comunicación

1

Completar Indicate the correct verb for each sentence.

1. Mis hermanos (conocen/**saben**) conducir, pero yo no (**sé**/conozco).
2. —¿(Conocen/**Saben**) ustedes dónde está el estadio? —No, no lo (conocemos/**sabemos**).
3. —¿(**Conoces**/Sabes) a Lady Gaga? —Bueno, (**sé**/conozco) quién es, pero no la (**conozco**/sé).
4. Mi profesora (sabe/**conoce**) Cuba y también (conoce/**sabe**) bailar salsa.

2

Combinar Combine elements from each column to create sentences. Answers will vary.

A	B	C
Shakira	(no) conocer	Jimmy Fallon
los Yankees	(no) saber	cantar y bailar
el primer ministro de Canadá		La Habana Vieja
mis amigos y yo		muchas personas importantes
tú		hablar dos lenguas extranjeras
		jugar al béisbol

NATIONAL communication STANDARDS

3

Preguntas In pairs, ask each other these questions. Answer with complete sentences. Answers will vary.

1. ¿Conoces a un(a) cantante famoso/a? ¿Te gusta cómo canta?
2. En tu familia, ¿quién sabe cantar bien? ¿Tu opinión es objetiva?
3. Y tú, ¿conduces bien o mal? ¿Y tus amigos?
4. Si un(a) amigo/a no conduce muy bien, ¿le ofreces crítica constructiva?
5. ¿Cómo parece estar el/la profesor(a) hoy? ¿Y tus compañeros de clase?

4

Entrevista Jot down three things you know how to do, three people you know, and three places you are familiar with. Then, in a small group, find out what you have in common. Answers will vary.

modelo

Estudiante 1: *¿Conocen ustedes a David Lomas?*
Estudiante 2: *Sí, conozco a David. Vivimos en la misma residencia estudiantil.*
Estudiante 3: *No, no lo conozco. ¿Cómo es?*

5

Anuncio In groups, read the ad and answer these questions. Answers will vary.

1. Busquen ejemplos de los verbos **saber** y **conocer**.
2. ¿Qué saben del Centro Comercial Málaga?
3. ¿Qué pueden hacer en el Centro Comercial Málaga?
4. ¿Conocen otros centros comerciales similares? ¿Cómo se llaman? ¿Dónde están?
5. ¿Conocen un centro comercial en otro país? ¿Cómo es?...

Él sabe dónde comer lo que más le gusta.
Él sabe cómo jugar cuatro horas seguidas.
Él sabe dónde está su regalo de cumpleaños.
Él sabe dónde divertirse...
... y usted sabe dónde puede encontrar un poco de todo.
¿Conoce algún otro lugar como éste?
CENTRO COMERCIAL
MÁLAGA
SABE LO QUE TE GUSTA.

Practice more at **vhlcentral.com**.

1 Teaching Tip To challenge students, write this activity on the board as cloze sentences.

1 Expansion Give students these sentences as items 5–8: **5. No (sé/conozco) a qué hora es el examen. (sé) 6. (Conoces/Sabes) las cataratas del Iguazú, ¿verdad? (Conoces) 7. ¿Quieren (saber/conocer) dónde va a ser la fiesta? (saber) 8. Esta noche voy a salir con mi novia, pero mis padres no lo (conocen/saben). Todavía no la (conocen/saben)... ¡no (conocen/saben) quién es ella! (saben, conocen, saben)**

2 Teaching Tip To simplify, before beginning the activity, read through column C and have students determine whether each item takes the verb **saber** or **conocer**.

2 Expansion
- Add more elements to column A (Ex: **yo, mis padres, mi profesor(a) de español**) and continue the activity.
- Ask students questions about what certain celebrities know how to do or whom they know. Ex: **Brad Pitt, ¿conoce a Angelina Jolie? (Sí, la conoce.) Miguel Cabrera, ¿sabe jugar al béisbol? (Sí, sabe jugarlo.)**

3 Expansion In pairs, have students create three additional questions using the verbs **conducir, ofrecer,** and **traducir**. Then have pairs join other pairs to ask and answer their questions.

4 Teaching Tip To simplify, have students divide a sheet of paper into three columns with the headings **Sé, Conozco a,** and **Conozco**. Then have them complete their lists.

5 Expansion Ask each group to create an advertisement using two examples each of **saber** and **conocer**.

TEACHING OPTIONS

Extra Practice Use the Internet to research advertising slogans that use verbs from **Estructura 6.1.** In groups, have students guess the company or product for each slogan. Ex: **Sabemos por qué vuelas. (American Airlines)**

Small Groups Ask students to write down four sentences (two true, two false) using **saber** and **conocer**. In groups of three, have them read their sentences aloud. The group should ask questions to guess if the person is lying or telling the truth.

Large Group Ask students to write down six things they know how to do. Have them circulate around the room to find out who else knows how to do those things, jotting down the names of those that answer **sí**. Have students report back to the class. Ex: **Keisha y yo sabemos tocar el piano.**

6.2 Indirect object pronouns

Tutorial

ANTE TODO In **Lección 5**, you learned that a direct object receives the action of the verb directly. In contrast, an indirect object receives the action of the verb indirectly.

SUBJECT	I.O. PRONOUN	VERB	DIRECT OBJECT	INDIRECT OBJECT
Roberto	**le**	presta	cien pesos	**a Luisa**.
Roberto		*lends*	*100 pesos*	*to Luisa.*

An indirect object is a noun or pronoun that answers the question *to whom* or *for whom* an action is done. In the preceding example, the indirect object answers this question: **¿A quién le presta Roberto cien pesos?** *To whom does Roberto lend 100 pesos?*

Indirect object pronouns

Singular forms		Plural forms	
me	(to, for) *me*	**nos**	(to, for) *us*
te	(to, for) *you* (fam.)	**os**	(to, for) *you* (fam.)
le	(to, for) *you* (form.)	**les**	(to, for) *you*
	(to, for) *him; her*		(to, for) *them*

▶ **¡Atención!** The forms of indirect object pronouns for the first and second persons (**me**, **te**, **nos**, **os**) are the same as the direct object pronouns. Indirect object pronouns agree in number with the corresponding nouns, but not in gender.

Bueno, le doy un descuento.

Acabo de mostrarles que sí sabemos regatear.

Using indirect object pronouns

▶ Spanish speakers commonly use both an indirect object pronoun and the noun to which it refers in the same sentence. This is done to emphasize and clarify to whom the pronoun refers.

Ella **le** vende la ropa **a Elena**. (I.O. PRONOUN: le; INDIRECT OBJECT: a Elena)

Les prestamos el dinero **a Inés y a Álex**. (I.O. PRONOUN: Les; INDIRECT OBJECT: a Inés y a Álex)

▶ Indirect object pronouns are also used without the indirect object noun when the person for whom the action is being done is known.

Ana **le** presta la falda **a Elena**.
Ana lends her skirt to Elena.

También **le** presta unos jeans.
She also lends her a pair of jeans.

Section Goals

In **Estructura 6.2**, students will learn:
- to identify an indirect object noun
- how to use indirect object pronouns

Instructional Resources
Supersite: Audio (Lab MP3 Files); Resources (Grammar Presentation Slides, Activity Pack, Scripts, Answer Keys); Testing Program (Quizzes)
WebSAM
Workbook, pp. 62–63
Lab Manual, p. 34

Teaching Tips

- Write on the board: **Mi novio me escribe un mensaje de texto.** Ask students what the direct object of the verb is. Then tell them that an indirect object answers the questions *to whom* or *for whom.*
- Write the indirect object pronouns on the board. Ask how their forms differ from those of direct object pronouns.
- Ask volunteers to read aloud the video-still captions, and have the class identify the indirect object pronoun in each.
- Point out that the redundant use of both an indirect object pronoun and an indirect object noun is common in Spanish and that, unlike in English, it is the indirect object noun that is optional, not the pronoun.

NATIONAL STANDARDS comparisons

TEACHING OPTIONS

Extra Practice Write sentences like these on the board: **1. Ana te prepara unos tacos. 2. Le presto dinero a Luisa. 3. Les compramos unos regalos a los niños.** Ask students to come to the board and underline the direct objects and circle the indirect objects.

Small Groups Have students work in groups of three. Have Student A "lend" an object to Student B and say: **Te presto mi...** Student B responds: **Me prestas tu...** Student C says: ____ **le presta a** ____ **su...** Have groups practice until each member has begun the chain twice. Practice plural pronouns by having two groups join together and two students "lend" something to two other students.

- Indirect object pronouns are usually placed before the conjugated form of the verb. In negative sentences the pronoun is placed between **no** and the conjugated verb.

Martín **me** compra un regalo.
Martín is buying me a gift.

Eva **no me** escribe cartas.
Eva doesn't write me letters.

CONSULTA

For more information on accents, see **Lección 4, Pronunciación**, p. 115, **Lección 10, Ortografía**, p. 315, and **Lección 11, Ortografía**, p. 349.

- When a conjugated verb is followed by an infinitive or the present progressive, the indirect object pronoun may be placed before the conjugated verb or attached to the infinitive or present participle. **¡Atención!** When an indirect object pronoun is attached to a present participle, an accent mark is added to maintain the proper stress.

Él no quiere **pagarte**./
Él no **te** quiere pagar.
He does not want to pay you.

Él está **escribiéndole** una postal a ella./
Él **le** está escribiendo una postal a ella.
He is writing a postcard to her.

- Because the indirect object pronouns **le** and **les** have multiple meanings, Spanish speakers often clarify to whom the pronouns refer with the preposition **a** + [*pronoun*] or **a** + [*noun*].

UNCLARIFIED STATEMENTS	CLARIFIED STATEMENTS
Yo **le** compro un abrigo.	Yo **le** compro un abrigo **a usted/él/ella**.
Ella **le** describe un libro.	Ella **le** describe un libro **a Juan**.

UNCLARIFIED STATEMENTS	CLARIFIED STATEMENTS
Él **les** vende unos sombreros.	Él **les** vende unos sombreros **a ustedes/ellos/ellas**.
Ellos **les** hablan muy claro.	Ellos **les** hablan muy claro **a los clientes**.

- The irregular verbs **dar** (*to give*) and **decir** (*to say; to tell*) are often used with indirect object pronouns.

The verbs dar and decir

Singular forms	dar	decir	Plural forms	dar	decir
yo	**doy**	**digo**	nosotros/as	**damos**	**decimos**
tú	**das**	**dices**	vosotros/as	**dais**	**decís**
Ud./él/ella	**da**	**dice**	Uds./ellos/ellas	**dan**	**dicen**

Me dan una fiesta cada año.
They give (throw) me a party every year.

Te digo la verdad.
I'm telling you the truth.

Voy a **darle** consejos.
I'm going to give her advice.

No **les digo** mentiras a mis padres.
I don't tell lies to my parents.

recursos
WB pp. 62–63
LM p. 34
vhlcentral.com Lección 6

¡INTÉNTALO! Use the cues in parentheses to provide the correct indirect object pronoun for each sentence.

1. Juan ___le___ quiere dar un regalo. (*to Elena*)
2. María ___nos___ prepara un café. (*for us*)
3. Beatriz y Felipe ___me___ escriben desde (*from*) Cuba. (*to me*)
4. Marta y yo ___les___ compramos unos guantes. (*for them*)
5. Los vendedores ___te___ venden ropa. (*to you, fam. sing.*)
6. La dependienta ___nos___ muestra los guantes. (*to us*)

Teaching Tips

- Point out that the position of indirect object pronouns in a sentence is the same as that of direct object pronouns.
- Ask individuals questions using indirect object pronouns. Ex: **¿A quién le ofreces ayuda? ¿Les das consejos a tus amigos? ¿Qué te dicen tus padres que no debes hacer? ¿Les dices mentiras a tus padres? ¿Cuándo vas a escribirles a tus abuelos?** Have students respond with complete sentences and ask follow-up questions if necessary.
- After going over the **¡Inténtalo!** orally with the class, ask students which items might require clarification (items 1 and 4). Ask them what they would add to each sentence in order to clarify **le** or **les**.
- As a comprehension check, have students write answers to these questions: **1. Es el cumpleaños de tu mejor amigo. ¿Qué vas a comprarle? 2. ¿A quiénes les hablas todos los días? 3. ¿Quién te presta dinero cuando lo necesitas? 4. ¿Quién les está enseñando español a ustedes?**
- In pairs, have students write the dialogue of an argument between two roommates, using **dar** and **decir**. Have volunteers role-play their conversations for the class. Encourage them to be creative and act out the argument with props, if possible.

TEACHING OPTIONS

Video Replay the **Fotonovela**. Ask students to note each time an indirect object pronoun is used. Then, have students find each use of **le** and state to whom it refers.

Game Give each student an envelope and a sheet of paper. Ask them to write a sentence using an indirect object pronoun, cut the paper into strips (one word per strip), shuffle them, and place them in the envelope. Then have students pass their envelopes to the person sitting behind them. Allow thirty seconds for them to unscramble the sentence and write it down, before placing the shuffled strips back into the envelope and passing it on. After three minutes, the row with the most correctly deciphered sentences wins.

Práctica

1 Completar Fill in the blanks with the correct pronouns to complete Mónica's description of her family's holiday shopping.

1. Juan y yo __le__ damos una blusa a nuestra hermana Gisela.
2. Mi tía __nos__ da a nosotros una mesa para la casa.
3. Gisela __le__ da dos corbatas a su novio.
4. A mi mamá yo __le__ doy un par de guantes negros.
5. A mi profesora __le__ doy dos libros de José Martí.
6. Juan __les__ da un regalo a mis padres.
7. Mis padres __me__ dan un traje nuevo a mí.
8. Y a ti, yo __te__ doy un regalo también. ¿Quieres verlo?

2 En La Habana Describe what happens on Pascual's trip to Cuba based on the cues provided.

1. ellos / cantar / canción / (mí)
Ellos me cantan una canción (a mí).

2. él / comprar / libros / (sus hijos) / Plaza de Armas
Él les compra libros (a sus hijos) en la Plaza de Armas.

3. yo / preparar el almuerzo (*lunch*) / (ti)
Yo te preparo el almuerzo (a ti).

4. él / explicar cómo llegar / (conductor)
Él le explica cómo llegar (al conductor).

5. mi novia / sacar / foto / (nosotros)
Mi novia nos saca una foto (a nosotros).

6. el guía (*guide*) / mostrar / catedral de San Cristóbal / (ustedes)
El guía les muestra la catedral de San Cristóbal (a ustedes).

3 Combinar Use an item from each column and an indirect object pronoun to create logical sentences. Answers will vary.

modelo

Mis padres les dan regalos a mis primos.

A	B	C	D
yo	comprar	mensajes electrónicos	mí
el dependiente	dar	corbata	ustedes
el profesor Arce	decir	dinero en efectivo	clienta
la vendedora	escribir	tarea	novia
mis padres	explicar	problemas	primos
tú	pagar	regalos	ti
nosotros/as	prestar	ropa	nosotros
¿?	vender	¿?	¿?

Practice more at **vhlcentral.com**.

NOTA CULTURAL

Cuban writer and patriot **José Martí** (1853–1895) was born in **La Habana Vieja**, the old colonial center of Havana. Founded by Spanish explorers in the early 1500s, Havana, along with San Juan, Puerto Rico, served as a major stopping point for Spaniards traveling to Mexico and South America.

NOTA CULTURAL

La Habana Vieja, Cuba, is the site of another well-known outdoor market. Located in the **Plaza de la Catedral**, it is a place where Cuban painters, artists, and sculptors sell their work, and other vendors offer handmade crafts and clothing.

1 Teaching Tip Before beginning the activity, have students identify the indirect object in each sentence.

1 Expansion Have students write four sentences about themselves, leaving out the indirect object pronoun. Ex: **Yo ____ doy un regalo a mis padres. Mi tío ____ compra una moto a mí...** Then have them exchange papers with a classmate and complete the sentences.

2 Teaching Tips

- To simplify, read through the cues for each item and have students identify the indirect object pronoun that is needed. Then have them write the complete sentences.
- Point out that students will need to add articles to some sentences.

2 Expansion Divide the class into small groups. Have each student pick a photo (photos 1, 2, 4, and 5 are most appropriate) to present to the group as a verbal portrait, including an introductory sentence that sets the scene, followed by a body and conclusion. The verbal portrait should answer the questions *who, what, where, when,* and *why* with regard to what is seen in the photo. After each group member has presented his or her photo, the group chooses one to present to the class.

3 Expansion Have students convert three of their statements into questions, using **¿Quién?**, **¿A quién?**, and **¿Qué?** Have pairs take turns asking and answering their questions. Ex: **¿Quién les vende la ropa? (el dependiente) ¿A quiénes les das regalos? (a mis primos) ¿Qué te explican tus padres? (los problemas)**

TEACHING OPTIONS

Heritage Speakers Ask heritage speakers to share any typical words or phrases that one would hear in a radio ad. Then have students work in pairs to create a radio commercial for their favorite clothing store. Have them tell customers what they can buy, for whom, and at what price.

Pairs Ask students to write five questions that elicit indirect object pronouns. In pairs, have students ask their questions and write down their partner's answers. Then ask pairs to review the questions and answers for accuracy.

Pairs Brainstorm on the board a list of things that parents tell high school-age or college-age children they should or should not do. Then have pairs ask each other if their parents tell them these things and summarize their findings for the class. Ex: **Nuestros padres nos dicen que no debemos tomar mucho café.**

NATIONAL communication STANDARDS

Comunicación

4 **Entrevista** In pairs, take turns asking and answering to or for whom you do these activities. Use the model as a guide. Answers will vary.

cantar canciones de amor (*love songs*)	escribir mensajes electrónicos
comprar ropa	mostrar fotos de un viaje
dar una fiesta	pedir dinero
decir mentiras	preparar comida (*food*) mexicana

modelo

escribir mensajes electrónicos
Estudiante 1: *¿A quién le escribes mensajes electrónicos?*
Estudiante 2: *Le escribo mensajes electrónicos a mi hermano.*

5 **¡Somos ricos!** You and your classmates chipped in on a lottery ticket and you won! Now you want to spend money on your loved ones. In groups of three, discuss what each person is buying for family and friends. Answers will vary.

modelo

Estudiante 1: *Quiero comprarle un vestido de Carolina Herrera a mi madre.*
Estudiante 2: *Y yo voy a darles un automóvil nuevo a mis padres.*
Estudiante 3: *Voy a comprarles una casa a mis padres, pero a mis amigos no les voy a dar nada.*

6 **Entrevista** Use these questions to interview a classmate. Answers will vary.

1. ¿Qué tiendas, almacenes o centros comerciales prefieres?
2. ¿A quién le compras regalos cuando hay rebajas?
3. ¿A quién le prestas dinero cuando lo necesita?
4. Quiero ir de compras. ¿Cuánto dinero me puedes prestar?
5. ¿Te dan tus padres su tarjeta de crédito cuando vas de compras?

NATIONAL communication STANDARDS

Síntesis

7 **Minidrama** In groups of three, take turns playing the roles of two shoppers and a clerk in a clothing store. The shoppers should talk about the articles of clothing they are looking for and for whom they are buying the clothes. The clerk should recommend several items based on the shoppers' descriptions. Use these expressions and also look at **Expresiones útiles** on page 179. Answers will vary.

Me queda grande/pequeño. *It's big/small on me.*	¿Está en rebaja? *Is it on sale?*
¿Tiene otro color? *Do you have another color?*	También estoy buscando... *I'm also looking for...*

TEACHING OPTIONS

Small Groups Have students write a conversation. One friend tries to convince the other to go shopping with him or her this weekend. The other friend explains that he or she cannot and lists all the things he or she is going to do. Students should include as many different indirect object pronouns as possible.

Pairs Ask students to imagine that they are going on an extended trip. Have them make a list of five things they are going to do (e.g., things they are going to buy for themselves or others) before leaving. Ex: **Voy a comprarme unos zapatos.**

Extra Practice Add a visual aspect to this grammar practice. Bring in personal or magazine photos that elicit statements with indirect object pronouns. Have students write descriptions of what is happening in each image. Ex: **La mujer está diciéndole a su hijo que tiene que comer el brócoli....**

4 Teaching Tips

- Have two volunteers read the model aloud. Then go through the phrases in the word bank and model question formation.
- To challenge students, have them ask follow-up questions for each item. Ex: **¿A quién le compras ropa? ¿Qué ropa le compras? ¿Dónde la compras?**

4 Expansion In pairs, give students five minutes to brainstorm as many questions as they can using different forms of the verbs in the word bank. Invite two pairs to come to the front of the class. Each pair takes a turn asking the other its questions. Encourage students to ask follow-up questions.

5 Teaching Tip Give each group a different lottery pay-out. Remind students they have to split it equally among the group members.

5 Expansion Have students research one of the different lotteries in Spain, such as **el Gordo** or **ONCE**. Have them write a brief description of how the lottery works, what it costs, and how much recent winners received.

6 Teaching Tip Take a class survey of the answers and write the results on the board.

6 Expansion Have students work in pairs and write a conversation between a parent and a child, using item 4 as a starting point. Ask students to role-play their dialogues for the class.

7 Teaching Tip To simplify, have students begin by brainstorming phrases for their role. Remind them that, except for the dialogue *between* the two shoppers, they should use **usted** in their conversations.

Section Goals

In **Estructura 6.3**, students will learn:
- the preterite of regular verbs
- spelling changes in the preterite for different verbs
- words commonly used with the preterite tense

Instructional Resources
Supersite: Audio (Lab MP3 Files); Resources (Grammar Presentation Slides, Activity Pack, Scripts, Answer Keys); Testing Program (Quizzes)
WebSAM
Workbook, pp. 64–65
Lab Manual, p. 35

Teaching Tips

- Introduce the preterite by describing some things you did yesterday, using the first-person preterite of known regular verbs. Use adverbs that signal the preterite (page 191). Ex: **Ayer compré una chaqueta nueva. Bueno, entré en el almacén y compré una. Y de repente, vi un sombrero. Decidí comprarlo también.** Each time you introduce a preterite form, write it on the board.
- After you have used several regular first-person preterites, expand by asking students questions. Ex: **Ayer compré un sombrero. Y tú, ____, ¿qué compraste ayer? (Compré un libro.)** Ask other students about their classmates' answers. Ex: **¿Qué compró ____ ayer? (Compró un libro.)**

6.3 Preterite tense of regular verbs

Tutorial

NATIONAL STANDARDS comparisons

ANTE TODO In order to talk about events in the past, Spanish uses two simple tenses: the preterite and the imperfect. In this lesson, you will learn how to form the preterite tense, which is used to express actions or states completed in the past.

Preterite of regular -ar, -er, and -ir verbs

		-ar verbs **comprar**	-er verbs **vender**	-ir verbs **escribir**
SINGULAR FORMS	yo	compr**é** *I bought*	vend**í** *I sold*	escrib**í** *I wrote*
	tú	compr**aste**	vend**iste**	escrib**iste**
	Ud./él/ella	compr**ó**	vend**ió**	escrib**ió**
PLURAL FORMS	nosotros/as	compr**amos**	vend**imos**	escrib**imos**
	vosotros/as	compr**asteis**	vend**isteis**	escrib**isteis**
	Uds./ellos/ellas	compr**aron**	vend**ieron**	escrib**ieron**

▶ **¡Atención!** The **yo** and **Ud./él/ella** forms of all three conjugations have written accents on the last syllable to show that it is stressed.

▶ As the chart shows, the endings for regular **-er** and **-ir** verbs are identical in the preterite.

¿Qué compraste?

Compré estos aretes.

▶ Note that the **nosotros/as** forms of regular **-ar** and **-ir** verbs in the preterite are identical to the present tense forms. Context will help you determine which tense is being used.

En invierno **compramos** ropa.
In the winter, we buy clothes.

Anoche **compramos** unos zapatos.
Last night we bought some shoes.

▶ **-Ar** and **-er** verbs that have a stem change in the present tense are regular in the preterite. They do *not* have a stem change.

	PRESENT	PRETERITE
cerrar (e:ie)	La tienda **cierra** a las seis.	La tienda **cerró** a las seis.
volver (o:ue)	Carlitos **vuelve** tarde.	Carlitos **volvió** tarde.
jugar (u:ue)	Él **juega** al fútbol.	Él **jugó** al fútbol.

▶ **¡Atención!** **-Ir** verbs that have a stem change in the present tense also have a stem change in the preterite.

CONSULTA
There are a few high-frequency irregular verbs in the preterite. You will learn more about them in **Estructura 9.1**, p. 286.

CONSULTA
You will learn about the preterite of **-ir** stem-changing verbs in **Estructura 8.1**, p. 254.

TEACHING OPTIONS

Extra Practice For practice with discrimination between preterite forms, call out preterite forms of regular verbs and point to individuals to provide the corresponding subject pronoun. Ex: **comimos (nosotros/as), creyeron (ustedes/ellos/ellas), llegué (yo), leíste (tú).**

Pairs Tell students to have a conversation about what they did last weekend. Make sure they include things they did by themselves and with others. Then, in groups of four, have them share their partner's weekend activities.

Small Groups Give each group of five a list of verbs, including some with spelling changes. Student A chooses a verb from the list and gives the **yo** form. Student B gives the **tú** form, and so on. Students work their way down the list, alternating who begins the conjugation chain.

- Verbs that end in **-car**, **-gar**, and **-zar** have a spelling change in the first person singular (**yo** form) in the preterite.

buscar	busc-	qu-	yo busqué
llegar	lleg-	gu-	yo llegué
empezar	empez-	c-	yo empecé

- Except for the **yo** form, all other forms of **-car**, **-gar**, and **-zar** verbs are regular in the preterite.

- Three other verbs—**creer**, **leer**, and **oír**—have spelling changes in the preterite. The **i** of the verb endings of **creer**, **leer**, and **oír** carries an accent in the **yo**, **tú**, **nosotros/as**, and **vosotros/as** forms, and changes to **y** in the **Ud./él/ella** and **Uds./ellos/ellas** forms.

creer	cre-	creí, creíste, creyó, creímos, creísteis, creyeron
leer	le-	leí, leíste, leyó, leímos, leísteis, leyeron
oír	o-	oí, oíste, oyó, oímos, oísteis, oyeron

- **Ver** is regular in the preterite, but none of its forms has an accent.

ver → vi, viste, vio, vimos, visteis, vieron

Words commonly used with the preterite

anoche	*last night*	**pasado/a (*adj.*)**	*last; past*
anteayer	*the day before yesterday*	**el año pasado**	*last year*
ayer	*yesterday*	**la semana pasada**	*last week*
de repente	*suddenly*	**una vez**	*once*
desde... hasta...	*from... until...*	**dos veces**	*twice*
		ya	*already*

Ayer llegué a Santiago de Cuba.
Yesterday I arrived in Santiago de Cuba.

Anoche oí un ruido extraño.
Last night I heard a strange noise.

- **Acabar de** + [*infinitive*] is used to say that something has just occurred. Note that **acabar** is in the present tense in this construction.

Acabo de comprar una falda.
I just bought a skirt.

Acabas de ir de compras.
You just went shopping.

recursos
WB pp. 64–65
LM p. 35
vhlcentral.com Lección 6

¡INTÉNTALO! Provide the appropriate preterite forms of the verbs.

	comer	salir	comenzar	leer
1. ellas	comieron	salieron	comenzaron	leyeron
2. tú	comiste	saliste	comenzaste	leíste
3. usted	comió	salió	comenzó	leyó
4. nosotros	comimos	salimos	comenzamos	leímos
5. yo	comí	salí	comencé	leí

Teaching Tips

- Point out that verbs ending in **-car** and **-gar** are regular and have logical spelling changes in the **yo** form in order to preserve the hard **c** and **g** sounds.
- Students will learn the preterite of **dar** in **Estructura 9.1**. If you wish to present it for recognition only at this point, you can tell them that the endings are identical to **ver** in the preterite.
- Provide sentence starters using the present indicative and have students complete them in a logical manner. Ex: **Todos los días los estudiantes llegan temprano, pero anteayer... (llegaron tarde.)**
- Practice verbs with spelling changes in the preterite by asking students about things they read, heard, and saw yesterday. Ex: **¿Leíste las noticias ayer? ¿Quiénes vieron el pronóstico del tiempo? Yo oí que va a llover hoy. ¿Qué oyeron ustedes?**
- Add a visual aspect to this grammar presentation. Use magazine pictures to demonstrate **acabar de**. Ex: **¿Quién acaba de ganar? (Serena Williams acaba de ganar.) ¿Qué acaban de ver ellos? (Acaban de ver una película.)**

TEACHING OPTIONS

Game Divide the class into teams of six and have them sit in rows. Call out the infinitive of a verb. The first person writes the preterite **yo** form on a sheet of paper and passes it to the second person, who writes the **tú** form, and so on. The sixth checks spelling. If all forms are correct, the team gets a point. Continue play, having team members rotate positions for each round. The team with the most points after six rounds wins.

Extra Practice Have students write down five things they did yesterday. Ask students questions about what they did to elicit as many different conjugations as possible. Ex: ____, **¿leíste las noticias ayer? ¿Quién más leyó las noticias ayer?...** ____ **y** ____, **ustedes dos leyeron las noticias ayer, ¿verdad? ¿Quiénes leyeron las noticias ayer?**

1 Teaching Tip To simplify, tell students to read through the items once and circle the correct infinitive for each sentence. Then ask them to read the sentences a second time and underline the subject for each verb. Finally, have them conjugate the infinitives.

1 Expansion Ask questions about **Andrea's** weekend. Have students answer with complete sentences. Ex: **¿Quién asistió a una reunión? ¿Qué compraron los amigos?**

2 Expansion Have students repeat the activity, using **ustedes** as the subject of the questions and **nosotros** in the answers.

Práctica

1 Completar Andrea is talking about what happened last weekend. Complete each sentence by choosing the correct verb and putting it in the preterite.

1. El viernes a las cuatro de la tarde, la profesora Mora __asistió__ (asistir, costar, usar) a una reunión (*meeting*) de profesores.
2. A la una, yo __llegué__ (llegar, bucear, llevar) a la tienda con mis amigos.
3. Mis amigos y yo __compramos__ (comprar, regatear, gastar) dos o tres cosas.
4. Yo __compré__ (costar, comprar, escribir) unos pantalones negros y mi amigo Mateo __compró__ (gastar, pasear, comprar) una camisa azul.
5. Después, nosotros __comimos__ (llevar, vivir, comer) cerca de un mercado.
6. A las tres, Pepe __habló__ (hablar, pasear, nadar) con su novia por teléfono.
7. El sábado por la tarde, mi mamá __escribió__ (escribir, beber, vivir) una carta.
8. El domingo mi tía __decidió__ (decidir, salir, escribir) comprarme un traje.
9. A las cuatro de la tarde, mi tía __encontró__ (beber, salir, encontrar) el traje y después nosotras __vimos__ (acabar, ver, salir) una película.

2 Preguntas Imagine that you have a pesky friend who keeps asking you questions. Respond that you already did or have just done what he/she asks. Make sure you and your partner take turns playing the role of the pesky friend and responding to his/her questions.

modelo

leer la lección
Estudiante 1: ¿Leíste la lección?
Estudiante 2: Sí, ya la leí./Sí, acabo de leerla.

1. escribir el mensaje electrónico
2. lavar (*to wash*) la ropa
3. oír las noticias (*news*)
4. comprar pantalones cortos
5. practicar los verbos
6. pagar la cuenta (*bill*)
7. empezar la composición
8. ver la película *Diarios de motocicleta*

Answers:
1. E1: ¿Escribiste el mensaje electrónico? E2: Sí, ya lo escribí./Acabo de escribirlo.
2. E1: ¿Lavaste la ropa? E2: Sí, ya la lavé./Acabo de lavarla.
3. E1: ¿Oíste las noticias? E2: Sí, ya las oí./Acabo de oírlas.
4. E1: ¿Compraste pantalones cortos? E2: Sí, ya los compré./Acabo de comprarlos.
5. E1: ¿Practicaste los verbos? E2: Sí, ya los practiqué./Acabo de practicarlos.
6. E1: ¿Pagaste la cuenta? E2: Sí, ya la pagué./Acabo de pagarla.
7. E1: ¿Empezaste la composición? E2: Sí, ya la empecé./Acabo de empezarla.
8. E1: ¿Viste la película *Diarios de motocicleta*? E2: Sí, ya la vi./Acabo de verla.

NOTA CULTURAL

Based on Ernesto "Che" Guevara's diaries, ***Diarios de motocicleta*** (2004) traces the road trip of Che (played by Gael García Bernal) with his friend Alberto Granado (played by Rodrigo de la Serna) through Argentina, Chile, Peru, Colombia, and Venezuela.

3 Teaching Tips
- To simplify, have students work with a partner to quickly review the preterite forms of the verbs in the activity.
- After students have completed item 7, discuss **las tres bes**. Ask students which one is most important to them when they go shopping.

3 Expansion Have students share their responses with a partner, who will ask follow-up questions. Ex: **—Mis padres vieron una película la semana pasada. —¿Qué película vieron? —Vieron *Gravity*. —¿Qué les pareció? —Les pareció muy buena.**

3 ¿Cuándo? Use the time expressions from the word bank to talk about when you and others did the activities listed. Answers will vary.

anoche	anteayer	el mes pasado	una vez
ayer	la semana pasada	el año pasado	dos veces

1. mi compañero/a de cuarto: llegar tarde a clase
2. mi mejor (*best*) amigo/a: salir con un(a) chico/a guapo/a
3. mis padres: ver una película
4. yo: llevar un traje/vestido
5. el presidente/primer ministro de mi país: asistir a una conferencia internacional
6. mis amigos y yo: comer en un restaurante
7. ¿?: comprar algo (*something*) bueno, bonito y barato

Practice more at **vhlcentral.com**.

TEACHING OPTIONS

TPR Have students stand in a circle. Begin by tossing a ball to a student and naming an infinitive and subject pronoun (Ex: **cerrar/tú**). The student who catches the ball has four seconds to provide the correct preterite form, toss the ball to another student, and name another infinitive and pronoun.

Extra Practice Ask students to imagine they have just visited an open-air market for the first time. Have them write a letter to a friend describing what they saw and did there. Then, ask students to exchange their letters with a classmate, who will respond.

Small Groups In groups of three, have students write down three sentences using verbs in the preterite. Then ask each group to act out its sentences for the class. When someone guesses the action, the group writes the sentence on the board.

NATIONAL STANDARDS communication

Comunicación

4 **Ayer** Jot down at what time you did these activities yesterday. Then get together with a classmate and find out at what time he or she did these activities. Be prepared to share your findings with the class. Answers will vary.

1. desayunar
2. empezar la primera clase
3. almorzar
4. ver a un(a) amigo/a
5. salir de clase
6. volver a la residencia/casa

5 **Las vacaciones** Imagine that you took these photos on a vacation with friends. Get together with a partner and use the pictures to tell him or her about your trip. Answers will vary.

6 **El fin de semana** Your instructor will give you and your partner different incomplete charts about what four employees at **Almacén Gigante** did last weekend. After you fill out the chart based on each other's information, you will fill out the final column about your partner. Answers will vary.

NATIONAL STANDARDS communication

Síntesis

7 **Conversación** Get together with a partner and have a conversation about what you did last week using verbs from the word bank. Don't forget to include school activities, shopping, and pastimes. Answers will vary.

acampar	comer	gastar	tomar
asistir	comprar	hablar	trabajar
bailar	correr	jugar	vender
beber	escribir	leer	ver
buscar	estudiar	oír	viajar

TEACHING OPTIONS

Large Group Have students stand up. Tell them to create a story chain about a student who had a very bad day. Begin the story by saying: **Ayer, Rigoberto pasó un día desastroso.** In order to sit down, students must contribute to the story. Call on a student to tell how **Rigoberto** began his day. The second person tells what happened next, and so on, until only one student remains. That person must conclude the story.

Extra Practice For homework, have students make a "to do" list at the beginning of their day. Then, ask students to return to their lists at the end of the day and write sentences stating which activities they completed. Ex: **limpiar mi habitación; No, no limpié mi habitación.**

4 Teaching Tips

- After forming pairs, model question formation and possible responses for the first two items.
- Encourage students to ask follow-up questions. Ex: **1. ¿Dónde desayunaste, en casa o en la cafetería? ¿Qué comiste?**

5 Teaching Tips

- You may wish to provide extra vocabulary. Ex: **los helados/las paletas, el picnic**
- Have students first state where they traveled and when. Then have them identify the people in the photos, stating their names and their relationship to them and describing their personalities. Finally, students should tell what everyone did on the trip. Encourage students to ask each other follow-up questions to learn more about their partner's trip.

5 Expansion After completing the activity orally, have students write a paragraph about their vacation, basing their account on the photos.

6 Teaching Tip Divide the class into pairs and distribute the handouts from the Activity Pack (Activity Pack/Supersite) that correspond to this Information Gap Activity. Give students ten minutes to complete the activity.

6 Expansion Have students tell the class about any activities that both their partner and one of the **Almacén Gigante** employees did. Ex: **La señora Zapata leyó un libro y ____ también. Los dos leyeron un libro.**

7 Teaching Tips

- Have volunteers rehearse their conversation, then present it to the class.
- Have volunteers report to the class what their partners did last week.

6.4 Demonstrative adjectives and pronouns

NATIONAL STANDARDS comparisons

Demonstrative adjectives

Tutorial

ANTE TODO In Spanish, as in English, demonstrative adjectives are words that "demonstrate" or "point out" nouns. Demonstrative adjectives precede the nouns they modify and, like other Spanish adjectives you have studied, agree with them in gender and number. Observe these examples and then study the chart below.

esta camisa	**ese** vendedor	**aquellos** zapatos
this shirt	*that salesman*	*those shoes (over there)*

Demonstrative adjectives

Singular: MASCULINE	Singular: FEMININE	Plural: MASCULINE	Plural: FEMININE	
este	**esta**	**estos**	**estas**	*this; these*
ese	**esa**	**esos**	**esas**	*that; those*
aquel	**aquella**	**aquellos**	**aquellas**	*that; those (over there)*

- There are three sets of demonstrative adjectives. To determine which one to use, you must establish the relationship between the speaker and the noun(s) being pointed out.
- The demonstrative adjectives **este**, **esta**, **estos**, and **estas** are used to point out things that are close to the speaker and the listener.

Me gustan estos zapatos.

- The demonstrative adjectives **ese**, **esa**, **esos**, and **esas** are used to point out things that are not close in space and time to the speaker. They may, however, be close to the listener.

Prefiero esos zapatos.

Section Goal

In **Estructura 6.4**, students will learn to use demonstrative adjectives and pronouns.

Instructional Resources
Supersite: Audio (Lab MP3 Files); Resources (Grammar Presentation Slides, Activity Pack, Scripts, Answer Keys); Testing Program (Quizzes)
WebSAM
Workbook, pp. 66–68
Lab Manual, p. 36

Teaching Tips

- Point to the book on your desk. Say: **Este libro está en la mesa.** Point to a book on a student's desk. Say: **Ese libro está encima del escritorio de** ____. Then point to a book on the window ledge. Say: **Aquel libro está cerca de la ventana**. Repeat the procedure with **tiza, papeles,** and **plumas**.
- Point out that although the masculine singular forms **este** and **ese** do not end in **–o**, their plural forms end in **–os**: **estos, esos**.
- Hold up or point to objects and have students give the plural: **este libro, esta mochila, este traje, este zapato.** Repeat with forms of **ese** and **aquel** with other nouns.
- You may want to have students associate **este** with **aquí**, **ese** with **allí**, and **aquel** with **allá**.

TEACHING OPTIONS

Extra Practice Hold up one or two items of clothing or classroom objects. Have students write all three forms of the demonstrative pronouns that would apply. Ex: **estos zapatos, esos zapatos, aquellos zapatos.**

Pairs Refer students to **Contextos** illustration on pages 174–175. Have them work with a partner to comment on the articles of clothing pictured. Ex: **Este suéter es bonito, ¿no? (No, ese suéter no es bonito. Es feo.) Aquella camiseta es muy cara. (Sí, aquella camiseta es cara.)**

▶ The demonstrative adjectives **aquel**, **aquella**, **aquellos**, and **aquellas** are used to point out things that are far away from the speaker and the listener.

Aquel auto es
de mi hermana.

Demonstrative pronouns

▶ Demonstrative pronouns are identical to their corresponding demonstrative adjectives, with the exception that they traditionally carry an accent mark on the stressed vowel. The **Real Academia** no longer requires this accent, but it is still commonly used.

Demonstrative pronouns

Singular		Plural	
MASCULINE	FEMININE	MASCULINE	FEMININE
éste	**ésta**	**éstos**	**éstas**
ése	**ésa**	**ésos**	**ésas**
aquél	**aquélla**	**aquéllos**	**aquéllas**

—¿Quieres comprar **este suéter**?
Do you want to buy this sweater?

—No, no quiero **éste**. Quiero **ése**.
No, I don't want this one. I want that one.

—¿Vas a leer **estas revistas**?
Are you going to read these magazines?

—Sí, voy a leer **éstas**. También voy a leer **aquéllas**.
Yes, I'm going to read these. I'll also read those (over there).

▶ **¡Atención!** Like demonstrative adjectives, demonstrative pronouns agree in gender and number with the corresponding noun.

Este libro es de Pablito. **Éstos** son de Juana.

▶ There are three neuter demonstrative pronouns: **esto**, **eso**, and **aquello**. These forms refer to unidentified or unspecified things, situations, ideas, and concepts. They do not change in gender or number and never carry an accent mark.

—¿Qué es **esto**?
What's this?

—**Eso** es interesante.
That's interesting.

—**Aquello** es bonito.
That's pretty.

recursos
WB pp. 66–68
LM p. 36
vhlcentral.com Lección 6

¡INTÉNTALO! Provide the correct form of the demonstrative adjective for these nouns.

1. la falda / este *esta falda*
2. los estudiantes / este *estos estudiantes*
3. los países / aquel *aquellos países*
4. la ventana / ese *esa ventana*
5. los periodistas / ese *esos periodistas*
6. el chico / aquel *aquel chico*
7. las sandalias / este *estas sandalias*
8. las chicas / aquel *aquellas chicas*

TEACHING OPTIONS

Small Groups Ask students to bring in fashion magazines. Have students work in small groups and give their opinions about the clothing they see in the magazines. Students should tell which items they like and which they do not, using demonstrative adjectives and pronouns. Encourage students to comment on other group members' comments. Ex: **¿Te gusta esa falda roja? Pienso que ésa es muy fea.**

Video Have students listen for the use of demonstrative pronouns as you replay the **Fotonovela**. Ask students to write each pronoun and the noun to which it refers. Then, have students look at a copy of the **Fotonovela** Videoscript (Supersite) to see if they were correct.

Teaching Tips

- Introduce demonstrative pronouns by having a volunteer stand next to you in front of the class. Place one book close to you and two more at varying distances. Say: **Necesito un libro.** Depending on the book the student hands to you, respond: **No, [éste] no. Quiero [ése].** Then place several books at each location. Say: **Necesito unos libros.** If needed, prompt the student to ask: **¿Cuáles? ¿Éstos?** Say: **No, quiero [aquéllos].** Repeat the process with pens **(plumas)** to elicit feminine forms.
- Engage students in short conversations about classroom objects and items of clothing. Ex: Pick up a student's backpack and ask him or her: **¿Es ésta mi mochila? (No, ésta es mi mochila.)** Turn to another student and ask about the same backpack: **¿Es ésa mi mochila? (No, ésa es la mochila de ____.)** Point to a student's pencil you have placed on the windowsill. Ask: **¿Es aquél tu lápiz? (No, aquél es su lápiz.)**
- Note that, since the **Real Academia Española** no longer requires written accents on demonstrative pronouns even for clarification, students may encounter publications that choose not to use them.
- To practice the neuter forms, write these expressions on the board: **¡Eso es fenomenal!**, **¡Esto es horrible!**, **¡Esto es estupendo!**, and **¿Qué es esto?** Then state situations and have students respond with one of the expressions. Ex: **1. Voy a cancelar el próximo examen. 2. La cafetería va a cerrar los lunes, miércoles y viernes. 3. Aquí te tengo un regalo.**
- Redo the **¡Inténtalo!** activity, using demonstrative pronouns.

1 Expansion To challenge students, ask them to expand each sentence with a phrase that includes a demonstrative pronoun. Ex: **Aquellos sombreros son muy elegantes, pero éstos son más baratos.**

2 Teaching Tips
- To simplify, have students underline the nouns that will be replaced by demonstrative pronouns.
- As you go over the activity, write each demonstrative pronoun on the board so students may verify that they have placed the accent marks correctly. You may choose to have your students leave out the accents.

3 Expansion
Ask students to find a photo featuring different articles of clothing or to draw several articles of clothing. Have them write five statements like that of the **Estudiante 1** model in part one of this activity. Then have students exchange their statements and photo/drawing with a partner to write responses like that of the **Estudiante 2** model.

Práctica

1 **Cambiar** Make the singular sentences plural and the plural sentences singular.

modelo
Estas camisas son blancas.
Esta camisa es blanca.

1. Aquellos sombreros son muy elegantes. Aquel sombrero es muy elegante.
2. Ese abrigo es muy caro. Esos abrigos son muy caros.
3. Estos cinturones son hermosos. Este cinturón es hermoso.
4. Esos precios son muy buenos. Ese precio es muy bueno.
5. Estas faldas son muy cortas. Esta falda es muy corta.
6. ¿Quieres ir a aquel almacén? ¿Quieres ir a aquellos almacenes?
7. Esas blusas son baratas. Esa blusa es barata.
8. Esta corbata hace juego con mi traje. Estas corbatas hacen juego con mis trajes.

2 **Completar** Here are some things people might say while shopping. Complete the sentences with the correct demonstrative pronouns.

1. No me gustan esos zapatos. Voy a comprar __éstos__. (*these*)
2. ¿Vas a comprar ese traje o __éste__? (*this one*)
3. Esta guayabera es bonita, pero prefiero __ésa__. (*that one*)
4. Estas corbatas rojas son muy bonitas, pero __ésas__ son fabulosas. (*those*)
5. Estos cinturones cuestan demasiado. Prefiero __aquéllos__. (*those over there*)
6. ¿Te gustan esas botas o __éstas__? (*these*)
7. Esa bolsa roja es bonita, pero prefiero __aquélla__. (*that one over there*)
8. No voy a comprar estas botas; voy a comprar __aquéllas__. (*those over there*)
9. ¿Prefieres estos pantalones o __ésos__? (*those*)
10. Me gusta este vestido, pero voy a comprar __ése__. (*that one*)
11. Me gusta ese almacén, pero __aquél__ es mejor (*better*). (*that one over there*)
12. Esa blusa es bonita, pero cuesta demasiado. Voy a comprar __ésta__. (*this one*)

3 **Describir** With your partner, look for two items in the classroom that are one of these colors: **amarillo**, **azul**, **blanco**, **marrón**, **negro**, **verde**, **rojo**. Take turns pointing them out to each other, first using demonstrative adjectives, and then demonstrative pronouns. Answers will vary.

modelo
azul
Estudiante 1: *Esta silla es azul. Aquella mochila es azul.*
Estudiante 2: *Ésta es azul. Aquélla es azul.*

Now use demonstrative adjectives and pronouns to discuss the colors of your classmates' clothing. One of you can ask a question about an article of clothing, using the wrong color. Your partner will correct you and point out that color somewhere else in the room.

modelo
Estudiante 1: *¿Esa camisa es negra?*
Estudiante 2: *No, ésa es azul. Aquélla es negra.*

Practice more at **vhlcentral.com**.

TEACHING OPTIONS

Pairs Have pairs role-play a dialogue between friends shopping for clothes. Student A tries to convince the friend that the clothes he or she wants to buy are not attractive. Student A suggests other items of clothing, but the friend does not agree. Students should use as many demonstrative adjectives and pronouns as possible.

Game Divide the class into two teams. Post pictures of different versions of the same object (Ex: sedan, sports car, all-terrain vehicle) on the board. Assign each a dollar figure, but do not share the prices with the class. Team A guesses the price of each object, using demonstrative adjectives and pronouns. Team B either agrees or guesses a higher or lower price. The team that guesses the closest price, wins. Ex: **Este carro cuesta $20.000, ése cuesta $35.000 y aquél cuesta $18.000.**

Comunicación

4 **Conversación** With a classmate, use demonstrative adjectives and pronouns to ask each other questions about the people around you. Use expressions from the word bank and/or your own ideas.
Answers will vary.

¿A qué hora...?	¿Cuántos años tiene(n)...?
¿Cómo es/son...?	¿De dónde es/son...?
¿Cómo se llama...?	¿De quién es/son...?
¿Cuándo...?	¿Qué clases toma(n)...?

modelo

Estudiante 1: *¿Cómo se llama esa chica?*
Estudiante 2: *Se llama Rebeca.*
Estudiante 1: *¿A qué hora llegó aquel chico a la clase?*
Estudiante 2: *A las nueve.*

5 **En una tienda** Imagine that you and a classmate are in Madrid shopping at Zara. Study the floor plan, then have a conversation about your surroundings. Use demonstrative adjectives and pronouns.
Answers will vary.

modelo

Estudiante 1: *Me gusta este suéter azul.*
Estudiante 2: *Yo prefiero aquella chaqueta.*

NOTA CULTURAL

Zara is an international clothing company based in Spain. Its innovative processes take a product from the design room to the manufacturing shelves in less than a month. This means that the merchandise is constantly changing to keep up with the most current trends.

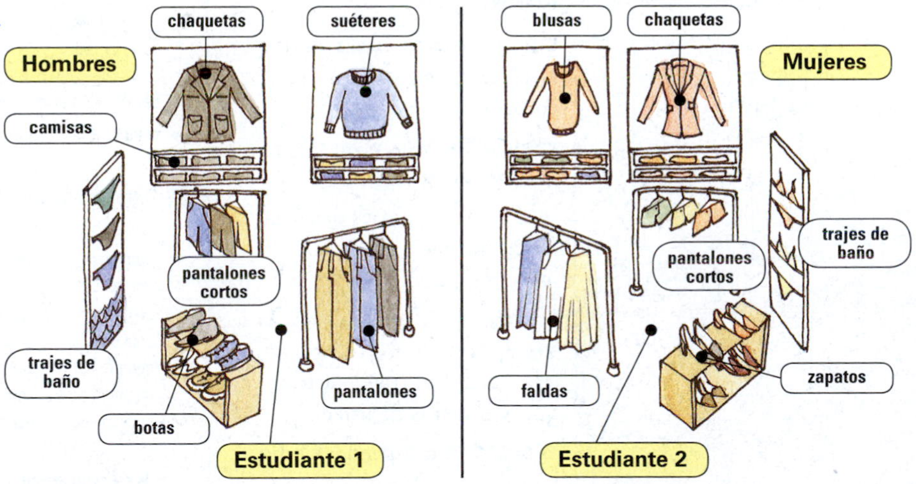

Síntesis

6 **Diferencias** Your instructor will give you and a partner each a drawing of a store. They are almost identical, but not quite. Use demonstrative adjectives and pronouns to find seven differences.
Answers will vary.

modelo

Estudiante 1: *Aquellas gafas de sol son feas, ¿verdad?*
Estudiante 2: *No. Aquellas gafas de sol son hermosas.*

4 Teaching Tip To challenge students, have both partners ask a question for each item in the word bank and at least one other question using an interrogative expression that is not included. Encourage students to ask follow-up questions.

5 Expansion Divide the class into small groups and have students role-play a situation between a salesperson and two customers. The customers should ask about the different items of clothing pictured and the salesperson will answer. They talk about how the items fit and their cost. The customers then express their preferences and decide which items to buy.

6 Teaching Tip Divide the class into pairs and distribute the handouts from the Activity Pack (Activity Pack/Supersite) that correspond with this Information Gap Activity. Give students ten minutes to complete the activity.

6 Expansion Have pairs work together with another pair to compare the seven responses that confirmed the seven differences. Ex: **No. Aquellas gafas de sol no son feas. Aquéllas son hermosas.** Ask a few groups to share some of the sentences with the class.

TEACHING OPTIONS

Pairs Ask students to write a conversation between two people sitting at a busy sidewalk café in the city. They are watching the people who walk by, asking each other questions about what the passersby are doing, and making comments on their clothing. Students should use as many demonstrative adjectives and pronouns as possible in their conversations. Invite several pairs to present their conversations to the class.

Small Groups Ask students to bring in pictures of their families, a sports team, a group of friends, etc. Have them take turns asking about and identifying the people in the pictures. Ex: **—¿Quién es aquella mujer? —¿Cuál? —Aquélla con la camiseta roja. —Es mi...**

Section Goal

In **Recapitulación**, students will review the grammar concepts from this lesson.

Instructional Resource
Supersite

1 Teaching Tips
- Before beginning the activity, ask students which preterite forms usually require accent marks.
- Ask a volunteer to identify which verbs have a spelling change in the preterite (**pagar, leer**).

1 Expansion Ask students to provide the **tú** and **nosotros** forms for these verbs.

2 Teaching Tip To simplify this activity, have students start by identifying whether a blank needs an adjective or a pronoun. If the blank requires an adjective, have them underline the corresponding noun. If the blank calls for a pronoun, have them identify the noun it replaces.

2 Expansion
Have students write their own dialogue in a department store using Activity 2 as a model. Have them role-play the conversations for the class, and encourage them to ad-lib new material as they go along.

Recapitulación

S Diagnostics

Review the grammar concepts you have learned in this lesson by completing these activities.

1 Completar Complete the chart with the correct preterite or infinitive form of the verbs. 30 pts.

Infinitive	yo	ella	ellos
tomar	tomé	tomó	**tomaron**
abrir	abrí	**abrió**	abrieron
comprender	comprendí	comprendió	comprendieron
leer	**leí**	leyó	leyeron
pagar	pagué	pagó	pagaron

2 En la tienda Look at the drawing and complete the conversation with demonstrative adjectives and pronouns. 14 pts.

CLIENTE Buenos días, señorita. Deseo comprar (1) ___esta___ corbata.

VENDEDORA Muy bien, señor. ¿No le interesa mirar (2) ___aquellos___ trajes que están allá? Hay unos que hacen juego con la corbata.

CLIENTE (3) ___Aquéllos___ de allá son de lana, ¿no? Prefiero ver (4) ___ese___ traje marrón que está detrás de usted.

VENDEDORA Estupendo. Como puede ver, es de seda. Cuesta seiscientos cincuenta dólares.

CLIENTE Ah… eh… no, creo que sólo voy a comprar la corbata, gracias.

VENDEDORA Bueno… si busca algo más económico, hay rebaja en (5) ___aquellos___ sombreros. Cuestan sólo treinta dólares.

CLIENTE ¡Magnífico! Me gusta (6) ___aquél___, el blanco que está hasta arriba (*at the top*). Y quiero pagar todo con (7) ___esta___ tarjeta.

VENDEDORA Sí, señor. Ahora mismo le traigo el sombrero.

RESUMEN GRAMATICAL

6.1 Saber and conocer *p. 184*

saber	conocer
sé	conozco
sabes	conoces
sabe	conoce
sabemos	conocemos
sabéis	conocéis
saben	conocen

- **saber** = to know facts/how to do something
- **conocer** = to know a person, place, or thing

6.2 Indirect object pronouns *pp. 186–187*

Indirect object pronouns

Singular	Plural
me	nos
te	os
le	les

- **dar** = doy, das, da, damos, dais, dan
- **decir (e:i)** = digo, dices, dice, decimos, decís, dicen

6.3 Preterite tense of regular verbs *pp. 190–191*

comprar	vender	escribir
compré	vendí	escribí
compraste	vendiste	escribiste
compró	vendió	escribió
compramos	vendimos	escribimos
comprasteis	vendisteis	escribisteis
compraron	vendieron	escribieron

Verbs with spelling changes in the preterite
- **-car:** buscar → yo busqué
- **-gar:** llegar → yo llegué
- **-zar:** empezar → yo empecé
- **creer:** creí, creíste, creyó, creímos, creísteis, creyeron
- **leer:** leí, leíste, leyó, leímos, leísteis, leyeron
- **oír:** oí, oíste, oyó, oímos, oísteis, oyeron
- **ver:** vi, viste, vio, vimos, visteis, vieron

TEACHING OPTIONS

Game Divide the class into two teams. Indicate a team member. Give an infinitive and a subject, and have the team member supply the correct preterite form. Award one point for each correct answer. Award a bonus point for correctly writing the verb on the board. The team with the most points wins.

TPR Write **presente** and **pretérito** on the board and have a volunteer stand in front of each word. Call out sentences using the present or the preterite. The student whose tense corresponds to the sentence has three seconds to step forward. Ex: **Compramos una chaqueta anteayer. (pretérito)**

Small Groups Ask students to write a description of a famous person, using **saber**, **conocer**, and one verb in the preterite. In small groups, have students read their descriptions aloud for the group to guess.

3 **¿Saber o conocer?** Complete each dialogue with the correct form of **saber** or **conocer**. 20 pts.

1. —¿Qué sabes hacer tú?
   —(Yo) Sé jugar al fútbol.
2. —¿Conoces tú esta tienda de ropa?
   —No, (yo) no la conozco. ¿Es buena?
3. —¿Tus padres no conocen a tu novio?
   —No, ¡ellos no saben que tengo novio!
4. —Mi compañero de cuarto todavía no me conoce bien.
   —Y tú, ¿lo quieres conocer a él?
5. —¿Saben ustedes dónde está el mercado?
   —No, nosotros no conocemos bien esta ciudad.

6.4 Demonstrative adjectives and pronouns *pp. 194–195*

Demonstrative adjectives

Singular		Plural	
Masc.	**Fem.**	**Masc.**	**Fem.**
este	esta	estos	estas
ese	esa	esos	esas
aquel	aquella	aquellos	aquellas

Demonstrative pronouns

Singular		Plural	
Masc.	**Fem.**	**Masc.**	**Fem.**
éste	ésta	éstos	éstas
ése	ésa	ésos	ésas
aquél	aquélla	aquéllos	aquéllas

4 **Oraciones** Form complete sentences using the information provided. Use indirect object pronouns and the present tense of the verbs. 10 pts.

1. Javier / prestar / el abrigo / a Maripili
   Javier le presta el abrigo a Maripili.
2. nosotros / vender / ropa / a los clientes
   Nosotros les vendemos ropa a los clientes.
3. el vendedor / traer / las camisetas / a mis amigos y a mí
   El vendedor nos trae las camisetas (a mis amigos y a mí).
4. yo / querer dar / consejos / a ti
   Yo quiero darte consejos (a ti)./Yo te quiero dar consejos (a ti).
5. ¿tú / ir a comprar / un regalo / a mí?
   ¿Tú vas a comprarme un regalo (a mí)?/¿Tú me vas a comprar un regalo (a mí)?

5 **Mi última compra** Write a short paragraph describing the last time you went shopping. Use at least four verbs in the preterite tense. 26 pts. Answers will vary.

modelo
El viernes pasado, busqué unos zapatos en el centro comercial...

6 **Poema** Write the missing words to complete the excerpt from the poem *Romance sonámbulo* by Federico García Lorca. 4 EXTRA points!

"Verde que te quiero verde.
Verde viento. Verdes ramas°.
El barco sobre la mar
y el caballo en la montaña, [...]
Verde que te quiero verde (*green*)."

ramas *branches*

Practice more at **vhlcentral.com**.

3 Teaching Tip Ask students to explain why they chose **saber** or **conocer** in each case.

3 Expansion Have students choose one dialogue from this activity and write a continuation. Encourage them to use at least one more example each of **saber** and **conocer**.

4 Teaching Tips
- Ask a volunteer to model the first sentence for the class.
- Before forming sentences, have students identify the indirect object in each item.
- Remind students of the possible positions for indirect object pronouns when using an infinitive.

4 Expansion
- Ask students to create three dehydrated sentences similar to those in **Actividad 4**. Have them exchange papers with a classmate and form complete sentences.
- For items 1–4, have students write questions that would elicit these statements. Ex: **1. ¿A quién le presta el abrigo Javier?/¿Qué le presta Javier a Maripili?** For item 5, have them write a response.

5 Teaching Tip To add a visual aspect to this activity, have students create a time line of what they did when they went shopping.

6 Teaching Tips
- Tell students to read through the whole excerpt before filling in the blanks.
- Have a volunteer read the excerpt aloud.

TEACHING OPTIONS

Extra Practice Add an auditory aspect to this grammar review. Read each of these sentences twice, pausing after the second time for students to write: **1. Ayer empecé a leer sobre los diseñadores hispanos. 2. Ellas buscaron unas bolsas en el mercado al aire libre. 3. El dependiente vendió cinco camisetas. 4. Nosotras oímos una explosión. 5. El joven le leyó el libro a su hermanito. 6. Raúl vio una película anoche.**

Game Divide the class into two teams. Indicate a member of each team and call out a color. The first student to find an object or article of clothing in the room, point to it, and use the correct form of a demonstrative adjective earns a point for their team. Ex: **¡Aquella camiseta es morada!** The team with the most points at the end wins.

Audio: Reading
Additional Reading

Section Goals

In **Lectura**, students will:

- learn to skim a text
- use what they know about text format to predict a document's content
- read a text rich in cognates and recognizable format elements

Instructional Resource
Supersite

Estrategia Tell students that they can often predict the content of an unfamiliar document in Spanish by skimming it and looking for recognizable format elements.

Examinar el texto Have students skim the text at the top of the ad. Point out the cognate **Liquidación** and the series of percentages. Ask them to predict what type of document it is. (It is an advertisement for a liquidation sale.) Then ask students to scan the rest of the ad.

Buscar cognados Ask volunteers to point out cognates.

Impresiones generales Ask students to sum up their general impression of the document by answering the three questions at the bottom.

Teaching Tips

- Point out the store's hours of operation. Remind students that many schedules and store hours are given using the 24-hour clock. Ask a volunteer to provide the times using the 12-hour clock.
- Remind students that, for these prices, periods are used where one would see a comma in English.
- Point out the shoe sizes and explain that they are European sizes. Then point out clothing sizes and ask students to guess what **P**, **M**, **G**, and **XG** stand for.

Lectura

NATIONAL STANDARDS communication cultures

Antes de leer

Estrategia
Skimming

Skimming involves quickly reading through a document to absorb its general meaning. This allows you to understand the main ideas without having to read word for word. When you skim a text, you might want to look at its title and subtitles. You might also want to read the first sentence of each paragraph.

Examinar el texto

Look at the format of the reading selection. How is it organized? What does the organization of the document tell you about its content?

Buscar cognados

Scan the reading selection to locate at least five cognates. Based on the cognates, what do you think the reading selection is about? Answers will vary. Suggested answers for 1-5: elegancia, blusas, accesorios, pantalones, precio.

1. ______________ 4. ______________
2. ______________ 5. ______________
3. ______________

The reading selection is about a sale in a store.

Impresiones generales

Now skim the reading selection to understand its general meaning. Jot down your impressions. What new information did you learn about the document by skimming it? Based on all the information you now have, answer these questions in Spanish.

1. Who created this document? un almacén/una tienda
2. What is its purpose? vender ropa
3. Who is its intended audience? gente que quiere comprar ropa

Practice more at **vhlcentral.com**.

Corona
http://corona.cl
Corona
¡Corona tiene las ofertas más locas del verano!
La tienda más elegante de la ciudad con precios increíbles
niños
mujeres
casa
baño
equipaje
Faldas largas
ROPA BONITA
Algodón. De distintos colores
Talla mediana
Precio especial: 8.000 pesos
Blusas de seda
BAMBÚ
De cuadros y de lunares
Ahora: 21.000 pesos
40% de rebaja
Vestido de algodón
PANAMÁ
Colores blanco, azul y verde
Ahora: 18.000 pesos
30% de rebaja
Accesorios
BELLEZA
Cinturones, gafas de sol, sombreros, medias
Diversos estilos
Todos con un 40% de rebaja
Carteras
ELEGANCIA
Colores anaranjado, blanco, rosado y amarillo
Ahora: 15.000 pesos
50% de rebaja
Sandalias de playa
GINO
Números del 35 al 38
A sólo 12.000 pesos
50% de descuento
Lunes a sábado de 9 a 21 horas.
Domingo de 10 a 14 horas.

TEACHING OPTIONS

Large Groups Ask students to create an ad for one or two items of clothing. Then, in groups, have them combine their ads into a "catalogue." Have groups exchange catalogues and discuss what items they would like to buy.

Small Groups Have small groups of students work together to write a cloze paragraph about shopping for clothing, modeled on the **Completar** paragraph. Ask each group member to contribute two sentences to the paragraph. Then have the group make a clean copy, omitting several words or phrases, and writing the omitted words and phrases below the paragraph. Have groups exchange paragraphs and complete them.

Real° Liquidación°

¡La rebaja está de moda en Corona!

¡Grandes rebajas!

y con la tarjeta de crédito más conveniente del mercado.

bebé | **hombres** | jardín | joyas | electrónica

Chaquetas
CASINO
Microfibra. Colores negro, café y gris
Tallas: P, M, G, XG
Ahora: 22.500 pesos

Traje inglés
GALES
Modelos originales
Ahora: 105.000 pesos
30% de rebaja

Pantalones
OCÉANO
Colores negro, gris y café
Ahora: 11.500 pesos
30% de rebaja

Accesorios
GUAPO
Gafas de sol, corbatas, cinturones, calcetines
Diversos estilos
Todos con un 40% de rebaja

Zapatos
COLOR
Italianos y franceses
Números del 40 al 45
A sólo 20.000 pesos

Ropa interior
ATLÁNTICO
Tallas: P, M, G
Colores blanco, negro y gris
40% de rebaja

Real *Royal* Liquidación *Clearance sale*

Por la compra de 40.000 pesos, puede llevar un regalo gratis.

- Un hermoso cinturón de mujer
- Un par de calcetines
- Una corbata de seda
- Una bolsa para la playa
- Una mochila
- Unas medias

Después de leer

Completar

Complete this paragraph about the reading selection with the correct forms of the words from the word bank.

almacén	hacer juego	tarjeta de crédito
caro	increíble	tienda
dinero	pantalones	verano
falda	rebaja	zapato

En este anuncio, el __almacén__ Corona anuncia la liquidación de __verano__ con grandes __rebajas__. Con muy poco __dinero__ usted puede conseguir ropa fina y elegante. Si no tiene dinero en efectivo, puede utilizar su __tarjeta de crédito__ y pagar luego. Para el caballero con gustos refinados, hay __zapatos__ importados de París y Roma. La señora elegante puede encontrar blusas de seda que __hacen juego__ con todo tipo de __pantalones/faldas__ o __faldas/pantalones__. Los precios de esta liquidación son realmente __increíbles__.

¿Cierto o falso?

Indicate whether each statement is **cierto** or **falso**. Correct the false statements.

1. Hay sandalias de playa. Cierto.
2. Las corbatas tienen una rebaja del 30%. Falso. Tienen una rebaja del 40%.
3. El almacén Corona tiene un departamento de zapatos. Cierto.
4. Normalmente las sandalias cuestan 22.000 pesos. Falso. Normalmente cuestan 24.000 pesos.
5. Cuando gastas 30.000 pesos en la tienda, llevas. un regalo gratis. Falso. Cuando gastas 40.000 pesos en la tienda, llevas un regalo gratis.
6. Tienen carteras amarillas. Cierto.

Preguntas

In pairs, take turns asking and answering these questions. Answers will vary.

1. Imagina que vas a ir a la tienda Corona. ¿Qué departamentos vas a visitar? ¿El departamento de ropa para señoras, el departamento de ropa para caballeros...?
2. ¿Qué vas a buscar en Corona?
3. ¿Hay tiendas similares a la tienda Corona en tu pueblo o ciudad? ¿Cómo se llaman? ¿Tienen muchas gangas?

Completar Have students quickly review the lesson vocabulary on pages 174–176 and 179 before they do this activity. Make sure that they understand the meaning of **el caballero con gustos refinados.**

¿Cierto o falso? Give students these sentences as items 7–10: **7. Las sandalias de playa no tienen una rebaja grande. (Falso. Tienen una rebaja del 50%.) 8. El almacén Corona está cerrado los domingos. (Falso. El almacén Corona está abierto de 10:00 a 14:00 los domingos.) 9. Se pueden conseguir carteras rosadas y blancas en rebaja. (Cierto.) 10. Un señor puede comprar una chaqueta gris de talla pequeña. (Cierto.)**

Preguntas Have small groups put together an ad for a department store where they shop. Have them use the **Almacén Corona** ad as a model. If two or more groups chose the same store, compare their ads in a follow-up discussion with the class.

TEACHING OPTIONS

TPR Write items of clothing on slips of paper. Have a volunteer choose a slip and mime putting on the item of clothing that he or she draws. The first student to correctly identify the item receives a point. The student with the most points at the end wins.

Heritage Speakers Ask heritage speakers to share phrases they know to ask the price of items. Ex: **¿Cuánto vale?** or **¿A cómo está(n)...?**

Game In pairs, have students play a modified version of **20 Preguntas**. Student A thinks of an item of clothing. Student B asks questions and guesses the name of the item. Student A keeps track of the number of questions and guesses. Allow partners to ask a total of ten questions and attempt to guess three times before moving on to the next item. The pair with the fewest questions overall wins.

Section Goals

In **Escritura**, students will:

- conduct an interview
- integrate vocabulary and structures taught in **Lección 6** into a written report
- report on an interview

Instructional Resource
Supersite

Estrategia Model an interview for students by asking a volunteer a few of the questions on this page. Then model how to report on an interview by transcribing verbatim a section of the dialogue on the board. Then give an example each of summarizing and summarizing but quoting occasionally.

Tema Tell students that they may interview a classmate or another Spanish-speaking student they know. Encourage them to take notes as they conduct the interview or record it. They might want to brainstorm additional questions with a classmate that they are not planning to interview. Introduce terms such as **entrevista, entrevistar, diálogo,** and **citas** as you present the activity.

Escritura

Estrategia

How to report an interview

There are several ways to prepare a written report about an interview. For example, you can transcribe the interview verbatim, you can simply summarize it, or you can summarize it but quote the speakers occasionally. In any event, the report should begin with an interesting title and a brief introduction, which may include the five Ws (*what, where, when, who, why*) and the H (*how*) of the interview. The report should end with an interesting conclusion. Note that when you transcribe dialogue in Spanish, you should pay careful attention to format and punctuation.

Writing dialogue in Spanish

- If you need to transcribe an interview verbatim, you can use speakers' names to indicate a change of speaker.

CARMELA	¿Qué compraste? ¿Encontraste muchas gangas?
ROBERTO	Sí, muchas. Compré un suéter, una camisa y dos corbatas. Y tú, ¿qué compraste?
CARMELA	Una blusa y una falda muy bonitas. ¿Cuánto costó tu camisa?
ROBERTO	Sólo diez dólares. ¿Cuánto costó tu blusa?
CARMELA	Veinte dólares.

- You can also use a dash (*raya*) to mark the beginning of each speaker's words.

—¿Qué compraste?

—Un suéter y una camisa muy bonitos. Y tú, ¿encontraste muchas gangas?

—Sí... compré dos blusas, tres camisetas y un par de zapatos.

—¡A ver!

Tema

Escribe un informe

Write a report for the school newspaper about an interview you conducted with a student about his or her shopping habits and clothing preferences. First, brainstorm a list of interview questions. Then conduct the interview using the questions below as a guide, but feel free to ask other questions as they occur to you.

Examples of questions:

- ¿Cuándo vas de compras?
- ¿Adónde vas de compras?
- ¿Con quién vas de compras?
- ¿Qué tiendas, almacenes o centros comerciales prefieres?
- ¿Compras ropa de catálogos o por Internet?
- ¿Prefieres comprar ropa cara o barata? ¿Por qué? ¿Te gusta buscar gangas?
- ¿Qué ropa llevas cuando vas a clase?
- ¿Qué ropa llevas cuando sales a bailar?
- ¿Qué ropa llevas cuando practicas un deporte?
- ¿Cuáles son tus colores favoritos? ¿Compras mucha ropa de esos colores?
- ¿Les das ropa a tu familia o a tus amigos/as?

EVALUATION: Informe

Criteria	Scale
Content	1 2 3 4 5
Organization	1 2 3 4 5
Accuracy	1 2 3 4 5
Creativity	1 2 3 4 5

Scoring	
Excellent	18–20 points
Good	14–17 points
Satisfactory	10–13 points
Unsatisfactory	< 10 points

Escuchar

Audio

Estrategia

Listening for linguistic cues

You can enhance your listening comprehension by listening for specific linguistic cues. For example, if you listen for the endings of conjugated verbs, or for familiar constructions, such as **acabar de** + [*infinitive*] or **ir a** + [*infinitive*], you can find out whether an event already took place, is taking place now, or will take place in the future. Verb endings also give clues about who is participating in the action.

To practice listening for linguistic cues, you will now listen to four sentences. As you listen, note whether each sentence refers to a past, present, or future action. Also jot down the subject of each sentence.

Preparación

Based on the photograph, what do you think Marisol has recently done? What do you think Marisol and Alicia are talking about? What else can you guess about their conversation from the visual clues in the photograph?

Ahora escucha

Now you are going to hear Marisol and Alicia's conversation. Make a list of the clothing items that each person mentions. Then put a check mark after the item if the person actually purchased it.

Marisol	Alicia
1. pantalones ✔	1. falda
2. blusa ✔	2. blusa
3. ________	3. zapatos
4. ________	4. cinturón

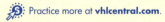

Practice more at **vhlcentral.com**.

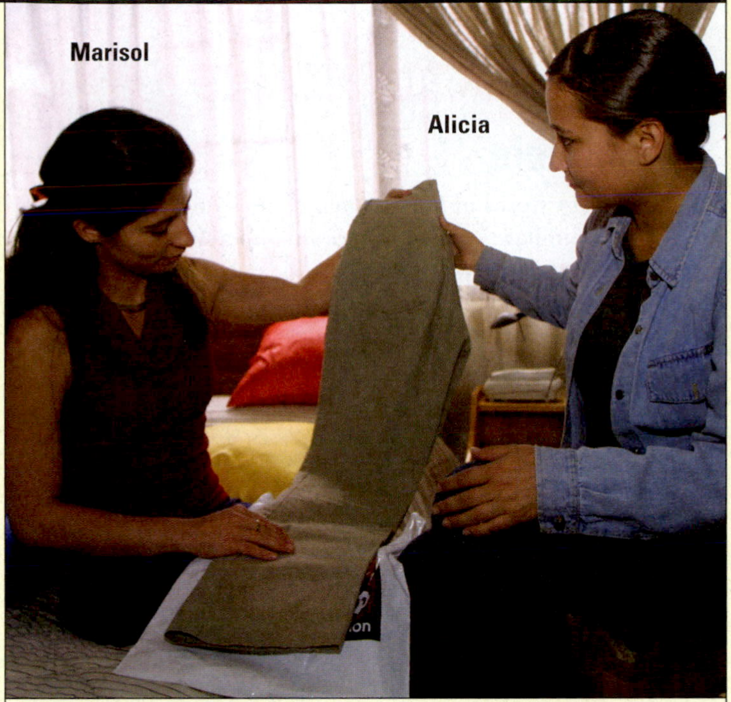

Comprensión

NATIONAL communication STANDARDS

¿Cierto o falso?

Indicate whether each statement is **cierto** or **falso.** Then correct the false statements.

1. Marisol y Alicia acaban de ir de compras juntas (*together*). Falso. Marisol acaba de ir de compras.
2. Marisol va a comprar unos pantalones y una blusa mañana. Falso. Marisol ya los compró.
3. Marisol compró una blusa de cuadros. Cierto.
4. Alicia compró unos zapatos nuevos hoy. Falso. Alicia va a comprar unos zapatos nuevos.
5. Alicia y Marisol van a ir al café. Cierto.
6. Marisol gastó todo el dinero de la semana en ropa nueva. Cierto.

Preguntas

Discuss the following questions with a classmate. Be sure to explain your answers. Answers will vary.

1. ¿Crees que Alicia y Marisol son buenas amigas? ¿Por qué?
2. ¿Cuál de las dos estudiantes es más ahorradora (*frugal*)? ¿Por qué?
3. ¿Crees que a Alicia le gusta la ropa que Marisol compró?
4. ¿Crees que la moda es importante para Alicia? ¿Para Marisol? ¿Por qué?
5. ¿Es importante para ti estar a la moda? ¿Por qué?

Section Goals

In **Escuchar**, students will:
- listen for specific linguistic cues in oral sentences
- answer questions based on a recorded conversation

Instructional Resources
Supersite: Audio (Textbook MP3s); Resources (Scripts)

Estrategia
Script 1. Acabamos de pasear por la ciudad y encontramos unos monumentos fenomenales. 2. Estoy haciendo las maletas. 3. Carmen y Alejandro decidieron ir a un restaurante. 4. Mi familia y yo vamos a ir a la playa.

Teaching Tip Ask students to look at the photo of **Marisol** and **Alicia** and predict what they are talking about.

Ahora escucha
Script MARISOL: Oye, Alicia, ¿qué estás haciendo?
ALICIA: Estudiando no más. ¿Qué hay de nuevo?
M: Acabo de comprarme esos pantalones que andaba buscando.
A: ¿Los encontraste en el centro comercial? ¿Y cuánto te costaron?
M: Míralos. ¿Te gustan? En el almacén Melo tienen tremenda rebaja. Como estaban baratos me compré una blusa también. Es de cuadros, pero creo que hace juego con los pantalones por el color rojo. ¿Qué piensas?
A: Es de los mismos colores que la falda y la blusa que llevaste cuando fuimos al cine anoche. La verdad es que te quedan muy bien esos colores. ¿No encontraste unos zapatos y un cinturón para completar el juego?
M: No lo digas ni de chiste. Mi tarjeta de crédito está que no aguanta más. Y trabajé poco la semana pasada. ¡Acabo de gastar todo el dinero para la semana!
A: ¡Ay, chica! Fui al centro comercial el mes pasado y encontré unos zapatos muy, pero muy de moda. Muy caros… pero buenos. No me los compré porque no los tenían en mi número. Voy a comprarlos cuando lleguen más… el vendedor me va a llamar.
M: Ajá… ¿Y va a invitarte a salir con él?
A: ¡Ay! ¡No seas así! Ven, vamos al café. Te ves muy bien y no hay que gastar eso aquí.
M: De acuerdo. Vamos.

(Script continues at far left in the bottom panels.)

Section Goals

In **En pantalla**, students will:

- read about **supermercados** in Mexico
- watch a television commercial for **Comercial Mexicana**, a Mexican supermarket chain
- read about the short film *Chicas day*
- watch the short film *Chicas day*

Instructional Resources
Supersite: Video (*En pantalla*); Resources (Scripts, Translations)

Introduction

To check comprehension, have pairs discuss the differences between grocery shopping in the U.S./Canada and Mexico. Then as a class, discuss the pros and cons of "one-stop" shopping and write their responses on the board.

Antes de ver

- Have students look at the video stills and read the captions aloud with a partner. Then ask students to predict what type of store is being advertised.
- Model pronunciation of the words in **Vocabulario útil** and have students repeat.
- Assure students that they do not need to understand every word they hear. Tell them to rely on visual cues, including gestures and facial expressions, and to listen for shopping-related vocabulary and words from **Vocabulario útil**.

Comprensión

- Have students read through the sentences before they watch the video.
- Have students correct the false statements.

Conversar

Give students a different context, such as a mother and her teenage daughter, and have them repeat the conversation.

En pantalla

NATIONAL STANDARDS communication cultures

Anuncio

Grocery stores in Mexico make one-stop shopping easy! Similar to the concept of a *Super-Walmart* in the U.S., most **supermercados**° in Mexico sell appliances, clothing, medicine, gardening supplies, electronics, and toys in addition to groceries. Large chains, like **Comercial Mexicana**, and smaller grocery stores alike typically sell a variety of products, allowing customers to satisfy all of their routine weekly shopping needs in one trip. Watch the **En pantalla** videoclip to see how one customer takes advantage of one-stop shopping at his local supermarket.

Vocabulario útil

con lo que ahorré	*with what I saved*
corazón	*sweetheart*
de peluche	*stuffed (toy)*
dragón	*dragon*
¿Me lo compras?	*Would you buy it for me?*

Comprensión

Indicate whether each statement is **cierto** or **falso**.

	Cierto	Falso
1. El niño quiere un elefante de peluche.	❍	✓
2. La señora usa zapatos negros.	❍	✓
3. El niño sigue a la señora hasta la caja.	✓	❍
4. La señora no es la mamá del niño.	✓	❍

Conversar

With a partner, use these cues to create a conversation in Spanish between two friends at a clothing store. Answers will vary.

Estudiante 1: Would you buy me a(n)...?
Estudiante 2: No, because it costs...
Estudiante 1: Please! I always (**siempre**) buy you...
Estudiante 2: OK, I will buy you this... How much does it cost?
Estudiante 1: It's on sale! It only costs....

supermercados *supermarkets*

Comercial mexicana

¿Me lo compras?

No, corazón.

¿Me lo compras, me lo compras, me lo compras?

Video: TV Clip

Practice more at **vhlcentral.com.**

TEACHING OPTIONS

Small Groups Have small groups of students write a conversation between the woman from the **Comercial Mexicana** ad and her husband or friend, in which she shares what happened on her shopping trip. Provide additional vocabulary as needed.

Pairs Write a list of situations on the board. (Ex: **el matrimonio de tu hermano/a, una cita a ciegas** [*blind date*], **un partido de béisbol, una fiesta en una residencia de la universidad**) Tell pairs to pick one of the situations and imagine that one student is clothes shopping for the event, and the other is a friend who is helping him/her shop. Have them write the conversation between the friends. Ask a few volunteers to role-play their conversations for the class.

Cortometraje

The short film *Chicas day* takes place on a sunny afternoon. A woman and a girl enjoy some time together at the swimming pool of a big house. Pay attention to the things they share and joke about, and how they interact. When the father arrives, everything comes to an abrupt end. What kind of relationship did you think the girl and the woman had at the beginning of the film? What were your expectations about the ending?

Preparación

Answer the following questions. Answers will vary.

1. ¿Te gusta disfrazarte (*to dress up*)? ¿Por qué?
2. ¿Cómo es un día ideal para ti?
3. ¿A quién admiras más? ¿Por qué?

Después de ver

Place these events in chronological order.

__6__ a. La niña dice que está enferma.
__5__ b. El padre llega a casa.
__1__ c. La mujer se pone (*puts on*) el traje de baño.
__7__ d. El padre habla por teléfono.
__3__ e. La niña y la mujer nadan en la piscina.
__2__ f. La mujer lleva gafas de sol.
__4__ g. La niña baila.

Conversar

With a partner, imagine that you know the woman in this short film. Talk about her: what you know about her life, what her name is, what she likes to wear, her relationships, etc. Make a list of traits based on what you imagined and what you saw in the film. Compare your list with another pair. Answers will vary.

Expresiones útiles

No seas pesada.	*Don't be a pain.*
cuando sea mayor	*when I grow up*
Me encuentro mal.	*I feel sick.*
¡Que sea la última vez!	*Let this be the last time!*
Ya era hora.	*It's about time.*
Pasa totalmente de la niña.	*She doesn't care about the girl at all.*

Para hablar del corto

el anillo	*ring*
la criada	*maid*
disfrazarse	*to dress up*
desatendido/a	*neglected*
fingir	*to pretend*
ocultar	*to hide*

Video: Short Film

Practice more at **vhlcentral.com.**

Antes de ver
- Have students look at the poster, and ask them what they think the short film will be about.
- Read through the **Expresiones útiles** and **Para hablar del corto** vocabulary with students to model pronunciation and practice using the terms.
- Reassure students that they do not need to understand every word they hear in the short film. Tell them to rely on visual cues and listen for cognates and words from **Expresiones útiles**.

Preparación Give students time to think about their answers. Allow them to ask you for additional vocabulary.

Después de ver Check the activity by having volunteers read the sentences aloud in order, one sentence per student.

Conversar
- Alternatively, have small groups imagine an alternate ending; they can write a short script and role-play it for the class. Have students vote on their favorite ending.
- Ask students to explain the title of this short film. Have them suggest other titles that might point to a different aspect of the film.

TEACHING OPTIONS

Small Groups Ask small groups to write a story about a special day in which the main characters dress up in order to have some fun and take a break from daily life (by crashing a wedding, attending a sci-fi convention, etc.).

Large Groups Divide the class into two groups, one that says the relationship between the woman and the girl is healthy and one that says that it is not. Hold a debate. Some questions to consider: Is the role-playing harmless? Is the woman filling a role that would otherwise be empty? Is she a bad influence? Is the little girl too attached to her?

Video: *Panorama cultural*
Interactive map

Section Goal

In **Panorama**, students will read about the geography, culture, history, and economy of Cuba.

Instructional Resources
Supersite: Video (***Panorama cultural***); Resources (Scripts, Translations, Digital Image Bank, Answer Keys)
WebSAM
Workbook, pp. 69–70
Video Manual, pp. 41–42

Teaching Tips

- Use the **Lección 6** digital images to assist with this presentation.
- Ask students to look at the map. Ask volunteers to read the captions on each call-out photo. Then discuss the photos with the class.

The Affective Dimension

Some students may have strong feelings about Cuba. Encourage students to discuss their points of view.

El país en cifras

- After reading about **La Habana Vieja**, show students images of this part of the city.
- Draw attention to the design and colors of the Cuban flag. Compare the Cuban flag to the Puerto Rican flag (page 170). Explain that Puerto Rico and Cuba, the last Spanish colonies in the western hemisphere, both gained their independence from Spain in 1898, in part through the intervention of the U.S.

¡Increíble pero cierto! Due to the patterns of evolution and adaptation common to islands, Cuba has many examples of unique flora and fauna. Have students research other examples.

Cuba

NATIONAL STANDARDS connections cultures

El país en cifras

- **Área:** 110.860 km² (42.803 millas²), *aproximadamente el área de Pensilvania*
- **Población:** 11.061.886
- **Capital:** La Habana—2.116.000

La Habana Vieja fue declarada° Patrimonio° Cultural de la Humanidad por la UNESCO en 1982. Este distrito es uno de los lugares más fascinantes de Cuba. En La Plaza de Armas, se puede visitar el majestuoso Palacio de Capitanes Generales, que ahora es un museo. En la calle° Obispo, frecuentada por el autor Ernest Hemingway, hay hermosos cafés, clubes nocturnos y tiendas elegantes.

- **Ciudades principales:** Santiago de Cuba; Camagüey; Holguín; Guantánamo
- **Moneda:** peso cubano
- **Idiomas:** español (oficial)

Bandera de Cuba

Cubanos célebres

- **Carlos Finlay,** doctor y científico (1833–1915)
- **José Martí,** político y poeta (1853–1895)
- **Fidel Castro,** ex primer ministro, ex comandante en jefe° de las fuerzas armadas (1926–)
- **Zoé Valdés,** escritora (1959–)
- **Ibrahim Ferrer,** músico (1927–2005)
- **Carlos Acosta,** bailarín (1973–)

Gran Teatro de La Habana

Plaza del Capitolio

Los coco taxis son un medio de transporte cubano muy popular.

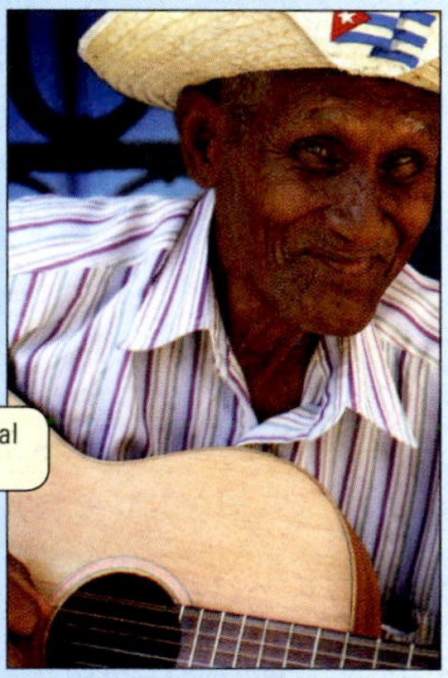

La música es parte esencial de la vida en Cuba.

fue declarada *was declared* Patrimonio *Heritage* calle *street*
comandante en jefe *commander in chief* liviano *light*
colibrí abeja *bee hummingbird* ave *bird* mundo *world*
miden *measure* pesan *weigh*

recursos

WB pp. 69–70	VM pp. 41–42	vhlcentral.com Lección 6

¡Increíble pero cierto!

Pequeño y liviano°, el colibrí abeja° de Cuba es una de las más de 320 especies de colibrí y es también el ave° más pequeña del mundo°. Menores que muchos insectos, estas aves minúsculas miden° 5 centímetros y pesan° sólo 1,95 gramos.

TEACHING OPTIONS

Variación léxica An item of clothing that you will see everywhere if you visit Cuba (or the Caribbean in general) is the **guayabera**. A loose-fitting, short-sleeved shirt made of natural fibers, the **guayabera** is perfect for hot, humid climates. **Guayaberas** generally have large pockets and may be decorated with embroidery. They are worn open at the neck and never tucked in.

Extra Practice Give students two stanzas of the first poem from **José Martí's** collection ***Versos sencillos***. Some students may recognize these as verses from the song ***Guantanamera***.

Yo soy un hombre sincero
de donde crece la palma;
y, antes de morirme, quiero
echar mis versos del alma.

Yo vengo de todas partes,
y hacia todas partes voy;
arte soy entre las artes;
en los montes, monte soy.

Baile • Ballet Nacional de Cuba

La bailarina Alicia Alonso fundó el Ballet Nacional de Cuba en 1948, después de° convertirse en una estrella° internacional en el Ballet de Nueva York y en Broadway. El Ballet Nacional de Cuba es famoso en todo el mundo por su creatividad y perfección técnica.

Economía • La caña de azúcar y el tabaco

La caña de azúcar° es el producto agrícola° que más se cultiva en la isla y su exportación es muy importante para la economía del país. El tabaco, que se usa para fabricar los famosos puros° cubanos, es otro cultivo° de mucha importancia.

Gente • Población

La población cubana tiene raíces° muy heterogéneas. La inmigración a la isla fue determinante° desde la colonia hasta mediados° del siglo° XX. Los cubanos de hoy son descendientes de africanos, europeos, chinos y antillanos, entre otros.

Música • Buena Vista Social Club

En 1997 nace° el fenómeno musical conocido como *Buena Vista Social Club*. Este proyecto reúne° a un grupo de importantes músicos de Cuba, la mayoría ya mayores, con una larga trayectoria interpretando canciones clásicas del son° cubano. Ese mismo año ganaron un *Grammy*. Hoy en día estos músicos son conocidos en todo el mundo, y personas de todas las edades bailan al ritmo° de su música.

¿Qué aprendiste? Responde a las preguntas con una oración completa.

1. ¿Qué autor está asociado con la Habana Vieja? Ernest Hemingway está asociado con la Habana Vieja.
2. ¿Por qué es famoso el Ballet Nacional de Cuba? Es famoso por su creatividad y perfección técnica.
3. ¿Cuáles son los dos cultivos más importantes para la economía cubana? Los cultivos más importantes son la caña de azúcar y el tabaco.
4. ¿Qué fabrican los cubanos con la planta del tabaco? Los cubanos fabrican puros.
5. ¿De dónde son muchos de los inmigrantes que llegaron a Cuba? Son de África, de Europa, de China y de las Antillas, entre otros lugares.
6. ¿En qué año ganó un *Grammy* el disco *Buena Vista Social Club*? Ganó un *Grammy* en 1997.

Conexión Internet Investiga estos temas en **vhlcentral.com**.

Practice more at **vhlcentral.com**.

1. Busca información sobre un(a) cubano/a célebre. ¿Por qué es célebre? ¿Qué hace? ¿Todavía vive en Cuba?
2. Busca información sobre una de las ciudades principales de Cuba. ¿Qué atracciones hay en esta ciudad?

después de *after* **estrella** *star* **caña de azúcar** *sugar cane* **agrícola** *farming* **puros** *cigars* **cultivo** *crop* **raíces** *roots* **determinante** *deciding* **mediados** *halfway through* **siglo** *century* **nace** *is born* **reúne** *gets together* **son** *Cuban musical genre* **ritmo** *rhythm*

Ballet Nacional de Cuba
Although the **Ballet Nacional de Cuba** specializes in classical dance, Cuban popular dances (**habanera, mambo, rumba**) have gained worldwide popularity. Students can interview grandparents or other adults to see what they remember about Cuban dances.

La caña de azúcar y el tabaco
With the collapse of the Soviet bloc and the end of subsidies, Cuba's economy suffered. In 1990, Cuba entered **el período especial en tiempo de paz**. Government planners have developed tourism, which formerly was seen as bourgeois and corrupting, as a means of gaining badly needed foreign currency.

Población
Have students pick an immigrant group and research its history in Cuba. Have them note general dates of arrival, what their community contributed to Cuban culture, and current demographics.

Buena Vista Social Club
If students are not familiar with the film or the music of ***Buena Vista Social Club***, play some songs from the sound track for students to hear. Read some song titles and have students make predictions about the music before they listen.

Conexión Internet Students will find supporting Internet activities and links at **vhlcentral.com**.

Teaching Tip You may want to wrap up this section by playing the ***Panorama cultural*** video footage for this lesson.

TEACHING OPTIONS

Language Notes Some Cuban songs mention beings with names that do not sound Spanish, such as **Obatalá, Elegguá,** and **Babaluayé**. These are divinities (**orichas**) of the Afro-Cuban religion, which has its origins in Yoruba-speaking West Africa. Forcibly converted to Catholicism upon their arrival in Cuba, Africans developed a syncretized religion in which they worshiped the gods they had brought from Africa in the form of Catholic saints. **Babaluayé,** for instance, is worshiped as **San Lázaro**. **Obatalá** is **Nuestra Señora de las Mercedes**. Cuban popular music is deeply rooted in the songs and dances with which Afro-Cubans expressed their devotion to the **orichas.**

Instructional Resources
Supersite: Audio (Textbook & Lab MP3s); Testing Program (Tests, MP3s)
WebSAM
Lab Manual, p. 36

La ropa

el abrigo	*coat*
los (blue)jeans	*jeans*
la blusa	*blouse*
la bolsa	*purse; bag*
la bota	*boot*
los calcetines (el calcetín)	*sock(s)*
la camisa	*shirt*
la camiseta	*t-shirt*
la cartera	*wallet*
la chaqueta	*jacket*
el cinturón	*belt*
la corbata	*tie*
la falda	*skirt*
las gafas (de sol)	*(sun)glasses*
los guantes	*gloves*
el impermeable	*raincoat*
las medias	*pantyhose; stockings*
los pantalones	*pants*
los pantalones cortos	*shorts*
la ropa	*clothes*
la ropa interior	*underwear*
las sandalias	*sandals*
el sombrero	*hat*
el suéter	*sweater*
el traje	*suit*
el traje de baño	*bathing suit*
el vestido	*dress*
los zapatos de tenis	*sneakers*

Verbos

conducir	*to drive*
conocer	*to know; to be acquainted with*
dar	*to give*
ofrecer	*to offer*
parecer	*to seem*
saber	*to know; to know how*
traducir	*to translate*

Ir de compras

el almacén	*department store*
la caja	*cash register*
el centro comercial	*shopping mall*
el/la cliente/a	*customer*
el/la dependiente/a	*clerk*
el dinero	*money*
(en) efectivo	*cash*
el mercado (al aire libre)	*(open-air) market*
un par (de zapatos)	*a pair (of shoes)*
el precio (fijo)	*(fixed; set) price*
la rebaja	*sale*
el regalo	*gift*
la tarjeta de crédito	*credit card*
la tienda	*store*
el/la vendedor(a)	*salesperson*
costar (o:ue)	*to cost*
gastar	*to spend (money)*
hacer juego (con)	*to match (with)*
llevar	*to wear; to take*
pagar	*to pay*
regatear	*to bargain*
usar	*to wear; to use*
vender	*to sell*

Adjetivos

barato/a	*cheap*
bueno/a	*good*
cada	*each*
caro/a	*expensive*
corto/a	*short (in length)*
elegante	*elegant*
hermoso/a	*beautiful*
largo/a	*long*
loco/a	*crazy*
nuevo/a	*new*
otro/a	*other; another*
pobre	*poor*
rico/a	*rich*

Los colores

el color	*color*
amarillo/a	*yellow*
anaranjado/a	*orange*
azul	*blue*
blanco/a	*white*
gris	*gray*
marrón, café	*brown*
morado/a	*purple*
negro/a	*black*
rojo/a	*red*
rosado/a	*pink*
verde	*green*

Palabras adicionales

acabar de (+ *inf.*)	*to have just done something*
anoche	*last night*
anteayer	*the day before yesterday*
ayer	*yesterday*
de repente	*suddenly*
desde	*from*
dos veces	*twice*
hasta	*until*
pasado/a (*adj.*)	*last; past*
el año pasado	*last year*
la semana pasada	*last week*
prestar	*to lend; to loan*
una vez	*once*
ya	*already*

Indirect object pronouns	*See page 186.*
Demonstrative adjectives and pronouns	*See page 194.*
Expresiones útiles	*See page 179.*

recursos
LM p. 36 | vhlcentral.com Lección 6

Vocabulary Tools

La rutina diaria

7

Communicative Goals

You will learn how to:

- **Describe your daily routine**
- **Talk about personal hygiene**
- **Reassure someone**

A PRIMERA VISTA
- **¿Está él en casa o en una tienda?**
- **¿Está contento o enojado?**
- **¿Cómo es él?**
- **¿Qué colores hay en la foto?**

Lesson Goals

In **Lección 7**, students will be introduced to the following:
- terms for daily routines
- reflexive verbs
- adverbs of time
- the custom of **la siesta**
- drinking **mate** as part of a daily routine
- indefinite and negative words
- preterite of **ser** and **ir**
- verbs like **gustar**
- predicting content from the title
- a video about **tapas**
- cultural, geographic, and historical information about Peru

A primera vista Here are some additional questions you can ask to personalize the photo: **¿Con quién vives? ¿Qué le dices antes de salir de casa? ¿Qué tipo de ropa llevas para ir a tus clases? ¿Les prestas esta ropa a tus amigos/as? ¿Qué ropa usaste en el verano? ¿Y en el invierno?**

Teaching Tip Look for these icons for additional communicative practice:

→👤←	Interpretive communication
←👤→	Presentational communication
👤↔👤	Interpersonal communication

INSTRUCTIONAL RESOURCES

Supersite (vhlcentral.com)
Video: ***Fotonovela, Flash cultura, Panorama cultural***
Audio: Textbook and Lab MP3 Files
Activity Pack: Information Gap Activities, games, additional activity handouts
Resources: SAM Answer Key, Scripts, Translations, **Vocabulario adicional**, sample lesson plan, Grammar Presentation Slides, Digital Image Bank
Testing Program: Quizzes, Tests, Exams, MP3s
Student Activities Manual: Workbook/Video Manual/Lab Manual
WebSAM (online Student Activities Manual)

Vocabulary Tools

Section Goals

In **Contextos**, students will learn and practice:

- vocabulary to talk about daily routines
- reflexive verbs to talk about daily routines
- adverbs of time

Instructional Resources

Supersite: Audio (Textbook and Lab MP3 Files); Resources (Digital Image Bank, **Vocabulario adicional**, Activity Pack, Scripts, Answer Keys); Testing Program (Quizzes)
WebSAM
Workbook, pp. 73–74
Lab Manual, p. 37

Teaching Tips

- Write **levantarse por la mañana** on the board and explain that it means *to get up in the morning*. Ask: **¿A qué hora te levantas por la mañana los lunes?** Ask another student: **¿A qué hora se levanta ____?** Then ask about Saturdays. Write **acostarse (o:ue)** on the board and explain that it means *to go to bed*. Follow the same procedure as for **levantarse**.
- Reflexives will only be used in the infinitive and third-person forms until **Estructura 7.1.**
- Use the **Lección 7 Contextos** digital images to assist with this presentation.
- Make true/false statements about the illustrations in **Contextos**. Have students correct any false statements. Ex: **Hay una chica que se peina por la noche en la habitación.** (**Cierto.**)
- If students ask, explain that **el pelo** is never used with **peinarse**, only with **cepillarse**.

Note: At this point you may want to present ***Vocabulario adicional: Más vocabulario para la vida diaria*** from the Supersite.

La rutina diaria

Más vocabulario

el baño, el cuarto de baño	*bathroom*
el inodoro	*toilet*
el jabón	*soap*
el despertador	*alarm clock*
el maquillaje	*makeup*
la rutina diaria	*daily routine*
bañarse	*to take a bath*
cepillarse el pelo	*to brush one's hair*
dormirse (o:ue)	*to go to sleep; to fall asleep*
lavarse la cara	*to wash one's face*
levantarse	*to get up*
maquillarse	*to put on makeup*
antes (de)	*before*
después	*afterwards; then*
después (de)	*after*
durante	*during*
entonces	*then*
luego	*then*
más tarde	*later (on)*
por la mañana	*in the morning*
por la noche	*at night*
por la tarde	*in the afternoon; in the evening*
por último	*finally*

Variación léxica

afeitarse ↔	rasurarse (*Méx., Amér. C.*)
ducha ↔	regadera (*Col., Méx., Venez.*)
ducharse ↔	bañarse (*Amér. L.*)
pantuflas ↔	chancletas (*Méx., Col.*); zapatillas (*Esp.*)

En la habitación por la mañana

En el baño por la mañana

recursos

WB pp. 73–74	LM p. 37	vhlcentral.com Lección 7

TEACHING OPTIONS

TPR In groups of three, have students take turns miming actions involving daily routines. The other group members should guess the verb or verb phrase. You may want to have students use only the infinitive form at this point. Ex: A student mimes washing his/her hands (**lavarse las manos**).

Variación léxica Ask heritage speakers if they use any of the words in **Variación léxica** and if they know of other words used to describe daily routines (Ex: **lavarse la boca/los dientes**). You may want to point out that other words for *bedroom* include **la alcoba, el aposento, el cuarto, el dormitorio, la pieza,** and **la recámara**.

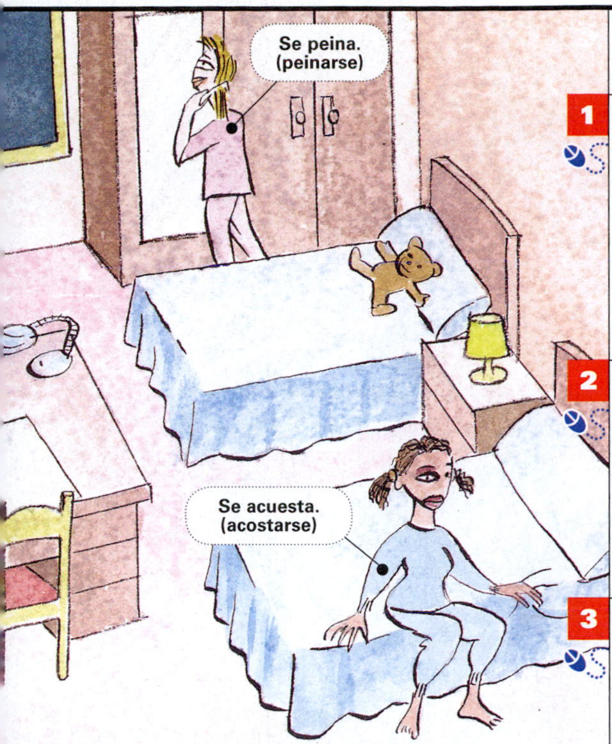

En la habitación por la noche

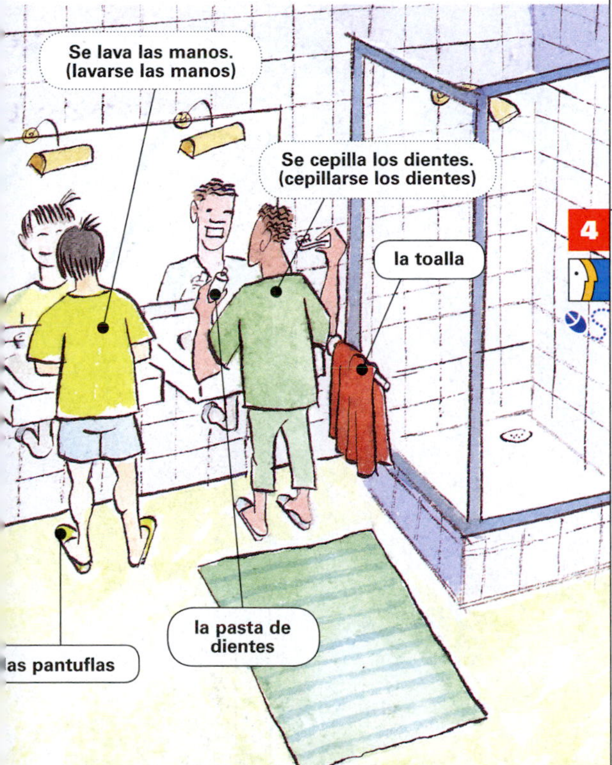

En el baño por la noche

Práctica

1 **Escuchar** Escucha las oraciones e indica si cada oración es **cierta** o **falsa**, según el dibujo.

1. falsa
2. cierta
3. falsa
4. cierta
5. falsa
6. falsa
7. falsa
8. cierta
9. falsa
10. cierta

2 **Ordenar** Escucha la rutina diaria de Marta. Después ordena los verbos según lo que escuchaste.

5 a. almorzar
2 b. ducharse
4 c. peinarse
7 d. ver la televisión
3 e. desayunar
8 f. dormirse
1 g. despertarse
6 h. estudiar en la biblioteca

3 **Seleccionar** Selecciona la palabra que no está relacionada con cada grupo.

1. lavabo • toalla • despertador • jabón despertador
2. manos • antes de • después de • por último manos
3. acostarse • jabón • despertarse • dormirse jabón
4. espejo • lavabo • despertador • entonces entonces
5. dormirse • toalla • vestirse • levantarse toalla
6. pelo • cara • manos • inodoro inodoro
7. espejo • champú • jabón • pasta de dientes espejo
8. maquillarse • vestirse • peinarse • dientes dientes
9. baño • dormirse • despertador • acostarse baño
10. ducharse • luego • bañarse • lavarse luego

4 **Identificar** Con un(a) compañero/a, identifica las cosas que cada persona necesita. Sigue el modelo. Some answers will vary.

modelo

Jorge / lavarse la cara
Estudiante 1: *¿Qué necesita Jorge para lavarse la cara?*
Estudiante 2: *Necesita jabón y una toalla.*

1. Mariana / maquillarse maquillaje y un espejo
2. Gerardo / despertarse un despertador
3. Celia / bañarse jabón y una toalla
4. Gabriel / ducharse una ducha, una toalla y jabón
5. Roberto / afeitarse un espejo y crema de afeitar
6. Sonia / lavarse el pelo champú y una toalla
7. Vanesa / lavarse las manos un lavabo, jabón y una toalla
8. Manuel / vestirse su ropa/una camiseta/unos pantalones/etc.
9. Simón / acostarse una cama
10. Daniela / cepillarse los dientes pasta de dientes y cepillo de dientes

TEACHING OPTIONS

Pairs Have students write out three daily routine activities without showing them to their partner. The partner will ask questions that contain adverbs of time in order to guess the action. Ex: **—¿Es antes o después de ducharse? —Antes de ducharse. —¿Es levantarse? —Sí.**

Small Groups Write verbs and verb phrases used to describe daily routines on separate note cards. Divide the class into small groups and give each group a set of cards. Students should work together to determine the most logical sequence in which the actions may occur.

1 Teaching Tip Go over **Actividad 1** with the class. Then, have volunteers correct the false statements.

1 Script 1. Hay dos despertadores en la habitación de las chicas. 2. Un chico se pone crema de afeitar en la cara. 3. Una de las chicas se ducha. 4. Uno de los chicos se afeita. 5. Hay una toalla en la habitación de las chicas. 6. Una de las chicas se maquilla. 7. Las chicas están en el baño. 8. Uno de los chicos se cepilla los dientes en el baño. 9. Uno de los chicos se viste. 10. Una de las chicas se despierta. *Textbook MP3s*

2 Teaching Tip To simplify, point out that the verbs in the list are in the infinitive form and tell students that they will hear them in conjugated (third-person singular) form. Before listening, have volunteers provide the third-person singular form of each verb.

2 Script Normalmente, Marta por la mañana se despierta a las siete, pero no puede levantarse hasta las siete y media. Se ducha y después se viste. Luego desayuna y se cepilla los dientes. Después, se peina y se maquilla. Entonces sale para sus clases. Después de las clases almuerza con sus amigos y por la tarde estudia en la biblioteca. Regresa a casa, cena y ve un poco la televisión. Por la noche, generalmente se acuesta a las diez y por último, se duerme. *Textbook MP3s*

3 Expansion Go over the answers and explain why a particular item does not belong. Ex: **El lavabo, la toalla y el jabón son para lavarse. El despertador es para despertarse.**

4 Expansion Have students make statements about the people's actions, then ask a question. Ex: **Jorge se lava la cara. ¿Qué necesita?**

5 Teaching Tip To simplify, first ask students to identify the adverbs of time in the sentences. Then have them read through all the items before attempting to put them in order.

5 Expansion Ask students if **Andrés's** schedule represents that of a "typical" student. Ask: **Un estudiante típico, ¿se despierta normalmente a las seis y media de la mañana? ¿A qué hora se despiertan ustedes?**

6 Expansion
- Ask brief comprehension questions about the actions in the drawings. Ex: **¿Quién se maquilla? (Lupe) ¿Quién se cepilla el pelo? (Ángel)**
- If students ask, point out that in drawing number 7, **Ángel se mira en el espejo**. Reflexive pronouns and verbs will be formally presented in **Estructura 7.1.** For now it is enough just to explain that *he is looking at himself,* hence the use of the pronoun **se**.

5 **La rutina de Andrés** Ordena esta rutina de una manera lógica.

a. Se afeita después de cepillarse los dientes. 4
b. Se acuesta a las once y media de la noche. 9
c. Por último, se duerme. 10
d. Después de afeitarse, sale para las clases. 5
e. Asiste a todas sus clases y vuelve a su casa. 6
f. Andrés se despierta a las seis y media de la mañana. 1
g. Después de volver a casa, come un poco. Luego estudia en su habitación. 7
h. Se viste y entonces se cepilla los dientes. 3
i. Se cepilla los dientes antes de acostarse. 8
j. Se ducha antes de vestirse. 2

6 **La rutina diaria** Con un(a) compañero/a, mira los dibujos y describe lo que hacen Ángel y Lupe.
Some answers may vary. Suggested answers:

1.

Ángel se afeita y mira la televisión.

2.

Lupe se maquilla y escucha la radio.

3.

Ángel se ducha y canta.

4.

Lupe se baña y lee.

5.

Ángel se lava la cara con jabón.

6.

Lupe se lava el pelo con champú en la ducha.

7.

Ángel se cepilla el pelo.

8.

Lupe se cepilla los dientes.

Practice more at **vhlcentral.com**.

TEACHING OPTIONS

Extra Practice Name daily routine activities and have students list all the words that they associate with each activity, such as things, places, and parts of the body. Ex: **lavarse las manos: el jabón, el cuarto de baño, el agua, la toalla**.

Small Groups In groups of three or four, have students think of a famous person or character and describe his or her daily routine. In their descriptions, students may use names of friends or family of the famous person or character. Have groups read their descriptions aloud for the rest of the class to guess.

NATIONAL communication STANDARDS

Comunicación

7 **La farmacia** Lee el anuncio y responde a las preguntas con un(a) compañero/a.
Answers will vary.

LA FARMACIA NUEVO SOL tiene todo lo que necesitas para la vida diaria.

Esta semana tenemos grandes rebajas.

Con poco dinero puedes comprar lo que necesitas para el cuarto de baño ideal.

Para los hombres ofrecemos...
Excelentes cremas de afeitar de Guapo y Máximo

Para las mujeres ofrecemos...
Nuevo maquillaje de Marisol y jabones de baño Ilusiones y Belleza

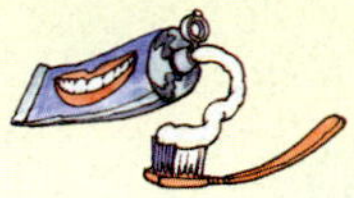

Y para todos tenemos los mejores jabones, pastas de dientes y cepillos de dientes.

¡Visita LA FARMACIA NUEVO SOL!
Tenemos los mejores precios. Visita nuestra tienda muy cerca de tu casa.

1. ¿Qué tipo de tienda es? Es una farmacia.
2. ¿Qué productos ofrecen para las mujeres? maquillaje, jabones de baño
3. ¿Qué productos ofrecen para los hombres? cremas de afeitar
4. Haz (*Make*) una lista de los verbos que asocias con los productos del anuncio. Suggested answers: afeitarse, maquillarse, cepillarse los dientes, ducharse/bañarse
5. ¿Dónde compras tus productos de higiene? Answers will vary.
6. ¿Tienes una tienda favorita? ¿Cuál es? Answers will vary.

8 **Rutinas diarias** Trabajen en parejas para describir la rutina diaria de dos o tres de estas personas. Pueden usar palabras de la lista. Answers will vary.

antes (de)	entonces	primero
después (de)	luego	tarde
durante el día	por último	temprano

- un(a) profesor(a) de la universidad
- un(a) turista
- un hombre o una mujer de negocios (*businessman/woman*)
- un vigilante nocturno (*night watchman*)
- un(a) jubilado/a (*retired person*)
- el presidente/primer ministro de tu país
- un niño de cuatro años
- Daniel Espinosa

NOTA CULTURAL

Daniel Espinosa (México, 1961) es un famoso diseñador de joyería (*jewelry*). Su trabajo es vanguardista (*avant-garde*), arriesgado (*risky*) e innovador. Su material favorito es la plata (*silver*). Entre sus clientes están Nelly Furtado, Eva Longoria, Salma Hayek, Shakira y Daisy Fuentes.

7 Expansion
- Ask small groups to write a competing ad for another pharmacy. Have each group present its ad to the class, who will vote for the most persuasive one.
- In pairs, have students write a conversation between a customer and an employee at **La Farmacia Nuevo Sol**. Encourage creativity. Have a few volunteers role-play their conversations for the class.

8 Teaching Tip To add a presentational and interpretive element to this activity, tell students to write descriptions without saying the name of the person they are describing. Have pairs exchange papers, read each other's work, and guess the identity of each person.

8 Expansion Ask volunteers to read their descriptions aloud. Ask other pairs who chose the same people if their descriptions are similar or how they differ.

TEACHING OPTIONS

Small Groups In small groups, have students write and act out a brief skit. Tell them to imagine that they are roommates who are trying to get ready for their morning classes at the same time, but there is only one bathroom in the house or apartment. Have the class vote for the most original or funniest skit.

Heritage Speakers Ask heritage speakers to write paragraphs in which they describe their daily routine when at home with their family. If they are not talking about their current situation, be sure that they keep their narration in the historical present. Have students present their paragraphs orally to the class. Verify comprehension by asking other students to paraphrase portions of each speaker's description.

Section Goals

In **Fotonovela**, students will:

- receive comprehensible input from free-flowing discourse
- learn functional phrases that preview lesson grammatical structures

Instructional Resources
Supersite: Video (***Fotonovela***); Resources (Scripts, Translations, Answer Keys)
WebSAM
Video Manual, pp. 13–14

Video Recap: Lección 6
Before doing this **Fotonovela** section, review the previous episode with these questions: **1. ¿Quién regateó con don Guillermo? ¿Recibió un buen descuento? (Maru regateó con don Guillermo. Sí, recibió un buen descuento.) 2. ¿Quiénes miraron faldas, blusas, bolsas y zapatos? (Jimena, Marissa y Maru los miraron.) 3. ¿Qué compró Miguel y para quién? (Miguel le compró unos aretes a Maru.) 4. Según don Guillermo, ¿quién ganó? (Miguel ganó.)**

Video Synopsis **Marissa, Felipe,** and **Jimena** all have plans to go out on a Friday night, but must compete for space in front of the mirror as they get ready. **Felipe** wins and manages to shave. **Marissa** convinces **Jimena** to skip the library and go with her to the movies.

Teaching Tip
Have students skim the **Fotonovela** captions and write down their impressions. Ask a few volunteers to share their impressions with the class.

¡Necesito arreglarme!

Es viernes por la tarde y Marissa, Jimena y Felipe se preparan para salir.

PERSONAJES

MARISSA

JIMENA

Video: *Fotonovela*

1

MARISSA ¿Hola? ¿Está ocupado?
JIMENA Sí. Me estoy lavando la cara.
MARISSA Necesito usar el baño.

2

MARISSA Tengo que terminar de arreglarme. Voy al cine esta noche.
JIMENA Yo también tengo que salir. ¿Te importa si me maquillo primero? Me voy a encontrar con mi amiga Elena en una hora.

3

JIMENA ¡Felipe! ¿Qué estás haciendo?
FELIPE Me estoy afeitando. ¿Hay algún problema?
JIMENA ¡Siempre haces lo mismo!
FELIPE Pues, yo no vi a nadie aquí.

4

JIMENA ¿Por qué no te afeitaste por la mañana?
FELIPE Porque cada vez que quiero usar el baño, una de ustedes está aquí. O bañándose o maquillándose.

5

JIMENA No te preocupes, Marissa. Llegaste primero. Entonces, te arreglas el pelo y después me maquillo.
FELIPE ¿Y yo? Tengo crema de afeitar en la cara. No me voy a ir. Estoy aquí y aquí me quedo.

6

MARISSA Tú ganas. ¿Adónde vas a ir esta noche, Felipe?
FELIPE Juan Carlos y yo vamos a ir a un café en el centro. Siempre hay música en vivo. (*Sale.*) Me siento guapísimo. Todavía me falta cambiarme la camisa.

TEACHING OPTIONS

Video Tips General suggestions for using video clips in the classroom can be found in the front matter of this Instructor's Annotated Edition.

¡Necesito arreglarme! Play the **¡Necesito arreglarme!** episode one time and have students jot down notes on what they see and hear. Then have them work in small groups to compare notes and prepare a brief plot summary. Play the segment again. Have students return to their groups to refine their summaries. Finally, discuss the plot with the entire class and correct any errors of fact or sequencing.

FELIPE

7

MARISSA ¿Adónde vas esta noche?

JIMENA A la biblioteca.

MARISSA ¡Es viernes! ¡Nadie debe estudiar los viernes! Voy a ver una película de Pedro Almodóvar con unas amigas.

8

MARISSA ¿Por qué no vienen tú y Elena al cine con nosotras? Después, podemos ir a ese café y molestar a Felipe.

9

JIMENA No sé.

MARISSA ¿Cuándo fue la última vez que viste a Juan Carlos?

JIMENA Cuando fuimos a Mérida.

10

MARISSA A ti te gusta ese chico.

JIMENA No tengo idea de qué estás hablando. Si no te importa, nos vemos en el cine.

Expresiones útiles

Talking about getting ready

Necesito arreglarme.
I need to get ready.
Me estoy lavando la cara.
I'm washing my face.
¿Te importa si me maquillo primero?
Is it OK with you if I put on my makeup first?
Tú te arreglas el pelo y después yo me maquillo.
You fix your hair and then I'll put on my makeup.
Todavía me falta cambiarme la camisa.
I still have to change my shirt.

Reassuring someone

Tranquilo/a.
Relax.
No te preocupes.
Don't worry.

Talking about past actions

¿Cuándo fue la última vez que viste a Juan Carlos?
When was the last time you saw Juan Carlos?
Cuando fuimos a Mérida.
When we went to Mérida.

Talking about likes and dislikes

Me fascinan las películas de Almodóvar.
I love Almodóvar's movies.
Me encanta la música en vivo.
I love live music.
Me molesta compartir el baño.
It bothers me to share the bathroom.

Additional vocabulary

encontrarse con *to meet up with*
molestar *to bother*
nadie *no one*

recursos

VM pp. 13–14	vhlcentral.com Lección 7

Expresiones útiles Draw attention to the verb forms **fue** and **fuimos** in the caption of video still 9. Tell students that these are preterite forms of the verbs **ser** and **ir**, respectively. Then explain that the context clarifies which verb is used. Point out the phrases **Me estoy lavando, me maquillo, te arreglas,** and **No te preocupes**. Tell the class that these are forms of the reflexive verbs **lavarse, maquillarse, arreglarse,** and **preocuparse**. Then, point out the phrases **Me fascinan, Me encanta**, and **Me molesta**. Explain that these are examples of verbs that have constructions similar to that of **gustar**. Finally, draw attention to the caption for video still 3 and point out the words **algún, Siempre,** and **nadie**. Explain that **algún** and **Siempre** are indefinite words and **nadie** is a negative word. Tell students that they will learn more about these concepts in **Estructura**.

Teaching Tip Have students get together in groups of three to role-play the episode. Encourage students to ad-lib when possible. Then, ask one or two groups to present the episode to the class.

Nota cultural In the Spanish-speaking world, young people tend to dress more formally than their U.S. counterparts, not only for parties, but also to go see a movie or attend class. This concept is known as **lucir bien** (*to look good*). In some countries, for people of all ages, dressing in an overly casual manner may result in poorer service at certain establishments.

TEACHING OPTIONS

TPR Ask students to write **Marissa, Jimena,** and **Felipe** on separate pieces of paper. Read aloud statements from the perspective of the characters and have students hold up the corresponding name. Ex: **Me quiero arreglar el pelo. (Marissa) Mi hermano se está afeitando. (Jimena)**

Small Groups Ask students to select one of the characters and write a short description about what they think his or her daily routine is like. Then have students who picked the same character get together to find similarities and differences in their descriptions.

Pairs Ask pairs of students to work together to create six true/false sentences about the **Fotonovela**. Have pairs exchange papers and complete the activity.

¿Qué pasó?

1 **¿Cierto o falso?** Indica si lo que dicen estas oraciones es **cierto** o **falso**. Corrige las oraciones falsas.

1. Marissa va a ver una película de Pedro Almodóvar con unas amigas.
   Cierto.
2. Jimena se va a encontrar con Elena en dos horas.
   Falso. Jimena se va a encontrar con Elena en una hora.
3. Felipe se siente muy feo después de afeitarse.
   Falso. Felipe se siente guapísimo después de afeitarse.
4. Jimena quiere maquillarse.
   Cierto.
5. Marissa quiere ir al café para molestar a Juan Carlos.
   Falso. Marissa quiere ir al café para molestar a Felipe.

2 **Identificar** Identifica quién puede decir estas oraciones. Puedes usar cada nombre más de una vez.

1. No puedo usar el baño porque siempre están aquí, o bañándose o maquillándose. ___Felipe___
2. Quiero arreglarme el pelo porque voy al cine esta noche. ___Marissa___
3. Hoy voy a ir a la biblioteca. ___Jimena___
4. ¡Necesito arreglarme! ___Marissa/Jimena/Felipe___
5. Te gusta Juan Carlos. ___Marissa___
6. ¿Por qué quieres afeitarte cuando estamos en el baño? ___Jimena/Marissa___

MARISSA

FELIPE

JIMENA

3 **Ordenar** Ordena correctamente los planes que tiene Marissa.

___5___ a. Voy al café.
___2___ b. Me arreglo el pelo.
___6___ c. Molesto a Felipe.
___3___ d. Me encuentro con unas amigas.
___1___ e. Entro al baño.
___4___ f. Voy al cine.

4 **En el baño** Trabajen en parejas para representar los papeles de dos compañeros/as de cuarto que deben usar el baño al mismo tiempo para hacer su rutina diaria. Usen las instrucciones como guía.
Answers will vary.

Estudiante 1	Estudiante 2
Di (*Say*) que quieres arreglarte porque vas a ir al cine.	→ Di (*Say*) que necesitas arreglarte porque te vas a encontrar con tus amigos/as.
Pregunta si puedes secarte (*dry*) el pelo.	→ Responde que no porque necesitas lavarte la cara.
Di que puede lavarse la cara, pero que después necesitas secarte el pelo.	→ Di que puede secarse el pelo, pero que después necesitas peinarte.

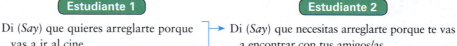

Practice more at **vhlcentral.com**.

1 Expansion Give students these true/false statements as items 6–7: **6. Felipe va a encontrarse con Juan Carlos en una discoteca. (Falso. Ellos van a encontrarse en un café.) 7. La última vez que Jimena vio a Juan Carlos fue ayer. (Falso. Fue en Mérida.)**

Nota cultural Internationally renowned, Spanish filmmaker **Pedro Almodóvar's** films are generally characterized by complex narratives and themes of family, identity, and desire. His movie ***Todo sobre mi madre*** (1999) won the Best Foreign Language Film Oscar. The 1988 film ***Mujeres al borde de un ataque de nervios***, his first movie to have major international success, was adapted as a musical.

2 Expansion Give students these sentences as items 7–8: **7. Quiero ponerme otra camisa. (Felipe) 8. Debes venir al cine. (Marissa)**

3 Expansion Ask pairs to imagine another character's plans and list them using the **yo** form of the verbs, as in the activity. Then have pairs share their lists with the class.

4 Possible Conversation
E1: Quiero arreglarme porque voy a ir al cine.
E2: Pues, necesito arreglarme porque voy a encontrarme con mis amigos.
E1: ¿Puedo secarme el pelo?
E2: No, porque necesito lavarme la cara.
E1: Está bien. Puedes lavarte la cara, pero después necesito secarme el pelo.
E2: De acuerdo. Puedes secarte el pelo, pero después necesito peinarme.

TEACHING OPTIONS

Extra Practice Add an auditory aspect to this vocabulary practice. Ask students to close their books. Then read aloud the sentences from **Actividad 3**, in the correct order. Read each sentence twice slowly to give students an opportunity to write them down. Then read them again at normal speed, without pausing, to allow students to check for accuracy or fill in any gaps. Ask comprehension questions as a follow-up.

Small Groups Have students get together in small groups to discuss and compare their daily routines. Have them use as many of the words and expressions from this lesson as they can. Then ask for a few volunteers to describe the daily routine of one of their group members.

NATIONAL STANDARDS comparisons

Pronunciación

Audio

The consonant r

ropa **rutina** **rico** **Ramón**

In Spanish, **r** has a strong trilled sound at the beginning of a word. No English words have a trill, but English speakers often produce a trill when they imitate the sound of a motor.

gustar **durante** **primero** **crema**

In any other position, **r** has a weak sound similar to the English *tt* in *better* or the English *dd* in *ladder*. In contrast to English, the tongue touches the roof of the mouth behind the teeth.

pizarra **corro** **marrón** **aburrido**

The letter combination **rr**, which only appears between vowels, always has a strong trilled sound.

caro **carro** **pero** **perro**

Between vowels, the difference between the strong trilled **rr** and the weak **r** is very important, as a mispronunciation could lead to confusion between two different words.

Práctica Lee las palabras en voz alta, prestando (*paying*) atención a la pronunciación de la **r** y la **rr**.

1. Perú
2. Rosa
3. borrador
4. madre
5. comprar
6. favor
7. rubio
8. reloj
9. Arequipa
10. tarde
11. cerrar
12. despertador

Oraciones Lee las oraciones en voz alta, prestando atención a la pronunciación de la **r** y la **rr**.

1. Ramón Robles Ruiz es programador. Su esposa Rosaura es artista.
2. A Rosaura Robles le encanta regatear en el mercado.
3. Ramón nunca regatea… le aburre regatear.
4. Rosaura siempre compra cosas baratas.
5. Ramón no es rico, pero prefiere comprar cosas muy caras.
6. ¡El martes Ramón compró un carro nuevo!

Refranes Lee en voz alta los refranes, prestando atención a la **r** y a la **rr**.

Perro que ladra no muerde.[1]

No se ganó Zamora en una hora.[2]

1 A dog's bark is worse than its bite.
2 Rome wasn't built in a day.

recursos
LM p. 38 | vhlcentral.com Lección 7

Section Goal

In **Pronunciación**, students will be introduced to the pronunciation of the consonant **r** and the letter combination **rr**.

Instructional Resources

Supersite: Audio (Textbook and Lab MP3 Files); Resources (Scripts, Answer Keys)
WebSAM
Lab Manual, p. 38

Teaching Tips

- Explain that **r** is trilled at the beginning of a word, and that there are no words that have a trill in American English. Model the pronunciation of **ropa, rutina, rico,** and **Ramón** and have the class repeat.
- Point out that in any other position, **r** is pronounced like the *tt* in American English *better*. Write the words **gustar, durante, primero,** and **crema** on the board and ask a volunteer to pronounce each word.
- Point out that **rr** always has a strong trilled sound and that it only appears between vowels. Pronounce the words **pizarra, corro, marrón,** and **aburrido** and have the class repeat.
- To help students discriminate between **r** and **rr**, write on the board the pairs **caro/carro** and **pero/perro**. Then pronounce each pair several times in random order, pausing after each for students to repeat. Ex: **caro, carro, caro, carro, carro, caro**
- If students struggle with the trill of **rr**, have them repeat the phrases *better butter* or *I edited it* in rapid succession.

Práctica/Oraciones/Refranes

These exercises are recorded on the *Textbook MP3s*. You may want to play the audio so that students practice listening to Spanish spoken by speakers other than yourself.

TEACHING OPTIONS

Extra Practice Write the names of a few Peruvian cities on the board and ask for a volunteer to pronounce each name. Ex: **Huaraz, Cajamarca, Trujillo, Puerto Maldonado, Cerro de Pasco, Piura**. Then write the names of a few Peruvian literary figures on the board and repeat the process. Ex: **Ricardo Palma, Ciro Alegría, Mario Vargas Llosa, César Vallejo.**

Small Groups Have students work in small groups and take turns reading aloud sentences from the **Fotonovela** episode in this lesson and in previous lessons, focusing on the correct pronunciation of **r** and **rr**.

Extra Practice Write this rhyme on the board and have students practice trilling: **Erre con erre, cigarro, erre con erre, barril, rápido corren los carros, sobre los rieles del ferrocarril.**

Flash CULTURA

Section Goals

In **Cultura**, students will:

- read about the custom of **la siesta**
- learn terms related to personal hygiene
- read about how drinking **mate** is part of a daily routine
- read about special customs in Mexico, El Salvador, Costa Rica, and Argentina

Instructional Resources
Supersite: Video (***Flash cultura***); Resources (Scripts, Translations, Answer Keys)
WebSAM
Video Manual, pp. 85–86

En detalle

Antes de leer Ask students about their sleep habits. **¿Cuántas horas duermes al día? ¿Tu horario te permite volver a casa y descansar al mediodía? Si no duermes bien durante la noche, ¿te duermes en clase?**

Lectura

- Point out that observance of the **siesta** is not universal. For example, when Spain entered the European Union, businesspeople began to adjust their work schedules to mirror those of their counterparts in other European countries.
- Explain that, as a result of the midday rest, a typical workday might end at 7 or 8 p.m.

Después de leer

- Have students share what facts in this reading are new or surprising to them.
- Ask students if they think the **siesta** should be incorporated into academic and business schedules in the United States or Canada. What sort of impact would this have? Have students write 3 to 4 sentences explaining their answers.

1 Expansion Ask students to create questions related to the corrected statements. Ex: **1. ¿Dónde empezó la costumbre de la siesta?**

EN DETALLE

Video: *Flash cultura*

NATIONAL STANDARDS connections cultures

La siesta

¿Sientes cansancio° después de comer?

¿Te cuesta° volver al trabajo° o a clase después del almuerzo? Estas sensaciones son normales. A muchas personas les gusta relajarse° después de almorzar. Este momento de descanso es **la siesta**. La siesta es popular en los países hispanos y viene de una antigua costumbre° del área del Mediterráneo. La palabra *siesta* viene del latín, es una forma corta de decir "sexta hora". La sexta hora del día es después del mediodía, el momento de más calor. Debido al° calor y al cansancio, los habitantes de España, Italia, Grecia y Portugal tienen la costumbre de dormir la siesta desde hace° más de° dos mil años. Los españoles y los portugueses llevaron la costumbre a los países americanos.

Aunque° hoy día esta costumbre está desapareciendo° en las grandes ciudades, la siesta todavía es importante en la cultura hispana. En pueblos pequeños, por ejemplo, muchas oficinas° y tiendas tienen la costumbre de cerrar por dos o tres horas después del mediodía. Los empleados van a su casa, almuerzan con sus familias, duermen la siesta o hacen actividades, como ir al gimnasio, y luego regresan al trabajo entre las 2:30 y las 4:30 de la tarde.

Los estudios científicos explican que una siesta corta después de almorzar ayuda° a trabajar más y mejor° durante la tarde. Pero ¡cuidado! Esta siesta debe durar° sólo entre veinte y cuarenta minutos. Si dormimos más, entramos en la fase de sueño profundo y es difícil despertarse.

Hoy, algunas empresas° de los EE.UU., Canadá, Japón, Inglaterra y Alemania tienen salas° especiales donde los empleados pueden dormir la siesta.

¿Dónde duermen la siesta?

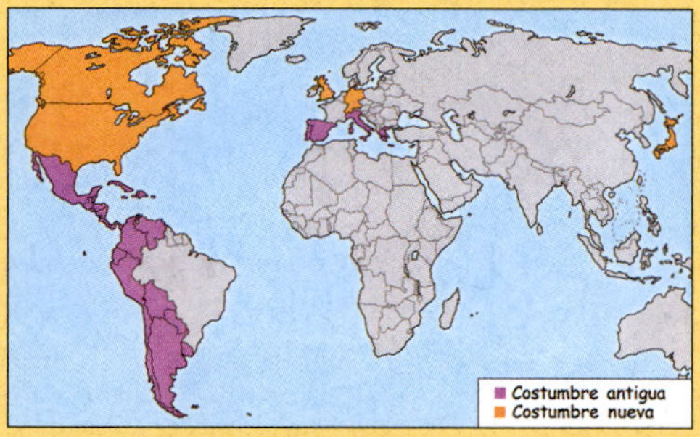

En los lugares donde la siesta es una costumbre antigua, las personas la duermen en su casa. En los países donde la siesta es una costumbre nueva, la gente duerme en sus lugares de trabajo o en centros de siesta.

Sientes cansancio *Do you feel tired* **Te cuesta** *Is it hard for you* **trabajo** *work* **relajarse** *to relax* **antigua costumbre** *old custom* **Debido al** *Because (of)* **desde hace** *for* **más de** *more than* **Aunque** *Although* **está desapareciendo** *is disappearing* **oficinas** *offices* **ayuda** *helps* **mejor** *better* **durar** *last* **algunas empresas** *some businesses* **salas** *rooms*

ACTIVIDADES

1 ¿Cierto o falso? Indica si lo que dicen las oraciones es **cierto** o **falso**. Corrige la información falsa.

1. La costumbre de la siesta empezó en Asia. Falso. La costumbre de la siesta empezó en el área del Mediterráneo.
2. La palabra *siesta* está relacionada con la sexta hora del día. Cierto.
3. Los españoles y los portugueses llevaron la costumbre de la siesta a Latinoamérica. Cierto.
4. La siesta ayuda a trabajar más y mejor durante la tarde. Cierto.
5. Los horarios de trabajo de las grandes ciudades hispanas son los mismos que los pueblos pequeños. Falso. En las grandes ciudades hispanas la costumbre de la siesta está desapareciendo.
6. Una siesta larga siempre es mejor que una siesta corta. Falso. La siesta debe durar entre veinte y cuarenta minutos.
7. En los Estados Unidos, los empleados de algunas empresas pueden dormir la siesta en el trabajo. Cierto.
8. Es fácil despertar de un sueño profundo. Falso. Es difícil despertar de un sueño profundo.

TEACHING OPTIONS

Small Groups Have students work in small groups to invent an original product related to the **siesta**. Then have them present an ad for their product to the class. Encourage creativity. Ex: **¿Tienes problemas para despertarte después de la siesta? Necesitas el nuevo despertador "AguaSiestas". Si no quieres entrar en la fase de sueño profundo, sólo pones el despertador y a los veinte minutos, se convierte en una mini-ducha de agua fría.** Have the class vote for the products they would most likely buy.

Cultural Comparison Divide the class into two groups. Have students debate the advantages and disadvantages of the **siesta** in the workplace and university life. Allow each group time to prepare their arguments, and provide additional vocabulary as needed.

ASÍ SE DICE

El cuidado personal

el aseo; el excusado; el servicio; el váter (Esp.)	el baño
el cortaúñas	*nail clippers*
el desodorante	*deodorant*
el enjuague bucal	*mouthwash*
el hilo dental/ la seda dental	*dental floss*
la máquina de afeitar/ de rasurar (Méx.)	*electric razor*

EL MUNDO HISPANO

Costumbres especiales

- **México y El Salvador** Los vendedores pasan por las calles anunciando a gritos° su mercancía°: tanques de gas y flores° en México; pan y tortillas en El Salvador.
- **Costa Rica** Para encontrar las direcciones°, los costarricenses usan referencias a anécdotas, lugares o características geográficas. Por ejemplo: *200 metros norte de la iglesia Católica, frente al° supermercado Mi Mega.*
- **Argentina** En Tigre, una ciudad junto al Río° de la Plata, la gente usa barcos particulares°, barcos colectivos y barcos-taxi para ir de una isla a otra. Todas las mañanas, un barco colectivo recoge° a los niños y los lleva a la escuela.

gritos *shouts* **mercancía** *merchandise* **flores** *flowers* **direcciones** *addresses* **frente al** *opposite* **Río** *River* **particulares** *private* **recoge** *picks up*

PERFIL

El mate

El mate es una parte muy importante de la rutina diaria en muchos países. Es una bebida° muy similar al té que se consume en Argentina, Uruguay y Paraguay. Tradicionalmente se bebe caliente° con una *bombilla*° y en un recipiente° que también se llama *mate*. Por ser amarga°, algunos le agregan° azúcar para suavizar su sabor°. El mate se puede tomar a cualquier° hora y en cualquier lugar, aunque en Argentina las personas prefieren sentarse en círculo e ir pasando el mate de mano en mano mientras° conversan. Los uruguayos, por otra parte, acostumbran llevar el agua° caliente para el mate en un termo° bajo el brazo° y lo beben mientras caminan. Si ves a una persona con un termo bajo el brazo y un mate en la mano, ¡es casi seguro que es de Uruguay!

bebida *drink* **caliente** *hot* **bombilla** *straw (in Argentina)* **recipiente** *container* **amarga** *bitter* **agregan** *add* **suavizar su sabor** *soften its flavor* **cualquier** *any* **mientras** *while* **agua** *water* **termo** *thermos* **bajo el brazo** *under their arm*

Conexión Internet

¿Qué costumbres son populares en los países hispanos?

Go to **vhlcentral.com** to find more cultural information related to this **Cultura** section.

ACTIVIDADES

2 Comprensión Completa las oraciones.

1. Uso <u>el hilo dental/la seda dental</u> para limpiar (*to clean*) entre los dientes.
2. En <u>El Salvador</u> las personas compran pan y tortillas a los vendedores que pasan por la calle.
3. El <u>mate</u> es una bebida similar al té.
4. Los uruguayos beben mate mientras <u>caminan</u>.

3 ¿Qué costumbres tienes? Escribe cuatro oraciones sobre una costumbre que compartes con tus amigos o con tu familia (por ejemplo: ir al cine, ir a eventos deportivos, leer, comer juntos, etc.). Explica qué haces, cuándo lo haces y con quién. Answers will vary.

recursos
VM pp. 85–86
vhlcentral.com Lección 7

Practice more at **vhlcentral.com**.

TEACHING OPTIONS

TPR On slips of paper, write phrases related to daily routines and hygiene from **Así se dice** and **Contextos** (Ex: **usar desodorante, usar enjuague bucal, afeitarse con una máquina de afeitar**). Divide the class into two teams. Have a member of team A draw out a slip of paper and mime the activity for team B to guess. Have teams alternate miming activities. Give one point for each correct answer.

Heritage Speakers Ask heritage speakers to describe customs from their cultural communities that have since changed or been adapted for U.S./Canadian culture.

Cultural Activity Ask pairs to choose a country not mentioned in **Perfil** or **El mundo hispano** and use the Internet to research a custom or tradition that affects daily life (Ex: **las onces,** the routine of eating an afternoon snack in Colombia and Chile). Have pairs present the custom to the class.

Así se dice
- Point out that **cortaúñas** is a compound word.
- To challenge students, add these hygiene-related words to the list: **el acondicionador, el suavizante (Esp.)** (*conditioner*); **la bañera, la tina** (*bathtub*); **el cabello** (*hair*); **la crema (hidratante), la loción** (*lotion*); **el dentífrico, la crema dental (Col.), la pasta dental (Perú, P. Rico)** (*toothpaste*); **las pinzas** (*tweezers*).
- Ask volunteers to create sentences using words from the list. Ex: **El aseo de mujeres está lejos de la sala de clase.**

Perfil
- Tell students that **mate** is also referred to as **yerba mate**.
- Explain that **mate** has a stimulating effect similar to that of the caffeine found in coffee or tea. **Mate** also has a high nutritional value, as it contains vitamins, minerals, and antioxidants.
- Draw attention to the photos. Explain that the **bombilla**, which is traditionally made of silver, serves as both a straw and a sieve. **Mate** containers are usually hollowed-out gourds, but can also be made of ceramic or metal.

El mundo hispano Ask students to create three true/false statements based on the information in **El mundo hispano**. Have pairs exchange papers and complete the activity.

2 Expansion Give students these sentences as items 5–6: **5. Venden ____ y ____ en las calles de México. (tanques de gas, flores) 6. El ____ es una bebida amarga; por eso, algunas personas lo toman con ____. (mate, azúcar)**

3 Teaching Tip To simplify, write time expressions on the board for students to use in their descriptions (Ex: **siempre, todos los años, cada mes**).

Section Goals

In **Estructura 7.1**, students will learn:
- the conjugation of reflexive verbs
- common reflexive verbs

Instructional Resources
Supersite: Audio (Lab MP3 Files); Resources (Grammar Presentation Slides, Activity Pack, Scripts, Answer Keys); Testing Program (Quizzes)
WebSAM
Workbook, pp. 75–76
Lab Manual, p. 39

Teaching Tips

- Model the first-person reflexive by talking about yourself. Ex: **Me levanto muy temprano. Me levanto a las cinco de la mañana.** Then model the second person by asking questions with a verb you have already used in the first person. Ex: **Y tú, ____, ¿a qué hora te levantas? (Me levanto a las ocho.)**
- Introduce the third person by making statements and asking questions about what a student has told you. Ex: ____ **se levanta muy tarde, ¿no? (Sí, se levanta muy tarde.)**
- Add a visual aspect to this grammar presentation. Use magazine pictures to clarify meanings between third-person singular and third-person plural forms. Ex: **Se lava las manos** and **Se lavan las manos.**
- On the board summarize the three possible positions for reflexive pronouns. You may want to demonstrate this visually by using an **X** to represent the reflexive pronoun: **X verbo conjugado, infinitivoX, gerundioX.** Remind students that they have already learned these positions for direct and indirect object pronouns.

7.1 Reflexive verbs

Tutorial

NATIONAL STANDARDS comparisons

ANTE TODO A reflexive verb is used to indicate that the subject does something to or for himself or herself. In other words, it "reflects" the action of the verb back to the subject. Reflexive verbs always use reflexive pronouns.

SUBJECT	REFLEXIVE VERB
Joaquín	**se ducha** por la mañana.

The verb lavarse (*to wash oneself*)

SINGULAR FORMS	yo	**me lavo**	*I wash (myself)*
	tú	**te lavas**	*you wash (yourself)*
	Ud.	**se lava**	*you wash (yourself)*
	él/ella	**se lava**	*he/she washes (himself/herself)*
PLURAL FORMS	nosotros/as	**nos lavamos**	*we wash (ourselves)*
	vosotros/as	**os laváis**	*you wash (yourselves)*
	Uds.	**se lavan**	*you wash (yourselves)*
	ellos/ellas	**se lavan**	*they wash (themselves)*

- The pronoun **se** attached to an infinitive identifies the verb as reflexive: **lavarse.**
- When a reflexive verb is conjugated, the reflexive pronoun agrees with the subject.

Me afeito. **Te despiertas** a las siete.

¿Te importa si me maquillo primero?

A las chicas les encanta maquillarse durante horas y horas.

- Like object pronouns, reflexive pronouns generally appear before a conjugated verb. With infinitives and present participles, they may be placed before the conjugated verb or attached to the infinitive or present participle.

Ellos **se** van a vestir.
Ellos van a vestir**se**.
They are going to get dressed.

Nos estamos lavando las manos.
Estamos lavándo**nos** las manos.
We are washing our hands.

- **¡Atención!** When a reflexive pronoun is attached to a present participle, an accent mark is added to maintain the original stress.

bañando → bañ**á**ndo**se** durmiendo → durmi**é**ndo**se**

AYUDA

Except for **se**, reflexive pronouns have the same forms as direct and indirect object pronouns.

Se is used for both singular and plural subjects—there is no individual plural form:
Pablo **se** lava.
Ellos **se** lavan.

TEACHING OPTIONS

Extra Practice To provide oral practice with reflexive verbs, create sentences that follow the pattern of the sentences in the examples. Say the sentence, have students repeat it, then say a different subject, varying the gender and number. Have students then say the sentence with the new subject, changing pronouns and verb forms as necessary.

Extra Practice Have students describe daily routines in their families. Encourage heritage speakers to use their own linguistic variation of words presented in this lesson. Ex: **regarse** (e:ie), **pintarse**. Have students work together to compare and contrast activities as well as lexical variations.

AYUDA

You have already learned several adjectives that can be used with **ponerse** when it means *to become*:

alegre, cómodo/a, contento/a, elegante, guapo/a, nervioso/a, rojo/a, and **triste**.

Common reflexive verbs

acordarse (de) (o:ue)	*to remember*	**llamarse**	*to be called; to be named*
acostarse (o:ue)	*to go to bed*	**maquillarse**	*to put on makeup*
afeitarse	*to shave*	**peinarse**	*to comb one's hair*
bañarse	*to take a bath*	**ponerse**	*to put on*
cepillarse	*to brush*	**ponerse (+ *adj.*)**	*to become (+ adj.)*
despertarse (e:ie)	*to wake up*	**preocuparse (por)**	*to worry (about)*
dormirse (o:ue)	*to go to sleep; to fall asleep*	**probarse** (o:ue)	*to try on*
ducharse	*to take a shower*	**quedarse**	*to stay*
enojarse (con)	*to get angry (with)*	**quitarse**	*to take off*
irse	*to go away; to leave*	**secarse**	*to dry (oneself)*
lavarse	*to wash (oneself)*	**sentarse** (e:ie)	*to sit down*
levantarse	*to get up*	**sentirse** (e:ie)	*to feel*
		vestirse (e:i)	*to get dressed*

COMPARE & CONTRAST

Unlike English, a number of verbs in Spanish can be reflexive or non-reflexive. If the verb acts upon the subject, the reflexive form is used. If the verb acts upon something other than the subject, the non-reflexive form is used. Compare these sentences.

Lola **lava** los platos.

Lola **se lava** la cara.

As the preceding sentences show, reflexive verbs sometimes have different meanings than their non-reflexive counterparts. For example, **lavar** means *to wash*, while **lavarse** means *to wash oneself, to wash up*.

▶ **¡Atención!** Parts of the body or clothing are generally not referred to with possessives, but with articles.

La niña se quitó **un** zapato.

Necesito cepillarme **los** dientes.

recursos

WB pp. 75–76

LM p. 39

vhlcentral.com Lección 7

¡INTÉNTALO! Indica el presente de estos verbos reflexivos.

despertarse

1. Mis hermanos se despiertan tarde.
2. Tú te despiertas tarde.
3. Nosotros nos despertamos tarde.
4. Benito se despierta tarde.
5. Yo me despierto tarde.

ponerse

1. Él se pone una chaqueta.
2. Yo me pongo una chaqueta.
3. Usted se pone una chaqueta.
4. Nosotras nos ponemos una chaqueta.
5. Las niñas se ponen una chaqueta.

Teaching Tips

- Go through the list of common reflexive verbs asking students closed-answer questions. Ex: **¿Te acuerdas de tu primer día en la universidad? (Sí, me acuerdo.) ¿Los niños se acuestan tarde o temprano? (Los niños se acuestan temprano.)**
- Emphasize that, with reflexive verbs, the person *doing* the action also *receives* the action. Contrast the difference between reflexive and non-reflexive verbs by giving examples from your life. Ex: **Los lunes, me despierto muy temprano, a las cinco. A las seis, despierto a mi hijo. Primero, me ducho y después baño a mi hijo…** (You may want to use a doll or other visual aspect for this presentation.)
- To practice reflexive verbs in the preterite and periphrastic future (**ir a** + [*infinitive*]), talk about what you did yesterday and plan to do tomorrow. Ex: **Ayer me levanté a las seis. Pero el sábado me voy a levantar a las nueve.** Then ask volunteers to talk about what they did and plan to do.
- Survey the class about the products they use daily, using reflexive verbs. Ex: ____, **¿te cepillas los dientes con *Crest* o *Colgate*? ¿Te lavas el pelo con *Pantene*? ¿Te lavas con *Dove* o *Lever 2000*?** Practice other forms by having students summarize the results. Ex: **Nick, Kim y Antoine se lavan con *Irish Spring*. Lucas y yo nos cepillamos los dientes con *Tom's*.**
- Ask volunteers to translate sentences such as: *He dresses the children at seven. He gets dressed at seven.*

¡Atención! Point out that the possessive article is not used with parts of the body and clothing. Especially with reflexive verbs, the pronoun eliminates any ambiguity.

TEACHING OPTIONS

TPR Model gestures for a few of the reflexive verbs. Ex: **acordarse** (tap side of head), **acostarse** (lay head on folded hands). Have students stand. Begin by practicing as a class using only the **nosotros** form, saying expressions at random. (Ex: **Nos lavamos la cara.**) Then vary the verb forms and point to the student who should perform the appropriate gesture. Keep a brisk pace. Vary by pointing to more than one student. (Ex: **Ustedes se peinan.**)

Pairs Have students write a short account of their daily routine. Then have pairs compare and contrast their routines using a Venn diagram (see **Lección 9, Escritura**). Have the pair label the circles with their names and write **Los/Las dos** where they overlap. Then have them list their activities in the appropriate section. Remind them to use the **nosotros/as** form for verbs under **Los/Las dos**.

1 Teaching Tip Before assigning the activity, review reflexive verbs by asking questions about weekday versus weekend routines. Ex: **¿Te levantas tarde o temprano los sábados? ¿Te acuestas tarde o temprano los domingos?**

1 Expansion To practice the formal register, describe situations and have students tell you what you are going to do. Ex: **Hace frío y nieva, pero necesito salir. (Usted va a ponerse el abrigo.) Acabo de levantarme. (Usted se va a lavar la cara.)**

2 Teaching Tip Before assigning the activity, review reflexive and non-reflexive verbs by asking questions using both forms. Ex: **¿Cuándo nos lavamos? (Nos lavamos todos los días.) ¿Cuándo lavamos el coche? (Lavamos el coche los fines de semana.)**

2 Expansion Ask students to write five sentence pairs that contrast reflexive and non-reflexive forms. Ex: **Me despierto a las siete. Despierto a mi compañero de cuarto a las ocho.**

3 Expansion
- Repeat the activity as a pattern drill, supplying different subjects for each drawing. Ex: **Número uno, yo. (Me quito los zapatos.) Número cinco, nosotras. (Nosotras nos maquillamos.)**
- Repeat the activity using the present progressive. Ask students to provide both possible sentences. Ex: **1. El joven se está quitando los zapatos./ El joven está quitándose los zapatos.**

Práctica

1 **Nuestra rutina** La familia de Blanca sigue la misma rutina todos los días. Según Blanca, ¿qué hacen ellos?

modelo
mamá / despertarse a las 5:00
Mamá se despierta a las cinco.

1. Roberto y yo / levantarse a las 7:00 Roberto y yo nos levantamos a las siete.
2. papá / ducharse primero y / luego afeitarse Papá se ducha primero y luego se afeita.
3. yo / lavarse la cara y / vestirse antes de tomar café Yo me lavo la cara y me visto antes de tomar café.
4. mamá / peinarse y / luego maquillarse Mamá se peina y luego se maquilla.
5. todos (nosotros) / sentarse a la mesa para comer Todos nos sentamos a la mesa para comer.
6. Roberto / cepillarse los dientes después de comer Roberto se cepilla los dientes después de comer.
7. yo / ponerse el abrigo antes de salir Yo me pongo el abrigo antes de salir.
8. nosotros / irse Nosotros nos vamos.

NOTA CULTURAL

Como en los EE.UU., **tomar café** en el desayuno es muy común en los países hispanos.

En muchas familias, incluso los niños toman café con leche (*milk*) en el desayuno antes de ir a la escuela.

El café en los países hispanos generalmente es más fuerte que en los EE.UU., y el descafeinado no es muy popular.

2 **La fiesta elegante** Selecciona el verbo apropiado y completa las oraciones con la forma correcta.

1. Tú ___lavas___ (lavar / lavarse) el auto antes de ir a la fiesta.
2. Nosotros ___nos bañamos___ (bañar / bañarse) antes de ir a la fiesta.
3. Para llegar a tiempo, Raúl y Marta ___acuestan___ (acostar / acostarse) a los niños antes de salir.
4. Cecilia ___se maquilla___ (maquillar / maquillarse) antes de salir.
5. Mis amigos siempre ___se visten___ (vestir / vestirse) con ropa muy elegante.
6. Julia y Ana ___se ponen___ (poner / ponerse) los vestidos nuevos.
7. Usted ___va___ (ir / irse) a llegar antes que (*before*) los demás invitados, ¿no?
8. En general, ___me afeito___ (afeitar / afeitarse) yo mismo, pero hoy es un día especial y el barbero (*barber*) me ___afeita___ (afeitar / afeitarse). ¡Será una fiesta inolvidable!

¡LENGUA VIVA!

In Spain a car is called **un coche**, while in many parts of Latin America it is known as **un carro**. Although you'll be understood using either of these terms, using **auto (automóvil)** will surely get you where you want to go.

3 **Describir** Mira los dibujos y describe lo que estas personas hacen. Some answers may vary.

1. el joven El joven se quita/se pone los zapatos.

2. Carmen Carmen se duerme./se acuesta./se despierta.

3. Juan Juan se pone/se quita la camiseta.

4. los pasajeros Los pasajeros se van.

5. Estrella Estrella se maquilla.

6. Toni Toni se enoja con el perro.

TEACHING OPTIONS

Extra Practice Tell students that the **Ramírez** family has just one bathroom that they share. Then have students figure out the family's morning schedule. Say: **El señor Ramírez se afeita antes que Alberto, pero después que Rafael. La señora Ramírez es la primera en ducharse y Montse es la última. Lolita se peina cuando su padre sale del cuarto de baño y antes que uno de sus hermanos. Nuria se maquilla después que Lolita, pero no inmediatamente después. (Primero se ducha la señora Ramírez. Después se afeita Rafael seguido por el señor Ramírez. Luego se peina Lolita. Alberto se afeita y después Nuria se maquilla. Finalmente Montse se ducha.)** You should also write the names on the board so students can keep track of the order of the family on paper.

NATIONAL communication STANDARDS

Comunicación

4 **Preguntas personales** En parejas, túrnense para hacerse estas preguntas. Answers will vary.

1. ¿A qué hora te levantas durante la semana?
2. ¿A qué hora te levantas los fines de semana?
3. ¿Prefieres levantarte tarde o temprano? ¿Por qué?
4. ¿Te enojas frecuentemente con tus amigos?
5. ¿Te preocupas fácilmente? ¿Qué te preocupa?
6. ¿Qué te pone contento/a?
7. ¿Qué haces cuando te sientes triste?
8. ¿Y cuando te sientes alegre?
9. ¿Te acuestas tarde o temprano durante la semana?
10. ¿A qué hora te acuestas los fines de semana?

5 **Charadas** En grupos, jueguen a las charadas. Cada persona debe pensar en dos oraciones con verbos reflexivos. La primera persona que adivina la charada dramatiza la siguiente. Answers will vary.

6 **Debate** En grupos, discutan este tema: ¿Quiénes necesitan más tiempo para arreglarse (*to get ready*) antes de salir, los hombres o las mujeres? Hagan una lista de las razones (*reasons*) que tienen para defender sus ideas e informen a la clase. Answers will vary.

7 **La coartada** Hoy se cometió un crimen entre las 7 y las 11 de la mañana. En parejas, imaginen que uno de ustedes es un sospechoso y el otro un policía investigador. El policía le pregunta al sospechoso qué hace habitualmente a esas horas y el sospechoso responde. Luego, el policía presenta las respuestas del sospechoso ante el jurado (la clase) y entre todos deciden si es culpable o no. Answers will vary.

NATIONAL communication STANDARDS

Síntesis

8 **La familia ocupada** Tú y tu compañero/a asisten a un programa de verano en Lima, Perú. Viven con la familia Ramos. Tu profesor(a) te va a dar la rutina incompleta que la familia sigue en las mañanas. Trabaja con tu compañero/a para completarla. Answers will vary.

modelo

Estudiante 1: ¿Qué hace el señor Ramos a las seis y cuarto?
Estudiante 2: El señor Ramos se levanta.

Practice more at **vhlcentral.com**.

4 Expansion Ask volunteers to call out some of their answers. The class should add information by speculating on the reason behind each answer. Ex: **Hablas por teléfono con tus amigos cuando te sientes triste porque ellos te comprenden muy bien.** Have the volunteer confirm or refute the speculation.

5 Teaching Tip Ask each group to present their best **charada** to the class.

6 Teaching Tip Before assigning groups, go over some of the things men and women do to get ready to go out. Ex: **Las mujeres se maquillan. Los hombres se afeitan.** Then ask students to indicate their opinion on the question, and divide the class into groups accordingly.

7 Teaching Tip You may want to give students more details of the crime.

8 Teaching Tip Divide the class into pairs and distribute the handouts from the Activity Pack (Activity Pack/Supersite) that correspond to this Information Gap Activity. Give students ten minutes to complete this activity.

8 Expansion Ask small groups to imagine that they all live in the same house, and have them put together a message board to reflect their different schedules.

TEACHING OPTIONS

Game Working in teams, students should tell each other about the strangest, funniest, or most exciting thing they have done. The team then chooses one account and writes it down. Collect the papers, shuffle them, and read the descriptions aloud. The class has two minutes to ask team members questions to find out who did the activity.

Extra Practice Add an auditory aspect to this grammar practice. Prepare descriptions of five celebrities or fictional characters, using reflexives. Write their names in random order on the board. Then read the descriptions aloud and have students match each one to a name. Ex: **Es seria; se preocupa por temas importantes, como la justicia. Siempre se viste de rojo. Quiere a su hermano, pero con frecuencia se enoja con él. Tiene una hermana menor que se llama Maggie. (Lisa Simpson)**

Section Goals

In **Estructura 7.2**, students will learn:
- high-frequency indefinite and negative words
- the placement and use of indefinite and negative words

Instructional Resources
Supersite: Audio (Lab MP3 Files); Resources (Grammar Presentation Slides, Activity Pack, Scripts, Answer Keys); Testing Program (Quizzes)
WebSAM
Workbook, pp. 77–78
Lab Manual, p. 40

Teaching Tips

- Write **alguien** and **nadie** on the board and ask questions about what students are wearing. Ex: **Hoy alguien lleva una camiseta verde. ¿Quién es? ¿Alguien lleva pantalones anaranjados?**
- Present negative words by complaining dramatically in a whining tone. Ex: **Nadie me llama por teléfono. Nunca recibo un mensaje electrónico de ningún estudiante. Ni mi esposo ni mis hijos se acuerdan de mi cumpleaños.** Then smile radiantly and state the opposite. Ex: **Alguien me llama por teléfono.**
- Add a visual aspect to this grammar presentation. Use magazine pictures to compare and contrast indefinite and negative words. Ex: **La señora tiene algo en las manos. ¿El señor tiene algo también? No, el señor no tiene nada.**
- Have students say they do the opposite of what you do. Ex: **Yo siempre canto en la ducha. (Nosotros no cantamos nunca en la ducha.)**
- Point out that **uno/a(s)** can be used as an indefinite pronoun. Ex: **¿Tienes un lápiz? Sí, tengo uno.**

7.2 Indefinite and negative words

Tutorial

NATIONAL STANDARDS comparisons

ANTE TODO Indefinite words refer to people and things that are not specific, for example, *someone* or *something*. Negative words deny the existence of people and things or contradict statements, for instance, *no one* or *nothing*. Spanish indefinite words have corresponding negative words, which are opposite in meaning.

Indefinite and negative words

Indefinite words		Negative words	
algo	*something; anything*	**nada**	*nothing; not anything*
alguien	*someone; somebody; anyone*	**nadie**	*no one; nobody; not anyone*
alguno/a(s), algún	*some; any*	**ninguno/a, ningún**	*no; none; not any*
o... o	*either... or*	**ni... ni**	*neither... nor*
siempre	*always*	**nunca, jamás**	*never, not ever*
también	*also; too*	**tampoco**	*neither; not either*

▶ There are two ways to form negative sentences in Spanish. You can place the negative word before the verb, or you can place **no** before the verb and the negative word after.

Nadie se levanta temprano.
No one gets up early.

No se levanta nadie temprano.
No one gets up early.

Ellos **nunca gritan**.
They never shout.

Ellos **no gritan nunca**.
They never shout.

¿Hay algún problema?

Siempre haces esto.

▶ Because they refer to people, **alguien** and **nadie** are often used with the personal **a**. The personal **a** is also used before **alguno/a, algunos/as,** and **ninguno/a** when these words refer to people and they are the direct object of the verb.

—Perdón, señor, ¿busca usted **a alguien**?
—No, gracias, señorita, no busco **a nadie**.

—Tomás, ¿buscas **a alguno** de tus hermanos?
—No, mamá, no busco **a ninguno**.

▶ **¡Atención!** Before a masculine singular noun, **alguno** and **ninguno** are shortened to **algún** and **ningún**.

—¿Tienen ustedes **algún** amigo peruano?

—No, no tenemos **ningún** amigo peruano.

AYUDA

Alguno/a, algunos/as are not always used in the same way English uses *some* or *any*. Often, **algún** is used where *a* would be used in English.

¿Tienes algún libro que hable de los incas?
Do you have a book that talks about the Incas?

Note that **ninguno/a** is rarely used in the plural.

—¿Visitaste algunos museos?
—No, no visité ninguno.

TEACHING OPTIONS

Extra Practice Write cloze sentences on the board and have the students complete them with an indefinite or negative word. Ex: **Los vegetarianos no comen hamburguesas ____. (nunca) Las madres ____ se preocupan por sus hijos. (siempre) En las fiestas ella no es sociable, ____ baila ____ habla con ____. (ni, ni, nadie)**

Pairs Have students take turns giving one-word indefinite and negative word prompts and having the other respond in complete sentences. Ex: **E1: siempre E2: Siempre le mando un mensaje electrónico a mi madre por la mañana.**

COMPARE & CONTRAST

In English, it is incorrect to use more than one negative word in a sentence. In Spanish, however, sentences frequently contain two or more negative words. Compare these Spanish and English sentences.

Nunca le escribo a **nadie**.
I never write to anyone.

No me preocupo **nunca** por **nada**.
I do not ever worry about anything.

As the preceding sentences show, once an English sentence contains one negative word (for example, *not* or *never*), no other negative word may be used. Instead, indefinite (or affirmative) words are used. In Spanish, however, once a sentence is negative, no other affirmative (that is, indefinite) word may be used. Instead, all indefinite ideas must be expressed in the negative.

- **Pero** is used to mean *but*. The meaning of **sino** is *but rather* or *on the contrary*. It is used when the first part of the sentence is negative and the second part contradicts it.

Los estudiantes no se acuestan temprano **sino** tarde.
The students don't go to bed early, but rather late.

Esas gafas son caras, **pero** bonitas.
Those glasses are expensive, but pretty.

María no habla francés **sino** español.
María doesn't speak French, but rather Spanish.

José es inteligente, **pero** no saca buenas notas.
José is intelligent but doesn't get good grades.

¡INTÉNTALO! Cambia las oraciones para que sean negativas.

1. Siempre se viste bien.
   Nunca se viste bien.
   No se viste bien nunca.
2. Alguien se ducha.
   Nadie se ducha.
   No se ducha nadie.
3. Ellas van también.
   Ellas tampoco van.
   Ellas no van tampoco.
4. Alguien se pone nervioso.
   Nadie se pone nervioso.
   No se pone nervioso nadie.
5. Tú siempre te lavas las manos.
   Tú nunca / jamás te lavas las manos.
   Tú no te lavas las manos nunca / jamás.
6. Voy a traer algo.
   No voy a traer nada.
7. Juan se afeita también.
   Juan tampoco se afeita.
   Juan no se afeita tampoco.
8. Mis amigos viven en una residencia o en casa.
   Mis amigos no viven ni en una residencia ni en casa.
9. La profesora hace algo en su escritorio.
   La profesora no hace nada en su escritorio.
10. Tú y yo vamos al mercado.
    Ni tú ni yo vamos al mercado.
11. Tienen un espejo en su casa.
    No tienen ningún espejo en su casa.
12. Algunos niños se ponen los abrigos.
    Ningún niño se pone el abrigo.

recursos
WB pp. 77–78
LM p. 40
vhlcentral.com Lección 7

Teaching Tips

- Emphasize that there is no limit to the number of negative words that can be strung together in a sentence in Spanish. Ex: **No hablo con nadie nunca de ningún problema, ni con mi familia ni con mis amigos.**
- Ask volunteers questions about their activities since the last class, reiterating the answers. Ex: **¿Quién compró algo nuevo? Sólo dos personas. Nadie más compró algo nuevo. Yo no compré nada nuevo tampoco.**
- Elicit negative responses by asking questions whose answers will clearly be negative. Ex: **¿Alguien lleva zapatos de lunares? (No, nadie lleva zapatos de lunares.) ¿Piensas comprar un barco mañana? (No, no pienso comprar ninguno/ningún barco.) ¿Tienes nietos? (No, no tengo ninguno/ningún nieto.)**
- Give examples of **pero** and **sino** using the seating of the students. Ex: ____ **se sienta al lado de** ____**, pero no al lado de** ____**. No se sienta a la izquierda de** ____**, sino a la derecha.** ____ **no se sienta al lado de la ventana, pero está cerca de la puerta.**

TEACHING OPTIONS

Video Show the **Fotonovela** again to give students more input containing indefinite and negative words. Stop the video where appropriate to discuss how these words are used.

Pairs Have pairs create sentences about your community using indefinite and negative words. Ex: **En nuestra ciudad no hay ningún mercado al aire libre. Hay algunos restaurantes de tapas.**

Small Groups Give small groups five minutes to write a description of **un señor muy, pero muy antipático**. Tell them to use as many indefinite and negative words as possible to describe what makes this person so unpleasant. Encourage exaggeration and creativity.

1 Teaching Tips
- To challenge students, ask them to change each sentence so that the opposite choice (**pero** or **sino**) would be correct. Ex: **Muchos estudiantes no viven en la residencia estudiantil, sino en apartamentos.**
- Display a magazine picture that shows a group of people involved in a specific activity. Then talk about the picture, modeling the types of constructions required in **Actividad 1**. Ex: **Todos trabajan en la oficina, pero ninguno tiene computadora.**

1 Expansion Have pairs create four sentences, two with **sino** and two with **pero**. Have them "dehydrate" their sentences and exchange papers with another pair, who will write the complete sentences.

2 Teaching Tip Review indefinite and negative words by using them in short sentences and asking volunteers to contradict your statements. Ex: **Veo a alguien en la puerta. (No, usted no ve a nadie en la puerta.) Nunca vengo a clase con el libro. (No, usted siempre viene a clase con el libro.)**

2 Expansion After students have role-played the conversation, ask them to summarize it. **Ana María no encontró ningún regalo para Eliana. Tampoco vio a ninguna amiga en el centro comercial....**

Práctica

1 **¿Pero o sino?** Forma oraciones sobre estas personas usando **pero** o **sino**.

modelo

muchos estudiantes viven en residencias estudiantiles / muchos de ellos quieren vivir fuera del (*off*) campus

Muchos estudiantes viven en residencias estudiantiles, pero muchos de ellos quieren vivir fuera del campus.

1. Marcos nunca se despierta temprano / siempre llega puntual a clase
   Marcos nunca se despierta temprano, pero siempre llega puntual a clase.
2. Lisa y Katarina no se acuestan temprano / muy tarde
   Lisa y Katarina no se acuestan temprano sino muy tarde.
3. Alfonso es inteligente / algunas veces es antipático
   Alfonso es inteligente, pero algunas veces es antipático.
4. los directores de la residencia no son ecuatorianos / peruanos
   Los directores de la residencia no son ecuatorianos sino peruanos.
5. no nos acordamos de comprar champú / compramos jabón
   No nos acordamos de comprar champú, pero compramos jabón.
6. Emilia no es estudiante / profesora
   Emilia no es estudiante sino profesora.
7. no quiero levantarme / tengo que ir a clase
   No quiero levantarme, pero tengo que ir a clase.
8. Miguel no se afeita por la mañana / por la noche
   Miguel no se afeita por la mañana sino por la noche.

2 **Completar** Completa esta conversación. Usa expresiones negativas en tus respuestas. Luego, dramatiza la conversación con un(a) compañero/a. Answers will vary.

AURELIO Ana María, ¿encontraste algún regalo para Eliana?
ANA MARÍA (1) No, no encontré ningún regalo/nada para Eliana.
AURELIO ¿Viste a alguna amiga en el centro comercial?
ANA MARÍA (2) No, no vi a ninguna amiga/ninguna/nadie en el centro comercial.
AURELIO ¿Me llamó alguien?
ANA MARÍA (3) No, nadie te llamó./No, no te llamó nadie.
AURELIO ¿Quieres ir al teatro o al cine esta noche?
ANA MARÍA (4) No, no quiero ir ni al teatro ni al cine.
AURELIO ¿No quieres salir a comer?
ANA MARÍA (5) No, no quiero salir a comer (tampoco).
AURELIO ¿Hay algo interesante en la televisión esta noche?
ANA MARÍA (6) No, no hay nada interesante en la televisión.
AURELIO ¿Tienes algún problema?
ANA MARÍA (7) No, no tengo ningún problema/ninguno.

Practice more at **vhlcentral.com**.

TEACHING OPTIONS

Small Groups Add a visual aspect to this grammar practice. Have students bring in pairs of photos or magazine pictures, such as two photos of different family members, to compare and contrast. Divide the class into groups of three and have each student present his or her pictures to the group. Ex: **Éste es mi tío Ignacio. Siempre viene a casa los domingos. Ésta es mi tía Yolanda. Vive en Lima y por eso nunca viene a casa.**

Extra Practice To provide oral practice with indefinite and negative words, create prompts that follow the pattern of the sentences in **Actividad 1** and **Actividad 2**. Say the first part of the sentence, then have students repeat it and finish the sentence. Ex: **1.** ____ **no se viste de azul hoy, sino** ____. **(de verde) 2.** ____ **no llegó temprano a clase hoy, sino** ____. **(tarde)**

NATIONAL communication STANDARDS

Comunicación

3

Opiniones Completa estas oraciones de una manera lógica. Luego, compara tus respuestas con las de un(a) compañero/a. Answers will vary.

1. Mi habitación es ________, pero ________.
2. Por la noche me gusta ________, pero ________.
3. Un(a) profesor(a) ideal no es ________, sino ________.
4. Mis amigos son ________, pero ________.

4

En el campus En parejas, háganse preguntas sobre qué hay en su universidad: residencias bonitas, departamento de ingeniería, cines, librerías baratas, estudiantes guapos/as, equipo de fútbol, playa, clases fáciles, museo, profesores/as estrictos/as. Sigan el modelo. Answers will vary.

modelo

Estudiante 1: ¿Hay algunas residencias bonitas?
Estudiante 2: Sí, hay una/algunas. Está(n) detrás del estadio.
Estudiante 1: ¿Hay algún museo?
Estudiante 2: No, no hay ninguno.

5

Quejas En parejas, hagan una lista de cinco quejas (*complaints*) comunes que tienen los estudiantes. Usen expresiones negativas. Answers will vary.

modelo

Nadie me entiende.

Ahora hagan una lista de cinco quejas que los padres tienen de sus hijos.

modelo

Nunca limpian sus habitaciones.

6

Anuncios En parejas, lean el anuncio y contesten las preguntas.

1. ¿Es el anuncio positivo o negativo? ¿Por qué? Some answers will vary. Answers will vary.
2. ¿Qué palabras indefinidas hay? algún, siempre, algo
3. Escriban el texto del anuncio cambiando todo por expresiones negativas. ¿No buscas ningún producto especial? ¡Nunca hay nada para nadie en las tiendas García!

Ahora preparen su propio (*own*) anuncio usando expresiones indefinidas y negativas.

¿Buscas algún producto especial?
¡Siempre hay algo para todos en las tiendas García!

NATIONAL communication STANDARDS

Síntesis

7

Encuesta Tu profesor(a) te va a dar una hoja de actividades para hacer una encuesta. Circula por la clase y pídeles a tus compañeros que comparen las actividades que hacen durante la semana con las que hacen durante los fines de semana. Escribe las respuestas. Answers will vary.

3 Teaching Tip Before assigning the activity, give some personal examples using different subjects. Ex: **Mi hijo es inteligente, pero no le gusta estudiar. Mi amiga no es norteamericana, sino española.**

3 Expansion Give students these sentences as items 5–6: **5. Mis padres no son ____ sino ____. 6. Mi compañero/a de cuarto es ____ pero ____.**

4 Teaching Tip To simplify, before beginning the activity, practice question formation for each topic as a class.

4 Expansion Have pairs of students create three additional sentences about your school.

5 Expansion Divide the class into all-male and all-female groups. Then have each group make two different lists: **Quejas que tienen los hombres de las mujeres** and **Quejas que tienen las mujeres de los hombres.** After five minutes, compare and contrast the answers and perceptions.

6 Expansion Have pairs work with another pair to create an ad that combines the best aspects of each of their individual ads. Then have them present their final product to the class.

7 Teaching Tip Distribute the ***Hojas de actividades*** from the Activity Pack/Supersite that correspond to this activity.

7 Expansion Have students write a short paragraph summarizing the information obtained through the **encuesta**. Ex: **Nadie va a la biblioteca durante el fin de semana, pero muchos vamos durante la semana. No estudiamos los sábados sino los domingos....**

TEACHING OPTIONS

Large Groups Write the names of four vacation spots on four slips of paper and post them in different corners of the room. Ask students to pick their vacation preference by going to one of the corners. Then, have each group produce a short paragraph describing the five reasons for their choice as well as one complaint about each of the other places.

Extra Practice Have students complete this cloze activity using **pero, sino,** and **tampoco: Yo me levanto temprano y hago mi tarea, ____ mi compañera de apartamento prefiere hacerla por la noche y acostarse muy tarde. (pero) Ella no tiene exámenes este semestre ____ proyectos. (sino) Yo no tengo exámenes ____. (tampoco) Sólo tengo mucha, mucha tarea.**

Section Goal

In **Estructura 7.3**, students will learn the preterite of **ser** and **ir**.

Instructional Resources
Supersite: Audio (Lab MP3 Files); Resources (Grammar Presentation Slides, Activity Pack, Scripts, Answer Keys); Testing Program (Quizzes)
WebSAM
Workbook, p. 79
Lab Manual, p. 41

Teaching Tips

- Ask volunteers to answer questions such as: **¿Fuiste al cine el sábado pasado? ¿Cómo fue la película? ¿Fueron tus amigos y tú a alguna fiesta durante el fin de semana? ¿Fue agradable la fiesta? ¿Quiénes fueron?**
- Contrast the preterite of **ser** and **ir** by saying pairs of sentences. Ex: **1. Anteayer fue sábado. Fui al supermercado el sábado. 2. Ayer fue domingo. No fui al supermercado ayer. 3. ¿Fueron ustedes al partido de fútbol el sábado? ¿Fue divertido el partido?**
- Point out that although the preterite forms of **ser** and **ir** are identical, there is rarely any confusion because context clarifies which verb is used.

7.3 Preterite of ser and ir

Tutorial

NATIONAL STANDARDS comparisons

ANTE TODO In **Lección 6**, you learned how to form the preterite tense of regular **-ar**, **-er**, and **-ir** verbs. The following chart contains the preterite forms of **ser** (*to be*) and **ir** (*to go*). Since these forms are irregular, you will need to memorize them.

Preterite of ser and ir

		ser (*to be*)	ir (*to go*)
SINGULAR FORMS	yo	fui	fui
	tú	fuiste	fuiste
	Ud./él/ella	fue	fue
PLURAL FORMS	nosotros/as	fuimos	fuimos
	vosotros/as	fuisteis	fuisteis
	Uds./ellos/ellas	fueron	fueron

AYUDA
Note that, whereas regular **-er** and **-ir** verbs have accent marks in the **yo** and **Ud./él/ella** forms of the preterite, **ser** and **ir** do not.

▶ Since the preterite forms of **ser** and **ir** are identical, context clarifies which of the two verbs is being used.

Él **fue** a comprar champú y jabón.
He went to buy shampoo and soap.

¿Cómo **fue** la película anoche?
How was the movie last night?

¿Cuándo fue la última vez que viste a Juan Carlos?

Cuando fuimos a Mérida.

¡INTÉNTALO! Completa las oraciones usando el pretérito de **ser** e **ir**.

ir

1. Los viajeros __fueron__ a Perú.
2. Patricia __fue__ a Cuzco.
3. Tú __fuiste__ a Iquitos.
4. Gregorio y yo __fuimos__ a Lima.
5. Yo __fui__ a Trujillo.
6. Ustedes __fueron__ a Arequipa.
7. Mi padre __fue__ a Lima.
8. Nosotras __fuimos__ a Cuzco.
9. Él __fue__ a Machu Picchu.
10. Usted __fue__ a Nazca.

ser

1. Usted __fue__ muy amable.
2. Yo __fui__ muy cordial.
3. Ellos __fueron__ simpáticos.
4. Nosotros __fuimos__ muy tontos.
5. Ella __fue__ antipática.
6. Tú __fuiste__ muy generoso.
7. Ustedes __fueron__ cordiales.
8. La gente __fue__ amable.
9. Tomás y yo __fuimos__ muy felices.
10. Los profesores __fueron__ buenos.

recursos
WB p. 79
LM p. 41
vhlcentral.com Lección 7

TEACHING OPTIONS

Video Replay the **Fotonovela** segment and have students listen for preterite forms of **ser** and **ir**. Stop the video with each example to illustrate how context makes the meaning of the verb clear.

Pairs Have pairs of students work together to solve this logical reasoning problem. **Mis compañeros de casa, Julia y Fernando, y yo fuimos de vacaciones durante el mes de julio a Puerto Rico, a Chile y a México. Julia fue a un viaje de esquí, pero Fernando y yo fuimos a lugares donde hace sol. El viaje de Fernando fue desagradable porque pasó un huracán y fue imposible nadar en el Pacífico durante esos días. Por suerte, mi viaje fue muy agradable. ¿Adónde fui? (a Puerto Rico) ¿Adónde fueron Julia y Fernando? (Julia fue a Chile y Fernando fue a México.)**

Práctica y Comunicación

NOTA CULTURAL

La ciudad peruana de **El Callao**, fundada en 1537, fue por muchos años el puerto (*port*) más activo de la costa del Pacífico en Suramérica. En el siglo XVIII, se construyó (*was built*) una fortaleza allí para proteger (*protect*) la ciudad de los ataques de piratas y bucaneros.

1 **Completar** Completa estas conversaciones con la forma correcta del pretérito de **ser** o **ir**. Indica el infinitivo de cada forma verbal.

Conversación 1

		ser	ir
RAÚL	¿Adónde (1) fueron ustedes de vacaciones?	○	✓
PILAR	(2) Fuimos a Perú.	○	✓
RAÚL	¿Cómo (3) fue el viaje?	✓	○
▶ PILAR	¡(4) Fue estupendo! Machu Picchu y El Callao son increíbles.	✓	○
RAÚL	¿(5) Fue caro el viaje?	✓	○
PILAR	No, el precio (6) fue muy bajo. Sólo costó tres mil dólares.	✓	○

Conversación 2

		ser	ir
ISABEL	Tina y Vicente (7) fueron novios, ¿no?	✓	○
LUCÍA	Sí, pero ahora no. Anoche Tina (8) fue a comer con Gregorio	○	✓
	y la semana pasada ellos (9) fueron al partido de fútbol.	○	✓
ISABEL	¿Ah sí? Javier y yo (10) fuimos al partido y no los vimos.	○	✓

2 **Descripciones** Forma oraciones con estos elementos. Usa el pretérito. Answers will vary.

A	B	C	D
yo	(no) ir	a un restaurante	ayer
tú	(no) ser	en autobús	anoche
mi compañero/a		estudiante	anteayer
nosotros		muy simpático/a	la semana pasada
mis amigos		a la playa	año pasado
ustedes		dependiente/a en una tienda	

3 **Preguntas** En parejas, túrnense para hacerse estas preguntas. Answers will vary.

1. ¿Cuándo fuiste al cine por última vez? ¿Con quién fuiste?
2. ¿Fuiste en auto, en autobús o en metro? ¿Cómo fue el viaje?
3. ¿Cómo fue la película?
4. ¿Fue una película de terror, de acción o un drama?
5. ¿Fue una de las mejores películas que viste? ¿Por qué?
6. ¿Fueron buenos los actores o no? ¿Cuál fue el mejor?
7. ¿Adónde fuiste/fueron después?
8. ¿Fue una buena idea ir al cine?
9. ¿Fuiste feliz ese día?

4 **El viaje** En parejas, escriban un diálogo de un(a) viajero/a hablando con el/la agente de viajes sobre un viaje que hizo recientemente. Usen el pretérito de **ser** e **ir**. Answers will vary.

modelo

Agente: *¿Cómo fue el viaje?*
Viajero: *El viaje fue maravilloso/horrible…*

Practice more at **vhlcentral.com**.

1 Teaching Tip Before assigning the activity, write cloze sentences on the board and ask volunteers to fill in the blanks. Ex: **¿Cómo ____ los guías turísticos durante tu viaje? (fueron) ¿Quién ____ con Marcela al baile? (fue)**

1 Expansion Ask small groups to write four questions based on the conversations. Have groups exchange papers to discuss and answer the questions they receive. Then have them confirm their answers with the group who wrote the questions.

2 Expansion Ask a volunteer to say one of his or her sentences aloud. Point to another student, and call out an interrogative word in order to cue a question. Ex: **E1: No fui a un restaurante anoche.** Say: **¿Adónde? E2: ¿Adónde fuiste? E1: Fui al cine.**

3 Expansion Have students form new pairs and describe the movie that their first partner saw, based on the information they learned from items 3–6. The other student should guess what movie it was, asking for more information as needed.

4 Expansion Ask pairs to write a similar conversation within a different context (Ex: **un día horrible**).

TEACHING OPTIONS

Small Groups Have small groups of students role-play a TV interview with astronauts who have just returned from a long stay on Mars. Have students review previous lesson vocabulary lists as necessary in preparation. Give groups sufficient time to plan and practice their skits. When all groups have completed the activity, ask a few of them to perform their role-play for the class.

TPR Read aloud a series of sentences using **ser** and **ir** in the preterite. Have students raise their right hand if the verb is **ser**, and their left hand for **ir**. Ex: **Yo fui camerero a los dieciocho años.** (right hand)

Section Goal

In **Estructura 7.4**, students will learn verbs that follow the pattern of **gustar**.

Instructional Resources
Supersite: Audio (Lab MP3 Files); Resources (Grammar Presentation Slides, Activity Pack, Scripts, Answer Keys); Testing Program (Quizzes)
WebSAM
Workbook, pp. 80–82
Lab Manual, p. 42

Teaching Tips

- Review the verb **gustar**. Write the headings **Les gusta(n)** and **No les gusta(n)** on the board. Have the class brainstorm a list of likes and dislikes among the college population including music, artists, movies, clothes, or hobbies. Use the lists to form statements and questions illustrating the use of the verb **gustar**. Use different indirect object pronouns. Ex: **A los estudiantes universitarios no les gusta el jazz. A mis amigos y a mí, sí nos gusta el jazz.**
- Use the previously generated lists of likes and dislikes to present verbs like **gustar**. Ex: **A los estudiantes les aburren los documentales. A mí tampoco me interesan esas películas. A muchos estudiantes les encanta la ropa de *J.Crew*.**

NATIONAL STANDARDS comparisons

7.4 Verbs like gustar

S Tutorial

ANTE TODO In **Lección 2**, you learned how to express preferences with **gustar**. You will now learn more about the verb **gustar** and other similar verbs. Observe these examples.

Me gusta ese champú.

ENGLISH EQUIVALENT
I like that shampoo.
LITERAL MEANING
That shampoo is pleasing to me.

¿**Te gustaron** las clases?

ENGLISH EQUIVALENT
Did you like the classes?
LITERAL MEANING
Were the classes pleasing to you?

- As the examples show, constructions with **gustar** do not have a direct equivalent in English. The literal meaning of this construction is *to be pleasing to* (*someone*), and it requires the use of an indirect object pronoun.

INDIRECT OBJECT PRONOUN	VERB	SUBJECT	SUBJECT	VERB	DIRECT OBJECT
Me	**gusta**	ese champú.	*I*	*like*	*that shampoo.*

- In the diagram above, observe how in the Spanish sentence the object being liked **(ese champú)** is really the subject of the sentence. The person who likes the object, in turn, is an indirect object because it answers the question: *To whom is the shampoo pleasing?*

¿Te gusta Juan Carlos?

Me gustan los cafés que tienen música en vivo.

- Other verbs in Spanish are used in the same way as **gustar**. Here is a list of the most common ones.

Verbs like gustar

aburrir	*to bore*	**importar**	*to be important to; to matter*
encantar	*to like very much; to love* (inanimate objects)	**interesar**	*to be interesting to; to interest*
faltar	*to lack; to need*	**molestar**	*to bother; to annoy*
fascinar	*to fascinate; to like very much*	**quedar**	*to be left over; to fit* (clothing)

¡ATENCIÓN!

Faltar expresses what is lacking or missing.
Me falta una página. *I'm missing one page.*
Quedar expresses how much of something is left.
Nos quedan tres pesos. *We have three pesos left.*

• • •

Quedar also means *to fit*. It can be used to tell how something looks (on someone).
Estos zapatos me quedan bien. *These shoes fit me well.*
Esa camisa te queda muy bien. *That shirt looks good on you.*

TEACHING OPTIONS

Pairs Have students work in pairs to compare and contrast activities they like to do with activities their parents/grandparents like to do. Encourage them to use the verb **gustar** and others that follow the same pattern.

Game Divide the class into small teams. Give a prompt including subject and object (Ex: **ella/películas de horror**). Allow teams one minute to construct a sentence using one of the verbs that follow the pattern of **gustar**. Then one member from each team will write the sentence on the board. Award one point to each team for each correct response.

▶ The most commonly used verb forms of **gustar** and similar verbs are the third person (singular and plural). When the object or person being liked is singular, the singular form (**gusta**) is used. When two or more objects or persons are being liked, the plural form (**gustan**) is used. Observe the following diagram:

me, te, le, nos, os, les	SINGULAR	encanta / interesó	la película / el concierto
	PLURAL	importan / fascinaron	las vacaciones / los museos de Lima

▶ To express what someone likes or does not like to do, use an appropriate verb followed by an infinitive. The singular form is used even if there is more than one infinitive.

Nos molesta comer a las nueve.
It bothers us to eat at nine o'clock.

Les encanta bailar y **cantar** en las fiestas.
They love to dance and sing at parties.

▶ As you learned in **Lección 2**, the construction **a** + [*pronoun*] (**a mí, a ti, a usted, a él,** etc.) is used to clarify or to emphasize who is pleased, bored, etc. The construction **a** + [*noun*] can also be used before the indirect object pronoun to clarify or to emphasize who is pleased.

A los turistas les gustó mucho Machu Picchu.
The tourists liked Machu Picchu a lot.

A ti te gusta cenar en casa, pero **a mí** me aburre.
You like eating dinner at home, but I get bored.

▶ **¡Atención! Mí** (*me*) has an accent mark to distinguish it from the possessive adjective **mi** (*my*).

AYUDA

Note that the **a** must be repeated if there is more than one person.
A Armando y a Carmen les molesta levantarse temprano.

¡INTÉNTALO! Indica el pronombre de objeto indirecto y la forma del tiempo presente adecuados en cada oración.

fascinar

1. A él <u>le fascina</u> viajar.
2. A mí <u>me fascina</u> bailar.
3. A nosotras <u>nos fascina</u> cantar.
4. A ustedes <u>les fascina</u> leer.
5. A ti <u>te fascina</u> correr y patinar.
6. A ellos <u>les fascinan</u> los aviones.
7. A mis padres <u>les fascina</u> caminar.
8. A usted <u>le fascina</u> jugar al tenis.
9. A mi esposo y a mí <u>nos fascina</u> dormir.
10. A Alberto <u>le fascina</u> dibujar y pintar.
11. A todos <u>nos/les fascina</u> opinar.
12. A Pili <u>le fascinan</u> los sombreros.

aburrir

1. A ellos <u>les aburren</u> los deportes.
2. A ti <u>te aburren</u> las películas.
3. A usted <u>le aburren</u> los viajes.
4. A mí <u>me aburren</u> las revistas.
5. A Jorge y a Luis <u>les aburren</u> los perros.
6. A nosotros <u>nos aburren</u> las vacaciones.
7. A ustedes <u>les aburre</u> el béisbol.
8. A Marcela <u>le aburren</u> los libros.
9. A mis amigos <u>les aburren</u> los museos.
10. A ella <u>le aburre</u> el ciclismo.
11. A Omar <u>le aburre</u> ir de compras.
12. A ti y a mí <u>nos aburre</u> el baile.

recursos
WB pp. 80–82
LM p. 42
vhlcentral.com Lección 7

Teaching Tips

- Write a model sentence on the board such as those found in the examples. Ex: **A Carlos le encanta la pasta de dientes *Crest*.** Then change the noun and ask volunteers to say the new sentence. Ex: **A nosotros (A nosotros nos encanta la pasta de dientes *Crest*.)**
- Ask students about their preferences, using verbs that follow the pattern of **gustar**. Ex: **A mí me encantan las lenguas, pero me aburren las matemáticas. ¿Qué les interesa a ustedes? ¿Qué les aburre?**
- Point out the third bullet on this page. Give students some sample phrases to complete. Ex: **A ____ me encantan las películas. A ____ les aburre ir de compras. A ____ le gusta viajar.** Explain that some phrases have many possible answers.

TEACHING OPTIONS

Large Group Have the class sit in a circle. Student A begins by saying **Me encanta** and an activity he or she enjoys. Ex: **Me encanta correr.** Student B reports what student A said and adds his or her own favorite activity. **A Frank le encanta correr. A mí me fascina bailar.** Student C reports the preferences of the first two students and adds his or her own, and so forth. This activity may be used with any verb that follows the pattern of **gustar**.

Extra Practice To add an auditory aspect to this grammar presentation, read a series of sentences aloud, pausing for students to write. Ex: **1. A todos en mi familia nos encanta viajar. 2. Nos gusta viajar en avión, pero nos molestan los aviones pequeños. 3. A mi hijo le interesan las culturas latinoamericanas, a mi esposo le encantan los países de Asia y a mí me fascina Europa.** Ask comprehension questions as a follow-up.

1 Teaching Tip To simplify, have students identify the subject in each sentence before filling in the blanks.

1 Expansion Have students use the verbs in the activity to write a paragraph describing their own musical tastes.

2 Expansion Repeat the activity using the preterite. Invite students to provide additional details. Ex: **1. A Ramón le molestó el despertador ayer. 2. A nosotros nos encantó esquiar en Vail.**

3 Teaching Tip To challenge students, have them add new items to columns A and C and then complete the activity.

3 Expansion Ask students to create two additional sentences using verbs from column B. Have students read their sentences aloud. After everyone has had a turn, ask the class how many similar or identical sentences they heard and what they were.

Práctica

1 **Completar** Completa las oraciones con todos los elementos necesarios.

1. ___A___ Adela ___le encanta___ (encantar) la música de Tito "El Bambino".
2. A ___mí___ me ___interesa___ (interesar) la música de otros países.
3. A mis amigos ___les encantan___ (encantar) las canciones (*songs*) de Calle 13.
4. A Juan y ___a___ Rafael no les ___molesta___ (molestar) la música alta (*loud*).
5. ___A___ nosotros ___nos fascinan___ (fascinar) los grupos de pop latino.
6. ___Al___ señor Ruiz ___le interesa___ (interesar) más la música clásica.
7. A ___mí___ me ___aburre___ (aburrir) la música clásica.
8. ¿A ___ti___ te ___falta___ (faltar) dinero para el concierto de Carlos Santana?
9. No. Ya compré el boleto y ___me quedan___ (quedar) cinco dólares.
10. ¿Cuánto dinero te ___queda___ (quedar) a ___ti___?

NOTA CULTURAL

Hoy día, la música latina es popular en los EE.UU. gracias a artistas como **Shakira**, de nacionalidad colombiana, y **Tito "El Bambino"**, puertorriqueño. Otros artistas, como **Carlos Santana** y **Gloria Estefan**, difundieron (*spread*) la música latina en los años 60, 70, 80 y 90.

2 **Describir** Mira los dibujos y describe lo que está pasando. Usa los verbos de la lista. Answers will vary. Suggested answers:

aburrir	faltar	molestar
encantar	interesar	quedar

1. a Ramón A Ramón le molesta despertarse temprano.

2. a nosotros A nosotros nos encanta esquiar.

3. a ti A ti no te queda bien este vestido. A ti te queda mal/grande este vestido.

4. a Sara A Sara le interesan los libros de arte moderno.

3 **Gustos** Forma oraciones con los elementos de las columnas. Answers will vary.

modelo

A ti te interesan las ruinas de Machu Picchu.

A	B	C
yo	aburrir	despertarse temprano
tú	encantar	mirarse en el espejo
mi mejor amigo/a	faltar	la música rock
mis amigos y yo	fascinar	las pantuflas rosadas
Bart y Homero Simpson	interesar	la pasta de dientes con menta (*mint*)
Shakira	molestar	las ruinas de Machu Picchu
Antonio Banderas		los zapatos caros

Practice more at **vhlcentral.com**.

TEACHING OPTIONS

Large Groups Have students stand and form a circle. Begin by tossing a ball to a student, who should state a complaint using a verb like **gustar** (Ex: **Me falta dinero para comprar los libros**) and then toss the ball to another student. The next student should offer advice (Ex: **Debes pedirle dinero a tus padres**) and throw the ball to another person, who will air another complaint. Repeat the activity with positive statements (**Me fascinan las películas cómicas**) and advice (**Debes ver las películas de Will Ferrell**).

Extra Practice Write sentences like these on the board. Have students copy them and draw faces (☺/☹) to indicate the feelings expressed. Ex: **1. Me encantan las enchiladas verdes. 2. Me aburren las matemáticas. 3. Me fascina la ópera italiana. 4. No me falta dinero para comprar un auto. 5. Me queda pequeño el sombrero.**

Comunicación

4 **Preguntas** En parejas, túrnense para hacer y contestar estas preguntas. Answers will vary.

1. ¿Te gusta levantarte temprano o tarde? ¿Por qué? ¿Y a tu compañero/a de cuarto?
2. ¿Te gusta acostarte temprano o tarde? ¿Y a tu compañero/a de cuarto?
3. ¿Te gusta dormir la siesta?
4. ¿Te encanta acampar o prefieres quedarte en un hotel cuando estás de vacaciones?
5. ¿Qué te gusta hacer en el verano?
6. ¿Qué te fascina de esta universidad? ¿Qué te molesta?
7. ¿Te interesan más las ciencias o las humanidades? ¿Por qué?
8. ¿Qué cosas te aburren?

5 **Completar** Trabajen en parejas. Túrnense para completar estas frases de una manera lógica. Answers will vary.

1. A mi novio/a le fascina(n)...
2. A mi mejor (*best*) amigo/a no le interesa(n)...
3. A mis padres les importa(n)...
4. A nosotros nos molesta(n)...
5. A mis hermanos les aburre(n)...
6. A mi compañero/a de cuarto le aburre(n)...
7. A los turistas les interesa(n)...
8. A los jugadores profesionales les encanta(n)...
9. A nuestro/a profesor(a) le molesta(n)...
10. A mí me importa(n)...

6 **La residencia** Tú y tu compañero/a de clase son los directores de una residencia estudiantil en Perú. Su profesor(a) les va a dar a cada uno de ustedes las descripciones de cinco estudiantes. Con la información tienen que escoger quiénes van a ser compañeros de cuarto. Después, completen la lista. Answers will vary.

Síntesis

7 **Situación** Trabajen en parejas para representar los papeles de un(a) cliente/a y un(a) dependiente/a en una tienda de ropa. Usen las instrucciones como guía. Answers will vary.

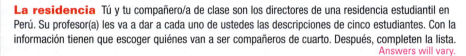

Dependiente/a	Cliente/a
Saluda al/a la cliente/a y pregúntale en qué le puedes servir.	→ Saluda al/a la dependiente/a y dile (*tell him/her*) qué quieres comprar y qué colores prefieres.
Pregúntale si le interesan los estilos modernos y empieza a mostrarle la ropa.	→ Explícale que los estilos modernos te interesan. Escoge las cosas que te interesan.
Habla de los gustos del/de la cliente/a.	→ Habla de la ropa (me queda(n) bien/mal, me encanta(n)...).
Da opiniones favorables al/a la cliente/a (las botas te quedan fantásticas...).	→ Decide cuáles son las cosas que te gustan y qué vas a comprar.

TEACHING OPTIONS

Pairs Have pairs prepare short TV commercials in which they use the target verbs presented in **Estructura 7.4** to sell a particular product. Group three pairs together to present their skits.

Extra Practice Add a visual aspect to this grammar practice. Bring in magazine pictures of people enjoying or not enjoying what they are doing. Have students create sentences with verbs like **gustar**. Ex: **A los chicos no les interesa estudiar.**

Game Give groups of students five minutes to write a description of social life during a specific historical period, such as the French Revolution or prehistoric times, using as many of the target verbs presented in **Estructura 7.4** as possible. When finished, ask groups how many of these verbs they used in their descriptions. Have the top three read their descriptions for the class, who vote for their favorite description.

4 Teaching Tip Take a class survey of the answers and write the results on the board. Ask volunteers to use verbs like **gustar** to summarize them.

5 Teaching Tip For items that start with **A mi(s)...** , have pairs compare their answers and then report to the class: first, the answers they had in common; then, the answers that differed. Ex: **A mis padres les importan los estudios, pero a los padres de ____ les importa más el dinero.**

6 Teaching Tip Divide the class into pairs and distribute the handouts from the Activity Pack (Activity Pack/Supersite) that correspond to this Information Gap Activity. Give students ten minutes to complete this activity.

6 Expansion
- Have pairs circulate around the classroom and compare their matches.
- Have pairs choose one of the students and write his or her want ad looking for a suitable roommate.

7 Teaching Tip To simplify, have students prepare for their roles by brainstorming a list of words and phrases. Remind students to use the formal register in this conversation.

7 Expansion Ask pairs to role-play their conversation for the class, or have them record it.

Section Goal

In **Recapitulación**, students will review the grammar concepts from this lesson.

Instructional Resource
Supersite

1 Expansion To challenge students, ask them to provide the infinitive and the third-person singular form of each verb.

2 Expansion Ask students to create four additional sentences using the preterite of **ser** and **ir**. Then have pairs exchange papers for peer editing.

3 Teaching Tips
- To simplify, have students begin by identifying the subject in each sentence.
- Remind students of the different positions for reflexive pronouns and the need for an infinitive after a phrase like **antes de** or a conjugated verb, such as **puedo**.

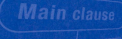

Recapitulación

Diagnostics

Completa estas actividades para repasar los conceptos de gramática que aprendiste en esta lección.

1 Completar Completa la tabla con la forma correcta de los verbos. 24 pts.

yo	tú	nosotros	ellas
me levanto	te levantas	nos levantamos	se levantan
me afeito	**te afeitas**	nos afeitamos	se afeitan
me visto	te vistes	**nos vestimos**	se visten
me seco	te secas	nos secamos	**se secan**

2 Hoy y ayer Cambia los verbos del presente al pretérito. 10 pts.

1. Vamos de compras hoy. Fuimos de compras hoy.
2. Por último, voy a poner el despertador. Por último, fui a poner el despertador.
3. Lalo es el primero en levantarse. Lalo fue el primero en levantarse.
4. ¿Vas a tu habitación? ¿Fuiste a tu habitación?
5. ¿Ustedes son profesores. Ustedes fueron profesores.

3 Reflexivos Completa cada conversación con la forma correcta de los verbos reflexivos. 22 pts.

TOMÁS Yo siempre (1) me baño (bañarse) antes de (2) acostarme (acostarse). Esto me relaja porque no (3) me duermo (dormirse) fácilmente. Y así puedo (4) levantarme (levantarse) más tarde. Y tú, ¿cuándo (5) te duchas (ducharse)?

LETI Pues por la mañana, para poder (6) despertarme (despertarse).

DAVID ¿Cómo (7) se siente (sentirse) Pepa hoy?

MARÍA Todavía está enojada.

DAVID ¿De verdad? Ella nunca (8) se enoja (enojarse) con nadie.

BETO ¿(Nosotros) (9) Nos vamos (Irse) de esta tienda? Estoy cansado.

SARA Pero antes vamos a (10) probarnos (probarse) estos sombreros. Si quieres, después (nosotros) (11) nos sentamos (sentarse) un rato.

RESUMEN GRAMATICAL

7.1 Reflexive verbs *pp. 220–221*

lavarse	
me lavo	nos lavamos
te lavas	os laváis
se lava	se lavan

7.2 Indefinite and negative words *pp. 224–225*

Indefinite words	Negative words
algo	nada
alguien	nadie
alguno/a(s), algún	ninguno/a, ningún
o... o	ni... ni
siempre	nunca, jamás
también	tampoco

7.3 Preterite of ser and ir *p. 228*

- The preterite of **ser** and **ir** are identical. Context will determine the meaning.

ser and ir	
fui	fuimos
fuiste	fuisteis
fue	fueron

7.4 Verbs like gustar *pp. 230–231*

aburrir	importar
encantar	interesar
faltar	molestar
fascinar	quedar

me, te, le, nos, os, les — SINGULAR: encanta / interesó — la película / el concierto; PLURAL: importan / fascinaron — las vacaciones / los museos

- Use the construction a + [*noun/pronoun*] to clarify the person in question.

A mí me encanta ver películas, ¿y a ti?

TEACHING OPTIONS

TPR Divide the class into two teams, **ser** and **ir**, and have them line up. Indicate the first member of each team and call out a sentence in Spanish. Ex: **Fuimos al parque.** The team member whose verb corresponds to the sentence has five seconds to step forward and provide the English translation.

Game Play **Concentración**. On eight note cards, write simple sentences using a variety of reflexive and non-reflexive verbs. (Ex: **Nos cepillamos los dientes. Lavamos el auto los sábados.**) On another eight cards, draw or paste a picture of an item that matches each description (Ex: a tube of toothpaste, a car). Place the cards face-down in four rows of four. Have pairs take turns selecting two cards; if they match, the pair keeps them, and if not, they return the cards to their original positions. The pair with the most cards at the end wins.

4 **Conversaciones** Completa cada conversación de manera lógica con palabras de la lista. No tienes que usar todas las palabras. **18 pts.**

algo	nada	ningún	siempre
alguien	nadie	nunca	también
algún	ni... ni	o... o	tampoco

1. —¿Tienes __algún__ plan para esta noche?
   —No, prefiero quedarme en casa. Hoy no quiero ver a __nadie__.
   —Yo __también__ me quedo. Estoy muy cansado.
2. —¿Puedo entrar? ¿Hay __alguien__ en el cuarto de baño?
   —Sí. ¡Un momento! Ahora mismo salgo.
3. —¿Puedes prestarme __algo__ para peinarme? No encuentro __ni__ mi cepillo __ni__ mi peine.
   —Lo siento, yo __tampoco__ encuentro los míos (*mine*).
4. —¿Me prestas tu maquillaje?
   —Lo siento, no tengo. __Nunca__ me maquillo.

5 **Oraciones** Forma oraciones completas con los elementos dados (*given*). Usa el presente de los verbos. **8 pts.**

1. David y Juan / molestar / levantarse temprano A David y a Juan les molesta levantarse temprano.
2. Lucía / encantar / las películas de terror A Lucía le encantan las películas de terror.
3. todos (nosotros) / importar / la educación A todos nos importa la educación.
4. tú / aburrir / ver / la televisión. A ti te aburre ver la televisión.

6 **Rutinas** Escribe seis oraciones que describan las rutinas de dos personas que conoces. **18 pts.**
Answers will vary.

modelo
Mi tía se despierta temprano, pero mi primo...

7 **Adivinanza** Completa la adivinanza con las palabras que faltan y adivina la respuesta. **¡4 puntos EXTRA!**

"Cuanto más° __te seca__ (*it dries you*), más se moja°."
¿Qué es? __La toalla__

Cuanto más *The more* se moja *it gets wet*

Practice more at **vhlcentral.com**.

4 Expansion Have students write additional mini-conversations using the remaining indefinite and negative words from the word bank.

5 Expansion Give students these sentences as items 5–8: **5. yo / faltar / dinero (A mí me falta dinero.) 6. Pedro y yo / fascinar / cantar y bailar (A Pedro y a mí nos fascina cantar y bailar.) 7. usted / quedar / muy bien / esas gafas de sol (A usted le quedan muy bien esas gafas de sol.) 8. ¿ / ustedes / interesar / conocer / otros países / ? (¿A ustedes les interesa conocer otros países?)**

6 Expansion Have volunteers share their sentences with the class. Encourage classmates to ask them follow-up questions. Ex: **¿Por qué se despierta temprano tu tía?**

7 Expansion To challenge students, have them work in small groups to create a riddle using grammar and/or vocabulary from this lesson. Have groups share their riddles with the class.

TEACHING OPTIONS

Game Play a game of **Diez Preguntas**. Ask a volunteer to think of a person in the class. Other students get one chance each to ask a question using indefinite and negative words. Ex: **¿Es alguien que siempre llega temprano a clase?**

Extra Practice Have students imagine they are a famous singer or actor. Then have them write eight sentences from the point of view of that person using verbs like **gustar** and indefinite and negative words. Ex: **Jennifer López: Me encanta la música pop pero me aburre la música clásica. Tampoco me interesa la música *country*....** Ask volunteers to share some of their sentences and see if the rest of the class agrees with their statements.

Audio: Reading
Additional Reading

Section Goals

In **Lectura**, students will:

- learn the strategy of predicting content from the title
- read an e-mail in Spanish

Instructional Resource
Supersite

Estrategia Tell students that they can often predict the content of a newspaper article from its headline. Display or make up several cognate-rich headlines from Spanish newspapers. Ex: **Decenas de miles recuerdan la explosión atómica en Hiroshima; Lanzamiento de musicahoy.net, sitio para profesionales y aficionados a la música; Científicos anuncian que Plutón ya no es planeta**. Ask students to predict the content of each article.

Examinar el texto Survey the class to find out the most common predictions. Were most of them about a positive or negative experience?

Compartir
Have pairs discuss how they are able to tell what the content will be by looking at the format of the text.

Cognados Discuss how scanning the text for cognates can help predict the content.

Lectura

NATIONAL STANDARDS communication cultures

Antes de leer

Estrategia
Predicting content from the title

Prediction is an invaluable strategy in reading for comprehension. For example, we can usually predict the content of a newspaper article from its headline. We often decide whether to read the article based on its headline. Predicting content from the title will help you increase your reading comprehension in Spanish.

Examinar el texto

Lee el título de la lectura y haz tres predicciones sobre el contenido. Escribe tus predicciones en una hoja de papel. Answers will vary.

Compartir

Comparte tus ideas con un(a) compañero/a de clase.

Cognados

Haz una lista de seis cognados que encuentres en la lectura. Answers will vary.

1. ______
2. ______
3. ______
4. ______
5. ______
6. ______

¿Qué te dicen los cognados sobre el tema de la lectura?

Practice more at **vhlcentral.com**.

Mensaje

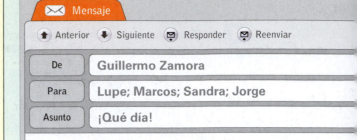

Anterior | Siguiente | Responder | Reenviar

De	Guillermo Zamora
Para	Lupe; Marcos; Sandra; Jorge
Asunto	¡Qué día!

Hola, chicos:

La semana pasada me di cuenta° de que necesito organizar mejor° mi rutina... pero especialmente debo prepararme mejor para los exámenes. Me falta disciplina, me molesta no tener control de mi tiempo y nunca deseo repetir los eventos de la semana pasada.

El miércoles pasé todo el día y toda la noche estudiando para el examen de biología del jueves por la mañana. Me aburre la biología y no empecé a estudiar hasta el día antes del examen. El jueves a las 8, después de no dormir en toda la noche, fui exhausto al examen. Fue difícil, pero afortunadamente° me acordé de todo el material. Esa noche me acosté temprano y dormí mucho.

Me desperté a las 7, y fue extraño° ver a mi compañero de cuarto, Andrés, preparándose para ir a dormir. Como° siempre se enferma°, tiene problemas para dormir y no hablamos mucho, no le comenté nada. Fui al baño a cepillarme los dientes para ir a clase. ¿Y Andrés? Él se acostó. "Debe estar enfermo°, ¡otra vez!", pensé.

TEACHING OPTIONS

Extra Practice Ask students to skim the selection and find sentences with verbs like **gustar**. Have them use the **le** and **les** pronouns to rewrite the sentences and talk about **Guillermo** and **Andrés**. Encourage students to say more about the characters by creating additional sentences of the **gustar** type.

Extra Practice Ask heritage speakers if they use e-mail regularly to keep in touch with friends and family in their families' countries of origin. Ask them if they have ever used Spanish-language versions of popular web-based e-mail applications. Then have the class log on to some Spanish-language versions of e-mail providers, such as Yahoo. Have them list cognates and loan words from English. Then ask students to compare pages from different countries (such as **ar.yahoo.com** and **pe.yahoo.com**) and note any differences in wording.

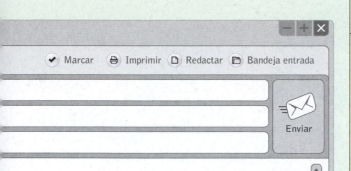

Marcar Imprimir Redactar Bandeja entrada

Enviar

Mi clase es a las 8, y fue necesario hacer las cosas rápido. Todo empezó a ir mal... eso pasa siempre cuando uno tiene prisa. Cuando busqué mis cosas para el baño, no las encontré. Entonces me duché sin jabón, me cepillé los dientes sin cepillo de dientes y me peiné con las manos. Tampoco encontré ropa limpia y usé la sucia. Rápido, tomé mis libros. ¿Y Andrés? Roncando°... ¡a las 7:50!

Cuando salí corriendo para la clase, la prisa no me permitió ver el campus desierto. Cuando llegué a la clase, no vi a nadie. No vi al profesor ni a los estudiantes. Por último miré mi reloj, y vi la hora. Las 8 en punto... ¡de la noche!

¡Dormí 24 horas!

Guillermo

me di cuenta *I realized* mejor *better* afortunadamente *fortunately* extraño *strange* Como *Since* se enferma *he gets sick* enfermo *sick* Roncando *Snoring*

Después de leer

Seleccionar

Selecciona la respuesta correcta.

1. ¿Quién es el/la narrador(a)? c
   a. Andrés
   b. una profesora
   c. Guillermo
2. ¿Qué le molesta al narrador? b
   a. Le molestan los exámenes de biología.
   b. Le molesta no tener control de su tiempo.
   c. Le molesta mucho organizar su rutina.
3. ¿Por qué está exhausto? c
   a. Porque fue a una fiesta la noche anterior.
   b. Porque no le gusta la biología.
   c. Porque pasó la noche anterior estudiando.
4. ¿Por qué no hay nadie en clase? a
   a. Porque es de noche.
   b. Porque todos están de vacaciones.
   c. Porque el profesor canceló la clase.
5. ¿Cómo es la relación de Guillermo y Andrés? b
   a. Son buenos amigos.
   b. No hablan mucho.
   c. Tienen una buena relación.

Ordenar

Ordena los sucesos de la narración. Utiliza los números del 1 al 9.

a. Toma el examen de biología. 2
b. No encuentra sus cosas para el baño. 5
c. Andrés se duerme. 7
d. Pasa todo el día y toda la noche estudiando para un examen. 1
e. Se ducha sin jabón. 6
f. Se acuesta temprano. 3
g. Vuelve a su cuarto después de las 8 de la noche. 9
h. Se despierta a las 7 y su compañero de cuarto se prepara para dormir. 4
i. Va a clase y no hay nadie. 8

Contestar

Contesta estas preguntas. Answers will vary.

1. ¿Cómo es tu rutina diaria? ¿Muy organizada?
2. ¿Cuándo empiezas a estudiar para los exámenes?
3. ¿Tienes compañero/a de cuarto? ¿Es tu amigo/a?
4. Para comunicarte con tus amigos/as, ¿prefieres el teléfono o el correo electrónico? ¿Por qué?

Seleccionar Before beginning the activity, have students summarize the reading selection by listing all the verbs in the preterite. Then, have them use these verbs to talk about **Guillermo's** day.

Ordenar

- Before beginning, ask a volunteer to summarize in Spanish, using the third-person present tense, the first two sentences of the reading selection.
- As writing practice, have students use the sentence in each item as the topic sentence of a short paragraph about **Guillermo** or **Andrés**.

Contestar

Have students work in small groups to tell each other about a day when everything turned out wrong due to a miscalculation. Have groups vote for the most unusual story to share with the class.

TEACHING OPTIONS

Pairs Add a visual aspect to this reading. Have pairs reconstruct **Guillermo's** confusing day graphically by means of one or more time lines (or other graphic representation). They should compare what **Guillermo** assumed was going on with what was actually occurring.

Pairs Have pairs of students work together to read the selection and write two questions about each paragraph. When they have finished, have them exchange papers with another pair, who can work together to answer the questions.

Video: *Panorama cultural*
Interactive map

Section Goal
In **Panorama**, students will read about the geography, culture, and history of Peru.

Instructional Resources
Supersite: Video (***Panorama cultural***); Resources (Scripts, Translations, Digital Image Bank, Answer Keys)
WebSAM
Workbook, pp. 83–84
Video Manual, pp. 43–44

Teaching Tips
- Use the **Lección 7 Panorama** digital images to assist with this presentation.
- Have students look at the map of Peru and ask them to find the **Río Amazonas** and the **Cordillera de los Andes**, and to speculate about the types of climate found in Peru. As a mountainous country near the equator, climate varies according to elevation, and ranges from tropical to arctic. Point out that well over half of the territory of Peru lies within the Amazon Basin. Encourage students to share what they know about Peru.

El país en cifras After each section, pause to ask students questions about the content. Point out that Iquitos, Peru's port city on the Amazon River, is a destination for ships that travel 2,300 miles up the Amazon from the Atlantic Ocean.

¡Increíble pero cierto! In recent years, the **El Niño** weather phenomenon has caused flooding in the deserts of southern Peru. The Peruvian government is working to preserve the **Líneas de Nazca** from further deterioration in the hope that someday scientists will discover more about their origins and meaning.

Perú

NATIONAL STANDARDS connections cultures

El país en cifras

- **Área:** 1.285.220 km² (496.224 millas²), *un poco menos que el área de Alaska*
- **Población:** 30.147.000
- **Capital:** Lima —8.769.000
- **Ciudades principales:** Arequipa —778.000, Trujillo, Chiclayo, Callao, Iquitos

Iquitos es un puerto muy importante en el río Amazonas. Desde Iquitos se envían° muchos productos a otros lugares, incluyendo goma°, nueces°, madera°, arroz°, café y tabaco. Iquitos es también un destino popular para los ecoturistas que visitan la selva°.

- **Moneda:** nuevo sol
- **Idiomas:** español (oficial); quechua, aimara y otras lenguas indígenas (oficiales en los territorios donde se usan)

Bandera de Perú

Bailando marinera norteña en Trujillo

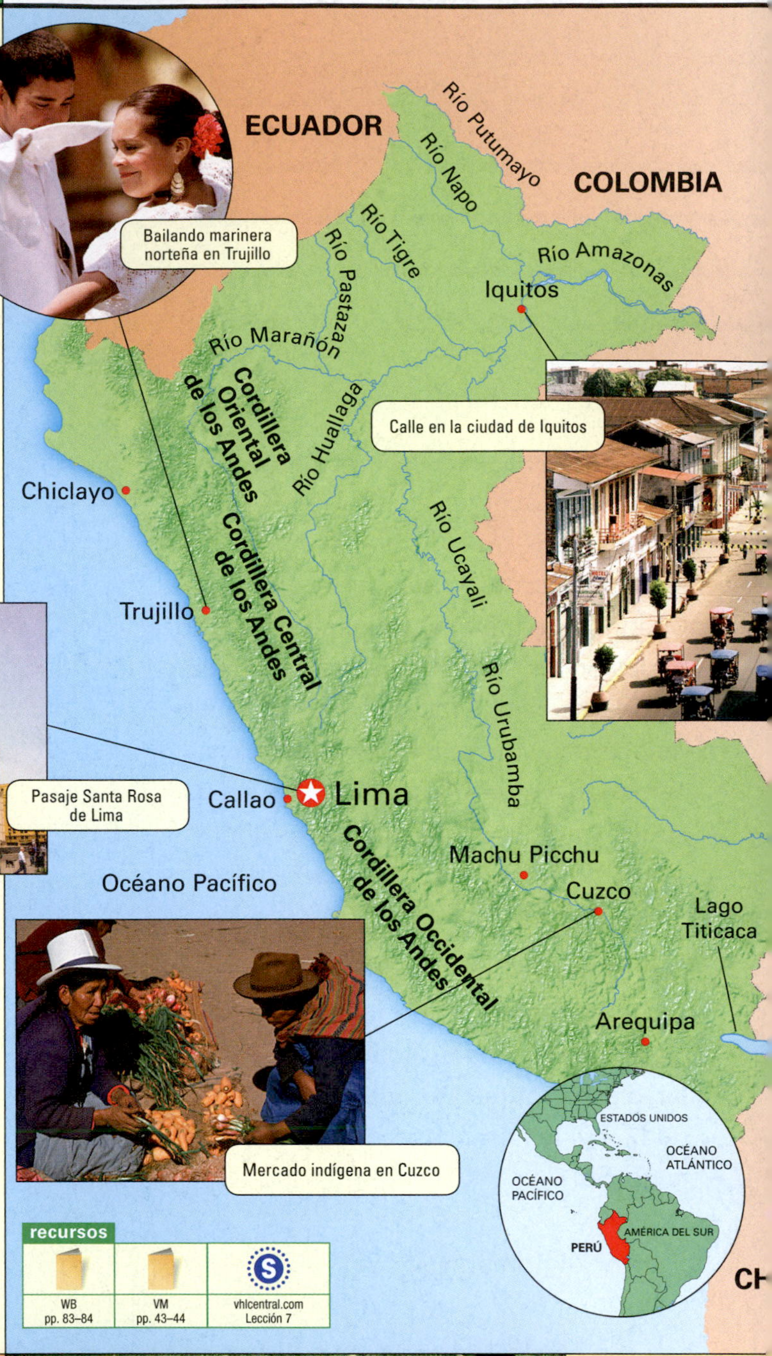

Calle en la ciudad de Iquitos

Pasaje Santa Rosa de Lima

Mercado indígena en Cuzco

Peruanos célebres
- **Clorinda Matto de Turner,** escritora (1854–1909)
- **César Vallejo,** poeta (1892–1938)
- **Javier Pérez de Cuéllar,** diplomático (1920–)
- **Juan Diego Flórez,** cantante de ópera (1973–)
- **Mario Vargas Llosa,** escritor (1936–)

Mario Vargas Llosa, Premio Nobel de Literatura 2010

se envían *are shipped* goma *rubber* nueces *nuts* madera *timber* arroz *rice* selva *jungle* Hace más de *More than... ago* grabó *engraved* tamaño *size*

recursos
WB pp. 83–84 | VM pp. 43–44 | vhlcentral.com Lección 7

¡Increíble pero cierto!

Hace más de° dos mil años la civilización nazca de Perú grabó° más de dos mil kilómetros de líneas en el desierto. Los dibujos sólo son descifrables desde el aire. Uno de ellos es un cóndor del tamaño° de un estadio. Las Líneas de Nazca son uno de los grandes misterios de la humanidad.

TEACHING OPTIONS

Heritage Speakers Ask heritage speakers of Peruvian origin or students who have visited Peru to make a short presentation to the class about their impressions. Encourage them to speak of the region they are from or have visited and how it differs from other regions in this vast country. If they have photographs, ask them to bring them to class to illustrate their talk.

TPR Invite students to take turns guiding the class on tours of Peru's waterways: one student gives directions, and the others follow by tracing the route on their map of Peru. For example: **Comenzamos en el río Amazonas, pasando por Iquitos hasta llegar al río Ucayali....**

Lugares • Lima

Lima es una ciudad moderna y antigua° a la vez°. La Iglesia de San Francisco es notable por su arquitectura barroca colonial. También son fascinantes las exhibiciones sobre los incas en el Museo Oro del Perú y en el Museo Nacional de Antropología y Arqueología. Barranco, el barrio° bohemio de la ciudad, es famoso por su ambiente cultural y sus bares y restaurantes.

BRASIL

Historia • Machu Picchu

A 80 kilómetros al noroeste de Cuzco está Machu Picchu, una ciudad antigua del Imperio inca. Está a una altitud de 2.350 metros (7.710 pies), entre dos cimas° de los Andes. Cuando los españoles llegaron a Perú y recorrieron la región, nunca encontraron Machu Picchu. En 1911, el arqueólogo estadounidense Hiram Bingham la redescubrió. Todavía no se sabe ni cómo se construyó° una ciudad a esa altura, ni por qué los incas la abandonaron. Sin embargo°, esta ciudad situada en desniveles° naturales es el ejemplo más conocido de la arquitectura inca.

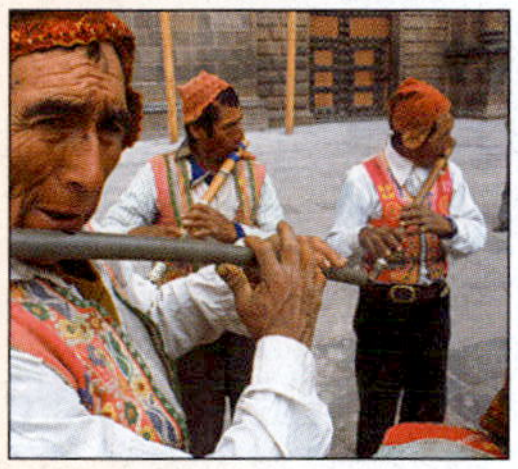

Artes • La música andina

Machu Picchu aún no existía° cuando se originó la música cautivadora° de las culturas indígenas de los Andes. Los ritmos actuales de la música andina tienen influencias españolas y africanas. Varios tipos de flauta°, entre ellos la quena y la zampoña, caracterizan esta música. En las décadas de los sesenta y los setenta se popularizó un movimiento para preservar la música andina, y hasta° Simon y Garfunkel incorporaron a su repertorio la canción *El cóndor pasa*.

Economía • Llamas y alpacas

Perú se conoce por sus llamas, alpacas, guanacos y vicuñas, todos ellos animales mamíferos° parientes del camello. Estos animales todavía tienen una enorme importancia en la economía del país. Dan lana para exportar a otros países y para hacer ropa, mantas°, bolsas y otros artículos artesanales. La llama se usa también para la carga y el transporte.

BOLIVIA

¿Qué aprendiste? Responde a las preguntas con una oración completa.

1. ¿Qué productos envía Iquitos a otros lugares? Iquitos envía goma, nueces, madera, arroz, café y tabaco a otros lugares.
2. ¿Cuáles son las lenguas oficiales de Perú? Las lenguas oficiales de Perú son el español, el quechua, el aimara y otras lenguas indígenas.
3. ¿Por qué es notable la Iglesia de San Francisco en Lima? Es notable por su arquitectura barroca colonial.
4. ¿Qué información sobre Machu Picchu no se sabe todavía? No se sabe ni cómo se construyó ni por qué la abandonaron.
5. ¿Qué son la quena y la zampoña? Son tipos de flauta.
6. ¿Qué hacen los peruanos con la lana de sus llamas y alpacas? La exportan a otros países y hacen ropa, mantas, bolsas y otros artículos artesanales.

Conexión Internet Investiga estos temas en **vhlcentral.com**.

1. Investiga la cultura incaica. ¿Cuáles son algunos de los aspectos interesantes de su cultura?
2. Busca información sobre dos artistas, escritores o músicos peruanos y presenta un breve informe a tu clase.

Practice more at **vhlcentral.com**.

antigua *old* a la vez *at the same time* barrio *neighborhood* cimas *summits* se construyó *was built* Sin embargo *However* desniveles *uneven pieces of land* aún no existía *didn't exist yet* cautivadora *captivating* flauta *flute* hasta *even* mamíferos *mammalian* mantas *blankets*

Lima Lima, rich in colonial architecture, is also home to the **Universidad de San Marcos,** which was established in 1551 and is the oldest university in South America.

Machu Picchu Another invention of the Incas was the **quipus**, clusters of knotted strings that were a means of keeping records and sending messages. A **quipu** consisted of a series of small, knotted cords attached to a larger cord. Each cord's color, place, size, and the knots it contained all had significance.

La música andina Ancient tombs belonging to pre-Columbian cultures like the **Nazca** and **Moche** have yielded instruments and other artifacts indicating that the precursors of Andean music go back at least two millennia.

Llamas y alpacas Of the camel-like animals of the Andes, only the sturdy **llama** has been domesticated as a pack animal. Its long, thick coat also provides fiber that is woven into a coarser grade of cloth. The more delicate **alpaca** and **vicuña** are raised only for their beautiful coats, which are used to create extremely high-quality cloth. The **guanaco** has never been domesticated.

Conexión Internet Students will find supporting Internet activities and links at **vhlcentral.com**.

Teaching Tip You may want to wrap up this section by playing the ***Panorama cultural*** video footage for this lesson.

TEACHING OPTIONS

Variación léxica Some of the most familiar words to have entered Spanish from the Quechua language are the names of animals native to the Andean region, such as **el cóndor, la llama, el puma,** and **la vicuña**. These words later passed from Spanish to a number of European languages, including English. **La alpaca** comes not from Quechua (the language of the Incas and their descendants, who inhabit most of the Andean region), but from Aymara, the language of indigenous people who live near Lake Titicaca on the Peruvian-Bolivian border. Some students may be familiar with the traditional Quechua tune, ***El cóndor pasa***, which was popularized in a version by Simon and Garfunkel.

Instructional Resources
Supersite: Audio (Textbook & Lab MP3s); Testing Program (Tests, MP3s)
WebSAM
Lab Manual, p. 42

Los verbos reflexivos

acordarse (de) (o:ue)	*to remember*
acostarse (o:ue)	*to go to bed*
afeitarse	*to shave*
bañarse	*to take a bath*
cepillarse el pelo	*to brush one's hair*
cepillarse los dientes	*to brush one's teeth*
despertarse (e:ie)	*to wake up*
dormirse (o:ue)	*to go to sleep; to fall asleep*
ducharse	*to take a shower*
enojarse (con)	*to get angry (with)*
irse	*to go away; to leave*
lavarse la cara	*to wash one's face*
lavarse las manos	*to wash one's hands*
levantarse	*to get up*
llamarse	*to be called; to be named*
maquillarse	*to put on makeup*
peinarse	*to comb one's hair*
ponerse	*to put on*
ponerse (+ *adj.*)	*to become (+ adj.)*
preocuparse (por)	*to worry (about)*
probarse (o:ue)	*to try on*
quedarse	*to stay*
quitarse	*to take off*
secarse	*to dry (oneself)*
sentarse (e:ie)	*to sit down*
sentirse (e:ie)	*to feel*
vestirse (e:i)	*to get dressed*

Palabras de secuencia

antes (de)	*before*
después	*afterwards; then*
después (de)	*after*
durante	*during*
entonces	*then*
luego	*then*
más tarde	*later (on)*
por último	*finally*

Palabras indefinidas y negativas

algo	*something; anything*
alguien	*someone; somebody; anyone*
alguno/a(s), algún	*some; any*
jamás	*never; not ever*
nada	*nothing; not anything*
nadie	*no one; nobody; not anyone*
ni... ni	*neither... nor*
ninguno/a, ningún	*no; none; not any*
nunca	*never; not ever*
o... o	*either... or*
siempre	*always*
también	*also; too*
tampoco	*neither; not either*

En el baño

el baño, el cuarto de baño	*bathroom*
el champú	*shampoo*
la crema de afeitar	*shaving cream*
la ducha	*shower*
el espejo	*mirror*
el inodoro	*toilet*
el jabón	*soap*
el lavabo	*sink*
el maquillaje	*makeup*
la pasta de dientes	*toothpaste*
la toalla	*towel*

Verbos similares a *gustar*

aburrir	*to bore*
encantar	*to like very much; to love (inanimate objects)*
faltar	*to lack; to need*
fascinar	*to fascinate; to like very much*
importar	*to be important to; to matter*
interesar	*to be interesting to; to interest*
molestar	*to bother; to annoy*
quedar	*to be left over; to fit (clothing)*

Palabras adicionales

el despertador	*alarm clock*
las pantuflas	*slippers*
la rutina diaria	*daily routine*
por la mañana	*in the morning*
por la noche	*at night*
por la tarde	*in the afternoon; in the evening*

Expresiones útiles	*See page 215.*

recursos
LM p. 42
vhlcentral.com Lección 7

Vocabulary Tools

La comida

8

Communicative Goals

You will learn how to:

- **Order food in a restaurant**
- **Talk about and describe food**

A PRIMERA VISTA

- **¿Dónde está ella?**
- **¿Qué hace?**
- **¿Es parte de su rutina diaria?**
- **¿Qué colores hay en la foto?**

Lesson Goals

In **Lección 8**, students will be introduced to the following:
- food terms
- meal-related words
- fruits and vegetables native to the Americas
- Spanish chef **Ferran Adrià**
- preterite of stem-changing verbs
- double object pronouns
- converting **le** and **les** to **se** with double object pronouns
- comparisons
- superlatives
- reading for the main idea
- a video about Latin food in the U.S.
- cultural, geographic, and historical information about Guatemala

A primera vista Here are some additional questions you can ask to personalize the photo: **¿Dónde te encanta comer? ¿Por qué? ¿Fuiste a algún lugar especial para comer la semana pasada? ¿Compras comida? ¿Dónde? ¿Prefieres cocinar o comer en un restaurante?**

Teaching Tip Look for these icons for additional communicative practice:

→•←	Interpretive communication
←•→	Presentational communication
•↔•	Interpersonal communication

INSTRUCTIONAL RESOURCES

Supersite (vhlcentral.com)
Video: ***Fotonovela, Flash cultura, Panorama cultural***
Audio: Textbook and Lab MP3 Files
Activity Pack: Information Gap Activities, games, additional activity handouts
Resources: SAM Answer Key, Scripts, Translations, **Vocabulario adicional**, sample lesson plan, Grammar Presentation Slides, Digital Image Bank
Testing Program: Quizzes, Tests, Exams, MP3s
Student Activities Manual: Workbook/Video Manual/Lab Manual
WebSAM (online Student Activities Manual)

Vocabulary Tools

Section Goals

In **Contextos**, students will learn and practice:
- food names
- meal-related vocabulary

Instructional Resources
Supersite: Audio (Textbook and Lab MP3 Files); Resources (Digital Image Bank, **Vocabulario adicional**, Activity Pack, Scripts, Answer Keys); Testing Program (Quizzes)
WebSAM
Workbook, pp. 85–86
Lab Manual, p. 43

Teaching Tips

- Tell what you are going to have for lunch, writing food vocabulary on the board. Ex: **Tengo hambre y voy a preparar una hamburguesa. ¿Qué ingredientes necesito? Pues, carne de res, queso, tomates, lechuga y mayonesa. También voy a preparar una ensalada. ¿Con qué ingredientes preparo la ensalada? A ver, lechuga, tomates, zanahorias...**
- Use the **Lección 8 Contextos** digital images to assist with this presentation.
- Have students look at the illustrations in **Contextos** and ask these questions: **¿Sí o no? ¿Hay bananas en el mercado? (Sí.) ¿Qué otras frutas hay? (Hay peras, uvas, naranjas y limones.) Y ¿hay cerveza? (No.)** Then mention typical dishes and ask students to tell what ingredients are used to make them. Ex: **una ensalada mixta, una ensalada de fruta, un sándwich**
- Ask students what some of their favorite foods are. Ex: **Y a ti, ____, ¿qué te gusta comer?**

La comida

Más vocabulario

el/la camarero/a	*waiter/waitress*
la comida	*food; meal*
la cuenta	*bill*
el/la dueño/a	*owner*
los entremeses	*appetizers*
el menú	*menu*
el plato (principal)	*(main) dish*
la propina	*tip*
la sección de (no) fumar	*(non) smoking section*
el agua (mineral)	*(mineral) water*
la bebida	*drink*
la cerveza	*beer*
la leche	*milk*
el refresco	*soft drink*
el ajo	*garlic*
las arvejas	*peas*
los cereales	*cereal; grains*
los frijoles	*beans*
el melocotón	*peach*
el pollo (asado)	*(roast) chicken*
el queso	*cheese*
el sándwich	*sandwich*
el yogur	*yogurt*
el aceite	*oil*
la margarina	*margarine*
la mayonesa	*mayonnaise*
el vinagre	*vinegar*
delicioso/a	*delicious*
sabroso/a	*tasty; delicious*
saber (a)	*to taste (like)*

Variación léxica

camarones ⟷ gambas (*Esp.*)
camarero ⟷ mesero (*Amér. L.*), mesonero (*Ven.*), mozo (*Arg., Chile, Urug., Perú*)
refresco ⟷ gaseosa (*Amér. C., Amér. S.*)

recursos
WB pp. 85–86
LM p. 43
vhlcentral.com Lección 8

TEACHING OPTIONS

Extra Practice To review vocabulary for colors, ask students what colors these food items are: **las bananas (amarillas), las uvas (verdes o moradas), las zanahorias (anaranjadas), los tomates (rojos, verdes o amarillos), los frijoles (blancos, marrones, verdes, rojos o negros), la lechuga (verde), las cebollas (blancas o moradas).**

Heritage Speakers Point out that food vocabulary varies according to region in the Spanish-speaking world. Ask heritage speakers to share food-related terms with which they are familiar and where the terms are used. Possible responses: **el guisante (Esp.), el chícaro (Méx.), el banano (Col.), el cambur (Ven.), el choclo (Chile, Perú), el elote (Méx.), la patata (Esp.)**

¡LENGUA VIVA!

You learned the verb **saber** in **Lección 6.** This verb is also used to describe food.

Use **saber** + [*adjective*] to explain how something *tastes.*

Ex: **Este plato sabe dulce/rico/amargo.**

(*This dish tastes sweet/delicious/bitter.*)

Use **saber** + **a** to say what something *tastes like.*

Ex: **Sabe a ajo.**

(*It tastes like garlic.*)

Estas langostas no saben a nada.

(*These lobsters don't taste like anything./ These lobsters don't have any flavor.*)

Práctica

1 **Escuchar** Indica si las oraciones que vas a escuchar son **ciertas** o **falsas**, según el dibujo. Después, corrige las falsas.

1. Cierta
2. Falsa. El hombre compra una naranja.
3. Cierta
4. Falsa. El pollo es una carne y la zanahoria es una verdura.
5. Cierta
6. Falsa. El hombre y la mujer no compran vinagre.
7. Falsa. La naranja es una fruta.
8. Falsa. La chuleta de cerdo es una carne.
9. Falsa. El limón es una fruta y el jamón es una carne.
10. Cierta

2 **Seleccionar** Paulino y Pilar van a cenar a un restaurante. Escucha la conversación y selecciona la respuesta que mejor completa cada oración.

1. Paulino le pide el __menú__ (menú / plato) al camarero.
2. El plato del día es (atún / salmón) __atún__.
3. Pilar ordena __agua mineral__ (leche / agua mineral) para beber.
4. Paulino quiere un refresco de __naranja__ (naranja / limón).
5. Paulino hoy prefiere __la chuleta__ (el salmón / la chuleta).
6. Dicen que la carne en ese restaurante es muy __sabrosa__ (sabrosa / mala).
7. Pilar come salmón con __zanahorias__ (zanahorias / champiñones).

3 **Identificar** Identifica la palabra que no está relacionada con cada grupo.

1. champiñón • cebolla • propina • zanahoria propina
2. camarones • ajo • atún • salmón ajo
3. aceite • leche • refresco • agua mineral aceite
4. jamón • chuleta de cerdo • vinagre • carne de res vinagre
5. cerveza • lechuga • arvejas • frijoles cerveza
6. carne • pescado • mariscos • camarero camarero
7. pollo • naranja • limón • melocotón pollo
8. maíz • queso • tomate • champiñón queso

4 **Completar** Completa las oraciones con las palabras más lógicas.

1. ¡Me gusta mucho este plato! Sabe __b__.
   a. mal b. delicioso c. antipático
2. Camarero, ¿puedo ver el __c__, por favor?
   a. aceite b. maíz c. menú
3. Carlos y yo bebemos siempre agua __b__.
   a. cómoda b. mineral c. principal
4. El plato del día es __a__.
   a. pollo asado b. mayonesa c. ajo
5. Margarita es vegetariana. Ella come __a__.
   a. frijoles b. chuletas c. jamón
6. Mi hermana le da __c__ a su niña.
   a. ajo b. vinagre c. yogur

TEACHING OPTIONS

Game Add a visual aspect to this vocabulary practice by playing **Concentración.** On eight cards, write names of food items. On another eight cards, draw or paste a picture that matches each food item. Place the cards face-down in four rows of four. In pairs, students select two cards. If the two cards match, the pair keeps them. If the two cards do not match, students replace them in their original positions. The pair with the most cards at the end wins.

Game Play a modified version of **20 Preguntas**. Ask a volunteer to think of a food item from the drawing or vocabulary list. Other students get one chance each to ask a yes/no question until someone guesses the item correctly. Limit attempts to ten questions per item. You may want to write some phrases on the board to cue students' questions. Ex: **¿Es una fruta? ¿Es roja?**

1 Expansion Have students write three additional true/false statements for a partner to answer.

1 Script 1. La langosta está cerca de los camarones. 2. El hombre compra una pera. 3. La lechuga es una verdura. 4. El pollo y la zanahoria son carnes. 5. La cebolla está cerca del maíz. 6. El hombre y la mujer compran vinagre. 7. La naranja es una verdura. 8. La chuleta de cerdo es pescado. 9. El limón y el jamón son frutas. 10. El pavo está cerca del pollo. *Textbook MP3s*

2 Teaching Tip To challenge students, write the cloze sentences on the board without the choices in parentheses. Have students copy them and complete them as they listen.

2 Script PAULINO: Camarero, ¿puedo ver el menú, por favor? CAMARERO: Sí, señor. Hoy el plato del día es atún con champiñones. ¿Qué les traigo de beber? PILAR: Yo voy a beber agua mineral. PA: Para mí, un refresco de naranja, por favor. C: ¿Quieren unos entremeses? El queso es muy sabroso. PA: Sí, queremos el queso. PI: Mira, Paulino, tienen el salmón en salsa de tomate que te gusta. PA: Sí, pero hoy prefiero la chuleta de cerdo. Dicen que la carne en este restaurante sabe deliciosa. PI: Muy bien, entonces yo voy a comer el salmón en salsa de tomate y zanahorias. *Textbook MP3s*

3 Expansion Have students indicate why a particular item does not belong. Ex: **El champiñón, la cebolla y la zanahoria son verduras. La propina no es una verdura.**

4 Expansion Give additional statements. Ex: **Un vegetariano no come ____. (carne)**

el desayuno

el almuerzo

la cena

Más vocabulario

escoger	*to choose*
merendar (e:ie)	*to snack*
probar (o:ue)	*to taste; to try*
recomendar (e:ie)	*to recommend*
servir (e:i)	*to serve*
el té	*tea*
el vino blanco	*white wine*

NOTA CULTURAL

En Guatemala, un desayuno típico incluye huevos, frijoles, fruta, tortillas, jugo y café.

Otros desayunos populares son:

madalenas (*muffins*) España

pan dulce (*assorted breads/pastries*) México

champurradas (*sugar cookies*) Guatemala

gallo pinto (*fried rice and beans*) Costa Rica

perico (*scrambled eggs with peppers and onions*) Venezuela

Teaching Tips

- Involve the class in a conversation about meals. Say: **Por lo general, desayuno sólo café con leche y pan tostado, pero cuando tengo mucha hambre desayuno dos huevos y una salchicha también. ____, ¿qué desayunas tú?** Ask follow-up questions to continue the discussion.
- Use the **Lección 8 Contextos** digital images to assist with this vocabulary presentation.
- Have students look at the illustrations on this page and say: **Mira el desayuno aquí. ¿Qué desayuna esta persona?** Then continue to **el almuerzo** and **la cena.** Have students identify the food items and talk about their eating habits, including what, when, and where they eat. Say: **Yo siempre desayuno en casa, pero casi nunca almuerzo en casa. ¿A qué hora almuerzan ustedes por lo general?**
- Ask students to tell you their favorite foods to eat for each of the three meals. Ex: ____, **¿qué te gusta desayunar?** Introduce additional items such as **los espaguetis, la pasta, la pizza.**

Nota cultural Point out that in Spanish-speaking countries, **el almuerzo**, also called **la comida**, usually is the main meal of the day, consists of several courses, and is enjoyed at a leisurely pace. **La cena** is typically much lighter than **el almuerzo**.

Note: At this point you may want to present ***Vocabulario adicional: Más vocabulario relacionado con la comida*** from the Supersite.

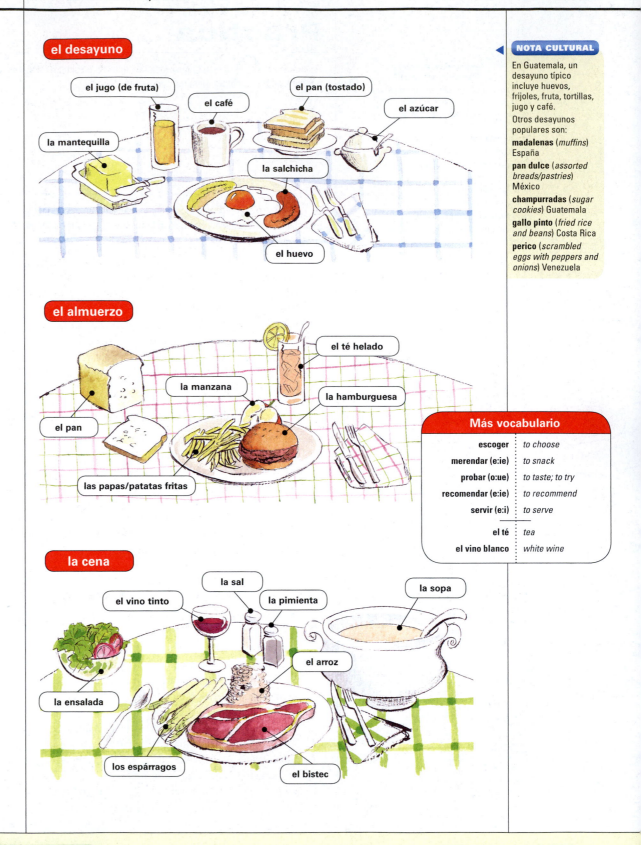

TEACHING OPTIONS

Small Groups In small groups, have students create a menu for a special occasion. Ask them to describe what they are going to serve for **el entremés, el plato principal**, and **bebidas**. Write **el postre** on the board and explain that it means *dessert*. Explain that in Spanish-speaking countries fresh fruit and cheese are common as dessert, but you may also want to introduce the words **el pastel** (*pie, cake*) and **el helado** (*ice cream*). Have groups present their menus to the class.

Extra Practice Add an auditory aspect to this vocabulary presentation. Prepare descriptions of five to seven different meals, with a mix of breakfasts, lunches, and dinners. As you read each description aloud, have students write down what you say as a dictation and then guess the meal it describes.

5 **Completar** Trabaja con un(a) compañero/a de clase para relacionar cada producto con el grupo alimenticio (*food group*) correcto.

modelo

La carne es del grupo uno.

el aceite	las bananas	los cereales	la leche
el arroz	el café	los espárragos	el pescado
el azúcar	la carne	los frijoles	el vino

1. La leche y el queso son del grupo cuatro.
2. Los frijoles son del grupo ocho.
3. El pescado y el pollo son del grupo tres.
4. El aceite es del grupo cinco.
5. El azúcar es del grupo dos.
6. Las manzanas y las bananas son del grupo siete.
7. El café es del grupo seis.
8. Los cereales son del grupo diez.
9. Los espárragos y los tomates son del grupo nueve.
10. El pan y el arroz son del grupo diez.

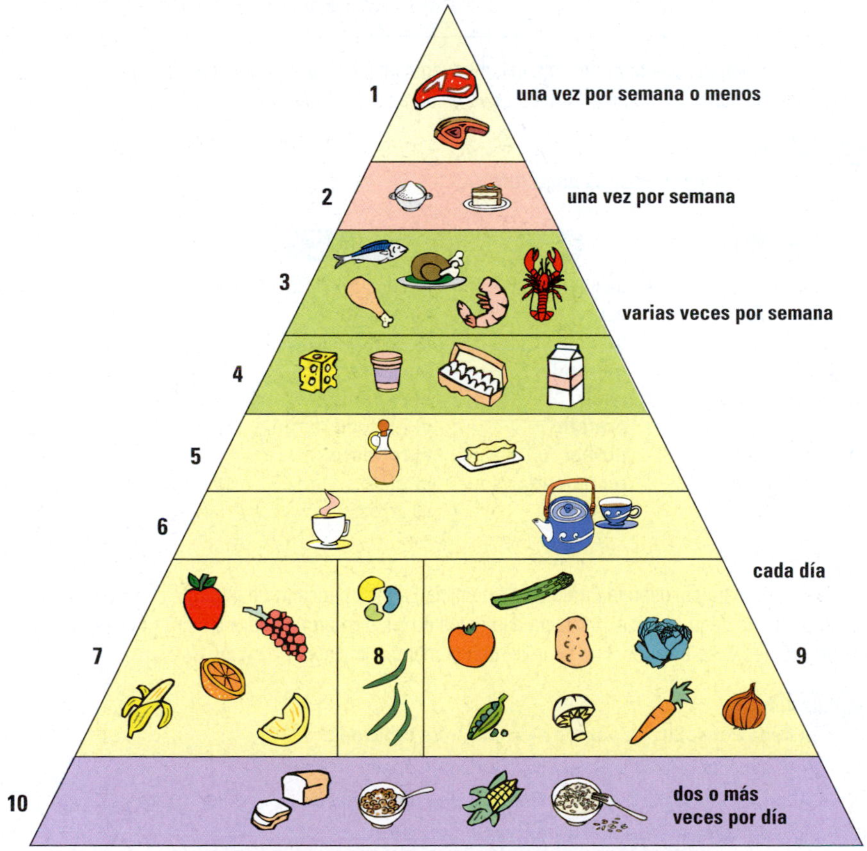

La Pirámide Alimenticia Latinoamericana

5 Teaching Tip Ask students to compare foods at the base of the pyramid with those at the top. (The foods at the bottom of the pyramid are essential dietary requirements. Closer to the top, the food items become less essential to daily requirements but help to balance out a diet.)

5 Expansion

- Ask additional questions about the **pirámide alimenticia.** Ask: **¿Qué se debe comer varias veces por semana? ¿Qué se debe comer todos los días? ¿Cuáles son los productos que aparecen en el grupo cuatro? ¿Y en el grupo siete?** Get students to have a discussion about what they eat. **¿Comen ustedes carne sólo una vez a la semana o menos? ¿Qué comidas comen ustedes dos veces o más al día? ¿Toman café todos los días?**
- Ask students if they know which food groups and food products are represented in the MyPlate system now used in the United States. Have pairs compare the dietary requirements of MyPlate and the Latin American food pyramid.

TEACHING OPTIONS

Heritage Speakers Ask heritage speakers to talk about food items or dishes unique to their families' countries of origin that are not typically found in this country. Have them describe what the item looks and tastes like. If the item is a dish, they should briefly describe how to prepare it if they know how to do so. Have the class ask follow-up questions to find out more information, such as when and where these items are eaten.

Extra Practice Have students draw food pyramids based not on what they should eat, but on what they actually do eat. Encourage them to include drawings or magazine cutouts to enhance the visual presentation. Then have students present their pyramids to the class.

6 Expansion Have students create three additional true/false statements for their partners to answer. Then ask volunteers to present their sentences for the rest of the class to answer.

6 **¿Cierto o falso?** Consulta la Pirámide Alimenticia Latinoamericana de la página 245 e indica si lo que dice cada oración es **cierto** o **falso**. Si la oración es falsa, escribe las comidas que sí están en el grupo indicado.

modelo
El queso está en el grupo diez.
Falso. En ese grupo están el maíz, el pan, los cereales y el arroz.

1. La manzana, la banana, el limón y las arvejas están en el grupo siete.
   Falso. En ese grupo están la manzana, las uvas, la banana, la naranja y el limón.
2. En el grupo cuatro están los huevos, la leche y el aceite.
   Falso. En ese grupo están los huevos, la leche, el queso y el yogur.
3. El azúcar está en el grupo dos.
   Cierto.
4. En el grupo diez están el pan, el arroz y el maíz.
   Cierto.
5. El pollo está en el grupo uno.
   Falso. En ese grupo están la carne de res/el bistec/el jamón y la chuleta de cerdo.
6. En el grupo nueve están la lechuga, el tomate, las arvejas, la naranja, la papa, los espárragos y la cebolla. Falso. En ese grupo están la lechuga, el tomate, las arvejas, la zanahoria, la papa, los espárragos, la cebolla y el champiñón.
7. El café y el té están en el mismo grupo.
   Cierto.
8. En el grupo cinco está el arroz.
   Falso. En ese grupo están el aceite y la mantequilla.
9. El pescado, el yogur y el bistec están en el grupo tres.
   Falso. En ese grupo están el pescado, el pollo, el pavo, los camarones y la langosta.

7 Expansion To simplify, ask individual students what people in the activity logically do. Point out that there are many possible answers to your questions. Ex: **¿Qué hace la camarera en el restaurante? ¿Qué hace el dueño?**

Nota cultural Ask students what they consider to be the staples of the North American diet. Ask them if there are any essential items in their personal diets they cannot live without.

7 **Combinar** Combina palabras de cada columna, en cualquier (*any*) orden, para formar diez oraciones lógicas sobre las comidas. Añade otras palabras si es necesario. Answers will vary.

modelo
La camarera nos sirve la ensalada.

A	B	C
el/la camarero/a	almorzar	la sección de no fumar
el/la dueño/a	escoger	el desayuno
mi familia	gustar	la ensalada
mi novio/a	merendar	las uvas
mis amigos y yo	pedir	el restaurante
mis padres	preferir	el jugo de naranja
mi hermano/a	probar	el refresco
el/la médico/a	recomendar	el plato
yo	servir	el arroz

NOTA CULTURAL
El arroz es un alimento básico en el Caribe, Centroamérica y México, entre otros países. Aparece frecuentemente como acompañamiento del plato principal y muchas veces se sirve con frijoles. Un plato muy popular en varios países es **el arroz con pollo** *(chicken and rice casserole)*.

8 Teaching Tip Emphasize that students must include at least one item from each group in the **pirámide alimenticia**.

8 Expansion Ask students why they chose their food items—because they are personal preferences, for their health benefits, or because they go well with other foods. Ex: **¿Por qué escogieron espárragos? ¿Les gustan mucho? ¿Son saludables? Van bien con el pescado, ¿verdad?**

8 **Un menú** En parejas, usen la Pirámide Alimenticia Latinoamericana de la página 245 para crear un menú para una cena especial. Incluyan alimentos de los diez grupos para los entremeses, los platos principales y las bebidas. Luego presenten el menú a la clase. Answers will vary.

modelo
La cena especial que vamos a preparar es deliciosa. Primero, hay dos entremeses: ensalada César y sopa de langosta. El plato principal es salmón con salsa de ajo y espárragos. También vamos a servir arroz...

Practice more at **vhlcentral.com**.

TEACHING OPTIONS

Extra Practice To review and practice the preterite along with food vocabulary, have students write a paragraph in which they describe what they ate yesterday. Students should also indicate whether this collection of meals represents a typical day for them. If not, they should explain why.

Small Groups In small groups, have students role-play a situation in a restaurant. Two students play the customers and the other plays the **camarero/a**. Write these sentences on the board as suggested phrases: **¿Están listos/as para pedir?, ¿Qué nos recomienda usted?, ¿Me trae ____, por favor?, ¿Y para empezar?, A sus órdenes, La especialidad de la casa.**

Comunicación

NATIONAL communication STANDARDS

9 **Conversación** En parejas, túrnense para hacerse estas preguntas. Answers will vary.

1. ¿Qué te gusta cenar?
2. ¿A qué hora, dónde y con quién almuerzas?
3. ¿Cuáles son las comidas más (*most*) típicas de tu almuerzo?
4. ¿Desayunas? ¿Qué comes y bebes por la mañana?
5. ¿Qué comida te gusta más? ¿Qué comida no conoces y quieres probar?
6. ¿Comes cada día alimentos de los diferentes grupos de la pirámide alimenticia? ¿Cuáles son las comidas y bebidas más frecuentes en tu dieta?
7. ¿Qué comida recomiendas a tus amigos? ¿Por qué?
8. ¿Eres vegetariano/a? ¿Crees que ser vegetariano/a es una buena idea? ¿Por qué?
9. ¿Te gusta cocinar (*to cook*)? ¿Qué comidas preparas para tus amigos? ¿Para tu familia?

10 **Describir** Con dos compañeros/as de clase, describe las dos fotos, contestando estas preguntas. Answers will vary.

- ¿Quiénes están en las fotos?
- ¿Dónde están?
- ¿Qué hora es?
- ¿Qué comen y qué beben?

11 **Crucigrama** Tu profesor(a) les va a dar a ti y a tu compañero/a un crucigrama (*crossword puzzle*) incompleto. Tú tienes las palabras que necesita tu compañero/a y él/ella tiene las palabras que tú necesitas. Tienen que darse pistas (*clues*) para completarlo. No pueden decir la palabra; deben utilizar definiciones, ejemplos y frases. Answers will vary.

modelo

6 vertical: Es un condimento que normalmente viene con la sal.
12 horizontal: Es una fruta amarilla.

9 Teaching Tip Ask the same questions of individual students. Ask other students to restate what their partners answered.

9 Expansion Have pairs join other pairs and share their answers to items 6 and 7. Then have them decide which student is the most adventurous eater of the group and report back to the class. You may wish to teach the phrase **el/la más aventurero/a del grupo,** thus previewing superlatives, which are presented in **Estructura 8.4.**

10 Expansion Add an additional visual aspect to this vocabulary practice. Using magazine pictures that show dining situations, have students describe what is going on: who the people are, what they are eating and drinking, and so forth.

11 Teaching Tip Divide the class into pairs and distribute the handouts from the Activity Pack (Activity Pack/ Supersite) that correspond to this Information Gap Activity. Give students ten minutes to complete this activity.

11 Expansion Have groups create another type of word puzzle, such as a word-find, to share with the class. It should contain additional food- and meal-related vocabulary.

TEACHING OPTIONS

Small Groups In small groups, ask students to prepare brief skits related to food. The skits may involve being in a market, in a restaurant, in a café, inviting people over for dinner, and so forth. Allow groups time to rehearse before performing their skits for the class, who will vote for the most creative one.

Game Play a game of continuous narration. One student begins with: **Voy a preparar** (*name of dish*) **y voy al mercado. Necesito comprar...** and names one food item. The next student then repeats the entire narration, adding another food item. Continue on with various students. When the possibilities for that particular dish are used up, have another student begin with another dish.

Section Goals

In **Fotonovela**, students will:

- receive comprehensible input from free-flowing discourse
- learn functional phrases that preview lesson grammatical structures

Instructional Resources
Supersite: Video (***Fotonovela***); Resources (Scripts, Translations, Answer Keys)
WebSAM
Video Manual, pp. 15–16

Video Recap: Lección 7
Before doing this **Fotonovela** section, review the previous episode with these questions: **1. ¿Adónde va a ir Marissa? (Va al cine.) 2. ¿Qué necesita hacer antes de salir? (Necesita arreglarse el pelo.) 3. ¿Qué está haciendo Felipe en el baño? (Está afeitándose.) 4. ¿Qué planes tiene Jimena? ¿Adónde decide ir al final? (Tiene que estudiar en la biblioteca. Decide ir al cine con Marissa.)**

Video Synopsis **Miguel** and **Maru** are at one of Mexico City's best restaurants enjoying a romantic dinner to celebrate their second anniversary. **Felipe** and **Juan Carlos** show up and, while **Juan Carlos** distracts the waiter, **Felipe** serves the couple their food, making a mess of the table. To set things right with the manager, they must pay for dinner and wash the dishes.

Teaching Tips

- Have the class predict the content of this episode based on its title and the video stills.
- Quickly review the predictions and ask the class a few questions to help them summarize this episode.

Una cena... romántica

Maru y Miguel quieren tener una cena romántica, pero les espera una sorpresa.

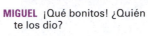

PERSONAJES

MARU

MIGUEL

Video: *Fotonovela*

MARU No sé qué pedir. ¿Qué me recomiendas?
MIGUEL No estoy seguro. Las chuletas de cerdo se ven muy buenas.
MARU ¿Vas a pedirlas?
MIGUEL No sé.

MIGUEL ¡Qué bonitos! ¿Quién te los dio?
MARU Me los compró un chico muy guapo e inteligente.
MIGUEL ¿Es tan guapo como yo?
MARU Sí, como tú, guapísimo.

(El camarero llega a la mesa.)
CAMARERO ¿Les gustaría saber nuestras especialidades del día?
MARU Sí, por favor.
CAMARERO Para el entremés, tenemos ceviche de camarón. De plato principal ofrecemos bistec con verduras a la plancha.

MARU Voy a probar el jamón.
CAMARERO Perfecto. ¿Y para usted, caballero?
MIGUEL Pollo asado con champiñones y papas, por favor.
CAMARERO Excelente.

MIGUEL Por nosotros.
MARU Dos años.

(en otra parte del restaurante)
JUAN CARLOS Disculpe. ¿Qué me puede contar del pollo? ¿Dónde lo consiguió el chef?
CAMARERO ¡Oiga! ¿Qué está haciendo?

TEACHING OPTIONS

Video Tips General suggestions for using video clips in the classroom can be found in the front matter of this Instructor's Annotated Edition.
Una cena... romántica Play the first half of the **Una cena... romántica** segment and have the class give you a description of what they see. Write their observations on the board, pointing out any inaccuracies. Repeat this process to allow the class to pick up more details of the plot. Then ask students to use the information they have accumulated to guess what happens in the rest of the segment. Write their predictions on the board. Then play the entire segment and, through discussion, help the class summarize the plot.

CAMARERO

JUAN CARLOS

FELIPE

GERENTE

7

FELIPE Los espárragos están sabrosísimos esta noche. Usted pidió el pollo, señor. Estos champiñones saben a mantequilla.

8

GERENTE ¿Qué pasa aquí, Esteban?

CAMARERO Lo siento, señor. Me quitaron la comida.

GERENTE (*a Felipe*) Señor, ¿quién es usted? ¿Qué cree que está haciendo?

9

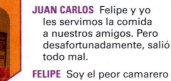

JUAN CARLOS Felipe y yo les servimos la comida a nuestros amigos. Pero desafortunadamente, salió todo mal.

FELIPE Soy el peor camarero del mundo. ¡Lo siento! Nosotros vamos a pagar la comida.

JUAN CARLOS ¿Nosotros?

10

FELIPE Todo esto fue idea tuya, Juan Carlos.

JUAN CARLOS ¿Mi idea? ¡Felipe! (*al gerente*) Señor, él es más responsable que yo.

GERENTE Tú y tú, vamos.

Expresiones útiles

Ordering food

¿Qué me recomiendas?
What do you recommend?
Las chuletas de cerdo se ven muy buenas.
The pork chops look good.
¿Les gustaría saber nuestras especialidades del día?
Would you like to hear our specials?
Para el entremés, tenemos ceviche de camarón.
For an appetizer, we have shrimp ceviche.
De plato principal ofrecemos bistec con verduras a la plancha.
For a main course, we have beef with grilled vegetables.
Voy a probar el jamón.
I am going to try the ham.

Describing people and things

¡Qué bonitos! ¿Quién te los dio?
How pretty! Who gave them to you?
Me los compró un chico muy guapo e inteligente.
A really handsome, intelligent guy bought them for me.
¿Es tan guapo como yo?
Is he as handsome as I am?
Sí, como tú, guapísimo.
Yes, like you, gorgeous.
Soy el peor camarero del mundo.
I am the worst waiter in the world.
Él es más responsable que yo.
He is more responsible than I am.

Additional vocabulary

el/la gerente *manager*
caballero *gentleman, sir*

recursos
VM pp. 15–16
vhlcentral.com Lección 8

Expresiones útiles Point out some of the unfamiliar structures, which will be taught in detail in **Estructura**. Have the class read the caption for video still 2, and draw attention to the double object pronouns **te los** and **Me los.** Explain that these are examples of indirect object pronouns and direct object pronouns used together. Then point out that **tan guapo como** is an example of a comparison of two things that are equal. Have the class read the caption for video still 10, and tell them that **más responsable que** is an example of a comparison of two unequal things. Then, for video still 9, point out **el peor camarero del mundo** and explain that this is an example of a superlative. Finally, draw attention to **guapísimo** in video still 2, and **sabrosísimos** in video still 7, and explain that these are absolute superlatives. Tell students that they will learn more about these concepts in **Estructura**.

Teaching Tips

- Have the class read through the entire **Fotonovela**, with volunteers playing the parts of **Miguel, Maru, Felipe, Juan Carlos,** the waiter, and the manager. Have students take turns playing the roles so more students participate.
- For video still 2, point out the question **¿Quién te los dio?** and explain that **dio** is the third-person preterite form of the verb **dar**. You may want to tell them that **dar** has the same preterite endings as **ver**. Students will learn the remaining preterite forms of **dar** in **Lección 9**.

Nota cultural The precise origins of **ceviche** are unknown, but each former Spanish colony has its own version of this dish, which consists of seafood marinated in citrus juices, usually lemon or lime, which "cook" the protein.

TEACHING OPTIONS

Pairs Have students work in pairs to create original mini-dialogues, using phrases from **Expresiones útiles** with other words and expressions they know. Ex: **—¿Qué tal el jamón? —Perdón, pero no sabe a nada. ¿Me puede recomendar otro plato? —Por supuesto. ¿Le gustaría un bistec con cebolla?**

Extra Practice Photocopy the **Fotonovela** Videoscript (Supersite) and white out words related to food, meals, and other key vocabulary in order to create a master for a cloze activity. Distribute the photocopies and have students fill in the target words as they watch the episode.

1 Teaching Tip To challenge students, give them these items as cloze sentences.

2 Teaching Tip Add an auditory aspect to this exercise. Have students close their books. Then read each item aloud and have the class identify the character.

2 Expansion Give the class these sentences as items 7–9: **7. ¡Qué ricos están los espárragos! (Felipe, Maru) 8. No sé qué pasó. Me quitaron la comida. (camarero) 9. Quiero saber dónde consigue el pollo el chef. ¿Me lo puede explicar? (Juan Carlos)**

3 Expansion In pairs, have students write a follow-up question for each item, and exchange papers with another pair. Ex: **1. ¿Cuánto tiempo llevan juntos? 2. ¿Cuál es el otro especial del día?**

4 Possible Conversations
Conversation 1:
E1: Oye, María, ¿conoces un buen restaurante en esta ciudad?
E2: Sí… el restaurante El Pescador sirve comida riquísima.
E1: ¿Por qué no vamos a El Pescador esta noche?
E2: ¿A qué hora?
E1: ¿A las ocho?
E2: Perfecto.
E1: Está bien. Nos vemos a las ocho.
E2: Adiós.
Conversation 2:
E1: ¿Qué le puedo traer?
E2: Bueno, ¿cuáles son los especiales del día?
E1: Hay ceviche de atún. También le recomiendo la langosta con arroz y verduras.
E2: Mmm… voy a pedir el ceviche y el bistec con verduras. De tomar, voy a pedir el jugo de piña.
E1: Gracias, señor.

¿Qué pasó?

1 Escoger Escoge la respuesta que completa mejor cada oración.

1. Miguel lleva a Maru a un restaurante para __c__.
   a. almorzar b. desayunar c. cenar
2. El camarero les ofrece __b__ como plato principal.
   a. ceviche de camarón b. bistec con verduras a la plancha
   c. pescado, arroz y ensalada
3. Miguel va a pedir __a__.
   a. pollo asado con champiñones y papas
   b. langosta al horno c. pescado con verduras a la mantequilla
4. Felipe les lleva la comida a sus amigos y prueba __c__.
   a. el jamón y los vinos b. el atún y la lechuga
   c. los espárragos y los champiñones

NOTA CULTURAL
El **ceviche** es un plato típico de varios países hispanos como México, Perú y Costa Rica. En México, se prepara con pescado o mariscos frescos, jugo de limón, jitomate, cebolla, chile y cilantro. Se puede comer como plato fuerte, pero también como entremés o botana (*snack*). Casi siempre se sirve con tostadas (*fried tortillas*) o galletas saladas (*crackers*).

2 Identificar Indica quién puede decir estas oraciones.

1. ¡Qué desastre! Soy un camarero muy malo. Felipe
2. Les recomiendo el bistec con verduras a la plancha. camarero
3. Tal vez escoja las chuletas de cerdo, creo que son muy sabrosas. Miguel
4. ¿Qué pasa aquí? gerente
5. Dígame las especialidades del día, por favor. Maru/Miguel
6. No fue mi idea. Felipe es más responsable que yo. Juan Carlos

3 Preguntas Contesta estas preguntas sobre la **Fotonovela**. Some answers may vary. Sample answers:

1. ¿Por qué fueron Maru y Miguel a un restaurante?
   Maru y Miguel fueron a un restaurante para tener una cena romántica.
2. ¿Qué entremés es una de las especialidades del día?
   El ceviche de camarón es el entremés del día.
3. ¿Qué pidió Maru?
   Maru pidió vino, sopa de frijoles y jamón con espárragos.
4. ¿Quiénes van a pagar la cuenta?
   Juan Carlos y Felipe van a pagar la cuenta.

4 En el restaurante Answers will vary.

1. Prepara con un(a) compañero/a una conversación en la que le preguntas si conoce algún buen restaurante en tu comunidad. Tu compañero/a responde que él/ella sí conoce un restaurante que sirve una comida deliciosa. Lo/La invitas a cenar y tu compañero/a acepta. Determinan la hora para verse en el restaurante.
2. Trabaja con un(a) compañero/a para representar los papeles de un(a) cliente/a y un(a) camarero/a en un restaurante. El/La camarero/a te pregunta qué te puede servir y tú preguntas cuál es la especialidad de la casa. El/La camarero/a te dice cuál es la especialidad y te recomienda algunos platos del menú. Tú pides entremeses, un plato principal y escoges una bebida. El/La camarero/a te sirve la comida y tú le das las gracias.

CONSULTA
To review indefinite words like **algún**, see **Estructura 7.2**, p. 224.

NATIONAL communication STANDARDS

Practice more at **vhlcentral.com**.

TEACHING OPTIONS

Extra Practice Ask students questions about the **Fotonovela** episode. Ex: **1. ¿Qué pidió de entremés Miguel? (Pidió ensalada de pera y queso.) 2. ¿Pidió Maru algún plato de pescado o mariscos? (No, pidió el jamón.) 3. ¿Se enoja Maru durante la cena? (No, no se enoja.) 4. ¿Es romántico Miguel? (Sí, es romántico.) 5. ¿Quién creen que es más responsable del problema en el restaurante, Juan Carlos o Felipe? (Answers will vary.)**

Large Groups Have students work in groups of five or six to prepare a skit in which a family goes to a restaurant, is seated by a server, reads and discusses the menu, and orders dinner. Each family member should ask a question about the menu and then order an entree and a drink. Encourage students to use humor and incorporate into the skit a mishap that threatens to ruin dinner. Ask one or two groups to perform the skit for the class.

NATIONAL STANDARDS comparisons

Pronunciación Audio

ll, ñ, c, and z

pollo **llave** **ella** **cebolla**

Most Spanish speakers pronounce **ll** like the *y* in *yes*.

mañana **señor** **baño** **niña**

The letter **ñ** is pronounced much like the *ny* in *canyon*.

café **colombiano** **cuando** **rico**

Before **a**, **o**, or **u**, the Spanish **c** is pronounced like the *c* in *car*.

cereales **delicioso** **conducir** **conocer**

Before **e** or **i**, the Spanish **c** is pronounced like the *s* in *sit*. (In parts of Spain, **c** before **e** or **i** is pronounced like the *th* in *think*.)

zeta **zanahoria** **almuerzo** **cerveza**

The Spanish **z** is pronounced like the *s* in *sit*. (In parts of Spain, **z** is pronounced like the *th* in *think*.)

Práctica Lee las palabras en voz alta.

1. mantequilla
2. cuñado
3. aceite
4. manzana
5. español
6. cepillo
7. zapato
8. azúcar
9. quince
10. compañera
11. almorzar
12. calle

Oraciones Lee las oraciones en voz alta.

1. Mi compañero de cuarto se llama Toño Núñez. Su familia es de la ciudad de Guatemala y de Quetzaltenango.
2. Dice que la comida de su mamá es deliciosa, especialmente su pollo al champiñón y sus tortillas de maíz.
3. Creo que Toño tiene razón porque hoy cené en su casa y quiero volver mañana para cenar allí otra vez.

Refranes Lee los refranes en voz alta.

Panza llena, corazón contento.2

Las apariencias engañan.1

1 Looks can be deceiving.
2 A full belly makes a happy heart.

recursos
LM p. 44 | vhlcentral.com Lección 8

Section Goal

In **Pronunciación**, students will be introduced to the pronunciation of the letter combination **ll** and the letters **ñ**, **c**, and **z**.

Instructional Resources
Supersite: Audio (Textbook and Lab MP3 Files); Resources (Scripts, Answer Keys)
WebSAM
Lab Manual, p. 44

Teaching Tips

- Point out that the Spanish letter combination **ll** is usually pronounced like the English *y* in *you*.
- Ask the class how the letter **ñ** is pronounced (like the *ny* in *canyon*).
- Tell the class that **c** is pronounced like the English *c* in *car* before **a**, **o**, or **u**.
- Ask the class how most Spanish speakers pronounce the letter **c** when it appears before **e** or **i** (like the English *s* in *sit*). Then point out that **c** before **e** or **i** is pronounced like the English *th* in *think* in some parts of Spain.
- Explain that the Spanish **z** is usually pronounced like the English *s* in *some*. Mention that in parts of Spain, **z** is pronounced like the English *th* in *think*.
- As you explain the pronunciation of these sounds, write a few of the example words on the board and have students pronounce them.

Práctica/Oraciones/Refranes These exercises are recorded on the *Textbook MP3s*. You may want to play the audio so that students practice listening to Spanish spoken by speakers other than yourself.

TEACHING OPTIONS

Extra Practice Write the names of a few distinguished Guatemalans on the board and ask for a volunteer to pronounce each one. Ex: **Luis Cardoza y Aragón** (writer), **Carlos Mérida** (painter), **Enrique Gómez Carrillo** (writer), **José Milla** (writer), **Alonso de la Paz** (sculptor). Repeat the process with a few city names: **Villanueva, Zacapa, Escuintla, Cobán.**

Pairs Have the class work in pairs to practice the pronunciation of the **Fotonovela** captions. Assign different episodes to different pairs. Encourage students to help their partner if he or she has trouble pronouncing a particular word. Circulate around the class and model correct pronunciation as needed, focusing on the letter combination **ll** and the letters **ñ**, **c**, and **z**.

Section Goals

In **Cultura**, students will:

- read about fruits and vegetables native to the Americas
- learn food-related terms
- read about Spanish chef **Ferran Adrià**
- read about typical dishes from Peru, Spain, and Colombia

Instructional Resources
Supersite: Video (***Flash cultura***); Resources (Scripts, Translations, Answer Keys)
WebSAM
Video Manual, pp. 87–88

En detalle

Antes de leer Ask students if they can name any fruits and vegetables that are native to the Americas.

Lectura

- The Aztec and Maya's beverage made of cacao, chile, and other spices was far thicker and more bitter than the hot chocolate most North Americans consume today.
- Point out that many words, such as **tomate, chocolate, aguacate, tamale,** and **mole,** come from Nahuatl, the language of the Aztecs. **Papa** comes from the Quechua word for *potato.* Explain that **salsa** is a general term for *sauce.*
- Explain that **tamales** are corn dough (usually filled with meat or cheese), which is wrapped in plant leaves or corn husks and steamed. **Arepas** are a type of thin corn cake, and **mole** is a Mexican sauce made of chile peppers, spices, and unsweetened chocolate.

Después de leer Ask students if they were surprised to learn that these foods were unknown to Europe and the rest of the world until about 500 years ago. Ask them to name dishes they would miss without these fruits and vegetables.

1 Expansion Ask students to write three additional true/false statements for a classmate to answer.

EN DETALLE

Video: *Flash cultura*

Frutas y verduras de América

Imagínate una pizza sin salsa° de tomate o una hamburguesa sin papas fritas. Ahora piensa que quieres ver una película, pero las palomitas de maíz° y el chocolate no existen. ¡Qué mundo° tan insípido°! Muchas de las comidas más populares del mundo tienen ingredientes esenciales que son originarios del continente llamado Nuevo Mundo. Estas frutas y verduras no fueron introducidas en Europa sino hasta° el siglo° XVI.

El tomate, por ejemplo, era° usado como planta ornamental cuando llegó por primera vez a Europa porque pensaron que era venenoso°. El maíz, por su parte, era ya la base de la comida de muchos países latinoamericanos muchos siglos antes de la llegada de los españoles.

La papa fue un alimento° básico para los incas. Incluso consiguieron deshidratarla para almacenarla° por largos períodos de tiempo. El cacao (planta con la que se hace el chocolate) fue muy importante para los aztecas y los mayas. Ellos usaban sus semillas° como moneda° y como ingrediente de diversas salsas. También las molían° para preparar una bebida, mezclándolas° con agua ¡y con chile!

El aguacate°, la guayaba°, la papaya, la piña y el maracuyá (o fruta de la pasión) son otros ejemplos de frutas originarias de América que son hoy día conocidas en todo el mundo.

Mole

¿En qué alimentos encontramos estas frutas y verduras?

Tomate: pizza, ketchup, salsa de tomate, sopa de tomate

Maíz: palomitas de maíz, tamales, tortillas, arepas (Colombia y Venezuela), pan

Papa: papas fritas, frituras de papa°, puré de papas°, sopa de papas, tortilla de patatas (España)

Cacao: mole (México), chocolatinas°, cereales, helados°, tartas°

Aguacate: guacamole (México), coctel de camarones, sopa de aguacate, nachos, enchiladas hondureñas

salsa *sauce* **palomitas de maíz** *popcorn* **mundo** *world* **insípido** *flavorless* **hasta** *until* **siglo** *century* **era** *was* **venenoso** *poisonous* **alimento** *food* **almacenarla** *to store it* **semillas** *seeds* **moneda** *currency* **las molían** *they used to grind them* **mezclándolas** *mixing them* **aguacate** *avocado* **guayaba** *guava* **frituras de papa** *chips* **puré de papas** *mashed potatoes* **chocolatinas** *chocolate bars* **helados** *ice cream* **tartas** *cakes*

ACTIVIDADES

1 ¿Cierto o falso? Indica si lo que dicen las oraciones es **cierto** o **falso**. Corrige la información falsa.

1. El tomate se introdujo a Europa como planta ornamental.
   Cierto.
2. Los incas sólo consiguieron almacenar las papas por poco tiempo.
   Falso. Los incas pudieron almacenar las papas por largo tiempo.
3. Los aztecas y los mayas usaron las papas como moneda. Falso.
   Los aztecas y los mayas usaron las semillas de cacao como moneda.
4. El maíz era una comida poco popular en Latinoamérica.
   Falso. El maíz era muy popular en Latinoamérica.
5. El aguacate era el alimento básico de los incas.
   Falso. El maíz era muy popular en Latinoamérica.
6. En México se hace una salsa con chocolate.
   Cierto.
7. El aguacate, la guayaba, la papaya, la piña y el maracuyá son originarios de América.
   Cierto.
8. Las arepas se hacen con cacao.
   Falso. Las arepas se hacen con maíz.
9. El aguacate es un ingrediente del cóctel de camarones.
   Cierto.
10. En España hacen una tortilla con papas.
    Cierto.

TEACHING OPTIONS

Game Have students make a *Bingo* card of fruits and vegetables mentioned in **Contextos** and on page 252, with one "free" square in the middle. Draw cards with different dishes and call them out. Have students cover the square on their card of the fruit or vegetable that is used in that dish. Ex: **tortilla de patatas** (Student covers **la papa**). The winner is the first student to fill a row (horizontally, vertically, or diagonally) and yell **¡*Bingo*!**

Extra Practice Tell students to imagine they are Europeans who traveled to the Americas 500 years ago and are tasting a fruit or vegetable for the first time. Have them write a letter to a friend or family member describing the look and taste of the fruit or vegetable. Encourage them to use verbs like **gustar** in the letter. You may want to brainstorm a list of possible adjectives on the board for students to use in their descriptions.

ASÍ SE DICE

La comida

el banano (Col.), el cambur (Ven.), el guineo (Nic.), el plátano (Amér. L., Esp.)	la banana
el choclo (Amér. S.), el elote (Méx.), el jojoto (Ven.), la mazorca (Esp.)	*corncob*
las caraotas (Ven.), los porotos (Amér. S.), las habichuelas (P. R.)	los frijoles
el durazno (Méx.)	el melocotón
el jitomate (Méx.)	el tomate

EL MUNDO HISPANO

Algunos platos típicos

- **Ceviche peruano:** Es un plato de pescado crudo° que se marina° en jugo de limón, con sal, pimienta, cebolla y ají°. Se sirve con lechuga, maíz, camote° y papa amarilla.
- **Gazpacho andaluz:** Es una sopa fría típica del sur de España. Se hace con verduras crudas y molidas°: tomate, ají, pepino° y ajo. También lleva pan, sal, aceite y vinagre.
- **Sancocho colombiano:** Es una sopa de pollo, pescado o carne con plátano, maíz, zanahoria, yuca, papas, cebolla, cilantro y ajo. Se sirve con arroz blanco.

crudo *raw* se marina *gets marinated* ají *pepper*
camote *sweet potato* molidas *mashed* pepino *cucumber*

PERFIL

Ferran Adrià: arte en la cocina°

¿Qué haces si un amigo te invita a comer croquetas líquidas o paella de *Kellogg's*? ¿Piensas que es una broma°? ¡Cuidado! Puedes estar perdiendo la oportunidad de probar los platos de uno de los chefs más innovadores del mundo°: **Ferran Adrià.**

Aire de zanahorias

Este artista de la cocina basa su éxito° en la creatividad y en la química. Adrià modifica combinaciones de ingredientes y juega con contrastes de gustos y sensaciones: frío-caliente, crudo-cocido°, dulce°-salado°... A partir de nuevas técnicas, altera la textura de los alimentos sin alterar su sabor°. Sus platos sorprendentes° y divertidos atraen a muchos nuevos chefs a su academia de cocina experimental. Quizás un día compraremos° en el supermercado té esférico°, carne líquida y espuma° de tomate.

cocina *kitchen* broma *joke* mundo *world* éxito *success* cocido *cooked*
dulce *sweet* salado *savory* sabor *taste* sorprendentes *surprising*
compraremos *we will buy* esférico *spheric* espuma *foam*

Conexión Internet

¿Qué platos comen los hispanos en los Estados Unidos?

Go to vhlcentral.com to find more cultural information related to this **Cultura** section.

ACTIVIDADES

2 Comprensión Empareja cada palabra con su definición.

1. fruta amarilla d
2. sopa típica de Colombia c
3. ingrediente del ceviche e
4. chef español d

a. gazpacho
b. Ferran Adrià
c. sancocho
d. guineo
e. pescado

3 ¿Qué plato especial hay en tu región? Escribe cuatro oraciones sobre un plato típico de tu región. Explica los ingredientes que contiene y cómo se sirve. Answers will vary.

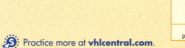

recursos
VM pp. 87–88
vhlcentral.com Lección 8

Practice more at **vhlcentral.com**.

TEACHING OPTIONS

Large Group Get students out of their seats. Give volunteers each a name of a fruit or vegetable (tell them to keep it secret) and have them stand at different points in the classroom. Then have the rest of the class circulate around the room and ask questions to guess what the volunteer represents. Ex: **¿Es fruta o verdura? ¿De qué color? ¿En qué platos se come?**

Game Play a *Jeopardy*-style game. Divide the class into three teams and have one representative from each team stand up. Read a definition and the first team representative to raise his or her hand must answer in the form of a question. Ex: **Es una sopa típica de Colombia.** (**¿Qué es el sancocho?**) Each correct answer earns one point. The team with the most points at the end wins.

Así se dice
- Model the pronunciation of each term and have students repeat it.
- To challenge students, add these words to the list: **el chícharo, el guisante** (*pea*); **el hongo, la seta** (*mushroom*); **el melón de agua (Cuba), la patilla (Col.)** (*watermelon*).
- Point out that **plátano** is also used for *plantain*.

Perfil *Time Magazine* named **Ferran Adrià** one of the most innovative people of the twenty-first century for his unique food creations and cooking style, known as molecular gastronomy. According to his philosophy, a successful marriage of two flavors is often achieved tapping into the "psychological palate" or memory of different food experiences. In 2006, 2007, 2008, and 2009, *Restaurant* magazine named **El Bulli** the number one restaurant in the world. The restaurant closed in 2011. Since then, he has been focusing on the **El Bulli** Foundation, a culinary laboratory and exhibition space.

El mundo hispano
- Point out that in **ceviche**, the fish or seafood gets "cooked" by the acidity of the lemon or lime juice.
- Ask: **¿Alguna vez probaron el ceviche, el gazpacho o el sancocho? De los ingredientes que tienen, ¿cuáles son originarios de América? ¿Conocen platos similares?**

2 Expansion Have pairs choose one of the dishes or ingredients from the activity and create a recipe using the item.

3 Expansion Ask students to create a **menu del día** in which they describe the dishes and suggest complementary dishes (appetizers, drinks, or dessert).

Section Goal

In **Estructura 8.1**, students will be introduced to the preterite of stem-changing verbs.

Instructional Resources
Supersite: Audio (Lab MP3 Files); Resources (Grammar Presentation Slides, Activity Pack, Scripts, Answer Keys); Testing Program (Quizzes)
WebSAM
Workbook, pp. 87–88
Lab Manual, p. 45

Teaching Tips

- Review present-tense forms of **–ir** stem-changing verbs like **pedir** and **dormir**. Also review formation of the preterite of regular **–ir** verbs, using **escribir** and **recibir**.
- Give model sentences that use these verbs in the preterite, emphasizing stem-changing forms. Ex: **Me dormí temprano anoche, pero mi compañero de cuarto se durmió muy tarde.**
- Ask students questions using stem-changing **–ir** verbs in the preterite. Ex: **¿Cuántas horas dormiste anoche?** Then have other students summarize the answers. Ex: ____ **durmió seis horas, pero** ____ **durmió ocho.** ____ **y** ____ **durmieron cinco horas.**
- Point out that **morir** means *to die* and provide sample sentences using third-person preterite forms of the verb. Ex: **No tengo bisabuelos. Ya murieron.**
- Other **–ir** verbs that change their stem vowel in the preterite are **conseguir, despedirse, divertirse, pedir, preferir, repetir, seguir, sentir, sugerir,** and **vestirse.**

8.1 Preterite of stem-changing verbs

Tutorial

ANTE TODO As you learned in **Lección 6**, **–ar** and **–er** stem-changing verbs have no stem change in the preterite. **–Ir** stem-changing verbs, however, do have a stem change. Study the following chart and observe where the stem changes occur.

Preterite of –ir stem-changing verbs

		servir *(to serve)*	**dormir** *(to sleep)*
SINGULAR FORMS	yo	serví	dormí
	tú	serviste	dormiste
	Ud./él/ella	s**i**rvió	d**u**rmió
PLURAL FORMS	nosotros/as	servimos	dormimos
	vosotros/as	servisteis	dormisteis
	Uds./ellos/ellas	s**i**rvieron	d**u**rmieron

▶ Stem-changing **–ir** verbs, in the preterite only, have a stem change in the third-person singular and plural forms. The stem change consists of either **e** to **i** or **o** to **u**.

(e → i) pedir: p**i**dió, p**i**dieron (o → u) morir (*to die*): m**u**rió, m**u**rieron

¿Quién pidió el jamón?

Yo lo pedí.

CONSULTA
There are a few high-frequency irregular verbs in the preterite. You will learn more about them in **Estructura 9.1**, p. 286.

¡INTÉNTALO! Cambia cada infinitivo al pretérito.

1. Yo *serví, dormí, pedí...* (servir, dormir, pedir, preferir, repetir, seguir)
   preferí, repetí, seguí
2. Usted ____________. (morir, conseguir, pedir, sentirse, servir, vestirse)
   murió, consiguió, pidió, se sintió, sirvió, se vistió
3. Tú ____________. (conseguir, servir, morir, pedir, dormir, repetir)
   conseguiste, serviste, moriste, pediste, dormiste, repetiste
4. Ellas ____________. (repetir, dormir, seguir, preferir, morir, servir)
   repitieron, durmieron, siguieron, prefirieron, murieron, sirvieron
5. Nosotros ____________. (seguir, preferir, servir, vestirse, pedir, dormirse)
   seguimos, preferimos, servimos, nos vestimos, pedimos, nos dormimos
6. Ustedes ____________. (sentirse, vestirse, conseguir, pedir, repetir, dormirse)
   se sintieron, se vistieron, consiguieron, pidieron, repitieron, se durmieron
7. Él ____________. (dormir, morir, preferir, repetir, seguir, pedir)
   durmió, murió, prefirió, repitió, siguió, pidió

recursos
WB pp. 87–88
LM p. 45
vhlcentral.com Lección 8

TEACHING OPTIONS

Large Groups Have the class stand and form a circle. Call out a name or subject pronoun and an infinitive that has a stem change in the preterite (Ex: **Miguel/seguir**). Toss a ball to a student, who will say the correct form (Ex: **siguió**) and toss the ball back to you. Then name another pronoun and infinitive and throw the ball to another student. To challenge students, include some infinitives without a stem change in the preterite.

Pairs Ask students to work in pairs to come up with ten original sentences in which they use the **Ud./él/ella** and **Uds./ellos/ellas** preterite forms of stem-changing **–ir** verbs. Point out that students should try to use vocabulary items from **Contextos** in their sentences. Ask pairs to share their sentences with the class.

Práctica

1

Completar Completa estas oraciones para describir lo que pasó anoche en el restaurante El Famoso.

NOTA CULTURAL

El horario de las comidas en España es distinto al de los EE.UU. El desayuno es ligero (*light*). La hora del almuerzo es entre las 2 y las 3 de la tarde. Es la comida más importante del día. Mucha gente merienda o come unas tapas por la tarde. La cena, normalmente ligera, suele (*tends*) ser entre las 9 y las 11 de la noche.

1. Paula y Humberto Suárez llegaron al restaurante El Famoso a las ocho y ___siguieron___ (seguir) al camarero a una mesa en la sección de no fumar.
2. El señor Suárez ___pidió___ (pedir) una chuleta de cerdo.
3. La señora Suárez ___prefirió___ (preferir) probar los camarones.
4. De tomar, los dos ___pidieron___ (pedir) vino tinto.
5. El camarero ___repitió___ (repetir) el pedido (*the order*) para confirmarlo.
6. La comida tardó mucho (*took a long time*) en llegar y los señores Suárez ___se durmieron___ (dormirse) esperando la comida.
7. A las nueve y media el camarero les ___sirvió___ (servir) la comida.
8. Después de comer la chuleta, el señor Suárez ___se sintió___ (sentirse) muy mal.
9. Pobre señor Suárez... ¿por qué no ___pidió___ (pedir) los camarones?

2

El camarero loco En el restaurante La Hermosa trabaja un camarero muy distraído que siempre comete muchos errores. Indica lo que los clientes pidieron y lo que el camarero les sirvió.

modelo

Armando / papas fritas
Armando pidió papas fritas, pero el camarero le sirvió maíz.

1. nosotros / jugo de naranja Nosotros pedimos jugo de naranja, pero el camarero nos sirvió papas.
2. Beatriz / queso Beatriz pidió queso, pero el camarero le sirvió uvas.
3. tú / arroz Tú pediste arroz, pero el camarero te sirvió arvejas/sopa.

4. Elena y Alejandro / atún Elena y Alejandro pidieron atún, pero el camarero les sirvió camarones/mariscos.
5. usted / agua mineral Usted pidió agua mineral, pero el camarero le sirvió vino tinto.
6. yo / hamburguesa Yo pedí una hamburguesa, pero el camarero me sirvió zanahorias.

Practice more at **vhlcentral.com**.

1 Teaching Tip To challenge students, provide two infinitives per blank.

1 Expansion Ask students to work in pairs to come up with an alternate ending to the narration, using stem-changing **–ir** verbs in the preterite. Pairs then share their endings with the class. The class can vote on the most original ending.

2 Teaching Tip As a transition to this activity, have students form small groups and share stories about when they or someone they know had a mishap while dining or serving food in a restaurant.

2 Expansion In pairs, have students redo the activity, this time role-playing the customer and the server. Model the possible interaction between the students. Ex: **E1: Perdón, pero pedí papas fritas y usted me sirvió maíz. E2: ¡Ay, perdón! Le traigo papas fritas enseguida.** Have students take turns playing the role of the customer and server.

TEACHING OPTIONS

Video Show the **Fotonovela** again to give students more input with stem-changing **–ir** verbs in the preterite. Have them write down the stem-changing forms they hear. Stop the video where appropriate to discuss how certain verbs were used and to ask comprehension questions. Ex: **¿Qué pidió Maru? ¿Quién les sirvió la comida a Maru y a Miguel?**

Extra Practice Prepare descriptions of five easily recognizable people in which you use the stem-changing forms of **–ir** verbs in the preterite. Write their names on the board in random order. Then read the descriptions aloud and have students match each one to the appropriate name. Ex: **Murió por sobredosis de medicamentos y heroína en 2014. Los aficionados al actor se sintieron muy mal cuando oyeron la noticia. (Philip Seymour Hoffman)**

3 Expansion Have students share their sentences with the class. Ask other students comprehension questions based on what was said.

4 Expansion
- To practice the formal register, have students ask you the same questions.
- After interviewing a classmate, have students form new pairs and report on their interviewee's answers.

5 Expansion
- Have groups present their description to the class in the form of a narration.
- Have students imagine that, in the middle of the date, either **César** or **Libertad** goes to the restroom to make a cellphone call to a friend. In pairs, have students write the dialogue of the phone call. Have a few volunteers role-play their conversations for the class.

Consulta In addition to pointing out words and expressions that may signal the preterite, remind students about transition words that help to move the flow of a narration (Ex: **primero, después, luego, también**).

Comunicación

NATIONAL communication STANDARDS

3 **El almuerzo** Trabajen en parejas. Túrnense para completar las oraciones de César de una manera lógica. Answers will vary.

modelo

Mi compañero de cuarto se despertó temprano, pero yo...
Mi compañero de cuarto se despertó temprano, pero yo me desperté tarde.

1. Yo llegué al restaurante a tiempo, pero mis amigos...
2. Beatriz pidió la ensalada de frutas, pero yo...
3. Yolanda les recomendó el bistec, pero Eva y Paco...
4. Nosotros preferimos las papas fritas, pero Yolanda...
5. El camarero sirvió la carne, pero yo...
6. Beatriz y yo pedimos café, pero Yolanda y Paco...
7. Eva se sintió enferma, pero Paco y yo...
8. Nosotros repetimos postre (*dessert*), pero Eva...
9. Ellos salieron tarde, pero yo...
10. Yo me dormí temprano, pero mi compañero de cuarto...

¡LENGUA VIVA!
In Spanish, the verb **repetir** is used to express *to have a second helping (of something).*
Cuando mi mamá prepara sopa de champiñones, yo siempre repito.
When my mom makes mushroom soup, I always have a second helping.

4 **Entrevista** Trabajen en parejas y túrnense para entrevistar a su compañero/a. Answers will vary.

1. ¿Te acostaste tarde o temprano anoche? ¿A qué hora te dormiste? ¿Dormiste bien?
2. ¿A qué hora te despertaste esta mañana? Y, ¿a qué hora te levantaste?
3. ¿A qué hora vas a acostarte esta noche?
4. ¿Qué almorzaste ayer? ¿Quién te sirvió el almuerzo?
5. ¿Qué cenaste ayer?
6. ¿Cenaste en un restaurante recientemente? ¿Con quién(es)?
7. ¿Qué pediste en el restaurante? ¿Qué pidieron los demás?
8. ¿Se durmió alguien en alguna de tus clases la semana pasada? ¿En qué clase?

Síntesis

5 **Describir** En grupos, estudien la foto y las preguntas. Luego, describan la primera (¿y la última?) cita de César y Libertad. Answers will vary.

- ¿Adónde salieron a cenar?
- ¿Qué pidieron?
- ¿Les gustó la comida?
- ¿Quién prefirió una cena vegetariana? ¿Por qué?
- ¿Cómo se vistieron?
- ¿De qué hablaron? ¿Les gustó la conversación?
- ¿Van a volver a verse? ¿Por qué?

CONSULTA
To review words commonly associated with the preterite, such as **anoche**, see **Estructura 6.3**, p. 191.

NATIONAL communication STANDARDS

TEACHING OPTIONS

Pairs In pairs, have students take turns telling each other about a memorable experience in a restaurant (a date, dinner with family or friends, etc.). Encourage students to take notes as their partners narrate. Then have students reveal to the class what their partners told them.

Extra Practice Add a visual aspect to this grammar practice. As you hold up magazine pictures that show restaurant scenes, have students describe them in the past tense, using the preterite. You may want to write on the board some stem-changing **–ir** verbs that might apply to the situations pictured in the photographs.

8.2 Double object pronouns

Tutorial

comparisons NATIONAL STANDARDS

ANTE TODO In **Lecciones 5** and **6**, you learned that direct and indirect object pronouns replace nouns and that they often refer to nouns that have already been referenced. You will now learn how to use direct and indirect object pronouns together. Observe the following diagram.

Indirect Object Pronouns			Direct Object Pronouns	
me	nos	+	lo	los
te	os		la	las
le (se)	les (se)			

▶ When direct and indirect object pronouns are used together, the indirect object pronoun always precedes the direct object pronoun.

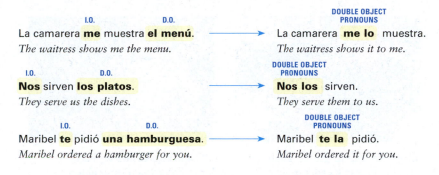

La camarera **me** (I.O.) muestra **el menú** (D.O.). → La camarera **me lo** (DOUBLE OBJECT PRONOUNS) muestra.
The waitress shows me the menu. → *The waitress shows it to me.*

Nos (I.O.) sirven **los platos** (D.O.). → **Nos los** (DOUBLE OBJECT PRONOUNS) sirven.
They serve us the dishes. → *They serve them to us.*

Maribel **te** (I.O.) pidió **una hamburguesa** (D.O.). → Maribel **te la** (DOUBLE OBJECT PRONOUNS) pidió.
Maribel ordered a hamburger for you. → *Maribel ordered it for you.*

¿Quién te los dio?

Me los compró un chico muy guapo.

▶ In Spanish, two pronouns that begin with the letter **l** cannot be used together. Therefore, the indirect object pronouns **le** and **les** always change to **se** when they are used with **lo, los, la,** and **las**.

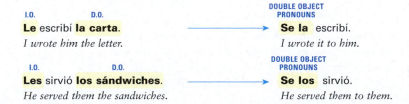

Le (I.O.) escribí **la carta** (D.O.). → **Se la** (DOUBLE OBJECT PRONOUNS) escribí.
I wrote him the letter. → *I wrote it to him.*

Les (I.O.) sirvió **los sándwiches** (D.O.). → **Se los** (DOUBLE OBJECT PRONOUNS) sirvió.
He served them the sandwiches. → *He served them to them.*

Section Goals

In **Estructura 8.2**, students will be introduced to:
- the use of double object pronouns
- converting **le** and **les** into **se** when used with direct object pronouns **lo, la, los,** and **las**

Instructional Resources

Supersite: Audio (Lab MP3 Files); Resources (Grammar Presentation Slides, Activity Pack, Scripts, Answer Keys); Testing Program (Quizzes)
WebSAM
Workbook, pp. 89–90
Lab Manual, p. 46

Teaching Tips

- Briefly review direct object pronouns (**Estructura 5.4**) and indirect object pronouns (**Estructura 6.2**). Give sentences and have students convert objects into object pronouns. Ex: **Sara escribió la carta. (Sara la escribió.) Mis padres escribieron una carta. (yo) (Mis padres me escribieron una carta.)**
- Model additional examples for students, asking them to make the conversion with **se**. Ex: **Le pedí papas fritas. (Se las pedí.) Les servimos café. (Se lo servimos.)**
- Emphasize that, with double object pronouns, the indirect object pronoun always precedes the direct object pronoun.

TEACHING OPTIONS

Extra Practice Write six sentences on the board for students to restate using double object pronouns. Ex: **Rita les sirvió la cena a los clientes. (Rita se la sirvió.)**
Pairs In pairs, ask students to write five sentences that contain both direct and indirect objects (not pronouns). Have them exchange papers with another pair, who will restate the sentences using double object pronouns.

Video Show the **Fotonovela** again to give students more input containing double object pronouns. Stop the video where appropriate to discuss how double object pronouns were used and to ask comprehension questions.

Teaching Tips

- Ask students questions to which they respond with third-person double object pronouns. Ex: **¿Le recomiendas el ceviche a ____ ? (Sí, se lo recomiendo.) ¿Les traes sándwiches a tus compañeros? (Sí, se los traigo.)**
- Practice pronoun placement with infinitives and present participles by giving sentences that show one method of pronoun placement and asking students to restate them another way. Ex: **Se lo voy a preparar. (Voy a preparárselo.)**
- Have students hand each other items in full view of the class; then ask comprehension questions. Ex: **¿Quién le dio el libro a Kevin? (____ se lo dio.)**

▶ Because **se** has multiple meanings, Spanish speakers often clarify to whom the pronoun refers by adding **a usted, a él, a ella, a ustedes, a ellos,** or **a ellas.**

¿El sombrero? Carlos **se** lo vendió **a ella**.
The hat? Carlos sold it to her.

¿Las verduras? Ellos **se** las compran **a usted**.
The vegetables? They are buying them for you.

▶ Double object pronouns are placed before a conjugated verb. With infinitives and present participles, they may be placed before the conjugated verb or attached to the end of the infinitive or present participle.

DOUBLE OBJECT PRONOUNS
Te lo voy a mostrar.

DOUBLE OBJECT PRONOUNS
Voy a mostrár**telo**.

DOUBLE OBJECT PRONOUNS
Nos las están comprando.

DOUBLE OBJECT PRONOUNS
Están comprándo**noslas**.

Mi abuelo **me lo** está leyendo.
Mi abuelo está leyéndo**melo**.

El camarero **se los** va a servir.
El camarero va a servír**selos**.

▶ As you can see above, when double object pronouns are attached to an infinitive or a present participle, an accent mark is added to maintain the original stress.

¡INTÉNTALO! Escribe el pronombre de objeto directo o indirecto que falta en cada oración.

Objeto directo

1. ¿La ensalada? El camarero nos ___la___ sirvió.
2. ¿El salmón? La dueña me ___lo___ recomienda.
3. ¿La comida? Voy a preparárte___la___.
4. ¿Las bebidas? Estamos pidiéndose___las___.
5. ¿Los refrescos? Te ___los___ puedo traer ahora.
6. ¿Los platos de arroz? Van a servírnos___los___ después.

Objeto indirecto

1. ¿Puedes traerme tu plato? No, no ___te___ lo puedo traer.
2. ¿Quieres mostrarle la carta? Sí, voy a mostrár___se___la ahora.
3. ¿Les serviste la carne? No, no ___se___ la serví.
4. ¿Vas a leerle el menú? No, no ___se___ lo voy a leer.
5. ¿Me recomiendas la langosta? Sí, ___te___ la recomiendo.
6. ¿Cuándo vas a prepararnos la cena? ___Se___ la voy a preparar en una hora.

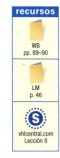

recursos
WB pp. 89–90
LM p. 46
vhlcentral.com Lección 8

TEACHING OPTIONS

Pairs Have students create five dehydrated sentences for their partner to complete. They should include the following elements: subject / action / direct object / indirect object (name or pronoun). Ex: **Carlos / escribe / carta / Marta** Their partners should "hydrate" the sentences using double object pronouns. Ex: **Carlos se la escribe (a Marta).**

Large Groups Split the class into two groups. Give cards that contain verbs that can take a direct object to one group. The other group gets cards containing nouns. Then select one member from each group to stand up and show his or her card. Another student converts the two elements into a sentence using double object pronouns. Ex: **mostrar / el libro →** [*Name of student*] **se lo va a mostrar.**

Práctica

1 **Responder** Imagínate que trabajas de camarero/a en un restaurante. Responde a los pedidos (*requests*) de estos clientes usando pronombres.

modelo
Sra. Gómez: Una ensalada, por favor.
Sí, señora. Enseguida (Right away) se la traigo.

1. Sres. López: La mantequilla, por favor. Sí, señores. Enseguida se la traigo.
2. Srta. Rivas: Los camarones, por favor. Sí, señorita. Enseguida se los traigo.
3. Sra. Lugones: El pollo asado, por favor. Sí, señora. Enseguida se lo traigo.
4. Tus compañeros/as de cuarto: Café, por favor. Sí, chicos/as. Enseguida se lo traigo.
5. Tu profesor(a) de español: Papas fritas, por favor. Sí, profesor(a). Enseguida se las traigo.
6. Dra. González: La chuleta de cerdo, por favor. Sí, doctora. Enseguida se la traigo.
7. Tu padre: Los champiñones, por favor. Sí, papá. Enseguida te los traigo.
8. Dr. Torres: La cuenta, por favor. Sí, doctor. Enseguida se la traigo.

AYUDA
Here are some other useful expressions:
ahora mismo *right now*
inmediatamente *immediately*
¡A la orden! *At your service!*
¡Ya voy! *I'm on my way!*

2 **¿Quién?** La señora Cevallos está planeando una cena. Se pregunta cómo va a resolver ciertas situaciones. En parejas, túrnense para decir lo que ella está pensando. Cambien los sustantivos subrayados por pronombres de objeto directo y hagan los otros cambios necesarios.

modelo
¡No tengo carne! ¿Quién va a traerme <u>la carne</u> del supermercado? (mi esposo)
Mi esposo va a traérmela./Mi esposo me la va a traer.

1. ¡Las invitaciones! ¿Quién les manda <u>las invitaciones</u> a los invitados (*guests*)? (mi hija) Mi hija se las manda.
2. No tengo tiempo de ir a la bodega. ¿Quién me puede comprar <u>el vino</u>? (mi hijo) Mi hijo puede comprármelo./Mi hijo me lo puede comprar.
3. ¡Ay! No tengo suficientes platos (*plates*). ¿Quién puede prestarme <u>los platos</u> que necesito? (mi mamá) Mi mamá puede prestármelos./Mi mamá me los puede prestar.
4. Nos falta mantequilla. ¿Quién nos trae <u>la mantequilla</u>? (mi cuñada) Mi cuñada nos la trae.
5. ¡Los entremeses! ¿Quién está preparándonos <u>los entremeses</u>? (Silvia y Renata) Silvia y Renata están preparándonoslos./Silvia y Renata nos los están preparando.
6. No hay suficientes sillas. ¿Quién nos trae <u>las sillas</u> que faltan? (Héctor y Lorena) Héctor y Lorena nos las traen.
7. No tengo tiempo de pedirle el aceite a Mónica. ¿Quién puede pedirle <u>el aceite</u>? (mi hijo) Mi hijo puede pedírselo./Mi hijo se lo puede pedir.
8. ¿Quién va a servirles <u>la cena</u> a los invitados? (mis hijos) Mis hijos van a servírsela./Mis hijos se la van a servir.
9. Quiero poner buena música de fondo (*background*). ¿Quién me va a recomendar <u>la música</u>? (mi esposo) Mi esposo va a recomendármela./Mi esposo me la va a recomendar.
10. ¡Los postres! ¿Quién va a preparar <u>los postres</u> para los invitados? (Sra. Villalba) La señora Villalba va a preparárselos./La señora Villalba se los va a preparar.

NOTA CULTURAL
Los vinos de Chile son conocidos internacionalmente. **Concha y Toro** es el productor y exportador más grande de vinos de Chile. Las zonas más productivas de vino están al norte de Santiago, en el Valle Central.

Practice more at **vhlcentral.com**.

1 Teaching Tip Do the activity with the whole class, selecting a student to play the role of customer and another to play the role of server for each item.

Ayuda Model the helpful phrases in sentences. Point out that **Ahora mismo, Inmediatamente,** and **Ya** can replace **Enseguida** in the **modelo** for **Actividad 1.**

2 Expansion
- For each item, change the subject in parentheses so that students practice different forms of the verbs.
- Add a visual aspect to this activity. Hold up magazine pictures and ask students to state who is doing what to or for whom. Ex: **La señora les muestra la casa a los jóvenes. Se la muestra a los jóvenes.**

TEACHING OPTIONS

Heritage Speakers Ask heritage speakers to talk about a favorite gift they received. Write **regalar** on the board and explain that it means *to give (a gift)*. Have students talk about what they received, who gave it to them (**regalar**), and why. Ask the rest of the class comprehension questions.

Game Play **Concentración**. Write sentences that use double object pronouns on each of eight cards. Ex: **Óscar se las muestra.** On another eight cards, draw or paste a picture that matches each sentence. Ex: A photo of a boy showing photos to his grandparents. Place the cards face-down in four rows of four. In pairs, students select two cards. If the two cards match, the pair keeps them. If they do not match, students replace them in their original position. The pair with the most cards at the end wins.

Comunicación

3

Contestar Trabajen en parejas. Túrnense para hacer preguntas, usando las palabras interrogativas **¿Quién?** o **¿Cuándo?**, y para responderlas. Sigan el modelo. Answers will vary.

modelo

nos enseña español
Estudiante 1: *¿Quién nos enseña español?*
Estudiante 2: *La profesora Camacho nos lo enseña.*

1. te puede explicar la tarea cuando no la entiendes
2. les vende el almuerzo a los estudiantes
3. vas a comprarme boletos (*tickets*) para un concierto
4. te escribe mensajes de texto
5. nos prepara los entremeses
6. me vas a prestar tu computadora
7. te compró esa bebida
8. nos va a recomendar el menú de la cafetería
9. le enseñó español al/a la profesor(a)
10. me vas a mostrar tu casa o apartamento

4

Preguntas En parejas, túrnense para hacerse estas preguntas. Answers will vary.

modelo

Estudiante 1: *¿Les prestas tu casa a tus amigos? ¿Por qué?*
Estudiante 2: *No, no se la presto a mis amigos porque no son muy responsables.*

1. ¿Me prestas tu auto? ¿Ya le prestaste tu auto a otro/a amigo/a?
2. ¿Quién te presta dinero cuando lo necesitas?
3. ¿Les prestas dinero a tus amigos? ¿Por qué?
4. ¿Nos compras el almuerzo a mí y a los otros compañeros de clase?
5. ¿Les mandas correo electrónico a tus amigos? ¿Y a tu familia?
6. ¿Les das regalos a tus amigos? ¿Cuándo?
7. ¿Quién te va a preparar la cena esta noche?
8. ¿Quién te va a preparar el desayuno mañana?

Síntesis

5

Regalos de Navidad Tu profesor(a) te va a dar a ti y a un(a) compañero/a una parte de la lista de los regalos de Navidad (*Christmas*) que Berta pidió y los regalos que sus parientes le compraron. Conversen para completar sus listas. Answers will vary.

modelo

Estudiante 1: *¿Qué le pidió Berta a su mamá?*
Estudiante 2: *Le pidió una computadora. ¿Se la compró?*
Estudiante 1: *Sí, se la compró.*

NOTA CULTURAL

Las fiestas navideñas (*Christmas season*) en los países hispanos duran hasta enero. En muchos lugares celebran **la Navidad** (*Christmas*), pero no se dan los regalos hasta el seis de enero, **el Día de los Reyes Magos** (*Three Kings' Day/The Feast of the Epiphany*).

3 Teaching Tips
- To simplify, begin by reading through the items and guiding students in choosing **quién** or **cuándo** for each one.
- Continue the **modelo** exchange by asking: **¿Cuándo nos lo enseña? (Nos lo enseña los lunes, miércoles, jueves y viernes.)**
- To challenge students, have them ask follow-up questions using other interrogative words.

3 Expansion Ask questions of individual students. Then ask them why they answered as they did. Students answer using double object pronouns. Ex: **¿Quién te enseña español? (Usted me lo enseña.) ¿Por qué? (Usted me lo enseña porque es profesor(a) de español.)**

4 Teaching Tip Ask the questions of individual students. Then verify class comprehension by asking other students to repeat the information given.

5 Teaching Tip Divide the class into pairs and distribute the handouts from the Activity Pack (Activity Pack/Supersite) that correspond to this Information Gap Activity. Give students ten minutes to complete this activity.

5 Expansion Ask students to find a new partner and make a list of the gifts they each received for their last birthday or other occasion. Then have students point to each item on their list and, using double object pronouns, tell their partner who bought it for them. Ex: **zapatos nuevos (Me los compró mi prima.)**

TEACHING OPTIONS

Heritage Speakers Ask heritage speakers if they or their families celebrate **el Día de los Reyes Magos** (The Feast of the Epiphany, January 6). Ask them to expand on the information given in the **Nota cultural** box and to tell whether **el Día de los Reyes** is more important for them than **la Navidad**.

Large Groups Divide the class into two groups. Give each member of the first group a strip of paper with a question on it. Ex: **¿Te compró ese suéter tu novia?** Give each member of the second group a piece of paper with an answer to one of the questions. Ex: **Sí, ella me lo compró.** Students must find their partners. Take care not to create sentences that can have more than one match.

8.3 Comparisons

Tutorial

NATIONAL STANDARDS comparisons

ANTE TODO Both Spanish and English use comparisons to indicate which of two people or things has a lesser, equal, or greater degree of a quality.

Comparisons

menos interesante	**más grande**	**tan sabroso como**
less interesting	*bigger*	*as delicious as*

Comparisons of inequality

▶ Comparisons of inequality are formed by placing **más** (*more*) or **menos** (*less*) before adjectives, adverbs, and nouns and **que** (*than*) after them.

más/menos + [*adjective* / *adverb* / *noun*] + **que**

▶ **¡Atención!** Note that while English has a comparative form for short adjectives (*tall**er***), such forms do not exist in Spanish (**más** alto).

adjectives

Los bistecs son **más caros que** el pollo.
Steaks are more expensive than chicken.

Estas uvas son **menos ricas que** esa pera.
These grapes are less tasty than that pear.

adverbs

Me acuesto **más tarde que** tú.
I go to bed later than you (do).

Luis se despierta **menos temprano que** yo.
Luis wakes up less early than I (do).

nouns

Juan prepara **más platos que** José.
Juan prepares more dishes than José (does).

Susana come **menos carne que** Enrique.
Susana eats less meat than Enrique (does).

La ensalada es menos cara que la sopa.

¿El pollo es más rico que el jamón?

▶ When the comparison involves a numerical expression, **de** is used before the number instead of **que**.

Hay más **de** cincuenta naranjas.
There are more than fifty oranges.

Llego en menos **de** diez minutos.
I'll be there in less than ten minutes.

▶ With verbs, this construction is used to make comparisons of inequality.

[*verb*] + **más/menos que**

Mis hermanos **comen más que** yo.
My brothers eat more than I (do).

Arturo **duerme menos que** su padre.
Arturo sleeps less than his father (does).

Section Goals

In **Estructura 8.3**, students will be introduced to:
- comparisons of inequality
- comparisons of equality
- irregular comparative words

Instructional Resources

Supersite: Audio (Lab MP3 Files); Resources (Grammar Presentation Slides, Activity Pack, Scripts, Answer Keys); Testing Program (Quizzes)
WebSAM
Workbook, pp. 91–92
Lab Manual, p. 47

Teaching Tips

- Write **más** + [*adjective*] + **que** and **menos** + [*adjective*] + **que** on the board, explaining their meaning. Illustrate with examples. Ex: **Esta clase es más grande que la clase de la tarde. La clase de la tarde es menos trabajadora que ésta.**
- Practice the structures by asking volunteers questions about classroom objects. **El lápiz de ____ , ¿es más largo que el lápiz de ____? (No, es menos largo que el lápiz de ____ .)**
- Point out that **que** and what follows it are optional if the items being compared are evident. Ex: **Los bistecs son más caros (que el pollo).**

TEACHING OPTIONS

Extra Practice Ask students questions that make comparisons of inequality using adjectives, adverbs, and nouns. Ex: **¿Qué es más sabroso que una ensalada de frutas? ¿Quién se despierta más tarde que tú? ¿Quién tiene más libros que yo?** Then ask questions that use verbs in their construction. Ex: **¿Quién habla más que yo en la clase?**

Heritage Speakers Ask heritage speakers to give four to five sentences in which they compare themselves to members of their families. Make sure that they use comparisons of inequality. To verify comprehension, ask other students in the class to report what the heritage speakers said.

Teaching Tips

- Ask the class questions to elicit comparisons of equality. Ex: **¿Quién es tan guapa como Scarlett Johansson? ¿Quién tiene tanto dinero como David Beckham?**
- Ask questions that involve comparisons with yourself. Ex: **¿Quién es tan alto/a como yo? ¿Quién se acostó tan tarde como yo?**
- Involve the class in a conversation about themselves and classroom objects. Ex: _____, **¿por qué tienes tantas plumas?** _____, **¡tu mochila es tan grande! Puedes llevar muchos libros, ¿no? ¿Quién más tiene una mochila tan grande?** Ask additional questions as needed to carry on the conversation.

Comparisons of equality

▶ This construction is used to make comparisons of equality.

tan + [*adjective* / *adverb*] + **como**   **tanto/a(s)** + [*singular noun* / *plural noun*] + **como**

¿Es tan guapo como yo?

¿Aquí vienen tantos mexicanos como extranjeros?

▶ **¡Atención!** Note that unlike **tan**, **tanto** acts as an adjective and therefore agrees in number and gender with the noun it modifies.

Estas uvas son **tan ricas como** aquéllas.
These grapes are as tasty as those ones (are).

Yo probé **tantos platos como** él.
I tried as many dishes as he did.

▶ **Tan** and **tanto** can also be used for emphasis, rather than to compare, with these meanings: **tan** *so*, **tanto** *so much*, **tantos/as** *so many*.

¡Tu almuerzo es **tan** grande!
Your lunch is so big!

¡Comes **tantas** manzanas!
You eat so many apples!

¡Comes **tanto**!
You eat so much!

¡Preparan **tantos** platos!
They prepare so many dishes!

▶ Comparisons of equality with verbs are formed by placing **tanto como** after the verb. Note that in this construction **tanto** does not change in number or gender.

[*verb*] + **tanto como**

Tú viajas **tanto como** mi tía.
You travel as much as my aunt (does).

Ellos hablan **tanto como** mis hermanas.
They talk as much as my sisters.

Sabemos **tanto como** ustedes.
We know as much as you (do).

No estudio **tanto como** Felipe.
I don't study as much as Felipe (does).

TEACHING OPTIONS

Extra Practice Have students write three original comparative sentences that describe themselves. Ex: **Soy tan baja como Ellen Page.** Then collect the papers, shuffle them, and read the sentences aloud. See if the rest of the class can guess who wrote each description.

Game Divide the class into two teams, A and B. Place the names of twenty famous people into a hat. Select a member from each team to draw a name. The student from team A then has ten seconds to compare those two famous people. If the student has made a logical comparison, team A gets a point. Then it is team B's turn to make a different comparison. The team with the most points at the end wins.

Irregular comparisons

▶ Some adjectives have irregular comparative forms.

Irregular comparative forms

Adjective		Comparative form	
bueno/a	*good*	**mejor**	*better*
malo/a	*bad*	**peor**	*worse*
grande	*grown, adult*	**mayor**	*older*
pequeño/a	*young*	**menor**	*younger*
joven	*young*	**menor**	*younger*
viejo/a	*old*	**mayor**	*older*

CONSULTA

To review how descriptive adjectives like **bueno**, **malo**, and **grande** are shortened before nouns, see **Estructura 3.1**, p. 82.

▶ When **grande** and **pequeño/a** refer to age, the irregular comparative forms, **mayor** and **menor**, are used. However, when these adjectives refer to size, the regular forms, **más grande** and **más pequeño/a**, are used.

Yo soy **menor** que tú.
I'm younger than you.

Pedí un plato **más pequeño.**
I ordered a smaller dish.

Nuestro hijo es **mayor** que el hijo de los Andrade.
Our son is older than the Andrades' son.

La ensalada de Isabel es **más grande** que ésa.
Isabel's salad is bigger than that one.

▶ The adverbs **bien** and **mal** have the same irregular comparative forms as the adjectives **bueno/a** and **malo/a**.

Julio nada **mejor** que los otros chicos.
Julio swims better than the other boys.

Ellas cantan **peor** que las otras chicas.
They sing worse than the other girls.

recursos

WB pp. 91–92

LM p. 47

vhlcentral.com Lección 8

¡INTÉNTALO! Escribe el equivalente de las palabras en inglés.

1. Ernesto mira más televisión ___que___ (*than*) Alberto.
2. Tú eres ___menos___ (*less*) simpático que Federico.
3. La camarera sirve ___tanta___ (*as much*) carne como pescado.
4. Recibo ___más___ (*more*) propinas que tú.
5. No estudio ___tanto como___ (*as much as*) tú.
6. ¿Sabes jugar al tenis tan bien ___como___ (*as*) tu hermana?
7. ¿Puedes beber ___tantos___ (*as many*) refrescos como yo?
8. Mis amigos parecen ___tan___ (*as*) simpáticos como ustedes.

Teaching Tips

- Practice the differences between **grande—mayor** and **pequeño/a—menor** when referring to age by having two students stand. Ask **E1: ____ , ¿cuántos años tienes? (E1: Tengo dieciocho años.)** Then ask **E2: Y tú, ____ , ¿cuántos años tienes? (E2: Tengo diecinueve años.)** Now ask the class: **¿Quién es mayor? ¿Y quién es más grande?**
- Ask questions and give examples to practice irregular comparative forms. Ex: (pointing to two students) **Lisa tiene diecinueve años y Shawn tiene veintiún años. ¿Lisa es mayor que Shawn? (No, Lisa es menor que Shawn.)** Then ask questions about celebrities. Ex: **¿Quién canta mejor, Adele o Rihanna?** Have students state their opinions in complete sentences. Ex: **Adele canta mejor que Rihanna.**

TEACHING OPTIONS

Large Groups Divide the class into groups of six. Give cards with adjectives listed on page 263 to one group. Give cards with the corresponding irregular comparative form to another group. Students must find their partners. To avoid confusion, make duplicate cards of **mayor** and **menor**.

Pairs Write on the board the heading **Nuestra universidad vs.** [*another nearby university*]. Underneath, write a list of categories. Ex: **la ciudad universitaria, los estudiantes, las residencias estudiantiles, el equipo de fútbol americano** Have pairs take turns making comparisons about the universities. Encourage them to be creative and to use a variety of comparative forms. Ex: **Los estudiantes de nuestra universidad estudian tanto como los estudiantes de** [*other university*].

1 Teaching Tip Quickly review the use of **de** before numerals in comparisons.

1 Expansion
- Ask two students a question, then have another student compare them. Ex: **¿Cuántas horas de televisión miras cada día? ¿Y tú, ____? ____, haz una comparación.**
- Ask several pairs of students different types of questions for later comparison. Ex: **¿Cuáles prefieres, las películas de aventuras o los dramas? ¿Estudias más para la clase de español o para la clase de matemáticas?**

2 Expansion Turn the activity statements into questions and ask them of students. Have them make up answers that involve comparisons. Ex: **¿Cómo es Mario?**

3 Teaching Tips
- Have a student read the **modelo** aloud. Emphasize that students' comparisons can begin with an element from either column A or C.
- To simplify, guide students in pairing up elements from columns A and C and brainstorming possible infinitives for each pair of elements.

Práctica

1 **Escoger** Escoge la palabra correcta para comparar a dos hermanas muy diferentes. Haz los cambios necesarios.

1. Lucila es más alta y más bonita __que__ Tita. (de, más, menos, que)
2. Tita es más delgada porque come __más__ verduras que su hermana. (de, más, menos, que)
3. Lucila es más __simpática__ que Tita porque es alegre. (listo, simpático, bajo)
4. A Tita le gusta comer en casa. Va a __menos__ restaurantes que su hermana. (más, menos, que) Es tímida, pero activa. Hace __más__ ejercicio (*exercise*) que su hermana. (más, tanto, menos) Todos los días toma más __de__ cinco vasos (*glasses*) de agua mineral. (que, tan, de)
5. Lucila come muchas papas fritas y se preocupa __menos__ que Tita por comer frutas. (de, más, menos) ¡Son __tan__ diferentes! Pero se llevan (*they get along*) muy bien. (como, tan, tanto)

2 **Emparejar** Compara a Mario y a Luis, los novios de Lucila y Tita, completando las oraciones de la columna A con las palabras o frases de la columna B.

A

1. Mario es __tan interesante__ como Luis.
2. Mario viaja tanto __como__ Luis.
3. Luis toma __tantas__ clases de cocina (*cooking*) como Mario.
4. Luis habla __francés__ tan bien como Mario.
5. Mario tiene tantos __amigos extranjeros__ como Luis.
6. ¡Qué casualidad (*coincidence*)! Mario y Luis también son hermanos, pero no hay tanta __diferencia__ entre ellos como entre Lucila y Tita.

B

tantas
diferencia
tan interesante
amigos extranjeros
como
francés

3 **Oraciones** Combina elementos de las columnas A, B y C para hacer comparaciones. Escribe oraciones completas. Answers will vary.

modelo
Chris Hemsworth tiene tantos autos como Jennifer Aniston.
Jennifer Aniston es menos musculosa que Chris Hemsworth.

A	B	C
la comida japonesa	costar	la gente de Montreal
el fútbol	saber	la música *country*
Chris Hemsworth	ser	el brócoli
el pollo	tener	el presidente de los EE.UU.
la gente de Vancouver	¿?	la comida italiana
la primera dama (*lady*) de los EE.UU.		el hockey
las universidades privadas		Jennifer Aniston
las espinacas		las universidades públicas
la música rap		la carne de res

Practice more at **vhlcentral.com**.

TEACHING OPTIONS

Extra Practice Add a visual aspect to this grammar practice. Using magazine pictures or drawings, show a family whose members vary widely in different aspects: age (write a number on each person that indicates how old he or she is), height, weight, and so forth. Ask students to make comparisons about that family. Give names to each family member so that the people are easier to identify.

Large Groups Divide the class into two groups. Survey each group to get information about various topics. Ex: **¿Quiénes hacen ejercicio todos los días? ¿Quiénes van al cine cada fin de semana? ¿Quiénes comen comida rápida tres veces a la semana?** Ask for a show of hands and tally the number of hands. Then have students make comparisons between the two groups based on the information given.

Comunicación

4

Intercambiar En parejas, hagan comparaciones sobre diferentes cosas. Pueden usar las sugerencias de la lista u otras ideas. Answers will vary.

modelo

Estudiante 1: *Los pollos de Pollitos del Corral son muy ricos.*
Estudiante 2: *Pues yo creo que los pollos de Rostipollos son tan buenos como los pollos de Pollitos del Corral.*
Estudiante 1: *Ummm... no tienen tanta mantequilla como los pollos de Pollitos del Corral. Tienes razón. Son muy sabrosos.*

restaurantes en tu ciudad/pueblo
cafés en tu comunidad
tiendas en tu ciudad/pueblo

periódicos en tu ciudad/pueblo
revistas favoritas
libros favoritos

comidas favoritas
los profesores
los cursos que toman

AYUDA

You can use these adjectives in your comparisons:
bonito/a
caro/a
elegante
interesante
inteligente

5

Conversar En grupos, túrnense para hacer comparaciones entre ustedes mismos (*yourselves*) y una persona de cada categoría de la lista. Answers will vary.

- una persona de tu familia
- un(a) amigo/a especial
- una persona famosa

Síntesis

6

La familia López En grupos, túrnense para hablar de Sara, Sabrina, Cristina, Ricardo y David y hacer comparaciones entre ellos. Answers will vary.

modelo

Estudiante 1: *Sara es tan alta como Sabrina.*
Estudiante 2: *Sí, pero David es más alto que ellas.*
Estudiante 3: *En mi opinión, él es guapo también.*

4 Expansion Ask pairs of volunteers to present one of their conversations to the class. Then survey the class to see with which of the students the class agrees more.

5 Teaching Tip Model the activity by making a few comparisons between yourself and a celebrity.

5 Expansion Ask a volunteer to share his or her comparisons. Then make comparisons between yourself and the student or yourself and the person the student mentioned. Continue to do this with different students, asking them to make similar comparisons as well.

6 Expansion Add an interpretive aspect to this activity. Have students create a drawing of a family similar to the one on this page. Tell them not to let anyone see their drawings. Then divide the class into pairs and have them describe their drawings to one another. Each student must draw the family described by his or her partner.

TEACHING OPTIONS

Extra Practice Add an auditory aspect to this grammar practice. Prepare short descriptions of five easily recognizable people in which you compare them to other well-known people. Write their names on the board in random order. Then read the descriptions aloud and have students match them to the appropriate name. Ex: **Esta persona trabaja en películas de Hollywood. Es tan buen actor como Matt Damon, pero tiene más hijos que él. Su pareja es más bonita que Jennifer Aniston. (Brad Pitt)**

TPR Give the same types of objects to different students but in different numbers. For example, hand out three books to one student, one book to another, and four to another. Then call on individuals to make comparisons between the students based on the number of objects they have.

Section Goals

In **Estructura 8.4**, students will be introduced to:
- superlatives
- irregular superlative forms

Instructional Resources
Supersite: Audio (Lab MP3 Files); Resources (Grammar Presentation Slides, Activity Pack, Scripts, Answer Keys); Testing Program (Quizzes)
WebSAM
Workbook, pp. 93–94
Lab Manual, p. 48

Teaching Tips

- Give names of famous people or places and have students make superlative statements about their most obvious quality. Ex: **Bill Gates (Es uno de los hombres más ricos del mundo.); el monte McKinley (Es la montaña más alta de Norteamérica.)**
- Ask questions and give examples to practice irregular superlative forms. Ex: **¿Quién es el menor de tu familia? ¿Ah, sí? ¿Cuántos hermanos mayores tienes?**
- Practice superlative questions by asking for students' opinions. Ex: **¿Cuál es la clase más difícil de esta universidad? ¿Y la más fácil?**
- Use magazine pictures to compare and contrast absolute superlatives. Ex: **Este edificio parece modernísimo, pero éste no. Parece viejísimo.**
- Ask volunteers to identify people you describe using absolute superlatives. Ex: **Tiene un canal y varios programas de televisión. Se le conoce por ser una filántropa muy generosa. Es riquísima. (Oprah Winfrey)**

8.4 Superlatives

Tutorial

NATIONAL STANDARDS comparisons

ANTE TODO Both English and Spanish use superlatives to express the highest or lowest degree of a quality.

el/la mejor	**el/la peor**	**el/la más alto/a**
the best	*the worst*	*the tallest*

▶ This construction is used to form superlatives. Note that the noun is always preceded by a definite article and that **de** is equivalent to the English *in* or *of*.

el/la/los/las + [*noun*] + **más/menos** + [*adjective*] + **de**

▶ The noun can be omitted if the person, place, or thing referred to is clear.

¿El restaurante Las Delicias?
Es **el más elegante** de la ciudad.
The restaurant Las Delicias?
It's the most elegant (one) in the city.

Recomiendo el pollo asado.
Es **el más sabroso** del menú.
I recommend the roast chicken.
It's the most delicious on the menu.

▶ Here are some irregular superlative forms.

Irregular superlatives

Adjective		Superlative form	
bueno/a	*good*	**el/la mejor**	*(the) best*
malo/a	*bad*	**el/la peor**	*(the) worst*
grande	*grown, adult*	**el/la mayor**	*(the) oldest*
pequeño/a	*young*	**el/la menor**	*(the) youngest*
joven	*young*	**el/la menor**	*(the) youngest*
viejo/a	*old*	**el/la mayor**	*(the) oldest*

▶ The absolute superlative is equivalent to *extremely*, *super*, or *very*. To form the absolute superlative of most adjectives and adverbs, drop the final vowel, if there is one, and add **-ísimo/a(s)**.

malo → **mal-** → **malísimo**
¡El bistec está **malísimo**!

mucho → **much-** → **muchísimo**
Comes **muchísimo**.

▶ Note these spelling changes.

rico → **riquísimo** **largo** → **larguísimo** **feliz** → **felicísimo**
fácil → **facilísimo** **joven** → **jovencísimo** **trabajador** → **trabajadorcísimo**

¡ATENCIÓN!
While **más** alone means *more*, after **el, la, los,** or **las**, it means *most*. Likewise, **menos** can mean *less* or *least*.
Es **el café más rico del** país.
It's the most delicious coffee in the country.
Es **el menú menos caro de** todos éstos.
It is the least expensive menu of all of these.

CONSULTA
The rule you learned in **Estructura 8.3** (p. 263) regarding the use of **mayor/menor** with age, but not with size, is also true with superlative forms.

recursos
WB pp. 93–94
LM p. 48
vhlcentral.com Lección 8

¡INTÉNTALO! Escribe el equivalente de las palabras en inglés.

1. Marisa es ___la más inteligente___ (*the most intelligent*) de todas.
2. Ricardo y Tomás son ___los menos aburridos___ (*the least boring*) de la fiesta.
3. Miguel y Antonio son ___los peores___ (*the worst*) estudiantes de la clase.
4. Mi profesor de biología es ___el mayor___ (*the oldest*) de la universidad.

TEACHING OPTIONS

Heritage Speakers Ask heritage speakers to discuss whether absolute superlatives are common in their culture (some regions and countries use them less frequently than others). Also have them discuss under what circumstances absolute superlatives are most frequently used, such as when talking about food, people, events, and so forth. Then have the class work in pairs to create mini-conversations based on the superlatives mentioned.

Extra Practice Ask students questions with superlatives about things and places at your university, in your community, in the class, and so forth. Include a mix of regular and irregular superlative forms. Ex: **¿Cuál es el edificio más grande del campus? ¿Cuál es la peor clase de la universidad?**

Práctica y Comunicación

1

El más... Responde a las preguntas afirmativamente. Usa las palabras entre paréntesis.

modelo

El cuarto está sucísimo, ¿no? (residencia)
Sí, es el más sucio de la residencia.

1. El almacén Velasco es buenísimo, ¿no? (centro comercial) Sí, es el mejor del centro comercial.
2. La silla de tu madre es comodísima, ¿no? (casa) Sí, es la más cómoda de la casa.
3. Ángela y Julia están nerviosísimas por el examen, ¿no? (clase) Sí, son las más nerviosas de la clase.
4. Jorge es jovencísimo, ¿no? (mis amigos) Sí, es el menor de mis amigos.

2

Completar Tu profesor(a) te va a dar una hoja de actividades con descripciones de José Valenzuela Carranza y Ana Orozco Hoffman. Completa las oraciones con las palabras de la lista.
Some answers may vary. Suggested answers:

altísima	del	mayor	peor
atlética	guapísimo	mejor	periodista
bajo	la	menor	trabajadorcísimo
de	más	Orozco	Valenzuela

1. José tiene 22 años; es el ___menor___ y el más ___bajo___ de su familia. Es ___guapísimo___ y ___trabajadorcísimo___. Es el mejor ___periodista___ de la ciudad y el ___peor___ jugador de baloncesto.
2. Ana es la más ___atlética___ y ___la___ mejor jugadora de baloncesto del estado. Es la ___mayor___ de sus hermanos (tiene 28 años) y es ___altísima___. Estudió la profesión ___más___ difícil ___de___ todas: medicina.
3. Jorge es el ___mejor___ jugador de videojuegos de su familia.
4. Mauricio es el menor de la familia ___Orozco___.
5. El abuelo es el ___mayor___ de todos los miembros de la familia Valenzuela.
6. Fifí es la perra más antipática ___del___ mundo.

3

Superlativos Trabajen en parejas para hacer comparaciones. Usen los superlativos.
Answers will vary.

modelo

Angelina Jolie, Bill Gates, Jimmy Carter
Estudiante 1: *Bill Gates es el más rico de los tres.*
Estudiante 2: *Sí, ¡es riquísimo! Y Jimmy Carter es el mayor de los tres.*

NATIONAL communication STANDARDS

1. Guatemala, Argentina, España
2. Jaguar, Prius, Smart
3. la comida mexicana, la comida francesa, la comida árabe
4. Amy Adams, Meryl Streep, Jennifer Lawrence
5. Ciudad de México, Buenos Aires, Nueva York
6. *Don Quijote de la Mancha*, *Cien años de soledad*, *Como agua para chocolate*
7. el fútbol americano, el golf, el béisbol
8. las películas románticas, las películas de acción, las películas cómicas

Practice more at **vhlcentral.com**.

1 Expansion

- Give these sentences to students as items 5–7: **5. Esas películas son malísimas, ¿no? (Hollywood) (Sí, son las peores de Hollywood.) 6. El centro comercial Galerías es grandísimo, ¿no? (ciudad) (Sí, es el más grande de la ciudad.) 7. Tus bisabuelos son viejísimos, ¿no? (familia) (Sí, son los mayores de mi familia.)**
- To challenge students, after they have completed the activity, have them repeat it by answering in the negative. Ex: **1. No, es el peor del centro comercial.**

2 Teaching Tip Distribute the ***Hojas de actividades*** (Activity Pack/Supersite) that correspond to this activity.

2 Expansion

In pairs, have students select a family member or a close friend and describe him or her using comparatives and superlatives. Ask volunteers to share their descriptions with the class.

3 Teaching Tips

- To simplify, read through the items with students and, in English, brainstorm points of comparison between the three people or things. For item 6, briefly describe these novels for students who are not familiar with them.
- Encourage students to create as many superlatives as they can for each item. Have volunteers share their most creative statements with the class.

TEACHING OPTIONS

Extra Practice Add an auditory aspect to this grammar practice. Prepare ten superlative sentences and read them aloud slowly, pausing after each sentence to allow students to write the direct opposite. Ex: **Ernesto es el menor de la familia. (Ernesto es el mayor de la familia.)**

Pairs Bring in clothing catalogs and have students work in pairs to create superlative statements about the prices of different items. Ask volunteers to share some of their statements with the class. You may want to have students review clothing-related vocabulary from **Lección 6.**

Section Goal

In **Recapitulación**, students will review the grammar concepts from this lesson.

Instructional Resource
Supersite

1 Teaching Tip Before beginning the activity, ask students to identify which verb forms have stem changes.

1 Expansion To challenge students, add columns for **tú** and **nosotros**.

2 Expansion Have students create questions about the dialogue. Ex: **¿Cómo se vistieron Marta y Daniel el sábado? ¿Por qué?** Call on volunteers to answer the questions.

3 Teaching Tips
- Remind students that indirect object pronouns always precede direct object pronouns.
- To simplify, have students underline the direct object and circle the indirect object in each question.

3 Expansion
For additional practice, have pairs write a brief dialogue from the point of view of two of the restaurant's customers, using indirect and direct object pronouns. Then have pairs role-play their dialogues for the class.

Recapitulación

Diagnostics

Completa estas actividades para repasar los conceptos de gramática que aprendiste en esta lección.

1 Completar Completa la tabla con la forma correcta del pretérito. 18 pts.

Infinitive	yo	usted	ellos
dormir	dormí	durmió	durmieron
servir	serví	sirvió	sirvieron
vestirse	me vestí	se vistió	se vistieron

2 La cena Completa la conversación con el pretérito de los verbos. 14 pts.

PAULA ¡Hola, Daniel! ¿Qué tal el fin de semana?

DANIEL Muy bien. Marta y yo (1) conseguimos (conseguir) hacer muchas cosas, pero lo mejor fue la cena del sábado.

PAULA Ah, ¿sí? ¿Adónde fueron?

DANIEL Al restaurante Vistahermosa. Es elegante, así que (nosotros) (2) nos vestimos (vestirse) bien.

PAULA Y, ¿qué platos (3) pidieron (pedir, ustedes)?

DANIEL Yo (4) pedí (pedir) camarones y Marta (5) prefirió (preferir) el pollo. Y al final, el camarero nos (6) sirvió (servir) flan.

PAULA ¡Qué rico!

DANIEL Sí. Pero después de la cena Marta no (7) se sintió (sentirse) bien.

3 Camareros Genaro y Úrsula son camareros en un restaurante. Completa la conversación que tienen con su jefe usando pronombres. 8 pts.

JEFE Úrsula, ¿le ofreciste agua fría al cliente de la mesa 22?

ÚRSULA Sí, (1) se la ofrecí de inmediato.

JEFE Genaro, ¿los clientes de la mesa 5 te pidieron ensaladas?

GENARO Sí, (2) me las pidieron.

ÚRSULA Genaro, ¿recuerdas si ya me mostraste los vinos nuevos?

GENARO Sí, ya (3) te los mostré.

JEFE Genaro, ¿van a pagarte la cuenta los clientes de la mesa 5?

GENARO Sí, (4) me la van a pagar/van a pagármela ahora mismo.

RESUMEN GRAMATICAL

8.1 Preterite of stem-changing verbs p. 254

servir	dormir
serví	dormí
serviste	dormiste
sirvió	durmió
servimos	dormimos
servisteis	dormisteis
sirvieron	durmieron

8.2 Double object pronouns pp. 257–258

Indirect Object Pronouns: **me, te, le (se), nos, os, les (se)**

Direct Object Pronouns: **lo, la, los, las**

Le escribí la carta. → Se la escribí.
Nos van a servir los platos. → Nos los van a servir./ Van a servírnoslos.

8.3 Comparisons pp. 261–263

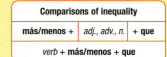

Comparisons of inequality

más/menos + *adj., adv., n.* **+ que**

verb **+ más/menos + que**

Comparisons of equality

tan + *adj., adv.,* **+ como**
tanto/a(s) + *noun* **+ como**

verb **+ tanto como**

Irregular comparative forms

bueno/a	mejor
malo/a	peor
grande	mayor
pequeño/a	menor
joven	menor
viejo/a	mayor

TEACHING OPTIONS

Game Divide the class into two teams and have them line up. Name a preterite stem-changing verb in the infinitive as well as a subject pronoun (Ex: **conseguir/ustedes**). The first team member to reach the board and correctly write the subject pronoun and the conjugated verb form earns one point (Ex: **ustedes consiguieron**). The team with the most points at the end wins.

TPR Have the class stand in a circle. Point to two students to step forward into the circle. Toss a ball to another student, who must make a comparison between the students inside the circle. Ex: **Ian es más alto que Omar.** Have students continue tossing the ball to each other and making original comparisons, until you indicate to them to pause. Then have another student join the middle of the circle, and have students make superlative statements. Repeat the process by indicating two new students to stand inside the circle.

8.4 Superlatives p. 266

el/la/ los/las +	noun	+ más/ menos +	adjective	+ de

► Irregular superlatives follow the same pattern as irregular comparatives.

4 El menú Observa el menú y sus características. Completa las oraciones basándote en los elementos dados. Usa comparativos y superlativos. 14 pts.

Ensaladas	*Precio*	*Calorías*
Ensalada de tomates	$9.00	170
Ensalada de mariscos	$12.99	325
Ensalada de zanahorias	$9.00	200
Platos principales		
Pollo con champiñones	$13.00	495
Cerdo con papas	$10.50	725
Atún con espárragos	$18.95	495

1. ensalada de mariscos / otras ensaladas / costar
   La ensalada de mariscos __cuesta más que__ las otras ensaladas.
2. pollo con champiñones / cerdo con papas / calorías
   El pollo con champiñones tiene __menos calorías que__ el cerdo con papas.
3. atún con espárragos / pollo con champiñones / calorías
   El atún con espárragos tiene __tantas calorías como__ el pollo con champiñones.
4. ensalada de tomates / ensalada de zanahorias / caro
   La ensalada de tomates es __tan cara como__ la ensalada de zanahorias.
5. cerdo con papas / platos principales / caro
   El cerdo con papas es __el menos caro de__ los platos principales.
6. ensalada de zanahorias / ensalada de tomates / costar
   La ensalada de zanahorias __cuesta tanto como__ la ensalada de tomates.
7. ensalada de mariscos / ensaladas / caro
   La ensalada de mariscos es __la más cara de__ las ensaladas.

5 Dos restaurantes ¿Cuál es el mejor restaurante que conoces? ¿Y el peor? Escribe un párrafo de por lo menos (*at least*) seis oraciones donde expliques por qué piensas así. Puedes hablar de la calidad de la comida, el ambiente, los precios, el servicio, etc. 46 pts. Answers will vary.

6 Adivinanza Completa la adivinanza y adivina la respuesta. ¡4 puntos EXTRA!

"En el campo yo nací°,
mis hermanos son
los __ajos__ (*garlic, pl.*),
y aquél que llora° por mí
me está partiendo°
en pedazos°."
¿Quién soy? __La cebolla__

nací *was born* llora *cries* partiendo *cutting* pedazos *pieces*

Practice more at **vhlcentral.com**.

4 Teaching Tips
- Remind students that the comparative **tanto/a** must agree in gender and number with the noun it modifies.
- To challenge students, have pairs ask each other questions about the menu using comparatives and superlatives. Ex: **¿Qué ensalada cuesta tanto como la ensalada de tomates? (La ensalada de zanahorias cuesta tanto como la ensalada de tomates.)**

5 Teaching Tip To help students organize their ideas, have them divide their paper into two columns: **mejor** and **peor.** Under each category, have students list the different reasons why their chosen restaurants are the best or worst.

6 Expansion Have students work in small groups to create an original riddle related to food. Have groups read their riddles for the class to guess.

TEACHING OPTIONS

TPR Have students write a celebrity's name, a place, and a thing on separate slips of paper. Collect the papers in three envelopes, separated by category. Then divide the class into two teams, **comparativos** and **superlativos**, and have them line up. Draw out two or three slips of paper (alternate randomly) and read the terms aloud. The corresponding team member has five seconds to step forward and create a logical comparison or superlative statement.

Pairs Have pairs imagine they went to a restaurant where the server mixed up all the orders. Call on pairs to share their experiences, using **pedir** and **servir** as well as double object pronouns. Ex: **Fui a un restaurante italiano. Pedí la pasta primavera. ¡El camarero me sirvió la sopa de mariscos! ¡Y me la sirvió fría! Mi compañero pidió langosta, pero el camarero no se la sirvió. ¡Le sirvió una chuleta de cerdo!**

Audio: Reading
Additional Reading

Section Goals

In **Lectura**, students will:
- learn to identify the main idea in a text
- read a content-rich menu and restaurant review

Instructional Resource
Supersite

Estrategia Tell students that recognizing the main idea of a text will help them unlock the meaning of unfamiliar words and phrases they come across while reading. Tell them to first check the title, where the main idea is often expressed. Then have them read the topic sentence of each paragraph before they read the full text to get a sense of the main idea.

Examinar el texto First, have students scan the menu. Ask how the title and subheadings help predict the content. Ask volunteers to state the meaning of each category of food served. Then have students scan the newspaper article. Ask them how the title and the format (the box with ratings) of the text give clues to the content.

Identificar la idea principal Ask students to read the column heading and the title of the article and predict the subject of the article and the author's purpose. Then have students read the topic sentence of the first paragraph and state the main idea. Finally, have them read the entire paragraph.

Lectura

NATIONAL STANDARDS communication cultures

Antes de leer

Estrategia
Reading for the main idea

As you know, you can learn a great deal about a reading selection by looking at the format and looking for cognates, titles, and subtitles. You can skim to get the gist of the reading selection and scan it for specific information. Reading for the main idea is another useful strategy; it involves locating the topic sentences of each paragraph to determine the author's purpose for writing a particular piece. Topic sentences can provide clues about the content of each paragraph, as well as the general organization of the reading. Your choice of which reading strategies to use will depend on the style and format of each reading selection.

Examinar el texto

En esta sección tenemos dos textos diferentes. ¿Qué estrategias puedes usar para leer la crítica culinaria°? ¿Cuáles son las apropiadas para familiarizarte con el menú? Utiliza las estrategias más eficaces° para cada texto. ¿Qué tienen en común? ¿Qué tipo de comida sirven en el restaurante?

Identificar la idea principal

Lee la primera oración de cada párrafo de la crítica culinaria del restaurante **La feria del maíz.** Apunta° el tema principal de cada párrafo. Luego lee todo el primer párrafo. ¿Crees que el restaurante le gustó al autor de la crítica culinaria? ¿Por qué? Ahora lee la crítica entera. En tu opinión, ¿cuál es la idea principal de la crítica? ¿Por qué la escribió el autor? Compara tus opiniones con las de un(a) compañero/a.

crítica culinaria *restaurant review* eficaces *effective*
Apunta *Jot down*

Practice more at **vhlcentral.com**.

M E N Ú

Entremeses

Tortilla servida con
• Ajiaceite (chile, aceite) • Ajicomino (chile, comino)

Pan tostado servido con
• Queso frito a la pimienta • Salsa de ajo y mayonesa

Sopas

• Tomate • Cebolla • Verduras • Pollo y huevo
• Carne de res • Mariscos

Entradas

Tomaticán
(tomate, papas, maíz, chile, arvejas y zanahorias)

Tamales
(maíz, azúcar, ajo, cebolla)

Frijoles enchilados
(frijoles negros, carne de cerdo o de res, arroz, chile)

Chilaquil
(tortilla de maíz, queso, hierbas y chile)

Tacos
(tortillas, pollo, verduras y salsa)

Cóctel de mariscos
(camarones, langosta, vinagre, sal, pimienta, aceite)

Postres°

• Plátanos caribeños • Cóctel de frutas al ron°
• Uvate (uvas, azúcar de caña y ron) • Flan napolitano
• Helado° de piña y naranja • Pastel° de yogur

Después de leer

Preguntas

En parejas, contesten estas preguntas sobre la crítica culinaria de **La feria del maíz.**

1. ¿Quién es el dueño y chef de **La feria del maíz**? Ernesto Sandoval
2. ¿Qué tipo de comida se sirve en el restaurante? tradicional
3. ¿Cuál es el problema con el servicio? Se necesitan más camareros
4. ¿Cómo es el ambiente del restaurante? agradable
5. ¿Qué comidas probó el autor? las tortillas, el ajiaceite, la sopa de mariscos, los tamales, los tacos de pollo y los plátanos caribeños
6. ¿Quieren ir ustedes al restaurante **La feria del maíz**? ¿Por qué? Answers will vary.

TEACHING OPTIONS

Small Groups Ask groups to create a dinner menu featuring their favorite dishes, including lists of ingredients similar to those in the menu above. Have groups present their menus to the class.

Heritage Speakers Ask a heritage speaker of Guatemalan origin or a student who has visited Guatemala and dined in restaurants or cafés to prepare a short presentation about his or her experiences there. Of particular interest would be a comparison and contrast of city vs. small-town restaurants. If possible, the presentation should be illustrated with menus from the restaurants, advertisements, or photos of and articles about the country.

23F

Gastronomía

Por Eduardo Fernández

La feria del maíz

Sobresaliente°. En el nuevo restaurante **La feria del maíz** va a encontrar la perfecta combinación entre la comida tradicional y el encanto° de la vieja ciudad de Antigua. Ernesto Sandoval, antiguo jefe de cocina° del famoso restaurante **El fogón**, está teniendo mucho éxito° en su nueva aventura culinaria.

El gerente°, el experimentado José Sierra, controla a la perfección la calidad del servicio. El camarero que me atendió esa noche fue muy amable en todo momento. Sólo hay que comentar que,

La feria del maíz
13 calle 4-41 Zona 1
La Antigua, Guatemala
2329912

lunes a sábado
10:30am-11:30pm
domingo 10:00am-10:00pm

Comida

Servicio

Ambiente

Precio

debido al éxito inmediato de **La feria del maíz**, se necesitan más camareros para atender a los clientes de una forma más eficaz. En esta ocasión, el mesero se tomó unos veinte minutos en traerme la bebida.

Afortunadamente, no me importó mucho la espera entre plato y plato, pues el ambiente es tan agradable que me sentí como en casa. El restaurante mantiene el estilo colonial de Antigua. Por dentro°, es elegante y rústico a la vez. Cuando el tiempo lo permite, se puede comer también en el patio, donde hay muchas flores.

El servicio de camareros y el ambiente agradable del local pasan a un segundo plano cuando llega la comida, de una calidad extraordinaria. Las tortillas de casa se sirven con un ajiaceite delicioso. La sopa de mariscos es excelente y los tamales, pues, tengo que confesar que son mejores que los de mi abuelita. También recomiendo los tacos de pollo, servidos con un mole buenísimo. De postre, don Ernesto me preparó su especialidad, unos plátanos caribeños sabrosísimos.

Los precios pueden parecer altos° para una comida tradicional, pero la calidad de los productos con que se cocinan los platos y el exquisito ambiente de **La feria del maíz** garantizan° una experiencia inolvidable°.

Bebidas

- Cerveza negra
- Chilate (bebida de maíz, chile y cacao)
- Jugos de fruta
- Agua mineral
- Té helado
- Vino tinto/blanco
- Ron

Postres *Desserts* ron *rum* Helado *Ice cream* Pastel *Cake* Sobresaliente *Outstanding* encanto *charm* jefe de cocina *head chef* éxito *success* gerente *manager* Por dentro *Inside* altos *high* garantizan *guarantee* inolvidable *unforgettable*

Preguntas

- Have students quickly review the article before answering the questions. Suggest that pairs take turns answering them. The student who does not answer a question should find the line of text that contains the answer.
- Give students these questions as items 7–9: **7. ¿Cómo fue el camarero que atendió al crítico? (Fue muy amable, pero estaba muy ocupado con otros clientes del restaurante.) 8. ¿Cuál fue la opinión del crítico con respecto a la comida? (La encontró toda de muy alta calidad.) 9. ¿Cómo son los precios de La feria del maíz? (Son altos, pero la calidad de la comida los justifica.)**

Un(a) guía turístico/a

Tú eres un(a) guía turístico/a en Guatemala. Estás en el restaurante **La feria del maíz** con un grupo de turistas norteamericanos. Ellos no hablan español y quieren pedir de comer, pero necesitan tu ayuda. Lee nuevamente el menú e indica qué error comete cada turista.

1. La señora Johnson es diabética y no puede comer azúcar. Pide sopa de verduras y tamales. No pide nada de postre.
   No debe pedir los tamales porque tienen azúcar.
2. Los señores Petit son vegetarianos y piden sopa de tomate, frijoles enchilados y plátanos caribeños.
   No deben pedir los frijoles enchilados porque tienen carne.
3. El señor Smith, que es alérgico al chocolate, pide tortilla servida con ajiaceite, chilaquil y chilate para beber.
   No debe pedir chilate porque tiene cacao.
4. La adorable hija del señor Smith tiene sólo cuatro años y le gustan mucho las verduras y las frutas naturales. Su papá le pide tomaticán y un cóctel de frutas.
   No debe pedir el cóctel de frutas porque tiene ron.
5. La señorita Jackson está a dieta y pide uvate, flan napolitano y helado.
   No debe pedir postres porque está a dieta.

Un(a) guía turístico/a Have students select an alternative food for the customer to order that would better suit his/her dietary needs.

The Affective Dimension
A source of discomfort in travel can be unfamiliar foods. Tell students that by learning about the foods of a country they are going to visit they can make that part of their visit even more enjoyable.

TEACHING OPTIONS

Large Groups Ask students to review the items in **Un(a) guía turístico/a**, write a conversation, and role-play the scene involving a tour guide eating lunch in a Guatemalan restaurant with several tourists. Have them work in groups of eight to assign the following roles: **camarero, guía turístico/a, la señora Johnson, los señores Petit, el señor Smith, la hija del señor Smith,** and **la señorita Jackson**. Have groups perform their skits for the class.

Variación léxica Tell students that the adjective of place or nationality for Guatemala is **guatemalteco/a**. Guatemalans often use a more colloquial term, **chapín**, as a synonym for **guatemalteco/a**.

Video: *Panorama cultural*
Interactive map

Section Goal

In **Panorama**, students will read about the geography, history, and culture of Guatemala.

Instructional Resources
Supersite: Video (***Panorama cultural***); Resources (Scripts, Translations, Digital Image Bank, Answer Keys)
WebSAM
Workbook, pp. 95–96
Video Manual, pp. 45–46

Teaching Tips

- Use the **Lección 8 Panorama** digital images to assist with this presentation.
- As students examine the map in their books, point out that Guatemala has three main climatic regions: the tropical Pacific and Caribbean coasts, the highlands (southwest), and jungle lowlands (north). Ask volunteers to read aloud the names of the cities, mountains, and rivers of Guatemala. Point out that indigenous languages are the source of many place names.

El país en cifras As you read about the languages of Guatemala, you might point out that while some Guatemalans are monolingual in either Spanish or a Mayan language, many are bilingual, speaking an indigenous language and Spanish.

¡Increíble pero cierto! Guatemala is internationally renowned for the wealth and diversity of its textile arts. Each village has a traditional, "signature" weaving style that allows others to quickly identify where each beautiful piece comes from.

Guatemala

NATIONAL STANDARDS connections cultures

El país en cifras

- **Área:** 108.890 km² (42.042 millas²), *un poco más pequeño que Tennessee*
- **Población:** 14.647.000
- **Capital:** Ciudad de Guatemala—1.075.000
- **Ciudades principales:** Quetzaltenango, Escuintla, Mazatenango, Puerto Barrios
- **Moneda:** quetzal
- **Idiomas:** español (oficial), lenguas mayas, xinca, garífuna

El español es la lengua de un 60 por ciento° de la población; el otro 40 por ciento tiene como lengua materna el xinca, el garífuna o, en su mayoría°, una de las lenguas mayas (cakchiquel, quiché y kekchícomo, entre otras). Una palabra que las lenguas mayas tienen en común es ixim, que significa 'maíz', un cultivo° de mucha importancia en estas culturas.

Mujeres indígenas limpiando cebollas

Bandera de Guatemala

Guatemaltecos célebres

- **Carlos Mérida,** pintor (1891–1984)
- **Miguel Ángel Asturias,** escritor (1899–1974)
- **Margarita Carrera,** poeta y ensayista (1929–)
- **Rigoberta Menchú Tum,** activista (1959–), Premio Nobel de la Paz° en 1992
- **Jaime Viñals Massanet,** montañista (1966–)

por ciento *percent* en su mayoría *most of them* cultivo *crop* Paz *Peace* telas *fabrics* tinte *dye* aplastados *crushed* hace... destiñan *keeps the colors from running*

Palacio Nacional de la Cultura en la Ciudad de Guatemala

Iglesia de la Merced en Antigua Guatemala

recursos
WB pp. 95–96 | VM pp. 45–46 | vhlcentral.com Lección 8

¡Increíble pero cierto!

¿Qué "ingrediente" secreto se encuentra en las telas° tradicionales de Guatemala? ¡El mosquito! El excepcional tinte° de estas telas es producto de una combinación de flores y de mosquitos aplastados°. El insecto hace que los colores no se destiñan°. Quizás es por esto que los artesanos representan la figura del mosquito en muchas de sus telas.

TEACHING OPTIONS

Worth Noting Although the indigenous population of Guatemala is Mayan, many place names in southwestern Guatemala are in Nahuatl, the language of the Aztecs of central Mexico. In the sixteenth century, Guatemala was conquered by Spaniards who came from the Valley of Mexico after having overthrown the Aztec rulers there. The Spanish were accompanied by large numbers of Nahuatl-speaking allies, who renamed the captured Mayan strongholds with Nahuatl names. The suffix **–tenango**, which appears in many of these names, means *place with a wall,* that is, a fortified place. **Quetzaltenango**, then, means *fortified place of the quetzal bird;* **Mazatenango** means *fortified place of the deer.*

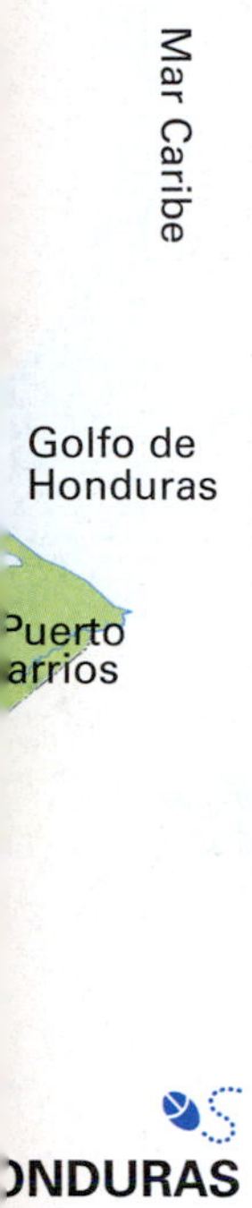

Ciudades • Antigua Guatemala

Antigua Guatemala fue fundada en 1543. Fue una capital de gran importancia hasta 1773, cuando un terremoto° la destruyó. Sin embargo, conserva el carácter original de su arquitectura y hoy es uno de los centros turísticos del país. Su celebración de la Semana Santa° es, para muchas personas, la más importante del hemisferio.

Naturaleza • El quetzal

El quetzal simbolizó la libertad para los antiguos° mayas porque creían° que este pájaro° no podía° vivir en cautiverio°. Hoy el quetzal es el símbolo nacional. El pájaro da su nombre a la moneda nacional y aparece también en los billetes° del país. Desafortunadamente, está en peligro° de extinción. Para su protección, el gobierno mantiene una reserva ecológica especial.

Historia • Los mayas

Desde 1500 a.C. hasta 900 d.C., los mayas habitaron gran parte de lo que ahora es Guatemala. Su civilización fue muy avanzada. Los mayas fueron arquitectos y constructores de pirámides, templos y observatorios. También descubrieron° y usaron el cero antes que los europeos, e inventaron un calendario complejo° y preciso.

Artesanía • La ropa tradicional

La ropa tradicional de los guatemaltecos se llama *huipil* y muestra el amor° de la cultura maya por la naturaleza. Ellos se inspiran en las flores°, plantas y animales para crear sus diseños° de colores vivos° y formas geométricas. El diseño y los colores de cada *huipil* indican el pueblo de origen y a veces también el sexo y la edad° de la persona que lo lleva.

¿Qué aprendiste? Responde a cada pregunta con una oración completa.

1. ¿Qué significa la palabra *ixim*?
   La palabra *ixim* significa "maíz".
2. ¿Quién es Rigoberta Menchú?
   Rigoberta Menchú es una activista de Guatemala.
3. ¿Qué pájaro representa a Guatemala?
   El quetzal representa a Guatemala.
4. ¿Qué simbolizó el quetzal para los mayas?
   El quetzal simbolizó la libertad para los mayas.
5. ¿Cuál es la moneda nacional de Guatemala?
   La moneda nacional de Guatemala es el quetzal.
6. ¿De qué fueron arquitectos los mayas?
   Los mayas fueron arquitectos de pirámides, templos y observatorios.
7. ¿Qué celebración de la Antigua Guatemala es la más importante del hemisferio para muchas personas? La celebración de la Semana Santa de la Antigua Guatemala es la más importante del hemisferio.
8. ¿Qué descubrieron los mayas antes que los europeos? Los mayas descubrieron el cero antes que los europeos.
9. ¿Qué muestra la ropa tradicional de los guatemaltecos? La ropa muestra el amor a la naturaleza.
10. ¿Qué indica un *huipil* con su diseño y sus colores? Con su diseño y colores, un *huipil* indica el pueblo de origen, el sexo y la edad de la persona.

Conexión Internet Investiga estos temas en **vhlcentral.com**.

1. Busca información sobre Rigoberta Menchú. ¿De dónde es? ¿Qué libros publicó? ¿Por qué es famosa?
2. Estudia un sitio arqueológico de Guatemala para aprender más sobre los mayas y prepara un breve informe para tu clase.

Practice more at **vhlcentral.com**.

terremoto *earthquake* **Semana Santa** *Holy Week* **antiguos** *ancient* **creían** *they believed* **pájaro** *bird* **no podía** *couldn't* **cautiverio** *captivity* **los billetes** *bills* **peligro** *danger* **descubrieron** *they discovered* **complejo** *complex* **amor** *love* **flores** *flowers* **diseños** *designs* **vivos** *bright* **edad** *age*

Antigua Guatemala Have students use tour books and the Internet to read more about **Semana Santa** celebrations in this Guatemalan city, usually referred to simply as Antigua. Also, you may want to play the ***Panorama cultural*** video footage for this lesson that focuses on Antigua and Chichicastenango.

El quetzal Recent conservation efforts in Guatemala, Costa Rica, and other Central American nations have focused on preserving the cloud forests (**bosques nubosos**) that are home to the **quetzal**.

Los mayas Today ethnobotanists work with Mayan traditional healers to learn about medicinal uses of plants of the region.

La ropa tradicional Many indigenous Guatemalans still wear traditional clothing richly decorated with embroidery. The **huipil** is a long, sleeveless tunic worn by women. A distinctively woven **faja**, or waist sash, identifies the town or village each woman comes from.

Conexión Internet Students will find supporting Internet activities and links at **vhlcentral.com**.

TEACHING OPTIONS

Worth Noting Spanish is a second language for more than 40% of Guatemalans. Students may be interested to learn that Guatemala has many bilingual education programs, where native languages are used in addition to Spanish for instructional purposes. There are also many government-sponsored Spanish as a Second Language (SSL) programs, offered through schools and radio or television. Speakers of Guatemala's indigenous languages often encounter problems similar to those found by other learners of Spanish: difficulty with agreement of number and gender.

Instructional Resources
Supersite: Audio (Textbook & Lab MP3s); Testing Program (Tests, MP3s)
WebSAM
Lab Manual, p. 48

Las comidas

el/la camarero/a	*waiter/waitress*
la comida	*food; meal*
la cuenta	*bill*
el/la dueño/a	*owner*
el menú	*menu*
la propina	*tip*
la sección de (no) fumar	*(non) smoking section*
el almuerzo	*lunch*
la cena	*dinner*
el desayuno	*breakfast*
los entremeses	*appetizers*
el plato (principal)	*(main) dish*
delicioso/a	*delicious*
rico/a	*tasty; delicious*
sabroso/a	*tasty; delicious*

Las frutas

la banana	*banana*
las frutas	*fruits*
el limón	*lemon*
la manzana	*apple*
el melocotón	*peach*
la naranja	*orange*
la pera	*pear*
la uva	*grape*

Las verduras

las arvejas	*peas*
la cebolla	*onion*
el champiñón	*mushroom*
la ensalada	*salad*
los espárragos	*asparagus*
los frijoles	*beans*
la lechuga	*lettuce*
el maíz	*corn*
las papas/patatas (fritas)	*(fried) potatoes; French fries*
el tomate	*tomato*
las verduras	*vegetables*
la zanahoria	*carrot*

La carne y el pescado

el atún	*tuna*
el bistec	*steak*
los camarones	*shrimp*
la carne	*meat*
la carne de res	*beef*
la chuleta (de cerdo)	*(pork) chop*
la hamburguesa	*hamburger*
el jamón	*ham*
la langosta	*lobster*
los mariscos	*shellfish*
el pavo	*turkey*
el pescado	*fish*
el pollo (asado)	*(roast) chicken*
la salchicha	*sausage*
el salmón	*salmon*

Otras comidas

el aceite	*oil*
el ajo	*garlic*
el arroz	*rice*
el azúcar	*sugar*
los cereales	*cereal; grains*
el huevo	*egg*
la mantequilla	*butter*
la margarina	*margarine*
la mayonesa	*mayonnaise*
el pan (tostado)	*(toasted) bread*
la pimienta	*black pepper*
el queso	*cheese*
la sal	*salt*
el sándwich	*sandwich*
la sopa	*soup*
el vinagre	*vinegar*
el yogur	*yogurt*

Las bebidas

el agua (mineral)	*(mineral) water*
la bebida	*drink*
el café	*coffee*
la cerveza	*beer*
el jugo (de fruta)	*(fruit) juice*
la leche	*milk*
el refresco	*soft drink*
el té (helado)	*(iced) tea*
el vino (blanco/tinto)	*(white/red) wine*

Verbos

escoger	*to choose*
merendar (e:ie)	*to snack*
morir (o:ue)	*to die*
pedir (e:i)	*to order (food)*
probar (o:ue)	*to taste; to try*
recomendar (e:ie)	*to recommend*
saber (a)	*to taste (like)*
servir (e:i)	*to serve*

Las comparaciones

como	*like; as*
más de (+ *number*)	*more than*
más... que	*more... than*
menos de (+ *number*)	*fewer than*
menos... que	*less... than*
tan... como	*as... as*
tantos/as... como	*as many... as*
tanto... como	*as much... as*
el/la mayor	*the oldest*
el/la mejor	*the best*
el/la menor	*the youngest*
el/la peor	*the worst*
mejor	*better*
peor	*worse*

Expresiones útiles	*See page 249.*

recursos
LM p. 48 | vhlcentral.com Lección 8

Vocabulary Tools

Las fiestas

9

Communicative Goals

You will learn how to:

- **Express congratulations**
- **Express gratitude**
- **Ask for and pay the bill at a restaurant**

A PRIMERA VISTA

- ¿Se conocen ellos?
- ¿Cómo se sienten, alegres o tristes?
- ¿Está el hombre más contento que la mujer?
- ¿De qué color es su ropa?

Lesson Goals

In **Lección 9**, students will be introduced to the following:

- terms for parties and celebrations
- words for stages of life and personal relationships
- **Semana Santa** celebrations
- Chile's International Music Festival in **Viña del Mar**
- irregular preterites
- verbs that change meaning in the preterite
- uses of **¿qué?** and **¿cuál?**
- pronouns after prepositions
- recognizing word families
- using a Venn diagram to organize information
- writing a comparative analysis
- using context to infer the meaning of unfamiliar words
- a television commercial about **Las Fiestas Patrias** and other celebrations in Chile
- the short film ***Iker pelos tiesos***
- a video about **las fiestas de la calle San Sebastián** in San Juan, Puerto Rico
- cultural, geographic, and economic information about Chile

A primera vista Here are some additional questions you can ask to personalize the photo: **¿Fuiste a una fiesta importante el año pasado? ¿Cuál fue la ocasión? ¿Sirvieron comida en la fiesta? ¿Qué sirvieron?**

Teaching Tip Look for these icons for additional communicative practice:

	Interpretive communication
	Presentational communication
	Interpersonal communication

INSTRUCTIONAL RESOURCES

Supersite (vhlcentral.com)
Video: ***Fotonovela, Flash cultura, Anuncio, Cortometraje, Panorama cultural***
Audio: Textbook and Lab MP3 Files
Activity Pack: Information Gap Activities, games, additional activity handouts
Resources: SAM Answer Key, Scripts, Translations, **Vocabulario adicional**, sample lesson plan, Grammar Presentation Slides, Digital Image Bank
Testing Program: Quizzes, Tests, Exams, MP3s
Student Activities Manual: Workbook/Video Manual/Lab Manual
WebSAM (online Student Activities Manual)

Vocabulary Tools

Section Goals

In **Contextos**, students will learn and practice:

- vocabulary related to parties and celebrations
- vocabulary used to talk about stages of life and personal relationships

Instructional Resources

Supersite: Audio (Textbook and Lab MP3 Files); Resources (Digital Image Bank, **Vocabulario adicional**, Activity Pack, Scripts, Answer Keys); Testing Program (Quizzes)
WebSAM
Workbook, pp. 97–98
Lab Manual, p. 49

Teaching Tips

- Ask about parties. Ex: **¿Fuiste a una fiesta el fin de semana pasado? ¿Qué tomaste allí? ¿Comiste algo? ¿Bailaste? ¿Escuchaste música?** Write **divertirse** on the board and explain what it means. Ask: **¿Te divertiste?** Also write **pasarlo bien** on the board. Say: **Ah, te divertiste mucho allí. Entonces, lo pasaste bien, ¿no? No lo pasaste mal.**
- Use the **Lección 9 Contextos** digital images to assist with this presentation.
- Have students respond to true/false statements about the illustrations in **Contextos**. Ex: **1. Es una fiesta de cumpleaños. (Cierto.) 2. Muchas personas lo pasan mal en la fiesta. (Falso.)** Next, ask students about parties. Ex: **¿Qué tipo de fiesta te gusta más? ¿Te gusta recibir regalos?**

Note: At this point you may want to present ***Vocabulario adicional: Más vocabulario para las celebraciones*** from the Supersite.

Las fiestas

Más vocabulario

la alegría	*happiness*
la amistad	*friendship*
el amor	*love*
el beso	*kiss*
la sorpresa	*surprise*
el aniversario (de bodas)	*(wedding) anniversary*
la boda	*wedding*
el cumpleaños	*birthday*
el día de fiesta	*holiday*
el divorcio	*divorce*
el matrimonio	*marriage*
la Navidad	*Christmas*
la quinceañera	*young woman celebrating her fifteenth birthday*
el/la recién casado/a	*newlywed*
cambiar (de)	*to change*
celebrar	*to celebrate*
divertirse (e:ie)	*to have fun*
graduarse (de/en)	*to graduate (from/in)*
invitar	*to invite*
jubilarse	*to retire (from work)*
nacer	*to be born*
odiar	*to hate*
pasarlo bien/mal	*to have a good/bad time*
reírse (e:i)	*to laugh*
relajarse	*to relax*
sonreír (e:i)	*to smile*
sorprender	*to surprise*
juntos/as	*together*
¡Felicidades!/ ¡Felicitaciones!	*Congratulations!*

Variación léxica

pastel ⟷ torta (*Arg., Col., Venez.*)
comprometerse ⟷ prometerse (*Esp.*)

recursos

WB pp. 97–98	LM p. 49	vhlcentral.com Lección 9

TEACHING OPTIONS

Extra Practice Ask students questions about birthdays and other celebrations and what days and months they fall on. Ask: ____, **¿cuándo es tu cumpleaños? (¿Qué día naciste?) ¿Estás casado/a? ¿Cuándo es tu aniversario de bodas?** Verify comprehension by asking other students to repeat. Then ask more general questions: **¿Cuándo es la Navidad?**

Worth Noting Point out that in addition to or instead of celebrating their birthday, many Hispanics celebrate their **día del santo**, or Saint's Day. This is the day that celebrates the saint for whom a person was named. In many Hispanic countries, the **día del santo** is just as important and significant in an individual's life as his or her birthday.

Relaciones personales

casarse (con)	*to get married (to)*
comprometerse (con)	*to get engaged (to)*
divorciarse (de)	*to get divorced (from)*
enamorarse (de)	*to fall in love (with)*
llevarse bien/mal (con)	*to get along well/ badly (with)*
romper (con)	*to break up (with)*
salir (con)	*to go out (with); to date*
separarse (de)	*to separate (from)*
tener una cita	*to have a date; to have an appointment*

Práctica

1 Escuchar Escucha la conversación e indica si las oraciones son **ciertas** o **falsas**.

1. A Silvia no le gusta mucho el chocolate. Falsa.
2. Silvia sabe que sus amigos le van a hacer una fiesta. Falsa.
3. Los amigos de Silvia le compraron un pastel de chocolate. Cierta.
4. Los amigos brindan por Silvia con refrescos. Falsa.
5. Silvia y sus amigos van a comer helado. Cierta.
6. Los amigos de Silvia le van a servir flan y galletas. Falsa.

2 Ordenar Escucha la narración y ordena las oraciones de acuerdo con los eventos de la vida de Beatriz.

__5__ a. Beatriz se compromete con Roberto.
__4__ b. Beatriz se gradúa.
__3__ c. Beatriz sale con Emilio.
__2__ d. Sus padres le hacen una gran fiesta.
__6__ e. La pareja se casa.
__1__ f. Beatriz nace en Montevideo.

3 Emparejar Indica la letra de la frase que mejor completa cada oración.

a. cambió de	d. nos divertimos	g. se llevan bien
b. lo pasaron mal	e. se casaron	h. sonrió
c. nació	f. se jubiló	i. tenemos una cita

1. María y sus compañeras de cuarto __g__. Son buenas amigas.
2. Pablo y yo __d__ en la fiesta. Bailamos y comimos mucho.
3. Manuel y Felipe __b__ en el cine. La película fue muy mala.
4. ¡Tengo una nueva sobrina! Ella __c__ ayer por la mañana.
5. Mi madre __a__ profesión. Ahora es artista.
6. Mi padre __f__ el año pasado. Ahora no trabaja.
7. Jorge y yo __i__ esta noche. Vamos a ir a un restaurante muy elegante.
8. Jaime y Laura __e__ el septiembre pasado. La boda fue maravillosa.

4 Definiciones En parejas, definan las palabras y escriban una oración para cada ejemplo. Answers will vary. Suggested answers below.

modelo

romper (con) *una pareja termina la relación*
Marta rompió con su novio.

1. regalar dar un regalo
2. helado una comida fría y dulce
3. pareja dos personas enamoradas
4. invitado una persona que va a una fiesta
5. casarse ellos deciden estar juntos para siempre
6. pasarlo bien divertirse
7. sorpresa la persona no sabe lo que va a pasar
8. amistad la relación entre dos personas que se llevan bien

1 Teaching Tip Before playing the audio, have students read through the statements.

1 Script E1: ¿Estamos listos, amigos? E2: Creo que sí. Aquí tenemos el pastel y el helado… E3: De chocolate, espero. Ustedes saben cómo le encanta a Silvia el chocolate… E2: Por supuesto, el chocolate para Silvia. Bueno, un pastel de chocolate, el helado… *Script continues on page 278.*

2 Teaching Tip Before listening, point out that although the items are in the present tense, students will hear a mix of present indicative and preterite in the audio.

2 Script Beatriz García nace en Montevideo, Uruguay. Siempre celebra su cumpleaños con pastel y helado. Para su cumpleaños número veinte, sus padres la sorprendieron y le organizaron una gran fiesta. Beatriz se divirtió muchísimo y conoció a Emilio, un chico muy simpático. Después de varias citas, Beatriz rompió con Emilio porque no fueron compatibles. Luego de dos años Beatriz conoció a Roberto en su fiesta de graduación y se enamoraron. En Navidad se comprometieron y celebraron su matrimonio un año más tarde al que asistieron más de cien invitados. Los recién casados son muy felices juntos y ya están planeando otra gran fiesta para celebrar su primer aniversario de bodas. *Textbook MP3s*

3 Expansion Have students write three cloze sentences based on the drawing on pages 276–277 for a partner to complete.

4 Expansion Ask students questions using verbs from the **Relaciones personales** box. Ex: **¿Con quién te llevas mal?**

TEACHING OPTIONS

Heritage Speakers Ask heritage speakers about some Hispanic holidays or other celebrations that they or their families typically celebrate, such as **el Día de los Reyes Magos, el día del santo, la fiesta de quince años, Carnaval,** and **el Día de los Muertos**. Ask speakers to elaborate on what the celebrations are like: who attends, what they eat and drink, why those days are celebrated, and so forth.

Game Play **Concentración**. Write vocabulary items that pertain to parties and celebrations on each of eight cards. On another eight cards, draw or paste a picture that matches each description. Place the cards face-down in four rows of four. In pairs, students select two cards. If the two cards match, the pair keeps them. If the two cards do not match, students replace them in their original position. The pair with the most cards at the end wins.

1 Script (continued) E3: ¿El helado es de la cafetería o lo compraste cerca de la residencia estudiantil? E2: Lo compré en la tienda que está al lado de nuestra residencia. Es mejor que el helado de la cafetería. E1: Psstt… aquí viene Silvia… E1, E2, E3: ¡Sorpresa! ¡Sorpresa, Silvia! ¡Felicidades! E4: ¡Qué sorpresa! ¡Gracias, amigos, muchas gracias! E1: Y ahora, ¡brindamos por nuestra amiga! E3: ¿Con qué brindamos? ¿Con el champán? E1: ¡Cómo no! ¡Por nuestra amiga Silvia, la más joven de todos nosotros! *Textbook MP3s*

Teaching Tips

- Engage students in a conversation about the stages in **Sergio's** life. Say: **Miren al bebé en el primer dibujo. ¡Qué contento está! ¿Qué hace en el segundo dibujo? Está paseando en un triciclo, ¿no? ¿Quiénes se acuerdan de su niñez?**
- Make true/false statements and have students correct the false ones. Ex: **La vejez ocurre antes de la niñez. (Falso. La vejez ocurre después de la madurez.)**

5 Expansion Have students create original sentences that describe events from **Más vocabulario** on page 276. Their partner has to name the event described. Ex: **Lourdes y Mario llevan diez años de casados. (el aniversario de bodas)**

¡Lengua viva! In the United States, **fiestas de quince años** have become big business. For many immigrants, giving an elaborate party represents a way to affirm both cultural identity and socioeconomic status.

6 Expansion In pairs, have students take turns making statements about celebrities, using the answers. Ex: **La muerte de Leonard Nimoy fue en el 2015.**

Las etapas de la vida de Sergio

el nacimiento

la niñez

la adolescencia

la juventud

la madurez

la vejez

Más vocabulario

la edad	*age*
el estado civil	*marital status*
las etapas de la vida	*the stages of life*
la muerte	*death*
casado/a	*married*
divorciado/a	*divorced*
separado/a	*separated*
soltero/a	*single*
viudo/a	*widower/widow*

5 **Las etapas de la vida** Identifica las etapas de la vida que se describen en estas oraciones.

1. Mi abuela se jubiló y se mudó (*moved*) a Viña del Mar. la vejez
2. Mi padre trabaja para una compañía grande en Santiago. la madurez
3. ¿Viste a mi nuevo sobrino en el hospital? Es precioso y ¡tan pequeño! el nacimiento
4. Mi abuelo murió este año. la vejez/la muerte
5. Mi hermana celebró su fiesta de quince años. la adolescencia
6. Mi hermana pequeña juega con muñecas (*dolls*). la niñez

6 **Cambiar** En parejas, imaginen que son dos hermanos/as de diferentes edades. Cada vez que el/la hermano/a menor dice algo, se equivoca. El/La hermano/a mayor lo/la corrige (*corrects him/her*), cambiando las expresiones subrayadas (*underlined*). Túrnense para ser mayor y menor, decir algo equivocado y corregir.

modelo

Estudiante 1: La niñez es cuando trabajamos mucho.
Estudiante 2: No, te equivocas (*you're wrong*). La madurez es cuando trabajamos mucho.

1. El nacimiento es el fin de la vida. la muerte
2. La juventud es la etapa cuando nos jubilamos. la vejez
3. A los sesenta y cinco años, muchas personas comienzan a trabajar. se jubilan
4. Julián y nuestra prima se divorcian mañana. se casan
5. Mamá odia a su hermana. quiere/se lleva bien con
6. El abuelo murió, por eso la abuela es separada. viuda
7. Cuando te gradúas de la universidad, estás en la etapa de la adolescencia. la juventud
8. Mi tío nunca se casó; es viudo. soltero

Practice more at **vhlcentral.com**.

NOTA CULTURAL

Viña del Mar es una ciudad en la costa de Chile, situada al oeste de Santiago. Tiene playas hermosas, excelentes hoteles, casinos y buenos restaurantes. El poeta Pablo Neruda pasó muchos años allí.

¡LENGUA VIVA!

The term **quinceañera** refers to a girl who is celebrating her 15th birthday. The party is called **la fiesta de quince años**.

AYUDA

Other ways to contradict someone:
No es verdad. *It's not true.*
Creo que no. *I don't think so.*
¡Claro que no! *Of course not!*
¡Qué va! *No way!*

TEACHING OPTIONS

Small Groups In small groups, have students perform a skit whose content describes and/or displays a particular stage of life (youth, old age, etc.) or marital status (married, single, divorced). The rest of the class has to try to figure out what the group is displaying.

Game Play a modified version of **20 Preguntas**. Ask a volunteer to think of a famous person. Other students get one chance each to ask a yes/no question until someone guesses the name correctly. Limit attempts to ten questions per famous person. Point out that students can narrow down their selection by using vocabulary about the stages of life and marital status.

Comunicación

7 **Una fiesta** Trabaja con un(a) compañero/a para planear una fiesta. Recuerda incluir la siguiente información. Answers will vary.

1. ¿Qué tipo de fiesta es? ¿Dónde va a ser? ¿Cuándo va a ser?
2. ¿A quiénes van a invitar?
3. ¿Qué van a comer? ¿Quiénes van a llevar o a preparar la comida?
4. ¿Qué van a beber? ¿Quiénes van a traer las bebidas?
5. ¿Cómo planean entretener a los invitados? ¿Van a bailar o a jugar algún juego?
6. Después de la fiesta, ¿quiénes van a limpiar (*to clean*)?

8 **Encuesta** Tu profesor(a) va a darte una hoja de actividades. Haz las preguntas de la hoja a dos o tres compañeros/as de clase para saber qué actitudes tienen en sus relaciones personales. Luego comparte los resultados de la encuesta con la clase y comenta tus conclusiones. Answers will vary.

Preguntas	Nombres	Actitudes
1. ¿Te importa la amistad? ¿Por qué?		
2. ¿Es mejor tener un(a) buen(a) amigo/a o muchos/as amigos/as?		
3. ¿Cuáles son las características que buscas en tus amigos/as?		
4. ¿Tienes novio/a? ¿A qué edad es posible enamorarse?		
5. ¿Deben las parejas hacer todo juntos? ¿Deben tener las mismas opiniones? ¿Por qué?		

¡LENGUA VIVA!

While a **buen(a) amigo/a** is a *good friend*, the term **amigo/a íntimo/a** refers to a *close friend*, or a very good friend, without any romantic overtones.

9 **Minidrama** En parejas, consulten la ilustración de la página 278 y luego, usando las palabras de la lista, preparen un minidrama para representar las etapas de la vida de Sergio. Pueden inventar más información sobre su vida. Answers will vary.

amor	celebrar	enamorarse	romper
boda	comprometerse	graduarse	salir
cambiar	cumpleaños	jubilarse	separarse
casarse	divorciarse	nacer	tener una cita

7 Teaching Tip To simplify, create a seven-column chart on the board with the headings **Lugar, Fecha y hora, Invitados, Comida, Bebidas, Actividades,** and **Limpieza**. Have groups brainstorm a few items for each category.

7 Expansion
- Ask volunteer groups to describe the party they have just planned.
- Have students make invitations for their party. Ask the class to judge which invitation is the cleverest, funniest, most elegant, etc.

8 Teaching Tip Distribute the ***Hojas de actividades*** (Activity Pack/Supersite). Give students ten minutes to ask other group members the questions.

8 Expansion Take a survey of the attitudes found in the entire class. Ex: **¿Quiénes creen que es más importante tener un buen amigo que muchos amigos? ¿Quiénes creen que es más importante tener muchos amigos que un buen amigo?**

9 Teaching Tip To simplify, read through the word list as a class and have students name the stage or stages of life that correspond to each word.

9 Expansion After all skits have been presented, have the class vote on the most original, funniest, truest to life, etc.

TEACHING OPTIONS

Extra Practice Add a visual aspect to this vocabulary practice. Using magazine pictures, display images that pertain to parties or celebrations, stages of life, or interpersonal relations. Have students describe the pictures and make guesses about who the people are, how they are feeling, and so forth.

Extra Practice Add an auditory aspect to this vocabulary practice. As a listening comprehension activity, prepare short descriptions of five easily recognizable people. Use as much active lesson vocabulary as possible. Write their names on the board in random order. Then read the descriptions aloud and have students match each one to the appropriate name. Ex: **Me divorcié tres veces, la última vez de otro cantante latino. Yo canto, pero también soy actriz y tengo mi propia marca de perfumes. (Jennifer López)**

Section Goals

In **Fotonovela**, students will:

- receive comprehensible input from free-flowing discourse
- learn functional phrases that preview lesson grammatical structures

Instructional Resources
Supersite: Video (***Fotonovela***); Resources (Scripts, Translations, Answer Keys)
WebSAM
Video Manual, pp. 17–18

Video Recap: Lección 8 Before doing this **Fotonovela** section, review the previous episode with these questions:
1. ¿Cuáles son los especiales del día en el restaurante? (El ceviche de camarón y el bistec con verduras a la plancha.) 2. ¿Qué pidió de plato principal Maru? ¿Y Miguel? (Maru pidió el jamón y Miguel pidió el pollo asado con champiñones y papas.) 3. ¿Quiénes le quitaron la comida al camarero? (Juan Carlos y Felipe se la quitaron.) 4. ¿Quiénes pagaron la comida de Maru y Miguel? (Felipe y Juan Carlos la pagaron.)

Video Synopsis The **Díaz** family gets ready for their annual **Día de Muertos** celebration. The whole family participates in the preparations, and **Ana María** shows **Marissa** and **Jimena** how to make **mole**. **Juan Carlos** is invited to accompany the family to the cemetery, where **Ana María, Ramón,** and **Roberto** remember their parents.

Teaching Tip Have students read the first line of dialogue in each caption and guess what happens in this episode.

El Día de Muertos

NATIONAL STANDARDS communication cultures

La familia Díaz conmemora el Día de Muertos.

PERSONAJES

MARISSA JIMENA FELIPE JUAN CARLOS

Video: *Fotonovela*

MAITE FUENTES El Día de Muertos se celebra en México el primero y el segundo de noviembre. Como pueden ver, hay calaveras de azúcar, flores, música y comida por todas partes. Ésta es una fiesta única que todos deben ver por lo menos una vez en la vida.

MARISSA *Holy moley!* ¡Está delicioso!

TÍA ANA MARÍA Mi mamá me enseñó a prepararlo. El mole siempre fue el plato favorito de mi papá. Mi hijo Eduardo nació el día de su cumpleaños. Por eso le pusimos su nombre.

TÍO RAMÓN ¿Dónde están mis hermanos?

JIMENA Mi papá y Felipe están en el otro cuarto. Esos dos antipáticos no quieren decirnos qué están haciendo. Y la tía Ana María...

TÍO RAMÓN ... está en la cocina.

TÍA ANA MARÍA Marissa, ¿le puedes llevar esa foto que está ahí a Carolina? La necesita para el altar.

MARISSA Sí. ¿Son sus padres?

TÍA ANA MARÍA Sí, el día de su boda.

MARISSA ¿Cómo se conocieron?

TÍA ANA MARÍA En la fiesta de un amigo. Fue amor a primera vista.

MARISSA (*Señala la foto.*) La voy a llevar al altar.

TÍA ANA MARÍA Ramón, ¿cómo estás?

TÍO RAMÓN Bien, gracias. ¿Y Mateo? ¿No vino contigo?

TÍA ANA MARÍA No. Ya sabes que me casé con un doctor y, pues, trabaja muchísimo.

TEACHING OPTIONS

Video Tips General suggestions for using video clips in the classroom can be found in the front matter of this Instructor's Annotated Edition.
El Día de Muertos Ask students to brainstorm a list of things that might happen during a celebration honoring deceased ancestors. Then play the **El Día de Muertos** episode once, asking students to take notes about what they see and hear. After viewing, have students use their notes to tell you what happened in this episode. Then play the segment again to allow students to refine their notes. Repeat the discussion process and guide the class to an accurate summary of the plot.

SRA. DÍAZ | SR. DÍAZ | TÍA ANA MARÍA | TÍO RAMÓN | TÍA NAYELI | DON DIEGO | MARTA | VALENTINA | MAITE FUENTES

SR. DÍAZ Familia Díaz, deben prepararse...

FELIPE ... ¡para la sorpresa de sus vidas!

JUAN CARLOS Gracias por invitarme.

SR. DÍAZ Juan Carlos, como eres nuestro amigo, ya eres parte de la familia.

(En el cementerio)

JIMENA Yo hice las galletas y el pastel. ¿Dónde los puse?

MARTA Postres... ¿Cuál prefiero? ¿Galletas? ¿Pastel? ¡Dulces!

VALENTINA Me gustan las galletas.

SR. DÍAZ Brindamos por ustedes, mamá y papá.

TÍO RAMÓN Todas las otras noches estamos separados. Pero esta noche estamos juntos.

TÍA ANA MARÍA Con gratitud y amor.

Expresiones útiles

Discussing family history

El mole siempre fue el plato favorito de mi papá.
Mole was always my dad's favorite dish.
Mi hijo Eduardo nació el día de su cumpleaños.
My son Eduardo was born on his birthday.
Por eso le pusimos su nombre.
That's why we named him after him (after my father).
¿Cómo se conocieron sus padres?
How did your parents meet?
En la fiesta de un amigo. Fue amor a primera vista.
At a friend's party. It was love at first sight.

Talking about a party/celebration

Ésta es una fiesta única que todos deben ver por lo menos una vez.
This is a unique celebration that everyone should see at least once.
Gracias por invitarme.
Thanks for inviting me.
Brindamos por ustedes.
A toast to you.

Additional vocabulary

alma *soul*
altar *altar*
ángel *angel*
calavera de azúcar *skull made out of sugar*
cementerio *cemetery*
cocina *kitchen*
disfraz *costume*

recursos

VM pp. 17–18 | vhlcentral.com Lección 9

Expresiones útiles Draw attention to **pusimos** and explain that it is an irregular preterite form of the verb **poner**. Then point out the forms **vino** (video still 6) and **hice** and **puse** (video still 9) and tell students that these are irregular preterite forms of the verbs **venir, hacer,** and **poner**. Finally, draw attention to the phrase **Cómo se conocieron** and explain that **conocer** in the preterite means *to meet*. Tell students that they will learn more about these concepts in **Estructura**.

Teaching Tip Go through the **Fotonovela**, asking volunteers to read the various parts.

Nota cultural **El Día de Muertos** is an example of a holiday that blends indigenous and Catholic customs and beliefs. In pre-Columbian times, this celebration of deceased ancestors was a month-long festival that fell in the ninth month of the Aztec calendar, in August. The Spaniards moved it to coincide with the Catholic holidays of All Saints' Day and All Souls' Day.

TEACHING OPTIONS

Extra Practice Photocopy the **Fotonovela** Videoscript (Supersite) and white out words related to celebrations and personal relationships, in order to make a master for a cloze activity. Have students fill in the missing words as they watch the episode.

Extra Practice Have students research a **Día de Muertos** celebration in another Spanish-speaking country, such as Bolivia, Ecuador, or Guatemala, and prepare a brief report in which they compare it to Mexico's celebration of **Día de Muertos**.

Game Divide the class into two teams, A and B. Give a member from team A a card with the name of an item from the **Fotonovela** or **Expresiones útiles** (Ex: **flores, cocina, foto**). He or she has thirty seconds to draw the item, while team A has to guess what it is. Award one point per correct answer. If team A cannot guess the item within the time limit, team B may try to "steal" the point.

¿Qué pasó?

1 Completar Completa las oraciones con la información correcta, según la **Fotonovela**.

1. El Día de Muertos es una ___fiesta___ única que todos deben ver.
2. La tía Ana María preparó ___mole___ para celebrar.
3. Marissa lleva la ___foto___ al altar.
4. Jimena hizo las ___galletas___ y el ___pastel___.
5. Marta no sabe qué ___postre___ prefiere.

2 Identificar Identifica quién puede decir estas oraciones. Vas a usar un nombre dos veces.

1. Mis padres se conocieron en la fiesta de un amigo. tía Ana María
2. El Día de Muertos se celebra con flores, calaveras de azúcar, música y comida. Maite Fuentes
3. Gracias por invitarme a celebrar este Día de Muertos. Juan Carlos
4. Los de la foto son mis padres el día de su boda. tía Ana María
5. A mí me gustan mucho las galletas. Valentina
6. ¡Qué bueno que estás aquí, Juan Carlos! Eres uno más de la familia. Sr. Díaz

SR. DÍAZ

MAITE FUENTES

JUAN CARLOS

VALENTINA

TÍA ANA MARÍA

3 Seleccionar Selecciona algunas de las opciones de la lista para completar las oraciones.

amor	días de fiesta	pasarlo bien	salieron
el champán	divorciarse	postres	se enamoraron
cumpleaños	flan	la quinceañera	una sorpresa

1. El Sr. Díaz y Felipe prepararon ___una sorpresa___ para la familia.
2. Los ___días de fiesta___, como el Día de Muertos, se celebran con la familia.
3. Eduardo, el hijo de Ana María, nació el día del ___cumpleaños___ de su abuelo.
4. La tía Ana María siente gratitud y ___amor___ hacia (*toward*) sus padres.
5. Los días de fiesta también son para ___pasarlo bien___ con los amigos.
6. El Día de Muertos se hacen muchos ___postres___.
7. Los padres de la tía Ana María ___se enamoraron___ a primera vista.

4 Una cena Trabajen en grupos para representar una conversación en una cena de Año Nuevo. Answers will vary.

- Una persona brinda por el año que está por comenzar y por estar con su familia y amigos.
- Cada persona del grupo habla de cuál es su comida favorita en año nuevo.
- Después de la cena, una persona del grupo dice que es hora de (*it's time to*) comer las uvas.
- Cada persona del grupo dice qué desea para el año que empieza.
- Después, cada persona del grupo debe desear Feliz Año Nuevo a las demás.

Practice more at **vhlcentral.com**.

NOTA CULTURAL

Comer doce uvas a las doce de la noche del 31 de diciembre de cada año es una costumbre que nació en España y que también se observa en varios países de Latinoamérica. Se debe comer una uva por cada una de las 12 campanadas (*strokes*) del reloj y se cree que (*it's believed that*) quien lo hace va a tener un año próspero.

1 Expansion Have students work in pairs or small groups to write questions that would have elicited these statements.

Nota cultural **Mole** is a thick, rich sauce usually served over chicken. Though recipes can vary greatly, it generally includes dried chili peppers, ground nuts or seeds, chocolate, onions, garlic, and crushed toasted tortillas. Due to the labor involved, homemade **mole** is reserved for special occasions, such as religious holidays, birthdays, or weddings.

2 Teaching Tip To simplify, ask these questions before doing this activity: **¿Quién trabaja en la televisión? (Maite Fuentes) ¿Quién no forma parte de la familia Díaz? (Juan Carlos/ Maite Fuentes)**

2 Expansion Give these sentences to students as items 7–8: **7. Mi esposo trabaja demasiado. (tía Ana María) 8. Con la ayuda de mi hijo, preparé una sorpresa para la familia. (Sr. Díaz)**

3 Teaching Tip Before doing this activity, have the class review the vocabulary on pages 276–277.

3 Expansion Have pairs create additional sentences with the leftover items from the word bank.

4 Teaching Tip Read through the bulleted items with the class and brainstorm two verbs, words, or phrases for each one. Then remind students of "filler" words that help conversation flow, such as **pues** and **bueno**.

TEACHING OPTIONS

Large Groups In groups, have students ad-lib the **Fotonovela** episode. Assure them that it is not necessary to memorize the episode or stick strictly to its content. They should try to get the general meaning across with the vocabulary and expressions they know, and they should also feel free to be creative. Then have volunteers act out the episode for the class.

Pairs Have students work in pairs to tell each other about celebrations they have with their own families. Remind them to use as many expressions as possible from the **Expresiones útiles** on page 281, as well as the vocabulary on pages 276–277. Follow up by asking a few students to describe celebrations in their partners' families.

NATIONAL STANDARDS comparisons

Pronunciación

Audio

The letters h, j, and g

helado **hombre** **hola** **hermosa**

The Spanish **h** is always silent.

José **jubilarse** **dejar** **pareja**

The letter **j** is pronounced much like the English *h* in *his*.

agencia **general** **Gil** **Gisela**

The letter **g** can be pronounced three different ways. Before **e** or **i**, the letter **g** is pronounced much like the English *h*.

Gustavo, gracias por llamar el domingo.

At the beginning of a phrase or after the letter **n**, the Spanish **g** is pronounced like the English *g* in *girl*.

Me gradué en agosto.

In any other position, the Spanish **g** has a somewhat softer sound.

Guerra **conseguir** **guantes** **agua**

In the combinations **gue** and **gui**, the **g** has a hard sound and the **u** is silent. In the combination **gua**, the **g** has a hard sound and the **u** is pronounced like the English *w*.

Práctica Lee las palabras en voz alta, prestando atención a la **h**, la **j** y la **g**.

1. hamburguesa	5. geografía	9. seguir	13. Jorge
2. jugar	6. magnífico	10. gracias	14. tengo
3. oreja	7. espejo	11. hijo	15. ahora
4. guapa	8. hago	12. galleta	16. guantes

Oraciones Lee las oraciones en voz alta, prestando atención a la **h**, la **j** y la **g**.

1. Hola. Me llamo Gustavo Hinojosa Lugones y vivo en Santiago de Chile.
2. Tengo una familia grande; somos tres hermanos y tres hermanas.
3. Voy a graduarme en mayo.
4. Para celebrar mi graduación, mis padres van a regalarme un viaje a Egipto.
5. ¡Qué generosos son!

Refranes Lee los refranes en voz alta, prestando atención a la **h**, la **j** y la **g**.

A la larga, lo más dulce amarga.[1]
El hábito no hace al monje.[2]

1 Too much of a good thing.
2 The clothes don't make the man.

recursos

LM p. 50

vhlcentral.com Lección 9

Section Goal

In **Pronunciación**, students will be introduced to the pronunciation of **h**, **j**, and **g**.

Instructional Resources

Supersite: Audio (Textbook and Lab MP3 Files); Resources (Scripts, Answer Keys)
WebSAM
Lab Manual, p. 50

Teaching Tips

- Ask the class how the Spanish **h** is pronounced. Ask volunteers to pronounce the example words. Contrast the pronunciations of the English *hotel* and the Spanish **hotel.**
- Explain that **j** is pronounced much like the English *h*.
- Draw attention to the fact that the letter **g** is pronounced like the English *h* before **e** or **i**. Write the example words on the board and ask volunteers to pronounce them.
- Point out that the letter **g** is pronounced like the English *g* in *good* at the beginning of a phrase or after the letter **n**.
- Explain that in any other position, particularly between vowels, **g** has a softer sound.
- Tell the class that in the combinations **gue** and **gui**, **g** has a hard sound and **u** is not pronounced. Explain that in the combination **gua,** the **u** sounds like the English *w*.

Práctica/Oraciones/Refranes

These exercises are recorded on the *Textbook MP3s.* You may want to play the audio so that students practice listening to Spanish spoken by speakers other than yourself.

TEACHING OPTIONS

Extra Practice Write the names of these Chilean cities on the board and ask for a volunteer to pronounce each one: **Santiago, Antofagasta, Rancagua, Coihaique.** Repeat the process with the names of these Chilean writers: **Alberto Blest Gana, Vicente Huidobro, Gabriela Mistral, Juan Modesto Castro.**

Pairs Have students work in pairs to read aloud the sentences in **Actividad 6, Cambiar,** page 278. Remind them to pay attention to the pronunciation of the letters **h**, **j**, and **g**. Encourage students to help their partners if they have trouble pronouncing a particular word.

Section Goals

In **Cultura**, students will:
- read about **Semana Santa** celebrations in the Spanish-speaking world
- learn terms related to parties and celebrations
- read about the International Music Festival in **Viña del Mar**, Chile
- read about Latin American celebrations

Instructional Resources
Supersite: Video (***Flash cultura***); Resources (Scripts, Translations, Answer Keys)
WebSAM
Video Manual, pp. 89–90

En detalle

Antes de leer Ask students what times of year they usually have vacation and if they have any traditions related to winter and spring break.

Lectura
- Point out that most Spanish-speaking countries have a Catholic background and that many national holidays coincide with Catholic holidays.
- As students read, have them make a list of traditional **Semana Santa** activities.
- Point out that the processions of **Sevilla** and **Antigua** not only attract the locals, but also international tourists.

Después de leer Have students share the **Semana Santa** traditions that are most interesting to them. Ask: **Si un amigo quiere ir a un país hispano durante Semana Santa, ¿qué le recomiendas? ¿Adónde debe ir?**

1 Expansion Give students these true/false statements as items 11–13: **11. La Pascua conmemora la Pasión de Jesucristo. (Cierto.) 12. En Antigua hay una tradición llamada "quema de la chamiza". (Falso. En Ayacucho, Perú, hay una tradición llamada "quema de la chamiza".) 13. Sevilla es conocida por las procesiones con penitentes**

EN DETALLE

Video: *Flash cultura*

Semana Santa: vacaciones y tradición

¿Te imaginas pasar veinticuatro horas tocando un tambor° entre miles de personas? Así es como mucha gente celebra el Viernes Santo° en el pequeño pueblo de **Calanda**, España.

De todas las celebraciones hispanas, la Semana Santa° es una de las más espectaculares y únicas.

Procesión en Sevilla, España

Semana Santa es la semana antes de Pascua°, una celebración religiosa que conmemora la Pasión de Jesucristo. Generalmente, la gente tiene unos días de vacaciones en esta semana. Algunas personas aprovechan° estos días para viajar, pero otras prefieren participar en las tradicionales celebraciones religiosas en las calles. En **Antigua**, Guatemala, hacen alfombras° de flores° y altares; también organizan Vía Crucis° y danzas. En las famosas procesiones y desfiles° religiosos de **Sevilla**, España, los fieles° sacan a las calles imágenes religiosas. Las imágenes van encima de plataformas ricamente decoradas con abundantes flores y velas°. En la procesión, los penitentes llevan túnicas y unos sombreros cónicos que les cubren° la cara°. En sus manos llevan faroles° o velas encendidas.

Si visitas algún país hispano durante la Semana Santa, debes asistir a un desfile. Las playas y las discotecas pueden esperar hasta la semana siguiente.

Alfombra de flores en Antigua, Guatemala

Otras celebraciones famosas

Ayacucho, Perú: Además de alfombras de flores y procesiones, aquí hay una antigua tradición llamada "quema de la chamiza"°.

Iztapalapa, Ciudad de México: Es famoso el Vía Crucis del cerro° de la Estrella. Es una representación del recorrido° de Jesucristo con la cruz°.

Popayán, Colombia: En las procesiones "chiquitas" los niños llevan imágenes que son copias pequeñas de las que llevan los mayores.

tocando un tambor *playing a drum* **Viernes Santo** *Good Friday* **Semana Santa** *Holy Week* **Pascua** *Easter Sunday* **aprovechan** *take advantage of* **alfombras** *carpets* **flores** *flowers* **Vía Crucis** *Stations of the Cross* **desfiles** *parades* **fieles** *faithful* **velas** *candles* **cubren** *cover* **cara** *face* **faroles** *lamps* **quema de la chamiza** *burning of brushwood* **cerro** *hill* **recorrido** *route* **cruz** *cross*

ACTIVIDADES

1 **¿Cierto o falso?** Indica si lo que dicen las oraciones sobre Semana Santa en países hispanos es **cierto** o **falso**. Corrige las falsas.

1. La Semana Santa se celebra después de Pascua.
   Falso. La Semana Santa es la semana antes de Pascua.
2. Las personas tienen días libres durante la Semana Santa.
   Cierto.
3. Todas las personas asisten a las celebraciones religiosas.
   Falso. Algunas personas aprovechan estos días para viajar.
4. En los países hispanos, las celebraciones se hacen en las calles.
   Cierto.
5. En Antigua y en Ayacucho es típico hacer alfombras de flores.
   Cierto.
6. En Sevilla, sacan imágenes religiosas a las calles.
   Cierto.
7. En Sevilla, las túnicas cubren la cara.
   Falso. Los sombreros cónicos cubren la cara.
8. En la procesión en Sevilla algunas personas llevan flores en sus manos.
   Falso. En sus manos llevan faroles o velas encendidas.
9. El Vía Crucis de Iztapalapa es en el interior de una iglesia.
   Falso. Es en el cerro de la Estrella.
10. Las procesiones "chiquitas" son famosas en Sevilla, España.
    Falso. Son famosas en Popayán, Colombia.

TEACHING OPTIONS

Large Groups Make two or three sets of six cards, each with the name of a place noted for its **Semana Santa** celebration (**Calanda, Antigua, Sevilla, Ayacucho, Iztapalapa, Popayán**). Shuffle the cards, hand them out, and have students stand. In order to find their partners, students must circulate around the classroom, asking questions without mentioning the city. Ex: **¿Hay alfombras de flores? ¿La gente lleva túnicas y sombreros cónicos?**

Pairs In pairs, have students research one of the **Semana Santa** celebrations on the Internet. Students should present their findings to the class. Ask them to include typical activities that take place that week, and encourage them to bring in maps or photos.

Heritage Speakers Ask heritage speakers to share **Semana Santa** traditions from their families' countries of origin.

ASÍ SE DICE

Fiestas y celebraciones

la despedida de soltero/a	*bachelor(ette) party*
el día feriado/festivo	el día de fiesta
disfrutar	*to enjoy*
festejar	celebrar
los fuegos artificiales	*fireworks*
pasarlo en grande	divertirse mucho
la vela	*candle*

EL MUNDO HISPANO

Celebraciones latinoamericanas

- **Oruro, Bolivia** Durante el carnaval de Oruro se realiza la famosa Diablada, una antigua danza° que muestra la lucha° entre el Bien y el Mal: ángeles contra° demonios.
- **Panchimalco, El Salvador** La primera semana de mayo, Panchimalco se cubre de flores y de color. También hacen el Desfile de las palmas° y bailan danzas antiguas.
- **Quito, Ecuador** El mes de agosto es el Mes de las Artes. Danza, teatro, música, cine, artesanías° y otros eventos culturales inundan la ciudad.
- **San Pedro Sula, Honduras** En junio se celebra la Feria Juniana. Hay comida típica, bailes, desfiles, conciertos, rodeos, exposiciones ganaderas° y eventos deportivos y culturales.

danza *dance* lucha *fight* contra *versus* palmas *palm leaves* artesanías *handcrafts* exposiciones ganaderas *cattle shows*

PERFIL

Festival de Viña del Mar

En 1959 unos estudiantes de **Viña del Mar**, Chile, celebraron una fiesta en una casa de campo conocida como la Quinta Vergara donde hubo° un espectáculo° musical. En 1960 repitieron el evento. Asistió tanta gente que muchos vieron el espectáculo parados° o sentados en el suelo°. Algunos se subieron a los árboles°.

Años después, se convirtió en el **Festival Internacional de la Canción**. Este evento se celebra en febrero, en el mismo lugar donde empezó. ¡Pero ahora nadie necesita subirse a un árbol para verlo! Hay un anfiteatro con capacidad para quince mil personas.

En el festival hay concursos° musicales y conciertos de artistas famosos como Calle 13 y Nelly Furtado.

Nelly Furtado

hubo *there was* espectáculo *show* parados *standing* suelo *floor* se subieron a los árboles *climbed trees* concursos *competitions*

Conexión Internet

¿Qué celebraciones hispanas hay en los Estados Unidos y Canadá?

Go to **vhlcentral.com** to find more cultural information related to this **Cultura** section.

ACTIVIDADES

2 Comprensión Responde a las preguntas.

1. ¿Cuántas personas por día pueden asistir al Festival de Viña del Mar? quince mil
2. ¿Qué es la Diablada? Es una antigua danza que muestra la lucha entre el bien y el mal.
3. ¿Qué celebran en Quito en agosto? Celebran el Mes de las Artes.
4. Nombra dos atracciones en la Feria Juniana de San Pedro Sula. Answers will vary.
5. ¿Qué es la Quinta Vergara? una casa de campo donde empezó el Festival de Viña del Mar.

3 ¿Cuál es tu celebración favorita? Escribe un pequeño párrafo sobre la celebración que más te gusta de tu comunidad. Explica cómo se llama, cuándo ocurre y cómo es. Answers will vary.

Practice more at **vhlcentral.com**.

recursos: VM pp. 89–90; vhlcentral.com Lección 9

Así se dice
- Explain that it is common in the Spanish-speaking world to **hacer puente** (have a four-day weekend, literally *to make a bridge*) if a holiday falls on a Thursday or Tuesday.
- To challenge students, add these celebration-related words to the list: **la carroza** (*float*); **el desfile** (*parade*); **la feria** (*fair*); **pasarlo bomba/pipa (Esp.)** (*to have a great time, to enjoy oneself*).

Perfil **Viña del Mar,** commonly called **Viña** or **La Ciudad Jardín,** is a thriving coastal city in central Chile and, apart from the **Festival Internacional de la Canción,** it is best known for its beaches. During the six days of the festival, lesser-known artists participate in musical competitions, with winners receiving the coveted statuette **La Gaviota de Plata**. International superstars of all musical genres also make special appearances.

El mundo hispano Ask students to compare the festivals. Ex: **¿Qué festival les parece el más interesante? ¿Creen que el carnaval de Oruro es tan divertido como el desfile de Panchimalco? ¿Por qué?**

2 Expansion Give students these questions as items 6–7: **6. ¿Qué fiesta puede celebrar una mujer antes de casarse? (la despedida de soltera) 7. ¿Cuándo es el festival de Panchimalco? (la primera semana de mayo)**

3 Expansion Have students exchange papers with a classmate for peer editing. When finished, have a few volunteers read their paragraphs aloud for the class.

TEACHING OPTIONS

Pairs Have students work in pairs to research and plan a trip to a festival mentioned in the reading. Students should explain why they want to visit that particular festival, how they will get there, and present an itinerary to the class.

TPR Divide the class into five groups: **Viña del Mar, Oruro, Panchimalco, Quito,** and **San Pedro Sula**. Call out a series of statements about the festivals without mentioning the city in which they take place. Have groups stand up when the festival refers to their city. Ex: **Su festival tiene lugar la primera semana de mayo.** (Group **Panchimalco** stands.)

Section Goal

In **Estructura 9.1**, students will be introduced to the irregular preterites of several common verbs.

Instructional Resources
Supersite: Audio (Lab MP3 Files); Resources (Grammar Presentation Slides, Activity Pack, Scripts, Answer Keys); Testing Program (Quizzes)
WebSAM
Workbook, pp. 99–100
Lab Manual, p. 51

Teaching Tips

- Quickly review the present tense of a stem-changing verb such as **pedir**. Write the paradigm on the board and ask volunteers to point out the stem-changing forms.
- Work through the preterite paradigms of **tener**, **venir**, and **decir**, modeling the pronunciation.
- Add a visual aspect to this grammar presentation. Use magazine pictures to ask about social events in the past. Ex: **¿Con quién vino este chico a la fiesta? (Vino con esa chica rubia.) ¿Qué se puso esta señora para ir a la boda? (Se puso un sombrero.) ¿Qué trajo esta chica a clase? (Trajo una mochila.) ¿Y qué hizo? (Se durmió.)**
- Write the preterite paradigm for **estar** on the board. Then erase the initial **es-** for each form and point out that the preterite of **estar** and **tener** are identical except for the initial **es-**.

9.1 Irregular preterites

Tutorial

ANTE TODO You already know that the verbs **ir** and **ser** are irregular in the preterite. You will now learn other verbs whose preterite forms are also irregular.

Preterite of tener, venir, and decir

		tener (u-stem)	**venir** (i-stem)	**decir** (j-stem)
SINGULAR FORMS	yo	tuve	vine	dije
	tú	tuviste	viniste	dijiste
	Ud./él/ella	tuvo	vino	dijo
PLURAL FORMS	nosotros/as	tuvimos	vinimos	dijimos
	vosotros/as	tuvisteis	vinisteis	dijisteis
	Uds./ellos/ellas	tuvieron	vinieron	dijeron

▶ **¡Atención!** The endings of these verbs are the regular preterite endings of **-er/-ir** verbs, except for the **yo** and **usted/él/ella** forms. Note that these two endings are unaccented.

▶ These verbs observe similar stem changes to **tener, venir,** and **decir**.

INFINITIVE	U-STEM	PRETERITE FORMS
poder	pud-	pude, pudiste, pudo, pudimos, pudisteis, pudieron
poner	pus-	puse, pusiste, puso, pusimos, pusisteis, pusieron
saber	sup-	supe, supiste, supo, supimos, supisteis, supieron
estar	estuv-	estuve, estuviste, estuvo, estuvimos, estuvisteis, estuvieron

INFINITIVE	I-STEM	PRETERITE FORMS
querer	quis-	quise, quisiste, quiso, quisimos, quisisteis, quisieron
hacer	hic-	hice, hiciste, hizo, hicimos, hicisteis, hicieron

¡ATENCIÓN! Note the **c** → **z** spelling change in the third-person singular form of **hacer**: **hizo**.

INFINITIVE	J-STEM	PRETERITE FORMS
traer	traj-	traje, trajiste, trajo, trajimos, trajisteis, trajeron
conducir	conduj-	conduje, condujiste, condujo, condujimos, condujisteis, condujeron
traducir	traduj-	traduje, tradujiste, tradujo, tradujimos, tradujisteis, tradujeron

▶ **¡Atención!** Most verbs that end in **-cir** are **j**-stem verbs in the preterite. For example, **producir** → **produje, produjiste,** etc.

Produjimos un documental sobre los accidentes en la casa.
We produced a documentary about accidents in the home.

▶ Notice that the preterites with **j**-stems omit the letter **i** in the **ustedes/ellos/ellas** form.

Mis amigos **trajeron** comida a la fiesta.
My friends brought food to the party.

Ellos **dijeron** la verdad.
They told the truth.

NATIONAL STANDARDS comparisons

TEACHING OPTIONS

Extra Practice Do a pattern practice drill. Name an infinitive and ask individuals to provide conjugations for the different subject pronouns and/or names you provide. Reverse the activity by saying a conjugated form and asking students to give an appropriate subject pronoun.

Game Divide the class into two teams. Indicate one team member at a time, alternating between teams. Give a verb in its infinitive form and a subject pronoun (Ex: **querer/tú**). The team member should give the correct preterite form (Ex: **quisiste**). Give one point per correct answer. Deduct one point for each wrong answer. The team with the most points at the end wins.

The preterite of dar

yo	**di**	nosotros/as	**dimos**
tú	**diste**	vosotros/as	**disteis**
Ud./él/ella	**dio**	Uds./ellos/ellas	**dieron**
SINGULAR FORMS		PLURAL FORMS	

▶ The endings for **dar** are the same as the regular preterite endings for **-er** and **-ir** verbs, except that there are no accent marks.

La camarera me **dio** el menú.
The waitress gave me the menu.

Los invitados le **dieron** un regalo.
The guests gave him/her a gift.

Le **di** a Juan algunos consejos.
I gave Juan some advice.

Nosotros **dimos** una gran fiesta.
We gave a great party.

▶ The preterite of **hay** (*inf.* **haber**) is **hubo** (*there was; there were*).

CONSULTA
Note that there are other ways to say *there was* or *there were* in Spanish. See **Estructura 10.1**, p. 318.

Marissa le dio la foto a la Sra. Díaz.

Hubo una celebración en casa de los Díaz.

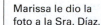

¡INTÉNTALO! Escribe la forma correcta del pretérito de cada verbo que está entre paréntesis.

1. (querer) tú quisiste
2. (decir) usted dijo
3. (hacer) nosotras hicimos
4. (traer) yo traje
5. (conducir) ellas condujeron
6. (estar) ella estuvo
7. (tener) tú tuviste
8. (dar) ella y yo dimos
9. (traducir) yo traduje
10. (haber) ayer hubo
11. (saber) usted supo
12. (poner) ellos pusieron
13. (venir) yo vine
14. (poder) tú pudiste
15. (querer) ustedes quisieron
16. (estar) nosotros estuvimos
17. (decir) tú dijiste
18. (saber) ellos supieron
19. (hacer) él hizo
20. (poner) yo puse
21. (traer) nosotras trajimos
22. (tener) yo tuve
23. (dar) tú diste
24. (poder) ustedes pudieron

recursos
WB pp. 99–100
LM p. 51
vhlcentral.com Lección 9

Teaching Tips

- Use the preterite forms of these verbs by talking about what you did in the recent past and then asking students questions that involve them in a conversation about what they did in the recent past. You may want to avoid the preterite of **poder, saber**, and **querer** for the moment. Ex: **El sábado pasado tuve que ir a la fiesta de cumpleaños de mi sobrina. Cumplió siete años. Le di un bonito regalo. ____, ¿tuviste que ir a una fiesta el sábado? ¿No? Pues, ¿qué hiciste el sábado?**
- Point out that **dar** has the same preterite endings as **ver**.
- Drill the preterite of **dar** by asking students about what they gave their family members for their last birthdays or other special occasion. Ex: **¿Qué le diste a tu hermano para su cumpleaños?** Then ask what other family members gave them. Ex: **¿Qué te dio tu padre? ¿Y tu madre?**
- In a dramatically offended tone, say: **Di una fiesta el sábado. Los invité a todos ustedes y ¡no vino nadie!** Complain about all the work you did to prepare for the party. Ex: **Limpié toda la casa, preparé tortilla española, fui al supermercado y compré refrescos, puse la mesa con platos bonitos, puse música salsa...** Then write **¿Por qué no viniste a mi fiesta?** and **Lo siento, profesor(a), no pude venir a su fiesta porque tuve que...** on the board and give students one minute to write a creative or humorous excuse. Have volunteers read their excuses aloud. Ex: **Lo siento, profesor, no pude venir a su fiesta porque tuve que lavarme el pelo....**

TEACHING OPTIONS

Video Show the **Fotonovela** again to give students more input containing irregular preterite forms. Stop the video where appropriate to discuss how certain verbs were used and to ask comprehension questions.

Extra Practice Have students write down six things they brought to class today. Then have them circulate around the room, asking other students if they also brought those items (**¿Trajiste tus llaves a clase hoy?**). When they find a student that answers **sí**, they ask that student to sign his or her name next to that item (**Firma aquí, por favor.**). Can students get signatures for all the items they brought to class?

1 Teaching Tip
To simplify, have students begin by identifying the subject in each sentence. Help them see that, for item 1, the subject is implied.

1 Expansion
- Ask individual students about the last time they threw a party. Ex: **La última vez que diste una fiesta, ¿quiénes estuvieron allí? ¿Fue alguien que no invitaste? ¿Qué llevaron los invitados?**
- Assign students to groups of three. Tell them they are going to write a narrative about a wedding. You will begin the story, then each student will add a sentence using an irregular verb in the preterite. Each group member should have at least two turns. Ex: **El domingo se casaron Carlos y Susana. (E1: Tuvieron una boda muy grande. E2: Vinieron muchos invitados. E3: Hubo un pastel enorme y elegante.)**

2 Teaching Tip
To challenge students, have them see how many sentences they can come up with to describe each drawing using the target verbs.

2 Expansion
Using magazine pictures, show images similar to those in the activity. Have students narrate what happened in the images using irregular preterite verb forms.

Práctica

1 **Completar** Completa estas oraciones con el pretérito de los verbos entre paréntesis.

1. El sábado ___hubo___ (haber) una fiesta sorpresa para Elsa en mi casa.
2. Sofía ___hizo___ (hacer) un pastel para la fiesta y Miguel ___trajo___ (traer) un flan.
3. Los amigos y parientes de Elsa ___vinieron___ (venir) y ___trajeron___ (traer) regalos.
4. El hermano de Elsa no ___vino___ (venir) porque ___tuvo___ (tener) que trabajar.
5. Su tía María Dolores tampoco ___pudo___ (poder) venir.
6. Cuando Elsa abrió la puerta, todos gritaron: "¡Feliz cumpleaños!" y su esposo le ___dio___ (dar) un beso.
7. Elsa no ___supo___ (saber) cómo reaccionar (*react*). ___Estuvo___ (Estar) un poco nerviosa al principio, pero pronto sus amigos ___pusieron___ (poner) música y ella ___pudo___ (poder) relajarse bailando con su esposo.
8. Al final de la noche, todos ___dijeron___ (decir) que se divirtieron mucho.

NOTA CULTURAL
El **flan** es un postre muy popular en los países de habla hispana. Se prepara con huevos, leche y azúcar y se sirve con salsa de caramelo. Existen variedades deliciosas como el flan de chocolate o el flan de coco.

2 **Describir** En parejas, usen verbos de la lista para describir lo que estas personas hicieron. Deben dar por lo menos dos oraciones por cada dibujo. Some answers may vary. Suggested answers:

dar	hacer	tener	traer
estar	poner	traducir	venir

1. el señor López
El señor López le dio/trajo dinero a su hijo.

2. Norma
Norma puso el pavo en la mesa. /Norma trajo el pavo a la mesa.

3. anoche nosotros
Anoche nosotros tuvimos/hicimos/dimos una fiesta de Navidad./Anoche nosotros estuvimos en una fiesta de Navidad.

4. Roberto y Elena
Roberto y Elena le trajeron/dieron un regalo a su amigo.

Practice more at **vhlcentral.com**.

TEACHING OPTIONS

Extra Practice Ask students to write a description of a party they once attended. They should include information on what kind of party it was, who was there, what people brought, what the guests did, and so forth. Have students exchange papers with a classmate for peer editing.

Small Groups In small groups, have each student write three sentences using irregular preterites. Two of the sentences should be true and the third should be false. As students read their sentences aloud to the group, the other members have to guess which of the sentences is the false one, discussing their reasoning with the group.

Comunicación

3

Preguntas En parejas, túrnense para hacerse y responder a estas preguntas. Answers will vary.

1. ¿Fuiste a una fiesta de cumpleaños el año pasado? ¿De quién?
2. ¿Quiénes fueron a la fiesta?
3. ¿Quién condujo el auto?
4. ¿Cómo estuvo el ambiente de la fiesta?
5. ¿Quién llevó regalos, bebidas o comida? ¿Llevaste algo especial?
6. ¿Hubo comida? ¿Quién la hizo? ¿Hubo champán?
7. ¿Qué regalo hiciste tú? ¿Qué otros regalos trajeron los invitados?
8. ¿Cuántos invitados hubo en la fiesta?
9. ¿Qué tipo de música hubo?
10. ¿Qué te dijeron algunos invitados de la fiesta?

4

Encuesta Tu profesor(a) va a darte una hoja de actividades. Para cada una de las actividades de la lista, encuentra a alguien que hizo esa actividad. Answers will vary.

modelo

traer dulces a clase
Estudiante 1: ¿Trajiste dulces a clase?
Estudiante 2: Sí, traje galletas y helado a la fiesta del fin del semestre.

Actividades	Nombres
1. ponerse un disfraz (*costume*) de Halloween	
2. traer dulces a clase	
3. conducir su auto a clase	
4. estar en la biblioteca ayer	
5. dar un regalo a alguien ayer	
6. poder levantarse temprano esta mañana	
7. hacer un viaje a un país hispano en el verano	
8. tener una cita anoche	
9. ir a una fiesta el fin de semana pasado	
10. tener que trabajar el sábado pasado	

Síntesis

5

Conversación En parejas, preparen una conversación en la que uno/a de ustedes va a visitar a su hermano/a para explicarle por qué no fue a su fiesta de graduación y para saber cómo estuvo la fiesta. Incluyan esta información en la conversación: Answers will vary.

- cuál fue el menú
- quiénes vinieron a la fiesta y quiénes no pudieron venir
- quiénes prepararon la comida o trajeron algo
- si él/ella tuvo que preparar algo
- lo que la gente hizo antes y después de comer
- cómo lo pasaron, bien o mal

3 Teaching Tip Instead of having students take turns, ask them to go through all the questions with their partner, taking notes about the information the partner gives them. Later, have them write a third-person description of their partner's experiences.

3 Expansion To practice the formal register, call on different students to ask you the questions in the activity. Ex: **¿Fue usted a una fiesta de cumpleaños el año pasado? (Sí, fui a la fiesta de cumpleaños de Lisa.)**

4 Teaching Tip Distribute the ***Hojas de actividades*** (Activity Pack/Supersite). Point out that to get information, students must form questions using the **tú** forms of the infinitives. Ex: **¿Trajiste dulces a clase?**

4 Expansion Write items 1–10 on the board and ask for a show of hands for each item. Ex: **¿Quién trajo dulces a clase?** Write tally marks next to each item to find out which activity was the most popular.

Nota cultural Halloween is celebrated in some Spanish-speaking countries, but it is not part of Hispanic culture. However, **El Día de todos los Santos** (November 1st) and **el Día de los Muertos** (November 2nd), which was featured in the **Fotonovela**, are two fall holidays that are deeply rooted in the culture.

5 Expansion Have pairs work in groups of four to write a paragraph combining the most interesting or unusual aspects of each pair's conversation. Ask a group representative to read the paragraph to the class, who will vote for the most creative or funniest paragraph.

TEACHING OPTIONS

Extra Practice Ask students to write a brief composition on the **Fotonovela** from this lesson. Students should write about where the characters went, what they did, what they said to each other, and so forth. (Note: Students should stick to completed actions in the past [*preterite*]. The use of the imperfect for narrating a story will not be presented until **Lección 10.**)

Large Groups Divide the class into two groups. To each member of the first group, give a strip of paper with a question. Ex: **¿Quién me trajo el pastel de cumpleaños?** To each member of the second group, give a strip of paper with the answer to that question. Ex: **Marta te lo trajo.** Students must find their partners.

Section Goal

In **Estructura 9.2**, students will be introduced to verbs that change meaning in the preterite tense.

Instructional Resources
Supersite: Audio (Lab MP3 Files); Resources (Grammar Presentation Slides, Activity Pack, Scripts, Answer Keys); Testing Program (Quizzes)
WebSAM
Workbook, p. 101
Lab Manual, p. 52

Teaching Tips

- Introduce the preterite of **conocer**. Say: **Ahora conozco a ustedes muy bien. Pero me acuerdo del día en que los conocí. ¿Ustedes se acuerdan del día en que nos conocimos? ¿Cuándo fue?** Ask volunteers to compare and contrast the meanings of **conocer** in your example.
- Stress the meaning of **poder** in the preterite by giving both affirmative (*to manage; to succeed*) and negative (*to try and fail*) examples. Ex: **Pude leer todas sus composiciones anoche, pero no pude leer las composiciones de la otra clase.**
- Stress the meaning of **querer** in the preterite by giving both affirmative (*to try*) and negative (*to refuse*) examples. Ex: **Quisimos ver una película el sábado, pero no quise ver ninguna película violenta.**

9.2 Verbs that change meaning in the preterite

Tutorial

NATIONAL STANDARDS comparisons

ANTE TODO The verbs **conocer, saber, poder,** and **querer** change meanings when used in the preterite. Because of this, each of them corresponds to more than one verb in English, depending on its tense.

Verbs that change meaning in the preterite

	Present	Preterite
conocer	*to know; to be acquainted with* **Conozco** a esa pareja. *I know that couple.*	*to meet* **Conocí** a esa pareja ayer. *I met that couple yesterday.*
saber	*to know information; to know how to do something* **Sabemos** la verdad. *We know the truth.*	*to find out; to learn* **Supimos** la verdad anoche. *We found out (learned) the truth last night.*
poder	*to be able; can* **Podemos** hacerlo. *We can do it.*	*to manage; to succeed (could and did)* **Pudimos** hacerlo ayer. *We managed to do it yesterday.*
querer	*to want; to love* **Quiero** ir, pero tengo que trabajar. *I want to go, but I have to work.*	*to try* **Quise** evitarlo, pero fue imposible. *I tried to avoid it, but it was impossible.*

¡ATENCIÓN!

In the preterite, the verbs **poder** and **querer** have different meanings, depending on whether they are used in affirmative or negative sentences.

pude *I succeeded*
no pude *I failed (to)*
quise *I tried (to)*
no quise *I refused (to)*

¡INTÉNTALO! Elige la respuesta más lógica.

1. Yo no hice lo que me pidieron mis padres. ¡Tengo mis principios! a
   a. No quise hacerlo. b. No supe hacerlo.
2. Hablamos por primera vez con Nuria y Ana en la boda. a
   a. Las conocimos en la boda. b. Les dijimos en la boda.
3. Por fin hablé con mi hermano después de llamarlo siete veces. b
   a. No quise hablar con él. b. Pude hablar con él.
4. Josefina se acostó para relajarse. Se durmió inmediatamente. a
   a. Pudo relajarse. b. No pudo relajarse.
5. Después de mucho buscar, encontraste la definición en el diccionario. b
   a. No supiste la respuesta. b. Supiste la respuesta.
6. Las chicas fueron a la fiesta. Cantaron y bailaron mucho. a
   a. Ellas pudieron divertirse. b. Ellas no supieron divertirse.

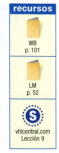

recursos
WB p. 101
LM p. 52
vhlcentral.com Lección 9

TEACHING OPTIONS

Extra Practice Prepare sentences using **conocer, saber, poder,** and **querer** in the present tense that will be logical when converted into the preterite. Have students convert them and explain how the meanings of the sentences change. Ex: **Sé la fecha de la fiesta. (Supe la fecha de la fiesta.)**

Heritage Speakers Ask heritage speakers to talk about one of these situations in the past: (1) when they found out there was no Santa Claus (**saber**), (2) when they met their best friend (**conocer**), or (3) something they tried to do but could not (**querer/no poder**). Verify student comprehension by asking other students to relate what was said.

Práctica y Comunicación

1

Carlos y Eva Forma oraciones con los siguientes elementos. Usa el pretérito y haz todos los cambios necesarios. Al final, inventa la razón del divorcio de Carlos y Eva.

1. anoche / mi esposa y yo / saber / que / Carlos y Eva / divorciarse
   Anoche mi esposa y yo supimos que Carlos y Eva se divorciaron.
2. los / conocer / viaje / isla de Pascua
   Los conocimos en un viaje a la isla de Pascua.
3. no / poder / hablar / mucho / con / ellos / ese día
   No pudimos hablar mucho con ellos ese día.
4. pero / ellos / ser / simpático / y / nosotros / hacer planes / vernos / con más / frecuencia
   Pero ellos fueron simpáticos y nosotros hicimos planes para vernos con más frecuencia.
5. yo / poder / encontrar / su / número / teléfono / páginas / amarillo
   Yo pude encontrar su número de teléfono en las páginas amarillas.
6. (yo) querer / llamar / los / ese día / pero / no / tener / tiempo
   Quise llamarlos ese día, pero no tuve tiempo.
7. cuando / los / llamar / nosotros / poder / hablar / Eva
   Cuando los llamé, nosotros pudimos hablar con Eva.
8. nosotros / saber / razón / divorcio / después / hablar / ella
   Nosotros supimos la razón del divorcio después de hablar con ella.
9. ____________________
   Answers will vary.

NOTA CULTURAL

La isla de Pascua es un remoto territorio chileno situado en el océano Pacífico Sur. Sus inmensas estatuas son uno de los mayores misterios del mundo: nadie sabe cómo o por qué se crearon. Para más información, véase **Panorama**, p. 305.

2

Completar Completa estas frases de una manera lógica. Answers will vary.

1. Ayer mi compañero/a de cuarto supo…
2. Esta mañana no pude…
3. Conocí a mi mejor amigo/a en…
4. Mis padres no quisieron…
5. Mi mejor amigo/a no pudo…
6. Mi novio/a y yo nos conocimos en…
7. La semana pasada supe…
8. Ayer mis amigos quisieron…

3

Telenovela En parejas, escriban el diálogo para una escena de una telenovela (*soap opera*). La escena trata de una situación amorosa entre tres personas: Mirta, Daniel y Raúl. Usen el pretérito de **conocer, poder, querer** y **saber** en su diálogo. Answers will vary.

Síntesis

4

Conversación En una hoja de papel, escribe dos listas: las cosas que hiciste durante el fin de semana y las cosas que quisiste hacer, pero no pudiste. Luego, compara tu lista con la de un(a) compañero/a, y expliquen ambos por qué no pudieron hacer esas cosas. Answers will vary.

Practice more at **vhlcentral.com**.

1 Expansion

- In pairs, students create five additional dehydrated sentences for their partners to complete, using the verbs **conocer, saber, poder**, and **querer**. After pairs have finished, ask volunteers to share some of their dehydrated sentences. Write them on the board and have the rest of the class "hydrate" them.
- To challenge students, have pairs use preterite forms of **conocer, saber, poder**, and **querer** to role-play **Carlos** and **Eva** explaining their separate versions of the divorce to their friends.

2 Teaching Tip Before assigning the activity, share with the class some recent things you found out, tried to do but could not, or the names of people you met, inviting students to respond.

3 Teaching Tips

- Explain that **telenovelas** are soap operas aired in a miniseries format. They typically run for a limited duration (averaging 120 episodes) and have a conclusion. In Mexico, historical romances are very popular, usually set in the colonial or revolutionary periods.
- Before students begin writing, brainstorm as a class some of the characteristics of soap operas, including how they create suspense and melodrama. You may wish to provide some extra vocabulary or key expressions.

4 Expansion Have pairs repeat the activity, this time describing another person. Ask students to share their descriptions with the class, who will guess the person being described.

TEACHING OPTIONS

Video Show the **Fotonovela** again to give students more input containing verbs that change meaning in the preterite. Stop the video where appropriate to discuss how certain verbs were used and to ask comprehension questions.

Pairs In pairs, have each student write three sentences using verbs that change meaning in the preterite. Two of the sentences should be true and the third should be false. Partners have to guess which of the sentences is the false one.

Section Goals

In **Estructura 9.3**, students will review:
- the uses of **¿qué?** and **¿cuál?**
- interrogative words and phrases

Instructional Resources
Supersite: Audio (Lab MP3 Files); Resources (Grammar Presentation Slides, Activity Pack, Scripts, Answer Keys); Testing Program (Quizzes)
WebSAM
Workbook, p. 102
Lab Manual, p. 53

Teaching Tips

- Review the question words **¿qué?** and **¿cuál?** Write incomplete questions on the board and ask students which interrogative word best completes each sentence. Ex: **1. ¿____ es tu número de teléfono? (Cuál) 2. ¿____ es esto? (Qué)**
- Point out that while both question words mean *what?* or *which?*, **¿qué?** is used with a noun, whereas **¿cuál?** is used with a verb. Ex: **¿Qué clase te gusta más? ¿Cuál es tu clase favorita?**
- Review the chart of interrogative words and phrases. Ask students personalized questions and invite them to ask you questions. Ex: **¿Cuál es tu película favorita? (*Como agua para chocolate*) ¿Qué director es su favorito? (Pedro Almodóvar)**
- Give students pairs of questions and have them explain the difference in meaning. Ex: **¿Qué es tu número de teléfono? ¿Cuál es tu número de teléfono?** Emphasize that the first question would be asked by someone who has no idea what a phone number is (asking for a definition) and, in the second question, someone wants to know *which* number (out of all the phone numbers in the world) is yours.

9.3 ¿Qué? and ¿cuál?

Tutorial

NATIONAL STANDARDS comparisons

ANTE TODO You've already learned how to use interrogative words and phrases. As you know, **¿qué?** and **¿cuál?** or **¿cuáles?** mean *what?* or *which?* However, they are not interchangeable.

▶ **¿Qué?** is used to ask for a definition or an explanation.

¿**Qué** es el flan?
What is flan?

¿**Qué** estudias?
What do you study?

▶ **¿Cuál(es)?** is used when there is more than one possibility to choose from.

¿**Cuál** de los dos prefieres, el vino o el champán?
Which of these (two) do you prefer, wine or champagne?

¿**Cuáles** son tus medias, las negras o las blancas?
Which ones are your socks, the black ones or the white ones?

▶ **¿Cuál?** should not be used before a noun; in this case, **¿qué?** is used.

¿**Qué** sorpresa te dieron tus amigos?
What surprise did your friends give you?

¿**Qué** colores te gustan?
What colors do you like?

▶ **¿Qué?** used before a noun has the same meaning as **¿cuál?**

¿**Qué regalo** te gusta?
What (Which) gift do you like?

¿**Qué dulces** quieren ustedes?
What (Which) sweets do you want?

Review of interrogative words and phrases

¿a qué hora?	*at what time?*	**¿cuántos/as?**	*how many?*
¿adónde?	*(to) where?*	**¿de dónde?**	*from where?*
¿cómo?	*how?*	**¿dónde?**	*where?*
¿cuál(es)?	*what?; which?*	**¿por qué?**	*why?*
¿cuándo?	*when?*	**¿qué?**	*what?; which?*
¿cuánto/a?	*how much?*	**¿quién(es)?**	*who?*

¡INTÉNTALO! Completa las preguntas con **¿qué?** o **¿cuál(es)?**, según el contexto.

1. ¿ Cuál de los dos te gusta más?
2. ¿ Cuál es tu teléfono?
3. ¿ Qué tipo de pastel pediste?
4. ¿ Qué es una galleta?
5. ¿ Qué haces ahora?
6. ¿ Cuáles son tus platos favoritos?
7. ¿ Qué bebidas te gustan más?
8. ¿ Qué es esto?
9. ¿ Cuál es el mejor?
10. ¿ Cuál es tu opinión?
11. ¿ Qué fiestas celebras tú?
12. ¿ Qué botella de vino prefieres?
13. ¿ Cuál es tu helado favorito?
14. ¿ Qué pones en la mesa?
15. ¿ Qué restaurante prefieres?
16. ¿ Qué estudiantes estudian más?
17. ¿ Qué quieres comer esta noche?
18. ¿ Cuál es la sorpresa mañana?
19. ¿ Qué postre prefieres?
20. ¿ Qué opinas?

recursos
WB p. 102
LM p. 53
vhlcentral.com Lección 9

TEACHING OPTIONS

Extra Practice Ask questions of individual students, using **¿qué?** and **¿cuál?** Make sure a portion of the questions are general and information-seeking in nature (**¿qué?**). Ex: **¿Qué es una guitarra? ¿Qué es un elefante?** This is also a good way for students to practice circumlocution (**Es algo que…**).

Pairs Ask students to write one question using each of the interrogative words on this page. Then have them ask those questions of a partner, who must answer in complete sentences. Students should ask follow-up questions when possible.

Game Divide the class into two teams, **qué** and **cuál**, and have them line up. Indicate the first member of each team and call out a question in English that uses *what* or *which*. Ex: What is your favorite ice cream? The first team member who steps forward and can provide a correct Spanish translation earns a point for his or her team.

Práctica y Comunicación

1 **Completar** Tu clase de español va a crear un sitio web. Completa estas preguntas con alguna(s) palabra(s) interrogativa(s). Luego, con un(a) compañero/a, hagan y contesten las preguntas para obtener la información para el sitio web.

1. ¿ Cuál es la fecha de tu cumpleaños?
2. ¿ Dónde/Cuándo/A qué hora naciste?
3. ¿ Cuál es tu estado civil?
4. ¿ Cómo/Cuándo/Dónde te relajas?
5. ¿ Quién/Cómo es tu mejor amigo/a?
6. ¿ Qué cosas te hacen reír?
7. ¿ Qué postres te gustan? ¿ Cuál te gusta más?
8. ¿ Qué problemas tuviste en la primera cita con alguien?

NATIONAL communication STANDARDS

2 **Una invitación** En parejas, lean esta invitación. Luego, túrnense para hacer y contestar preguntas con **qué** y **cuál** basadas en la información de la invitación. Answers will vary.

modelo

Estudiante 1: ¿Cuál es el nombre del padre de la novia?
Estudiante 2: Su nombre es Fernando Sandoval Valera.

Fernando Sandoval Valera
Isabel Arzipe de Sandoval
Lorenzo Vásquez Amaral
Elena Soto de Vásquez

tienen el agrado de invitarlos
a la boda de sus hijos
María Luisa y José Antonio
La ceremonia religiosa tendrá lugar
el sábado 10 de junio a las dos de la tarde
en el Templo de Santo Domingo
(Calle Santo Domingo, 961).

Después de la ceremonia, sírvanse pasar a la recepción en el salón de baile del Hotel Metrópoli (Sotero del Río, 465).

¡LENGUA VIVA!
The word **invitar** is not always used exactly like *invite*. Sometimes, if you say **Te invito un café**, it means that you are offering to buy that person a coffee.

3 **Quinceañera** Trabaja con un(a) compañero/a. Uno/a de ustedes es el/la director(a) del salón de fiestas "Renacimiento". La otra persona es el padre/la madre de Sandra, quien quiere hacer la fiesta de quince años de su hija gastando menos de $25 por invitado. Su profesor(a) va a darles la información necesaria para confirmar la reservación. Answers will vary.

modelo

Estudiante 1: ¿Cuánto cuestan los entremeses?
Estudiante 2: Depende. Puede escoger champiñones por 50 centavos o camarones por dos dólares.
Estudiante 1: ¡Uf! A mi hija le gustan los camarones, pero son muy caros.
Estudiante 2: Bueno, también puede escoger quesos por un dólar por invitado.

Practice more at **vhlcentral.com**.

1 Expansion Conduct a conversation with the whole class to find consensus on some of the questions.

2 Expansion
- Add a visual aspect to this activity. Bring in images showing a group of people at a wedding reception. Have pairs of students imagine they are sitting at a table at the reception, and have them ask each other questions about the attendees. Encourage creativity. Ex: **¿Quién es esa mujer que baila con el señor alto y delgado? ¿Qué postres van a servir? ¿Dónde está el novio?**
- Have pairs design an invitation to a party, wedding, **fiesta de quince años**, or other social event. Then have them answer questions from the class about their invitation without showing it. The class guesses what kind of social event is announced. Ex: **¿Dónde es el evento? (en el salón de baile "Cosmopolita") ¿A qué hora es? (a las ocho de la noche) ¿De quiénes es la invitación? (de los señores López Pujol) Es una fiesta de quince años. (Sí.)** Finally, have pairs reveal their design to the class.

3 Teaching Tip Divide the class into pairs and distribute the handouts from the Activity Pack (Activity Pack/Supersite) that correspond to this Information Gap Activity. Give students ten minutes to complete this activity.

3 Expansion With the same partner, have students prepare a **telenovela** skit with characters from the **Quinceañera** activity. Encourage them to use interrogative words and verbs that change meaning in the preterite. Ask pairs to role-play their skits for the class.

TEACHING OPTIONS

Pairs In pairs, students prepare a conversation between two friends. One of the friends is planning a surprise party (**fiesta sorpresa**) for a mutual friend. However, the other person reveals that he or she does not care much for the party honoree and tells why. The class can vote for the funniest or most original skit.

Game Play a *Jeopardy*-style game. Prepare five answers for each of six categories (30 answers in all), in varying degrees of difficulty. Ex: **una celebración para una quinceañera.** Ask for three volunteers to play. Students must give their answers in the form of a question. Ex: **¿Qué es una fiesta de quince años?** You may want to decrease the number of questions and have additional volunteers participate in the game.

Section Goals

In **Estructura 9.4**, students will be introduced to:
- pronouns as objects of prepositions
- the pronoun-preposition combinations **conmigo** and **contigo**

Instructional Resources
Supersite: Audio (Lab MP3 Files); Resources (Grammar Presentation Slides, Activity Pack, Scripts, Answer Keys); Testing Program (Quizzes)
WebSAM
Workbook, pp. 103–104
Lab Manual, p. 54

Teaching Tips

- Review the prepositions often used with **estar** in **Estructura 2.3**. Use prepositional pronouns as you describe yourself and others in relation to people and things. Say: **¿Quién está delante de mí? Sí, ____ está delante de mí. ¿Y quién está detrás de ella? Sí, ____ está detrás de ella.**
- Ask students which pronouns they recognize and which are new. Ask the class to deduce the rules for pronouns after prepositions.
- Point out that students have been using these pronouns with the preposition **a** since **Lección 2**, when they learned the verb **gustar**.
- Practice **conmigo** and **contigo** by making invitations and having students decline. Ex: ____, **¿quieres ir conmigo al museo? (No, no quiero ir contigo.)** In a sad tone, say: **Nadie quiere ir conmigo a ningún lado.**

9.4 Pronouns after prepositions

Tutorial

NATIONAL STANDARDS comparisons

ANTE TODO In Spanish, as in English, the object of a preposition is the noun or pronoun that follows a preposition. Observe the following diagram.

PREPOSITION	NOUN	PREPOSITION	PRONOUN
La sopa es para	Alicia	y para	él.

Prepositional pronouns

	Singular		Plural	
preposition +	**mí**	*me*	**nosotros/as**	*us*
	ti	*you (fam.)*	**vosotros/as**	*you (fam.)*
	Ud.	*you (form.)*	**Uds.**	*you*
	él	*him*	**ellos**	*them (m.)*
	ella	*her*	**ellas**	*them (f.)*

- Note that, except for **mí** and **ti,** these pronouns are the same as the subject pronouns. **¡Atención! Mí** (*me*) has an accent mark to distinguish it from the possessive adjective **mi** (*my*).

- The preposition **con** combines with **mí** and **ti** to form **conmigo** and **contigo**, respectively.

  —¿Quieres venir **conmigo** a Concepción?
  Do you want to come with me to Concepción?

  —Sí, gracias, me gustaría ir **contigo**.
  Yes, thanks, I would like to go with you.

- The preposition **entre** is followed by **tú** and **yo** instead of **ti** and **mí**.

  Papá va a sentarse **entre tú y yo**.
  Dad is going to sit between you and me.

CONSULTA
For more prepositions, refer to **Estructura 2.3,** p. 56.

¡INTÉNTALO! Completa estas oraciones con las preposiciones y los pronombres apropiados.

1. (*with him*) No quiero ir con él.
2. (*for her*) Las galletas son para ella.
3. (*for me*) Los mariscos son para mí.
4. (*with you*, pl.) Preferimos estar con ustedes.
5. (*with you*, sing. fam.) Me gusta salir contigo.
6. (*with me*) ¿Por qué no quieres tener una cita conmigo?
7. (*for her*) La cuenta es para ella.
8. (*for them*, m.) La habitación es muy pequeña para ellos.
9. (*with them*, f.) Anoche celebré la Navidad con ellas.
10. (*for you*, sing. fam.) Este beso es para ti.
11. (*with you*, sing. fam.) Nunca me aburro contigo.
12. (*with you*, pl.) ¡Qué bien que vamos con ustedes!
13. (*for you*, sing. fam.) Para ti la vida es muy fácil.
14. (*for them*, f.) Para ellas no hay sorpresas.

recursos
WB pp. 103–104
LM p. 54
vhlcentral.com Lección 9

TEACHING OPTIONS

Extra Practice Describe someone in the classroom using prepositions of location, without saying the student's name. Ex: **Esta persona está entre la ventana y ____. No está al lado de____.** The rest of the class has to guess the person being described. Once students have this model, ask individuals to create similar descriptions so that their classmates may guess.

Game Divide the class into two teams. One student from the first team chooses an item in the classroom and writes it down. Call on five students from the other team to ask questions about the item's location. Ex: **¿Está cerca de mí?** The first student can respond with **sí, no, caliente,** or **frío**. If a team guesses the item within five tries, give it a point. If not, give the other team a point. The team with the most points wins.

Práctica y Comunicación

1

Completar David sale con sus amigos a comer. Para saber quién come qué, lee el mensaje electrónico que David le envió (*sent*) a Cecilia dos días después y completa el diálogo en el restaurante con los pronombres apropiados.

modelo

Camarero: Los camarones en salsa verde, ¿para quién son?
David: Son para ella.

Para: Cecilia | Asunto: El menú

Hola, Cecilia:
¿Recuerdas la comida del viernes? Quiero repetir el menú en mi casa el miércoles. Ahora voy a escribir lo que comimos, luego me dices si falta algún plato. Yo pedí el filete de pescado y Maribel camarones en salsa verde. Tatiana pidió un plato grandísimo de machas a la parmesana. Diana y Silvia pidieron langostas, ¿te acuerdas? Y tú, ¿qué pediste? Ah, sí, un bistec grande con papas. Héctor también pidió un bistec, pero más pequeño. Miguel pidió pollo y vino tinto para todos. Y la profesora comió ensalada verde porque está a dieta. ¿Falta algo? Espero tu mensaje. Hasta pronto. David.

CAMARERO El filete de pescado, ¿para quién es?
DAVID Es para (1) mí.
CAMARERO Aquí está. ¿Y las machas a la parmesana y las langostas?
DAVID Las machas son para (2) ella.
SILVIA Y DIANA Las langostas son para (3) nosotras.
CAMARERO Tengo un bistec grande...
DAVID Cecilia, es para (4) ti, ¿no es cierto? Y el bistec más pequeño es para (5) él.
CAMARERO ¿Y la botella de vino?
MIGUEL Es para todos (6) nosotros, y el pollo es para (7) mí.
CAMARERO (*a la profesora*) Entonces la ensalada verde es para (8) usted.

NOTA CULTURAL

Las **machas a la parmesana** son un plato muy típico de Chile. Se prepara con machas, un tipo de almeja (*clam*) que se encuentra en Suramérica. Las machas a la parmesana se hacen con queso parmesano, limón, sal, pimienta y mantequilla, y luego se ponen en el horno (*oven*).

NATIONAL communication STANDARDS

2

Compartir Tu profesor(a) va a darte una hoja de actividades en la que hay un dibujo. En parejas, hagan preguntas para saber dónde está cada una de las personas en el dibujo. Ustedes tienen dos versiones diferentes de la ilustración. Al final deben saber dónde está cada persona. Answers will vary.

modelo

Estudiante 1: ¿Quién está al lado de Óscar?
Estudiante 2: Alfredo está al lado de él.

Alfredo	Dolores	Graciela	Raúl
Sra. Blanco	Enrique	Leonor	Rubén
Carlos	Sra. Gómez	Óscar	Yolanda

AYUDA

Here are some other useful prepositions: **al lado de, debajo de, a la derecha de, a la izquierda de, cerca de, lejos de, delante de, detrás de, entre.**

Practice more at **vhlcentral.com**.

1 Teaching Tips

- Remind students that they are to fill in the blanks with prepositional pronouns, not names of the characters in the conversation.
- To simplify, have students begin by scanning the e-mail message. On the board, list the people who ate at the restaurant (starting with the sender of the e-mail and its recipient). Then guide students in matching each name with the dish ordered. Have students refer to the list as they complete the dialogue.

1 Expansion

In small groups, have students play the roles of the people mentioned in the e-mail message. Ex: **E1: ¿Para quién son los camarones? E2: Son para mí. E1: ¿Y el bistec? E2: Es para él.**

2 Teaching Tip Divide the class into pairs and distribute the handouts from the Activity Pack (Activity Pack/Supersite) that correspond to this Information Gap Activity. Give students ten minutes to complete this activity.

2 Expansion

- Using both versions of the drawing as a guide, ask questions of the class to find out where the people are. Ex: **¿Quién sabe dónde está la señora Blanco?**
- Verify that all students labeled the characters correctly by suggesting changes to the drawing and using prepositions to ask about their new locations. Ex: **Yolanda y Carlos cambian de lugar. ¿Quién está al lado de Yolanda ahora? (Rubén)**

TEACHING OPTIONS

Video Show the **Fotonovela** again to refresh the class's memory of the lesson's episode. Then, have pairs write three sentences from the point of view of the characters in the video, using prepositional pronouns. Have them exchange papers with another pair, who will identify the character. Ex: **Marissa trajo una foto para mí. (Carolina)**

Large Groups Divide the class into two groups. Give group A cards that contain an activity (Ex: **jugar al baloncesto**) and give group B cards that contain a place (Ex: **el gimnasio**). Have students circulate around the room to find places that match their activities. Ex: **E1: Voy a jugar al baloncesto. ¿Puedo ir contigo? E2: Pues, yo voy al museo. No puedes ir conmigo.** or **Voy al gimnasio. Sí, puedes ir conmigo.**

Section Goal

In **Recapitulación**, students will review the grammar concepts from this lesson.

Instructional Resource
Supersite

1 Teaching Tip Ask students to identify which verb changes meaning in the preterite.

1 Expansion
- To challenge students, ask them to provide the **tú** and **ustedes** forms of the verbs.
- Have students provide the conjugations of **conocer, dar,** and **venir**.

2 Teaching Tip To simplify, have students circle the subject of each verb before filling in the blanks.

2 Expansion
Have students work in pairs to write a response e-mail from **Omar**. Tell them to use the preterite tense to ask for more details about the party. Ex: **¿Qué más tuviste que hacer para preparar la fiesta? ¿Qué regalos te dieron tus amigos?**

Recapitulación

Diagnostics

Completa estas actividades para repasar los conceptos de gramática que aprendiste en esta lección.

1 Completar Completa la tabla con el pretérito de los verbos. **18 pts.**

Infinitive	yo	ella	nosotros
conducir	conduje	condujo	condujimos
hacer	hice	hizo	hicimos
saber	supe	supo	supimos

2 Mi fiesta Completa este mensaje electrónico con el pretérito de los verbos de la lista. Vas a usar cada verbo sólo una vez. **20 pts.**

dar	haber	tener
decir	hacer	traer
estar	poder	venir
	poner	

Hola, Omar:

Como tú no (1) pudiste venir a mi fiesta de cumpleaños, quiero contarte cómo fue. El día de mi cumpleaños, muy temprano por la mañana, mis hermanos me (2) dieron una gran sorpresa: ellos (3) pusieron un regalo delante de la puerta de mi habitación: ¡una bicicleta roja preciosa! Mi madre nos preparó un desayuno riquísimo. Después de desayunar, mis hermanos y yo (4) tuvimos que limpiar toda la casa, así que (*therefore*) no (5) hubo más celebración hasta la tarde. A las seis y media (nosotros) (6) hicimos una barbacoa en el patio de la casa. Todos los invitados (7) trajeron bebidas y regalos. (8) Vinieron todos mis amigos, excepto tú, ¡qué pena! :-(La fiesta (9) estuvo muy animada hasta las diez de la noche, cuando mis padres (10) dijeron que los vecinos (*neighbors*) iban a (*were going to*) protestar y entonces todos se fueron a sus casas.

RESUMEN GRAMATICAL

9.1 Irregular preterites *pp. 286–287*

u-stem	estar poder poner saber tener	estuv- pud- pus- sup- tuv-	-e, -iste, -o, -imos, -isteis, -(i)eron
i-stem	hacer querer venir	hic- quis- vin-	
j-stem	conducir decir traducir traer	conduj- dij- traduj- traj-	

- Preterite of **dar**: **di, diste, dio, dimos, disteis, dieron**
- Preterite of **hay** (*inf.* **haber**): **hubo**

9.2 Verbs that change meaning in the preterite *p. 290*

Present	Preterite
conocer	
to know; to be acquainted with	*to meet*
saber	
to know info.; to know how to do something	*to find out; to learn*
poder	
to be able; can	*to manage; to succeed*
querer	
to want; to love	*to try*

9.3 ¿Qué? and ¿cuál? *p. 292*

- Use **¿qué?** to ask for a definition or an explanation.
- Use **¿cuál(es)?** when there is more than one possibility to choose from.
- **¿Cuál?** should not be used before a noun; use **¿qué?** instead.
- **¿Qué?** used before a noun has the same meaning as **¿cuál?**

TEACHING OPTIONS

TPR Have students stand and form a circle. Call out an infinitive from **Resumen gramatical** and a subject pronoun (Ex: **poder/nosotros**) and toss a ball to a student, who will give the correct preterite form (Ex: **pudimos**). He or she then tosses the ball to another student, who must use the verb correctly in a sentence before throwing the ball back to you. Ex: **No pudimos comprar los regalos.**

Small Groups Tell small groups to imagine that one of them has received an anonymous birthday gift from a secret admirer. Have them create a dialogue in which friends ask questions about the gift and the potential admirer. Students must use at least two irregular preterites, two examples of **¿qué?** or **¿cuál?**, and three pronouns after prepositions.

9.4 Pronouns after prepositions *p. 294*

Prepositional pronouns

	Singular	Plural
Preposition +	mí	nosotros/as
	ti	vosotros/as
	Ud.	Uds.
	él	ellos
	ella	ellas

► Exceptions: **conmigo, contigo, entre tú y yo**

3 **¿Presente o pretérito?** Escoge la forma correcta de los verbos en paréntesis. **12 pts.**

1. Después de muchos intentos (*tries*), (podemos/(pudimos)) hacer una piñata.
2. —¿Conoces a Pepe?
   —Sí, lo (conozco/(conocí)) en tu fiesta.
3. Como no es de aquí, Cristina no ((sabe)/supo) mucho de las celebraciones locales.
4. Yo no ((quiero)/quise) ir a un restaurante grande, pero tú decides.
5. Ellos (quieren/(quisieron)) darme una sorpresa, pero Nina me lo dijo todo.
6. Mañana se terminan las vacaciones; por fin ((podemos)/pudimos) volver a la escuela.

4 **Preguntas** Escribe una pregunta para cada respuesta con los elementos dados. Empieza con **qué**, **cuál** o **cuáles** de acuerdo con el contexto y haz los cambios necesarios. **8 pts.**

1. —¿? / pastel / querer —Quiero el pastel de chocolate. 1. ¿Qué pastel quieres?
2. —¿? / ser / sangría —La sangría es una bebida típica española. 2. ¿Qué es la sangría?
3. —¿? / ser / restaurante favorito —Mis restaurantes favoritos son Dalí y Jaleo. 3. ¿Cuáles son tus restaurantes favoritos?
4. —¿? / ser / dirección electrónica —Mi dirección electrónica es paco@email.com. 4. ¿Cuál es tu dirección electrónica?

5 **¿Dónde me siento?** Completa la conversación con los pronombres apropiados. **14 pts.**

JUAN A ver, te voy a decir dónde te vas a sentar. Manuel, ¿ves esa silla? Es para ___ti___. Y esa otra silla es para tu novia, que todavía no está aquí.
MANUEL Muy bien, yo la reservo para ___ella___.
HUGO ¿Y esta silla es para ___mí___ (*me*)?
JUAN No, Hugo. No es para ___ti___. Es para Carmina, que viene con Julio.
HUGO No, Carmina y Julio no pueden venir. Hablé con ___ellos___ y me avisaron.
JUAN Pues ellos se lo pierden (*it's their loss*). ¡Más comida para ___nosotros___ (*us*)!
CAMARERO Aquí tienen el menú. Les doy un minuto y enseguida estoy con ___ustedes___.

6 **Cumpleaños feliz** Escribe cinco oraciones que describan cómo celebraste tu último cumpleaños. Usa el pretérito y los pronombres que aprendiste en esta lección. **28 pts.** Answers will vary.

7 **Poema** Completa este fragmento del poema *Elegía nocturna* de Carlos Pellicer con el pretérito de los verbos entre paréntesis. **¡4 puntos EXTRA!**

“Ay de mi corazón° que nadie ___quiso___ (querer)
tomar de entre mis manos desoladas.
Tú ___viniste___ (venir) a mirar sus llamaradas°
y le miraste arder° claro° y sereno.”

corazón *heart* llamaradas *flames* arder *to burn* claro *clear*

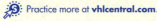

Practice more at **vhlcentral.com**.

3 Teaching Tip To challenge students, ask them to explain why they chose the preterite or present tense in each case.

4 Expansion Give students these answers as items 5–8: **5. —¿? / libro / comprar —Voy a comprar el libro de viajes. (¿Qué libro vas a comprar?) 6. —¿? / ser / última película / ver —Vi la película *Los abrazos rotos*. (¿Cuál fue la última película que viste?) 7. —¿? / ser / número de la suerte —Mi número de la suerte es el ocho. (¿Cuál es tu número de la suerte?) 8. —¿? / ser / nacimiento —El nacimiento es la primera etapa de la vida. (¿Qué es el nacimiento?)**

5 Expansion
Have four volunteers role-play the dialogue for the class. Encourage them to ad-lib as they present.

6 Teaching Tip To simplify, have students begin by making an idea map. In the center circle, have them write **Mi último cumpleaños**. Help them brainstorm labels for the surrounding circles, such as **lugar, invitados, comida, regalos**. You also may want to provide a list of infinitives that students may use in their descriptions.

7 Teaching Tip You may want to point out the example of **leísmo** in line 4 (**le miraste**). Explain that some Spanish speakers tend to use **le** or **les** as direct object pronouns. In this case, **le** replaces the direct object pronoun **lo**, which refers to **mi corazón**.

Nota cultural Mexican poet **Carlos Pellicer** mixes in his works the splendor of nature with the most intimate emotions. Some of his most important works are ***Práctica de vuelo, Hora de junio,*** and ***Camino***. Also a museologist, he helped create the **Museo Casa de Frida Kahlo** and the **Anahuacalli**, which exhibits pre-Hispanic art donated by **Diego Rivera**.

TEACHING OPTIONS

Game Divide the class into two teams and have them line up. Indicate the first member of each team and call out a sentence. Ex: **Me gusta el color gris.** The first student to reach the board and write a corresponding question using the proper interrogative form earns a point for his or her team. Ex: **¿Qué color te gusta?** or **¿Cuál es tu color preferido?** The team with the most points at the end wins.

Pairs Add a visual aspect to this grammar review. Have pairs choose a photo of a person from a magazine and invent an imaginary list of the ten most important things that happened to that person in his or her lifetime. Tell them to use at least four preterites from this lesson. Ex: **Conoció al presidente de los Estados Unidos. Ganó la lotería y le dio todo el dinero a su mejor amigo.** Have pairs present their photos and lists to the class, who will ask follow-up questions. Ex: **¿Por qué le dio todo el dinero a un amigo?**

Audio: Reading
Additional Reading

Section Goals

In **Lectura**, students will:

- learn to use word families to infer meaning in context
- read content-rich texts

Instructional Resource
Supersite

Estrategia Write **conocer** on the board and remind students of the meaning *to know, be familiar with*. Next to it, write **conocimiento** and **conocido**. Tell students that recognizing the family relationship between a known word and unfamiliar words can help them infer the meaning of the words they do not yet know. Guide students to see that **conocimiento** is a noun meaning *knowledge, familiarity* and **conocido** is an adjective form of the verb meaning *known* or *well-known*.

Examinar el texto Have students scan the text for clues to its contents. Ask volunteers to tell what kind of text it is and how they know. Headlines (**titulares**), photos, and layout (**diseño de la página**) reveal that it is the society section (**notas sociales**) of a newspaper.

Raíces Have students fill in the rest of the chart after they have read **Vida social**.

Lectura

NATIONAL STANDARDS communication cultures

Antes de leer

Estrategia

Recognizing word families

Recognizing root words can help you guess the meaning of words in context, ensuring better comprehension of a reading selection. Using this strategy will enrich your Spanish vocabulary as you will see below.

Examinar el texto

Familiarízate con el texto usando las estrategias de lectura más efectivas para ti. ¿Qué tipo de documento es? ¿De qué tratan° las cuatro secciones del documento? Explica tus respuestas.

Raíces°

Completa el siguiente cuadro° para ampliar tu vocabulario. Usa palabras de la lectura de esta lección y vocabulario de las lecciones anteriores. ¿Qué significan las palabras que escribiste en el cuadro? Some answers may vary. Suggested answers:

Verbos	Sustantivos	Otras formas
1. agradecer *to thank, to be grateful for*	agradecimiento/gracias *gratitude/thanks*	agradecido *grateful, thankful*
2. estudiar	estudiante *student*	estudiado *studied*
3. celebrar *to celebrate*	celebración *celebration*	celebrado
4. bailar *to dance*	baile	bailable *danceable*
5. bautizar	bautismo *baptism*	bautizado *baptized*

¿De qué tratan...? *What are... about?* Raíces *Roots* cuadro *chart*

Practice more at **vhlcentral.com**.

Vida social

Matrimonio Espinoza Álvarez-Reyes Salazar

El día sábado 17 de junio a las 19 horas, se celebró el matrimonio de Silvia Reyes y Carlos Espinoza en la catedral de Santiago. La ceremonia fue oficiada por el pastor Federico Salas y participaron los padres de los novios, el señor Jorge Espinoza y señora y el señor José Alfredo Reyes y señora. Después de la ceremonia, los padres de los recién casados ofrecieron una fiesta bailable en el restaurante La Misión.

Bautismo

José María recibió el bautismo el 26 de junio.

Sus padres, don Roberto Lagos Moreno y doña María Angélica Sánchez, compartieron la alegría de la fiesta con todos sus parientes y amigos. La ceremonia religiosa tuvo lugar° en la catedral de Aguas Blancas. Después de la ceremonia, padres, parientes y amigos celebraron una fiesta en la residencia de la familia Lagos.

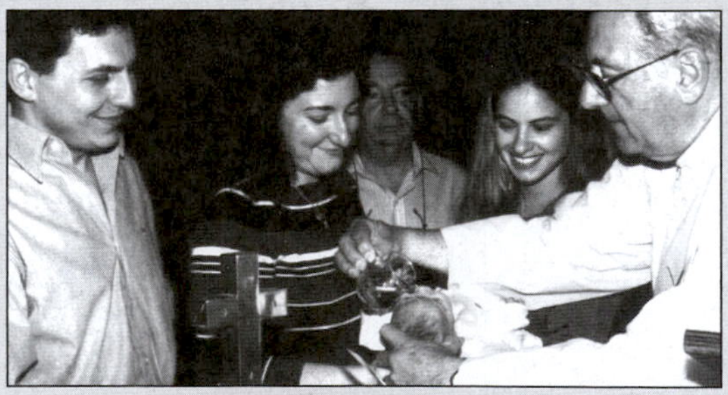

TEACHING OPTIONS

Heritage Speakers Ask heritage speakers to share with the class other terms they use to refer to various types of celebrations. Possible responses: wedding: **boda, casamiento**; graduation: **graduación, promoción**; baptism: **bautizo**; birthday: **cumpleaños, día del santo.**

Extra Practice Here are some related words of which at least one form will be familiar to students. Guide them to recognize the relationship between words and meanings. **idea, ideal, idealismo, idealizar, idear, ideario, idealista • conservar, conservación, conserva, conservador • bueno, bondad, bondadoso, bonito • habla, hablador, hablar, hablante, hablado**

32B

Fiesta de quince años

El doctor don Amador Larenas Fernández y la señora Felisa Vera de Larenas celebraron los quince años de su hija Ana Ester junto a sus parientes y amigos. La quinceañera reside en la ciudad de Valparaíso y es estudiante del Colegio Francés. La fiesta de presentación en sociedad de la señorita Ana Ester fue el día viernes 2 de mayo a las 19 horas en el Club Español. Entre los invitados especiales asistieron el alcalde° de la ciudad, don Pedro Castedo, y su esposa. La música estuvo a cargo de la Orquesta Americana. ¡Feliz cumpleaños, le deseamos a la señorita Ana Ester en su fiesta bailable!

Expresión de gracias

Carmen Godoy Tapia

Agradecemos° sinceramente a todas las personas que nos acompañaron en el último adiós a nuestra apreciada esposa, madre, abuela y tía, la señora Carmen Godoy Tapia. El funeral tuvo lugar el día 28 de junio en la ciudad de Viña del Mar. La vida de Carmen Godoy fue un ejemplo de trabajo, amistad, alegría y amor para todos nosotros. Su esposo, hijos y familia agradecen de todo corazón° su asistencia° al funeral a todos los parientes y amigos.

tuvo lugar *took place* alcalde *mayor* Agradecemos *We thank* de todo corazón *sincerely* asistencia *attendance*

Después de leer

Corregir

Escribe estos comentarios otra vez para corregir la información errónea.

1. El alcalde y su esposa asistieron a la boda de Silvia y Carlos. El alcalde y su esposa asistieron a la fiesta de quince años de Ana Ester.
2. Todos los anuncios (*announcements*) describen eventos felices. Tres de los anuncios tratan de eventos felices. Uno trata de una muerte.
3. Felisa Vera de Larenas cumple quince años. Ana Ester Larenas cumple quince años.
4. Roberto Lagos y María Angélica Sánchez son hermanos. Roberto Lagos y María Angélica Sánchez están casados/son esposos.
5. Carmen Godoy Tapia les dio las gracias a las personas que asistieron al funeral. La familia de Carmen Godoy Tapia les dio las gracias a las personas que asistieron al funeral.

Identificar

Escribe el nombre de la(s) persona(s) descrita(s) (*described*).

1. Dejó viudo a su esposo el 28 de junio. Carmen Godoy Tapia
2. Sus padres y todos los invitados brindaron por él, pero él no entendió por qué. José María
3. El Club Español les presentó una cuenta considerable. don Amador Larenas Fernández y doña Felisa Vera de Larenas
4. Unió a los novios en santo matrimonio. el pastor Federico Salas
5. Su fiesta de cumpleaños se celebró en Valparaíso. Ana Ester

Un anuncio

Trabajen en grupos pequeños para inventar un anuncio breve sobre una celebración importante. Puede ser una graduación, un matrimonio o una gran fiesta en la que ustedes participan. Incluyan la siguiente información. Answers will vary.

1. nombres de los participantes
2. la fecha, la hora y el lugar
3. qué se celebra
4. otros detalles de interés

Teaching Tip You may want to discuss other aspects of **fiesta de quince años** celebrations. Point out that the celebration has elements of a Sweet Sixteen or bat mitzvah, a prom, and a wedding. For example, often there is a church ceremony followed by a reception with a catered dinner, live music or DJ, and dancing. The birthday girl may have a court made up of **damas de honor** and **chambelanes**. In some cases, the girl may wear flat shoes at the church mass and then later, at the reception, to symbolize her transition into adulthood, her father will change the shoes to high heels. Ask students if they have seen elements related to this celebration in North America, such as Hallmark cards, **quinceañera** Barbie dolls, or the 2006 film ***Quinceañera***.

Corregir Ask volunteers to correct each false statement and point out the location in the text where they found the correct answer.

Identificar

- If students have trouble inferring the meaning of any word or phrase, help them identify the corresponding context clues.
- Have pairs write one question for each of the five items and exchange them with another pair, who will answer the questions.

Un anuncio

- Provide students with additional examples of announcements from Spanish-language newspapers to analyze and use as models.
- Have heritage speakers work with students who are being exposed to Spanish for the first time. When students have finished writing, ask them to read their announcements aloud. Have students combine the articles to create their own **Vida social** page for a class newspaper.

TEACHING OPTIONS

Extra Practice Have pairs visit the website of a Spanish-language newspaper, such as ***El Tiempo*** (Colombia), ***El Universal*** (Mexico), or the magazine ***Hola*** (Mexico). Tell them to look for sections called **Gente, Sociedad,** or **Sociales**. Have them print the photos and present the events to the class, using the preterite tense and vocabulary from this lesson.

Game Have students describe the people mentioned in the announcements they wrote for the above activity **Un anuncio**; their classmates will guess the event they are describing.

Section Goals

In **Escritura**, students will:

- create a Venn diagram to organize information
- learn words and phrases that signal similarity and difference
- write a comparative analysis

Instructional Resource
Supersite

Estrategia Explain that a graphic organizer, such as a Venn diagram, is a useful way to record information and visually organize details to be compared and contrasted in a comparative analysis. On the board, draw a Venn diagram with the headings **La boda de mi hermano, El bautismo de mi sobrina,** and the subheadings **Diferencias** and **Similitudes**. Tell students they are going to complete a Venn diagram to compare two celebrations. Discuss with the class how these events are alike and how they are different, using some of the terms to signal similarities and differences.

Tema Explain to students that to write a comparative analysis, they will need to use words or phrases that signal similarities **(similitudes)** and differences **(diferencias)**. Model the pronunciation of the words and expressions under **Escribir una composición**. Then have volunteers use them in sentences to express the similarities and differences listed in the Venn diagram.

Escritura

Estrategia

Planning and writing a comparative analysis

Writing any kind of comparative analysis requires careful planning. Venn diagrams are useful for organizing your ideas visually before comparing and contrasting people, places, objects, events, or issues. To create a Venn diagram, draw two circles that overlap one another and label the top of each circle. List the differences between the two elements in the outer rings of the two circles, then list their similarities where the two circles overlap. Review the following example.

Diferencias y similitudes

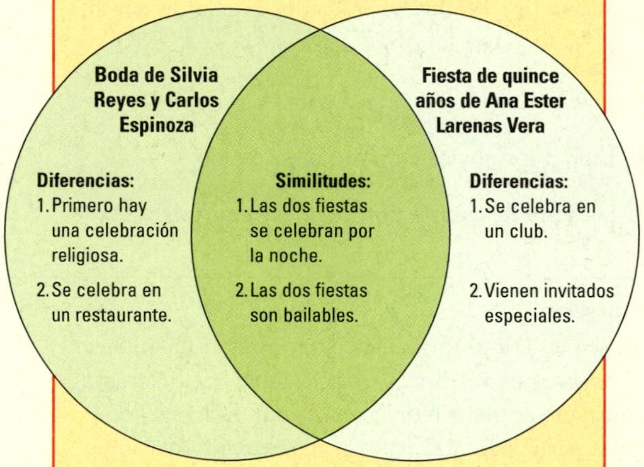
Boda de Silvia Reyes y Carlos Espinoza
Diferencias:
1. Primero hay una celebración religiosa.
2. Se celebra en un restaurante.
Similitudes:
1. Las dos fiestas se celebran por la noche.
2. Las dos fiestas son bailables.
Fiesta de quince años de Ana Ester Larenas Vera
Diferencias:
1. Se celebra en un club.
2. Vienen invitados especiales.

La lista de palabras y expresiones a la derecha puede ayudarte a escribir este tipo de ensayo (*essay*).

Tema

Escribir una composición

Compara una celebración familiar (como una boda, una fiesta de cumpleaños o una graduación) a la que tú asististe recientemente con otro tipo de celebración. Utiliza palabras y expresiones de esta lista.

Para expresar similitudes

además; también	*in addition; also*
al igual que	*the same as*
como	*as; like*
de la misma manera	*in the same manner (way)*
del mismo modo	*in the same manner (way)*
tan + [*adjetivo*] + como	*as* + [adjective] + *as*
tanto/a(s) + [*sustantivo*] + como	*as many/much* + [noun] + *as*

Para expresar diferencias

a diferencia de	*unlike*
a pesar de	*in spite of*
aunque	*although*
en cambio	*on the other hand*
más/menos... que	*more/less . . . than*
no obstante	*nevertheless; however*
por el contrario	*on the contrary*
por otro lado	*on the other hand*
sin embargo	*nevertheless; however*

EVALUATION: Composición

Criteria	Scale
Content	1 2 3 4
Organization	1 2 3 4
Use of comparisons/contrasts	1 2 3 4
Use of vocabulary	1 2 3 4
Accuracy	1 2 3 4

Scoring	
Excellent	18–20 points
Good	14–17 points
Satisfactory	10–13 points
Unsatisfactory	< 10 points

Escuchar

Audio

Estrategia

Guessing the meaning of words through context

When you hear an unfamiliar word, you can often guess its meaning by listening to the words and phrases around it.

To practice this strategy, you will now listen to a paragraph. Jot down the unfamiliar words that you hear. Then listen to the paragraph again and jot down the word or words that give the most useful clues to the meaning of each unfamiliar word.

Preparación

Lee la invitación. ¿De qué crees que van a hablar Rosa y Josefina?

Ahora escucha

Ahora escucha la conversación entre Josefina y Rosa. Cuando oigas una de las palabras de la columna A, usa el contexto para identificar el sinónimo o la definición en la columna B.

A	B
d 1. festejar	a. conmemoración religiosa de una muerte
c 2. dicha	b. tolera
h 3. bien parecido	c. suerte
g 4. finge (fingir)	d. celebrar
b 5. soporta (soportar)	e. me divertí
e 6. yo lo disfruté (disfrutar)	f. horror
	g. crea una ficción
	h. guapo

Practice more at **vhlcentral.com**.

Margarita Robles de García
y Roberto García Olmos

Piden su presencia en la celebración
del décimo aniversario de bodas
el día 13 de marzo
con una misa en la Iglesia Virgen del Coromoto
a las 6:30

seguida por cena y baile
en el restaurante El Campanero,
Calle Principal, Las Mercedes
a las 8:30

Comprensión

NATIONAL communication STANDARDS

¿Cierto o falso?

Lee cada oración e indica si lo que dice es **cierto** o **falso**. Corrige las oraciones falsas.

1. No invitaron a mucha gente a la fiesta de Margarita y Roberto porque ellos no conocen a muchas personas. Falso. Fueron muchos invitados.
2. Algunos fueron a la fiesta con pareja y otros fueron sin compañero/a. Cierto.
3. Margarita y Roberto decidieron celebrar el décimo aniversario porque no hicieron una fiesta el día de su boda. Falso. Celebraron el décimo aniversario porque les gustan las fiestas.
4. Rafael les parece interesante a Rosa y a Josefina. Cierto.
5. Josefina se divirtió mucho en la fiesta porque bailó toda la noche con Rafael. Falso. Josefina se divirtió mucho, pero bailó con otros, no con Rafael.

Preguntas

Responde a estas preguntas con oraciones completas. Answers will vary.

1. ¿Son solteras Rosa y Josefina? ¿Cómo lo sabes?
2. ¿Tienen las chicas una amistad de mucho tiempo con la pareja que celebra su aniversario? ¿Cómo lo sabes?

Section Goals

In **Escuchar**, students will:
- use context to infer meaning of unfamiliar words
- answer questions based on a recorded conversation

Instructional Resources
Supersite: Audio (Textbook MP3s); Resources (Scripts)

Estrategia
Script Hoy mi sobrino Gabriel cumplió seis años. Antes de la fiesta, ayudé a mi hermana a decorar la sala con globos de todos los colores, pero ¡qué bulla después!, cuando los niños se pusieron a estallarlos todos. El pastel de cumpleaños estaba riquísimo, y cuando Gabriel sopló las velas, apagó las seis. Los otros niños le regalaron un montón de juguetes, y nos divertimos mucho.

Teaching Tip
Have students read the invitation and guess what **Rosa** and **Josefina** will be talking about in the audio.

Ahora escucha
Script JOSEFINA: Rosa, ¿te divertiste anoche en la fiesta?
ROSA: Sí, me divertí más en el aniversario que en la boda. ¡La fiesta estuvo fenomenal! Fue buena idea festejar el aniversario en un restaurante. Así todos pudieron relajarse.
J: En parte, yo lo disfruté porque son una pareja tan linda; qué dicha que estén tan enamorados después de diez años de matrimonio. Me gustaría tener una relación como la de ellos. Y también saberlo celebrar con tanta alegría. ¡Pero qué cantidad de comida y bebida!
R: Es verdad que Margarita y Roberto exageran un poco con sus fiestas, pero son de la clase de gente que le gusta celebrar los eventos de la vida. Y como tienen tantas amistades y dos familias tan grandes...
J: Oye, Rosa, hablando de

(Script continues at far left in the bottom panels.)

familia, ¿llegaste a conocer al cuñado de Magali? Es soltero, ¿no? Quise bailar con él, pero no me sacó a bailar.
R: Hablas de Rafael. Es muy bien parecido; ¡ese pelo...! Estuve hablando con él después del brindis. Me dijo que no le gusta ni el champán ni el vino; él finge tomar cuando brindan porque no lo soporta. No te sacó a bailar porque él y Susana estaban juntos en la fiesta.
J: De todos modos, aun sin Rafael, bailé toda la noche. Lo pasé muy, pero muy bien.

Section Goals

In **En pantalla**, students will:

- read about **las Fiestas Patrias** in Chile
- watch a television commercial about **las Fiestas Patrias** and other celebrations in Chile

Instructional Resources
Supersite: Video (***En pantalla***); Resources (Scripts, Translations)

Introduction To check comprehension, have students indicate whether these statements are **cierto** or **falso** and correct the false statements. **1. Durante las Fiestas Patrias todos los niños tienen que ir a la escuela. (Falso. Durante las Fiestas Patrias se cierran casi todas las escuelas.) 2. Las empanadas y los asados son bailes típicos de Chile. (Falso. Son platos tradicionales de Chile.) 3. Los chilenos vuelan volantines durante las Fiestas Patrias. (Cierto.)**

Antes de ver

- Have students look at the video stills, read the captions, and predict what is being celebrated in each visual.
- Read through the **Vocabulario útil** with students and model the pronunciation.

Seleccionar

- For items 1–3, have students name a holiday that they associate with the three related words.
- Have students write a sentence using each of the words that doesn't belong.

Fiesta

Have students imagine that one of their friends is timid and reluctant to come to the party. Ask them to write a dialogue in which they try to convince their friend to come.

En pantalla

NATIONAL STANDARDS communication cultures

Anuncio

Desfiles°, música, asados°, fuegos artificiales° y baile son los elementos de una buena fiesta. ¿Celebrar durante toda una semana? ¡Eso sí que es una fiesta espectacular! El 18 de septiembre Chile conmemora su independencia de España y los chilenos demuestran su orgullo° nacional durante una semana llena de celebraciones. Durante las Fiestas Patrias° casi todas las oficinas° y escuelas se cierran para que la gente se reúna° a festejar. Desfiles y rodeos representan la tradición de los vaqueros° del país, y la gente baila cueca, el baile nacional. Las familias y los amigos se reúnen para preparar y comer platos tradicionales como las empanadas y asados. Otra de las tradiciones de estas fiestas es hacer volar cometas°, llamadas volantines. Mira el video para descubrir cómo se celebran otras fiestas en Chile.

Vocabulario útil

conejo	*bunny*
disfraces	*costumes*
mariscal	*traditional Chilean soup with raw seafood*
sustos	*frights*
vieja (Chi.)	*mother*

Seleccionar

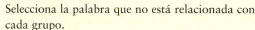

Selecciona la palabra que no está relacionada con cada grupo.

1. disfraces • noviembre • arbolito • sustos arbolito
2. volantines • arbolito • regalos • diciembre volantines
3. conejo • enero • huevitos • chocolates enero
4. septiembre • volantines • disfraces • asado disfraces

Fiesta

Trabajen en grupos de tres. Imaginen que van a organizar una fiesta para celebrar el 4 de julio. Escriban una invitación electrónica para invitar a sus parientes y amigos a la fiesta. Describan los planes que tienen para la fiesta y díganles a sus amigos qué tiene que traer cada uno. Answers will vary.

Desfiles/Paradas *Parades* **asados** *barbecues* **fuegos artificiales** *fireworks* **orgullo** *pride* **Fiestas Patrias** *Independence Day celebrations* **oficinas** *offices* **se reúna** *would get together* **vaqueros** *cowboys* **cometas/volantines** *kites*

CHV FIESTAS PATRIAS
CHILEVISION

Noviembre: disfraces, dulces...

Mayo: besito, tarjeta, tecito con la mamá...

Septiembre... Septiembre: familia, parada militar...

Video: TV Clip

Practice more at **vhlcentral.com**.

TEACHING OPTIONS

Small Groups Have small groups create a commercial similar to the one for **Chilevisión**, but that includes other important holidays. Allow groups to choose any Spanish-speaking country they want, including the U.S. and Canada. Have groups bring in visuals to represent each celebration and hold up the visuals as they read the script aloud for the class. Each group member should read a portion of the script.

Heritage Speakers If heritage speakers have attended parties for young people in a Spanish-speaking country (such as a **miniteca** in Colombia), have them describe certain aspects of the party. Is it common to bring food or drink to a friend's party? Are parties more or less formal than in the U.S.? Do people dance or just listen to music? Have the rest of the class compare and contrast these customs with their own.

Cortometraje

Para Iker, cada persona se parece a un animal. Por ejemplo, su papá es un oso°. A Iker le habría gustado° ser un oso también, pero él es otro animal. Y eso es algo que nadie sabe en la escuela. ¿Qué puede pasar si° sus compañeros descubren el secreto de Iker?

Preparación

En parejas, túrnense para hacerse estas preguntas. Answers will vary.

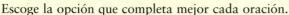

1. ¿Tienes rasgos particulares? ¿Cuáles son de tu apariencia física? ¿Cuáles son de tu personalidad?
2. ¿Cuáles de tus rasgos son buenos? ¿Cuáles son malos? ¿Cómo determinas que son buenos o malos?
3. ¿Qué rasgos te hacen una persona única?
4. ¿Es común alguno de esos rasgos en tu familia? ¿Cuál?
5. ¿Qué animal crees que serías (*you would be*) según (*according to*) tus rasgos? Explica tu respuesta.

Después de ver

Escoge la opción que completa mejor cada oración.

1. En la familia de Iker, __b__ el mismo rasgo.
   a. no hay dos personas con
   b. él y su abuelo comparten
   c. el abuelo y Tito tienen
2. Para Iker, su __b__ es un perico.
   a. hermana b. mamá c. maestra (*teacher*)
3. Iker se sintió __a__ cuando su compañero le dijo que le gustaba su peinado.
   a. aliviado (*relieved*) b. cohibido c. enojado
4. Al final, Iker estaba __c__ de mostrar su pelo tal y como es.
   a. avergonzado b. nervioso c. orgulloso

Conversar

En parejas, respondan a estas preguntas con oraciones completas. Answers will vary.

1. ¿Se han sentido ustedes cohibidos/as alguna vez? ¿Qué pasó?
2. ¿Cuáles son las ventajas (*advantages*) de presentarse ante el mundo tal y como son?
3. ¿Creen que la percepción que tienen de ustedes mismos/as influye en (*influences*) la manera en que ven a los demás? Expliquen su respuesta.

oso *bear* le habría gustado *he would have liked* si *if*

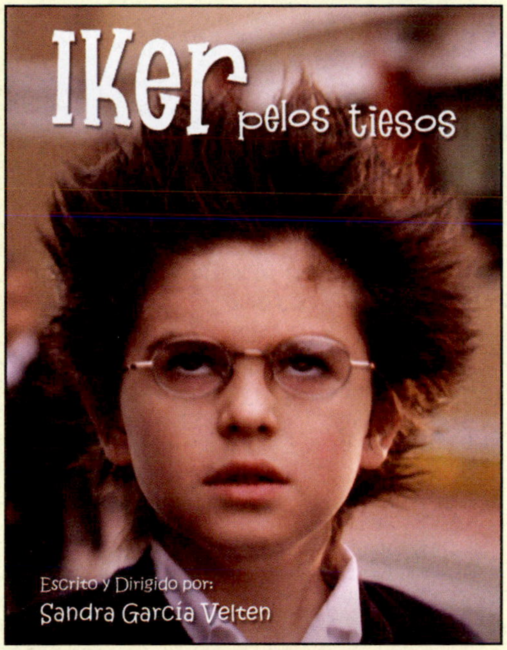

Expresiones útiles

devolver	*to return, to give back*
disimular	*to hide, to disguise*
me hubiera gustado	*I would have liked*
meter	*to put (something) in, to introduce*
el peinado	*hairstyle*
salir (igual) a	*to take after*
si supieran	*if they knew*
tieso/a	*stiff*

Para hablar del corto

burlarse (de)	*to make fun (of)*
esconder(se)	*to hide (oneself)*
la fuerza	*strength*
orgulloso/a	*proud*
pelear(se)	*to fight (with one another)*
el rasgo	*feature, characteristic*
sentirse cohibido/a	*to feel self-conscious*

Video: Short Film

Practice more at **vhlcentral.com**.

Antes de ver

- Have students look at the poster, and ask them if the boy's hair reminds them of any animal.
- Read through the **Expresiones útiles** and **Para hablar del corto** vocabulary with students to model pronunciation and practice using the terms.
- Reassure students that they do not need to understand every word they hear in the short film. Tell them to rely on visual cues and to listen for cognates and words from **Expresiones útiles**.
- Ask students to predict how the film will end.

Preparación Have pairs ask each other questions 1–4. Then have them assess their partner's answers up to that point and predict what their partner will answer for item 5.

Después de ver As a variant, have students close their books. Then provide these items as cloze sentences. Rather than the multiple-choice options, give students a word bank.

Conversar Once pairs have completed the activity, have students debate the notion that we all, to some extent, conform to society with regard to our physical appearance.

TEACHING OPTIONS

Small Groups Teach students the Mexican slang expressions that they will hear in the film, such as **órale**. In small groups, have them write mini-conversations that incorporate the expressions. Have volunteers read their dialogues to the class.

Large Groups Divide the class into two groups and tell them to imagine that they are administrators at Iker's school. Some parents have complained about the school uniform policy. Have one group argue for the abolishment of school uniforms and one group argue that the dress code should remain in effect. As part of their arguments, students should consider the increase in bullying incidents at the school over the past year.

Video: *Panorama cultural*
Interactive map

Section Goal

In **Panorama**, students will read about the geography, culture, and economy of Chile.

Instructional Resources
Supersite: Video (***Panorama cultural***); Resources (Scripts, Translations, Digital Image Bank, Answer Keys)
WebSAM
Workbook, pp. 105–106
Video Manual, pp. 47–48

Teaching Tips

- Use the **Lección 9 Panorama** digital images to assist with this presentation.
- Ask students to look at the map of Chile, and have them talk about the physical features of the country. Point out that Chile is about 2,700 miles from north to south, but no more than 276 miles from east to west. Point out that Chile has a variety of climates.

El país en cifras After reading **Chilenos célebres,** give students more information about **Bernardo O'Higgins**. They can probably guess correctly that his father was an Irish immigrant, but should also know that he is considered one of the founders of modern Latin America, along with **Simón Bolívar** and **José de San Martín**. These "founding fathers" are called **los próceres**.

¡Increíble pero cierto! The Atacama Desert covers the northern third of the country. It is considered one of the best places in the world for astronomical observations, due to its high altitude, absence of cloud cover, dry air, and lack of light pollution and radio interference.

Chile

NATIONAL STANDARDS connections cultures

El país en cifras

- **Área:** 756.950 km² (292.259 millas²), *dos veces el área de Montana*
- **Población:** 17.363.000 *Aproximadamente el 80 por ciento de la población del país es urbana.*
- **Capital:** Santiago de Chile—6.034.000
- **Ciudades principales:** Valparaíso—865.000, Concepción, Viña del Mar, Temuco
- **Moneda:** peso chileno
- **Idiomas:** español (oficial), mapuche

El puerto de Valparaíso

Bandera de Chile

Chilenos célebres

- **Bernardo O'Higgins,** militar° y héroe nacional (1778–1842)
- **Gabriela Mistral,** Premio Nobel de Literatura, 1945; poeta y diplomática (1889–1957)
- **Pablo Neruda,** Premio Nobel de Literatura, 1971; poeta (1904–1973)
- **Isabel Allende,** novelista (1942–)
- **Ana Tijoux,** cantante (1977–)

Torres del Paine

Pablo Neruda

militar *soldier* desierto *desert* el más seco *the driest* mundo *world* han tenido *have had* ha sido usado *has been used* Marte *Mars*

La costa de Viña del Mar

Edificio antiguo en Santiago

Una celebración en Temuco

recursos

WB	VM	vhlcentral.com
pp. 105–106	pp. 47–48	Lección 9

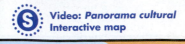

¡Increíble pero cierto!

El desierto° de Atacama, en el norte de Chile, es el más seco° del mundo°. Con más de cien mil km² de superficie, algunas zonas de este desierto nunca han tenido° lluvia. Atacama ha sido usado° como escenario para representar a Marte° en películas y series de televisión.

TEACHING OPTIONS

Heritage Speakers Invite heritage speakers to select a poem by **Pablo Neruda** to read aloud for the class. Many of the ***Odas elementales,*** such as ***Oda a la alcachofa, Oda al tomate,*** and ***Oda a la cebolla,*** are written in simple language. Prepare copies of the poem beforehand and go over unfamiliar vocabulary.

Worth Noting Though Chile is one of the smallest Spanish-speaking countries in South America, it has about 2,700 miles of coastline. Some of the highest peaks in the Andes lie on the border with Argentina, and the volcanoes that lie along the Atacama Desert are the tallest in the world. Chile's agricultural region is a valley the size of central California's. The southern archipelago is cool, foggy, and rainy, like the Alaska panhandle. It is estimated that Chile has about 6,000 islands.

Lugares • La isla de Pascua

La isla de Pascua° recibió ese nombre porque los exploradores holandeses° llegaron a la isla por primera vez el día de Pascua de 1722. Ahora es parte del territorio de Chile. La isla de Pascua es famosa por los *moái*, estatuas enormes que representan personas con rasgos° muy exagerados. Estas estatuas las construyeron los *rapa nui*, los antiguos habitantes de la zona. Todavía no se sabe mucho sobre los *rapa nui*, ni tampoco se sabe por qué decidieron abandonar la isla.

Deportes • Los deportes de invierno

Hay muchos lugares para practicar deportes de invierno en Chile porque las montañas nevadas de los Andes ocupan gran parte del país. El Parque Nacional Villarrica, por ejemplo, situado al pie de un volcán y junto a° un lago, es un sitio popular para el esquí y el *snowboard*. Para los que prefieren deportes más extremos, el centro de esquí Valle Nevado organiza excursiones para practicar heliesquí.

Ciencias • Astronomía

Los observatorios chilenos, situados en los Andes, son lugares excelentes para las observaciones astronómicas. Científicos° de todo el mundo van a Chile para estudiar las estrellas° y otros cuerpos celestes. Hoy día Chile está construyendo nuevos observatorios y telescopios para mejorar las imágenes del universo.

Economía • El vino

La producción de vino comenzó en Chile en el siglo° XVI. Ahora la industria del vino constituye una parte importante de la actividad agrícola del país y la exportación de sus productos está aumentando° cada vez más. Los vinos chilenos son muy apreciados internacionalmente por su gran variedad, sus ricos y complejos sabores° y su precio moderado. Los más conocidos son los vinos de Aconcagua y del valle del Maipo.

¿Qué aprendiste? Responde a cada pregunta con una oración completa.

1. ¿Qué porcentaje (*percentage*) de la población chilena es urbana? El 80 por ciento de la población chilena es urbana.
2. ¿Qué son los *moái*? ¿Dónde están? Los *moái* son estatuas enormes. Están en la isla de Pascua.
3. ¿Qué deporte extremo ofrece el centro de esquí Valle Nevado? Ofrece la práctica de heliesquí.
4. ¿Por qué van a Chile científicos de todo el mundo? Porque los observatorios chilenos son excelentes para las observaciones astronómicas.
5. ¿Cuándo comenzó la producción de vino en Chile? Comenzó en el siglo XVI.
6. ¿Por qué son apreciados internacionalmente los vinos chilenos? Son apreciados por su variedad, sus ricos y complejos sabores y su precio moderado.

Conexión Internet Investiga estos temas en **vhlcentral.com**.

1. Busca información sobre Pablo Neruda e Isabel Allende. ¿Dónde y cuándo nacieron? ¿Cuáles son algunas de sus obras (*works*)? ¿Cuáles son algunos de los temas de sus obras?
2. Busca información sobre sitios donde los chilenos y los turistas practican deportes de invierno en Chile. Selecciona un sitio y descríbeselo a tu clase.

Practice more at **vhlcentral.com**.

La isla de Pascua *Easter Island* **holandeses** *Dutch* **rasgos** *features* **junto a** *beside* **Científicos** *Scientists* **estrellas** *stars* **siglo** *century* **aumentando** *increasing* **complejos sabores** *complex flavors*

TEACHING OPTIONS

Worth Noting The native Mapuche people of southern Chile are a small minority of the Chilean population today, but have maintained a strong cultural identity since the time of their first contact with Europeans. In fact, they resisted conquest so well that it was only in the late nineteenth century that the government of Chile could assert sovereignty over the region south of the Bío-Bío River. However, the majority of Chileans are of European descent. Chilean Spanish is much less infused with indigenous lexical items than the Spanish of countries such as Guatemala and Mexico, where the larger indigenous population has made a greater impact on the language.

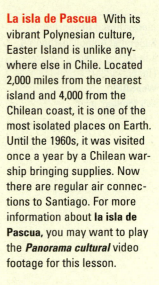

La isla de Pascua With its vibrant Polynesian culture, Easter Island is unlike anywhere else in Chile. Located 2,000 miles from the nearest island and 4,000 from the Chilean coast, it is one of the most isolated places on Earth. Until the 1960s, it was visited once a year by a Chilean warship bringing supplies. Now there are regular air connections to Santiago. For more information about **la isla de Pascua**, you may want to play the ***Panorama cultural*** video footage for this lesson.

Los deportes de invierno Remind students that some of the highest mountains in South America lie along the border Chile shares with Argentina. In the south is the **Parque Nacional Torres del Paine**, a national park featuring ice caverns, deep glacial trenches, and other spectacular features.

Astronomía In 1962, the Cerro Tololo Inter-American Observatory was founded as a joint project between Chilean and U.S. astronomers. Since that time, so many other major telescopes have been installed for research purposes that Chile is home to the highest concentration of telescopes in the world.

El vino Invite students to research the wine-growing regions of Chile and to compare them to those of California, Spain, or other wine-producing areas. Encourage students to share their findings with the class.

Conexión Internet Students will find supporting Internet activities and links at **vhlcentral.com**.

Instructional Resources
Supersite: Audio (Textbook & Lab MP3s); Testing Program (Tests, MP3s)
WebSAM
Lab Manual, p. 54

Las celebraciones

el aniversario (de bodas)	*(wedding) anniversary*
la boda	*wedding*
el cumpleaños	*birthday*
el día de fiesta	*holiday*
la fiesta	*party*
el/la invitado/a	*guest*
la Navidad	*Christmas*
la quinceañera	*young woman celebrating her fifteenth birthday*
la sorpresa	*surprise*
brindar	*to toast* (drink)
celebrar	*to celebrate*
divertirse (e:ie)	*to have fun*
invitar	*to invite*
pasarlo bien/mal	*to have a good/bad time*
regalar	*to give* (a gift)
reírse (e:i)	*to laugh*
relajarse	*to relax*
sonreír (e:i)	*to smile*
sorprender	*to surprise*

Los postres y otras comidas

la botella (de vino)	*bottle (of wine)*
el champán	*champagne*
los dulces	*sweets; candy*
el flan (de caramelo)	*baked (caramel) custard*
la galleta	*cookie*
el helado	*ice cream*
el pastel (de chocolate)	*(chocolate) cake; pie*
el postre	*dessert*

Las relaciones personales

la amistad	*friendship*
el amor	*love*
el divorcio	*divorce*
el estado civil	*marital status*
el matrimonio	*marriage*
la pareja	*(married) couple; partner*
el/la recién casado/a	*newlywed*
casarse (con)	*to get married (to)*
comprometerse (con)	*to get engaged (to)*
divorciarse (de)	*to get divorced (from)*
enamorarse (de)	*to fall in love (with)*
llevarse bien/mal (con)	*to get along well/ badly (with)*
odiar	*to hate*
romper (con)	*to break up (with)*
salir (con)	*to go out (with); to date*
separarse (de)	*to separate (from)*
tener una cita	*to have a date; to have an appointment*
casado/a	*married*
divorciado/a	*divorced*
juntos/as	*together*
separado/a	*separated*
soltero/a	*single*
viudo/a	*widower/widow*

Las etapas de la vida

la adolescencia	*adolescence*
la edad	*age*
las etapas de la vida	*the stages of life*
la juventud	*youth*
la madurez	*maturity; middle age*
la muerte	*death*
el nacimiento	*birth*
la niñez	*childhood*
la vejez	*old age*
cambiar (de)	*to change*
graduarse (de/en)	*to graduate (from/in)*
jubilarse	*to retire (from work)*
nacer	*to be born*

Palabras adicionales

la alegría	*happiness*
el beso	*kiss*
conmigo	*with me*
contigo	*with you*
¡Felicidades!/ ¡Felicitaciones!	*Congratulations!*
¡Feliz cumpleaños!	*Happy birthday!*

Expresiones útiles	*See page 281.*

recursos
LM p. 54 | vhlcentral.com Lección 9

Vocabulary Tools

En el consultorio 10

Communicative Goals

You will learn how to:

- **Describe how you feel physically**
- **Talk about health and medical conditions**

A PRIMERA VISTA

- **¿Están en una farmacia o en un hospital?**
- **¿La mujer es médica o dentista?**
- **¿Qué hace ella, una operación o un examen médico?**
- **¿Crees que la paciente está nerviosa?**

contextos

fotonovela

cultura

estructura

adelante

Lesson Goals

In **Lección 10**, students will be introduced to the following:

- names of parts of the body
- health-related terms
- medical-related vocabulary
- health services in Spanish-speaking countries
- healers and shamans
- the imperfect tense
- uses of the preterite and imperfect tenses
- impersonal **se** constructions
- using **se** for unplanned events
- forming adverbs using [*adjective*] + **–mente**
- common adverbs and adverbial expressions
- activating background knowledge
- a video about hospitals in Argentina
- cultural, geographic, and economic information about Costa Rica and Nicaragua

A primera vista Ask these additional questions: **¿Cuándo fue la última vez que viste a tu médico/a? ¿Estuviste en su consultorio la semana pasada? ¿Cuáles son las mejores comidas para sentirte bien?**

Teaching Tip Look for these icons for additional communicative practice:

→•←	Interpretive communication
←•→	Presentational communication
•↔•	Interpersonal communication

INSTRUCTIONAL RESOURCES

Supersite (vhlcentral.com)
Video: ***Fotonovela, Flash cultura, Panorama cultural***
Audio: Textbook and Lab MP3 Files
Activity Pack: Information Gap Activities, games, additional activity handouts
Resources: SAM Answer Key, Scripts, Translations, **Vocabulario adicional**, sample lesson plan, Grammar Presentation Slides, Digital Image Bank
Testing Program: Quizzes, Tests, Exams, MP3s
Student Activities Manual: Workbook/Video Manual/Lab Manual
WebSAM (online Student Activities Manual)

Vocabulary Tools

Section Goals

In **Contextos**, students will learn and practice:

- names of parts of the body
- vocabulary for talking about illnesses and accidents
- vocabulary associated with medical visits

Instructional Resources
Supersite: Audio (Textbook and Lab MP3 Files); Resources (Digital Image Bank, **Vocabulario adicional**, Activity Pack, Scripts, Answer Keys); Testing Program (Quizzes)
WebSAM
Workbook, pp. 109–110
Lab Manual, p. 55

Teaching Tips

- Pretend to have had an accident-filled day. Ex: **Ayer pasé un día horrible. Fui a pasear en bicicleta y me caí. Me lastimé las rodillas y los brazos. Luego, cuando llegué a casa, me di con la puerta y me lastimé el ojo. Esta mañana cerré la puerta del auto y me lastimé el dedo.** Then ask comprehension questions about what hurts. Ex: **¿Me duele la garganta? (No.)** Finally, ask students about likely treatment options.
- Use the **Lección 10 Contextos** digital images to assist with this presentation.
- Have students refer to the scene and the vocabulary boxes as you give yes/no statements about the new vocabulary. Ex: **¿Sí o no? La enfermera le toma la temperatura a la paciente. (Sí.) La doctora le pone una inyección al hombre. (No.)** Then ask volunteers to describe what is going on in the scene, using as much of the new vocabulary as possible.

En el consultorio

Más vocabulario

la clínica	*clinic*
el consultorio	*doctor's office*
el/la dentista	*dentist*
el examen médico	*physical exam*
la farmacia	*pharmacy*
el hospital	*hospital*
la operación	*operation*
la sala de emergencia(s)	*emergency room*
el cuerpo	*body*
el oído	*(sense of) hearing; inner ear*
el accidente	*accident*
la salud	*health*
el síntoma	*symptom*
caerse	*to fall (down)*
darse con	*to bump into; to run into*
doler (o:ue)	*to hurt*
enfermarse	*to get sick*
estar enfermo/a	*to be sick*
lastimarse (el pie)	*to injure (one's foot)*
poner una inyección	*to give an injection*
recetar	*to prescribe*
romperse (la pierna)	*to break (one's leg)*
sacar(se) un diente	*to have a tooth removed*
sufrir una enfermedad	*to suffer an illness*
torcerse (o:ue) (el tobillo)	*to sprain (one's ankle)*
toser	*to cough*

Variación léxica

gripe ↔	gripa (*Col., Gua., Méx.*)
resfriado ↔	catarro (*Cuba, Esp., Gua.*)
sala de emergencia(s) ↔	sala de urgencias (*Arg., Col., Esp., Méx.*)
romperse ↔	quebrarse (*Arg., Gua.*)

recursos: WB pp. 109–110 | LM p. 55 | vhlcentral.com Lección 10

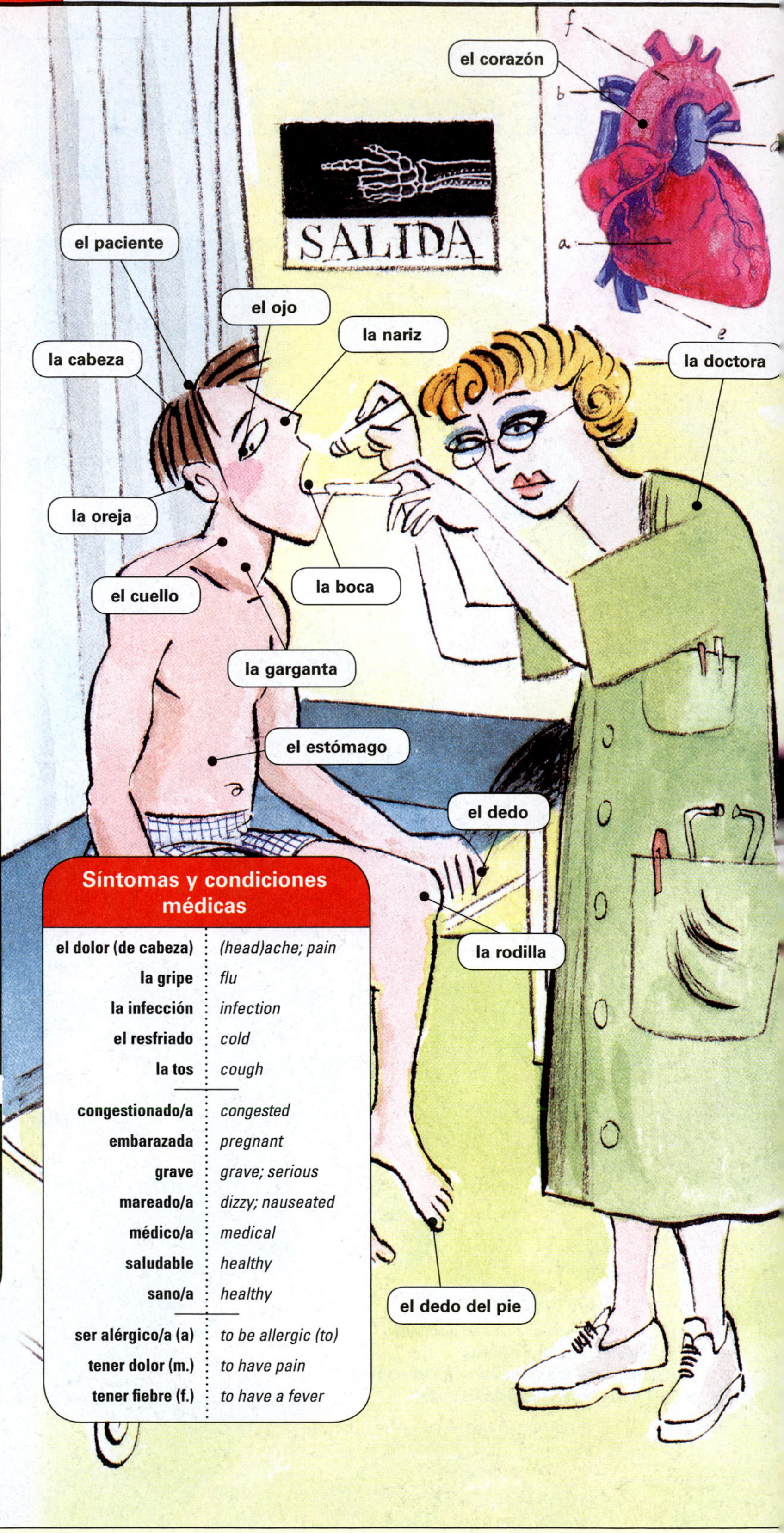

Síntomas y condiciones médicas

el dolor (de cabeza)	*(head)ache; pain*
la gripe	*flu*
la infección	*infection*
el resfriado	*cold*
la tos	*cough*
congestionado/a	*congested*
embarazada	*pregnant*
grave	*grave; serious*
mareado/a	*dizzy; nauseated*
médico/a	*medical*
saludable	*healthy*
sano/a	*healthy*
ser alérgico/a (a)	*to be allergic (to)*
tener dolor (m.)	*to have pain*
tener fiebre (f.)	*to have a fever*

TEACHING OPTIONS

TPR Play a game of **Simón dice.** Write **toquen** on the board and explain that it means *touch.* Start by saying: **Simón dice… que toquen la nariz.** Students are to touch their noses and keep their hands there until instructed to do otherwise. Work through various parts of the body. Be sure to give instructions occasionally without saying **Simón dice…**

Variación léxica Point out differences in health-related vocabulary, as well as some false cognates. **Embarazada** means *pregnant*, not *embarrassed.* You may also want to present **constipado/a** and explain that it does not mean *constipated*, but rather *congested* or *stuffed up.* Point out that, whereas in English people have ten fingers and ten toes, in Spanish people have twenty **dedos: diez dedos de las manos y diez de los pies.**

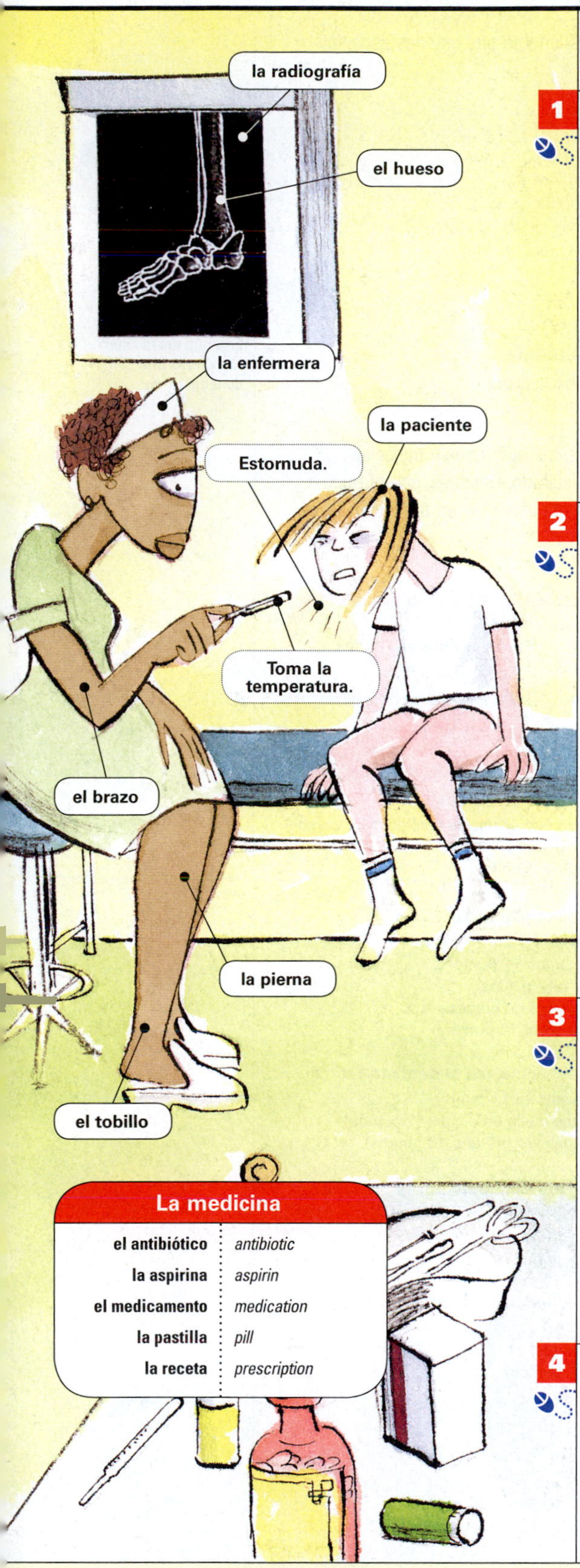

La medicina

el antibiótico	*antibiotic*
la aspirina	*aspirin*
el medicamento	*medication*
la pastilla	*pill*
la receta	*prescription*

Práctica

1 Escuchar Escucha las preguntas y selecciona la respuesta más adecuada.

a. Tengo dolor de cabeza y fiebre.
b. No fui a la clase porque estaba (*I was*) enfermo.
c. Me caí la semana pasada jugando al tenis.
d. Debes ir a la farmacia.
e. Porque tengo gripe.
f. Sí, tengo mucha tos por las noches.
g. Lo llevaron directamente a la sala de emergencia.
h. No sé. Todavía tienen que tomarme la temperatura.

1. ___c___ 3. ___g___ 5. ___f___ 7. ___a___
2. ___e___ 4. ___d___ 6. ___h___ 8. ___b___

2 Seleccionar Escucha la conversación entre Daniel y su doctor y selecciona la respuesta que mejor complete cada oración.

1. Daniel cree que tiene _a_.
 a. gripe b. un resfriado c. la temperatura alta
2. A Daniel le duele la cabeza, estornuda, tose y _c_.
 a. se cae b. tiene fiebre c. está congestionado
3. El doctor le _b_.
 a. pone una inyección b. toma la temperatura
 c. mira el oído
4. A Daniel no le gustan _a_.
 a. las inyecciones b. los antibióticos c. las visitas al doctor
5. El doctor dice que Daniel tiene _b_.
 a. gripe b. un resfriado c. fiebre
6. Después de la consulta Daniel va a _c_.
 a. la sala de emergencia b. la clínica c. la farmacia

3 Completar Completa las oraciones con una palabra de la misma familia de la palabra subrayada. Usa la forma correcta de cada palabra.

1. Cuando oyes algo, usas el ___oído___.
2. Cuando te enfermas, te sientes ___enfermo/a___ y necesitas ir al consultorio para ver a la ___enfermera___.
3. ¿Alguien ___estornudó___? Creo que oí un estornudo (*sneeze*).
4. No puedo arrodillarme (*kneel down*) porque me lastimé la ___rodilla___ en un accidente de coche.
5. ¿Vas al ___consultorio___ para consultar al médico?
6. Si te rompes un diente, vas al ___dentista___.

4 Contestar Mira el dibujo y contesta las preguntas. Answers will vary.

1. ¿Qué hace la doctora?
2. ¿Qué hay en la pared (*wall*)?
3. ¿Qué hace la enfermera?
4. Qué hace el paciente?
5. ¿A quién le duele la garganta?
6. ¿Qué tiene la paciente?

TEACHING OPTIONS

Game Play **Concentración**. On eight cards, write names for parts of the body or items found in a doctor's office. On another eight cards, draw or paste a picture that matches each word. Place the cards facedown in four rows of four. In pairs, students select two cards. If the cards match, the pair keeps them. If the cards do not match, students replace them in their original position. The pair with the most cards at the end wins.

Heritage Speakers Ask heritage speakers to describe a visit they made to a doctor's office. Verify comprehension by having students relate what was said. On the board, write any nonactive vocabulary that students may use, such as **auscultar los pulmones, sacar la lengua, tomar la presión arterial, la sangre,** and so forth.

1 Teaching Tip Before playing the audio, have students read through the list of responses. Explain that not all the questions are directed at the same person.

1 Script 1. ¿Cuándo te caíste? 2. ¿Por qué vas al médico? 3. ¿Adónde llevaron a Juan después del accidente? 4. ¿Adónde debo ir para conseguir estas pastillas? 5. ¿Tienes mucha tos? 6. ¿Tienes fiebre? 7. ¿Cuáles son sus síntomas, señor? 8. Ayer no te vi en la clase de biología. ¿Por qué? *Textbook MP3s*

2 Teaching Tip To challenge students, write the activity items on the board as cloze sentences. Have students complete them as they listen to the audio.

2 Script DANIEL: Hola, doctor. Me siento enfermo. Creo que tengo gripe. DOCTOR: ¿Cuándo te enfermaste? DA: La semana pasada. DO: ¿Cuáles son tus síntomas? DA: Me duele la cabeza, estornudo y tengo mucha tos por las noches. Ah, y también estoy congestionado. DO: Voy a tomarte la temperatura. DA: ¿Me va a poner una inyección, doctor? No me gustan las inyecciones. DO: No tienes fiebre y, tranquilo, no necesitas inyecciones. Esto es un simple resfriado. Voy a recetarte unas pastillas y pronto tu salud va a mejorar. DA: Gracias, doctor. Voy a pasar por la farmacia al salir de la consulta. *Textbook MP3s*

3 Teaching Tip Have students identify the part of speech of each underlined word and each fill-in-the-blank answer.

3 Expansion Have students write two additional cloze sentences for a partner to complete.

4 Teaching Tip Have pairs play a memory game. Have them study the drawing for 30 seconds, then ask each other the questions.

5 Teaching Tip Point out that there are several parts of the body that may be associated with each activity. Encourage students to list as many as they can.

5 Expansion Do the activity in reverse. Name parts of the body and ask students to associate them with as many activities as they can.

6 Expansion
- Ask for a show of hands for those who fall into the different health levels based on point totals. Analyze the trends of the class—are your students healthy or unhealthy?
- Ask for volunteers from each of the three groups to explain whether they think the results of the survey are accurate or not. Ask them to give examples based on their own eating, exercise, and other health habits.
- You may want to have students brainstorm a few additional health-related questions and responses, and adjust the point totals accordingly. Ex: **¿Con qué frecuencia te lavas las manos? ¿Con qué frecuencia usas seda dental? ¿Tomas el sol sin bloqueador solar? ¿Comes comida rápida (McDonald's, etc.)? ¿Fumas cigarros? ¿Consumes mucha cafeína?**

Note: At this point you may want to present ***Vocabulario adicional: Más vocabulario para el consultorio*** from the Supersite.

5 **Asociaciones** Trabajen en parejas para identificar las partes del cuerpo que ustedes asocian con estas actividades. Sigan el modelo. Answers will vary.

modelo

nadar
Estudiante 1: Usamos los brazos para nadar.
Estudiante 2: Usamos las piernas también.

1. hablar por teléfono
2. tocar el piano
3. correr en el parque
4. escuchar música
5. ver una película
6. toser
7. llevar zapatos
8. comprar perfume
9. estudiar biología
10. comer pollo asado

AYUDA

Remember that in Spanish, parts of the body are usually referred to with an article and not a possessive adjective: **Me duelen los pies.** The indirect object pronoun **me** is used to express the concept of *my*.

6 **Cuestionario** Contesta el cuestionario seleccionando las respuestas que reflejen mejor tus experiencias. Suma (*Add*) los puntos de cada respuesta y anota el resultado. Después, con el resto de la clase, compara y analiza los resultados del cuestionario y comenta lo que dicen de la salud y de los hábitos de todo el grupo. Answers will vary.

¿Tienes buena salud?

27–30 puntos	Salud y hábitos excelentes
23–26 puntos	Salud y hábitos buenos
22 puntos o menos	Salud y hábitos problemáticos

1. **¿Con qué frecuencia te enfermas? (resfriados, gripe, etc.)**
   Cuatro veces por año o más. (1 punto)
   Dos o tres veces por año. (2 puntos)
   Casi nunca. (3 puntos)
2. **¿Con qué frecuencia tienes dolores de estómago o problemas digestivos?**
   Con mucha frecuencia. (1 punto)
   A veces. (2 puntos)
   Casi nunca. (3 puntos)
3. **¿Con qué frecuencia sufres de dolores de cabeza?**
   Frecuentemente. (1 punto)
   A veces. (2 puntos)
   Casi nunca. (3 puntos)
4. **¿Comes verduras y frutas?**
   No, casi nunca como verduras ni frutas. (1 punto)
   Sí, a veces. (2 puntos)
   Sí, todos los días. (3 puntos)
5. **¿Eres alérgico/a a algo?**
   Sí, a muchas cosas. (1 punto)
   Sí, a algunas cosas. (2 puntos)
   No. (3 puntos)
6. **¿Haces ejercicios aeróbicos?**
   No, casi nunca hago ejercicios aeróbicos. (1 punto)
   Sí, a veces. (2 puntos)
   Sí, con frecuencia. (3 puntos)
7. **¿Con qué frecuencia te haces un examen médico?**
   Nunca o casi nunca. (1 punto)
   Cada dos años. (2 puntos)
   Cada año y/o antes de empezar a practicar un deporte. (3 puntos)
8. **¿Con qué frecuencia vas al dentista?**
   Nunca voy al dentista. (1 punto)
   Sólo cuando me duele un diente. (2 puntos)
   Por lo menos una vez por año. (3 puntos)
9. **¿Qué comes normalmente por la mañana?**
   No como nada por la mañana. (1 punto)
   Tomo una bebida dietética. (2 puntos)
   Como cereal y fruta. (3 puntos)
10. **¿Con qué frecuencia te sientes mareado/a?**
    Frecuentemente. (1 punto)
    A veces. (2 puntos)
    Casi nunca. (3 puntos)

Practice more at **vhlcentral.com**.

TEACHING OPTIONS

Small Groups On the board, write popular expressions related to parts of the body and guide students in guessing their meanings. Ex: **tomarle el pelo (a alguien), no tener pelos en la lengua, salvarse por un pelo, costar un ojo de la cara, no tener dos dedos de frente, ponerle los pelos de punta, hablar hasta por los codos.** In small groups, have students create a sentence about a famous person or classmate for each expression. Ex: **El presidente no tiene pelos en la lengua.**

Game Play a modified version of **20 Preguntas**. Ask a volunteer to think of a part of the body. Other students get one chance each to ask a yes/no question until someone guesses the correct body part. Limit attempts to ten questions per item. Encourage students to guess by associating activities with various parts of the body.

Comunicación

7 **¿Qué les pasó?** Trabajen en un grupo de dos o tres personas. Hablen de lo que les pasó y de cómo se sienten las personas que aparecen en los dibujos. Answers will vary.

1. Adela
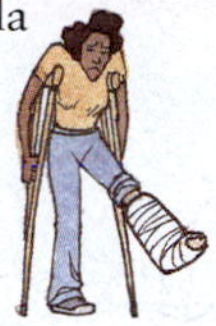

2. Francisco

3. Pilar

4. Pedro

5. Cristina

6. Félix
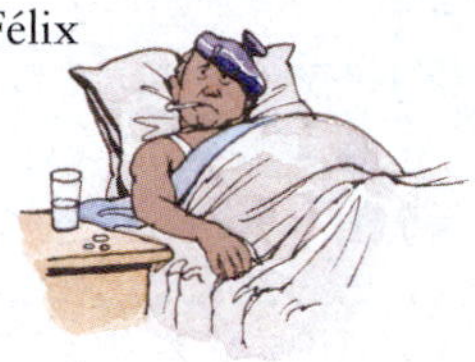

8 **Un accidente** Cuéntale a un(a) compañero/a de un accidente o una enfermedad que tuviste. Incluye información que conteste estas preguntas. Answers will vary.

- ✓ ¿Qué ocurrió?
- ✓ ¿Dónde ocurrió?
- ✓ ¿Cuándo ocurrió?
- ✓ ¿Cómo ocurrió?
- ✓ ¿Quién te ayudó y cómo?
- ✓ ¿Tuviste algún problema después del accidente o después de la enfermedad?
- ✓ ¿Cuánto tiempo tuviste el problema?

9 **Crucigrama** Tu profesor(a) les va a dar a ti y a un(a) compañero/a un crucigrama (*crossword*) incompleto. Tú tienes las palabras que necesita tu compañero/a y él/ella tiene las palabras que tú necesitas. Tienen que darse pistas para completarlo. No pueden decir la palabra necesaria; deben utilizar definiciones, ejemplos y frases. Answers will vary.

modelo

10 horizontal: La usamos para hablar.
14 vertical: Es el médico que examina los dientes.

Successful Language Learning Tell students to imagine situations in which they commonly see a doctor and to think about what they would say in Spanish in each of these situations.

7 Expansion
- Ask students to list the various possibilities of what happened to these people and how they feel. Have them name possible treatments for each.
- Bring in magazine pictures related to illness, medicine, and medical appointments. Have students describe what is going on in the images.

8 Teaching Tip Model this activity by talking about an illness or accident you had.

8 Expansion
To practice more verb forms, have students discuss with a partner illnesses or accidents that someone they know had.

9 Teaching Tip Divide the class into pairs and distribute the handouts from the Activity Pack (Activity Pack/Supersite) that correspond to this Information Gap Activity. Give students ten minutes to complete this activity.

9 Expansion
Have pairs use words from the crossword to role-play a visit to a doctor's office.

TEACHING OPTIONS

Pairs For homework, ask students to draw an alien or other fantastic being. In the next class period, have students describe the alien to a classmate, who will draw it according to the description. Ex: **Tiene una cabeza grande y tres piernas delgadas con pelo en las rodillas. Encima de la cabeza tiene ocho ojos pequeños y uno grande...** Then have students compare the drawings for accuracy.

Extra Practice Write **Mido ____ pies y ____ pulgadas** on the board and explain what it means. Then have students write physical descriptions of themselves using as much vocabulary from this lesson as they can. Collect the papers, shuffle them, and read the descriptions aloud. The rest of the class has to guess who is being described.

Section Goals

In **Fotonovela**, students will:

- receive comprehensible input from free-flowing discourse
- learn functional phrases that preview lesson grammatical structures

Instructional Resources
Supersite: Video (***Fotonovela***); Resources (Scripts, Translations, Answer Keys)
WebSAM
Video Manual, pp. 19–20

Video Recap: Lección 9
Before doing this **Fotonovela** section, review the previous episode with these questions:
1. ¿Qué les enseñó a hacer la tía Ana María a Jimena y a Marissa? (Les enseñó a hacer mole.) 2. ¿Quiénes prepararon una sorpresa para llevar al cementerio? (El Sr. Díaz y Felipe la prepararon.) 3. ¿Qué postres hizo Jimena? (Ella hizo galletas y pastel.) 4. ¿Por quiénes brindaron Ana María, Roberto y Ramón? (Ellos brindaron por sus padres.)

Video Synopsis While out with her friend **Elena, Jimena's** cold symptoms start bothering her. Despite taking **don Diego's** and **Elena's** home remedies, the cold symptoms persist. At her mother's insistence, **Jimena** goes to the doctor, who prescribes some medicine.

Teaching Tips

- Have students scan the **Fotonovela** for words and expressions related to illness, injury, and health care. Then have them predict what will happen in this episode.
- Review the predictions and ask a few questions to guide students in summarizing this episode.

¡Qué dolor!

Jimena no se siente bien y tiene que ir al doctor.

NATIONAL STANDARDS communication cultures

PERSONAJES

ELENA

JIMENA

Video: *Fotonovela*

ELENA ¿Cómo te sientes?
JIMENA Me duele un poco la garganta. Pero no tengo fiebre.
ELENA Creo que tienes un resfriado. Te voy a llevar a casa.

ELENA ¿Don Diego ya fue a la farmacia? ¿Cuánto tiempo hace que lo llamaste?
JIMENA Hace media hora. Ay, qué cosas, de niña apenas me enfermaba. No perdí ni un solo día de clases.
ELENA Yo tampoco.

ELENA Nunca tenía resfriados, pero me rompí el brazo dos veces. Mi hermana y yo estábamos paseando en bicicleta y casi me di con un señor que caminaba por la calle. Me caí y me rompí el brazo.

JIMENA ¿Qué es esto?
ELENA Es té de jengibre. Cuando me dolía el estómago, mi mamá siempre me hacía tomarlo. Se dice que es bueno para el dolor de estómago.
JIMENA Pero no me duele el estómago.

JIMENA Hola, don Diego. Gracias por venir.
DON DIEGO Fui a la farmacia. Aquí están las pastillas para el resfriado. Se debe tomar una cada seis horas con las comidas. Y no se deben tomar más de seis pastillas al día.

(La Sra. Díaz llama a Jimena.)
JIMENA Hola, mamá. Don Diego me trajo los medicamentos... ¿Al doctor? ¿Estás segura? Allá nos vemos. (*A Elena*) Mi mamá ya hizo una cita para mí con el Dr. Meléndez.

TEACHING OPTIONS

Video Tips General suggestions for using video clips in the classroom can be found in the front matter of this Instructor's Annotated Edition.

¡Qué dolor! Play the **¡Qué dolor!** episode and have students jot down key words that they hear. Then have them work in small groups to prepare a brief plot summary based on their lists of key words. Play the segment again and have students return to their groups to refine their summaries. Finally, discuss the plot of this episode with the entire class and correct any errors of fact or sequencing.

Extra Practice Photocopy the **Fotonovela** Videoscript (Supersite) and white out words related to injuries and illnesses in order to make a master for a cloze activity. Have students fill in the missing words as they watch the episode.

DON DIEGO

SRA. DÍAZ

DR. MELÉNDEZ

7

SRA. DÍAZ ¿Te pusiste un suéter anoche?

JIMENA No, mamá. Se me olvidó.

SRA. DÍAZ Doctor, esta jovencita salió anoche, se le olvidó ponerse un suéter y parece que le dio un resfriado.

8

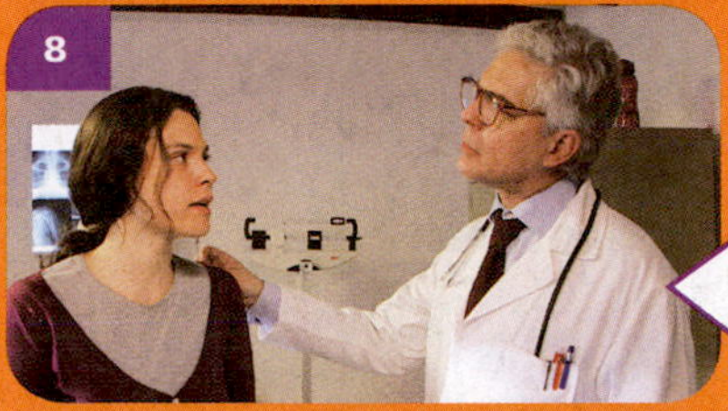

DR. MELÉNDEZ Jimena, ¿cuáles son tus síntomas?

JIMENA Toso con frecuencia y me duele la garganta.

DR. MELÉNDEZ ¿Cuánto tiempo hace que tienes estos síntomas?

JIMENA Hace dos días que me duele la garganta.

9

DR. MELÉNDEZ Muy bien. Aquí no tienes infección. No tienes fiebre. Te voy a mandar algo para la garganta. Puedes ir por los medicamentos inmediatamente a la farmacia.

10

SRA. DÍAZ Doctor, ¿cómo está? ¿Es grave?

DR. MELÉNDEZ No, no es nada grave. Jimena, la próxima vez, escucha a tu mamá. ¡Tienes que usar suéter!

Expresiones útiles

Discussing medical conditions

¿Cómo te sientes?
How do you feel?
Me duele un poco la garganta.
My throat hurts a little.
No me duele el estómago.
My stomach doesn't hurt.
De niño/a apenas me enfermaba.
As a child, I rarely got sick.
¡Soy alérgico/a a chile!
I'm allergic to chili powder!

Discussing remedies

Se dice que el té de jengibre es bueno para el dolor de estómago.
They say ginger tea is good for stomachaches.
Aquí están las pastillas para el resfriado.
Here are the pills for your cold.
Se debe tomar una cada seis horas.
You should take one every six hours.

Expressions with hacer

Hace + [*period of time*] **que** + [*present /preterite*]
¿Cuánto tiempo hace que tienes estos síntomas?
How long have you had these symptoms?
Hace dos días que me duele la garganta.
My throat has been hurting for two days.
¿Cuánto tiempo hace que lo llamaste?
How long has it been since you called him?
Hace media hora.
It's been a half hour (since I called).

Additional vocabulary

canela *cinnamon*
miel *honey*
terco *stubborn*

recursos

VM pp. 19–20	vhlcentral.com Lección 10

Expresiones útiles Point out the phrase **apenas me enfermaba**. Explain that **apenas** is an adverb, and that **me enfermaba** is an imperfect tense form, used here to talk about habitual events in the past. Then draw attention to **Se dice que** and **Se debe tomar** and explain that these are examples of impersonal constructions with **se**. Finally, point out **Se me olvidó** and **se le olvidó** under video still 7 and tell students that **se** is also used to describe unplanned or accidental events. Tell students that they will learn more about these concepts in **Estructura**.

Teaching Tip Ask students to read the **Fotonovela** captions in groups of five. Ask one or two groups to role-play the dialogue for the class.

Nota cultural In Celsius, normal body temperature is 37 degrees. If a temperature reading is above 37 but below 38, it is considered **febrícula**, or low-grade fever. Any temperature from 38 to 40 degrees Celsius is considered a fever (**fiebre**).

TEACHING OPTIONS

Pairs On the board, write the paradigms for **hace** + [*time period*] + **que** + [*present*] and **hace** + [*time period*] + **que** + [*preterite*]. Ask a few comprehension questions to contrast their uses. Ex: **¿Cuánto tiempo hace que te graduaste de la escuela secundaria? ¿Cuánto tiempo hace que eres estudiante universitario?** Then write two lists on the board, one with activities (Ex: **ir al dentista, leer un buen libro, ver una película extranjera, hacerse un examen médico, comer comida orgánica**) and one with time expressions (Ex: **un año, un mes, una semana, dos días, una hora**). Then have pairs interview each other to find out how long it has been since they have done these activities. Ex: —**¿Cuánto tiempo hace que fuiste al dentista?** —**Hace dos años que fui al dentista./Fui al dentista hace dos años.** Have students report to the class about their partners' activities.

¿Qué pasó?

1 ¿Cierto o falso? Decide si lo que dicen estas oraciones sobre Jimena es **cierto** o **falso**. Corrige las oraciones falsas.

	Cierto	Falso	
1. Dice que de niña apenas se enfermaba.	✓	○	
2. Tiene dolor de garganta y fiebre.	○	✓	Tiene dolor de garganta, pero no tiene fiebre.
3. Olvidó ponerse un suéter anoche.	✓	○	
4. Hace tres días que le duele la garganta.	○	✓	Hace dos días que le duele la garganta.
5. El doctor le dice que tiene una infección.	○	✓	El doctor le dice que no tiene una infección.

2 Identificar Identifica quién puede decir estas oraciones.

1. Como dice tu mamá, tienes que usar suéter. Dr. Meléndez
2. Por pasear en bicicleta me rompí el brazo dos veces. Elena
3. ¿Cuánto tiempo hace que toses y te duele la garganta? Dr. Meléndez
4. Tengo cita con el Dr. Meléndez. Jimena
5. Dicen que el té de jengibre es muy bueno para los dolores de estómago. Elena
6. Nunca perdí un día de clases porque apenas me enfermaba. Jimena

DR. MELÉNDEZ

ELENA

JIMENA

3 Ordenar Pon estos sucesos en el orden correcto.

a. Jimena va a ver al doctor. 4
b. El doctor le dice a la Sra. Díaz que no es nada serio. 6
c. Elena le habla a Jimena de cuando se rompió el brazo. 2
d. El doctor le receta medicamentos. 5
e. Jimena le dice a Elena que le duele la garganta. 1
f. Don Diego le trae a Jimena las pastillas para el resfriado. 3

4 En el consultorio Trabajen en parejas para representar los papeles de un(a) médico/a y su paciente. Usen las instrucciones como guía.

El/La médico/a	El/La paciente
Pregúntale al / a la paciente qué le pasó.	→ Dile que te caíste en casa. Describe tu dolor.
Pregúntale cuánto tiempo hace que se cayó.	→ Describe la situación. Piensas que te rompiste el dedo.
Mira el dedo. Debes recomendar un tratamiento (*treatment*) al / a la paciente.	→ Debes hacer preguntas al / a la médico/a sobre el tratamiento (*treatment*).

Practice more at **vhlcentral.com**.

AYUDA

Here are some useful expressions:
¿Cómo se lastimó...?
¿Qué le pasó?
¿Cuánto tiempo hace que...?
Tengo...
Estoy...
¿Es usted alérgico/a a algún medicamento?
Usted debe...

1 Expansion Give students these sentences as items 6–7: **6. Toma té de jengibre porque le duele el estómago. (Falso. No le duele el estómago.) 7. Tose con frecuencia. (Cierto.)**

2 Expansion Give students these sentences as items 7–8: **7. Si quieres, ya puedes ir a la farmacia. (Dr. Meléndez) 8. De pequeña nunca tenía resfriados. (Elena/Jimena)**

Nota cultural In the Dominican Republic, drinking **té de jengibre** is a Christmas tradition. It is made with fresh ginger root, cinnamon sticks, and sugar, and served hot.

3 Teaching Tip Write each sentence from this activity on separate strips of paper and shuffle them. Divide the class into groups of three and distribute a set of sentences to each group; each student should receive two sentences. Have groups put the sentences in correct order and then return them to a group representative, who will read them aloud.

4 Possible Conversation
E1: Buenos días. ¿Cómo se lastimó?
E2: Doctor, me caí en casa. Me duele mucho la mano.
E1: ¿Y cuánto tiempo hace que se cayó?
E2: Hace más de dos horas. Creo que me rompí el dedo.
E1: ¿Ah, sí? ¿Le duele mucho?
E2: Me duele muchísimo, doctor. Y estoy mareada.
E1: Bueno, le voy a sacar una radiografía primero.
E2: ¿Está roto el dedo?
E1: No se preocupe. No está roto. Como le duele mucho, le voy a recetar unas pastillas.
E2: Sí, doctor. Gracias.

TEACHING OPTIONS

Heritage Speakers Ask heritage speakers to prepare a poster about the health care system of their families' countries of origin or other Spanish-speaking countries they have visited. Have them present their posters to the class, and invite students to ask questions about the information.

Extra Practice Ask students questions about the **Fotonovela**. Ex: **1. ¿Quién fue a la farmacia para conseguirle unas pastillas a Jimena? (Don Diego fue a la farmacia.) 2. ¿Quién se rompió el mismo brazo dos veces? (Elena se lo rompió dos veces.) 3. ¿Por qué la mamá de Elena le daba té de jengibre? (Porque le dolía el estómago.) 4. ¿Cuáles son los síntomas de Jimena? (Tose mucho y le duele la garganta.)**

Ortografía

Audio

El acento y las sílabas fuertes

In Spanish, written accent marks are used on many words. Here is a review of some of the principles governing word stress and the use of written accents.

as-pi-ri-na **gri-pe** **to-man** **an-tes**

In Spanish, when a word ends in a vowel, **-n**, or **-s**, the spoken stress usually falls on the next-to-last syllable. Words of this type are very common and do not need a written accent.

a-sí **in-glés** **in-fec-ción** **hé-ro-e**

When a word ends in a vowel, **-n**, or **-s**, and the spoken stress does *not* fall on the next-to-last syllable, then a written accent is needed.

hos-pi-tal **na-riz** **re-ce-tar** **to-ser**

When a word ends in any consonant *other* than **-n** or **-s**, the spoken stress usually falls on the last syllable. Words of this type are very common and do not need a written accent.

lá-piz **fút-bol** **hués-ped** **sué-ter**

When a word ends in any consonant *other* than **-n** or **-s** and the spoken stress does *not* fall on the last syllable, then a written accent is needed.

far-ma-cia **bio-lo-gí-a** **su-cio** **frí-o**

Diphthongs (two weak vowels or a strong and weak vowel together) are normally pronounced as a single syllable. A written accent is needed when a diphthong is broken into two syllables.

sol **pan** **mar** **tos**

Spanish words of only one syllable do not usually carry a written accent (unless it is to distinguish meaning: **se** and **sé**).

CONSULTA

In Spanish, **a**, **e**, and **o** are considered strong vowels while **i** and **u** are weak vowels. To review this concept, see **Lección 3, Pronunciación**, p. 77.

Práctica Busca las palabras que necesitan acento escrito y escribe su forma correcta.

1. sal-mon salmón
2. ins-pec-tor
3. nu-me-ro número
4. fa-cil fácil
5. ju-go
6. a-bri-go
7. ra-pi-do rápido
8. sa-ba-do sábado
9. vez
10. me-nu menú
11. o-pe-ra-cion operación
12. im-per-me-a-ble
13. a-de-mas además
14. re-ga-te-ar
15. an-ti-pa-ti-co antipático
16. far-ma-cia
17. es-qui esquí
18. pen-sion pensión
19. pa-is país
20. per-don perdón

El ahorcado Juega al ahorcado (*hangman*) para adivinar las palabras.

1. __ l __ __ __ __ a — Vas allí cuando estás enfermo. clínica
2. __ __ __ e __ c __ __ n — Se usa para poner una vacuna (*vaccination*). inyección
3. __ __ d __ o __ __ __ __ __ __ a — Permite ver los huesos. radiografía
4. __ __ __ i __ o — Trabaja en un hospital. médico
5. a __ __ __ b __ __ __ __ __ __ __ — Es una medicina. antibiótico

recursos

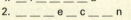

LM p. 56	vhlcentral.com Lección 10

Section Goals

In **Ortografía**, students will review:

- word stress
- the use of written accent marks

Instructional Resources

Supersite: Audio (Lab MP3 Files); Resources (Scripts, Answer Keys)
WebSAM
Lab Manual, p. 56

Teaching Tips

- You may want to explain that all words in which the spoken stress falls on the antepenultimate or preantepenultimate syllable will carry a written accent, regardless of the word's final letter.
- As you go through each point in the explanation, write the example words on the board, pronounce them, and have students repeat. Then, ask students to provide words they learned in previous lessons that exemplify each point.
- Make a list of unfamiliar words on the board, leaving out any written accent marks. Pronounce them, and ask students if a written accent mark is needed, and if so, where it should be placed. Include words that carry a written accent mark as well as some that do not.
- Point out that **Ortografía** replaces **Pronunciación** in the Student Edition for **Lecciones 10–18**, but not in the Lab Manual. The **Recursos** box references the **Pronunciación** sections found in all lessons of the Lab Manual.

TEACHING OPTIONS

Extra Practice Add an auditory aspect to this **Ortografía** section. Have students close their books. Then read aloud the questions in **Actividad 6, Cuestionario,** page 310. Say each sentence twice slowly and once at normal speed to give students enough time to write. Then have them open their books and check their work.

Pairs Ask students to work in pairs and explain why each word in the **Práctica** activity does or does not have a written accent mark. The same process can be followed with the words in the **El ahorcado** activity.

Section Goals

In **Cultura**, students will:

- read about health services in Spanish-speaking countries
- learn health-related terms
- read about **curanderos** and **chamanes**
- read about home remedies and medicinal plants

Instructional Resources

Supersite: Video (***Flash cultura***); Resources (Scripts, Translations, Answer Keys)
WebSAM
Video Manual, pp. 91–92

En detalle

Antes de leer Ask students about their experiences with health care while traveling. Ex: **¿Alguna vez te enfermaste durante un viaje? ¿Dónde? ¿Fuiste al hospital o al médico? ¿Quién lo pagó?**

Lectura

- Point out that many over-the-counter health care products in the U.S. are available by request at pharmacies in Spanish-speaking countries (e.g., facial cleansers, sunscreen, contact lens solution).
- Tell students that most pharmacies are closed on Sundays.
- While traditional pharmacies are privately owned and consist of a small counter and retail space, large chain pharmacies are entering the market, especially in Latin America.

Después de leer

- Ask students which three factors described in the article would be most important in devising an ideal health care system.

1 Expansion Give students these true/false statements as items 9–10: **9. El sistema de salud en Cuba no es muy desarrollado. (Falso. Es muy desarrollado.) 10. Las farmacias generalmente tienen un horario comercial. (Cierto.)**

Flash CULTURA

EN DETALLE

Video: *Flash cultura*

NATIONAL STANDARDS connections cultures

Servicios de salud

¿Sabías que en los países hispanos no necesitas pagar por los servicios de salud? Ésta es una de las diferencias que hay entre países como los Estados Unidos y los países hispanos.

En la mayor parte de estos países, el gobierno ofrece servicios médicos muy baratos o gratuitos° a sus ciudadanos°. Los turistas y extranjeros también pueden tener acceso a los servicios médicos a bajo° costo. La Seguridad Social y organizaciones similares son las responsables de gestionar° estos servicios.

Naturalmente, esto no funciona igual° en todos los países. En Ecuador, México y Perú, la situación varía según las regiones. Los habitantes de las ciudades y pueblos grandes tienen acceso a más servicios médicos, mientras que quienes viven en pueblos remotos sólo cuentan con° pequeñas clínicas.

Por su parte, Costa Rica, Colombia, Cuba y España tienen sistemas de salud muy desarrollados°.

Cruz verde de farmacia en Madrid, España

En España, por ejemplo, la mayoría de la gente tiene acceso a ellos y en muchos casos son completamente gratuitos. Según un informe de la Organización Mundial de la Salud, el sistema de salud español ocupa uno de los primeros diez lugares del mundo. Esto se debe no sólo al buen funcionamiento° del sistema, sino también al nivel de salud general de la población. Impresionante, ¿no?

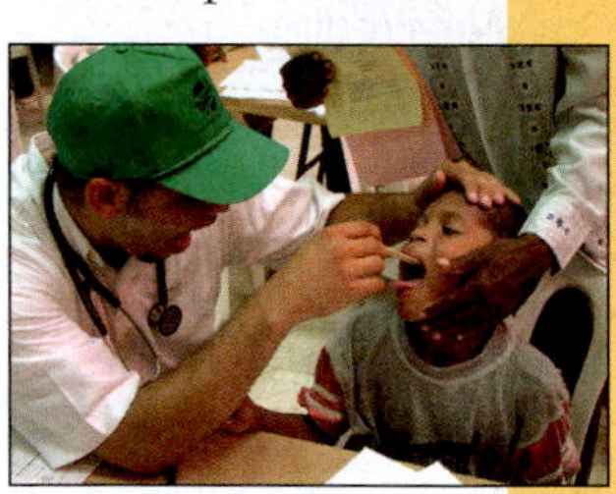

Consulta médica en la República Dominicana

Las farmacias

Farmacia de guardia: Las farmacias generalmente tienen un horario comercial. Sin embargo°, en cada barrio° hay una farmacia de guardia que abre las veinticuatro horas del día.

Productos farmacéuticos: Todavía hay muchas farmacias tradicionales que están más especializadas en medicinas y productos farmacéuticos. No venden una gran variedad de productos.

Recetas: Muchos medicamentos se venden sin receta médica. Los farmacéuticos aconsejan° a las personas sobre problemas de salud y les dan las medicinas.

Cruz° verde: En muchos países, las farmacias tienen como símbolo una cruz verde. Cuando la cruz verde está encendida°, la farmacia está abierta.

gratuitos *free (of charge)* **ciudadanos** *citizens* **bajo** *low* **gestionar** *to manage* **igual** *in the same way* **cuentan con** *have* **desarrollados** *developed* **funcionamiento** *operation* **Sin embargo** *However* **barrio** *neighborhood* **aconsejan** *advise* **Cruz** *Cross* **encendida** *lit (up)*

ACTIVIDADES

1 **¿Cierto o falso?** Indica si lo que dicen las oraciones es cierto o falso. Corrige la información falsa.

1. En los países hispanos los gobiernos ofrecen servicios de salud accesibles a sus ciudadanos. Cierto.
2. En los países hispanos los extranjeros tienen que pagar mucho dinero por los servicios médicos. Falso. Los extranjeros tienen acceso a los servicios médicos a bajo costo.
3. El sistema de salud español es uno de los mejores del mundo. Cierto.
4. Las farmacias de guardia abren sólo los sábados y domingos. Falso. Las farmacias de guardia abren las 24 horas del día.
5. En los países hispanos las farmacias venden una gran variedad de productos. Falso. En los países hispanos las farmacias están más especializadas en medicinas y productos farmacéuticos.
6. Los farmacéuticos de los países hispanos aconsejan a los enfermos y venden algunas medicinas sin necesidad de receta. Cierto.
7. En México y otros países, los pueblos remotos cuentan con grandes centros médicos. Falso. Cuentan con pequeñas clínicas.
8. Muchas farmacias usan una cruz verde como símbolo. Cierto.

TEACHING OPTIONS

Cultural Comparison Ask students to write a short paragraph in which they compare the health care systems in the U.S. or Canada with those of different Spanish-speaking countries. You may want to have students review comparisons (**Estructura 8.3**) before writing.

Pairs Ask pairs to write a dialogue in which a foreign tourist in Costa Rica goes to the emergency room due to an injury. Have them use vocabulary from **Contextos** and **Expresiones útiles**. Have students role-play their dialogues for the class.

ASÍ SE DICE

La salud

el chequeo (Esp., Méx.)	el examen médico
la droguería (Col.)	la farmacia
la herida	*injury; wound*
la píldora	la pastilla
los primeros auxilios	*first aid*
la sangre	*blood*

EL MUNDO HISPANO

Remedios caseros° y plantas medicinales

- **Achiote°** En Suramérica se usa para curar inflamaciones de garganta. Las hojas° de achiote se cuecen° en agua, se cuelan° y se hacen gárgaras° con esa agua.
- **Ají** En Perú se usan cataplasmas° de las semillas° de ají para aliviar los dolores reumáticos y la tortícolis°.
- **Azúcar** En Nicaragua y otros países centroamericanos se usa el azúcar para detener° la sangre en pequeñas heridas.
- **Sábila (aloe vera)** En Latinoamérica, el jugo de las hojas de sábila se usa para reducir cicatrices°. Se recomienda aplicarlo sobre la cicatriz dos veces al día, durante varios meses.

Remedios caseros *Home remedies* **Achiote** *Annatto* **hojas** *leaves* **se cuecen** *are cooked* **se cuelan** *they are drained* **gárgaras** *gargles* **cataplasmas** *pastes* **semillas** *seeds* **tortícolis** *stiff neck* **detener** *to stop* **cicatrices** *scars*

PERFILES

Curanderos° y chamanes

¿Quieres ser doctor(a), juez(a)°, político/a o psicólogo/a? En algunas sociedades de las Américas **los curanderos** y **los chamanes** no tienen que escoger entre estas profesiones porque ellos son mediadores de conflictos y dan consejos a la comunidad. Su opinión es muy respetada.

Códice Florentino, México, siglo XVI

Desde las culturas antiguas° de las Américas muchas personas piensan que la salud del cuerpo y de la mente sólo puede existir si hay un equilibrio entre el ser humano y la naturaleza. Los curanderos y los chamanes son quienes cuidan este equilibrio.

Los curanderos se especializan más en enfermedades físicas, mientras que los chamanes están más relacionados con los males° de la mente y el alma°. Ambos° usan plantas, masajes y rituales y sus conocimientos se basan en la tradición, la experiencia, la observación y la intuición.

Cuzco, Perú

Curanderos *Healers* **juez(a)** *judge* **antiguas** *ancient* **males** *illnesses* **alma** *soul* **Ambos** *Both*

Conexión Internet

¿Cuáles son algunos hospitales importantes del mundo hispano?

Go to **vhlcentral.com** to find more cultural information related to this **Cultura** section.

ACTIVIDADES

2 Comprensión Contesta las preguntas.

1. ¿Cómo se les llama a las farmacias en Colombia? droguerías
2. ¿Qué parte del achiote se usa para curar la garganta? las hojas
3. ¿Cómo se aplica la sábila para reducir cicatrices? Se aplica sobre la cicatriz dos veces al día.
4. En algunas partes de las Américas, ¿quiénes mantienen el equilibrio entre el ser humano y la naturaleza? los chamanes y curanderos
5. ¿Qué usan los curanderos y chamanes para curar? Usan plantas, masajes y rituales.

3 ¿Qué haces cuando tienes gripe? Escribe cuatro oraciones sobre las cosas que haces cuando tienes gripe. Explica si vas al médico, si tomas medicamentos o si sigues alguna dieta especial. Después, comparte tu texto con un(a) compañero/a. Answers will vary.

Practice more at **vhlcentral.com**.

recursos: VM pp. 91–92 | vhlcentral.com Lección 10

TEACHING OPTIONS

TPR Divide the class into two teams, **remedios naturales** and **medicina moderna**, and have them stand at opposite sides of the room. Read a medical scenario aloud. The team whose name defines the situation most accurately has five seconds to step forward. Ex: **1. Juan sufre de dolores de cabeza. Hoy tiene una migraña. Decide comprar vitamina B2. (remedios naturales) 2. María tiene mucha ansiedad. Además siente estrés por su trabajo. Toma pastillas calmantes. (medicina moderna)**

Small Groups Have small groups create a television commercial for a new natural product. Encourage them to include a customer testimonial stating how long they have had these symptoms (**hace** + [*time period*] + **que** + [*present*]), when they started using the product (**hace** + [*time period*] + **que** + [*preterite*]), and how they feel now.

Así se dice

- You may want to point out that in Spain a **droguería** is not a pharmacy, but rather a shop selling cleaning and decorating materials, as well as cosmetics.
- To challenge students, add these health-related words to the list: **la espalda** (*back*); **la fractura** (*fracture*); **el hombro** (*shoulder*); **el jarabe** (*cough syrup*); **la lengua** (*tongue*); **la muñeca** (*wrist*); **sangrar** (*to bleed*); **tener escalofríos** (*to have chills*); **el vendaje** (*bandage*).
- Practice new vocabulary by asking questions. Ex: **¿Vas todos los años a hacerte un chequeo?**

Perfiles **Curanderos** sometimes experience discrimination in the medical field. However, recently, some medical doctors have grown to understand the beliefs of **los curanderos** and are working with them to help support their ceremonies and natural care while providing additional modern medical attention.

El mundo hispano

- Ask students: **¿Conocen otros remedios caseros o naturales?**
- Ask heritage speakers to describe home remedies used in their families.

2 Expansion Give students these questions as items 6–8: **6. ¿Para qué se usa el azúcar en Centroamérica? (para detener la sangre) 7. ¿Quiénes curan los males de la mente y el alma? (los chamanes) 8. ¿En qué se basan los conocimientos de los curanderos y chamanes? (en la tradición, la experiencia, la observación y la intuición)**

3 Teaching Tip As a variant, have students create a list of recommendations for a friend who has the flu. Ex: **Debes tomar sopa de pollo con verduras.**

Section Goal

In **Estructura 10.1**, students will learn the imperfect tense.

Instructional Resources
Supersite: Audio (Lab MP3 Files); Resources (Grammar Presentation Slides, Activity Pack, Scripts, Answer Keys); Testing Program (Quizzes)
WebSAM
Workbook, pp. 111–112
Lab Manual, p. 57

Teaching Tips

- Explain to students that they can already express the past with the preterite tense, and now they are learning the imperfect tense, which also expresses the past but in a different way.
- As you work through the discussion of the imperfect, test comprehension by asking volunteers to supply the correct form of verbs for the subjects you name. Ex: **romper/nosotros (rompíamos)**
- Point out that **había** is impersonal and can be followed by a singular or plural noun. Ex: **Había una enfermera. Había muchos pacientes.**

¡Atención! To demonstrate that the accents on –**er** and –**ir** verbs break diphthongs, write **farmacia** and **vendia** on the board. Ask volunteers to pronounce each word, and have the class identify which needs a written accent to break the diphthong (**vendía**).

10.1 The imperfect tense

S Tutorial

ANTE TODO In **Lecciones 6–9,** you learned the preterite tense. You will now learn the imperfect, which describes past activities in a different way.

The imperfect of regular verbs

		cantar	beber	escribir
SINGULAR FORMS	yo	cant**aba**	beb**ía**	escrib**ía**
	tú	cant**abas**	beb**ías**	escrib**ías**
	Ud./él/ella	cant**aba**	beb**ía**	escrib**ía**
PLURAL FORMS	nosotros/as	cant**ábamos**	beb**íamos**	escrib**íamos**
	vosotros/as	cant**abais**	beb**íais**	escrib**íais**
	Uds./ellos/ellas	cant**aban**	beb**ían**	escrib**ían**

De niña apenas me enfermaba.

Cuando me dolía el estómago, mi mamá me daba té de jengibre.

- There are no stem changes in the imperfect.

entender (e:ie)	**Entendíamos** japonés. *We used to understand Japanese.*
servir (e:i)	El camarero les **servía** el café. *The waiter was serving them coffee.*
doler (o:ue)	A Javier le **dolía** el tobillo. *Javier's ankle was hurting.*

- The imperfect form of **hay** is **había** *(there was; there were; there used to be).*
- **¡Atención!** **Ir, ser,** and **ver** are the only verbs that are irregular in the imperfect.

The imperfect of irregular verbs

		ir	ser	ver
SINGULAR FORMS	yo	**iba**	**era**	**veía**
	tú	**ibas**	**eras**	**veías**
	Ud./él/ella	**iba**	**era**	**veía**
PLURAL FORMS	nosotros/as	**íbamos**	**éramos**	**veíamos**
	vosotros/as	**ibais**	**erais**	**veíais**
	Uds./ellos/ellas	**iban**	**eran**	**veían**

NATIONAL STANDARDS comparisons

¡ATENCIÓN!

Note that the imperfect endings of **-er** and **-ir** verbs are the same. Also note that the **nosotros** form of **-ar** verbs always carries an accent mark on the first **a** of the ending. All forms of **-er** and **-ir** verbs in the imperfect carry an accent on the first **i** of the ending.

AYUDA

Like **hay, había** can be followed by a singular or plural noun.
Había un solo médico en la sala.
Había dos pacientes allí.

TEACHING OPTIONS

Extra Practice To provide oral practice with the imperfect tense, change the subjects in **¡Inténtalo!** on page 319. Have students give the appropriate forms for each infinitive listed.

Large Groups Write a list of activities on the board. Ex: **1. tenerle miedo a la oscuridad 2. ir a la escuela en autobús 3. llevar el almuerzo a la escuela 4. comer brócoli 5. ser atrevido/a en clase 6. creer en Santa Claus** Have students copy the list on a sheet of paper and check off the items that they used to do when they were in the second grade. Then have them circulate around the room and find other students that used to do the same activities. Ex: **¿Le tenías miedo a la oscuridad?** When they find a student who used to do the same activity, have them write that student's name next to the item. Then have students report back to the class. Ex: **Mark y yo creíamos en Santa Claus.**

CONSULTA

You will learn more about the contrast between the preterite and the imperfect in **Estructura 10.2**, pp. 322–323.

Uses of the imperfect

- As a general rule, the imperfect is used to describe actions that are seen by the speaker as incomplete or "continuing," while the preterite is used to describe actions that have been completed. The imperfect expresses what was happening at a certain time or how things used to be. The preterite, in contrast, expresses a completed action.

—¿Qué te **pasó**? *What happened to you?*	—Me **torcí** el tobillo. *I sprained my ankle.*
—¿Dónde **vivías** de niño? *Where did you live as a child?*	—**Vivía** en San José. *I lived in San José.*

- These expressions are often used with the imperfect because they express habitual or repeated actions: **de niño/a** (*as a child*), **todos los días** (*every day*), **mientras** (*while*).

Uses of the imperfect

1. Habitual or repeated actions	**Íbamos** al parque los domingos. *We used to go to the park on Sundays.*
2. Events or actions that were in progress	Yo **leía** mientras él **estudiaba**. *I was reading while he was studying.*
3. Physical characteristics	**Era** alto y guapo. *He was tall and handsome.*
4. Mental or emotional states	**Quería** mucho a su familia. *He loved his family very much.*
5. Telling time	**Eran** las tres y media. *It was 3:30.*
6. Age	Los niños **tenían** seis años. *The children were six years old.*

¡INTÉNTALO! Indica la forma correcta de cada verbo en el imperfecto.

1. Mis hermanos ___veían___ (ver) televisión todas las tardes.
2. Yo ___viajaba___ (viajar) en el tren de las 3:30.
3. ¿Dónde ___vivía___ (vivir) Samuel de niño?
4. Tú ___hablabas___ (hablar) con Javier.
5. Leonardo y yo ___corríamos___ (correr) por el parque.
6. Ustedes ___iban___ (ir) a la clínica.
7. Nadia ___bailaba___ (bailar) merengue.
8. ¿Cuándo ___asistías___ (asistir) tú a clase de español?
9. Yo ___era___ (ser) muy feliz.
10. Nosotras ___comprendíamos___ (comprender) las preguntas.

recursos

WB pp. 111–112

LM p. 57

vhlcentral.com Lección 10

Teaching Tips

- Ask students to compare and contrast a home video with a snapshot in the family picture album. Then call their attention to the brief description of the uses of the imperfect. Which actions would be best captured by a home video? (Continuing actions; incomplete actions; what was happening; how things used to be.) Which actions are best captured in a snapshot? (A completed action.)
- Ask students to answer questions about themselves in the past. Ex: **Y tú, ____, ¿ibas al parque los domingos cuando eras niño/a? ¿Qué hacías mientras tu madre preparaba la comida? ¿Cómo eras de niño/a?**
- Ask questions about the **Fotonovela** characters using the imperfect. Ex: **De niña, ¿Jimena se enfermaba mucho o poco? (Se enfermaba poco.) ¿Elena tenía muchos resfriados? (No, no tenía muchos resfriados.) ¿Qué tomaban para los dolores de estómago en la casa de Elena? (Tomaban té de jengibre.) ¿Qué remedio para la garganta usaban en la casa de don Diego? (Usaban miel con canela.)**

Successful Language Learning Ask students to think about what they used to do when they were younger and imagine how to say it in Spanish. This is good practice for real-life conversations because people often talk about their childhood when making new friends.

TEACHING OPTIONS

Extra Practice Prepare a list of sentences in the present tense. Ex: **Todos los días jugamos al tenis.** Read each sentence twice, pausing to allow students to convert the present tense to the imperfect. Ex: **Todos los días jugábamos al tenis.**

Extra Practice Ask students to write a description of their first-grade classroom and teacher, using the imperfect. Ex: **En la sala de clases había... La maestra se llamaba... Ella era...** Have students share their descriptions with a classmate.

Large Groups Have the class stand and form a circle. Call out a name or subject pronoun and an infinitive (Ex: **ellas/ver**). Toss a ball to a student, who will say the correct imperfect form (Ex: **veían**). He or she should then name a new subject and infinitive and throw the ball to another student.

1 Teaching Tips

- Before assigning the activity, review the forms of the imperfect by calling out an infinitive and a series of subject pronouns. Ask volunteers to give the corresponding forms. Ex: **querer: usted (quería); yo (quería); nosotras (queríamos).** Include irregular verbs.
- As a model, write these sentences on the board and have volunteers supply the verb forms and then reorder the sentences. **No ____ (dormir) bien. (dormía/1) ____ (Ser) la una de la mañana cuando llamé al doctor. (Era/3) Me desperté a las once porque ____ (sentirse) mal. (me sentía/2)**

1 Expansion Have students write a conversation between **Miguelito** and his friends in which he relates what happened after the accident.

2 Expansion To challenge students, ask them to state the reason the imperfect is used in each sentence.

3 Expansion Write these sentences on the board, and have students work in pairs to complete them. **1. Fui al doctor porque ____. 2. Tuvo que ir al dentista porque ____. 3. El médico le dio unas pastillas porque ____. 4. La enfermera le tomó la temperatura porque ____.**

Práctica

1

Completar Primero, completa las oraciones con el imperfecto de los verbos. Luego, pon las oraciones en orden lógico y compáralas con las de un(a) compañero/a.

a. El doctor dijo que no __era__ (ser) nada grave. __7__
b. El doctor __quería__ (querer) ver la nariz del niño. __6__
c. Su mamá __estaba__ (estar) dibujando cuando Miguelito entró llorando. __3__
d. Miguelito __tenía__ (tener) la nariz hinchada (*swollen*). Fueron al hospital. __4__
e. Miguelito no __iba__ (ir) a jugar más. Ahora quería ir a casa a descansar. __8__
f. Miguelito y sus amigos __jugaban__ (jugar) al béisbol en el patio. __2__
g. __Eran__ (Ser) las dos de la tarde. __1__
h. Miguelito le dijo a la enfermera que __le dolía__ (dolerle) la nariz. __5__

2

Transformar Forma oraciones completas para describir lo que hacían Julieta y César. Usa las formas correctas del imperfecto y añade todas las palabras necesarias.

1. Julieta y César / ser / paramédicos
   Julieta y César eran paramédicos.
2. trabajar / juntos y / llevarse / muy bien
   Trabajaban juntos y se llevaban muy bien.
3. cuando / haber / accidente, / siempre / analizar / situación / con cuidado
   Cuando había un accidente, siempre analizaban la situación con cuidado.
4. preocuparse / mucho / por / pacientes
   Se preocupaban mucho por los pacientes.
5. si / paciente / tener / mucho / dolor, / ponerle / inyección
   Si el paciente tenía mucho dolor, le ponían una inyección.

3

En la escuela de medicina Usa los verbos de la lista para completar las oraciones con las formas correctas del imperfecto. Algunos verbos se usan más de una vez. Some answers may vary. Suggested answers:

caerse	enfermarse	ir	querer	tener
comprender	estornudar	pensar	sentirse	tomar
doler	hacer	poder	ser	toser

1. Cuando Javier y Victoria __eran__ estudiantes de medicina, siempre __tenían__ que ir al médico.
2. Cada vez que él __tomaba__ un examen, a Javier le __dolía__ mucho la cabeza.
3. Cuando Victoria __hacía__ ejercicios aeróbicos, siempre __se sentía__ mareada.
4. Todas las primaveras, Javier __estornudaba/tosía__ mucho porque es alérgico al polen.
5. Victoria también __se caía__ de su bicicleta camino a la escuela.
6. Después de comer en la cafetería, a Victoria siempre le __dolía__ el estómago.
7. Javier __quería/pensaba__ ser médico para ayudar a los demás.
8. Pero no __comprendía__ por qué él __se enfermaba__ con tanta frecuencia.
9. Cuando Victoria __tenía__ fiebre, no __podía__ ni leer el termómetro.
10. A Javier __le dolían__ los dientes, pero nunca __quería__ ir al dentista.
11. Victoria __tosía/estornudaba__ mucho cuando __se sentía__ congestionada.
12. Javier y Victoria __pensaban__ que nunca __iban__ a graduarse.

Practice more at **vhlcentral.com.**

TEACHING OPTIONS

TPR Model gestures for physical or emotional states using the imperfect. Ex: **Me dolía la cabeza.** (Furrow your brow and rub your forehead.) **Tenía fiebre.** (Fan yourself.) Have students stand. Say an expression at random (Ex: **Estornudabas**) and signal a student to perform the appropriate gesture. Keep a brisk pace. Vary by pointing to multiple students. (Ex: **Ustedes se enfermaban.**)

Small Groups In small groups, have students talk about doctors or dentists that they used to visit. Tell each group to select the best and worst experience and write a description of each to share with the class.

Extra Practice If possible, have students bring in video clips from popular movies or *YouTube*. Choose three or four clips and have the students describe the events after viewing each one.

Comunicación

communication NATIONAL STANDARDS

4

Entrevista Trabajen en parejas. Un(a) estudiante usa estas preguntas para entrevistar a su compañero/a. Luego compartan los resultados de la entrevista con la clase. Answers will vary.

1. Cuando eras estudiante de primaria, ¿te gustaban tus profesores/as?
2. ¿Veías mucha televisión cuando eras niño/a?
3. Cuando tenías diez años, ¿cuál era tu programa de televisión favorito?
4. Cuando eras niño/a, ¿qué hacía tu familia durante las vacaciones?
5. ¿Cuántos años tenías en 2010?
6. Cuando estabas en el quinto año escolar, ¿qué hacías con tus amigos/as?
7. Cuando tenías once años, ¿cuál era tu grupo musical favorito?
8. Antes de tomar esta clase, ¿sabías hablar español?

5

Describir En parejas, túrnense para describir cómo eran sus vidas cuando eran niños. Pueden usar las sugerencias de la lista u otras ideas. Luego informen a la clase sobre la vida de su compañero/a. Answers will vary.

modelo

De niña, mi familia y yo siempre íbamos a Tortuguero. Tomábamos un barco desde Limón, y por las noches mirábamos las tortugas (turtles) en la playa. Algunas veces teníamos suerte, porque las tortugas venían a poner (lay) huevos. Otras veces, volvíamos al hotel sin ver ninguna tortuga.

- las vacaciones
- ocasiones especiales
- qué hacías durante el verano
- celebraciones con tus amigos/as
- celebraciones con tu familia
- cómo era tu escuela
- cómo eran tus amigos/as
- los viajes que hacías
- a qué jugabas
- qué hacías cuando te sentías enfermo/a

NOTA CULTURAL

El Parque Nacional Tortuguero está en la costa del Caribe, al norte de la ciudad de Limón, en Costa Rica. Varias especies de tortuga (*turtle*) van a las playas del parque para poner (*lay*) sus huevos. Esto ocurre de noche, y hay guías que llevan pequeños grupos de turistas a observar este fenómeno biológico.

Síntesis

communication NATIONAL STANDARDS

6

En el consultorio Tu profesor(a) te va a dar una lista incompleta con los pacientes que fueron al consultorio del doctor Donoso ayer. En parejas, conversen para completar sus listas y saber a qué hora llegaron las personas al consultorio y cuáles eran sus problemas. Answers will vary.

4 Teaching Tip To simplify, have students record the results of their interviews in a Venn diagram, which they can use to present the information to the class.

5 Teaching Tips
- After students have completed the activity in pairs, divide the class into small groups. Then, after each student reports to the class, have groups decide on a follow-up question to ask.
- You may want to assign this activity as a short written composition.

6 Teaching Tip Divide the class into pairs and distribute the handouts from the Activity Pack (Activity Pack/Supersite) that correspond to this Information Gap Activity. Give students ten minutes to complete this activity.

6 Expansion Have pairs write Dr. Donoso's advice for three of the patients. Then have them read the advice to the class and compare it with what other pairs wrote for the same patients.

TEACHING OPTIONS

Large Groups Label the four corners of the room **La Revolución Americana, Tiempos prehistóricos, El Imperio Romano,** and **El Japón de los samurai.** Have students go to the corner that best represents the historical period they would visit if they could. Each group should then discuss their reasons for choosing that period using the imperfect tense. A spokesperson will report the group's responses to the rest of the class.

Game Divide the class into teams of three. Each team should choose a historical or fictional villain. When it is their turn, they will give the class one hint. The other teams are allowed three questions, which must be answered truthfully. At the end of the question/answer session, teams must guess the person's identity. Award one point for each correct guess and two to any team able to stump the class.

10.2 The preterite and the imperfect

Tutorial

NATIONAL STANDARDS comparisons

ANTE TODO Now that you have learned the forms of the preterite and the imperfect, you will learn more about how they are used. The preterite and the imperfect are not interchangeable. In Spanish, the choice between these two tenses depends on the context and on the point of view of the speaker.

Me rompí el brazo cuando estaba paseando en bicicleta.

Tenía dolor de cabeza, pero me tomé una aspirina y se me fue.

COMPARE & CONTRAST

Use the preterite to...

1. Express actions that are viewed by the speaker as completed

Sandra **se rompió** la pierna.
Sandra broke her leg.

Fueron a Buenos Aires ayer.
They went to Buenos Aires yesterday.

2. Express the beginning or end of a past action

La película **empezó** a las nueve.
The movie began at nine o'clock.

Ayer **terminé** el proyecto para la clase de química.
Yesterday I finished the project for chemistry class.

3. Narrate a series of past actions or events

La doctora me **miró** los oídos, me **hizo** unas preguntas y **escribió** la receta.
The doctor looked in my ears, asked me some questions, and wrote the prescription.

Me di con la mesa, **me caí** y **me lastimé** el pie.
I bumped into the table, I fell, and I injured my foot.

Use the imperfect to...

1. Describe an ongoing past action with no reference to its beginning or end

Sandra **esperaba** al doctor.
Sandra was waiting for the doctor.

El médico **se preocupaba** por sus pacientes.
The doctor worried about his patients.

2. Express habitual past actions and events

Cuando **era** joven, **jugaba** al tenis.
When I was young, I used to play tennis.

De niño, Eduardo **se enfermaba** con mucha frecuencia.
As a child, Eduardo used to get sick very frequently.

3. Describe physical and emotional states or characteristics

La chica **quería** descansar. **Se sentía** mal y **tenía** dolor de cabeza.
The girl wanted to rest. She felt ill and had a headache.

Ellos **eran** altos y **tenían** ojos verdes.
They were tall and had green eyes.

Estábamos felices de ver a la familia.
We were happy to see our family.

AYUDA

These words and expressions, as well as similar ones, commonly occur with the preterite: **ayer, anteayer, una vez, dos veces, tres veces, el año pasado, de repente**.

They usually imply that an action has happened at a specific point in time. For a review, see **Estructura 6.3**, p. 191.

AYUDA

These words and expressions, as well as similar ones, commonly occur with the imperfect: **de niño/a, todos los días, mientras, siempre, con frecuencia, todas las semanas.** They usually express habitual or repeated actions in the past.

Section Goal

In **Estructura 10.2**, students will compare and contrast the uses and meanings of the preterite and imperfect tenses.

Instructional Resources
Supersite: Audio (Lab MP3 Files); Resources (Grammar Presentation Slides, Activity Pack, Scripts, Answer Keys); Testing Program (Quizzes)
WebSAM
Workbook, pp. 113–116
Lab Manual, p. 58

Teaching Tips

- Draw a simple time line on the board. Mark the year you were born and the present year. Invite students to guess how old you were at key points in your life. Ex: **¿Qué creen ustedes? ¿Cuántos años tenía yo cuando aprendí a conducir?** Mark the appropriate spot on the time line and write the corresponding phrase (**Aprendí a conducir.**).
- Give personalized examples as you contrast the preterite and the imperfect. Ex: **La semana pasada tuve que ir al dentista. Me dolía mucho el diente.**
- Involve the class in a conversation about what they did in the past. Ask: ____, **¿paseabas en bicicleta cuando eras niño/a? ¿Te caíste alguna vez?** ____, **¿iba tu familia de vacaciones todos los años cuando eras niño/a? ¿Adónde iban?**
- Add a visual aspect to this grammar presentation. Create or bring in a series of simple drawings. As you hold up each one, have students narrate the events in English and say whether they would use the preterite or imperfect in each case. Ex: 1. The man was sleeping (imperfect). It was midnight (imperfect). The door was open (imperfect). 2. It was 12:05. (imperfect). The man heard a noise (preterite)… Then have volunteers narrate the scenes in Spanish.

TEACHING OPTIONS

Extra Practice Write in English a simple, humorous retelling of a well-known fairy tale. Read it to the class, pausing after each verb in the past to ask the class whether the imperfect or preterite would be used in Spanish. Ex: *Once upon a time there was a girl named Little Red Riding Hood. She wanted to take lunch to her ailing grandmother. She put a loaf of bread, a wedge of cheese, and a bottle of Beaujolais in a basket and set off through the woods. Meanwhile, farther down the path, a big, ugly, snaggle-toothed wolf was leaning against a tree, filing his nails…*

Pairs On separate slips of paper, have students write six personalized statements, one for each of the uses of the preterite and imperfect in **Compare & Contrast**. Have them shuffle the slips and exchange them with a partner, who will identify which preterite or imperfect use each of the sentences illustrates.

▶ The preterite and the imperfect often appear in the same sentence. In such cases, the imperfect describes what *was happening*, while the preterite describes the action that "interrupted" the ongoing activity.

Miraba la tele cuando **sonó** el teléfono.
I was watching TV when the phone rang.

Felicia **leía** el periódico cuando **llegó** Ramiro.
Felicia was reading the newspaper when Ramiro arrived.

▶ You will also see the preterite and the imperfect together in narratives such as fiction, news, and the retelling of events. The imperfect provides background information, such as time, weather, and location, while the preterite indicates the specific events that occurred.

Eran las dos de la mañana y el detective ya no **podía** mantenerse despierto. **Se bajó** lentamente del coche, **estiró** las piernas y **levantó** los brazos hacia el cielo oscuro.
It was two in the morning, and the detective could no longer stay awake. He slowly stepped out of the car, stretched his legs, and raised his arms toward the dark sky.

La luna **estaba** llena y no **había** en el cielo ni una sola nube. De repente, el detective **escuchó** un grito espeluznante proveniente del parque.
The moon was full and there wasn't a single cloud in the sky. Suddenly, the detective heard a piercing scream coming from the park.

Un médico colombiano desarrolló una vacuna contra la malaria

En 1986, el doctor colombiano Manuel Elkin Patarroyo creó la primera vacuna sintética para combatir la malaria. Esta enfermedad parecía haberse erradicado hacía décadas en muchas partes del mundo. Sin embargo, justo cuando Patarroyo terminó de elaborar la inmunización, los casos de malaria empezaban a aumentar de nuevo. En mayo de 1993, el doctor colombiano cedió la patente de la vacuna a la Organización Mundial de la Salud en nombre de Colombia. Los grandes laboratorios farmacéuticos presionaron a la OMS porque querían la vacuna. Las presiones no tuvieron éxito y, en 1995, el doctor Patarroyo y la OMS pactaron continuar con el acuerdo inicial: la vacuna seguía siendo propiedad de la OMS.

¡INTÉNTALO! Elige el pretérito o el imperfecto para completar la historia. Explica por qué se usa ese tiempo verbal en cada ocasión. Answers for the second part will vary.

1. Eran (Fueron/Eran) las doce.
2. Había (Hubo/Había) mucha gente en la calle.
3. A las doce y media, Tomás y yo entramos (entramos/entrábamos) en el restaurante Tárcoles.
4. Todos los días yo almorzaba (almorcé/almorzaba) con Tomás al mediodía.
5. El camarero llegó (llegó/llegaba) inmediatamente con el menú.
6. Nosotros empezamos (empezamos/empezábamos) a leerlo.
7. Yo pedí (pedí/pedía) el pescado.
8. De repente, el camarero volvió (volvió/volvía) a nuestra mesa.
9. Y nos dio (dio/daba) una mala noticia.
10. Desafortunadamente, no tenían (tuvieron/tenían) más pescado.
11. Por eso Tomás y yo decidimos (decidimos/decidíamos) comer en otro lugar.
12. Llovía (Llovió/Llovía) mucho cuando salimos (salimos/salíamos) del restaurante.
13. Así que regresamos (regresamos/regresábamos) al restaurante Tárcoles.
14. Esta vez, pedí (pedí/pedía) arroz con pollo.

recursos
WB pp. 113–116
LM p. 58
vhlcentral.com Lección 10

Teaching Tips

- Give further examples from your own experiences that contrast the imperfect and the preterite. Ex: **Quería ver la nueva película ____, pero anoche sólo pude ir a las diez de la noche. La película fue buena, pero terminó muy tarde. Era la una cuando llegué a casa. Me acosté muy tarde y esta mañana, cuando me levanté, estaba cansadísimo/a.**
- Have students find the example of an interrupted action in the realia.
- Create a slide presentation or text document of a simple narration in Spanish, in such a way that the first screen shows only the sentences with imperfect verbs and the second screen has only the preterite. Show the first group of sentences and read it aloud. Ask students what tense is used (imperfect) and if they know what happened and why not (no, it only sets the scene). Then show the second set of sentences. After reading through the sentences, ask students the tense (preterite), if they know what happened (yes), and if this is an interesting story (no). Then show a final screen that combines the tenses and read through the complete narration. Explain that, now that students have learned both the imperfect and the preterite, they are able to communicate in a more complete, interesting way.
- After completing **¡Inténtalo!**, have students explain why the preterite or imperfect was used in each case. Then call on different students to create new sentences illustrating the same uses.

TEACHING OPTIONS

Pairs Ask students to narrate the most interesting, embarrassing, exciting, or annoying thing that has happened to them recently. Tell them to describe what happened and how they felt, using the preterite and the imperfect.

Video Show the **Fotonovela** again to give students more input about the use of the imperfect. Stop the video at appropriate moments to contrast the use of preterite and imperfect tenses.

Heritage Speakers Have heritage speakers work with other students in pairs to write a simple summary of this lesson's **Fotonovela**. First, as a class, briefly summarize the episode in English and write which verbs would be in the imperfect or preterite. Then have pairs write their paragraphs. They should set the scene, and describe where the characters were, what they were doing, and what happened.

1 Expansion Ask comprehension questions about the article. Ex: **¿Qué pasó ayer? (Hubo un accidente.) ¿Dónde hubo un accidente? (en el centro de San José) ¿Qué tiempo hacía? (Estaba muy nublado y llovía.) ¿Qué le pasó a la mujer que manejaba? (Murió al instante.) ¿Y a su pasajero? (Sufrió varias fracturas.) ¿Qué hizo el conductor del autobús? (Intentó dar un viraje brusco y perdió control del autobús.) ¿Qué les pasó a los pasajeros del autobús? (Nada; no se lastimó ninguno.)**

2 Teaching Tip To simplify, begin by reading through the items as a class. Have students label each blank with an *I* for *imperfect* or *P* for *preterite*.

2 Expansion Have volunteers explain why they chose the preterite or imperfect in each case. Ask them to point out any words or expressions that triggered one tense or the other.

3 Expansion
- After students compare their sentences, ask them to report to the class the most interesting things their partners said.
- To challenge students, ask them to expand on one of their sentences, creating a paragraph about an imaginary or actual past experience.

Práctica

1 **En el periódico** Completa esta noticia con las formas correctas del pretérito o el imperfecto.

Un accidente trágico

Ayer temprano por la mañana (1) hubo (haber) un trágico accidente en el centro de San José cuando el conductor de un autobús no (2) vio (ver) venir un carro. La mujer que (3) manejaba (manejar) el carro (4) murió (morir) al instante y los paramédicos (5) tuvieron (tener) que llevar al pasajero al hospital porque (6) sufrió (sufrir) varias fracturas. El conductor del autobús (7) dijo (decir) que no (8) vio (ver) el carro hasta el último momento porque (9) estaba (estar) muy nublado y (10) llovía (llover). Él (11) intentó (intentar) (*to attempt*) dar un viraje brusco (*to swerve*), pero (12) perdió (perder) el control del autobús y no (13) pudo (poder) evitar (*to avoid*) el accidente. Según nos informaron, no (14) se lastimó (lastimarse) ningún pasajero del autobús.

AYUDA

Reading Spanish-language newspapers is a good way to practice verb tenses. You will find that both the imperfect and the preterite occur with great regularity. Many newsstands carry international papers, and many Spanish-language newspapers (such as Spain's ***El País***, Mexico's ***Reforma***, and Argentina's ***Clarín***) are on the Web.

2 **Seleccionar** Utiliza el tiempo verbal adecuado, según el contexto. Answers will vary. Suggested answers:

1. La semana pasada, Manolo y Aurora querían (querer) dar una fiesta. Decidieron (Decidir) invitar a seis amigos y servirles mucha comida.
2. Manolo y Aurora estaban (estar) preparando la comida cuando Elena llamó (llamar). Como siempre, tenía (tener) que estudiar para un examen.
3. A las seis, volvió (volver) a sonar el teléfono. Su amigo Francisco tampoco podía (poder) ir a la fiesta, porque tenía (tener) fiebre. Manolo y Aurora se sentían (sentirse) muy tristes, pero tenían (tener) que preparar la comida.
4. Después de otros quince minutos, sonó (sonar) el teléfono. Sus amigos, los señores Vega, estaban (estar) en camino (*en route*) al hospital: a su hijo le dolía (doler) mucho el estómago. Sólo dos de los amigos podían (poder) ir a la cena.
5. Por supuesto, iban (ir) a tener demasiada comida. Finalmente, cinco minutos antes de las ocho, llamaron (llamar) Ramón y Javier. Ellos pensaban (pensar) que la fiesta era (ser) la próxima semana.
6. Tristes, Manolo y Aurora se sentaron (sentarse) a comer solos. Mientras comían (comer), pronto llegaron (llegar) a la conclusión de que era (ser) mejor estar solos: ¡La comida estaba (estar) malísima!

3 **Completar** Completa las frases de una manera lógica. Usa el pretérito o el imperfecto. En parejas, comparen sus respuestas. Answers will vary.

1. De niño/a, yo...
2. Yo conducía el auto mientras...
3. Anoche mi novio/a...
4. Ayer el/la profesor(a)...
5. La semana pasada un(a) amigo/a...
6. Con frecuencia mis padres...
7. Esta mañana en la cafetería...
8. Hablábamos con el doctor cuando...

Practice more at **vhlcentral.com**.

TEACHING OPTIONS

Small Groups In groups of four, have students write a short article about an imaginary trip they took last summer. Students should use the imperfect to set the scene and the preterite to narrate the events. Each student should contribute three sentences to the article. When finished, have students read their articles to the class.

Heritage Speakers Ask heritage speakers to write a brief narration of a well-known fairy tale, such as *Little Red Riding Hood* (***Caperucita Roja***). Allow them to change details as they see fit, modernizing the story or setting it in another country, for example, but tell them to pay special attention to the use of preterite and imperfect verbs. Have them share their retellings with the class.

Comunicación

4

Entrevista Usa estas preguntas para entrevistar a un(a) compañero/a acerca de su primer(a) novio/a. Si quieres, puedes añadir otras preguntas. Answers will vary.

1. ¿Quién fue tu primer(a) novio/a?
2. ¿Cuántos años tenías cuando lo/la conociste?
3. ¿Cómo era él/ella?
4. ¿Qué le gustaba hacer? ¿Tenían ustedes los mismos pasatiempos?
5. ¿Por cuánto tiempo salieron ustedes?
6. ¿Adónde iban cuando salían?
7. ¿Pensaban casarse?
8. ¿Cuándo y por qué rompieron?

5

La sala de emergencias En parejas, miren la lista e inventen qué les pasó a estas personas que están en la sala de emergencias. Answers will vary.

modelo

Eran las tres de la tarde. Como todos los días, Pablo jugaba al fútbol con sus amigos. Estaba muy contento. De repente, se cayó y se rompió el brazo. Entonces fue a la sala de emergencias.

Paciente	Edad	Hora	Estado
1. Pablo Romero	9 años	15:20	hueso roto (el brazo)
2. Estela Rodríguez	45 años	15:25	tobillo torcido
3. Lupe Quintana	29 años	15:37	embarazada, dolores
4. Manuel López	52 años	15:45	infección de garganta
5. Marta Díaz	3 años	16:00	congestión, fiebre
6. Roberto Salazar	32 años	16:06	dolor de oído
7. Marco Brito	18 años	16:18	daño en el cuello, posible fractura
8. Ana María Ortiz	66 años	16:29	reacción alérgica a un medicamento

6

Situación Anoche alguien robó (*stole*) el examen de la **Lección 10** de la oficina de tu profesor(a) y tú tienes que averiguar quién lo hizo. Pregúntales a tres compañeros dónde estaban, con quién estaban y qué hicieron entre las ocho y las doce de la noche. Answers will vary.

Síntesis

7

La primera vez En grupos, cuéntense cómo fue la primera vez que les pusieron una inyección, se rompieron un hueso, pasaron la noche en un hospital, estuvieron mareados/as, etc. Incluyan estos datos en su conversación: una descripción del tiempo que hacía, sus edades, qué pasó y cómo se sentían. Answers will vary.

TEACHING OPTIONS

Small Groups Have small groups write a skit and perform it for the class. Three students walk into the campus clinic. Each explains to the nurse what happened and why he or she should be seen first. Students should use the preterite and imperfect.

Game Create a short narrative in the past based on a well-known story. Allow space between sentences so they may be easily cut into strips. Then make a copy of the narrative and edit it, changing all preterites to imperfects and vice versa. Make two copies of each version and cut the sentences apart. Place a complete set of both the versions into two separate bags, mix the strips up, and challenge two teams to reconstruct the correct version. The team that does so first wins.

4 Teaching Tips

- In order to be sensitive to those who haven't had a romantic relationship, you may wish to change the context to a first friendship. Items 5–8 should be adjusted accordingly (Ex: **¿Por cuánto tiempo fueron amigos/as?**).
- To simplify, have students prepare a few notes to help them with their responses.

4 Expansion Have students write a summary of their partners' responses, omitting all names. Collect the summaries, then read them to the class. Have students guess who had the relationship described in the summary.

5 Teaching Tip Remind students that the 24-hour clock is often used for schedules. Go through a few of the times and ask volunteers to provide the equivalent in the 12-hour clock.

5 Expansion Have pairs share their answers with the class, without mentioning the patient's name. The class must guess who it is.

6 Expansion Have groups decide who is the most likely thief. Ask them to prepare a police report explaining why they believe their suspect is the culprit.

7 Teaching Tip To simplify, before assigning groups, have students list information they can include in their descriptions, such as their age, the time, the date, what the weather was like, and so forth. Then have them list the events of the day in the order they happened.

7 Expansion Have students decide who in their group is the most accident-prone on the basis of his or her responses. Ask the group to prepare a doctor's account of his or her treatments.

Section Goals

In **Estructura 10.3**, students will be introduced to:
- impersonal constructions with **se**
- using **se** for unplanned events

Instructional Resources
Supersite: Audio (Lab MP3 Files); Resources (Grammar Presentation Slides, Activity Pack, Scripts, Answer Keys); Testing Program (Quizzes)
WebSAM
Workbook, pp. 117–118
Lab Manual, p. 59

Teaching Tips

- Have students look at the three signs in the grammar explanation, and ask simple questions about the situations. Ex: **¿Podemos nadar en esta playa? (No, se prohíbe nadar.)**
- Test comprehension by asking questions based on similar **se** constructions. Ex: **¿Se habla español en Inglaterra? (No, se habla inglés.) ¿Dónde se hacen las películas norteamericanas? (Se hacen en Hollywood.)**
- Divide the board into two columns, labeled **Sí** and **No**. Ask volunteers to describe what is and is not allowed in Spanish class, using impersonal constructions with **se**. Ex: **Se debe hablar español. Se prohíben las gafas de sol.**

10.3 Constructions with se

Tutorial

ANTE TODO In **Lección 7**, you learned how to use **se** as the third person reflexive pronoun (**Él se despierta. Ellos se visten. Ella se baña.**). **Se** can also be used to form constructions in which the person performing the action is not expressed or is de-emphasized.

NATIONAL STANDARDS comparisons

Impersonal constructions with se

▶ In Spanish, verbs that are not reflexive can be used with **se** to form impersonal constructions. These are statements in which the person performing the action is not defined.

Se habla español en Costa Rica.
Spanish is spoken in Costa Rica.

Se puede leer en la sala de espera.
You can read in the waiting room.

Se hacen operaciones aquí.
They perform operations here.

Se necesitan medicinas enseguida.
They need medicine right away.

AYUDA
In English, the passive voice or indefinite subjects (*you, they, one*) are used where Spanish uses impersonal constructions with **se**.

▶ **¡Atención!** Note that the third person singular verb form is used with singular nouns and the third person plural form is used with plural nouns.

Se vende ropa. **Se venden** camisas.

▶ You often see the impersonal **se** in signs, advertisements, and directions.

SE PROHÍBE
NADAR

Se necesitan programadores
Grupo Tecno
Tel. 778-34-34

ENTRADA
Se entra por la izquierda

Se for unplanned events

¿Te pusiste un suéter anoche?

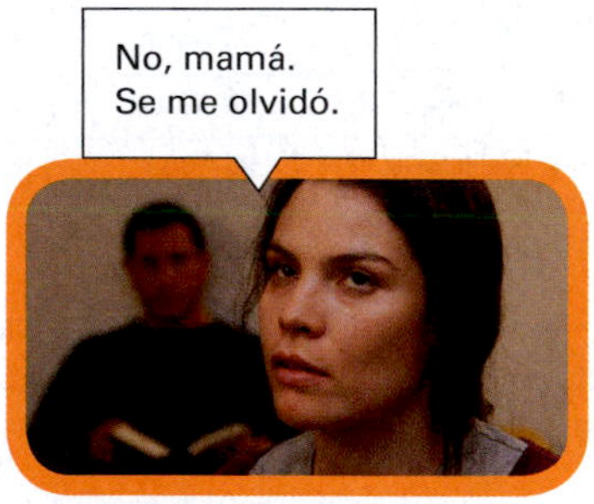
No, mamá.
Se me olvidó.

▶ **Se** also describes accidental or unplanned events. In this construction, the person who performs the action is de-emphasized, implying that the accident or unplanned event is not his or her direct responsibility. Note this construction.

se	+	[INDIRECT OBJECT PRONOUN]	+	[VERB]	+	[SUBJECT]
Se		me		cayó		la pluma.

TEACHING OPTIONS

TPR Use impersonal constructions with **se** to have students draw what you say. Ex: You say: **Se prohíbe entrar,** and students draw a door with a diagonal line through it. Other possible expressions: **Se sale por la derecha. Se permiten perros. Se prohíben botellas.**

Extra Practice For homework, have students search the Internet for common icons or international signs. Then, in pairs, have students write directions using **se** for each image. Ex: **Se prohíbe pasear en bicicleta. Se prohíbe pasar. Se habla español.**

Extra Practice Mime activities and have students state what happened, using **se**. Ex: Leave your keys out on the table, wave goodbye, and head for the door. (**Se le olvidaron/quedaron las llaves.**) Mime turning a key in the ignition, but the car does not start. (**Se le dañó el auto.**)

▶ In this type of construction, what would normally be the direct object of the sentence becomes the subject, and it agrees with the verb, not with the indirect object pronoun.

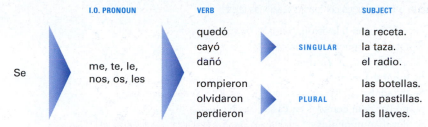

	I.O. PRONOUN	VERB		SUBJECT
Se	me, te, le, nos, os, les	quedó cayó dañó	SINGULAR	la receta. la taza. el radio.
		rompieron olvidaron perdieron	PLURAL	las botellas. las pastillas. las llaves.

▶ These verbs are the ones most frequently used with **se** to describe unplanned events.

Verbs commonly used with se

caer	*to fall; to drop*	**perder (e:ie)**	*to lose*
dañar	*to damage; to break down*	**quedar**	*to be left behind*
olvidar	*to forget*	**romper**	*to break*

Se me perdió el teléfono de la farmacia.
I lost the pharmacy's phone number.

Se nos olvidaron los pasajes.
We forgot the tickets.

▶ **¡Atención!** While Spanish has a verb for *to fall* (**caer**), there is no direct translation for *to drop*. **Dejar caer** (*To let fall*) or a **se** construction is often used to mean *to drop*.

El médico **dejó caer** la aspirina.
The doctor dropped the aspirin.

A mí **se me cayeron** los cuadernos.
I dropped the notebooks.

CONSULTA
For an explanation of prepositional pronouns, refer to **Estructura 9.4**, p. 294.

▶ To clarify or emphasize who the person involved in the action is, this construction commonly begins with the preposition **a** + [*noun*] or **a** + [*prepositional pronoun*].

Al paciente se le perdió la receta.
The patient lost his prescription.

A ustedes se les quedaron los libros en casa.
You left the books at home.

¡INTÉNTALO! Completa las oraciones con **se** impersonal y los verbos en presente.

A

1. Se enseñan (enseñar) cinco lenguas en esta universidad.
2. Se come (comer) muy bien en Las Delicias.
3. Se venden (vender) muchas camisetas allí.
4. Se sirven (servir) platos exquisitos cada noche.

Completa las oraciones con **se** y los verbos en pretérito.

B

1. Se me rompieron (*I broke*) las gafas.
2. Se te cayeron (*You* (fam., sing.) *dropped*) las pastillas.
3. Se les perdió (*They lost*) la receta.
4. Se le quedó (*You* (form., sing.) *left*) aquí la radiografía.

recursos
WB pp. 117–118
LM p. 59
vhlcentral.com Lección 10

Teaching Tips

- Test comprehension by asking volunteers to change sentences from plural to singular and vice versa. Ex: **Se me perdieron las llaves. (Se me perdió la llave.)**
- Have students finish sentences using a construction with **se** to express an unplanned event. Ex: **1. Al doctor ____. (se le cayó el termómetro) 2. A la profesora ____. (se le quedaron los papeles en casa)**
- Involve students in a conversation about unplanned events that happened to them recently. Say: **Se me olvidaron las gafas de sol esta mañana. Y a ti, ____, ¿se te olvidó algo esta mañana? ¿Qué se te olvidó?** Continue with other verbs. Ex: **¿A quién se le perdió algo importante esta semana? ¿Qué se te perdió?**

Successful Language Learning Tell students that this construction has no exact equivalent in English. Tell them to examine the examples in the textbook and make up some of their own in order to get a feel for how this construction works.

TEACHING OPTIONS

Video Show the **Fotonovela** again to give students more input containing constructions with **se**. Have students write down as many of the examples as they can. After viewing, have students edit their lists and cross out any reflexive verbs that they mistakenly understood to be constructions with **se**.

Heritage Speakers Ask heritage speakers to write a fictional or true account of a day in which everything went wrong. Ask them to include as many constructions with **se** as possible. Have them read their accounts aloud to the class, who will summarize the events.

Extra Practice Have students use **se** constructions to make excuses in different situations. Ex: You did not bring in a composition to class. (**Se me dañó la computadora.**)

1 Expansion

- Change the date from 1901 to 2011 and go through the exercise again orally.
- In pairs, have students use constructions with **se** to write a description of a period in history such as the French or American Revolution, the Sixties, and Prohibition. Then have pairs form groups of six and read their descriptions aloud to their group.
- Have pairs use **se** constructions to note cultural differences between Spanish-speaking countries and their own. Ex: **Aquí se habla inglés, pero en ____ se habla español.**

2 Teaching Tips

- Model the activity by asking volunteers to translate similar phrases. Ex: Nurse sought **(Se busca enfermero/a)**; Used books bought **(Se compran libros usados)**
- Ask students to discuss with a partner where these signs could be found locally.

3 Teaching Tip To simplify, have students work in pairs to brainstorm verbs that could be used to complete this activity.

3 Expansion

Add another visual aspect to this activity. Use magazine pictures to have students continue describing past events using constructions with **se**.

Práctica

1 **¿Cierto o falso?** Lee estas oraciones sobre la vida en 1901. Indica si lo que dice cada oración es **cierto** o **falso**. Luego corrige las oraciones falsas.

1. Se veía mucha televisión. Falso. No se veía televisión. Se leía mucho.
2. Se escribían muchos libros. Cierto.
3. Se viajaba mucho en tren. Cierto.
4. Se montaba a caballo. Cierto.
5. Se mandaba correo electrónico. Falso. No se mandaba correo electrónico. Se mandaban cartas y postales.
6. Se preparaban comidas en casa. Cierto.
7. Se llevaban minifaldas. Falso. No se llevaban minifaldas. Se llevaban faldas largas.
8. Se pasaba mucho tiempo con la familia. Cierto.

2 **Traducir** Traduce estos letreros (*signs*) y anuncios al español.

1. Nurses needed Se necesitan enfermeros/as
2. Eating and drinking prohibited Se prohíbe comer y beber
3. Programmers sought Se buscan programadores
4. English is spoken Se habla inglés
5. Computers sold Se venden computadoras
6. No talking Se prohíbe hablar
7. Teacher needed Se necesita profesor(a)
8. Books sold Se venden libros
9. Do not enter Se prohíbe entrar
10. Spanish is spoken Se habla español

3 **¿Qué pasó?** Mira los dibujos e indica lo que pasó en cada uno. Some answers will vary. Suggested answers:

1. camarero / pastel
Al camarero se le cayó el pastel.

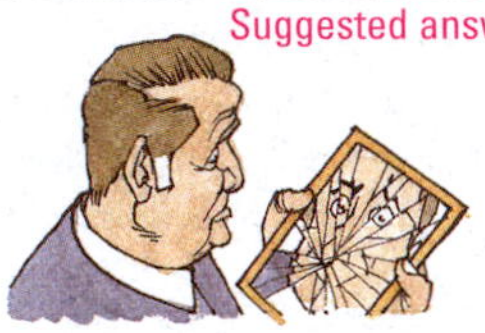

2. Sr. Álvarez / espejo
Al señor Álvarez se le rompió el espejo.

3. Arturo / tarea
A Arturo se le olvidó la tarea.

4. Sra. Domínguez / llaves
A la Sra. Domínguez se le perdieron las llaves.

5. Carla y Lupe / botellas de vino
A Carla y a Lupe se les rompieron las botellas de vino.

6. Juana / platos
A Juana se le rompieron los platos.

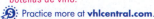

Practice more at **vhlcentral.com**.

TEACHING OPTIONS

Extra Practice Have students imagine that they have just seen a movie about the future. Have them work in groups to prepare a description of the way of life portrayed in the movie using the imperfect tense and constructions with **se**. Ex: **No se necesitaba trabajar. Se usaban robots para hacer todo. Se viajaba por telepatía. No se comía nada sino en los fines de semana.**

Game Divide the class into teams of four. Have each team think of a famous place or public building and compose four signs that could be found on the premises. Teams will take turns reading their signs aloud. Each team that correctly identifies the place or building receives one point. The team with the most points wins.

NATIONAL communication STANDARDS

Comunicación

4 **¿Distraído/a yo?** Trabajen en parejas y usen estas preguntas para averiguar cuál de los/las dos es más distraído/a (*absentminded*). Answers will vary.

¿Alguna vez...
1. se te olvidó invitar a alguien a una fiesta o comida? ¿A quién?
2. se te quedó algo importante en la casa? ¿Qué?
3. se te perdió algo importante durante un viaje? ¿Qué?
4. se te rompió algo muy caro? ¿Qué?

¿Sabes...
5. si se permite el ingreso (*admission*) de perros al parque cercano a la universidad?
6. si en el supermercado se aceptan cheques?
7. dónde se arreglan zapatos y botas?
8. qué se sirve en la cafetería de la universidad los lunes?

5 **Opiniones** En parejas, terminen cada oración con ideas originales. Después, comparen los resultados con la clase para ver qué pareja tuvo las mejores ideas. Answers will vary.

1. No se tiene que dejar propina cuando...
2. Antes de viajar, se debe...
3. Si se come bien, ...
4. Para tener una vida sana, se debe...
5. Se sirve la mejor comida en...
6. Se hablan muchas lenguas en...

NATIONAL communication STANDARDS

Síntesis

6 **Anuncios** En grupos, preparen dos anuncios de televisión para presentar a la clase. Usen el imperfecto y por lo menos dos construcciones con **se** en cada uno. Answers will vary.

modelo

Se me cayeron unos libros en el pie y me dolía mucho. Pero ahora no, gracias a SuperAspirina 500. ¡Dos pastillas y se me fue el dolor! Se puede comprar SuperAspirina 500 en todas las farmacias Recetamax.

4 Teaching Tip Encourage students to give detailed responses. Model this by choosing from the first set of questions and providing as many details as possible. Ex: **Una vez cuando era adolescente se me rompió un plato muy caro de mi abuela. Pero ella no se enojó. Me dijo: No te preocupes por el plato. ¿Te lastimaste?**

4 Expansion Have each pair decide on the most unusual answer to the questions. Ask the student who gave it to describe the event to the class.

5 Expansion Ask pairs to write similar beginnings to three different statements using **se** constructions. Have pairs exchange papers and finish each other's sentences.

6 Expansion After all the groups have presented their ads, have each group write a letter of complaint. Their letter should be directed to one of the other groups, claiming false advertising.

TEACHING OPTIONS

Extra Practice Write these sentence fragments on the board and ask students to supply at least two logical endings using a construction with **se**. **1. Una vez, cuando yo comía en un restaurante elegante, ____. (se me rompió un vaso; se me perdió la tarjeta de crédito) 2. Ayer cuando yo venía a clase, ____. (se me dañó la bicicleta; me caí y se me rompió el brazo) 3. Cuando era niño/a, siempre ____. (se me olvidaban las cosas; se me perdían las cosas) 4. El otro día cuando yo lavaba los platos, ____. (se me rompieron tres vasos; se me acabó el detergente)**

Section Goals

In **Estructura 10.4**, students will learn:
- the formation of adverbs using [*adjective*] + **–mente**
- common adverbs and adverbial expressions

Instructional Resources
Supersite: Audio (Lab MP3 Files); Resources (Grammar Presentation Slides, Activity Pack, Scripts, Answer Keys); Testing Program (Quizzes)
WebSAM
Workbook, pp. 119–120
Lab Manual, p. 60

Teaching Tips

- Add a visual aspect to this grammar presentation. Use magazine pictures to review known adverbs. Ex: **Miren la foto que tengo *aquí*. *Hoy* esta chica se siente *bien*, pero *ayer* se sentía *mal*.** Write the adverbs on the board as you proceed.
- After presenting the formation of adverbs that end in **–mente**, ask volunteers to convert known adjectives into adverbs and then use them in a sentence. Ex: **cómodo/cómodamente: Alberto se sentó cómodamente en la silla.**
- Name celebrities and have students create sentences about them, using adverbs. Ex: **Shakira (Shakira baila maravillosamente.)**

10.4 Adverbs

Tutorial

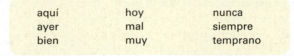

ANTE TODO Adverbs are words that describe how, when, and where actions take place. They can modify verbs, adjectives, and even other adverbs. In previous lessons, you have already learned many Spanish adverbs, such as the ones below.

aquí	hoy	nunca
ayer	mal	siempre
bien	muy	temprano

- The most common adverbs end in **-mente**, equivalent to the English ending *-ly*.

verdaderamente *truly, really* **generalmente** *generally* **simplemente** *simply*

- To form these adverbs, add **-mente** to the feminine form of the adjective. If the adjective does not have a special feminine form, just add **-mente** to the standard form. **¡Atención!** Adjectives do not lose their accents when adding **-mente**.

ADJECTIVE	FEMININE FORM	SUFFIX	ADVERB
seguro	segura	-mente	seguramente
fabuloso	fabulosa	-mente	fabulosamente
enorme		-mente	enormemente
fácil		-mente	fácilmente

- Adverbs that end in **-mente** generally follow the verb, while adverbs that modify an adjective or another adverb precede the word they modify.

Maira dibuja **maravillosamente**.
Maira draws wonderfully.

Sergio está **casi siempre** ocupado.
Sergio is almost always busy.

Common adverbs and adverbial expressions

a menudo	*often*	**así**	*like this; so*	**menos**	*less*
a tiempo	*on time*	**bastante**	*enough; rather*	**muchas veces**	*a lot; many times*
a veces	*sometimes*	**casi**	*almost*	**poco**	*little*
además (de)	*furthermore; besides*	**con frecuencia**	*frequently*	**por lo menos**	*at least*
apenas	*hardly; scarcely*	**de vez en cuando**	*from time to time*	**pronto**	*soon*
		despacio	*slowly*	**rápido**	*quickly*

¡ATENCIÓN!
When a sentence contains two or more adverbs in sequence, the suffix **-mente** is dropped from all but the last adverb.
Ex: **El médico nos habló simple y abiertamente.** *The doctor spoke to us simply and openly.*

¡ATENCIÓN!
Rápido functions as an adjective (**Ella tiene una computadora rápida.**) as well as an adverb (**Ellas corren rápido.**). Note that as an adverb, **rápido** does not need to agree with any other word in the sentence. You can also use the adverb **rápidamente** (**Ella corre rápidamente.**).

recursos
WB pp. 119–120
LM p. 60
vhlcentral.com Lección 10

¡INTÉNTALO! Transforma los adjetivos en adverbios.

1. alegre alegremente
2. constante constantemente
3. gradual gradualmente
4. perfecto perfectamente
5. real realmente
6. frecuente frecuentemente
7. tranquilo tranquilamente
8. regular regularmente
9. maravilloso maravillosamente
10. normal normalmente
11. básico básicamente
12. afortunado afortunadamente

TEACHING OPTIONS

Heritage Speakers Have heritage speakers talk about daily life when they were children or adolescents. Tell them to use at least eight of the common adverbs and adverbial expressions listed. Then have the rest of the class write sentences comparing and contrasting their experiences with those of the heritage speakers.

Extra Practice Have pairs of students write sentences using adverbs such as **nunca, hoy,** and **despacio.** When they have finished, ask volunteers to dictate their sentences to you to write on the board. After you have written a sentence and checked it for accuracy, ask a volunteer to create a sentence that uses the antonym of the adverb.

Práctica

1

Escoger Completa la historia con los adverbios adecuados.

1. La cita era a las dos, pero llegamos ___tarde___. (menos, nunca, tarde)
2. El problema fue que ___ayer___ se nos dañó el despertador. (aquí, ayer, despacio)
3. La recepcionista no se enojó porque sabe que normalmente llego ___a tiempo___. (a veces, a tiempo, poco)
4. ___Por lo menos___ el doctor estaba listo. (Por lo menos, Muchas veces, Casi)
5. ___Apenas___ tuvimos que esperar cinco minutos. (Así, Además, Apenas)
6. El doctor dijo que nuestra hija Irene necesitaba cambiar su rutina diaria ___inmediatamente___. (temprano, menos, inmediatamente)
7. El doctor nos explicó ___bien___ las recomendaciones del Cirujano General (*Surgeon General*) sobre la salud de los jóvenes. (de vez en cuando, bien, apenas)
8. ___Afortunadamente___ nos dijo que Irene estaba bien, pero tenía que hacer más ejercicio y comer mejor. (Bastante, Afortunadamente, A menudo)

NOTA CULTURAL

La doctora Antonia Novello, de Puerto Rico, fue la primera mujer y la primera hispana en tomar el cargo de **Cirujana General** de los Estados Unidos (1990–1993).

Comunicación

2

NATIONAL communication STANDARDS

Aspirina Lee el anuncio y responde a las preguntas con un(a) compañero/a. Answers will vary.

No hay tiempo para el dolor de cabeza.
Si tienes prisa, o simplemente quieres que tu dolor de cabeza se vaya muy pronto, piensa en Capalivia. Se asimila mejor y actúa rápidamente. Ya no se puede perder tiempo por un dolor de cabeza.
ASPIRINA
masticable
ASPIRINA
masticable

1. ¿Cuáles son los adverbios que aparecen en el anuncio?
2. Según el anuncio, ¿cuáles son las ventajas (*advantages*) de este tipo de aspirina?
3. ¿Tienen ustedes dolores de cabeza? ¿Qué toman para curarlos?
4. ¿Qué medicamentos ven con frecuencia en los anuncios de televisión? Escriban descripciones de varios de estos anuncios. Usen adverbios en sus descripciones.

Practice more at **vhlcentral.com**.

1 Teaching Tip Review common adverbs and adverbial expressions by drawing a three-column chart on the board. Label the columns **¿Cómo?**, **¿Cuándo?**, and **¿Dónde?** Ask volunteers to call out adverbs for each column. Write the correct answers on the board. Ex: **¿Cómo? (despacio, fácilmente) ¿Cuándo? (nunca, siempre, a menudo) ¿Dónde? (aquí, allí)**

2 Teaching Tip Before assigning the activity, ask some general questions about the ad. Ex: **¿Qué producto se vende? (aspirina) ¿Dónde se encuentra un anuncio de este tipo? (en una revista)**

2 Expansion Have pairs create a similar ad for a different pharmaceutical product. Collect the ads and read the descriptions aloud. The rest of the class should try to identify the product.

TEACHING OPTIONS

Extra Practice Add an auditory aspect to this grammar practice. Prepare sentences using adverbs and read them aloud slowly to allow students time to write. Ex: **A mi profesor de español siempre se le olvidan las cosas. Con frecuencia se pone dos medias diferentes por la mañana. Habla despacio cuando es necesario. De vez en cuando se le pierden los papeles.** Ask comprehension questions as a follow-up.

Game Divide the class into teams of three. Each team should have a piece of paper. Say the name of a historical figure and give teams three minutes to write down as many facts as they can about that person, using adverbs and adverbial expressions. At the end of each round, have teams read their answers aloud. Award one point to the team with the most correct answers for each historical figure.

Section Goal

In **Recapitulación**, students will review the grammar concepts from this lesson.

Instructional Resource
Supersite

1 Teaching Tip Ask students to identify the infinitive for each row.

1 Expansion Ask students to provide the forms for **ir**, **ver**, and **doler**.

2 Expansion
- To challenge students, have them create sentences to express the opposite meaning for each item. Ex: **1. Pablito se cae muy poco.**
- Ask students to write a paragraph in which they use at least five of the listed adverbs. Then have them exchange papers with a partner for peer editing.

Recapitulación

Diagnostics

Completa estas actividades para repasar los conceptos de gramática que aprendiste en esta lección.

1 Completar Completa el cuadro con la forma correcta del imperfecto. 24 pts.

yo/Ud./él/ella	tú	nosotros	Uds./ellos/ellas
era	eras	éramos	eran
cantaba	**cantabas**	cantábamos	cantaban
venía	venías	**veníamos**	venían
quería	querías	queríamos	**querían**

2 Adverbios Escoge el adverbio correcto de la lista para completar estas oraciones. Lee con cuidado las oraciones; los adverbios sólo se usan una vez. No vas a usar uno de los adverbios. 16 pts.

a menudo	apenas	fácilmente
a tiempo	casi	maravillosamente
además	despacio	por lo menos

1. Pablito se cae __a menudo__; un promedio (*average*) de cuatro veces por semana.
2. No me duele nada y no sufro de ninguna enfermedad; me siento __maravillosamente__ bien.
3. —Doctor, ¿cómo supo que tuve una operación de garganta?
—Muy __fácilmente__, lo leí en su historial médico (*medical history*).
4. ¿Le duele mucho la espalda (*back*)? Entonces tiene que levantarse __despacio__.
5. Ya te sientes mucho mejor, ¿verdad? Mañana puedes volver al trabajo; tu temperatura es __casi__ normal.
6. Es importante hacer ejercicio con regularidad, __por lo menos__ tres veces a la semana.
7. El examen médico no comenzó ni tarde ni temprano. Comenzó __a tiempo__, a las tres de la tarde.
8. Parece que ya te estás curando del resfriado. __Apenas__ estás congestionada.

RESUMEN GRAMATICAL

10.1 The imperfect tense pp. 318–319

The imperfect of regular verbs

cantar	beber	escribir
cantaba	bebía	escribía
cantabas	bebías	escribías
cantaba	bebía	escribía
cantábamos	bebíamos	escribíamos
cantabais	bebíais	escribíais
cantaban	bebían	escribían

- There are no stem changes in the imperfect: **entender (e:ie) → entendía; servir (e:i) → servía; doler (o:ue) → dolía**
- The imperfect of **hay** is **había**.
- Only three verbs are irregular in the imperfect.
ir: **iba, ibas, iba, íbamos, ibais, iban**
ser: **era, eras, era, éramos, erais, eran**
ver: **veía, veías, veía, veíamos, veíais, veían**

10.2 The preterite and the imperfect pp. 322–323

Preterite	Imperfect
1. Completed actions **Fueron a Buenos Aires ayer.**	1. Ongoing past action **Usted miraba el fútbol.**
2. Beginning or end of past action **La película empezó a las nueve.**	2. Habitual past actions **Todos los domingos yo visitaba a mi abuela.**
3. Series of past actions or events **Me caí y me lastimé el pie.**	3. Description of states or characteristics **Ella era alta. Quería descansar.**

10.3 Constructions with se pp. 236–327

Impersonal constructions with se

Se	prohíbe fumar.
	habla español.
	hablan varios idiomas.

TEACHING OPTIONS

TPR Divide the class into three groups: **-ar** verbs, **-er** verbs, and **-ir** verbs. Read a series of sentences that contain the imperfect tense. Have groups stand up when their verb form is used. Ex: **Mi escuela primaria tenía un patio grande.** (**-er** verb group stands)

Extra Practice Ask students to use the preterite and imperfect to write a paragraph about an imaginary scenario in which a celebrity got injured and went to the emergency room. Have students describe the person's age, where he or she was, the weather, the time, what he or she was doing when the accident occurred, and what happened at the hospital. Ask volunteers to read their paragraphs aloud.

Se for unplanned events		
Se	me, te, le, nos, os, les	cayó la taza.
		dañó el radio.
		rompieron las botellas.
		olvidaron las llaves.

10.4 **Adverbs** p. 330

Formation of adverbs	
fácil →	fácilmente
seguro →	seguramente
verdadero →	verdaderamente

3 **Un accidente** Escoge el imperfecto o el pretérito según el contexto para completar esta conversación. 20 pts.

NURIA Hola, Felipe. ¿Estás bien? ¿Qué es eso? ¿(1) (**Te lastimaste**/Te lastimabas) el pie?

FELIPE Ayer (2) (**tuve**/tenía) un pequeño accidente.

NURIA Cuéntame. ¿Cómo (3) (**pasó**/pasaba)?

FELIPE Bueno, (4) (fueron/**eran**) las cinco de la tarde y (5) (llovió/**llovía**) mucho cuando (6) (**salí**/salía) de la casa en mi bicicleta. No (7) (**vi**/veía) a una chica que (8) (caminó/**caminaba**) en mi dirección, y los dos (9) (**nos caímos**/nos caíamos) al suelo (*ground*).

NURIA Y la chica, ¿está bien ella?

FELIPE Sí. Cuando llegamos al hospital, ella sólo (10) (tuvo/**tenía**) dolor de cabeza.

4 **Oraciones** Escribe oraciones con **se** a partir de los elementos dados (*given*). Usa el tiempo especificado entre paréntesis y añade pronombres cuando sea necesario. 10 pts.

modelo

Carlos / quedar / la tarea en casa (pretérito)

A Carlos se le quedó la tarea en casa.

1. en la farmacia / vender / medicamentos (presente) En la farmacia se venden medicamentos.
2. ¿(tú) / olvidar / las llaves / otra vez? (pretérito) ¿Se te olvidaron las llaves otra vez?
3. (yo) / dañar / la computadora (pretérito) Se me dañó la computadora.
4. en esta clase / prohibir / hablar inglés (presente) En esta clase se prohíbe hablar inglés.
5. ellos / romper / las gafas / en el accidente (pretérito) A ellos se les rompieron las gafas en el accidente.

5 **En la consulta** Escribe al menos cinco oraciones sobre tu última visita al médico. Incluye cinco verbos en pretérito y cinco en imperfecto. Habla de qué te pasó, cómo te sentías, cómo era el/la doctor(a), qué te dijo, etc. Usa tu imaginación. 30 pts. Answers will vary.

6 **Refrán** Completa el refrán con las palabras que faltan. ¡4 puntos EXTRA!

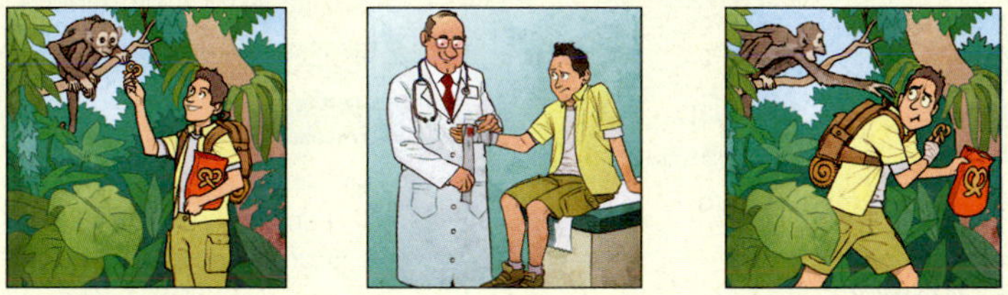

"Lo que __bien__ (*well*) se aprende, nunca __se__ pierde."

Practice more at **vhlcentral.com**.

3 Teaching Tip To challenge students, have them explain why they used the preterite and imperfect in each case and how the meaning might change if the other tense were used.

4 Teaching Tip For items 2, 3, and 5, have volunteers rewrite the sentences on the board using other pronouns. Ex: **2. (nosotros) ¿Se nos olvidaron las llaves otra vez?**

4 Expansion Give students these additional items: **6. (yo) / caer / el vaso de cristal (pretérito) (Se me cayó el vaso de cristal.) 7. (ustedes) / quedar / las maletas en el aeropuerto (pretérito) (A ustedes se les quedaron las maletas en el aeropuerto.) 8. en esta tienda / hablar / español e italiano (presente) (En esta tienda se hablan español e italiano.)**

5 Teaching Tip After writing their paragraphs, have students work in pairs and ask each other follow-up questions about their visits.

6 Teaching Tips
- Have volunteers give additional examples of situations in which one might use this expression.
- Ask students to give the English equivalent of this phrase. (*What is well learned is never lost.*) Ask them how this expression might relate to their own lives and studies.

TEACHING OPTIONS

Extra Practice Write questions on the board that elicit the impersonal **se**. Have pairs write two responses for each question. Ex: **¿Qué se hace para mantener la salud? ¿Dónde se come bien en esta ciudad? ¿Cuándo se dan fiestas en esta universidad? ¿Dónde se consiguen los jeans más baratos?**

Game Divide the class into two teams and have them line up. Point to the first member of each team and call out an adjective that can be changed into an adverb (Ex: **lento**). The first student to reach the board and correctly write the adverb (**lentamente**) earns a point for his or her team. If the student can also write an "opposite" adverb (Ex: **rápidamente**), he or she earns a bonus point. The team with the most points at the end wins.

Audio: Reading
Additional Reading

Section Goals

In **Lectura**, students will:
- learn to activate background knowledge to understand a reading selection
- read a content-rich text on health care while traveling

Instructional Resource
Supersite

Estrategia Tell students that they will find it easier to understand the content of a reading selection on a particular topic by reviewing what they know about the subject before reading. Then ask students to brainstorm ways to stay healthy while traveling. Possible responses: do not drink tap water, do not eat raw fruit or vegetables, pack personal medical supplies that may not be available at the destination.

Examinar el texto Students should mention that the text is an interview (**entrevista**) by a journalist (**periodista**) of an author (**autora**) whose book is about staying healthy while traveling.

Conocimiento previo Have small groups write a paragraph summarizing ways to safeguard health while traveling. Their recommendations should be based on their collective experiences. If no one in the group can relate personally to a given situation, encourage students to draw on the experiences of people they know. Have groups share their paragraphs with the class.

The Affective Dimension Remind students that they will probably feel less anxious about reading in Spanish if they follow the suggestions in the **Estrategia** sections, which are designed to reinforce and increase reading comprehension skills.

Lectura

NATIONAL STANDARDS communication cultures

Antes de leer

Estrategia
Activating background knowledge

Using what you already know about a particular subject will often help you better understand a reading selection. For example, if you read an article about a recent medical discovery, you might think about what you already know about health in order to understand unfamiliar words or concepts.

Examinar el texto

Utiliza las estrategias de lectura que tú consideras más efectivas para hacer algunas observaciones preliminares acerca del texto. Después trabajen en parejas para comparar sus observaciones acerca del texto. Luego contesten estas preguntas:

- Analicen el formato del texto: ¿Qué tipo de texto es? ¿Dónde creen que se publicó este artículo?
- ¿Quiénes son Carla Baron y Tomás Monterrey?
- Miren la foto del libro. ¿Qué sugiere el título del libro sobre su contenido?

Conocimiento previo

Ahora piensen en su conocimiento previo° sobre el cuidado de la salud en los viajes. Consideren estas preguntas:

- ¿Viajaron alguna vez a otro estado o a otro país?
- ¿Tuvieron problemas durante sus viajes con el agua, la comida o el clima del lugar?
- ¿Olvidaron poner en su maleta algún medicamento que después necesitaron?
- Imaginen que su compañero/a se va de viaje. Díganle por lo menos cinco cosas que debe hacer para prevenir cualquier problema de salud.

conocimiento previo *background knowledge*

Practice more at **vhlcentral.com**.

Libro de la semana

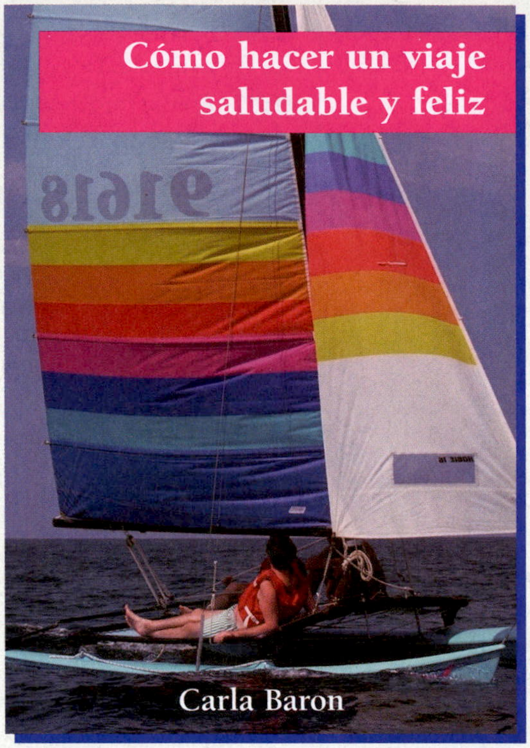

Después de leer

Correspondencias

Busca las correspondencias entre los problemas y las recomendaciones.

Problemas

1. el agua __b__
2. el sol __d__
3. la comida __a__
4. la identificación __e__
5. el clima __c__

Recomendaciones

a. Hay que adaptarse a los ingredientes desconocidos (*unknown*).
b. Toma sólo productos purificados (*purified*).
c. Es importante llevar ropa adecuada cuando viajas.
d. Lleva loción o crema con alta protección solar.
e. Lleva tu pasaporte.

TEACHING OPTIONS

Heritage Speakers Ask heritage speakers to state consequences for a tourist who does not follow the recommendations in **Correspondencias**. Ex: **a. La persona prueba una comida picante y le da dolor de estómago.** After each consequence is stated, have volunteers suggest an appropriate course of action or treatment. Ex: **Debe ir a una farmacia y comprar unas pastillas, como *Tums*.** Encourage heritage speakers to respond to the students' suggestions.

Small Groups Ask small groups to select a country they would like to visit. Have them research and write a report about what food and beverage precautions should be taken (**precauciones que se deben tomar**) by visitors to that country. They should mention precautions such as not eating undercooked meat or unwashed fruits, and not drinking tap water.

Entrevista a Carla Baron

por Tomás Monterrey

Tomás: ¿Por qué escribió su libro *Cómo hacer un viaje saludable y feliz*?

Carla: Me encanta viajar, conocer otras culturas y escribir. Mi primer viaje lo hice cuando era estudiante universitaria. Todavía recuerdo el día en que llegamos a San Juan, Puerto Rico. Era el panorama ideal para unas vacaciones maravillosas, pero al llegar a la habitación del hotel, bebí mucha agua de la llave° y luego pedí un jugo de frutas con mucho hielo°. El clima en San Juan es tropical y yo tenía mucha sed y calor. Los síntomas llegaron en menos de media hora: pasé dos días con dolor de estómago y corriendo al cuarto de baño cada diez minutos. Desde entonces, siempre que viajo sólo bebo agua mineral y llevo un pequeño bolso con medicinas necesarias, como pastillas para el dolor y también bloqueador solar, una crema repelente de mosquitos y un desinfectante.

Tomás: ¿Son reales° las situaciones que se narran en su libro?

Carla: Sí, son reales y son mis propias° historias°. A menudo los autores crean caricaturas divertidas de un turista en dificultades. ¡En mi libro la turista en dificultades soy yo!

Tomás: ¿Qué recomendaciones puede encontrar el lector en su libro?

Carla: Bueno, mi libro es anecdótico y humorístico, pero el tema de la salud se trata° de manera seria. En general, se dan recomendaciones sobre ropa adecuada para cada sitio, consejos para protegerse del sol, y comidas y bebidas adecuadas para el turista que viaja al Caribe o Suramérica.

Tomás: ¿Tiene algún consejo para las personas que se enferman cuando viajan?

Carla: Muchas veces los turistas toman el avión sin saber nada acerca del país que van a visitar. Ponen toda su ropa en la maleta, toman el pasaporte, la cámara fotográfica y ¡a volar°! Es necesario tomar precauciones porque nuestro cuerpo necesita adaptarse al clima, al sol, a la humedad, al agua y a la comida. Se trata de° viajar, admirar las maravillas del mundo y regresar a casa con hermosos recuerdos. En resumen, el secreto es "prevenir en vez de° curar".

llave *faucet* hielo *ice* reales *true* propias *own* historias *stories* se trata *is treated* ¡a volar! *Off they go!* Se trata de *It's a question of* en vez de *instead of*

Seleccionar

Selecciona la respuesta correcta.

1. El tema principal de este libro es __d__.
   a. Puerto Rico b. la salud y el agua c. otras culturas
   d. el cuidado de la salud en los viajes
2. Las situaciones narradas en el libro son __a__.
   a. autobiográficas b. inventadas c. ficticias
   d. imaginarias
3. ¿Qué recomendaciones no vas a encontrar en este libro? __d__
   a. cómo vestirse adecuadamente
   b. cómo prevenir las quemaduras solares
   c. consejos sobre la comida y la bebida
   d. cómo dar propina en los países del Caribe o de Suramérica
4. En opinión de la señorita Baron, __b__.
   a. es bueno tomar agua de la llave y beber jugo de frutas con mucho hielo
   b. es mejor tomar solamente agua embotellada (*bottled*)
   c. los minerales son buenos para el dolor abdominal
   d. es importante visitar el cuarto de baño cada diez minutos
5. ¿Cuál de estos productos no lleva la autora cuando viaja a otros países? __c__
   a. desinfectante
   b. crema repelente
   c. detergente
   d. pastillas medicinales

Correspondencias Ask students to work together in pairs and use cognates or context clues to match **Problemas** with **Recomendaciones**.

Seleccionar
- Have students check their work by locating the sections in the text where the information can be found.
- Ask the class the questions. Have volunteers answer orally or write their answers on the board.

TEACHING OPTIONS

Pairs Ask pairs to use the items in **Correspondencias** on page 334 as a model. Have them work together to write additional possibilities for **Problemas** and **Recomendaciones**. Ex: **Problema: el dinero; Recomendación: Lleva cheques de viajero o una tarjeta de crédito internacional.** When pairs have completed five more items, have them exchange their items with another pair, who will match them.

Heritage Speakers Ask heritage speakers to describe a few health tips for traveling in their families' countries of origin, such as any immunizations that may be required; appropriate clothing; spicy regional foods or dishes that may cause digestive problems; and so forth. Have the rest of the class ask follow-up questions.

Video: *Panorama cultural*
Interactive map

Section Goal

In **Panorama**, students will read about the geography, culture, and economy of Costa Rica.

Instructional Resources
Supersite: Video (***Panorama cultural***); Resources (Scripts, Translations, Digital Image Bank, Answer Keys)
WebSAM
Workbook, pp. 121–122
Video Manual, pp. 49–50

Teaching Tips

- Use the **Lección 10 Panorama** digital images to assist with this presentation.
- Have students look at the map of Costa Rica. Encourage them to mention the physical features that they notice. Discuss the map and the images in the call-out photos.

El país en cifras After each section, ask students questions about the content. Ex: **¿Entre qué masas de agua está Costa Rica? Las ciudades principales, ¿en qué lado de la cordillera Central están?** When reading about Costa Rica's population, point out that the country has a 96% literacy rate, the best in Latin America. Point out that **Óscar Arias** received the Nobel Peace Prize for his work in resolving civil wars in the other Central American countries during the 1970s and 1980s.

¡Increíble pero cierto! Costa Rica has one of the most long-standing democratic traditions in the Americas. Although it has no army, it does have a national police force and a rural guard.

Costa Rica

NATIONAL STANDARDS connections cultures

El país en cifras

- **Área:** 51.100 km² (19.730 millas²), *aproximadamente el área de Virginia Occidental°*
- **Población:** 4.755.000

Costa Rica es el país de Centroamérica con la población más homogénea. El 94% de sus habitantes es blanco y mestizo°. Más del 50% de la población es de ascendencia° española y un alto porcentaje tiene sus orígenes en otros países europeos.

- **Capital:** San José —1.515.000
- **Ciudades principales:** Alajuela, Cartago, Puntarenas, Heredia
- **Moneda:** colón costarricense
- **Idioma:** español (oficial)

Bandera de Costa Rica

Costarricenses célebres

- **Carmen Lyra,** escritora (1888–1949)
- **Chavela Vargas,** cantante (1919–2012)
- **Óscar Arias Sánchez,** ex presidente de Costa Rica (1941–)
- **Laura Chinchilla Miranda,** ex presidenta de Costa Rica (1959–)
- **Claudia Poll,** nadadora° olímpica (1972–)

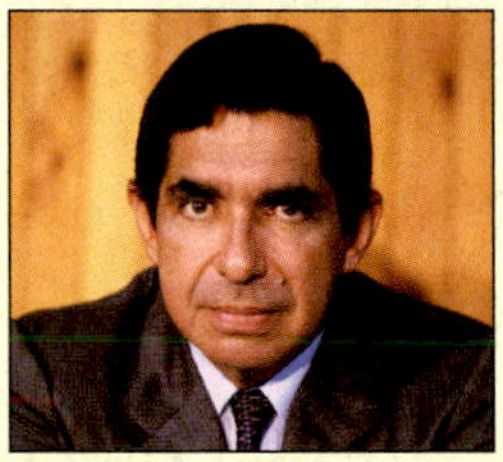

Óscar Arias recibió el Premio Nobel de la Paz en 1987.

Virginia Occidental *West Virginia* mestizo *of indigenous and white parentage* ascendencia *descent* nadadora *swimmer* ejército *army* gastos *expenditures* invertir *to invest* cuartel *barracks*

Mercado Central en San José

Vista del volcán Arenal

Edificio Metálico en San José

Basílica de Nuestra Señora de los Ángeles en Cartago

recursos

WB	VM	vhlcentral.com
pp. 121–122	pp. 49–50	Lección 10

¡Increíble pero cierto!

Costa Rica no tiene ejército°. Sin gastos° militares, el gobierno puede invertir° más dinero en la educación y las artes. En la foto aparece el Museo Nacional de Costa Rica, antiguo cuartel° del ejército.

TEACHING OPTIONS

Heritage Speakers Invite students of Costa Rican background or whose families are from Central America to share information about the national nicknames that Central Americans use for each other. Costa Ricans are called **ticos**, Nicaraguans are referred to as **nicas**, and Guatemalans are known as **chapines**.

Variación léxica Tell students that if they visit Costa Rica, they may hear a few interesting colloquialisms. For example, **pulpería** is the word for *corner grocery store*. A gas station is called a **bomba**, literally *pump*. A city block is called **cien metros**, literally *a hundred meters*.

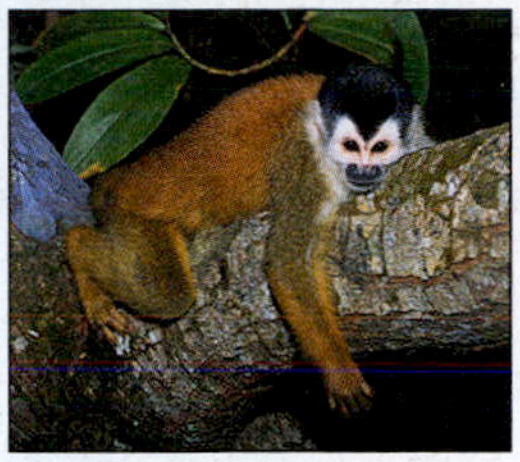

Lugares • Los parques nacionales

El sistema de parques nacionales de Costa Rica ocupa aproximadamente el 12% de su territorio y fue establecido° para la protección de su biodiversidad. En los parques, los ecoturistas pueden admirar montañas, cataratas° y una gran variedad de plantas exóticas. Algunos ofrecen también la oportunidad de ver quetzales°, monos°, jaguares, armadillos y mariposas° en su hábitat natural.

Economía • Las plantaciones de café

Costa Rica fue el primer país centroamericano en desarrollar° la industria del café. En el siglo° XIX, los costarricenses empezaron a exportar esta semilla a Inglaterra°, lo que significó una contribución importante a la economía de la nación. Actualmente, más de 50.000 costarricenses trabajan en el cultivo del café. Este producto representa cerca del 15% de sus exportaciones anuales.

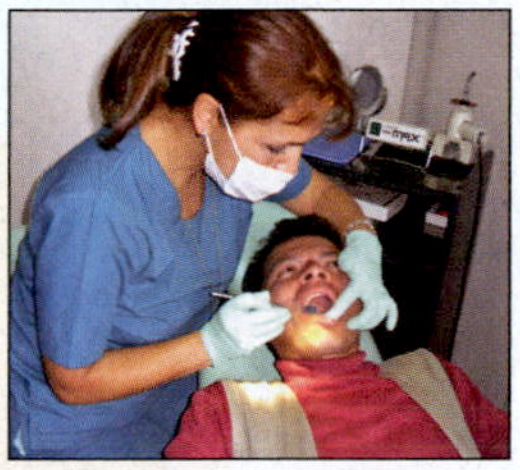

Sociedad • Una nación progresista

Costa Rica es un país progresista. Tiene un nivel de alfabetización° del 96%, uno de los más altos de Latinoamérica. En 1871, esta nación centroamericana abolió la pena de muerte° y en 1948 eliminó el ejército e hizo obligatoria y gratuita° la educación para todos sus ciudadanos.

Parque Morazán en San José

¿Qué aprendiste? Contesta las preguntas con oraciones completas.

1. ¿Cómo se llama la capital de Costa Rica?
   La capital de Costa Rica se llama San José.
2. ¿Quién es Claudia Poll?
   Claudia Poll es una nadadora olímpica.
3. ¿Qué porcentaje del territorio de Costa Rica ocupan los parques nacionales?
   Los parques nacionales ocupan aproximadamente el 12% del territorio de Costa Rica.
4. ¿Para qué se establecieron los parques nacionales? Los parques nacionales se establecieron para proteger los ecosistemas de la región y su biodiversidad.
5. ¿Qué pueden ver los turistas en los parques nacionales? En los parques nacionales, los turistas pueden ver cataratas, montañas y muchas plantas exóticas.
6. ¿Cuántos costarricenses trabajan en las plantaciones de café hoy día?
   Más de 50.000 costarricenses trabajan en las plantaciones de café hoy día.
7. ¿Cuándo eliminó Costa Rica la pena de muerte?
   Costa Rica eliminó la pena de muerte en 1871.

Conexión Internet Investiga estos temas en **vhlcentral.com**.

Practice more at **vhlcentral.com**.

1. Busca información sobre Óscar Arias Sánchez. ¿Quién es? ¿Por qué se le considera (*is he considered*) un costarricense célebre?
2. Busca información sobre los artistas de Costa Rica. ¿Qué artista, escritor o cantante te interesa más? ¿Por qué?

establecido *established* cataratas *waterfalls* quetzales *type of tropical bird* monos *monkeys* mariposas *butterflies* en desarrollar *to develop* siglo *century* Inglaterra *England* nivel de alfabetización *literacy rate* pena de muerte *death penalty* gratuita *free*

Los parques nacionales Costa Rica's system of national parks was begun in the 1960s. With the addition of buffer zones in which some logging and farming are allowed, the percentage of Costa Rica's territory protected by environmental legislation rose to 27%.

Las plantaciones de café Invite students to prepare a coffee-tasting session, where they sample the coffees of Central America. You may wish to compare them to South American or African coffees as well. Teach vocabulary to describe the flavors: **rico, amargo, fuerte,** and so forth.

Una nación progresista Because of its mild climate (in terms of weather *and* politics), Costa Rica has become a major destination for retired and expatriate North Americans. Survey students to see how many have visited Costa Rica already, and how many know of friends or family who have visited or live there.

Conexión Internet Students will find supporting Internet activities and links at **vhlcentral.com**.

Teaching Tip You may want to wrap up this section by playing the ***Panorama cultural*** video footage for this lesson.

TEACHING OPTIONS

Worth Noting Costa Rica has three types of lands protected by ecological legislation: **parques nacionales, refugios silvestres,** and **reservas biológicas**. Costa Rica's most famous protected area is the **Reserva Biológica Bosque Nuboso Monteverde** (Monteverde Cloud Forest Biological Reserve), where over 400 different species of birds have been recorded. The town of Monteverde was founded in 1950 by Quakers from the United States, who began dairy farming and cheese-making there. In order to protect the watershed, the settlers decided to preserve about a third of their property as a biological reserve. In 1972 this area more than doubled, and then became the **Reserva Biológica**. Today Monteverde still has a cheese factory (**La Fábrica de Quesos Monteverde**) and its cheeses are sold throughout the country.

Section Goal

In **Panorama**, students will read about the geography, history, and culture of Nicaragua.

Instructional Resources
Supersite: Video (***Panorama cultural***); Resources (Scripts, Translations, Digital Image Bank, Answer Keys)
WebSAM
Workbook, pp. 123–124
Video Manual, pp. 51–52

Teaching Tips

- Use the **Lección 10 Panorama** digital images to assist with this presentation.
- Have students look at the map of Nicaragua and talk about the geographical features of the country. Point out the concentration of cities along the country's Pacific Coast, and note the sparse settlement in the eastern part of the country and along the Caribbean coast. Tell students that, nearly 100 years after the construction of the Panama Canal, a proposal has been made for a new interoceanic canal, utilizing the San Juan River and Lake Nicaragua.

El país en cifras Tell students that Nicaragua's national slogan is **"El país de lagos y volcanes."** After students read about the capital, ask: **Aproximadamente, ¿qué porcentaje de nicaragüenses vive en Managua? (el 15%)** Tell students that many Nicaraguans have chosen to live in the capital in part due to devastation from war and natural disasters, such as Hurricane Mitch in 1998, and earthquakes and volcanic eruptions in 1999.

¡Increíble pero cierto! **Concepción** is considered an active volcano even though its last major eruption occurred in 1957. Pressure building up in the volcano caused a 6.2 earthquake in 2005.

Nicaragua

NATIONAL STANDARDS connections cultures

El país en cifras

- **Área:** 129.494 km² (49.998 millas²), *aproximadamente el área de Nueva York. Nicaragua es el país más grande de Centroamérica. Su terreno es muy variado e incluye bosques tropicales, montañas, sabanas° y marismas°, además de unos 40 volcanes.*
- **Población:** 5.848.000
- **Capital:** Managua—934.000 *Managua está en una región de una notable inestabilidad geográfica, con muchos volcanes y terremotos°. En décadas recientes, los nicaragüenses han decidido° que no vale la pena° construir rascacielos° porque no resisten los terremotos.*
- **Ciudades principales:** León, Masaya, Granada
- **Moneda:** córdoba
- **Idiomas:** español (oficial); lenguas indígenas y criollas (oficiales); inglés

Bandera de Nicaragua

Nicaragüenses célebres

- **Rubén Darío,** poeta (1867–1916)
- **Violeta Barrios de Chamorro,** política y expresidenta (1929–)
- **Daniel Ortega,** político y presidente (1945–)
- **Gioconda Belli,** poeta (1948–)
- **Luis Enrique,** cantante y compositor (1962–)

sabanas *grasslands* marismas *marshes* terremotos *earthquakes* han decidido *have decided* no vale la pena *it's not worthwhile* rascacielos *skyscrapers* agua dulce *fresh water* Surgió *Emerged* maravillas *wonders*

Iglesia en León

Teatro Nacional Rubén Darío en Managua

Calle en Granada

Violeta Barrios de Chamorro

recursos
WB pp. 123–124 | VM pp. 51–52 | vhlcentral.com Lección 10

¡Increíble pero cierto!

Ometepe, que en náhuatl significa "dos montañas", es la isla más grande del mundo en un lago de agua dulce°. Surgió° en el lago de Nicaragua por la actividad de los volcanes Maderas y Concepción. Por su valor natural y arqueológico, fue nominada para las siete nuevas maravillas° del mundo en 2009.

TEACHING OPTIONS

Worth Noting Managua is a city that has been destroyed and rebuilt multiple times due to wars and natural disasters. This has contributed to the unusual method used for listing street addresses in this capital city. Many places do not have an address that includes an actual building number and street name. Instead, the address includes a reference to a local landmark, and its relationship to other permanent features of the landscape, such as Lake Managua. Here is a typical Managua address: **De la Clínica Don Bosco, 2 cuadras al norte, 3 al sur.**

Extra Practice Invite students to compare the romantic poetry of **Rubén Darío** to the contemporary work of **Ernesto Cardenal** and **Gioconda Belli.** Students can choose several poems to read aloud to the class, and then comment on differences in style and content.

Historia • Las huellas° de Acahualinca

La región de Managua se caracteriza por tener un gran número de sitios prehistóricos. Las huellas de Acahualinca son uno de los restos° más famosos y antiguos°. Se formaron hace más de 6.000 años, a orillas° del lago de Managua. Las huellas, tanto de humanos como de animales, se dirigen° hacia una misma dirección, hacia el lago.

Artes • Ernesto Cardenal (1925–)

Ernesto Cardenal, poeta, escultor y sacerdote° católico, es uno de los escritores más famosos de Nicaragua, país conocido° por sus grandes poetas. Ha escrito° más de 35 libros y es considerado uno de los principales autores de Latinoamérica. Desde joven creyó en el poder de la poesía para mejorar la sociedad y trabajó por establecer la igualdad° y la justicia en su país. En los años 60, Cardenal estableció la comunidad artística del archipiélago de Solentiname en el lago de Nicaragua. Fue ministro de cultura del país desde 1979 hasta 1988 y participó en la fundación de Casa de los Tres Mundos, una organización creada para el intercambio cultural internacional.

Naturaleza • El lago de Nicaragua

El lago de Nicaragua, con un área de más de 8.000 km^2 (3.100 $millas^2$), es el lago más grande de Centroamérica. Tiene más de 400 islas e islotes° de origen volcánico, entre ellas la isla Zapatera. Allí se han encontrado° numerosos objetos de cerámica y estatuas prehispánicos. Se cree que la isla era un centro ceremonial indígena.

¿Qué aprendiste? Responde a cada pregunta con una oración completa.

1. ¿Por qué no hay muchos rascacielos en Managua?
   No hay muchos rascacielos en Managua porque no resisten los terremotos.
2. Nombra dos poetas de Nicaragua.
   Rubén Darío y Gioconda Belli/Ernesto Cardenal son dos poetas de Nicaragua.
3. Qué significa Ometepe en náhuatl?
   Ometepe significa "dos montañas" en náhuatl.
4. ¿Cuándo y dónde se formaron las huellas de Acahualinca?
   Las huellas de Acahualinca se formaron hace más de 6.000 años, a orillas del lago de Managua.
5. ¿Por qué es famoso el archipiélago de Solentiname?
   El archipiélago de Solentiname es famoso porque es el sitio de la comunidad artística establecida por Cardenal.
6. ¿Qué cree Ernesto Cardenal acerca de la poesía?
   Cardenal cree que la poesía puede mejorar la sociedad.
7. ¿Cómo se formaron las islas del lago de Nicaragua?
   Las islas se formaron por erupciones volcánicas.
8. ¿Qué hay de interés arqueológico en la isla Zapatera?
   En la isla Zapatera hay muchos objetos de cerámica y estatuas prehispánicos./Se cree que la isla era un centro ceremonial indígena.

Conexión Internet Investiga estos temas en **vhlcentral.com.**

1. ¿Dónde se habla inglés en Nicaragua y por qué?
2. ¿Qué información hay ahora sobre la economía y/o los derechos humanos en Nicaragua?

Practice more at **vhlcentral.com.**

huellas *footprints* **restos** *remains* **antiguos** *ancient* **orillas** *shores* **se dirigen** *are headed* **sacerdote** *priest* **conocido** *known* **Ha escrito** *He has written* **igualdad** *equality* **islotes** *islets* **se han encontrado** *have been found*

Las huellas de Acahualinca
The **huellas de Acahualinca** consist of the prints of bison, otter, deer, lizards, and birds—as well as humans. The prints were preserved in soft mud, then covered with volcanic ash, which became petrified.

Ernesto Cardenal After completing undergraduate courses in Nicaragua, **Ernesto Cardenal** studied in Mexico and in the United States, where he worked with the religious poet Thomas Merton at the Trappist seminary in Kentucky. He later studied theology in Colombia and was ordained in Nicaragua in 1965. Shortly after that, **Cardenal** founded the faith-based community of artists on the Solentiname Islands.

El lago de Nicaragua
Environmental groups in Nicaragua have been concerned about the recent introduction of a variety of **tilapia** into Lake Nicaragua. Although **tilapia** are native to the lake, this variety is a more prolific species. Environmentalists are concerned that the Nicaraguan-Norwegian joint venture responsible for this initiative has not done an adequate environmental impact study, and that the delicate and unique ecology of the lake may be negatively impacted.

Conexión Internet Students will find supporting Internet activities and links at **vhlcentral.com**.

Teaching Tip You may want to wrap up this section by playing the ***Panorama cultural*** video footage for this lesson.

TEACHING OPTIONS

Worth Noting On July 19, 1979, the **FSLN** (**Frente Sandinista de Liberación Nacional**), known as the **Sandinistas**, came to power in Nicaragua after winning a revolutionary struggle against the dictatorship of **Anastasio Somoza**. The **Sandinistas** began a program of economic and social reform that threatened the power of Nicaragua's traditional elite, leading to a civil war known as the **Contra** war. The United States became enmeshed in this conflict, illegally providing funding and arms to the **Contras**, who fought to oust the **Sandinistas**. The **Sandinistas** were voted out in 1990 but returned to power in the 2006 elections. President Daniel Ortega was reelected in 2011.

Instructional Resources
Supersite: Audio (Textbook & Lab MP3s); Testing Program (Tests, MP3s)
WebSAM
Lab Manual, p. 60

El cuerpo

la boca	*mouth*
el brazo	*arm*
la cabeza	*head*
el corazón	*heart*
el cuello	*neck*
el cuerpo	*body*
el dedo	*finger*
el dedo del pie	*toe*
el estómago	*stomach*
la garganta	*throat*
el hueso	*bone*
la nariz	*nose*
el oído	*(sense of) hearing; inner ear*
el ojo	*eye*
la oreja	*(outer) ear*
el pie	*foot*
la pierna	*leg*
la rodilla	*knee*
el tobillo	*ankle*

La salud

el accidente	*accident*
el antibiótico	*antibiotic*
la aspirina	*aspirin*
la clínica	*clinic*
el consultorio	*doctor's office*
el/la dentista	*dentist*
el/la doctor(a)	*doctor*
el dolor (de cabeza)	*(head)ache; pain*
el/la enfermero/a	*nurse*
el examen médico	*physical exam*
la farmacia	*pharmacy*
la gripe	*flu*
el hospital	*hospital*
la infección	*infection*
el medicamento	*medication*
la medicina	*medicine*
la operación	*operation*
el/la paciente	*patient*
la pastilla	*pill*
la radiografía	*X-ray*
la receta	*prescription*
el resfriado	*cold (illness)*
la sala de emergencia(s)	*emergency room*
la salud	*health*
el síntoma	*symptom*
la tos	*cough*

Verbos

caerse	*to fall (down)*
dañar	*to damage; to break down*
darse con	*to bump into; to run into*
doler (o:ue)	*to hurt*
enfermarse	*to get sick*
estar enfermo/a	*to be sick*
estornudar	*to sneeze*
lastimarse (el pie)	*to injure (one's foot)*
olvidar	*to forget*
poner una inyección	*to give an injection*
prohibir	*to prohibit*
recetar	*to prescribe*
romper	*to break*
romperse (la pierna)	*to break (one's leg)*
sacar(se) un diente	*to have a tooth removed*
ser alérgico/a (a)	*to be allergic (to)*
sufrir una enfermedad	*to suffer an illness*
tener dolor (*m.*)	*to have pain*
tener fiebre (*f.*)	*to have a fever*
tomar la temperatura	*to take someone's temperature*
torcerse (o:ue) (el tobillo)	*to sprain (one's ankle)*
toser	*to cough*

Adjetivos

congestionado/a	*congested*
embarazada	*pregnant*
grave	*grave; serious*
mareado/a	*dizzy; nauseated*
médico/a	*medical*
saludable	*healthy*
sano/a	*healthy*

Adverbios

a menudo	*often*
a tiempo	*on time*
a veces	*sometimes*
además (de)	*furthermore; besides*
apenas	*hardly; scarcely*
así	*like this; so*
bastante	*enough; rather*
casi	*almost*
con frecuencia	*frequently*
de niño/a	*as a child*
de vez en cuando	*from time to time*
despacio	*slowly*
menos	*less*
muchas veces	*a lot; many times*
poco	*little*
por lo menos	*at least*
pronto	*soon*
rápido	*quickly*
todos los días	*every day*

Conjunción

mientras	*while*

Expresiones útiles	*See page 313.*

Vocabulary Tools

recursos

LM p. 60 | vhlcentral.com Lección 10

La tecnología 11

Communicative Goals

You will learn how to:

- **Talk about using technology and electronics**
- **Use common expressions on the telephone**
- **Talk about car trouble**

A PRIMERA VISTA

- **¿Qué hacen las chicas?**
- **¿Crees que usan sus teléfonos con frecuencia?**
- **¿Son unas chicas saludables?**
- **¿Qué partes del cuerpo se ven en la foto?**

Lesson Goals

In **Lección 11**, students will be introduced to the following:

- terms related to technology, electronics, and the Internet
- terms related to cars and their accessories
- social networks in Spanish-speaking countries
- text messaging
- familiar (**tú**) commands
- uses of **por** and **para**
- reciprocal reflexive verbs
- stressed possessive adjectives and pronouns
- recognizing borrowed words
- a video about technology in Peru
- cultural, geographic, and historical information about Argentina and Uruguay

A primera vista Here are some additional questions you can ask: **¿Te gustan los teléfonos celulares? ¿Para qué usas tu teléfono celular? ¿Cómo te comunicas con tus amigos? ¿Por chat, por teléfono o se escriben mensajes electrónicos?**

Teaching Tip Look for these icons for additional communicative practice:

→●←	Interpretive communication
←●→	Presentational communication
●↔●	Interpersonal communication

INSTRUCTIONAL RESOURCES

Supersite (vhlcentral.com)
Video: ***Fotonovela, Flash cultura, Panorama cultural***
Audio: Textbook and Lab MP3 Files
Activity Pack: Information Gap Activities, games, additional activity handouts
Resources: SAM Answer Key, Scripts, Translations, **Vocabulario adicional**, sample lesson plan, Grammar Presentation Slides, Digital Image Bank
Testing Program: Quizzes, Tests, Exams, MP3s
Student Activities Manual: Workbook/Video Manual/Lab Manual
WebSAM (online Student Activities Manual)

Section Goals

In **Contextos**, students will learn and practice:
- vocabulary related to technology, electronics, and the Internet
- terms related to cars and their accessories

Instructional Resources
Supersite: Audio (Textbook and Lab MP3 Files); Resources (Digital Image Bank, **Vocabulario adicional**, Activity Pack, Scripts, Answer Keys); Testing Program (Quizzes)
WebSAM
Workbook, pp. 125–126
Lab Manual, p. 61

Teaching Tips

- To engage students in a conversation, ask them about electronic items they have. Ex: **¿Quiénes tienen cámara digital? ¿Quiénes tienen teléfono celular? ¿Cuántas veces al día lo usas? ¿Para qué lo usas?**
- Use the **Lección 11 Contextos** digital images to assist with this presentation.
- As students look at the illustration, ask questions to elicit computer vocabulary and ask them about their computer use. Ex: **¿Es portátil la computadora? ¿Qué se usa para mover el cursor? ¿Quiénes navegan en la red? ¿Cuál es tu sitio web favorito?**
- Give students true/false statements about electronic devices and have them react. Ex: **El control remoto se usa con el televisor. (Cierto.)**
- Explain to students that Spanish speakers sometimes adopt and use English words in place of their Spanish counterparts. This is especially true with words having to do with technology. For example, in Argentina, Chile, and Puerto Rico, **el mouse** is heard more frequently than **el ratón**. **El email** is also often used instead of **el correo electrónico** by many Spanish speakers.

La tecnología

Más vocabulario

la cámara digital/de video	*digital/video camera*
el canal	*(TV) channel*
el cargador	*charger*
el correo de voz	*voice mail*
el estéreo	*stereo*
el reproductor de CD	*CD player*
la aplicación	*app*
el archivo	*file*
la arroba	*@ symbol*
el blog	*blog*
el buscador	*browser*
la conexión inalámbrica	*wireless connection*
la dirección electrónica	*e-mail address*
Internet	*Internet*
el mensaje de texto	*text message*
la página principal	*home page*
el programa de computación	*software*
la red	*network; Web*
el sitio web	*website*
apagar	*to turn off*
borrar	*to erase*
chatear	*to chat*
descargar	*to download*
escanear	*to scan*
funcionar	*to work*
grabar	*to record*
guardar	*to save*
imprimir	*to print*
llamar	*to call*
navegar (en Internet)	*to surf (the Internet)*
poner, prender	*to turn on*
sonar (o:ue)	*to ring*
descompuesto/a	*not working; out of order*
lento/a	*slow*
lleno/a	*full*

Variación léxica

computadora ↔ ordenador (*Esp.*), computador (*Col.*)
descargar ↔ bajar (*Arg., Col., Esp., Ven.*)

recursos
WB pp. 125–126 | LM p. 61 | vhlcentral.com Lección 11

TEACHING OPTIONS

Large Group Ask students to write down a list of six electronic devices they have or use frequently. If possible, have them specify the brand name. Then have students circulate around the room and ask others if they have the same items. If someone answers affirmatively, the student should get the person's signature (**Firma aquí, por favor**). Students should try to get a different signature for each item.

Game Add a visual aspect to this vocabulary practice. Play **Concentración**. On eight cards, write names of electronic items. On another eight cards, draw or paste a picture that matches each name. Place the cards facedown in four rows of four. In pairs, students select two cards. If the cards match, the pair keeps them. If the cards do not match, students replace them in their original position. The pair with the most cards at the end wins.

Práctica

1 Escuchar Escucha la conversación entre dos amigas. Después completa las oraciones.

1. María y Ana están en __b__.
   a. una tienda b. un cibercafé c. un restaurante
2. A María le encantan __b__.
   a. los celulares b. las cámaras digitales c. los cibercafés
3. Ana y María __c__ las fotos.
   a. escanean b. borran c. imprimen
4. María quiere tomar un café y __c__.
   a. poner la computadora b. sacar fotos digitales
   c. navegar en Internet
5. Ana paga por el café y __a__.
   a. el uso de Internet b. la impresora c. la cámara

2 ¿Cierto o falso? Escucha las oraciones e indica si lo que dice cada una es **cierto** o **falso**, según el dibujo.

1. cierto
2. falso
3. falso
4. cierto
5. cierto
6. falso
7. cierto
8. falso

3 Oraciones Escribe oraciones usando estos elementos. Usa el pretérito y añade las palabras necesarias.

1. yo / descargar / fotos / Internet
   Yo descargué las fotos digitales por Internet.
2. tú / apagar / televisor / diez / noche
   Tú apagaste el televisor a las diez de la noche.
3. Daniel y su esposa / comprar / computadora portátil / ayer
   Daniel y su esposa compraron una computadora portátil ayer.
4. Sara y yo / ir / cibercafé / para / navegar en Internet
   Sara y yo fuimos al cibercafé para navegar en Internet.
5. Jaime / decidir / comprar / reproductor de MP3
   Jaime decidió comprar un reproductor de MP3.
6. teléfono celular / sonar / pero / yo / no contestar
   El teléfono celular sonó, pero yo no contesté.

4 Preguntas Mira el dibujo y contesta las preguntas. Answers will vary.

1. ¿Qué tipo de café es?
2. ¿Cuántas impresoras hay? ¿Cuántos ratones?
3. ¿Por qué vinieron estas personas al café?
4. ¿Qué hace el camarero?
5. ¿Qué hace la mujer en la computadora? ¿Y el hombre?
6. ¿Qué máquinas están cerca del televisor?
7. ¿Dónde hay un cibercafé en tu comunidad?
8. ¿Por qué puedes tú necesitar un cibercafé?

TEACHING OPTIONS

Pairs Have pairs of students role-play one of these situations in a cybercafé. 1. An irate customer claims to have been overcharged for brief Internet use. The employee, who insists on being paid the full amount, claims that the customer spent quite a bit of time online. 2. A customer has been waiting over an hour to use a computer and must ask another customer to log off and give him or her a chance. The second customer becomes annoyed at the request and the two must sort it out.

Heritage Speakers Ask heritage speakers to describe their experiences with Spanish-language Web applications, such as e-mail, instant messenger, or websites. Do they or their families regularly visit Spanish-language websites? Which ones?

1 Teaching Tip To simplify, have students read through the items before listening to the audio.

1 Script ANA: ¿María? ¿Qué haces aquí en el cibercafé? ¿No tienes Internet en casa? MARÍA: Pues, sí, pero la computadora está descompuesta. Tengo que esperar unos días más. A: Te entiendo. Me pasó lo mismo con la computadora portátil hace poco. Todavía no funciona bien ... por eso vine aquí. M: ¿Recibiste algún mensaje interesante? A: Sí. Mi hijo está de vacaciones con unos amigos en Argentina. Tiene una cámara digital y me mandó unas fotos digitales. M: ¡Qué bien! Me encantan las cámaras digitales. Normalmente imprimimos las fotos con nuestra impresora y no tenemos que ir a ninguna tienda. Es muy conveniente. *Script continues on page 344.*

2 Teaching Tip To challenge students, have them provide the correct information.

2 Script 1. Hay dos personas navegando en Internet. 2. El camarero está hablando por su teléfono celular. 3. Dos señoras están usando la impresora. 4. En la pantalla del televisor se puede ver un partido de fútbol. 5. Un hombre habla por teléfono mientras navega en la red. 6. Hay cuatro computadoras portátiles en el cibercafé. 7. Hay dos discos compactos encima de una mesa. 8. El cibercafé tiene impresora pero no tiene reproductor de DVD. *Textbook MP3s*

3 Expansion Have students create three dehydrated sentences for a partner to complete.

4 Teaching Tips
- For item 7, if there aren't any cybercafés in the community, ask students if they think one is needed and why.
- For item 8, survey the class for overall trends.

1 Script (continued)
A: Claro que sí. También imprimo fotos, pero no voy a imprimirlas ahora. M: Ahí está mi café. Voy a navegar en Internet mientras tomo mi cafecito. A: Bueno. Tengo que irme. Voy a pagar por el café y el uso de Internet. ¿No es muy caro, verdad? M: Para nada, es muy barato. Hasta luego. A: Chau. Nos vemos.
Textbook MP3s

Teaching Tips

- Using cognate vocabulary, ask students about cars. Ex: **¿Quiénes tienen carro? ¿Qué tipo de carro es? ¿Cuántas veces al mes tienes que llenar el tanque? ¿Cuánto cuesta la gasolina ahora?**
- Use the **Lección 11 Contextos** digital images to assist with this vocabulary presentation.
- Have students refer to the illustration on this page as you give true/false statements. Ex: **Un mecánico limpia el parabrisas. (Falso.)**

5 Teaching Tip Before beginning the activity, ask several brief yes/no questions to test comprehension. Ex: **¿Sí o no? ¿Se usa el baúl para llenar el tanque? (No.)**

5 Expansion Have students create three similar sentence starters for a partner to complete. Write some on the board and have the class complete them.

6 Expansion
Ask groups to discuss car troubles they have had. Possible subjects: a visit to the mechanic, a car accident, getting a speeding ticket, etc. Write helpful vocabulary on the board. Ex: **ponerle una multa, exceder la velocidad máxima**. Have each group pick the strangest or funniest story to share with the class.

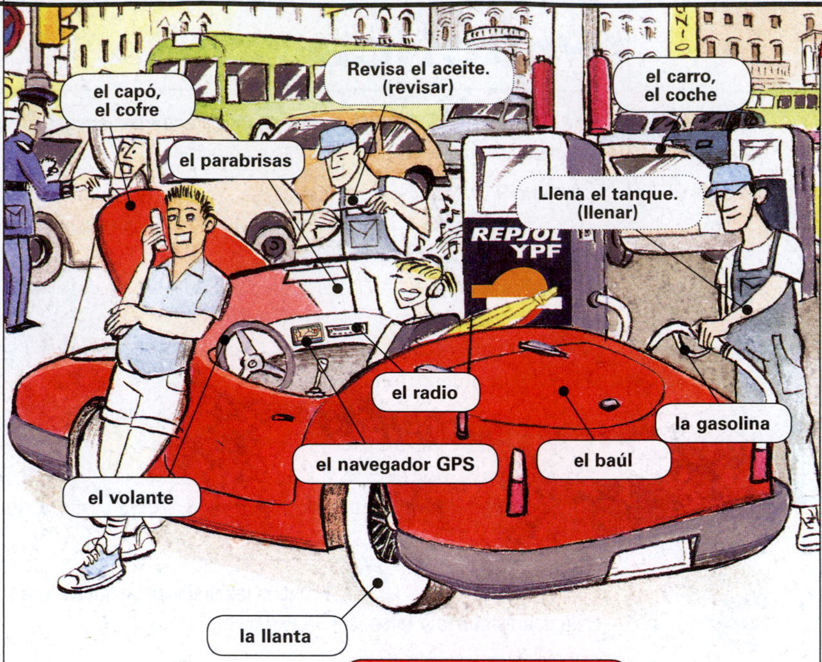

En la gasolinera

Más vocabulario

la autopista	*highway*
la calle	*street*
la carretera	*highway; (main) road*
la circulación, el tráfico	*traffic*
el garaje, el taller (mecánico)	*garage; (mechanic's) repair shop*
la licencia de conducir	*driver's license*
el/la mecánico/a	*mechanic*
la policía	*police (force)*
la velocidad máxima	*speed limit*
arrancar	*to start*
arreglar	*to fix; to arrange*
bajar(se) de	*to get off of/out of (a vehicle)*
conducir, manejar	*to drive*
estacionar	*to park*
parar	*to stop*
subir(se) a	*to get on/into (a vehicle)*

5 Completar Completa estas oraciones con las palabras correctas.

1. Para poder conducir legalmente, necesitas... una licencia de conducir.
2. Puedes poner las maletas en... el baúl.
3. Si tu carro no funciona, debes llevarlo a... un mecánico/taller/garaje.
4. Para llenar el tanque de tu coche, necesitas ir a... la gasolinera.
5. Antes de un viaje largo, es importante revisar... el aceite.
6. Otra palabra para autopista es... carretera.
7. Mientras hablas por teléfono celular, no es buena idea... manejar/conducir.
8. Otra palabra para coche es... carro.

¡LENGUA VIVA!
Aunque **carro** es el término que se usa en la mayoría de países hispanos, no es el único. En España, por ejemplo, se dice **coche**, y en Argentina, Chile y Uruguay se dice **auto**.

6 Conversación Completa la conversación con las palabras de la lista.

el aceite	la gasolina	llenar	el parabrisas	el taller
el baúl	las llantas	manejar	revisar	el volante

EMPLEADO Bienvenido al (1) ___taller___ mecánico *Óscar*. ¿En qué le puedo servir?
JUAN Buenos días. Quiero (2) ___llenar___ el tanque y revisar (3) ___el aceite___, por favor.
EMPLEADO Con mucho gusto. Si quiere, también le limpio (4) ___el parabrisas___.
JUAN Sí, gracias. Está un poquito sucio. La próxima semana tengo que (5) ___manejar___ hasta Buenos Aires. ¿Puede cambiar (6) ___las llantas___? Están gastadas (*worn*).
EMPLEADO Claro que sí, pero voy a tardar (*it will take me*) un par de horas.
JUAN Mejor regreso mañana. Ahora no tengo tiempo. ¿Cuánto le debo por (7) ___la gasolina___?
EMPLEADO Sesenta pesos. Y veinticinco por (8) ___revisar___ y cambiar el aceite.

Practice more at **vhlcentral.com**.

CONSULTA
For more information about **Buenos Aires**, see **Panorama**, p. 370.

TEACHING OPTIONS

TPR Draw a car on the board. Be sure to include identifiable parts (windshield, steering wheel, etc.). Make sticky notes that contain the Spanish names for these items. Have students place the notes on the corresponding parts of the car.

Variación léxica Ask students if they can explain why a trunk is called **maletera** in Peru (it is where one puts the **maletas**) or a **cajuela** in Mexico (it is related to the words **caja** and **cajón**).

TPR Divide the class into small groups. Have students take turns miming actions involving technology or parts of a car. The other group members should guess the object being used. Ex: A student mimes clicking a mouse. (**el ratón**)

Heritage Speakers Ask heritage speakers to describe car trends in their families' countries of origin. What brands are available? What size models are most popular?

Comunicación

7 **Preguntas** Trabajen en parejas y túrnense para contestar estas preguntas. Después compartan sus respuestas con la clase. Answers will vary.

1. a. ¿Tienes un teléfono celular? ¿Para qué lo usas?
   b. ¿Qué utilizas más: el teléfono o el correo electrónico? ¿Por qué?
   c. En tu opinión, ¿cuáles son las ventajas (*advantages*) y desventajas de los diferentes modos de comunicación?
2. a. ¿Con qué frecuencia usas la computadora?
   b. ¿Para qué usas Internet?
   c. ¿Tienes tu propio blog? ¿Cómo es?
3. a. ¿Miras la televisión con frecuencia? ¿Qué programas ves?
   b. ¿Dónde miras tus programas favoritos, en la tele o en la computadora?
   c. ¿Ves películas en la computadora? ¿Cuál es tu película favorita de todos los tiempos (*of all time*)?
   d. ¿A través de (*By*) qué medio escuchas música? ¿Radio, estéreo, reproductor de MP3 o computadora?
4. a. ¿Tienes licencia de conducir?
   b. ¿Tienes carro? Descríbelo.

NOTA CULTURAL

Algunos sitios web utilizan códigos para identificar su país de origen. Éstos son los códigos para algunos países hispanohablantes:

Argentina	.ar
Colombia	.co
España	.es
México	.mx
Venezuela	.ve

8 **Postal** En parejas, lean la tarjeta postal. Después contesten las preguntas. Answers will vary.

19 julio de 1979

Hola, Paco:

¡Saludos! Estamos de viaje por unas semanas. La Costa del Sol es muy bonita. No hemos encontrado (*we haven't found*) a tus amigos porque nunca están en casa cuando llamamos. El teléfono suena y suena y nadie contesta. Vamos a seguir llamando.

Sacamos muchas fotos muy divertidas. Cuando regresemos y las revelemos (*get them developed*), te las voy a enseñar. Las playas son preciosas. Hasta ahora el único problema fue que la oficina en la cual reservamos un carro perdió nuestros papeles y tuvimos que esperar mucho tiempo.

También tuvimos un pequeño problema con el hotel. La agencia de viajes nos reservó una habitación en un hotel que está muy lejos de todo. No podemos cambiarla, pero no me importa mucho. A pesar de eso, estamos contentos.

Tu hermana, Gabriela

Francisco Jiménez
San Lorenzo 3250
Rosario, Argentina 2000

1. ¿Cuáles son los problemas que ocurren en el viaje de Gabriela?
2. Con la tecnología de hoy, ¿existen los mismos problemas cuando se viaja? ¿Por qué?
3. Hagan una comparación entre la tecnología de los años 70 y 80 y la de hoy.
4. Imaginen que la hija de Gabriela escribe un mensaje electrónico sobre el mismo tema con fecha de hoy. Escriban ese mensaje, incorporando la tecnología actual (teléfonos celulares, Internet, cámaras digitales, etc.). Inventen nuevos problemas.

7 Teaching Tip For item 2, if few or no students have their own blogs, ask them if they follow any and what they are about. Encourage them to seek out some blogs related to learning Spanish as a foreign language.

7 Expansion Write names of different communication devices on the board (Ex: **teléfono celular, computadora**). Then survey the class to find out how many people own or use these items. Analyze the trends of the class.

8 Teaching Tip Possible answers: **1. Gabriela no encuentra a los amigos de Paco porque nunca están en casa, tuvo que esperar mucho por el carro y su hotel estaba muy lejos de todo. 2. No existen los mismos problemas porque existen el correo de voz y los teléfonos celulares, se puede reservar un carro en Internet y se puede buscar información sobre un hotel en la red antes del viaje.**

8 Expansion Ask groups to write a postcard similar to the one in the activity, except that in theirs the problems encountered during the trip are a direct result of the existence of technology, not its absence.

Note: At this point you may want to present ***Vocabulario adicional: Más vocabulario para el carro y la tecnología*** from the Supersite.

TEACHING OPTIONS

Extra Practice For homework, have students do an Internet research project on technology and technology terminology in the Spanish-speaking world. Suggest possible topics and websites where students may look for information. Have students write out their reports and present them to the class.

Large Groups Stage a debate about the role of technology in today's world. Divide the class into two groups and assign each side a position. Propose this debate topic: **La tecnología: ¿beneficio o no?** Allow groups time to plan their arguments before staging the debate.

Section Goals

In **Fotonovela**, students will:

- receive comprehensible input from free-flowing discourse
- learn functional phrases that preview lesson grammatical structures

Instructional Resources
Supersite: Video (***Fotonovela***); Resources (Scripts, Translations, Answer Keys)
WebSAM
Video Manual, pp. 21–22

Video Recap: Lección 10
Before doing this **Fotonovela** section, review the previous episode with these questions: **1. ¿Qué estaba haciendo Jimena cuando empezó a sentirse mal? (Estaba estudiando con Elena.) 2. ¿Quién llevó a Jimena al médico? (Elena la llevó.) 3. ¿Cuáles eran los síntomas de Jimena? (Tosía, le dolía la garganta y estaba congestionada.) 4. ¿Qué le recetó el médico? (Algo / Una medicina para la garganta.)**

Video Synopsis **Miguel's** car has broken down again, and he has to take it to his friend **Jorge's** repair shop. In the meantime, **Maru** has bad luck with her computer. Their friends do their best to help them with their technological problems. **Miguel's** car is saved one last time, but **Maru** may not be so lucky with her computer.

Teaching Tips

- Have students predict the content of this episode based on the video stills only.
- Quickly review students' predictions and ask a few questions to guide them in summarizing this episode.

En el taller

El coche de Miguel está descompuesto y Maru tiene problemas con su computadora.

PERSONAJES

MIGUEL

JORGE

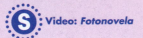

Video: *Fotonovela*

MIGUEL ¿Cómo lo ves?
JORGE Creo que puedo arreglarlo. ¿Me pasas la llave?

JORGE ¿Y dónde está Maru?
MIGUEL Acaba de enviarme un mensaje de texto: "Última noticia sobre la computadora portátil: todavía está descompuesta. Moni intenta arreglarla. Voy para allá".

JORGE ¿Está descompuesta tu computadora?
MIGUEL No, la mía no, la suya. Una amiga la está ayudando.
JORGE Un mal día para la tecnología, ¿no?

MIGUEL Ella está preparando un proyecto para ver si puede hacer sus prácticas profesionales en el Museo de Antropología.
JORGE ¿Y todo está en la computadora?
MIGUEL Y claro.

MARU Buenos días, Jorge.
JORGE ¡Qué gusto verte, Maru! ¿Cómo está la computadora?
MARU Mi amiga Mónica recuperó muchos archivos, pero muchos otros se borraron.

MARU Estamos en una triste situación. Yo necesito una computadora nueva, y Miguel necesita otro coche.
JORGE Y un televisor nuevo para mí, por favor.

TEACHING OPTIONS

Video Tips General suggestions for using video clips in the classroom can be found in the front matter of this Instructor's Annotated Edition.

En el taller Show the **En el taller** episode once without sound and have the class create a plot summary based on the visual cues. Then show the episode with sound and have the class make corrections and fill in any gaps in the plot summary.

MARU

7

MARU ¿Qué vamos a hacer, Miguel?

MIGUEL Tranquila, cariño. Por eso tenemos amigos como Jorge y Mónica. Nos ayudamos los unos a los otros.

8

JORGE ¿No te sientes afortunada, Maru? No te preocupes. Sube.

MIGUEL ¡Por fin!

MARU Gracias, Jorge. Eres el mejor mecánico de la ciudad.

9

MIGUEL ¿Cuánto te debo por el trabajo?

JORGE Hombre, no es nada. Guárdalo para el coche nuevo. Eso sí, recomiéndame con tus amigos.

MIGUEL Gracias, Jorge.

10

JORGE No manejes en carretera. Revisa el aceite cada 1.500 kilómetros y asegúrate de llenarle el tanque... No manejes con el cofre abierto. Nos vemos.

Expresiones útiles

Giving instructions to a friend

¿Me pasas la llave?
Can you pass me the wrench?
No lo manejes en carretera.
Don't drive it on the highway.
Revisa el aceite cada 1.500 kilómetros.
Check the oil every 1,500 kilometers.
Asegúrate de llenar el tanque.
Make sure to fill up the tank.
No manejes con el cofre abierto.
Don't drive with the hood open.
Recomiéndame con tus amigos.
Recommend me to your friends.

Taking a phone call

Aló./Bueno./Diga.
Hello.
¿Quién habla?/¿De parte de quién?
Who is speaking/calling?
Con él/ella habla.
Speaking.
¿Puedo dejar un recado?
May I leave a message?

Reassuring someone

Tranquilo/a, cariño.
Relax, sweetie.
Nos ayudamos los unos a los otros.
We help each other out.
No te preocupes.
Don't worry.

Additional vocabulary

entregar *to hand in*
el intento *attempt*
la noticia *news*
el proyecto *project*
recuperar *to recover*

recursos
VM pp. 21–22
vhlcentral.com Lección 11

Expresiones útiles Point out the phrases **No lo manejes, Revisa, Asegúrate, No manejes, Recomiéndame,** and **No te preocupes.** Explain that these are **tú** commands, a direct way of telling someone to do or not to do something. Then draw attention to the words **Nos ayudamos** and tell students that this is a reciprocal reflexive construction that expresses a shared action. Point out the words **la mía** and **la suya** in the caption of video still 3 and tell the class that these are examples of possessive pronouns. Tell students that they will learn more about these concepts in **Estructura**.

Teaching Tip Ask students to read the **Fotonovela** captions aloud in groups of three. Then have one or two groups role-play the dialogue for the class. Encourage them to ad-lib whenever possible.

Nota cultural **Prácticas profesionales** are similar to unpaid internships in the U.S. Normally, they are carried out as a requirement for a study program, in the form of a professional practicum or fieldwork.

TEACHING OPTIONS

Extra Practice Make a photocopy of the **Fotonovela** Videoscript (Supersite) and white out key words to create a master for a cloze activity. Hand out photocopies of the master to students and have them fill in the missing words as they watch the **En el taller** episode. You may have students share their answers in small groups and help each other fill in any gaps.

Pairs Write some phone call scenarios on the board. Ex: **1. Llamas a la casa de tu mejor amigo/a, pero no está. 2. Llamas a tu novio/a para contarle un problema que tienes.** Ask students to sit or stand back-to-back in pairs, and have them role-play the conversations, using phrases from **Expresiones útiles**. To simplify, you may want to have students brainstorm phrases for each situation. If nearly all students have cell phones, have them use phones as props for this activity.

¿Qué pasó?

1 **Seleccionar** Selecciona las respuestas que completan correctamente estas oraciones.

1. Jorge intenta arreglar __b__.
   a. la computadora de Maru b. el coche de Miguel c. el teléfono celular de Felipe
2. Maru dice que se borraron muchos __a__ de su computadora.
   a. archivos b. sitios web c. mensajes de texto
3. Jorge dice que necesita un __c__.
   a. navegador GPS b. reproductor de DVD c. televisor
4. Maru dice que Jorge es el mejor __a__.
   a. mecánico de la ciudad b. amigo del mundo c. compañero de la clase
5. Jorge le dice a Miguel que no maneje su coche en __c__.
   a. el tráfico b. el centro de la ciudad c. la carretera

2 **Identificar** Identifica quién puede decir estas oraciones.

1. Cómprate un coche nuevo y recomiéndame con tus amigos. Jorge
2. El mensaje de texto de Maru dice que su computadora todavía está descompuesta. Miguel
3. Mi amiga Mónica me ayudó a recuperar muchos archivos, pero necesito una computadora nueva. Maru
4. No conduzcas con el cofre abierto y recuerda que el tanque debe estar lleno. Jorge
5. Muchos de los archivos de mi computadora se borraron. Maru

MARU

MIGUEL

JORGE

3 **Problema mecánico** Trabajen en parejas para representar los papeles de un(a) mecánico/a y un(a) cliente/a que está llamando al taller porque su carro está descompuesto. Usen las instrucciones como guía. Answers will vary.

Mecánico/a	Cliente/a
Contesta el teléfono con un saludo y el nombre del taller.	→ Saluda y explica que tu carro está descompuesto.
Pregunta qué tipo de problema tiene exactamente.	→ Explica que tu carro no arranca cuando hace frío.
Di que debe traer el carro al taller.	→ Pregunta cuándo puedes llevarlo.
Ofrece una hora para revisar el carro.	→ Acepta la hora que ofrece el/la mecánico/a.

Ahora cambien los papeles y representen otra conversación. Ustedes son un(a) técnico/a y un(a) cliente/a. Usen estas ideas:

el celular no guarda mensajes	la impresora imprime muy lentamente
la computadora no descarga fotos	el reproductor de DVD está descompuesto

Practice more at **vhlcentral.com**.

1 Teaching Tip Read the activity items to the class as true/false statements. Ask students to correct the false statements. Ex: **Jorge intenta arreglar el coche de Miguel. (Cierto.)**

2 Expansion Give students these sentences as items 6–8: **6. No me tienes que pagar nada. (Jorge) 7. No sé si voy a poder entregar el proyecto. (Maru) 8. Hoy me siento afortunado porque me ayudó mi amigo. (Miguel)**

3 Possible Conversation
E1: ¿Bueno? Taller Mendoza.
E2: Buenos días. Tengo un problema con mi carro.
E1: ¿Qué pasó? ¿Cuál es el problema exactamente?
E2: El carro no arranca cuando hace frío.
E1: Tengo que revisarlo. ¿Puede venir al taller?
E2: Creo que sí. ¿A qué hora debo pasar?
E1: Tengo tiempo esta tarde a las tres.
E2: Muy bien. Es una buena hora para mí también.
E1: Nos vemos a las tres. Gracias, y hasta esta tarde.
E2: Hasta luego.

3 Teaching Tip For the second conversation, have students brainstorm a list of phrases for their roles. Encourage them to follow a similar outline to that of the first conversation.

The Affective Dimension Talking on the phone can be more stressful than talking with someone in person because one does not see the other person's facial expressions or gestures. Remind students that they do not need to understand every word, and that they should ask the other person to repeat if necessary.

TEACHING OPTIONS

Extra Practice Have each student choose one of the **Fotonovela** characters and prepare a five-sentence summary of the day's events from that person's point of view. As volunteers read their summaries to the class, have the class guess which character would have given each summary.

Small Groups Have the class work in small groups to write questions about the **Fotonovela**. Have each group hand its questions to another group to write the answers. Ex: **G1: ¿A quién le mandó un mensaje de texto Maru? G2: Maru le mandó un mensaje de texto a Miguel.**

Ortografía

Audio

La acentuación de palabras similares

Although accent marks usually indicate which syllable in a word is stressed, they are also used to distinguish between words that have the same or similar spellings.

Él maneja el coche. **Sí, voy si quieres.**

Although one-syllable words do not usually carry written accents, some *do* have accent marks to distinguish them from words that have the same spelling but different meanings.

Sé cocinar. **Se baña.** **¿Tomas té?** **Te duermes.**

Sé (*I know*) and **té** (*tea*) have accent marks to distinguish them from the pronouns **se** and **te**.

para mí **mi cámara** **Tú lees.** **tu estéreo**

Mí (*Me*) and **tú** (*you*) have accent marks to distinguish them from the possessive adjectives **mi** and **tu**.

¿Por qué vas? **Voy porque quiero.**

Several words of more than one syllable also have accent marks to distinguish them from words that have the same or similar spellings.

Éste es rápido. **Este tren es rápido.**

Demonstrative pronouns may have accent marks to distinguish them from demonstrative adjectives.

¿Cuándo fuiste? **Fui cuando me llamó.**
¿Dónde trabajas? **Voy al taller donde trabajo.**

Adverbs have accent marks when they are used to convey a question.

Práctica Marca los acentos en las palabras que los necesitan.

ANA Alo, soy Ana. ¿Que tal? Aló/¿Qué?
JUAN Hola, pero… ¿por que me llamas tan tarde? ¿por qué?
ANA Porque mañana tienes que llevarme a la universidad. Mi auto esta dañado. está
JUAN ¿Como se daño? ¿Cómo?/dañó
ANA Se daño el sabado. Un vecino (*neighbor*) choco con (*crashed into*) el. dañó/sábado/chocó/él

Crucigrama Utiliza las siguientes pistas (*clues*) para completar el crucigrama. ¡Ojo con los acentos!

Horizontales

1. Él _________ levanta.
4. No voy _________ no puedo.
7. Tú _________ acuestas.
9. ¿ _________ es el examen?
10. Quiero este video y _________.

Verticales

2. ¿Cómo _________ usted?
3. Eres _________ mi hermano.
5. ¿ _________ tal?
6. Me gusta _________ suéter.
8. Navego _________ la red.

	1 S	2 E			3 C				
		S		4 P	O	R	5 Q	U	6 E
		7 T	8 E		M		U		S
9 C	U	Á	N	D	O		10 É	S	E

recursos
LM p. 62
vhlcentral.com Lección 11

Section Goal

In **Ortografía**, students will learn about the use of accent marks to distinguish between words that have the same or similar spellings.

Instructional Resources
Supersite: Audio (Lab MP3 Files); Resources (Scripts, Answer Keys)
WebSAM
Lab Manual, p. 62

Teaching Tips

- As you go through each point in the explanation, pronounce the example sentences, as well as some of your own, and have students write them on the board.
- Write the example sentences, as well as some of your own, on the board without accent marks. Ask students where the written accents should go.
- Use gestures and tone to emphasize the difference in stress between **por qué** and **porque**.
- Ask students to provide words they learned in previous lessons that exemplify each point. Have them make a two-column chart of words they know. Ex: **mi/mí, tu/tú, te/té, el/él, si/sí, se/sé,** etc.
- Point out that **Ortografía** replaces **Pronunciación** in the Student Edition for **Lecciones 10–15**, but not in the Lab Manual. The **Recursos** box references the **Pronunciación** sections found in all lessons of the Lab Manual.

TEACHING OPTIONS

Small Groups Have students work in groups to discuss which words in the **Práctica** activity need written accents and why. If necessary, have them quickly review the information about accents in the **Ortografía** section of **Lección 10**, page 315.

Extra Practice Prepare a series of mini-dialogues. Slowly read each one aloud, pausing to allow students to write. Then, in pairs, have students check their work. Ex: **1. —¿Ésta es tu cámara? —Sí, ¿por qué? —Porque es idéntica a la que mi papá me compró. 2. —¿Dónde encontraste mi mochila? —¡Pues, donde la dejaste! —Ah, es verdad. ¡Qué tonta soy! Se me olvidó detrás del sofá. 3. —¿Cuándo visitó Buenos Aires Mario? —Yo sé que Laura fue el año pasado, ¿pero cuándo fue él? —¡Ni idea! Por eso te lo pregunté a ti.** Ask comprehension questions as a follow-up.

Section Goals

In **Cultura**, students will:
- read about social networks in Spanish-speaking countries
- learn technology-related terms
- read about different types of **bicimotos**
- read about text messaging

Instructional Resources
Supersite: Video (***Flash cultura***); Resources (Scripts, Translations, Answer Keys)
WebSAM
Video Manual, pp. 93–94

En detalle

Antes de leer
Survey the class about social networks. Ask: **¿Usan las redes sociales? ¿Cuáles? ¿Con qué frecuencia usan las redes sociales?**

Lectura
Point out the boxed feature on page 350. Ask students what they think are the two languages used most on social networks. (English, Chinese)

Después de leer
Ask students: **En tu opinión, ¿nos comunicábamos mejor antes o después del invento de las redes sociales? ¿Por qué?** Have students write their answers in a short paragraph, and encourage volunteers to share their responses with the class.

1 Expansion Ask students to write three additional true/false statements. Then have them exchange papers with a classmate and complete the activity.

Flash CULTURA

EN DETALLE

Video: *Flash cultura*

NATIONAL STANDARDS connections cultures

Las redes sociales

¿Cómo te comunicas con tu familia y con tus amigos? Al igual que° en los Estados Unidos, en los países hispanohablantes las redes sociales han tenido° un gran impacto en los últimos años. Los usos básicos de los teléfonos celulares ya no son las llamadas° y los mensajes de texto, sino el contacto entre amigos y familiares por medio de° redes sociales y de aplicaciones como Facebook, Twitter, Tuenti o Instagram.

La mayoría de los hispanos tiene un perfil° en Facebook o en Twitter, pero el método de comunicación más popular en los países hispanohablantes es Whatsapp. Por medio de esta aplicación de mensajería los usuarios° pueden crear grupos y enviarse° un número ilimitado de imágenes, videos y mensajes de texto y de audio. Su popularidad se debe a que es una forma rápida y prácticamente gratuita° de comunicarse.

Hoy en día, los teléfonos inteligentes y los contratos telefónicos son más asequibles°, por lo que la mayoría de los hispanos disfruta de estos celulares y de sus ventajas tecnológicas. Gracias a las redes sociales y a las aplicaciones, las personas pueden estar en constante comunicación con sus seres queridos° más lejanos°. La inevitable pregunta es: ¿Qué ocurre con los seres queridos que están cerca? La influencia que tienen las redes sociales en las relaciones humanas es cada vez un tema más polémico.

El español en las redes sociales

- El español es la tercera lengua más utilizada en las redes sociales.
- El español es la segunda lengua más usada en Twitter, con un crecimiento° de más de 800% en los últimos diez años.
- Facebook tiene 80 millones de usuarios hispanohablantes.
- Sólo en España, Whatsapp tiene 20 millones de usuarios que usan la aplicación un promedio° de 150 veces al día.

Al igual que *Like* **han tenido** *have had* **llamadas** *calls* **por medio de** *through* **perfil** *profile* **usuarios** *users* **enviarse** *send each other* **gratuita** *free* **asequibles** *affordable* **seres queridos** *loved ones* **lejanos** *distant* **crecimiento** *growth* **promedio** *average*

ACTIVIDADES

1 **¿Cierto o falso?** Indica si lo que dicen estas oraciones es **cierto** o **falso**. Corrige la información falsa.

1. Los hispanos prefieren las llamadas para comunicarse con sus familias y con sus amigos. Falso. Los hispanos prefieren comunicarse por medio de redes sociales y de aplicaciones.
2. Twitter no se usa en Latinoamérica. Falso. La mayoría de los hispanos tiene un perfil en Facebook o en Twitter.
3. Whatsapp es un método de comunicación muy común en los países hispanos. Cierto.
4. Whatsapp permite enviar fotos a los contactos del celular. Cierto.
5. Pocos hispanos pueden comprar un teléfono inteligente. Falso. Hoy en día los teléfonos inteligentes son más asequibles.
6. Una ventaja de las redes sociales es el contacto con las personas que están lejos. Cierto.
7. El español es la segunda lengua más utilizada en las redes sociales. Falso. El español es la tercera lengua más utilizada en las redes sociales.
8. Los españoles visitan constantemente la aplicación de Whatsapp. Cierto.

TEACHING OPTIONS

Extra Practice Tell students to imagine that they are writing to a friend who refuses to use social networks. Have students persuade their friend by describing how it has changed their own lives. If necessary, review comparatives and superlatives, **hace** + [*time period*] + **que** + [*present*] and **hace** + [*time period*] + **que** + [*preterite*].

Heritage Speakers Ask heritage speakers to describe social network use in their families.

Pairs In pairs, have students list, in order of importance, the top five reasons to use social networks. Have pairs share their lists with the class to see if a consensus can be reached. Make sure students write their lists in Spanish.

ASÍ SE DICE

La tecnología

los audífonos (Méx., Col.), los auriculares (Arg.), los cascos (Esp.)	*headset; earphones*
el móvil (Esp.)	el celular
el manos libres (Amér. S.)	*hands-free system*
la memoria	*memory*
mensajear (Méx.)	enviar y recibir mensajes de texto

EL MUNDO HISPANO

Las bicimotos

- **Argentina** El *ciclomotor* se usa mayormente° para repartir a domicilio° comidas y medicinas.
- **Perú** La *motito* se usa mucho para el reparto a domicilio de pan fresco todos los días.
- **México** La *Vespa* se usa para evitar° el tráfico en grandes ciudades.
- **España** La población usa el *Vespino* para ir y volver al trabajo cada día.
- **Puerto Rico** Una *scooter* es el medio de transporte favorito en las zonas rurales.
- **República Dominicana** Las *moto-taxis* son el medio de transporte más económico, ¡pero no olvides el casco°!

mayormente *mainly* **repartir a domicilio** *home delivery of* **evitar** *to avoid* **casco** *helmet*

PERFIL

Los mensajes de texto

¿Qué tienen en común un **mensaje de texto** y un telegrama?: la necesidad de decir lo máximo en el menor espacio posible —y rápidamente—. Así como los abuelos se las arreglaron° para hacer más baratos sus telegramas, que se cobraban° por número de palabras, ahora los jóvenes buscan ahorrar° espacio, tiempo y dinero, en sus mensajes de texto. Esta economía del lenguaje dio origen al **lenguaje chat**, una forma de escritura muy creativa y compacta. Olvídate de la gramática, la puntuación y la ortografía: es tan flexible que evoluciona° todos los días con el uso que cada quien° le da, aunque° hay muchas palabras y expresiones ya establecidas°. Fácilmente encontrarás° abreviaturas (**xq?**, "¿Por qué?"; **tkm**, "Te quiero mucho."), sustitución de sonidos por números (**a2**, "Adiós."; **5mntrios**, "Sin comentarios."), símbolos (**ad+**, "además") y omisión de vocales y acentos (**tb**, "también"; **k tl?**, "¿Qué tal?"). Ahora que lo sabes, si un amigo te envía: **cont xfa, m dbs $!**°, puedes responderle: **ntp, ns vms + trd**°.

se las arreglaron *they managed to* **se cobraban** *were charged* **ahorrar** *to save* **evoluciona** *evolves* **cada quien** *each person* **aunque** *although* **establecidas** *fixed* **encontrarás** *you will find* **cont xfa, m dbs $!** Contesta, por favor, ¡me debes dinero! **ntp, ns vms +trd** No te preocupes, nos vemos más tarde.

Conexión Internet

¿Qué sitios web son populares entre los jóvenes hispanos?

Go to **vhlcentral.com** to find more cultural information related to this **Cultura** section.

ACTIVIDADES

2 Comprensión Responde a las preguntas.

1. ¿Cuáles son tres formas de decir *headset*? los audífonos, los auriculares, los cascos
2. ¿Para qué se usan las bicimotos en Argentina? para repartir a domicilio comidas y medicinas
3. ¿Qué dio origen al "lenguaje chat"? la necesidad de ahorrar espacio, tiempo y dinero
4. ¿Es importante escribir los acentos en los mensajes de texto? No. La gramática, la ortografía y la puntuación no importan en un mensaje de texto.

3 ¿Cómo te comunicas? Escribe un párrafo breve en donde expliques qué utilizas para comunicarte con tus amigos/as (correo electrónico, redes sociales, teléfono, etc.) y de qué hablan cuando se llaman por teléfono. Answers will vary.

recursos: VM pp. 93–94; vhlcentral.com Lección 11

Practice more at **vhlcentral.com**.

Así se dice

- Model the pronunciation of each term.
- To challenge students, add these words to the list: **la señal** (*signal*); **tener la batería baja** (*to have a low battery*).
- Ask students questions using these terms. Ex: **Si hablas por teléfono mientras manejas, ¿usas un manos libres? Nunca mensajeas mientras conduces, ¿verdad?**

Perfil

- Have students look up additional Spanish text messaging abbreviations in an online Spanish SMS dictionary. Ask them to decipher the meaning of the phrase **hexo x ti y xa ti** (**hecho por ti y para ti**) with regard to an online dictionary in which anyone can make entries. Then, have students make a list of the abbreviations they would use most when texting.

El mundo hispano

- Ask: **¿Alguna vez paseaste en bicimoto? ¿Qué te parece este modo de transporte?**
- Have students write three fill-in-the-blank sentences about this section for a partner to complete.

2 Expansion Ask additional comprehension questions. Ex: **¿Para qué necesita memoria un móvil? (para guardar fotos, videos y mensajes de texto)**

3 Teaching Tip Allow students ten minutes to write a rough draft of their paragraph without looking up any words or grammar. Then have students work with a classmate to peer-edit their text and consult any necessary resources.

3 Expansion To challenge students, have them also explain how they expect their methods of communication will be different in ten years, using **ir a +** [*infinitive*].

TEACHING OPTIONS

Pairs For homework, ask student pairs to write a short dialogue between two people using text messages. If necessary, have them research additional text message abbreviations on the Internet. Encourage humor and creativity. In the next class period, have pairs exchange dialogues with another pair, who will decipher the conversation.

TPR Call out true/false statements about the information presented on pages 350–351. If the statement is true, have students raise their right hand, and if it is false, have students raise their left hand. To challenge students, have volunteers correct the false statements.

Heritage Speakers If heritage speakers have family in Spanish-speaking countries, ask them to discuss social network use there.

Section Goals

In **Estructura 11.1**, students will learn:

- affirmative **tú** commands
- negative **tú** commands

Instructional Resources

Supersite: Audio (Lab MP3 Files); Resources (Grammar Presentation Slides, Activity Pack, Scripts, Answer Keys); Testing Program (Quizzes)
WebSAM
Workbook, pp. 127–128
Lab Manual, p. 63

Teaching Tips

- Model the use of informal commands with simple examples using TPR and gestures. Ex: Point to a student and say: ____, **levántate. Gracias, ahora siéntate.** Give other commands using **camina, vuelve, toca,** and **corre**.
- Help students recognize that the affirmative **tú** command forms of regular verbs are the same as the third-person singular forms.
- Emphasize that **tú** commands are spoken to people one addresses as **tú**.

NATIONAL STANDARDS comparisons

11.1 Familiar commands

Tutorial

ANTE TODO In Spanish, the command forms are used to give orders or advice. You use **tú** commands (**mandatos familiares**) when you want to give an order or advice to someone you normally address with the familiar **tú**.

Affirmative tú commands

Infinitive	Present tense él/ella form	Affirmative tú command
hablar	habla	**habla** (tú)
guardar	guarda	**guarda** (tú)
prender	prende	**prende** (tú)
volver	vuelve	**vuelve** (tú)
pedir	pide	**pide** (tú)
imprimir	imprime	**imprime** (tú)

- Affirmative **tú** commands usually have the same form as the **él/ella** form of the present indicative.

Guarda el documento antes de cerrarlo.
Save the document before closing it.

Imprime tu tarea para la clase de inglés.
Print your homework for English class.

- The following verbs have irregular affirmative **tú** commands.

Irregular affirmative tú commands

decir	**di**	salir	**sal**
hacer	**haz**	ser	**sé**
ir	**ve**	tener	**ten**
poner	**pon**	venir	**ven**

¡**Sal** ahora mismo!
Leave at once!

Haz los ejercicios.
Do the exercises.

- Since **ir** and **ver** have the same **tú** command (**ve**), context will determine the meaning.

Ve al cibercafé con Yolanda.
Go to the cybercafé with Yolanda.

Ve ese programa... es muy interesante.
See that program... it's very interesting.

Súbete al coche y préndelo.

No lo manejes en la carretera.

TEACHING OPTIONS

TPR Ask individual students to comply with a series of commands requiring them to perform actions or move around the room. While the student follows the command, the class writes it down as a volunteer writes it on the board. Be sure to use both affirmative and negative commands. Ex: **Recoge ese papel. Ponlo en la basura. Regresa a tu escritorio. No te sientes. Siéntate ahora.**

Pairs Ask students to imagine they are starting a computer club. Have them make a list of five things to do in order to get ready for the first meeting and five things not to do to make sure everything runs smoothly, using infinitives. Then have students take turns telling partners what to do or not do.

- The negative **tú** commands are formed by dropping the final **-o** of the **yo** form of the present tense. For **-ar** verbs, add **-es**. For **-er** and **-ir** verbs, add **-as**.

Negative tú commands

Infinitive	Present tense yo form	Negative tú command
hablar	hablo	**no hables** (tú)
guardar	guardo	**no guardes** (tú)
prender	prendo	**no prendas** (tú)
volver	vuelvo	**no vuelvas** (tú)
pedir	pido	**no pidas** (tú)

Héctor, **no pares** el carro aquí.
Héctor, don't stop the car here.

No prendas la computadora todavía.
Don't turn on the computer yet.

- Verbs with irregular **yo** forms maintain the same irregularity in their negative **tú** commands. These verbs include **conducir, conocer, decir, hacer, ofrecer, oír, poner, salir, tener, traducir, traer, venir,** and **ver**.

No pongas el disco en la computadora.
Don't put the disk in the computer.

No conduzcas tan rápido.
Don't drive so fast.

- Note also that stem-changing verbs keep their stem changes in negative **tú** commands.

No p**ie**rdas tu celular.
Don't lose your cell phone.

No v**ue**lvas a esa gasolinera.
Don't go back to that gas station.

No rep**i**tas las instrucciones.
Don't repeat the instructions.

- Verbs ending in **-car**, **-gar**, and **-zar** have a spelling change in the negative **tú** commands.

sa**car**	**c** → **qu**	no sa**qu**es
apa**gar**	**g** → **gu**	no apa**gu**es
almor**zar**	**z** → **c**	no almuer**c**es

- The following verbs have irregular negative **tú** commands.

Irregular negative tú commands

dar	**no des**
estar	**no estés**
ir	**no vayas**
saber	**no sepas**
ser	**no seas**

¡ATENCIÓN!

In affirmative commands, reflexive, indirect, and direct object pronouns are always attached to the end of the verb. In negative commands, these pronouns always precede the verb.

Bórralos./No los borres.

Escríbeles un mensaje electrónico./**No les escribas** un mensaje electrónico.

•••

When a pronoun is attached to an affirmative command that has two or more syllables, an accent mark is added to maintain the original stress:

borra → **bórralos**
prende → **préndela**
imprime → **imprímelo**

recursos
WB pp. 127–128
LM p. 63
vhlcentral.com Lección 11

¡INTÉNTALO! Indica los mandatos familiares afirmativos y negativos de estos verbos.

1. correr ___Corre___ más rápido. No ___corras___ más rápido.
2. llenar ___Llena___ el tanque. No ___llenes___ el tanque.
3. salir ___Sal___ ahora. No ___salgas___ ahora.
4. descargar ___Descarga___ ese documento. No ___descargues___ ese documento.
5. levantarse ___Levántate___ temprano. No ___te levantes___ temprano.
6. hacerlo ___Hazlo___ ya. No ___lo hagas___ ahora.

Teaching Tips

- Contrast the negative forms of **tú** commands by giving an affirmative command followed by a negative command. Ex: ____, **camina a la puerta. No camines rápidamente.** Write the examples on the board as you go along.
- Test comprehension and practice negative **tú** commands by calling out the infinitives of a variety of regular verbs the students already know and asking individual students to convert them into negative commands. Ex: **toser: no tosas; pedir: no pidas; pensar: no pienses.**
- Ask volunteers to convert affirmative **tú** commands with reflexive and object pronouns into negative forms. Ex: **Imprímelo. (No lo imprimas.) Vete. (No te vayas.)**

TEACHING OPTIONS

Heritage Speakers Ask heritage speakers to bring in a Spanish advertisement that uses informal commands. Ask them to explain why they think informal commands were used instead of formal ones.

Pairs As a class, brainstorm one or two unique situations in which **tú** commands may be used, such as an owner talking to his pet. Have pairs write and act out a situation for the class.

Pairs Have pairs imagine that they are in charge of a computer lab at a university in a Spanish-speaking country. Have them write down four things students must do and four things they must not do while in the lab. Instruct them to use **tú** commands throughout. Then, write **Mandatos afirmativos** and **Mandatos negativos** on the board and ask individuals to write one of their commands in the appropriate column.

1 Expansion Continue this activity orally with the class, using regular verbs. Call out a negative command and designate individuals to make corresponding affirmative commands. Ex: **No sirvas la comida ahora. (Sirve la comida ahora./Sírvela ahora.)**

2 Expansion Ask volunteers to role-play the exchanges between **Pedro** and **Marina**. Encourage them to ad-lib and add more to the exchanges as they go along.

3 Teaching Tip To simplify, review the vocabulary in the word bank by asking students to make associations with each word. Ex: **imprimir (documento), descargar (programa)**

Práctica

1

Completar Tu mejor amigo no entiende nada de tecnología y te pide ayuda. Completa los comentarios de tu amigo con el mandato de cada verbo.

1. No vengas en una hora. Ven ahora mismo. (venir)
2. Haz tu tarea después. No la hagas ahora. (hacer)
3. No vayas a la tienda a comprar papel para la impresora. Ve a la cafetería a comprarme algo de comer. (ir)
4. No me digas que no puedes abrir un archivo. Dime que el programa de computación funciona sin problemas. (decirme)
5. Sé generoso con tu tiempo y no seas antipático si no entiendo fácilmente. (ser)
6. Ten mucha paciencia y no tengas prisa. (tener)
7. Apaga tu teléfono celular, pero no apagues la computadora. (apagar)

2

Cambiar Pedro y Marina no pueden ponerse de acuerdo (*agree*) cuando viajan en su carro. Cuando Pedro dice que algo es necesario, Marina expresa una opinión diferente. Usa la información entre paréntesis para formar las órdenes que Marina le da a Pedro.

modelo

Pedro: Necesito revisar el aceite del carro. (seguir hasta el próximo pueblo)
Marina: *No revises el aceite del carro. Sigue hasta el próximo pueblo.*

1. Necesito conducir más rápido. (parar el carro) No conduzcas más rápido. Para el carro.
2. Necesito poner el radio. (hablarme) No pongas el radio. Háblame.
3. Necesito almorzar ahora. (comer más tarde) No almuerces ahora. Come más tarde.
4. Necesito sacar los discos compactos. (manejar con cuidado) No saques… Maneja…
5. Necesito estacionar el carro en esta calle. (pensar en otra opción) No estaciones… Piensa…
6. Necesito volver a esa gasolinera. (arreglar el carro en un taller) No vuelvas… Arregla…
7. Necesito leer el mapa. (pedirle ayuda a aquella señora) No leas… Pídele…
8. Necesito dormir en el carro. (acostarse en una cama) No duermas… Acuéstate…

3

Problemas Tú y tu compañero/a trabajan en el centro de computadoras de la universidad. Muchos estudiantes están llamando con problemas. Denles órdenes para ayudarlos a resolverlos.

Answers will vary. Suggested answers:

modelo

Problema: *No veo nada en la pantalla.*
Tu respuesta: *Prende la pantalla de tu computadora.*

apagar…	descargar…	grabar…	imprimir…	prender…
borrar…	funcionar…	guardar…	navegar…	volver…

1. No me gusta este programa de computación. Descarga otro.
2. Tengo miedo de perder mi documento. Guárdalo.
3. Prefiero leer este sitio web en papel. Imprímelo.
4. Mi correo electrónico funciona muy lentamente. Borra los mensajes más viejos.
5. Busco información sobre los gauchos de Argentina. Navega en Internet.
6. Tengo demasiados archivos en mi computadora. Borra algunos archivos.
7. Mi computadora se congeló (*froze*). Apaga la computadora y luego préndela.
8. Quiero ver las fotos del cumpleaños de mi hermana. Descárgalas.

Practice more at **vhlcentral.com**.

NOTA CULTURAL

Los gauchos (*nomadic cowboys*), conocidos por su habilidad (*skill*) para montar a caballo y utilizar el lazo, viven en la Región Pampeana, una llanura muy extensa ubicada en el centro de Argentina y dedicada a la agricultura (*agriculture*).

TEACHING OPTIONS

TPR Have pairs of students brainstorm a list of actions that can be mimed. Then have them give each other **tú** commands based on the actions. Call on several pairs to demonstrate their actions for the class. When a repertoire of mimable actions is established, do TPR with the class using these commands/actions.

Pairs Tell students to imagine that they belong to their grandparents' generation and are not very familiar with new technology. Have them write three questions about electronic devices to ask a partner, who will answer using affirmative and negative commands. If the response uses a negative command, it should be followed by an affirmative command. Ex: **¿Debo apagar la computadora cada vez que salgo de la casa? (No, no la apagues. Pero guarda todos tus documentos.)** Students should ask follow-up questions when necessary.

Comunicación

4 **Órdenes** Intercambia mandatos negativos y afirmativos con tu compañero/a. Debes seguir las órdenes que él o ella te da o reaccionar apropiadamente. Answers will vary.

modelo

Estudiante 1: *Dame todo tu dinero.*
Estudiante 2: *No, no quiero dártelo. Muéstrame tu cuaderno.*
Estudiante 1: *Aquí está.*
Estudiante 2: *Ve a la pizarra y escribe tu nombre.*
Estudiante 1: *No quiero. Hazlo tú.*

5 **Anuncios** Miren este anuncio. Luego, en grupos pequeños, preparen tres anuncios adicionales para tres escuelas que compiten (*compete*) con ésta. Answers will vary.

INFORMÁTICA ARGENTINA
Toma nuestros cursos y aprende a usar la computadora
abre y lee tus archivos
imprime tus documentos
entra al campo de la tecnología
¡Ponte en contacto con nosotros llamando al 11-4-129-1508 HOY!

Síntesis

6 **¡Tanto que hacer!** Tu profesor(a) te va a dar una lista de diligencias (*errands*). Algunas las hiciste tú y algunas las hizo tu compañero/a. Las diligencias que ya hicieron tienen esta marca ✔. Pero quedan cuatro diligencias por hacer. Dale órdenes a tu compañero/a y él/ella responde para confirmar si hay que hacerla o si ya la hizo. Answers will vary.

modelo

Estudiante 1: *Llena el tanque.*
Estudiante 2: *Ya llené el tanque. / ¡Ay, no! Tenemos que llenar el tanque.*

4 Teaching Tip To simplify, ask students to brainstorm a list of what they might ask their classmates to do.

4 Expansion Have volunteers report to the class what they were asked to do, what they did, and what they did not do.

5 Teaching Tip Ask comprehension questions about the ad. **¿Qué se anuncia? (cursos de informática) ¿Cómo puedes informarte? (llamar por teléfono) ¿Dónde se encuentra este tipo de anuncio? (en periódicos y revistas)**

5 Expansion Post the finished ads in different places around the classroom. Have groups circulate and write one question for each poster. Then have group members ask their questions. Group answers should include a **tú** command.

6 Teaching Tips
- Divide the class into pairs and distribute the handouts from the Activity Pack (Activity Pack/Supersite) that correspond to this Information Gap Activity. Give students ten minutes to complete this activity.
- Ask volunteers to give examples of **tú** commands that college students usually give to their roommates. Ex: **Apaga la tele. No te acuestes en el sofá.**

TEACHING OPTIONS

Pairs Have pairs prepare a conversation between two roommates who are getting ready for a party. Students should use affirmative and negative **tú** commands. Ex: **E1: ¡Sal del baño ya! E2: ¡No me grites!...**

Large Group Have the class stand in a circle. Name an infinitive and toss a ball to a student. He or she will give the affirmative **tú** command and throw the ball to another student, who will provide the negative form.

Extra Practice Add an auditory aspect to this grammar practice. Prepare series of commands that would be said to certain individuals. Write the names on the board and read each series aloud. Have students match the commands to each name. Ex: **No comas eso. Dame el periódico. No te subas al sofá. Tráeme las pantuflas. (un perro)**

Section Goal

In **Estructura 11.2**, students will learn when to use **por** and **para**.

Instructional Resources
Supersite: Audio (Lab MP3 Files); Resources (Grammar Presentation Slides, Activity Pack, Scripts, Answer Keys); Testing Program (Quizzes)
WebSAM
Workbook, pp. 129–130
Lab Manual, p. 64

Teaching Tips

- Bring in magazine advertisements or write popular sayings on the board and have students identify the uses of **por** and **para**. Ex: **Habla hasta por los codos; Para un mundo más justo; Calabaza, calabaza, cada uno para su casa; Por la boca muere el pez.**
- Ask students to translate phrases requiring **por**. Ex: *talk by phone, send information by e-mail, walk across campus, walk along Bécquer Street, arrive in the afternoon/in the morning, be worried about the accident/about your friend, drive 30 miles per hour, study for four hours.*

11.2 Por and para

Tutorial

NATIONAL STANDARDS comparisons

ANTE TODO Unlike English, Spanish has two words that mean *for*: **por** and **para**. These two prepositions are not interchangeable. Study the following charts to see how they are used.

▶ **Por** and **para** are most commonly used to describe aspects of movement, time, and action, but in different circumstances.

Por	Para
Movement	
Through or by a place La excursión nos llevó **por** el centro. *The tour took us through downtown.*	**Toward a destination** Mis amigos van **para** el estadio. *My friends are going to the stadium.*
Time	
Duration of an event Ana navegó la red **por** dos horas. *Ana surfed the net for two hours.*	**Action deadline** Tengo que escribir un ensayo **para** mañana. *I have to write an essay by tomorrow.*
Action	
Reason or motive for an action or circumstance Llegué a casa tarde **por** el tráfico. *I got home late because of the traffic.*	**Indication of for whom something is intended or done** Estoy preparando una sorpresa **para** Eduardo. *I'm preparing a surprise for Eduardo.*

▶ Here is a list of the uses of **por** and **para**.

Por is used to indicate...

1. **Movement: Motion or a general location** . . *(around, through, along, by)*	Pasamos **por** el parque y **por** el río. *We passed by the park and along the river.*
2. **Time: Duration of an action** . . . . *(for, during, in)*	Estuve en la Patagonia **por** un mes. *I was in Patagonia for a month.*
3. **Action: Reason or motive for an action** . . *(because of, on account of, on behalf of)*	Lo hizo **por** su familia. *She did it on behalf of her family.*
4. **Object of a search** . . . . *(for, in search of)*	Vengo **por** ti a las ocho. *I'm coming for you at eight.* Manuel fue **por** su cámara digital. *Manuel went in search of his digital camera.*
5. **Means by which something is done** . . . *(by, by way of, by means of)*	Ellos viajan **por** la autopista. *They travel by (by way of) the highway.*
6. **Exchange or substitution** . . . . *(for, in exchange for)*	Le di dinero **por** el reproductor de MP3. *I gave him money for the MP3 player.*
7. **Unit of measure** . . . . *(per, by)*	José manejaba a 120 kilómetros **por** hora. *José was driving 120 kilometers per hour.*

¡ATENCIÓN!

Por is also used in several idiomatic expressions, including:
por aquí *around here*
por ejemplo *for example*
por eso *that's why; therefore*
por fin *finally*

AYUDA

Remember that when giving an exact time, **de** is used instead of **por** before **la mañana, la tarde,** or **la noche**.
La clase empieza a las nueve **de** la mañana.

•••

In addition to **por**, **durante** is also commonly used to mean *for* when referring to time.
Esperé al mecánico **durante** cincuenta minutos.

TEACHING OPTIONS

TPR Call out a sentence, omitting either **por** or **para**. If students think **por** should be used in the sentence, they raise one hand. If they think **para** should be used, they raise two hands. Avoid cases where either **por** or **para** could be used. Ex: **Tengo que leer el capítulo 11 ____ mañana.** (two hands) **Elena trabaja ____ la noche.** (one hand) **Estuve en Buenos Aires ____ el mes de marzo.** (one hand)

Extra Practice Ask students to write a paragraph about a time when communication technology failed them. Remind them to include new vocabulary and at least two uses each of **por** and **para**. Have students exchange their papers for peer editing.

Para is used to indicate...

1. **Movement: Destination** (*toward, in the direction of*)	Salimos **para** Córdoba el sábado. *We are leaving for Córdoba on Saturday.*
2. **Time: Deadline or a specific time in the future** (*by, for*)	Él va a arreglar el carro **para** el viernes. *He will fix the car by Friday.*
3. **Action: Purpose or goal + [*infinitive*]** (*in order to*)	Juan estudia **para** (ser) mecánico. *Juan is studying to be a mechanic.*
4. **Purpose + [*noun*]** (*for, used for*)	Es una llanta **para** el carro. *It's a tire for the car.*
5. **The recipient of something** (*for*)	Compré una impresora **para** mi hijo. *I bought a printer for my son.*
6. **Comparison with others or an opinion** (*for, considering*)	**Para** un joven, es demasiado serio. *For a young person, he is too serious.* **Para** mí, esta lección no es difícil. *For me, this lesson isn't difficult.*
7. **In the employment of** (*for*)	Sara trabaja **para** Telecom Argentina. *Sara works for Telecom Argentina.*

▶ In many cases it is grammatically correct to use either **por** or **para** in a sentence. The meaning of the sentence is different, however, depending on which preposition is used.

Caminé **por** el parque. *I walked through the park.*	Caminé **para** el parque. *I walked to (toward) the park.*
Trabajó **por** su padre. *He worked for (in place of) his father.*	Trabajó **para** su padre. *He worked for his father('s company).*

¡INTÉNTALO! Completa estas oraciones con las preposiciones **por** o **para**.

1. Fuimos al cibercafé ___por___ la tarde.
2. Necesitas un navegador GPS ___para___ encontrar la casa de Luis.
3. Entraron ___por___ la puerta.
4. Quiero un pasaje ___para___ Buenos Aires.
5. ___Para___ arrancar el carro, necesito la llave.
6. Arreglé el televisor ___para___ mi amigo.
7. Estuvieron nerviosos ___por___ el examen.
8. ¿No hay una gasolinera ___por___ aquí?
9. El reproductor de MP3 es ___para___ usted.
10. Juan está enfermo. Tengo que trabajar ___por___ él.
11. Estuvimos en Canadá ___por___ dos meses.
12. ___Para___ mí, el español es fácil.
13. Tengo que estudiar la lección ___para___ el lunes.
14. Voy a ir ___por___ la carretera.
15. Compré dulces ___para___ mi novia.
16. Compramos el auto ___por___ un buen precio.

recursos
WB pp. 129–130
LM p. 64
vhlcentral.com Lección 11

Teaching Tips

- Create a matching activity for the uses of **para**. Write sentences exemplifying each use of **para** listed, but not in the order they are given in the text. Ex: **1. Maru escribió un mensaje para Miguel. 2. Este autobús va para Mérida. 3. Para Jimena, los estudios son importantes. 4. Jorge trabaja para un taller. 5. Estudia para llegar a ser doctora. 6. El baúl es para las maletas. 7. Tengo que entregar el proyecto para la semana que viene.** Call on individual students to match each sentence with its usage.
- Have students make two flash-cards. On one they write **por** and on the other **para**. Call out one of the uses for either word. Students hold up the appropriate card. Then call on a volunteer to write a sentence illustrating that use on the board. The class verifies the accuracy of the sentence.
- Add a visual aspect to this grammar presentation. Use magazine pictures to practice sentences demonstrating the uses of **por** and **para**. Ex: **Este señor hace la cena para su esposa. Los novios montan a caballo por el campo.**

TEACHING OPTIONS

Large Group Give each student in the class a strip of paper on which you have written one of the uses of **por** or **para**, or a sentence that exemplifies one of the uses. Have students circulate around the room until they find the person who has the match for their use or sentence. After everyone has found a partner, the pairs read their sentences and uses to the class.

Game Play **Concentración**. Create one card for each use of **por** and **para**, and one card with a sentence illustrating each use, for a total of 28 cards. Shuffle the cards and lay them face down. Then, taking turns, students uncover two cards at a time, trying to match a use to a sentence. The student with the most matches wins.

Práctica

1 **Completar** Completa este párrafo con las preposiciones **por** o **para**.

El mes pasado mi esposo y yo hicimos un viaje a Buenos Aires y sólo pagamos dos mil dólares (1) por los pasajes. Estuvimos en Buenos Aires (2) por una semana y paseamos por toda la ciudad. Durante el día caminamos (3) por la plaza San Martín, el microcentro y el barrio de La Boca, donde viven muchos artistas. (4) Por la noche fuimos a una tanguería, que es una especie de teatro, (5) para mirar a la gente bailar tango. Dos días después decidimos hacer una excursión (6) por las pampas (7) para ver el paisaje y un rodeo con gauchos. Alquilamos (*We rented*) un carro y manejamos (8) por todas partes y pasamos unos días muy agradables. El último día que estuvimos en Buenos Aires fuimos a Galerías Pacífico (9) para comprar recuerdos (*souvenirs*) (10) para nuestros hijos y nietos. Compramos tantos regalos que tuvimos que pagar impuestos (*duties*) en la aduana al regresar.

2 **Oraciones** Crea oraciones originales con los elementos de las columnas. Une los elementos usando **por** o **para**. Answers will vary.

modelo

Fuimos a Mar del Plata por razones de salud para visitar a un especialista.

(no) fue al mercado	por/para	comprar frutas	por/para	¿?
(no) fuimos a las montañas	por/para	tres días	por/para	¿?
(no) fuiste a Mar del Plata	por/para	razones de salud	por/para	¿?
(no) fueron a Buenos Aires	por/para	tomar el sol	por/para	¿?

3 **Describir** Usa **por** o **para** y el tiempo presente para describir estos dibujos. Answers will vary.

1. ______________________

2. ______________________

3. ______________________

4. ______________________

5. ______________________

6. ______________________

Practice more at **vhlcentral.com**.

1 Expansion
To challenge students, have them list the uses of **por** and **para** in the paragraph. Then ask them to work in pairs to add sentences to the paragraph, employing the remaining uses of **por** and **para**. (Remaining uses of **por**: reason or motive, object of search, means, unit of measure; remaining uses of **para**: destination, deadline, purpose + [*noun*], comparison, employment)

2 Teaching Tips
- Model the activity by creating a sentence with an element from each column. Ask a volunteer to explain your choice of **por** or **para**. Possible sentences: **Fuimos al mercado para comprar frutas por la mañana. No fueron a Buenos Aires por tres días para divertirse.**
- Divide the class into groups of three. Groups should write as many sentences as they can by combining elements from each column in a given amount of time. The group with the most correct sentences wins.

3 Expansion
Have students take turns with a partner to expand their descriptions to a short oral narrative. After each drawing has been described, ask students to pick two or three of their narratives and link them into a story.

NOTA CULTURAL

Mar del Plata es un centro turístico en la costa de Argentina. La ciudad es conocida como "la perla del Atlántico" y todos los años muchos turistas visitan sus playas y casinos.

TEACHING OPTIONS

Large Group Have students create ten questions for a survey about the use of modern technology. Questions should include as many uses of **por** and **para** as possible. When finished, have students administer their survey to five different people in the room, then compile their results. Ex: **¿Por cuántos minutos al día hablas por teléfono celular?** Ask students to present a summary of their findings to the class.

Extra Practice Ask students to imagine they are explaining to a younger sibling how to take care of the family car and why certain types of maintenance are necessary. Students should employ as many different uses of **por** and **para** in their explanations as possible.

NATIONAL communication STANDARDS

Comunicación

4 **Descripciones** Usa **por** o **para** y completa estas frases de manera lógica. Luego, compara tus respuestas con las de un(a) compañero/a. Answers will vary.

1. En casa, hablo con mis amigos...
2. Mi padre/madre trabaja...
3. Ayer fui al taller...
4. Los miércoles tengo clases...
5. A veces voy a la biblioteca...
6. Esta noche tengo que estudiar...
7. Necesito... dólares...
8. Compré un regalo...
9. Mi mejor amigo/a estudia...
10. Necesito hacer la tarea...

5 **Situación** En parejas, dramaticen esta situación. Utilicen muchos ejemplos de **por** y **para.** Answers will vary.

Hijo/a	Padre/Madre
Pídele dinero a tu padre/madre.	Pregúntale a tu hijo/a para qué lo necesita.
Dile que quieres comprar un carro.	Pregúntale por qué necesita un carro.
Explica tres razones por las que necesitas un carro.	Explica por qué sus razones son buenas o malas.
Dile que por no tener un carro tu vida es muy difícil.	Decide si vas a darle el dinero y explica por qué.

NATIONAL communication STANDARDS

Síntesis

6 **Una subasta (*auction*)** Cada estudiante debe traer a la clase un objeto o una foto del objeto para vender. En grupos, túrnense para ser el/la vendedor(a) y los postores (*bidders*). Para empezar, el/la vendedor(a) describe el objeto y explica para qué se usa y por qué alguien debe comprarlo. Answers will vary.

modelo

Vendedora: *Aquí tengo un reproductor de CD. Pueden usarlo para escuchar su música favorita o para escuchar canciones en español. Sólo hace un año que lo compré y todavía funciona perfectamente. ¿Quién ofrece $ 1.500 para empezar?*
Postor(a) 1: *Pero los reproductores de CD son anticuados. Te doy $ 20.*
Vendedora: *Ah, pero éste es muy especial porque viene con el CD que grabé cuando quería ser cantante de ópera.*
Postor(a) 2: *Ah, ¡entonces te doy $ 100!*

4 Teaching Tip Model the activity by completing item 1 in two different ways.

4 Expansion Have students create new sentences, employing additional uses of **por** and **para**.

5 Teaching Tip
Ask students questions about the car in the picture. Ex: **¿Te gusta este carro? ¿Cuánto se paga por un carro así? ¿A cuántas millas por hora corre este carro?** Have students write their answers using complete sentences.

5 Expansion
- Ask volunteers to role-play their conversation for the class.
- Show a picture of an old used car and ask students to create a new conversation. The parents are offering to buy their son/daughter this car instead of the one shown in the activity.

6 Teaching Tips
- Before the bidding begins, display the items to be auctioned off and name them. Invite students to walk around with their group members and discuss what the items are, their purposes, and how much they will pay for them.
- Have groups prepare the opening statements for the items their members brought. Students then take turns opening up the bidding for the entire class. Non-group members may bid on each item. Group members should place bids to keep the bidding alive.

TEACHING OPTIONS

Small Groups Have students create a television advertisement for a car or piece of technological equipment. Students should describe the item; explain why the customer should buy it; tell how much it costs; explain that the item is on sale only until a certain date; and detail any possible trade-ins. Students should use **por** and **para** as much as possible in their ad.

Extra Practice For students still having trouble distinguishing between **por** and **para**, have them create a mnemonic device, like a story or chant, for remembering the different uses. Ex: **Vine por la tarde y busqué por el parque, por el río y por el centro. Busqué por horas. Viajé por carro, por tren y por avión.** Do the same for **para**.

Section Goal

In **Estructura 11.3**, students will learn the use of reciprocal reflexives.

Instructional Resources
Supersite: Audio (Lab MP3 Files); Resources (Grammar Presentation Slides, Activity Pack, Scripts, Answer Keys); Testing Program (Quizzes)
WebSAM
Workbook, pp. 131–132
Lab Manual, p. 65

Teaching Tips

- Ask a volunteer to explain what reflexive verbs are. Ask other students to provide examples. Review reflexive verbs and pronouns by asking students questions about their personal routine. Ex: **Yo me desperté a las seis de la mañana. Y tú, ____ , ¿a qué hora te despertaste?**
- After going over the example sentences, ask students questions that contain or require reciprocal constructions. Ex: **¿Los estudiantes y los profesores siempre se saludan? ¿Se ven ustedes con frecuencia durante la semana? En las elecciones, ¿los candidatos siempre se respetan?**
- Add a visual aspect to this grammar presentation. Hold up images of pairs of celebrities and have students write descriptions about them, using reciprocal reflexives. Remind students they can use the present, preterite, or imperfect tense. Ex: Photos of Jennifer Aniston and Brad Pitt (**Antes se querían mucho, pero ahora no se hablan....**)

NATIONAL STANDARDS comparisons

11.3 Reciprocal reflexives

S Tutorial

ANTE TODO In **Lección 7**, you learned that reflexive verbs indicate that the subject of a sentence does the action to itself. Reciprocal reflexives, on the other hand, express a shared or reciprocal action between two or more people or things. In this context, the pronoun means *(to) each other* or *(to) one another*.

Luis y Marta **se** miran en el espejo.
Luis and Marta look at themselves in the mirror.

Luis y Marta **se** miran.
Luis and Marta look at each other.

▶ Only the plural forms of the reflexive pronouns (**nos, os, se**) are used to express reciprocal actions because the action must involve more than one person or thing.

Cuando **nos vimos** en la calle, **nos abrazamos**.
When we saw each other on the street, we hugged (one another).

Ustedes **se** van a **encontrar** en el cibercafé, ¿no?
You are meeting (each other) at the cybercafé, right?

Nos ayudamos cuando usamos la computadora.
We help each other when we use the computer.

Las amigas **se saludaron** y **se besaron**.
The friends greeted each other and kissed (one another).

¡ATENCIÓN!
Here is a list of common verbs that can express reciprocal actions:
abrazar(se) *to hug; to embrace (each other)*
ayudar(se) *to help (each other)*
besar(se) *to kiss (each other)*
encontrar(se) *to meet (each other); to run into (each other)*
saludar(se) *to greet (each other)*

¡INTÉNTALO! Indica el reflexivo recíproco adecuado de estos verbos en el presente o el pretérito.

presente

1. (escribir) Los novios *se escriben*.
   Nosotros nos escribimos.
   Ana y Ernesto se escriben.
2. (escuchar) Mis tíos se escuchan.
   Nosotros nos escuchamos.
   Ellos se escuchan.
3. (ver) Nosotros nos vemos.
   Fernando y Tomás se ven.
   Ustedes se ven.
4. (llamar) Ellas se llaman.
   Mis hermanos se llaman.
   Pepa y yo nos llamamos.

pretérito

1. (saludar) Nicolás y tú *se saludaron*.
   Nuestros vecinos se saludaron.
   Nosotros nos saludamos.
2. (hablar) Los amigos se hablaron.
   Elena y yo nos hablamos.
   Ustedes se hablaron.
3. (conocer) Alberto y yo nos conocimos.
   Ustedes se conocieron.
   Ellos se conocieron.
4. (encontrar) Ana y Javier se encontraron.
   Los primos se encontraron.
   Mi hermana y yo nos encontramos.

recursos
WB pp. 131–132
LM p. 65
vhlcentral.com Lección 11

TEACHING OPTIONS

Extra Practice Have students describe what they and their significant other or best friend do together, or what their friends do together. Have them use these verbs: **llamarse por teléfono, verse, decirse, ayudarse, encontrarse, reunirse.** Ex: **Mi amigo y yo siempre nos ayudamos con las tareas. Nos reunimos en la biblioteca o en mi casa y estudiamos por horas. Cuando hay examen de español, nos hacemos preguntas sobre el vocabulario y la gramática.**

Pairs Have students write a conversation in which they discuss two friends who are romantically involved, but have had a misunderstanding. Ask them to incorporate these verbs: **conocerse, encontrarse, quererse, hablarse, enojarse, besarse, mirarse,** and **entenderse.** Have pairs role-play their conversations for the class.

Práctica y Comunicación

1

Un amor recíproco Describe a Laura y a Elián usando los verbos recíprocos.

modelo

Laura veía a Elián todos los días. Elián veía a Laura todos los días.
Laura y Elián se veían todos los días.

1. Laura conocía bien a Elián. Elián conocía bien a Laura.
   Laura y Elián se conocían bien.
2. Laura miraba a Elián con amor. Elián la miraba con amor también.
   Laura y Elián se miraban con amor.
3. Laura entendía bien a Elián. Elián entendía bien a Laura.
   Laura y Elián se entendían bien.
4. Laura hablaba con Elián todas las noches por teléfono. Elián hablaba con Laura todas las noches por teléfono.
   Laura y Elián se hablaban todas las noches por teléfono.
5. Laura ayudaba a Elián con sus problemas. Elián la ayudaba también con sus problemas.
   Laura y Elián se ayudaban con sus problemas.

2

Describir Mira los dibujos y describe lo que estas personas hicieron. Answers will vary. Suggested answers:

1. Las hermanas se abrazaron.

2. Ellos se besaron.

3. Gilberto y Mercedes no se miraron / no se hablaron / se enojaron.

4. Tú y yo nos saludamos / nos encontramos en la calle.

NATIONAL communication STANDARDS

3

Preguntas En parejas, túrnense para hacerse estas preguntas. Answers will vary.

1. ¿Se vieron tú y tu mejor amigo/a ayer? ¿Cuándo se ven ustedes normalmente?
2. ¿Dónde se encuentran tú y tus amigos?
3. ¿Se ayudan tú y tu mejor amigo/a con sus problemas?
4. ¿Se entienden bien tus compañeros de clase?
5. ¿Dónde se conocieron tú y tu mejor amigo/a? ¿Cuánto tiempo hace que se conocen ustedes?
6. ¿Cuándo se dan regalos tú y tu novio/a?
7. ¿Se escriben tú y tus amigos mensajes de texto o prefieren llamarse por teléfono?
8. ¿Siempre se llevan bien tú y tu compañero/a de cuarto? Explica.

Practice more at **vhlcentral.com**.

1 Teaching Tip To simplify, before beginning the activity, review conjugations of the imperfect tense.

1 Expansion

- Have students expand upon the sentences to create a story about **Laura** and **Elián** falling in love.
- Have students rewrite the sentences, imagining that they are talking about themselves and their significant other, a close friend, or a relative.

2 Teaching Tip

Have pairs choose a drawing and create the story of what the characters did leading up to the moment pictured and what they did after that. Ask pairs to share their stories, and have the class vote for the most original or funniest one.

3 Teaching Tips

- To simplify, ask students to read through the questions and prepare short answers before talking to their partners.
- Have students ask follow-up questions. Ex: **¿A qué hora se vieron ayer? ¿Dónde se vieron? ¿Por qué se vieron ayer? ¿Para qué se ven ustedes normalmente?**
- Encourage students to verify what they hear by paraphrasing or summarizing their partner's responses.

TEACHING OPTIONS

Game Divide the class into small teams and write a verb on the board. Teams have twenty seconds to come up with a famous couple or two famous people or entities that behave or feel that way toward each other. The verb may be conjugated in the present, imperfect, or preterite tense. Ex: **quererse (Romeo y Julieta se querían.)** All teams with a correct answer earn one point. The team with the most points at the end wins.

Extra Practice Call on volunteers to act out a reciprocal action. The class will guess the action, using the correct verb in a sentence.

Heritage Speakers Ask heritage speakers to summarize the action of their favorite love story, soap opera, or television drama. They should use as many reciprocal reflexives as possible in their summaries. Ask the class comprehension questions as a follow-up.

Section Goals

In **Estructura 11.4**, students will learn:

- the stressed possessive adjectives and pronouns
- placement of stressed possessive adjectives

Instructional Resources

Supersite: Audio (Lab MP3 Files); Resources (Grammar Presentation Slides, Activity Pack, Scripts, Answer Keys); Testing Program (Quizzes)
WebSAM
Workbook, pp. 133–134
Lab Manual, p. 66

Teaching Tips

- Ask questions that involve unstressed possessive adjectives and respond to student answers with statements that involve the stressed possessive adjectives. Write each stressed possessive adjective you introduce on the board as you say it. Ex: ____, **¿es éste tu lápiz? (Sí.) Pues, este lápiz es tuyo,** ____ . Show your own pencil. **Éste es mi lápiz. Este lápiz es mío.**
- Write the masculine forms of the stressed possessive adjectives/pronouns on the board, and ask volunteers to give the feminine and plural forms. Emphasize that when a stressed possessive adjective is used, the word it modifies is preceded by an article.

11.4 Stressed possessive adjectives and pronouns

NATIONAL STANDARDS comparisons

S Tutorial

ANTE TODO Spanish has two types of possessive adjectives: the unstressed (or short) forms you learned in **Lección 3** and the stressed (or long) forms. The stressed forms are used for emphasis or to express *of mine*, *of yours*, and so on.

Stressed possessive adjectives

Masculine singular	Feminine singular	Masculine plural	Feminine plural	
mío	**mía**	**míos**	**mías**	*my; (of) mine*
tuyo	**tuya**	**tuyos**	**tuyas**	*your; (of) yours* (fam.)
suyo	**suya**	**suyos**	**suyas**	*your; (of) yours* (form.)*; his; (of) his; her; (of) hers; its*
nuestro	**nuestra**	**nuestros**	**nuestras**	*our; (of) ours*
vuestro	**vuestra**	**vuestros**	**vuestras**	*your; (of) yours* (fam.)
suyo	**suya**	**suyos**	**suyas**	*your; (of) yours; their; (of) theirs*

▶ **¡Atención!** Used with **un/una**, these possessives are similar in meaning to the English expression *of mine/yours/*etc.

Juancho es **un** amigo **mío**.
Juancho is a friend of mine.

Ella es **una** compañera **nuestra**.
She is a classmate of ours.

▶ Stressed possessive adjectives agree in gender and number with the nouns they modify. While unstressed possessive adjectives are placed before the noun, stressed possessive adjectives are placed after the noun they modify.

su impresora
her printer
→ la impresora **suya**
her printer

nuestros televisores
our television sets
→ los televisores **nuestros**
our television sets

▶ A definite article, an indefinite article, or a demonstrative adjective usually precedes a noun modified by a stressed possessive adjective.

Me encantan
- **unos** discos compactos **tuyos**. *I love some of your CDs.*
- **los** discos compactos **tuyos**. *I love your CDs.*
- **estos** discos compactos **tuyos**. *I love these CDs of yours.*

▶ Since **suyo, suya, suyos,** and **suyas** have more than one meaning, you can avoid confusion by using the construction: [*article*] + [*noun*] + **de** + [*subject pronoun*].

el teclado **suyo** → el teclado **de él/ella/usted**
el teclado **de ustedes/ellos/ellas**

CONSULTA

This is the same construction you learned in **Lección 3** for clarifying **su** and **sus**. To review unstressed possessive adjectives, see **Estructura 3.2,** p. 85.

TEACHING OPTIONS

Large Groups Have the class stand in a circle. Call out a sentence using a possessive adjective (Ex: **Nuestros radios son nuevos.**). Toss a ball to a student, who restates the sentence with a stressed possessive adjective (Ex: **Los radios nuestros son nuevos.**) and throws the ball to another student. He or she must restate it using a possessive pronoun (Ex: **Los nuestros son nuevos.**) and toss the ball back to you.

Extra Practice Call out a noun and subject pronoun, then ask students to say which stressed possessive adjective they would use. Ex: **discos compactos, ustedes (suyos)**

TPR Place photos of objects in a bag. Ask students to retrieve one photo and mime how to use the item. Have volunteers use stressed possessives to guess the item. Ex: **Es el carro de ____ y ____. Es el carro suyo.**

Possessive pronouns

- Possessive pronouns are used to replace a noun + [*possessive adjective*]. In Spanish, the possessive pronouns have the same forms as the stressed possessive adjectives, but they are preceded by a definite article.

la cámara **nuestra**	**la nuestra**
el navegador GPS **tuyo**	**el tuyo**
los archivos **suyos**	**los suyos**

- A possessive pronoun agrees in number and gender with the noun it replaces.

—Aquí está **mi coche**. ¿Dónde está **el tuyo**?
Here's my car. Where is yours?

—**El mío** está en el taller de mi hermano.
Mine is at my brother's garage.

—¿Tienes **las revistas** de Carlos?
Do you have Carlos' magazines?

—No, pero tengo **las nuestras**.
No, but I have ours.

¿También está descompuesta tu computadora?

No, la mía no, la suya.

¡INTÉNTALO! Indica las formas tónicas (*stressed*) de estos adjetivos posesivos y los pronombres posesivos correspondientes.

	adjetivos	pronombres
1. su cámara digital	la cámara digital suya	la suya
2. mi televisor	el televisor mío	el mío
3. nuestros discos compactos	los discos compactos nuestros	los nuestros
4. tus aplicaciones	las aplicaciones tuyas	las tuyas
5. su monitor	el monitor suyo	el suyo
6. mis videos	los videos míos	los míos
7. nuestra impresora	la impresora nuestra	la nuestra
8. tu estéreo	el estéreo tuyo	el tuyo
9. nuestro blog	el blog nuestro	el nuestro
10. mi computadora	la computadora mía	la mía

recursos
WB pp. 133–134
LM p. 66
vhlcentral.com Lección 11

Teaching Tips

- Ask students questions using unstressed possessive adjectives or the [*article*] + [*noun*] + **de** construction before a name, having them answer with a possessive pronoun. Ex: **¿Tienes tu cuaderno? Sí, tengo el mío.**
- Point out that the function of the stressed possessives is to give emphasis. They are often used to point out contrasts. Ex: **¿Tu carro es azul? Pues, el carro mío es rojo. ¿Tu cámara digital no es buena? La mía es excelente.**

TEACHING OPTIONS

Video Replay the **Fotonovela**, having students listen for each use of an unstressed possessive adjective and write down the sentence in which it occurs. Next, have students rewrite those sentences using a stressed possessive adjective. Then, discuss how the use of stressed possessive adjectives affected the meaning or fluidity of the sentences.

Pairs Tell students that their laundry has gotten mixed up with their roommate's and since they are the same size and have the same tastes in clothing, they cannot tell what belongs to whom. Have them ask each other questions about different articles of clothing. Ex: **—¿Son tuyos estos pantalones de rayas? —Sí, son míos. —Y, ¿estos calcetines rojos son tuyos? —Sí, son míos, pero esta camisa grandísima no es mía.**

Práctica

1

Oraciones Forma oraciones con estas palabras. Usa el presente y haz los cambios necesarios.

1. un / amiga / suyo / vivir / Mendoza Una amiga suya vive en Mendoza.
2. ¿me / prestar / calculadora / tuyo? ¿Me prestas la calculadora tuya?
3. el / coche / suyo / nunca / funcionar / bien El coche suyo nunca funciona bien.
4. no / nos / interesar / problemas / suyo No nos interesan los problemas suyos.
5. yo / querer / cámara digital / mío / ahora mismo Yo quiero la cámara digital mía ahora mismo.
6. un / amigos / nuestro / manejar / como / loco Unos amigos nuestros manejan como locos.

2

¿Es suyo? Un policía ha capturado (*has captured*) al hombre que robó (*robbed*) en tu casa. Ahora quiere saber qué cosas son tuyas. Túrnate con un(a) compañero/a para hacer el papel del policía y usa las pistas (*clues*) para contestar las preguntas.

modelo

no/viejo

Policía: Esta impresora, ¿es suya?

Estudiante: No, no es mía. La mía era más vieja.

1. sí E1: Este estéreo, ¿es suyo? E2: Sí, es mío.

2. no/pequeño E1: Este televisor, ¿es suyo? E2: No, no es mío. El mío era más pequeño.

3. sí E1: Estos teléfonos celulares, ¿son suyos? E2: Sí, son míos.

4. sí E1: Esta computadora portátil, ¿es suya? E2:Sí, es mía.

5. no/grande E1: Esta cámara de video, ¿es suya? E2: No, no es mía. La mía era más grande.

6. no/caro E1: Estos reproductores de MP3, ¿son suyos? E2: No, no son míos. Los míos eran más caros.

3

Conversaciones Completa estas conversaciones con las formas adecuadas de los pronombres posesivos.

1. —La casa de ellos estaba en la Avenida Alvear. ¿Dónde estaba la casa de ustedes?
   —__La nuestra__ estaba en la calle Bolívar.
2. —A Carmen le encanta su monitor nuevo.
   —¿Sí? A José no le gusta __el suyo__.
3. —Puse mis discos aquí. ¿Dónde pusiste __los tuyos__, Alfonso?
   —Puse __los míos__ en el escritorio.
4. —Se me olvidó traer mis llaves. ¿Trajeron ustedes __las suyas__?
   —No, dejamos __las nuestras__ en casa.
5. —Yo compré mi computadora en una tienda y Marta compró __la suya__ en Internet. Y __la tuya__, ¿dónde la compraste?
   —__La mía__ es de Cíbermax.

Practice more at **vhlcentral.com**.

1 Expansion Have students write four additional dehydrated sentences that use stressed possessive adjectives or pronouns. Have them exchange papers with a classmate, who will "rehydrate" them.

2 Expansion Have students continue the activity, using these items: **el navegador GPS, las calculadoras, el reproductor de DVD, los ratones.**

3 Teaching Tip To simplify, have students begin by scanning the conversations and writing the English translation of the word for each blank. Ex: 1. *Ours.* Then have them underline the noun that the pronoun refers to and state its gender and number. Ex: 1. **la casa**; feminine singular.

3 Expansion Have students create conversations modeled after the ones in the activity and perform them for the class. Each one should consist of at least six lines and use as many stressed possessive adjectives and pronouns as possible.

TEACHING OPTIONS

Large Groups Have students bring in a photo of their favorite car, and tell them to imagine that everyone in town is picking up his or her car at the mechanic's shop at the same time. Have students role-play a scene between the mechanic and several customers. The mechanic tries to determine to whom each car belongs.

Pairs Have pairs make a wish list consisting of ten items that they need for next year, then give it to another pair. Students must then divide the items between themselves, deciding who gets what on the list, and justifying their claim. Ex: **—La bicicleta nueva es mía. La necesito para ir a la universidad. —Bueno, entonces el navegador GPS es mío porque acabo de comprar un automóvil nuevo.** Students should try to use at least one possessive adjective or pronoun in their claims.

Comunicación

4 **Vendedores competitivos** Trabajen en grupos de tres. Uno/a de ustedes va a una tienda a comprar un aparato tecnológico (reproductor de MP3, computadora portátil, monitor, etc.). Los/Las otros/as dos son empleados/as de dos marcas rivales y compiten para convencer al/a la cliente/a de que compre su producto. Usen los adjetivos posesivos y túrnense para comprar y vender. ¿Quién es el/la mejor vendedor/a? Answers will vary.

modelo

Estudiante 1: Buenos días, quiero comprar un reproductor de MP3.
Estudiante 2: Tengo lo que necesita. El mío, tiene capacidad para 500 canciones.
Estudiante 3: El tuyo es muy viejo, con el mío también puedes ver videos…

5 **Comparar** Trabajen en parejas. Intenta (*Try to*) convencer a tu compañero/a de que algo que tú tienes es mejor que lo que él/ella tiene. Pueden hablar de sus carros, reproductores de MP3, teléfonos celulares, clases, horarios o trabajos. Answers will vary.

modelo

Estudiante 1: Mi computadora tiene una pantalla de quince pulgadas (*inches*). ¿Y la tuya?
Estudiante 2: La mía es mejor porque tiene una pantalla de diecisiete pulgadas.
Estudiante 1: Pues la mía…

Síntesis

6 **Inventos locos** En grupos pequeños, imaginen que construyeron un aparato tecnológico revolucionario. Dibujen su invento y descríbanlo contestando estas preguntas. Incluyan todos los detalles que crean (*that you believe*) necesarios. Luego, compártanlo con la clase. Utilicen los posesivos, **por** y **para** y el vocabulario de **Contextos**. Answers will vary.

modelo

Nuestro aparato se usa para cocinar huevos y funciona de una manera muy fácil…

- ¿Para qué se usa?
- ¿Cómo es?
- ¿Cuánto cuesta?
- ¿Qué personas van a comprar este aparato?

4 Teaching Tip Encourage students to bring in personal items to use as props, or have them print out photos of the items.

5 Teaching Tip Before beginning the activity, have students make a list of objects to compare. Then have them brainstorm as many different qualities or features of those objects as they can. Finally, have them list adjectives that they might use to compare the objects they have chosen.

5 Expansion Have pairs who had a heated discussion perform it for the class.

6 Expansion To challenge students, have them create a television or radio ad for their invention.

Extra Practice

- Write the names of four different means of communication on slips of paper and post them in different corners of the room: **el correo electrónico, el teléfono, el mensaje de texto, una carta.** Tell students to pick their preferred means of communication and go to that corner. Then have each group write five reasons for their choice as well as one reason why they did not choose any of the others, using stressed possessive adjectives and pronouns.
- Write a cloze paragraph on the board and have students complete it with the correct stressed possessive adjectives and pronouns. To simplify, add a word bank.

TEACHING OPTIONS

Large Group Add a visual aspect to this grammar practice. Ask each student to bring in a photo of an object. Tell students not to tell anyone what their object is, and place it in a bag. Call students up one at a time to choose a photo. Students then circulate around the classroom, trying to find the owner of their photo. Ex: **¿Es tuyo este control remoto? (No, no es mío.** or **Sí, es mío.)**

Extra Practice Have students imagine that they are salespersons at a car dealership and they are writing a letter to a customer explaining why their cars are better than those of the other two dealerships in town. Students should compare several attributes of the cars and use stressed possessive adjectives and pronouns when appropriate.

Section Goal

In **Recapitulación**, students will review the grammar concepts from this lesson.

Instructional Resource
Supersite

1 Teaching Tip Remind students that the **–s** ending is only present in negative familiar commands.

1 Expansion To challenge students, have them write mini-dialogues that include these command forms.

2 Teaching Tip Ask students to identify the rule associated with each use of **por** or **para** in the sentences.

2 Expansion Ask questions using **por** and **para**. Ex: **¿Hablan mucho por *Skype*? ¿Para qué clase estudian más, la clase de español o la clase de matemáticas?**

3 Expansion Make plural nouns singular and singular nouns plural in each question and have students repeat the activity. Ex: **1. ¿Éstos son mis videos? (Sí, son los tuyos.)**

Recapitulación

Diagnostics

Completa estas actividades para repasar los conceptos de gramática que aprendiste en esta lección.

1 Completar Completa la tabla con las formas de los mandatos familiares. **16 pts.**

Infinitivo	Mandato	
	Afirmativo	Negativo
comer	come	no comas
hacer	haz	no hagas
sacar	saca	no saques
venir	ven	no vengas
ir	ve	no vayas

2 Por y para Completa el diálogo con **por** o **para**. **20 pts.**

MARIO Hola, yo trabajo (1) __para__ el periódico de la universidad. ¿Puedo hacerte unas preguntas?

INÉS Sí, claro.

MARIO ¿Navegas mucho (2) __por__ la red?

INÉS Sí, todos los días me conecto a Internet (3) __para__ leer mi correo y navego (4) __por__ una hora. También me gusta hablar (5) __por__ *Skype* con mis amigos. Es muy bueno y, (6) __para__ mí, es divertido.

MARIO ¿Y qué piensas sobre hacer la tarea en la computadora?

INÉS En general, me parece bien, pero (7) __por__ ejemplo, anoche hice unos ejercicios (8) __para__ la clase de álgebra y al final me dolieron los ojos. (9) __Por__ eso a veces prefiero hacer la tarea a mano.

MARIO Muy bien. Muchas gracias (10) __por__ tu tiempo.

3 Posesivos Completa las oraciones y confirma de quién son las cosas. **12 pts.**

1. —¿Éste es mi video? —Sí, es el __tuyo__ (*fam.*).
2. —¿Ésta es la cámara de tu papá? —Sí, es la __suya__.
3. —¿Ese teléfono es de Pilar? —Sí, es el __suyo__.
4. —¿Éstos son los cargadores de ustedes? —No, no son __nuestros__.
5. —¿Ésta es tu computadora portátil? —No, no es __mía__.
6. —¿Ésas son mis fotos? —Sí, son las __suyas__ (*form.*).

RESUMEN GRAMATICAL

11.1 Familiar commands pp. 352–353

tú commands

Infinitive	Affirmative	Negative
guardar	**guarda**	**no guardes**
volver	**vuelve**	**no vuelvas**
imprimir	**imprime**	**no imprimas**

- Irregular **tú** command forms

dar → **no des**	saber → **no sepas**
decir → **di**	salir → **sal**
estar → **no estés**	ser → **sé, no seas**
hacer → **haz**	tener → **ten**
ir → **ve, no vayas**	venir → **ven**
poner → **pon**	

- Verbs ending in **-car, -gar, -zar** have a spelling change in the negative **tú** commands:

sacar → no saques
apagar → no apagues
almorzar → no almuerces

11.2 Por and para pp. 356–357

- Uses of **por**:

motion or general location; duration; reason or motive; object of a search; means by which something is done; exchange or substitution; unit of measure

- Uses of **para**:

destination; deadline; purpose or goal; recipient of something; comparison or opinion; in the employment of

11.3 Reciprocal reflexives p. 360

- Reciprocal reflexives express a shared or reciprocal action between two or more people or things. Only the plural forms (**nos, os, se**) are used.

Cuando **nos vimos** en la calle, **nos abrazamos.**

- Common verbs that can express reciprocal actions:

abrazar(se), ayudar(se), besar(se), conocer(se), encontrar(se), escribir(se), escuchar(se), hablar(se), llamar(se), mirar(se), saludar(se), ver(se)

TEACHING OPTIONS

Pairs Have pairs create a short survey about technology use. Encourage them to use **por** and **para**, as well as adverbs like **a menudo, normalmente**, etc. Then have them exchange their surveys with another pair and complete them. Ask volunteers to share their survey results with the class.

Extra Practice Tell students that you are a new student in class who likes to take people's things. Go around the room and gather students' belongings (books, pens, bags, etc.). In each case, insist that the item is yours. Ex: **Esta mochila es mía.** Have students protest and take their item back. Ex: **Esta mochila no es tuya, es mía.** Have other students contribute by asking, **¿Esta mochila es suya o es mía?**

11.4 Stressed possessive adjectives and pronouns

pp. 362–363

Stressed possessive adjectives

Masculine	Feminine
mío(s)	mía(s)
tuyo(s)	tuya(s)
suyo(s)	suya(s)
nuestro(s)	nuestra(s)
vuestro(s)	vuestra(s)
suyo(s)	suya(s)

la impresora **suya** → **la suya**

las llaves **mías** → **las mías**

4 Ángel y diablito A Juan le gusta pedir consejos a su ángel y a su diablito imaginarios. Completa las respuestas con mandatos familiares desde las dos perspectivas. **16 pts.**

1. Estoy manejando. ¿Voy más rápido?
   Á No, no ___vayas___ más rápido.
   D Sí, ___ve___ más rápido.
2. Es el reproductor de MP3 de mi hermana. ¿Lo pongo en mi mochila?
   Á No, no ___lo pongas___ en tu mochila.
   D Sí, ___ponlo___ en tu mochila.
3. Necesito estirar (*to stretch*) las piernas. ¿Doy un paseo?
   Á Sí, ___da___ un paseo.
   D No, no ___des___ un paseo.
4. Mi amigo necesita imprimir algo. ¿Apago la impresora?
   Á No, no ___apagues___ la impresora.
   D Sí, ___apaga___ la impresora.

5 Oraciones Forma oraciones para expresar acciones recíprocas con el tiempo indicado. **12 pts.**

modelo

tú y yo / conocer / bien (presente) *Tú y yo nos conocemos bien.*

1. José y Paco / llamar / una vez por semana (imperfecto)
   José y Paco se llamaban una vez por semana.
2. mi novia y yo / ver / todos los días (presente)
   Mi novia y yo nos vemos todos los días.
3. los compañeros de clase / ayudar / con la tarea (pretérito)
   Los compañeros de clase se ayudaron con la tarea.
4. tú y tu mamá / escribir / por correo electrónico / cada semana (imperfecto)
   Tú y tu mamá se escribían por correo electrónico cada semana.
5. mis hermanas y yo / entender / perfectamente (presente)
   Mis hermanas y yo nos entendemos perfectamente.
6. los profesores / saludar / con mucho respeto (pretérito)
   Los profesores se saludaron con mucho respeto.

6 La tecnología Escribe al menos seis oraciones diciéndole a un(a) amigo/a qué hacer para tener "una buena relación" con la tecnología. Usa mandatos familiares afirmativos y negativos. **24 pts.**

Answers will vary.

7 Saber compartir Completa la expresión con los dos pronombres posesivos que faltan. **¡4 puntos EXTRA!**

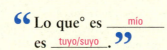

"Lo que° es ___mío___ es ___tuyo/suyo___."

Lo que *What*

Practice more at **vhlcentral.com**.

4 Teaching Tip Have volunteers role-play each exchange for the class. Encourage them to ad-lib as they go.

4 Expansion Give students these situations as items 5–8: **5. Mi amigo tiene las respuestas del examen final de historia. ¿Se las pido? (No, no se las pidas.; Sí, pídeselas.) 6. Es el cumpleaños de mi compañero de cuarto. ¿Le compro algo? (Sí, cómprale algo.; No, no le compres nada.) 7. Rompí la computadora portátil de mi padre. ¿Se lo digo? (Sí, díselo.; No, no se lo digas.) 8. No tengo nada de dinero. ¿Busco trabajo? (Sí, búscalo.; No, no lo busques.)**

5 Expansion Have students create two additional dehydrated sentences. Then have them exchange papers with a classmate and complete the exercise.

6 Teaching Tip To challenge students, have them first write a letter from the point of view of the friend who needs help with technology. Then have students write their suggestions according to the problems outlined in the letter.

7 Teaching Tip Explain that this expression takes the masculine possessive form because it does not refer to anything specific, as denoted by **lo que**.

TEACHING OPTIONS

Game Divide the class into two teams, **por** and **para**, and have them line up. Choose a volunteer to go first from each team, and say an English sentence using an equivalent of **por** or **para**. Ex: Yesterday I got sick and my brother worked *for* me. The student whose team corresponds to the correct Spanish equivalent of *for* has five seconds to step forward and give the Spanish translation. Ex: **Ayer me enfermé y mi hermano trabajó *por* mí.** Award one point for every correct answer. The team with the most points at the end wins.

Small Groups As a class, brainstorm a list of infinitives that can be made reciprocal (**llamar, abrazar, conocer**, etc.) and write them on the board. In small groups, have students create a dialogue using at least six of these infinitives. Then have students act out their dialogues for the class. Encourage students to use lesson vocabulary.

Audio: Reading
Additional Reading

Section Goals

In **Lectura**, students will:

- learn to recognize borrowed words
- increase their reading comprehension in Spanish by using borrowed words to predict content
- read a content-rich text with borrowed words

Instructional Resource
Supersite

Estrategia Tell students that recognizing words borrowed from English will help them understand unfamiliar texts.

Examinar el texto If students struggle answering these questions, have them focus on the character in red shorts and what he is holding and saying.

Buscar Invite students to speculate as to why so many words related to technology are loan words from English.

Sobre el autor **Juan Matías Loiseau** has also made two award-winning short films, ***El Ángel de Dorotea*** (2005) and ***Abismos*** (2006).

Lectura

NATIONAL STANDARDS communication cultures

Antes de leer

Estrategia

Recognizing borrowed words

One way languages grow is by borrowing words from each other. English words that relate to technology often are borrowed by Spanish and other languages throughout the world. Sometimes the words are modified slightly to fit the sounds of the languages that borrow them. When reading in Spanish, you can often increase your understanding by looking for words borrowed from English or other languages you know.

Examinar el texto

Observa la tira cómica°. ¿De qué trata°? ¿Cómo lo sabes? Answers will vary.

Buscar

Esta lectura contiene una palabra tomada° del inglés. Trabaja con un(a) compañero/a para encontrarla.

el celular

Repasa° las palabras nuevas relacionadas con la tecnología que aprendiste en **Contextos** y expande la lista de palabras tomadas del inglés. Answers will vary.

__________ __________
__________ __________
__________ __________

Sobre el autor

Juan Matías Loiseau (1974–). Más conocido como Tute, este artista nació en Buenos Aires, Argentina. Estudió diseño gráfico, humorismo y cine. Sus tiras cómicas se publican en Estados Unidos, Francia y toda Latinoamérica.

tira cómica *comic strip* ¿De qué trata? *What is it about?* tomada *taken* Repasa *Review*

Practice more at **vhlcentral.com**.

TEACHING OPTIONS

Pairs Have pairs of students work together to create an alternate ending to this comic. Then have students get together in groups and share their new endings. Have the group select one to present to the class.

Game Have students write a short description of a type of new technology that has changed their lives. Tell them to present the most general clues first, moving toward more specific clues. Ex: **Con esto puedo enviarles mensajes cortos a mis amigos. Y los amigos míos pueden contestarme inmediatamente. Uso el celular sin usar minutos. (mensajes de texto)** Have students read their descriptions for the class to guess.

Después de leer

Comprensión

Indica si las oraciones son **ciertas** o **falsas**. Corrige las falsas.

Cierto	Falso	
✓		1. Hay tres personajes en la tira cómica: un usuario de teléfono, un amigo y un empleado de la empresa (*company*) telefónica.
	✓	2. El nuevo servicio de teléfono incluye las llamadas telefónicas únicamente. También viene con un tipo que te sigue a todos lados.
	✓	3. El empleado duerme en su casa. Duerme al lado de la cama del usuario.
✓		4. El contrato de teléfono dura (*lasts*) un año.
	✓	5. El usuario y el amigo están trabajando (*working*). Están de vacaciones.

Preguntas

Responde a estas preguntas con oraciones completas. Usa el pretérito y el imperfecto.

1. ¿Al usuario le gustaba usar el teléfono celular todo el tiempo?
   No, al usuario le molestaba usar el celular todo el tiempo.
2. ¿Por qué el usuario decidió tirar el teléfono al mar?
   Porque el celular y el tipo lo tenían harto.
3. Según el amigo, ¿para qué tenía el usuario que tirar el teléfono celular al mar?
   El usuario tenía que tirar el teléfono al mar para recuperar su libertad.
4. ¿Qué ocurrió cuando el usuario tiró el teléfono?
   El empleado fue a buscar el teléfono.
5. ¿Qué le dijo el empleado al usuario cuando salió del mar?
   El empleado le dijo que tenía una llamada perdida.

Conversar

En grupos pequeños, hablen de estos temas. Answers will vary.

1. ¿Se sienten identificados/as con el usuario de teléfono de la tira cómica? ¿Por qué?
2. ¿Cuáles son los aspectos positivos y los negativos de tener teléfono celular?
3. ¿Cuál es para ustedes el límite que debe tener la tecnología en nuestras vidas?

te viene *comes with* tipo *guy, dude* te avisa *alerts you* escuchás *listen (Arg.)* distraídos *careless* piso *floor* bolsa de dormir *sleeping bag* darle de baja *to suspend* harto *fed up* revolear *throw it away with energy (S. America)* bien hecho *well done* llamada perdida *missed call*

Comprensión Have students write three additional true/false statements for a classmate to complete.

Preguntas
- Have students work in pairs to answer these questions.
- Assign a number to each panel in the comic. Then have students identify the panel(s) where they found the information needed for their answers.

Conversar For item 2, survey the class and write their answers on the board in a two-column chart with the headings **Lo positivo** and **Lo negativo**. Then ask the class to determine which column wins out overall.

TEACHING OPTIONS

Large Groups Ask students to work in groups of six. Tell them to improvise and create a humorous story as a group. Ask one person in the group to start it off by giving an introductory sentence, such as: **Ayer estuvimos en el coche y ocurrió algo muy raro.** Have the others add sentences with additional details to complete the story. Encourage students to be creative and make the story as long as they wish.

Pairs In pairs, have students create a comic strip about cars or car accessories. Tell them that they may use the same main character as the comic on these pages, or they may develop new character(s). Have students present their comics to the class.

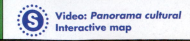

Video: *Panorama cultural*
Interactive map

Section Goal

In **Panorama**, students will read about the geography, history, and culture of Argentina.

Instructional Resources
Supersite: Video (***Panorama cultural***); Resources (Scripts, Translations, Digital Image Bank, Answer Keys)
WebSAM
Workbook, pp. 135–136
Video Manual, pp. 53–54

Teaching Tips

- Use the **Lección 11 Panorama** digital images to assist with this presentation.
- Have students look at the map of Argentina, and guide them to recognize Argentina's great size and the variety of topographical features, such as mountains (**los Andes**), vast plains (**las pampas**), and large rivers.
- Point out that Argentina is one of the largest beef producers in the world and that **gauchos** have played an important role in the culture of the country. Bariloche is an important winter recreation area. Remind students that June–August is winter in the southern hemisphere.

El país en cifras Patagonia is very sparsely populated, but Buenos Aires is a metropolis about the size of New York City. Invite students to mention anything they know about Argentina.

¡Increíble pero cierto! **Avenida 9 de Julio** is so wide that pedestrians need a few minutes and several green lights to cross it (there are stoplights to control pedestrian traffic). To help alleviate this, some urban planners have advocated making the central part of the avenue subterranean.

Argentina

NATIONAL STANDARDS: connections, cultures

El país en cifras

- **Área:** 2.780.400 km² (1.074.000 millas²)
  Argentina es el país de habla española más grande del mundo. Su territorio es dos veces el tamaño° de Alaska.
- **Población:** 43.024.000
- **Capital:** Buenos Aires (y su área metropolitana) —13.528.000
  En el gran Buenos Aires vive más del treinta por ciento de la población total del país. La ciudad es conocida° como el "París de Suramérica" por su estilo parisino°.

Buenos Aires

- **Ciudades principales:** Córdoba —1.493.000, Rosario —1.231.000, Mendoza —917.000
- **Moneda:** peso argentino
- **Idiomas:** español (oficial), lenguas indígenas

Bandera de Argentina

Argentinos célebres

- **Jorge Luis Borges,** escritor (1899–1986)
- **María Eva Duarte de Perón ("Evita"),** primera dama° (1919–1952)
- **Mercedes Sosa,** cantante (1935–2009)
- **Leandro "Gato" Barbieri,** saxofonista (1932–)
- **Adolfo Pérez Esquivel,** activista (1931–), Premio Nobel de la Paz en 1980

tamaño *size* conocida *known* parisino *Parisian* primera dama *First Lady* anchas *wide* mide *it measures* campo *field*

Monte Fitz Roy (Chaltén)

recursos
WB pp. 135–136 | VM pp. 53–54 | vhlcentral.com Lección 11

¡Increíble pero cierto!

La Avenida 9 de Julio en Buenos Aires es una de las calles más anchas° del mundo. De lado a lado mide° cerca de 140 metros, lo que es equivalente a un campo° y medio de fútbol. Su nombre conmemora el Día de la Independencia de Argentina.

TEACHING OPTIONS

Worth Noting The Argentinian cowboy, the **gaucho**, has played as significant a role in the folklore of Argentina as the cowboy of the Old West has played in that of the United States. Two classic works of Argentinian literature focus on the **gaucho**. ***El gaucho Martín Fierro***, an epic poem by **José Hernández** (1834–1886), celebrates the **gaucho's** fiercely independent way of life, whereas **Domingo Sarmiento's** (1811–1888) biography, ***Facundo: Civilización y barbarie***, describes the nomadic, uneducated **gauchos** as hindrances in Argentina's pursuit of economic, social, and political progress.

Extra Practice Have students listen to a song on one of the many recordings by singer **Mercedes Sosa**. Then, have pairs work together to transcribe the lyrics. Invite volunteers to share their work with the class.

BRASIL

Historia • Inmigración europea

Se dice que Argentina es el país más "europeo" de toda Latinoamérica. Después del año 1880, inmigrantes italianos, alemanes, españoles e ingleses llegaron para establecerse en esta nación. Esta diversidad cultural ha dejado° una profunda huella° en la música, el cine y la arquitectura argentinos.

Artes • El tango

El tango es uno de los símbolos culturales más importantes de Argentina. Este género° musical es una mezcla de ritmos de origen africano, italiano y español, y se originó a finales del siglo XIX entre los porteños°. Poco después se hizo popular entre el resto de los argentinos y su fama llegó hasta París. Como baile, el tango en un principio° era provocativo y violento, pero se hizo más romántico durante los años 30. Hoy día, este estilo musical tiene adeptos° en muchas partes del mundo°.

Lugares • Las cataratas del Iguazú

Las famosas cataratas° del Iguazú se encuentran entre las fronteras de Argentina, Paraguay y Brasil, al norte de Buenos Aires. Cerca de ellas confluyen° los ríos Iguazú y Paraná. Estas extensas caídas de agua tienen hasta 80 metros (262 pies) de altura° y en época° de lluvias llegan a medir 4 kilómetros (2,5 millas) de ancho. Situadas en el Parque Nacional Iguazú, las cataratas son un destino° turístico muy visitado.

¿Qué aprendiste? Responde a cada pregunta con una oración completa.

Artesano en Buenos Aires

1. ¿Qué porcentaje de la población de Argentina vive en el gran Buenos Aires?
   Más del treinta por ciento de la población de Argentina vive en el gran Buenos Aires.
2. ¿Quién era Mercedes Sosa?
   Mercedes Sosa era una cantante argentina.
3. Se dice que Argentina es el país más europeo de Latinoamérica. ¿Por qué? Se dice que Argentina es el país más europeo de Latinoamérica porque muchos inmigrantes europeos se establecieron allí.
4. ¿Qué tipo de baile es uno de los símbolos culturales más importantes de Argentina?
   El tango es uno de los símbolos culturales más importantes de Argentina.
5. ¿Dónde y cuándo se originó el tango?
   El tango se originó entre los porteños a finales del siglo XIX.
6. ¿Cómo era el baile del tango originalmente?
   El tango era un baile provocativo y violento.
7. ¿En qué parque nacional están las cataratas del Iguazú?
   Las cataratas del Iguazú están en el Parque Nacional Iguazú.

Conexión Internet Investiga estos temas en **vhlcentral.com**.

1. Busca información sobre el tango. ¿Te gustan los ritmos y sonidos del tango? ¿Por qué? ¿Se baila el tango en tu comunidad?
2. ¿Quiénes fueron Juan y Eva Perón y qué importancia tienen en la historia de Argentina?

Practice more at **vhlcentral.com**.

ha dejado *has left* **huella** *mark* **género** *genre* **porteños** *people of Buenos Aires* **en un principio** *at first* **adeptos** *followers* **mundo** *world* **cataratas** *waterfalls* **confluyen** *converge* **altura** *height* **época** *season* **destino** *destination*

Inmigración europea Among the waves of immigrants were thousands of European Jews. An interesting chapter in the history of the **pampas** features Jewish **gauchos**. A generous, pre-Zionist philanthropist purchased land for Jews who settled on the Argentine grasslands. At one time, the number of Yiddish-language newspapers in Argentina was second only to that in New York City.

El tango **Carlos Gardel** (1890–1935) is considered the great classic interpreter of **tango**. If possible, bring in a recording of his version of a **tango** such as ***Cuesta abajo*** or ***Volver.*** **Astor Piazzola** (1921–1992) was a modern exponent of **tango**. His **tango nuevo** has found interpreters such as cellist Yo-Yo Ma and the Kronos Quartet. For more information about **el tango**, you may want to play the ***Panorama cultural*** video footage for this lesson.

Las cataratas del Iguazú At just over ten miles away, **Puerto Iguazú** is the closest city to the falls. Other nearby attractions include the **Itaipú** dam, which is the world's biggest hydroelectric facility, and the **Parque de las Aves,** where one can observe many near-extinct and exotic species of birds.

Conexión Internet Students will find supporting Internet activities and links at **vhlcentral.com.**

TEACHING OPTIONS

Variación léxica Argentinians frequently use the word **¡che!** to get the attention of someone they are talking to. **Che** also serves as a kind of spoken exclamation point with which Argentinians pepper their speech. This is so noticeable to outsiders that Argentinians are often given the nickname **Che** in other parts of the Spanish-speaking world. Another notable feature of Argentine Spanish is the existence, alongside **tú**, of **vos** as the second-person singular familiar pronoun. **Vos** is also heard in other parts of Latin America, and it is accompanied by corresponding verb forms in the present tense. Here are some equivalents: **vos contás / tú cuentas, vos pensás / tú piensas, vos sos / tú eres, vos ponés / tú pones, vos venís / tú vienes.**

Section Goal

In **Panorama**, students will read about the geography and culture of Uruguay.

Instructional Resources
Supersite: Video (***Panorama cultural***); Resources (Scripts, Translations, Digital Image Bank, Answer Keys)
WebSAM
Workbook, 137–138
Video Manual, pp. 55–56

Teaching Tips

- Use the **Lección 11 Panorama** digital images to assist with this presentation.
- Have students look at the map of Uruguay and talk about the country's geographical features. Point out the long coastline that runs along the **Río de la Plata,** separating Uruguay from Argentina. Point out that Uruguay and Argentina have a great deal in common culturally.

El país en cifras After reading the paragraph under **Capital,** tell students that at the time of European contact, the area from **Punta del Este** northward up the coast of Brazil to Rio Grande do Sul was one enormous, uninterrupted beach. Early explorers were awestruck by the natural beauty of the Uruguayan landscape, which had rich and varied wildlife. After reading **Uruguayos célebres,** point out that **Horacio Quiroga's *Cuentos de la selva*** are set amidst Uruguay's natural flora and fauna.

¡Increíble pero cierto! One **ñandú** egg can measure more than five inches, weigh one pound, and equal twelve chicken eggs. Males typically incubate the eggs and then watch fiercely over the chicks. Their paternal instinct is so intense that they might even raise other males' chicks as if they were their own.

Uruguay

NATIONAL STANDARDS connections cultures

El país en cifras

- **Área:** 176.220 km² (68.039 millas²), *el tamaño° del estado de Washington*
- **Población:** 3.332.000
- **Capital:** Montevideo—1.672.000

Casi la mitad° de la población de Uruguay vive en Montevideo. Situada en la desembocadura° del famoso Río de la Plata, esta ciudad cosmopolita e intelectual es también un destino popular para las vacaciones, debido a sus numerosas playas de arena° blanca que se extienden hasta la ciudad de Punta del Este.

- **Ciudades principales:** Salto, Paysandú, Las Piedras, Rivera
- **Moneda:** peso uruguayo
- **Idiomas:** español (oficial)

Bandera de Uruguay

Uruguayos célebres

- **Horacio Quiroga,** escritor (1878–1937)
- **Juana de Ibarbourou,** escritora (1892–1979)
- **Mario Benedetti,** escritor (1920–2009)
- **Cristina Peri Rossi,** escritora y profesora (1941–)
- **Jorge Drexler,** cantante y compositor (1964–)

tamaño *size* mitad *half* desembocadura *mouth* arena *sand* avestruz *ostrich* no voladora *flightless* medir *measure* cotizado *valued*

Gaucho uruguayo

Entrada a la Ciudad Vieja, Colonia del Sacramento

recursos

WB pp. 137–138	VM pp. 55–56	vhlcentral.com Lección 11

¡Increíble pero cierto!

En Uruguay hay muchos animales curiosos, entre ellos el ñandú. De la misma familia del avestruz°, el ñandú es el ave no voladora° más grande del hemisferio occidental. Puede llegar a medir° dos metros. Normalmente, va en grupos de veinte o treinta y vive en el campo. Es muy cotizado° por su carne, sus plumas y sus huevos.

TEACHING OPTIONS

Variación léxica Montevideo looks out across the wide estuary of the **Río de la Plata** toward Buenos Aires, Argentina. Uruguay and Argentina have many cultural elements in common, including linguistic similarities. When speaking, Uruguayans tend to use **vos** as frequently as **tú,** as well as the corresponding verb forms. The plural of both forms is **ustedes,** as in the rest of Latin America. In the northern part of Uruguay, along the border with Brazil, the majority of residents are bilingual in Portuguese and Spanish.

Costumbres • La carne y el mate

En Uruguay y Argentina, la carne es un elemento esencial de la dieta diaria. Algunos platillos representativos de estas naciones son el asado°, la parrillada° y el chivito°. El mate, una infusión similar al té, también es típico de la región. Esta bebida de origen indígena está muy presente en la vida social y familiar de estos países aunque, curiosamente, no se puede consumir en bares o restaurantes.

Deportes • El fútbol

El fútbol es el deporte nacional de Uruguay. El primer equipo de balompié uruguayo se formó en 1891 y en 1930 el país suramericano fue la sede° de la primera Copa Mundial de esta disciplina. El equipo nacional ha conseguido grandes éxitos° a lo largo de los años: dos campeonatos olímpicos, en 1923 y 1928, y dos campeonatos mundiales, en 1930 y 1950. De hecho, Uruguay y Argentina han presentado su candidatura binacional para que la Copa Mundial de Fútbol de 2030 se celebre en sus países.

Costumbres • El Carnaval

El Carnaval de Montevideo es el de mayor duración en el mundo. A lo largo de 40 días, los uruguayos disfrutan de° los desfiles° y la música que inundan las calles de su capital. La celebración más conocida es el Desfile de Llamadas, en el que participan bailarines al ritmo del candombe, una danza de tradición africana.

Edificio del Parlamento en Montevideo

¿Qué aprendiste? Contesta cada pregunta con una oración completa.

1. ¿Qué tienen en común cuatro de los uruguayos célebres mencionados en la página anterior (*previous*)?
   Son escritores.
2. ¿Cuál es el elemento esencial de la dieta uruguaya?
   La carne es esencial en la dieta uruguaya.
3. ¿Qué es el ñandú?
   El ñandú es un ave no voladora que vive en Uruguay.
4. ¿Qué es el mate?
   El mate es una bebida indígena que es similar al té.
5. ¿Cuándo se formó el primer equipo uruguayo de fútbol?
   En 1891 se formó el primer equipo de fútbol uruguayo.
6. ¿Cuándo se celebró la primera Copa Mundial de fútbol?
   La primera Copa Mundial se celebró en 1930.
7. ¿Cómo se llama la celebración más conocida del Carnaval de Montevideo?
   La celebración más conocida del Carnaval de Montevideo se llama el Desfile de Llamadas.
8. ¿Cuántos días dura el Carnaval de Montevideo?
   El Carnaval de Montevideo dura unos cuarenta días.

Conexión Internet Investiga estos temas en **vhlcentral.com.**

1. Uruguay es conocido como un país de muchos escritores. Busca información sobre uno de ellos y escribe una biografía.
2. Investiga cuáles son las comidas y bebidas favoritas de los uruguayos. Descríbelas e indica cuáles te gustaría probar y por qué.

Practice more at **vhlcentral.com**.

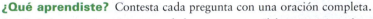

asado *barbecued beef* parrillada *barbecue* chivito *goat in Argentina; steak sandwich in Uruguay* sede *site* éxitos *successes* disfrutan de *enjoy* desfiles *parades*

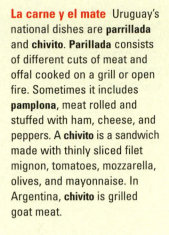

La carne y el mate Uruguay's national dishes are **parrillada** and **chivito**. **Parillada** consists of different cuts of meat and offal cooked on a grill or open fire. Sometimes it includes **pamplona**, meat rolled and stuffed with ham, cheese, and peppers. A **chivito** is a sandwich made with thinly sliced filet mignon, tomatoes, mozzarella, olives, and mayonnaise. In Argentina, **chivito** is grilled goat meat.

El fútbol Uruguayan women have begun to make their mark in soccer. Although the International Federation of Football Association (FIFA) established a women's league in 1982, it was not until 1985 that the first women's league—from Brazil—was formally established. The women's league of Uruguay was formed in 1996 and now participates in international soccer play.

El Carnaval Along with the rest of Latin America, Uruguay participated in the slave trade during the colonial period. African-influenced **candombe** music is popular with Uruguayans from all sectors of society.

Conexión Internet Students will find supporting Internet activities and links at **vhlcentral.com**.

Teaching Tip You may want to wrap up this section by playing the ***Panorama cultural*** video footage for this lesson.

TEACHING OPTIONS

Worth Noting Uruguay is similar to its larger, more powerful neighbor, Argentina, in many ways: Uruguayans also love the **tango** and **yerba mate,** many play the Argentine card game **truco,** and most are devoted carnivores. Historically, raising cattle, the culture of the **gaucho,** and the great cattle ranches called **estancias** have been important elements in the Uruguayan culture. Another, less pleasant, similarity was in the Dirty War (**Guerra sucia**) waged by an Uruguayan military dictatorship against domestic dissidents during the 1970s and 80s. In 1984 the military allowed the election of a civilian government. Today, presidential and parliamentary elections are held every five years. Uruguay has a multi-party system in which three political parties dominate.

Instructional Resources
Supersite: Audio (Textbook & Lab MP3s); Testing Program (Tests, MP3s)
WebSAM
Lab Manual, p. 66

La tecnología

la aplicación	*app*
la cámara digital/de video	*digital/video camera*
el canal	*(TV) channel*
el cargador	*charger*
el cibercafé	*cybercafé*
el control remoto	*remote control*
el correo de voz	*voice mail*
el disco compacto	*CD*
el estéreo	*stereo*
el radio	*radio (set)*
el reproductor de CD	*CD player*
el reproductor de MP3	*MP3 player*
el (teléfono) celular	*(cell) phone*
el televisor	*television set*
apagar	*to turn off*
funcionar	*to work*
llamar	*to call*
poner, prender	*to turn on*
sonar (o:ue)	*to ring*
descompuesto/a	*not working; out of order*
lento/a	*slow*
lleno/a	*full*

Verbos

abrazar(se)	*to hug; to embrace (each other)*
ayudar(se)	*to help (each other)*
besar(se)	*to kiss (each other)*
encontrar(se) (o:ue)	*to meet (each other); to run into (each other)*
saludar(se)	*to greet (each other)*

La computadora

el archivo	*file*
la arroba	*@ symbol*
el blog	*blog*
el buscador	*browser*
la computadora (portátil)	*(portable) computer; (laptop)*
la conexión inalámbrica	*wireless connection*
la dirección electrónica	*e-mail address*
la impresora	*printer*
Internet	*Internet*
el mensaje de texto	*text message*
el monitor	*(computer) monitor*
la página principal	*home page*
la pantalla	*screen*
el programa de computación	*software*
el ratón	*mouse*
la red	*network; Web*
el reproductor de DVD	*DVD player*
el sitio web	*website*
el teclado	*keyboard*
borrar	*to erase*
chatear	*to chat*
descargar	*to download*
escanear	*to scan*
grabar	*to record*
guardar	*to save*
imprimir	*to print*
navegar (en Internet)	*to surf (the Internet)*

El carro

la autopista	*highway*
el baúl	*trunk*
la calle	*street*
la carretera	*highway; (main) road*
el capó, el cofre	*hood*
el carro, el coche	*car*
la circulación, el tráfico	*traffic*
el garaje, el taller (mecánico)	*garage; (mechanic's) repair shop*
la gasolina	*gasoline*
la gasolinera	*gas station*
la licencia de conducir	*driver's license*
la llanta	*tire*
el/la mecánico/a	*mechanic*
el navegador GPS	*GPS*
el parabrisas	*windshield*
la policía	*police (force)*
la velocidad máxima	*speed limit*
el volante	*steering wheel*
arrancar	*to start*
arreglar	*to fix; to arrange*
bajar(se) de	*to get off of/out of (a vehicle)*
conducir, manejar	*to drive*
estacionar	*to park*
llenar (el tanque)	*to fill (the tank)*
parar	*to stop*
revisar (el aceite)	*to check (the oil)*
subir(se) a	*to get on/into (a vehicle)*

Otras palabras y expresiones

por aquí	*around here*
por ejemplo	*for example*
por eso	*that's why; therefore*
por fin	*finally*

Por and **para**	*See pages 356–357.*
Stressed possessive adjectives and pronouns	*See pages 362–363.*
Expresiones útiles	*See page 347.*

recursos
LM p. 66
vhlcentral.com Lección 11

Vocabulary Tools

La vivienda

12

Communicative Goals

You will learn how to:

- **Welcome people to your home**
- **Describe your house or apartment**
- **Talk about household chores**
- **Give instructions**

A PRIMERA VISTA

- ¿Están los chicos en casa?
- ¿Viven en una casa o en un apartamento?
- ¿Ya comieron o van a comer?
- ¿Están de buen humor o de mal humor?

Lesson Goals

In **Lección 12**, students will be introduced to the following:

- terms for parts of a house
- names of common household objects
- terms for household chores
- central patios
- floating islands in Lake Titicaca
- relative pronouns
- formal (**usted/ustedes**) commands
- object pronouns with formal commands
- present subjunctive
- subjunctive with verbs and expressions of will and influence
- locating the main parts of a sentence
- using linking words
- writing a lease agreement
- using visual cues while listening
- a commercial for **Carrefour** supermarkets
- the short film ***036***
- a video about the **Museo Casa de Frida Kahlo**
- cultural and geographic information about Panama and El Salvador

A primera vista Here are some additional questions you can ask to personalize the photo: **¿Dónde vives? ¿Con quién vives? ¿Cómo es tu casa? ¿Qué haces en casa por la noche? ¿Qué haces los fines de semana? ¿Tienes computadora en casa? ¿Qué otros aparatos tecnológicos tienes?**

Teaching Tip Look for these icons for additional communicative practice:

	Interpretive communication
	Presentational communication
	Interpersonal communication

INSTRUCTIONAL RESOURCES

Supersite (vhlcentral.com)
Video: ***Fotonovela, Flash cultura, Anuncio, Cortometraje, Panorama cultural***
Audio: Textbook and Lab MP3 Files
Activity Pack: Information Gap Activities, games, additional activity handouts
Resources: SAM Answer Key, Scripts, Translations, **Vocabulario adicional**, sample lesson plan, Grammar Presentation Slides, Digital Image Bank
Testing Program: Quizzes, Tests, Exams, MP3s
Student Activities Manual: Workbook/Video Manual/Lab Manual
WebSAM (online Student Activities Manual)

Vocabulary Tools

Section Goals

In **Contextos**, students will learn and practice:
- names of rooms in a house
- names of common household objects
- terms for household chores

Instructional Resources
Supersite: Audio (Textbook and Lab MP3 Files); Resources (Digital Image Bank, **Vocabulario adicional**, Activity Pack, Scripts, Answer Keys); Testing Program (Quizzes)
WebSAM
Workbook, pp. 139–140
Lab Manual, p. 67

Teaching Tips

- Use the **Lección 12 Contextos** digital images to assist with this presentation.
- As students look at the illustration in their books, describe the house, naming the kinds of rooms and introducing those that are not shown. Ex: **Ésta es la casa de los Hernández. Hay una sala grande, un dormitorio, una oficina, una cocina y un altillo. También hay un cuarto de baño, un sótano, un patio y un garaje, pero no vemos estos cuartos en la ilustración.**
- Ask open-ended questions about the house and housework pictured in the illustration. Ex: **¿Dónde se pone la comida después de regresar del supermercado?** Ask personalized questions. Ex: **____, ¿vives en una residencia o en un apartamento? ¿Cuántos cuartos hay?**

Note: At this point you may want to present ***Vocabulario adicional: Más vocabulario para el hogar*** from the Supersite.

La vivienda

Más vocabulario

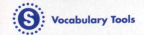

las afueras	*suburbs; outskirts*
el alquiler	*rent (payment)*
el ama (*m., f.*) de casa	*housekeeper; caretaker*
el barrio	*neighborhood*
el edificio de apartamentos	*apartment building*
el/la vecino/a	*neighbor*
la vivienda	*housing*
el balcón	*balcony*
la entrada	*entrance*
la escalera	*stairs*
el garaje	*garage*
el jardín	*garden; yard*
el patio	*patio; yard*
el pasillo	*hallway*
el sótano	*basement*
la cafetera	*coffee maker*
el electrodoméstico	*electrical appliance*
el horno (de microondas)	*(microwave) oven*
la lavadora	*washing machine*
la luz	*light; electricity*
la secadora	*clothes dryer*
la tostadora	*toaster*
el cartel	*poster*
la mesita de noche	*night stand*
los muebles	*furniture*
alquilar	*to rent*
mudarse	*to move (from one house to another)*

Variación léxica

dormitorio ↔ alcoba (*Arg.*); aposento (*Rep. Dom.*); recámara (*Méx.*)
apartamento ↔ departamento (*Arg., Chile, Méx.*); piso (*Esp.*)
lavar los platos ↔ lavar/fregar los trastes (*Amér. C., Rep. Dom.*)

recursos
WB pp. 139–140 | LM p. 67 | vhlcentral.com Lección 12

Los quehaceres domésticos

arreglar	*to straighten up*
barrer el suelo	*to sweep the floor*
cocinar	*to cook*
ensuciar	*to get (something) dirty*
hacer quehaceres domésticos	*to do household chores*
lavar (el suelo, los platos)	*to wash (the floor, the dishes)*
limpiar la casa	*to clean the house*
planchar la ropa	*to iron the clothes*
quitar la mesa	*to clear the table*
quitar el polvo	*to dust*

TEACHING OPTIONS

Extra Practice Ask students to complete these analogies.
1. **aspiradora : ____ :: lavadora : ropa (alfombra)** (***Aspiradora* es a ____ como *lavadora* es a *ropa*.**)
2. **frío : calor :: congelador : ____ (horno)**
3. **cama : dormitorio :: ____ : oficina (escritorio)**
4. **platos : cocina :: carro : ____ (garaje)**

Heritage Speakers Ask heritage speakers to tell the class any other terms their families use to refer to rooms in a home or household appliances. Ex: **el lavaplatos = el lavavajillas; el altillo = el ático, el desván.**

Práctica

1 Escuchar Escucha la conversación y completa las oraciones.

1. Pedro va a limpiar primero __la sala__.
2. Paula va a comenzar en __la cocina__.
3. Pedro va a __planchar la ropa__ en el sótano.
4. Pedro también va a limpiar __la oficina__.
5. Ellos están limpiando la casa porque __la madre de Pedro viene a visitarlos__.

2 Respuestas Escucha las preguntas y selecciona la respuesta más adecuada. Una respuesta no se va a usar.

__3__ a. Sí, la alfombra estaba muy sucia.
__5__ b. No, porque todavía se están mudando.
__1__ c. Sí, sacudí la mesa y el estante.
____ d. Sí, puse el pollo en el horno.
__2__ e. Hice la cama, pero no limpié los muebles.
__4__ f. Sí, después de sacarla de la secadora.

3 Escoger Escoge la letra de la respuesta correcta.

1. Cuando quieres tener una lámpara y un despertador cerca de tu cama, puedes ponerlos en __c__.
   a. el barrio b. el cuadro c. la mesita de noche
2. Si no quieres vivir en el centro de la ciudad, puedes mudarte __b__.
   a. al alquiler b. a las afueras c. a la vivienda
3. Guardamos (*We keep*) los pantalones, las camisas y los zapatos en __b__.
   a. la secadora b. el armario c. el patio
4. Para subir de la planta baja al primer piso, usas __c__.
   a. la entrada b. el cartel c. la escalera
5. Ponemos cuadros y pinturas en __a__.
   a. las paredes b. los quehaceres c. los jardines

4 Definiciones En parejas, identifiquen cada cosa que se describe. Luego inventen sus propias descripciones de algunas palabras y expresiones de **Contextos**.

modelo

Estudiante 1: *Es donde pones los libros.*
Estudiante 2: *el estante*

1. Es donde pones la cabeza cuando duermes. la/una almohada
2. Es el quehacer doméstico que haces después de comer. lavar los platos/quitar la mesa
3. Algunos de ellos son las cómodas y los sillones. los muebles
4. Son las personas que viven en tu barrio. los vecinos
5. ______
6. ______

TEACHING OPTIONS

Small Groups Have groups of three interview each other about their dream house, one conducting the interview, one answering, and one taking notes. At three-minute intervals have students switch roles until each has been interviewer, interviewee, and note-taker. Then have a volunteer from each group use the notes to tell the class about their team members' dream houses.

Game Ask students to bring in pictures of mansions, castles, or palaces. Divide the class into teams of three, and have each team write a description of parts of the residence that are not visible in the photos. Have each team read its description aloud. To determine the winner, ask the students to vote for the best description.

1 Teaching Tip Help students check their answers by converting each sentence into a question. Ex: **1. ¿Qué va a limpiar Pedro primero?**

1 Script PEDRO: Paula, tenemos que limpiar toda la casa esta mañana. ¿Por dónde podemos empezar? PAULA: Pienso empezar por la cocina. Voy a lavar los platos, sacar la basura y barrer el suelo. PE: Pues, primero voy a limpiar la sala. Necesito pasar la aspiradora y sacudir los muebles. PA: Después de la sala, ¿qué cuarto quieres limpiar? PE: Después quiero limpiar la oficina. PA: Entonces yo voy a limpiar el dormitorio de huéspedes. PE: Bueno. Debes hacer la cama en ese dormitorio también. PA: Ya lo sé. Ah, ¿puedes planchar la ropa en el sótano, Pedro? PE: Sí… Espero que todo vaya bien durante la visita de mi madre. PA: Sí. Pues yo espero que ella no venga hasta que todo esté limpio. ¡No nos queda mucho tiempo para terminar!
Textbook MP3s

2 Teaching Tip To simplify, before listening, have students read through the items and brainstorm questions that could have elicited these answers.

2 Script 1. ¿Sacudiste los muebles de la oficina? 2. ¿Arreglaste tu dormitorio? 3. ¿Pasaste la aspiradora? 4. ¿Planchaste la ropa? 5. ¿Visitaste a los nuevos vecinos?
Textbook MP3s

3 Expansion To challenge students, write these items on the board as a cloze activity.

4 Expansion Have pairs give each other words from **Contextos** for their partners to define. Ex: **el pasillo (Pasas por este lugar cuando vas de un cuarto al otro.)**

Teaching Tips

- Use the **Lección 12 Contextos** digital images to assist with this vocabulary presentation.
- Ask volunteers to name the items on the table. Then talk about the uses of the silverware (**cubiertos**), glassware (**cristalería**), and china (**vajilla**) pictured. Ex: **La copa sirve para tomar vino.** Also ask questions, such as: **Tomamos café en un vaso, ¿verdad? (No, tomamos café en una taza.)**
- Add a visual aspect to this vocabulary presentation. Bring in silverware, plates, and glasses. As you hold up each item, engage students in a conversation. Have them name each item and guide you in setting the table. Ex: **¿Dónde pongo el tenedor, a la derecha o a la izquierda del plato?** Then model table manners common to many Spanish-speaking countries and contrast them to dining in the U.S. Ex: resting wrists (never elbows!) on the table, rather than placing one hand in your lap

5 Expansion

- Ask students additional questions modeled on the sentence starters in **Actividad 5**. Ex: **¿Qué se necesita para comer la carne?**
- Add a visual aspect to this activity. Using pictures of different foods or dishes, ask students what utensils are needed. Ex: **¿Qué se necesita para comer este plato de espaguetis? (un tenedor y una cuchara)**

6 Teaching Tip

Before forming groups, model the activity with your own information. Ex: **En casa, mi esposa siempre pasa la aspiradora, pero yo sacudo los muebles. Mi hijo...**

5 **Completar** Completa estas frases con las palabras más adecuadas.

1. Para tomar vino necesitas... una copa
2. Para comer una ensalada necesitas... un tenedor/un plato
3. Para tomar café necesitas... una taza
4. Para poner la comida en la mesa necesitas... un plato/poner la mesa
5. Para limpiarte la boca después de comer necesitas... una servilleta
6. Para cortar (*to cut*) un bistec necesitas... un cuchillo (y un tenedor)
7. Para tomar agua necesitas... un vaso/una copa
8. Para tomar sopa necesitas... una cuchara/un plato

6 **Los quehaceres** Trabajen en grupos para indicar quién hace estos quehaceres domésticos en sus casas. Luego contesten las preguntas. Answers will vary.

barrer el suelo	lavar los platos	planchar la ropa
cocinar	lavar la ropa	sacar la basura
hacer las camas	pasar la aspiradora	sacudir los muebles

modelo

Estudiante 1: *¿Quién pasa la aspiradora en tu casa?*
Estudiante 2: *Mi hermano y yo pasamos la aspiradora.*

1. ¿Quién hace más quehaceres, tú o tus compañeros/as?
2. ¿Quiénes hacen la mayoría de los quehaceres, los hombres o las mujeres?
3. ¿Piensas que debes hacer más quehaceres? ¿Por qué?

Practice more at **vhlcentral.com**.

TEACHING OPTIONS

Heritage Speakers Ask heritage speakers to talk about special features, details, or areas of their homes that are particular to their family's culture. Ex: In Colombian homes, decorating the dining room with a **bodegón** (still-life painting of fruit). Also, if their families have told them about houses and apartments in their countries of origin, have them share these details with the class.

Extra Practice Write these sentence starters on the board, and have the students complete them with appropriate chores. **1. Antes de pasar la aspiradora, tienes que... (sacudir los muebles.) 2. Después de lavar y secar la ropa, normalmente... (tienes que plancharla.) 3. Después de comer, tienes que... (lavar los platos.) 4. Tienes que levantarte antes de... (hacer la cama.) 5. Antes de sentarte a comer, tienes que... (poner la mesa.)**

Comunicación

7

La vida doméstica En parejas, describan las habitaciones que ven en estas fotos. Identifiquen y describan cinco muebles o adornos (*accessories*) de cada foto y digan dos quehaceres que se pueden hacer en cada habitación. Answers will vary.

8

Mi apartamento Dibuja el plano (*floor plan*) de un apartamento amueblado (*furnished*) imaginario y escribe los nombres de las habitaciones y de los muebles. En parejas, siéntense espalda contra espalda (*sit back to back*). Uno/a de ustedes describe su apartamento mientras su compañero/a lo dibuja según la descripción. Cuando terminen, miren el segundo dibujo. ¿Es similar al dibujo original? Hablen de los cambios que se necesitan hacer para mejorar el dibujo. Repitan la actividad intercambiando papeles. Answers will vary.

CONSULTA

To review bathroom-related vocabulary, see **Lección 7, Contextos,** p. 210.

9

¡Corre, corre! Tu profesor(a) va a darte una serie incompleta de dibujos que forman una historia. Tú y tu compañero/a tienen dos series diferentes. Descríbanse los dibujos para completar la historia. Answers will vary.

modelo

Estudiante 1: Marta quita la mesa.
Estudiante 2: Francisco...

7 Teaching Tip

Model the activity using magazine pictures. Have students guess which photo you are describing. Ex: **¡Qué comedor más desordenado! ¡Es un desastre! Alguien debe quitar los platos sucios de la mesa. También es necesario sacudir los muebles y pasar la aspiradora.**

8 Teaching Tips

- Draw a floor plan of a four-room apartment on the board. Ask volunteers to describe it.
- Have students draw their floor plans before you assign pairs. Make sure they understand the activity so that their floor plans do not become too complicated.

8 Expansion

- Have students make the suggested changes to their floor plans and repeat the activity again with a different partner.
- Have pairs repeat the activity, drawing floor plans of their actual homes or apartments.
- In pairs, tell students to imagine that they are interior decorators. Give each pair the same catalogue from IKEA or Pottery Barn, but set different budgets. Tell them they must design the apartment of their dreams without going over the spending limit. Have students describe their dream houses to the class while volunteers draw them on the board.

9 Teaching Tip Divide the class into pairs and distribute the handouts from the Activity Pack (Activity Pack/Supersite) that correspond to this Information Gap Activity.

9 Expansion

Have pairs tell each other about an occasion when they have had to clean up their home for a particular reason. Encourage pairs to ask each other questions to find out additional information. Then ask volunteers to share their partners' stories with the class.

TEACHING OPTIONS

Extra Practice Have students complete this cloze activity. **La vida doméstica de un estudiante universitario puede ser un desastre, ¿no? Nunca hay tiempo para hacer los ____ (quehaceres) domésticos. Sólo ____ (pasa) la aspiradora una vez al semestre y nunca ____ (sacude) los muebles. Los ____ (platos) sucios se acumulan en la ____ (cocina). Saca la ropa de la ____ (secadora) y se la pone sin ____ (planchar). Y, ¿por qué hacer la ____ (cama)? Se va a acostar en ella de nuevo este mismo día, ¿no?**

Game Have students bring in real estate ads. Ask teams of three to write a description of a property. Teams then take turns reading their descriptions aloud. Other teams guess the price. The team that guesses the amount closest to the real price without going over scores one point.

Section Goals

In **Fotonovela**, students will:
- receive comprehensible input from free-flowing discourse
- learn functional phrases that preview lesson grammatical structures

Instructional Resources
Supersite: Video (***Fotonovela***); Resources (Scripts, Translations, Answer Keys)
WebSAM
Video Manual, pp. 23–24

Video Recap: Lección 11
Before doing this **Fotonovela** section, review the previous episode with these questions:
1. ¿Qué se borró de la computadora de Maru? (Se borraron muchos archivos.) 2. ¿Quién intenta arreglar la computadora de Maru? (Mónica intenta arreglarla.) 3. ¿Dónde está Miguel? (Él está en el taller de Jorge.) 4. ¿Cuánto le pagó Miguel a Jorge para arreglar su coche? (No le pagó nada.)

Video Synopsis **Felipe** and **Jimena** have promised to clean the apartment in exchange for permission to take a trip to the **Yucatán** Peninsula. **Marissa, Juan Carlos**, and **don Diego** help them finish on time.

Teaching Tips
- Have students predict the content of this episode, based on the title and video stills.
- Ask the class if this episode was what they expected, based on the predictions they made.

Los quehaceres

Jimena y Felipe deben limpiar el apartamento para poder ir de viaje con Marissa.

PERSONAJES

JIMENA

FELIPE

Video: *Fotonovela*

1

SR. DÍAZ Quieren ir a Yucatán con Marissa, ¿verdad?
SRA. DÍAZ Entonces, les sugiero que arreglen este apartamento. Regresamos más tarde.
SR. DÍAZ Les aconsejo que preparen la cena para las 8:30.

2

MARISSA ¿Qué pasa?
JIMENA Nuestros papás quieren que Felipe y yo arreglemos toda la casa.
FELIPE Y que, además, preparemos la cena.
MARISSA ¡Pues, yo les ayudo!

3

MARISSA Mis padres siempre quieren que mis hermanos y yo ayudemos con los quehaceres. No me molesta ayudar. Pero odio limpiar el baño.
JIMENA Lo que más odio yo es sacar la basura.

4

JUAN CARLOS Hola, Jimena. ¿Está Felipe? (*a Felipe*) Te olvidaste del partido de fútbol.
FELIPE Juan Carlos, ¿verdad que mi papá te considera como de la familia?
JUAN CARLOS Sí.

5

(*Don Diego llega a ayudar a los chicos.*)
FELIPE Tenemos que limpiar la casa hoy.
JIMENA ¿Nos ayuda, don Diego?
DON DIEGO Claro. Recomiendo que se organicen en equipos para limpiar.

6

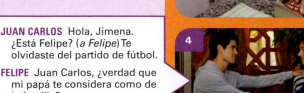

MARISSA Yo lleno el lavaplatos... después de vaciarlo.
DON DIEGO Juan Carlos, ¿por qué no terminas de pasar la aspiradora? Y Felipe, tú limpia el polvo. ¡Ya casi acaban!

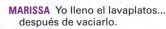

TEACHING OPTIONS

Video Tips General suggestions for using video clips in the classroom can be found in the front matter of this Instructor's Annotated Edition.

Los quehaceres Play the last half of the **Los quehaceres** episode and have students summarize what they see and hear. Then, have the class predict what happens in the first half of the episode, based on their observations. Write their predictions on the board. Then play the entire episode and through discussion, guide the class to a correct summary of the plot.

SRA. DÍAZ SR. DÍAZ MARISSA JUAN CARLOS DON DIEGO

7

(Los chicos preparan la cena y ponen la mesa.)

JUAN CARLOS ¿Dónde están los tenedores?

JIMENA Allá.

JUAN CARLOS ¿Y las servilletas?

MARISSA Aquí están.

8

FELIPE La sala está tan limpia. Le pasamos la aspiradora al sillón y a las cortinas. ¡Y también a las almohadas!

JIMENA Yucatán, ¡ya casi llegamos!

9

(Papá y mamá regresan a casa.)

SRA. DÍAZ ¡Qué bonita está la casa!

SR. DÍAZ Buen trabajo, muchachos. ¿Qué hay para cenar?

JIMENA Quesadillas. Vengan.

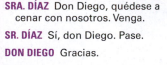

10

SRA. DÍAZ Don Diego, quédese a cenar con nosotros. Venga.

SR. DÍAZ Sí, don Diego. Pase.

DON DIEGO Gracias.

Expresiones útiles

Making recommendations

Le(s) sugiero que arregle(n) este apartamento.
I suggest you tidy up this apartment.
Le(s) aconsejo que prepare(n) la cena para las ocho y media.
I recommend that you have dinner ready for eight thirty.

Organizing work

Recomiendo que se organicen en equipos para limpiar.
I recommend that you divide yourselves into teams to clean.
Yo lleno el lavaplatos… después de vaciarlo.
I'll fill the dishwasher… after I empty it.
¿Por qué no terminas de pasar la aspiradora?
Why don't you finish vacuuming?
¡Ya casi acaban!
You're almost finished!
Felipe, tú quita el polvo.
Felipe, you dust.

Making polite requests

Don Diego, quédese a cenar con nosotros.
Don Diego, stay and have dinner with us.
Venga.
Come on.
Don Diego, pase.
Don Diego, come in.

Additional vocabulary

el plumero *duster*

recursos

VM pp. 23–24 | vhlcentral.com Lección 12

Expresiones útiles Draw attention to the sentences that begin with **Le(s) sugiero que…**, **Le(s) aconsejo que…**, and **Recomiendo que…** Explain that these sentences are examples of the present subjunctive with verbs of will or influence. Write one of these sentences on the board. Point out that the main clause contains a verb of will or influence, while the subordinate clause contains a verb in the present subjunctive. Then point out that the verbs **quédese, Venga,** and **pase** are formal commands. Have students guess whether they are **usted** or **ustedes** commands. Finally, point out the command **Vengan** next to video still 9. Explain that this is an example of an **ustedes** command. Tell students that they will learn more about these concepts in **Estructura**.

Teaching Tip Have the class read through the entire **Fotonovela**, with volunteers playing the various parts. Then, ask different volunteers to read through the dialogue a second time. Encourage them to ad-lib when possible, use gestures, and be expressive when reading their roles.

TEACHING OPTIONS

Extra Practice Photocopy the **Fotonovela** Videoscript (Supersite) and white out words related to houses and household chores in order to create a master for a cloze activity. Distribute the photocopies and tell students to fill in the missing words as they view the episode.

Pairs Have students imagine that the **Díaz** family has decided to sell their apartment. Ask pairs to write a real estate advertisement for the apartment. Encourage creativity. Have volunteers read their ads for the class.

¿Qué pasó?

1 **¿Cierto o falso?** Indica si lo que dicen estas oraciones es **cierto** o **falso**. Corrige las oraciones falsas.

	Cierto	Falso
1. Felipe y Jimena tienen que preparar el desayuno. *Felipe y Jimena tienen que preparar la cena.*	❍	✔
2. Don Diego ayuda a los chicos organizando los quehaceres domésticos.	✔	❍
3. Jimena le dice a Juan Carlos dónde están los tenedores.	✔	❍
4. A Marissa no le molesta limpiar el baño. *Marissa odia limpiar el baño.*	❍	✔
5. Juan Carlos termina de lavar los platos. *Juan Carlos termina de pasar la aspiradora.*	❍	✔

2 **Identificar** Identifica quién puede decir estas oraciones.

1. Yo les ayudo, no me molesta hacer quehaceres domésticos. *Marissa*
2. No me gusta sacar la basura, pero es necesario hacerlo. *Jimena*
3. Es importante que termines de pasar la aspiradora, Juan Carlos. *Don Diego*
4. ¡La casa está muy limpia! ¡Qué bueno que pasamos la aspiradora! *Felipe*
5. ¡Buen trabajo, chicos! ¿Qué vamos a cenar? *Sr. Díaz*

3 **Completar** Los chicos y don Diego están haciendo los quehaceres. Adivina en qué cuarto está cada uno de ellos.

1. Jimena limpia el congelador. Jimena está en *la cocina*.
2. Don Diego limpia el escritorio. Don Diego está en *la oficina*.
3. Felipe pasa la aspiradora debajo de la mesa y las sillas. Felipe está en *el comedor*.
4. Juan Carlos sacude el sillón. Juan Carlos está en *la sala*.
5. Marissa hace la cama. Marissa está en *el dormitorio*.

4 **Mi casa** Dibuja el plano de una casa o de un apartamento. Puede ser el plano de la casa o del apartamento donde vives o de donde te gustaría (*you would like*) vivir. Después, trabajen en parejas y describan lo que se hace en cuatro de las habitaciones. Para terminar, pídanse (*ask for*) ayuda para hacer dos quehaceres domésticos. Pueden usar estas frases en su conversación. *Answers will vary.*

Quiero mostrarte...	Al fondo hay...
Ésta es (la cocina).	Quiero que me ayudes a (sacar la basura).
Allí yo (preparo la comida).	Por favor, ayúdame con...

Practice more at **vhlcentral.com**.

1 Expansion Give students these true/false statements as items 6–7: **6. Marissa lleva seis platos a la mesa. (Falso. Marissa lleva seis vasos a la mesa.) 7. Después de terminar con la limpieza, don Diego se va a su casa. (Falso. Don Diego se queda a cenar.)**

Nota cultural In Mexico, **quesadillas** are typically made with corn tortillas and Oaxacan cheese. Other ingredients may be added, such as **chorizo** or **huitlacoche** (a type of corn fungus). In northern regions, **quesadillas** are also made with wheat flour tortillas and any cheese that melts easily.

2 Teaching Tip Before beginning this activity, have the class skim the **Fotonovela** captions on pages 380–381.

2 Expansion Give students these sentences as items 6–7: **6. No puedo ver el partido de fútbol hoy. (Felipe) 7. ¡Vengan a comer las quesadillas! (Jimena)**

3 Expansion Ask pairs to come up with lists of other household chores that can be done in each of the rooms. Have them share their answers with the class. Keep count of the items on their lists to find out which pair came up with the most correct possibilities.

4 Possible Conversation
E1: Quiero mostrarte mi casa. Ésta es la sala. Me gusta mirar la televisión allí. Aquí está la oficina. Allí hablo por teléfono y trabajo en la computadora. Éste es el garaje. Es donde tengo mis dos coches. Y aquí está la cocina, donde preparo las comidas. Quiero que me ayudes a sacudir los muebles y pasar la aspiradora.
E2: Está bien. Ahora quiero mostrarte mi apartamento...

TEACHING OPTIONS

Small Groups Have the class label various parts of the classroom with the names of rooms one would typically find in a house. If possible, rearrange the classroom desks and chairs to represent the different rooms and their furniture. Then have students work in small groups to write a skit about a family that is cleaning up the house in preparation for a dinner party. Have groups perform their skits for the class. Be sure to give them time to rehearse.

Game Have students write a few sentences that one of the characters in this **Fotonovela** episode would say. They can look at the captions on pages 380–381 for ideas, but they should not copy sentences word for word. Then have students read their sentences to the class. The class will guess which character would say those sentences.

Ortografía

Audio

Mayúsculas y minúsculas

Here are some of the rules that govern the use of capital letters (**mayúsculas**) and lowercase letters (**minúsculas**) in Spanish.

Los estudiantes llegaron al aeropuerto a las dos.
Luego fueron al hotel.

In both Spanish and English, the first letter of every sentence is capitalized.

Rubén Blades **Panamá** **Colón** **los Andes**

The first letter of all proper nouns (names of people, countries, cities, geographical features, etc.) is capitalized.

Cien años de soledad ***Don Quijote de la Mancha***
El País ***Muy Interesante***

The first letter of the first word in titles of books, films, and works of art is generally capitalized, as well as the first letter of any proper names. In newspaper and magazine titles, as well as other short titles, the initial letter of each word is often capitalized.

la señora Ramos **don Francisco**
el presidente **Sra. Vives**

Titles associated with people are *not* capitalized unless they appear as the first word in a sentence. Note, however, that the first letter of an abbreviated title is capitalized.

Último **Álex** **MENÚ** **PERDÓN**

Accent marks should be retained on capital letters. In practice, however, this rule is often ignored.

lunes **viernes** **marzo** **primavera**

The first letter of days, months, and seasons is not capitalized.

español **estadounidense** **japonés** **panameños**

The first letter of nationalities and languages is not capitalized.

Profesor Herrera, ¿es cierto que somos venenosas°?
Sí, Pepito. ¿Por qué lloras?

Práctica Corrige las mayúsculas y minúsculas incorrectas.

1. soy lourdes romero. Soy Colombiana. Soy Lourdes Romero. Soy colombiana.
2. éste Es mi Hermano álex. Éste es mi hermano Álex.
3. somos De panamá. Somos de Panamá.
4. ¿es ud. La sra. benavides? ¿Es Ud. la Sra. Benavides?
5. ud. Llegó el Lunes, ¿no? Ud. llegó el lunes, ¿no?

Palabras desordenadas Lee el diálogo de las serpientes. Ordena las letras para saber de qué palabras se trata. Después escribe las letras indicadas para descubrir por qué llora Pepito.

m n a a P á _ _ _ _ _ _

s t e m r a _ _ _ _ _ _

i g s l é n _ _ _ _ _ _

y a U r u g u _ _ _ _ _ _ _

r o ñ e s a _ _ _ _ _ _

¡ _ orque _ e acabo de morder° la _ en _ u _ !

Respuestas: Panamá, martes, inglés, Uruguay, señora.
¡Porque me acabo de morder la lengua!

recursos
LM p. 68
vhlcentral.com Lección 12

venenosas *venomous* morder *to bite*

Section Goal

In **Ortografía**, students will learn about the rules for capitalization in Spanish.

Instructional Resources
Supersite: Audio (Lab MP3 Files); Resources (Scripts, Answer Keys)
WebSAM
Lab Manual, p. 68

Teaching Tips

- Explain that in a few Spanish city and country names the definite article is considered part of the name, and is thus capitalized. Ex: **La Habana, La Coruña, La Haya, El Salvador**.
- As in English, Spanish titles of books, films, and works of art are italicized in print; however, capitalization rules differ. In Spanish, only the first word and any proper noun gets an initial capital. Spanish treatment of the names of newspapers and magazines is the same as in English; they are italicized in print and each word is capitalized. Tell students that ***El País*** is a Spanish newspaper and ***Muy Interesante*** is a popular science magazine.
- After going through the explanation, write example titles, names, sentences, etc., all in lowercase on the board. Then, ask pairs to decide which letters should be capitalized.
- Point out that **Ortografía** replaces **Pronunciación** in the Student Edition for **Lecciones 10–15**, but not in the Lab Manual. The **Recursos** box references the **Pronunciación** sections found in all lessons of the Lab Manual.

TEACHING OPTIONS

Extra Practice Have students scan the reading on the next page. Have them circle all the capital letters and explain why each is capitalized. Then point out the words **árabe, españoles,** and **islámica** and have volunteers explain why they are not capitalized.

Extra Practice Add an auditory aspect to this **Ortografía** section. Read this sentence aloud for students to write down: **El doctor Guzmán, el amigo panameño de la señorita Rivera, llegó a Quito el lunes, doce de mayo.** To allow students time to write, read the sentence twice slowly and once at full speed. Tell the class to abbreviate all titles. Have volunteers write their version of the sentence on the board, and as a class correct any mistakes they may have made.

Flash CULTURA

Section Goals

In **Cultura**, students will:

- read about central patios, courtyards, and colonial architecture in Spanish-speaking countries
- learn terms related to the home
- read about the floating islands of Lake Titicaca
- read about unique furniture pieces

Instructional Resources
Supersite: Video (***Flash cultura***); Resources (Scripts, Translations, Answer Keys)
WebSAM
Video Manual, pp. 95–96

En detalle

Antes de leer Have students look at the photos and predict the content of this reading. Ask students if they have seen similar architecture in North America or abroad.

Lectura

- Explain that Spanish homes with central patios are most common in the southern region of the country.
- Point out that university and administrative buildings often have central patios as well.
- As students read, have them make a list of characteristics of central patios.

Después de leer

Ask pairs to discuss possible reasons why this architecture is not as common in the U.S. and Canada.

1 Expansion Give students these true/false statements as items 11–13: **11. Los patios centrales son comunes en las casas de México, España y Colombia. (Cierto.) 12. Las casas con patio central generalmente tienen tres pisos o más. (Falso. Tienen dos o tres pisos.) 13. Estas casas tienden (*tend*) a ser calientes porque les entra mucha luz del sol. (Falso. El patio da ventilación a los cuartos y el agua y la vegetación mantienen la temperatura fresca.)**

EN DETALLE

Video: *Flash cultura*

NATIONAL STANDARDS connections cultures

El patio central

En las tardes cálidas° de Oaxaca, México; Córdoba, España, o Popayán, Colombia, es un placer sentarse en **el patio central** de una casa y tomar un refresco disfrutando de° una buena conversación. De influencia árabe, esta característica arquitectónica° fue traída° a las Américas por los españoles. En la época° colonial, se construyeron casas, palacios, monasterios, hospitales y escuelas con patio central. Éste es un espacio privado e íntimo en donde se puede disfrutar del sol y de la brisa° estando aislado° de la calle.

El centro del patio es un espacio abierto. Alrededor de° él, separado por columnas, hay un pasillo cubierto°. Así, en el patio hay zonas de sol y de sombra°. El patio es una parte importante de la vivienda familiar y su decoración se cuida° mucho. En el centro del patio muchas veces hay una fuente°, plantas e incluso árboles°. El agua es un elemento muy importante en la cultura islámica porque simboliza la purificación del cuerpo y del alma°. Por esta razón y para disminuir° la temperatura, el agua en estas construcciones es muy importante. El agua y la vegetación ayudan a mantener la temperatura fresca y el patio proporciona° luz y ventilación a todas las habitaciones.

La distribución

Las casas con patio central eran usualmente las viviendas de familias adineradas°. Son casas de dos o tres pisos. Los cuartos de la planta baja son las áreas comunes: cocina, comedor, sala, etc., y tienen puertas al patio. En los pisos superiores están las habitaciones privadas de la familia.

cálidas *hot* **disfrutando de** *enjoying* **arquitectónica** *architectural* **traída** *brought* **época** *era* **brisa** *breeze* **aislado** *isolated* **Alrededor de** *Surrounding* **cubierto** *covered* **sombra** *shade* **se cuida** *is looked after* **fuente** *fountain* **árboles** *trees* **alma** *soul* **disminuir** *lower* **proporciona** *provides* **adineradas** *wealthy*

ACTIVIDADES

1 **¿Cierto o falso?** Indica si lo que dicen las oraciones es cierto o falso. Corrige las falsas.

1. Los patios centrales de Latinoamérica tienen su origen en la tradición indígena. **Falso.** Los patios centrales tienen su origen en la arquitectura árabe.
2. Los españoles llevaron a América el concepto del patio. **Cierto.**
3. En la época colonial las casas eran las únicas construcciones con patio central. **Falso.** Se construyeron casas, palacios, monasterios, hospitales y escuelas.
4. El patio es una parte importante en estas construcciones, y es por eso que se le presta atención a su decoración. **Cierto.**
5. El patio central es un lugar de descanso que da luz y ventilación a las habitaciones. **Cierto.**
6. Las fuentes en los patios tienen importancia por razones culturales y porque bajan la temperatura. **Cierto.**
7. En la cultura española el agua simboliza salud y bienestar del cuerpo y del alma. **Falso.** En la cultura islámica el agua simboliza salud y bienestar del cuerpo y del alma.
8. Las casas con patio central eran para personas adineradas. **Cierto.**
9. Los cuartos de la planta baja son privados. **Falso.** Los cuartos de la planta baja son las áreas comunes.
10. Los dormitorios están en los pisos superiores. **Cierto.**

TEACHING OPTIONS

Cultural Comparison Discuss other features of homes in Spanish-speaking countries. For example, in Spain, washing machines are typically the front-loading type and are located in the kitchen. Most families do not own clothes dryers; they hang their clothing to air-dry on a balcony or patio. Also, in Spain, it is very uncommon to see **armarios empotrados** (built-in closets); most people store their clothing in wardrobes. Have students write descriptions of how their lives would be different if they lived in homes with these features.

Small Groups Have students work in groups of three and compare a house with a central patio to a house with a backyard. Tell them to make a list of **similitudes** and **diferencias**. After completing their charts, have two groups get together and compare their lists.

ASÍ SE DICE

La vivienda

el ático, el desván	el altillo
la cobija (Col., Méx.), la frazada (Arg., Cuba, Ven.)	la manta
el escaparate (Cuba, Ven.), el ropero (Méx.)	el armario
el fregadero	*kitchen sink*
el frigidaire (Perú); el frigorífico (Esp.), la nevera	el refrigerador
el lavavajillas (Arg., Esp., Méx.)	el lavaplatos

EL MUNDO HISPANO

Los muebles

- **Mecedora°** La mecedora es un mueble típico de Latinoamérica, especialmente de la zona del Caribe. A las personas les gusta relajarse mientras se mecen° en el patio.
- **Mesa camilla** Era un mueble popular en España hasta hace algunos años. Es una mesa con un bastidor° en la parte inferior° para poner un brasero°. En invierno, las personas se sentaban alrededor de la mesa camilla para conversar, jugar a las cartas o tomar café.

- **Hamaca** Se cree que los taínos hicieron las primeras hamacas con fibras vegetales. Su uso es muy popular en toda Latinoamérica para dormir y descansar.

Mecedora *Rocking chair* se mecen *they rock themselves* bastidor *frame* inferior *bottom* brasero *container for hot coals*

PERFIL

Las islas flotantes del lago Titicaca

Bolivia y Perú comparten el **lago Titicaca**, donde viven **los uros**, uno de los pueblos indígenas más antiguos de América. Hace muchos años, los uros fueron a vivir al lago escapando de **los incas.** Hoy en día, siguen viviendo allí en **islas flotantes** que ellos mismos hacen con unos juncos° llamados **totora**. Primero tejen° grandes plataformas. Luego, con el mismo material, construyen sus casas sobre las plataformas. La totora es resistente, pero con el tiempo el agua la pudre°. Los habitantes de las islas necesitan renovar continuamente las plataformas y las casas. Sus muebles y sus barcos también están hechos° de juncos. Los uros viven de la pesca y del turismo; en las islas hay unas tiendas donde venden artesanías° hechas con totora.

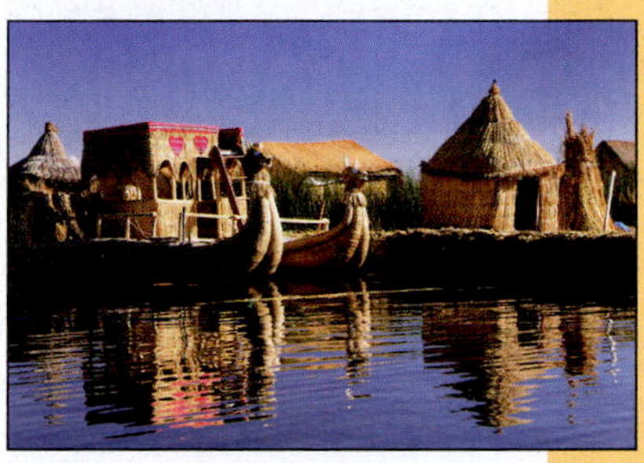

juncos *reeds* tejen *they weave* la pudre *rots it* hechos *made* artesanías *handcrafts*

Conexión Internet

¿Cómo son las casas modernas en los países hispanos?

Go to **vhlcentral.com** to find more cultural information related to this **Cultura** section.

ACTIVIDADES

2 Comprensión Responde a las preguntas.

1. Tu amigo mexicano te dice: "La **cobija** azul está en el **ropero**". ¿Qué quiere decir? La manta azul está en en el armario.
2. ¿Quiénes hicieron las primeras hamacas? ¿Qué material usaron? los taínos; fibras vegetales
3. ¿Qué grupo indígena vive en el lago Titicaca? Los uros viven en el lago Titicaca.
4. ¿Qué pueden comprar los turistas en las islas flotantes del lago Titicaca? Pueden comprar artesanías hechas con totora.

3 Viviendas tradicionales Escribe cuatro oraciones sobre una vivienda tradicional que conoces. Explica en qué lugar se encuentra, de qué materiales está hecha y cómo es. Answers will vary.

Practice more at **vhlcentral.com**.

recursos: VM pp. 95–96; vhlcentral.com Lección 12

TEACHING OPTIONS

Small Groups In small groups, have students research the floating islands of Lake Titicaca and make a poster or collage. Tell them to include information about the **uro** way of life, tourism, and any other significant details about the islands. Have groups present their posters to the class.

Extra Practice Ask students to write a short description of their favorite room in their family's house or apartment. Encourage them to give details about the furniture and decorations. Have them share their paragraphs with a partner, who will ask clarifying questions about the room.

Así se dice
- Model the pronunciation of each term and have students repeat it.
- Explain that compound words like **lavavajillas** are often masculine: **el lavavajillas, los lavavajillas**.
- To challenge students, add these household-related words to the list: **arrendar (Chi., Col.), rentar (Cuba, Méx, P. Rico)** (*to rent*); **la chimenea** (*fireplace*); **el corredor** (*hallway*); **el gavetero (Cuba, Pan., P. Rico)** (*dresser, bureau*); **la licuadora, la batidora (Cuba, Esp., Rep. Dom., Ven.)** (*blender*); **las persianas** (*blinds*); **el plato hondo, el tazón** (*bowl*); **el tragaluz, la claraboya** (*skylight*).

Perfil
- Have students share any facts from the reading that are new or surprising to them.
- Ask students: **¿Les interesa visitar estas islas? ¿Cuáles son las ventajas y desventajas de vivir en un sitio así?**

El mundo hispano
- If possible, bring in photos of the three pieces of furniture.
- Ask students if they have similar furniture in their homes.

2 Expansion Give students these questions as items 5–7: **5. ¿Por qué los uros se fueron a vivir al lago Titicaca? (Para escapar de los incas.) 6. ¿Cómo se hace la base de las casas flotantes? (Se tejen con totora.) 7. ¿Por qué se usaba una mesa camilla en invierno y no en verano? (Daba calor a los pies.)**

3 Teaching Tip To add a visual aspect to this activity, have students find a photo of a traditional dwelling and use the photo as a basis for their written description.

Section Goal

In **Estructura 12.1**, students will learn the relative pronouns **que, quien(es), lo que** and their uses.

Instructional Resources
Supersite: Audio (Lab MP3 Files); Resources (Grammar Presentation Slides, Activity Pack, Scripts, Answer Keys); Testing Program (Quizzes)
WebSAM
Workbook, pp. 141–142
Lab Manual, p. 69

Teaching Tips

- Have students look at the **Fotonovela** on pages 380–381. Ask questions about the episode. Restate each student response as a sentence using a relative pronoun. Write the sentences on the board and underline the relative pronouns. Ex: **1. ¿Quiénes van a arreglar la casa? (Felipe y Jimena) Sí, ellos son las personas que van a limpiar la casa. 2. ¿Qué cuarto tiene lavaplatos? (la cocina) Sí, la cocina es el cuarto que tiene lavaplatos.**
- Compare and contrast the use of **que** and **quien** by writing some examples on the board. Ex: **Es la chica que vino con Carlos a mi fiesta. Es la chica a quien conocí en mi fiesta.** Have students deduce the rule.

12.1 Relative pronouns

Tutorial

ANTE TODO In both English and Spanish, relative pronouns are used to combine two sentences or clauses that share a common element, such as a noun or pronoun. Study this diagram.

Mis padres me regalaron **la aspiradora**.
My parents gave me the vacuum cleaner.

La aspiradora funciona muy bien.
The vacuum cleaner works really well.

La aspiradora **que** mis padres me regalaron funciona muy bien.
The vacuum cleaner that my parents gave me works really well.

Lourdes es muy inteligente.
Lourdes is very intelligent.

Lourdes estudia español.
Lourdes is studying Spanish.

Lourdes, **quien** estudia español, es muy inteligente.
Lourdes, who studies Spanish, is very intelligent.

Eso fue todo lo que dijimos.

Mi papá se lleva bien con Juan Carlos, quien es como mi hermano.

- Spanish has three frequently used relative pronouns. **¡Atención!** Even though interrogative words (**qué**, **quién**, etc.) always carry an accent, relative pronouns never carry a written accent.

que	*that; which; who*
quien(es)	*who; whom; that*
lo que	*that which; what*

- **Que** is the most frequently used relative pronoun. It can refer to things or to people. Unlike its English counterpart, *that*, **que** is never omitted.

¿Dónde está la cafetera **que** compré?
Where is the coffee maker (that) I bought?

El hombre **que** limpia es Pedro.
The man who is cleaning is Pedro.

- The relative pronoun **quien** refers only to people, and is often used after a preposition or the personal **a**. **Quien** has only two forms: **quien** (singular) and **quienes** (plural).

¿Son las chicas **de quienes** me hablaste la semana pasada?
Are they the girls (that) you told me about last week?

Eva, **a quien** conocí anoche, es mi nueva vecina.
Eva, whom I met last night, is my new neighbor.

TEACHING OPTIONS

Extra Practice Write these sentences on the board, and have students supply the correct relative pronoun.
1. **Hay una escalera ____ sube al primer piso. (que)**
2. **Elena es la muchacha a ____ le presté la aspiradora. (quien)**
3. **¿Dónde pusiste la ropa ____ acabas de quitarte? (que)**
4. **¿Cuáles son los estudiantes a ____ les alquilas tu casa? (quienes)**
5. **La cómoda ____ compramos la semana pasada está en el dormitorio de mi hermana. (que)**

Heritage Speakers Using complex sentences with relative pronouns, have heritage speakers describe a location in their families' communities where people can get together. Ex: town square, park, café, etc.

¡LENGUA VIVA!

In English, it is generally recommended that *who(m)* be used to refer to people, and that *that* and *which* be used to refer to things. In Spanish, however, it is perfectly acceptable to use **que** when referring to people.

▶ **Quien(es)** is occasionally used instead of **que** in clauses set off by commas.

Lola, **quien** es cubana, es médica.
Lola, who is Cuban, is a doctor.

Su tía, **que** es alemana, ya llegó.
His aunt, who is German, already arrived.

▶ Unlike **que** and **quien(es), lo que** doesn't refer to a specific noun. It refers to an idea, a situation, or a past event and means *what, that which,* or *the thing that.*

Lo que me molesta es el calor.
What bothers me is the heat.

Lo que quiero es una casa.
What I want is a house.

Este supermercado tiene todo **lo que** necesito.

A Samuel no le gustó **lo que** le dijo Violeta.

¡INTÉNTALO! Completa estas oraciones con pronombres relativos.

1. Voy a utilizar los platos _que_ me regaló mi abuela.
2. Ana comparte un apartamento con la chica a _quien_ conocimos en la fiesta de Jorge.
3. Esta oficina tiene todo _lo que_ necesitamos.
4. Puedes estudiar en el dormitorio _que_ está a la derecha de la cocina.
5. Los señores _que_ viven en esa casa acaban de llegar de Centroamérica.
6. Los niños a _quienes_ viste en nuestro jardín son mis sobrinos.
7. La piscina _que_ ves desde la ventana es la piscina de mis vecinos.
8. Úrsula, _que/quien_ ayudó a mamá a limpiar el refrigerador, es muy simpática.
9. El hombre de _quien_ hablo es mi padre.
10. _Lo que_ te dijo Pablo no es cierto.
11. Tengo que sacudir los muebles _que_ están en el altillo una vez al mes.
12. No entiendo por qué no lavaste los vasos _que_ te dije.
13. La mujer a _quien_ saludaste vive en las afueras.
14. ¿Sabes _lo que_ necesita este dormitorio? ¡Unas cortinas!
15. No quiero volver a hacer _lo que_ hice ayer.
16. No me gusta vivir con personas a _quienes_ no conozco.

recursos
WB pp. 141–142
LM p. 69
vhlcentral.com Lección 12

Teaching Tips

- Test comprehension as you proceed by asking volunteers to answer questions about students and objects in the classroom. Ex: **¿Cómo se llama la estudiante que se sienta detrás de ____? ¿Cómo se llaman los estudiantes a quienes acabo de hacer una pregunta? ¿Dónde está la tarea que ustedes hicieron para hoy?**
- Add a visual aspect to this grammar presentation. Line up four to five pictures. Ask questions that use relative pronouns or elicit them in student answers. Ex: **¿Quién está comiendo una hamburguesa? (El muchacho que está en la playa está comiendo una hamburguesa.) ¿Quién sabe lo que está haciendo esta muchacha? (Está quitando la mesa.)**
- Ask students to make two short lists: **Lo que tengo en mi dormitorio** and **Lo que quiero tener en mi dormitorio.** Ask volunteers to read part of their lists to the class. Encourage a conversation by asking questions such as: **¿Es esto lo que tienes en tu dormitorio? ¿Es un ____ lo que quieres tú?**

TEACHING OPTIONS

Video Show the **Fotonovela** again to give students more input containing relative pronouns. Stop the video where appropriate to discuss how relative pronouns were used.

Game Ask students to bring in some interesting pictures from magazines or the Internet, but tell them not to show these photos to one another. Divide the class into teams of three. Each team should pick a picture. One student will write an accurate description of it, and the others will write imaginary descriptions. Tell them to use relative pronouns in the descriptions. Each team will read its three descriptions aloud without showing the picture. Give the rest of the class two minutes to ask questions about the descriptions before guessing which is the accurate one. Award one point for a correct guess and two points to the team able to fool the class.

1 Expansion Ask students to write alternate endings for each of the sentences. Then ask several volunteers to read their sentences aloud.

2 Expansion Ask questions about the content of the activity. Ex: **1. ¿Quiénes quieren comprar una casa? (Jaime y Tina) 2. ¿Qué casa quieren comprar? (una casa que está en las afueras de la ciudad) 3. ¿De quién era la casa? (de una artista famosa) 4. ¿Cómo venden la casa? (con todos los muebles que tenía) 5. ¿Qué tipo de alfombra tiene la sala? (una alfombra que la artista trajo de Kuwait)**

3 Teaching Tip Ask a volunteer to read the **modelo** aloud. Ask another volunteer to explain what word is replaced by the relative pronoun **que**.

3 Expansion Have pairs write three more sentences that contain relative pronouns and refer to **Javier** and **Ana's** new home.

Práctica

1 Combinar Combina elementos de la columna A y la columna B para formar oraciones lógicas.

A

1. Ése es el hombre __d__.
2. Rubén Blades, __c__.
3. No traje __e__.
4. ¿Te gusta la manta __b__?
5. ¿Cómo se llama el programa __g__?
6. La mujer __a__.

B

a. con quien bailaba es mi vecina
b. que te compró Cecilia
c. quien es de Panamá, es un cantante muy bueno
d. que arregló mi lavadora
e. lo que necesito para la clase de matemáticas
f. que comiste en el restaurante
g. que escuchaste en la radio anoche

NOTA CULTURAL

Rubén Blades es un cantante, compositor y actor panameño muy famoso. Este versátil abogado fue también Ministro de Turismo en su país (2004–2009) y fue nombrado Embajador contra el racismo por las Naciones Unidas en el 2000.

2 Completar Completa la historia sobre la casa que Jaime y Tina quieren comprar, usando los pronombres relativos **que, quien, quienes** o **lo que**.

1. Jaime y Tina son los chicos a __quienes__ conocí la semana pasada.
2. Quieren comprar una casa __que__ está en las afueras de la ciudad.
3. Es una casa __que__ era de una artista famosa.
4. La artista, a __quien__ yo conocía, murió el año pasado y no tenía hijos.
5. Ahora se vende la casa con todos los muebles __que__ ella tenía.
6. La sala tiene una alfombra __que__ ella trajo de Kuwait.
7. La casa tiene muchos estantes, __lo que__ a Tina le encanta.

3 Oraciones Javier y Ana acaban de casarse y han comprado (*they have bought*) una casa y muchas otras cosas. Combina sus declaraciones para formar una sola oración con los pronombres relativos **que, quien(es)** y **lo que**.

modelo

Vamos a usar los vasos nuevos mañana. Los pusimos en el comedor.
Mañana vamos a usar los vasos nuevos que pusimos en el comedor.

1. Tenemos una cafetera nueva. Mi prima nos la regaló.
   Tenemos una cafetera nueva que mi prima nos regaló.
2. Tenemos una cómoda nueva. Es bueno porque no hay espacio en el armario.
   Tenemos una cómoda nueva, lo que es bueno porque no hay espacio en el armario.
3. Esos platos no nos costaron mucho. Están encima del horno.
   Esos platos que están encima del horno no nos costaron mucho.
4. Esas copas me las regaló mi amiga Amalia. Ella viene a visitarme mañana.
   Esas copas me las regaló mi amiga Amalia, quien/que viene a visitarme mañana.
5. La lavadora está casi nueva. Nos la regalaron mis suegros.
   La lavadora que nos regalaron mis suegros está casi nueva.
6. La vecina nos dio una manta de lana. Ella la compró en México.
   La vecina nos dio una manta de lana que compró en México.

Practice more at **vhlcentral.com**.

TEACHING OPTIONS

Extra Practice Have students use relative pronouns to complete this series. **1. ____ tenemos que hacer es buscar otro apartamento. (Lo que) 2. El apartamento ____ tenemos sólo tiene dos dormitorios. (que) 3. Ayer hablamos con un compañero ____ alquila una casa cerca de aquí. (que) 4. Buscamos algo similar a ____ él tiene: tres dormitorios, dos cuartos de baño, una cocina, una sala, un comedor... ¡y un alquiler bajo! (lo que) 5. Nos dio el nombre de unos agentes a ____ podemos contactar. (quienes)**

Pairs Ask pairs of students to write a description of a new household gadget, using relative pronouns. Their descriptions should include the purpose of the gadget and how it is used.

communication NATIONAL STANDARDS

Comunicación

4

Entrevista En parejas, túrnense para hacerse estas preguntas. Answers will vary.

1. ¿Qué es lo que más te gusta de vivir en las afueras o en la ciudad?
2. ¿Cómo son las personas que viven en tu barrio?
3. ¿Cuál es el quehacer doméstico que pagarías (*you would pay*) por no hacer?
4. ¿Quién es la persona que hace los quehaceres domésticos en tu casa?
5. ¿Hay vecinos que te caen bien? ¿Quiénes?
6. ¿De qué vecino es el coche que más te gusta?
7. ¿Cuál es el barrio de tu ciudad que más te gusta y por qué?
8. ¿Quién es la persona a quien le pedirías (*you would ask*) que te ayude con los quehaceres?
9. ¿Cuál es el lugar de la casa donde te sientes más cómodo/a? ¿Por qué?
10. ¿Qué es lo que más te gusta de tu barrio?
11. ¿Qué hace el vecino que más llama la atención?
12. ¿Qué es lo que menos te gusta de tu barrio?

5

Adivinanza En grupos, túrnense para describir distintas partes de una vivienda usando pronombres relativos. Los demás compañeros tienen que hacer preguntas hasta que adivinen (*they guess*) la palabra. Answers will vary.

modelo

Estudiante 1: Es lo que tenemos en el dormitorio.
Estudiante 2: ¿Es el mueble que usamos para dormir?
Estudiante 1: No. Es lo que usamos para guardar la ropa.
Estudiante 3: Lo sé. Es la cómoda.

communication NATIONAL STANDARDS

Síntesis

6

Definir En parejas, definan las palabras. Usen los pronombres relativos **que, quien(es)** y **lo que**. Luego compartan sus definiciones con la clase. Answers will vary.

alquiler	flan	patio	tenedor
amigos	guantes	postre	termómetro
aspiradora	jabón	sillón	vaso
enfermera	manta	sótano	vecino

modelo

lavadora Es lo que se usa para lavar la ropa.
pastel Es un postre que comes en tu cumpleaños.

AYUDA

Remember that **de**, followed by the name of a material, means *made of*.
Es de algodón.
It's made of cotton.
• • •
Es un tipo de means *It's a kind/sort of...*
Es un tipo de flor.
It's a kind of flower.

4 Teaching Tip Have students take notes on the answers provided by their partners to use in expansion activities.

4 Expansion

- Have pairs team up to form groups of four. Each student will report on his or her partner, using the information obtained in the interview.
- Have pairs of students write four additional questions. Ask pairs to exchange their questions with another pair, and then interview each other using the new set of questions. Students should ask their partner follow-up questions as needed.

5 Expansion
Have groups choose their three best **adivinanzas** and present them to the class.

6 Expansion
Have pairs choose one of the items listed in the activity and develop a magazine ad. Their ad should include at least three sentences with relative pronouns.

TEACHING OPTIONS

Small Groups Have students bring in pictures of houses (exterior only). Have them work in groups of three to write a description of what they imagine the interiors to be like. Remind them to use relative pronouns in their descriptions.
Extra Practice Add an auditory aspect to this grammar practice. Prepare short descriptions of easily recognizable residences, such as the White House, Hearst Castle, Alcatraz prison, Graceland, and Buckingham Palace. Write their names on the board in random order. Then read your descriptions aloud and have students match each one to the appropriate name.
Ex: **Es un castillo que está situado en una pequeña montaña cerca del océano Pacífico de California. Lo construyó un norteamericano considerado bastante excéntrico. Es un sitio que visitan muchos turistas cada año. (Hearst Castle)**

Section Goals

In **Estructura 12.2**, students will learn:

- formal **(usted/ustedes)** commands
- use of object pronouns with formal commands

Instructional Resources

Supersite: Audio (Lab MP3 Files); Resources (Grammar Presentation Slides, Activity Pack, Scripts, Answer Keys); Testing Program (Quizzes)
WebSAM
Workbook, pp. 143–144
Lab Manual, p. 70

Teaching Tips

- Model the use of formal commands with simple examples using TPR and gestures. Ex: **Levántense. Siéntense.** Then point to individual students and give commands in an exaggerated formal tone. Ex: **Señor(ita) ____, levántese.** Give other commands using **salga/salgan, vuelva/vuelvan,** and **venga/vengan.**
- Write these sentences on the board, contrasting their meaning with the examples in the text: **Habla con ellos. Come frutas y verduras. Lavan los platos ahora mismo. Beben menos té y café.**
- Have volunteers give the command forms for other verbs, such as **alquilar, correr,** or **imprimir.**

12.2 Formal (usted/ustedes) commands

S Tutorial

ANTE TODO As you learned in **Lección 11**, the command forms are used to give orders or advice. Formal commands are used with people you address as **usted** or **ustedes**. Observe these examples, then study the chart.

Hable con ellos, don Francisco.
Talk with them, Don Francisco.

Coma frutas y verduras.
Eat fruits and vegetables.

Laven los platos ahora mismo.
Wash the dishes right now.

Beban menos té y café.
Drink less tea and coffee.

Formal commands (Ud. and Uds.)

Infinitive	Present tense yo form	Ud. command	Uds. command
limpiar	limpi**o**	limpie	limpi**en**
barrer	barr**o**	barra	barr**an**
sacudir	sacud**o**	sacuda	sacud**an**
decir (e:i)	dig**o**	diga	dig**an**
pensar (e:ie)	piens**o**	piense	piens**en**
volver (o:ue)	vuelv**o**	vuelva	vuelv**an**
servir (e:i)	sirv**o**	sirva	sirv**an**

▶ The **usted** and **ustedes** commands, like the negative **tú** commands, are formed by dropping the final **-o** of the **yo** form of the present tense. For **-ar** verbs, add **-e** or **-en**. For **-er** and **-ir** verbs, add **-a** or **-an**.

Don Diego, quédese a cenar con nosotros.

No se preocupen, yo los ayudo.

▶ Verbs with irregular **yo** forms maintain the same irregularity in their formal commands. These verbs include **conducir, conocer, decir, hacer, ofrecer, oír, poner, salir, tener, traducir, traer, venir,** and **ver**.

Oiga, don Manolo...
Listen, Don Manolo...

¡**Salga** inmediatamente!
Leave immediately!

Ponga la mesa, por favor.
Set the table, please.

Hagan la cama antes de salir.
Make the bed before leaving.

▶ Note also that verbs maintain their stem changes in **usted** and **ustedes** commands.

e:ie	o:ue	e:i
No **pierda** la llave.	**Vuelva** temprano, joven.	**Sirva** la sopa, por favor.
Cierren la puerta.	**Duerman** bien, chicos.	**Repitan** las frases.

AYUDA

By learning formal commands, it will be easier for you to learn the subjunctive forms that are presented in **Estructura 12.3**, p. 394.

TEACHING OPTIONS

Video Replay the **Fotonovela**, having students focus on formal commands. Ask them to write down each formal command that they hear. Then form groups of three and have students compare their lists.

Extra Practice Describe situations and have students call out **ustedes** commands that would be used. Ex: A mother sending her kids off to overnight camp. (**Cepíllense los dientes antes de dormir.**)

TPR Have students stand. Using the verbs presented in the discussion of formal commands, give commands at random (Ex: **Barra el suelo.**) and point to a student who should perform the appropriate gesture. Keep a brisk pace. Vary by pointing to more than one student. Ex: **Pongan la mesa.**

AYUDA

These spelling changes are necessary to ensure that the words are pronounced correctly. See **Lección 8, Pronunciación,** p. 251, and **Lección 9, Pronunciación,** p. 283.

• • •

It may help you to study the following series of syllables. Note that, within each series, the consonant sound doesn't change.

ca que qui co cu
za ce ci zo zu
ga gue gui go gu
ja ge gi jo ju

▶ Verbs ending in **-car**, **-gar**, and **-zar** have a spelling change in the command forms.

sa**car**	**c → qu**	sa**qu**e, sa**qu**en
ju**gar**	**g → gu**	jue**gu**e, jue**gu**en
almor**zar**	**z → c**	almuer**c**e, almuer**c**en

▶ These verbs have irregular formal commands.

Infinitive	Ud. command	Uds. command
dar	**dé**	**den**
estar	**esté**	**estén**
ir	**vaya**	**vayan**
saber	**sepa**	**sepan**
ser	**sea**	**sean**

▶ To make a formal command negative, simply place **no** before the verb.

No ponga las maletas en la cama.
Don't put the suitcases on the bed.

No ensucien los sillones.
Don't dirty the armchairs.

▶ In affirmative commands, reflexive, indirect, and direct object pronouns are always attached to the end of the verb.

Siénten**se**, por favor.
Sígame**,** Laura.

Acuésten**se** ahora.
Póngan**las** en el suelo, por favor.

▶ **¡Atención!** When a pronoun is attached to an affirmative command that has two or more syllables, an accent mark is added to maintain the original stress.

limpie → límpielo
diga → dígamelo

lean → léanlo
sacudan → sacúdanlos

▶ In negative commands, these pronouns always precede the verb.

No **se** preocupe.
No **me lo** dé.

No **los** ensucien.
No **nos las** traigan.

▶ **Usted** and **ustedes** can be used with the command forms to strike a more formal tone. In such instances, they follow the command form.

Muéstrele usted la foto a su amigo.
Show the photo to your friend.

Tomen ustedes esta mesa.
Take this table.

recursos

WB pp. 143–144
LM p. 70
vhlcentral.com Lección 12

¡INTÉNTALO! Indica los mandatos (*commands*) afirmativos y negativos correspondientes.

1. escucharlo (Ud.) Escúchelo. No lo escuche.
2. decírmelo (Uds.) Díganmelo. No me lo digan.
3. salir (Ud.) Salga. No salga.
4. servírnoslo (Uds.) Sírvannoslo. No nos lo sirvan.
5. barrerla (Ud.) Bárrala. No la barra.
6. hacerlo (Ud.) Hágalo. No lo haga.

Teaching Tips

- Ask volunteers to write formal command forms of other verbs with spelling changes on the board. Ex: **empezar (empiece); comenzar (comience); buscar (busque); pagar (pague); llegar (llegue)**.
- Test comprehension as you proceed by asking volunteers to supply the correct form of other infinitives you name.
- Point out that the written accent mark on **dé** serves to distinguish the verb form from the preposition **de**.
- Point out that the affirmative answer for item 4 of **¡Inténtalo!** is spelled with a double **n**: **Sírvannoslo.**

TEACHING OPTIONS

Extra Practice Write a list of situations on the board using singular and plural forms. Ex: **La cocina está sucia. Mis amigos y yo tenemos hambre. Tenemos miedo.** Then have students write responses in the form of commands. Ex: **Límpiela. Hagan la cena. No tengan miedo.**

Heritage Speakers Ask heritage speakers to make a list of ten commands they would hear in their homes that may not be heard elsewhere. Ex: **Sírvale el café al niño. Acuéstese después de almorzar.**

1 Expansion
- Ask volunteers to give additional organizational tips for **señora González**.
- To challenge students, have them work in pairs to formulate a list of instructions for the movers. Ex: **Tengan cuidado con los platos. No pongan los cuadros en una caja.** Then, with the class, compare and contrast the commands the pairs have formulated.

2 Teaching Tip
To simplify, before starting the activity, have volunteers describe the situation in each of the drawings and identify who is speaking to whom.

2 Expansion Continue the exercise by using magazine pictures. Ex: **Tengan paciencia con los niños.**

Extra Practice
To add an auditory aspect to this grammar practice, prepare several different series of formal commands that would be expressed in particular circumstances. After you read each set of commands aloud, students should guess the situation. Ex: **Por favor, siéntense todos. Abróchense los cinturones de seguridad y apaguen todos los aparatos electrónicos. Ahora coloquen el respaldo de su asiento en posición vertical y aseguren la mesa de servicio. (un avión)**

Práctica

1 **Completar** La señora González quiere mudarse de casa. Ayúdala a organizarse. Indica el mandato formal de cada verbo.

1. ___Lea___ los anuncios del periódico y ___guárdelos___. (Leer, guardarlos)
2. ___Vaya___ personalmente y ___vea___ las casas usted misma. (Ir, ver)
3. Decida qué casa quiere y ___llame___ al agente. ___Pídale___ un contrato de alquiler. (llamar, Pedirle)
4. ___Contrate___ un camión (*truck*) para ese día y ___pregúnteles___ la hora exacta de llegada. (Contratar, preguntarles)
5. El día de la mudanza (*On moving day*) ___esté___ tranquila. ___Vuelva___ a revisar su lista para completar todo lo que tiene que hacer. (estar, Volver)
6. Primero, ___dígales___ a todos en casa que usted va a estar ocupada. No ___les diga___ que usted va a hacerlo todo. (decirles, decirles)
7. ___Saque___ tiempo para hacer las maletas tranquilamente. No ___les haga___ las maletas a los niños más grandes. (Sacar, hacerles)
8. No ___se preocupe___. ___Sepa___ que todo va a salir bien. (preocuparse, Saber)

2 **¿Qué dicen?** Mira los dibujos y escribe un mandato lógico para cada uno. Usa palabras que aprendiste en **Contextos**. Answers will vary. Suggested answers:

1. Abran sus libros, por favor.

2. Cierre la puerta. ¡Hace frío!

3. Traiga usted la cuenta, por favor.

4. La cocina está sucia. Bárranla, por favor.

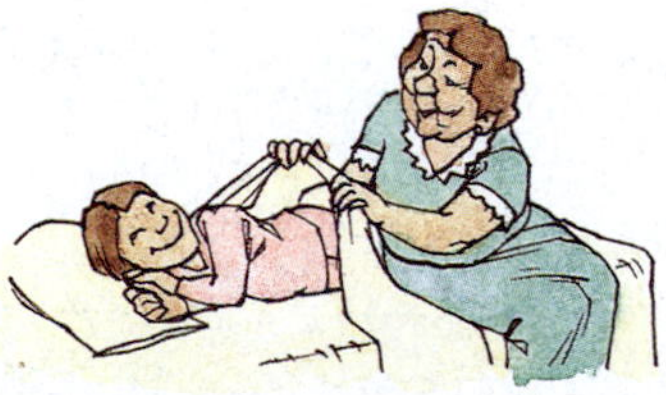

5. Duerma bien, niña.

6. Arreglen el cuarto, por favor. Está desordenado.

Practice more at **vhlcentral.com**.

TEACHING OPTIONS

Small Groups Form small groups of students who have similar living arrangements, such as dormitories, at home, or in an apartment. Then have the groups write suggestions for a newly arrived resident, using formal commands. Ex: **No ponga usted la tele después de las diez. Saque la basura temprano. No estacione el carro en la calle. No invite a sus amigos a la casa después de las once.**

Extra Practice Add an auditory aspect to this grammar practice. Prepare a series of sentences that contain formal commands. Read each twice, pausing after the second time for students to write. Then ask volunteers to write their sentences on the board and correct them as a class. Ex: **1. Saquen la basura a la calle. 2. Almuerce usted conmigo hoy. 3. Niños, jueguen en el patio. 4. Váyase inmediatamente. 5. Esté usted aquí a las diez.**

NATIONAL communication STANDARDS

Comunicación

3

Solucionar Trabajen en parejas. Un(a) estudiante presenta los problemas de la columna A y el/la otro/a los de la columna B. Usen mandatos formales y túrnense para ofrecer soluciones. Answers will vary.

modelo

Estudiante 1: Vilma se torció un tobillo jugando al tenis. Es la tercera vez.
Estudiante 2: *No juegue más al tenis. / Vaya a ver a un especialista.*

A	B
1. Se me perdió el libro de español con todas mis notas.	1. Mis hijas no se levantan temprano. Siempre llegan tarde a la escuela.
2. A Vicente se le cayó la botella de vino para la cena.	2. A mi abuela le robaron (*stole*) las maletas. Era su primer día de vacaciones.
3. ¿Cómo? ¿Se le olvidó traer el traje de baño a la playa?	3. Nuestra casa es demasiado pequeña para nuestra familia.
4. Se nos quedaron los pasaportes en la casa. El avión sale en una hora.	4. Me preocupo constantemente por Roberto. Trabaja demasiado.

4

Conversaciones En parejas, escojan dos situaciones y preparen conversaciones para presentar a la clase. Usen mandatos formales. Answers will vary.

modelo

Lupita: Señor Ramírez, siento mucho llegar tan tarde. Mi niño se enfermó. ¿Qué debo hacer?
Sr. Ramírez: *No se preocupe. Siéntese y descanse un poco.*

SITUACIÓN 1 Profesor Rosado, no vine la semana pasada porque el equipo jugaba en Boquete. ¿Qué debo hacer para ponerme al día (*catch up*)?

SITUACIÓN 2 Los invitados de la boda llegan a las cuatro de la tarde, las mesas están sin poner y el champán sin servir. Son las tres de la tarde y los camareros apenas están llegando. ¿Qué deben hacer los camareros?

SITUACIÓN 3 Mi novio es un poco aburrido. No le gustan ni el cine, ni los deportes, ni salir a comer. Tampoco habla mucho. ¿Qué puedo hacer?

▶**SITUACIÓN 4** Tengo que preparar una presentación para mañana sobre el Canal de Panamá. ¿Por dónde comienzo?

NOTA CULTURAL

El 31 de diciembre de 1999, los Estados Unidos cedió el control del **Canal de Panamá** al gobierno de Panamá, terminando así con casi cien años de administración estadounidense.

NATIONAL communication STANDARDS

Síntesis

5

Presentar En grupos, preparen un anuncio de televisión para presentar a la clase. El anuncio debe tratar de un detergente, un electrodoméstico o una agencia inmobiliaria (*real estate agency*). Usen mandatos, los pronombres relativos (**que, quien(es)** o **lo que**) y el **se** impersonal. Answers will vary.

modelo

Compre el lavaplatos Destellos. Tiene todo lo que usted desea. Es el lavaplatos que mejor funciona. Venga a verlo ahora mismo... No pierda ni un minuto más. Se aceptan tarjetas de crédito.

3 Teaching Tip Ask volunteers to offer other suggestions for the problem in the **modelo**. Ex: **Tenga usted más cuidado. Compre nuevos zapatos de tenis.**

3 Expansion Ask pairs to pick their most humorous or unusual response to present to the class.

4 Expansion Have pairs write an additional scenario on a sheet of paper. Then ask them to exchange papers with another pair, and give them two minutes to prepare a new dialogue. Have them act out their dialogues for the authors.

5 Teaching Tip Divide the class into small groups. Have them choose a product or business and brainstorm positive attributes that they want to advertise.

5 Expansion
- Ask groups to present their commercials to the class.
- Have groups make a video of their ads outside of class. Encourage them to be as creative as possible.

The Affective Dimension When presenting the television commercial, students may feel more comfortable speaking if they assume the personae of celebrity endorsers.

TEACHING OPTIONS

Heritage Speakers Have heritage speakers write a brief description of a kitchen item commonly found in their homes, but not typically in other communities. Ex: **comal, molcajete, cafetera exprés, paellera**. Ask the rest of the class to write a description of the most unusual kitchen item in their homes. Collect all the descriptions, shuffle them, and read them aloud. Have the class guess which items are more typical of Spanish-speaking households. Then, have heritage speakers use formal commands to give the basic steps of a recipe that uses one of the items.

Pairs Have pairs of students write a list of commands for the president of your school. Ex: **Por favor, no suba el costo de la matrícula. Permita más fiestas en las residencias.** Then have them write a list of plural commands for their fellow students. Ex: **No hablen en la biblioteca.**

Section Goals

In **Estructura 12.3**, students will learn:

- the present subjunctive of regular verbs
- the present subjunctive of stem-changing verbs
- irregular verbs in the present subjunctive

Instructional Resources

Supersite: Audio (Lab MP3 Files); Resources (Grammar Presentation Slides, Activity Pack, Scripts, Answer Keys); Testing Program (Quizzes)
WebSAM
Workbook, pp. 145–146
Lab Manual, p. 71

Teaching Tips

- On the board, make two columns labeled **Indicativo** and **Subjuntivo,** and write sentences like these under each column: Column 1: **Mi esposo lava los platos. Mi esposo barre el suelo. Mi esposo cocina.** Column 2: **Es importante que mi esposo lave los platos. Es urgente que mi esposo barra el suelo. Es bueno que mi esposo cocine.** Underline **mi esposo lave,** guiding students to notice the difference between the indicative and subjunctive forms. Do the same for the other sentences.
- Check for understanding by asking volunteers to give subjunctive forms of other regular verbs from this lesson such as **planchar, barrer,** and **sacudir.**
- Emphasize that the formation of the subjunctive is very similar to formal commands and negative **tú** commands.

12.3 The present subjunctive

Tutorial

NATIONAL STANDARDS comparisons

ANTE TODO With the exception of commands, all the verb forms you have been using have been in the indicative mood. The indicative is used to state facts and to express actions or states that the speaker considers to be real and definite. In contrast, the subjunctive mood expresses the speaker's attitudes toward events, as well as actions or states the speaker views as uncertain or hypothetical.

Por favor, quiten los platos de la mesa.

Les aconsejo que preparen la cena.

▶ The present subjunctive is formed very much like **usted, ustedes,** and *negative* **tú** commands. From the **yo** form of the present indicative, drop the **-o** ending, and replace it with the subjunctive endings.

INFINITIVE	PRESENT INDICATIVE	VERB STEM	PRESENT SUBJUNCTIVE
hablar	**hablo**	**habl-**	**hable**
comer	**como**	**com-**	**coma**
escribir	**escribo**	**escrib-**	**escriba**

▶ The present subjunctive endings are:

-ar verbs		-er and -ir verbs	
-e	**-emos**	**-a**	**-amos**
-es	**-éis**	**-as**	**-áis**
-e	**-en**	**-a**	**-an**

Present subjunctive of regular verbs

		hablar	comer	escribir
SINGULAR FORMS	yo	hable	coma	escriba
	tú	hables	comas	escribas
	Ud./él/ella	hable	coma	escriba
PLURAL FORMS	nosotros/as	hablemos	comamos	escribamos
	vosotros/as	habléis	comáis	escribáis
	Uds./ellos/ellas	hablen	coman	escriban

AYUDA

Note that, in the present subjunctive, **-ar** verbs use endings normally associated with present tense **-er** and **-ir** verbs. Likewise, **-er** and **-ir** verbs in the present subjunctive use endings normally associated with **-ar** verbs in the present tense. Note also that, in the present subjunctive, the **yo** form is the same as the **Ud./él/ella** form.

¡LENGUA VIVA!

You may think that English has no subjunctive, but it does! While once common, it now survives mostly in set expressions such as *If I were you...* and *Be that as it may...*

TEACHING OPTIONS

Large Group Have the class stand in a circle. Name an infinitive of a regular verb and subject pronoun (Ex: **alquilar/yo**), and toss a ball to a student. He or she must provide the correct subjunctive form (Ex: **alquile**) and toss the ball back. You may want to have students give an entire phrase (Ex: **que yo alquile**) so that they become accustomed to this structure.

Extra Practice Read aloud sentences that use the subjunctive, and have students repeat. Then call out a different subject for the subordinate clause, and have students say the new sentence, making all the necessary changes. Ex: **Es malo que ustedes trabajen mucho. Javier. (Es malo que Javier trabaje mucho.) Es necesario que lleguen temprano. Nosotras. (Es necesario que lleguemos temprano.)**

▶ Verbs with irregular **yo** forms show the same irregularity in all forms of the present subjunctive.

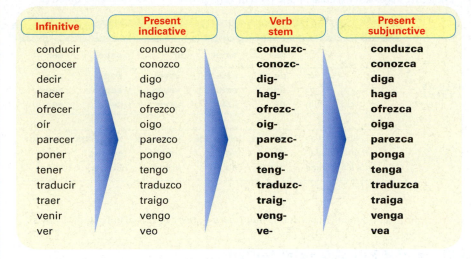

Infinitive	Present indicative	Verb stem	Present subjunctive
conducir	conduzco	**conduzc-**	**conduzca**
conocer	conozco	**conozc-**	**conozca**
decir	digo	**dig-**	**diga**
hacer	hago	**hag-**	**haga**
ofrecer	ofrezco	**ofrezc-**	**ofrezca**
oír	oigo	**oig-**	**oiga**
parecer	parezco	**parezc-**	**parezca**
poner	pongo	**pong-**	**ponga**
tener	tengo	**teng-**	**tenga**
traducir	traduzco	**traduzc-**	**traduzca**
traer	traigo	**traig-**	**traiga**
venir	vengo	**veng-**	**venga**
ver	veo	**ve-**	**vea**

▶ To maintain the **c, g,** and **z** sounds, verbs ending in **-car, -gar,** and **-zar** have a spelling change in all forms of the present subjunctive.

sacar: sa**qu**e, sa**qu**es, sa**qu**e, sa**qu**emos, sa**qu**éis, sa**qu**en

jugar: jue**gu**e, jue**gu**es, jue**gu**e, ju**gu**emos, ju**gu**éis, jue**gu**en

almorzar: almuer**c**e, almuer**c**es, almuer**c**e, almor**c**emos, almor**c**éis, almuer**c**en

Present subjunctive of stem-changing verbs

▶ **-Ar** and **-er** stem-changing verbs have the same stem changes in the subjunctive as they do in the present indicative.

pensar (e:ie): p**ie**nse, p**ie**nses, p**ie**nse, pensemos, penséis, p**ie**nsen

mostrar (o:ue): m**ue**stre, m**ue**stres, m**ue**stre, mostremos, mostréis, m**ue**stren

entender (e:ie): ent**ie**nda, ent**ie**ndas, ent**ie**nda, entendamos, entendáis, ent**ie**ndan

volver (o:ue): v**ue**lva, v**ue**lvas, v**ue**lva, volvamos, volváis, v**ue**lvan

AYUDA

Note that stem-changing verbs and verbs that have a spelling change have the same ending as regular verbs in the present subjunctive.

▶ **-Ir** stem-changing verbs have the same stem changes in the subjunctive as they do in the present indicative, but in addition, the **nosotros/as** and **vosotros/as** forms undergo a stem change. The unstressed **e** changes to **i**, while the unstressed **o** changes to **u**.

pedir (e:i): p**i**da, p**i**das, p**i**da, p**i**damos, p**i**dáis, p**i**dan

sentir (e:ie): s**ie**nta, s**ie**ntas, s**ie**nta, s**i**ntamos, s**i**ntáis, s**ie**ntan

dormir (o:ue): d**ue**rma, d**ue**rmas, d**ue**rma, d**u**rmamos, d**u**rmáis, d**ue**rman

Teaching Tips

- It may be helpful for students to be aware how English uses the subjunctive mood. Ex: *I wish she were here. I insist that he take notes. I suggest you be there tomorrow. If it were me, I would be happy.*
- Point out the stem changes that occur in the **nosotros/as** and **vosotros/as** forms of **–ir** stem-changing verbs.
- Write a few simple cloze sentences on the board and have students complete them in a logical manner. Ex: **Es bueno que mis padres ____. Es importante que yo ____. Es urgente que la profesora ____.** Then have students write three original sentences using the same impersonal expressions.

TEACHING OPTIONS

Pairs Have pairs of students role-play a conversation between a landlord and his/her new tenant. Give pairs sufficient time to plan and practice. When all pairs have completed the activity, ask a few of them to introduce their characters and perform the conversation for the class.

Extra Practice Ask students to compare family members' attitudes toward domestic life using the subjunctive. Ex: **Según los padres, es necesario que los hijos... Según los hijos, es malo que...** You may wish to repeat this activity several times, varying the age group of the children (**niños pequeños, adolescentes, adultos**). Make a three-column chart on the board and write students' sentences under the appropriate age group.

Irregular verbs in the present subjunctive

▶ These five verbs are irregular in the present subjunctive.

Irregular verbs in the present subjunctive

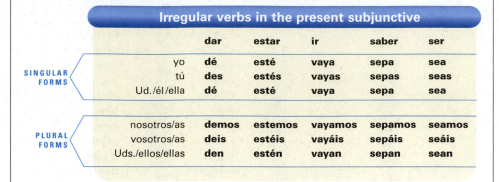

		dar	estar	ir	saber	ser
SINGULAR FORMS	yo	**dé**	**esté**	**vaya**	**sepa**	**sea**
	tú	**des**	**estés**	**vayas**	**sepas**	**seas**
	Ud./él/ella	**dé**	**esté**	**vaya**	**sepa**	**sea**
PLURAL FORMS	nosotros/as	**demos**	**estemos**	**vayamos**	**sepamos**	**seamos**
	vosotros/as	**deis**	**estéis**	**vayáis**	**sepáis**	**seáis**
	Uds./ellos/ellas	**den**	**estén**	**vayan**	**sepan**	**sean**

▶ **¡Atención!** The subjunctive form of **hay** (*there is, there are*) is also irregular: **haya**.

General uses of the subjunctive

▶ The subjunctive is mainly used to express: 1) will and influence, 2) emotion, 3) doubt, disbelief, and denial, and 4) indefiniteness and nonexistence.

▶ The subjunctive is most often used in sentences that consist of a main clause and a subordinate clause. The main clause contains a verb or expression that triggers the use of the subjunctive. The conjunction **que** connects the subordinate clause to the main clause.

Main clause	Connector	Subordinate clause
Es muy importante	que	**vayas** al hotel ahora mismo.

▶ These impersonal expressions are always followed by clauses in the subjunctive:

Es bueno que... *It's good that...*	**Es mejor que...** *It's better that...*	**Es malo que...** *It's bad that...*
Es importante que... *It's important that...*	**Es necesario que...** *It's necessary that...*	**Es urgente que...** *It's urgent that...*

¡INTÉNTALO! Indica el presente de subjuntivo de estos verbos.

1. (alquilar, beber, vivir) que yo alquile, beba, viva
2. (estudiar, aprender, asistir) que tú estudies, aprendas, asistas
3. (encontrar, poder, tener) que él encuentre, pueda, tenga
4. (hacer, pedir, dormir) que nosotras hagamos, pidamos, durmamos
5. (dar, hablar, escribir) que ellos den, hablen, escriban
6. (pagar, empezar, buscar) que ustedes paguen, empiecen, busquen
7. (ser, ir, saber) que yo sea, vaya, sepa
8. (estar, dar, oír) que tú estés, des, oigas

recursos

WB pp. 145–146

LM p. 71

vhlcentral.com Lección 12

Teaching Tips

- Give examples of sentences for one or two forms of each verb, using the impersonal expressions introduced in this section: Ex: ____, **es bueno que le des tu lápiz a ____. Es importante que ustedes estén en la clase a las ____ en punto. Es bueno que mi hija vaya de compras conmigo esta tarde. Es necesario que ustedes sepan todas las formas del subjuntivo.**
- Check understanding by writing on the board main clauses ending in **que** that require a subjunctive in the subordinate clause. Invite volunteers to suggest several endings for each, using verbs they have just gone over. Ex: **Es importante que... (aprendamos español, yo entienda la lección, los estudiantes traigan sus libros).**
- Point out that, in order to use the subjunctive in the subordinate clause, the conjunction **que** must be present and there must be a change of subject. Write these sentences on the board: **Es importante que limpies la cocina. Es importante limpiar la cocina.** Have a volunteer explain why the subjunctive is used only in the first sentence. Emphasize that, while the first example states one person's responsibility, the second is a broad statement about the importance of cleaning kitchens.
- Reiterate that, whereas the word *that* is usually optional in English, **que** is required in Spanish. As in the **¡Inténtalo!**, you may want to have students practice subjunctive forms with **que**, so that its use becomes routine.

TEACHING OPTIONS

Video Show the **Fotonovela** again to give students more comprehensible input that uses the present subjunctive. Stop the video where appropriate and ask students to say which of the four principal uses of the subjunctive (will and influence; emotion; doubt, disbelief, and denial; indefiniteness and nonexistence) is expressed in each instance.

Extra Practice Prepare a short paragraph containing sentences in the present subjunctive. Read each sentence twice, pausing after the second time for students to write. Ex: **Es urgente que encontremos una casa nueva. Es mejor que cada uno tenga su propio dormitorio. Necesitamos una casa que esté cerca de la universidad. No es urgente que nos mudemos inmediatamente. Es importante que empecemos a buscar la casa ya.** Then, ask the class comprehension questions.

Práctica y Comunicación

1

Completar Completa las oraciones con el presente de subjuntivo de los verbos entre paréntesis. Luego empareja las oraciones del primer grupo con las del segundo grupo.

A

1. Es mejor que cenemos en casa. (nosotros, cenar) b
2. Es importante que visites las casas colgadas de Cuenca. (tú, visitar) c
3. Señora, es urgente que le saque el diente. Tiene una infección. (yo, sacar) e
4. Es malo que Ana les dé tantos dulces a los niños. (dar) a
5. Es necesario que lleguen a la una de la tarde. (ustedes, llegar) f
6. Es importante que nos acostemos temprano. (nosotros, acostarse) d

NOTA CULTURAL

Las casas colgadas (*hanging*) de Cuenca, España, son muy famosas. Situadas en un acantilado (*cliff*), forman parte del paisaje de la ciudad.

B

a. Es importante que coman más verduras. (ellos, comer)
b. No, es mejor que salgamos a comer. (nosotros, salir)
c. Y yo creo que es bueno que vaya a Madrid después. (yo, ir)
d. En mi opinión, no es necesario que durmamos tanto. (nosotros, dormir)
e. ¿Ah, sí? ¿Es necesario que me tome un antibiótico también? (yo, tomar)
f. Para llegar a tiempo, es necesario que almorcemos temprano. (nosotros, almorzar)

2

NATIONAL communication STANDARDS

Minidiálogos En parejas, completen los minidiálogos con expresiones impersonales de una manera lógica. Answers will vary.

modelo

Miguelito: Mamá, no quiero arreglar mi cuarto.
Sra. Casas: Es necesario que lo arregles. Y es importante que sacudas los muebles también.

1. **MIGUELITO** Mamá, no quiero estudiar. Quiero salir a jugar con mis amigos.
   SRA. CASAS ______
2. **MIGUELITO** Mamá, es que no me gustan las verduras. Prefiero comer pasteles.
   SRA. CASAS ______
3. **MIGUELITO** ¿Tengo que poner la mesa, mamá?
   SRA. CASAS ______
4. **MIGUELITO** No me siento bien, mamá. Me duele todo el cuerpo y tengo fiebre.
   SRA. CASAS ______

3

Entrevista Trabajen en parejas. Entrevístense usando estas preguntas. Expliquen sus respuestas. Answers will vary.

1. ¿Es importante que las personas sepan una segunda lengua? ¿Por qué?
2. ¿Es urgente que los norteamericanos aprendan otras lenguas?
3. Si un(a) norteamericano/a quiere aprender francés, ¿es mejor que lo aprenda en Francia?
4. ¿Es necesario que una persona sepa decir "te amo" en la lengua nativa de su pareja?
5. ¿Es importante que un cantante de ópera entienda italiano?

Practice more at **vhlcentral.com**.

1 Expansion
After students have paired the sentences from each group, have them continue a couple of the short conversations with three more sentences using the subjunctive. Ex: **No es posible que encontremos un restaurante con mesas disponibles a las siete. Es mejor que salgamos ahora mismo para no tener ese problema. Sin embargo, es importante que no manejemos muy rápido; no quiero causar un accidente.**

2 Teaching Tip To simplify, before assigning the activity, have students brainstorm impersonal expressions that a mother would say to her young son.

2 Expansion
- Ask volunteers to share their mini-dialogues with the rest of the class. Encourage them to ad-lib as they go.
- Ask questions about **Miguelito** and his mother. Ex: **Para la señora Casas, ¿es necesario que Miguelito coma pasteles? (No. Es necesario que Miguelito coma las verduras.) ¿Qué quiere Miguelito? (Quiere salir a jugar con sus amigos.)** Have a volunteer explain why the second response does not take the subjunctive. (There isn't a change of subject and **que** is absent.)

3 Expansion
Ask students to report on their partner's answers using complete sentences and explanations. Ex: **¿Qué opina ____ sobre los cantantes de ópera? ¿Cree que es importante que entiendan italiano?** Ask follow-up questions as necessary.

TEACHING OPTIONS

Heritage Speakers Have heritage speakers think of any major social differences between their own cultural communities and mainstream culture. Invite them to share these comparisons with the class using impersonal expressions. Ex: **Aquí, es necesario que llames antes de ir a visitar a un amigo. En mi cultura, es normal que lleguemos sin llamar a la casa de un amigo....**

Small Groups Divide the class into groups of four. Assign each group one of these personal characteristics: **apariencia física, dinero, inteligencia, personalidad.** Have groups use the subjunctive to write a short paragraph about the importance or unimportance of this trait for certain individuals. Ex: **Para ser presidente, es importante que la persona tenga carisma....**

Section Goals

In **Estructura 12.4**, students will learn:

- the subjunctive with verbs and expressions of will and influence
- common verbs of will and influence

Instructional Resources
Supersite: Audio (Lab MP3 Files); Resources (Grammar Presentation Slides, Digital Image Bank, Activity Pack, Scripts, Answer Keys); Testing Program (Quizzes)
WebSAM
Workbook, pp. 147–148
Lab Manual, p. 72

Teaching Tips

- Write the word **Recomendaciones** on the board. Ask volunteers for household tips and write them on the board in the infinitive form, followed by the student's name in parentheses. Ex: **hacer todos los quehaceres los sábados** (Paul); **lavar los platos a mano** (Sara) When you have approximately ten suggestions, begin rephrasing them using verbs of will and influence with subordinate clauses. Ex: **Paul nos aconseja que hagamos todos los quehaceres los sábados. Sara recomienda que lavemos los platos a mano.** After you have modeled several responses, ask volunteers to continue. Give them cues such as: **¿Qué sugiere ____?**
- Go through the lists of verbs of will and influence and impersonal expressions that generally take the subjunctive, giving examples of their use.
- Have a volunteer read the advertisement for **Dentabrit** and explain what the subject of each clause is.

12.4 Subjunctive with verbs of will and influence

Tutorial

ANTE TODO You will now learn how to use the subjunctive with verbs and expressions of will and influence.

¡ATENCIÓN!
In English, verbs or expressions of will and influence often use a construction with an infinitive, such as *I want you to go.* This is not the case in Spanish, where the subjunctive would be used in a subordinate clause.

▶ Verbs of will and influence are often used when someone wants to affect the actions or behavior of other people.

Enrique **quiere** que salgamos a cenar.
Enrique wants us to go out to dinner.

Paola **prefiere** que cenemos en casa.
Paola prefers that we have dinner at home.

▶ Here is a list of widely used verbs of will and influence.

Verbs of will and influence

aconsejar	*to advise*	**pedir** (e:i)	*to ask (for)*
desear	*to wish; to desire*	**preferir** (e:ie)	*to prefer*
importar	*to be important; to matter*	**prohibir**	*to prohibit*
		querer (e:ie)	*to want*
insistir (en)	*to insist (on)*	**recomendar** (e:ie)	*to recommend*
mandar	*to order*	**rogar** (o:ue)	*to beg*
necesitar	*to need*	**sugerir** (e:ie)	*to suggest*

▶ Some impersonal expressions, such as **es necesario que, es importante que, es mejor que,** and **es urgente que,** are considered expressions of will or influence.

▶ When the main clause contains an expression of will or influence, the subjunctive is required in the subordinate clause, provided that the two clauses have different subjects.

Main clause — Connector — Subordinate clause

VERB OF WILL — SUBJUNCTIVE

Mi mamá **prefiere** que yo **saque** la basura.

TEACHING OPTIONS

Small Groups Have small groups write nine sentences, each of which uses a different verb of will and influence with the subjunctive. Ask volunteers to write some of their group's best sentences on the board. Work with the class to read the sentences and check for accuracy.

Extra Practice Have students finish these sentence starters. **1. Yo insisto en que mis amigos… 2. No quiero que mi familia… 3. Para mí es importante que el amor… 4. Prefiero que mi residencia… 5. Mi novio/a no quiere que yo… 6. Los profesores siempre recomiendan a los estudiantes que… 7. El doctor sugiere que nosotros… 8. Mi madre me ruega que… 9. El policía manda que los estudiantes… 10. El fotógrafo prefiere que la gente…**

Les sugiero que arreglen este apartamento.

Recomiendo que se organicen en equipos.

▶ Indirect object pronouns are often used with the verbs **aconsejar, importar, mandar, pedir, prohibir, recomendar, rogar,** and **sugerir**.

Te aconsejo que estudies.
I advise you to study.

Le sugiero que vaya a casa.
I suggest that he go home.

Les recomiendo que barran el suelo.
I recommend that you sweep the floor.

Le ruego que no venga.
I'm begging you not to come.

▶ Note that all the forms of **prohibir** in the present tense carry a written accent, except for the **nosotros/as** form: **prohíbo, prohíbes, prohíbe, prohibimos, prohibís, prohíben**.

Ella les **prohíbe** que miren la televisión.
She prohibits them from watching TV.

Nos **prohíben** que nademos en la piscina.
They prohibit us from swimming in the swimming pool.

▶ The infinitive is used with words or expressions of will and influence if there is no change of subject in the sentence.

No quiero **sacudir** los muebles.
I don't want to dust the furniture.

Paco prefiere **descansar**.
Paco prefers to rest.

Es importante **sacar** la basura.
It's important to take out the trash.

No es necesario **quitar** la mesa.
It's not necessary to clear the table.

¡INTÉNTALO! Completa cada oración con la forma correcta del verbo entre paréntesis.

1. Te sugiero que vayas (ir) con ella al supermercado.
2. Él necesita que yo le preste (prestar) dinero.
3. No queremos que tú hagas (hacer) nada especial para nosotros.
4. Mis papás quieren que yo limpie (limpiar) mi cuarto.
5. Nos piden que la ayudemos (ayudar) a preparar la comida.
6. Quieren que tú saques (sacar) la basura todos los días.
7. Quiero descansar (descansar) esta noche.
8. Es importante que ustedes limpien (limpiar) los estantes.
9. Su tía les manda que pongan (poner) la mesa.
10. Te aconsejo que no salgas (salir) con él.
11. Mi tío insiste en que mi prima haga (hacer) la cama.
12. Prefiero ir (ir) al cine.
13. Es necesario estudiar (estudiar).
14. Recomiendo que ustedes pasen (pasar) la aspiradora.

recursos
WB pp. 147–148
LM p. 72
vhlcentral.com Lección 12

Teaching Tips

- Elicit indirect object pronouns with verbs of influence by making statements that give advice and asking students for advice. Ex: **Yo siempre les aconsejo a mis estudiantes que estudien mucho. ¿Qué me recomiendan ustedes a mí?** Continue: **1. Mi coche no arranca cuando hace mucho frío. ¿Qué me recomiendas, ____? 2. Mi apartamento está siempre desordenado. ¿Qué me aconsejan? 3. Voy a tener huéspedes este fin de semana. ¿Qué nos sugieren que hagamos?** Ask follow-up questions as appropriate.
- Write these sentences on the board: **Quiero que almuerces en la cafetería. Quiero almorzar en la cafetería.** Ask a volunteer to explain why an infinitive is used in the second sentence instead of the subjunctive.

TEACHING OPTIONS

Extra Practice Create sentences that follow the pattern of the sentences in **¡Inténtalo!** Say the sentence, have students repeat it, then give a different subject pronoun for the subordinate clause, varying the person and number. Have students then say the sentence with the new subject, changing pronouns and verbs as necessary.

TPR Have students stand. At random, call out implied commands using statements with verbs of will or influence and actions that can be mimed. Ex: **Quiero que laves los platos. Insisto en que hagas la cama.** When you make a statement, point to a student to mime the action. Also use plural statements and point to more than one student. When you use negative statements, students should do nothing. Keep a brisk pace.

1 Teaching Tip Before beginning the activity, ask a volunteer to read the first line of the dialogue aloud. Guide students to see that the subject of the verb in the blank is **yo**, which is implied by **me** in the main clause.

1 Expansion Have pairs write a summary of the dialogue in the third person. Ask one or two volunteers to read their summaries to the class.

2 Teaching Tip Ask two volunteers to read the **modelo**. Then ask other volunteers to offer additional suggestions for **Isabel**.

2 Expansion Have students create two suggestions for each person. In the second they should use one of the impersonal expressions listed on page 396.

3 Expansion Have a conversation with the class about the information they learned in their interviews. Ask: **¿A quiénes siempre les dan consejos sus amigos? ¿Quiénes siempre les dan consejos a los amigos suyos? ¿Qué tipo de consejos ofrecen?**

Práctica

1 **Completar** Completa el diálogo con verbos de la lista.

cocina	haga	quiere	sea
comas	ponga	saber	ser
diga	prohíbe	sé	vaya

IRENE Tengo problemas con Vilma. Sé que debo hablar con ella. ¿Qué me recomiendas que le (1) diga ?
JULIA Pues, necesito (2) saber más antes de darte consejos.
IRENE Bueno, para empezar me (3) prohíbe que traiga dulces a la casa.
JULIA Pero chica, tiene razón. Es mejor que tú no (4) comas cosas dulces.
IRENE Sí, ya lo sé. Pero quiero que (5) sea más flexible. Además, insiste en que yo (6) haga todo en la casa.
JULIA Yo (7) sé que Vilma (8) cocina y hace los quehaceres todos los días.
IRENE Sí, pero siempre que hay fiesta me pide que (9) ponga los cubiertos (*silverware*) y las copas en la mesa y que (10) vaya al sótano por las servilletas y los platos. ¡Es lo que más odio: ir al sótano!
JULIA Mujer, ¡Vilma sólo (11) quiere que ayudes en la casa!

2 **Aconsejar** En parejas, lean lo que dice cada persona. Luego den consejos lógicos usando verbos como **aconsejar, recomendar** y **prohibir**. Sus consejos deben ser diferentes de lo que la persona quiere hacer. Answers will vary.

modelo

Isabel: Quiero conseguir un comedor con los muebles más caros del mundo.
Consejo: *Te aconsejamos que consigas unos muebles menos caros.*

1. **DAVID** Pienso poner el cuadro del lago de Maracaibo en la cocina.
2. **SARA** Voy en bicicleta a comprar unas copas de cristal.
3. **SR. ALARCÓN** Insisto en comenzar a arreglar el jardín en marzo.
4. **SRA. VILLA** Quiero ver las tazas y los platos de la tienda El Ama de Casa Feliz.
5. **DOLORES** Voy a poner servilletas de tela (*cloth*) para los cuarenta invitados.
6. **SR. PARDO** Pienso poner todos mis muebles nuevos en el altillo.
7. **SRA. GONZÁLEZ** Hay una fiesta en casa esta noche, pero no quiero limpiarla.
8. **CARLITOS** Hoy no tengo ganas de hacer las camas ni de quitar la mesa.

NOTA CULTURAL

En el **lago de Maracaibo**, en Venezuela, hay casas suspendidas sobre el agua que se llaman **palafitos**. Este tipo de construcciones les recordó a los conquistadores la ciudad de Venecia, Italia, de donde viene el nombre "Venezuela", que significa "pequeña Venecia".

3 **Preguntas** En parejas, túrnense para contestar las preguntas. Usen el subjuntivo. Answers will vary.

1. ¿Te dan consejos tus amigos/as? ¿Qué te aconsejan? ¿Aceptas sus consejos? ¿Por qué?
2. ¿Qué te sugieren tus profesores que hagas antes de terminar los cursos que tomas?
3. ¿Insisten tus amigos/as en que salgas mucho con ellos?
4. ¿Qué quieres que te regalen tu familia y tus amigos/as en tu cumpleaños?
5. ¿Qué le recomiendas tú a un(a) amigo/a que no quiere salir los sábados con su novio/a?
6. ¿Qué les aconsejas a los nuevos estudiantes de tu universidad?

Practice more at **vhlcentral.com**.

TEACHING OPTIONS

Small Groups Have small groups prepare skits in which a group of roommates is discussing how to divide the household chores equitably. Give groups time to prepare and practice their skits before presenting them to the class.

Pairs Give pairs of students five minutes to write a conversation in which they logically use as many of the verbs of will and influence with the subjunctive as they can. After the time is up, ask pairs to count the number of subjunctive constructions they used in their conversations. Have the top three or four perform their conversations for the class.

Comunicación

4 **Inventar** En parejas, preparen una lista de seis personas famosas. Un(a) estudiante da el nombre de una persona famosa y el/la otro/a le da un consejo. Answers will vary.

modelo

Estudiante 1: Judge Judy.
Estudiante 2: Le recomiendo que sea más simpática con la gente.
Estudiante 2: Bradley Cooper.
Estudiante 1: Le aconsejo que haga más películas.

5 **Hablar** En parejas, miren la ilustración. Imaginen que Gerardo es su hermano y necesita ayuda para arreglar su casa y resolver sus problemas románticos y económicos. Usen expresiones impersonales y verbos como **aconsejar**, **sugerir** y **recomendar**. Answers will vary.

modelo

Es mejor que arregles el apartamento más a menudo.
Te aconsejo que no dejes para mañana lo que puedes hacer hoy.

Síntesis

6 **La doctora Salvamórez** Hernán tiene problemas con su novia y le escribe a la doctora Salvamórez, columnista del periódico *Panamá y su gente*. Ella responde a las cartas de personas con problemas románticos. En parejas, lean el mensaje de Hernán y después usen el subjuntivo para escribir los consejos de la doctora. Answers will vary.

Estimada doctora Salvamórez:
Mi novia nunca quiere que yo salga de casa. No le molesta que vengan mis amigos a visitarme. Pero insiste en que nosotros sólo miremos los programas de televisión que ella quiere. Necesita saber dónde estoy en cada momento, y yo necesito que ella me dé un poco de independencia. ¿Qué hago?

Hernán

4 Teaching Tip Ask volunteers to read the **modelo** aloud and provide other suggestions for Judge Judy and Bradley Cooper.

4 Expansion Ask each pair to pick its favorite response and share it with the class, who will vote for the most clever, shocking, or humorous suggestion.

5 Teaching Tips
- Use the **Lección 12 Estructura** digital images to assist with the presentation of this activity.
- Ask volunteers to describe the drawing, naming everything they see and all the chores that need to be done.

5 Expansion
Have students change partners and take turns playing the roles of **Gerardo** and his sibling giving him advice. Ex: **Te sugiero que pongas la pizza en la basura....**

6 Expansion
- Have pairs compare their responses in groups of four. Ask groups to choose which among all of the suggestions are the most likely to work for **Hernán**, and have them share these with the class.
- Have pairs choose a famous couple in history or fiction. Ex: Elizabeth Bennet and Mr. Darcy or Napoleon and Josephine. Then have them write a letter from one of the couples to **doctora Salvamórez**. Finally, have them exchange their letters with another pair and write the corresponding responses from the doctor.

TEACHING OPTIONS

Heritage Speakers Have heritage speakers write a list of five suggestions for other class members participating in an exchange program in their cultural communities. Their suggestions should focus on participating in the daily life of their host family's home. Ask students to share their suggestions with the class. Facilitate conversation by having students respond to the suggestions or ask additional questions.

Small Groups Divide the class into small groups. Write the names of famous historical figures on slips of paper and place them in small paper bags; give each group a bag. Have students take turns drawing names and giving three pieces of "advice" about what the person should do. The other students will try to guess who it is. They are allowed to ask additional questions, if necessary, to figure out the person's identity.

Section Goal

In **Recapitulación**, students will review the grammar concepts from this lesson.

Instructional Resource
Supersite

1 Expansion Give students additional verbs to conjugate in the subjunctive. Ex: **comer, dar, estar, saber, traer**.

2 Expansion

- Have volunteers take turns reading aloud portions of the brochure.
- To challenge students, ask them to work in pairs to write four pieces of advice for a real estate agent, using impersonal expressions. Ex: **Es importante que sea honesto....** Have a few pairs read their sentences for the class.

Extra Practice

On note cards or sticky notes, write names of well-known characters from literature, film, or television. Making sure that students do not see the name assigned to them, stick a note on the back of each student's shirt. Have students circulate around the room, giving each other hints about the identity of their characters, using the subjunctive. Tell students to be sure to use only the present tense in the main clause. Ex: **Tu madre dice que es importante que te cases con el conde París. / Tu novio te pide que te cases con él en secreto. / Deseas que toda tu familia crea que estás muerta. (Julieta Capuleto)**

Recapitulación

Diagnostics

Completa estas actividades para repasar los conceptos de gramática que aprendiste en esta lección.

1 Completar Completa el cuadro con la forma correspondiente del presente de subjuntivo. 24 pts.

yo/él/ella	tú	nosotros/as	Uds./ellos/ellas
limpie	limpies	limpiemos	limpien
venga	**vengas**	vengamos	vengan
quiera	quieras	**queramos**	quieran
ofrezca	ofrezcas	ofrezcamos	**ofrezcan**

2 El apartamento ideal Completa este folleto (*brochure*) informativo con la forma correcta del presente de subjuntivo. 16 pts.

¿Eres joven y buscas tu primera vivienda? Te ofrezco estos consejos:

- Te sugiero que primero (tú) (1) __escribas__ (escribir) una lista de las cosas que quieres en un apartamento.
- Quiero que después (2) __pienses__ (pensar) muy bien cuáles son tus prioridades. Es necesario que cada persona (3) __tenga__ (tener) sus prioridades claras, porque el hogar (*home*) perfecto no existe.
- Antes de decidir en qué área quieren vivir, les aconsejo a ti y a tu futuro/a compañero/a de apartamento que (4) __salgan__ (salir) a ver la ciudad y que (5) __conozcan__ (conocer) los distintos barrios y las afueras.
- Pidan que el agente les (6) __muestre__ (mostrar) todas las partes de cada casa.
- Finalmente, como consumidores, es importante que nosotros (7) __sepamos__ (saber) bien nuestros derechos (*rights*); por eso, deben insistir en que todos los puntos del contrato (8) __estén__ (estar) muy claros antes de firmarlo (*signing it*).

¡Buena suerte!

RESUMEN GRAMATICAL

12.1 Relative pronouns *pp. 386–387*

Relative pronouns	
que	*that; which; who*
quien(es)	*who; whom; that*
lo que	*that which; what*

12.2 Formal commands *pp. 390–391*

Formal commands (**Ud.** and **Uds.**)

Infinitive	Present tense yo form	Ud(s). command
limpiar	limpio	limpie(n)
barrer	barro	barra(n)
sacudir	sacudo	sacuda(n)

► Verbs with stem changes or irregular **yo** forms maintain the same irregularity in the formal commands:

hacer: yo hago → Hagan la cama.

Irregular formal commands	
dar	dé (Ud.); den (Uds.)
estar	esté(n)
ir	vaya(n)
saber	sepa(n)
ser	sea(n)

12.3 The present subjunctive *pp. 394–396*

Present subjunctive of regular verbs

hablar	comer	escribir
hable	coma	escriba
hables	comas	escribas
hable	coma	escriba
hablemos	comamos	escribamos
habléis	comáis	escribáis
hablen	coman	escriban

TEACHING OPTIONS

TPR Add an auditory aspect to this grammar review. Have students imagine they are landlords with students as tenants. Prepare statements about the tenants, using impersonal expressions. As you read each statement, have students give a thumbs-up if they like what they hear or a thumbs-down if they do not. Ex: **Es importante que los estudiantes mantengan el apartamento limpio.** (thumbs-up) **Es urgente que den fiestas todos los sábados.** (thumbs-down)

Extra Practice Write items like these on the board and have students give the subjunctive forms: **1. barrer: yo/ella/ustedes (que yo barra, que ella barra, que ustedes barran) 2. mudarse: ellos/usted/tú (que ellos se muden, que usted se mude, que tú te mudes) 3. dormir: nosotros/tú/ella (que nosotros durmamos, que tú duermas, que ella duerma)**

Irregular verbs in the present subjunctive		
dar		dé, des, dé, demos, deis, den
estar	est- +	-é, -és, -é, -emos, -éis, -én
ir	vay- +	
saber	sep- +	-a, -as, -a, -amos, -áis, -an
ser	se- +	

12.4 Subjunctive with verbs of will and influence

pp. 398–399

▸ Verbs of will and influence: **aconsejar, desear, importar, insistir (en), mandar, necesitar, pedir** (e:i), **preferir** (e:ie), **prohibir, querer** (e:ie), **recomendar** (e:ie), **rogar** (o:ue), **sugerir** (e:ie)

3 **Relativos** Completa las oraciones con **lo que, que** o **quien(es)**. 16 pts.

1. Me encanta la alfombra __que__ está en el comedor.
2. Mi amiga Tere, con __quien__ trabajo, me regaló ese cuadro.
3. Todas las cosas __que__ tenemos vienen de la casa de mis abuelos.
4. Hija, no compres más cosas. __Lo que__ debes hacer ahora es organizarlo todo.
5. La agencia de decoración de __que__ le hablé se llama Casabella.
6. Esas flores las dejaron en la puerta mis nuevos vecinos, a __quienes__ aún (*yet*) no conozco.
7. Leonor no compró nada, porque __lo que__ le gustaba era muy caro.
8. Mi amigo Aldo, a __quien__ visité ayer, es un cocinero excelente.

4 **Preparando la casa** Martín y Ángela van a hacer un curso de verano en Costa Rica y una vecina va a cuidarles (*take care of*) la casa mientras ellos no están. Completa las instrucciones de la vecina con mandatos formales. Usa cada verbo una sola vez y agrega pronombres de objeto directo o indirecto si es necesario. 20 pts.

arreglar	dejar	hacer	pedir	sacudir
barrer	ensuciar	limpiar	poner	tener

Primero, (1) __hagan__ ustedes las maletas. Las cosas que no se llevan a Costa Rica, (2) __pónganlas__ en el altillo. Ángela, (3) __arregle/limpie__ las habitaciones y Martín, (4) __limpie/arregle__ usted la cocina y el baño. Después, los dos (5) __barran__ el suelo y (6) __sacudan__ los muebles de toda la casa. Ángela, no (7) __deje__ sus joyas (*jewelry*) en el apartamento. (8) __Tengan__ cuidado ¡y no (9) __ensucien__ nada antes de irse! Por último, (10) __pídanle__ a alguien que recoja (*pick up*) su correo.

5 **Los quehaceres** A tu compañero/a de cuarto no le gusta ayudar con los quehaceres. Escribe al menos seis oraciones dándole consejos para hacer más divertidos los quehaceres. 24 pts.

Answers will vary.

modelo

Te sugiero que pongas música mientras lavas los platos…

6 **El circo** Completa esta famosa frase que tiene su origen en el circo (*circus*). ¡4 puntos EXTRA!

"¡__Pasen__ (Pasar) ustedes y __vean__ (ver)! El espectáculo va a comenzar."

Practice more at **vhlcentral.com**.

3 Teaching Tip Have students circle the noun or idea to which each relative pronoun refers.

3 Expansion
- Ask volunteers to give the corresponding questions for each item. Ex: **1. ¿Qué alfombra te encanta?**
- Have students work in pairs to create four additional sentences using relative pronouns.

4 Teaching Tips
- To simplify, have students begin by scanning the paragraph and identifying which blanks call for **usted** commands and which call for **ustedes** commands.
- Tell students that some answers will contain object pronouns (items 2 and 10).

5 Teaching Tip Before beginning this activity, have pairs discuss their own habits regarding chores.

5 Expansion Have students imagine they have two roommates, and ask them to rewrite their sentences using **ustedes** commands.

6 Expansion To challenge students, ask them to write two **ustedes** commands for people attending a circus and one **usted** command for the master of ceremonies.

TEACHING OPTIONS

Extra Practice Call out formal commands. Ex: **Sacudan los muebles.** Have students respond by naming the infinitive and subject. Ex: **sacudir, ustedes**. Reverse the drill by calling out verb phrases and either **usted** or **ustedes**. Have students give the command form.

Large Groups Review present subjunctive and vocabulary from previous lessons. Divide the class into two teams and have them line up. Name a person or group of people. Ex: **estudiantes de computación, Katy Perry, un niño en su primer día de la escuela primaria**. Then point to the first member of team A, who has three seconds to create a piece of advice. Ex: **Quiero que apaguen las computadoras.** Then the first member of team B has to give another sentence. Continue until the chain is broken, then name a new person.

Audio: Reading
Additional Reading

Section Goals

In **Lectura**, students will:

- learn to locate the main parts of a sentence
- read a content-rich text with long sentences

Instructional Resource
Supersite

Estrategia Tell students that if they have trouble reading long sentences in Spanish, they should pause to identify the main verb of the sentence and its subject. They should then reread the entire sentence.

Examinar el texto Students should see from the layout (cover page with title, photo, and phone number; interior pages with an introduction and several headings followed by short paragraphs) that this is a brochure. Revealing cognates are: **información** (cover) and **residencia oficial del Presidente de Panamá** (introduction).

¿Probable o improbable? Ask volunteers to read aloud each item and give the answer. Have a volunteer rephrase the improbable statement so that it is probable.

Oraciones largas Ask pairs to create a couple of long sentences. Have them point out the main verb and subject.

Lectura

NATIONAL STANDARDS communication cultures

Antes de leer

Estrategia

Locating the main parts of a sentence

Did you know that a text written in Spanish is an average of 15% longer than the same text written in English? Since the Spanish language tends to use more words to express ideas, you will often encounter long sentences when reading in Spanish. Of course, the length of sentences varies with genre and with authors' individual styles. To help you understand long sentences, identify the main parts of the sentence before trying to read it in its entirety. First locate the main verb of the sentence, along with its subject, ignoring any words or phrases set off by commas. Then reread the sentence, adding details like direct and indirect objects, transitional words, and prepositional phrases.

Examinar el texto

Mira el formato de la lectura. ¿Qué tipo de documento es? ¿Qué cognados encuentras en la lectura? ¿Qué te dicen sobre el tema de la selección?

¿Probable o improbable?

Mira brevemente el texto e indica si estas oraciones son probables o improbables.

1. Este folleto° es de interés turístico. probable
2. Describe un edificio moderno cubano. improbable
3. Incluye algunas explicaciones de arquitectura. probable
4. Espera atraer° a visitantes al lugar. probable

Oraciones largas

Mira el texto y busca algunas oraciones largas. Con un(a) compañero/a, identifiquen las partes principales de la oración y después examinen las descripciones adicionales. ¿Qué significan las oraciones?

folleto *brochure* atraer *to attract* épocas *time periods*

Bienvenidos al Palacio de las Garzas

El palacio está abierto de martes a domingo.
Para más información,
llame al teléfono 507-226-7000.
También puede solicitar° un folleto
a la casilla° 3467,
Ciudad de Panamá, Panamá.

Después de leer

Ordenar

Pon estos eventos en el orden cronológico adecuado.

3 El palacio se convirtió en residencia presidencial.
2 Durante diferentes épocas°, maestros, médicos y banqueros ejercieron su profesión en el palacio.
4 El Dr. Belisario Porras ocupó el palacio por primera vez.
1 Los españoles construyeron el palacio.
5 Se renovó el palacio.
6 Los turistas pueden visitar el palacio de martes a domingo.

Practice more at **vhlcentral.com**.

TEACHING OPTIONS

Heritage Speakers Ask heritage speakers to give a brief presentation about a famous government building in their family's home country. Tell them to include recommendations about what rooms and objects are particularly noteworthy and should not be missed. If possible, they should illustrate their presentation with photographs or brochures.

Extra Practice Ask students to write ten statements using the subjunctive to describe their dream house (**la casa de mis sueños**). Ex: **Para mí es importante que haya una piscina de tamaño olímpico en la casa de mis sueños. Recomiendo que la cocina sea grande porque me gusta cocinar. Es necesario que tenga varios dormitorios porque siempre tengo huéspedes.** Have students share their sentences with a partner.

El Palacio de las Garzas° es la residencia oficial del Presidente de Panamá desde 1903. Fue construido en 1673 para ser la casa de un gobernador español. Con el paso de los años fue almacén, escuela, hospital, aduana, banco y por último, palacio presidencial.

En la actualidad el edificio tiene tres pisos, pero los planos originales muestran una construcción de un piso con un gran patio en el centro. La restauración del palacio comenzó en el año 1922 y los trabajos fueron realizados por el arquitecto Villanueva-Meyer y el pintor Roberto Lewis. El palacio, un monumento al estilo colonial, todavía conserva su elegancia y buen gusto, y es una de las principales atracciones turísticas del barrio Casco Viejo°.

Planta baja

El Patio de las Garzas

Una antigua puerta de hierro° recibe a los visitantes. El patio interior todavía conserva los elementos originales de la construcción: piso de mármol°, columnas cubiertas° de nácar° y una magnífica fuente° de agua en el centro. Aquí están las nueve garzas que le dan el nombre al palacio y que representan las nueve provincias de Panamá.

Primer piso

El Salón Amarillo

Aquí el turista puede visitar una galería de cuarenta y un retratos° de gobernadores y personajes ilustres de Panamá. La principal atracción de este salón es el sillón presidencial, que se usa especialmente cuando hay cambio de presidente. Otros atractivos de esta área son el comedor Los Tamarindos, que se destaca° por la elegancia de sus muebles y sus lámparas de cristal, y el Patio Andaluz, con sus coloridos mosaicos que representan la unión de la cultura indígena y la española.

El Salón Dr. Belisario Porras

Este elegante y majestuoso salón es uno de los lugares más importantes del Palacio de las Garzas. Lleva su nombre en honor al Dr. Belisario Porras, quien fue tres veces presidente de Panamá (1912–1916, 1918–1920 y 1920–1924).

Segundo piso

Es el área residencial del palacio y el visitante no tiene acceso a ella. Los armarios, las cómodas y los espejos de la alcoba fueron comprados en Italia y Francia por el presidente Porras, mientras que las alfombras, cortinas y frazadas° son originarias de España.

solicitar *request* **casilla** *post office box* **Garzas** *Herons* **Casco Viejo** *Old Quarter* **hierro** *iron* **mármol** *marble* **cubiertas** *covered* **nácar** *mother-of-pearl* **fuente** *fountain* **retratos** *portraits* **se destaca** *stands out* **frazadas** *blankets*

Ordenar Quickly go over the correct order by asking a volunteer to read the sentence he or she believes should be first, another volunteer to read the sentence that should be second, and so forth.

Preguntas

Contesta las preguntas.

1. ¿Qué sala es notable por sus muebles elegantes y sus lámparas de cristal? el comedor Los Tamarindos
2. ¿En qué parte del palacio se encuentra la residencia del presidente? en el segundo piso
3. ¿Dónde empiezan los turistas su visita al palacio? en el Patio de las Garzas
4. ¿En qué lugar se representa artísticamente la rica herencia cultural de Panamá? en el Patio Andaluz
5. ¿Qué salón honra la memoria de un gran panameño? el Salón Dr. Belisario Porras
6. ¿Qué partes del palacio te gustaría (*would you like*) visitar? ¿Por qué? Explica tu respuesta. Answers will vary.

Conversación

En grupos de tres o cuatro estudiantes, hablen sobre lo siguiente: Answers will vary.

1. ¿Qué tiene en común el Palacio de las Garzas con otras residencias presidenciales u otras casas muy grandes?
2. ¿Te gustaría vivir en el Palacio de las Garzas? ¿Por qué?
3. Imagina que puedes diseñar tu palacio ideal. Describe los planos para cada piso del palacio.

Preguntas
- Go over the answers as a class.
- To add a visual aspect to this reading, have students work in pairs to create a detailed floor plan of the **Palacio de las Garzas**. Then have volunteers use **usted** commands to tell you how to draw the floor plan on the board. Ex: **Dibuje la planta baja. Ponga una fuente de agua en el centro.**

Conversación
After groups have finished their conversations, encourage the class to discuss the three questions. Ask additional questions, such as: **¿En qué se diferencia el Palacio de las Garzas con otras casas? ¿A quién no le gustaría vivir en el Palacio de las Garzas? ¿Por qué? ¿Quién está de acuerdo?**

TEACHING OPTIONS

Variación léxica Point out that **piso** may mean *floor, flooring; apartment, flat;* or *story* (of a building). In Spanish, the **planta baja** of a building is its ground floor. The second story is called the **primer piso**; the third story is called the **segundo piso**, and so forth. The top floor in a building is called the **planta alta**. In the **Palacio de las Garzas,** the **segundo piso** is also the **planta alta**.

Large Groups Ask students to work in groups of five to role-play a guided tour of the **Palacio de las Garzas.** One group member plays the guide and the others play tourists. Encourage the guide to develop a script and the tourists to ask questions about the residence and its occupants. Give each group time to prepare and practice before performing its skit for the class.

Section Goals

In **Escritura**, students will:

- learn to use linking words
- integrate **Lección 12** vocabulary and structures
- write a lease agreement

Instructional Resource
Supersite

Estrategia Review the linking words. Point out that they are all words with which students are familiar. Have pairs use a few of them in sentences, and ask volunteers to share their sentences with the class.

Tema

- Review with students the details suggested for inclusion in the lease agreement. You may wish to present the following terms students can use in their agreements: **arrendatario** (*tenant*); **arrendador** (*landlord*); **propietario** (*owner*); **estipulaciones** (*stipulations*); **parte** (*party*); **de anticipación, de antelación** (*in advance*).
- Provide students with samples of legal documents in Spanish. (Many legal forms are downloadable from the Internet.) Go over the format of these documents with students, clarifying legal terminology as necessary.

Escritura

Estrategia

Using linking words

You can make your writing sound more sophisticated by using linking words to connect simple sentences or ideas and create more complex sentences. Consider these passages, which illustrate this effect:

Without linking words

En la actualidad el edificio tiene tres pisos. Los planos originales muestran una construcción de un piso con un gran patio en el centro. La restauración del palacio comenzó en el año 1922. Los trabajos fueron realizados por el arquitecto Villanueva-Meyer y el pintor Roberto Lewis.

With linking words

En la actualidad el edificio tiene tres pisos, pero los planos originales muestran una construcción de un piso con un gran patio en el centro. La restauración del palacio comenzó en el año 1922 y los trabajos fueron realizados por el arquitecto Villanueva-Meyer y el pintor Roberto Lewis.

Linking words

cuando	*when*
mientras	*while*
o	*or*
pero	*but*
porque	*because*
pues	*since*
que	*that; who; which*
quien(es)	*who*
sino	*but (rather)*
y	*and*

Tema

Escribir un contrato de arrendamiento°

communication STANDARDS

Eres el/la administrador(a)° de un edificio de apartamentos. Prepara un contrato de arrendamiento para los nuevos inquilinos°. El contrato debe incluir estos detalles:

- la dirección° del apartamento y del/de la administrador(a)
- las fechas del contrato
- el precio del alquiler y el día que se debe pagar
- el precio del depósito
- información y reglas° acerca de:
  - la basura
  - el correo
  - los animales domésticos
  - el ruido°
  - los servicios de electricidad y agua
  - el uso de electrodomésticos
- otros aspectos importantes de la vida comunitaria

contrato de arrendamiento *lease* administrador(a) *manager* inquilinos *tenants* dirección *address* reglas *rules* ruido *noise*

EVALUATION: Contrato

Criteria	Scale
Content	1 2 3 4
Organization	1 2 3 4
Use of vocabulary	1 2 3 4
Use of linking words	1 2 3 4
Grammatical accuracy	1 2 3 4

Scoring	
Excellent	18–20 points
Good	14–17 points
Satisfactory	10–13 points
Unsatisfactory	< 10 points

Escuchar

Audio

Estrategia

Using visual cues

Visual cues like illustrations and headings provide useful clues about what you will hear.

To practice this strategy, you will listen to a passage related to the following photo. Jot down the clues the photo gives you as you listen.

Preparación

Mira el dibujo. ¿Qué pistas te da para comprender la conversación que vas a escuchar? ¿Qué significa *bienes raíces?*

Ahora escucha

Mira los anuncios de esta página y escucha la conversación entre el señor Núñez, Adriana y Felipe. Luego indica si cada descripción se refiere a la casa ideal de Adriana y Felipe, a la casa del anuncio o al apartamento del anuncio.

Oraciones	La casa ideal	La casa del anuncio	El apartamento del anuncio
Es barato.	___	___	✔
Tiene cuatro dormitorios.	___	✔	___
Tiene una oficina.	✔	___	___
Tiene un balcón.	___	___	✔
Tiene una cocina moderna.	___	✔	___
Tiene un jardín muy grande.	___	✔	___
Tiene un patio.	✔	___	___

18G

Bienes raíces

Se vende.
4 dormitorios,
3 baños, cocina moderna, jardín con árboles frutales.
B/. 225.000

Se alquila.
2 dormitorios,
1 baño.
Balcón.
Urbanización Las Brisas. B/. 525

Comprensión

NATIONAL communication STANDARDS

Preguntas

1. ¿Cuál es la relación entre el señor Núñez, Adriana y Felipe? ¿Cómo lo sabes? El Sr. Núñez es el padre de Adriana y Felipe es su esposo.
2. ¿Qué diferencia de opinión hay entre Adriana y Felipe sobre dónde quieren vivir? Felipe prefiere vivir en la ciudad, pero Adriana quiere vivir en las afueras.
3. Usa la información de los dibujos y la conversación para entender lo que dice Adriana al final. ¿Qué significa "todo a su debido tiempo"? Answers will vary.

Conversación

En parejas, túrnense para hacer y contestar las preguntas. Answers will vary.

1. ¿Qué tienen en común el apartamento y la casa del anuncio con el lugar donde tú vives?
2. ¿Qué piensas de la recomendación del señor Núñez?
3. ¿Qué tipo de sugerencias te da tu familia sobre dónde vivir?
4. ¿Dónde prefieres vivir tú, en un apartamento o en una casa? Explica por qué.

Practice more at **vhlcentral.com**.

Section Goals

In **Escuchar**, students will:
- use visual cues to help them understand an oral passage
- answer questions based on the content of a recorded conversation

Instructional Resources
Supersite: Audio (Textbook MP3s); Resources (Scripts)

Estrategia
Script En mi niñez lo pasé muy bien. Vivíamos en una pequeña casa en la isla Colón con vistas al mar. Pasaba las horas buceando alrededor de los arrecifes de coral. A veces me iba a pasear por las plantaciones de bananos o a visitar el pueblo de los indios guayamí. Otros días iba con mi hermano al mar en una pequeña lancha para pescar. Era una vida feliz y tranquila. Ahora vivo en la Ciudad de Panamá. ¡Qué diferencia!

Ahora escucha
Script ADRIANA: Mira, papá, tienen una sección especial de bienes raíces en el periódico. Felipe, mira esta casa… tiene un jardín enorme.
FELIPE: ¡Qué linda! ¡Uy, qué cara! ¿Qué piensa usted? ¿Debemos buscar una casa o un apartamento?
SR. NÚÑEZ: Bueno, hijos, hay muchas cosas que deben considerar. Primero, ¿les gustaría vivir en las afueras o en el centro de la ciudad?
F: Pues, señor Núñez, yo prefiero vivir en la ciudad. Así tenemos el teatro, los parques, los centros comerciales… todo cerca de casa. Sé que Adriana quiere vivir en las afueras porque es más tranquilo.
S: De todos modos van a necesitar un mínimo de dos dormitorios, un baño, una sala grande… ¿Qué más?
A: Es importante que tengamos

(Script continues at far left in the bottom panels.)

una oficina para mí y un patio para las plantas.
S: Como no tienen mucho dinero ahorrado, es mejor que alquilen un apartamento pequeño por un tiempo. Así pueden ahorrar su dinero para comprar la casa ideal. Miren este apartamento. Tiene un balcón precioso y está en un barrio muy seguro y bonito. Y el alquiler es muy razonable.
F: Adriana, me parece que tu padre tiene razón. Con un alquiler tan barato, podemos comprar muebles y también ahorrar dinero cada mes.
A: ¡Ay!, quiero mi casa. Pero, bueno, ¡todo a su debido tiempo!

Section Goals

In **En pantalla**, students will:

- read about how the 2008 economic crisis has affected Spain
- watch a television commercial for **Carrefour** supermarkets
- read about the short film ***036***
- watch the short film ***036***

Instructional Resources
Supersite: Video (***En pantalla***); Resources (Scripts, Translations)

Introduction To check comprehension, ask these questions: **1. ¿Cuándo empezó la crisis económica en España? (Empezó en el año 2008.) 2. ¿Qué promueve la cadena de supermercados Carrefour? (Que es possible ahorrar y mantener el estilo al mismo tiempo.)**

Preparación
Ask students to share with the class any unusual experiences while doing the laundry they (or family members) have had. Was the experience related to a product that they used?

Antes de ver

- Have students look at the video stills, read the captions, and predict what is being sold in this commercial.
- Ask a volunteer to read the **Vocabulario útil** aloud.
- Tell students to rely on visual cues and to listen for cognates and words from **Vocabulario útil** as they watch the commercial.

Ordenar
Have students describe the decor, the clothes, and the women in the commercial.

Consejos
To practice more formal commands, have students write a list of the commands that might be overheard at a laundromat or dry cleaner's.

En pantalla

Anuncio

La crisis económica que vive España desde el año 2008 ha repercutido° notablemente en el estilo de vida de los españoles, y sobre todo en la cesta de la compra°, la que se ha visto reducida a productos básicos y de bajo precio. Con este anuncio, la cadena° de supermercados Carrefour promueve° que es posible ahorrar° y mantener el estilo al mismo tiempo, sin tener que prescindir de° productos de calidad a buen precio. Carrefour utiliza el humor y el optimismo ante el duro° tema de la crisis, haciendo que el cliente se sienta identificado y valorado.

Vocabulario útil

conjunto	*outfit*
cuidar	*to take care of*
prêt-à-porter (*Fr.*)	*ready-to-wear*
suavizante	*fabric softener*

Preparación

¿Lavas tu propia ropa? ¿Tienes lavadora y secadora en casa? ¿Utilizas algún producto especial, como suavizante? ¿Qué importancia tiene para ti el cuidado de la ropa? Answers will vary.

Ordenar

Pon en orden lo que ves en el anuncio de televisión. No vas a usar dos elementos.

5 a. medias	1 e. cortinas
2 b. alfombra	6 f. secadoras
___ c. copas	3 g. maquillaje
4 d. tazas	___ h. cuadros

Consejos

En parejas, preparen una lista de un mínimo de seis consejos para economizar en los siguientes quehaceres domésticos u otros. Utilicen el imperativo y el subjuntivo. Compartan sus consejos con la clase. Answers will vary.

- lavar ropa
- limpiar la casa
- cocinar
- lavar los platos

ha repercutido *has had an effect* **cesta de la compra** *shopping basket* **cadena** *chain* **promueve** *promotes* **ahorrar** *to save (money)* **prescindir de** *to do without* **duro** *tough* **bajamos** *we lower* **viene bien** *is just right*

Anuncio de Carrefour

La Asociación de mujeres que [...] quieren cuidar su ropa...

Le dicena "no" a la crisis y "sí" a Carrefour.

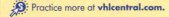

Porque bajamos° los precios [...], Carrefour te viene bien°.

Video: TV Clip

Practice more at **vhlcentral.com.**

TEACHING OPTIONS

Pairs Have students work in pairs to write another commercial for **Carrefour.**

Large Groups Divide the class into three groups and have each one create a survey consisting of eight questions about their classmates' lifestyles. One group should ask about students' living space, the second should ask about students' roommates, and the third should ask about daily chores and habits. Once groups have created their surveys, have them exchange surveys with other groups and complete them. Then ask volunteers from each group to summarize the survey results.

Cortometraje

La burocracia puede ser complicada y frustrante, con sus reglas° y su jerarquía impenetrables. En *036* vemos cómo una chica española llega a una oficina del gobierno preparada para presentar° todos los documentos necesarios para hacerse trabajadora autónoma. La chica "se bate en duelo°" con el oficinista° como si se tratara de° una película del Lejano Oeste°. Él cree que ella no tiene todos los documentos, pero la chica sabe lo que hace.

Preparación

En parejas, contesten estas preguntas. Answers will vary.

1. ¿Qué es la burocracia?
2. ¿En qué tipo de oficinas es común?
3. ¿En qué circunstancias es necesario presentar documentos?

Después de ver

Completa cada oración con una palabra de la lista.

un café	ganas	el impreso
la determinación	una grapadora	la oficina

1. Cuando llega la chica a __la oficina__, un chico sale frustrado.
2. El oficinista se sirve __un café__ antes de dejarla hablar.
3. El oficinista no tiene __ganas__ de ayudarla.
4. __La determinación__ de la chica es más fuerte que la del oficinista.
5. Al final la chica sorprende a todos cuando saca __una grapadora__.

Conversar

Entrevista a un(a) compañero/a y pregúntale cuándo tuvo que confrontarse con la burocracia. ¿Qué sucedió? Comparen sus experiencias con la de la chica del cortometraje. Answers will vary.

reglas *rules* presentar *submit* se bate en duelo *fights a duel* oficinista *office worker* como si se tratara de *as if it were* Lejano Oeste *Wild West*

Expresiones útiles

la casilla	*box (on a form)*
cumplimentar	*to fill out*
el DNI	Documento Nacional de Identidad
darse de alta	*to register*
grapado/a	*stapled*
la Hacienda	*IRS equivalent in Spain*
el impreso	*form*
el/la trabajador(a) autónomo/a	*self-employed worker*

Para hablar del corto

desafiar	*to challenge*
la grapadora	*stapler*
perseverar	*to persevere*
sellar	*to stamp*
terco/a	*stubborn*

Video: ***Short Film***

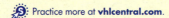

Practice more at **vhlcentral.com**.

Antes de ver

- Have students look at the poster and ask them what they think the short film will be about.
- Read through the **Expresiones útiles** and **Para hablar del corto** vocabulary with students to model pronunciation and practice using the terms. Explain that **el DNI** is the name of Spain's national identity card. In many Latin American countries it is called **cédula de identidad** or **carné de identidad**, among other terms. Point out that **grapar, la grapadora**, and **grapado/a** are used in Spain, while **engrapar, la engrapadora**, and **engrapado/a** are more commonly used in Latin America.
- Reassure students that they do not need to understand every word they hear in the short film. Tell them to rely on visual cues and listen for cognates and words from **Expresiones útiles**.

Preparación Allow students to ask you for additional vocabulary. Circulate around the room to help as they formulate their answers. Call upon pairs to share their ideas with the class.

Después de ver Have students write additional items using the **Expresiones útiles** and **Para hablar del corto** vocabulary.

Conversar After students have had time to discuss their experiences, make a list of the types of bureaucracy encountered and talk about them as a class.

TEACHING OPTIONS

Worth Noting The female protagonist in this short film, **Carolina Bang**, is an up-and-coming Spanish actress. She has appeared on TV and in other short films and has been in several of Álex de la Iglesia's films, including ***Balada triste de trompeta*** (2010) and ***Mi gran noche*** (2015). De la Iglesia is an acclaimed Spanish director.

Heritage Speakers Ask heritage speakers to share any experiences they may have had with bureaucracies in their families' countries of origin. Ask them to research the processes, if necessary, and compare them with U.S. systems. Some interesting comparisons might be made for obtaining driving licenses, passports, tax forms, etc.

Video: *Panorama cultural*
Interactive map

Section Goal

In **Panorama**, students will read about the geography and culture of Panama.

Instructional Resources
Supersite: Video (***Panorama cultural***); Resources (Scripts, Translations, Digital Image Bank, Answer Keys)
WebSAM
Workbook, pp. 149–150
Video Manual, pp. 57–58

Teaching Tips

- Use the **Lección 12 Panorama** digital images to assist with this presentation.
- Have students look at the map of Panama and discuss the physical features of the country. Point out the bodies of water that run along the coasts of Panama, and the canal that cuts through the isthmus (**istmo**). Then, have students look at the call-out photos and read the captions. Point out that the Kuna live on the San Blas Islands in the Caribbean Sea.

El país en cifras Mention that the national currency, the balboa, is named for **Vasco Núñez de Balboa**, who explored the Isthmus of Panama in 1501. Tell students that **chibcha** is a major indigenous language group, with dialects spoken by people from central Colombia through eastern Nicaragua. After reading about the **Panameños célebres**, ask students to share what they know about the individuals.

¡Increíble pero cierto! The opening of the Panama Canal not only dramatically reduced the distance ships had to travel to get from the Atlantic Ocean to the Pacific, it also provided a much safer route than the stormy, perilous route around Cape Horn and through the Straits of Magellan.

Panamá

NATIONAL STANDARDS connections cultures

El país en cifras

- **Área:** 75.420 km² (29.119 millas²), *aproximadamente el área de Carolina del Sur*
- **Población:** 3.608.000
- **Capital:** La Ciudad de Panamá —1.346.000
- **Ciudades principales:** Colón, David
- **Moneda:** balboa; es equivalente al dólar estadounidense.

En Panamá circulan los billetes de dólar estadounidense. El país centroamericano, sin embargo, acuña° su propia moneda. "El peso" es una moneda grande equivalente a cincuenta centavos°. La moneda de cinco centavos es llamada frecuentemente "real".

- **Idiomas:** español (oficial), lenguas indígenas, inglés *Muchos panameños son bilingües. La lengua materna del 14% de los panameños es el inglés.*

Mujer kuna lavando una mola

Un turista disfruta del bosque tropical colgado de un cable.

Bandera de Panamá

Panameños célebres

- **Mariano Rivera,** beisbolista (1969–)
- **Mireya Moscoso,** política (1946–)
- **Rubén Blades,** músico y político (1948–)
- **Danilo Pérez,** pianista (1966–)
- **Jorge Cham,** caricaturista (1976–)

Ruinas de un fuerte panameño

recursos: WB pp. 149–150 | VM pp. 57–58 | vhlcentral.com Lección 12

acuña *mints* centavos *cents*
promedio *average* peaje *toll*

¡Increíble pero cierto!

¿Conocías estos datos sobre el Canal de Panamá?

- Gracias al Canal de Panamá, el viaje en barco de Nueva York a Tokio es 3.000 millas más corto.
- Su construcción costó 639 millones de dólares.
- Hoy lo usan en promedio° 39 barcos al día.
- El peaje° promedio cuesta 54.000 dólares.

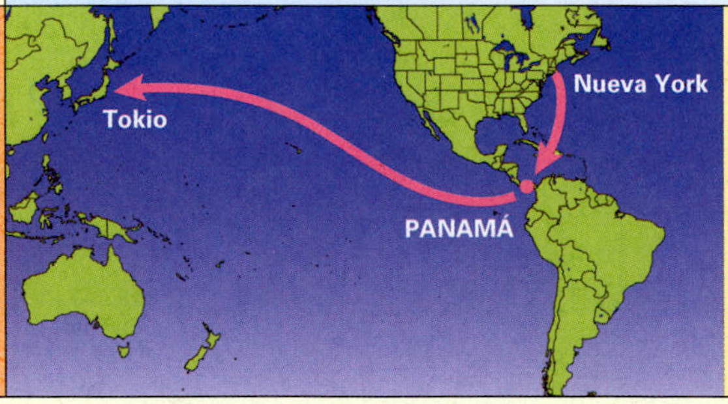

TEACHING OPTIONS

Extra Practice Discuss how **Rubén Blades** changed the world of salsa music by introducing lyrics with social commentary into what previously had been simply dance music. To add an interpretive element, bring in his recording ***Buscando América***, and have students listen to ***El padre Antonio y su monaguillo Andrés***, based on the story of Archbishop **Óscar Romero** of El Salvador. Or, listen to the story of ***Pedro Navaja*** on ***Siembra***, **Blades'** classic collaboration with **Willie Colón**. Have students write a summary of the song in English or describe how **Blades'** salsa differs from traditional "romantic" salsa.

Lugares • El Canal de Panamá

El Canal de Panamá conecta el océano Pacífico con el océano Atlántico. La construcción de este cauce° artificial empezó en 1903 y concluyó diez años después. Es una de las principales fuentes° de ingresos° del país, gracias al dinero que aportan los más de 14.000 buques° que transitan anualmente por esta ruta y a las actividades comerciales que se han desarrollado° en torno a° ella.

Artes • La mola

La mola es una forma de arte textil de los kunas, una tribu indígena que vive principalmente en las islas San Blas. Esta pieza artesanal se confecciona con fragmentos de tela° de colores vivos. Algunos de sus diseños son abstractos, inspirados en las formas del coral, y otros son geométricos, como en las molas más tradicionales. Antiguamente, estos tejidos se usaban sólo como ropa, pero hoy día también sirven para decorar las casas.

Naturaleza • El mar

Panamá, cuyo° nombre significa "lugar de muchos peces°", es un país muy frecuentado por los aficionados del buceo y la pesca. El territorio panameño cuenta con una gran variedad de playas en los dos lados del istmo°, con el mar Caribe a un lado y el océano Pacífico al otro. Algunas zonas costeras están destinadas al turismo. Otras están protegidas por la diversidad de su fauna marina, en la que abundan los arrecifes° de coral, como el Parque Nacional Marino Isla Bastimentos.

Vista de la Ciudad de Panamá

¿Qué aprendiste? Contesta cada pregunta con una oración completa.

1. ¿Cuál es la lengua materna del catorce por ciento de los panameños?
   El inglés es la lengua materna del catorce por ciento de los panameños.
2. ¿A qué unidad monetaria (*monetary unit*) es equivalente el balboa?
   El balboa es equivalente al dólar estadounidense.
3. ¿Qué océanos une el Canal de Panamá?
   El Canal de Panamá une los océanos Atlántico y Pacífico.
4. ¿Quién es Mariano Rivera?
   Mariano Rivera es un beisbolista panameño.
5. ¿Qué son las molas?
   Las molas son una forma de arte textil de los kunas.
6. ¿Cómo son los diseños de las molas?
   Algunos diseños son abstractos y otros son geométricos.
7. ¿Para qué se usan las molas?
   Las molas se usan como ropa y para decorar las casas.
8. ¿Cómo son las playas de Panamá?
   Son muy variadas; unas están destinadas al turismo, otras tienen valor ecológico.
9. ¿Qué significa "Panamá"?
   "Panamá" significa "lugar de muchos peces".

Conexión Internet Investiga estos temas en **vhlcentral.com**.

1. Investiga la historia de las relaciones entre Panamá y los Estados Unidos y la decisión de devolver (*give back*) el Canal de Panamá. ¿Estás de acuerdo con la decisión? Explica tu opinión.
2. Investiga sobre los kunas u otro grupo indígena de Panamá. ¿En qué partes del país viven? ¿Qué lenguas hablan? ¿Cómo es su cultura?

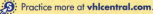

Practice more at **vhlcentral.com**.

cauce *channel* **fuentes** *sources* **ingresos** *income* **buques** *ships* **han desarrollado** *have developed* **en torno a** *around* **tela** *fabric* **cuyo** *whose* **peces** *fish* **istmo** *isthmus* **arrecifes** *reefs*

El Canal de Panamá The Panama Canal is a lake-and-lock type of canal, connecting the Atlantic and Pacific oceans at one of the lowest points on the Continental Divide. It is about 40 miles long and is one of the two most strategic man-made waterways on earth (the Suez Canal is the other).

La mola The Kuna originally lived on mainland Panama, but the majority chose to move to the San Blas Islands, where they could maintain their way of life. Elaborate traditions accompany every life-cycle event in Kuna culture, and many of these ceremonies are depicted on the elaborate appliqué **molas**.

El mar

- For more information about **el buceo** and other ocean sports, you may want to show the ***Panorama cultural*** video footage for this lesson.
- The **Parque Nacional Bastimentos** is located in the **Archipiélago de Bocas del Toro**. In this nature reserve, turtles nest on some of the beaches. Its coral reefs are home to more than 200 species of tropical fish, in addition to lobsters, manatees, and other marine life. The park is also known for its mangroves, which offer snorkelers another aquatic experience.

Conexión Internet Students will find supporting Internet activities and links at **vhlcentral.com**.

TEACHING OPTIONS

Worth Noting The Kuna people have a strong, rich oral tradition. During regular community meetings, ritual forms of speaking, including storytelling and speeches, are presented by community elders. It is only recently that a written form of the Kuna language has been developed by outsiders. However, as Spanish—and even English—begin to encroach more into **Kuna Yala** (the Kuna name for their homeland), linguistic anthropologists have highlighted the urgency of recording and preserving the rich Kuna oral tradition, fearing that the traditional Kuna language and culture will begin to be diluted by outside influences.

Section Goal

In **Panorama**, students will read about the geography and culture of El Salvador.

Instructional Resources
Supersite: Video (***Panorama cultural***); Resources (Scripts, Translations, Digital Image Bank, Answer Keys)
WebSAM
Workbook, pp. 151–152
Video Manual, pp. 59–60

Teaching Tips

- Use the **Lección 12 Panorama** digital images to assist with this presentation.
- Have students look at the map of El Salvador.
- Draw students' attention to the number of active volcanoes in El Salvador. Tell students that because of the fertility of El Salvador's volcanic soil, the country has a strong agricultural sector. Have students look at the inset map as you point out that El Salvador is the only Central American country without coastline on the Gulf of Mexico. Look at the photos and ask volunteers to read the captions.

El país en cifras In the early 1970s, El Salvador's overpopulation, chronic economic problems, and lack of social justice resulted in social disturbances that the government put down with brutal force.

¡Increíble pero cierto! In the town of Concepción de Ataco, another legend claims that on the **Cerro la Empalizada** there is a cave containing plants that disorient anyone who steps on them.

El Salvador

NATIONAL STANDARDS connections cultures

El país en cifras

- **Área:** 21.040 km² (8.124 millas²), *el tamaño° de Massachusetts*
- **Población:** 6.125.000
El Salvador es el país centroamericano más pequeño y el más densamente poblado°. Su población, al igual que la de Honduras, es muy homogénea: casi el 90 por ciento es mestiza.
- **Capital:** San Salvador—1.605.000
- **Ciudades principales:** Soyapango, Santa Ana, San Miguel, Mejicanos
- **Moneda:** dólar estadounidense
- **Idiomas:** español (oficial), náhuatl, lenca

Bandera de El Salvador

Salvadoreños célebres

- **Óscar Romero,** arzobispo° y activista por los derechos humanos° (1917–1980)
- **Claribel Alegría,** poeta, novelista y cuentista (1924–)
- **Roque Dalton,** poeta, ensayista y novelista (1935–1975)
- **María Eugenia Brizuela,** política (1956–)
- **Francesca Miranda,** diseñadora (1957–)

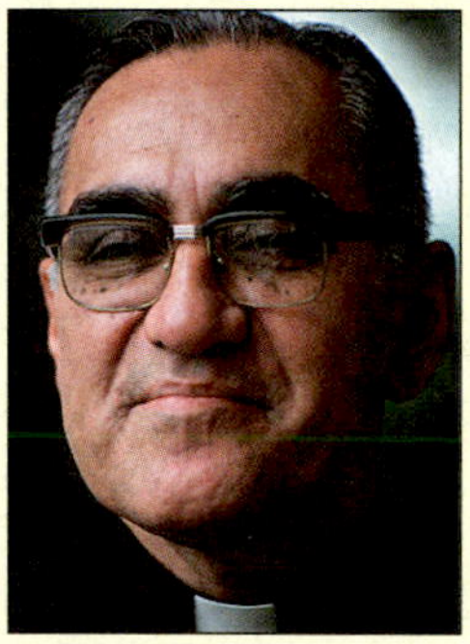

Óscar Romero

tamaño *size* arzobispo *archbishop* derechos humanos *human rights* laguna *lagoon* poblado *populated* sirena *mermaid*

Ruinas de Tazumal

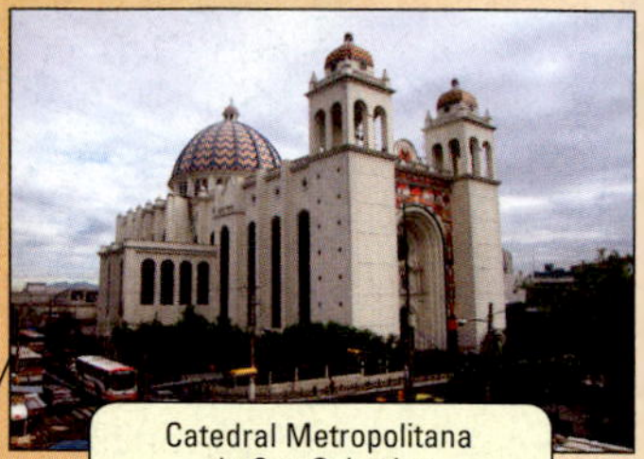

Catedral Metropolitana de San Salvador

Chorros de la Calera en Juayúa

recursos

WB pp. 151–152	VM pp. 59–60	vhlcentral.com Lección 12

¡Increíble pero cierto!

El rico folclor salvadoreño se basa sobre todo en sus extraordinarios recursos naturales. Por ejemplo, según una leyenda, las muertes que se producen en la laguna° de Alegría tienen su explicación en la existencia de una sirena° solitaria que vive en el lago y captura a los jóvenes atractivos.

TEACHING OPTIONS

Worth Noting Government repression in El Salvador intensified resistance, and by the mid-1970s a civil war was being fought between government forces and the **FMLN,** an armed guerrilla movement. Among the many martyrs of the war was the Archbishop of San Salvador, **Óscar Romero.** A descendent of the privileged class in El Salvador, **Romero** came to champion the cause of peace and social justice for the poor. This position made him the target of reactionary elements. On March 24, 1980, Archbishop **Romero** was assassinated while giving mass in the Cathedral of San Salvador. His life and death became an inspiration for those seeking social justice. Still, it was only in 1991 that a cease-fire brought an end to the civil war.

Deportes • El surfing

El Salvador es uno de los destinos favoritos en Latinoamérica para la práctica del surfing. Cuenta con 300 kilómetros de costa a lo largo del océano Pacífico y sus olas° altas son ideales para quienes practican este deporte. De sus playas, La Libertad es la más visitada por surfistas de todo el mundo, gracias a que está muy cerca de la capital salvadoreña. Sin embargo, los fines de semana muchos visitantes prefieren viajar a la Costa del Bálsamo, donde se concentra menos gente.

Naturaleza • El Parque Nacional Montecristo

El Parque Nacional Montecristo se encuentra en la región norte del país. Se le conoce también como El Trifinio porque se ubica° en el punto donde se unen las fronteras de Guatemala, Honduras y El Salvador. Este bosque reúne a muchas especies vegetales y animales, como orquídeas, monos araña°, pumas, quetzales y tucanes. Además, las copas° de sus enormes árboles forman una bóveda° que impide° el paso de la luz solar. Este espacio natural se encuentra a una altitud de 2.400 metros (7.900 pies) sobre el nivel del mar y recibe 200 centímetros (80 pulgadas°) de lluvia al año.

Artes • La artesanía de Ilobasco

Ilobasco es un pueblo conocido por sus artesanías. En él se elaboran objetos con arcilla° y cerámica pintada a mano, como juguetes°, adornos° y utensilios de cocina. Además, son famosas sus "sorpresas", que son pequeñas piezas° de cerámica en cuyo interior se representan escenas de la vida diaria. Los turistas realizan excursiones para ver la elaboración, paso a paso°, de estos productos.

¿Qué aprendiste? Contesta cada pregunta con una oración completa.

1. ¿Qué tienen en común las poblaciones de El Salvador y Honduras?
   Las poblaciones de los dos países son muy homogéneas.
2. ¿Qué es el náhuatl?
   El náhuatl es un idioma que se habla en El Salvador.
3. ¿Quién es María Eugenia Brizuela?
   Es una política salvadoreña.
4. Hay muchos lugares ideales para el surfing en El Salvador. ¿Por qué? Porque El Salvador recibe algunas de las mejores olas del océano Pacífico.
5. ¿A qué altitud se encuentra el Parque Nacional Montecristo? Se encuentra a una altitud de 2.400 metros.
6. ¿Cuáles son algunos de los animales y las plantas que viven en este parque?
   Hay orquídeas, monos araña, pumas, quetzales y tucanes.
7. ¿Por qué se le llama El Trifinio al Parque Nacional Montecristo? Porque es el punto donde se unen Guatemala, Honduras y El Salvador.
8. ¿Por qué es famoso el pueblo de Ilobasco?
   Es famoso por los objetos de arcilla y por los artículos de cerámica pintados a mano.
9. ¿Qué se puede ver en un viaje a Ilobasco?
   Se puede ver la fabricación de los artículos de cerámica paso a paso.
10. ¿Qué son las "sorpresas" de Ilobasco?
    Las "sorpresas" son pequeñas piezas de cerámica con escenas de la vida diaria en su interior.

Conexión Internet Investiga estos temas en **vhlcentral.com**.

1. El Parque Nacional Montecristo es una reserva natural; busca información sobre otros parques o zonas protegidas en El Salvador. ¿Cómo son estos lugares? ¿Qué tipos de plantas y animales se encuentran allí?
2. Busca información sobre museos u otros lugares turísticos en San Salvador (u otra ciudad de El Salvador).

Practice more at **vhlcentral.com**.

olas *waves* se ubica *it is located* monos araña *spider monkeys* copas *tops* bóveda *cap* impide *blocks* pulgadas *inches* arcilla *clay* juguetes *toys* adornos *ornaments* piezas *pieces* paso a paso *step by step*

El surfing Tell students that **La Libertad** is a relatively small town that sees a large influx of beachgoers, not just surfers, during the weekends and holidays. Black volcanic sand covers the beach of **La Libertad**. About five miles east lies Zunzal beach, which, during Holy Week (**Semana Santa**) each year, is the site of international surfing competitions.

El Parque Nacional Montecristo The Montecristo cloud forest (**bosque nuboso**) is a protected area at the point where El Salvador, Honduras, and Guatemala meet. The point, at the summit of Montecristo, is called **El Trifinio**. Visitors only have access to Montecristo between November 1st and June 1st. The rest of the year it is closed to visitors for the animals' reproductive season.

La artesanía de Ilobasco Ilobasco is a crafts village that specializes in ceramics. **Sorpresas** are one of the most famous items. They are miniscule, intricate scenes and figures inside egg-shaped shells about the size of a walnut.

Conexión Internet Students will find supporting Internet activities and links at **vhlcentral.com**.

TEACHING OPTIONS

Variación léxica **Pupusa** is the name given to the Salvadoran version of the **tortilla**. In fact, **pupusas** are made by putting a filling such as red beans, onions, garlic, and cheese on one uncooked **tortilla**, laying another **tortilla** over it, and pressing the two together so they adhere, and then frying both in hot oil until the **pupusa** is golden and crunchy. Served sizzling from the fryer, **pupusas** are delicious. They are so popular that in El Salvador there are many shops, called **pupuserías**, that specialize in them. And if you visit a neighborhood in the United States where Salvadorans have settled, you will inevitably find a **pupusería**. You may want to play the ***Panorama cultural*** video footage for this lesson that shows how **pupusas** are made.

Instructional Resources
Supersite: Audio (Textbook & Lab MP3s); Testing Program (Tests, MP3s)
WebSAM
Lab Manual, p. 72

Las viviendas

las afueras	*suburbs; outskirts*
el alquiler	*rent (payment)*
el ama (*m., f.*) de casa	*housekeeper; caretaker*
el barrio	*neighborhood*
el edificio de apartamentos	*apartment building*
el/la vecino/a	*neighbor*
la vivienda	*housing*
alquilar	*to rent*
mudarse	*to move (from one house to another)*

Los cuartos y otros lugares

el altillo	*attic*
el balcón	*balcony*
la cocina	*kitchen*
el comedor	*dining room*
el dormitorio	*bedroom*
la entrada	*entrance*
la escalera	*stairs*
el garaje	*garage*
el jardín	*garden; yard*
la oficina	*office*
el pasillo	*hallway*
el patio	*patio; yard*
la sala	*living room*
el sótano	*basement*

Los muebles y otras cosas

la alfombra	*carpet; rug*
la almohada	*pillow*
el armario	*closet*
el cartel	*poster*
la cómoda	*chest of drawers*
las cortinas	*curtains*
el cuadro	*picture*
el estante	*bookcase; bookshelves*
la lámpara	*lamp*
la luz	*light; electricity*
la manta	*blanket*
la mesita	*end table*
la mesita de noche	*night stand*
los muebles	*furniture*
la pared	*wall*
la pintura	*painting; picture*
el sillón	*armchair*
el sofá	*sofa*

Los electrodomésticos

la cafetera	*coffee maker*
la cocina, la estufa	*stove*
el congelador	*freezer*
el electrodoméstico	*electric appliance*
el horno (de microondas)	*(microwave) oven*
la lavadora	*washing machine*
el lavaplatos	*dishwasher*
el refrigerador	*refrigerator*
la secadora	*clothes dryer*
la tostadora	*toaster*

La mesa

la copa	*wineglass*
la cuchara	*(table or large) spoon*
el cuchillo	*knife*
el plato	*plate*
la servilleta	*napkin*
la taza	*cup*
el tenedor	*fork*
el vaso	*glass*

Los quehaceres domésticos

arreglar	*to straighten up*
barrer el suelo	*to sweep the floor*
cocinar	*to cook*
ensuciar	*to get (something) dirty*
hacer la cama	*to make the bed*
hacer quehaceres domésticos	*to do household chores*
lavar (el suelo, los platos)	*to wash (the floor, the dishes)*
limpiar la casa	*to clean the house*
pasar la aspiradora	*to vacuum*
planchar la ropa	*to iron the clothes*
poner la mesa	*to set the table*
quitar la mesa	*to clear the table*
quitar el polvo	*to dust*
sacar la basura	*to take out the trash*
sacudir los muebles	*to dust the furniture*

Verbos y expresiones verbales

aconsejar	*to advise*
insistir (en)	*to insist (on)*
mandar	*to order*
recomendar (e:ie)	*to recommend*
rogar (o:ue)	*to beg*
sugerir (e:ie)	*to suggest*
Es bueno que...	*It's good that...*
Es importante que...	*It's important that...*
Es malo que...	*It's bad that...*
Es mejor que...	*It's better that...*
Es necesario que...	*It's necessary that...*
Es urgente que...	*It's urgent that...*

Relative pronouns	*See page 386.*
Expresiones útiles	*See page 381.*

recursos
LM p. 72 | vhlcentral.com Lección 12

Vocabulary Tools

La naturaleza 13

Communicative Goals

You will learn how to:

- Talk about and discuss the environment
- Express your beliefs and opinions about issues

A PRIMERA VISTA

- ¿Está mareada esta mujer?
- ¿Es importante que use ropa cómoda?
- ¿Es necesario que tenga cuidado?
- ¿Le interesa la naturaleza?

Lesson Goals

In **Lección 13**, students will be introduced to the following:

- terms to describe nature, the environment, conservation, and recycling
- the Andes mountain range
- Colombia's Santa Marta mountain range
- subjunctive with verbs and expressions of emotion
- subjunctive with verbs and expressions of doubt, disbelief, and denial
- expressions of certainty
- subjunctive with conjunctions
- forming regular past participles
- irregular past participles
- past participles used as adjectives
- identifying a text's purpose
- a video about nature in Costa Rica
- cultural, geographic, and historical information about Colombia and Honduras

A primera vista Ask these additional questions: **¿Te interesa la ecología? ¿Te gusta entrar en contacto con la naturaleza? ¿Cómo te sientes cuando estás fuera de la ciudad? ¿Te preocupa la ecología de la región donde vives?**

Teaching Tip Look for these icons for additional communicative practice:

	Interpretive communication
	Presentational communication
	Interpersonal communication

INSTRUCTIONAL RESOURCES

Supersite (vhlcentral.com)
Video: ***Fotonovela, Flash cultura, Panorama cultural***
Audio: Textbook and Lab MP3 Files
Activity Pack: Information Gap Activities, games, additional activity handouts
Resources: SAM Answer Key, Scripts, Translations, **Vocabulario adicional**, sample lesson plan, Grammar Presentation Slides, Digital Image Bank
Testing Program: Quizzes, Tests, Exams, MP3s
Student Activities Manual: Workbook/Video Manual/Lab Manual
WebSAM (online Student Activities Manual)

Vocabulary Tools

Section Goals

In **Contextos**, students will learn and practice:

- terms to describe nature and the environment
- conservation terms

Instructional Resources
Supersite: Audio (Textbook and Lab MP3 Files); Resources (Digital Image Bank, **Vocabulario adicional**, Activity Pack, Scripts, Answer Keys); Testing Program (Quizzes)
WebSAM
Workbook, pp. 155–156
Lab Manual, p. 73

Teaching Tips

- Write the headings **la naturaleza** and **la conservación** on the board and ask students to guess what they mean. Then, have two volunteers come to the board and write down all the English words the class can brainstorm pertaining to nature and conservation. After the class has produced at least fifteen words under each heading, have students look in their texts to see how many Spanish equivalents they can find.
- Use the **Lección 13 Contextos** digital images to assist with this presentation.
- Point to vocabulary items illustrated and ask volunteers to identify each item. Then ask questions about the items in **Más vocabulario**. Ex: **¿Cuáles son los recursos naturales de nuestra región? ¿Cuáles son los problemas de contaminación del medio ambiente de nuestra región? ¿Cómo se llama el río en nuestra ciudad? ¿Se puede nadar allí? ¿Por qué no? ¿Se debe pescar allí? ¿Por qué no?**

Note: At this point you may want to present ***Vocabulario adicional: Más vocabulario para la naturaleza*** from the Supersite.

La naturaleza

Más vocabulario

el bosque (tropical)	*(tropical; rain) forest*
el desierto	*desert*
la naturaleza	*nature*
la planta	*plant*
la selva, la jungla	*jungle*
la tierra	*land; soil*
el cielo	*sky*
la estrella	*star*
la luna	*moon*
el calentamiento global	*global warming*
el cambio climático	*climate change*
la conservación	*conservation*
la contaminación (del aire; del agua)	*(air; water) pollution*
la deforestación	*deforestation*
la ecología	*ecology*
el/la ecologista	*ecologist*
el ecoturismo	*ecotourism*
la energía (nuclear; solar)	*(nuclear; solar) energy*
la extinción	*extinction*
la fábrica	*factory*
el medio ambiente	*environment*
el peligro	*danger*
el recurso natural	*natural resource*
la solución	*solution*
el gobierno	*government*
la ley	*law*
la (sobre)población	*(over)population*
ecológico/a	*ecological*
puro/a	*pure*
renovable	*renewable*

Variación léxica

hierba ⟷ pasto (*Perú*); grama (*Venez., Col.*); zacate (*Méx.*)

recursos

WB pp. 155–156	LM p. 73	vhlcentral.com Lección 13

TEACHING OPTIONS

Heritage Speakers Tell students that they might see **hierba** spelled **yerba**, but the pronunciation is the same. Ask heritage speakers to think of things found in nature that have more than one name. Ex: **culebra/serpiente/víbora** (*snake*); **piedra/roca** (*rock*); **bosque tropical/selva tropical** (*rain forest*).

Extra Practice Write a vocabulary word on a scrap of paper and show it to a volunteer. That student should draw on the board pictures that represent the word. The class must guess the word, then spell it in Spanish as another volunteer writes it on the board.

Large Groups Have students stand in a circle. Pronounce a word from **Contextos**, use it in a sentence, then repeat the word. Toss a ball to a student, who must spell the word (including accents) and toss the ball back. Students who misspell are eliminated.

Más vocabulario

el animal	*animal*
la ballena	*whale*
el mono	*monkey*
la tortuga (marina)	*(sea) turtle*

Práctica

1 **Escuchar** Mientras escuchas estas oraciones, anota los sustantivos (*nouns*) que se refieren a las plantas, los animales, la tierra y el cielo.

Plantas	Animales	Tierra	Cielo
flores	perro	desiertos	sol
hierba	tortugas marinas	volcán	nubes
árboles	peces	bosques tropicales	estrellas

2 **¿Cierto o falso?** Escucha las oraciones e indica si lo que dice cada una es **cierto** o **falso**, según el dibujo.

1. cierto
2. falso
3. falso
4. cierto
5. cierto
6. falso

3 **Seleccionar** Selecciona la palabra que no está relacionada.

1. estrella • gobierno • luna • sol gobierno
2. lago • río • mar • peligro peligro
3. vaca • ballena • pájaro • población población
4. cielo • cráter • aire • nube cráter
5. desierto • solución • selva • bosque solución
6. flor • hierba • renovable • árbol renovable

4 **Definir** Trabaja con un(a) compañero/a para definir o describir cada palabra. Sigue el modelo. Answers will vary.

modelo

Estudiante 1: *¿Qué es el cielo?*
Estudiante 2: *El cielo está sobre la tierra y tiene nubes.*

1. la población
2. un mono
3. el calentamiento global
4. la naturaleza
5. un desierto
6. la extinción
7. la ecología
8. un sendero

5 **Describir** Trabajen en parejas para describir estas fotos. Answers will vary.

1 Teaching Tip To simplify, have students brainstorm a few words for each category before listening.

1 Script 1. Mi novio siempre me compra flores para nuestro aniversario. 2. Cuando era pequeño, jugaba con mi perro todo el tiempo. 3. En los desiertos casi no hay hierba. 4. Algunos científicos dicen que la temperatura del sol va a aumentar en los próximos años. 5. Hoy día, en Latinoamérica hay seis especies de tortugas marinas en peligro de extinción. *Script continues on page 418.*

2 Teaching Tip To challenge students, have them correct the false statements.

2 Script 1. Hay un gato jugando con un perro. 2. La vaca está en un sendero de la montaña. 3. No hay nubes sobre el valle. 4. La vaca está comiendo hierba. 5. Una pareja come sobre la hierba. 6. Las piedras están lejos del río.
Textbook MP3s

3 Expansion Have students state a category for the related words. Ex: **1. cosas que están en el cielo**

4 Expansion Have pairs read their definitions aloud in random order for the class to guess which term is being described.

5 Teaching Tip To simplify, give students these guidelines to help them prepare their descriptions: objects in the photos, colors, what the weather is like, the time of day, the location where the photo was taken.

5 Expansion Ask students to imagine the photos were taken on a recent vacation. Have them write a brief essay about their vacation, incorporating their descriptions.

TEACHING OPTIONS

TPR Make a series of true/false statements related to the lesson theme using the vocabulary. Tell students to remain seated if a statement is true and to stand if it is false. Ex: **A los gatos les gusta nadar en los lagos.** (Students stand.) **Los carros son responsables en parte de la contaminación del aire.** (Students remain seated.)

Game Have students fold a sheet of paper in half four times to create 16 squares and choose one vocabulary word to write in each square. Call out definitions for the vocabulary words. If students have the defined word, they mark their paper. The first student to mark four words in a row (across, down, or diagonally) calls out **¡Loto!** Have the student read aloud his or her words to check if the definitions have been given.

1 Script (continued)

6. Durante la tormenta, las nubes grises cubrían toda la ciudad. 7. En el mar Caribe hay muchos peces exóticos. 8. Algunas noches vamos al campo para ver las estrellas. 9. El Puracé es un volcán activo en los Andes colombianos. 10. Los árboles de los bosques tropicales contienen las curas para muchas enfermedades.
Textbook MP3s

Teaching Tips

- Use the **Lección 13 Contextos** digital images to assist with this vocabulary presentation.
- Involve students in a discussion about recycling and conservation. Ask volunteers to describe what is happening in the drawing. Ask: **¿Qué hace la señora de la izquierda? (Recicla una lata de aluminio.)** Cover the active vocabulary, then ask about students' own experiences and opinions. Ex: **¿Tiene un buen programa de reciclaje nuestra ciudad? ¿Qué hacen ustedes para reducir la contaminación del medio ambiente? ¿Qué hace la universidad? ¿Cómo estamos afectados por la contaminación en nuestra ciudad/región? ¿Cuál es el mayor problema ecológico de nuestra región? ¿Qué evitan ustedes por razones ecológicas?**

6 Expansion

- Ask questions to engage students in a conversation that requires them to recycle the activity vocabulary. Ex: **¿Qué debemos hacer para mantener las calles limpias? ¿Para qué trabajan los científicos? ¿Por qué es necesario que trabajemos para proteger el medio ambiente?**
- Have students write five additional sentences, using different forms of the verbs. Ask volunteers to share their sentences with the class.

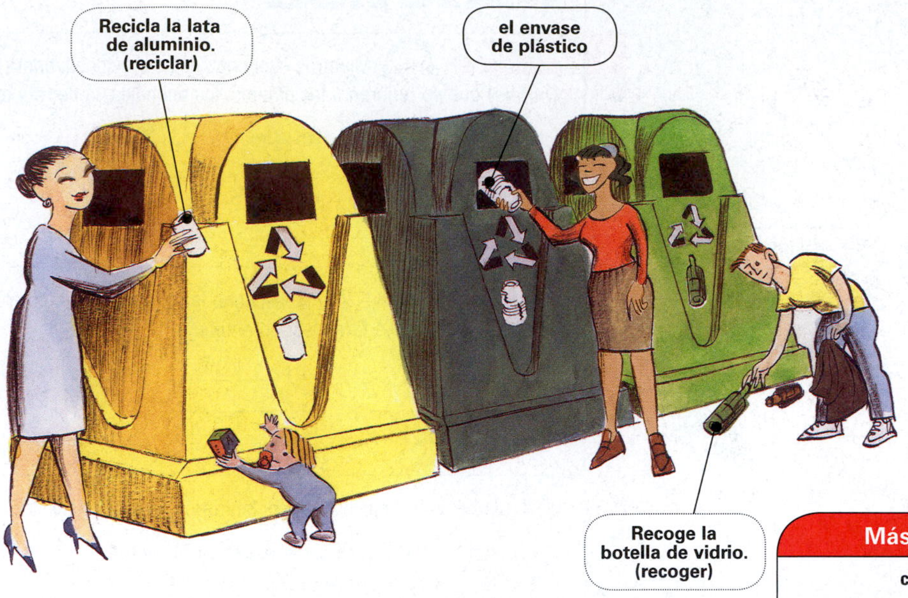

El reciclaje

Más vocabulario

cazar	to hunt
conservar	to conserve
contaminar	to pollute
controlar	to control
cuidar	to take care of
dejar de (+ *inf.*)	to stop (doing something)
desarrollar	to develop
descubrir	to discover
destruir	to destroy
estar afectado/a (por)	to be affected (by)
estar contaminado/a	to be polluted
evitar	to avoid
mejorar	to improve
proteger	to protect
reducir	to reduce
resolver (o:ue)	to resolve; to solve
respirar	to breathe

6 Completar Selecciona la palabra o la expresión adecuada para completar cada oración.

contaminar	destruyen	reciclamos
controlan	están afectadas	recoger
cuidan	mejoramos	resolver
descubrir	proteger	se desarrollaron

1. Si vemos basura en las calles, la debemos ___recoger___.
2. Los científicos trabajan para ___descubrir___ nuevas soluciones.
3. Es necesario que todos trabajemos juntos para ___resolver___ los problemas del medio ambiente.
4. Debemos ___proteger___ el medio ambiente porque hoy día está en peligro.
5. Muchas leyes nuevas ___controlan___ el nivel de emisiones que producen las fábricas.
6. Las primeras civilizaciones ___se desarrollaron___ cerca de los ríos y los mares.
7. Todas las personas ___están afectadas___ por la contaminación.
8. Los turistas deben tener cuidado de no ___contaminar___ los lugares que visitan.
9. Podemos conservar los recursos si ___reciclamos___ el aluminio, el vidrio y el plástico.
10. La contaminación y la deforestación ___destruyen___ el medio ambiente.

Practice more at **vhlcentral.com**.

TEACHING OPTIONS

Pairs Have pairs of students write each vocabulary word from this page on index cards. Pairs then shuffle the cards and take turns drawing from the stack. The student who draws a card then must make a comment about conservation or the environment, using the word he or she has drawn. The other student writes down the comment. After students finish the stack, call on volunteers to share their comments.

Small Groups Divide the class into groups of three or four. Have each group make a list of eight environmental problems in the region. Ask groups to trade lists. Have them write solutions to the problems on the list they receive, and then give the lists back to the original group. After reading the solutions, the original groups should give reasons why the solutions are viable or not.

Comunicación

7

¿Es importante? En parejas, lean este párrafo y contesten las preguntas.
Some answers will vary. Suggested answers:

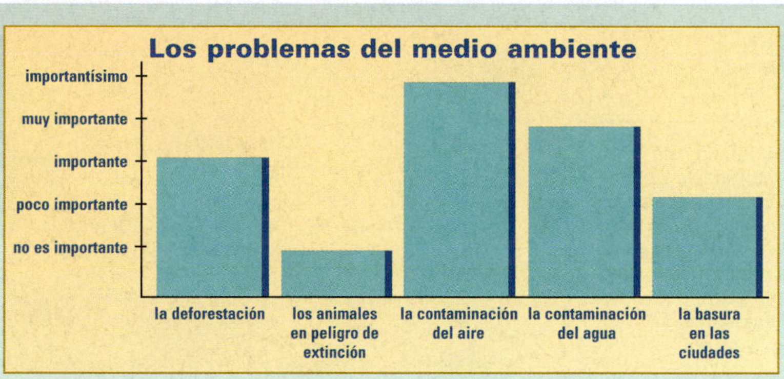

Para celebrar El día de la Tierra, una estación de radio colombiana hizo una pequeña encuesta entre estudiantes universitarios, donde les preguntaron sobre los problemas del medio ambiente. Se les preguntó cuáles creían que eran los cinco problemas más importantes del medio ambiente. Ellos también tenían que decidir el orden de importancia de estos problemas, del uno al cinco.

Los resultados probaron (*proved*) que la mayoría de los estudiantes están preocupados por la contaminación del aire. Muchos mencionaron que no hay aire puro en las ciudades. El problema número dos para los estudiantes es que los ríos y los lagos están afectados por la contaminación. La deforestación quedó como el problema número tres, la basura en las ciudades como el número cuatro y los animales en peligro de extinción como el cinco.

1. Según la encuesta, ¿qué problema consideran más grave? ¿Qué problema consideran menos grave? la contaminación del aire; los animales en peligro de extinción
2. ¿Cómo creen ustedes que se puede evitar o resolver el problema más importante?
3. ¿Es necesario resolver el problema menos importante? ¿Por qué?
4. ¿Consideran ustedes que existen los mismos problemas en su comunidad? Den algunos ejemplos.

8

Situaciones Trabajen en grupos pequeños para representar estas situaciones. Answers will vary.

1. Unos/as representantes de una agencia ambiental (*environmental*) hablan con el/la presidente/a de una fábrica que está contaminando el aire o el río de la zona.
2. Un(a) guía de ecoturismo habla con un grupo sobre cómo disfrutar (*enjoy*) de la naturaleza y conservar el medio ambiente.
3. Un(a) representante de la universidad habla con un grupo de nuevos estudiantes sobre la campaña (*campaign*) ambiental de la universidad y trata de reclutar (*tries to recruit*) miembros para un club que trabaja para la protección del medio ambiente.

9

Escribir una carta Trabajen en parejas para escribir una carta a una fábrica real o imaginaria que esté contaminando el medio ambiente. Expliquen las consecuencias que sus acciones van a tener para el medio ambiente. Sugiéranle algunas ideas para que solucione el problema. Utilicen por lo menos diez palabras de **Contextos.** Answers will vary.

7 Expansion
Divide the class into groups of five to discuss questions 2–4. Groups should reach a consensus for each question, then report back to the class.

8 Teaching Tip
Divide the class into small groups. Have each group choose a situation, but make sure that each situation is selected by at least one group. Have students take turns playing each role. After groups have had time to prepare their situations, ask volunteers to present them to the class.

9 Teaching Tips
- Remind students that a business letter in Spanish begins with a salutation, such as **Estimado(s) señor(es)**, and ends with a closing such as **Atentamente**.
- With the class, brainstorm a list of agencies or companies that are known not to be environmentally conscious. Ask the class to categorize the companies by how they harm the environment. Then divide the class into pairs and have them choose a company for the activity. Alternately, you can vary the activity to have it focus on green companies.

TEACHING OPTIONS

Heritage Speakers Ask heritage speakers to interview family members or people in their community about the environmental challenges in their families' countries of origin. Encourage them to find out how the problems affect the land and the people. Have students report their findings to the class.

Large Groups Prepare two sets of index cards, one with environmental problems and the other with possible solutions. Ex: **la destrucción de los bosques – reducir las áreas de deforestación; la contaminación de los ríos – controlar el tipo de sustancias que hay en el agua**. Shuffle the two sets of cards and distribute them. Have students with problem cards circulate around the room, asking their classmates questions until they find a viable solution.

Section Goals

In **Fotonovela**, students will:

- receive comprehensible input from free-flowing discourse
- learn functional phrases that preview lesson grammatical structures

Instructional Resources
Supersite: Video (***Fotonovela***); Resources (Scripts, Translations, Answer Keys)
WebSAM
Video Manual, pp. 25–26

Video Recap: Lección 12
Before doing this **Fotonovela** section, review the previous episode with these questions:
1. ¿Por qué tuvieron que arreglar la casa Felipe y Jimena? (Porque querían ir a la Yucatán con Marissa.) 2. ¿Quiénes ayudaron a los hermanos a limpiar la casa? (Juan Carlos, Marissa y don Diego) 3. ¿Qué recomendación les hizo don Diego a los chicos para limpiar la casa más rápido? (organizarse en equipos) 4. ¿Pudieron terminar la cena a tiempo? (Sí, la terminaron a tiempo.) ¿A quién invitaron a cenar? (Invitaron a don Diego.)

Video Synopsis **Jimena**, **Felipe**, **Juan Carlos**, and **Marissa** take a trip to the **Yucatán** Peninsula. While **Marissa** and **Jimena** visit a turtle sanctuary and the Mayan ruins of **Tulum**, the boys take a guided tour of the jungle, where **Felipe** has a mishap.

Teaching Tips

- Have students scan the **Fotonovela** captions and list words related to nature and the environment. Then have them predict what will happen in this episode. Write their predictions on the board.
- Quickly review the guesses students made about the episode. Through discussion, guide the class to an accurate summary of the plot.

Aventuras en la naturaleza

NATIONAL STANDARDS communication cultures

Las chicas visitan un santuario de tortugas, mientras los chicos pasean por la selva.

PERSONAJES

MARISSA

JIMENA

Video: *Fotonovela*

1

MARISSA Querida tía Ana María, lo estoy pasando muy bien. Es maravilloso que México tenga tantos programas estupendos para proteger a las tortugas. Hoy estamos en Tulum, y ¡el paisaje es espectacular! Con cariño, Marissa.

2

MARISSA Estoy tan feliz de que estés aquí conmigo.

JIMENA Es mucho más divertido cuando se viaja con amigos.

(Llegan Felipe y Juan Carlos)

JIMENA ¿Qué pasó?

JUAN CARLOS No lo van a creer.

3

GUÍA A menos que protejamos a los animales de la contaminación y la deforestación, en poco tiempo muchos de ellos van a estar extintos. Por favor, síganme y eviten pisar las plantas.

4

FELIPE Nos retrasamos sólo cinco minutos... Qué extraño. Estaban aquí hace unos minutos.

JUAN CARLOS ¿Adónde se fueron?

FELIPE No creo que puedan ir muy lejos.

(Se separan para buscar al grupo.)

5

FELIPE Juan Carlos encontró al grupo. ¡Yo esperaba encontrarlos también! ¡Pero nunca vinieron por mí! Yo estaba asustado. Regresé al lugar de donde salimos y esperé. Me perdí todo el recorrido.

6

FELIPE Decidí seguir un río y...

MARISSA No es posible que un guía continúe el recorrido cuando hay dos personas perdidas.

JIMENA Vamos a ver, chicos, ¿qué pasó? Dígannos la verdad.

TEACHING OPTIONS

Video Tips General suggestions for using video clips in the classroom can be found in the front matter of this Instructor's Annotated Edition.

Aventuras en la naturaleza Play the **Aventuras en la naturaleza** episode and have students give you a "play-by-play" description of the action. Write their descriptions on the board. Then replay it, asking the class to list any key words they hear. Write some of the key words on the board. Finally, discuss the material on the board with the class and guide students toward an accurate summary of the plot.

JUAN CARLOS

FELIPE

GUÍA

7

JUAN CARLOS Felipe se cayó. Él no quería contarles.

JIMENA ¡Lo sabía!

8

FELIPE Y ustedes, ¿qué hicieron hoy?

JIMENA Marissa y yo fuimos al santuario de las tortugas.

9

MARISSA Aprendimos sobre las normas que existen para proteger a las tortugas marinas.

JIMENA Pero no cabe duda de que necesitamos aprobar más leyes para mantenerlas protegidas.

MARISSA Fue muy divertido verlas tan cerca.

10

JUAN CARLOS Entonces se divirtieron. ¡Qué bien!

JIMENA Gracias, y tú, pobrecito, pasaste todo el día con mi hermano. Siempre te mete en problemas.

Expresiones útiles

Talking about the environment

Aprendimos sobre las normas que existen para proteger a las tortugas marinas.
We learned about the regulations that exist to protect sea turtles.

Afortunadamente, ahora la población está aumentando.
Fortunately, the population is now growing.

No cabe duda de que necesitamos aprobar más leyes para mantenerlas protegidas.
There is no doubt that we need to pass more laws to keep them protected.

Es maravilloso que México tenga tantos programas estupendos para proteger a las tortugas.
It's marvelous that Mexico has so many wonderful programs to protect the turtles.

A menos que protejamos a los animales de la contaminación y la deforestación, en poco tiempo muchos de ellos van a estar extintos.
Unless we protect animals from pollution and habitat loss, soon many of them will be extinct.

Additional vocabulary

aumentar
to grow; to get bigger

meterse en problemas
to get into trouble

perdido/a
lost

el recorrido
tour

sobre todo
above all

recursos

VM pp. 25–26

vhlcentral.com Lección 13

Expresiones útiles

- Point out the sentence that begins with **A menos que protejamos...** and explain that **a menos que** is a conjunction that is always followed by the subjunctive. Then draw attention to the captions for video stills 1 and 2. Tell students that **Es maravilloso que México tenga...** and **Estoy tan feliz de que estés aquí conmigo** are examples of the subjunctive used with expressions of emotion. Finally, draw attention to the sentence **No creo que puedan ir muy lejos** under video still 4. Explain that this is an example of the subjunctive used with an expression of doubt.
- Draw attention to the words **asustado, perdidas,** and **protegidas** in the captions for video stills 5, 6, and 9. Tell students that these are examples of past participles used as adjectives, and when used with **estar**, they describe a condition or state that results from an action.

Teaching Tips

- Continue the conversation that you began in **Contextos** about the state of the environment in your area. Integrate **Expresiones útiles** into the conversation.
- Have the class work in groups to read through the entire **Fotonovela** aloud, with volunteers playing the various parts.

Nota cultural Mexico is believed to be the home of roughly ten percent of all known species. These include 500 species of mammals, 300 species of birds, and 25,000 species of plants. Human interference with natural habitats as well as climate changes have, however, placed many of these species in danger. Among those threatened by extinction are the jaguar, the golden eagle, and the **vaquita** (the world's smallest porpoise).

TEACHING OPTIONS

TPR As you play the episode, have students raise their hands each time they hear the subjunctive.

Extra Practice Photocopy the **Fotonovela** Videoscript (Supersite) and white out target vocabulary and expressions in order to create a master for a cloze activity. Have students fill in the blanks as they watch the episode.

Large Groups Divide the class into four groups and assign each one a nature reserve **(reserva natural)** in a Spanish-speaking country. (Ex: **La Pedregoza** in Colombia, **Reserva Marina de Galápagos** in Ecuador, Costa Rica's **Reserva Ecológica Manuel Antonio**, and Mexico's **Reserva Natural Cuatro Ciénagas**.) For homework, have each group prepare a presentation, including size, flora and fauna, environmental issues the reserve faces, and any other significant information.

¿Qué pasó?

1 Teaching Tip To challenge students, write these sentences on the board without the multiple choice items and have students complete them.

2 Expansion Have pairs of students write questions or statements that could have elicited these comments.

Nota cultural **Tulum** is the third most visited archeological site in Mexico, after **Teotihuacán** and **Chichén Itzá**.

3 Expansion Ask students to write three additional questions for a classmate to answer.

4 Possible Conversation
E1: ¿Hay problemas de contaminación donde vives?
E2: Sí, tenemos un problema muy grave de contaminación en los ríos. Hay muchos papeles, botellas y latas en ellos. En las montañas, los ríos no están tan afectados por la contaminación pero en las ciudades, sí. ¿En tu región hay problemas de contaminación?
E1: Sí, tenemos un problema gravísimo de contaminación del aire. Esto causa enfermedades para los habitantes.
E2: Qué terrible. ¿Cómo podemos resolver los problemas de la contaminación?
E1: Bueno, nosotros ahora tenemos un programa de reciclaje. También algunas personas tratan de no usar el auto. Usan el metro o caminan.

The Affective Dimension Many students feel nervous when called on to give an answer or to read aloud. You can minimize anxiety by asking for volunteers and by having students work in pairs or groups.

1 **Seleccionar** Selecciona la respuesta más lógica para completar cada oración.

1. México tiene muchos programas para __c__ a las tortugas.
   a. destruir b. reciclar c. proteger
2. Según la guía, muchos animales van a estar en peligro de __b__ si no los protegemos.
   a. reciclaje b. extinción c. deforestación
3. La guía les pide a los visitantes que eviten pisar __a__.
   a. las plantas b. las piedras c. la tierra
4. Felipe no quería contarles a las chicas que se __c__.
   a. divirtió b. alegró c. cayó
5. Jimena dice que debe haber más __b__ para proteger a las tortugas.
   a. playas b. leyes c. gobiernos

2 **Identificar** Identifica quién puede decir estas oraciones. Puedes usar algunos nombres más de una vez.

1. Fue divertido ver a las tortugas y aprender las normas para protegerlas. Marissa/Jimena
2. Tenemos que evitar la contaminación y la deforestación. guía
3. Estoy feliz de estar aquí, Tulum es maravilloso. Marissa
4. Es una lástima que me pierda el recorrido. Felipe
5. No es posible que esa historia que nos dices sea verdad. Jimena/Marissa
6. No van a creer lo que le sucedió a Felipe. Juan Carlos
7. Tenemos que cuidar las plantas y los animales. guía
8. Ojalá que mi hermano no se meta en más problemas. Jimena

NOTA CULTURAL
Tulum es una importante zona arqueológica que se localiza en la costa del estado de Quintana Roo, México. La ciudad amurallada (*walled*), construida (*built*) por los mayas, es famosa por su ubicación (*location*) dramática en un acantilado (*cliff*) frente al mar.

3 **Preguntas** Contesta estas preguntas usando la información de **Fotonovela**.

1. ¿Qué lugar visitan Marissa y Jimena?
   Marissa y Jimena visitan un santuario de tortugas.
2. ¿Adónde fueron Juan Carlos y Felipe?
   Juan Carlos y Felipe fueron a la selva.
3. Según la guía, ¿por qué muchos animales están en peligro de extinción?
   Muchos animales están en peligro de extinción por la contaminación y la deforestación.
4. ¿Por qué Jimena y Marissa no creen la historia de Felipe?
   Porque no es posible que un guía continúe el recorrido cuando hay dos personas perdidas.
5. ¿Qué esperaba Felipe cuando se perdió?
   Felipe esperaba encontrar al grupo.

4 **El medio ambiente** En parejas, discutan algunos problemas ambientales y sus posibles soluciones. Usen estas preguntas y frases en su conversación.
Answers will vary.

- ¿Hay problemas de contaminación donde vives?
- Tenemos un problema muy grave de contaminación de...
- ¿Cómo podemos resolver los problemas de la contaminación?

NATIONAL communication STANDARDS

Practice more at **vhlcentral.com**.

TEACHING OPTIONS

Extra Practice Add an auditory aspect to this vocabulary practice. Use the sentences in **Actividad 1** or **Actividad 2** for a dictation activity. Have students close their books; then read each sentence twice slowly and once at regular speed. Then have students open their books and check their work for accuracy. Ask comprehension questions as a follow-up.

Small Groups Have students work in groups of three to write a short article about their environmental concerns for a local newsletter (**boletín informativo**). Their articles should include a description of a few environmental problems and some suggestions for solving them. Have groups share their articles with the class.

Ortografía

Audio

Los signos de puntuación

In Spanish, as in English, punctuation marks are important because they help you express your ideas in a clear, organized way.

No podía ver las llaves. Las buscó por los estantes, las mesas, las sillas, el suelo; minutos después, decidió mirar por la ventana. Allí estaban...

The **punto y coma** (;), **the tres puntos** (...), and the **punto** (.) are used in very similar ways in Spanish and English.

Argentina, Brasil, Paraguay y Uruguay son miembros de Mercosur.

In Spanish, the **coma** (,) is not used before **y** or **o** in a series.

13,5% **29,2°** **3.000.000** **$2.999,99**

In numbers, Spanish uses a **coma** where English uses a decimal point and a **punto** where English uses a comma.

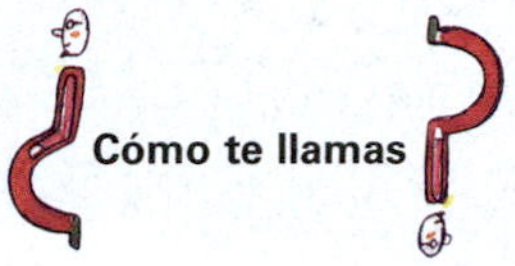

¿Dónde está? **¡Ven aquí!**

Questions in Spanish are preceded and followed by **signos de interrogación** (¿ ?), and exclamations are preceded and followed by **signos de exclamación** (¡ !).

Práctica Lee el párrafo e indica los signos de puntuación necesarios. Answers will vary.

Ayer recibí la invitación de boda de Marta mi amiga colombiana inmediatamente empecé a pensar en un posible regalo fui al almacén donde Marta y su novio tenían una lista de regalos había de todo copas cafeteras tostadoras finalmente decidí regalarles un perro ya sé que es un regalo extraño pero espero que les guste a los dos

¿Palabras de amor? El siguiente diálogo tiene diferentes significados (*meanings*) dependiendo de los signos de puntuación que utilices y el lugar donde los pongas. Intenta encontrar los diferentes significados. Answers will vary.

JULIÁN me quieres
MARISOL no puedo vivir sin ti
JULIÁN me quieres dejar
MARISOL no me parece mala idea
JULIÁN no eres feliz conmigo
MARISOL no soy feliz

recursos

LM p. 74	vhlcentral.com Lección 13

Section Goal

In **Ortografía**, students will learn the use of punctuation marks in Spanish.

Instructional Resources
Supersite: Audio (Lab MP3 Files); Resources (Scripts, Answer Keys)
WebSAM
Lab Manual, p. 74

Teaching Tips

- Explain that there is no space before or between ellipsis marks in Spanish. There is, however, a space after the third ellipsis point when used within a sentence.
- Model reading the numerical examples. Ex: **13,5% = trece coma cinco por ciento.** Write numbers on the board for translations into Spanish. Ex: 89.3%; 5,020,307; $13.50
- Explain that the inverted question mark or exclamation point does not always come at the beginning of a sentence, but where the question or exclamation begins. Ex:
  —¿Cómo estás, Mirta?
  —¡Bien! Y tú, ¿cómo estás?
  —Ay, ¡me duele la cabeza!
- Point out that **Ortografía** replaces **Pronunciación** in the Student Edition for **Lecciones 10–15**, but not in the Lab Manual. The **Recursos** box references the **Pronunciación** sections found in all lessons of the Lab Manual.

¿Palabras de amor? Two possibilities for punctuation:

J: ¿Me quieres?
M: ¡No puedo vivir sin ti!
J: ¿Me quieres dejar?
M: No. Me parece mala idea.
J: ¿No eres feliz conmigo?
M: No. Soy feliz.

J: ¿Me quieres?
M: No. Puedo vivir sin ti.
J: ¡Me quieres dejar!
M: No me parece mala idea.
J: ¿No eres feliz conmigo?
M: No soy feliz.

TEACHING OPTIONS

Pairs Have pairs write example sentences for each of the four punctuation rules in **Ortografía**. Ask volunteers to write their sentences on the board and have the class identify the rules.

Video Photocopy the **Fotonovela** Videoscript (Supersite) and white out the punctuation in order to make a master for a cloze activity. Distribute the photocopies and, as you replay the episode, have students mark the punctuation.

Extra Practice To simplify the **¿Palabras de amor?** activity, write *A woman without her man is nothing* on the board and point out how it can be punctuated in two ways to express opposite meanings. After completing the dialogues, have students work in pairs to dramatize both versions. Ask a few pairs to role-play the contrasting dialogues for the class.

Flash CULTURA

Section Goals

In **Cultura**, students will:

- read about the Andes mountain range
- learn nature-related terms
- read about Colombia's **Sierra Nevada de Santa Marta**
- read about important bodies of water in Latin America

Instructional Resources
Supersite: Video (***Flash cultura***); Resources (Scripts, Translations, Answer Keys)
WebSAM
Video Manual, pp. 97–98

En detalle

Antes de leer Preview the reading by asking these questions: **¿Qué montañas conocen? ¿Qué les parece más interesante, pasar tiempo en la playa o en las montañas? ¿Por qué?**

Lectura

- Point out that the Andes pass through seven different countries.
- Tell students that the highest area of the Andes is known as the **altiplano**, where farmers raise sheep, llamas, alpacas, and vicuñas. They use these animals' wool to make clothing and blankets.
- Add a visual aspect to this reading. Bring in topographic maps of Spain, Central America, and South America and indicate other important mountain ranges in Spanish-speaking countries, such as **los Pirineos** (Spain), or **la Sierra Madre Occidental** and **Oriental** (Mexico).

Después de leer
Ask students to discuss with a partner what facts from this reading are new or surprising to them.

1 Teaching Tip To challenge students, rephrase the items as comprehension questions. Ex: **2. ¿Qué es "la espina dorsal de Suramérica"?**

EN DETALLE

Video: *Flash cultura*

NATIONAL STANDARDS connections cultures

¡Los Andes se mueven!

Los Andes, la cadena° de montañas más extensa de América, son conocidos como "la espina dorsal° de Suramérica". Sus 7.240 kilómetros (4.500 millas) van desde el norte° de la región entre Venezuela y Colombia, hasta el extremo sur°, entre Argentina y Chile, y pasan por casi todos los países suramericanos. La cordillera° de los Andes, formada hace 27 millones de años, es la segunda más alta del mundo, después de la del Himalaya (aunque° esta última es mucho más "joven", ya que se formó hace apenas cinco millones de años).

Para poder atravesar° de un lado a otro de los Andes, existen varios pasos o puertos° de montaña. Situados a grandes alturas°, son generalmente estrechos° y peligrosos. En algunos de ellos hay, también, vías ferroviarias°.

De acuerdo con° varias instituciones científicas, la cordillera de los Andes se eleva° y se hace más angosta° cada año. La capital de Chile se acerca° a la capital de Argentina a un ritmo° de 19,4 milímetros por año. Si ese ritmo se mantiene°, Santiago y Buenos Aires podrían unirse° en unos... 63 millones de años, ¡casi el mismo tiempo que ha transcurrido° desde la extinción de los dinosaurios!

Arequipa, Perú

Los Andes en números

3 Cordilleras que forman los Andes: Las cordilleras Central, Occidental y Oriental
900 (A.C.°) Año aproximado en que empezó el desarrollo° de la cultura chavín, en los Andes peruanos
600 Número aproximado de volcanes que hay en los Andes
6.960 Metros (22.835 pies) de altura del Aconcagua (Argentina), el pico° más alto de los Andes

cadena *range* **espina dorsal** *spine* **norte** *north* **sur** *south* **cordillera** *mountain range* **aunque** *although* **atravesar** *to cross* **puertos** *passes* **alturas** *heights* **estrechos** *narrow* **vías ferroviarias** *railroad tracks* **De acuerdo con** *According to* **se eleva** *rises* **angosta** *narrow* **se acerca** *gets closer* **ritmo** *rate* **se mantiene** *keeps going* **podrían unirse** *could join together* **ha transcurrido** *has gone by* **A.C.** *Before Christ* **desarrollo** *development* **pico** *peak*

ACTIVIDADES

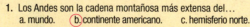

1 **Escoger** Escoge la opción que completa mejor cada oración.

1. Los Andes son la cadena montañosa más extensa del…
   a. mundo. b. continente americano. c. hemisferio norte.
2. "La espina dorsal de Suramérica" es…
   a. los Andes. b. el Himalaya. c. el Aconcagua.
3. La cordillera de los Andes se extiende…
   a. de este a oeste. b. de sur a oeste. c. de norte a sur.
4. El Himalaya y los Andes tienen…
   a. diferente altura. b. la misma altura. c. el mismo color.
5. Es posible atravesar los Andes por medio de…
   a. montañas b. puertos c. metro
6. En algunos de los puertos de montaña de los Andes hay…
   a. puertas. b. vías ferroviarias. c. cordilleras.
7. En 63 millones de años, Buenos Aires y Santiago podrían…
   a. separarse. b. desarrollarse. c. unirse.
8. El Aconcagua es…
   a. una montaña. b. un grupo indígena. c. un volcán.

TEACHING OPTIONS

Extra Practice List on the board: **3; 900; 600; 6.960; 27 millones; 63 millones; 7.240; 19,4; 4.500**. Have students form sentences about the reading using each number. Ex: **Hay tres cordilleras que forman los Andes.**

Cultural Comparison For homework, ask students to research a North American mountain range and compare and contrast it with one of the ranges mentioned on these pages. To simplify, brainstorm a list of research categories, such as climate, local industries, tourism, flora and fauna, and inhabitants.

Pairs Have pairs create questions and corresponding answers about the reading. One student should create the answers. The other student then develops the questions. After five minutes, have partners switch roles.

ASÍ SE DICE

La naturaleza

el arco iris	*rainbow*
la cascada; la catarata	*waterfall*
el cerro; la colina; la loma	*hill, hillock*
la cima; la cumbre; el tope (Col.)	*summit; mountaintop*
la maleza; los rastrojos (Col.); la yerba mala (Cuba); los hierbajos (Méx.); los yuyos (Arg.)	*weeds*
la niebla	*fog*

EL MUNDO HISPANO

Cuerpos° de agua

- **Lago de Maracaibo** es el lago natural más grande de Suramérica y tiene una conexión directa y natural con el mar.
- **Lago Titicaca** es el lago navegable más alto del mundo. Se encuentra a más de 3.800 metros de altitud.
- **Bahía Mosquito** es una bahía bioluminiscente. En sus aguas viven unos microorganismos que emiten luz° cuando sienten que algo agita° el agua.

Cuerpos *Bodies* emiten luz *emit light* agita *shakes*

PERFIL

La Sierra Nevada de Santa Marta

La Sierra Nevada de Santa Marta es una cadena de montañas en la costa norte de Colombia. Se eleva abruptamente desde las costas del mar Caribe y en apenas 42 kilómetros llega a una altura de 5.775 metros (18.947 pies) en sus picos nevados°. Tiene las montañas más altas de Colombia y es la formación montañosa costera° más alta del mundo.

Los pueblos indígenas que habitan allí lograron° mantener los frágiles ecosistemas de estas montañas a través de° un sofisticado sistema de terrazas° y senderos empedrados° que permitieron° el control de las aguas en una región de muchas lluvias, evitando así la erosión de la tierra. La Sierra fue nombrada Reserva de la Biosfera por la UNESCO en 1979.

nevados *snowcapped* costera *coastal* lograron *managed* a través de *by means of* terrazas *terraces* empedrados *cobblestone* permitieron *allowed*

Conexión Internet

¿Dónde se puede hacer ecoturismo en Latinoamérica?

Go to **vhlcentral.com** to find more cultural information related to this **Cultura** section.

ACTIVIDADES

2 Comprensión Indica si lo que dice cada oración es **cierto** o **falso**. Corrige la información falsa.

1. En Colombia, *weeds* se dice **hierbajos**. Falso. Se dice rastrojos.
2. El lago Titicaca es el más grande del mundo. Falso. Es el lago navegable más alto del mundo.
3. La Sierra Nevada de Santa Marta es la formación montañosa costera más alta del mundo. Cierto.
4. Los indígenas destruyeron el ecosistema de Santa Marta. Falso. Lograron mantener los ecosistemas de las montañas.

3 Maravillas de la naturaleza Escribe un párrafo breve donde describas alguna maravilla de la naturaleza que has (*you have*) visitado y que te impresionó. Puede ser cualquier (*any*) sitio natural: un río, una montaña, una selva, etc. Answers will vary.

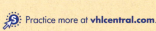

Practice more at **vhlcentral.com**.

recursos: VM pp. 97–98 | vhlcentral.com Lección 13

Así se dice
- Model the pronunciation of each term and have students repeat it.
- To challenge students, add these nature-related words to the list: **el acantilado** (*cliff*); **la marisma, el pantano** (*swamp; wetlands*).
- Ask questions using the terms. Ex: **¿Es fácil manejar cuando hay niebla?**

Perfil
- Point out the **Sierra Nevada de Santa Marta** on the map on page 444.
- As students read, have them think about the similarities and differences between the **Sierra Nevada de Santa Marta** and the Andes.

El mundo hispano
- Use a map to point out the locations (Venezuela; between Peru and Bolivia; and Vieques, Puerto Rico, respectively) of these bodies of water.
- Ask the class to name important bodies of water in the U.S. and Canada. Have students compare and contrast them with those mentioned in the reading.

2 Expansion Give students these statements as items 5–7: **5. La Sierra Nevada de Santa Marta es más extensa que la cordillera de los Andes. (Falso. La cordillera de los Andes es más extensa.) 6. El lago Titicaca está a más de 3.000 metros de altitud. (Cierto.) 7. Un arco iris se ve cuando hay precipitación y sol a la vez. (Cierto.)**

3 Teaching Tips
- To add a visual aspect to this activity, have students make a simple drawing or collage.
- If students have not visited any place in nature that impressed them, give them the option of researching a place that they would like to visit.

TEACHING OPTIONS

TPR Add an auditory aspect to this **Cultura** presentation. Prepare descriptions of the bodies of water and mountain ranges mentioned on these pages. Ex: **Es la formación montañosa más alta del mundo. Cada año se eleva un poco más. Está formada por tres cordilleras.** Give each student a set of cards with the names of geographical features, and have them hold up the corresponding name for each sentence you read.

Large Groups Give five volunteers each a slip of paper with a different body of water or mountain range: **el lago Titicaca, el lago de Maracaibo, la Bahía Mosquito, los Andes,** and **la Sierra Nevada de Santa Marta**. Then have the class circulate around the room and ask questions to find out what body of water or mountain range each volunteer represents. Ex: **¿Eres un cuerpo de agua o una montaña? ¿En qué país(es) estás?**

Section Goals

In **Estructura 13.1**, students will learn:
- to use the subjunctive with verbs and expressions of emotion
- common verbs and expressions of emotion

Instructional Resources
Supersite: Audio (Lab MP3 Files); Resources (Grammar Presentation Slides, Activity Pack, Scripts, Answer Keys); Testing Program (Quizzes)
WebSAM
Workbook, pp. 157–158
Lab Manual, p. 75

Teaching Tips
- Ask students to call out some of the verbs that, when placed in the main clause, trigger the subjunctive in the subordinate clause (see **Estructura 12.4**). List the verbs on the board and ask students to use them in sentences as a review of the conjugation of regular **–ar, –er,** and **–ir** verbs.
- Model the use of some common verbs and expressions of emotion. Ex: **Me molesta mucho que recojan la basura sólo una vez a la semana. Me sorprende que algunas personas no se preocupen por el medio ambiente.** Then ask volunteers to use other verbs and expressions in sentences.

13.1 The subjunctive with verbs of emotion

S Tutorial

NATIONAL comparisons STANDARDS

ANTE TODO In the previous lesson, you learned how to use the subjunctive with expressions of will and influence. You will now learn how to use the subjunctive with verbs and expressions of emotion.

Main clause: Marta **espera** — que — Subordinate clause: yo **vaya** al lago este fin de semana.

▶ When the verb in the main clause of a sentence expresses an emotion or feeling, such as hope, fear, joy, pity, or surprise, the subjunctive is required in the subordinate clause.

Nos alegramos de que te **gusten** las flores.
We are happy that you like the flowers.

Temo que Ana no **pueda** ir mañana con nosotros.
I'm afraid that Ana won't be able to go with us tomorrow.

Siento que tú no **puedas** venir mañana.
I'm sorry that you can't come tomorrow.

Le **sorprende** que Juan **sea** tan joven.
It surprises him that Juan is so young.

Es una lástima que ellos no estén aquí con nosotros.

Me alegro de que te diviertas.

Common verbs and expressions of emotion

alegrarse (de)	*to be happy*	**tener miedo (de)**	*to be afraid (of)*
esperar	*to hope; to wish*	**es extraño**	*it's strange*
gustar	*to like*	**es una lástima**	*it's a shame*
molestar	*to bother*	**es ridículo**	*it's ridiculous*
sentir (e:ie)	*to be sorry; to regret*	**es terrible**	*it's terrible*
sorprender	*to surprise*	**es triste**	*it's sad*
temer	*to be afraid*	**ojalá (que)**	*I hope (that); I wish (that)*

CONSULTA
Certain verbs of emotion, like **gustar, molestar,** and **sorprender,** require indirect object pronouns. For more examples, see **Estructura 7.4,** pp. 230–231.

Me molesta que la gente no **recicle** el plástico.
It bothers me that people don't recycle plastic.

Es triste que **tengamos** problemas como el cambio climático.
It's sad that we have problems like climate change.

TEACHING OPTIONS

Large Groups Have students circulate around the room, interviewing each other about their hopes and fears for the future of the environment. Ex: **¿Qué deseas para el futuro del medio ambiente? (Deseo que encontremos una solución al problema de la contaminación.) ¿Qué es lo que más temes? (Temo que destruyamos los bosques tropicales.)** Encourage students to use the common verbs and expressions of emotion.

Extra Practice Ask students to imagine that they have just finished watching a documentary about the effects of pollution. Have them write five responses to what they saw and heard, using different verbs or expressions of emotion in each sentence. Ex: **Me sorprende que el río esté contaminado...**

▶ As with expressions of will and influence, the infinitive, not the subjunctive, is used after an expression of emotion when there is no change of subject. Compare these sentences.

Temo **llegar** tarde. *I'm afraid I'll arrive late.*	Temo que mi novio **llegue** tarde. *I'm afraid my boyfriend will arrive late.*

▶ The expression **ojalá (que)** means *I hope* or *I wish*, and it is always followed by the subjunctive. Note that the use of **que** with this expression is optional.

Ojalá (que) se conserven nuestros recursos naturales. *I hope (that) our natural resources will be conserved.*	**Ojalá (que) recojan** la basura hoy. *I hope (that) they collect the garbage today.*

Ojalá que
su aseguradora escuche sus necesidades con la misma atención.
COLMENA
salud - medicina
Con su familia, por su futuro.
Por fin usted se puede poner en manos de una compañía confiable.

¡INTÉNTALO! Completa las oraciones con las formas correctas de los verbos.

1. Ojalá que ellos descubran (descubrir) nuevas formas de energía.
2. Espero que Ana nos ayude (ayudar) a recoger la basura en la carretera.
3. Es una lástima que la gente no recicle (reciclar) más.
4. Esperamos proteger (proteger) a las tortugas marinas que llegan a esta playa.
5. Me alegro de que mis amigos quieran (querer) conservar la naturaleza.
6. Espero que tú vengas (venir) a la reunión (*meeting*) del Club de Ecología.
7. Es malo contaminar (contaminar) el medio ambiente.
8. A mis padres les gusta que nosotros participemos (participar) en la reunión.
9. Es terrible que nuestras ciudades estén (estar) afectadas por la contaminación.
10. Ojalá que yo pueda (poder) hacer algo para reducir el calentamiento global.

recursos
WB pp. 157–158
LM p. 75
vhlcentral.com Lección 13

Teaching Tip Compare and contrast the use of the infinitive and the subjunctive with examples like these: **Juan espera hacer algo para aliviar el problema de la contaminación ambiental. Juan espera que el gobierno haga algo para aliviar el problema de la contaminación ambiental.** Then ask: **¿Es terrible no reciclar? ¿Es terrible que yo no recicle?**

The Affective Dimension Encourage students to start each class by making a list of what they want to accomplish in class that day, using the subjunctive. Explain that, in doing this, they will gradually feel more comfortable with the subjunctive.

Extra Practice Bring in single-frame cartoons (such as those found in *The New Yorker*) with the captions removed, and/or photos from magazines. Have students write a statement for each one about what the cartoon character or person is thinking, using the subjunctive with verbs of emotion. Encourage students to use creativity and humor. Then, in small groups, have students explain their captions and choose the funniest ones to share with the class.

TEACHING OPTIONS

Extra Practice Have students look at the drawing for **Contextos** on pages 416–417. Ask them to imagine they are one of the people pictured. Then have them write five sentences about how they feel from the point of view of that person. Ex: **Ojalá Gustavo no olvide el sendero para regresar al carro...**

Pairs Have pairs tell each other three things that bother them and three things they are happy about. Encourage students to comment on their partners' answers.

Large Groups Expand the **¡Inténtalo!** activity. Read the beginning of one of the sentences (stop just before the blank) and throw a ball to a student. He or she must complete the sentence in an original manner, using the correct subjunctive form or an infinitive.

Práctica

1 Completar Completa el diálogo con palabras de la lista. Compara tus respuestas con las de un(a) compañero/a.

Bogotá, Colombia

alegro	molesta	salga
encuentren	ojalá	tengo miedo de
estén	puedan	vayan
lleguen	reduzcan	visitar

OLGA Me alegro de que Adriana y Raquel (1) vayan a Colombia. ¿Van a estudiar?
SARA Sí. Es una lástima que (2) lleguen una semana tarde. Ojalá que la universidad las ayude a buscar casa. (3) Tengo miedo de que no consigan dónde vivir.
OLGA Me (4) molesta que seas tan pesimista, pero sí, yo también espero que (5) encuentren gente simpática y que hablen mucho español.
SARA Sí, ojalá. Van a hacer un estudio sobre la deforestación en las costas. Es triste que en tantos países los recursos naturales (6) estén en peligro.
OLGA Pues, me (7) alegro de que no se queden mucho en la capital por la contaminación. (8) Ojalá tengan tiempo de viajar por el país.
SARA Sí, espero que (9) puedan ir a Medellín. Sé que también quieren (10) visitar la Catedral de Sal de Zipaquirá.

NOTA CULTURAL
Los principales factores que determinan la temperatura de **Bogotá, Colombia,** son su proximidad al ecuador y su altitud, 2.640 metros (8.660 pies) sobre el nivel (*level*) del mar. Con un promedio (*average*) de 13° C (56° F), Bogotá disfruta de un clima templado (*mild*) durante la mayor parte del año. Hay, sin embargo, variaciones considerables entre el día (18° C) y la noche (7° C).

2 Transformar Transforma estos elementos en oraciones completas para formar un diálogo entre Juan y la madre de Raquel. Añade palabras si es necesario. Luego, con un(a) compañero/a, presenta el diálogo a la clase.

1. Juan, / esperar / (tú) escribirle / Raquel. / Ser / tu / novia. / Ojalá / no / sentirse / sola Juan, espero que (tú) le escribas a Raquel. Es tu novia. Ojalá (que) no se sienta sola.
2. molestarme / (usted) decirme / lo que / tener / hacer. / Ahora / mismo / le / estar / escribiendo Me molesta que (Ud.) me diga lo que tengo que hacer. Ahora mismo le estoy escribiendo.
3. alegrarme / oírte / decir / eso. / Ser / terrible / estar / lejos / cuando / nadie / recordarte Me alegro de oírte decir eso. Es terrible estar lejos cuando nadie te recuerda.
4. señora, / ¡yo / tener / miedo de / (ella) no recordarme / mí! / Ser / triste / estar / sin / novia Señora, ¡yo tengo miedo de que (ella) no me recuerde a mí! Es triste estar sin novia.
5. ser / ridículo / (tú) sentirte / así. / Tú / saber / ella / querer / casarse / contigo Es ridículo que te sientas así. Tú sabes que ella quiere casarse contigo.
6. ridículo / o / no, / sorprenderme / (todos) preocuparse / ella / y / (nadie) acordarse de / mí Ridículo o no, me sorprende que todos se preocupen por ella y nadie se acuerde de mí.

Practice more at **vhlcentral.com**.

1 Teaching Tips
- To simplify, start by having students read the items listed in the word bank. Ask volunteers to point out which verbs are in the subjunctive and which words trigger it.
- Ask individuals to explain why they chose the verbs or expressions they did.

1 Expansion
Ask pairs to write a new conversation based on the one in the activity. Students should use the subjunctive at least six times. Call on pairs to perform their conversations for the class. Have the class vote for the funniest or most original one.

2 Teaching Tip Have volunteers look at the dehydrated sentences and name elements that could trigger the subjunctive in a following clause.
Ex: **esperar, ojalá, molestarme**

TEACHING OPTIONS

Game Write each of the common verbs and expressions of emotion on slips of paper and put them in a large bag. On separate strips, write an equal number of infinitives and subject pronouns. Place these in a separate bag and divide the class into two teams. One member of each team draws a slip of paper from each bag and writes a sentence on the board using the elements on both slips. If the sentence makes sense and the grammar is correct, that team gets one point. The team with the most points at the end wins.

Pairs Have students write five sentences describing nature or the environment. Students then read their sentences to a partner who will respond to each one, expressing a feeling or hope.
Ex: **Hay muchos animales que están en peligro de extinción. (Es terrible que haya muchos animales en peligro de extinción.)**

Comunicación

3 **Comentar** En parejas, túrnense para formar oraciones sobre su comunidad, sus clases, su gobierno o algún otro tema, usando expresiones como **me alegro de que**, **temo que** y **es extraño que.** Luego, reaccionen a los comentarios de su compañero/a. Answers will vary.

modelo

Estudiante 1: *Me alegro de que vayan a limpiar el río.*
Estudiante 2: *Yo también. Me preocupa que el agua del río esté tan sucia.*

4 **Contestar** Lee el mensaje electrónico que Raquel le escribió a su novio, Juan. Luego, en parejas, contesten el mensaje usando expresiones como **me sorprende que**, **me molesta que** y **es una lástima que.** Answers will vary.

De: Raquel
Para: Juan
Asunto: ¡Hola!

Hola, Juan:

Mi amor, siento no escribirte más frecuentemente. La verdad es que estoy muy ocupada todo el tiempo. No sabes cuánto me estoy divirtiendo en Colombia. Me sorprende haber podido adaptarme tan bien. Es bueno tener tanto trabajo. Aprendo mucho más aquí que en el laboratorio de la universidad. Me encanta que me den responsabilidades y que compartan sus muchos conocimientos conmigo. Ay, pero pienso mucho en ti. Qué triste es que no podamos estar juntos por tanto tiempo. Ojalá que los días pasen rápido. Bueno, querido, es todo por ahora. Escríbeme pronto.

Te quiero y te extraño mucho,

Raquel

AYUDA

Echar de menos (a alguien) and **extrañar (a alguien)** are two ways of saying *to miss (someone)*.

Síntesis

5 **No te preocupes** Estás muy preocupado/a por los problemas del medio ambiente y le comentas a tu compañero/a todas tus preocupaciones. Él/Ella va a darte la solución adecuada para tus preocupaciones. Su profesor(a) les va a dar una hoja distinta a cada uno/a con la información necesaria para completar la actividad. Answers will vary.

modelo

Estudiante 1: *Me molesta que las personas tiren basura en las calles.*
Estudiante 2: *Por eso es muy importante que los políticos hagan leyes para conservar las ciudades limpias.*

3 Teaching Tips
- To simplify, have students divide a sheet of paper into four columns, with these headings: **Nuestra ciudad, Las clases, El gobierno**, and another subject of their choosing. Ask them to brainstorm topics or issues for each column.
- Have groups write statements about these issues and exchange them with another group, who will write down their reactions.

4 Expansion In pairs, have students tell each other about a memorable event in their lives, such as a recent trip, birthday celebration, or exciting purchase they made. Using verbs and expressions of emotion, partners should draft an e-mail to express their reactions.

5 Teaching Tip Divide the class into pairs and distribute the handouts from the Activity Pack (Activity Pack/Supersite) that correspond to this Information Gap Activity. Give students ten minutes to complete the activity.

5 Expansion Have students work in groups of three to create a public service announcement. Groups should choose one of the ecological problems they mentioned in the activity, and include the proposed solutions for that problem in their announcement.

TEACHING OPTIONS

Small Groups Divide the class into groups of three. Have students write three predictions about the future on separate pieces of paper and put them in a bag. Students take turns drawing predictions and reading them to the group. Each group member should respond with an appropriate expression of emotion. Ex: **Voy a ganar millones de dólares algún día. (—Me alegro de que vayas a ganar millones de dólares. —Yo también.**

¡Ojalá que a mí me pase lo mismo!)
Extra Practice Ask students to imagine that they are world leaders speaking at an environmental summit. Have students deliver a short speech to the class addressing one or two of the world's environmental problems and how they hope to solve them. Students should use as many verbs and expressions of emotion as possible.

Section Goals

In **Estructura 13.2**, students will learn:

- to use the subjunctive with verbs and expressions of doubt, disbelief, and denial
- common verbs and expressions of doubt, disbelief, and denial
- expressions of certainty

Instructional Resources
Supersite: Audio (Lab MP3 Files); Resources (Grammar Presentation Slides, Activity Pack, Scripts, Answer Keys); Testing Program (Quizzes)
WebSAM
Workbook, pp. 159–160
Lab Manual, p. 76

Teaching Tips

- Introduce a few of the expressions of doubt, disbelief, or denial by talking about a topic familiar to the class. Ex: **Dudo que el equipo de baloncesto vaya a ganar el partido este fin de semana. Es probable que el otro equipo gane.** As you introduce each expression of doubt, disbelief, or denial, write it on the board, making sure that students understand its meaning and recognize the subjunctive verb in the subordinate clause.
- Ask volunteers to read the captions to the video stills, having them identify the phrase that triggers the subjunctive and the verb in the subjunctive.
- Add a visual aspect to this grammar presentation. Bring in articles and photos from Spanish-language tabloids. As you hold up each one, have students react, using expressions of doubt, disbelief, and denial. Ex: **Es improbable que una señora hable con extraterrestres.**

13.2 The subjunctive with doubt, disbelief, and denial

S Tutorial

NATIONAL STANDARDS comparisons

ANTE TODO Just as the subjunctive is required with expressions of emotion, influence, and will, it is also used with expressions of doubt, disbelief, and denial.

Main clause		Subordinate clause
Dudan	que	su hijo les **diga** la verdad.

- The subjunctive is always used in a subordinate clause when there is a change of subject and the expression in the main clause implies negation or uncertainty.

No creo que puedan ir muy lejos.

No es posible que el guía continúe el recorrido sin ustedes.

- Here is a list of some common expressions of doubt, disbelief, or denial.

Expressions of doubt, disbelief, or denial

dudar	*to doubt*	**no es seguro**	*it's not certain*
negar (e:ie)	*to deny*	**no es verdad**	*it's not true*
no creer	*not to believe*	**es imposible**	*it's impossible*
no estar seguro/a (de)	*not to be sure*	**es improbable**	*it's improbable*
no es cierto	*it's not true; it's not certain*	**(no) es posible**	*it's (not) possible*
		(no) es probable	*it's (not) probable*

El gobierno **niega** que el agua **esté** contaminada.
The government denies that the water is contaminated.

Dudo que el gobierno **resuelva** el problema.
I doubt that the government will solve the problem.

Es probable que **haya** menos bosques y selvas en el futuro.
It's probable that there will be fewer forests and jungles in the future.

No es verdad que mi hermano **estudie** ecología.
It's not true that my brother studies ecology.

¡LENGUA VIVA!
In English, the expression *it is probable* indicates a fairly high degree of certainty. In Spanish, however, **es probable** implies uncertainty and therefore triggers the subjunctive in the subordinate clause: **Es probable que venga Elena (pero quizás no puede).**

TEACHING OPTIONS

Extra Practice Write these statements on the board. Ask students to write their reactions using a different expression of doubt, disbelief, or denial for each. **1. Muchos tipos de peces viven en el desierto. 2. El cielo se está cayendo. 3. Los carros pequeños no contaminan. 4. No hay ningún animal en peligro de extinción.** Then have students discuss their answers with a partner.

Pairs Ask students to write five absurd statements and read them aloud to a partner, who will react with an expression of doubt, disbelief, or denial. Ex: **Unos hombres verdes me visitan todos los días. (No creo que unos hombres verdes te visiten todos los días.)** Students should respond to their partner's reactions.

▶ The indicative is used in a subordinate clause when there is no doubt or uncertainty in the main clause. Here is a list of some expressions of certainty.

Expressions of certainty

no dudar	*not to doubt*	**estar seguro/a (de)**	*to be sure*
no cabe duda de	*there is no doubt*	**es cierto**	*it's true; it's certain*
no hay duda de	*there is no doubt*	**es seguro**	*it's certain*
no negar (e:ie)	*not to deny*	**es verdad**	*it's true*
creer	*to believe*	**es obvio**	*it's obvious*

No negamos que **hay** demasiados carros en las carreteras.
We don't deny that there are too many cars on the highways.

Es verdad que Colombia **es** un país bonito.
It's true that Colombia is a beautiful country.

No hay duda de que el Amazonas **es** uno de los ríos más largos.
There is no doubt that the Amazon is one of the longest rivers.

Es obvio que las ballenas **están** en peligro de extinción.
It's obvious that whales are in danger of extinction.

▶ In affirmative sentences, the verb **creer** expresses belief or certainty, so it is followed by the indicative. In negative sentences, however, when doubt is implied, **creer** is followed by the subjunctive.

Creo que **debemos** usar exclusivamente la energía solar.
I believe we should use solar energy exclusively.

No creo que **haya** vida en el planeta Marte.
I don't believe that there is life on the planet Mars.

▶ The expressions **quizás** and **tal vez** are usually followed by the subjunctive because they imply doubt about something.

Quizás haga sol mañana.
Perhaps it will be sunny tomorrow.

Tal vez veamos la luna esta noche.
Perhaps we will see the moon tonight.

¡INTÉNTALO! Completa estas oraciones con la forma correcta del verbo.

1. Dudo que ellos <u>trabajen</u> (trabajar).
2. Es cierto que él <u>come</u> (comer) mucho.
3. Es imposible que ellos <u>salgan</u> (salir).
4. Es probable que ustedes <u>ganen</u> (ganar).
5. No creo que ella <u>vuelva</u> (volver).
6. Es posible que nosotros <u>vayamos</u> (ir).
7. Dudamos que tú <u>recicles</u> (reciclar).
8. Creo que ellos <u>juegan</u> (jugar) al fútbol.
9. No niego que ustedes <u>estudian</u> (estudiar).
10. Es posible que ella no <u>venga</u> (venir) a casa.
11. Es probable que Lucio y Carmen <u>duerman</u> (dormir).
12. Es posible que mi prima Marta <u>llame</u> (llamar).
13. Tal vez Juan no nos <u>oiga</u> (oír).
14. No es cierto que Paco y Daniel nos <u>ayuden</u> (ayudar).

recursos
WB pp. 159–160
LM p. 76
vhlcentral.com Lección 13

Teaching Tips

- Have students respond to statements that elicit expressions of doubt, disbelief, or denial and expressions of certainty. Ex: **Terminan la nueva residencia antes del próximo año. (Es seguro que la terminan antes del próximo año.) La universidad va a tener un nuevo presidente pronto. (No es verdad que la universidad vaya a tener un nuevo presidente pronto.)**
- Have students change the items in **¡Inténtalo!**, making the affirmative verbs in the main clauses negative, and the negative ones affirmative, and making all corresponding changes. Ex: **1. No dudo que ellos trabajan.**

TEACHING OPTIONS

TPR Call out a series of sentences, using either an expression of certainty or an expression of doubt, disbelief, or denial. Have students stand if they hear an expression of certainty or remain seated if they hear an expression of doubt. Ex: **Es cierto que algunos pájaros hablan.** (Students stand.)

Heritage Speakers Ask heritage speakers to jot down a few statements about things unique to their cultural communities. Ex: **Como chiles en el desayuno.** Have the class react using expressions of doubt, disbelief, denial, or certainty. Ex: **Dudo que comas chiles en el desayuno.**

Extra Practice Ask students to write sentences about three things of which they are certain and three things they doubt or cannot believe. Have students share some of their sentences with the class.

1 Expansion

Have pairs prepare another conversation between **Raúl** and his father using expressions of doubt, disbelief, and denial, as well as expressions of certainty. This time, **Raúl** is explaining the advantages of the Internet to his reluctant father and trying to persuade him to use it. Have pairs role-play their conversations for the class.

Práctica

1 **Escoger** Escoge las respuestas correctas para completar el diálogo. Luego dramatiza el diálogo con un(a) compañero/a.

RAÚL Ustedes dudan que yo realmente (1) estudie (estudio/estudie). No niego que a veces me (2) divierto (divierto/divierta) demasiado, pero no cabe duda de que (3) tomo (tomo/tome) mis estudios en serio. Estoy seguro de que cuando me vean graduarme van a pensar de manera diferente. Creo que no (4) tienen (tienen/tengan) razón con sus críticas.

PAPÁ Es posible que tu mamá y yo no (5) tengamos (tenemos/tengamos) razón. Es cierto que a veces (6) dudamos (dudamos/dudemos) de ti. Pero no hay duda de que te (7) pasas (pasas/pases) toda la noche en Internet y oyendo música. No es nada seguro que (8) estés (estás/estés) estudiando.

RAÚL Es verdad que (9) uso (uso/use) mucho la computadora pero, ¡piensen! ¿No es posible que (10) sea (es/sea) para buscar información para mis clases? ¡No hay duda de que Internet (11) es (es/sea) el mejor recurso del mundo! Es obvio que ustedes (12) piensan (piensan/piensen) que no hago nada, pero no es cierto.

PAPÁ No dudo que esta conversación nos (13) va (va/vaya) a ayudar. Pero tal vez esta noche (14) puedas (puedes/puedas) trabajar sin música. ¿Está bien?

2 Expansion

- Continue the activity by making other false statements. Ex: **Voy a hacer una excursión a la Patagonia mañana. Mi abuela sólo come pasteles y cebollas.**
- Tell students to write five statements about themselves or people they know, three of which should be false and two of which should be true. Have them read their sentences to a partner, who will react using statements of certainty or disbelief, and try to determine which statements are true.

2 **Dudas** Carolina es una chica que siempre miente. Expresa tus dudas sobre lo que Carolina está diciendo ahora. Usa las expresiones entre paréntesis para tus respuestas.

modelo

El próximo año Marta y yo vamos de vacaciones por diez meses. (dudar)
¡Ja! Dudo que vayan de vacaciones por ese tiempo. ¡Ustedes no son ricas!

1. Estoy escribiendo una novela en español. (no creer)
   No creo que estés escribiendo una novela en español.
2. Mi tía es la directora de PETA. (no ser verdad)
   No es verdad que tu tía sea la directora de PETA.
3. Dos profesores míos juegan para los Osos (*Bears*) de Chicago. (ser imposible)
   Es imposible que dos profesores tuyos jueguen para los Osos de Chicago.
4. Mi mejor amiga conoce al chef Guy Fieri. (no ser cierto)
   No es cierto que tu mejor amiga conozca al chef Guy Fieri.
5. Mi padre es dueño del Centro Rockefeller. (no ser posible)
   No es posible que tu padre sea dueño del Centro Rockefeller.
6. Yo ya tengo un doctorado (*doctorate*) en lenguas. (ser improbable)
   Es improbable que ya tengas un doctorado en lenguas.

AYUDA

Here are some useful expressions to say that you don't believe someone.
¡Qué va!
¡Imposible!
¡No te creo!
¡Es mentira!

Practice more at **vhlcentral.com**.

TEACHING OPTIONS

Large Groups Divide the class into large groups to stage an environmental debate. Some groups should play the role of environmental advocates while others represent industrialists and big business. Have students take turns presenting a policy platform for the group they represent. When they are finished, opposing groups express their doubt, disbelief, and denial.

Heritage Speakers Ask heritage speakers to write a paragraph about a current event or political issue in their cultural community. Ask them to be sure to include expressions of certainty as well as expressions of doubt, disbelief, or denial. Have them read their paragraphs to the class, who will react using the subjunctive with emotions, doubt, or disbelief.

Comunicación

3 **Entrevista** En parejas, imaginen que trabajan para un periódico y que tienen que hacerle una entrevista a la ecologista Mary Axtmann, quien colaboró en la fundación de la organización Ciudadanos Pro Bosque San Patricio, en Puerto Rico. Escriban seis preguntas para la entrevista después de leer las declaraciones de Mary Axtmann. Al final, inventen las respuestas de Axtmann.
Answers will vary.

NOTA CULTURAL

La asociación de **Mary Axtmann** trabaja para la conservación del Bosque San Patricio. También ofrece conferencias sobre temas ambientales, hace un censo anual de pájaros y tiene un grupo de guías voluntarios. La comunidad hace todo el trabajo; la asociación no recibe ninguna ayuda del gobierno.

Declaraciones de Mary Axtmann:

"... que el bosque es un recurso ecológico educativo para la comunidad."

"El Bosque San Patricio es un pulmón (*lung*) que produce oxígeno para la ciudad."

"El Bosque San Patricio está en medio de la ciudad de San Juan. Por eso digo que este bosque es una esmeralda (*emerald*) en un mar de concreto."

"El bosque pertenece (*belongs*) a la comunidad."

"Nosotros salvamos este bosque mediante la propuesta (*proposal*) y no la protesta."

4 **Adivinar** Escribe cinco oraciones sobre tu vida presente y futura. Cuatro deben ser falsas y sólo una debe ser cierta. Presenta tus oraciones al grupo. El grupo adivina cuál es la oración cierta y expresa sus dudas sobre las oraciones falsas. Answers will vary.

AYUDA

Here are some useful verbs for talking about plans.
esperar → *to hope*
querer → *to want*
pretender → *to intend*
pensar → *to plan*
Note that **pretender** and *pretend* are false cognates. To express *to pretend*, use the verb **fingir**.

modelo

Estudiante 1: *Quiero irme un año a la selva a trabajar.*
Estudiante 2: *Dudo que te guste vivir en la selva.*
Estudiante 3: *En cinco años voy a ser presidente de los Estados Unidos.*
Estudiante 2: *No creo que seas presidente de los Estados Unidos en cinco años. ¡Tal vez en treinta!*

Síntesis

5 **Intercambiar** En grupos, escriban un párrafo sobre los problemas del medio ambiente en su estado o en su comunidad. Compartan su párrafo con otro grupo, que va a ofrecer opiniones y soluciones. Luego presenten su párrafo, con las opiniones y soluciones del otro grupo, a la clase.
Answers will vary.

3 Teaching Tip Before starting, have the class brainstorm different topics that might be discussed with Mary Axtmann.

3 Expansion Ask pairs to role-play their interviews for the class.

4 Teaching Tip Tell groups to choose a secretary, who will write down the group members' true statements and present them to the class.

5 Teaching Tip Assign students to groups of four. Ask group members to appoint a mediator to lead the discussion, a secretary to write the paragraph, a proofreader to check what was written, and a stenographer to take notes on the opinions and solutions of the other group.

5 Expansion Have students create a poster illustrating the environmental problems in their community and proposing possible solutions.

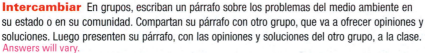

TEACHING OPTIONS

Small Groups In groups of three, have students pretend they are filming a live newscast on a local news station. Give each group a breaking news story and have one student play the reporter that interviews the other two about what is happening. The interviewees should use the expressions from the lesson when responding to the reporter's questions. Possible news stories: protest in favor of animal rights, a volcano about to erupt, a local ecological problem.

Game Divide the class into two teams. Team A writes sentences with expressions of certainty, while team B writes sentences with expressions of doubt, disbelief, or denial. Put all the sentences in a hat. Each team takes turns drawing sentences and stating the opposite of what the sentence says. The team with the most correct sentences at the end wins.

Section Goals

In **Estructura 13.3**, students will learn:

- conjunctions that require the subjunctive
- conjunctions followed by the subjunctive or the indicative

Instructional Resources

Supersite: Audio (Lab MP3 Files); Resources (Grammar Presentation Slides, Activity Pack, Scripts, Answer Keys); Testing Program (Quizzes)
WebSAM
Workbook, pp. 161–162
Lab Manual, p. 77

Teaching Tips

- To introduce conjunctions that require the subjunctive, make a few statements about yourself. Ex: **Nunca llego a clase tarde a menos que tenga un problema con mi carro. Siempre leo mi correo electrónico antes de que empiece mi primera clase. Camino a clase con tal de que no llueva.** Write each conjunction on the board as you go.
- Have volunteers read the captions to the video stills. Help them identify the conjunctions in the sentences and the subjunctive verbs in the subordinate clauses.

13.3 The subjunctive with conjunctions

S Tutorial

NATIONAL STANDARDS comparisons

ANTE TODO Conjunctions are words or phrases that connect other words and clauses in sentences. Certain conjunctions commonly introduce adverbial clauses, which describe *how, why, when,* and *where* an action takes place.

Main clause	Conjunction	Adverbial clause
Vamos a visitar a Carlos	**antes de que**	**regrese** a California.

Muchos animales van a estar en peligro de extinción, a menos que los protejamos.

Marissa habla con Jimena antes de que lleguen los chicos.

- With certain conjunctions, the subjunctive is used to express a hypothetical situation, uncertainty as to whether an action or event will take place, or a condition that may or may not be fulfilled.

Voy a dejar un recado **en caso de que Gustavo me llame**.
I'm going to leave a message in case Gustavo calls me.

Voy al supermercado **para que tengas** algo de comer.
I'm going to the store so that you'll have something to eat.

- Here is a list of the conjunctions that always require the subjunctive.

Conjunctions that require the subjunctive

a menos que	*unless*	**en caso (de) que**	*in case (that)*
antes (de) que	*before*	**para que**	*so that*
con tal (de) que	*provided that*	**sin que**	*without*

Algunos animales van a morir **a menos que** haya leyes para protegerlos.
Some animals are going to die unless there are laws to protect them.

Ellos nos llevan a la selva **para que** veamos las plantas tropicales.
They are taking us to the jungle so that we may see the tropical plants.

- The infinitive, not **que** + [*subjunctive*], is used after the prepositions **antes de, para,** and **sin** when there is no change of subject. **¡Atención!** While you may use a present participle with the English equivalent of these phrases, in Spanish you cannot.

Te llamamos **antes de salir** de la casa.
We will call you before leaving the house.

Te llamamos mañana **antes de que salgas**.
We will call you tomorrow before you leave.

TEACHING OPTIONS

Extra Practice Write these partial sentences on the board. Have students complete them with true or invented information about their own lives. **1. Voy a terminar los estudios con tal de que..., 2. Necesito $500 en caso de que..., 3. Puedo salir este sábado a menos que..., 4. El mundo cambia sin que..., 5. Debo... antes de que..., 6. Mis padres... para que yo...** Encourage students to expand on their answers with additional information when possible.

Video Have students divide a sheet of paper into four columns, labeling them **Voluntad, Emoción, Duda,** and **Conjunción**. Replay the **Fotonovela** episode. Have them listen for each use of the subjunctive, marking the example they hear in the appropriate column.

Extra Practice Play the episode again, then have students write a short summary that includes each use of the subjunctive.

Conjunctions with subjunctive or indicative

Voy a formar un club de ecología tan pronto como vuelva al D.F.

Cuando veo basura, la recojo.

Conjunctions used with subjunctive or indicative

cuando	*when*	**hasta que**	*until*
después de que	*after*	**tan pronto como**	*as soon as*
en cuanto	*as soon as*		

- With the conjunctions above, use the subjunctive in the subordinate clause if the main clause expresses a future action or command.

Vamos a resolver el problema **cuando desarrollemos** nuevas tecnologías.
We are going to solve the problem when we develop new technologies.

Después de que ustedes **tomen** sus refrescos, reciclen las botellas.
After you drink your soft drinks, recycle the bottles.

- With these conjunctions, the indicative is used in the subordinate clause if the verb in the main clause expresses an action that habitually happens, or that happened in the past.

Contaminan los ríos **cuando construyen** nuevos edificios.
They pollute the rivers when they build new buildings.

Contaminaron el río **cuando construyeron** ese edificio.
They polluted the river when they built that building.

¡INTÉNTALO! Completa las oraciones con las formas correctas de los verbos.

1. Voy a estudiar ecología cuando ___vuelva___ (volver) a la universidad.
2. No podemos evitar el cambio climático, a menos que todos ___trabajemos___ (trabajar) juntos.
3. No podemos conducir sin ___contaminar___ (contaminar) el aire.
4. Siempre recogemos mucha basura cuando ___vamos___ (ir) al parque.
5. Elisa habló con el presidente del Club de Ecología después de que ___terminó___ (terminar) la reunión.
6. Vamos de excursión para ___observar___ (observar) los animales y las plantas.
7. La contaminación va a ser un problema muy serio hasta que nosotros ___cambiemos___ (cambiar) nuestros sistemas de producción y transporte.
8. El gobierno debe crear más parques nacionales antes de que los bosques y ríos ___estén___ (estar) completamente contaminados.
9. La gente recicla con tal de que no ___sea___ (ser) difícil.

recursos
WB pp. 161–162
LM p. 77
vhlcentral.com Lección 13

Teaching Tips

- Write sentences that use **antes de** and **para** and ask volunteers to rewrite them so that they end with subordinate clauses instead of a preposition and an infinitive. Ex: **Voy a hablar con Paula antes de ir a clase. (... antes de que ella vaya a clase; ... antes de que Sergio le hable; ... antes de que ella compre esas botas.)**
- As students complete the **¡Inténtalo!** activity, have them circle the conjunctions that always require the subjunctive.

TEACHING OPTIONS

TPR Have students write **I** for **infinitivo** on one piece of paper and **S** for **subjuntivo** on another. Make several statements, some with prepositions followed by the infinitive and some with conjunctions followed by the subjunctive. Students should hold up the paper that represents what they heard. Ex: **Juan habla despacio para que todos lo entiendan. (S) No necesitan un carro para ir a la universidad. (I)**

Extra Practice Have students use these prepositions and conjunctions to make statements about the environment: **para, para que, sin, sin que, antes de,** and **antes de que.** Ex: **Es importante empezar un programa de reciclaje antes de que tengamos demasiada basura. No es posible conservar los bosques sin que se deje de cortar tantos árboles...**

1 Expansion
- Ask students to write new endings for each sentence. Ex: **Voy a llevar a mis hijos al parque para que... (hagan más ejercicio/jueguen con sus amigos/pasen más tiempo fuera de la casa).**
- Ask pairs to write six original sentences about a trip they plan to take. Have them use one conjunction that requires the subjunctive in each sentence.

2 Teaching Tip As you go through the items, ask students which conjunctions require the subjunctive and which could be followed by the subjunctive or the indicative. For those that could take both, discuss which one students used and why.

3 Expansion
- Ask students to identify the natural resources and environmental problems mentioned in the reading.
- Have students create an advertisement for an environmental agency that protects one of the natural resources mentioned in the reading. Students should state the name and goals of the agency, how these goals serve the public interest, and where and how donations can be made.

Práctica

1 **Completar** La señora Montero habla de una excursión que quiere hacer con su familia. Completa las oraciones con la forma correcta de cada verbo.

1. Voy a llevar a mis hijos al parque para que aprendan (aprender) sobre la naturaleza.
2. Voy a pasar todo el día allí a menos que haga (hacer) mucho frío.
3. Podemos explorar el parque en bicicleta sin caminar (caminar) demasiado.
4. Vamos a bajar al cráter con tal de que no se prohíba (prohibir).
5. Siempre llevamos al perro cuando vamos (ir) al parque.
6. No pensamos ir muy lejos en caso de que llueva (llover).
7. Vamos a almorzar a la orilla (*shore*) del río cuando nosotros terminemos (terminar) de preparar la comida.
8. Mis hijos van a dejar todo limpio antes de salir (salir) del parque.

2 **Frases** Completa estas frases de una manera lógica. Answers will vary.

1. No podemos controlar la contaminación del aire a menos que...
2. Voy a reciclar los productos de papel y de vidrio en cuanto...
3. Debemos comprar coches eléctricos tan pronto como...
4. Protegemos los animales en peligro de extinción para que...
5. Mis amigos y yo vamos a recoger la basura de la universidad después de que...
6. No podemos desarrollar nuevas fuentes (*sources*) de energía sin...
7. Hay que eliminar la contaminación del agua para...
8. No podemos proteger la naturaleza sin que...

3 **Organizaciones colombianas** En parejas, lean las descripciones de las organizaciones de conservación. Luego expresen en sus propias (*own*) palabras las opiniones de cada organización. Answers will vary.

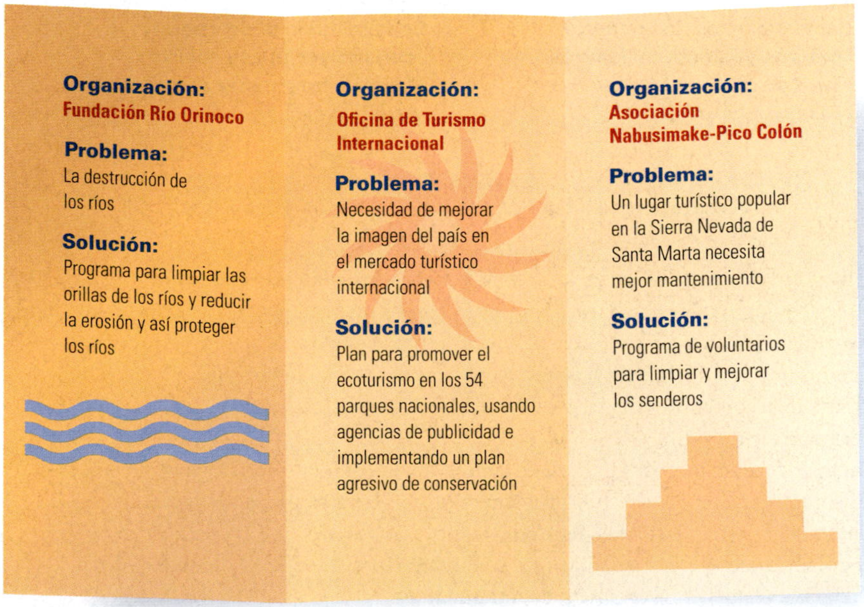

Organización:
Fundación Río Orinoco
Problema:
La destrucción de los ríos
Solución:
Programa para limpiar las orillas de los ríos y reducir la erosión y así proteger los ríos
Organización:
Oficina de Turismo Internacional
Problema:
Necesidad de mejorar la imagen del país en el mercado turístico internacional
Solución:
Plan para promover el ecoturismo en los 54 parques nacionales, usando agencias de publicidad e implementando un plan agresivo de conservación
Organización:
Asociación Nabusimake-Pico Colón
Problema:
Un lugar turístico popular en la Sierra Nevada de Santa Marta necesita mejor mantenimiento
Solución:
Programa de voluntarios para limpiar y mejorar los senderos

Practice more at **vhlcentral.com**.

AYUDA

Here are some expressions you can use as you complete **Actividad 3**.

Se puede evitar... con tal de que...
Es necesario... para que...
Debemos prohibir... antes de que...
No es posible... sin que...
Vamos a... tan pronto como...
A menos que... no vamos a...

TEACHING OPTIONS

Pairs Ask students to imagine that, unless some dramatic environmental actions are taken, the world as we know it will end in five days. It is their responsibility as community leaders to give a speech warning people what will happen unless everyone takes action. Have students work with a partner to prepare a three-minute presentation for the class, using as many different conjunctions that require the subjunctive as possible.

Small Groups Divide the class into groups of four. The first student begins a sentence, the second picks a conjunction, and the third student finishes the sentence. The fourth student writes the sentence down. Students should take turns playing the different roles until they have created eight sentences.

Comunicación

4 **Preguntas** En parejas, túrnense para hacerse estas preguntas. Answers will vary.

1. ¿Qué haces cada noche antes de acostarte?
2. ¿Qué haces después de salir de la universidad?
3. ¿Qué hace tu familia para que puedas asistir a la universidad?
4. ¿Qué piensas hacer tan pronto como te gradúes?
5. ¿Qué quieres hacer mañana, a menos que haga mal tiempo?
6. ¿Qué haces en tus clases sin que los profesores lo sepan?

5 **Comparar** En parejas, comparen una actividad rutinaria que ustedes hacen con algo que van a hacer en el futuro. Usen palabras de la lista. Answers will vary.

antes de	después de que	hasta que	sin (que)
antes de que	en caso de que	para (que)	tan pronto como

modelo

Estudiante 1: *El sábado vamos al lago. Tan pronto como volvamos, vamos a estudiar para el examen.*
Estudiante 2: *Todos los sábados llevo a mi primo al parque para que juegue. Pero el sábado que viene, con tal de que no llueva, lo voy a llevar a las montañas.*

Síntesis

6 **Tres en raya (*Tic-Tac-Toe*)** Formen dos equipos. Con el vocabulario de esta lección, una persona comienza una frase y otra persona de su equipo la termina usando palabras de la gráfica. El primer equipo que forme tres oraciones seguidas (*in a row*) gana el tres en raya. Hay que usar la conjunción o la preposición y el verbo correctamente. Si no, ¡no cuenta! Answers will vary.

modelo

Equipo 1
Estudiante 1: *Dudo que podamos eliminar la deforestación…*
Estudiante 2: *sin que nos ayude el gobierno.*
Equipo 2
Estudiante 1: *Creo que podemos conservar nuestros recursos naturales…*
Estudiante 2: *con tal de que todos hagamos algo para ayudar.*

cuando	con tal de que	para que
antes de que	para	sin que
hasta que	en caso de que	antes de

¡LENGUA VIVA!

Tic-Tac-Toe has various names in the Spanish-speaking world, including **tres en raya, tres en línea, ta-te-ti, gato, la vieja,** and **triqui-triqui**.

4 Expansion When pairs have finished asking and answering the questions, work with the whole class, asking several individuals each of the questions and asking other students to react to their responses.
Ex: ____ **hace ejercicios aeróbicos antes de acostarse. ¿Quién más hace ejercicio? ¡Uf! Hacer ejercicio a esa hora me parece excesivo. ¿Quiénes ven la tele? ¿Nadie lee un libro antes de acostarse?**

5 Teaching Tip
Have partners compare the routines of other people they know and what they are going to do in the future. Have them do the same with celebrities, making guesses about their routines.

6 Teaching Tips
- Have groups prepare *Tic-Tac-Toe* cards like the one shown in the activity.
- Regroup the students to do a second round of *Tic-Tac-Toe*.

TEACHING OPTIONS

Heritage Speakers Ask heritage speakers if they played *Tic-Tac-Toe* when growing up. What did they call it? Have them look at the names listed in **¡Lengua viva!** to see if any are familiar. Ask them the names of other childhood games they played and to describe them. Are the games similar to those played by other students in the class?

Pairs Ask partners to interview each other about what they must do today for their future goals to become a reality. Students should state what their goals are, the necessary conditions to achieve them, and obstacles they may encounter. Students should use as many conjunctions as possible in their interviews. Have pairs present their interviews to the class.

Section Goals

In **Estructura 13.4** students will learn:
- how to form regular past participles
- how to form irregular past participles
- how to use past participles as adjectives

Instructional Resources
Supersite: Audio (Lab MP3 Files); Resources (Grammar Presentation Slides, Activity Pack, Scripts, Answer Keys); Testing Program (Quizzes)
WebSAM
Workbook, pp. 163–164
Lab Manual, p. 78

Teaching Tips

- Use magazine pictures to review some of the regular past participles that students have learned as adjectives: **aburrido, afectado, avergonzado, cansado, casado, cerrado, desordenado, enamorado, enojado, equivocado, mareado, ocupado, ordenado, preocupado.** As you review these forms, have students indicate the corresponding infinitives.
- Check for understanding by calling out known infinitives and asking volunteers to give their past participles. Ex: **mirar (mirado), comprender (comprendido), cumplir (cumplido)**
- Practice irregular forms by asking students to finish incomplete sentences. Ex: **Esas piñatas son ____ en México. (hechas) El problema de deforestación no está ____. (resuelto)**
- See if students can find the use of past participles used as adjectives from the **Fotonovela** video. If they correctly identify **asustado** from still 5, ask them to supply the infinitive of this verb.

13.4 Past participles used as adjectives

Tutorial

NATIONAL STANDARDS comparisons

ANTE TODO In **Lección 5**, you learned about present participles (**estudiando**). Both Spanish and English have past participles. The past participles of English verbs often end in **-ed** (*to turn* → *turned*), but many are also irregular (*to buy* → *bought; to drive* → *driven*).

- In Spanish, regular **-ar** verbs form the past participle with **-ado.** Regular **-er** and **-ir** verbs form the past participle with **-ido.**

INFINITIVE	STEM	PAST PARTICIPLE
bailar	bail-	**bailado**
comer	com-	**comido**
vivir	viv-	**vivido**

- **¡Atención!** The past participles of **-er** and **-ir** verbs whose stems end in **-a, -e,** or **-o** carry a written accent mark on the **i** of the **-ido** ending.

caer	**caído**	reír	**reído**
creer	**creído**	sonreír	**sonreído**
leer	**leído**	traer	**traído**
oír	**oído**		

Irregular past participles

abrir	**abierto**	morir	**muerto**
decir	**dicho**	poner	**puesto**
describir	**descrito**	resolver	**resuelto**
descubrir	**descubierto**	romper	**roto**
escribir	**escrito**	ver	**visto**
hacer	**hecho**	volver	**vuelto**

AYUDA
You already know several past participles used as adjectives: **aburrido, interesado, nublado, perdido,** etc.
•••
Note that all irregular past participles except **dicho** and **hecho** end in **-to.**

- In Spanish, as in English, past participles can be used as adjectives. They are often used with the verb **estar** to describe a condition or state that results from an action. Like other Spanish adjectives, they must agree in gender and number with the nouns they modify.

Me gusta usar papel **reciclado.**
I like to use recycled paper.

La mesa está **puesta** y la cena está **servida.**
The table is set and dinner is served.

¡INTÉNTALO! Indica la forma correcta del participio pasado de estos verbos.

1. hablar hablado
2. beber bebido
3. decidir decidido
4. romper roto
5. escribir escrito
6. cantar cantado
7. oír oído
8. traer traído
9. correr corrido
10. leer leído
11. ver visto
12. hacer hecho

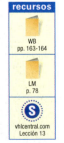

recursos
WB pp. 163-164
LM p. 78
vhlcentral.com Lección 13

TEACHING OPTIONS

Extra Practice Create oral substitution drills. Say a sentence and have students repeat (Ex: **Felipe está enojado.**). Provide a new subject (**Sara e Isabel**). Have students replace the original subject with the new one, making all necessary changes (**Sara e Isabel están enojadas.**).

Game Divide the class into teams of five and have each team sit in a row. The first person in the row has a blank piece of paper. Have five infinitives in mind. Call out one of them. Allow the student with the paper five seconds to write down the past participle of the infinitive and pass the paper to the next student in his or her row. The team with the most correct responses wins.

Práctica

1 **Completar** Completa las oraciones con la forma adecuada del participio pasado del verbo que está entre paréntesis.

1. Nuestra excursión a la selva ya está preparada (preparar).
2. Todos los detalles están escritos (escribir) en español.
3. Tenemos que comprar los pasajes, pero Sara no encuentra el mapa. ¡Ay no! Creo que estamos perdidos (perder).
4. Sabemos que la agencia de viajes está en una plaza muy conocida (conocer), la Plaza Bolívar. Está abierta (abrir) de nueve a tres.
5. El nombre de la agencia está escrito (escribir) en la entrada y en la acera (*sidewalk*).
6. Pero ya son las tres y diez... qué mala suerte. Seguramente la oficina ya está cerrada (cerrar).

NOTA CULTURAL

Simón Bolívar (1783–1830) es considerado el "libertador" de cinco países de Suramérica: Venezuela, Perú, Bolivia, Colombia y Ecuador. Su apellido se ve en nombres como Bolivia, Ciudad Bolívar, la Universidad Simón Bolívar, el bolívar (la moneda venezolana) y en los nombres de plazas y calles.

2 **Preparativos** Tú y tu compañero/a van a hacer un viaje. Túrnense para hacerse estas preguntas sobre los preparativos (*preparations*). Usen el participio pasado en sus respuestas.

modelo

Estudiante 1: ¿Compraste los pasajes de avión?
Estudiante 2: Sí, los pasajes ya están comprados.

1. ¿Hiciste las maletas?
   Sí, las maletas ya están hechas.
2. ¿Confirmaste las reservaciones para el hotel?
   Sí, las reservaciones ya están confirmadas.
3. ¿Compraste tus medicinas?
   Sí, las/mis medicinas ya están compradas.
4. ¿Lavaste la ropa?
   Sí, la ropa ya está lavada.
5. ¿Apagaste todas las luces?
   Sí, las luces ya están apagadas.
6. ¿Cerraste bien la puerta?
   Sí, la puerta ya está cerrada.

Comunicación

NATIONAL communication STANDARDS

3 **Describir** Tú y un(a) compañero/a son agentes de policía y tienen que investigar un crimen. Miren el dibujo y describan lo que encontraron en la habitación del señor Villalonga. Usen el participio pasado en la descripción. Luego, comparen su descripción con la de otra pareja. Answers will vary.

modelo

La puerta del baño no estaba cerrada.

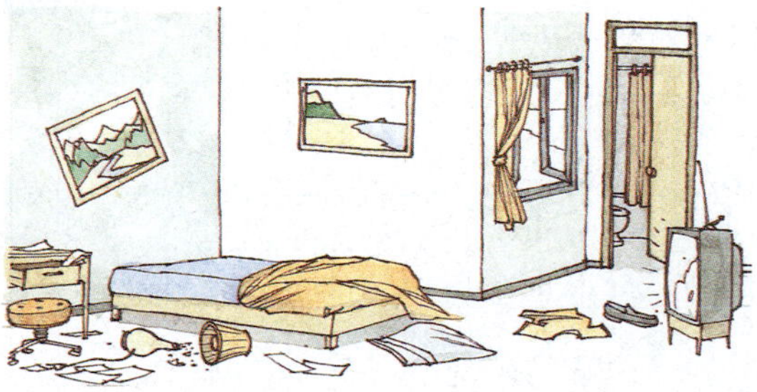

AYUDA

You may want to use the past participles of these verbs to describe the illustration: **abrir, desordenar** (*to make untidy*), **hacer, poner, romper, tirar** (*to throw*).

1 Expansion Have pairs make a list of new nouns of different gender and/or number, one for each item in the activity, to replace the original nouns being modified by past participles. They should double-check that the new sentences will make sense. Have them exchange their list with another pair, who should rewrite the sentences, then return them to the first pair for correction.

2 Expansion Have students redo the activity using a negative response and a different past participle used as an adjective to provide a reason. Ex: **1. No, no están hechas porque la ropa no está limpia. 2. No, no están confirmadas porque el teléfono del hotel está ocupado.**

3 Teaching Tip To simplify, before assigning the activity to pairs, allow students a couple of minutes to make notes about the crime scene.

3 Expansion Have students give their answers in round-robin format. Remind them that each contribution has to contain new information not previously supplied.

TEACHING OPTIONS

Pairs Have pairs make a promotional flyer for a new environmentally friendly business in town. Their flyers should include at least three past participles used as adjectives. When they have finished, circulate the flyers in the class. Have the students say which businesses they would most like to visit and why.

Game Divide the class into teams of three. Each team should think of a famous place or a historical monument. The other teams will take turns asking questions about the place. Questions can only be answered with **sí/no** and each one should have a past participle used as an adjective. Ex: **¿Está abierto al público? ¿Es conocido solamente en ese país?** The first team to guess the identity of the site wins a point.

Section Goal

In **Recapitulación**, students will review the grammar concepts from this lesson.

Instructional Resource
Supersite

1 Teaching Tip Before beginning the activity, ask students to identify any verbs that have irregular past participles.

1 Expansion Ask students to create sentences using the past participles from the chart. Remind them that they must agree with the noun they modify. Ex: **Las cartas ya están escritas.**

2 Teaching Tip To simplify, have students underline the conjunction in each sentence. Then have them determine which conjunctions must take the subjunctive and which may take either subjunctive or indicative. Finally, have them complete the activity.

2 Expansion Ask students to create three additional sentences using conjunctions.

3 Teaching Tips

- Before students complete the activity, have them underline expressions of doubt, disbelief, or denial that take the subjunctive.
- Have volunteers role-play each dialogue for the class. Encourage them to ad-lib as they go.

3 Expansion Have students rewrite the dialogue using expressions that convey similar meanings. Ex: **1. No cabe duda de que debemos escribir nuestra presentación sobre el reciclaje.**

Recapitulación

Diagnostics

Completa estas actividades para repasar los conceptos de gramática que aprendiste en esta lección.

1 Completar Completa la tabla con la forma correcta de los verbos. 12 pts.

Infinitivo	Participio (f.)	Infinitivo	Participio (m.)
completar	completada	hacer	hecho
cubrir	cubierta	pagar	pagado
decir	dicha	perder	perdido
escribir	escrita	poner	puesto

2 Subjuntivo con conjunciones Escoge la forma correcta del verbo para completar las oraciones. 12 pts.

1. En cuanto (empiecen/empiezan) las vacaciones, vamos a viajar.
2. Por favor, llámeme a las siete y media en caso de que no (me despierto/me despierte).
3. Toni va a usar su bicicleta hasta que los coches híbridos (cuesten/cuestan) menos dinero.
4. Estudiantes, pueden entrar al parque natural con tal de que (van/vayan) todos juntos.
5. Debemos conservar el agua antes de que no (queda/quede) nada para beber.
6. Siempre quiero vender mi coche cuando (yo) (piense/pienso) en la contaminación.

3 Creer o no creer Completa esta conversación con la forma correcta del presente de indicativo o de subjuntivo, según el contexto. 12 pts.

CAROLA Creo que (1) debemos (nosotras, deber) escribir nuestra presentación sobre el reciclaje.

MÓNICA Hmm, no estoy segura de que el reciclaje (2) sea (ser) un buen tema. No hay duda de que la gente ya (3) sabe (saber) reciclar.

CAROLA Sí, pero dudo que todos lo (4) practiquen (practicar).

MÓNICA ¿Sabes, Néstor? El sábado vamos a ir a limpiar la playa con un grupo de voluntarios. ¿Quieres ir?

NÉSTOR No creo que (5) pueda (yo, poder) ir, tengo que estudiar.

CAROLA ¿Estás seguro? ¡Es imposible que (6) vayas (tú, ir) a estudiar todo el fin de semana!

NÉSTOR Bueno, sí, tengo un par de horas en la tarde para ir a la playa...

RESUMEN GRAMATICAL

13.1 The subjunctive with verbs of emotion pp. 426-427

Verbs and expressions of emotion	
alegrarse (de)	tener miedo (de)
esperar	es extraño
gustar	es una lástima
molestar	es ridículo
sentir (e:ie)	es terrible
sorprender	es triste
temer	ojalá (que)

Main clause		Subordinate clause
Marta espera	que	yo **vaya** al lago mañana.
Ojalá	que	**comamos** en casa.

13.2 The subjunctive with doubt, disbelief, and denial pp. 430-431

Expressions of doubt, disbelief, or denial (used with subjunctive)	
dudar	no es verdad
negar (e:ie)	es imposible
no creer	es improbable
no estar seguro/a (de)	(no) es posible
no es cierto	(no) es probable
no es seguro	

Expressions of certainty (used with indicative)	
no dudar	estar seguro/a (de)
no cabe duda de	es cierto
no hay duda de	es seguro
no negar (e:ie)	es verdad
creer	es obvio

► The infinitive is used after these expressions when there is no change of subject.

13.3 The subjunctive with conjunctions pp. 434-435

Conjunctions that require the subjunctive	
a menos que	en caso (de) que
antes (de) que	para que
con tal (de) que	sin que

TEACHING OPTIONS

TPR Divide the class into two teams, **indicativo** and **subjuntivo**, and have them line up. Point to the first member of each team and call out an expression of doubt, disbelief, denial, or certainty. The student whose team corresponds to the mood has ten seconds to step forward and give an example sentence. Ex: **es posible** (The student from the **subjuntivo** team steps forward. Example sentence: **Es posible que el río esté contaminado.**)

Extra Practice Tell students to imagine they are the president of their school's nature club. Have them prepare a short speech in which they try to convince new students about the importance of the environment and nature. Have them use at least three expressions with the subjunctive.

Extra Practice Call out infinitives and have volunteers give the correct past participle.

4 **Oraciones** Escribe oraciones con estos elementos. Usa el subjuntivo y el participio pasado cuando sea necesario. 20 pts.

1. ser ridículo / los coches / contaminar tanto
Es ridículo que los coches contaminen tanto.
2. el gobierno / ir a proteger / las ciudades / afectar / por los tornados El gobierno va a proteger las ciudades afectadas por los tornados.
3. no caber duda de / tú y yo / poder / hacer mucho más
No cabe duda de que tú y yo podemos hacer mucho más.
4. los ecologistas / temer / no conservarse / los recursos naturales Los ecologistas temen que no se conserven los recursos naturales.
5. (yo) no estar seguro / los niños / poder ir / porque / el parque / estar / cerrar No estoy seguro de que los niños puedan ir porque el parque está cerrado.
6. (yo) alegrarse de / en mi ciudad / reciclarse / el plástico y el vidrio Me alegro de que en mi ciudad se reciclen el plástico y el vidrio.
7. (nosotros) no creer que / la casa / estar / abrir
No creemos que la casa esté abierta.
8. estar prohibido / tocar o dar de comer a / estos animales / proteger Está prohibido tocar o dar de comer a estos animales protegidos.
9. es improbable / existir / leyes / contra la deforestación
Es improbable que existan leyes contra la deforestación.
10. ojalá que / la situación / mejorar / día a día
Ojalá que la situación mejore día a día.

► The infinitive is used after the prepositions **antes de**, **para**, and **sin** when there is no change of subject.

Te llamamos **antes de salir** de casa.

Te llamamos mañana **antes de que salgas**.

Conjunctions used with subjunctive or indicative	
cuando después de que en cuanto	hasta que tan pronto como

13.4 Past participles used as adjectives p. 438

Past participles

Infinitive	Stem	Past participle
bailar	bail-	**bailado**
comer	com-	**comido**
vivir	viv-	**vivido**

Irregular past participles

abrir	**abierto**	morir	**muerto**
decir	**dicho**	poner	**puesto**
describir	**descrito**	resolver	**resuelto**
descubrir	**descubierto**	romper	**roto**
escribir	**escrito**	ver	**visto**
hacer	**hecho**	volver	**vuelto**

► Like common adjectives, past participles must agree with the noun they modify.

Hay unas postales escritas en español.

5 **Escribir** Escribe un diálogo de al menos seis oraciones en el que un(a) amigo/a hace comentarios pesimistas sobre la situación del medio ambiente en tu ciudad o región y tú respondes con comentarios y reacciones optimistas. Usa verbos y expresiones de esta lección. 44 pts. Answers will vary.

6 **Canción** Completa estos versos de una canción de Juan Luis Guerra. ¡4 puntos EXTRA!

"Ojalá que ___llueva___ (llover)
café en el campo.
Pa'° que todos los niños
___canten___ (cantar) en el campo."

Pa' *short for* Para

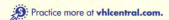

Practice more at **vhlcentral.com.**

4 Expansion Ask students to create three additional dehydrated sentences. Then have them exchange papers with a classmate and hydrate the sentences.

5 Teaching Tip Remind students that, with the exception of **ojalá**, the word **que** must be present and there must be a change of subject in order to use the subjunctive.

6 Expansion Have students create their own song verse by replacing **llueva café** and **canten** with other verbs in the subjunctive. Ex: **nieve helado** and **bailen**

TEACHING OPTIONS

Game Have students make *Bingo* cards of different verbs, expressions, and conjunctions that require the subjunctive. Read aloud sentences using the subjunctive. If students have the verb, expression, or phrase on their card, they should cover the space. The first student to complete a horizontal, vertical, or diagonal row is the winner.

Pairs Ask students to write down two true sentences and two false ones. Encourage them to write sentences that are all very likely. In pairs, have students take turns reading their sentences. Their partner should react, using expressions of doubt, disbelief, denial, or certainty. The student who stumps his or her partner with all four statements wins. Have pairs share their most challenging sentences with the class.

Section Goals

In **Lectura**, students will:

- learn that recognizing the purpose of a text can help them understand it
- read two fables

Instructional Resource
Supersite

Estrategia Tell students that recognizing the writer's purpose will help them comprehend an unfamiliar text.

Examinar los textos Have students scan the texts, using the reading strategies they have learned to determine the authors' purposes. Then have them work with a partner to answer the questions. Students should recognize that the texts are fables because the characters are animals.

Predicciones

- Tell pairs that where their predictions differ they should refer back to the texts for resolution.
- Give students these additional predictions: **5. Los textos son infantiles. 6. Se trata de una historia romántica.**

Determinar el propósito

- Tell students to take notes about the characters as they read. Remind students that they should be able to retell the stories in their own words.
- Ask students who generally reads fables. Ex: **Por lo general, ¿las fábulas se escriben para niños, adultos o ambos?** Then have them write a few sentences explaining their answer.

Lectura

NATIONAL STANDARDS communication cultures

Antes de leer

Estrategia

Recognizing the purpose of a text

When you are faced with an unfamiliar text, it is important to determine the writer's purpose. If you are reading an editorial in a newspaper, for example, you know that the journalist's objective is to persuade you of his or her point of view. Identifying the purpose of a text will help you better comprehend its meaning.

Examinar los textos

Primero, utiliza la estrategia de lectura para familiarizarte con los textos. Después contesta estas preguntas y compara tus respuestas con las de un(a) compañero/a. Answers will vary.

- ¿De qué tratan los textos?°
- ¿Son fábulas°, poemas, artículos de periódico...?
- ¿Cómo lo sabes?

Predicciones

Lee estas predicciones sobre la lectura e indica si estás de acuerdo° con ellas. Después compara tus opiniones con las de un(a) compañero/a. Answers will vary.

1. Los textos son del género° de ficción.
2. Los personajes son animales.
3. La acción de los textos tiene lugar en un zoológico.
4. Hay alguna moraleja°.

Determinar el propósito

Con un(a) compañero/a, hablen de los posibles propósitos° de los textos. Consideren estas preguntas: Answers will vary.

- ¿Qué te dice el género de los textos sobre los posibles propósitos de los textos?
- ¿Piensas que los textos pueden tener más de un propósito? ¿Por qué?

¿De qué tratan los textos? *What are the texts about?*
fábulas *fables* estás de acuerdo *you agree*
género *genre* moraleja *moral* propósitos *purposes*

Practice more at **vhlcentral.com**.

Sobre los autores

Félix María Samaniego (1745–1801) nació en España y escribió las *Fábulas morales* que ilustran de manera humorística el carácter humano. Los protagonistas de muchas de sus fábulas son animales que hablan.

El perro y el cocodrilo

Bebiendo un perro en el Nilo°,
al mismo tiempo corría.
"Bebe quieto°", le decía
un taimado° cocodrilo.

Díjole° el perro prudente:
"Dañoso° es beber y andar°;
pero ¿es sano el aguardar
a que me claves el diente°? "

¡Oh qué docto° perro viejo!
Yo venero° su sentir°
en esto de no seguir
del enemigo el consejo.

TEACHING OPTIONS

Pairs Pair more advanced students with those who have weaker language skills. Ask pairs to write a short description of the events in one of the fables presented here. Encourage them to use transitional words and expressions, such as **primero, finalmente, por eso,** and **entonces**.

Heritage Speakers Ask heritage speakers to describe any fables in Spanish with which they are familiar. If possible, have them bring in copies of the text. Then have a class discussion comparing the protagonists and moral of the fable to those in this **Lectura** section.

Tomás de Iriarte (1750–1791) nació en las islas Canarias y tuvo gran éxito° con su libro *Fábulas literarias*. Su tendencia a representar la lógica a través de° símbolos de la naturaleza fue de gran influencia para muchos autores de su época°.

El pato° y la serpiente

A orillas° de un estanque°,
diciendo estaba un pato:
"¿A qué animal dio el cielo°
los dones que me ha dado°?

"Soy de agua, tierra y aire:
cuando de andar me canso°,
si se me antoja, vuelo°;
si se me antoja, nado".

Una serpiente astuta
que le estaba escuchando,
le llamó con un silbo°,
y le dijo "¡Seo° guapo!

"No hay que echar tantas plantas°;
pues ni anda como el gamo°,
ni vuela como el sacre°,
ni nada como el barbo°;

"y así tenga sabido
que lo importante y raro°
no es entender de todo,
sino ser diestro° en algo".

Nilo *Nile* quieto *in peace* taimado *sly* Díjole *Said to him* Dañoso *Harmful* andar *to walk* ¿es sano... diente? *Is it good for me to wait for you to sink your teeth into me?* docto *wise* venero *revere* sentir *wisdom* éxito *success* a través de *through* época *time* pato *duck* orillas *banks* estanque *pond* cielo *heaven* los dones... dado *the gifts that it has given me* me canso *I get tired* si se... vuelo *if I feel like it, I fly* silbo *hiss* Seo *Señor* No hay... plantas *There's no reason to boast* gamo *deer* sacre *falcon* barbo *barbel (a type of fish)* raro *rare* diestro *skillful*

Después de leer

Comprensión

Escoge la mejor opción para completar cada oración.

1. El cocodrilo _____ perro.
   a. está preocupado por el (b.) quiere comerse al
   c. tiene miedo del
2. El perro _____ cocodrilo.
   (a.) tiene miedo del b. es amigo del
   c. quiere quedarse con el
3. El pato cree que es un animal _____.
   a. muy famoso b. muy hermoso
   (c.) de muchos talentos
4. La serpiente cree que el pato es _____.
   a. muy inteligente (b.) muy tonto c. muy feo

Comprensión
- To simplify, before beginning the activity, call on volunteers to explain the fables in their own words using Spanish.
- Encourage students to justify their answers by citing the text.

Preguntas

Contesta las preguntas. Answers will vary.

1. ¿Qué representa el cocodrilo?
   ____
2. ¿Qué representa el pato?
   ____
3. ¿Cuál es la moraleja (*moral*) de "El perro y el cocodrilo"?
   ____
4. ¿Cuál es la moraleja de "El pato y la serpiente"?
   ____

Preguntas For items 1 and 2, have the class brainstorm a list of adjectives to describe each animal.

Coméntalo

En parejas, túrnense para hacerse estas preguntas. ¿Estás de acuerdo con las moralejas de estas fábulas? ¿Por qué? ¿Cuál de estas fábulas te gusta más? ¿Por qué? ¿Conoces otras fábulas? ¿Cuál es su propósito? Answers will vary.

Coméntalo
For additional class discussion, have students imagine they must rewrite fables with the same morals, but using other animals as the protagonists. Ask students: **¿Qué animales escogen para sustituir a estos animales? ¿Cómo cambia la historia?**

Escribir

Escribe una fábula para compartir con la clase. Puedes escoger algunos animales de la lista o escoger otros. ¿Qué características deben tener estos animales? Answers will vary.

- una abeja (*bee*)
- un gato
- un mono
- un burro
- un perro
- una tortuga
- un águila (*eagle*)
- un pavo real (*peacock*)

Escribir
- Before writing, encourage students to outline their fables. Have them include the characters, the setting, the basic plot, and the moral in their outlines.
- If needed, supply additional vocabulary for students to describe the animals' characteristics. Ex: **sabio, perezoso, terco, fiel, lento, inquieto, orgulloso, egoísta, (im)paciente**

TEACHING OPTIONS

Extra Practice To challenge students, have them write a story from the viewpoint of the dog, the crocodile, the duck, or the snake, in which they explain their encounter with another animal and what they learned from the experience. You may want to review the imperfect and preterite tenses before assigning this activity.

Small Groups If time and resources permit, bring in other fables in Spanish, such as **Samaniego's *El herrero y el perro*** or ***La abeja haragana*** by **Horacio Quiroga**. Have students work in small groups to read and analyze one fable in terms of its characters and moral. Then have volunteers summarize their analyses for the class.

Section Goal

In **Panorama**, students will read about the geography, history, and culture of Colombia.

Instructional Resources
Supersite: Video (***Panorama cultural***); Resources (Scripts, Translations, Digital Image Bank, Answer Keys)
WebSAM
Workbook, pp. 165–166
Video Manual, pp. 61–62

Teaching Tips
- Use the **Lección 13 Panorama** digital images to assist with this presentation.
- Have students look at the map of Colombia and talk about the physical features of the country. Point out the three parallel ranges of the Andes in the west. After students look at the call-out photos and read the captions, point out that there are no major cities in the eastern half of the country. Ask students to suggest reasons for the lack of population in that area.

El país en cifras After reading the **Población** section, ask students what the impact might be of having 55% of the nation's territory unpopulated, and the sort of problems this might create for a national government. Point out that, although Spanish is the official language, some indigenous peoples speak **chibcha** and **araucano**.

¡Increíble pero cierto! In their desperation to recover the gold from Lake Guatavita, Spaniards made several attempts to drain the lake. Around 1545, **Hernán Pérez de Quesada** set up a bucket brigade that lowered the water level by a few meters, allowing a small amount of gold to be gathered.

Video: *Panorama cultural*
Interactive map

Colombia

NATIONAL STANDARDS connections cultures

El país en cifras

- **Área:** 1.138.910 km² (439.734 millas²), *tres veces el área de Montana*
- **Población:** 46.245.000

De todos los países de habla hispana, sólo México tiene más habitantes que Colombia. Casi toda la población colombiana vive en las áreas montañosas y la costa occidental° del país. Aproximadamente el 55% de la superficie° del país está sin poblar°.

- **Capital:** Bogotá —8.744.000
- **Ciudades principales:** Medellín —3.497.000, Cali —2.352.000, Barranquilla —1.836.000, Cartagena —978.600

Medellín

- **Moneda:** peso colombiano
- **Idiomas:** español (oficial); lenguas indígenas, criollas y gitanas

Bandera de Colombia

Palacio de San Francisco, Bogotá

Desfile en Cartagena

Feria de Cali

Colombianos célebres

- **Édgar Negret,** escultor°, pintor (1920–2012)
- **Juan Pablo Montoya,** automovilista (1975–)
- **Fernando Botero,** pintor, escultor (1932–)
- **Shakira,** cantante (1977–)
- **Sofía Vergara,** actriz (1972–)

occidental *western* superficie *surface* sin poblar *unpopulated* escultor *sculptor* dioses *gods* arrojaban *threw* oro *gold* cacique *chief* llevó *led*

recursos
WB pp. 165–166 | VM pp. 61–62 | vhlcentral.com Lección 13

¡Increíble pero cierto!

En el siglo XVI los exploradores españoles oyeron la leyenda de El Dorado. Esta leyenda cuenta que los indios, como parte de un ritual en honor a los dioses°, arrojaban° oro° a la laguna de Guatavita y el cacique° se sumergía en sus aguas cubierto de oro. Aunque esto era cierto, muy pronto la exageración llevó° al mito de una ciudad de oro.

Laguna de Guatavita

TEACHING OPTIONS

La música One of Colombia's contributions to Latin popular music is the dance called the **cumbia**. The **cumbia** was born out of the fusion of musical elements contributed by each of Colombia's three main ethnic groups: indigenous Andeans, Africans, and Europeans. According to ethnomusicologists, the flutes and wind instruments characteristically used in the **cumbia** derive from indigenous Andean music, the rhythms have their origin in African music, and the melodies are shaped by popular Spanish melodies. **Cumbias** are popular outside of Colombia, particularly in Mexico. Another Colombian dance, native to the Caribbean coast, is the **vallenato**, a fusion of African and European elements. If possible, bring in examples of **cumbias** and **vallenatos** for the class to listen to and compare and contrast.

Lugares • El Museo del Oro

El famoso Museo del Oro del Banco de la República fue fundado° en Bogotá en 1939 para preservar las piezas de orfebrería° de la época precolombina. Tiene más de 30.000 piezas de oro y otros materiales; en él se pueden ver joyas°, ornamentos religiosos y figuras que representaban ídolos. El cuidado con el que se hicieron los objetos de oro refleja la creencia° de las tribus indígenas de que el oro era la expresión física de la energía creadora° de los dioses.

Literatura • Gabriel García Márquez (1927–2014)

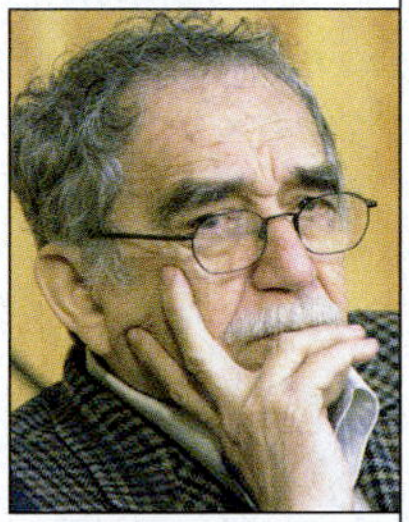

Gabriel García Márquez, ganador del Premio Nobel de Literatura en 1982, es considerado uno de los escritores más importantes de la literatura universal. García Márquez publicó su primer cuento° en 1947, cuando era estudiante universitario. Su libro más conocido, *Cien años de soledad*, está escrito en el estilo° literario llamado "realismo mágico", un estilo que mezcla° la realidad con lo irreal y lo mítico°.

Historia • Cartagena de Indias

Los españoles fundaron la ciudad de Cartagena de Indias en 1533 y construyeron a su lado la fortaleza° más grande de las Américas, el Castillo de San Felipe de Barajas. En la ciudad de Cartagena se conservan muchos edificios de la época colonial, como iglesias, monasterios, palacios y mansiones. Cartagena es conocida también por el Festival Internacional de Música y su prestigioso Festival Internacional de Cine.

Costumbres • El Carnaval

Durante el Carnaval de Barranquilla, la ciudad vive casi exclusivamente para esta fiesta. Este festival es una fusión de las culturas que han llegado° a las costas caribeñas de Colombia y de sus grupos autóctonos°. El evento más importante es la Batalla° de Flores, un desfile° de carrozas° decoradas con flores. En 2003, la UNESCO declaró este carnaval como Patrimonio de la Humanidad°.

¿Qué aprendiste? Contesta cada pregunta con una oración completa.

1. ¿Cuáles son las principales ciudades de Colombia? Bogotá, Medellín, Cali, Barranquilla y Cartagena son las ciudades principales de Colombia.
2. ¿Qué país de habla hispana tiene más habitantes que Colombia? México tiene más habitantes que Colombia.
3. ¿Quién era Édgar Negret? Édgar Negret era un escultor y pintor colombiano.
4. ¿Cuándo oyeron los españoles la leyenda de El Dorado? En el siglo XVI los españoles oyeron la leyenda.
5. ¿Para qué fue fundado el Museo del Oro? El museo fue fundado para preservar las piezas de orfebrería de la época precolombina.
6. ¿Quién ganó el Premio Nobel de Literatura en 1982? Gabriel García Márquez lo ganó.
7. ¿Qué construyeron los españoles al lado de la ciudad de Cartagena de Indias? Construyeron el Castillo de San Felipe de Barajas.
8. ¿Cuál es el evento más importante del Carnaval de Barranquilla? El evento más importante es la Batalla de Flores.

Conexión Internet Investiga estos temas en **vhlcentral.com**.

Practice more at **vhlcentral.com**.

1. Busca información sobre las ciudades más grandes de Colombia. ¿Qué lugares de interés hay en estas ciudades? ¿Qué puede hacer un(a) turista en estas ciudades?
2. Busca información sobre pintores y escultores colombianos como Édgar Negret, Débora Arango o Fernando Botero. ¿Cuáles son algunas de sus obras más conocidas? ¿Cuáles son sus temas?

fundado *founded* **orfebrería** *goldsmithing* **joyas** *jewelry* **creencia** *belief* **creadora** *creative* **cuento** *story* **estilo** *style* **mezcla** *mixes* **mítico** *mythical* **fortaleza** *fortress* **han llegado** *have arrived* **autóctonos** *indigenous* **Batalla** *Battle* **desfile** *parade* **carrozas** *floats* **Patrimonio de la Humanidad** *World Heritage*

TEACHING OPTIONS

Worth Noting Colombia, like other mountainous countries near the equator, does not experience the four seasons that are known in parts of the United States and Canada. The average temperature of a given location does not vary much during the course of a year. Climate, however, changes dramatically with elevation, the higher altitudes being cooler than the low-lying ones. While the average temperature at sea level is 86°, 57° is the average temperature in Bogotá, the third highest capital in the world, behind La Paz, Bolivia, and Quito, Ecuador. When Colombians speak of **verano** or **invierno**, they are referring to the dry season (**verano**) and the rainy season (**invierno**). When these seasons occur varies from one part of the country to another. In the Andean region, the **verano**, or dry season, generally falls between December and March.

El Museo del Oro In pre-Columbian times, the native peoples from different regions of Colombia developed distinct styles of working with gold. Some preferred to melt copper into the metal before working it, some pounded the gold, while others poured it into molds. If possible, bring additional photos of pre-Columbian gold-work.

Gabriel García Márquez (1927–2014) **García Márquez** was raised primarily by his maternal grandparents, who made a profound impression upon his life and literature. His grandfather was a man of strong ideals and a military hero. His grandmother, who held many superstitious beliefs, regaled the young **García Márquez** with fantastical stories.

Cartagena de Indias Since Cartagena de Indias was the point of departure for shipments of Andean gold to Spain, it was the frequent target of pirate attacks from the sixteenth through the eighteenth centuries. The most famous siege was led by the English pirate Sir Francis Drake, in 1586. He held the city for 100 days, until the residents surrendered to him some 100,000 pieces of gold.

El Carnaval The many events that make up the **Carnaval de Barranquilla** are spread out over about a month. Although the carnival queen is crowned at the beginning of the festivities, the real opening act is the **Guacherna**, which is a nighttime street parade involving **comparsas** (live bands) and costumed dancers. The **Carnaval's** official slogan is **¡Quien lo vive es quien lo goza!**

Conexión Internet Students will find supporting Internet activities and links at **vhlcentral.com**.

Section Goal

In **Panorama**, students will read about the geography, economy, and culture of Honduras.

Instructional Resources
Supersite: Video (***Panorama cultural***); Resources (Scripts, Translations, Digital Image Bank, Answer Keys)
WebSAM
Workbook, pp. 167–168
Video Manual, pp. 63–64

Teaching Tips

- Use the **Lección 13 Panorama** digital images to assist with this presentation.
- Have students look at the map of Honduras and talk about the geographical features of the country. Hills and mountains cover three quarters of Honduras, with lowlands found only along coastal areas and in major river valleys. Deforestation is a major environmental challenge in Honduras. If deforestation continues at the current rate the country will have no trees in the next decade.

El país en cifras After reading about the indigenous populations of Honduras, tell students that the **misquito** people also live along the Caribbean coast of Nicaragua.

¡Increíble pero cierto! Although the Honduran justice system is not known for its fairness, the case of the artisan prisoners at the **Penitenciaría Central de Tegucigalpa** is a surprising example of business ethics. All profits from the sale of the crafts went directly to the creators: the prisoners themselves.

Honduras

NATIONAL STANDARDS connections cultures

El país en cifras

- **Área:** 112.492 km² (43.870 millas²), *un poco más grande que Tennessee*
- **Población:** 8.598.000

Cerca del 90 por ciento de la población de Honduras es mestiza. Todavía hay pequeños grupos indígenas como los jicaque, los misquito y los paya, que han mantenido su cultura sin influencias exteriores y que no hablan español.

- **Capital:** Tegucigalpa—1.088.000

Tegucigalpa

- **Ciudades principales:** San Pedro Sula, El Progreso, La Ceiba
- **Moneda:** lempira
- **Idiomas:** español (oficial), lenguas indígenas, inglés

Bandera de Honduras

Hondureños célebres

- **José Antonio Velásquez,** pintor (1906–1983)
- **Argentina Díaz Lozano,** escritora (1912–1999)
- **Carlos Roberto Reina,** juez° y presidente del país (1926–2003)
- **Roberto Sosa,** escritor (1930–2011)
- **Salvador Moncada,** científico (1944–)

juez *judge* presos *prisoners* madera *wood* hamacas *hammocks*

Guacamayo

Mercado en San Pedro Sula

Lago de Yojoa

recursos
WB pp. 167–168 | VM pp. 63–64 | vhlcentral.com Lección 13

¡Increíble pero cierto!

¿Irías de compras a una prisión? Hace un tiempo, cuando la Penitenciaría Central de Tegucigalpa aún funcionaba, los presos° hacían objetos de madera°, hamacas° y hasta instrumentos musicales y los vendían en una tienda dentro de la prisión. Allí, los turistas podían regatear con este especial grupo de artesanos.

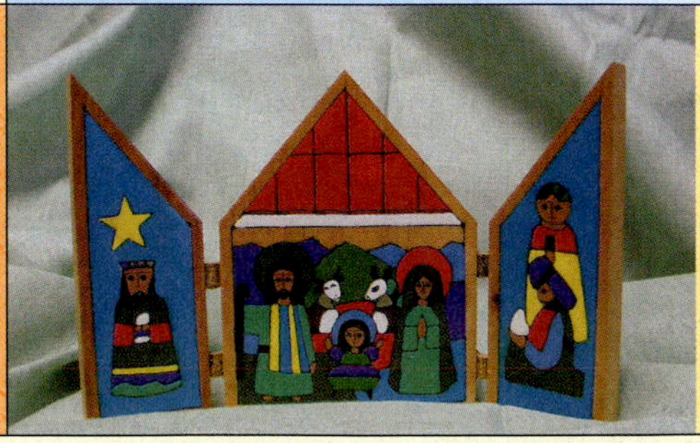

TEACHING OPTIONS

Worth Noting It was in Honduras, on his fourth voyage, that Christopher Columbus first set foot on the mainland of the continent now known as the Americas. On August 14, 1502, the navigator landed at a site near the town of Trujillo and named the country **Honduras** (*Depths*) because of the deep waters along the northern Caribbean coast.

Extra Practice Have students choose one of the people listed in **Hondureños célebres** and find out more about his or her work. They should report their findings to the class.

Lugares • Copán

Copán es una zona arqueológica muy importante de Honduras. Fue construida por los mayas y se calcula que en el año 400 d. C. albergaba° a una ciudad con más de 150 edificios y una gran cantidad de plazas, patios, templos y canchas° para el juego de pelota°. Las ruinas más famosas del lugar son los edificios adornados con esculturas pintadas a mano, los cetros° ceremoniales de piedra y el templo Rosalila.

Economía • Las plantaciones de bananas

Desde hace más de cien años, las bananas son la exportación principal de Honduras y han tenido un papel fundamental en su historia. En 1899, la Standard Fruit Company empezó a exportar bananas del país centroamericano hacia Nueva Orleans. Esta fruta resultó tan popular en los Estados Unidos que generó grandes beneficios° para esta compañía y para la United Fruit Company, otra empresa norteamericana. Estas trasnacionales intervinieron muchas veces en la política hondureña debido° al enorme poder° económico que alcanzaron° en la nación.

San Antonio de Oriente, 1957, José Antonio Velásquez

Artes • José Antonio Velásquez (1906–1983)

José Antonio Velásquez fue un famoso pintor hondureño. Es catalogado como primitivista° porque sus obras° representan aspectos de la vida cotidiana. En la pintura° de Velásquez es notorio el énfasis en los detalles°, la falta casi total de los juegos de perspectiva y la pureza en el uso del color. Por todo ello, el artista ha sido comparado con importantes pintores europeos del mismo género° como Paul Gauguin o Emil Nolde.

¿Qué aprendiste? Contesta cada pregunta con una oración completa.

1. ¿Qué es el lempira?
   El lempira es la moneda nacional de Honduras.
2. ¿Por qué es famoso Copán?
   Porque es el sitio arqueológico más importante de Honduras.
3. ¿Dónde está el templo Rosalila?
   El templo Rosalila está en Copán.
4. ¿Cuál es la exportación principal de Honduras?
   Las bananas son la exportación principal de Honduras.
5. ¿Qué fue la Standard Fruit Company? La Standard Fruit Company fue una compañía estadounidense que exportaba bananas de Honduras e intervino muchas veces en la política hondureña.
6. ¿Cómo es el estilo de José Antonio Velásquez?
   El estilo de Velásquez es primitivista.
7. ¿Qué temas trataba Velásquez en su pintura?
   Velásquez pintaba aspectos de la vida cotidiana.

Conexión Internet Investiga estos temas en **vhlcentral.com**.

1. ¿Cuáles son algunas de las exportaciones principales de Honduras, además de las bananas? ¿A qué países exporta Honduras sus productos?
2. Busca información sobre Copán u otro sitio arqueológico en Honduras. En tu opinión, ¿cuáles son los aspectos más interesantes del sitio?

Practice more at **vhlcentral.com**.

albergaba *housed* canchas *courts* juego de pelota *pre-Columbian ceremonial ball game* cetros *scepters* beneficios *profits* debido a *due to* poder *power* alcanzaron *reached* primitivista *primitivist* obras *works* pintura *painting* detalles *details* género *genre*

Copán Recent archeological studies have focused on the abrupt disappearance of the Mayans from Copán around the ninth century C.E. Findings indicate that the Mayan dynasty suffered a sudden collapse that left the Copán valley virtually depopulated within a century. For more information about Copán, you may want to play the ***Panorama cultural*** video footage for this lesson.

Las plantaciones de bananas When Hurricane Mitch struck Central America in October 1998, it not only wiped out much of the infrastructure of Honduras, but also destroyed 60% of the projected agricultural exports. Today's agricultural problems are due to rampant deforestation and consequent drought and soil erosion.

José Antonio Velásquez The primitive style established by **José Antonio Velásquez** is now being carried on by his son, **Tulio Velásquez. Tulio**, who was taught by his father, had his first exhibition in 1959. Since then, his primitive art has been exhibited throughout the Americas, in Europe, and in Asia. Have students view works by each artist and then write a brief comparison of their styles.

Conexión Internet Students will find supporting Internet activities and links at **vhlcentral.com**.

TEACHING OPTIONS

Worth Noting Honduras was among the hardest hit of the Central American nations when Hurricane Mitch struck in late October 1998. Major roadways and bridges were destroyed, entire communities were covered in mud, and an air of hopelessness and desperation pervaded the country. With one of the lowest per capita income levels and one of the highest illiteracy rates in Central America, Hondurans were already struggling before the devastation of the hurricane. Since then, the economy has grown about 7% per year, but half of the population still remains below the poverty line.

Heritage Speakers Ask heritage speakers to research one of the Honduran topics mentioned in **Panorama** and write a three-paragraph essay about it. They may then present their findings orally to the class.

Instructional Resources
Supersite: Audio (Textbook & Lab MP3s); Testing Program (Tests, MP3s)
WebSAM
Lab Manual, p. 78

La naturaleza

el árbol	*tree*
el bosque (tropical)	*(tropical; rain) forest*
el cielo	*sky*
el cráter	*crater*
el desierto	*desert*
la estrella	*star*
la flor	*flower*
la hierba	*grass*
el lago	*lake*
la luna	*moon*
la naturaleza	*nature*
la nube	*cloud*
la piedra	*stone*
la planta	*plant*
el río	*river*
la selva, la jungla	*jungle*
el sendero	*trail; path*
el sol	*sun*
la tierra	*land; soil*
el valle	*valley*
el volcán	*volcano*

Los animales

el animal	*animal*
el ave, el pájaro	*bird*
la ballena	*whale*
el gato	*cat*
el mono	*monkey*
el perro	*dog*
el pez (sing.), los peces (pl.)	*fish*
la tortuga (marina)	*(sea) turtle*
la vaca	*cow*

Vocabulary Tools

recursos

LM p. 78 | vhlcentral.com Lección 13

El medio ambiente

el calentamiento global	*global warming*
el cambio climático	*climate change*
la conservación	*conservation*
la contaminación (del aire; del agua)	*(air; water) pollution*
la deforestación	*deforestation*
la ecología	*ecology*
el/la ecologista	*ecologist*
el ecoturismo	*ecotourism*
la energía (nuclear, solar)	*(nuclear, solar) energy*
el envase	*container*
la extinción	*extinction*
la fábrica	*factory*
el gobierno	*government*
la lata	*(tin) can*
la ley	*law*
el medio ambiente	*environment*
el peligro	*danger*
la (sobre)población	*(over)population*
el reciclaje	*recycling*
el recurso natural	*natural resource*
la solución	*solution*
cazar	*to hunt*
conservar	*to conserve*
contaminar	*to pollute*
controlar	*to control*
cuidar	*to take care of*
dejar de (+ *inf.*)	*to stop (doing something)*
desarrollar	*to develop*
descubrir	*to discover*
destruir	*to destroy*
estar afectado/a (por)	*to be affected (by)*
estar contaminado/a	*to be polluted*
evitar	*to avoid*
mejorar	*to improve*
proteger	*to protect*
reciclar	*to recycle*
recoger	*to pick up*
reducir	*to reduce*
resolver (o:ue)	*to resolve; to solve*
respirar	*to breathe*
de aluminio	*(made) of aluminum*
de plástico	*(made) of plastic*
de vidrio	*(made) of glass*
ecológico/a	*ecological*
puro/a	*pure*
renovable	*renewable*

Las emociones

alegrarse (de)	*to be happy*
esperar	*to hope; to wish*
sentir (e:ie)	*to be sorry; to regret*
temer	*to be afraid*
es extraño	*it's strange*
es una lástima	*it's a shame*
es ridículo	*it's ridiculous*
es terrible	*it's terrible*
es triste	*it's sad*
ojalá (que)	*I hope (that); I wish (that)*

Las dudas y certezas

(no) creer	*(not) to believe*
(no) dudar	*(not) to doubt*
(no) negar (e:ie)	*(not) to deny*
es imposible	*it's impossible*
es improbable	*it's improbable*
es obvio	*it's obvious*
no cabe duda de	*there is no doubt that*
no hay duda de	*there is no doubt that*
(no) es cierto	*it's (not) certain*
(no) es posible	*it's (not) possible*
(no) es probable	*it's (not) probable*
(no) es seguro	*it's (not) certain*
(no) es verdad	*it's (not) true*

Conjunciones

a menos que	*unless*
antes (de) que	*before*
con tal (de) que	*provided (that)*
cuando	*when*
después de que	*after*
en caso (de) que	*in case (that)*
en cuanto	*as soon as*
hasta que	*until*
para que	*so that*
sin que	*without*
tan pronto como	*as soon as*

Past participles used as adjectives	*See page 438.*
Expresiones útiles	*See page 421.*

En la ciudad 14

Communicative Goals

You will learn how to:

- **Give advice to others**
- **Give and receive directions**
- **Discuss daily errands and city life**

contextos

pages 450–453

- City life
- Daily chores
- Money and banking
- At a post office

fotonovela

pages 454–457

Maru is racing against the clock to turn in her application for an internship at the **Museo de Antropología**. Between a car that won't start and long lines all over town, she'll need some help if she wants to meet her deadline.

cultura

pages 458–459

- City transportation
- Luis Barragán

estructura

pages 460–473

- The subjunctive in adjective clauses
- **Nosotros/as** commands
- The future
- **Recapitulación**

adelante

pages 474–479

Lectura: A short story
Panorama: Venezuela y la República Dominicana

A PRIMERA VISTA

- **¿Viven estas personas en un bosque, un pueblo o una ciudad?**
- **¿Dónde están, en una calle o en un sendero?**
- **¿Es posible que estén afectadas por la contaminación? ¿Por qué?**
- **¿Está limpio o sucio el lugar donde están?**

Lesson Goals

In **Lección 14**, students will be introduced to the following:

- names of commercial establishments
- banking terminology
- citing locations
- city transportation
- Mexican architect **Luis Barragán**
- subjunctive in adjective clauses
- **nosotros/as** commands
- future tense
- identifying point of view
- a video about Mexico City's subway system
- geographic, economic, and historical information about Venezuela and the Dominican Republic

A primera vista Here are some additional questions you can ask based on the photo: **¿Cómo es la vida en la ciudad? ¿Y en el campo? ¿Dónde prefieres vivir? ¿Por qué? ¿Es posible que una ciudad esté completamente libre de contaminación? ¿Cómo? ¿Qué responsabilidades tienen las personas que viven en una ciudad para proteger el medio ambiente?**

Teaching Tip Look for these icons for additional communicative practice:

	Interpretive communication
	Presentational communication
	Interpersonal communication

INSTRUCTIONAL RESOURCES

Supersite (vhlcentral.com)
Video: ***Fotonovela, Flash cultura, Panorama cultural***
Audio: Textbook and Lab MP3 Files
Activity Pack: Information Gap Activities, games, additional activity handouts
Resources: SAM Answer Key, Scripts, Translations, **Vocabulario adicional**, sample lesson plan, Grammar Presentation Slides, Digital Image Bank
Testing Program: Quizzes, Tests, Exams, MP3s
Student Activities Manual: Workbook/Video Manual/Lab Manual
WebSAM (online Student Activities Manual)

Section Goals

In **Contextos**, students will learn and practice:

- names of commercial establishments
- banking terminology
- citing locations

Instructional Resources
Supersite: Audio (Textbook and Lab MP3 Files); Resources (Digital Image Bank, **Vocabulario adicional**, Activity Pack, Scripts, Answer Keys); Testing Program (Quizzes)
WebSAM
Workbook, pp. 169–170
Lab Manual, p. 79

Teaching Tips

- Using realia or magazine pictures, ask volunteers to identify the items. Ex: **carne, zapato, pan**. As students give their answers, write the names of corresponding establishments on the board (**carnicería, zapatería, panadería**). Then present banking vocabulary by miming common transactions. Ex: **Cuando necesito dinero, voy al banco. Escribo un cheque y lo cobro.**
- Use the **Lección 14 Contextos** digital images to assist with this presentation.
- Ask the class questions about the illustrations in **Contextos**. Ex: **¿Qué tienda queda entre la lavandería y la carnicería? Las dos señoras al lado de la estatua, ¿de qué hablan? ¿Qué tipo de transacciones pueden hacerse en un banco?**

Successful Language Learning Ask students to imagine how they would use this vocabulary when traveling.

Note: At this point you may want to present ***Vocabulario adicional: Más vocabulario para la ciudad*** from the Supersite.

En la ciudad

Más vocabulario

la frutería	*fruit store*
la heladería	*ice cream shop*
la pastelería	*pastry shop*
la pescadería	*fish market*
la cuadra	*(city) block*
la dirección	*address*
la esquina	*corner*
el estacionamiento	*parking lot*
derecho	*straight (ahead)*
enfrente de	*opposite; facing*
hacia	*toward*
cruzar	*to cross*
doblar	*to turn*
hacer diligencias	*to run errands*
quedar	*to be located*
el cheque (de viajero)	*(traveler's) check*
la cuenta corriente	*checking account*
la cuenta de ahorros	*savings account*
ahorrar	*to save (money)*
cobrar	*to cash (a check)*
depositar	*to deposit*
firmar	*to sign*
llenar (un formulario)	*to fill out (a form)*
pagar a plazos	*to pay in installments*
pagar al contado/ en efectivo	*to pay in cash*
pedir prestado/a	*to borrow*
pedir un préstamo	*to apply for a loan*
ser gratis	*to be free of charge*

Variación léxica

cuadra ←→ manzana (*Esp.*)
estacionamiento ←→ aparcamiento (*Esp.*)
doblar ←→ girar; virar; dar vuelta
hacer diligencias ←→ hacer mandados

recursos
WB pp. 169–170 | LM p. 79 | vhlcentral.com Lección 14

TEACHING OPTIONS

Extra Practice Add an auditory aspect to this vocabulary presentation. Prepare and read aloud a series of mini-dialogues; have students name the place or activity. Ex: **1. —Señorita, ¿tienen números más grandes? —Sí, creo que le queda un 42. —Gracias. ¿Me los puedo probar aquí? (la zapatería) 2. —Perdón, ¿cómo llego a la carnicería? —Cruzas la plaza y está allá, en la esquina. —Ah, sí... ya la veo, al lado de la zapatería. Gracias. (indicar cómo llegar)** This activity may also be done in pairs.

Pairs Have students draw schematic maps of a city square and the surrounding blocks, labeling all establishments and streets. Then have them write a description of each establishment's location and exchange it with a partner. Have students re-create the map, based on the description. Finally have partners verify the accuracy of the two sets of maps.

Práctica

1 Escuchar Mira el dibujo. Luego escucha las oraciones e indica si lo que dice cada una es **cierto** o **falso**.

	Cierto	Falso		Cierto	Falso
1.	❍	✓	6.	✓	❍
2.	✓	❍	7.	✓	❍
3.	❍	✓	8.	❍	✓
4.	✓	❍	9.	❍	✓
5.	❍	✓	10.	✓	❍

2 ¿Quién la hizo? Escucha la conversación entre Telma y Armando. Escribe el nombre de la persona que hizo cada diligencia o una X si nadie la hizo. Una diligencia la hicieron los dos.

1. abrir una cuenta corriente Armando
2. abrir una cuenta de ahorros Telma
3. ir al banco Armando, Telma
4. ir a la panadería X
5. ir a la peluquería Telma
6. ir al supermercado Armando

3 Seleccionar Indica dónde haces estas diligencias.

banco	joyería	pescadería
carnicería	lavandería	salón de belleza
frutería	pastelería	zapatería

1. comprar galletas pastelería
2. comprar manzanas frutería
3. lavar la ropa lavandería
4. comprar mariscos pescadería
5. comprar pollo carnicería
6. comprar sandalias zapatería

4 Completar Completa las oraciones con las palabras más adecuadas.

1. El banco me regaló un reloj. Fue gratis.
2. Me gusta ahorrar dinero, pero no me molesta gastarlo.
3. La cajera me dijo que tenía que firmar el cheque en el dorso (*on the back*) para cobrarlo.
4. Para pagar con un cheque, necesito tener dinero en mi cuenta corriente.
5. Mi madre va a un cajero automático para obtener dinero en efectivo cuando el banco está cerrado.
6. Cada viernes, Julio lleva su cheque al banco y lo cobra para tener dinero en efectivo.
7. Ana deposita su cheque en su cuenta de ahorros.
8. Cuando viajas, es buena idea llevar cheques de viajero.

1 Teaching Tip Have students check their answers by reading each statement in the script to the class and asking volunteers to say whether it is true or false. To challenge students, have them correct the false statements.

1 Script 1. El supermercado queda al este de la plaza, al lado de la joyería. 2. La zapatería está al lado de la carnicería. 3. El banco queda al sur de la plaza. 4. Cuando sales de la zapatería, la lavandería está a su lado. 5. La carnicería está al lado del banco. *Script continues on page 452.*

2 Teaching Tip Do this listening exercise as a TPR activity. Have students raise their right hand if **Armando** did the errand, their left hand if it was **Telma**, or both hands if both people did it.

2 Script TELMA: Hola, Armando, ¿qué tal? ARMANDO: Pues bien. Acabo de hacer unas diligencias. Fui a la carnicería y al supermercado. ¿Y tú? Estás muy guapa. ¿Fuiste a la peluquería? T: Sí, fui al nuevo salón de belleza que está enfrente de la panadería. También fui al banco. A: ¿A qué banco fuiste? T: Fui al banco Mercantil. Está aquí en la esquina. A: Ah, ¿sí? Yo abrí una cuenta corriente ayer, ¡y fue gratis! T: Sí, yo abrí una cuenta de ahorros esta mañana y no me cobraron nada. *Textbook MP3s*

3 Expansion After students finish, ask them what else can be bought or done in each establishment. Ex: **¿Qué más podemos comprar en la pastelería?**

4 Expansion Ask students to compare and contrast aspects of banking. Ex: ATM vs. traditional tellers; paying bills online vs. by check; savings account vs. checking account. Have them work in groups of three to make a list of **Ventajas** and **Desventajas**.

TEACHING OPTIONS

Game Add a visual aspect to this vocabulary presentation by playing **Concentración**. On eight cards, write names of types of commercial establishments. On another eight cards, draw or paste a picture that matches each commercial establishment. Place the cards facedown in four rows of four. In pairs, students select two cards. If the cards match, the pair keeps them. If the cards do not match, students replace them in their original position. The pair with the most cards at the end wins.

Pairs Have each student write a shopping list with ten items. Have students include items found in different stores. Then have them exchange their shopping list with a partner. Each student tells his or her partner where to go to get each item. Ex: **unas botas (Para comprar unas botas, tienes que ir a la zapatería que queda en la calle ____.)**

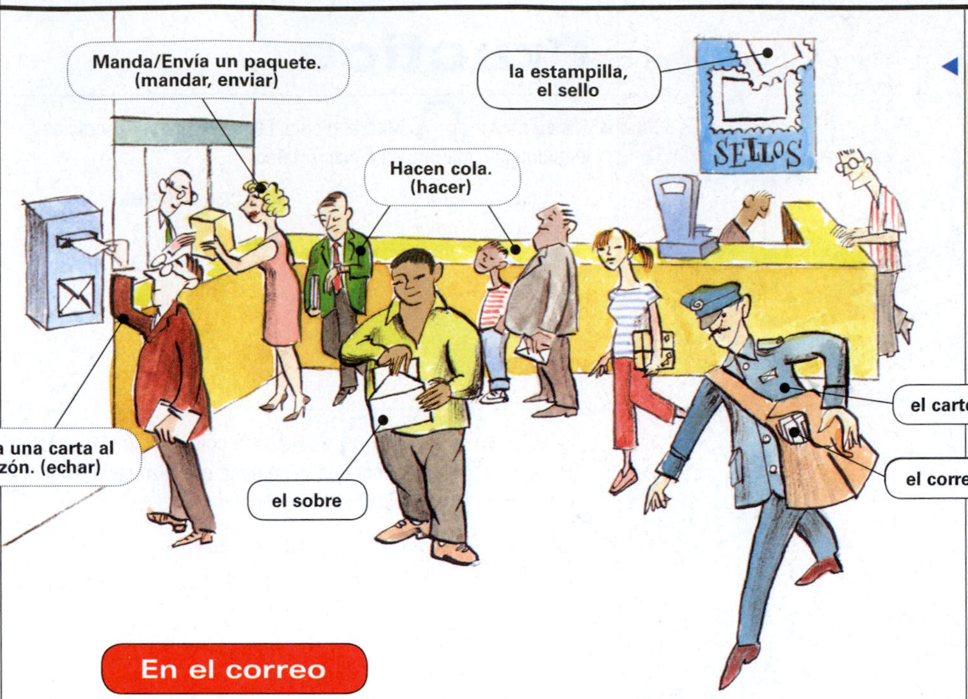

En el correo

¡LENGUA VIVA! Note that **correo** can mean either *mail* or *post office*. Other ways to say *post office* are **la oficina de correos** and **correos.**

5 Conversación Completa la conversación entre Juanita y el cartero con las palabras más adecuadas.

CARTERO Buenas tardes, ¿es usted la señorita Ramírez? Le traigo un (1) ___paquete___.
JUANITA Sí, soy yo. ¿Quién lo envía?
CARTERO La señora Brito. Y también tiene dos (2) ___cartas___.
JUANITA Ay, pero ¡ninguna es de mi novio! ¿No llegó nada de Manuel Fuentes?
CARTERO Sí, pero él echó la carta al (3) ___buzón___ sin poner un (4) ___sello___ en el sobre.
JUANITA Entonces, ¿qué recomienda usted que haga?
CARTERO Sugiero que vaya al (5) ___correo___. Con tal de que pague el costo del sello, se le puede dar la carta sin ningún problema.
JUANITA Uy, otra diligencia, y no tengo mucho tiempo esta tarde para (6) ___hacer___ cola en el correo, pero voy enseguida. ¡Ojalá que sea una carta de amor!

¡LENGUA VIVA! In Spanish, **Soy yo** means *That's me or It's me.* **¿Eres tú?/ ¿Es usted?** means *Is that you?*

6 En el banco Tú eres un(a) empleado/a de banco y tu compañero/a es un(a) estudiante universitario/a que necesita abrir una cuenta corriente. En parejas, hagan una lista de las palabras que pueden necesitar para la conversación. Después lean estas situaciones y modifiquen su lista original según la situación. Answers will vary.

- una pareja de recién casados quiere pedir un préstamo para comprar una casa
- una persona quiere información de los servicios que ofrece el banco
- un(a) estudiante va a estudiar al extranjero (*abroad*) y quiere saber qué tiene que hacer para llevar su dinero de una forma segura
- una persona acaba de ganar 50 millones de dólares en la lotería y quiere saber cómo invertirlos (*invest them*)

Ahora, escojan una de las cuatro situaciones y represéntenla para la clase.

Practice more at **vhlcentral.com**.

1 Script (continued)
6. Cuando sales de la joyería, el cajero automático está a su lado. 7. No hay ninguna heladería cerca de la plaza. 8. La joyería está al oeste de la peluquería. 9. Hay una frutería al norte de la plaza. 10. No hay ninguna pastelería cerca de la plaza. *Textbook MP3s*

Teaching Tips
- Use the **Lección 14 Contextos** digital images to assist with this vocabulary presentation.
- Ask students questions about the scene to elicit active vocabulary. Ex: **¿Qué hace la señora en la ventanilla? Y las personas que esperan detrás de ella, ¿qué hacen?** Then, involve students in a conversation about sending mail and the post office. Ex: **Necesito estampillas. ¿Dónde está el correo que está más cerca de aquí? A mí me parece que la carta es una forma de escritura en vías de extinción. Desde que uso el correo electrónico y los mensajes de texto, casi nunca escribo cartas. ¿Quiénes todavía escriben cartas?**

5 Expansion
- After you have gone over the activity, have pairs role-play the conversation, encouraging them to ad-lib as they go.
- Have pairs create short conversations similar to the one presented in the activity, but set in a different place of business. Ex: **el salón de belleza, la pescadería**

6 Teaching Tips
- To simplify, create a word bank of useful phrases on the board. Ask volunteers to suggest expressions.
- Go over the new vocabulary by asking questions. Ex: **¿Cuándo pedimos un préstamo? ¿Los cheques son para una cuenta corriente o una cuenta de ahorros?**

TEACHING OPTIONS

Extra Practice Ask students to research specific information about a bank in a Spanish-speaking country. Have them write a summary of branches, services, rates, and hours.
Pairs Have pairs list the five best places for local students. Ex: **la mejor pizza, el mejor corte de pelo**. Then have them write directions to each place from campus. Expand by having students debate their choices.

Game Divide the class into two teams and have them sit in two rows facing one another, so that a person from team A is directly across from a person from team B. Begin with the first two students and work your way down the rows. Say a word, and the first student to say an associated word wins a point for his or her team. Ex: You say: **correo**. The first person from team B answers: **sello**. Team B wins one point.

Comunicación

7

Diligencias En parejas, decidan quién va a hacer cada diligencia y cuál es la manera más rápida de llegar a los diferentes lugares desde el campus. Answers will vary.

modelo

cobrar unos cheques
Estudiante 1: *Yo voy a cobrar unos cheques. ¿Cómo llego al banco?*
Estudiante 2: *Conduce hacia el norte hasta cruzar la calle Oak. El banco queda en la esquina a la izquierda.*

1. enviar un paquete
2. comprar botas nuevas
3. comprar un pastel de cumpleaños
4. lavar unas camisas
5. comprar helado
6. cortarse (*to cut*) el pelo

AYUDA

Note these different meanings:
quedar *to be located; to be left over; to fit*
quedarse *to stay, to remain*

8

El Hatillo Trabajen en parejas para representar los papeles de un(a) turista que está perdido/a en El Hatillo y de un(a) residente de la ciudad que quiere ayudarlo/la. Answers will vary.

modelo

Plaza Sucre, café Primavera
Estudiante 1: *Perdón, ¿por dónde queda la Plaza Sucre?*
Estudiante 2: *Del café Primavera, camine derecho por la calle Sucre hasta cruzar la calle Comercio…*

1. Plaza Bolívar, farmacia
2. Casa de la Cultura, Plaza Sucre
3. banco, terminal
4. estacionamiento (este), escuela
5. Plaza Sucre, estacionamiento (oeste)
6. joyería, banco
7. farmacia, joyería
8. zapatería, iglesia

NOTA CULTURAL

El Hatillo es un municipio del área metropolitana de Caracas. Forma parte del Patrimonio Cultural de Venezuela y es muy popular por su arquitectura pintoresca, sus restaurantes y sus tiendas de artesanía.

9

Cómo llegar En grupos, escriban un minidrama en el que unos/as turistas están preguntando cómo llegar a diferentes sitios de la comunidad en la que ustedes viven. Answers will vary.

7 Teaching Tip

Draw a map of your campus and nearby streets that includes symbols of public buildings. Ask students to use the map to answer your questions and direct you to different locations. Ex: **¿En qué calle queda el banco más cercano? Estoy en la esquina de ____ y ____. ¿Me pueden indicar cómo llegar a ______?**

8 Teaching Tips

- Go over the icons in the map's legend, finding the place each represents.
- Explain that the task is to give directions to the first place from the second place. Ask students to find **Plaza Sucre** and **café Primavera** on the map.

8 Expansion

Ask students to read about **El Hatillo** on the Internet and report back to the class with their findings.

9 Teaching Tips

- As a class, brainstorm different tourist sites in and around your area. Write them on the board.
- Using one of the places listed on the board, model the activity by asking volunteers to give driving directions from campus.

TEACHING OPTIONS

TPR Have students work in pairs. One partner is blindfolded and the other gives directions for getting from one place in the classroom to another. Ex: **¿Quieres llegar de tu escritorio a la puerta? Bueno, camina derecho cinco pasos. Da tres pasos a la izquierda. Luego dobla a la derecha y camina cuatro pasos para que no choques con el escritorio. Estás cerca de la puerta. Sigue derecho dos pasos más. Allí está la puerta.**

Game Divide the class into teams of three. Each must write directions to a particular commercial establishment close to campus. The teams read their directions, and the other teams try to guess what errand they are running. Each team that guesses correctly wins a point. The team with the most points wins.

Section Goals

In **Fotonovela**, students will:

- receive comprehensible input from free-flowing discourse
- learn functional phrases that preview lesson grammatical structures

Instructional Resources
Supersite: Video (***Fotonovela***); Resources (Scripts, Translations, Answer Keys)
WebSAM
Video Manual, pp. 27–28

Video Recap: Lección 13
Before doing this **Fotonovela** section, review the previous one with these questions:
1. ¿Adónde fueron Marissa y Jimena? (Fueron al santuario de tortugas.) 2. ¿Qué aprendieron allí? (Aprendieron sobre las normas para proteger a las tortugas.) 3. ¿Qué le pasó a Felipe durante el recorrido por la selva? (Se cayó.) 4. ¿Qué mentira les dijo Felipe a las chicas? (Les dijo que se perdió todo el recorrido.)

Video Synopsis **Maru** is racing against the clock to deliver her application for an internship at the **Museo de Antropología**. However, with **Miguel's** car broken down again, long lines at the bank, and heavy traffic, **Maru** needs her friend **Mónica's** help to meet the deadline.

Teaching Tip Ask students to predict what they would see and hear in an episode in which one of the characters runs into trouble when trying to get somewhere on time in a big city. Then, ask them a few questions to help them summarize this episode.

Corriendo por la ciudad

NATIONAL STANDARDS communication cultures

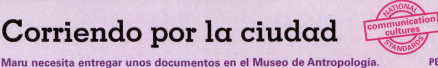

Maru necesita entregar unos documentos en el Museo de Antropología.

PERSONAJES

MARU

MIGUEL

Video: *Fotonovela*

1
MARU Miguel, ¿estás seguro de que tu coche está estacionado en la calle de Independencia? Estoy en la esquina de Zaragoza y Francisco Sosa. OK. Estoy enfrente del salón de belleza.

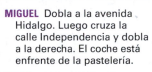

2
MIGUEL Dobla a la avenida Hidalgo. Luego cruza la calle Independencia y dobla a la derecha. El coche está enfrente de la pastelería.

MARU ¡Ahí está! Gracias, cariño. Hablaremos luego.

3
MARU Vamos, arranca. Pensé que podías aguantar unos kilómetros más. Necesito un coche que funcione bien. (*en el teléfono*) Miguel, tu coche está descompuesto. Voy a pasar al banco porque necesito dinero, y luego me iré en taxi al museo.

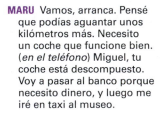

4
MARU Hola, Moni. Lo siento, tengo que ir a entregar un paquete y todavía tengo que ir a un cajero.

MÓNICA ¡Uf! Y la cola está súper larga.

5
MARU ¿Me puedes prestar algo de dinero?

MÓNICA Déjame ver cuánto tengo. Estoy haciendo diligencias, y me gasté casi todo el efectivo en la carnicería y en la panadería y en la frutería.

6
MÓNICA ¿Estás bien? Te ves pálida. Sentémonos un minuto.

MARU ¡No tengo tiempo! Tengo que llegar al Museo de Antropología. Necesito entregar...

MÓNICA ¡Ah, sí, tu proyecto!

TEACHING OPTIONS

Video Tips General suggestions for using video clips in the classroom can be found in the front matter of this Instructor's Annotated Edition.

Corriendo por la ciudad Play the **Corriendo por la ciudad** episode without sound and ask the class to summarize what they see. Then, ask them to predict the content of the episode and write their predictions on the board. Then play the entire episode with sound. Finally, through questions and discussion, lead the class to an accurate summary of the plot.

MÓNICA

7

MÓNICA ¿Puedes mandarlo por correo? El correo está muy cerca de aquí.

MARU El plazo para mandarlo por correo se venció la semana pasada. Tengo que entregarlo personalmente.

8

MARU ¿Me podrías prestar tu coche?

MÓNICA Estás muy nerviosa para manejar con este tráfico. Te acompaño. ¡No!, mejor, yo te llevo. Mi coche está en el estacionamiento de la calle Constitución.

9

MARU En esta esquina dobla a la derecha. En el semáforo, a la izquierda y sigue derecho.

MÓNICA Hay demasiado tráfico. No sé si podemos...

10

MARU Hola, Miguel. No, no hubo más problemas. Lo entregué justo a tiempo. Nos vemos más tarde. (*a Mónica*) ¡Vamos a celebrar!

recursos

VM pp. 27–28 | vhlcentral.com Lección 14

Expresiones útiles

Getting/giving directions

Estoy en la esquina de Zaragoza y Francisco Sosa.
I'm at the corner of Zaragoza and Francisco Sosa.
Dobla a la avenida Hidalgo.
Turn on Hidalgo Avenue.
Luego cruza la calle Independencia y dobla a la derecha.
Then cross Independencia Street and turn right.
El coche está enfrente de la pastelería.
The car is in front of the bakery.
En el semáforo, a la izquierda y sigue derecho.
Left at the light, then straight ahead.

Talking about errands

Voy a pasar al banco porque necesito dinero.
I'm going to the bank because I need money.
No tengo tiempo.
I don't have time.
Estoy haciendo diligencias, y me gasté casi todo el efectivo.
I'm running errands, and I spent most of my cash.

Asking for a favor

¿Me puedes prestar algo de dinero?
Could you lend me some money?
¿Me podrías prestar tu coche?
Could I borrow your car?

Talking about deadlines

Tengo que entregar mi proyecto.
I have to turn in my project.
El plazo para mandarlo por correo se venció la semana pasada.
The deadline to mail it in passed last week.

Additional vocabulary

acompañar *to accompany*
aguantar *to endure, to hold up*
ándale *come on*
pálido/a *pale*
¿Qué onda? *What's up?*

Expresiones útiles In the caption for video still 2, explain that **Hablaremos** is a future tense form. Have the class scan the caption for video still 3 for another example of the future (**iré**). Tell students that they will learn more about these structures in **Estructura**. Then point out the statement **Necesito un coche que funcione bien.** Explain that the subordinate clause functions as an adjective, and in this case requires the subjunctive because the existence of the car is unknown or indefinite. Finally, draw attention to the verb **Sentémonos** under video still 6 and explain that this is an example of a **nosotros/as** command. Tell students that they will learn more about these concepts in **Estructura**.

Teaching Tip Have students work in pairs to read the **Fotonovela** captions aloud. (Have the same student read both **Miguel** and **Mónica's** roles.) Then have volunteers ad-lib this episode for the class.

Nota cultural Taxis are cheap, quick, and easy to find in Mexico City. In fact, there are more than 250,000 taxis regulated by the government. Riders should be wary of the approximately 45,000 illegal taxis, or **taxis pirata**.

TEACHING OPTIONS

Extra Practice Photocopy the **Fotonovela** Videoscript (Supersite) and white out key vocabulary in order to make a master for a cloze activity. Distribute the copies and, as you play the **Corriendo por la ciudad** episode, have students fill in the blanks.

Pairs Ask pairs to create a skit in which a tourist asks for directions in a Spanish-speaking country. Tell them to use phrases from **Expresiones útiles**. Give the class sufficient time to prepare and rehearse the skits; then ask a few volunteers to role-play their skits for the class.

1 Expansion Give students these true/false statements as items 5–6: **5. Maru va al museo en taxi. (Falso. Mónica la lleva en su coche.) 6. Hay mucha gente en el cajero. (Cierto.)**

Nota cultural For timely delivery of correspondence in Mexico City, courier services are often used within the city limits, rather than the postal service. Some companies even have their own in-house messengers for such purposes.

2 Teaching Tip Write these sentences on separate slips of paper so that students can arrange them in the correct sequence.

3 Expansion Have pairs come up with an additional situation and then make a list of the errands that **Maru, Mónica,** and **Miguel** need to do in order to complete the task. Then have them read the list of errands aloud so the class can guess what the situation might be.

4 Possible Conversation
E1: Voy al supermercado y a la heladería. ¿Quieres ir conmigo?
E2: Sí, en cuanto termine mi almuerzo, te acompaño.
E1: Tengo que pasar por el banco porque necesito dinero.
E2: Yo también necesito ir al banco. ¿Hay un banco por aquí con cajero automático?
E1: Hay un cajero automático a tres cuadras de aquí. Queda en la calle Libertad.
E2: También necesito ir a la lavandería y al correo para mandar unas cartas.
E1: No hay problema… el correo y la lavandería están cerca del banco.
E2: Oye, ¿qué vas a hacer esta noche?
E1: Voy a ir a la fiesta que celebran para un amigo. ¿Quieres ir?
E2: ¡Sí, gracias!

¿Qué pasó?

1 **¿Cierto o falso?** Decide si lo que dicen estas oraciones es **cierto** o **falso**. Corrige las oraciones falsas.

	Cierto	Falso	
1. Miguel dice que su coche está estacionado enfrente de la carnicería.	○	✔	Miguel dice que su coche está estacionado enfrente de la pastelería.
2. Maru necesita pasar al banco porque necesita dinero.	✔	○	
3. Mónica gastó el efectivo en la joyería y el supermercado.	○	✔	Mónica gastó el efectivo en la carnicería, la panadería y la frutería.
4. Maru puede mandar el paquete por correo.	○	✔	Maru no puede mandar el paquete por correo.

2 **Ordenar** Pon los sucesos de la **Fotonovela** en el orden correcto.

a. Maru le pide dinero prestado a Mónica. 3
b. Maru entregó el paquete justo a tiempo (*just in time*). 6
c. Mónica dice que hay una cola súper larga en el banco. 2
d. Mónica lleva a Maru en su coche. 4
e. Maru dice que se irá en taxi al museo. 1
f. Maru le dice a Mónica que doble a la derecha en la esquina. 5

3 **Otras diligencias** En parejas, hagan una lista de las diligencias que Miguel, Maru y Mónica necesitan hacer para completar estas actividades. Answers will vary.

1. enviar un paquete por correo
2. pedir una beca (*scholarship*)
3. visitar una nueva ciudad
4. abrir una cuenta corriente
5. celebrar el cumpleaños de Mónica
6. comprar una nueva computadora portátil

MARU

MIGUEL

MÓNICA

4 **Conversación** Un(a) compañero/a y tú son vecinos/as. Uno/a de ustedes acaba de mudarse y necesita ayuda porque no conoce la ciudad. Los/Las dos tienen que hacer algunas diligencias y deciden hacerlas juntos/as. Preparen una conversación breve incluyendo planes para ir a estos lugares. Answers will vary.

modelo
Estudiante 1: Necesito lavar mi ropa. ¿Sabes dónde queda una lavandería?
Estudiante 2: Sí. Aquí a dos cuadras hay una. También tengo que lavar mi ropa. ¿Qué te parece si vamos juntos?

- un banco
- una lavandería
- un supermercado
- una heladería
- una panadería

AYUDA
primero *first*
luego *then*
¿Sabes dónde queda…? *Do you know where…is?*
¿Qué te parece? *What do you think?*
¡Cómo no! *But of course!*

Practice more at **vhlcentral.com.**

TEACHING OPTIONS

Extra Practice Add an auditory aspect to this vocabulary practice. Prepare several sets of directions that explain how to get to well-known places on campus or in your community, without mentioning the destinations by name. Read each set of directions aloud and ask the class to tell you where they would end up if they followed your directions.

Pairs Tell pairs of students to imagine that one of them is a new student who is having trouble navigating the campus while doing some errands (Ex: mailing letters, getting cash from the ATM, and going to the bookstore). Ask them to write a dialogue between the new student and a passerby who helps him or her. Have a few pairs perform their dialogues for the class.

NATIONAL STANDARDS comparisons

Ortografía

Audio

Las abreviaturas

In Spanish, as in English, abbreviations are often used in order to save space and time while writing. Here are some of the most commonly used abbreviations in Spanish.

usted → **Ud.** **ustedes** → **Uds.**

As you have already learned, the subject pronouns **usted** and **ustedes** are often abbreviated

don → **D.** **doña** → **Dña.** **doctor(a)** → **Dr(a).**
señor → **Sr.** **señora** → **Sra.** **señorita** → **Srta.**

These titles are frequently abbreviated.

centímetro → **cm** **metro** → **m** **kilómetro** → **km**
litro → **l** **gramo** → **g** **kilogramo** → **kg**

The abbreviations for these units of measurement are often used, but without periods.

por ejemplo → **p. ej.** **página(s)** → **pág(s).**

These abbreviations are often seen in books.

derecha → **dcha.** **izquierda** → **izq., izqda.**
código postal → **C.P.** **número** → **n.º**

These abbreviations are often used in mailing addresses.

Banco → **Bco.** **Compañía** → **Cía.**
cuenta corriente → **c/c.** **Sociedad Anónima (*Inc.*)** → **S.A.**

These abbreviations are frequently used in the business world.

Práctica Escribe otra vez esta información usando las abreviaturas adecuadas.

1. doña María Dña. María
2. señora Pérez Sra. Pérez
3. Compañía Mexicana de Inversiones Cía. Mexicana de Inversiones
4. usted Ud.
5. Banco de Santander Bco. de Santander
6. doctor Medina Dr. Medina
7. Código Postal 03697 C.P. 03697
8. cuenta corriente número 20-453 c/c., n.º 20-453

Emparejar En la tabla hay nueve abreviaturas. Empareja los cuadros necesarios para formarlas. S.A., Bco., cm, Dña., c/c., dcha., Srta., C.P., Ud.

S.	c.	C.	c	co.	U
B	c/	Sr	A.	D	dc
ta.	P.	ña.	ha.	m	d.

recursos

LM p. 80 | vhlcentral.com Lección 14

Section Goal

In **Ortografía**, students will learn some common Spanish abbreviations.

Instructional Resources
Supersite: Audio (Lab MP3 Files); Resources (Scripts, Answer Keys)
WebSAM
Lab Manual, p. 80

Teaching Tips

- Point out that the abbreviations **Ud.** and **Uds.** begin with a capital letter, though the spelled-out forms do not.
- Write **D., Dña., Dr., Dra., Sr., Sra.,** and **Srta.** on the board. Again, point out that the abbreviations begin with a capital letter, though the spelled-out forms do not.
- Point out that the period in **n.º** does not appear at the end of the abbreviation.
- Point out that **Ortografía** replaces **Pronunciación** in the Student Edition for **Lecciones 10–15**, but not in the Lab Manual. The **Recursos** box references the **Pronunciación** sections found in all lessons of the Lab Manual.

Successful Language Learning Tell students that the ability to recognize common abbreviations will make it easier for them to interpret written information in a Spanish-speaking country.

TEACHING OPTIONS

Pairs Working in pairs, have students write an imaginary mailing address that uses as many abbreviations as possible. Then have a few pairs write their work on the board, and ask for volunteers to read the addresses aloud.

Extra Practice Write a list of abbreviations on the board; each abbreviation should have one letter missing. Have the class fill in the missing letters and tell you what each abbreviation stands for. Ex: **U__., D__a., Bc__., d__ha., p__gs., __zq., S.__.**

Flash CULTURA

Section Goals

In **Cultura**, students will:

- read about city transportation
- learn transportation-related terms
- read about Mexican architect **Luis Barragán**
- read about nicknames for Latin American and Spanish cities

Instructional Resources
Supersite: Video (***Flash cultura***); Resources (Scripts, Translations, Answer Keys)
WebSAM
Video Manual, pp. 99–100

En detalle

Antes de leer Ask students to predict the content of this reading based on the title, photo, and map. Have them share with the class their experiences with public transportation.

Lectura

- Explain that most bus and subway stations have detailed maps with colors and station names in order to facilitate system use. Many stations are named after a neighborhood, an important building, or a monument in the area.
- Of the 195 stations in Mexico City's subway system, at least two downtown stations are attractions in themselves. **Insurgentes** is packed with market stalls and is a popular place for shopping. Near the national palace, **Pino Suárez** houses an Aztec pyramid, which was unearthed during the **metro's** construction.

Después de leer Ask students to give examples of U.S. or Canadian cities that have transit systems, and if possible what type (**autobús, metro, tranvía,** or **tren**).

1 Expansion Ask students to write three additional true/false statements for a partner to complete.

EN DETALLE

Video: *Flash cultura*

NATIONAL STANDARDS connections cultures

Paseando en metro

Hoy es el primer día de Teresa en la Ciudad de México. Debe tomar el metro para ir del centro de la ciudad a Coyoacán, en el sur. Llega a la estación Zócalo y compra un pasaje por el equivalente a treinta y nueve centavos° de dólar, ¡qué ganga! Con este pasaje puede ir a cualquier° parte de la ciudad o del área metropolitana.

No sólo en México, sino también en ciudades de Venezuela, Chile, Argentina y España, hay sistemas de transporte público eficientes y muy económicos. También suele haber° varios tipos de transporte: autobús, metro, tranvía°, microbús y tren. Generalmente se pueden comprar abonos° de uno o varios días para un determinado tipo de transporte. En algunas ciudades también existen abonos de transporte combinados que permiten usar, por ejemplo, el metro y el autobús o el autobús y el tren. En estas ciudades, los metros, autobuses y trenes pasan con mucha frecuencia. Las paradas° y estaciones están bien señalizadas°.

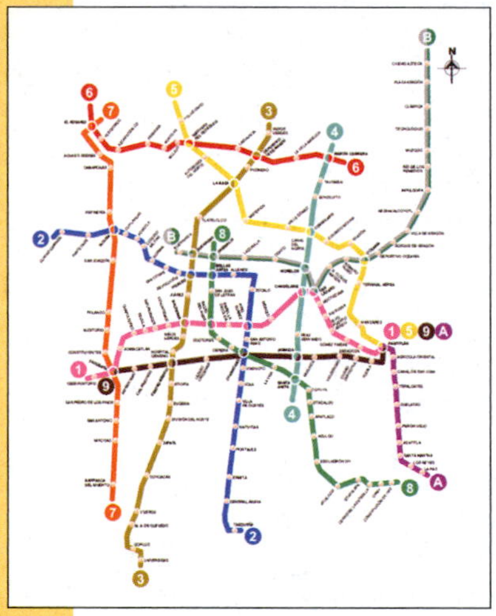

Vaya°, Teresa ya está llegando a Coyoacán. Con lo que ahorró en el pasaje del metro, puede comprarse un helado de mango y unos esquites° en el jardín Centenario.

El metro

El primer metro de Suramérica que se abrió al público fue el de Buenos Aires, Argentina (1913); el último, el de Lima, Perú (2011).

Ciudad	Pasajeros/Día (aprox.)
México D.F., México	5.200.000
Madrid, España	2.500.000
Santiago, Chile	2.400.000
Caracas, Venezuela	1.800.000
Buenos Aires, Argentina	1.000.000
Medellín, Colombia	770.000
Guadalajara, México	206.000

centavos *cents* **cualquier** *any* **suele haber** *there usually are* **tranvía** *streetcar* **abonos** *passes* **paradas** *stops* **señalizadas** *labeled* **Vaya** *Well* **esquites** *toasted corn kernels*

ACTIVIDADES

1 ¿Cierto o falso? Indica si lo que dice cada oración es cierto o falso. Corrige la información falsa.

1. En la Ciudad de México, el pasaje de metro cuesta 39 dólares. Falso. Cuesta 39 centavos de dólar.
2. En México, un pasaje se puede usar sólo para ir al centro de la ciudad. Falso. Se puede ir a cualquier parte de la ciudad o del área metropolitana.
3. En Chile hay varios tipos de transporte público. Cierto.
4. En ningún caso los abonos de transporte sirven para más de un tipo de transporte. Falso. Hay abonos combinados que permiten usar distintos tipos de transporte.
5. Los trenes, autobuses y metros pasan con mucha frecuencia. Cierto.
6. Hay pocos letreros en las paradas y estaciones. Falso. Las paradas y estaciones están bien señalizadas.
7. Los servicios de metro de México y España son los que mayor cantidad de viajeros transporta cada día. Cierto.
8. La ciudad de Buenos Aires tiene el sistema de metro más viejo de Latinoamérica. Cierto.
9. El metro que lleva menos tiempo en servicio es el de la ciudad de Medellín, Colombia. Falso. Es el de Lima, Perú.

TEACHING OPTIONS

Small Groups Have students work in small groups, research one of the transportation systems mentioned in the reading, and create an informational poster. Tell them to include a system map, the pricing scheme, a brief history, and any other significant information. Have groups present their posters to the class.

Pairs In pairs, have students use the Internet to research a map of a Spanish-speaking city's subway system and write a dialogue between a tourist trying to get to a museum and a subway ticket agent. Encourage students to use formal commands. Have pairs role-play their dialogues for the class.

ASÍ SE DICE

En la ciudad

el parqueadero (Col., Pan.) el parqueo (Bol., Cuba, Amér. C.)	el estacionamiento
dar un aventón (Méx.); dar botella (Cuba)	*to give (someone) a ride*
el subterráneo, el subte (Arg.)	el metro

EL MUNDO HISPANO

Apodos de ciudades

Así como Nueva York es la Gran Manzana, muchas ciudades hispanas tienen un apodo°.

- **La tacita de plata°** A Cádiz, España, se le llama así por sus edificios blancos de estilo árabe.
- **Ciudad de la eterna primavera** Arica, Chile; Cuernavaca, México, y Medellín, Colombia, llevan este sobrenombre por su clima templado° durante todo el año.
- **La docta°** Así se conoce a la ciudad argentina de Córdoba por su gran tradición universitaria.
- **La ciudad de los reyes** Así se conoce Lima, Perú, porque fue la capital del Virreinato° del Perú y allí vivían los virreyes°.
- **La arenosa** Barranquilla, Colombia, se le llama así por sus orillas del río cubiertas° de arena.

apodo *nickname* **plata** *silver* **templado** *mild* **docta** *erudite* **Virreinato** *Viceroyalty* **virreyes** *viceroys* **cubiertas** *covered*

PERFIL

Luis Barragán: arquitectura y emoción

Para el arquitecto mexicano **Luis Barragán** (1902–1988) los sentimientos° y emociones que despiertan sus diseños eran muy importantes. Afirmaba° que la arquitectura tiene una dimensión espiritual. Para él, era belleza, inspiración, magia°, serenidad, misterio, silencio, privacidad, asombro°...

Casa Barragán, Ciudad de México, 1947-1948

Las obras de Barragán muestran un suave° equilibrio entre la naturaleza y la creación humana. Su estilo también combina la arquitectura tradicional mexicana con conceptos modernos. Una característica de sus casas son las paredes envolventes° de diferentes colores con muy pocas ventanas.

En 1980, Barragán obtuvo° el Premio Pritzker, algo así como el Premio Nobel de Arquitectura. Está claro que este artista logró° que sus casas transmitieran sentimientos especiales.

sentimientos *feelings* **Afirmaba** *He stated* **magia** *magic* **asombro** *amazement* **suave** *smooth* **envolventes** *enveloping* **obtuvo** *received* **logró** *managed*

Conexión Internet

¿Qué otros arquitectos combinan las construcciones con la naturaleza?

Go to **vhlcentral.com** to find more cultural information related to this **Cultura** section.

ACTIVIDADES

2 Comprensión Contesta las preguntas.

1. ¿En qué país estás si te dicen "Dame botella al parqueo"? en Cuba
2. ¿Qué ciudades tienen clima templado todo el año? Arica, Chile; Cuernavaca, México, y Medellín, Colombia
3. ¿Qué es más importante en los diseños de Barragán: la naturaleza o la creación humana? Son igual de importantes.
4. ¿Qué premio obtuvo Barragán y cuándo? Barragán obtuvo el Premio Pritzker en 1980.

3 ¿Qué ciudad te gusta? Escribe un párrafo breve sobre el sentimiento que despiertan las construcciones que hay en una ciudad o un pueblo que te guste mucho. Explica cómo es y cómo te sientes cuando estás allí. Inventa un apodo para este lugar. Answers will vary.

Practice more at **vhlcentral.com**.

recursos: VM pp. 99–100 | vhlcentral.com Lección 14

Así se dice To challenge students, add these words to the list: **el estanco (Esp.)** (*shop where tobacco, stamps, and postcards are sold*); **llevar** (*to give [someone] a ride*); **la nevería (Méx.)** (*ice cream shop*); **el parquímetro** (*parking meter*); **la perfumería** (*perfume shop*); **el quiosco** (*newsstand*); **la relojería** (*clock and watch shop*); **la tienda de abarrotes (Méx., Andes), la abarrotería (Guat., Méx., Pan.), la bodega (Cuba, Perú, Ven.), el colmado (R. Dom., P. Rico)** (*grocery store*).

Perfil **Luis Barragán** traveled extensively in Spain, France, and Morocco. These experiences inspired him to relate the architecture of North Africa and the Mediterranean to that of Mexico. In 2004, **Barragán's** home and studio were named a UNESCO World Heritage site.

El mundo hispano

- You may want to include other city nicknames. Ex: **Curramba, La Bella (Barranquilla, Colombia), La Atenas suramericana (Bogotá, Colombia), La ciudad blanca (Arequipa, Perú), La ciudad imperial (Cuzco, Perú), La perla del Pacífico (Guayaquil, Ecuador), La ciudad del Sol (Quilpué, Chile).**
- Ask students what city they would like to visit. They can share their responses with the class or write 3–4 sentences explaining their reasoning.

2 Expansion Give students these questions as items 5–6: **5. ¿En qué país estás si un amigo te da aventón a un lugar? (México) 6. ¿Qué ciudad argentina es conocida por su gran tradición universitaria? (Córdoba)**

3 Teaching Tip To simplify, have students work in small groups to brainstorm a list of descriptive adjectives and verbs of emotion.

TEACHING OPTIONS

Large Groups Divide the class into two groups. Give each member of the first group a card with a nickname from **El mundo hispano**. Give each member of the second group a card with the reason for the nickname. Have students circulate around the room, asking questions until they find their partners. Finally, have the class form a "map" of the cities. Ask pairs to read their cards aloud.

Extra Practice If time and resources permit, have students use the Internet or library to find and copy a picture of one of **Luis Barragán's** buildings or spaces. Ask them to write five sentences describing the photo. Also tell them to include their personal opinions. Encourage students to compare the work to another building or space with which they are familiar.

Section Goal

In **Estructura 14.1**, students will learn the use of the subjunctive in adjective clauses.

Instructional Resources
Supersite: Audio (Lab MP3 Files); Resources (Grammar Presentation Slides, Activity Pack, Scripts, Answer Keys); Testing Program (Quizzes)
WebSAM
Workbook, pp. 171–172
Lab Manual, p. 81

Teaching Tips

- Add a visual aspect to this grammar presentation. Use magazine pictures to compare and contrast the uses of the indicative and subjunctive in adjective clauses. Ex: **Esta casa tiene una fuente en el jardín. Yo busco una casa que tenga piscina. Este señor come insectos vivos. ¿Conocen a alguien que coma insectos vivos?**
- Ask volunteers to answer questions that describe their wishes. Ex: **¿Qué buscas en una casa? ¿Qué buscas en un(a) compañero/a de cuarto?**
- Ask volunteers to read the captions to the video stills and point out the subordinate adjective clause and its antecedent, then indicate whether the indicative or subjunctive is used in the clause, and why.
- Make sure to point out the role of the indefinite article vs. the definite article in determining the use of the subjunctive in adjective clauses. Show students the two sentences in **¡Atención!** and have them explain why the subjunctive is used in one, but not the other.

14.1 The subjunctive in adjective clauses

Tutorial

comparisons

ANTE TODO In **Lección 13**, you learned that the subjunctive is used in adverbial clauses after certain conjunctions. You will now learn how the subjunctive can be used in adjective clauses to express that the existence of someone or something is uncertain or indefinite.

¿Conoces una joyería que esté cerca?

No, no conozco ninguna joyería que esté cerca de aquí.

- The subjunctive is used in an adjective (or subordinate) clause that refers to a person, place, thing, or idea that either does not exist or whose existence is uncertain or indefinite. In the examples below, compare the differences in meaning between the statements using the indicative and those using the subjunctive.

Indicative	Subjunctive
Necesito **el libro** que **tiene** información sobre Venezuela. *I need **the book** that has information about Venezuela.*	Necesito **un libro** que **tenga** información sobre Venezuela. *I need **a book** that has information about Venezuela.*
Quiero vivir en **esta casa** que **tiene** jardín. *I want to live in **this house** that has a garden.*	Quiero vivir en **una casa** que **tenga** jardín. *I want to live in **a house** that has a garden.*
En mi barrio, hay **una heladería** que **vende** helado de mango. *In my neighborhood, **there's an ice cream shop** that sells mango ice cream.*	En mi barrio no hay **ninguna heladería** que **venda** helado de mango. *In my neighborhood, **there is no ice cream shop** that sells mango ice cream.*

- When the adjective clause refers to a person, place, thing, or idea that is clearly known, certain, or definite, the indicative is used.

Quiero ir **al supermercado** que **vende** productos venezolanos.
I want to go to the supermarket that sells Venezuelan products.

Busco **al profesor** que **enseña** japonés.
I'm looking for the professor who teaches Japanese.

Conozco **a alguien** que **va** a esa peluquería.
I know someone who goes to that beauty salon.

Tengo **un amigo** que **vive** cerca de mi casa.
I have a friend who lives near my house.

¡ATENCIÓN!

Adjective clauses are subordinate clauses that modify a noun or pronoun in the main clause of a sentence. That noun or pronoun is called the *antecedent*.

¡ATENCIÓN!

Observe the important role that the indefinite article vs. the definite article plays in determining the use of the subjunctive in adjective clauses. Read the following sentences and notice why they are different:

¿Conoces *un* restaurante italiano que *esté* cerca de mi casa?

¿Conoces *el* restaurante italiano que *está* cerca de mi casa?

TEACHING OPTIONS

Extra Practice To provide oral practice with adjective clauses in the subjunctive and indicative, create sentences that follow the pattern of the sentences in the examples. Say a sentence, have students repeat it, then change the main clause. Have students then say the sentence with the new clause, changing the subordinate clause as necessary. **Conozco una tienda donde venden helados riquísimos. (Busco una tienda donde...)**

Heritage Speakers Ask heritage speakers to describe business establishments in their cultural communities. They should use both the indicative and the subjunctive, varying the verbs in the main clause as much as possible. Have the rest of the class compare and contrast these establishments with those around your university.

▶ The personal **a** is not used with direct objects that are hypothetical people. However, as you learned in **Lección 7**, **alguien** and **nadie** are always preceded by the personal **a** when they function as direct objects.

Necesitamos **un empleado** que **sepa** usar computadoras.
We need an employee who knows how to use computers.

Necesitamos **al empleado** que **sabe** usar computadoras.
We need the employee who knows how to use computers.

Buscamos **a alguien** que **pueda** cocinar.
We're looking for someone who can cook.

No conocemos **a nadie** que **pueda** cocinar.
We don't know anyone who can cook.

▶ The subjunctive is commonly used in questions with adjective clauses when the speaker is trying to find out information about which he or she is uncertain. However, if the person who responds to the question knows the information, the indicative is used.

—¿Hay un parque que **esté** cerca de nuestro hotel?
Is there a park that's near our hotel?

—Sí, hay un parque que **está** muy cerca del hotel.
Yes, there's a park that's very near the hotel.

▶ **¡Atención!** Here are some verbs that are commonly followed by adjective clauses in the subjunctive:

Verbs commonly used with subjunctive

buscar	**haber**
conocer	**necesitar**
encontrar	**querer**

SECCIÓN AMARILLA
Busque cualquier información que necesite.

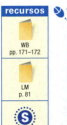

¡INTÉNTALO! Escoge entre el subjuntivo y el indicativo para completar cada oración.

recursos
WB pp. 171–172
LM p. 81
vhlcentral.com Lección 14

1. Necesito una persona que __pueda__ (puede/pueda) cantar bien.
2. Buscamos a alguien que __tenga__ (tiene/tenga) paciencia.
3. ¿Hay restaurantes aquí que __sirvan__ (sirven/sirvan) comida japonesa?
4. Tengo una amiga que __saca__ (saca/saque) fotografías muy bonitas.
5. Hay una carnicería que __está__ (está/esté) cerca de aquí.
6. No vemos ningún apartamento que nos __interese__ (interesa/interese).
7. Conozco a un estudiante que __come__ (come/coma) hamburguesas todos los días.
8. ¿Hay alguien que __diga__ (dice/diga) la verdad?

Teaching Tips

- Ask closed-ended questions, repeating the answer using complete sentences and the subjunctive. Ex: ____, **¿conoces a alguien que sepa hablar japonés? (No.) ____ no conoce a nadie que sepa japonés, pero ____ conoce a una joven japonesa que estudia inglés.**
- Test comprehension as you proceed by asking volunteers to supply the correct form of verbs for adjective clauses you suggest. Ex: **Prefiero la playa donde ____ menos gente. (hay) Prefiero una playa donde ____ menos gente. (haya)**
- Suggest main clauses with the verbs listed and ask students to write the adjective clause. Ex: **Necesito un coche que... ; Busco al señor que... ; No hay nadie que...**
- Ask a volunteer to read the Yellow Pages ad and explain why the verb **necesite** is in the subjunctive.

TEACHING OPTIONS

Pairs Ask pairs to rewrite the sentences in the **¡Inténtalo!** activity with the unused verbs **(puede, tiene, sirven, saque, esté, interesa, coma, dice)** and change the main clauses accordingly.

Extra Practice Ask students to imagine that they have the opportunity to build their ideal community. Have them write a paragraph describing what they need, want, and are looking for in this place, taking into account the climate, inhabitants, cultural and employment opportunities, architecture, leisure activities, geography, and so on. Their descriptions should include only sentences in the subjunctive. Refer them to the verbs in the list to help them develop their ideas.

1 Teaching Tip Briefly review the use of the indicative and subjunctive in adjective clauses. Write two contrasting sentences on the board. Ex: **Conozco una pastelería donde sirven café. No hay ninguna pastelería en este barrio donde sirvan café.** Then ask volunteers to explain why the indicative or subjunctive was used in each sentence.

2 Teaching Tip Have volunteers write each "rehydrated" sentence on the board. Ask other volunteers to point out why the subjunctive or indicative was used in each sentence.

2 Expansion Ask pairs to invent an ending to **Marta's** day of running errands by writing a few sentences using the subjunctive in adjective clauses. Ex: **No encuentro una estación de metro que quede cerca...**

3 Teaching Tips
- Ask volunteers to discuss the types of information found in classified ads. Write them on the board.
- Have students do the activity by studying the ads for a few minutes and then discussing them with a partner with their books closed.

3 Expansion Have pairs compose their own classified ad for one of the topics listed on the board but not covered in the activity.

Práctica

1

Completar Completa estas oraciones con la forma correcta del indicativo o del subjuntivo de los verbos entre paréntesis.

1. Buscamos un hotel que ___tenga___ (tener) piscina.
2. ¿Sabe usted dónde ___queda___ (quedar) el Correo Central?
3. ¿Hay algún buzón por aquí donde yo ___pueda___ (poder) echar una carta?
4. Ana quiere ir a la carnicería que ___está___ (estar) en la avenida Lecuna.
5. Encontramos un restaurante que ___sirve___ (servir) comida típica venezolana.
6. ¿Conoces a alguien que ___sepa___ (saber) mandar un *fax* por computadora?
7. Llamas al empleado que ___entiende___ (entender) este nuevo programa de computación.
8. No hay nada en este mundo que ___sea___ (ser) gratis.

2

Oraciones Marta está haciendo diligencias en Caracas con una amiga. Forma oraciones con estos elementos, usando el presente de indicativo o de subjuntivo. Haz los cambios que sean necesarios.

1. yo / conocer / un / panadería / que / vender / pan / cubano
   Yo conozco una panadería que vende pan cubano.
2. ¿hay / alguien / que / saber / dirección / de / un / buen / carnicería?
   ¿Hay alguien que sepa la dirección de una buena carnicería?
3. yo / querer / comprarle / mi / hija / un / zapatos / que / gustar
   Yo quiero comprarle a mi hija unos zapatos que le gusten.
4. ella / no / encontrar / nada / que / gustar / en / ese / zapatería
   Ella no encuentra nada que le guste en esa zapatería.
5. ¿tener / dependientas / algo / que / ser / más / barato?
   ¿Tienen las dependientas algo que sea más barato?
6. ¿conocer / tú / alguno / banco / que / ofrecer / cuentas / corrientes / gratis?
   ¿Conoces tú algún banco que ofrezca cuentas corrientes gratis?
7. nosotras / no / conocer / nadie / que / hacer / tanto / diligencias / como / nosotras
   Nosotras no conocemos a nadie que haga tantas diligencias como nosotras.
8. nosotras / necesitar / un / línea / de / metro / que / nos / llevar / a / casa
   Nosotras necesitamos una línea de metro que nos lleve a casa.

NOTA CULTURAL

El **metro** de Caracas empezó a funcionar en 1983, después de varios años de intensa publicidad para promoverlo (*promote it*). El arte fue un recurso importante en la promoción del metro. En las estaciones se pueden admirar obras (*works*) de famosos escultores venezolanos como Carlos Cruz-Diez y Jesús Rafael Soto.

3

Anuncios clasificados En parejas, lean estos anuncios y luego describan el tipo de persona u objeto que se busca. Answers will vary.

CLASIFICADOS

VENDEDOR(A) Se necesita persona dinámica y responsable con buena presencia. Experiencia mínima de un año. Horario de trabajo flexible. Llamar a Joyería Aurora de 10 a 13h y de 16 a 18h. Tel: 263-7553

PELUQUERÍA UNISEX Se busca persona con experiencia en peluquería y maquillaje para trabajar tiempo completo. Llamar de 9 a 13: 30h. Tel: 261-3548

COMPARTIR APARTAMENTO Se necesita compañera para compartir apartamento de 2 dormitorios en el Chaco. Alquiler $500 por mes. No fumar. Llamar al 951-3642 entre 19 y 22h.

CLASES DE INGLÉS Profesor de Inglaterra con diez años de experiencia ofrece clases para grupos o instrucción privada para individuos. Llamar al 933-4110 de 16:30 a 18:30.

SE BUSCA CONDOMINIO Se busca condominio en Sabana Grande con 3 dormitorios, 2 baños, sala, comedor y aire acondicionado. Tel: 977-2018.

EJECUTIVO DE CUENTAS Se requiere joven profesional con al menos dos años de experiencia en el sector financiero. Se ofrecen beneficios excelentes. Enviar currículum vitae al Banco Unión, Avda. Urdaneta 263, Caracas.

TEACHING OPTIONS

Pairs Have students write a description of the kind of place where they would like to vacation, using the subjunctive. Then have them exchange papers and suggest places that satisfy the desired characteristics. Ex: **Quiero ir de vacaciones a un lugar donde pueda esquiar en julio.... (Bariloche, Argentina, es un lugar donde puedes esquiar en julio.)**

Extra Practice Add an auditory aspect to this grammar practice. Prepare a series of sentences. Read each one twice, pausing to allow students time to write. Ex: **1. ¿Conoces una peluquería donde un corte de pelo no sea muy caro? 2. Sí, el salón de belleza que está al lado del banco tiene precios bajos. 3. No hay otra peluquería que tenga tan buen servicio. 4. Gracias, tú siempre me das consejos que me ayudan.** After, ask students to explain why the subjunctive was or wasn't used in each example.

Comunicación

4 **Subjuntivo** Completa estas frases de una manera lógica. Luego, con un(a) compañero/a, túrnense para comparar sus respuestas. Answers will vary.

modelo

Estudiante 1: *Tengo una novia que sabe bailar tango. ¿Y tú?*
Estudiante 2: *Yo tengo un novio que habla alemán.*

1. Deseo un trabajo (*job*) que...
2. Algún día espero tener un apartamento/una casa que...
3. Mis padres buscan un carro que..., pero yo quiero un carro que...
4. Tengo un(a) novio/a que...
5. Un(a) consejero/a (*advisor*) debe ser una persona que...
6. Me gustaría (*I would like*) conocer a alguien que...
7. En esta clase no hay nadie que...
8. No tengo ningún profesor que...

5 **Encuesta** Tu profesor(a) va a darte una hoja de actividades. Circula por la clase y pregúntales a tus compañeros/as si conocen a alguien que haga cada actividad de la lista. Si responden que sí, pregúntales quién es y anota sus respuestas. Luego informa a la clase de los resultados de tu encuesta. Answers will vary.

6 **¿Compatibles?** Vas a mudarte a un apartamento con dos dormitorios. Como no quieres pagar el alquiler tú solo/a, estás buscando a un(a) compañero/a para que viva contigo. Escribe un anuncio buscando a alguien con cuatro características que consideres importantes y pégalo en la pared de la clase. Puedes usar algunas de estas opciones u otras en tu anuncio y no olvides usar el subjuntivo. Answers will vary.

- cocinar
- escuchar hip-hop
- estar informado/a
- gustarle la política/el arte/los deportes
- llevarse bien con los animales
- ser vegetariano/a / limpio/a / optimista
- tener paciencia

modelo

Busco a alguien a quien no le guste el fútbol, que sea vegetariano, juegue videojuegos y le fascine la ciencia ficción.

Luego lee los anuncios de tus compañeros/as. ¿Con quién(es) podrías compartir tu apartamento? Busca tres candidatos/as y entrevístalos/las en dos minutos. Túrnate para entrevistar y ser entrevistado. ¿Encontraste a la persona ideal para que viva contigo? Answers will vary.

Síntesis

7 **Busca los cuatro** Tu profesor(a) te va a dar una hoja con ocho anuncios clasificados y a tu compañero/a otra hoja con ocho anuncios distintos a los tuyos. Háganse preguntas para encontrar los cuatro anuncios de cada hoja que tienen su respuesta en la otra. Answers will vary.

Practice more at **vhlcentral.com**.

TEACHING OPTIONS

Video Show the **Fotonovela** episode again and have students summarize it, using the subjunctive with adjective clauses. Ex: **Según Maru, Miguel necesita un carro que funcione bien. Mónica busca una joyería que esté cerca...**

Small Groups Ask students to bring in travel brochures or tourist information from the Internet. Divide the class into groups of four and have them write a short radio spot for one of the tourist locations using only the subjunctive and formal commands.

4 Teaching Tip Model the activity by giving a personal example. Write a sentence starter on the board and then complete it. Ex: **No conozco ningún restaurante cercano que... (No conozco ningún restaurante cercano que tenga un patio grande.)**

4 Expansion Assign students to groups of six and ask them to pick two responses and make a visual representation of them. Designate a student from each group to show the visual for the class to guess what the response was. Guesses should include an adjective clause.

5 Teaching Tip Distribute the ***Hojas de actividades*** (Activity Pack/Supersite) that correspond to this activity.

5 Expansion Have pairs write six original sentences with adjective clauses based on the answers of the **encuesta**. Three sentences should have subordinate clauses in the subjunctive.

6 Teaching Tip During the interview phase of the activity, encourage students to ask follow-up questions to gather more information that will aid them in determining compatibility. For example, if the interviewee generally likes animals and the interviewer has a cat, they should make sure that the potential roommate doesn't have any issues with cats.

7 Teaching Tip Divide the class into pairs and distribute the handouts from the Activity Pack (Activity Pack/Supersite) that correspond to this Information Gap Activity.

7 Expansion Have pairs write counterparts for two of the ads that do not have them. One ad should be for someone seeking to buy something and the other should be a "for sale" ad.

Section Goal
In **Estructura 14.2**, students will learn **nosotros/as** commands.

Instructional Resources
Supersite: Audio (Lab MP3 Files); Resources (Grammar Presentation Slides, Activity Pack, Scripts, Answer Keys); Testing Program (Quizzes)
WebSAM
Workbook, pp. 173–174
Lab Manual, p. 82

Teaching Tips
- Model the **nosotros/as** commands by making suggestions to the class. Begin by having students respond to **tú** and **ustedes** commands, and then add commands for the class as a whole. Ex: ____ **, abre el libro.** ____ **y** ____ **, abran el libro. Ahora todos, abramos el libro. Abrámoslo.**
- Check comprehension by asking volunteers to convert **vamos a** + [*infinitive*] suggestions into **nosotros/as** commands.

Successful Language Learning Ask students to think about how they might use the **nosotros/as** commands when they are out with a group of Spanish speakers.

14.2 Nosotros/as commands

Tutorial

NATIONAL comparisons STANDARDS

ANTE TODO You have already learned familiar (**tú**) commands and formal (**usted/ustedes**) commands. You will now learn **nosotros/as** commands, which are used to give orders or suggestions that include yourself and other people.

▶ **Nosotros/as** commands correspond to the English *Let's*.

***Nosotros/as* commands**

Infinitive	*Nosotros/as* form of present subjunctive	*Nosotros/as* command
cruzar	crucemos	**(no) crucemos**
comer	comamos	**(no) comamos**
escribir	escribamos	**(no) escribamos**
pedir	pidamos	**(no) pidamos**
salir	salgamos	**(no) salgamos**
volver	volvamos	**(no) volvamos**

▶ As the chart shows, both affirmative and negative **nosotros/as** commands are generally formed by using the first-person plural form of the present subjunctive.

Crucemos la calle.
Let's cross the street.

No crucemos la calle.
Let's not cross the street.

CONSULTA
Remember that stem-changing **–ir** verbs have an additional stem change in the **nosotros/as** and **vosotros/as** forms of the present subjunctive. To review these forms, see **Estructura 12.3**, p. 395.

▶ The affirmative *Let's* + [*verb*] command may also be expressed with **vamos a** + [*infinitive*]. Remember, however, that **vamos a** + [*infinitive*] can also mean *we are going to (do something)*. Context and tone of voice determine which meaning is being expressed.

Vamos a cruzar la calle.
Let's cross the street.

Vamos a trabajar mucho.
We're going to work a lot.

▶ To express *Let's go*, the present indicative form of **ir** (**vamos**) is used, not the subjunctive. For the negative command, however, the subjunctive is used.

Vamos a la pescadería.
Let's go to the fish market.

No **vayamos** a la pescadería.
Let's not go to the fish market.

Pensemos, ¿adónde fuiste hoy?

¡Eso es! ¡El carro de Miguel! Vamos.

TEACHING OPTIONS

TPR Brainstorm gestures related to this lesson's vocabulary. Have students stand. At random, call out **nosotros/as** commands. All students should perform the appropriate gesture. Keep a brisk pace. Ex: **Echemos una carta al buzón. Hagamos cola. Firmemos un cheque. Paguemos en efectivo. Llenemos un formulario.**

Extra Practice To provide oral practice with **nosotros/as** commands, create sentences with **vamos a** before the name of a business. Ex: **Vamos al banco. Vamos a la peluquería.** Say the sentence, have students repeat it, then call on individual students to add an appropriate **nosotros/as** command form. Ex: **Saquemos dinero. Cortémonos el pelo.**

▶ Object pronouns are always attached to affirmative **nosotros/as** commands. A written accent is added to maintain the original stress.

Firmemos el cheque. → **Firmémoslo.**
Let's sign the check. *Let's sign it.*

Escribamos a Ana y Raúl. → **Escribámosles.**
Let's write Ana and Raúl. *Let's write them.*

▶ Object pronouns are placed in front of negative **nosotros/as** commands.

No **les paguemos** el préstamo.
Let's not pay them the loan.

No **se lo digamos** a ellos.
Let's not tell them.

No **lo compremos.**
Let's not buy it.

No **se la presentemos.**
Let's not introduce her to him.

▶ When **nos** or **se** is attached to an affirmative **nosotros/as** command, the final **-s** is dropped from the verb ending.

Sentémonos allí.
Let's sit there.

Démoselo a ella.
Let's give it to her.

▶ The **nosotros/as** command form of **irse** is **vámonos**. Its negative form is **no nos vayamos**.

¡**Vámonos** de vacaciones!
Let's go away on vacation!

No nos vayamos de aquí.
Let's not go away from here.

¡Hagamos un viaje!
¡Pidamos un préstamo!
¡Compremos un caballo!
BANCOSUR. LLÁMANOS.

Teaching Tips
- Call out affirmative commands and point to individuals to convert them into negative commands (and vice versa).
- Call out commands with object nouns and ask volunteers to repeat the commands with the appropriate pronouns.

recursos
WB pp. 173–174
LM p. 82
vhlcentral.com Lección 14

¡INTÉNTALO! Indica los mandatos afirmativos y negativos de la primera persona del plural (**nosotros/as**) de estos verbos.

1. estudiar *estudiemos, no estudiemos*
2. cenar cenemos, no cenemos
3. leer leamos, no leamos
4. decidir decidamos, no decidamos
5. decir digamos, no digamos
6. cerrar cerremos, no cerremos
7. levantarse levantémonos, no nos levantemos
8. irse vámonos, no nos vayamos
9. depositar depositemos, no depositemos
10. quedarse quedémonos, no nos quedemos
11. pedir pidamos, no pidamos
12. vestirse vistámonos, no nos vistamos

TEACHING OPTIONS

Pairs Have pairs create an ad similar to the one on this page, using **nosotros/as** commands. Then have them exchange their ads with another pair who corrects them. Finally, have some pairs share their ads with the class.

Small Groups Divide the class into groups of three. Student A writes a sentence that contains a **nosotros/as** command with direct or indirect objects. Ex: **Firmemos el cheque.** Student B must rewrite the sentence using pronouns. Ex: **Firmémoslo.** Then, student C must express the statement negatively. Ex: **No lo firmemos.** Have them switch roles and continue writing sentences until each has played student A twice.

1 Teaching Tip Encourage pairs performing in front of the class to ad-lib additional material as they see fit.

1 Expansion In pairs, have students write three cloze mini-conversations between two friends in which they use **nosotros/as** commands. Each dialogue should take place in a different commercial establishment, but students should leave out details that explicitly give away the friends' location. Then, have pairs exchange papers with another pair, who will fill in the blanks and try to identify the setting of each mini-conversation. They should end by acting it out for the class.

2 Expansion To challenge students, have pairs create another logical **nosotros/as** command for each item.
Ex: **1. Vamos a levantarnos a las seis. (Sí, levantémonos a las seis. Y acostémonos temprano por la noche.)**

Práctica

1 **Completar** Completa esta conversación con mandatos de **nosotros/as.** Luego, representa la conversación con un(a) compañero/a.

MARÍA Sergio, ¿quieres hacer diligencias ahora o por la tarde?
SERGIO No (1) las dejemos (dejarlas) para más tarde. (2) Hagámoslas (Hacerlas) ahora. ¿Qué tenemos que hacer?
MARÍA Necesito comprar sellos.
SERGIO Yo también. (3) Vamos (Ir) al correo.
MARÍA Pues, antes de ir al correo, necesito sacar dinero de mi cuenta corriente.
SERGIO Bueno, (4) busquemos (buscar) un cajero automático.
MARÍA ¿Tienes hambre?
SERGIO Sí. (5) Crucemos (Cruzar) la calle y (6) entremos (entrar) en ese café.
MARÍA Buena idea.
SERGIO ¿Nos sentamos aquí?
MARÍA No, no (7) nos sentemos (sentarse) aquí; (8) sentémonos (sentarse) enfrente de la ventana.
SERGIO ¿Qué pedimos?
MARÍA (9) Pidamos (Pedir) café y pan dulce.

2 **Responder** Responde a cada mandato de **nosotros/as** según las indicaciones entre paréntesis. Sustituye los sustantivos por los objetos directos e indirectos.

modelo
Vamos a vender el carro.
Sí, vendámoslo./No, no lo vendamos.

1. Vamos a levantarnos a las seis. (sí)
   Sí, levantémonos a las seis.
2. Vamos a enviar los paquetes. (no)
   No, no los enviemos.
3. Vamos a depositar el cheque. (sí)
   Sí, depositémoslo.
4. Vamos al supermercado. (no)
   No, no vayamos al supermercado.
5. Vamos a mandar esta postal a nuestros amigos. (no)
   No, no se la mandemos.
6. Vamos a limpiar la habitación. (sí)
   Sí, limpiémosla.
7. Vamos a mirar la televisión. (no)
   No, no la miremos.
8. Vamos a bailar. (sí)
   Sí, bailemos.
9. Vamos a pintar la sala. (no)
   No, no la pintemos.
10. Vamos a comprar estampillas. (sí)
    Sí, comprémoslas.

Practice more at **vhlcentral.com.**

TEACHING OPTIONS

Heritage Speakers Ask heritage speakers to write a conversation using **nosotros/as** commands. The topic of the conversation should be typical errands they run in their communities. Have them read their conversations to the class, making sure to note any new vocabulary on the board.

Game Divide the class into teams of three. Teams will take turns responding to your cues with a **nosotros/as** command. Ex: **Necesitamos pan. (Vamos a la panadería.)** Give the cue. Allow the team members to confer and come up with a team answer, and then call on a team. Each correct answer earns one point. The team with the most points at the end wins.

NATIONAL communication STANDARDS

Comunicación

3 **Preguntar** Tú y tu compañero/a están de vacaciones en Caracas y se hacen sugerencias para resolver las situaciones que se presentan. Inventen mandatos afirmativos o negativos de **nosotros/as.** Answers will vary.

modelo

Se nos olvidaron las tarjetas de crédito.
Paguemos en efectivo./No compremos más regalos.

A	B
1. El museo está a sólo una cuadra de aquí.	1. Tenemos muchos cheques de viajero.
2. Tenemos hambre.	2. Tenemos prisa para llegar al cine.
3. Hay una cola larga en el cine.	3. Estamos cansados y queremos dormir.

4 **Decisiones** Trabajen en grupos pequeños. Ustedes están en Caracas por dos días. Lean esta página de una guía turística sobre la ciudad y decidan qué van a hacer hoy por la mañana, por la tarde y por la noche. Hagan oraciones con mandatos afirmativos o negativos de **nosotros/as.** Answers will vary.

modelo

Visitemos el Museo de Arte Contemporáneo de Caracas esta tarde. Quiero ver las esculturas de Jesús Rafael Soto.

NOTA CULTURAL

Jesús Rafael Soto (1923–2005) fue un escultor y pintor venezolano. Sus obras cinéticas (*kinetic works*) frecuentemente incluyen formas que brillan (*shimmer*) y vibran. En muchas de ellas el espectador se puede integrar a la obra.

GUÍA DE Caracas

MUSEOS
- **Museo de Arte Colonial** Avenida Panteón
- **Museo de Arte Contemporáneo de Caracas** Parque Central. Esculturas de Jesús Rafael Soto y pinturas de Miró, Chagall y Picasso.
- **Galería de Arte Nacional** Parque Central. Colección de más de 4.000 obras de arte venezolano.

SITIOS DE INTERÉS
- **Plaza Bolívar**
- **Jardín Botánico** Avenida Interna UCV. De 8:00 a 5:00.
- **Parque del Este** Avenida Francisco de Miranda. Parque más grande de la ciudad con terrario.
- **Casa Natal de Simón Bolívar** Esquina de Sociedad de la avenida Universitaria. Casa colonial donde nació El Libertador.

RESTAURANTES
- **El Barquero** Avenida Luis Roche
- **Restaurante El Coyuco** Avenida Urdaneta
- **Restaurante Sorrento** Avenida Francisco Solano
- **Café Tonino** Avenida Andrés Bello

NATIONAL communication STANDARDS

Síntesis

5 **Situación** Tú y un(a) compañero/a viven juntos/as en un apartamento y tienen problemas económicos. Describan los problemas y sugieran algunas soluciones. Hagan oraciones con mandatos afirmativos o negativos de **nosotros/as.** Answers will vary.

modelo

Hagamos un presupuesto (budget).
No gastemos tanto dinero.

3 Expansion To challenge students, ask them to expand their answers with a reason for their choice. Ex: **Paguemos en efectivo porque tenemos suficiente dinero.**

4 Expansion Have groups bring in tourist information for another city in the Spanish-speaking world and repeat the activity. Encourage them to make copies of this information for the class. They should then present to the class their suggestions for what to do, using **nosotros/as** commands.

5 Teaching Tip To simplify, have students brainstorm different financial problems and solutions encountered by roommates sharing an apartment. Write their responses on the board.

5 Expansion Call on pairs to perform their **Situación** for the class. Encourage them to ad-lib as they go.

TEACHING OPTIONS

Pairs Have pairs create a guide for their favorite city, based on the **Guía de Caracas** in **Actividad 4**. Have them exchange their guides with another pair. That pair should decide which places they will visit and which they will avoid. Have them express their preferences using **nosotros/as** commands.

Pairs Have students create a dialogue in which two friends are deciding which local restaurant to go to for dinner. Students should use **nosotros/as** commands as much as possible. Have pairs perform their role-plays for the class.

Section Goals

In **Estructura 14.3**, students will learn:
- the future tense
- irregular verbs in the future
- the future as a means of expressing conjecture or probability

Instructional Resources
Supersite: Audio (Lab MP3 Files); Resources (Grammar Presentation Slides, Activity Pack, Scripts, Answer Keys); Testing Program (Quizzes)
WebSAM
Workbook, pp. 175–176
Lab Manual, p. 83

Teaching Tips

- Review the **ir a** + [*infinitive*] construction to express the future in Spanish. Then, work through the paradigm for the formation of the future. Go over regular and irregular verbs in the future point by point, calling students' attention to the information in **¡Atención!**
- Ask students about their future activities using **ir a** + [*infinitive*]. After they answer, repeat the information using the future. Ex: **¿A qué hora van a almorzar ustedes? (Vamos a almorzar a la una.) Ustedes almorzarán a la una.**
- Check for understanding by asking volunteers to give different forms of verbs not listed. Ex: **ahorrar, ofrecer, vivir**

14.3 The future

Tutorial

NATIONAL STANDARDS comparisons

ANTE TODO You have already learned ways of expressing the near future in Spanish. You will now learn how to form and use the future tense. Compare the different ways of expressing the future in Spanish and English.

Present indicative

Voy al cine mañana.
I'm going to the movies tomorrow.

Present subjunctive

Ojalá **vaya al cine** mañana.
I hope I go to the movies tomorrow.

ir a + [*infinitive*]

Voy a ir al cine.
I'm going to go to the movies.

Future

Iré al cine.
I will go to the movies.

CONSULTA

To review **ir a** + [*infinitive*], see **Estructura 4.1**, p. 118.

▶ In Spanish, the future is a simple tense that consists of one word, whereas in English it is made up of the auxiliary verb *will* or *shall*, and the main verb.

Future tense

		estudiar	aprender	recibir
SINGULAR FORMS	yo	estudiar**é**	aprender**é**	recibir**é**
	tú	estudiar**ás**	aprender**ás**	recibir**ás**
	Ud./él/ella	estudiar**á**	aprender**á**	recibir**á**
PLURAL FORMS	nosotros/as	estudiar**emos**	aprender**emos**	recibir**emos**
	vosotros/as	estudiar**éis**	aprender**éis**	recibir**éis**
	Uds./ellos/ellas	estudiar**án**	aprender**án**	recibir**án**

¡ATENCIÓN!

Note that **-ar**, **-er**, and **-ir** verbs all have the same endings in the future tense.

▶ **¡Atención!** Note that all of the future endings have a written accent except the **nosotros/as** form.

¿Cuándo **recibirás** la carta?
When will you receive the letter?

Mañana **aprenderemos** más.
Tomorrow we will learn more.

▶ The future endings are the same for regular and irregular verbs. For regular verbs, simply add the endings to the infinitive. For irregular verbs, add the endings to the irregular stem.

Irregular verbs in the future

INFINITIVE	STEM	FUTURE FORMS
decir	dir-	dir**é**
hacer	har-	har**é**
poder	podr-	podr**é**
poner	pondr-	pondr**é**
querer	querr-	querr**é**
saber	sabr-	sabr**é**
salir	saldr-	saldr**é**
tener	tendr-	tendr**é**
venir	vendr-	vendr**é**

TEACHING OPTIONS

Extra Practice To provide oral practice, create sentences using the future. Say a sentence, have students repeat it, then change the subject. Have students then say the sentence with the new subject, changing the verb as necessary.

Heritage Speakers Ask heritage speakers to share any song excerpts they know that use the future, such as ***No seré*** by **Julieta Venegas, *El día de mi suerte*** by **Héctor Lavoe,** or ***Viviré*** by **Juan Luis Guerra**. Have the class analyze the use of the future.

Game Divide the class into teams of five. Each team should have a piece of paper. Give an infinitive in Spanish. The first team member will write the **yo** form of the verb and pass the paper to the second member, who will write the **tú** form, and so forth. The first team to finish the entire paradigm correctly wins a point. The team with the most points at the end wins.

▶ The future of **hay** (*inf.* **haber**) is **habrá** (*there will be*).

La próxima semana **habrá** un nuevo director.
Next week there will be a new director.

Habrá más formularios en el correo.
There will be more forms at the post office.

▶ Although the English word *will* can refer to future time, it also refers to someone's willingness to do something. In this case, Spanish uses **querer** + [*infinitive*], not the future tense.

¿Quieres llamarme, por favor?
Will you please call me?

¿Quieren ustedes escucharnos, por favor?
Will you please listen to us?

COMPARE & CONTRAST

In Spanish, the future tense has an additional use: expressing conjecture or probability. English sentences involving expressions such as *I wonder, I bet, must be, may, might,* and *probably* are often translated into Spanish using the *future of probability*.

—¿Dónde **estarán** mis llaves?
I wonder where my keys are.

—**Estarán** en la cocina.
They're probably in the kitchen.

—¿Qué hora **será**?
What time can it be? (I wonder what time it is.)

—**Serán** las once o las doce.
It must be (It's probably) eleven or twelve.

Note that although the future tense is used, these verbs express conjecture about *present* conditions, events, or actions.

CONSULTA

To review these conjunctions of time, see **Estructura 13.3**, p. 435.

▶ The future may also be used in the main clause of sentences in which the present subjunctive follows a conjunction of time such as **cuando, después (de) que, en cuanto, hasta que,** and **tan pronto como.**

Cuando llegues a casa, **hablaremos.**
When you get home, we will talk.

Nos verás en cuanto entres en la cafetería.
You'll see us as soon as you enter the cafeteria.

¡INTÉNTALO! Conjuga los verbos entre paréntesis en futuro.

1. (dejar, correr, pedir) yo *dejaré, correré, pediré*
2. (cobrar, beber, vivir) tú cobrarás, beberás, vivirás
3. (hacer, poner, venir) Lola hará, pondrá, vendrá
4. (tener, decir, querer) nosotros tendremos, diremos, querremos
5. (ir, ser, estar) ustedes irán, serán, estarán
6. (firmar, comer, repetir) usted firmará, comerá, repetirá
7. (saber, salir, poder) yo sabré, saldré, podré
8. (encontrar, jugar, servir) tú encontrarás, jugarás, servirás

recursos

WB pp. 175–176

LM p. 83

vhlcentral.com Lección 14

Teaching Tips

- Go over the future of **hay**. Remind students that **habrá** is the only form and does not agree with any element in a sentence.
- Go over the explanation of **querer** + [*infinitive*].
- Explain the use of the future for expressing conjecture, which English generally expresses with the present tense. Add a visual aspect to this grammar presentation. Use magazine pictures to get students to speculate about what people are thinking or going to do. Ex: **¿Qué estará pensando la mujer que hace cola en el banco? (Estará pensando en su cita en el salón de belleza.)**
- Go over the use of the future in the main clause of sentences in which the present subjunctive follows a conjunction of time. Check for understanding by asking individuals to supply the main clause to prompts of present subjunctive clauses. Ex: **En cuanto pueda...; Tan pronto como me lo digas...**
- Ask students to answer questions about the future of the **Fotonovela** characters. Ex: **¿Quién tendrá la profesión más interesante? ¿Por qué? ¿Quién será más feliz?**

TEACHING OPTIONS

Pairs Ask students to write ten academic resolutions for the upcoming semester, using the future. Ex: **Haré dos o tres borradores de cada composición. Practicaré el español con los estudiantes hispanos.** Have students share their resolutions with a partner, who will then report back to the class. Ex: ____ **hará dos o tres borradores de cada composición.**

Extra Practice Ask students to finish these sentences logically: **1. Tan pronto como termine mis estudios,... 2. El día que gane la lotería,... 3. Cuando lleguen las vacaciones,... 4. Hasta que tenga mi propio** (*own*) **apartamento,...** Encourage them to expand their answers with additional information where appropriate.

1 Teaching Tips
- Before beginning the activity, briefly explain the subtle difference between the near future, expressed by **ir a +** [*infinitive*] and the future tense.
- Have two volunteers read the **modelo**. Then change the subject of the sentence and ask another volunteer to say the new sentence. Ex: **Celia va a hacer unas compras. (Hará unas compras.)**

2 Expansion Have partners tell each other about a real person they have seen somewhere but to whom they have never spoken. Have them speculate about that person. Ex: **Será el dueño del restaurante. Trabajará hasta muy tarde cada noche. Vivirá en las afueras de la ciudad.** Then, have pairs share their speculations with the class.

3 Teaching Tip Before beginning the activity, give students a few minutes to brainstorm about the categories before assigning pairs.

3 Expansion
- After completing the activity, have students share their predictions with the class. Write some of the predictions on the board.
- Have pairs complete this activity predicting the future of a celebrity. Then have the class try to guess the identity of each celebrity.

Successful Language Learning Ask students to discuss with a partner how they could use Spanish in their present or future careers.

Práctica

1 **Planes** Celia está hablando de sus planes. Repite lo que dice, usando el tiempo futuro.

modelo

Hoy voy a hacer unas compras.
Hoy haré unas compras.

1. Voy a pasar por el banco a cobrar un cheque. Pasaré por el banco a cobrar un cheque.
2. Mi hermana va a venir conmigo al supermercado. Mi hermana vendrá conmigo al supermercado.
3. Vamos a buscar las mejores rebajas. Buscaremos las mejores rebajas.
4. Voy a comprarme unas botas. Me compraré unas botas.
5. Después voy a volver a casa y me voy a duchar. Después volveré a casa y me ducharé.
6. Seguramente mis amigos me van a llamar para salir esta noche. Seguramente mis amigos me llamarán para salir esta noche.

2 **¿Quién será?** En parejas, imaginen que están en un café y ven entrar a un hombre o una mujer. Imaginen cómo será su vida y utilicen el futuro de probabilidad en su conversación. Usen estas preguntas como guía y después lean su conversación delante de la clase. Answers will vary.

modelo

Estudiante 1: *¿Será simpático?*
Estudiante 2: *Creo que no, está muy serio. Será antipático.*

- ¿Estará soltero/a?
- ¿Cuántos años tendrá?
- ¿Vivirá por aquí cerca?
- ¿Será famoso/a?
- ¿Será de otro país?
- ¿Con quién vivirá?
- ¿Estará esperando a alguien? ¿A quién?

3 **¿Qué pasará?** Imagina que tienes que adivinar (*to predict*) el futuro de tu compañero/a. Túrnense para hablar sobre cada una de estas categorías usando el futuro. Answers will vary.

modelo

Estudiante 1: *¿Seré rico? ¿Tendré una casa grande?*
Estudiante 2: *Mmm... tendrás muy poco dinero durante los próximos cinco años, pero después serás muy, muy rico con una casa enorme. Luego te mudarás a una isla desierta donde conocerás a...*

- amor
- dinero
- salud
- trabajo
- vivienda

Practice more at **vhlcentral.com**.

TEACHING OPTIONS

Small Groups Divide the class into small groups. Have students take turns telling the group three things they will do next summer or next year. Ex: **Viajaré a Europa. Trabajaré en un banco.** Have students report back to the class what their group members will do.

Extra Practice To provide more practice with the future, give students oral prompts with a future date. Ex: **En el año 2025...** Provide the prompt and then call on individual students to complete the sentence using the future. **(...nadie manejará un coche. ... usted vivirá en Costa Rica.)**

Comunicación

4 **Conversar** Tú y tu compañero/a viajarán a la República Dominicana por siete días. Indiquen lo que harán y no harán. Digan dónde, cómo, con quién o en qué fechas lo harán, usando el anuncio (*ad*) como guía. Pueden usar sus propias ideas también. Answers will vary.

modelo

Estudiante 1: *¿Qué haremos el martes?*
Estudiante 2: *Visitaremos el Jardín Botánico.*
Estudiante 1: *Pues, tú visitarás el Jardín Botánico y yo caminaré por el Mercado Modelo.*

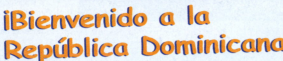

¡Bienvenido a la República Dominicana!

Se divertirá desde el momento en que llegue al **Aeropuerto Internacional de las Américas**.

- Visite la ciudad colonial de **Santo Domingo** con su interesante arquitectura.
- Vaya al **Jardín Botánico** y disfrute de nuestra abundante naturaleza.
- En el **Mercado Modelo** no va a poder resistir la tentación de comprar artesanías.
- No deje de escalar el **Pico Duarte** (se recomiendan 3 días).
- ¿Le gusta bucear? **Cabarete** tiene todo el equipo que usted necesita.
- ¿Desea nadar? **Punta Cana** le ofrece hermosas playas.

NOTA CULTURAL

En la **República Dominicana** están el punto más alto y el más bajo de las Antillas. El Pico Duarte mide (*measures*) 3.175 metros y el lago Enriquillo está a 45 metros bajo el nivel del mar (*sea level*).

5 **Planear** En parejas, hagan planes para empezar un negocio (*business*). Elijan una de las opciones y usen las preguntas como guía. Finalmente, presenten su plan a la clase. Answers will vary.

un supermercado | un salón de belleza | una heladería

1. ¿Cómo se llamará?
2. ¿Cuánta gente trabajará en este lugar? ¿Qué hará cada persona?
3. ¿En qué parte de la ciudad estará? ¿Cómo llegará la gente?
4. ¿Quién será el/la director(a)? ¿Por qué?
5. ¿Van a necesitar un préstamo? ¿Cómo lo pedirán?
6. Este/a supermercado / salón de belleza / heladería será el/la mejor de la ciudad porque...

Síntesis

6 **El futuro de Cristina** Tu profesor(a) va a darte una serie incompleta de dibujos sobre el futuro de Cristina. Tú y tu compañero/a tienen dos series diferentes. Háganse preguntas y respondan de acuerdo a los dibujos para completar la historia. Answers will vary.

modelo

Estudiante 1: *¿Qué hará Cristina en el año 2025?*
Estudiante 2: *Ella se graduará en el año 2025.*

4 Teaching Tips
- Give pairs time to read the ad before they complete the activity.
- If you have any students of Dominican heritage in your class or if any of your students have visited the Dominican Republic, ask them to share what they know about the places named in the ad.

4 Expansion Have several pairs role-play their conversations to the class.

5 Expansion Have groups develop visual aids to accompany their presentation.

6 Teaching Tip Divide the class into pairs and distribute the handouts from the Activity Pack (Activity Pack/Supersite) that correspond to this Information Gap Activity. Give students ten minutes to complete the activity.

6 Expansion
- Have students change partners, and have the new pairs use the future to retell the story without looking at the drawings. Later, ask students if the second version of the story differed from the first one.
- Have pairs pick a person who is currently in the news and write predictions about his or her future. Ask pairs to share their predictions with the class.

TEACHING OPTIONS

Large Groups Have students stand in a circle. Name an infinitive and subject pronoun. Ex: **tener/ustedes.** Throw a ball to a student, who must give the correct simple future form (Ex: **tendrán**) and toss the ball back to you. Keep a brisk pace.

Large Groups Assign a century to each corner of the room. Ex: 23rd century. Tell students they are going to go into the future in a time machine **(máquina del tiempo)**. They should pick which year they would like to visit and go to that corner. Once assembled, each group should develop a summary of life in their century. After groups have finished, call on a spokesperson in each group to report to the class.

Section Goal

In **Recapitulación**, students will review the grammar concepts from this lesson.

Instructional Resource
Supersite

1 Teaching Tip Complete this activity orally as a class.

1 Expansion To challenge students, add the verbs **saber, tener,** and **hacer** to the chart.

2 Teaching Tip Have students begin by identifying which commands are negative. Call on a volunteer to explain the difference in the formation of affirmative and negative **nosotros/as** commands.

2 Expansion Have students work in pairs to create an original dialogue using **nosotros/as** commands.

Recapitulación

Diagnostics

Completa estas actividades para repasar los conceptos de gramática que aprendiste en esta lección.

1 Completar Completa el cuadro con la forma correspondiente del futuro. **20 pts.**

Infinitive	yo	ella	nosotros
ahorrar	ahorraré	ahorrará	ahorraremos
decir	diré	dirá	diremos
poner	pondré	pondrá	pondremos
querer	querré	querrá	querremos
salir	saldré	saldrá	saldremos

2 Los novios Completa este diálogo entre dos novios con mandatos en la forma de **nosotros/as**. **20 pts.**

SIMÓN ¿Quieres ir al cine mañana?

CARLA Sí, ¡qué buena idea! (1) Compremos (Comprar) los boletos (*tickets*) por teléfono.

SIMÓN No, mejor (2) pidámoselos (pedírselos) gratis a mi prima, quien trabaja en el cine.

CARLA ¡Fantástico!

SIMÓN Y también quiero visitar la nueva galería de arte el fin de semana que viene.

CARLA ¿Por qué esperar? (3) Visitémosla (Visitarla) esta tarde.

SIMÓN Bueno, pero primero tengo que limpiar mi apartamento.

CARLA No hay problema. (4) Limpiémoslo (Limpiarlo) juntos.

SIMÓN Muy bien. ¿Y tú no tienes que hacer diligencias hoy? (5) Hagámoslas (Hacerlas) también.

CARLA Sí, tengo que ir al correo y al banco. (6) Vamos (Ir) al banco hoy, pero no (7) vayamos (ir) al correo todavía. Antes tengo que escribir una carta.

SIMÓN ¿Una carta misteriosa? (8) Escribámosla (Escribirla) ahora.

CARLA No, mejor no (9) la escribamos (escribirla) hasta que regresemos de la galería donde venden un papel reciclado muy lindo (*cute*).

SIMÓN ¿Papel lindo? ¿Pues para quién es la carta?

CARLA No importa. (10) Empecemos (Empezar) a limpiar.

RESUMEN GRAMATICAL

14.1 The subjunctive in adjective clauses pp. 460–461

- When adjective clauses refer to something that is known, certain, or definite, the indicative is used.

Necesito **el** libro que **tiene** fotos.

- When adjective clauses refer to something that is uncertain or indefinite, the subjunctive is used.

Necesito **un** libro que **tenga** fotos.

14.2 Nosotros/as commands pp. 464–465

- Same as **nosotros/as** form of present subjunctive.

Affirmative	Negative
Démosle un libro a Lola.	No le demos un libro a Lola.
Démoselo.	No se lo demos.

- While the subjunctive form of the verb **ir** is used for the negative **nosotros/as** command, the indicative is used for the affirmative command.

No **vayamos** a la plaza. **Vamos** a la plaza.

14.3 The future pp. 468–469

Future tense of **estudiar***	
estudiaré	estudiaremos
estudiarás	estudiaréis
estudiará	estudiarán

*Same ending for **-ar, -er,** and **-ir** verbs.

- The future of **hay** is **habrá** (*there will be*).
- The future can also express conjecture or probability.

TEACHING OPTIONS

Large Groups Have students stand and form a circle. Have one student step inside the circle and describe a situation. Ex: **Tenemos un examen mañana.** The student to the right should step forward and propose a solution, using a **nosotros/as** command form. Ex: **Estudiemos el subjuntivo.** Continue around the circle until each student has had a turn forming commands. Then have another student start the activity again with a new situation.

Large Groups Divide the class into two groups. Give one group cards with situations. Ex: **El profesor canceló la clase.** Give the other group cards with statements using the future to express conjecture or probability. Ex: **Llegaré a clase y no habrá nadie.** Students must find their partners.

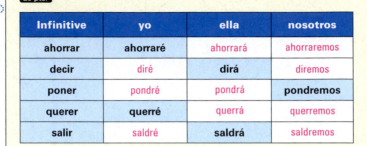

Irregular verbs in the future

Infinitive	Stem	Future forms
decir	dir-	diré
hacer	har-	haré
poder	podr-	podré
poner	pondr-	pondré
querer	querr-	querré
saber	sabr-	sabré
salir	saldr-	saldré
tener	tendr-	tendré
venir	vendr-	vendré

3 **Frases** Escribe oraciones con los elementos que se dan. Usa el tiempo futuro. 10 pts.

1. Lorenzo y yo / ir / al banco / mañana / y / pedir / un préstamo Lorenzo y yo iremos al banco mañana y pediremos un préstamo.
2. la empleada del banco / hacernos / muchas preguntas / y / también / darnos / un formulario La empleada del banco nos hará muchas preguntas y también nos dará un formulario.
3. Lorenzo / llenar / el formulario / y / yo / firmarlo Lorenzo llenará el formulario y yo lo firmaré.
4. nosotros / salir / del banco / contentos / porque el dinero / llegar / a nuestra cuenta / muy pronto Nosotros saldremos del banco contentos porque el dinero llegará a nuestra cuenta muy pronto.
5. los dos / tener / que trabajar mucho / para pagar el préstamo / pero nuestros padres / ayudarnos Los dos tendremos que trabajar mucho para pagar el préstamo, pero nuestros padres nos ayudarán.

4 **Verbos** Escribe los verbos en el presente de indicativo o de subjuntivo. 20 pts.

1. —¿Sabes dónde hay un restaurante donde nosotros (1) __podamos__ (poder) comer paella valenciana? —No, no conozco ninguno que (2) __sirva__ (servir) paella, pero conozco uno que (3) __se especializa__ (especializarse) en tapas españolas.
2. Busco vendedores que (4) __sean__ (ser) educados. No estoy seguro de conocer a alguien que (5) __tenga__ (tener) esa característica. Pero ahora que lo pienso, ¡sí! Tengo dos amigos que (6) __trabajan__ (trabajar) en el almacén Excelencia. Los voy a llamar. Y debo decirles que necesitamos que (ellos) (7) __sepan__ (saber) hablar inglés.
3. Se busca apartamento que (8) __esté__ (estar) bien situado, que (9) __cueste__ (costar) menos de $800 al mes y que (10) __permita__ (permitir) tener perros.

5 **La ciudad ideal** Escribe un párrafo de al menos cinco oraciones describiendo cómo es la comunidad ideal donde te gustaría (*you would like*) vivir en el futuro y compárala con la comunidad donde vives ahora. Usa cláusulas adjetivas y el vocabulario de esta lección. 30 pts. Answers will vary.

6 **Adivinanza** Completa la adivinanza y adivina la respuesta. ¡4 puntos EXTRA!

"Me llegan las cartas
y no sé __leer__ (*to read*)
y, aunque° me las como,
no mancho° el papel."
¿Quién soy? __el buzón__

aunque *although* no mancho *I don't stain*

Practice more at **vhlcentral.com.**

3 Teaching Tip Before beginning the activity, ask students to identify the irregular verbs in the future tense.

4 Teaching Tip Before students complete the activity, have them circle the verbs in the main clause of each sentence.

5 Teaching Tips
- Have students make a Venn diagram with the headings **Mi comunidad, Mi comunidad ideal,** and **Las dos**. Have them fill in each area with short phrases to include in their paragraphs.
- Have students exchange their papers for peer editing.

6 Expansion To challenge students, have them work in small groups to create a riddle about an object or place found in the city.

TEACHING OPTIONS

Heritage Speakers Ask heritage speakers to compare a city or town from their families' countries of origin with their current hometown. What forms of transportation are available? Is there a downtown area? Where do people tend to live and work? Encourage classmates to ask follow-up questions.

Game Divide the class into two teams. Write a main clause on the board. Ex: **Busco un apartamento...** and have one member from each team come to the board and complete the sentence with subordinate clauses in the indicative or subjunctive. Each correct answer earns one point. The team with the most points at the end wins.

Audio: Reading
Additional Reading

Section Goals

In **Lectura**, students will:

- learn the strategy of identifying a narrator's point of view
- read an authentic narrative in Spanish

Instructional Resource
Supersite

Estrategia Tell students that recognizing the point of view from which a narrative is told will help them comprehend it. Write examples of first-person and omniscient narratives on the board and ask students to identify the point of view in each.

Examinar el texto Ask students to read the first two paragraphs of ***Esquina peligrosa*** and determine whether the narrative is written from the first- or third-person point of view. Call on a volunteer to explain what clues in the text help reveal the narrator.

Punto de vista Have students complete this activity in pairs. First have them find the corresponding sentences in the text. Then have them fill in the blanks with the **yo** form of the verbs, the pronouns **yo** or **me**, or the possessive adjective **mi**.

Lectura

NATIONAL STANDARDS connections cultures

Antes de leer

Estrategia
Identifying point of view

You can understand a narrative more completely if you identify the point of view of the narrator. You can do this by simply asking yourself from whose perspective the story is being told. Some stories are narrated in the first person. That is, the narrator is a character in the story, and everything you read is filtered through that person's thoughts, emotions, and opinions. Other stories have an omniscient narrator who is not one of the story's characters and who reports the thoughts and actions of all the characters.

Examinar el texto

Lee brevemente este cuento escrito por Marco Denevi. ¿Crees que se narra en primera persona o tiene un narrador omnisciente? ¿Cómo lo sabes?
Answers will vary.
____
____

Punto de vista

Éstos son fragmentos de *Esquina peligrosa* en los que se cambió el punto de vista° a primera persona. Completa cada oración de manera lógica.

1. Le __ordené__ a mi chofer que me condujese hasta aquel barrio...
2. Al doblar la esquina __vi__ el almacén, el mismo viejo y sombrío almacén donde __yo__ había trabajado como dependiente...
3. El recuerdo de __mi__ niñez me puso nostálgico. Se __me__ humedecieron los ojos.
4. Yo __tomé__ la canasta de mimbre, __fui__ llenándola con paquetes [...] y __salí__ a hacer el reparto.

punto de vista *point of view*

Practice more at **vhlcentral.com**.

Marco Denevi (1922–1998) fue un escritor y dramaturgo argentino. Estudió derecho y más tarde se convirtió en escritor. Algunas de sus obras, como *Rosaura a las diez,* han sido° llevadas al cine. Denevi se caracteriza por su gran creatividad e ingenio, que jamás dejan de sorprender al lector°.

Esquina peligrosa

Marco Denevi

El señor Epidídimus, el magnate de las finanzas°, uno de los hombres más ricos del mundo, sintió un día el vehemente deseo de visitar el barrio donde había vivido cuando era niño y trabajaba como dependiente de almacén.

Le ordenó a su chofer que lo condujese hasta aquel barrio humilde° y remoto. Pero el barrio estaba tan cambiado que el señor Epidídimus no lo reconoció. En lugar de calles de tierra había bulevares asfaltados°, y las míseras casitas de antaño° habían sido reemplazadas por torres de departamentos°.

Al doblar una esquina vio el almacén, el mismo viejo y sombrío° almacén donde él había trabajado como dependiente cuando tenía doce años.

—Deténgase aquí—le dijo al chofer. Descendió del automóvil y entró en el almacén. Todo se conservaba igual que en la época de su infancia: las estanterías, la anticuada caja registradora°, la balanza de pesas° y, alrededor, el mudo asedio° de la mercadería.

El señor Epidídimus percibió el mismo olor de sesenta años atrás: un olor picante y agridulce a jabón

TEACHING OPTIONS

Pairs Have pairs of students reread ***Esquina peligrosa*** and write four discussion questions about the selection. When they have finished, have them exchange questions with another pair, who can work together to discuss and answer them.

Small Groups Have students generate a list of other short stories or excerpts of longer works that contain fantastical elements on the board. Then, in small groups, have students choose a text and compare and contrast its fantastical qualities with ***Esquina peligrosa***.

han sido *have been* lector *reader* finanzas *finance* humilde *humble, modest* asfaltados *paved with asphalt* antaño *yesteryear* torres de departamentos *apartment buildings* sombrío *somber* anticuada caja registradora *old-fashioned cash register* balanza de pesas *scale* mudo asedio *silent siege* aserrín *sawdust* acaroína *pesticide* penumbra del fondo *half-light from the back* reparto *delivery* lodazal *bog*

amarillo, a aserrín° húmedo, a vinagre, a aceitunas, a acaroína°. El recuerdo de su niñez lo puso nostálgico. Se le humedecieron los ojos. Le pareció que retrocedía en el tiempo.

Desde la penumbra del fondo° le llegó la voz ruda del patrón:

—¿Estas son horas de venir? Te quedaste dormido, como siempre.

El señor Epidídimus tomó la canasta de mimbre, fue llenándola con paquetes de azúcar, de yerba y de fideos, y salió a hacer el reparto°.

La noche anterior había llovido y las calles de tierra estaban convertidas en un lodazal°.

(1974)

Después de leer

Comprensión

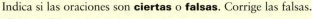

Indica si las oraciones son **ciertas** o **falsas**. Corrige las falsas.

Cierto	Falso	
	✓	1. El señor Epidídimus tiene una tienda con la que gana poco dinero. Es un magnate de las finanzas, uno de los hombres más ricos del mundo.
✓		2. Epidídimus vivía en un barrio humilde cuando era pequeño.
✓		3. Epidídimus le ordenó al chofer que lo llevara a un barrio de gente con poco dinero.
✓		4. Cuando Epidídimus entró al almacén se acordó de experiencias pasadas.
	✓	5. Epidídimus les dio órdenes a los empleados del almacén. Su patrón le ordenó hacer el reparto.

Comprensión Have students write five additional true/false statements for a partner to complete. Make sure students correct the false statements.

Interpretación

Contesta estas preguntas con oraciones completas. Answers will vary.

1. ¿Es rico o pobre Epidídimus? ¿Cómo lo sabes?
2. ¿Por qué Epidídimus va al almacén?
3. ¿De quién es la voz "ruda" que Epidídimus escucha? ¿Qué orden crees que le dio a Epidídimus?
4. ¿Qué hace Epidídimus al final?

Interpretación Have students work in pairs to complete this activity. Ask them to support their answers with fragments from the text.

Coméntalo

En parejas, hablen de sus impresiones y conclusiones. Tomen como guía estas preguntas. Answers will vary.

- ¿Te sorprendió el final de este cuento? ¿Por qué?
- ¿Qué va a hacer Epidídimus el resto del día?
- ¿Crees que Epidídimus niño estaba soñando o Epidídimus adulto estaba recordando?
- ¿Por qué crees que el cuento se llama *Esquina peligrosa*?

Coméntalo Ask students to explain their opinions. For the third question, survey the class to see which is the most popular interpretation.

TEACHING OPTIONS

Pairs Bring in another short story with a surprising ending, such as ***El eclipse*** by **Augusto Monterroso**. In pairs, have students compare and contrast the endings.

Extra Practice Ask students to write a short story about their own lives, using the framework of ***Esquina peligrosa***. Tell them to include the same ambiguity as to whether the story is a memory or a dream, and to use a surprise ending. Have volunteers read their stories aloud for the class.

Section Goal

In **Panorama**, students will read about the history, geography, and economy of Venezuela.

Instructional Resources
Supersite: Video (***Panorama cultural***); Resources (Scripts, Translations, Digital Image Bank, Answer Keys)
WebSAM
Workbook, pp. 177–178
Video Manual, pp. 65–66

Teaching Tips

- Use the **Lección 14 Panorama** digital images to assist with this presentation.
- Have students look at the map of Venezuela and talk about the physical features of the country. Have students trace the Orinoco River and notice the types of terrain it runs through. Note that the principal cities are all located along the Caribbean coast.

El país en cifras Point out that the national currency is named for **Simón Bolívar,** the Latin American hero who played a central role in the struggle for independence from Spain. Point out that **Bolívar's** birthplace was Caracas. After reading about the **yanomami,** point out the vastness of Venezuela's jungle area, and remind students that various indigenous groups inhabit this largely undeveloped area.

¡Increíble pero cierto! Angel Falls is located in the rugged, nearly inaccessible Guiana Highlands in southeastern Venezuela, and is most easily viewed from the air. In fact, that is how American pilot James C. Angel made the first non-native exploration of this natural wonder.

Video: *Panorama cultural*
Interactive map

Venezuela

NATIONAL STANDARDS connections cultures

El país en cifras

- **Área:** 912.050 km^2 (352.144 $millas^2$), *aproximadamente dos veces el área de California*
- **Población:** 28.868.000
- **Capital:** Caracas —3.051.000
- **Ciudades principales:** Maracaibo —2.153.000, Valencia —1.738.000, Barquisimeto —1.159.000, Maracay —1.040.000
- **Moneda:** bolívar
- **Idiomas:** español (oficial), lenguas indígenas (oficiales)

El yanomami es uno de los idiomas indígenas que se habla en Venezuela. La cultura de los yanomami tiene su centro en el sur de Venezuela, en el bosque tropical. Son cazadores° y agricultores y viven en comunidades de hasta 400 miembros.

Bandera de Venezuela

Venezolanos célebres

- **Teresa Carreño,** compositora y pianista (1853–1917)
- **Rómulo Gallegos,** escritor y político (1884–1969)
- **Andrés Eloy Blanco,** poeta (1896–1955)
- **Gustavo Dudamel,** director de orquesta (1981–)
- **Baruj Benacerraf,** científico (1920–2011)

En 1980, Baruj Benacerraf, junto con dos de sus colegas, recibió el Premio Nobel por sus investigaciones en el campo° de la inmunología y las enfermedades autoinmunes. Nacido en Caracas, Benacerraf también vivió en París y los Estados Unidos.

cazadores *hunters* campo *field* caída *drop* Salto Ángel *Angel Falls* catarata *waterfall* la dio a conocer *made it known*

Isla Margarita

Vista de Caracas

Una piragua

recursos

WB	VM	vhlcentral.com
pp. 177–178	pp. 65–66	Lección 14

¡Increíble pero cierto!

Con una caída° de 979 metros (3.212 pies) desde la meseta de Auyan Tepuy, Salto Ángel°, en Venezuela, es la catarata° más alta del mundo, ¡diecisiete veces más alta que las cataratas del Niágara! James C. Angel la dio a conocer° en 1935. Los indígenas de la zona la denominan "Kerepakupai Merú".

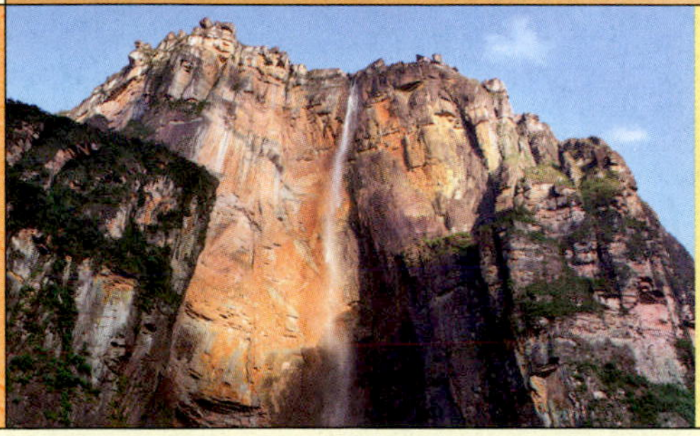

TEACHING OPTIONS

Variación léxica Venezuelan Spanish has a rich repertoire of regionalisms and colloquialisms. If students go to Caracas, they are certainly going to hear the word **pana**, which means both **amigo** and **amiga**. Ex: **¡Eso es chévere, pana!** The Venezuelan equivalent of *guy* or *girl* is **chamo/a**. An inhabitant of the city of Caracas is a **caraqueño/a**. Some other words that are specific to Venezuela are **cambur** for **banana** and **caraota** for **frijol**.

Worth Noting **Rómulo Gallegos's** great novel, ***Doña Bárbara***, is set in the **Llanos** of Venezuela, a region known for its cattle raising culture. The theme of the novel is one that has been explored by many Latin American writers—the struggle between **civilización y barbarie**.

Economía • El petróleo

La industria petrolera° es muy importante para la economía venezolana. La mayor concentración de petróleo del país se encuentra debajo del lago Maracaibo. En 1976 se nacionalizaron las empresas° petroleras y pasaron a ser propiedad° del estado con el nombre de *Petróleos de Venezuela*. Este producto representa más del 90% de las exportaciones del país, siendo los Estados Unidos su principal comprador°.

Actualidades • Caracas

El *boom* petrolero de los años cincuenta transformó a Caracas en una ciudad cosmopolita. Sus rascacielos° y excelentes sistemas de transporte la hacen una de las ciudades más modernas de Latinoamérica. El metro, construido en 1983, es uno de los más modernos del mundo y sus extensas carreteras y autopistas conectan la ciudad con el interior del país. El corazón de la capital es el Parque Central, una zona de centros comerciales, tiendas, restaurantes y clubes.

Historia • Simón Bolívar (1783–1830)

A principios del siglo° XIX, el territorio de la actual Venezuela, al igual que gran parte de América, todavía estaba bajo el dominio de la Corona° española. El general Simón Bolívar, nacido en Caracas, es llamado "El Libertador" porque fue el líder del movimiento independentista suramericano en el área que hoy es Venezuela, Colombia, Ecuador, Perú y Bolivia.

¿Qué aprendiste? Contesta cada pregunta con una oración completa.

1. ¿Cuál es la moneda de Venezuela?
   La moneda de Venezuela es el bolívar.
2. ¿Quién fue Rómulo Gallegos?
   Rómulo Gallegos fue un escritor y político venezolano.
3. ¿Cuándo se dio a conocer el Salto Ángel?
   El Salto Ángel se dio a conocer en 1935.
4. ¿Cuál es el producto más exportado de Venezuela?
   El producto más exportado de Venezuela es el petróleo.
5. ¿Qué ocurrió en 1976 con las empresas petroleras?
   En 1976 las empresas petroleras se nacionalizaron.
6. ¿Cómo se llama la capital de Venezuela?
   La capital de Venezuela se llama Caracas.
7. ¿Qué hay en el Parque Central de Caracas?
   Hay centros comerciales, tiendas, restaurantes y clubes.
8. ¿Por qué es conocido Simón Bolívar como "El Libertador"?
   Simón Bolívar es conocido como "El Libertador" porque fue el líder del movimiento independentista suramericano.

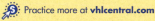

Sombreros y hamacas en Ciudad Bolívar

Conexión Internet Investiga estos temas en **vhlcentral.com**.

1. Busca información sobre Simón Bolívar. ¿Cuáles son algunos de los episodios más importantes de su vida? ¿Crees que Bolívar fue un estadista (*statesman*) de primera categoría? ¿Por qué?
2. Prepara un plan para un viaje de ecoturismo por el Orinoco. ¿Qué quieres ver y hacer durante la excursión?

Practice more at **vhlcentral.com**.

industria petrolera *oil industry* empresas *companies* propiedad *property* comprador *buyer* rascacielos *skyscrapers* siglo *century* Corona *Crown*

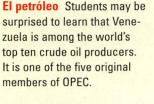

El petróleo Students may be surprised to learn that Venezuela is among the world's top ten crude oil producers. It is one of the five original members of OPEC.

Caracas Both Caracas and Houston, Texas, are major urban areas fueled by oil booms. Students may find it interesting to compare how these cities have developed. Houston's urban development is limited only by the coastline, allowing it to sprawl in all other directions; Caracas is hemmed into a narrow valley by two mountain ranges, leading to its dense development and its many high-rises.

Simón Bolívar The life of **Simón Bolívar** has inspired artists of every sort: from painters and sculptors to musicians and writers. In 1989, Colombian Nobel winner **Gabriel García Márquez** published ***El general en su laberinto***, his vision of **Bolívar** toward the end of his life, as he muses about his accomplishments and disappointments.

Conexión Internet Students will find supporting Internet activities and links at **vhlcentral.com**.

Teaching Tip You may want to wrap up this section by playing the ***Panorama cultural*** video footage for this lesson.

TEACHING OPTIONS

Worth Noting Tell students that the **Salto Ángel**, besides being the highest uninterrupted waterfall in the world, falls from a **tepuy**, a flat-topped, sandstone mountain with vertical sides. Because of the isolation that results from the great elevation and the vertical sides, the top of each **tepuy** is a unique ecosystem, featuring plants and animals of different species that grow nowhere else on earth, including the tops of neighboring **tepuyes**. The chilly, damp climate atop a **tepuy** differs so markedly from the tropical climate at its base that **tepuy**-dwelling species cannot survive on the **sabana** below and vice versa.

Heritage Speakers Ask heritage speakers whose families are of Venezuelan origin or students who have visited there to tell the class about their experiences in the country.

Section Goal

In **Panorama**, students will read about the geography and culture of the Dominican Republic.

Instructional Resources
Supersite: Video (***Panorama cultural***); Resources (Scripts, Translations, Digital Image Bank, Answer Keys)
WebSAM
Workbook, pp. 179–180
Video Manual, pp. 67–68

Teaching Tips

- Use the **Lección 14 Panorama** digital images to assist with this presentation.
- Have students look at the map of the Dominican Republic and talk about geographical features of the country. Have students note that the majority of cities are located along the coast or close to it and that there are few cities in the center of the island. Point out that there are rugged mountains through the center of the country, with fertile valleys interspersed.

El país en cifras After reading **Población,** point out that Haiti is the poorest country in the western hemisphere. Ask students to speculate about how that might affect the Dominican Republic. After reading **Idiomas**, emphasize the fact that Haitian Creole is widely spoken; this confirms a major Haitian presence in the Dominican Republic.

¡Increíble pero cierto! DNA research conducted by Spain in 2003 shows that the remains in Sevilla are indeed Columbus'. However, the Dominican Republic has not allowed their remains to be exhumed, so a comparative analysis has not been performed.

La República Dominicana

NATIONAL STANDARDS connections cultures

Músicos dominicanos

Catedral de Santa María la Menor

El país en cifras

- **Área:** 48.730 km² (18.815 millas²), *el área combinada de New Hampshire y Vermont*
- **Población:** 10.349.000

La isla La Española, llamada así tras° el primer viaje de Cristóbal Colón, estuvo bajo el completo dominio de la corona° española hasta 1697, cuando la parte oeste de la isla pasó a ser propiedad° francesa. Hoy día está dividida políticamente en dos países, la República Dominicana en la zona este y Haití en el oeste.

- **Capital:** Santo Domingo—2.191.000
- **Ciudades principales:** Santiago de los Caballeros, La Vega, Puerto Plata, San Pedro de Macorís
- **Moneda:** peso dominicano
- **Idiomas:** español (oficial), criollo haitiano

Bandera de la República Dominicana

Dominicanos célebres

- **Juan Pablo Duarte,** político y padre de la patria° (1813–1876)
- **Celeste Woss y Gil,** pintora (1891–1985)
- **Juan Luis Guerra,** compositor y cantante de merengue (1957–)
- **Pedro Martínez,** beisbolista (1971–)
- **Marcos Díaz,** nadador de ultradistancia (1975–)

Trabajadores del campo recogen la cosecha de ajos

recursos
WB pp. 179–180 | VM pp. 67–68 | vhlcentral.com Lección 14

tras *after* corona *crown* propiedad *property* padre de la patria *founding father* restos *remains* tumbas *graves* navegante *sailor* reemplazó *replaced*

¡Increíble pero cierto!

Los restos° de Cristóbal Colón pasaron por varias ciudades desde su muerte en el siglo XVI hasta el siglo XIX. Por esto, se conocen dos tumbas° de este navegante°: una en la Catedral de Sevilla, España y otra en el Museo Faro a Colón en Santo Domingo, que reemplazó° la tumba inicial en la catedral de la capital dominicana.

TEACHING OPTIONS

Language Notes Although the Arawak and Taíno people who were indigenous to Hispaniola were virtually eliminated following the European conquest, Caribbean Spanish continues to be marked by lexical items from these cultures. Point out these words of Native American origin that have entered Spanish: **ají** *(chili pepper)*, **cacique** *(political leader)*, **canoa** *(canoe)*, **hamaca** *(hammock)*, **huracán** *(hurricane)*.

Extra Practice Bring in recordings by **Juan Luis Guerra,** such as his 1998 album ***Ni es lo mismo ni es igual.*** Invite students to follow the printed lyrics as they listen to a track such as ***Mi PC.*** Then, have students work together to create an English translation of the song.

Ciudades • Santo Domingo

La zona colonial de Santo Domingo, ciudad fundada en 1496, posee° algunas de las construcciones más antiguas del hemisferio. Gracias a las restauraciones°, la arquitectura de la ciudad es famosa no sólo por su belleza sino también por el buen estado de sus edificios. Entre sus sitios más visitados se cuentan° la Calle de las Damas, llamada así porque allí paseaban las señoras de la corte del Virrey; el Alcázar de Colón, un palacio construido entre 1510 y 1514 por Diego Colón, hijo de Cristóbal; y la Fortaleza Ozama, la más vieja de las Américas, construida entre 1502 y 1508.

Deportes • El béisbol

El béisbol es un deporte muy practicado en el Caribe. Los primeros países hispanos en tener una liga fueron Cuba y México, donde se empezó a jugar al béisbol en el siglo° XIX. Hoy día este deporte es una afición° nacional en la República Dominicana. Albert Pujols (foto, derecha), Carlos Gómez y David Ortiz son sólo tres de los muchísimos beisbolistas dominicanos que han alcanzado° enorme éxito° e inmensa popularidad entre los aficionados.

Artes • El merengue

El merengue, un ritmo originario de la República Dominicana, tiene sus raíces° en el campo. Tradicionalmente las canciones hablaban de los problemas sociales de los campesinos°. Sus instrumentos eran la guitarra, el acordeón, el guayano° y la tambora, un tambor° característico del lugar. Entre 1930 y 1960, el merengue se popularizó en las ciudades; adoptó un tono más urbano, en el que se incorporaron instrumentos como el saxofón y el bajo°, y empezaron a formarse grandes orquestas. Uno de los cantantes y compositores de merengue más famosos es Juan Luis Guerra.

¿Qué aprendiste? Responde a cada pregunta con una oración completa.

1. ¿Quién es Juan Luis Guerra?
   Juan Luis Guerra es un compositor y cantante de merengue.
2. ¿Cuándo se fundó la ciudad de Santo Domingo?
   Santo Domingo se fundó en 1496.
3. ¿Qué es el Alcázar de Colón?
   El Alcázar de Colón es un palacio construido entre 1510 y 1514 por Diego Colón, hijo de Cristóbal.
4. Nombra dos beisbolistas famosos de la República Dominicana.
   Dos beisbolistas famosos de la República Dominicana son Pedro Martínez y David Ortiz/Albert Pujols/Carlos Gómez.
5. ¿De qué hablaban las canciones de merengue tradicionales?
   Las canciones de merengue tradicionales hablaban de los problemas sociales de los campesinos.
6. ¿Qué instrumentos se utilizaban para tocar (*play*) el merengue?
   Se utilizaban la guitarra, el acordeón, el guayano y la tambora.
7. ¿Cuándo se transformó el merengue en un estilo urbano?
   El merengue se transformó en un estilo urbano entre los años 1930 y 1960.
8. ¿Qué cantante ha ayudado a internacionalizar el merengue?
   Juan Luis Guerra ha ayudado a internacionalizar el merengue.

Conexión Internet Investiga estos temas en **vhlcentral.com.**

Practice more at **vhlcentral.com.**

1. Busca más información sobre la isla La Española. ¿Cómo son las relaciones entre la República Dominicana y Haití?
2. Busca más información sobre la zona colonial de Santo Domingo: la Catedral de Santa María, la Casa de Bastidas o el Panteón Nacional. ¿Cómo son estos edificios? ¿Te gustan? Explica tus respuestas.

posee *possesses* restauraciones *restorations* se cuentan *are included* siglo *century* afición *pastime* han alcanzado *have reached* éxito *success* raíces *roots* campesinos *rural people* guayano *metal scraper* tambor *drum* bajo *bass*

Santo Domingo UNESCO has declared Santo Domingo a World Heritage site because of the abundance of historical architecture. Efforts are being made to restore buildings to their original grandeur, and to "correct" restorations made in the past that were not true to original architectural styles.

El béisbol The Dominican Republic has the second-highest number of players in Major League Baseball (only the U.S. has more). The Dominican Republic has its own baseball league (with six teams), whose season lasts from October to January. Many major and minor league players play in the Dominican League during their off-season.

El merengue The **merengue** represents a fusion of the cultures that make up the Dominican Republic's heritage. The gourd scraper—or **güiro**—comes from the indigenous Arawak people, the **tambora**—a drum unique to the Dominican Republic—is part of the nation's African legacy, the stringed instruments were adapted from the Spanish guitar, and the accordion was introduced by German merchants. For more information about **merengue,** you may want to play the ***Panorama cultural*** video footage for this lesson.

Conexión Internet Students will find supporting Internet activities and links at **vhlcentral.com**.

TEACHING OPTIONS

Worth Noting Students may enjoy learning more about Latin American baseball. They can check out reports of Caribbean League baseball games on the Internet, which follow Dominican, Cuban, and Venezuelan teams among others. Encourage students to create a bilingual dictionary of baseball terms such as **jardinero** *(outfielder)*, **jardín** *(outfield)*, **cuadrangular/jonrón** *(home run)*, **batear** *(to hit)*, **pichear** *(to pitch)*, **anotar carreras** *(to score runs)*, **ponchar** *(to strike out)*, **la goma** *(home plate)*, **el montículo** *(mound)*, and so forth. Encourage sports fans to identify Latin Americans currently playing in the Major Leagues.

Instructional Resources
Supersite: Audio (Textbook & Lab MP3s); Testing Program (Tests, MP3s)
WebSAM
Lab Manual, p. 83

En la ciudad

el banco	*bank*
la carnicería	*butcher shop*
el correo	*post office*
el estacionamiento	*parking lot*
la frutería	*fruit store*
la heladería	*ice cream shop*
la joyería	*jewelry store*
la lavandería	*laundromat*
la panadería	*bakery*
la pastelería	*pastry shop*
la peluquería, el salón de belleza	*beauty salon*
la pescadería	*fish market*
el supermercado	*supermarket*
la zapatería	*shoe store*
hacer cola	*to stand in line*
hacer diligencias	*to run errands*

En el banco

el cajero automático	*ATM*
el cheque (de viajero)	*(traveler's) check*
la cuenta corriente	*checking account*
la cuenta de ahorros	*savings account*
ahorrar	*to save (money)*
cobrar	*to cash (a check)*
depositar	*to deposit*
firmar	*to sign*
llenar (un formulario)	*to fill out (a form)*
pagar a plazos	*to pay in installments*
pagar al contado/en efectivo	*to pay in cash*
pedir prestado/a	*to borrow*
pedir un préstamo	*to apply for a loan*
ser gratis	*to be free of charge*

Cómo llegar

la cuadra	*(city) block*
la dirección	*address*
la esquina	*corner*
el letrero	*sign*
cruzar	*to cross*
doblar	*to turn*
estar perdido/a	*to be lost*
indicar cómo llegar	*to give directions*
quedar	*to be located*
(al) este	*(to the) east*
(al) norte	*(to the) north*
(al) oeste	*(to the) west*
(al) sur	*(to the) south*
derecho	*straight (ahead)*
enfrente de	*opposite; facing*
hacia	*toward*

En el correo

el cartero	*mail carrier*
el correo	*mail; post office*
la estampilla, el sello	*stamp*
el paquete	*package*
el sobre	*envelope*
echar (una carta) al buzón	*to put (a letter) in the mailbox; to mail*
enviar, mandar	*to send; to mail*

Expresiones útiles	*See page 455.*

recursos

LM p. 83	vhlcentral.com Lección 14

Vocabulary Tools

El bienestar

15

Communicative Goals

You will learn how to:

- **Talk about health, well-being, and nutrition**
- **Talk about physical activities**

contextos

fotonovela

cultura

estructura

adelante

A PRIMERA VISTA

- **¿Está la chica en un gimnasio o en un lugar al aire libre?**
- **¿Practica ella deportes frecuentemente?**
- **¿Es activa o sedentaria?**
- **¿Es probable que le importe su salud?**

Lesson Goals

In **Lección 15**, students will be introduced to the following:

- terms for health and exercise
- nutrition terms
- natural spas
- the health benefits of quinoa
- conditional
- present perfect
- past perfect
- making inferences
- organizing information logically when writing
- writing a personal wellness plan
- listening for the gist and for cognates
- a public service ad for the **Asociación Parkinson Alicante**
- the short film ***Cloe***
- a video about places to relax and ways to deal with stress in Madrid, Spain
- cultural, geographic, and historical information about Bolivia and Paraguay

A primera vista Here are some additional questions you can ask: **¿Crees que tienes buena salud? ¿Vas al gimnasio regularmente? ¿Usas tu carro para hacer diligencias, o caminas? ¿Qué haces cuando te sientes nervioso/a o cansado/a? ¿Es importante que desayunes todas las mañanas? ¿Cuántas horas duermes cada noche?**

Teaching Tip Look for these icons for additional communicative practice:

	Interpretive communication
	Presentational communication
	Interpersonal communication

INSTRUCTIONAL RESOURCES

Supersite (vhlcentral.com)
Video: ***Fotonovela, Flash cultura, Anuncio, Cortometraje, Panorama cultural***
Audio: Textbook and Lab MP3 Files
Activity Pack: Information Gap Activities, games, additional activity handouts
Resources: SAM Answer Key, Scripts, Translations, **Vocabulario adicional**, sample lesson plan, Grammar Presentation Slides, Digital Image Bank
Testing Program: Quizzes, Tests, Exams, MP3s
Student Activities Manual: Workbook/Video Manual/Lab Manual
WebSAM (online Student Activities Manual)

Vocabulary Tools

Section Goals

In **Contextos**, students will learn and practice:

- vocabulary used to talk about health and exercise
- vocabulary used to discuss nutrition and a healthy diet

Instructional Resources

Supersite: Audio (Textbook and Lab MP3 Files); Resources (Digital Image Bank, **Vocabulario adicional**, Activity Pack, Scripts, Answer Keys); Testing Program (Quizzes)
WebSAM
Workbook, pp. 181–182
Lab Manual, p. 85

Teaching Tips

- Use the **Lección 15 Contextos** digital images to assist with this presentation.
- Write **hacer ejercicio** on the board, then ask personalized questions, writing new vocabulary on the board: Ex: **¿Quiénes hacen ejercicio regularmente? ¿Hacen ejercicios aeróbicos? ¿Quiénes levantan pesas?**
- Give the people in the illustration names and make statements and ask questions about their activities. Ex: **El señor Garza es teleadicto. Él no hace ejercicio. Ve televisión y come papitas. ¿Es activo o sedentario? ¿Lleva una vida sana?** After you have gone over the active vocabulary, ask students personalized questions to engage the class in a discussion about their exercise habits. Ex: **¿Qué hacen para aliviar el estrés? ¿Creen que se puede hacer demasiada gimnasia? ¿Creen que es más importante ser flexible o ser fuerte?**
- Point out the *No smoking* sign at the top right of the drawing. Explain that the infinitive, instead of a command form, is often found on public signs to express prohibitions or instructions.

El bienestar

Más vocabulario

adelgazar	*to lose weight; to slim down*
aliviar el estrés	*to reduce stress*
aliviar la tensión	*to reduce tension*
apurarse, darse prisa	*to hurry; to rush*
aumentar de peso, engordar	*to gain weight*
calentarse (e:ie)	*to warm up*
disfrutar (de)	*to enjoy; to reap the benefits (of)*
entrenarse	*to train*
estar a dieta	*to be on a diet*
estar en buena forma	*to be in good shape*
hacer gimnasia	*to work out*
llevar una vida sana	*to lead a healthy lifestyle*
mantenerse en forma	*to stay in shape*
sufrir muchas presiones	*to be under a lot of pressure*
tratar de (+ *inf.*)	*to try (to do something)*
la droga	*drug*
el/la drogadicto/a	*drug addict*
activo/a	*active*
débil	*weak*
en exceso	*in excess; too much*
flexible	*flexible*
fuerte	*strong*
sedentario/a	*sedentary*
tranquilo/a	*calm; quiet*
el bienestar	*well-being*

Variación léxica

hacer ejercicios aeróbicos ←→ hacer aeróbic *(Esp.)*
el/la entrenador(a) ←→ el/la monitor(a)

recursos
WB pp. 181–182 | LM p. 85 | vhlcentral.com Lección 15

TEACHING OPTIONS

TPR Ask students to stand. Call out commands based on the lesson vocabulary. Ex: **¡Levanten pesas! ¡Hagan ejercicios aeróbicos! ¡Apúrense! ¡Descansen!** Working with students, invent a gesture to mime each activity. When you have invented gestures to cover all the vocabulary, carry out a TPR activity with the class. Keep a brisk pace. Vary singular and plural commands.

Heritage Speakers Have volunteers read the words in the **Variación léxica** box aloud. Ask heritage speakers if they can name any additional terms related to fitness, health, and well-being. Ex: **tener mucho estrés, estar estresado/a; trotar**

Práctica

1 **Escuchar** Mira el dibujo. Luego escucha las oraciones e indica si lo que se dice en cada oración es **cierto** o **falso**.

	Cierto	Falso		Cierto	Falso
1.	❍	✓	6.	❍	✓
2.	❍	✓	7.	❍	✓
3.	✓	❍	8.	✓	❍
4.	✓	❍	9.	❍	✓
5.	✓	❍	10.	❍	✓

2 **Seleccionar** Escucha el anuncio del gimnasio Sucre. Marca con una **X** los servicios que se ofrecen.

__x__ 1. dietas para adelgazar
_____ 2. programa para aumentar de peso
__x__ 3. clases de gimnasia
__x__ 4. entrenador personal
__x__ 5. masajes
_____ 6. programa para dejar de fumar

3 **Identificar** Identifica el antónimo (*antonym*) de cada palabra.

apurarse	fuerte
disfrutar	mantenerse en forma
engordar	sedentario
estar enfermo	sufrir muchas presiones
flexible	tranquilo

1. activo sedentario
2. adelgazar engordar
3. aliviar el estrés sufrir muchas presiones
4. débil fuerte
5. ir despacio apurarse
6. estar sano estar enfermo
7. nervioso tranquilo
8. ser teleadicto mantenerse en forma

4 **Combinar** Combina elementos de cada columna para formar ocho oraciones lógicas sobre el bienestar.

1. David levanta pesas h
2. Estás en buena forma d
3. Felipe se lastimó f
4. José y Rafael e
5. Mi hermano a
6. Sara hace ejercicios de b
7. Mis primas están a dieta c
8. Para llevar una vida sana, g

a. aumentó de peso.
b. estiramiento.
c. porque quieren adelgazar.
d. porque haces ejercicio.
e. sudan mucho en el gimnasio.
f. un músculo de la pierna.
g. no se debe fumar.
h. y corre mucho.

1 Teaching Tip Check answers by reading each statement and asking volunteers to say whether it is true or false. To challenge students, have them provide the correct information for each false statement.

1 Script 1. Se puede fumar dentro del gimnasio. 2. El teleadicto está en buena forma. 3. Los músculos del entrenador son grandes. 4. La mujer que está corriendo también está sudando.
Script continues on page 484.

2 Teaching Tip Tell students to listen to the audio without looking at the drawing.

2 Script Si quieres estar en buena forma, aliviar el estrés o adelgazar, el gimnasio Sucre te ofrece una serie de programas que se adaptarán a tus gustos. Tenemos un equipo de entrenadores que te pueden ayudar a mantenerte en forma con las clases de ejercicios aeróbicos y de gimnasia. Si sufres muchas presiones y lo que necesitas es un servicio más especial, puedes trabajar con un entrenador personal en nuestros programas privados de pesas, masajes y dietas para adelgazar.
Textbook MP3s

3 Expansion Have students use each pair of opposite terms in sentences.
Ex: **José está muy nervioso porque no estudió para el examen. Roberto estudió por dos horas; por eso está tranquilo.**

4 Expansion Have students create original endings for the sentence starters in the left column.

Note: At this point you may want to present ***Vocabulario adicional: Más vocabulario para el bienestar*** from the Supersite.

TEACHING OPTIONS

Pairs Have pairs of students interview each other about what they do to stay fit. Interviewers should also find out how often their partner does these things and when he or she did them over the past week. Ask students to write a brief report summarizing the interview.

Game Divide the class into teams of three. Ask one team to stay outside the room while the class chooses a vocabulary word or expression. When the team returns, they must try to guess it by asking the class yes/no questions. If the team guesses the word within ten questions, they get a point. Ex: **¿Es un lugar? ¿Describe a una persona? ¿Es una acción? ¿Es algo que haces para estar en buena forma?**

1 Script (continued) 5. Se puede recibir un masaje en el gimnasio Sucre. 6. Hay cuatro hombres en la clase de ejercicios aeróbicos. 7. El hombre que levanta pesas lleva una vida muy sedentaria. 8. La instructora de la clase de ejercicios aeróbicos lleva una vida muy activa. 9. El hombre que mira televisión está a dieta. 10. No hay nadie en el gimnasio que haga ejercicios de estiramiento.
Textbook MP3s

Teaching Tips
- Use the **Lección 15 Contextos** digital images to assist with this vocabulary presentation.
- First, ask open-ended or yes/no questions that elicit the names of the foods depicted. Ex: **¿Qué es esto? (un huevo) Y esto al lado del queso, ¿son papas fritas?** Then ask students either/or questions to elicit the vocabulary in **La nutrición**. Ex: **¿La carne tiene proteínas o vitaminas?** Continue asking for information or opinions. Ex: **La cafeína, ¿creen que es una droga? ¿Por qué?**
- Point out that although English *alcohol* contains three syllables, Spanish **alcohol** is pronounced as two syllables.

5 Expansion
After checking each item, ask students personalized questions, or have them comment on the information. Ex: **¿Comen ustedes comidas con mucha proteína después de hacer ejercicio?** Ask follow-up questions when possible.

Ayuda Present the vocabulary using the words in sentences that describe your eating or physical activity patterns.

6 Expansion
As students share their answers with the class, write on the board any common themes that emerge. Have a class discussion about these themes and their origins.

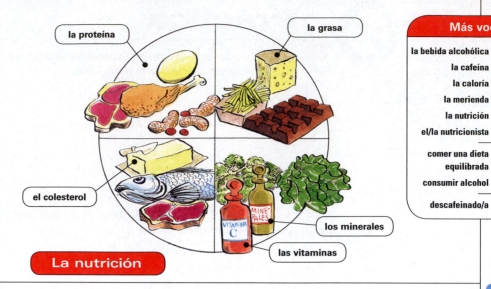

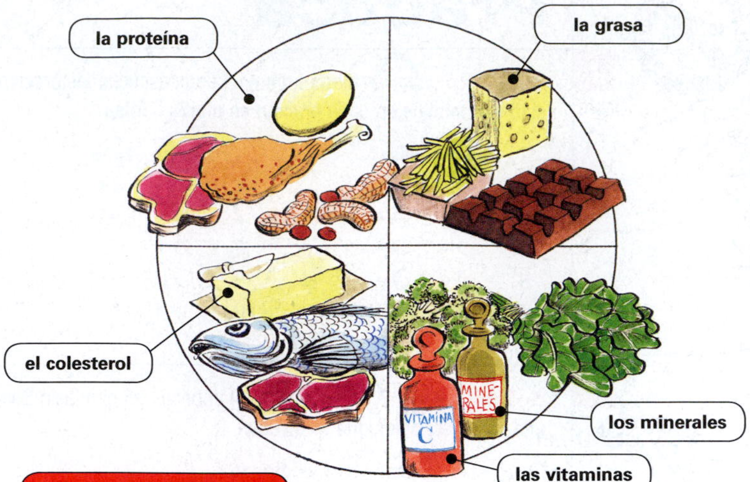

La nutrición

Más vocabulario

la bebida alcohólica	*alcoholic beverage*
la cafeína	*caffeine*
la caloría	*calorie*
la merienda	*afternoon snack*
la nutrición	*nutrition*
el/la nutricionista	*nutritionist*
comer una dieta equilibrada	*to eat a balanced diet*
consumir alcohol	*to consume alcohol*
descafeinado/a	*decaffeinated*

5 **Completar** Completa cada oración con la palabra adecuada.

1. Después de hacer ejercicio, como pollo o bistec porque contienen __b__.
   a. drogas b. proteínas c. grasa
2. Para __c__, es necesario consumir comidas de todos los grupos alimenticios (*nutrition groups*).
   a. aliviar el estrés b. correr c. comer una dieta equilibrada
3. Mis primas __a__ una buena comida.
   a. disfrutan de b. tratan de c. sudan
4. Mi entrenador no come queso ni papas fritas porque contienen __c__.
   a. dietas b. vitaminas c. mucha grasa
5. Mi padre no come mantequilla porque él necesita reducir __b__.
   a. la nutrición b. el colesterol c. el bienestar
6. Mi novio cuenta __c__ porque está a dieta.
   a. las pesas b. los músculos c. las calorías

CONSULTA
To review what you have learned about nutrition and food groups, see **Contextos, Lección 8**, pp. 242–245.

6 **La nutrición** En parejas, hablen de los tipos de comida que comen y las consecuencias que tienen para su salud. Luego compartan la información con la clase. Answers will vary.

1. ¿Cuántas comidas con mucha grasa comes regularmente? ¿Piensas que debes comer menos comidas de este tipo? ¿Por qué?
2. ¿Compras comidas con muchos minerales y vitaminas? ¿Necesitas consumir más comidas que los contienen? ¿Por qué?
3. ¿Algún miembro de tu familia tiene problemas con el colesterol? ¿Qué haces para evitar problemas con el colesterol?
4. ¿Eres vegetariano/a? ¿Conoces a alguien que sea vegetariano/a? ¿Qué piensas de la idea de no comer carne u otros productos animales? ¿Es posible comer una dieta equilibrada sin comer carne? Explica.
5. ¿Tomas cafeína en exceso? ¿Qué ventajas (*advantages*) y desventajas tiene la cafeína? Da ejemplos de productos que contienen cafeína y de productos descafeinados.
6. ¿Llevas una vida sana? ¿Y tus amigos? ¿Crees que, en general, los estudiantes llevan una vida sana? ¿Por qué?

Practice more at **vhlcentral.com**.

AYUDA
Some useful words:
sano = saludable
en general = por lo general
estricto
normalmente
muchas veces
a veces
de vez en cuando

TEACHING OPTIONS

TPR Add an auditory aspect to this vocabulary practice. Have students write **bueno** on one piece of paper and **malo** on another. Prepare a series of statements about healthy and unhealthy habits. As you read each statement, have students hold up the corresponding paper. Ex: **Antes de hacer ejercicio, siempre como comidas con mucha grasa. (malo) Consumo muy poco alcohol. (bueno)**

Small Groups In groups of three or four, have students take turns miming actions involving fitness, health, and well-being. The other group members should guess the verb or verb phrase. Ex: A student mimes lifting weights. (**Estás levantando pesas.**)

Comunicación

7 **Un anuncio** En grupos de cuatro, imaginen que son dueños/as de un gimnasio con un equipo (*equipment*) moderno, entrenadores cualificados y un(a) nutricionista. Preparen y presenten un anuncio para la televisión que hable del gimnasio y atraiga (*attracts*) a una gran variedad de nuevos clientes. No se olviden de presentar esta información: Answers will vary.

- las ventajas de estar en buena forma
- el equipo que tienen
- los servicios y clases que ofrecen
- las características únicas
- la dirección y el teléfono
- el precio para los socios (*members*)

8 **Recomendaciones para la salud** En parejas, imaginen que están preocupados/as por los malos hábitos de un(a) amigo/a que no está bien últimamente (*lately*). Escriban y representen una conversación en la cual hablen de lo que está pasando en la vida de su amigo/a y los cambios que necesita hacer para llevar una vida sana. Answers will vary.

9 **El teleadicto** Con un(a) compañero/a, representen los papeles de un(a) nutricionista y un(a) teleadicto/a. La persona sedentaria habla de sus malos hábitos para la comida y de que no hace ejercicio. También dice que toma demasiado café y que siente mucho estrés. El/La nutricionista le sugiere una dieta equilibrada con bebidas descafeinadas y una rutina para mantenerse en forma. El/La teleadicto/a le da las gracias por su ayuda. Answers will vary.

10 **El gimnasio perfecto** Tú y tu compañero/a quieren encontrar el gimnasio perfecto. Su profesor(a) les va a dar a cada uno/a de ustedes el anuncio de un gimnasio. Túrnense para hacerse preguntas sobre las actividades que se ofrecen en cada uno. Al final, decidan cuál es el mejor gimnasio y compartan su decisión con la clase. Answers will vary.

11 **¿Quién es?** Trabajen en grupos. Cada uno/a de ustedes va a elegir a una persona famosa por temas de salud y bienestar. Los demás miembros del grupo deben hacer preguntas hasta descubrir a quién eligió cada quien. Recuerden usar el vocabulario de la lección. Answers will vary.

modelo

Estudiante 1: ¿Haces ejercicio todos los días?
Estudiante 2: Sí, hago gimnasia y juego al baloncesto.
Estudiante 3: ¿Comes una dieta equilibrada?
Estudiante 2: Sí, y perdí más de 80 libras (*pounds*) de peso.
Estudiante 1: ¡Ya sé! ¡Eres Jennifer Hudson!

TEACHING OPTIONS

Pairs Tell students to imagine that they are personal wellness consultants. (If you wish, have them take on the persona of one of the people mentioned in **Actividad 11**.) Have them give their partner a set of ten guidelines on how to begin a comprehensive health program. Suggestions should be made regarding diet, aerobic exercise, strength training, flexibility training, and stress management. Have students switch roles.

Extra Practice Ask students to write down five personal goals for achieving or maintaining a healthy lifestyle. Then have them write a brief paragraph explaining why they want to attain these goals and how they plan to achieve them. Call on volunteers to share their goals with the class.

7 Teaching Tips
- Have students visit health clubs in your area to gather brochures and/or fitness magazines to help them brainstorm ideas.
- Have groups write their advertisement so that each student gets to speak for an equal amount of time.

8 Teaching Tips
- Suggest that students use expressions of doubt followed by the subjunctive or expressions of certainty. Review the expressions on pages 430–431 as needed.
- Have partners discuss at least five bad habits their friend has, explain why he or she has them, and what he or she tried to do to overcome them. Then, have students discuss ways of successfully overcoming each habit.

9 Teaching Tip Before doing this activity, review the verbs and expressions of will and influence on pages 398–399.

9 Expansion Have students conduct a follow-up interview that takes place one month after the initial meeting.

10 Teaching Tip Divide the class into pairs and distribute the handouts from the Activity Pack (Activity Pack/Supersite) that correspond to this activity.

10 Expansion
- Have pairs work in groups to discuss which gym they would join and why.
- Have groups compare these gyms with your campus gym.

11 Teaching Tip Encourage students to think of people from all areas of health, including nutrition, exercise, and mental well-being. To simplify, provide a list of names on the board. Ex: Richard Simmons, Jillian Michaels, Dr. Oz, Oprah, Dr. Phil, Billy Blanks, Bethenny Frankel, Jackie Warner, Michael Pollan

Section Goals

In **Fotonovela**, students will:

- receive comprehensible input from free-flowing discourse
- learn functional phrases that preview lesson grammatical structures

Instructional Resources
Supersite: Video (***Fotonovela***); Resources (Scripts, Translations, Answer Keys)
WebSAM
Video Manual, pp. 29–30

Video Recap: Lección 14
Before doing this **Fotonovela** section, review the previous episode with these questions:
1. ¿Por qué Maru no está en Yucatán con los otros chicos? (Tuvo que entregar su proyecto.)
2. ¿Por qué Maru dice que necesita un coche que funcione bien? (Porque el coche de Miguel está descompuesto.)
3. ¿Qué quiere Maru que Mónica le preste? (Quiere que Mónica le preste dinero para tomar un taxi.) 4. ¿Dónde dejó Maru el proyecto? (Lo dejó en el coche de Miguel.) 5. ¿Cómo llegó Maru al Museo de Antropología? (Mónica la llevó.)

Video Synopsis **Marissa, Felipe, Jimena,** and **Juan Carlos** visit the famous Mayan ruins of **Chichén Itzá.** After exploring the archeological site, they visit a spa to escape the sun and unwind. **Juan Carlos** and **Jimena** finally connect.

Teaching Tips

- Ask students to read only the first statement in each caption. Then have them predict the content of the episode, based only on those sentences. Write down their predictions.
- Quickly review the predictions students made about the episode. Through discussion, help the class summarize the plot.

Chichén Itzá

communication cultures — NATIONAL STANDARDS

Los chicos exploran Chichén Itzá y se relajan en un spa.

PERSONAJES

MARISSA

FELIPE

Video: *Fotonovela*

MARISSA ¡Chichén Itzá es impresionante! Qué lástima que Maru y Miguel no estén con nosotros. Sobre todo Maru.

FELIPE Ha estado bajo mucha presión.

MARISSA Podría quedarme aquí para siempre. ¿Ustedes ya habían venido antes?

FELIPE Sí. Nuestros papás nos trajeron cuando éramos niños.

(*en otro lugar de las ruinas*)

JUAN CARLOS ¡Hace calor!

JIMENA ¡Sí! Hay que estar en buena forma para recorrer las ruinas.

JUAN CARLOS Siempre había llevado una vida sana antes de entrar a la universidad.

JIMENA Tienes razón. La universidad hace que seamos muy sedentarios.

JUAN CARLOS ¡Busquemos a Felipe y a Marissa!

FELIPE El otro día le gané a Juan Carlos en el parque.

JUAN CARLOS Estaba mirando hacia otro lado, cuando me di cuenta, Felipe ya había empezado a correr.

FELIPE ¡Gané!

JIMENA Qué calor. Tengo una idea. Vamos.

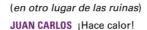

TEACHING OPTIONS

Video Tips General suggestions for using video clips in the classroom can be found in the front matter of this Instructor's Annotated Edition.

Chichén Itzá To introduce the class to this **Fotonovela** episode, first play the video without any sound so students can concentrate on the action. Have students tell you what they saw and make predictions about the content of the video. Then, play the episode with sound and have students jot down notes about the plot. Next, have the class work in small groups to compare notes and prepare summaries of the episode. Ask one or two groups to read their summaries to the class. Finally, discuss the plot with the class and check for accuracy.

JUAN CARLOS

JIMENA

EMPLEADA

7

EMPLEADA Ofrecemos varios servicios para aliviar el estrés: masajes, saunas...

8

FELIPE Me gustaría un masaje.

MARISSA Yo prefiero un baño mineral.

9

JUAN CARLOS ¿Crees que tendrías un poco de tiempo libre la semana que viene? Me gustaría invitarte a salir.

JIMENA ¿Sin Felipe?

JUAN CARLOS Sin Felipe.

10

EMPLEADA ¿Ya tomaron una decisión?

JIMENA Sí.

Expresiones útiles

Wishing a friend were with you

Qué lástima que no estén con nosotros.
What a shame that they aren't with us.
Sobre todo Maru.
Especially Maru.
Él/Ella ha estado bajo mucha presión.
He/She has been under a lot of pressure.
Creo que ellos ya habían venido antes.
I think they had already come (here) before.

Talking about trips

¿Ustedes ya habían venido antes?
Had you been (here) before?
Sí. He querido regresar desde que leí el *Chilam Balam*.
Yes. I have wanted to come back ever since I read the Chilam Balam.
¿Recuerdas cuando nos trajo papá?
Remember when Dad brought us?
Al llegar a la cima, comenzaste a llorar.
When we got to the top, you started to cry.

Talking about well-being

Siempre había llevado una vida sana antes de entrar a la universidad.
I had always maintained a healthy lifestyle before starting college.
Ofrecemos varios servicios para aliviar el estrés.
We offer many services to relieve stress.
Me gustaría un masaje.
I would like a massage.

Additional vocabulary

la cima *top, peak*
el escalón *step*
el muro *wall*
tomar una decisión *to make a decision*

recursos
VM pp. 29–30
vhlcentral.com Lección 15

Expresiones útiles Draw attention to the sentence **Me gustaría un masaje**. Tell students that **gustaría** is an example of the conditional, which they saw in **Lección 8** (**¿Les gustaría saber cuáles son las especialidades del día?**). The conditional is formed much like the future tense. Point out that **ha estado** and **He querido** are examples of the present perfect, which combines a present-tense form of the verb **haber** with the past participle of another verb. Finally, explain that **habían venido** and **había llevado** are examples of the past perfect, which combines an imperfect-tense form of **haber** with a past participle. Tell students that they will learn more about these concepts in **Estructura**.

Teaching Tips

- Have the class read through the entire **Fotonovela**, with volunteers playing the various parts.
- Point out **Me gustaría invitarte a salir** from the caption for video still 9. Ask students to translate it into English using the sentence **Me gustaría un masaje** from **Expresiones útiles** as a guide.
- Explain that the conditional is used to express *what you would do* or *what would happen* under certain circumstances and that they will learn more about its use in **Estructura**.

Nota cultural **Chichén Itzá** is a large pre-Columbian archeological site built by the Mayans in Mexico. Now a UNESCO World Heritage Site, it attracts thousands of tourists from all over the world each year. While at one time visitors were given open access to **Chichén Itzá**, this is now limited due to the erosion and destruction of many structures.

TEACHING OPTIONS

Pairs Have students work in pairs to write five true/false statements about the **Chichén Itzá** episode. Then, have pairs exchange papers with another pair, who will work together to complete the activity and correct the false information.

Extra Practice Photocopy the **Fotonovela** Videoscript (Supersite) and white out key vocabulary in order to make a master for a cloze activity. Distribute the copies and, as you play the **Chichén Itzá** episode, have students fill in the blanks.

1 Teaching Tip To challenge students, write the incomplete statements on the board. Have students close their books and finish them using their own words.

1 Expansion Have the class work in pairs or small groups to write a question that would elicit each statement.

2 Expansion
- Give the class these statements as items 7-8: **7. ¡Creo que papá no ha hecho ejercicio por mucho tiempo! (Felipe) 8. Es extraño que Juan Carlos no te invite a salir. (Marissa)**
- Have students close their books, then give them these sentences as a dictation. Read each sentence twice slowly. Ask volunteers to write their sentences on the board and correct them as a class.

3 Teaching Tip Remind students to use examples from the **Fotonovela** to help them support their answers.

3 Expansion
- Have pairs write sentences using any unused words from the word bank. Ask volunteers to share their sentences with the class.
- In pairs, have students ask each other questions using words from the list. Encourage partners to ask follow-up questions to learn more about their habits. Pairs should report their findings to the class.

¿Qué pasó?

1 Seleccionar Selecciona la respuesta que completa mejor cada oración.

1. Felipe y Marissa piensan que Maru __c__.
   a. debe hacer ejercicio b. aumentó de peso c. ha estado bajo mucha presión
2. Felipe y Jimena visitaron Chichén Itzá __b__.
   a. para aliviar el estrés b. cuando eran niños c. para llevar una vida sana
3. Jimena dice que la universidad hace a los estudiantes __b__.
   a. comer una dieta equilibrada b. ser sedentarios c. levantar pesas
4. En el spa ofrecen servicios para __b__.
   a. sudar b. aliviar el estrés c. ser flexibles
5. Felipe elige que le den un __c__.
   a. baño mineral b. almuerzo c. masaje

2 Identificar Identifica quién puede decir estas oraciones.

1. No me di cuenta (*I didn't realize*) de que habías empezado a correr, por eso ganaste. Juan Carlos
2. Miguel y Maru no visitaron Chichén Itzá, ¡qué lástima que no estén con nosotros! Marissa
3. Se necesita estar en buena forma para visitar este tipo de lugares. Jimena
4. Los masajes, saunas y baños minerales que ofrecemos alivian la tensión. empleada
5. Si salimos, no invites a Felipe. Jimena
6. Yo corro más rápido que Juan Carlos. Felipe

MARISSA

FELIPE

JIMENA

JUAN CARLOS

EMPLEADA

3 Inventar En parejas, hagan descripciones de los personajes de la **Fotonovela**. Utilicen las oraciones, la lista de palabras y otras expresiones que sepan. Answers will vary.

aliviar el estrés	hacer ejercicios de estiramiento	masaje
bienestar	llevar una vida sana	teleadicto/a
grasa	mantenerse en forma	vitamina

modelo

Estudiante 1: *Felipe es activo, flexible y fuerte.*
Estudiante 2: *Marissa siempre hace ejercicios de estiramiento. Está en buena forma y lleva una vida muy sana...*

1. A Juan Carlos le duelen los músculos después de hacer gimnasia.
2. Maru a veces sufre presiones y estrés en la universidad.
3. A Jimena le encanta salir con amigos o leer un buen libro.
4. Felipe trata de comer una dieta equilibrada.
5. Juan Carlos no es muy flexible.

Practice more at **vhlcentral.com.**

NATIONAL communication STANDARDS

TEACHING OPTIONS

Extra Practice Ask the class a few additional questions about the **Fotonovela**. Ex: **¿Por qué Jimena lloraba mientras subía los escalones de El Castillo? (Quería regresar al hotel y jugar en la playa.) ¿Qué servicios ofrece el spa para aliviar el estrés? (Ofrece masajes, saunas y tratamientos con vitaminas y minerales para la piel.)**

Pairs Have pairs prepare a television program in which travelers are interviewed about their recent trip to the Mayan ruins of **Chichén Itzá**. Allow students to research more about the archeological site online before writing their scripts. Make sure to give them enough time to prepare and rehearse; then ask volunteers to present their programs to the class. Alternately, you may want the students to make a video of their programs and play them for the class.

NATIONAL STANDARDS comparisons

Ortografía

Audio

Las letras b y v

Since there is no difference in pronunciation between the Spanish letters **b** and **v**, spelling words that contain these letters can be tricky. Here are some tips.

nombre **blusa** **absoluto** **descubrir**

The letter **b** is always used before consonants.

bonita **botella** **buscar** **bienestar**

At the beginning of words, the letter **b** is usually used when it is followed by the letter combinations **-on, -or, -ot, -u, -ur, -us, -ien,** and **-ene.**

adelgazaba **disfrutaban** **ibas** **íbamos**

The letter **b** is used in the verb endings of the imperfect tense for **-ar** verbs and the verb **ir.**

voy **vamos** **estuvo** **tuvieron**

The letter **v** is used in the present tense forms of **ir** and in the preterite forms of **estar** and **tener.**

octavo **huevo** **activa** **grave**

The letter **v** is used in these noun and adjective endings: **-avo/a, -evo/a, -ivo/a, -ave, -eve.**

Práctica Completa las palabras con las letras **b** o **v**.

1. Una _v_ez me lastimé el _b_razo cuando esta_b_a _b_uceando.
2. Manuela ol_v_idó sus li_b_ros en el auto_b_ús.
3. Ernesto tomó el _b_orrador y se puso todo _b_lanco de tiza.
4. Para tener una _v_ida sana y saluda_b_le, necesitas tomar _v_itaminas.
5. En mi pue_b_lo hay un _b_ule_v_ar que tiene muchos ár_b_oles.

El ahorcado (*Hangman*) Juega al ahorcado para adivinar las palabras.

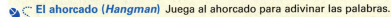

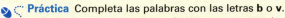

1. n u b e s — Están en el cielo. nubes
2. b u z ó n — Relacionado con el correo buzón
3. b o t e l l a — Está llena de líquido. botella
4. n i e v e — Fenómeno meteorológico nieve
5. v e n t a n a s — Los "ojos" de la casa ventanas

recursos

LM p. 86	vhlcentral.com Lección 15

Section Goal

In **Ortografía**, students will learn about the spelling of words that contain **b** and **v**.

Instructional Resources

Supersite: Audio (Lab MP3 Files); Resources (Scripts, Answer Keys)
WebSAM
Lab Manual, p. 86

Teaching Tips

- Ask the class if **b** or **v** is used before a consonant. Then say the words **nombre, blusa, absoluto,** and **descubrir** and have volunteers write them on the board.
- Write the words **bonita, botella, buscar,** and **bienestar** on the board. Ask the class to explain why these words start with a **b**.
- Ask the class if **b** or **v** is used in the endings of **-ar** verbs and the verb **ir** in the imperfect tense. Then say the words **adelgazaba, disfrutaban, ibas,** and **íbamos** and ask volunteers to write them on the board.
- Ask why the words **voy, vamos, estuvo,** and **tuvieron** are spelled with **v** and have volunteers write them on the board.
- Write the words **octavo, huevo, activa,** and **grave** on the board and ask the class to explain why these words are spelled with **v**.
- Point out that **Ortografía** replaces **Pronunciación** in the Student Edition for **Lecciones 10–15**, but not in the Lab Manual. The **Recursos** box references the **Pronunciación** sections found in all lessons of the Lab Manual.

TEACHING OPTIONS

Extra Practice Add an auditory aspect to this **Ortografía** presentation. Prepare a dictation exercise with words containing **b** and **v**. Slowly read each sentence twice, allowing time for students to write. Ex: **Doña Victoria era muy activa y llevaba una vida muy sana. Siempre almorzaba verduras y nunca tomaba vino ni refrescos. Nunca fumaba e iba al gimnasio todos los jueves, viernes y sábados para tomar clases de ejercicios aeróbicos.** Ask comprehension questions as a follow-up.

Pairs Have partners use **Vocabulario** at the back of the book to help them write five sentences that contain words with **b** and **v**. Encourage students to use as many of these words as they can. They should leave blanks in place of these letters, as in the **Práctica** activity. Then have pairs exchange papers with another pair, and complete the words.

Flash CULTURA

Section Goals

In **Cultura**, students will:
- read about natural spas
- learn exercise-related terms
- read about the health benefits of quinoa
- read about popular beliefs regarding health

Instructional Resources
Supersite: Video (***Flash cultura***); Resources (Scripts, Translations, Answer Keys)
WebSAM
Video Manual, pp. 101–102

En detalle
Antes de leer Have students look at the photos and describe what they see. Then ask: **¿Alguna vez han ido a un balneario? ¿Por qué creen que las personas van a los balnearios?**

Lectura
- While people of all ages visit spas, the elderly have discovered specific health benefits. In places like Villa Elisa, Argentina, many go to thermal baths to reduce swelling in their joints and relieve backaches.
- Point out the word **lodoterapia**. Have a volunteer explain what it means and how this word is formed.
- Point out the chart and ask students what information it shows.

Después de leer
Ask students which spa they would like to visit. Have them write a short paragraph of 3 to 4 sentences explaining why.

1 Expansion Have students rephrase each statement as a question. Ex: **2. ¿Desde cuándo se conocen los tratamientos con agua y lodo?**

EN DETALLE

Video: *Flash cultura*

Spas naturales

NATIONAL STANDARDS connections cultures

¿Hay algo mejor que un buen baño° para descansar y aliviar la tensión? Y si el baño se toma en una terma°, el beneficio° es mayor. Los tratamientos con agua y lodo° para mejorar la salud y el bienestar son populares en las Américas desde hace muchos siglos°. Las termas son manantiales° naturales de agua caliente. La temperatura facilita la absorción de minerales y otros elementos que contiene el agua y que son buenos para la salud. El agua de las termas se usa en piscinas, baños y duchas o en el sitio natural en el que surge°: pozas°, estanques° o cuevas°.

Volcán de lodo El Totumo, Colombia

En Baños de San Vicente, en Ecuador, son muy populares los tratamientos° con lodo volcánico.

El lodo caliente se extiende por el cuerpo; así la piel° absorbe los minerales beneficiosos para la salud; también se usa para dar masajes. La lodoterapia es útil para tratar varias enfermedades, además hace que la piel se vea radiante.

Ecotermales en Arenal, Costa Rica

En Costa Rica, la actividad volcánica también ha dado° origen a fuentes° y pozas termales. Si te gusta cuidarte y amas la naturaleza, recuerda estos nombres: Las Hornillas y Las Pailas. Son pozas naturales de aguas termales que están cerca del volcán Rincón de la Vieja. Un baño termal en medio de un paisaje tan hermoso es una experiencia única.

Otros balnearios°

Todos ofrecen piscinas, baños, pozas y duchas de aguas termales y además...

Lugar	Servicios
El Edén y Yanasara, Curgos (Perú)	cascadas° de aguas termales
Montbrió del Camp, Tarragona (España)	baños de algas°
Puyuhuapi (Chile)	duchas de agua de mar; baños de algas
Termas de Río Hondo, Santiago del Estero (Argentina)	baños de lodo
Tepoztlán, Morelos (México)	temazcales° aztecas
Uyuni, Potosí (Bolivia)	baños de sal

baño *bath* **terma** *hot spring* **beneficio** *benefit* **lodo** *mud* **siglos** *centuries* **manantiales** *springs* **surge** *springs forth* **pozas** *small pools* **estanques** *ponds* **cuevas** *caves* **tratamientos** *treatments* **piel** *skin* **ha dado** *has given* **fuentes** *springs* **balnearios** *spas* **cascadas** *waterfalls* **algas** *seaweed* **temazcales** *steam and medicinal herb baths*

ACTIVIDADES

1 **¿Cierto o falso?** Indica si lo que dicen las oraciones es cierto o falso. Corrige la información falsa.

1. Las aguas termales son beneficiosas para algunas enfermedades, incluido el estrés. **Cierto.**
2. Los tratamientos con agua y lodo se conocen sólo desde hace pocos años. **Falso.** Son populares desde hace muchos siglos.
3. Las termas son manantiales naturales de agua caliente. **Cierto.**
4. La lodoterapia es un tratamiento con barro (*mud*). **Cierto.**
5. La temperatura de las aguas termales no afecta la absorción de los minerales. **Falso.** Facilita la absorción de minerales y otros elementos.
6. Mucha gente va a Baños de San Vicente, Ecuador, por sus playas. **Falso.** Mucha gente va por los tratamientos con lodo.
7. Las Hornillas son pozas de aguas termales en Costa Rica. **Cierto.**
8. Montbrió del Camp ofrece baños de sal. **Falso.** Montbrió del Camp ofrece baños de algas.
9. Es posible ver aguas termales en forma de cascadas. **Cierto.**
10. Tepoztlán ofrece temazcales aztecas. **Cierto.**

TEACHING OPTIONS

TPR Call out true/false statements about the reading. If the statement is true, have students raise one hand. If the statement is false, have students raise both hands. To challenge students, have volunteers correct the false information.

Small Groups Have students work in small groups. Tell them to imagine that they are planning a trip to one of the spas mentioned in the reading. Have them do additional Internet research and find out how to travel there, the services offered, and the prices. Then have groups present their itineraries to the class.

ASÍ SE DICE

El ejercicio

los abdominales	*sit-ups*
la bicicleta estática	*stationary bicycle*
el calambre muscular	*(muscular) cramp*
el (fisi)culturismo; la musculación (Esp.)	*bodybuilding*
las flexiones de pecho; las lagartijas (Méx.; Col.); las planchas (Esp.)	*push-ups*
la cinta (trotadora) (Arg.; Chile)	**la cinta caminadora**

EL MUNDO HISPANO

Creencias° sobre la salud

- **Colombia** Como algunos suelos son de baldosas°, se cree que si uno anda descalzo° se enfrían° los pies y esto puede causar un resfriado o artritis.
- **Cuba** Por la mañana, muchas madres sacan a sus bebés a los patios y a las puertas de las casas. La creencia es que unos cinco minutos de sol ayudan a fijar° el calcio en los huesos y aumentan la inmunidad contra las enfermedades.
- **México** Muchas personas tienen la costumbre de tomar a diario un vaso de jugo del cactus conocido como "nopal". Se dice que es bueno para reducir el colesterol y el azúcar en la sangre y que ayuda a adelgazar.

Creencias *Beliefs* **baldosas** *tiles* **anda descalzo** *walks barefoot* **se enfrían** *get cold* **fijar** *to set*

PERFIL

La quinua

La quinua es una semilla° de gran valor° nutricional. Se produce en los Andes de Bolivia, Perú, Argentina, Colombia, Chile y Ecuador, y también en los Estados Unidos. Forma parte de la dieta básica de esos países andinos desde hace más de 5.000 años.

La quinua es rica en proteínas, hierro° y magnesio. Contiene los ocho aminoácidos básicos para el ser humano; por esto es un alimento muy completo, ideal para vegetarianos y veganos. Otra de las ventajas de la quinua es que no contiene gluten, por lo que la pueden consumir personas con alergias e intolerancia a esta proteína.

Aunque es técnicamente una semilla, la quinua es considerada un cereal por su composición y por su uso. Los granos° de la quinua pueden ser tostados para hacer harina° o se pueden cocinar de múltiples maneras. Se utiliza como reemplazo° del arroz o de la pasta, con verduras, carnes, etc., en ensaladas, o como reemplazo de la avena° en el desayuno.

semilla *seed* **valor** *value* **hierro** *iron* **granos** *grains* **harina** *flour* **reemplazo** *replacement* **avena** *oats*

Conexión Internet

¿Qué sistemas de ejercicio son más populares entre los hispanos?

Go to **vhlcentral.com** to find more cultural information related to this **Cultura** section.

ACTIVIDADES

2 Comprensión Responde a las preguntas.

1. Una argentina te dice: "Voy a usar la cinta." ¿Qué va a hacer? Va a usar la cinta caminadora.
2. Según los colombianos, ¿qué efectos negativos tiene el no usar zapatos en casa? Puede causar un resfriado o artritis.
3. ¿Qué es la quinua? Es una semilla de gran valor nutricional.
4. ¿Qué proteína no contiene la quinua? No contiene gluten.

3 Para sentirte mejor Entrevista a un(a) compañero/a sobre las cosas que hace todos los días y las cosas que hace al menos una o dos veces a la semana para sentirse mejor. Hablen sobre actividades deportivas, la alimentación y lo que hacen en sus ratos libres. Answers will vary.

Practice more at **vhlcentral.com**.

recursos: VM pp. 101–102; vhlcentral.com Lección 15

TEACHING OPTIONS

Heritage Speakers Ask heritage speakers to talk about popular health beliefs or foods with healing properties that they have encountered in their communities or heard from their relatives.

Pairs Divide the class into pairs. Have students take turns quizzing each other about the health beliefs and practices mentioned on these pages. Write a question on the board for students to use as a model. Ex: **¿Para qué sirve la lodoterapia?**

Game Play a *Jeopardy*-style game. Divide the class into three teams and have one member from each team stand up. Read a definition. Ex: **Es una semilla de gran valor nutricional.** The first student to raise his or her hand must answer in the form of a question. Ex: **¿Qué es la quinua?** Each correct answer earns one point. The team with the most points wins.

Así se dice

- Model the pronunciation of each term and have students repeat it.
- To challenge students, add these exercise-related words to the list: **estar cachas (Esp.)** (*to be very muscular*); **la (máquina) elíptica** (*elliptical machine*); **la fatiga** (*fatigue*); **rebajar** (*to lose weight*); **la resistencia** (*endurance*); **trotar, hacer footing (Esp.)** (*to jog*).
- Ask students personalized questions to involve them in a discussion using the new vocabulary. Ex: **¿Qué haces si te da un calambre muscular? (Hago ejercicios de estiramiento.)**

Perfil

- Quinoa's name is derived from the Quechua word *kinwa*. It has become very popular in the United States, Canada, Europe, Japan, and China, which has caused its prices to more than triple.
- The United Nations has designated nutrient-rich quinoa as a "super crop" for its potential to feed the world's poor because it grows well in poor soils and is drought resistant.

El mundo hispano Ask students if any of these popular beliefs are surprising to them.

2 Expansion Give students these questions as items 5–6: **5. ¿Qué contiene la quinua? (proteínas, hierro, magnesio, aminoácidos) 6. Si eres parte del ejército español, es probable que hagas planchas. ¿Qué haces? (flexiones de pecho)**

3 Teaching Tip

- Review vocabulary for daily routines from **Lección 7**.
- To simplify, before coming to class, have students brainstorm a list of interview questions to ask their partners.

3 Expansion Call on volunteers to summarize their partners' responses for the class.

Section Goals

In **Estructura 15.1** students will learn:
- to use the conditional
- to make polite requests and hypothesize about past conditions

Instructional Resources

Supersite: Audio (Lab MP3 Files); Resources (Grammar Presentation Slides, Activity Pack, Scripts, Answer Keys); Testing Program (Quizzes)
WebSAM
Workbook, pp. 183–184
Lab Manual, p. 87

Teaching Tips

- Ask students to imagine they are on the trip with the **Fotonovela** characters. Ask them what they would like to do there. Ex: **¿Qué te gustaría hacer o ver en México? A mí me gustaría ir de excursión. ¿Y a ti?** Tell students that **gustaría** is a polite form of **gustar** that they already know. The conditional can be used to make polite requests.
- Ask volunteers to read the captions to the video stills and indicate which verbs are in the conditional.
- Point out that, as in the future, there is only one set of endings in the conditional.
- Check for understanding by citing an infinitive and a subject pronoun while pointing to a specific student. The student should respond with the conditional form. Ex: **decir / nosotros (diríamos); venir / tú (vendrías)**
- Ask students what the future form of **hay** is. Then ask them what they would expect the conditional form to be **(habrá/ habría).**

NATIONAL STANDARDS comparisons

15.1 The conditional

Tutorial

ANTE TODO The conditional tense in Spanish expresses what you *would do* or what *would happen* under certain circumstances.

The conditional tense

		visitar	comer	escribir
SINGULAR FORMS	yo	visitar**ía**	comer**ía**	escribir**ía**
	tú	visitar**ías**	comer**ías**	escribir**ías**
	Ud./él/ella	visitar**ía**	comer**ía**	escribir**ía**
PLURAL FORMS	nosotros/as	visitar**íamos**	comer**íamos**	escribir**íamos**
	vosotros/as	visitar**íais**	comer**íais**	escribir**íais**
	Uds./ellos/ellas	visitar**ían**	comer**ían**	escribir**ían**

Me gustaría un masaje.

¿Crees que tendrías un poco de tiempo libre?

- The conditional tense is formed much like the future tense. The endings are the same for all verbs, both regular and irregular. For regular verbs, you simply add the appropriate endings to the infinitive. **¡Atención!** All forms of the conditional have an accent mark.

- For irregular verbs, add the conditional endings to the irregular stems.

INFINITIVE	STEM	CONDITIONAL	INFINITIVE	STEM	CONDITIONAL
decir	dir-	dir**ía**	querer	querr-	querr**ía**
hacer	har-	har**ía**	saber	sabr-	sabr**ía**
poder	podr-	podr**ía**	salir	saldr-	saldr**ía**
poner	pondr-	pondr**ía**	tener	tendr-	tendr**ía**
haber	habr-	habr**ía**	venir	vendr-	vendr**ía**

- While in English the conditional is a compound verb form made up of the auxiliary verb *would* and a main verb, in Spanish it is a simple verb form that consists of one word.

Yo no **iría** a ese gimnasio.
I would not go to that gym.

¿**Vendrías** conmigo a la clase de yoga?
Would you come to yoga class with me?

¡ATENCIÓN!

The polite expressions **Me gustaría...** (*I would like...*) and **Te gustaría** (*You would like...*) are commonly used examples of the conditional.

AYUDA

The infinitive of **hay** is **haber**, so its conditional form is **habría.**

TEACHING OPTIONS

TPR In teams of five, have students line up several feet from the board. Call out an infinitive. The first team members race to the board and write the **yo** form of the verb in the conditional, then pass the chalk to the next team members, who write the **tú** form, and so on. The team that finishes first and has all the forms correct wins the round.

Extra Practice Ask students to write a short paragraph describing what they would do over the next six months if they could do anything their hearts desired and money and time were no object. Ex: **Yo viajaría por todo el mundo...** Call on volunteers to read their paragraphs aloud, then ask the class comprehension questions about what was said. Ex: **¿Qué harían ____ y ____?**

▶ The conditional is commonly used to make polite requests.

¿**Podrías** abrir la ventana, por favor?	¿**Sería** tan amable de venir a mi oficina?
Would you open the window, please?	*Would you be so kind as to come to my office?*

▶ In Spanish, as in English, the conditional expresses the future in relation to a past action or state of being. In other words, the future indicates what *will happen* whereas the conditional indicates what *would happen.*

Creo que mañana **hará** sol.	**Creía** que hoy **haría** sol.
I think it will be sunny tomorrow.	*I thought it would be sunny today.*

▶ The English *would* is often used with a verb to express the conditional, but it can also mean *used to,* in the sense of past habitual action. To express past habitual actions, Spanish uses the imperfect, not the conditional.

Íbamos al parque los sábados.	Antes, me **entrenaba** todos los días.
We would go to the park on Saturdays.	*Before, I used to work out every day.*

AYUDA

Keep in mind the two parallel combinations shown in the example sentences:
1) present tense in main clause → future tense in subordinate clause
2) past tense in main clause → conditional tense in subordinate clause

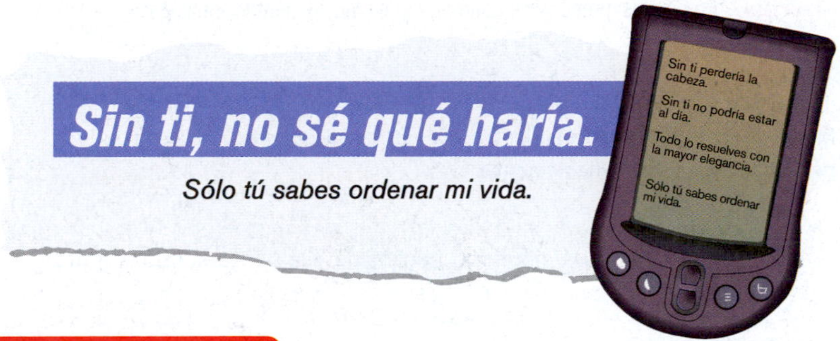

Sin ti, no sé qué haría.
Sólo tú sabes ordenar mi vida.
Sin ti perdería la cabeza.
Sin ti no podría estar al día.
Todo lo resuelves con la mayor elegancia.
Sólo tú sabes ordenar mi vida.

COMPARE & CONTRAST

In **Lección 14**, you learned the *future of probability.* Spanish also has the *conditional of probability,* which expresses conjecture or probability about a past condition, event, or action. Compare these Spanish and English sentences.

Serían las once de la noche cuando Elvira me llamó.	Sonó el teléfono. ¿**Llamaría** Emilio para cancelar nuestra cita?
It must have been (It was probably) 11 p.m. when Elvira called me.	*The phone rang. I wondered if it was Emilio calling to cancel our date.*

Note that English conveys conjecture or probability with phrases such as *I wondered if, probably,* and *must have been.* In contrast, Spanish gets these same ideas across with conditional forms.

¡INTÉNTALO! Indica la forma apropiada del condicional de los verbos.

1. Yo escucharía, leería, me apuraría (escuchar, leer, apurarse)
2. Tú te mantendrías, comprenderías, compartirías (mantenerse, comprender, compartir)
3. Marcos pondría, vendría, querría (poner, venir, querer)
4. Nosotras seríamos, sabríamos, iríamos (ser, saber, ir)
5. Ustedes adelgazarían, deberían, sufrirían (adelgazar, deber, sufrir)
6. Ella saldría, podría, haría (salir, poder, hacer)
7. Yo tendría, trataría, fumaría (tener, tratar, fumar)
8. Tú dirías, verías, engordarías (decir, ver, engordar)

recursos
WB pp. 183–184
LM p. 87
vhlcentral.com Lección 15

Teaching Tips

- Discuss the use of the conditional in polite requests. Remind students of the forms **me gustaría** and **te gustaría**, which they have already seen in the **Fotonovela**. You might point out that usage tends to occur in set expressions, such as **¿Podrías… ? ¿Sería usted tan amable de… ? ¿Tendrían ustedes la bondad de… ? ¿Me harías el favor de… ?**
- Explain the concept of the conditional as *the future of the past.* Explain that the conditional is used to express some action that was yet to occur at some past time, and give examples. Ex: **1. Creo que me mantendré en forma. Creía que me mantendría en forma. 2. Sé que adelgazarás. Sabía que adelgazarías.**
- Remind students of the future of probability. Point out that the conditional of probability functions just like it, but in the context of the past. Compare the second example in the Compare & Contrast box to the following: **Suena el teléfono. ¿Llamará Emilio para cancelar nuestra cita?**

TEACHING OPTIONS

Extra Practice Tell students to imagine that their families have come into a great deal of money. Ask them to write ten sentences describing what they and their family members would do with the money. Students should try to use as many different verbs and conjugations as possible. Ex: **Mi familia y yo ayudaríamos a los artistas de nuestra ciudad…**

Pairs Have students work together to role-play interviewing a personal trainer. Interviewers should ask the trainer what he or she would do to help get them in shape. Have students switch roles.

Práctica

1 Teaching Tips
- To simplify, have students begin by underlining the infinitives with irregular stems.
- Ask six volunteers to write the completed sentences on the board. Have the class check for accurate spelling and grammar.

1 **¡A ponerse en forma!** Víctor y Emilia quieren apuntarse (*enroll*) a un gimnasio y están hablando con el gerente. Completa las oraciones con el condicional del verbo.

VÍCTOR Buenas tardes. Necesitamos información sobre el gimnasio.
GERENTE Por supuesto. Me (1) encantaría (encantar) ayudar.
EMILIA Primero, ¿ (2) podría (poder) usted decirnos cuánto cuesta al mes?
GERENTE (3) Costaría (costar) setenta dólares por persona.
VÍCTOR Y además del uso de las máquinas, ¿qué otros servicios (4) estarían (estar) incluidos?
GERENTE Ustedes (5) tendrían (tener) un entrenador particular (*personal*) que los (6) ayudaría (ayudar) a estar en buena forma y les (7) recomendaría (recomendar) qué clases de ejercicios les (8) serían (ser) más beneficiosos.
EMILIA Víctor, ¿qué piensas? ¿Tú (9) irías (ir) al gimnasio dos veces por semana?

2 Expansion Ask questions about the responses to practice all forms of the conditional. Ex: **¿Qué le diría ____ a la persona de enfrente? (Le diría que no puede ver nada.) ¿Qué harían ____ y ____ en esta situación? (Asistirían a otra clase.)**

2 **¿Qué harías?** En parejas, pregúntense qué harían en las siguientes situaciones. Answers will vary.

modelo
¡No me perdería mi clase de ejercicios aeróbicos por nada del mundo! Me movería a un lado para poder ver bien al instructor y hablaría con la persona de enfrente amablemente.

Estás en una clase de ejercicios aeróbicos y la persona de enfrente no te deja ver.

Vas al banco a depositar un cheque y te das cuenta de (*you realize*) que en tu cuenta hay por error un millón de dólares que no es tuyo.

Estás manejando por el desierto y te quedas sin gasolina.

Vuelves a tu apartamento después de tus clases y tu ex novio/a no te deja entrar.

3 Teaching Tip Before you divide the class into pairs, allow individuals sufficient time to write out their eight ideas. Then have students work with a partner to give advice. Tell them to take turns sharing their ideas.

3 Expansion
Have partners choose their three best ideas to present to the class. Write them on the board, then ask the class to vote on which are the most creative or interesting.

3 **Presidente por un día** Imagina que eres el/la presidente/a de tu universidad por un día. Escribe ocho cosas que harías en esa situación. Usa el condicional. Luego compara tus ideas con las de un(a) compañero/a. Answers will vary.

modelo
Yo tendría un jet privado para mis viajes.

conocer	hacer	poner
dar	invitar	sufrir
disfrutar	mejorar	tener

Practice more at **vhlcentral.com.**

TEACHING OPTIONS

Pairs Have students take turns asking each other for favors, using courtesy expressions with the conditional. Partners respond by saying whether they will do the favor; if they cannot, they should make up an excuse. Ex: **¿Me podrías recoger del gimnasio a las cinco de la tarde? (Lo siento, pero no puedo. Tengo una clase de química hasta las cinco y media.)**

Large Groups Ask students to think about what they would do if they were training for the Olympics. Have them pick an event and a Spanish-speaking country to represent. Ex: **Sería de Paraguay. Nadaría los 200 metros.** Then go around asking each student to read his or her sentence aloud, but have them listen carefully to their classmates so they can first restate what their classmates said.

NATIONAL communication STANDARDS

Comunicación

4 **Conversaciones** Tu profesor(a) te dará una hoja de actividades. En ella se presentan dos listas con diferentes problemas que supuestamente tienen los estudiantes. En parejas, túrnense para explicar los problemas de su lista; uno/a cuenta lo que le pasa y el/la otro/a dice lo que haría en esa situación usando la frase "Yo en tu lugar..." (*If I were you...*). Answers will vary.

AYUDA
Here are two ways of saying *If I were you:*
Si yo fuera tú...
Yo en tu lugar...

modelo
Estudiante 1: ¡Qué problema! Mi novio/a no me habla desde el domingo.
Estudiante 2: Yo en tu lugar, no le diría nada por unos días para ver qué pasa.

5 **Roberto en el gimnasio** Roberto es una persona muy sedentaria. El médico le dice que tiene que adelgazar para mejorar su salud. Dile ocho cosas que tú harías si fueras él. Usa el condicional. Después, compara tus sugerencias con las de un(a) compañero/a. Answers will vary.

modelo
Si yo fuera tú, vería menos la televisión y haría gimnasia.

NATIONAL communication STANDARDS

Síntesis

6 **Encuesta** Tu profesor(a) te dará una hoja de actividades. Circula por la clase y pregúntales a tres compañeros/as qué actividad(es) de las que se describen les gustaría realizar. Usa el condicional de los verbos. Anota las respuestas e informa a la clase de los resultados de la encuesta. Answers will vary.

modelo
Estudiante 1: ¿Dejarías de fumar?
Estudiante 2: Claro que sí. Sería difícil al principio, pero podría hacerlo.

Actividades	Nombre de tu compañero/a y su respuesta	Nombre de tu compañero/a y su respuesta	Nombre de tu compañero/a y su respuesta
1. tomar vitaminas			
2. adelgazar			
3. levantar pesas			
4. entrenarse para un maratón			
5. comer una dieta equilibrada			
6. mantenerse en forma			

4 Teaching Tip Distribute the ***Hojas de actividades*** (Activity Pack/Supersite) that correspond to this activity.

4 Expansion Working as a class, name a problem from one of the lists and ask several volunteers to share the suggestions they received. Encourage other students to comment on the suggestions.

5 Teaching Tip Go over the directions with the class. Work with the class to brainstorm a list of Roberto's problems. Write them on the board. Then give students time to write eight pieces of advice.

6 Teaching Tip Distribute the ***Hojas de actividades*** (Activity Pack/Supersite) that correspond to this activity.

6 Expansion Encourage students to add two more activities to their list.

TEACHING OPTIONS

Game Have students each write down the name of a well-known person. Then, have them read it aloud to the student at their left. That student has to say what he or she would do if he or she were that person. Ex: **E1: Salma Hayek E2: Si yo fuera Salma Hayek, haría una película con Chris Pratt.**

Extra Practice Ask students to write a short paragraph answering this question: **¿Qué harías para cambiar tu vida?** Have students exchange papers with a classmate to check the paragraphs for accuracy.

Section Goal

In **Estructura 15.2**, students will learn the use of the present perfect.

Instructional Resources
Supersite: Audio (Lab MP3 Files); Resources (Grammar Presentation Slides, Activity Pack, Scripts, Answer Keys); Testing Program (Quizzes)
WebSAM
Workbook, pp. 185–186
Lab Manual, p. 88

Teaching Tips

- Have students turn to pages 486–487. Ask them to read the **Fotonovela** captions again and write down the past participles they find. Ask students if they are used as adjectives or as parts of verbs.
- Model the present perfect by making statements about what you and others in the class have done, or by asking students questions. Ex: **Yo he preparado una lección. Ustedes han leído la sección de Estructura, ¿verdad? ¿Quién no la ha leído?**

Consulta Tell students that while the present perfect is generally used in Spanish just as it is in English, the expression *to have just done something* is expressed in Spanish by **acabar de** + [*infinitive*]. Write these sentences on the board and contrast them: **Acabo de venir del gimnasio. He venido del gimnasio.**

Nota cultural
The ***Chilam Balam*** texts are considered a challenge for translators because of the archaic, idiomatic, and metaphorical nature of the Yucatec Maya language. Have students research more about the language online and see if they can find any similarities to Spanish. Then have students share their findings with the class.

15.2 The present perfect

Tutorial

ANTE TODO In **Lección 13**, you learned how to form past participles. You will now learn how to form the present perfect indicative (**el pretérito perfecto de indicativo**), a compound tense that uses the past participle. The present perfect is used to talk about what someone *has done*. In Spanish, it is formed with the present tense of the auxiliary verb **haber** and a past participle.

Maru ha estado bajo mucha presión.

He querido regresar desde que leí el *Chilam Balam.*

Present indicative of haber

Singular forms		Plural forms	
yo	**he**	nosotros/as	**hemos**
tú	**has**	vosotros/as	**habéis**
Ud./él/ella	**ha**	Uds./ellos/ellas	**han**

Tú no **has aumentado** de peso.
You haven't gained weight.

¿**Ha asistido** Juan a la clase de yoga?
Has Juan attended the yoga class?

Yo ya **he leído** esos libros.
I've already read those books.

Hemos conocido al entrenador.
We have met the trainer.

▶ The past participle does not change in form when it is part of the present perfect tense; it only changes in form when it is used as an adjective.

Clara **ha abierto** las ventanas.
Clara has opened the windows.

Las ventanas están **abiertas**.
The windows are open.

Yo **he cerrado** la puerta del gimnasio.
I've closed the door to the gym.

La puerta del gimnasio está **cerrada**.
The door to the gym is closed.

▶ In Spanish, the present perfect indicative generally is used just as in English: to talk about what someone has done or what has occurred. It usually refers to the recent past.

He trabajado cuarenta horas esta semana.
I have worked forty hours this week.

¿Cuál es el último libro que **has leído**?
What is the last book that you have read?

NATIONAL STANDARDS comparisons

NOTA CULTURAL
El ***Chilam Balam*** es un grupo de libros sobre la civilización maya. Hablan sobre historia, rituales, medicina, astronomía y literatura, entre otros temas. Fueron escritos en diferentes épocas (*times*) por autores anónimos y en lengua maya.

CONSULTA
To review what you have learned about past participles, see **Estructura 13.4**, p. 438.

CONSULTA
Remember that the Spanish equivalent of the English *to have just* (*done something*) is **acabar de** + [*infinitive*]. Do not use the present perfect to express that English structure.
Juan acaba de llegar.
Juan has just arrived.
See **Estructura 6.3**, p. 191.

TEACHING OPTIONS

Extra Practice Ask students what they have done over the past week to lead a healthy lifestyle. Ask follow-up questions to elicit a variety of different conjugations of the present perfect. Ex: **¿Qué han hecho esta semana para llevar una vida sana? Y tú, ____, ¿qué has hecho? ¿Qué ha hecho ____ esta semana?**

Pairs Ask students to tell their partners five things they have done in the past to stay in shape. Partners repeat back what the person has said, using the **tú** form of the present perfect. Ex: **He levantado pesas. (Muy bien. Has levantado pesas.)**

Large Groups Have the class stand in a circle. Call out a subject pronoun and an infinitive. Ex: **yo/sufrir**. Toss a ball to a student, who will say the correct present perfect form (Ex: **yo he sufrido**) and toss the ball to another student, who will use the verb in a sentence.

▶ In English, the auxiliary verb and the past participle are often separated. In Spanish, however, these two elements—**haber** and the past participle—cannot be separated by any word.

Siempre **hemos vivido** en Bolivia.
We have always lived in Bolivia.

Usted nunca **ha venido** a mi oficina.
You have never come to my office.

¿Y Juan Carlos todavía no te ha invitado a salir?

Últimamente hemos sufrido muchas presiones en la universidad.

▶ The word **no** and any object or reflexive pronouns are placed immediately before **haber**.

Yo **no he comido** la merienda.
I haven't eaten the snack.

¿Por qué **no la has comido**?
Why haven't you eaten it?

Susana ya **se ha entrenado**.
Susana has already trained.

Ellos **no lo han terminado**.
They haven't finished it.

▶ Note that *to have* can be either a main verb or an auxiliary verb in English. As a main verb, it corresponds to **tener,** while as an auxiliary, it corresponds to **haber**.

Tengo muchos amigos.
I have a lot of friends.

He sufrido muchas presiones.
I have been under a lot of pressure.

▶ To form the present perfect of **hay,** use the third-person singular of **haber (ha) + habido**.

Ha habido muchos problemas con la nueva entrenadora.
There have been a lot of problems with the new trainer.

Ha habido un accidente en la calle Central.
There has been an accident on Central Street.

¡INTÉNTALO! Indica el pretérito perfecto de indicativo de estos verbos.

1. (disfrutar, comer, vivir) yo he disfrutado, he comido, he vivido
2. (traer, adelgazar, compartir) tú has traído, has adelgazado, has compartido
3. (venir, estar, correr) usted ha venido, ha estado, ha corrido
4. (leer, resolver, poner) ella ha leído, ha resuelto, ha puesto
5. (decir, romper, hacer) ellos han dicho, han roto, han hecho
6. (mantenerse, dormirse) nosotros nos hemos mantenido, nos hemos dormido
7. (estar, escribir, ver) yo he estado, he escrito, he visto
8. (vivir, correr, morir) él ha vivido, ha corrido, ha muerto

recursos
WB pp. 185–186
LM p. 88
vhlcentral.com Lección 15

Teaching Tips

- Ask students questions in the present perfect with indirect and direct objects. Have students respond using the correct pronoun and placement. Ex: _____, **¿has estudiado bien la lección? (Sí, la he estudiado bien.)** _____, **¿has entendido todo lo que te he dicho? (No, no lo he entendido todo.) ¿Todos me han entregado el trabajo de hoy? (Sí, todos se lo hemos entregado.)**
- Explain that, although an adverb can never appear between **haber** and its past participle, it may appear in other positions in the sentence to change emphasis. Ex: **Hemos vivido siempre en Bolivia. Siempre hemos vivido en Bolivia.**
- Tell students that the present perfect used with **alguna vez** means *ever*. Ex: **¿Alguna vez has corrido un maratón?** *(Have you ever run a marathon?)* **¿Has ido alguna vez a la India?** *(Have you ever gone to India?)*
- Before assigning the **¡Inténtalo!** to the class, do a quick review of irregular past participles.
- Practice adverb placement by supplying an adverb for each item in the **¡Inténtalo!** activity. Ex: **siempre (Siempre he disfrutado./He disfrutado siempre.)**

TEACHING OPTIONS

Large Groups Divide the class into groups. Have students write down five fitness activities. Then have them ask each of their group members if they have ever done those activities and record their answers. Ex: **¿Has levantado pesas? ¿Has tomado clases en un gimnasio? ¿Has corrido en un maratón? ¿Has nadado en el océano?** Encourage students to ask follow-up questions.

Extra Practice Draw a time line on the board. On the far right of the line, write **el presente**. Just to the left of that point, write **el pasado muy reciente**. To the left of that, write **el pasado reciente**. Then to the far left, write **el pasado**. Make a statement using the preterite, the present perfect, or **acabar de** + [*infinitive*]. Have students indicate on the time line when the action took place.

1 Expansion
Have students write five original sentences using the present perfect to describe their past health and that of their friends and family members.

Ayuda Practice the expressions by using sentences that describe you and your students' lives.
Ex: **He comido ceviche un par de veces. ¿Quién ha comido ceviche muchas veces?**

2 Expansion
- Ask students follow-up questions about their responses.
- To challenge students, have partners elaborate on their responses by asking each other questions about what they have done.
Ex: **—¿Has buceado? —Sí, he buceado varias veces. —¡Qué suerte! ¿Dónde has buceado, en el Caribe?**

3 Expansion
- Take a survey of the answers given and write the results on the board. Then ask volunteers to summarize the results. Ex: **Casi todos hemos dejado de tomar refrescos.**
- Ask students to give examples of the benefits of adopting some of the healthy habits listed. Ex: **Ahora puedo subir la escalera hasta el quinto piso sin llegar cansado/a.**

Práctica

1

Completar Estas oraciones describen cómo es la vida de unos estudiantes. Completa las oraciones con el pretérito perfecto de indicativo de los verbos de la lista.

adelgazar	comer	llevar
aumentar	hacer	sufrir

1. Luisa ___ha sufrido___ muchas presiones este año.
2. Juan y Raúl ___han aumentado___ de peso porque no hacen ejercicio.
3. Pero María y yo ___hemos adelgazado___ porque trabajamos en exceso y nos olvidamos de comer.
4. Desde siempre, yo ___he llevado___ una vida muy sana.
5. Pero tú y yo no ___hemos hecho___ gimnasia este semestre.

2

¿Qué has hecho? Indica si has hecho lo siguiente. Answers will vary.

modelo
escalar una montaña
Sí, he escalado varias montañas./No, no he escalado nunca una montaña.

1. jugar al baloncesto
2. viajar a Bolivia
3. conocer a una persona famosa
4. levantar pesas
5. comer un insecto
6. recibir un masaje
7. aprender varios idiomas
8. bailar salsa
9. ver una película en español
10. escuchar música latina
11. estar despierto/a 24 horas
12. bucear

AYUDA
You may use some of these expressions in your answers:
una vez *once*
un par de veces *a couple of times*
algunas veces *a few times*
varias veces *several times*
muchas veces *many times, often*

3

La vida sana En parejas, túrnense para hacer preguntas sobre el tema de la vida sana. Sean creativos. Answers will vary.

modelo
encontrar un gimnasio
Estudiante 1: *¿Has encontrado un buen gimnasio cerca de tu casa?*
Estudiante 2: *Yo no he encontrado un gimnasio, pero sé que debo buscar uno.*

1. tratar de estar en forma
2. estar a dieta los últimos dos meses
3. dejar de tomar refrescos
4. hacerse una prueba del colesterol
5. entrenarse cinco días a la semana
6. cambiar de una vida sedentaria a una vida activa
7. tomar vitaminas por las noches y por las mañanas
8. hacer ejercicio para aliviar la tensión
9. consumir mucha proteína
10. dejar de fumar

Practice more at **vhlcentral.com**.

TEACHING OPTIONS

Small Groups Divide the class into groups of four to write and perform skits in which one student plays a personal trainer, another plays a nutritionist, and the other two play clients. The personal trainer and nutritionist ask the clients whether they have done the things they have recommended. The clients explain what they have done and make excuses for what they have not done.

Pairs Have students discuss with a classmate five things they have already done today. Ex: **He estudiado la lección para esta clase. He ido al gimnasio. He ido a una clase de ejercicios aeróbicos. He almorzado con unos amigos. He escrito un mensaje electrónico a mis abuelos. ¿Qué has hecho tú?**

Comunicación

4 **Descripción** En parejas, describan lo que han hecho y no han hecho estas personas. Usen la imaginación. Answers will vary.

1. Jorge y Raúl

2. Luisa

3. Jacobo

4. Natalia y Diego

5. Ricardo

6. Carmen

5 **Describir** En parejas, identifiquen a una persona que lleva una vida muy sana. Puede ser una persona que conocen o un personaje que aparece en una película o programa de televisión. Entre los dos, escriban una descripción de lo que esta persona ha hecho para llevar una vida sana. Answers will vary.

modelo

Mario López siempre ha hecho todo lo posible para mantenerse en forma. Él…

NOTA CULTURAL

Nacido en San Diego e hijo de padres mexicanos, el actor **Mario López** se mantiene en forma haciendo ejercicio todos los días.

Síntesis

6 **Situación** Trabajen en parejas para representar una conversación entre un(a) enfermero/a de la clínica de la universidad y un(a) estudiante. Answers will vary.

- El/La estudiante no se siente nada bien.
- El/La enfermero/a debe averiguar de dónde viene el problema e investigar los hábitos del/de la estudiante.
- El/La estudiante le explica lo que ha hecho en los últimos meses y cómo se ha sentido.
- Luego el/la enfermero/a le da recomendaciones de cómo llevar una vida más sana.

4 Teaching Tip To simplify, before beginning the activity, ask volunteers to describe the people in the drawings and how they think they feel.

4 Expansion In small groups, have students choose one of the drawings to elaborate on, using the preterite, present perfect, and present indicative. To begin, each student should take a turn telling a part of the story using the preterite, then as the story moves into the recent past, each group member should add to the story using the present perfect. To finish, the group should decide together what the people have just done and what they are going to do next. You may wish to assign one group member as the secretary to record the stories so that they can be shared with the class. Ex: **Carmen fue de vacaciones a Chile… En Portillo ella ha esquiado en una montaña… Carmen acaba de quitarse las botas de esquí y ahora va a almorzar en un restaurante.**

5 Teaching Tip Have pairs describe eight things their chosen person has done that exemplify a healthy lifestyle. Remind them to include introductory and concluding statements in their descriptions.

5 Expansion Have students choose someone who is the exact opposite of the healthy person they chose earlier and write a description of what that person has done that exemplifies an unhealthy lifestyle.

6 Expansion While pairs are performing their role-plays for the class, stop the action after the patient has described his or her symptoms and what he or she has done in the last few months. Ask the class to make a diagnosis. Then have the pair finish their presentation.

TEACHING OPTIONS

Game Have students write three important things they have done over the past year on a slip of paper and put it in a box. Ex: **Este año he creado un blog.** Have students draw a paper from the box, then circulate around the room, asking classmates if they have done the activities listed, until they find the person who wrote the slip of paper. The first person to find a match wins.

Heritage Speakers Have heritage speakers interview a Spanish-speaking immigrant to find out how that person's life has changed since moving to this country. Tell them to find out if the interviewee's physical activity and diet have changed and report this information to the class. Have the rest of the class react and state to what degree the interviewee's lifestyle is typical of this country.

Section Goal

In **Estructura 15.3**, students will learn the use of the past perfect tense.

Instructional Resources
Supersite: Audio (Lab MP3 Files); Resources (Grammar Presentation Slides, Activity Pack, Scripts, Answer Keys); Testing Program (Quizzes)
WebSAM
Workbook, pp. 187–188
Lab Manual, p. 89

Teaching Tips

- Introduce the past perfect tense by making statements about the past that are true for you. Write examples of the past perfect on the board as you use them. Ex: **Esta mañana vine a la universidad en la bicicleta de mi hijo. Nunca antes había venido en bicicleta. Muchas veces antes había caminado y también había venido en autobús cuando tenía prisa, pero nunca en bicicleta.**
- Check for comprehension of **ya** by contrasting it with **nunca**. Ex: **Antes del semestre pasado, nunca había enseñado este curso, pero ya había enseñado otros cursos de español.**

Successful Language Learning

Tell students to imagine how they might use the past perfect to tell someone about their lives.

15.3 The past perfect

Tutorial

NATIONAL STANDARDS comparisons

ANTE TODO The past perfect indicative (**el pretérito pluscuamperfecto de indicativo**) is used to talk about what someone *had done* or what *had occurred* before another past action, event, or state. Like the present perfect, the past perfect uses a form of **haber**—in this case, the imperfect—plus the past participle.

Past perfect indicative

		cerrar	perder	asistir
SINGULAR FORMS	yo	**había** cerrado	**había** perdido	**había** asistido
	tú	**habías** cerrado	**habías** perdido	**habías** asistido
	Ud./él/ella	**había** cerrado	**había** perdido	**había** asistido
PLURAL FORMS	nosotros/as	**habíamos** cerrado	**habíamos** perdido	**habíamos** asistido
	vosotros/as	**habíais** cerrado	**habíais** perdido	**habíais** asistido
	Uds./ellos/ellas	**habían** cerrado	**habían** perdido	**habían** asistido

Antes de 2014, **había vivido** en La Paz.
Before 2014, I had lived in La Paz.

Cuando llegamos, Luis ya **había salido.**
When we arrived, Luis had already left.

▶ The past perfect is often used with the word **ya** (*already*) to indicate that an action, event, or state had already occurred before another. Remember that, unlike its English equivalent, **ya** cannot be placed between **haber** and the past participle.

Ella **ya había salido** cuando llamaron.
She had already left when they called.

Cuando llegué, Raúl **ya se había acostado.**
When I arrived, Raúl had already gone to bed.

▶ **¡Atención!** The past perfect is often used in conjunction with **antes de** + [*noun*] or **antes de** + [*infinitive*] to describe when the action(s) occurred.

Antes de este año, nunca **había estudiado español.**
Before this year, I had never studied Spanish.

Luis **me había llamado antes de venir.**
Luis had called me before he came.

¡INTÉNTALO! Indica el pretérito pluscuamperfecto de indicativo de cada verbo.

1. Nosotros ya habíamos cenado (cenar) cuando nos llamaron.
2. Antes de tomar esta clase, yo no había estudiado (estudiar) nunca el español.
3. Antes de ir a México, ellos nunca habían ido (ir) a otro país.
4. Eduardo nunca se había entrenado (entrenarse) tanto en invierno.
5. Tú siempre habías llevado (llevar) una vida sana antes del año pasado.
6. Antes de conocerte, yo ya te había visto (ver) muchas veces.

recursos
WB pp. 187–188
LM p. 89
vhlcentral.com Lección 15

TEACHING OPTIONS

Extra Practice Have students write sentences, using the past perfect and each of the following twice: **antes de** + [*noun*], **antes de** + [*infinitive*], the preterite, and the imperfect. Have students peer edit their work before sharing their sentences with the class. Ex: **Nuestros bisabuelos ya habían muerto cuando éramos niños....**

TPR Make a series of statements about the past, using two different verbs. Make sure one of these verbs is in the past perfect indicative. After making a statement, call out the infinitive of one of the verbs. If that verb represents the action that occurred first in the sentence, have students raise one finger. If it occurred second, have them raise two fingers. Ex: **Tomás ya había bajado de la montaña cuando empezó a nevar. Empezar.** (two fingers)

Práctica

1 **Completar** Completa los minidiálogos con las formas correctas del pretérito pluscuamperfecto de indicativo.

1. **SARA** Antes de cumplir los 15 años, ¿ habías estudiado (estudiar) tú otra lengua?
   JOSÉ Sí, había tomado (tomar) clases de inglés y de italiano.
2. **DOLORES** Antes de ir a Argentina, ¿ habían probado (probar) tú y tu familia el mate?
   TOMÁS Sí, ya habíamos tomado (tomar) mate muchas veces.
3. **ANTONIO** Antes de este año, ¿ había corrido (correr) usted en un maratón?
   SRA. VERA No, nunca lo había hecho (hacer).
4. **SOFÍA** Antes de su enfermedad, ¿ había sufrido (sufrir) muchas presiones tu tío?
   IRENE Sí… y él nunca se había mantenido (mantenerse) en forma.

NOTA CULTURAL

El mate, una bebida similar al té, es muy popular en Argentina, Uruguay y Paraguay. Se dice que controla el estrés y la obesidad, y que estimula el sistema inmunológico.

2 **Tu vida** Indica si ya habías hecho estas cosas antes de cumplir los dieciséis años. Answers will vary.

1. hacer un viaje en avión
2. escalar una montaña
3. escribir un poema
4. filmar un video
5. enamorarte
6. tomar clases de ejercicios aeróbicos
7. montar a caballo
8. ir de pesca
9. manejar un carro
10. cantar frente a 50 o más personas

Comunicación

NATIONAL communication STANDARDS

3 **Gimnasio Olímpico** En parejas, lean el anuncio y contesten las preguntas.

Hasta el año pasado, siempre había mirado la tele sentado en el sofá durante mis ratos libres. ¡Era sedentario y teleadicto! Jamás había practicado ningún deporte y había aumentado mucho de peso.
Este año, he empezado a comer una dieta equilibrada y voy al gimnasio todos los días. He comenzado a ser una persona muy activa y he adelgazado. Disfruto de una vida sana. ¡Me siento muy feliz!
Manténgase en forma.
¡Acabo de descubrir una nueva vida!
¡Venga al Gimnasio Olímpico hoy mismo!

1. Identifiquen los elementos del pretérito pluscuamperfecto de indicativo en el anuncio. había mirado; había practicado; había aumentado
2. ¿Cómo era la vida del hombre cuando llevaba una vida sedentaria? ¿Cómo es ahora? Answers will vary.
3. ¿Se identifican ustedes con algunos de los hábitos, presentes o pasados, de este hombre? ¿Con cuáles? Answers will vary.
4. ¿Qué les recomienda el hombre del anuncio a los lectores? ¿Creen que les da buenos consejos? Answers will vary.

Practice more at **vhlcentral.com.**

1 Expansion
- Have students pick one of the exchanges and expand upon it to create a conversation with six lines.
- Have students create an original conversation like the ones in the activity. Call on volunteers to perform them for the class.

Nota cultural Traditionally, drinking **mate** is a social custom. The leaves are steeped in a decorative gourd and the beverage is sipped through a filtering straw called a **bombilla**. The **mate** is shared by all those present by passing the gourd from person to person. For more information on **mate**, refer students to **Lección 7**, page 219.

2 Teaching Tip Ask students questions to elicit the answers for the activity. Ex: **¿Quién había hecho un viaje en avión antes de cumplir los 16 años?** Ask follow-up questions to elicit other conjugations of the past perfect. Ex: **Entonces, de todos ustedes, ¿quiénes habían hecho un viaje en avión antes de cumplir los 16 años? (____ y ____ habían hecho...)**

3 Teaching Tip Before beginning the activity, survey the class to find out who exercises regularly and/or carefully watches what he or she eats. Ask these students to use the past perfect to say what they had done in their life prior to starting their fitness or diet program. Ex: **Había comido pastel de chocolate todos los días.**

3 Expansion Have groups create an ad for a different type of health-related business, such as a vegetarian restaurant.

TEACHING OPTIONS

Pairs Have students imagine that they have just joined a gym and are telling a friend about their new experiences. Ask students to tell their partners five things they had never done before. Ex: **Nunca había sudado tanto antes de empezar a ir al gimnasio.** Students should react to their partner's answers and ask follow-up questions if possible.

Large Groups Divide the class into large groups for a game of "one-upmanship." The first student states something he or she had done before a certain age. The second student tells what the first one had done, then counters with something even more outrageous that he or she had done, and so on, until everyone has participated. Ex: ____ **había viajado en avión antes de cumplir los cinco años, pero yo había viajado en barco antes de tener tres años.**

Section Goal

In **Recapitulación**, students will review the grammar concepts from this lesson.

Instructional Resource
Supersite

1 Teaching Tips
- Remind students that every verb form in the conditional carries an accent mark.
- Complete this activity orally as a class.

1 Expansion
- Ask students to provide the remaining forms of the verbs.
- Add **decir, tener,** and **venir** to the chart.

2 Teaching Tips
- Before beginning the activity, call on a volunteer to name the reflexive verb in the exercise. Remind students that the reflexive pronoun should appear before the conjugated verb.
- Complete this activity orally as a class.

2 Expansion To challenge students, have them provide the remaining verb forms.

3 Teaching Tip To simplify, have students indicate the subject for each item.

3 Expansion
- Have students compose questions about the conversation. Ex: **¿Nidia le dijo a Omar que Jaime y ella irían a la demostración de yoga?**
- To challenge students, ask them to identify which sentences from the conversation could be replaced by **ir a** + [*infinitive*] in the imperfect and retain the same meaning. Ex: **1. Yo creía que iba a llover, pero hizo sol.**

Recapitulación

Diagnostics

Completa estas actividades para repasar los conceptos de gramática que aprendiste en esta lección.

1 Verbos Completa el cuadro con la forma correcta de los verbos. 24 pts.

Infinitivo	tú	nosotros	ellas
tratar	tratarías	trataríamos	tratarían
querer	querrías	querríamos	querrían
poder	podrías	podríamos	podrían
haber	habrías	habríamos	habrían
vivir	vivirías	viviríamos	vivirían

2 Completar Completa el cuadro con el pretérito perfecto de los verbos. 12 pts.

Infinitivo	yo	él	ellas
tratar	he tratado	ha tratado	han tratado
entrenarse	me he entrenado	se ha entrenado	se han entrenado

3 Diálogo Completa la conversación con la forma adecuada del condicional de los verbos. 16 pts.

aconsejar	encantar	ir	poder
dejar	gustar	llover	volver

OMAR ¿Sabes? La demostración de yoga al aire libre fue un éxito. Yo creía que (1) llovería, pero hizo sol.

NIDIA Ah, me alegro. Te dije que Jaime y yo (2) iríamos, pero tuvimos un imprevisto (*something came up*) y no pudimos. Y a Laura, ¿la viste allí?

OMAR Sí, ella vino. Al contrario que tú, al principio me dijo que ella y su esposo no (3) podrían venir, pero al final aparecieron (*showed up*). Necesitaba relajarse un poco; está muy estresada con su trabajo.

NIDIA Yo le (4) aconsejaría que busque otra cosa. En su lugar, (5) dejaría esa compañía y (6) volvería a escribir un libro.

OMAR Estoy de acuerdo. Oye, esta noche voy a ir al gimnasio. ¿(7) Te gustaría venir conmigo?

NIDIA Sí, (8) me encantaría/me gustaría. ¿A qué hora vamos?

OMAR A las siete y media.

RESUMEN GRAMATICAL

15.1 The conditional pp. 492–493

The conditional tense* of **disfrutar**	
disfrutaría	disfrutaríamos
disfrutarías	disfrutaríais
disfrutaría	disfrutarían

*Same ending for **-ar, - er,** and **-ir** verbs.

► Verbs with irregular conditional: **decir, haber, hacer, poder, poner, querer, saber, salir, tener, venir**

15.2 The present perfect pp. 496–497

Present indicative of **haber**	
he	hemos
has	habéis
ha	han

Present perfect: present tense of **haber** + past participle

Present perfect indicative	
he empezado	hemos empezado
has empezado	habéis empezado
ha empezado	han empezado

He empezado a ir al gimnasio con regularidad.
***I have begun** to go to the gym regularly.*

15.3 The past perfect p. 500

Past perfect: imperfect tense of **haber** + past participle

Past perfect indicative	
había vivido	habíamos vivido
habías vivido	habíais vivido
había vivido	habían vivido

Antes de 2015, yo ya **había vivido** en tres países diferentes.
*Before 2015, **I had already lived** in three different countries.*

TEACHING OPTIONS

Extra practice Ask students to say which Spanish-speaking country they would visit and why. Ex: **Iría a Uruguay y visitaría Punta del Este.**

TPR Have students form a circle. Throw a foam or paper ball to a student and call out a time expression. Ex: **Antes de este semestre...** The student must complete the sentence using the past perfect (Ex: **Antes de este semestre, había estudiado japonés.**) and throw the ball to another student, who should do the same. Continue through a few more students, then provide a new sentence starter. Ex: **Antes de estudiar en esta universidad...**

4 **Preguntas** Completa las preguntas para estas respuestas usando el pretérito perfecto de indicativo. 16 pts.

modelo

—¿*Has llamado* a tus padres? —Sí, los llamé ayer.

1. —¿Tú has hecho ejercicio esta mañana en el gimnasio? —No, hice ejercicio en el parque.
2. —Y ustedes, ¿han desayunado ya? —Sí, desayunamos en el hotel.
3. —Y Juan y Felipe, ¿adónde han ido ? —Fueron al cine.
4. —Paco, ¿(nosotros) hemos recibido la cuenta del gimnasio? —Sí, la recibimos la semana pasada.
5. —Señor Martín, ¿ha pescado algo ya? —Sí, pesqué uno grande. Ya me puedo ir a casa contento.
6. —Inés, ¿has visto mi pelota de fútbol? —Sí, la vi esta mañana en el coche.
7. —Yo no he tomado café todavía. ¿Alguien quiere acompañarme? —No, gracias. Yo ya tomé mi café en casa.
8. —¿Ya te ha dicho el doctor que puedes comer chocolate? —Sí, me lo dijo ayer.

5 **Antes de graduarse** Di lo que cada una de estas personas ya había hecho o no había hecho todavía antes de graduarse de la universidad. Sigue el modelo. 12 pts.

modelo

yo / ya conocer a muchos amigos
Yo ya había conocido a muchos amigos.

1. Margarita / ya dejar de fumar
   Margarita ya había dejado de fumar.
2. tú / ya aprender a mantenerse en forma
   Tú ya habías aprendido a mantenerte en forma.
3. Julio / ya casarse
   Julio ya se había casado.
4. Mabel y yo / ya practicar yoga
   Mabel y yo ya habíamos practicado yoga.
5. los hermanos Falsero / todavía no perder un partido de vóleibol
   Los hermanos Falsero todavía no habían perdido un partido de vóleibol.
6. yo / ya entrenarse para el maratón
   Yo ya me había entrenado para el maratón.

6 **Manteniéndote en forma** Escribe al menos cinco oraciones para describir cómo te has mantenido en forma este semestre. Di qué cosas han cambiado este semestre en relación con el año pasado. Por ejemplo, ¿qué cosas has hecho o practicado este semestre que nunca habías probado antes? 20 pts. Answers will vary.

7 **Poema** Completa este fragmento de un poema de Nezahualcóyotl con el pretérito perfecto de indicativo de los verbos. ¡4 puntos EXTRA!

"He llegado (Llegar) aquí,
soy Yoyontzin.
Sólo busco las flores
sobre la tierra, he venido (venir)
a cortarlas."

Practice more at **vhlcentral.com.**

4 Teaching Tips
- Call on volunteers to read the model aloud.
- To simplify, have students begin by identifying the subject and infinitive for each blank.

4 Expansion Have students change the response for each item to the present perfect. Ex: **1. No, he hecho ejercicio en el parque.**

5 Expansion Give students these sentence cues as items 7-8: **7. nosotros / ya sufrir muchas presiones (Nosotros ya habíamos sufrido muchas presiones.) 8. Óscar / ya ir al gimnasio (Óscar ya había ido al gimnasio.)**

6 Teaching Tip To simplify, before students begin writing, encourage them to list their ideas under two columns: **El año pasado** and **Este semestre**. Have students brainstorm a few verbs in the past perfect for the first column and in the present perfect for the second.

7 Expansion Have students write a personalized version of the poem fragment. Ex: **He llegado aquí, soy ____. Sólo busco ____. He ____ a ____.**

TEACHING OPTIONS

Extra Practice Prepare sentences that use the present perfect. Say each sentence, have students repeat it, then say a different subject, varying the number. Have students then say the sentence with the new subject, making any necessary changes.

Game Divide the class into teams of five and have them sit in rows. Give the first student in each row a piece of paper. Call out an infinitive and have the first team member write the past perfect **yo** form of the verb and pass the paper to the second team member, who writes the **tú** form, and so forth. The first team to complete the paradigm correctly earns a point. The team with the most points at the end wins.

Audio: Reading
Additional Reading

Section Goals

In **Lectura**, students will:

- learn to make inferences and draw conclusions to understand a text
- read a short story and practice inferential reading

Instructional Resource
Supersite

Estrategia Tell students that authors may omit certain details or avoid making direct, explicit descriptions in order to make a story or poem more interesting. Explain that it is the reader's job to look for clues in the story and infer information left unstated.

El autor
Have students read the biography and list three important facts about the author.

El título Ask students to read the title and come up with an English equivalent for it. (*One of These Days*) Have pairs explain the different meanings this expression can convey. (revenge, hope)

El cuento Have students work in pairs to look up the words and answer the question. When they have finished, survey the class to see what most students think the story is about.

Lectura

NATIONAL STANDARDS
communication
cultures

Antes de leer

Estrategia
Making inferences

For dramatic effect and to achieve a smoother writing style, authors often do not explicitly supply the reader with all the details of a story or poem. Clues in the text can help you infer those things the writer chooses not to state in a direct manner. You simply "read between the lines" to fill in the missing information and draw conclusions. To practice making inferences, read these statements:

A Liliana le encanta ir al gimnasio. Hace años que empezó a levantar pesas.

Based on this statement alone, what inferences can you draw about Liliana?

El autor

Ve a la página 445 de tu libro y lee la biografía de Gabriel García Márquez.

El título

Sin leer el texto del cuento (*story*), lee el título. Escribe cinco oraciones que empiecen con la frase "Un día de éstos". Answers will vary.

El cuento

Éstas son algunas palabras que vas a encontrar al leer *Un día de éstos*. Busca su significado en el diccionario. Según estas palabras, ¿de qué piensas que trata (*is about*) el cuento? Answers will vary.

alcalde	lágrimas
dentadura postiza	muela
displicente	pañuelo
enjuto	rencor
guerrera	teniente

Practice more at **vhlcentral.com**.

Un día de éstos

Gabriel García Márquez

El lunes amaneció tibio° y sin lluvia. Don Aurelio Escovar, dentista sin título y buen madrugador°, abrió su gabinete° a las seis. Sacó de la vidriera° una dentadura postiza° montada aún° en el molde de yeso° y puso sobre la mesa un puñado° de instrumentos que ordenó de mayor a menor, como en una exposición. Llevaba una camisa a rayas, sin cuello, cerrada arriba con un botón dorado°, y los pantalones sostenidos con cargadores° elásticos. Era rígido, enjuto, con una mirada que raras veces correspondía a la situación, como la mirada de los sordos°.

Cuando tuvo las cosas dispuestas sobre la mesa rodó la fresa° hacia el sillón de resortes y se sentó a pulir° la dentadura postiza. Parecía no pensar en lo que hacía, pero trabajaba con obstinación, pedaleando en la fresa incluso cuando no se servía de ella.

Después de las ocho hizo una pausa para mirar el cielo por la ventana y vio dos gallinazos° pensativos que se secaban al sol en el caballete° de la casa vecina. Siguió trabajando con la idea de que antes del almuerzo volvería a llover°. La voz destemplada° de su hijo de once años lo sacó de su abstracción.

—Papá.

—Qué.

—Dice el alcalde que si le sacas una muela.

—Dile que no estoy aquí.

Estaba puliendo un diente de oro°. Lo retiró a la distancia del brazo y lo examinó con los ojos a medio cerrar. En la salita de espera volvió a gritar su hijo.

—Dice que sí estás porque te está oyendo.

El dentista siguió examinando el diente. Sólo cuando lo puso en la mesa con los trabajos terminados, dijo:

amaneció tibio *dawn broke warm* madrugador *early riser* gabinete *office* vidriera *glass cabinet* dentadura postiza *dentures* montada aún *still set* yeso *plaster* puñado *handful* dorado *gold* sostenidos con cargadores *held by suspenders* sordos *deaf* rodó la fresa *he turned the drill* pulir *to polish* gallinazos *vultures* caballete *ridge* volvería a llover *it would rain again* voz destemplada *harsh voice* oro *gold* cajita de cartón *small cardboard box* puente *bridge* te pega un tiro *he will shoot you* Sin apresurarse *Without haste* gaveta *drawer* Hizo girar *He turned* apoyada *resting* umbral *threshold* mejilla *cheek* hinchada *swollen* barba *beard* marchitos *faded* hervían *were boiling* pomos de loza *china bottles* cancel de tela *cloth screen* se acercaba *was approaching* talones *heels* mandíbula *jaw* cautelosa *cautious* cacerola *saucepan* pinzas *pliers* escupidera *spittoon* aguamanil *washstand* cordal *wisdom tooth* gatillo *pliers* se aferró *clung* barras *arms* descargó *unloaded* vacío helado *icy hollowness* riñones *kidneys* no soltó un suspiro *he didn't let out a sigh* muñeca *wrist* amarga ternura *bitter tenderness* teniente *lieutenant* crujido *crunch* a través de *through* sudoroso *sweaty* jadeante *panting* se desabotonó *he unbuttoned* a tientas *blindly* bolsillo *pocket* trapo *cloth* cielorraso desfondado *ceiling with the paint sagging* telaraña polvorienta *dusty spiderweb* haga buches de *rinse your mouth out with* vaina *thing*

TEACHING OPTIONS

Pairs Have students work in pairs to compare and contrast **don Aurelio Escovar** and **el alcalde**. Encourage them to use adjectives and descriptive phrases from the reading to make inferences about the personality of these characters. Have volunteers present their character analyses to the class.

Small Groups Have students work in groups of three to rewrite the story from a different point of view. Assign groups the point of view of the boy, the dentist, or the mayor. Have groups share their stories with the class to compare and contrast the different versions.

—Mejor.
Volvió a operar la fresa. De una cajita de cartón° donde guardaba las cosas por hacer, sacó un puente° de varias piezas y empezó a pulir el oro.
—Papá.
—Qué.
Aún no había cambiado de expresión.
—Dice que si no le sacas la muela te pega un tiro°.
Sin apresurarse°, con un movimiento extremadamente tranquilo, dejó de pedalear en la fresa, la retiró del sillón y abrió por completo la gaveta° inferior de la mesa. Allí estaba el revólver.
—Bueno —dijo—. Dile que venga a pegármelo.
Hizo girar° el sillón hasta quedar de frente a la puerta, la mano apoyada° en el borde de la gaveta. El alcalde apareció en el umbral°. Se había afeitado la mejilla° izquierda, pero en la otra, hinchada° y dolorida, tenía una barba° de cinco días. El dentista vio en sus ojos marchitos° muchas noches de desesperación. Cerró la gaveta con la punta de los dedos y dijo suavemente:
—Siéntese.
—Buenos días —dijo el alcalde.
—Buenos —dijo el dentista.
Mientras hervían° los instrumentos, el alcalde apoyó el cráneo en el cabezal de la silla y se sintió mejor. Respiraba un olor glacial. Era un gabinete pobre: una vieja silla de madera, la fresa de pedal y una vidriera con pomos de loza°. Frente a la silla, una ventana con un cancel de tela° hasta la altura de un hombre. Cuando sintió que el dentista se acercaba°, el alcalde afirmó los talones° y abrió la boca.
Don Aurelio Escovar le movió la cabeza hacia la luz. Después de observar la muela dañada, ajustó la mandíbula° con una presión cautelosa° de los dedos.
—Tiene que ser sin anestesia —dijo.
—¿Por qué?
—Porque tiene un absceso.
El alcalde lo miró en los ojos.
—Está bien —dijo, y trató de sonreír. El dentista no le correspondió. Llevó a la mesa de trabajo la cacerola° con los instrumentos hervidos y los sacó del agua con unas pinzas° frías, todavía sin apresurarse. Después rodó la escupidera° con la punta del zapato y fue a lavarse las manos en el aguamanil°. Hizo todo sin mirar al alcalde. Pero el alcalde no lo perdió de vista.
Era una cordal° inferior. El dentista abrió las piernas y apretó la muela con el gatillo° caliente. El alcalde se aferró° a las barras° de la silla, descargó° toda su fuerza en los pies y sintió un vacío helado° en los riñones°, pero no soltó un suspiro°. El dentista sólo movió la muñeca°. Sin rencor, más bien con una amarga ternura°, dijo:
—Aquí nos paga veinte muertos, teniente°.
El alcalde sintió un crujido° de huesos en la mandíbula y sus ojos se llenaron de lágrimas. Pero no suspiró hasta que no sintió salir la muela. Entonces la vio a través de° las lágrimas. Le pareció tan extraña a su dolor, que no pudo entender la tortura de sus cinco noches anteriores. Inclinado sobre la escupidera, sudoroso°, jadeante°, se desabotonó° la guerrera y buscó a tientas° el pañuelo en el bolsillo° del pantalón. El dentista le dio un trapo° limpio.
—Séquese las lágrimas —dijo.
El alcalde lo hizo. Estaba temblando. Mientras el dentista se lavaba las manos, vio el cielorraso desfondado° y una telaraña polvorienta° con huevos de araña e insectos muertos. El dentista regresó secándose. "Acuéstese —dijo— y haga buches de° agua de sal." El alcalde se puso de pie, se despidió con un displicente saludo militar, y se dirigió a la puerta estirando las piernas, sin abotonarse la guerrera.
—Me pasa la cuenta —dijo.
—¿A usted o al municipio?
El alcalde no lo miró. Cerró la puerta, y dijo, a través de la red metálica:
—Es la misma vaina°.

Después de leer

Comprensión

Completa las oraciones con la palabra o expresión correcta.

1. Don Aurelio Escovar es ___dentista___ sin título.
2. Al alcalde le duele ___una muela /una cordal___.
3. Aurelio Escovar y el alcalde se llevan ___mal___.
4. El alcalde amenaza (*threatens*) al dentista con pegarle un ___tiro___.
5. Finalmente, Aurelio Escovar ___le saca___ la muela al alcalde.
6. El alcalde llevaba varias noches sin ___dormir___.

Interpretación

En parejas, respondan a estas preguntas. Luego comparen sus respuestas con las de otra pareja. Answers will vary.

1. ¿Cómo reacciona don Aurelio cuando escucha que el alcalde amenaza con pegarle un tiro? ¿Qué les dice esta actitud sobre las personalidades del dentista y del alcalde?
2. ¿Por qué creen que don Aurelio y el alcalde no se llevan bien?
3. ¿Creen que era realmente necesario no usar anestesia?
4. ¿Qué piensan que significa el comentario "aquí nos paga veinte muertos, teniente"? ¿Qué les dice esto del alcalde y su autoridad en el pueblo?
5. ¿Cómo se puede interpretar el saludo militar y la frase final del alcalde "es la misma vaina"?

TEACHING OPTIONS

Pairs Have students work in pairs to invent two characters for a **minicomedia**: a dentist from New York and an easily frightened patient. Tell students to begin by writing a physical and psychological description of each character. Then have them write the dialogue for their **minicomedia**. Encourage humor and creativity. Have volunteers role-play their dialogues for the class.

Extra Practice To challenge students, have them work in pairs to write an alternate ending to the story, in which the dentist refuses to treat the mayor's toothache. Encourage students to share their alternate endings with the class.

Teaching Tips

- Explain that ***Un día de éstos*** is part of the short story collection ***Los funerales de la Mamá Grande***, which **García Márquez** finished writing in 1959.
- The events of ***Un día de éstos*** take place during **La Violencia**, an era of intense civil conflict in Colombian history, which started in 1946 and lasted over a decade. This complex conflict generally centered around supporters of the Liberal and Conservative political parties. The Liberal and Communist parties organized self-defense groups and guerrilla units, both of which fought against the Conservatives and each other.

Comprensión Have students work in pairs to complete the sentences. When they have finished, go over the answers orally with the class.

Interpretación Give students these questions as items 6–9: **6. ¿Creen que el dentista y el alcalde habían sido amigos antes de ese día? 7. En su opinión, ¿quién tiene más poder, el dentista o el alcalde? 8. ¿Cómo creen que es la relación entre el gobierno y la gente de este pueblo? 9. ¿Qué creen que va a pasar cuando el alcalde se mejore?**

Section Goals

In **Escritura**, students will:
- learn to organize information logically
- integrate lesson vocabulary and structures
- write a personal wellness plan in Spanish

Instructional Resource
Supersite

Estrategia Have students brainstorm details of maintaining a personal wellness plan that includes nutrition, exercise, and stress reduction. Then have a volunteer tell about his or her plan, and guide students in organizing the information in three different ways: chronologically, sequentially, and in order of importance.

Tema Review the three suggested categories of details to include. Then, have volunteers make up questions or use the ones on this page to interview you regarding your personal wellness plan.

Successful Language Learning Point out to students that this strategy will help them improve their writing in both Spanish and English.

Escritura

Estrategia

Organizing information logically

Many times a written piece may require you to include a great deal of information. You might want to organize your information in one of three different ways:

- chronologically (e.g., events in the history of a country)
- sequentially (e.g., steps in a recipe)
- in order of importance

Organizing your information beforehand will make both your writing and your message clearer to your readers. If you were writing a piece on weight reduction, for example, you would need to organize your ideas about two general areas: eating right and exercise. You would need to decide which of the two is more important according to your purpose in writing the piece. If your main idea is that eating right is the key to losing weight, you might want to start your piece with a discussion of good eating habits. You might want to discuss the following aspects of eating right in order of their importance:

- quantities of food
- selecting appropriate foods
- healthy recipes
- percentage of fat in each meal
- calorie count
- percentage of carbohydrates in each meal
- frequency of meals

You would then complete the piece by following the same process to discuss the various aspects of the importance of getting exercise.

Tema

NATIONAL communication STANDARDS

Escribir un plan personal de bienestar

Desarrolla un plan personal para mejorar tu bienestar, tanto físico como emocional. Tu plan debe describir:

1. lo que has hecho para mejorar tu bienestar y llevar una vida sana
2. lo que no has podido hacer todavía
3. las actividades que debes hacer en los próximos meses

Considera también estas preguntas:

La nutrición
- ¿Comes una dieta equilibrada?
- ¿Consumes suficientes vitaminas y minerales?
- ¿Consumes demasiada grasa?
- ¿Quieres aumentar de peso o adelgazar?
- ¿Qué puedes hacer para mejorar tu dieta?

El ejercicio
- ¿Haces ejercicio? ¿Con qué frecuencia?
- ¿Vas al gimnasio? ¿Qué tipo de ejercicios haces allí?
- ¿Practicas algún deporte?
- ¿Qué puedes hacer para mejorar tu bienestar físico?

El estrés
- ¿Sufres muchas presiones?
- ¿Qué actividades o problemas te causan estrés?
- ¿Qué haces (o debes hacer) para aliviar el estrés y sentirte más tranquilo/a?
- ¿Qué puedes hacer para mejorar tu bienestar emocional?

EVALUATION: Plan personal de bienestar

Criteria	Scale
Content	1 2 3 4
Organization	1 2 3 4
Use of vocabulary	1 2 3 4
Accuracy and mechanics	1 2 3 4
Creativity	1 2 3 4

Scoring	
Excellent	18–20 points
Good	14–17 points
Satisfactory	10–13 points
Unsatisfactory	< 10 points

Escuchar

Audio

Estrategia

Listening for the gist/ Listening for cognates

Combining these two strategies is an easy way to get a good sense of what you hear. When you listen for the gist, you get the general idea of what you're hearing, which allows you to interpret cognates and other words in a meaningful context. Similarly, the cognates give you information about the details of the story that you might not have understood when listening for the gist.

To practice these strategies, you will listen to a short paragraph. Write down the gist of what you hear and jot down a few cognates. Based on the gist and the cognates, what conclusions can you draw about what you heard?

Preparación

Mira la foto. ¿Qué pistas° te da de lo que vas a oír? Answers will vary.

Ahora escucha

Escucha lo que dice Ofelia Cortez de Bauer. Anota algunos de los cognados que escuchas y también la idea general del discurso°. Answers will vary.

____

____

____

____

Idea general: ______________________________

Ahora contesta las siguientes preguntas.

1. ¿Cuál es el género° del discurso?
2. ¿Cuál es el tema?
3. ¿Cuál es el propósito°?

pistas *clues* **discurso** *speech* **género** *genre* **propósito** *purpose* **público** *audience* **debía haber incluido** *should have included*

Practice more at **vhlcentral.com**.

Comprensión

¿Cierto o falso?

Indica si lo que dicen estas oraciones es **cierto** o **falso**. Corrige las oraciones falsas.

	Cierto	Falso
1. La señora Bauer habla de la importancia de estar en buena forma y de hacer ejercicio.	✓	○
2. Según ella, lo más importante es que lleves el programa sugerido por los expertos. Lo más importante es que lleves un programa variado que te guste.	○	✓
3. La señora Bauer participa en actividades individuales y de grupo.	✓	○
4. El único objetivo del tipo de programa que ella sugiere es adelgazar. Los objetivos de su programa son: condicionar el sistema cardiopulmonar, aumentar la fuerza muscular y mejorar la flexibilidad.	○	✓

Preguntas

Responde a las preguntas. Answers will vary.

1. Imagina que el programa de radio sigue. Según las pistas que ella dio, ¿qué vas a oír en la segunda parte?
2. ¿A qué tipo de público° le interesa el tema del que habla la señora Bauer?
3. ¿Sigues los consejos de la señora Bauer? Explica tu respuesta.
4. ¿Qué piensas de los consejos que ella da? ¿Hay otra información que ella debía haber incluido°?

Section Goals

In **Escuchar**, students will:
- listen for the gist and for cognates
- answer questions about a radio program

Instructional Resources
Supersite: Audio (Textbook MP3s); Resources (Scripts)

Estrategia
Script Cuando nos casamos le prometí a Magdalena que no íbamos a residir con su familia por más de un año. Y si Dios quiere, ¡así va a ser! Magdalena y yo encontramos un condominio absolutamente perfecto. Hoy pasamos por el banco para pedir el préstamo hipotecario. ¡Espero que no haya problema con el chequeo del crédito!

Teaching Tip
Have students write a description of what they see in the photo.

Ahora escucha
Script Buenos días, radioyentes, y bienvenidos a "Tu bienestar". Les habla Ofelia Cortez de Bauer. Hoy vamos a hablar de la importancia de estar en buena forma. Primero, quiero que entiendan que estar en buena forma no es sólo cosa de estar delgado o ser fuerte. Para mantenerse en forma deben tener tres objetivos: condicionar el sistema cardiopulmonar, aumentar la fuerza muscular y mejorar la flexibilidad. Cada persona tiene sus propios objetivos, y también sus propias limitaciones físicas, y debe diseñar su programa con un monitor de acuerdo con éstos. Pero óiganme bien, ¡lo más importante es tener una rutina variada, con ejercicios que les gusten, porque de otro modo no lo van a hacer! Mi rutina personal es la siguiente. Dos días por semana voy a la clase de ejercicios aeróbicos, claro con un buen calentamiento al comienzo. Tres días por semana corro en el parque, o si hace mal tiempo, uso una caminadora en el gimnasio. Luego levanto pesas y termino haciendo estiramientos de los músculos. Los fines de semana me mantengo activa pero hago una variedad de cosas de acuerdo a lo que quiere hacer la familia. A veces practico la natación; otras, vamos de excursión al campo, por ejemplo. Como les había dicho la semana pasada, como unas 1.600 calorías al día, mayormente alimentos con poca grasa y sin sal. Disfruto mucho del bienestar que estos hábitos me producen. Ahora iremos a unos anuncios de nuestros patrocinadores. Cuando regresemos, voy a contestar sus preguntas acerca del ejercicio, la dieta o el bienestar en general. El teléfono es el 43.89.76. No se vayan. Ya regresamos con mucha más información.

(Script continues at far left in the bottom panels.)

Section Goals

In **En pantalla**, students will:
- read about an association in Spain that promotes awareness of Parkinson's disease
- watch a public service ad for the **Asociación Parkinson Alicante**
- read about the short film ***Cloe***
- watch the short film ***Cloe***

Instructional Resources
Supersite: Video (***En pantalla***); Resources (Scripts, Translations)

Introduction Ask students what they know about Parkinson's disease. Do they know someone with Parkinson's? What do they know about Michael J. Fox, who starred in *Teen Wolf*, having Parkinson's?

Antes de ver
- Have students look at the video stills, read the captions, and predict how the man in the costume is promoting awareness of Parkinson's disease.
- Read through the **Vocabulario útil** with students and model the pronunciation.
- Before showing the ad, assure students that they do not need to understand every word they hear. Tell them to rely on visual cues and to listen for cognates and the words from **Vocabulario útil**.

Preparación Have students talk about the NGOs (non-governmental organizations) they know. An NGO is any nonprofit, voluntary citizens' group. Many NGOs focus on health, the environment, or human rights.

Escoger Ask students for their opinions about the ad. Do they like it? Do they think it's funny? Do they think it's effective?

Una campaña Have pairs present their campaigns to the class. Then have students vote for the best campaign.

En pantalla

NATIONAL STANDARDS communication cultures

Anuncio

El objetivo de esta original y divertida campaña es informar y sensibilizar° a la sociedad sobre la enfermedad del Parkinson y el sufrimiento que ocasiona° a los que la padecen°. Además de darse a conocer° y enfrentarse a° la indiferencia, con esta campaña también se pretende° recaudar fondos°, ya que la Asociación Parkinson Alicante se ha visto afectada por la crisis económica española, disminuyendo así el número de ayudas recibidas.

Vocabulario útil

aullar	*to howl*
hombre lobo	*werewolf*
lucha	*fight, battle*
manada	*pack (of wolves)*
subvenciones	*subsidies*
tiembla	*trembles, shakes*

Preparación

¿Conoces alguna ONG (organización no gubernamental)? ¿Cuál? ¿Qué cosas ha hecho esa organización para ayudar a los demás? Answers will vary.

Escoger

Elige la opción correcta.

1. Las __a__ a la asociación estaban fallando.
   a. subvenciones b. peticiones
2. La asociación decidió inventar una __b__ para el Parkinson.
   a. pastilla b. causa
3. Michael J. Fox hizo el papel de un __a__ y tiene Parkinson.
   a. hombre lobo b. hombre araña
4. La forma para llegar a todo el mundo es __b__ lo más fuerte (*loud*) posible.
   a. cantar b. aullar

Una campaña

En parejas, creen una campaña para transformar una organización, real o ficticia. Utilicen el condicional. Answers will vary.

sensibilizar *to raise awareness* ocasiona *causes* la padecen *suffer from it* darse a conocer *spreading the word* enfrentarse a *to fight against* se pretende *the hope is to* recaudar fondos *to raise money*

Asociación Parkinson Alicante

Hemos decidido inventarnos una causa para el Parkinson.

Tal vez la gente pueda creerse que ser hombre lobo provoque Parkinson.

Queremos que la gente conozca la asociación y nos ayude en esta lucha.

Video: TV Clip

Practice more at **vhlcentral.com.**

TEACHING OPTIONS

Extra Practice Have students imagine that they are sending a donation to the **Asociación Parkinson Alicante**. Tell them to write a letter to the association explaining what about the ad motivated them to send a donation. Encourage them to use the conditional, the present perfect, and the past perfect in their letter.

Extra Practice Have students research Parkinson's disease. What are the symptoms? How is it treated? Have them share their findings with the class.

Cortometraje

A veces, nos encontramos con alguien que conocemos, pero no nos acordamos muy bien de cómo. El chico protagonista de *Cloe*, Dani, toma esta idea y la utiliza para acercarse a hablar con una chica en un café. Según él, se conocieron hace un par de años: su amigo Coque dio una fiesta de disfraces en su apartamento en La Latina, un barrio de Madrid.

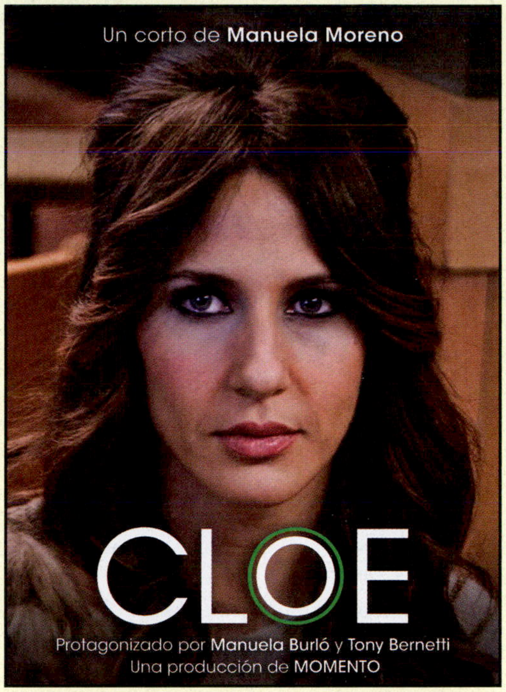

Preparación

¿Alguna vez le has hablado a un desconocido (*stranger*) que creías conocer? ¿Alguna vez te ha hablado un desconocido que creía conocerte? ¿Qué sucedió? Answers will vary.

Después de ver

Indica si lo que dice cada oración es **cierto** o **falso**. Corrige las oraciones falsas.

1. La chica protagonista se llama Cloe. Falso. Se llama Marta.
2. La chica dice que se conocieron en una fiesta de Navidad. Falso. La chica dice que se conocieron en una fiesta de disfraces.
3. El chico dice que en la fiesta iba disfrazado del Lobo Feroz. Falso. El chico dice que no iba disfrazado de nada.
4. La chica no conoce al chico. Cierto.
5. Al final, el chico se da cuenta de que ella también le ha mentido. Cierto.

Conversar

Imagina que la conversación entre el chico y la chica se desarrolla de otra manera y la historia acaba de manera diferente. En parejas, escriban un final diferente para el corto. Luego, compártanlo con la clase. Answers will vary.

Expresiones útiles

la Caperucita Roja	*Little Red Riding Hood*
en la punta de la lengua	*on the tip of one's tongue*
la fiesta de disfraces	*costume party*
ir vestido de algo	*to dress up as something*
el Lobo Feroz	*Big Bad Wolf*
se pasó un poco	*he went too far*
el tipo éste	*this guy*
la trenza	*braid*

Para hablar del corto

caradura	*cheeky*
encontrarse con (alguien)	*to run into (someone)*
fingir	*to pretend*
mentir (e:ie)	*to lie*

Video: Short Film

Practice more at **vhlcentral.com.**

Antes de ver

- Have students look at the poster, and ask them what they think the short film will be about.
- Read through the **Expresiones útiles** and **Para hablar del corto** vocabulary with students to model pronunciation and practice using the terms.
- Reassure students that they do not need to understand every word they hear in the short film. Tell them to rely on visual cues and listen for cognates and words from **Expresiones útiles**.

Preparación Give students a few moments to think of examples from their own experiences. Allow them to ask you for additional vocabulary.

Después de ver Have students write two additional true/false statements for a partner to answer.

Conversar After students have presented their alternate endings, have the class discuss their reactions and opinions.

TEACHING OPTIONS

Worth Noting ***Cloe*** (2011) was written and directed by Spanish filmmaker **Manuela Moreno**. She has several other short films: ***Lo sé*** (2013), ***Pipas*** (2013), ***Camas*** (2010), ***Quiero estar el resto de mi vida contigo*** (2009), and ***Dolores*** (2008). She has also directed a feature-length film, ***Cómo sobrevivir a una despedida*** (2015).

Pairs Have pairs role-play a conversation in which two strangers pretend to know each other. Tell them to think about where they run into each other and how they could have met before.

Video: Panorama cultural
Interactive map

Section Goal

In **Panorama**, students will read about the geography, culture, and history of Bolivia.

Instructional Resources
Supersite: Video (***Panorama cultural***); Resources (Scripts, Translations, Digital Image Bank, Answer Keys)
WebSAM
Workbook, pp. 189–190
Video Manual, pp. 69–70

Teaching Tips

- Use the **Lección 15 Panorama** digital images to assist with this presentation.
- Have students look at the map of Bolivia. Point out that Bolivia is a completely landlocked country. Have students name the five countries that share its borders. Point out Bolivia's three main regions: the Andes region, the high plain (**altiplano**), and the Amazon basin. Ask students to read aloud the places labeled on the map and to identify whether place names are in Spanish or in an indigenous language.

El país en cifras Have volunteers create a pie chart that represents Bolivia's ethnic makeup as described in the **Población** section. As students read about the **Ciudades principales**, have them locate each city on the map. As students read about **Idiomas**, point out that **quechua** was the language of the Incan empire.

¡Increíble pero cierto! Visitors to La Paz and other Andean cities often experience **soroche**, or altitude sickness. Andean natives typically develop increased lung capacity and a greater capacity for diffusing oxygen to the body, helping to compensate for decreased oxygen levels at these heights.

Bolivia

NATIONAL STANDARDS connections cultures

El país en cifras

- **Área:** 1.098.580 km² (424.162 millas²), *equivalente al área total de Francia y España*
- **Población:** 10.631.000

Los indígenas quechua y aimara constituyen más de la mitad° de la población de Bolivia. Estos grupos indígenas han mantenido sus culturas y lenguas tradicionales. Las personas de ascendencia° indígena y europea representan la tercera parte de la población. Los demás son de ascendencia europea nacida en Latinoamérica. Una gran mayoría de los bolivianos, más o menos el 70%, vive en el altiplano°.

- **Capital:** La Paz, sede° del gobierno, capital administrativa—1.715.000; Sucre, sede del Tribunal Supremo, capital constitucional y judicial
- **Ciudades principales:** Santa Cruz de la Sierra—1.584.000; Cochabamba, Oruro, Potosí
- **Moneda:** peso boliviano
- **Idiomas:** español (oficial), aimara (oficial), quechua (oficial)

Plaza Murillo

Vista de la ciudad de Sucre

Bandera de Bolivia

Vista de la ciudad de Oruro

Bolivianos célebres

- **Jesús Lara,** escritor (1898–1980)
- **Víctor Paz Estenssoro,** político y presidente (1907–2001)
- **María Luisa Pacheco,** pintora (1919–1982)
- **Matilde Casazola,** poeta (1942–)
- **Edmundo Paz Soldán,** escritor (1967–)

recursos: WB pp. 189–190 | VM pp. 69–70 | vhlcentral.com Lección 15

mitad *half* ascendencia *descent* altiplano *high plateau* sede *seat* paraguas *umbrella* cascada *waterfall*

¡Increíble pero cierto!

La Paz es la capital más alta del mundo. Su aeropuerto está situado a una altitud de 4.061 metros (13.325 pies). Ah, y si viajas en carro hasta La Paz, ¡no te olvides del paraguas°! En la carretera, que cruza 9.000 metros de densa selva, te encontrarás con una cascada°.

TEACHING OPTIONS

Cultural Note Another way to become acquainted with the traditions of Bolivia's different regions is through regional dances. The **cueca collasuyo** is a traditional dance from the **altiplano** region, while the **cueca chapaca** is from the **Chaco** area. The **chiringueros del Bení** is traditionally performed by rubber tappers from the Amazon area.

Cultural Activity To give students the opportunity to listen to the sounds of **quechua** or **aimara**, as well as the music of the Andes, bring in recordings made by Andean musicians, such as **Inti Illimani** or **Inkuyo**. Some recordings may include lyrics in the original language and in translation.

Lugares • El lago Titicaca

Titicaca, situado en los Andes de Bolivia y Perú, es el lago navegable más alto del mundo, a una altitud de 3.810 metros (12.500 pies). Con un área de más de 8.300 kilómetros^2 (3.200 millas^2), también es el segundo lago más grande de Suramérica, después del lago de Maracaibo (Venezuela). La mitología inca cuenta que los hijos del dios° Sol emergieron de las profundas aguas del lago Titicaca para fundar su imperio°.

Artes • La música andina

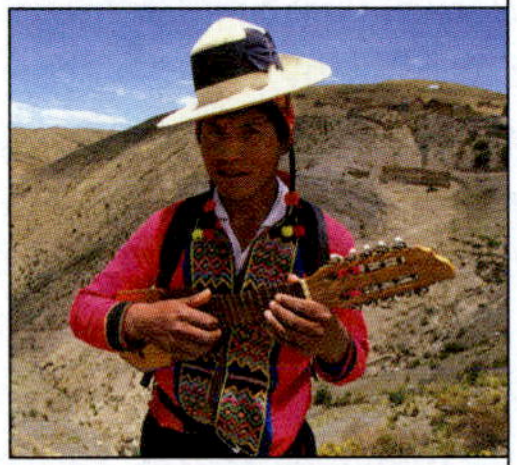

La música andina, compartida por Bolivia, Perú, Ecuador, Chile y Argentina, es el aspecto más conocido de su folclore. Hay muchos conjuntos° profesionales que dan a conocer° esta música popular, de origen indígena, alrededor° del mundo. Algunos de los grupos más importantes y que llevan más de treinta años actuando en escenarios internacionales son Los Kjarkas (Bolivia), Inti Illimani (Chile), Los Chaskis (Argentina) e Illapu (Chile).

Historia • Tiahuanaco

Tiahuanaco, que significa "Ciudad de los dioses", es un sitio arqueológico de ruinas preincaicas situado cerca de La Paz y del lago Titicaca. Se piensa que los antepasados° de los indígenas aimara fundaron este centro ceremonial hace unos 15.000 años. En el año 1100, la ciudad tenía unos 60.000 habitantes. En este sitio se pueden ver el Templo de Kalasasaya, el Monolito Ponce, el Templete Subterráneo, la Puerta del Sol y la Puerta de la Luna. La Puerta del Sol es un impresionante monumento que tiene tres metros de alto y cuatro de ancho° y que pesa unas 10 toneladas.

¿Qué aprendiste? Responde a las preguntas con una oración completa.

1. ¿Qué idiomas se hablan en Bolivia? En Bolivia se hablan español, quechua y aimara.
2. ¿Dónde vive la mayoría de los bolivianos? La mayoría de los bolivianos vive en el altiplano.
3. ¿Cuál es la capital administrativa de Bolivia? La capital administrativa de Bolivia es La Paz.
4. Según la mitología inca, ¿qué ocurrió en el lago Titicaca? Los hijos del dios Sol emergieron del lago para fundar el imperio inca.
5. ¿De qué países es la música andina? La música andina es de Bolivia, Perú, Ecuador, Chile y Argentina.
6. ¿Qué origen tiene esta música? Es música de origen indígena.
7. ¿Cómo se llama el sitio arqueológico situado cerca de La Paz y el lago Titicaca? El sitio arqueológico situado cerca de La Paz y el lago Titicaca se llama Tiahuanaco.
8. ¿Qué es la Puerta del Sol? La Puerta del Sol es un monumento que está en Tiahuanaco.

Conexión Internet Investiga estos temas en **vhlcentral.com**.

Practice more at **vhlcentral.com**.

1. Busca información sobre un(a) boliviano/a célebre. ¿Cuáles son algunos de los episodios más importantes de su vida? ¿Qué ha hecho esta persona? ¿Por qué es célebre?
2. Busca información sobre Tiahuanaco u otro sitio arqueológico en Bolivia. ¿Qué han descubierto los arqueólogos en ese sitio?

dios *god* imperio *empire* conjuntos *groups* dan a conocer *make known* alrededor *around* antepasados *ancestors* ancho *wide*

El lago Titicaca Sitting more than two miles above sea level, Lake Titicaca is larger than the area of Delaware and Rhode Island combined. Five major river systems feed into the lake, which has forty-one islands. Lake Titicaca is also the largest lake in South America as measured by water volume.

La música andina Andean music is characterized by its plaintive, haunting melodies, often based in a minor or pentatonic scale.

Tiahuanaco The pre-Incan civilization that flourished at **Tiahuanaco** was probably a theocracy, governed by priest-kings. The primary deity was **Viracocha**, a sky and thunder god worshipped throughout much of the Andean world. The Tiahuanacan head of state was viewed as **Viracocha's** embodiment on earth.

Conexión Internet Students will find supporting Internet activities and links at **vhlcentral.com**.

Teaching Tip You may want to wrap up this section by playing the ***Panorama cultural*** video footage for this lesson.

TEACHING OPTIONS

Worth Noting Teams of scientists have extracted sediment samples from Titicaca's lakebed to study the history of climatological change in the region. Such research helps scientists build models to analyze contemporary trends in global climate change.

Worth Noting Students might enjoy learning this indigenous riddle about the **armadillo**, the animal whose outer shell is used to make the **charango**, a small guitar used in Andean music.
Vive en el cerro, lejos del mar.
De concha el saco sin abrochar.
Cuando se muere... ¡pues a cantar!

Video: *Panorama cultural*
Interactive map

Section Goal

In **Panorama**, students will read about the geography and culture of Paraguay.

Instructional Resources
Supersite: Video (***Panorama cultural***); Resources (Scripts, Translations, Digital Image Bank, Answer Keys)
WebSAM
Workbook, pp. 191–192
Video Manual, pp. 71–72

Teaching Tips

- Use the **Lección 15 Panorama** digital images to assist with this presentation.
- Have students look at the map of Paraguay. Note that the major population centers lie east of the Paraguay River, which divides the country in two. West of the river is the **Gran Chaco,** a sparsely populated and largely infertile region.

El país en cifras As you read **Idiomas,** point out that **guaraní** is also spoken in neighboring Bolivia, Brazil, and Argentina. However, as an officially bilingual nation, Paraguay has the largest concentration of **guaraní** speakers. As students read **Paraguayos célebres,** let them know that writer **Augusto Roa Bastos** is well known throughout Latin America as both a poet and novelist. His novels ***Yo, el Supremo*** and ***Hijo de hombre*** deal with the turbulent and difficult history of Paraguay.

¡Increíble pero cierto! Like Paraguay, several other Spanish-speaking countries impose fines on citizens for not voting. Ask students to research and name these countries. Ask the class if they think that such a measure should be implemented here to improve voter turnout at the polls.

Paraguay

NATIONAL STANDARDS connections cultures

El país en cifras

- **Área:** 406.750 km² (157.046 millas²), *el tamaño° de California*
- **Población:** 6.703.000
- **Capital:** Asunción—2.139.000
- **Ciudades principales:** Ciudad del Este, San Lorenzo, Lambaré, Fernando de la Mora
- **Moneda:** guaraní
- **Idiomas:** español (oficial), guaraní (oficial)

Las tribus indígenas que habitaban la zona antes de la llegada de los españoles hablaban guaraní. Ahora el 90 por ciento de los paraguayos habla esta lengua, que se usa con frecuencia en canciones, poemas, periódicos y libros. Varios institutos y asociaciones, como el Teatro Guaraní, se dedican a preservar la cultura y la lengua guaraníes.

Bandera de Paraguay

Paraguayos célebres

- **Agustín Barrios,** guitarrista y compositor (1885–1944)
- **Josefina Plá,** escritora y ceramista (1903–1999)
- **Augusto Roa Bastos,** escritor (1917–2005)
- **Olga Blinder,** pintora (1921–2008)
- **Berta Rojas,** guitarrista (1966–)

Paraguayo con alfombras típicas del país

Agricultor indígena de la tribu maca

Itapúa

recursos

WB pp. 191–192	VM pp. 71–72	vhlcentral.com Lección 15

tamaño *size* multara *fined*

¡Increíble pero cierto!

¿Te imaginas qué pasaría si el gobierno multara° a los ciudadanos que no van a votar? En Paraguay es una obligación. Ésta es una ley nacional, que otros países también tienen, para obligar a los ciudadanos a participar en las elecciones. En Paraguay los ciudadanos que no van a votar tienen que pagar una multa al gobierno.

TEACHING OPTIONS

Worth Noting Give students exposure to the **guaraní** language by sharing the names of these typical Paraguayan dishes: **chipa** (a baked good flavored with **anís**), **kiveve** (a stew made from **andaí**, a type of squash), and **pastel mandi'o** (turnovers made with the South American staple, manioc flour, and filled with **so'o ku'i**, chopped meat). Invite students who have visited or lived in Paraguay to share other information about traditional Paraguayan fare. Be sure to have them mention the national drink of Paraguay (as well as Uruguay, Argentina, and Rio Grande do Sul in Brazil), **yerba mate.** This is an infusion made from the leaves of a tree native to Paraguay and is sometimes called *Paraguayan tea* in English.

Artesanía • El ñandutí

La artesanía° más famosa de Paraguay se llama ñandutí y es un encaje° hecho a mano originario de Itauguá. En guaraní, la palabra ñandutí significa telaraña° y esta pieza recibe ese nombre porque imita el trazado° que crean los arácnidos. Estos encajes suelen ser° blancos, pero también los hay de colores, con formas geométricas o florales.

Ciencias • La represa Itaipú

La represa° Itaipú es una instalación hidroeléctrica que se encuentra en la frontera entre Paraguay y Brasil. Su construcción inició en 1974 y duró 8 años. La cantidad de concreto que se utilizó durante los primeros cinco años de esta obra fue similar a la que se necesita para construir un edificio de 350 pisos. Cien mil trabajadores paraguayos participaron en el proyecto. En 1984 se puso en funcionamiento la Central Hidroeléctrica de Itaipú y gracias a su cercanía con las famosas cataratas del Iguazú, muchos turistas la visitan diariamente.

Naturaleza • Los ríos Paraguay y Paraná

Los ríos Paraguay y Paraná sirven de frontera natural entre Argentina y Paraguay, y son las principales rutas de transporte de este último país. El Paraná tiene unos 3.200 kilómetros navegables, y por esta ruta pasan barcos de más de 5.000 toneladas, los cuales viajan desde el estuario° del Río de la Plata hasta la ciudad de Asunción. El río Paraguay divide el Gran Chaco de la meseta° Paraná, donde vive la mayoría de los paraguayos.

¿Qué aprendiste? Contesta cada pregunta con una oración completa.

1. ¿Quién fue Augusto Roa Bastos?
   Augusto Roa Bastos fue un escritor paraguayo.
2. ¿Cómo se llama la moneda de Paraguay?
   La moneda de Paraguay se llama guaraní.
3. ¿Qué es el ñandutí?
   El ñandutí es un tipo de encaje.
4. ¿De dónde es originario el ñandutí?
   El ñandutí es originario de Itauguá.
5. ¿Qué forma imita el ñandutí?
   Imita la forma de una telaraña.
6. En total, ¿cuántos años tomó la construcción de la represa Itaipú?
   La construcción de la represa Itaipú tomó 8 años.
7. ¿A cuántos paraguayos dio trabajo la construcción de la represa?
   La construcción de la represa dio trabajo a 100.000 paraguayos.
8. ¿Qué países separan los ríos Paraguay y Paraná? Los ríos Paraguay y Paraná separan Argentina y Paraguay.
9. ¿Qué distancia se puede navegar por el Paraná?
   Se pueden navegar 3.200 kilómetros.

Conexión Internet Investiga estos temas en **vhlcentral.com**.

1. Busca información sobre Alfredo Stroessner, el ex presidente de Paraguay. ¿Por qué se le considera un dictador?
2. Busca información sobre la historia de Paraguay. En tu opinión, ¿cuáles fueron los episodios decisivos en su historia?

Practice more at **vhlcentral.com**.

artesanía *crafts* encaje *lace* telaraña *spiderweb* trazado *outline; design* suelen ser *are usually* represa *dam* estuario *estuary* meseta *plateau*

El ñandutí In recent years, the number of traditional **ñandutí** makers has been in serious decline. Many artisans of Itauguá have turned to more profitable sources of income. In an effort to keep this traditional art alive, formal instruction in the skill of making **ñandutí** has been incorporated in the curriculum of local handicraft schools.

La represa Itaipú The Itaipú dam project is a joint venture between Brazil and Paraguay, and has been remarkably successful. In 2013, the plant supplied 75% of Paraguay's energy and 17% of that consumed by Brazil.

Los ríos Paraguay y Paraná The Paraná River was a highway for the settlement of Paraguay. Along its banks, between the sixteenth and late eighteenth centuries, the Jesuits organized their **guaraní**-speaking parishioners into small, self-supporting city-states built around mission settlements, similar to the Franciscan mission system in California during the same period.

Conexión Internet Students will find supporting Internet activities and links at **vhlcentral.com**.

Teaching Tip You may want to wrap up this section by playing the ***Panorama cultural*** video footage for this lesson.

TEACHING OPTIONS

Worth Noting Paraguay has twelve national parks. In addition, there are ecological reserves dedicated to the preservation of endangered flora and fauna. The rich diversity of plant and animal life, and the government's commitment to preserving these natural wonders, have made Paraguay a popular destination for ecotourists. The parks cover a wide spectrum of ecology. The **Parque Nacional Defensores del Chaco** and **Parque Nacional Teniente Enciso** are located in the semi-arid Chaco. Other parks, like **Parque Nacional Caaguazú** southeast of Asunción, are covered with subtropical rainforest.

Instructional Resources
Supersite: Audio (Textbook & Lab MP3s); Testing Program (Tests, MP3s)
WebSAM
Lab Manual, p. 89

El bienestar

el bienestar	*well-being*
la droga	*drug*
el/la drogadicto/a	*drug addict*
el masaje	*massage*
el/la teleadicto/a	*couch potato*
adelgazar	*to lose weight; to slim down*
aliviar el estrés	*to reduce stress*
aliviar la tensión	*to reduce tension*
apurarse, darse prisa	*to hurry; to rush*
aumentar de peso, engordar	*to gain weight*
disfrutar (de)	*to enjoy; to reap the benefits (of)*
estar a dieta	*to be on a diet*
(no) fumar	*(not) to smoke*
llevar una vida sana	*to lead a healthy lifestyle*
sufrir muchas presiones	*to be under a lot of pressure*
tratar de (+ *inf.*)	*to try (to do something)*
activo/a	*active*
débil	*weak*
en exceso	*in excess; too much*
flexible	*flexible*
fuerte	*strong*
sedentario/a	*sedentary*
tranquilo/a	*calm; quiet*

En el gimnasio

la cinta caminadora	*treadmill*
la clase de ejercicios aeróbicos	*aerobics class*
el/la entrenador(a)	*trainer*
el músculo	*muscle*
calentarse (e:ie)	*to warm up*
entrenarse	*to train*
estar en buena forma	*to be in good shape*
hacer ejercicio	*to exercise*
hacer ejercicios aeróbicos	*to do aerobics*
hacer ejercicios de estiramiento	*to do stretching exercises*
hacer gimnasia	*to work out*
levantar pesas	*to lift weights*
mantenerse en forma	*to stay in shape*
sudar	*to sweat*

La nutrición

la bebida alcohólica	*alcoholic beverage*
la cafeína	*caffeine*
la caloría	*calorie*
el colesterol	*cholesterol*
la grasa	*fat*
la merienda	*afternoon snack*
el mineral	*mineral*
la nutrición	*nutrition*
el/la nutricionista	*nutritionist*
la proteína	*protein*
la vitamina	*vitamin*
comer una dieta equilibrada	*to eat a balanced diet*
consumir alcohol	*to consume alcohol*
descafeinado/a	*decaffeinated*

Expresiones útiles	*See page 487.*

recursos

LM p. 89	vhlcentral.com Lección 15

Vocabulary Tools

Plan de escritura

1 **Ideas y organización**

Begin by organizing your writing materials. If you prefer to write by hand, you may want to have a few spare pens and pencils on hand, as well as an eraser or correction fluid. If you prefer to use a word-processing program, make sure you know how to type Spanish accent marks, the **tilde**, and Spanish punctuation marks. Then make a list of the resources you can consult while writing. Finally, make a list of the basic ideas you want to cover. Beside each idea, jot down a few Spanish words and phrases you may want to use while writing.

2 **Primer borrador**

Write your first draft, using the resources and ideas you gathered in **Ideas y organización.**

3 **Comentario**

Exchange papers with a classmate and comment on each other's work, using these questions as a guide. Begin by mentioning what you like about your classmate's writing.

a. How can your classmate make his or her writing clearer, more logical, or more organized?
b. What suggestions do you have for making the writing more interesting or complete?
c. Do you see any spelling or grammatical errors?

4 **Redacción**

Revise your first draft, keeping in mind your classmate's comments. Also, incorporate any new information you may have. Before handing in the final version, review your work using these guidelines:

a. Make sure each verb agrees with its subject. Then check the gender and number of each article, noun, and adjective.
b. Check your spelling and punctuation.
c. Consult your **Anotaciones para mejorar la escritura** (see description below) to avoid repetition of previous errors.

5 **Evaluación y progreso**

You may want to share what you've written with a classmate, a small group, or the entire class. After your instructor has returned your paper, review the comments and corrections. On a separate sheet of paper, write the heading **Anotaciones para mejorar** (*Notes for improving*) **la escritura** and list your most common errors. Place this list and your corrected document in your writing portfolio (**Carpeta de trabajos**) and consult it from time to time to gauge your progress.

Spanish Terms for Direction Lines and Classroom Use

Below is a list of useful terms that you might hear your instructor say in class. It also includes Spanish terms that appear in the direction lines of your textbook.

En las instrucciones	*In direction lines*
Cambia/Cambien...	*Change...*
Camina/Caminen por la clase.	*Walk around the classroom.*
Ciertas o falsas	*True or false*
Cierto o falso	*True or false*
Circula/Circulen por la clase.	*Walk around the classroom.*
Completa las oraciones de una manera lógica.	*Complete the sentences logically.*
Con un(a) compañero/a...	*With a classmate...*
Contesta las preguntas.	*Answer the questions.*
Corrige las oraciones falsas.	*Correct the false statements.*
Cuenta/Cuenten...	*Tell...*
Di/Digan...	*Say...*
Discute/Discutan...	*Discuss...*
En grupos...	*In groups...*
En parejas...	*In pairs...*
Entrevista...	*Interview...*
Escúchala	*Listen to it*
Forma oraciones completas.	*Create/Make complete sentences.*
Háganse preguntas.	*Ask each other questions.*
Haz el papel de...	*Play the role of...*
Haz los cambios necesarios.	*Make the necessary changes.*
Indica/Indiquen si las oraciones...	*Indicate if the sentences...*
Intercambia/Intercambien...	*Exchange...*
Lee/Lean en voz alta.	*Read aloud.*
Pon/Pongan...	*Put...*
... que mejor completa...	*...that best completes...*
Reúnete...	*Get together...*
... se da/dan como ejemplo.	*...is/are given as a model.*
Toma nota...	*Take note...*
Tomen apuntes.	*Take notes.*
Túrnense...	*Take turns...*

Palabras útiles	*Useful words*
la adivinanza	*riddle*
el anuncio	*advertisement/ad*
los apuntes	*notes*
el borrador	*draft*
la canción	*song*
la concordancia	*agreement*
el contenido	*contents*
el cortometraje	*short film*
eficaz	*efficient; effective*
la encuesta	*survey*
el equipo	*team*
el esquema	*outline*
el folleto	*brochure*
las frases	*phrases*
la hoja de actividades	*activity sheet/handout*
la hoja de papel	*piece of paper*
la información errónea	*incorrect information*
el/la lector(a)	*reader*
la lectura	*reading*
las oraciones	*sentences*
la ortografía	*spelling*
el papel	*role*
el párrafo	*paragraph*
el paso	*step*
la(s) persona(s) descrita(s)	*the person (people) described*
la pista	*clue*
por ejemplo	*for example*
el propósito	*purpose*
los recursos	*resources*
el reportaje	*report*
los resultados	*results*
según	*according to*
siguiente	*following*
la sugerencia	*suggestion*
el sustantivo	*noun*
el tema	*topic*
último	*last*
el último recurso	*last resort*

Verbos útiles	*Useful verbs*
adivinar	*to guess*
anotar	*to jot down*
añadir	*to add*
apoyar	*to support*
averiguar	*to find out*
cambiar	*to change*
combinar	*to combine*
compartir	*to share*
comprobar (o:ue)	*to check*
contestar	*to answer*
corregir (e:i)	*to correct*
crear	*to create*
devolver (o:ue)	*to return*
doblar	*to fold*
dramatizar	*to act out*
elegir (e:i)	*to choose/select*
emparejar	*to match*
entrevistar	*to interview*
escoger	*to choose*
identificar	*to identify*
incluir	*to include*
informar	*to report*
intentar	*to try*
intercambiar	*to exchange*
investigar	*to research*
marcar	*to mark*
preguntar	*to ask*
recordar (o:ue)	*to remember*
responder	*to answer*
revisar	*to revise*
seguir (e:i)	*to follow*
seleccionar	*to select*
subrayar	*to underline*
traducir	*to translate*
tratar de	*to be about*

Expresiones útiles	*Useful expressions*
Ahora mismo.	*Right away.*
¿Cómo no?	*But of course.*
¿Cómo se dice ______ en español?	*How do you say ______ in Spanish?*
¿Cómo se escribe ______?	*How do you spell ______?*
¿Comprende(n)?	*Do you understand?*
Con gusto.	*With pleasure.*
Con permiso.	*Excuse me.*
De acuerdo.	*Okay.*
De nada.	*You're welcome.*
¿De veras?	*Really?*
¿En qué página estamos?	*What page are we on?*
¿En serio?	*Seriously?*
Enseguida.	*Right away.*
hoy día	*nowadays*
Más despacio, por favor.	*Slower, please.*
Muchas gracias.	*Thanks a lot.*
No entiendo.	*I don't understand.*
No hay de qué.	*Don't mention it.*
No importa.	*No problem./It doesn't matter.*
¡No me digas!	*You don't say!*
No sé.	*I don't know.*
¡Ojalá!	*Hopefully!*
Perdone.	*Pardon me.*
Por favor.	*Please.*
Por supuesto.	*Of course.*
¡Qué bien!	*Great!*
¡Qué gracioso!	*How funny!*
¡Qué pena!	*What a shame/pity!*
¿Qué significa ______?	*What does ______ mean?*
Repite, por favor.	*Please repeat.*
Tengo una pregunta.	*I have a question.*
¿Tiene(n) alguna pregunta?	*Do you have any questions?*
Vaya(n) a la página dos.	*Go to page 2.*

Glossary of Grammatical Terms

ADJECTIVE A word that modifies, or describes, a noun or pronoun.

muchos libros
many books

un hombre **rico**
*a **rich** man*

las mujeres **altas**
*the **tall** women*

Demonstrative adjective An adjective that specifies which noun a speaker is referring to.

esta fiesta
***this** party*

ese chico
***that** boy*

aquellas flores
***those** flowers*

Possessive adjective An adjective that indicates ownership or possession.

mi mejor vestido
***my** best dress*

Éste es **mi** hermano.
*This is **my** brother.*

Stressed possessive adjective A possessive adjective that emphasizes the owner or possessor.

Es un libro **mío.**
*It's **my book**./It's a book **of mine**.*

Es amiga **tuya**; yo no la conozco.
*She's a friend **of yours**; I don't know her.*

ADVERB A word that modifies, or describes, a verb, adjective, or other adverb.

Pancho escribe **rápidamente.**
*Pancho writes **quickly**.*

Este cuadro es **muy** bonito.
*This picture is **very** pretty.*

ARTICLE A word that points out a noun in either a specific or a non-specific way.

Definite article An article that points out a noun in a specific way.

el libro
***the** book*

la maleta
***the** suitcase*

los diccionarios
***the** dictionaries*

las palabras
***the** words*

Indefinite article An article that points out a noun in a general, non-specific way.

un lápiz
***a** pencil*

una computadora
***a** computer*

unos pájaros
***some** birds*

unas escuelas
***some** schools*

CLAUSE A group of words that contains both a conjugated verb and a subject, either expressed or implied.

Main (or Independent) clause A clause that can stand alone as a complete sentence.

Pienso ir a cenar pronto.
I plan to go to dinner soon.

Subordinate (or Dependent) clause A clause that does not express a complete thought and therefore cannot stand alone as a sentence.

Trabajo en la cafetería **porque necesito dinero para la escuela.**
*I work in the cafeteria **because I need money for school.***

COMPARATIVE A construction used with an adjective or adverb to express a comparison between two people, places, or things.

Este programa es **más interesante** que el otro.
*This program is **more interesting than** the other one.*

Tomás no es **tan alto como** Alberto.
*Tomás is not **as tall as** Alberto.*

CONJUGATION A set of the forms of a verb for a specific tense or mood or the process by which these verb forms are presented.

Preterite conjugation of **cantar:**

canté	cantamos
cantaste	cantasteis
cantó	cantaron

CONJUNCTION A word used to connect words, clauses, or phrases.

Susana es de Cuba **y** Pedro es de España.
*Susana is from Cuba **and** Pedro is from Spain.*

No quiero estudiar **pero** tengo que hacerlo.
*I don't want to study, **but** I have to.*

CONTRACTION The joining of two words into one. The only contractions in Spanish are **al** and **del**.

Mi hermano fue **al** concierto ayer.
*My brother went **to the** concert yesterday.*

Saqué dinero **del** banco.
*I took money **from the** bank.*

DIRECT OBJECT A noun or pronoun that directly receives the action of the verb.

Tomás lee **el libro.** *Tomás reads **the book**.*	**La** pagó ayer. *She paid **it** yesterday.*

GENDER The grammatical categorizing of certain kinds of words, such as nouns and pronouns, as masculine, feminine, or neuter.

Masculine
articles **el, un**
pronouns **él, lo, mío, éste, ése, aquél**
adjective **simpático**

Feminine
articles **la, una**
pronouns **ella, la, mía, ésta, ésa, aquélla**
adjective **simpática**

IMPERSONAL EXPRESSION A third-person expression with no expressed or specific subject.

Es muy importante. ***It's very important.***	**Llueve** mucho. ***It's raining** hard.*

Aquí **se habla** español.
*Spanish **is spoken** here.*

INDIRECT OBJECT A noun or pronoun that receives the action of the verb indirectly; the object, often a living being, to or for whom an action is performed.

Eduardo **le** dio un libro **a Linda**.
*Eduardo gave a book **to Linda**.*

La profesora **me** puso una C en el examen.
*The professor gave **me** a C on the test.*

INFINITIVE The basic form of a verb. Infinitives in Spanish end in **-ar**, **-er**, or **-ir**.

hablar ***to speak***	**correr** ***to run***	**abrir** ***to open***

INTERROGATIVE An adjective, adverb, or pronoun used to ask a question.

¿**Quién** habla? ***Who** is speaking?*	¿**Cuántos** compraste? ***How many** did you buy?*

¿**Qué** piensas hacer hoy?
***What** do you plan to do today?*

INVERSION Changing the word order of a sentence, often to form a question.

Statement: Elena pagó la cuenta del restaurante.

Inversion: ¿Pagó Elena la cuenta del restaurante?

MOOD A grammatical distinction of verbs that indicates whether the verb is intended to make a statement or command or to express a doubt, emotion, or condition contrary to fact.

Imperative mood Verb forms used to make commands.

Di la verdad. ***Tell** the truth.*	**Caminen** ustedes conmigo. ***Walk** with me.*

¡**Comamos** ahora!
***Let's eat** now!*

Indicative mood Verb forms used to state facts, actions, and states considered to be real.

Sé que **tienes** el dinero.
*I know that **you have** the money.*

Subjunctive mood Verb forms used principally in subordinate (dependent) clauses to express wishes, desires, emotions, doubts, and certain conditions, such as contrary-to-fact situations.

Prefieren que **hables** en español.
*They prefer that **you speak** in Spanish.*

Dudo que Luis **tenga** el dinero necesario.
*I doubt that Luis **has** the necessary money.*

NOUN A word that identifies people, animals, places, things, and ideas.

hombre ***man***	**gato** ***cat***
México ***Mexico***	**casa** ***house***
libertad ***freedom***	**libro** ***book***

NUMBER A grammatical term that refers to singular or plural. Nouns in Spanish and English have number. Other parts of a sentence, such as adjectives, articles, and verbs, can also have number.

Singular	Plural
una cosa *a thing*	**unas** cosas *some things*
el profesor *the professor*	**los** profesores *the professors*

NUMBERS Words that represent amounts.

Cardinal numbers Words that show specific amounts.

cinco minutos
five minutes

el año **dos mil veintitrés**
the year 2023

Ordinal numbers Words that indicate the order of a noun in a series.

el **cuarto** jugador
*the **fourth** player*

la **décima** hora
*the **tenth** hour*

PAST PARTICIPLE A past form of the verb used in compound tenses. The past participle may also be used as an adjective, but it must then agree in number and gender with the word it modifies.

Han **buscado** por todas partes.
*They have **searched** everywhere.*

Yo no había **estudiado** para el examen.
*I hadn't **studied** for the exam.*

Hay una **ventana abierta** en la sala.
*There is an **open window** in the living room.*

PERSON The form of the verb or pronoun that indicates the speaker, the one spoken to, or the one spoken about. In Spanish, as in English, there are three persons: first, second, and third.

Person	Singular	Plural
1st	**yo** *I*	**nosotros/as** *we*
2nd	**tú, Ud.** *you*	**vosotros/as, Uds.** *you*
3rd	**él, ella** *he, she*	**ellos, ellas** *they*

PREPOSITION A word or words that describe(s) the relationship, most often in time or space, between two other words.

Anita es **de** California.
*Anita is **from** California.*

La chaqueta está **en** el carro.
*The jacket is **in** the car.*

Marta se peinó **antes de** salir.
*Marta combed her hair **before** going out.*

PRESENT PARTICIPLE In English, a verb form that ends in *-ing*. In Spanish, the present participle ends in **-ndo**, and is often used with **estar** to form a progressive tense.

Mi hermana está **hablando** por teléfono ahora mismo.
*My sister is **talking** on the phone right now.*

PRONOUN A word that takes the place of a noun or nouns.

Demonstrative pronoun A pronoun that takes the place of a specific noun.

Quiero **ésta**.
*I want **this one**.*

¿Vas a comprar ése?
*Are you going to buy **that one**?*

Juan prefirió **aquéllos**.
*Juan preferred **those** (over there).*

Object pronoun A pronoun that functions as a direct or indirect object of the verb.

Te digo la verdad.
*I'm telling **you** the truth.*

Me lo trajo Juan.
*Juan brought **it** to **me**.*

Reflexive pronoun A pronoun that indicates that the action of a verb is performed by the subject on itself. These pronouns are often expressed in English with *-self*: *myself*, *yourself*, etc.

Yo **me bañé** antes de salir.
***I bathed (myself)** before going out.*

Elena **se acostó** a las once y media.
*Elena **went to bed** at eleven-thirty.*

Relative pronoun A pronoun that connects a subordinate clause to a main clause.

El chico **que** nos escribió viene de visita mañana.
*The boy **who** wrote us is coming to visit tomorrow.*

Ya sé **lo que** tenemos que hacer.
*I already know **what** we have to do.*

Subject pronoun A pronoun that replaces the name or title of a person or thing, and acts as the subject of a verb.

Tú debes estudiar más.
***You** should study more.*

Él llegó primero.
***He** arrived first.*

SUBJECT A noun or pronoun that performs the action of a verb and is often implied by the verb.

María va al supermercado.
***María** goes to the supermarket.*

(**Ellos**) Trabajan mucho.
***They** work hard.*

Esos **libros** son muy caros.
*Those **books** are very expensive.*

SUPERLATIVE A word or construction used with an adjective or adverb to express the highest or lowest degree of a specific quality among three or more people, places, or things.

De todas mis clases, ésta es la **más interesante**.
*Of all my classes, this is the **most interesting**.*

Raúl es el **menos simpático** de los chicos.
*Raúl is the **least likeable** of the boys.*

TENSE A set of verb forms that indicates the time of an action or state: past, present, or future.

Compound tense A two-word tense made up of an auxiliary verb and a present or past participle. In Spanish, **estar** and **haber** are auxiliary verbs.

En este momento, **estoy estudiando**.
*At this time, **I am studying**.*

El paquete no **ha llegado** todavía.
*The package **has** not **arrived** yet.*

Simple tense A tense expressed by a single verb form.

María **estaba** enferma anoche.
*María **was** sick last night.*

Juana **hablará** con su mamá mañana.
*Juana **will speak** with her mom tomorrow.*

VERB A word that expresses actions or states of being.

Auxiliary verb A verb used with a present or past participle to form a compound tense. **Haber** is the most commonly used auxiliary verb in Spanish.

Los chicos **han** visto los elefantes.
*The children **have** seen the elephants.*

Espero que **hayas** comido.
*I hope you **have** eaten.*

Reflexive verb A verb that describes an action performed by the subject on itself and is always used with a reflexive pronoun.

Me compré un carro nuevo.
*I **bought myself** a new car.*

Pedro y Adela **se levantan** muy temprano.
*Pedro and Adela **get (themselves) up** very early.*

Spelling change verb A verb that undergoes a predictable change in spelling, in order to reflect its actual pronunciation in the various conjugations.

practicar	c→qu	practico	practiqu**é**
dirigir	g→j	dirigí	diri**j**o
almorzar	z→c	almorzó	almor**c**é

Stem-changing verb A verb whose stem vowel undergoes one or more predictable changes in the various conjugations.

entender (e:ie)	ent**ie**ndo
pedir (e:i)	p**i**den
dormir (o:ue, u)	d**ue**rmo, d**u**rmieron

Verb Conjugation Tables

The verb lists

The list of verbs below, and the model-verb tables that start on page A-11 show you how to conjugate the verbs taught in **PANORAMA**. Each verb in the list is followed by a model verb conjugated according to the same pattern. The number in parentheses indicates where in the verb tables you can find the conjugated forms of the model verb. If you want to find out how to conjugate **divertirse**, for example, look up number 33, **sentir**, the model for verbs that follow the **e:ie** stem-change pattern.

How to use the verb tables

In the tables you will find the infinitive, present and past participles, and all the simple forms of each model verb. The formation of the compound tenses of any verb can be inferred from the table of compound tenses, pages A-11–12, either by combining the past participle of the verb with a conjugated form of **haber** or by combining the present participle with a conjugated form of **estar.**

abrazar (z:c) like cruzar (37)
abrir like vivir (3) *except* past participle is **abierto**
aburrir(se) like vivir (3)
acabar like hablar (1)
acampar like hablar (1)
acompañar like hablar (1)
aconsejar like hablar (1)
acordarse (o:ue) like contar (24)
acostarse (o:ue) like contar (24)
adelgazar (z:c) like cruzar (37)
afeitarse like hablar (1)
ahorrar like hablar (1)
alegrarse like hablar (1)
aliviar like hablar (1)
almorzar (o:ue) like contar (24) *except* (z:c)
alquilar like hablar (1)
andar like hablar (1) *except* preterite stem is **anduv-**
anunciar like hablar (1)
apagar (g:gu) like llegar (41)
aplaudir like vivir (3)
apreciar like hablar (1)
aprender like comer (2)
apurarse like hablar (1)
arrancar (c:qu) like tocar (44)
arreglar like hablar (1)
asistir like vivir (3)
aumentar like hablar (1)
ayudar(se) like hablar (1)
bailar like hablar (1)
bajar(se) like hablar (1)
bañarse like hablar (1)
barrer like comer (2)
beber like comer (2)
besar(se) like hablar (1)
borrar like hablar (1)
brindar like hablar (1)
bucear like hablar (1)
buscar (c:qu) like tocar (44)
caber (4)
caer(se) (5)
calentarse (e:ie) like pensar (30)
calzar (z:c) like cruzar (37)
cambiar like hablar (1)
caminar like hablar (1)
cantar like hablar (1)
casarse like hablar (1)
cazar (z:c) like cruzar (37)
celebrar like hablar (1)
cenar like hablar (1)
cepillarse like hablar (1)
cerrar (e:ie) like pensar (30)
chatear like hablar (1)
cobrar like hablar (1)
cocinar like hablar (1)
comenzar (e:ie) (z:c) like empezar (26)
comer (2)
compartir like vivir (3)
comprar like hablar (1)
comprender like comer (2)
comprometerse like comer (2)
comunicarse (c:qu) like tocar (44)
conducir (c:zc) (6)
confirmar like hablar (1)
conocer (c:zc) (35)
conseguir (e:i) (g:gu) like seguir (32)
conservar like hablar (1)
consumir like vivir (3)
contaminar like hablar (1)
contar (o:ue) (24)
contestar like hablar (1)
contratar like hablar (1)
controlar like hablar (1)
conversar like hablar (1)
correr like comer (2)
costar (o:ue) like contar (24)
creer (y) (36)
cruzar (z:c) (37)
cuidar like hablar (1)
dañar like hablar (1)
dar (7)
deber like comer (2)
decidir like vivir (3)
decir (e:i) (8)
declarar like hablar (1)
dejar like hablar (1)
depositar like hablar (1)
desarrollar like hablar (1)
desayunar like hablar (1)
descansar like hablar (1)
descargar like llegar (41)
describir like vivir (3) *except* past participle is descrito
descubrir like vivir (3) *except* past participle is descubierto
desear like hablar (1)
despedir(se) (e:i) like pedir (29)
despertarse (e:ie) like pensar (30)
destruir (y) (38)
dibujar like hablar (1)
dirigir (g:j) like vivir (3) *except* (g:j)
disfrutar like hablar (1)
divertirse (e:ie) like sentir (33)
divorciarse like hablar (1)
doblar like hablar (1)
doler (o:ue) like volver (34) *except* past participle is regular
dormir(se) (o:ue) (25)
ducharse like hablar (1)
dudar like hablar (1)
durar like hablar (1)
echar like hablar (1)
elegir (e:i) like pedir (29) *except* (g:j)

emitir like vivir (3)
empezar (e:ie) (z:c) (26)
enamorarse like hablar (1)
encantar like hablar (1)
encontrar(se) (o:ue) like contar (24)
enfermarse like hablar (1)
engordar like hablar (1)
enojarse like hablar (1)
enseñar like hablar (1)
ensuciar like hablar (1)
entender (e:ie) (27)
entrenarse like hablar (1)
entrevistar like hablar (1)
enviar (envío) (39)
escalar like hablar (1)
escanear like hablar (1)
escoger (g:j) like proteger (43)
escribir like vivir (3) *except* past participle is **escrito**
escuchar like hablar (1)
esculpir like vivir (3)
esperar like hablar (1)
esquiar (esquío) like enviar (39)
establecer (c:zc) like conocer (35)
estacionar like hablar (1)
estar (9)
estornudar like hablar (1)
estudiar like hablar (1)
evitar like hablar (1)
explicar (c:qu) like tocar (44)
faltar like hablar (1)
fascinar like hablar (1)
firmar like hablar (1)
fumar like hablar (1)
funcionar like hablar (1)
ganar like hablar (1)
gastar like hablar (1)
grabar like hablar (1)
graduarse (gradúo) (40)
guardar like hablar (1)
gustar like hablar (1)
haber (hay) (10)
hablar (1)
hacer (11)
importar like hablar (1)
imprimir like vivir (3)
indicar (c:qu) like tocar (44)
informar like hablar (1)
insistir like vivir (3)
interesar like hablar (1)
invertir (e:ie) like sentir (33)
invitar like hablar (1)
ir(se) (12)
jubilarse like hablar (1)
jugar (u:ue) (g:gu) (28)
lastimarse like hablar (1)
lavar(se) like hablar (1)
leer (y) like creer (36)
levantar(se) like hablar (1)
limpiar like hablar (1)
llamar(se) like hablar (1)
llegar (g:gu) (41)
llenar like hablar (1)
llevar(se) like hablar (1)
llover (o:ue) like volver (34) *except* past participle is regular
luchar like hablar (1)
mandar like hablar (1)
manejar like hablar (1)
mantener(se) (e:ie) like tener (20)
maquillarse like hablar (1)
mejorar like hablar (1)
merendar (e:ie) like pensar (30)
mirar like hablar (1)
molestar like hablar (1)
montar like hablar (1)
morir (o:ue) like dormir (25) *except* past participle is **muerto**
mostrar (o:ue) like contar (24)
mudarse like hablar (1)
nacer (c:zc) like conocer (35)
nadar like hablar (1)
navegar (g:gu) like llegar (41)
necesitar like hablar (1)
negar (e:ie) like pensar (30) *except* (g:gu)
nevar (e:ie) like pensar (30)
obedecer (c:zc) like conocer (35)
obtener (e:ie) like tener (20)
ocurrir like vivir (3)
odiar like hablar (1)
ofrecer (c:zc) like conocer (35)
oír (13)
olvidar like hablar (1)
pagar (g:gu) like llegar (41)
parar like hablar (1)
parecer (c:zc) like conocer (35)
pasar like hablar (1)
pasear like hablar (1)
patinar like hablar (1)
pedir (e:i) (29)
peinarse like hablar (1)
pensar (e:ie) (30)
perder (e:ie) like entender (27)
pescar (c:qu) like tocar (44)
pintar like hablar (1)
planchar like hablar (1)
poder (o:ue) (14)
poner(se) (15)
practicar (c:qu) like tocar (44)
preferir (e:ie) like sentir (33)
preguntar like hablar (1)
prender like comer (2)
preocuparse like hablar (1)
preparar like hablar (1)
presentar like hablar (1)
prestar like hablar (1)
probar(se) (o:ue) like contar (24)
prohibir (prohíbo) (42)
proteger (g:j) (43)
publicar (c:qu) like tocar (44)
quedar(se) like hablar (1)
querer (e:ie) (16)
quitar(se) like hablar (1)
recetar like hablar (1)
recibir like vivir (3)
reciclar like hablar (1)
recoger (g:j) like proteger (43)
recomendar (e:ie) like pensar (30)
recordar (o:ue) like contar (24)
reducir (c:zc) like conducir (6)
regalar like hablar (1)
regatear like hablar (1)
regresar like hablar (1)
reír(se) (e:i) (31)
relajarse like hablar (1)
renunciar like hablar (1)
repetir (e:i) like pedir (29)
resolver (o:ue) like volver (34)
respirar like hablar (1)
revisar like hablar (1)
rogar (o:ue) like contar (24) *except* (g:gu)
romper(se) like comer (2) *except* past participle is **roto**
saber (17)
sacar (c:qu) like tocar (44)
sacudir like vivir (3)
salir (18)
saludar(se) like hablar (1)
secar(se) (c:qu) like tocar (44)
seguir (e:i) (32)
sentarse (e:ie) like pensar (30)
sentir(se) (e:ie) (33)
separarse like hablar (1)
ser (19)
servir (e:i) like pedir (29)
solicitar like hablar (1)
sonar (o:ue) like contar (24)
sonreír (e:i) like reír(se) (31)
sorprender like comer (2)
subir like vivir (3)
sudar like hablar (1)
sufrir like vivir (3)
sugerir (e:ie) like sentir (33)
suponer like poner (15)
temer like comer (2)
tener (e:ie) (20)
terminar like hablar (1)
tocar (c:qu) (44)
tomar like hablar (1)
torcerse (o:ue) like volver (34) *except* (c:z) and past participle is regular; e.g., **yo tuerzo**
toser like comer (2)
trabajar like hablar (1)
traducir (c:zc) like conducir (6)
traer (21)
transmitir like vivir (3)
tratar like hablar (1)
usar like hablar (1)
vender like comer (2)
venir (e:ie) (22)
ver (23)
vestirse (e:i) like pedir (29)
viajar like hablar (1)
visitar like hablar (1)
vivir (3)
volver (o:ue) (34)
votar like hablar (1)

Regular verbs: simple tenses

	INDICATIVE					SUBJUNCTIVE		IMPERATIVE
Infinitive	Present	Imperfect	Preterite	Future	Conditional	Present	Past	
1 hablar	hablo	hablaba	hablé	hablaré	hablaría	hable	hablara	
	hablas	hablabas	hablaste	hablarás	hablarías	hables	hablaras	habla tú (no hables)
Participles:	habla	hablaba	habló	hablará	hablaría	hable	hablara	hable Ud.
hablando	hablamos	hablábamos	hablamos	hablaremos	hablaríamos	hablemos	habláramos	hablemos
hablado	habláis	hablabais	hablasteis	hablaréis	hablaríais	habléis	hablarais	hablad (no habléis)
	hablan	hablaban	hablaron	hablarán	hablarían	hablen	hablaran	hablen Uds.
2 comer	como	comía	comí	comeré	comería	coma	comiera	
	comes	comías	comiste	comerás	comerías	comas	comieras	come tú (no comas)
Participles:	come	comía	comió	comerá	comería	coma	comiera	coma Ud.
comiendo	comemos	comíamos	comimos	comeremos	comeríamos	comamos	comiéramos	comamos
comido	coméis	comíais	comisteis	comeréis	comeríais	comáis	comierais	comed (no comáis)
	comen	comían	comieron	comerán	comerían	coman	comieran	coman Uds.
3 vivir	vivo	vivía	viví	viviré	viviría	viva	viviera	
	vives	vivías	viviste	vivirás	vivirías	vivas	vivieras	vive tú (no vivas)
Participles:	vive	vivía	vivió	vivirá	viviría	viva	viviera	viva Ud.
viviendo	vivimos	vivíamos	vivimos	viviremos	viviríamos	vivamos	viviéramos	vivamos
vivido	vivís	vivíais	vivisteis	viviréis	viviríais	viváis	vivierais	vivid (no viváis)
	viven	vivían	vivieron	vivirán	vivirían	vivan	vivieran	vivan Uds.

All verbs: compound tenses

PERFECT TENSES											
INDICATIVE								SUBJUNCTIVE			
Present Perfect		Past Perfect		Future Perfect		Conditional Perfect		Present Perfect		Past Perfect	
he		había		habré		habría		haya		hubiera	
has	hablado	habías	hablado	habrás	hablado	habrías	hablado	hayas	hablado	hubieras	hablado
ha	comido	había	comido	habrá	comido	habría	comido	haya	comido	hubiera	comido
hemos	vivido	habíamos	vivido	habremos	vivido	habríamos	vivido	hayamos	vivido	hubiéramos	vivido
habéis		habíais		habréis		habríais		hayáis		hubierais	
han		habían		habrán		habrían		hayan		hubieran	

PROGRESSIVE TENSES											
INDICATIVE								SUBJUNCTIVE			
Present Progressive		Past Progressive		Future Progressive		Conditional Progressive		Present Progressive		Past Progressive	
estoy		estaba		estaré		estaría		esté		estuviera	
estás	hablando	estabas	hablando	estarás	hablando	estarías	hablando	estés	hablando	estuvieras	hablando
está	comiendo	estaba	comiendo	estará	comiendo	estaría	comiendo	esté	comiendo	estuviera	comiendo
estamos	viviendo	estábamos	viviendo	estaremos	viviendo	estaríamos	viviendo	estemos	viviendo	estuviéramos	viviendo
estáis		estabais		estaréis		estaríais		estéis		estuvierais	
están		estaban		estarán		estarían		estén		estuvieran	

Irregular verbs

		INDICATIVE					SUBJUNCTIVE		IMPERATIVE
	Infinitive	Present	Imperfect	Preterite	Future	Conditional	Present	Past	
4	caber	**quepo**	cabía	**cupe**	**cabré**	**cabría**	**quepa**	**cupiera**	
		cabes	cabías	**cupiste**	**cabrás**	**cabrías**	**quepas**	**cupieras**	cabe tú (no **quepas**)
	Participles:	cabe	cabía	**cupo**	**cabrá**	**cabría**	**quepa**	**cupiera**	**quepa** Ud.
	cabiendo	cabemos	cabíamos	**cupimos**	**cabremos**	**cabríamos**	**quepamos**	**cupiéramos**	**quepamos**
	cabido	cabéis	cabíais	**cupisteis**	**cabréis**	**cabríais**	**quepáis**	**cupierais**	cabed (no **quepáis**)
		caben	cabían	**cupieron**	**cabrán**	**cabrían**	**quepan**	**cupieran**	**quepan** Uds.
5	caer(se)	**caigo**	caía	caí	caeré	caería	**caiga**	**cayera**	
		caes	caías	**caíste**	caerás	caerías	**caigas**	**cayeras**	cae tú (no **caigas**)
	Participles:	cae	caía	**cayó**	caerá	caería	**caiga**	**cayera**	**caiga** Ud.
	cayendo	caemos	caíamos	**caímos**	caeremos	caeríamos	**caigamos**	**cayéramos**	**caigamos**
	caído	caéis	caíais	**caísteis**	caeréis	caeríais	**caigáis**	**cayerais**	caed (no **caigáis**)
		caen	caían	**cayeron**	caerán	caerían	**caigan**	**cayeran**	**caigan** Uds.
6	conducir	**conduzco**	conducía	**conduje**	conduciré	conduciría	**conduzca**	**condujera**	
	(c:zc)	conduces	conducías	**condujiste**	conducirás	conducirías	**conduzcas**	**condujeras**	conduce tú (no **conduzcas**)
		conduce	conducía	**condujo**	conducirá	conduciría	**conduzca**	**condujera**	**conduzca** Ud.
	Participles:	conducimos	conducíamos	**condujimos**	conduciremos	conduciríamos	**conduzcamos**	**condujéramos**	**conduzcamos**
	conduciendo	conducís	conducíais	**condujisteis**	conduciréis	conduciríais	**conduzcáis**	**condujerais**	conducid (no **conduzcáis**)
	conducido	conducen	conducían	**condujeron**	conducirán	conducirían	**conduzcan**	**condujeran**	**conduzcan** Uds.

	Infinitive	INDICATIVE					SUBJUNCTIVE		IMPERATIVE
		Present	Imperfect	Preterite	Future	Conditional	Present	Past	
7	dar	**doy**	daba	**di**	daré	daría	**dé**	**diera**	
		das	dabas	**diste**	darás	darías	**des**	**dieras**	da tú (no des)
	Participles:	da	daba	**dio**	dará	daría	**dé**	**diera**	**dé** Ud.
	dando	damos	dábamos	**dimos**	daremos	daríamos	**demos**	**diéramos**	**demos**
	dado	dais	dabais	**disteis**	daréis	daríais	**deis**	**dierais**	dad (no **deis**)
		dan	daban	**dieron**	darán	darían	**den**	**dieran**	**den** Uds.
8	decir (e:i)	**digo**	decía	**dije**	**diré**	**diría**	**diga**	**dijera**	
		dices	decías	**dijiste**	**dirás**	**dirías**	**digas**	**dijeras**	**di** tú (no **digas**)
	Participles:	**dice**	decía	**dijo**	**dirá**	**diría**	**diga**	**dijera**	**diga** Ud.
	diciendo	decimos	decíamos	**dijimos**	**diremos**	**diríamos**	**digamos**	**dijéramos**	**digamos**
	dicho	decís	decíais	**dijisteis**	**diréis**	**diríais**	**digáis**	**dijerais**	decid (no **digáis**)
		dicen	decían	**dijeron**	**dirán**	**dirían**	**digan**	**dijeran**	**digan** Uds.
9	estar	**estoy**	estaba	**estuve**	estaré	estaría	**esté**	**estuviera**	
		estás	estabas	**estuviste**	estarás	estarías	**estés**	**estuvieras**	**está** tú (no **estés**)
	Participles:	**está**	estaba	**estuvo**	estará	estaría	**esté**	**estuviera**	**esté** Ud.
	estando	estamos	estábamos	**estuvimos**	estaremos	estaríamos	estemos	**estuviéramos**	estemos
	estado	estáis	estabais	**estuvisteis**	estaréis	estaríais	estéis	**estuvierais**	estad (no estéis)
		están	estaban	**estuvieron**	estarán	estarían	**estén**	**estuvieran**	**estén** Uds.
10	haber	**he**	había	**hube**	**habré**	**habría**	**haya**	**hubiera**	
		has	habías	**hubiste**	**habrás**	**habrías**	**hayas**	**hubieras**	
	Participles:	**ha**	había	**hubo**	**habrá**	**habría**	**haya**	**hubiera**	
	habiendo	**hemos**	habíamos	**hubimos**	**habremos**	**habríamos**	**hayamos**	**hubiéramos**	
	habido	**habéis**	habíais	**hubisteis**	**habréis**	**habríais**	**hayáis**	**hubierais**	
		han	habían	**hubieron**	**habrán**	**habrían**	**hayan**	**hubieran**	
11	hacer	**hago**	hacía	**hice**	**haré**	**haría**	**haga**	**hiciera**	
		haces	hacías	**hiciste**	**harás**	**harías**	**hagas**	**hicieras**	**haz** tú (no **hagas**)
	Participles:	hace	hacía	**hizo**	**hará**	**haría**	**haga**	**hiciera**	**haga** Ud.
	haciendo	hacemos	hacíamos	**hicimos**	**haremos**	**haríamos**	**hagamos**	**hiciéramos**	**hagamos**
	hecho	hacéis	hacíais	**hicisteis**	**haréis**	**haríais**	**hagáis**	**hicierais**	haced (no **hagáis**)
		hacen	hacían	**hicieron**	**harán**	**harían**	**hagan**	**hicieran**	**hagan** Uds.
12	ir	**voy**	**iba**	**fui**	iré	iría	**vaya**	**fuera**	
		vas	**ibas**	**fuiste**	irás	irías	**vayas**	**fueras**	**ve** tú (no **vayas**)
	Participles:	**va**	**iba**	**fue**	irá	iría	**vaya**	**fuera**	**vaya** Ud.
	yendo	**vamos**	**íbamos**	**fuimos**	iremos	iríamos	**vayamos**	**fuéramos**	**vamos**
	ido	**vais**	**ibais**	**fuisteis**	iréis	iríais	**vayáis**	**fuerais**	id (no **vayáis**)
		van	**iban**	**fueron**	irán	irían	**vayan**	**fueran**	**vayan** Uds.
13	oír (y)	**oigo**	oía	**oí**	oiré	oiría	**oiga**	**oyera**	
		oyes	oías	**oíste**	oirás	oirías	**oigas**	**oyeras**	**oye** tú (no **oigas**)
	Participles:	**oye**	oía	**oyó**	oirá	oiría	**oiga**	**oyera**	**oiga** Ud.
	oyendo	**oímos**	oíamos	**oímos**	oiremos	oiríamos	**oigamos**	**oyéramos**	**oigamos**
	oído	**oís**	oíais	**oísteis**	oiréis	oiríais	**oigáis**	**oyerais**	oíd (no **oigáis**)
		oyen	oían	**oyeron**	oirán	oirían	**oigan**	**oyeran**	**oigan** Uds.

	INDICATIVE					SUBJUNCTIVE		IMPERATIVE
Infinitive	Present	Imperfect	Preterite	Future	Conditional	Present	Past	
14 poder (o:ue) **Participles:** **pudiendo** podido	**puedo** **puedes** **puede** podemos podéis **pueden**	podía podías podía podíamos podíais podían	**pude** **pudiste** **pudo** **pudimos** **pudisteis** **pudieron**	**podré** **podrás** **podrá** **podremos** **podréis** **podrán**	**podría** **podrías** **podría** **podríamos** **podríais** **podrían**	**pueda** **puedas** **pueda** podamos podáis **puedan**	**pudiera** **pudieras** **pudiera** **pudiéramos** **pudierais** **pudieran**	**puede** tú (no **puedas**) **pueda** Ud. podamos poded (no podáis) **puedan** Uds.
15 poner **Participles:** poniendo **puesto**	**pongo** pones pone ponemos ponéis ponen	ponía ponías ponía poníamos poníais ponían	**puse** **pusiste** **puso** **pusimos** **pusisteis** **pusieron**	**pondré** **pondrás** **pondrá** **pondremos** **pondréis** **pondrán**	**pondría** **pondrías** **pondría** **pondríamos** **pondríais** **pondrían**	**ponga** **pongas** **ponga** **pongamos** **pongáis** **pongan**	**pusiera** **pusieras** **pusiera** **pusiéramos** **pusierais** **pusieran**	**pon** tú (no **pongas**) **ponga** Ud. **pongamos** poned (no **pongáis**) **pongan** Uds.
16 querer (e:ie) **Participles:** queriendo querido	**quiero** **quieres** **quiere** queremos queréis **quieren**	quería querías quería queríamos queríais querían	**quise** **quisiste** **quiso** **quisimos** **quisisteis** **quisieron**	**querré** **querrás** **querrá** **querremos** **querréis** **querrán**	**querría** **querrías** **querría** **querríamos** **querríais** **querrían**	**quiera** **quieras** **quiera** queramos queráis **quieran**	**quisiera** **quisieras** **quisiera** **quisiéramos** **quisierais** **quisieran**	**quiere** tú (no **quieras**) **quiera** Ud. **queramos** quered (no queráis) **quieran** Uds.
17 saber **Participles:** sabiendo sabido	**sé** sabes sabe sabemos sabéis saben	sabía sabías sabía sabíamos sabíais sabían	**supe** **supiste** **supo** **supimos** **supisteis** **supieron**	**sabré** **sabrás** **sabrá** **sabremos** **sabréis** **sabrán**	**sabría** **sabrías** **sabría** **sabríamos** **sabríais** **sabrían**	**sepa** **sepas** **sepa** **sepamos** **sepáis** **sepan**	**supiera** **supieras** **supiera** **supiéramos** **supierais** **supieran**	sabe tú (no **sepas**) **sepa** Ud. **sepamos** sabed (no **sepáis**) **sepan** Uds.
18 salir **Participles:** saliendo salido	**salgo** sales sale salimos salís salen	salía salías salía salíamos salíais salían	salí saliste salió salimos salisteis salieron	**saldré** **saldrás** **saldrá** **saldremos** **saldréis** **saldrán**	**saldría** **saldrías** **saldría** **saldríamos** **saldríais** **saldrían**	**salga** **salgas** **salga** **salgamos** **salgáis** **salgan**	saliera salieras saliera saliéramos salierais salieran	**sal** tú (no **salgas**) **salga** Ud. **salgamos** salid (no **salgáis**) **salgan** Uds.
19 ser **Participles:** siendo sido	**soy** **eres** **es** **somos** **sois** **son**	**era** **eras** **era** **éramos** **erais** **eran**	**fui** **fuiste** **fue** **fuimos** **fuisteis** **fueron**	seré serás será seremos seréis serán	sería serías sería seríamos seríais serían	**sea** **seas** **sea** **seamos** **seáis** **sean**	**fuera** **fueras** **fuera** **fuéramos** **fuerais** **fueran**	**sé** tú (no **seas**) **sea** Ud. **seamos** sed (no **seáis**) **sean** Uds.
20 tener (e:ie) **Participles:** teniendo tenido	**tengo** **tienes** **tiene** tenemos tenéis **tienen**	tenía tenías tenía teníamos teníais tenían	**tuve** **tuviste** **tuvo** **tuvimos** **tuvisteis** **tuvieron**	**tendré** **tendrás** **tendrá** **tendremos** **tendréis** **tendrán**	**tendría** **tendrías** **tendría** **tendríamos** **tendríais** **tendrían**	**tenga** **tengas** **tenga** **tengamos** **tengáis** **tengan**	**tuviera** **tuvieras** **tuviera** **tuviéramos** **tuvierais** **tuvieran**	**ten** tú (no **tengas**) **tenga** Ud. **tengamos** tened (no **tengáis**) **tengan** Uds.

		INDICATIVE					SUBJUNCTIVE		IMPERATIVE
	Infinitive	**Present**	**Imperfect**	**Preterite**	**Future**	**Conditional**	**Present**	**Past**	
21	traer	**traigo**	traía	**traje**	traeré	traería	**traiga**	**trajera**	
		traes	traías	**trajiste**	traerás	traerías	**traigas**	**trajeras**	trae tú (no **traigas**)
	Participles:	trae	traía	**trajo**	traerá	traería	**traiga**	**trajera**	**traiga** Ud.
	trayendo	traemos	traíamos	**trajimos**	traeremos	traeríamos	**traigamos**	**trajéramos**	**traigamos**
	traído	traéis	traíais	**trajisteis**	traeréis	traeríais	**traigáis**	**trajerais**	traed (no **traigáis**)
		traen	traían	**trajeron**	traerán	traerían	**traigan**	**trajeran**	**traigan** Uds.
22	venir (e:ie)	**vengo**	venía	**vine**	**vendré**	**vendría**	**venga**	**viniera**	
		vienes	venías	**viniste**	**vendrás**	**vendrías**	**vengas**	**vinieras**	**ven** tú (no **vengas**)
	Participles:	**viene**	venía	**vino**	**vendrá**	**vendría**	**venga**	**viniera**	**venga** Ud.
	viniendo	venimos	veníamos	**vinimos**	**vendremos**	**vendríamos**	**vengamos**	**viniéramos**	**vengamos**
	venido	venís	veníais	**vinisteis**	**vendréis**	**vendríais**	**vengáis**	**vinierais**	venid (no **vengáis**)
		vienen	venían	**vinieron**	**vendrán**	**vendrían**	**vengan**	**vinieran**	**vengan** Uds.
23	ver	**veo**	**veía**	**vi**	veré	vería	**vea**	**viera**	
		ves	**veías**	**viste**	verás	verías	**veas**	**vieras**	**ve** tú (no **veas**)
	Participles:	ve	**veía**	**vio**	verá	vería	**vea**	**viera**	**vea** Ud.
	viendo	vemos	**veíamos**	**vimos**	veremos	veríamos	**veamos**	**viéramos**	**veamos**
	visto	veis	**veíais**	**visteis**	veréis	veríais	**veáis**	**vierais**	ved (no **veáis**)
		ven	**veían**	**vieron**	verán	verían	**vean**	**vieran**	**vean** Uds.

Stem-changing verbs

		INDICATIVE					SUBJUNCTIVE		IMPERATIVE
	Infinitive	**Present**	**Imperfect**	**Preterite**	**Future**	**Conditional**	**Present**	**Past**	
24	contar (o:ue)	**cuento**	contaba	conté	contaré	contaría	**cuente**	contara	
		cuentas	contabas	contaste	contarás	contarías	**cuentes**	contaras	**cuenta** tú (no **cuentes**)
	Participles:	**cuenta**	contaba	contó	contará	contaría	**cuente**	contara	**cuente** Ud.
	contando	contamos	contábamos	contamos	contaremos	contaríamos	contemos	contáramos	contemos
	contado	contáis	contabais	contasteis	contaréis	contaríais	contéis	contarais	contad (no contéis)
		cuentan	contaban	contaron	contarán	contarían	**cuenten**	contaran	**cuenten** Uds.
25	dormir (o:ue)	**duermo**	dormía	dormí	dormiré	dormiría	**duerma**	**durmiera**	
		duermes	dormías	dormiste	dormirás	dormirías	**duermas**	**durmieras**	**duerme** tú (no **duermas**)
	Participles:	**duerme**	dormía	**durmió**	dormirá	dormiría	**duerma**	**durmiera**	**duerma** Ud.
	durmiendo	dormimos	dormíamos	dormimos	dormiremos	dormiríamos	**durmamos**	**durmiéramos**	**durmamos**
	dormido	dormís	dormíais	dormisteis	dormiréis	dormiríais	**durmáis**	**durmierais**	dormid (no **durmáis**)
		duermen	dormían	**durmieron**	dormirán	dormirían	**duerman**	**durmieran**	**duerman** Uds.
26	empezar (e:ie) (z:c)	**empiezo**	empezaba	**empecé**	empezaré	empezaría	**empiece**	empezara	
		empiezas	empezabas	empezaste	empezarás	empezarías	**empieces**	empezaras	**empieza** tú (no **empieces**)
		empieza	empezaba	empezó	empezará	empezaría	**empiece**	empezara	**empiece** Ud.
	Participles:	empezamos	empezábamos	empezamos	empezaremos	empezaríamos	**empecemos**	empezáramos	**empecemos**
	empezando	empezáis	empezabais	empezasteis	empezaréis	empezaríais	**empecéis**	empezarais	empezad (no **empecéis**)
	empezado	**empiezan**	empezaban	empezaron	empezarán	empezarían	**empiecen**	empezaran	**empiecen** Uds.

	Infinitive	INDICATIVE Present	Imperfect	Preterite	Future	Conditional	SUBJUNCTIVE Present	Past	IMPERATIVE
27	entender	**entiendo**	entendía	entendí	entenderé	entendería	**entienda**	entendiera	
	(e:ie)	**entiendes**	entendías	entendiste	entenderás	entenderías	**entiendas**	entendieras	**entiende** tú (no **entiendas**)
		entiende	entendía	entendió	entenderá	entendería	**entienda**	entendiera	**entienda** Ud.
	Participles:	entendemos	entendíamos	entendimos	entenderemos	entenderíamos	entendamos	entendiéramos	entendamos
	entendiendo	entendéis	entendíais	entendisteis	entenderéis	entenderíais	entendáis	entendierais	entended (no entendáis)
	entendido	**entienden**	entendían	entendieron	entenderán	entenderían	**entiendan**	entendieran	**entiendan** Uds.
28	jugar (u:ue)	**juego**	jugaba	**jugué**	jugaré	jugaría	**juegue**	jugara	
	(g:gu)	**juegas**	jugabas	jugaste	jugarás	jugarías	**juegues**	jugaras	**juega** tú (no **juegues**)
		juega	jugaba	jugó	jugará	jugaría	**juegue**	jugara	**juegue** Ud.
	Participles:	jugamos	jugábamos	jugamos	jugaremos	jugaríamos	juguemos	jugáramos	juguemos
	jugando	jugáis	jugabais	jugasteis	jugaréis	jugaríais	juguéis	jugarais	jugad (no juguéis)
	jugado	**juegan**	jugaban	jugaron	jugarán	jugarían	**jueguen**	jugaran	**jueguen** Uds.
29	pedir (e:i)	**pido**	pedía	pedí	pediré	pediría	**pida**	**pidiera**	
		pides	pedías	pediste	pedirás	pedirías	**pidas**	**pidieras**	**pide** tú (no **pidas**)
	Participles:	**pide**	pedía	**pidió**	pedirá	pediría	**pida**	**pidiera**	**pida** Ud.
	pidiendo	pedimos	pedíamos	pedimos	pediremos	pediríamos	**pidamos**	**pidiéramos**	**pidamos**
	pedido	pedís	pedíais	pedisteis	pediréis	pediríais	**pidáis**	**pidierais**	pedid (no **pidáis**)
		piden	pedían	**pidieron**	pedirán	pedirían	**pidan**	**pidieran**	**pidan** Uds.
30	pensar (e:ie)	**pienso**	pensaba	pensé	pensaré	pensaría	**piense**	pensara	
		piensas	pensabas	pensaste	pensarás	pensarías	**pienses**	pensaras	**piensa** tú (no **pienses**)
	Participles:	**piensa**	pensaba	pensó	pensará	pensaría	**piense**	pensara	**piense** Ud.
	pensando	pensamos	pensábamos	pensamos	pensaremos	pensaríamos	pensemos	pensáramos	pensemos
	pensado	pensáis	pensabais	pensasteis	pensaréis	pensaríais	penséis	pensarais	pensad (no penséis)
		piensan	pensaban	pensaron	pensarán	pensarían	**piensen**	pensaran	**piensen** Uds.
31	reír(se) (e:i)	**río**	reía	**reí**	reiré	reiría	**ría**	**riera**	
		ríes	reías	**reíste**	reirás	reirías	**rías**	**rieras**	**ríe** tú (no **rías**)
	Participles:	**ríe**	reía	**rió**	reirá	reiría	**ría**	**riera**	**ría** Ud.
	riendo	**reímos**	reíamos	**reímos**	reiremos	reiríamos	**riamos**	**riéramos**	**riamos**
	reído	**reís**	reíais	**reísteis**	reiréis	reiríais	**riáis**	**rierais**	reíd (no **riáis**)
		ríen	reían	**rieron**	reirán	reirían	**rían**	**rieran**	**rían** Uds.
32	seguir (e:i)	**sigo**	seguía	seguí	seguiré	seguiría	**siga**	**siguiera**	
	(gu:g)	**sigues**	seguías	seguiste	seguirás	seguirías	**sigas**	**siguieras**	**sigue** tú (no **sigas**)
		sigue	seguía	**siguió**	seguirá	seguiría	**siga**	**siguiera**	**siga** Ud.
	Participles:	seguimos	seguíamos	seguimos	seguiremos	seguiríamos	**sigamos**	**siguiéramos**	**sigamos**
	siguiendo	seguís	seguíais	seguisteis	seguiréis	seguiríais	**sigáis**	**siguierais**	seguid (no **sigáis**)
	seguido	**siguen**	seguían	**siguieron**	seguirán	seguirían	**sigan**	**siguieran**	**sigan** Uds.
33	sentir (e:ie)	**siento**	sentía	sentí	sentiré	sentiría	**sienta**	**sintiera**	
		sientes	sentías	sentiste	sentirás	sentirías	**sientas**	**sintieras**	**siente** tú (no **sientas**)
	Participles:	**siente**	sentía	**sintió**	sentirá	sentiría	**sienta**	**sintiera**	**sienta** Ud.
	sintiendo	sentimos	sentíamos	sentimos	sentiremos	sentiríamos	**sintamos**	**sintiéramos**	**sintamos**
	sentido	sentís	sentíais	sentisteis	sentiréis	sentiríais	**sintáis**	**sintierais**	sentid (no **sintáis**)
		sienten	sentían	**sintieron**	sentirán	sentirían	**sientan**	**sintieran**	**sientan** Uds.

	Infinitive	INDICATIVE Present	Imperfect	Preterite	Future	Conditional	SUBJUNCTIVE Present	Past	IMPERATIVE
34	volver (o:ue)	**vuelvo**	volvía	volví	volveré	volvería	**vuelva**	volviera	
		vuelves	volvías	volviste	volverás	volverías	**vuelvas**	volvieras	**vuelve** tú (no **vuelvas**)
	Participles:	**vuelve**	volvía	volvió	volverá	volvería	**vuelva**	volviera	**vuelva** Ud.
	volviendo	volvemos	volvíamos	volvimos	volveremos	volveríamos	volvamos	volviéramos	volvamos
	vuelto	volvéis	volvíais	volvisteis	volveréis	volveríais	volváis	volvierais	volved (no volváis)
		vuelven	volvían	volvieron	volverán	volverían	**vuelvan**	volvieran	**vuelvan** Uds.

Verbs with spelling changes only

	Infinitive	INDICATIVE Present	Imperfect	Preterite	Future	Conditional	SUBJUNCTIVE Present	Past	IMPERATIVE
35	conocer (c:zc)	**conozco**	conocía	conocí	conoceré	conocería	**conozca**	conociera	
		conoces	conocías	conociste	conocerás	conocerías	**conozcas**	conocieras	conoce tú (no **conozcas**)
	Participles:	conoce	conocía	conoció	conocerá	conocería	**conozca**	conociera	**conozca** Ud.
	conociendo	conocemos	conocíamos	conocimos	conoceremos	conoceríamos	**conozcamos**	conociéramos	**conozcamos**
	conocido	conocéis	conocíais	conocisteis	conoceréis	conoceríais	**conozcáis**	conocierais	conoced (no **conozcáis**)
		conocen	conocían	conocieron	conocerán	conocerían	**conozcan**	conocieran	**conozcan** Uds.
36	creer (y)	creo	creía	**creí**	creeré	creería	crea	**creyera**	
		crees	creías	**creíste**	creerás	creerías	creas	**creyeras**	cree tú (no creas)
	Participles:	cree	creía	**creyó**	creerá	creería	crea	**creyera**	crea Ud.
	creyendo	creemos	creíamos	**creímos**	creeremos	creeríamos	creamos	**creyéramos**	creamos
	creído	creéis	creíais	**creísteis**	creeréis	creeríais	creáis	**creyerais**	creed (no creáis)
		creen	creían	**creyeron**	creerán	creerían	crean	**creyeran**	crean Uds.
37	cruzar (z:c)	cruzo	cruzaba	**crucé**	cruzaré	cruzaría	**cruce**	cruzara	
		cruzas	cruzabas	cruzaste	cruzarás	cruzarías	**cruces**	cruzaras	cruza tú (no **cruces**)
	Participles:	cruza	cruzaba	cruzó	cruzará	cruzaría	**cruce**	cruzara	**cruce** Ud.
	cruzando	cruzamos	cruzábamos	cruzamos	cruzaremos	cruzaríamos	**crucemos**	cruzáramos	**crucemos**
	cruzado	cruzáis	cruzabais	cruzasteis	cruzaréis	cruzaríais	**crucéis**	cruzarais	cruzad (no **crucéis**)
		cruzan	cruzaban	cruzaron	cruzarán	cruzarían	**crucen**	cruzaran	**crucen** Uds.
38	destruir (y)	**destruyo**	destruía	destruí	destruiré	destruiría	**destruya**	**destruyera**	
		destruyes	destruías	destruiste	destruirás	destruirías	**destruyas**	**destruyeras**	**destruye** tú (no **destruyas**)
	Participles:	**destruye**	destruía	**destruyó**	destruirá	destruiría	**destruya**	**destruyera**	**destruya** Ud.
	destruyendo	destruimos	destruíamos	destruimos	destruiremos	destruiríamos	**destruyamos**	**destruyéramos**	**destruyamos**
	destruido	destruís	destruíais	destruisteis	destruiréis	destruiríais	**destruyáis**	**destruyerais**	destruid (no **destruyáis**)
		destruyen	destruían	**destruyeron**	destruirán	destruirían	**destruyan**	**destruyeran**	**destruyan** Uds.
39	enviar (envío)	**envío**	enviaba	envié	enviaré	enviaría	**envíe**	enviara	
		envías	enviabas	enviaste	enviarás	enviarías	**envíes**	enviaras	**envía** tú (no **envíes**)
		envía	enviaba	envió	enviará	enviaría	**envíe**	enviara	**envíe** Ud.
	Participles:	enviamos	enviábamos	enviamos	enviaremos	enviaríamos	**enviemos**	enviáramos	enviemos
	enviando	enviáis	enviabais	enviasteis	enviaréis	enviaríais	**enviéis**	enviarais	enviad (no **enviéis**)
	enviado	**envían**	enviaban	enviaron	enviarán	enviarían	**envíen**	enviaran	**envíen** Uds.

	Infinitive	INDICATIVE					SUBJUNCTIVE		IMPERATIVE
		Present	Imperfect	Preterite	Future	Conditional	Present	Past	
40	graduarse (gradúo) **Participles:** graduando graduado	**gradúo** **gradúas** **gradúa** graduamos graduáis **gradúan**	graduaba graduabas graduaba graduábamos graduabais graduaban	gradué graduaste graduó graduamos graduasteis graduaron	graduaré graduarás graduará graduaremos graduaréis graduarán	graduaría graduarías graduaría graduaríamos graduaríais graduarían	**gradúe** **gradúes** **gradúe** graduemos graduéis **gradúen**	graduara graduaras graduara graduáramos graduarais graduaran	**gradúa** tú (no **gradúes**) **gradúe** Ud. graduemos graduad (no graduéis) **gradúen** Uds.
41	llegar (g:gu) **Participles:** llegando llegado	llego llegas llega llegamos llegáis llegan	llegaba llegabas llegaba llegábamos llegabais llegaban	**llegué** llegaste llegó llegamos llegasteis llegaron	llegaré llegarás llegará llegaremos llegaréis llegarán	llegaría llegarías llegaría llegaríamos llegaríais llegarían	**llegue** **llegues** **llegue** **lleguemos** **lleguéis** **lleguen**	llegara llegaras llegara llegáramos llegarais llegaran	llega tú (no **llegues**) **llegue** Ud. **lleguemos** llegad (no **lleguéis**) **lleguen** Uds.
42	prohibir (prohíbo) **Participles:** prohibiendo prohibido	**prohíbo** **prohíbes** **prohíbe** prohibimos prohibís **prohíben**	prohibía prohibías prohibía prohibíamos prohibíais prohibían	prohibí prohibiste prohibió prohibimos prohibisteis prohibieron	prohibiré prohibirás prohibirá prohibiremos prohibiréis prohibirán	prohibiría prohibirías prohibiría prohibiríamos prohibiríais prohibirían	**prohíba** **prohíbas** **prohíba** prohibamos prohibáis **prohíban**	prohibiera prohibieras prohibiera prohibiéramos prohibierais prohibieran	**prohíbe** tú (no **prohíbas**) **prohíba** Ud. prohibamos prohibid (no prohibáis) **prohíban** Uds.
43	proteger (g:j) **Participles:** protegiendo protegido	**protejo** proteges protege protegemos protegéis protegen	protegía protegías protegía protegíamos protegíais protegían	protegí protegiste protegió protegimos protegisteis protegieron	protegeré protegerás protegerá protegeremos protegeréis protegerán	protegería protegerías protegería protegeríamos protegeríais protegerían	**proteja** **protejas** **proteja** **protejamos** **protejáis** protejan	protegiera protegieras protegiera protegiéramos protegierais protegieran	protege tú (no **protejas**) **proteja** Ud. **protejamos** proteged (no **protejáis**) **protejan** Uds.
44	tocar (c:qu) **Participles:** tocando tocado	toco tocas toca tocamos tocáis tocan	tocaba tocabas tocaba tocábamos tocabais tocaban	**toqué** tocaste tocó tocamos tocasteis tocaron	tocaré tocarás tocará tocaremos tocaréis tocarán	tocaría tocarías tocaría tocaríamos tocaríais tocarían	**toque** **toques** **toque** **toquemos** **toquéis** **toquen**	tocara tocaras tocara tocáramos tocarais tocaran	toca tú (no **toques**) **toque** Ud. **toquemos** tocad (no **toquéis**) **toquen** Uds.

Guide to Vocabulary

Note on alphabetization

For purposes of alphabetization, **ch** and **ll** are not treated as separate letters, but **ñ** follows **n**. Therefore, in this glossary you will find that **año**, for example, appears after **anuncio.**

Abbreviations used in this glossary

adj.	adjective	*form.*	formal	*pl.*	plural
adv.	adverb	*indef.*	indefinite	*poss.*	possessive
art.	article	*interj.*	interjection	*prep.*	preposition
conj.	conjunction	*i.o.*	indirect object	*pron.*	pronoun
def.	definite	*m.*	masculine	*ref.*	reflexive
d.o.	direct object	*n.*	noun	*sing.*	singular
f.	feminine	*obj.*	object	*sub.*	subject
fam.	familiar	*p.p.*	past participle	*v.*	verb

Spanish-English

A

a *prep.* at; to 1
  ¿A qué hora...? At what time...? 1
  a bordo aboard
  a dieta on a diet 15
  a la derecha de to the right of 2
  a la izquierda de to the left of 2
  a la plancha grilled 8
  a la(s) + *time* at + *time* 1
  a menos que *conj.* unless 13
  a menudo *adv.* often 10
  a nombre de in the name of 5
  a plazos in installments 14
  A sus órdenes. At your service.
  a tiempo *adv.* on time 10
  a veces *adv.* sometimes 10
  a ver let's see
abeja *f.* bee
abierto/a *adj.* open 5, 14
abogado/a *m., f.* lawyer
abrazar(se) *v.* to hug; to embrace (each other) 11
abrazo *m.* hug
abrigo *m.* coat 6
abril *m.* April 5
abrir *v.* to open 3
abuelo/a *m., f.* grandfather/grandmother 3
abuelos *pl.* grandparents 3
aburrido/a *adj.* bored; boring 5
aburrir *v.* to bore 7
aburrirse *v.* to get bored
acabar de (+ *inf.*) *v.* to have just *done something* 6
acampar *v.* to camp 5
accidente *m.* accident 10
acción *f.* action
  de acción action (genre)
aceite *m.* oil 8
aceptar: ¡Acepto casarme contigo! I'll marry you!
acompañar *v.* to accompany 14
aconsejar *v.* to advise 12
acontecimiento *m.* event
acordarse (de) (o:ue) *v.* to remember 7
acostarse (o:ue) *v.* to go to bed 7
activo/a *adj.* active 15
actor *m.* actor
actriz *f.* actress
actualidades *f., pl.* news; current events
adelgazar *v.* to lose weight; to slim down 15
además (de) *adv.* furthermore; besides 10
adicional *adj.* additional
adiós *m.* goodbye 1
adjetivo *m.* adjective
administración de empresas *f.* business administration 2
adolescencia *f.* adolescence 9
¿adónde? *adv.* where (to)? (destination) 2
aduana *f.* customs
aeróbico/a *adj.* aerobic 15
aeropuerto *m.* airport 5
afectado/a *adj.* affected 13
afeitarse *v.* to shave 7
aficionado/a *m., f.* fan 4
afirmativo/a *adj.* affirmative
afuera *adv.* outside 5
afueras *f., pl.* suburbs; outskirts 12
agencia de viajes *f.* travel agency 5
agente de viajes *m., f.* travel agent 5
agosto *m.* August 5
agradable *adj.* pleasant
agua *f.* water 8
  agua mineral mineral water 8
aguantar *v.* to endure, to hold up 14
ahora *adv.* now 2
  ahora mismo right now 5
ahorrar *v.* to save (money) 14
ahorros *m., pl.* savings 14
aire *m.* air 13
ajo *m.* garlic 8
al (*contraction of* **a + el)** 4
  al aire libre open-air 6
  al contado in cash 14
  (al) este (to the) east 14
  al lado de next to; beside 2
  (al) norte (to the) north 14
  (al) oeste (to the) west 14
  (al) sur (to the) south 14
alcoba *f.* bedroom
alcohol *m.* alcohol 15
alcohólico/a *adj.* alcoholic 15
alegrarse (de) *v.* to be happy 13
alegre *adj.* happy; joyful 5
alegría *f.* happiness 9
alemán, alemana *adj.* German 3
alérgico/a *adj.* allergic 10
alfombra *f.* carpet; rug 12
algo *pron.* something; anything 7
algodón *m.* cotton 6
alguien *pron.* someone; somebody; anyone 7
algún, alguno/a(s) *adj.* any; some 7
alimento *m.* food
  alimentación *f.* diet
aliviar *v.* to reduce 15
  aliviar el estrés/la tensión to reduce stress/tension 15
allá *adv.* over there 2
allí *adv.* there 2
alma *f.* soul 9
almacén *m.* department store 6

almohada *f.* pillow 12
almorzar (o:ue) *v.* to have lunch 4
almuerzo *m.* lunch 4, 8
aló *interj.* hello (*on the telephone*) 11
alquilar *v.* to rent 12
alquiler *m.* rent (payment) 12
altar *m.* altar 9
altillo *m.* attic 12
alto/a *adj.* tall 3
aluminio *m.* aluminum 13
ama de casa *m., f.* housekeeper; caretaker 12
amable *adj.* nice; friendly 5
amarillo/a *adj.* yellow 6
amigo/a *m., f.* friend 3
amistad *f.* friendship 9
amor *m.* love 9
  amor a primera vista love at first sight 9
anaranjado/a *adj.* orange 6
ándale *interj.* come on 14
andar *v.* **en patineta** to skateboard 4
ángel *m.* angel 9
anillo *m.* ring
animal *m.* animal 13
aniversario (de bodas) *m.* (wedding) anniversary 9
anoche *adv.* last night 6
anteayer *adv.* the day before yesterday 6
antes *adv.* before 7
  antes (de) que *conj.* before 13
  antes de *prep.* before 7
antibiótico *m.* antibiotic 10
antipático/a *adj.* unpleasant 3
anunciar *v.* to announce; to advertise
anuncio *m.* advertisement
año *m.* year 5
  año pasado last year 6
apagar *v.* to turn off 11
aparato *m.* appliance
apartamento *m.* apartment 12
apellido *m.* last name 3
apenas *adv.* hardly; scarcely 10
aplaudir *v.* to applaud
aplicación *f.* app 11
apreciar *v.* to appreciate
aprender (a + *inf.*) *v.* to learn 3
apurarse *v.* to hurry; to rush 15
aquel, aquella *adj.* that (over there) 6
aquél, aquélla *pron.* that (over there) 6
aquello *neuter, pron.* that; that thing; that fact 6
aquellos/as *pl. adj.* those (over there) 6
aquéllos/as *pl. pron.* those (ones) (over there) 6
aquí *adv.* here 1
  Aquí está(n)... Here is/are... 5
árbol *m.* tree 13
archivo *m.* file 11
arete *m.* earring 6
argentino/a *adj.* Argentine 3
armario *m.* closet 12
arqueología *f.* archeology 2
arqueólogo/a *m., f.* archeologist
arquitecto/a *m., f.* architect
arrancar *v.* to start (*a car*) 11
arreglar *v.* to fix; to arrange 11; to neaten; to straighten up 12
arreglarse *v.* to get ready 7; to fix oneself (*clothes, hair, etc. to go out*) 7
arroba *f.* @ symbol 11
arroz *m.* rice 8
arte *m.* art 2
artes *f., pl.* arts
artesanía *f.* craftsmanship; crafts
artículo *m.* article
artista *m., f.* artist 3
artístico/a *adj.* artistic
arveja *f.* pea 8
asado/a *adj.* roast 8
ascenso *m.* promotion
ascensor *m.* elevator 5
así *adv.* like this; so (*in such a way*) 10
asistir (a) *v.* to attend 3
aspiradora *f.* vacuum cleaner 12
aspirante *m., f.* candidate; applicant
aspirina *f.* aspirin 10
atún *m.* tuna 8
aumentar *v.* to grow; to get bigger 13
aumentar *v.* **de peso** to gain weight 15
aumento *m.* increase
  aumento de sueldo pay raise
aunque although
autobús *m.* bus 1
automático/a *adj.* automatic
auto(móvil) *m.* auto(mobile) 5
autopista *f.* highway 11
ave *f.* bird 13
avenida *f.* avenue
aventura *f.* adventure
  de aventuras adventure (genre)
avergonzado/a *adj.* embarrassed 5
avión *m.* airplane 5
¡Ay! *interj.* Oh!
  ¡Ay, qué dolor! Oh, what pain!
ayer *adv.* yesterday 6
ayudar(se) *v.* to help (each other) 11
azúcar *m.* sugar 8
azul *adj. m., f.* blue 6

B

bailar *v.* to dance 2
bailarín/bailarina *m., f.* dancer
baile *m.* dance
bajar(se) de *v.* to get off of/out of (a vehicle) 11
bajo/a *adj.* short (*in height*) 3
balcón *m.* balcony 12
balde *m.* bucket 5
ballena *f.* whale 13
baloncesto *m.* basketball 4
banana *f.* banana 8
banco *m.* bank 14
banda *f.* band
bandera *f.* flag
bañarse *v.* to bathe; to take a bath 7
baño *m.* bathroom 7
barato/a *adj.* cheap 6
barco *m.* boat 5
barrer *v.* to sweep 12
  barrer el suelo *v.* to sweep the floor 12
barrio *m.* neighborhood 12
bastante *adv.* enough; rather 10
basura *f.* trash 12
baúl *m.* trunk 11
beber *v.* to drink 3
bebida *f.* drink 8
  bebida alcohólica *f.* alcoholic beverage 15
béisbol *m.* baseball 4
bellas artes *f., pl.* fine arts
belleza *f.* beauty 14
beneficio *m.* benefit
besar(se) *v.* to kiss (each other) 11
beso *m.* kiss 9
biblioteca *f.* library 2
bicicleta *f.* bicycle 4
bien *adv.* well 1
bienestar *m.* well-being 15
bienvenido(s)/a(s) *adj.* welcome 1
billete *m.* paper money; ticket
billón *m.* trillion
biología *f.* biology 2
bisabuelo/a *m., f.* great-grand-father/great-grandmother 3
bistec *m.* steak 8
blanco/a *adj.* white 6
blog *m.* blog 11
(blue)jeans *m., pl.* jeans 6
blusa *f.* blouse 6
boca *f.* mouth 10
boda *f.* wedding 9
boleto *m.* ticket 2
bolsa *f.* purse, bag 6
bombero/a *m., f.* firefighter
bonito/a *adj.* pretty 3
borrador *m.* eraser 2
borrar *v.* to erase 11
bosque *m.* forest 13
  bosque tropical tropical forest; rain forest 13

bota *f.* boot 6
botella *f.* bottle 9
botella de vino bottle of wine 9
botones *m., f. sing.* bellhop 5
brazo *m.* arm 10
brindar *v.* to toast (*drink*) 9
bucear *v.* to scuba dive 4
buen, bueno/a *adj.* good 3, 6
buena forma good shape (*physical*) 15
Buenas noches. Good evening; Good night. 1
Buenas tardes. Good afternoon. 1
Bueno. Hello. (*on telephone*) 11
Buenos días. Good morning. 1
bulevar *m.* boulevard
buscador *m.* browser 11
buscar *v.* to look for 2
buzón *m.* mailbox 14

C

caballero *m.* gentleman, sir 8
caballo *m.* horse 5
cabe: no cabe duda de there's no doubt 13
cabeza *f.* head 10
cada *adj. m., f.* each 6
caerse *v.* to fall (down) 10
café *m.* café 4; *adj. m., f.* brown 6; *m.* coffee 8
cafeína *f.* caffeine 15
cafetera *f.* coffee maker 12
cafetería *f.* cafeteria 2
caído/a *p.p.* fallen 14
caja *f.* cash register 6
cajero/a *m., f.* cashier
cajero automático *m.* ATM 14
calavera de azúcar *f.* skull made out of sugar 9
calcetín (calcetines) *m.* sock(s) 6
calculadora *f.* calculator 2
calentamiento global *m.* global warming 13
calentarse (e:ie) *v.* to warm up 15
calidad *f.* quality 6
calle *f.* street 11
calor *m.* heat
caloría *f.* calorie 15
calzar *v.* to take size... shoes 6
cama *f.* bed 5
cámara de video *f.* video camera 11
cámara digital *f.* digital camera 11
camarero/a *m., f.* waiter/ waitress 8
camarón *m.* shrimp 8
cambiar (de) *v.* to change 9
cambio: de cambio in change 2
cambio *m.* **climático** climate change 13
cambio *m.* **de moneda** currency exchange
caminar *v.* to walk 2
camino *m.* road
camión *m.* truck; bus
camisa *f.* shirt 6
camiseta *f.* t-shirt 6
campo *m.* countryside 5
canadiense *adj.* Canadian 3
canal *m.* (TV) channel 11
canción *f.* song
candidato/a *m., f.* candidate
canela *f.* cinnamon 10
cansado/a *adj.* tired 5
cantante *m., f.* singer
cantar *v.* to sing 2
capital *f.* capital city
capó *m.* hood 11
cara *f.* face 7
caramelo *m.* caramel 9
cargador *m.* charger 11
carne *f.* meat 8
carne de res *f.* beef 8
carnicería *f.* butcher shop 14
caro/a *adj.* expensive 6
carpintero/a *m., f.* carpenter
carrera *f.* career
carretera *f.* highway; (main) road 11
carro *m.* car; automobile 11
carta *f.* letter 4; (playing) card 5
cartel *m.* poster 12
cartera *f.* wallet 4, 6
cartero *m.* mail carrier 14
casa *f.* house; home 2
casado/a *adj.* married 9
casarse (con) *v.* to get married (to) 9
casi *adv.* almost 10
catorce fourteen 1
cazar *v.* to hunt 13
cebolla *f.* onion 8
cederrón *m.* CD-ROM
celebrar *v.* to celebrate 9
cementerio *m.* cemetery 9
cena *f.* dinner 8
cenar *v.* to have dinner 2
centro *m.* downtown 4
centro comercial shopping mall 6
cepillarse los dientes/el pelo *v.* to brush one's teeth/one's hair 7
cerámica *f.* pottery
cerca de *prep.* near 2
cerdo *m.* pork 8
cereales *m., pl.* cereal; grains 8
cero *m.* zero 1
cerrado/a *adj.* closed 5
cerrar (e:ie) *v.* to close 4
cerveza *f.* beer 8
césped *m.* grass
ceviche *m.* marinated fish dish 8
ceviche de camarón *m.* lemon-marinated shrimp 8
chaleco *m.* vest
champán *m.* champagne 9
champiñón *m.* mushroom 8
champú *m.* shampoo 7
chaqueta *f.* jacket 6
chatear *v.* to chat 11
chau *fam. interj.* bye 1
cheque *m.* (bank) check 14
cheque (de viajero) *m.* (traveler's) check 14
chévere *adj., fam.* terrific
chico/a *m., f.* boy/girl 1
chino/a *adj.* Chinese 3
chocar (con) *v.* to run into
chocolate *m.* chocolate 9
choque *m.* collision
chuleta *f.* chop (*food*) 8
chuleta de cerdo *f.* pork chop 8
cibercafé *m.* cybercafé 11
ciclismo *m.* cycling 4
cielo *m.* sky 13
cien(to) one hundred 2
ciencias *f., pl.* sciences 2
ciencias ambientales environmental science 2
de ciencia ficción *f.* science fiction (genre)
científico/a *m., f.* scientist
cierto/a *adj.* certain 13
es cierto it's certain 13
no es cierto it's not certain 13
cima *f.* top, peak 15
cinco five 1
cincuenta fifty 2
cine *m.* movie theater 4
cinta *f.* (audio)tape
cinta caminadora *f.* treadmill 15
cinturón *m.* belt 6
circulación *f.* traffic 11
cita *f.* date; appointment 9
ciudad *f.* city
ciudadano/a *m., f.* citizen
Claro (que sí). *fam.* Of course.
clase *f.* class 2
clase de ejercicios aeróbicos *f.* aerobics class 15
clásico/a *adj.* classical
cliente/a *m., f.* customer 6
clínica *f.* clinic 10
cobrar *v.* to cash (a check) 14
coche *m.* car; automobile 11
cocina *f.* kitchen; stove 9, 12
cocinar *v.* to cook 12
cocinero/a *m., f.* cook, chef
cofre *m.* hood 14
cola *f.* line 14
colesterol *m.* cholesterol 15
color *m.* color 6
comedia *f.* comedy; play
comedor *m.* dining room 12
comenzar (e:ie) *v.* to begin 4
comer *v.* to eat 3
comercial *adj.* commercial; business-related
comida *f.* food; meal 4, 8
como like; as 8
¿cómo? what?; how? 1, 2
¿Cómo es...? What's... like?

¿Cómo está usted? *form.* How are you? 1
¿Cómo estás? *fam.* How are you? 1
¿Cómo se llama usted? *(form.)* What's your name? 1
¿Cómo te llamas? *fam.* What's your name? 1
cómoda *f.* chest of drawers 12
cómodo/a *adj.* comfortable 5
compañero/a de clase *m., f.* classmate 2
compañero/a de cuarto *m., f.* roommate 2
compañía *f.* company; firm
compartir *v.* to share 3
compositor(a) *m., f.* composer
comprar *v.* to buy 2
compras *f., pl.* purchases
ir de compras to go shopping 5
comprender *v.* to understand 3
comprobar *v.* to check
comprometerse (con) *v.* to get engaged (to) 9
computación *f.* computer science 2
computadora *f.* computer 1
computadora portátil *f.* portable computer; laptop 11
comunicación *f.* communication
comunicarse (con) *v.* to communicate (with)
comunidad *f.* community 1
con *prep.* with 2
Con él/ella habla. Speaking. (*on telephone*) 11
con frecuencia *adv.* frequently 10
Con permiso. Pardon me; Excuse me. 1
con tal (de) que *conj.* provided (that) 13
concierto *m.* concert
concordar *v.* to agree
concurso *m.* game show; contest
conducir *v.* to drive 6, 11
conductor(a) *m., f.* driver 1
conexión *f.* **inalámbrica** wireless connection 11
confirmar *v.* to confirm 5
confirmar *v.* **una reservación** *f.* to confirm a reservation 5
confundido/a *adj.* confused 5
congelador *m.* freezer 12
congestionado/a *adj.* congested; stuffed-up 10
conmigo *pron.* with me 4, 9
conocer *v.* to know; to be acquainted with 6
conocido/a *adj.; p.p.* known
conseguir (e:i) *v.* to get; to obtain 4
consejero/a *m., f.* counselor; advisor
consejo *m.* advice
conservación *f.* conservation 13
conservar *v.* to conserve 13
construir *v.* to build
consultorio *m.* doctor's office 10
consumir *v.* to consume 15
contabilidad *f.* accounting 2
contador(a) *m., f.* accountant
contaminación *f.* pollution 13
contaminación del aire/del agua air/water pollution 13
contaminado/a *adj.* polluted 13
contaminar *v.* to pollute 13
contar (o:ue) *v.* to count; to tell 4
contento/a *adj.* content 5
contestadora *f.* answering machine
contestar *v.* to answer 2
contigo *fam. pron.* with you 5, 9
contratar *v.* to hire
control *m.* **remoto** remote control 11
controlar *v.* to control 13
conversación *f.* conversation 1
conversar *v.* to converse, to chat 2
copa *f.* wineglass; goblet 12
corazón *m.* heart 10
corbata *f.* tie 6
corredor(a) *m., f.* **de bolsa** stockbroker
correo *m.* mail; post office 14
correo de voz *m.* voice mail 11
correo electrónico *m.* e-mail 4
correr *v.* to run 3
cortesía *f.* courtesy
cortinas *f., pl.* curtains 12
corto/a *adj.* short (*in length*) 6
cosa *f.* thing 1
costar (o:ue) *v.* to cost 6
costarricense *adj.* Costa Rican 3
cráter *m.* crater 13
creer *v.* to believe 3, 13
creer (en) *v.* to believe (in) 3
no creer *v.* not to believe 13
creído/a *adj., p.p.* believed 14
crema de afeitar *f.* shaving cream 5, 7
crimen *m.* crime; murder
cruzar *v.* to cross 14
cuaderno *m.* notebook 1
cuadra *f.* (city) block 14
¿cuál(es)? which?; which one(s)? 2
¿Cuál es la fecha de hoy? What is today's date? 5
cuadro *m.* picture 12
cuando *conj.* when 7; 13
¿cuándo? when? 2
¿cuánto(s)/a(s)? how much/how many? 1, 2
¿Cuánto cuesta...? How much does... cost? 6
¿Cuántos años tienes? How old are you?
cuarenta forty 2
cuarto de baño *m.* bathroom 7
cuarto *m.* room 2; 7
cuarto/a *adj.* fourth 5
menos cuarto quarter to (time) 1
y cuarto quarter after (time) 1
cuatro four 1
cuatrocientos/as four hundred 2
cubano/a *adj.* Cuban 3
cubiertos *m., pl.* silverware
cubierto/a *p.p.* covered
cubrir *v.* to cover
cuchara *f.* (table or large) spoon 12
cuchillo *m.* knife 12
cuello *m.* neck 10
cuenta *f.* bill 8; account 14
cuenta corriente *f.* checking account 14
cuenta de ahorros *f.* savings account 14
cuento *m.* short story
cuerpo *m.* body 10
cuidado *m.* care
cuidar *v.* to take care of 13
cultura *f.* culture 2
cumpleaños *m., sing.* birthday 9
cumplir años *v.* to have a birthday
cuñado/a *m., f.* brother-in-law/sister-in-law 3
currículum *m.* résumé
curso *m.* course 2

D

danza *f.* dance
dañar *v.* to damage; to break down 10
dar *v.* to give 6
dar un consejo *v.* to give advice
darse con *v.* to bump into; to run into (something) 10
darse prisa *v.* to hurry; to rush 15
de *prep.* of; from 1
¿De dónde eres? *fam.* Where are you from? 1
¿De dónde es usted? *form.* Where are you from? 1
¿De parte de quién? Who is speaking/calling? (*on telephone*) 11
¿de quién...? whose...? (*sing.*) 1
¿de quiénes...? whose...? (*pl.*) 1
de algodón (made) of cotton 6
de aluminio (made) of aluminum 13
de buen humor in a good mood 5
de compras shopping 5
de cuadros plaid 6
de excursión hiking 4
de hecho in fact
de ida y vuelta roundtrip 5
de la mañana in the morning; A.M. 1
de la noche in the evening; at night; P.M. 1
de la tarde in the afternoon; in the early evening; P.M. 1
de lana (made) of wool 6
de lunares polka-dotted 6
de mal humor in a bad mood 5
de moda in fashion 6
De nada. You're welcome. 1
de niño/a as a child 10
de parte de on behalf of 11

de plástico (made) of plastic 13
de rayas striped 6
de repente suddenly 6
de seda (made) of silk 6
de vaqueros western (genre)
de vez en cuando from time to time 10
de vidrio (made) of glass 13
debajo de *prep.* below; under 2
deber (+ *inf.*) *v.* should; must; ought to 3
deber *m.* responsibility; obligation
debido a due to (the fact that)
débil *adj.* weak 15
decidir (+ *inf.*) *v.* to decide 3
décimo/a *adj.* tenth 5
decir (e:i) *v.* **(que)** to say (that); to tell (that) 4
decir la respuesta to say the answer 4
decir la verdad to tell the truth 4
decir mentiras to tell lies 4
declarar *v.* to declare; to say
dedo *m.* finger 10
dedo del pie *m.* toe 10
deforestación *f.* deforestation 13
dejar *v.* to let; to quit; to leave behind
dejar de (+ ***inf.***) *v.* to stop (*doing something*) 13
dejar una propina *v.* to leave a tip
del (*contraction of* **de + el**) of the; from the 1
delante de *prep.* in front of 2
delgado/a *adj.* thin; slender 3
delicioso/a *adj.* delicious 8
demás *adj.* the rest
demasiado *adv.* too much 6
dentista *m., f.* dentist 10
dentro de (diez años) within (ten years); inside
dependiente/a *m., f.* clerk 6
deporte *m.* sport 4
deportista *m.* sports person
deportivo/a *adj.* sports-related 4
depositar *v.* to deposit 14
derecha *f.* right 2
a la derecha de to the right of 2
derecho *adv.* straight (ahead) 14
derechos *m., pl.* rights
desarrollar *v.* to develop 13
desastre (natural) *m.* (natural) disaster
desayunar *v.* to have breakfast 2
desayuno *m.* breakfast 8
descafeinado/a *adj.* decaffeinated 15
descansar *v.* to rest 2
descargar *v.* to download 11
descompuesto/a *adj.* not working; out of order 11
describir *v.* to describe 3
descrito/a *p.p.* described 14
descubierto/a *p.p.* discovered 14
descubrir *v.* to discover 13
desde *prep.* from 6
desear *v.* to wish; to desire 2
desempleo *m.* unemployment
desierto *m.* desert 13
desigualdad *f.* inequality
desordenado/a *adj.* disorderly 5
despacio *adv.* slowly 10
despedida *f.* farewell; goodbye
despedir (e:i) *v.* to fire
despedirse (de) (e:i) *v.* to say goodbye (to)
despejado/a *adj.* clear (*weather*)
despertador *m.* alarm clock 7
despertarse (e:ie) *v.* to wake up 7
después *adv.* afterwards; then 7
después de after 7
después de que *conj.* after 13
destruir *v.* to destroy 13
detrás de *prep.* behind 2
día *m.* day 1
día de fiesta holiday 9
diario *m.* diary 1; newspaper
diario/a *adj.* daily 7
dibujar *v.* to draw 2
dibujo *m.* drawing
dibujos animados *m., pl.* cartoons
diccionario *m.* dictionary 1
dicho/a *p.p.* said 14
diciembre *m.* December 5
dictadura *f.* dictatorship
diecinueve nineteen 1
dieciocho eighteen 1
dieciséis sixteen 1
diecisiete seventeen 1
diente *m.* tooth 7
dieta *f.* diet 15
comer una dieta equilibrada to eat a balanced diet 15
diez ten 1
difícil *adj.* difficult; hard 3
Diga. Hello. (*on telephone*) 11
diligencia *f.* errand 14
dinero *m.* money 6
dirección *f.* address 14
dirección electrónica *f.* e-mail address 11
director(a) *m., f.* director; (*musical*) conductor
dirigir *v.* to direct
disco compacto compact disc (CD) 11
discriminación *f.* discrimination
discurso *m.* speech
diseñador(a) *m., f.* designer
diseño *m.* design
disfraz *m.* costume 9
disfrutar (de) *v.* to enjoy; to reap the benefits (of) 15
disminuir *v.* to reduce
diversión *f.* fun activity; entertainment; recreation 4
divertido/a *adj.* fun
divertirse (e:ie) *v.* to have fun 9
divorciado/a *adj.* divorced 9
divorciarse (de) *v.* to get divorced (from) 9
divorcio *m.* divorce 9
doblar *v.* to turn 14
doble *adj.* double 5
doce twelve 1
doctor(a) *m., f.* doctor 3; 10
documental *m.* documentary
documentos de viaje *m., pl.* travel documents
doler (o:ue) *v.* to hurt 10
dolor *m.* ache; pain 10
dolor de cabeza *m.* headache 10
doméstico/a *adj.* domestic 12
domingo *m.* Sunday 2
don *m.* Mr.; sir 1
doña *f.* Mrs.; ma'am 1
donde *adv.* where
¿Dónde está...? Where is...? 2
¿dónde? where? 1, 2
dormir (o:ue) *v.* to sleep 4
dormirse (o:ue) *v.* to go to sleep; to fall asleep 7
dormitorio *m.* bedroom 12
dos two 1
dos veces *f.* twice; two times 6
doscientos/as two hundred 2
drama *m.* drama; play
dramático/a *adj.* dramatic
dramaturgo/a *m., f.* playwright
droga *f.* drug 15
drogadicto/a *m., f.* drug addict 15
ducha *f.* shower 7
ducharse *v.* to shower; to take a shower 7
duda *f.* doubt 13
dudar *v.* to doubt 13
no dudar *v.* not to doubt 13
dueño/a *m., f.* owner 8
dulces *m., pl.* sweets; candy 9
durante *prep.* during 7
durar *v.* to last

E

e *conj.* (*used instead of* **y** *before words beginning with* **i** *and* **hi**) and
echar *v.* to throw
echar (una carta) al buzón *v.* to put (a letter) in the mailbox; to mail 14
ecología *f.* ecology 13
ecológico/a *adj.* ecological 13
ecologista *m., f.* ecologist 13
economía *f.* economics 2
ecoturismo *m.* ecotourism 13
ecuatoriano/a *adj.* Ecuadorian 3
edad *f.* age 9
edificio *m.* building 12
edificio de apartamentos apartment building 12
(en) efectivo *m.* cash 6

ejercer *v.* to practice/exercise (a degree/profession)
ejercicio *m.* exercise 15
  ejercicios aeróbicos aerobic exercises 15
  ejercicios de estiramiento stretching exercises 15
ejército *m.* army
el *m., sing., def. art.* the 1
él *sub. pron.* he 1; *obj. pron.* him
elecciones *f., pl.* election
electricista *m., f.* electrician
electrodoméstico *m.* electric appliance 12
elegante *adj. m., f.* elegant 6
elegir (e:i) *v.* to elect
ella *sub. pron.* she 1; *obj. pron.* her
ellos/as *sub. pron.* they 1; *obj. pron.* them
embarazada *adj.* pregnant 10
emergencia *f.* emergency 10
emitir *v.* to broadcast
emocionante *adj. m., f.* exciting
empezar (e:ie) *v.* to begin 4
empleado/a *m., f.* employee 5
empleo *m.* job; employment
empresa *f.* company; firm
en *prep.* in; on 2
  en casa at home
  en caso (de) que *conj.* in case (that) 13
  en cuanto *conj.* as soon as 13
  en efectivo in cash 14
  en exceso in excess; too much 15
  en línea in-line 4
  en punto on the dot; exactly; sharp (*time*) 1
  en qué in what; how
  ¿En qué puedo servirles? How can I help you? 5
  en vivo live 7
enamorado/a (de) *adj.* in love (with) 5
enamorarse (de) *v.* to fall in love (with) 9
encantado/a *adj.* delighted; pleased to meet you 1
encantar *v.* to like very much; to love (*inanimate objects*) 7
encima de *prep.* on top of 2
encontrar (o:ue) *v.* to find 4
encontrar(se) (o:ue) *v.* to meet (each other); to run into (each other) 11
  encontrarse con to meet up with 7
encuesta *f.* poll; survey
energía *f.* energy 13
  energía nuclear nuclear energy 13
  energía solar solar energy 13
enero *m.* January 5
enfermarse *v.* to get sick 10
enfermedad *f.* illness 10
enfermero/a *m., f.* nurse 10
enfermo/a *adj.* sick 10
enfrente de *adv.* opposite; facing 14
engordar *v.* to gain weight 15
enojado/a *adj.* angry 5
enojarse (con) *v.* to get angry (with) 7
ensalada *f.* salad 8
ensayo *m.* essay 3
enseguida *adv.* right away
enseñar *v.* to teach 2
ensuciar *v.* to get (something) dirty 12
entender (e:ie) *v.* to understand 4
enterarse *v.* to find out
entonces *adv.* so, then 5, 7
entrada *f.* entrance 12; ticket
entre *prep.* between; among 2
entregar *v.* to hand in 11
entremeses *m., pl.* hors d'oeuvres; appetizers 8
entrenador(a) *m., f.* trainer 15
entrenarse *v.* to practice; to train 15
entrevista *f.* interview
entrevistador(a) *m., f.* interviewer
entrevistar *v.* to interview
envase *m.* container 13
enviar *v.* to send; to mail 14
equilibrado/a *adj.* balanced 15
equipaje *m.* luggage 5
equipo *m.* team 4
equivocado/a *adj.* wrong 5
eres *fam.* you are 1
es he/she/it is 1
  Es bueno que… It's good that… 12
  es cierto it's certain 13
  es extraño it's strange 13
  es igual it's the same 5
  Es importante que… It's important that… 12
  es imposible it's impossible 13
  es improbable it's improbable 13
  Es malo que… It's bad that… 12
  Es mejor que… It's better that… 12
  Es necesario que… It's necessary that… 12
  es obvio it's obvious 13
  es posible it's possible 13
  es probable it's probable 13
  es ridículo it's ridiculous 13
  es seguro it's certain 13
  es terrible it's terrible 13
  es triste it's sad 13
  Es urgente que… It's urgent that… 12
  Es la una. It's one o'clock. 1
  es una lástima it's a shame 13
  es verdad it's true 13
esa(s) *f., adj.* that; those 6
ésa(s) *f., pron.* that (one); those (ones) 6
escalar *v.* to climb 4
  escalar montañas to climb mountains 4
escalera *f.* stairs; stairway 12
escalón *m.* step 15
escanear *v.* to scan 11
escoger *v.* to choose 8
escribir *v.* to write 3
  escribir un mensaje electrónico to write an e-mail 4
  escribir una carta to write a letter 4
escrito/a *p.p.* written 14
escritor(a) *m., f.* writer
escritorio *m.* desk 2
escuchar *v.* to listen (to) 2
  escuchar la radio to listen to the radio 2
  escuchar música to listen to music 2
escuela *f.* school 1
esculpir *v.* to sculpt
escultor(a) *m., f.* sculptor
escultura *f.* sculpture
ese *m., sing., adj.* that 6
ése *m., sing., pron.* that one 6
eso *neuter, pron.* that; that thing 6
esos *m., pl., adj.* those 6
ésos *m., pl., pron.* those (ones) 6
España *f.* Spain
español *m.* Spanish (*language*) 2
español(a) *adj. m., f.* Spanish 3
espárragos *m., pl.* asparagus 8
especialidad: las especialidades del día today's specials 8
especialización *f.* major 2
espectacular *adj.* spectacular
espectáculo *m.* show
espejo *m.* mirror 7
esperar *v.* to hope; to wish 13
  esperar (+ *inf.*) *v.* to wait (for); to hope 2
esposo/a *m., f.* husband/wife; spouse 3
esquí (acuático) *m.* (water) skiing 4
esquiar *v.* to ski 4
esquina *f.* corner 14
está he/she/it is, you are
  Está bien. That's fine.
  Está (muy) despejado. It's (very) clear. (*weather*)
  Está lloviendo. It's raining. 5
  Está nevando. It's snowing. 5
  Está (muy) nublado. It's (very) cloudy. (*weather*) 5
esta(s) *f., adj.* this; these 6
  esta noche tonight
ésta(s) *f., pron.* this (one); these (ones) 6
establecer *v.* to establish
estación *f.* station; season 5
  estación de autobuses bus station 5
  estación del metro subway station 5
  estación de tren train station 5

estacionamiento *m.* parking lot 14
estacionar *v.* to park 11
estadio *m.* stadium 2
estado civil *m.* marital status 9
Estados Unidos *m., pl.* (EE.UU.; E.U.) United States
estadounidense *adj. m., f.* from the United States 3
estampilla *f.* stamp 14
estante *m.* bookcase; bookshelves 12
estar *v.* to be 2
  estar a dieta to be on a diet 15
  estar aburrido/a to be bored 5
  estar afectado/a (por) to be affected (by) 13
  estar cansado/a to be tired 5
  estar contaminado/a to be polluted 13
  estar de acuerdo to agree
    Estoy de acuerdo. I agree.
    No estoy de acuerdo. I don't agree.
  estar de moda to be in fashion 6
  estar de vacaciones *f., pl.* to be on vacation 5
  estar en buena forma to be in good shape 15
  estar enfermo/a to be sick 10
  estar harto/a de... to be sick of...
  estar listo/a to be ready 5
  estar perdido/a to be lost 14
  estar roto/a to be broken
  estar seguro/a to be sure 5
  estar torcido/a to be twisted; to be sprained 10
  No está nada mal. It's not bad at all. 5
estatua *f.* statue
este *m.* east 14
este *m., sing., adj.* this 6
éste *m., sing., pron.* this (one) 6
estéreo *m.* stereo 11
estilo *m.* style
estiramiento *m.* stretching 15
esto *neuter pron.* this; this thing 6
estómago *m.* stomach 10
estornudar *v.* to sneeze 10
estos *m., pl., adj.* these 6
éstos *m., pl., pron.* these (ones) 6
estrella *f.* star 13
  estrella de cine *m., f.* movie star
estrés *m.* stress 15
estudiante *m., f.* student 1, 2
estudiantil *adj. m., f.* student 2
estudiar *v.* to study 2
estufa *f.* stove 12
estupendo/a *adj.* stupendous 5
etapa *f.* stage 9
evitar *v.* to avoid 13
examen *m.* test; exam 2
  examen médico physical exam 10
excelente *adj. m., f.* excellent 5
exceso *m.* excess 15
excursión *f.* hike; tour; excursion 4
excursionista *m., f.* hiker
éxito *m.* success
experiencia *f.* experience
explicar *v.* to explain 2
explorar *v.* to explore
expresión *f.* expression
extinción *f.* extinction 13
extranjero/a *adj.* foreign
extrañar *v.* to miss
extraño/a *adj.* strange 13

F

fábrica *f.* factory 13
fabuloso/a *adj.* fabulous 5
fácil *adj.* easy 3
falda *f.* skirt 6
faltar *v.* to lack; to need 7
familia *f.* family 3
famoso/a *adj.* famous
farmacia *f.* pharmacy 10
fascinar *v.* to fascinate 7
favorito/a *adj.* favorite 4
fax *m.* fax (machine)
febrero *m.* February 5
fecha *f.* date 5
¡Felicidades! Congratulations! 9
¡Felicitaciones! Congratulations! 9
feliz *adj.* happy 5
  ¡Feliz cumpleaños! Happy birthday! 9
fenomenal *adj.* great, phenomenal 5
feo/a *adj.* ugly 3
festival *m.* festival
fiebre *f.* fever 10
fiesta *f.* party 9
fijo/a *adj.* fixed, set 6
fin *m.* end 4
  fin de semana weekend 4
finalmente *adv.* finally
firmar *v.* to sign (*a document*) 14
física *f.* physics 2
flan (de caramelo) *m.* baked (caramel) custard 9
flexible *adj.* flexible 15
flor *f.* flower 13
folclórico/a *adj.* folk; folkloric
folleto *m.* brochure
forma *f.* shape 15
formulario *m.* form 14
foto(grafía) *f.* photograph 1
francés, francesa *adj. m., f.* French 3
frecuentemente *adv.* frequently
frenos *m., pl.* brakes
frente (frío) *m.* (cold) front 5
fresco/a *adj.* cool
frijoles *m., pl.* beans 8
frío/a *adj.* cold
frito/a *adj.* fried 8
fruta *f.* fruit 8
frutería *f.* fruit store 14
fuera *adv.* outside
fuerte *adj. m., f.* strong 15
fumar *v.* to smoke 15
  (no) fumar *v.* (not) to smoke 15
funcionar *v.* to work 11; to function
fútbol *m.* soccer 4
fútbol americano *m.* football 4
futuro/a *adj.* future
  en el futuro in the future

G

gafas (de sol) *f., pl.* (sun)glasses 6
gafas (oscuras) *f., pl.* (sun)glasses
galleta *f.* cookie 9
ganar *v.* to win 4; to earn (money)
ganga *f.* bargain 6
garaje *m.* garage; (mechanic's) repair shop 11; garage (*in a house*) 12
garganta *f.* throat 10
gasolina *f.* gasoline 11
gasolinera *f.* gas station 11
gastar *v.* to spend (*money*) 6
gato *m.* cat 13
gemelo/a *m., f.* twin 3
genial *adj.* great
gente *f.* people 3
geografía *f.* geography 2
gerente *m., f.* manager 8
gimnasio *m.* gymnasium 4
gobierno *m.* government 13
golf *m.* golf 4
gordo/a *adj.* fat 3
grabar *v.* to record 11
gracias *f., pl.* thank you; thanks 1
  Gracias por invitarme. Thanks for inviting me. 9
graduarse (de/en) *v.* to graduate (from/in) 9
grande *adj.* big; large 3
grasa *f.* fat 15
gratis *adj. m., f.* free of charge 14
grave *adj.* grave; serious 10
gripe *f.* flu 10
gris *adj. m., f.* gray 6
gritar *v.* to scream, to shout
grito *m.* scream 5
guantes *m., pl.* gloves 6
guapo/a *adj.* handsome; good-looking 3
guardar *v.* to save (on a computer) 11
guerra *f.* war
guía *m., f.* guide
gustar *v.* to be pleasing to; to like 2
  Me gustaría... I would like...
gusto *m.* pleasure 1
  El gusto es mío. The pleasure is mine. 1

Mucho gusto. Pleased to meet you. 1
¡Qué gusto verlo/la! *(form.) How nice to see you!*
¡Qué gusto verte! *(fam.) How nice to see you!*

H

haber *(auxiliar) v.* to have (done something) 15
habitación *f.* room 5
habitación doble double room 5
habitación individual single room 5
hablar *v.* to talk; to speak 2
hacer *v.* to do; to make 4
Hace buen tiempo. The weather is good. 5
Hace (mucho) calor. It's (very) hot. *(weather)* 5
Hace fresco. It's cool. *(weather)* 5
Hace (mucho) frío. It's (very) cold. *(weather)* 5
Hace mal tiempo. The weather is bad. 5
Hace (mucho) sol. It's (very) sunny. *(weather)* 5
Hace (mucho) viento. It's (very) windy. *(weather)* 5
hacer cola to stand in line 14
hacer diligencias to run errands 14
hacer ejercicio to exercise 15
hacer ejercicios aeróbicos to do aerobics 15
hacer ejercicios de estiramiento to do stretching exercises 15
hacer el papel (de) to play the role (of)
hacer gimnasia to work out 15
hacer juego (con) to match (with) 6
hacer la cama to make the bed 12
hacer las maletas to pack (one's) suitcases 5
hacer quehaceres domésticos to do household chores 12
hacer (wind)surf to (wind)surf 5
hacer turismo to go sightseeing
hacer un viaje to take a trip 5
¿Me harías el honor de casarte conmigo? Would you do me the honor of marrying me?
hacia *prep.* toward 14
hambre *f.* hunger
hamburguesa *f.* hamburger 8
hasta *prep.* until 6; toward
Hasta la vista. See you later. 1
Hasta luego. See you later. 1
Hasta mañana. See you tomorrow. 1
Hasta pronto. See you soon. 1
hasta que *conj.* until 13
hay there is; there are 1
Hay (mucha) contaminación. It's (very) smoggy.
Hay (mucha) niebla. It's (very) foggy.
Hay que It is necessary that
No hay de qué. You're welcome. 1
No hay duda de There's no doubt 13
hecho/a *p.p.* done 14
heladería *f.* ice cream shop 14
helado/a *adj.* iced 8
helado *m.* ice cream 9
hermanastro/a *m., f.* stepbrother/stepsister 3
hermano/a *m., f.* brother/sister 3
hermano/a mayor/menor *m., f.* older/younger brother/sister 3
hermanos *m., pl.* siblings (brothers and sisters) 3
hermoso/a *adj.* beautiful 6
hierba *f.* grass 13
hijastro/a *m., f.* stepson/stepdaughter 3
hijo/a *m., f.* son/daughter 3
hijo/a único/a *m., f.* only child 3
hijos *m., pl.* children 3
híjole *interj.* wow 6
historia *f.* history 2; story
hockey *m.* hockey 4
hola *interj.* hello; hi 1
hombre *m.* man 1
hombre de negocios *m.* businessman
hora *f.* hour 1; the time
horario *m.* schedule 2
horno *m.* oven 12
horno de microondas *m.* microwave oven 12
horror *m.* horror
de horror horror (genre)
hospital *m.* hospital 10
hotel *m.* hotel 5
hoy *adv.* today 2
hoy día *adv.* nowadays
Hoy es... Today is... 2
hueco *m.* hole 4
huelga *f.* strike *(labor)*
hueso *m.* bone 10
huésped *m., f.* guest 5
huevo *m.* egg 8
humanidades *f., pl.* humanities 2
huracán *m.* hurricane

I

ida *f.* one way *(travel)*
idea *f.* idea
iglesia *f.* church 4
igualdad *f.* equality
igualmente *adv.* likewise 1
impermeable *m.* raincoat 6
importante *adj. m., f.* important 3
importar *v.* to be important to; to matter 7
imposible *adj. m., f.* impossible 13
impresora *f.* printer 11
imprimir *v.* to print 11
improbable *adj. m., f.* improbable 13
impuesto *m.* tax
incendio *m.* fire
increíble *adj. m., f.* incredible 5
indicar cómo llegar *v.* to give directions 14
individual *adj.* single *(room)* 5
infección *f.* infection 10
informar *v.* to inform
informe *m.* report; paper *(written work)*
ingeniero/a *m., f.* engineer 3
inglés *m.* English *(language)* 2
inglés, inglesa *adj.* English 3
inodoro *m.* toilet 7
insistir (en) *v.* to insist (on) 12
inspector(a) de aduanas *m., f.* customs inspector 5
inteligente *adj. m., f.* intelligent 3
intento *m.* attempt 11
intercambiar *v.* to exchange
interesante *adj. m., f.* interesting 3
interesar *v.* to be interesting to; to interest 7
internacional *adj. m., f.* international
Internet Internet 11
inundación *f.* flood
invertir (e:ie) *v.* to invest
invierno *m.* winter 5
invitado/a *m., f.* guest 9
invitar *v.* to invite 9
inyección *f.* injection 10
ir *v.* to go 4
ir a (+ *inf.*) to be going to do something 4
ir de compras to go shopping 5
ir de excursión (a las montañas) to go on a hike (in the mountains) 4
ir de pesca to go fishing
ir de vacaciones to go on vacation 5
ir en autobús to go by bus 5
ir en auto(móvil) to go by auto(mobile); to go by car 5
ir en avión to go by plane 5
ir en barco to go by boat 5
ir en metro to go by subway
ir en moto(cicleta) to go by motorcycle 5
ir en taxi to go by taxi 5
ir en tren to go by train
irse *v.* to go away; to leave 7
italiano/a *adj.* Italian 3
izquierda *f.* left 2
a la izquierda de to the left of 2

J

jabón *m.* soap 7
jamás *adv.* never; not ever 7
jamón *m.* ham 8
japonés, japonesa *adj.* Japanese 3
jardín *m.* garden; yard 12
jefe, jefa *m., f.* boss
jengibre *m.* ginger 10
joven *adj. m., f., sing.* (**jóvenes** *pl.*) young 3
  joven *m., f., sing.* (**jóvenes** *pl.*) young person 1
joyería *f.* jewelry store 14
jubilarse *v.* to retire (*from work*) 9
juego *m.* game
jueves *m., sing.* Thursday 2
jugador(a) *m., f.* player 4
jugar (u:ue) *v.* to play 4
  jugar a las cartas *f., pl.* to play cards 5
jugo *m.* juice 8
  jugo de fruta *m.* fruit juice 8
julio *m.* July 5
jungla *f.* jungle 13
junio *m.* June 5
juntos/as *adj.* together 9
juventud *f.* youth 9

K

kilómetro *m.* kilometer 11

L

la *f., sing., def. art.* the 1; *f., sing., d.o. pron.* her, it, *form.* you 5
laboratorio *m.* laboratory 2
lago *m.* lake 13
lámpara *f.* lamp 12
lana *f.* wool 6
langosta *f.* lobster 8
lápiz *m.* pencil 1
largo/a *adj.* long 6
las *f., pl., def. art.* the 1; *f., pl., d.o. pron.* them; you 5
lástima *f.* shame 13
lastimarse *v.* to injure oneself 10
  lastimarse el pie to injure one's foot 10
lata *f.* (*tin*) can 13
lavabo *m.* sink 7
lavadora *f.* washing machine 12
lavandería *f.* laundromat 14
lavaplatos *m., sing.* dishwasher 12
lavar *v.* to wash 12
  lavar (el suelo, los platos) to wash (the floor, the dishes) 12
lavarse *v.* to wash oneself 7
  lavarse la cara to wash one's face 7
  lavarse las manos to wash one's hands 7
le *sing., i.o. pron.* to/for him, her, *form.* you 6
  Le presento a... *form.* I would like to introduce you to (name). 1
lección *f.* lesson 1
leche *f.* milk 8
lechuga *f.* lettuce 8
leer *v.* to read 3
  leer el correo electrónico to read e-mail 4
  leer un periódico to read a newspaper 4
  leer una revista to read a magazine 4
leído/a *p.p.* read 14
lejos de *prep.* far from 2
lengua *f.* language 2
  lenguas extranjeras *f., pl.* foreign languages 2
lentes de contacto *m., pl.* contact lenses
  lentes (de sol) (sun)glasses
lento/a *adj.* slow 11
les *pl., i.o. pron.* to/for them, you 6
letrero *m.* sign 14
levantar *v.* to lift 15
  levantar pesas to lift weights 15
levantarse *v.* to get up 7
ley *f.* law 13
libertad *f.* liberty; freedom
libre *adj. m., f.* free 4
librería *f.* bookstore 2
libro *m.* book 2
licencia de conducir *f.* driver's license 11
limón *m.* lemon 8
limpiar *v.* to clean 12
  limpiar la casa *v.* to clean the house 12
limpio/a *adj.* clean 5
línea *f.* line 4
listo/a *adj.* ready; smart 5
literatura *f.* literature 2
llamar *v.* to call 11
  llamar por teléfono to call on the phone
llamarse *v.* to be called; to be named 7
llanta *f.* tire 11
llave *f.* key 5; wrench 11
llegada *f.* arrival 5
llegar *v.* to arrive 2
llenar *v.* to fill 11, 14
  llenar el tanque to fill the tank 11
  llenar (un formulario) to fill out (a form) 14
lleno/a *adj.* full 11
llevar *v.* to carry 2; to wear; to take 6
  llevar una vida sana to lead a healthy lifestyle 15
  llevarse bien/mal (con) to get along well/badly (with) 9
llorar *v.* to cry 15
llover (o:ue) *v.* to rain 5
  Llueve. It's raining. 5
lluvia *f.* rain
lo *m., sing. d.o. pron.* him, it, *form.* you 5
  ¡Lo he pasado de película! I've had a fantastic time!
  lo mejor the best (thing)
  lo que that which; what 12
  Lo siento. I'm sorry. 1
loco/a *adj.* crazy 6
locutor(a) *m., f.* (TV or radio) announcer
lodo *m.* mud
los *m., pl., def. art.* the 1; *m. pl., d.o. pron.* them, you 5
luchar (contra/por) *v.* to fight; to struggle (against/for)
luego *adv.* then 7; later 1
lugar *m.* place 2, 4
luna *f.* moon 13
lunares *m.* polka dots
lunes *m., sing.* Monday 2
luz *f.* light; electricity 12

M

madrastra *f.* stepmother 3
madre *f.* mother 3
madurez *f.* maturity; middle age 9
maestro/a *m., f.* teacher
magnífico/a *adj.* magnificent 5
maíz *m.* corn 8
mal, malo/a *adj.* bad 3
maleta *f.* suitcase 1
mamá *f.* mom
mandar *v.* to order 12; to send; to mail 14
manejar *v.* to drive 11
manera *f.* way
mano *f.* hand 1
manta *f.* blanket 12
mantener *v.* to maintain 15
  mantenerse en forma to stay in shape 15
mantequilla *f.* butter 8
manzana *f.* apple 8
mañana *f.* morning, a.m. 1; tomorrow 1
mapa *m.* map 1, 2
maquillaje *m.* makeup 7
maquillarse *v.* to put on makeup 7
mar *m.* sea 5
maravilloso/a *adj.* marvelous 5
mareado/a *adj.* dizzy; nauseated 10
margarina *f.* margarine 8
mariscos *m., pl.* shellfish 8
marrón *adj. m., f.* brown 6
martes *m., sing.* Tuesday 2
marzo *m.* March 5
más *adv.* more 2
  más de (+ *number*) more than 8
  más tarde later (on) 7
  más... que more... than 8

masaje *m.* massage 15
matemáticas *f., pl.* mathematics 2
materia *f.* course 2
matrimonio *m.* marriage 9
máximo/a *adj.* maximum 11
mayo *m.* May 5
mayonesa *f.* mayonnaise 8
mayor *adj.* older 3
  el/la mayor *adj.* oldest 8
me *sing., d.o. pron.* me 5; *sing. i.o. pron.* to/for me 6
  Me gusta... I like... 2
  Me gustaría(n)... I would like... 15
  Me llamo... My name is... 1
  Me muero por... I'm dying to (for)...
mecánico/a *m., f.* mechanic 11
mediano/a *adj.* medium
medianoche *f.* midnight 1
medias *f., pl.* pantyhose, stockings 6
medicamento *m.* medication 10
medicina *f.* medicine 10
médico/a *m., f.* doctor 3; *adj.* medical 10
medio/a *adj.* half 3
  medio ambiente *m.* environment 13
  medio/a hermano/a *m., f.* half-brother/half-sister 3
  mediodía *m.* noon 1
  medios de comunicación *m., pl.* means of communication; media
  y media thirty minutes past the hour (time) 1
mejor *adj.* better 8
  el/la mejor *m., f.* the best 8
mejorar *v.* to improve 13
melocotón *m.* peach 8
menor *adj.* younger 3
  el/la menor *m., f.* youngest 8
menos *adv.* less 10
  menos cuarto..., menos quince... quarter to... (*time*) 1
  menos de (+ *number*) fewer than 8
  menos... que less... than 8
mensaje *m.* **de texto** text message 11
mensaje electrónico *m.* e-mail message 4
mentira *f.* lie 4
menú *m.* menu 8
mercado *m.* market 6
  mercado al aire libre open-air market 6
merendar (e:ie) *v.* to snack 8; to have an afternoon snack
merienda *f.* afternoon snack 15
mes *m.* month 5
mesa *f.* table 2
mesita *f.* end table 12
  mesita de noche night stand 12
meterse en problemas *v.* to get into trouble 13
metro *m.* subway 5
mexicano/a *adj.* Mexican 3
mí *pron., obj. of prep.* me 9
mi(s) *poss. adj.* my 3
microonda *f.* microwave 12
  horno de microondas *m.* microwave oven 12
miedo *m.* fear
miel *f.* honey 10
mientras *conj.* while 10
miércoles *m., sing.* Wednesday 2
mil *m.* one thousand 2
  mil millones billion
milla *f.* mile
millón *m.* million 2
millones (de) *m.* millions (of)
mineral *m.* mineral 15
minuto *m.* minute
mío(s)/a(s) *poss.* my; (of) mine 11
mirar *v.* to look (at); to watch 2
  mirar (la) televisión to watch television 2
mismo/a *adj.* same 3
mochila *f.* backpack 2
moda *f.* fashion 6
moderno/a *adj.* modern
molestar *v.* to bother; to annoy 7
monitor *m.* (computer) monitor 11
  monitor(a) *m., f.* trainer
mono *m.* monkey 13
montaña *f.* mountain 4
montar *v.* **a caballo** to ride a horse 5
montón: un montón de a lot of 4
monumento *m.* monument 4
morado/a *adj.* purple 6
moreno/a *adj.* brunet(te) 3
morir (o:ue) *v.* to die 8
mostrar (o:ue) *v.* to show 4
moto(cicleta) *f.* motorcycle 5
motor *m.* motor
muchacho/a *m., f.* boy/girl 3
mucho/a *adj.*, a lot of; much; many 3
  (Muchas) gracias. Thank you (very much); Thanks (a lot). 1
  muchas veces *adv.* a lot; many times 10
  Mucho gusto. Pleased to meet you. 1
mudarse *v.* to move (from one house to another) 12
muebles *m., pl.* furniture 12
muerte *f.* death 9
muerto/a *p.p.* died 14
mujer *f.* woman 1
  mujer de negocios *f.* business woman
  mujer policía *f.* female police officer
multa *f.* fine
mundial *adj. m., f.* worldwide
mundo *m.* world 8
muro *m.* wall 15
músculo *m.* muscle 15
museo *m.* museum 4
música *f.* music 2
musical *adj. m., f.* musical
músico/a *m., f.* musician
muy *adv.* very 1
  (Muy) bien, gracias. (Very) well, thanks. 1

N

nacer *v.* to be born 9
nacimiento *m.* birth 9
nacional *adj. m., f.* national
nacionalidad *f.* nationality 1
nada nothing 1; not anything 7
  nada mal not bad at all 5
nadar *v.* to swim 4
nadie *pron.* no one, nobody, not anyone 7
naranja *f.* orange 8
nariz *f.* nose 10
natación *f.* swimming 4
natural *adj. m., f.* natural 13
naturaleza *f.* nature 13
navegador *m.* **GPS** GPS 11
navegar (en Internet) *v.* to surf (the Internet) 11
Navidad *f.* Christmas 9
necesario/a *adj.* necessary 12
necesitar (+ *inf.*) *v.* to need 2
negar (e:ie) *v.* to deny 13
  no negar (e:ie) *v.* not to deny 13
negocios *m., pl.* business; commerce
negro/a *adj.* black 6
nervioso/a *adj.* nervous 5
nevar (e:ie) *v.* to snow 5
  Nieva. It's snowing. 5
ni...ni neither... nor 7
niebla *f.* fog
nieto/a *m., f.* grandson/granddaughter 3
nieve *f.* snow
ningún, ninguno/a(s) *adj.* no; none; not any 7
niñez *f.* childhood 9
niño/a *m., f.* child 3
no no; not 1
  ¿no? right? 1
  no cabe duda de there is no doubt 13
  no es seguro it's not certain 13
  no es verdad it's not true 13
  No está nada mal. It's not bad at all. 5
  no estar de acuerdo to disagree
  No estoy seguro. I'm not sure.
  no hay there is not; there are not 1
  No hay de qué. You're welcome. 1
  no hay duda de there is no doubt 13
  ¡No me diga(s)! You don't say!
  No me gustan nada. I don't like them at all. 2

no muy bien not very well 1
No quiero. I don't want to. 4
No sé. I don't know.
No te preocupes. (*fam.*) Don't worry. 7
no tener razón to be wrong 3
noche *f.* night 1
nombre *m.* name 1
norte *m.* north 14
norteamericano/a *adj.* (North) American 3
nos *pl., d.o. pron.* us 5; *pl., i.o. pron.* to/for us 6
Nos vemos. See you. 1
nosotros/as *sub. pron.* we 1; *obj. pron.* us
noticia *f.* news 11
noticias *f., pl.* news
noticiero *m.* newscast
novecientos/as nine hundred 2
noveno/a *adj.* ninth 5
noventa ninety 2
noviembre *m.* November 5
novio/a *m., f.* boyfriend/girlfriend 3
nube *f.* cloud 13
nublado/a *adj.* cloudy 5
Está (muy) nublado. It's very cloudy. 5
nuclear *adj. m. f.* nuclear 13
nuera *f.* daughter-in-law 3
nuestro(s)/a(s) *poss. adj.* our 3; our, (of) ours 11
nueve nine 1
nuevo/a *adj.* new 6
número *m.* number 1; (shoe) size 6
nunca *adv.* never; not ever 7
nutrición *f.* nutrition 15
nutricionista *m., f.* nutritionist 15

O

o or 7
o... o; either... or 7
obedecer *v.* to obey
obra *f.* work (*of art, literature, music, etc.*)
obra maestra *f.* masterpiece
obtener *v.* to obtain; to get
obvio/a *adj.* obvious 13
océano *m.* ocean
ochenta eighty 2
ocho eight 1
ochocientos/as eight hundred 2
octavo/a *adj.* eighth 5
octubre *m.* October 5
ocupación *f.* occupation
ocupado/a *adj.* busy 5
ocurrir *v.* to occur; to happen
odiar *v.* to hate 9
oeste *m.* west 14
oferta *f.* offer
oficina *f.* office 12
oficio *m.* trade
ofrecer *v.* to offer 6
oído *m.* (sense of) hearing; inner ear 10
oído/a *p.p.* heard 14
oír *v.* to hear 4
ojalá (que) *interj.* I hope (that); I wish (that) 13
ojo *m.* eye 10
olvidar *v.* to forget 10
once eleven 1
ópera *f.* opera
operación *f.* operation 10
ordenado/a *adj.* orderly 5
ordinal *adj.* ordinal (*number*)
oreja *f.* (outer) ear 10
organizarse *v.* to organize oneself 12
orquesta *f.* orchestra
ortografía *f.* spelling
ortográfico/a *adj.* spelling
os *fam., pl. d.o. pron.* you 5; *fam., pl. i.o. pron.* to/for you 6
otoño *m.* autumn 5
otro/a *adj.* other; another 6
otra vez again

P

paciente *m., f.* patient 10
padrastro *m.* stepfather 3
padre *m.* father 3
padres *m., pl.* parents 3
pagar *v.* to pay 6
pagar a plazos to pay in installments 14
pagar al contado to pay in cash 14
pagar en efectivo to pay in cash 14
pagar la cuenta to pay the bill
página *f.* page 11
página principal *f.* home page 11
país *m.* country 1
paisaje *m.* landscape 5
pájaro *m.* bird 13
palabra *f.* word 1
paleta helada *f.* popsicle 4
pálido/a *adj.* pale 14
pan *m.* bread 8
pan tostado *m.* toasted bread 8
panadería *f.* bakery 14
pantalla *f.* screen 11
pantalla táctil *f.* touch screen
pantalones *m., pl.* pants 6
pantalones cortos *m., pl.* shorts 6
pantuflas *f.* slippers 7
papa *f.* potato 8
papas fritas *f., pl.* fried potatoes; French fries 8
papá *m.* dad
papás *m., pl.* parents
papel *m.* paper 2; role
papelera *f.* wastebasket 2
paquete *m.* package 14
par *m.* pair 6
par de zapatos pair of shoes 6
para *prep.* for; in order to; by; used for; considering 11
para que *conj.* so that 13
parabrisas *m., sing.* windshield 11
parar *v.* to stop 11
parecer *v.* to seem 6
pared *f.* wall 12
pareja *f.* (married) couple; partner 9
parientes *m., pl.* relatives 3
parque *m.* park 4
párrafo *m.* paragraph
parte: de parte de on behalf of 11
partido *m.* game; match (*sports*) 4
pasado/a *adj.* last; past 6
pasado *p.p.* passed
pasaje *m.* ticket 5
pasaje de ida y vuelta *m.* roundtrip ticket 5
pasajero/a *m., f.* passenger 1
pasaporte *m.* passport 5
pasar *v.* to go through
pasar la aspiradora to vacuum 12
pasar por la aduana to go through customs
pasar tiempo to spend time
pasarlo bien/mal to have a good/bad time 9
pasatiempo *m.* pastime; hobby 4
pasear *v.* to take a walk; to stroll 4
pasear en bicicleta to ride a bicycle 4
pasear por to walk around
pasillo *m.* hallway 12
pasta *f.* **de dientes** toothpaste 7
pastel *m.* cake; pie 9
pastel de chocolate *m.* chocolate cake 9
pastel de cumpleaños *m.* birthday cake
pastelería *f.* pastry shop 14
pastilla *f.* pill; tablet 10
patata *f.* potato 8
patatas fritas *f., pl.* fried potatoes; French fries 8
patinar (en línea) *v.* to (inline) skate 4
patineta *f.* skateboard 4
patio *m.* patio; yard 12
pavo *m.* turkey 8
paz *f.* peace
pedir (e:i) *v.* to ask for; to request 4; to order (*food*) 8
pedir prestado *v.* to borrow 14
pedir un préstamo *v.* to apply for a loan 14
Todos me dijeron que te pidiera una disculpa de su parte. They all told me to ask you to excuse them/forgive them.
peinarse *v.* to comb one's hair 7

película *f.* movie 4
peligro *m.* danger 13
peligroso/a *adj.* dangerous
pelirrojo/a *adj.* red-haired 3
pelo *m.* hair 7
pelota *f.* ball 4
peluquería *f.* beauty salon 14
peluquero/a *m., f.* hairdresser
penicilina *f.* penicillin
pensar (e:ie) *v.* to think 4
  pensar (+ *inf.*) *v.* to intend to; to plan to (*do something*) 4
  pensar en *v.* to think about 4
pensión *f.* boardinghouse
peor *adj.* worse 8
  el/la peor *adj.* the worst 8
pequeño/a *adj.* small 3
pera *f.* pear 8
perder (e:ie) *v.* to lose; to miss 4
perdido/a *adj.* lost 13, 14
Perdón. Pardon me.; Excuse me. 1
perezoso/a *adj.* lazy
perfecto/a *adj.* perfect 5
periódico *m.* newspaper 4
periodismo *m.* journalism 2
periodista *m., f.* journalist 3
permiso *m.* permission
pero *conj.* but 2
perro *m.* dog 13
persona *f.* person 3
personaje *m.* character
  personaje principal *m.* main character
pesas *f. pl.* weights 15
pesca *f.* fishing
pescadería *f.* fish market 14
pescado *m.* fish (*cooked*) 8
pescar *v.* to fish 5
peso *m.* weight 15
pez *m., sing.* (**peces** *pl.*) fish (*live*) 13
pie *m.* foot 10
piedra *f.* stone 13
pierna *f.* leg 10
pimienta *f.* black pepper 8
pintar *v.* to paint
pintor(a) *m., f.* painter
pintura *f.* painting; picture 12
piña *f.* pineapple
piscina *f.* swimming pool 4
piso *m.* floor (*of a building*) 5
pizarra *f.* blackboard 2
placer *m.* pleasure
planchar la ropa *v.* to iron the clothes 12
planes *m., pl.* plans
planta *f.* plant 13
  planta baja *f.* ground floor 5
plástico *m.* plastic 13
plato *m.* dish (*in a meal*) 8; *m.* plate 12
  plato principal *m.* main dish 8
playa *f.* beach 5
plaza *f.* city or town square 4
plazos *m., pl.* periods; time 14
pluma *f.* pen 2
plumero *m.* duster 12
población *f.* population 13
pobre *adj. m., f.* poor 6
pobrecito/a *adj.* poor thing 3
pobreza *f.* poverty
poco *adv.* little 5, 10
poder (o:ue) *v.* to be able to; can 4
  ¿Podría pedirte algo? Could I ask you something?
  ¿Puedo dejar un recado? May I leave a message? 11
poema *m.* poem
poesía *f.* poetry
poeta *m., f.* poet
policía *f.* police (force) 11
política *f.* politics
político/a *m., f.* politician; *adj.* political
pollo *m.* chicken 8
  pollo asado *m.* roast chicken 8
poner *v.* to put; to place 4; to turn on (*electrical appliances*) 11
  poner la mesa to set the table 12
  poner una inyección to give an injection 10
  ponerle el nombre to name someone/something 9
ponerse (+ *adj.*) *v.* to become (+ *adj.*) 7; to put on 7
por *prep.* in exchange for; for; by; in; through; around; along; during; because of; on account of; on behalf of; in search of; by way of; by means of 11
  por aquí around here 11
  por ejemplo for example 11
  por eso that's why; therefore 11
  por favor please 1
  por fin finally 11
  por la mañana in the morning 7
  por la noche at night 7
  por la tarde in the afternoon 7
  por lo menos *adv.* at least 10
  ¿por qué? why? 2
  Por supuesto. Of course.
  por teléfono by phone; on the phone
  por último finally 7
porque *conj.* because 2
portátil *adj.* portable 11
portero/a *m., f.* doorman/doorwoman 1
porvenir *m.* future
  por el porvenir for/to the future
posesivo/a *adj.* possessive
posible *adj.* possible 13
  es posible it's possible 13
  no es posible it's not possible 13
postal *f.* postcard
postre *m.* dessert 9
practicar *v.* to practice 2
  practicar deportes *m., pl.* to play sports 4
precio (fijo) *m.* (fixed; set) price 6
preferir (e:ie) *v.* to prefer 4
pregunta *f.* question
preguntar *v.* to ask (*a question*) 2
premio *m.* prize; award
prender *v.* to turn on 11
prensa *f.* press
preocupado/a (por) *adj.* worried (about) 5
preocuparse (por) *v.* to worry (about) 7
preparar *v.* to prepare 2
preposición *f.* preposition
presentación *f.* introduction
presentar *v.* to introduce; to present; to put on (*a performance*)
  Le presento a... I would like to introduce you to (name). (*form.*) 1
  Te presento a... I would like to introduce you to (name). (*fam.*) 1
presiones *f., pl.* pressures 15
prestado/a *adj.* borrowed
préstamo *m.* loan 14
prestar *v.* to lend; to loan 6
primavera *f.* spring 5
primer, primero/a *adj.* first 5
primero *adv.* first 2
primo/a *m., f.* cousin 3
principal *adj. m., f.* main 8
prisa *f.* haste
  darse prisa *v.* to hurry; to rush 15
probable *adj. m., f.* probable 13
  es probable it's probable 13
  no es probable it's not probable 13
probar (o:ue) *v.* to taste; to try 8
probarse (o:ue) *v.* to try on 7
problema *m.* problem 1
profesión *f.* profession 3
profesor(a) *m., f.* teacher 1, 2
programa *m.* program 1
  programa de computación *m.* software 11
  programa de entrevistas *m.* talk show
  programa de realidad *m.* reality show
programador(a) *m., f.* computer programmer 3
prohibir *v.* to prohibit 10; to forbid
pronombre *m.* pronoun
pronto *adv.* soon 10
propina *f.* tip 8
propio/a *adj.* own
proteger *v.* to protect 13
proteína *f.* protein 15
próximo/a *adj.* next 3
proyecto *m.* project 11
prueba *f.* test; quiz 2
psicología *f.* psychology 2
psicólogo/a *m., f.* psychologist
publicar *v.* to publish

público *m.* audience
pueblo *m.* town
puerta *f.* door 2
puertorriqueño/a *adj.* Puerto Rican 3
pues *conj.* well
puesto *m.* position; job
puesto/a *p.p.* put 14
puro/a *adj.* pure 13

Q

que *pron.* that; which; who 12
  ¿En qué...? In which...?
  ¡Qué...! How...!
  ¡Qué dolor! What pain!
  ¡Qué ropa más bonita! What pretty clothes! 6
  ¡Qué sorpresa! What a surprise!
  ¿qué? what? 1, 2
  ¿Qué día es hoy? What day is it? 2
  ¿Qué hay de nuevo? What's new? 1
  ¿Qué hora es? What time is it? 1
  ¿Qué les parece? What do you (*pl.*) think?
  ¿Qué onda? What's up? 14
  ¿Qué pasa? What's happening? What's going on? 1
  ¿Qué pasó? What happened?
  ¿Qué precio tiene? What is the price?
  ¿Qué tal...? How are you?; How is it going? 1
  ¿Qué talla lleva/usa? What size do you wear? 6
  ¿Qué tiempo hace? How's the weather? 5
quedar *v.* to be left over; to fit (*clothing*) 7; to be located 14
quedarse *v.* to stay; to remain 7
quehaceres domésticos *m., pl.* household chores 12
quemar (un CD/DVD) *v.* to burn (a CD/DVD)
querer (e:ie) *v.* to want; to love 4
queso *m.* cheese 8
quien(es) *pron.* who; whom; that 12
¿quién(es)? who?; whom? 1, 2
  ¿Quién es...? Who is...? 1
  ¿Quién habla? Who is speaking/calling? (*telephone*) 11
química *f.* chemistry 2
quince fifteen 1
  menos quince quarter to (time) 1
  y quince quarter after (time) 1
quinceañera *f.* young woman celebrating her fifteenth birthday 9
quinientos/as five hundred 2
quinto/a *adj.* fifth 5
quisiera *v.* I would like
quitar el polvo *v.* to dust 12
quitar la mesa *v.* to clear the table 12
quitarse *v.* to take off 7
quizás *adv.* maybe 5

R

racismo *m.* racism
radio *f.* radio (*medium*) 2; *m.* radio (set) 11
radiografía *f.* X-ray 10
rápido *adv.* quickly 10
ratón *m.* mouse 11
ratos libres *m., pl.* spare (free) time 4
raya *f.* stripe
razón *f.* reason
rebaja *f.* sale 6
receta *f.* prescription 10
recetar *v.* to prescribe 10
recibir *v.* to receive 3
reciclaje *m.* recycling 13
reciclar *v.* to recycle 13
recién casado/a *m., f.* newlywed 9
recoger *v.* to pick up 13
recomendar (e:ie) *v.* to recommend 8, 12
recordar (o:ue) *v.* to remember 4
recorrer *v.* to tour an area
recorrido *m.* tour 13
recuperar *v.* to recover 11
recurso *m.* resource 13
  recurso natural *m.* natural resource 13
red *f.* network; Web 11
reducir *v.* to reduce 13
refresco *m.* soft drink 8
refrigerador *m.* refrigerator 12
regalar *v.* to give (a gift) 9
regalo *m.* gift 6
regatear *v.* to bargain 6
región *f.* region; area
regresar *v.* to return 2
regular *adv.* so-so; OK 1
reído *p.p.* laughed 14
reírse (e:i) *v.* to laugh 9
relaciones *f., pl.* relationships
relajarse *v.* to relax 9
reloj *m.* clock; watch 2
renovable *adj.* renewable 13
renunciar (a) *v.* to resign (from)
repetir (e:i) *v.* to repeat 4
reportaje *m.* report
reportero/a *m., f.* reporter
representante *m., f.* representative
reproductor de CD *m.* CD player 11
reproductor de DVD *m.* DVD player 11
reproductor de MP3 *m.* MP3 player 11
resfriado *m.* cold (*illness*) 10
residencia estudiantil *f.* dormitory 2
resolver (o:ue) *v.* to resolve; to solve 13
respirar *v.* to breathe 13
responsable *adj.* responsible 8
respuesta *f.* answer
restaurante *m.* restaurant 4
resuelto/a *p.p.* resolved 14
reunión *f.* meeting
revisar *v.* to check 11
  revisar el aceite *v.* to check the oil 11
revista *f.* magazine 4
rico/a *adj.* rich 6; *adj.* tasty; delicious 8
ridículo/a *adj.* ridiculous 13
río *m.* river 13
rodilla *f.* knee 10
rogar (o:ue) *v.* to beg; to plead 12
rojo/a *adj.* red 6
romántico/a *adj.* romantic
romper *v.* to break 10
  romperse la pierna *v.* to break one's leg 10
romper (con) *v.* to break up (with) 9
ropa *f.* clothing; clothes 6
  ropa interior *f.* underwear 6
rosado/a *adj.* pink 6
roto/a *adj.* broken 14
rubio/a *adj.* blond(e) 3
ruso/a *adj.* Russian 3
rutina *f.* routine 7
  rutina diaria *f.* daily routine 7

S

sábado *m.* Saturday 2
saber *v.* to know; to know how 6
  saber a to taste like 8
sabrosísimo/a *adj.* extremely delicious 8
sabroso/a *adj.* tasty; delicious 8
sacar *v.* to take out
  sacar buenas notas to get good grades 2
  sacar fotos to take photos 5
  sacar la basura to take out the trash 12
  sacar(se) un diente to have a tooth removed 10
sacudir *v.* to dust 12
  sacudir los muebles to dust the furniture 12
sal *f.* salt 8
sala *f.* living room 12; room
  sala de emergencia(s) emergency room 10
salario *m.* salary
salchicha *f.* sausage 8
salida *f.* departure; exit 5
salir *v.* to leave 4; to go out
  salir con to go out with; to date 4, 9
  salir de to leave from 4
  salir para to leave for (*a place*) 4
salmón *m.* salmon 8

salón de belleza *m.* beauty salon 14
salud *f.* health 10
saludable *adj.* healthy 10
saludar(se) *v.* to greet (each other) 11
saludo *m.* greeting 1
saludos a... greetings to... 1
sandalia *f.* sandal 6
sandía *f.* watermelon
sándwich *m.* sandwich 8
sano/a *adj.* healthy 10
se *ref. pron.* himself, herself, itself, *form.* yourself, themselves, yourselves 7
se *impersonal* one 10
Se hizo... He/she/it became...
secadora *f.* clothes dryer 12
secarse *v.* to dry (oneself) 7
sección de (no) fumar *f.* (non) smoking section 8
secretario/a *m., f.* secretary
secuencia *f.* sequence
sed *f.* thirst
seda *f.* silk 6
sedentario/a *adj.* sedentary; related to sitting 15
seguir (e:i) *v.* to follow; to continue 4
según according to
segundo/a *adj.* second 5
seguro/a *adj.* sure; safe; confident 5
seis six 1
seiscientos/as six hundred 2
sello *m.* stamp 14
selva *f.* jungle 13
semáforo *m.* traffic light 14
semana *f.* week 2
fin *m.* **de semana** weekend 4
semana *f.* **pasada** last week 6
semestre *m.* semester 2
sendero *m.* trail; path 13
sentarse (e:ie) *v.* to sit down 7
sentir (e:ie) *v.* to be sorry; to regret 13
sentirse (e:ie) *v.* to feel 7
señor (Sr.); don *m.* Mr.; sir 1
señora (Sra.); doña *f.* Mrs.; ma'am 1
señorita (Srta.) *f.* Miss 1
separado/a *adj.* separated 9
separarse (de) *v.* to separate (from) 9
septiembre *m.* September 5
séptimo/a *adj.* seventh 5
ser *v.* to be 1
ser aficionado/a (a) to be a fan (of)
ser alérgico/a (a) to be allergic (to) 10
ser gratis to be free of charge 14
serio/a *adj.* serious
servicio *m.* service 15
servilleta *f.* napkin 12
servir (e:i) *v.* to serve 8; to help 5
sesenta sixty 2
setecientos/as seven hundred 2
setenta seventy 2
sexismo *m.* sexism
sexto/a *adj.* sixth 5
sí *adv.* yes 1
si *conj.* if 4
SIDA *m.* AIDS
siempre *adv.* always 7
siete seven 1
silla *f.* seat 2
sillón *m.* armchair 12
similar *adj. m., f.* similar
simpático/a *adj.* nice; likeable 3
sin *prep.* without 13
sin duda without a doubt
sin embargo however
sin que *conj.* without 13
sino but (rather) 7
síntoma *m.* symptom 10
sitio *m.* place 3
sitio *m.* **web** website 11
situado/a *p.p.* located
sobre *m.* envelope 14; *prep.* on; over 2
sobre todo above all 13
(sobre)población *f.* (over)population 13
sobrino/a *m., f.* nephew/niece 3
sociología *f.* sociology 2
sofá *m.* couch; sofa 12
sol *m.* sun 13
solar *adj. m., f.* solar 13
soldado *m., f.* soldier
soleado/a *adj.* sunny
solicitar *v.* to apply (*for a job*)
solicitud (de trabajo) *f.* (job) application
sólo *adv.* only 6
solo/a *adj.* alone
soltero/a *adj.* single 9
solución *f.* solution 13
sombrero *m.* hat 6
Son las dos. It's two o'clock. 1
sonar (o:ue) *v.* to ring 11
sonreído *p.p.* smiled 14
sonreír (e:i) *v.* to smile 9
sopa *f.* soup 8
sorprender *v.* to surprise 9
sorpresa *f.* surprise 9
sótano *m.* basement; cellar 12
soy I am 1
Soy de... I'm from... 1
su(s) *poss. adj.* his; her; its; *form.* your; their 3
subir(se) a *v.* to get on/into (*a vehicle*) 11
sucio/a *adj.* dirty 5
sudar *v.* to sweat 15
suegro/a *m., f.* father-in-law/ mother-in-law 3
sueldo *m.* salary
suelo *m.* floor 12
sueño *m.* sleep
suerte *f.* luck
suéter *m.* sweater 6
sufrir *v.* to suffer 10
sufrir muchas presiones to be under a lot of pressure 15
sufrir una enfermedad to suffer an illness 10
sugerir (e:ie) *v.* to suggest 12
supermercado *m.* supermarket 14
suponer *v.* to suppose 4
sur *m.* south 14
sustantivo *m.* noun
suyo(s)/a(s) *poss.* (of) his/her; (of) hers; its; *form.* your, (of) yours, (of) theirs, their 11

T

tabla de (wind)surf *f.* surf board/sailboard 5
tal vez *adv.* maybe 5
talentoso/a *adj.* talented
talla *f.* size 6
talla grande *f.* large
taller *m.* **mecánico** garage; mechanic's repair shop 11
también *adv.* also; too 2; 7
tampoco *adv.* neither; not either 7
tan *adv.* so 5
tan... como as... as 8
tan pronto como *conj.* as soon as 13
tanque *m.* tank 11
tanto *adv.* so much
tanto... como as much... as 8
tantos/as... como as many... as 8
tarde *adv.* late 7; *f.* afternoon; evening; P.M. 1
tarea *f.* homework 2
tarjeta *f.* (post) card
tarjeta de crédito *f.* credit card 6
tarjeta postal *f.* postcard
taxi *m.* taxi 5
taza *f.* cup 12
te *sing., fam., d.o. pron.* you 5; *sing., fam., i.o. pron.* to/for you 6
Te presento a... *fam.* I would like to introduce you to (name). 1
¿Te gustaría? Would you like to?
¿Te gusta(n)...? Do you like...? 2
té *m.* tea 8
té helado *m.* iced tea 8
teatro *m.* theater
teclado *m.* keyboard 11
técnico/a *m., f.* technician
tejido *m.* weaving
teleadicto/a *m., f.* couch potato 15
(teléfono) celular *m.* (cell) phone 11
telenovela *f.* soap opera
teletrabajo *m.* telecommuting
televisión *f.* television 2
televisión por cable *f.* cable television
televisor *m.* television set 11
temer *v.* to fear; to be afraid 13
temperatura *f.* temperature 10
temporada *f.* period of time 5
temprano *adv.* early 7

tenedor *m.* fork 12
tener *v.* to have 3
tener... años to be... years old 3
tener (mucho) calor to be (very) hot 3
tener (mucho) cuidado to be (very) careful 3
tener dolor to have pain 10
tener éxito to be successful
tener fiebre to have a fever 10
tener (mucho) frío to be (very) cold 3
tener ganas de (+ *inf.*) to feel like (*doing something*) 3
tener (mucha) hambre *f.* to be (very) hungry 3
tener (mucho) miedo (de) to be (very) afraid (of); to be (very) scared (of) 3
tener miedo (de) que to be afraid that
tener planes *m., pl.* to have plans
tener (mucha) prisa to be in a (big) hurry 3
tener que (+ *inf.*) *v.* to have to (*do something*) 3
tener razón *f.* to be right 3
tener (mucha) sed *f.* to be (very) thirsty 3
tener (mucho) sueño to be (very) sleepy 3
tener (mucha) suerte to be (very) lucky 3
tener tiempo to have time 14
tener una cita to have a date; to have an appointment 9
tenis *m.* tennis 4
tensión *f.* tension 15
tercer, tercero/a *adj.* third 5
terco/a *adj.* stubborn 10
terminar *v.* to end; to finish 2
terminar de (+ *inf.*) *v.* to finish (*doing something*)
terremoto *m.* earthquake
terrible *adj. m., f.* terrible 13
ti *obj. of prep., fam.* you 9
tiempo *m.* time 14; weather 5
tiempo libre free time
tienda *f.* store 6
tierra *f.* land; soil 13
tinto/a *adj.* red (wine) 8
tío/a *m., f.* uncle/aunt 3
tíos *m., pl.* aunts and uncles 3
título *m.* title
tiza *f.* chalk 2
toalla *f.* towel 7
tobillo *m.* ankle 10
tocar *v.* to play (*a musical instrument*); to touch
todavía *adv.* yet; still 3, 5
todo *m.* everything 5
todo(s)/a(s) *adj.* all
todos *m., pl.* all of us; *m., pl.* everybody; everyone
todos los días *adv.* every day 10
tomar *v.* to take; to drink 2
tomar clases *f., pl.* to take classes 2
tomar el sol to sunbathe 4
tomar en cuenta to take into account
tomar fotos *f., pl.* to take photos 5
tomar la temperatura to take someone's temperature 10
tomar una decisión to make a decision 15
tomate *m.* tomato 8
tonto/a *adj.* foolish 3
torcerse (o:ue) (el tobillo) *v.* to sprain (one's ankle) 10
tormenta *f.* storm
tornado *m.* tornado
tortuga (marina) *f.* (sea) turtle 13
tos *f., sing.* cough 10
toser *v.* to cough 10
tostado/a *adj.* toasted 8
tostadora *f.* toaster 12
trabajador(a) *adj.* hard-working 3
trabajar *v.* to work 2
trabajo *m.* job; work
traducir *v.* to translate 6
traer *v.* to bring 4
tráfico *m.* traffic 11
tragedia *f.* tragedy
traído/a *p.p.* brought 14
traje *m.* suit 6
traje de baño *m.* bathing suit 6
trajinera *f.* type of barge 3
tranquilo/a *adj.* calm; quiet 15
Tranquilo/a. Relax. 7
Tranquilo/a, cariño. Relax, sweetie. 11
transmitir *v.* to broadcast
tratar de (+ *inf.*) *v.* to try (*to do something*) 15
trece thirteen 1
treinta thirty 1, 2
y treinta thirty minutes past the hour (time) 1
tren *m.* train 5
tres three 1
trescientos/as three hundred 2
trimestre *m.* trimester; quarter 2
triste *adj.* sad 5
tú *fam. sub. pron.* you 1
tu(s) *fam. poss. adj.* your 3
turismo *m.* tourism
turista *m., f.* tourist 1
turístico/a *adj.* touristic
tuyo(s)/a(s) *fam. poss. pron.* your; (of) yours 11

U

Ud. *form. sing.* you 1
Uds. *pl.* you 1
último/a *adj.* last 7
la última vez the last time 7
un, uno/a *indef. art.* a; one 1
a la una at one o'clock 1
una vez once 6
una vez más one more time
uno one 1
único/a *adj.* only 3; unique 9
universidad *f.* university; college 2
unos/as *m., f., pl. indef. art.* some 1
urgente *adj.* urgent 12
usar *v.* to wear; to use 6
usted (Ud.) *form. sing.* you 1
ustedes (Uds.) *pl.* you 1
útil *adj.* useful
uva *f.* grape 8

V

vaca *f.* cow 13
vacaciones *f. pl.* vacation 5
valle *m.* valley 13
vamos let's go 4
vaquero *m.* cowboy
de vaqueros *m., pl.* western (genre)
varios/as *adj. m. f., pl.* various; several
vaso *m.* glass 12
veces *f., pl.* times 6
vecino/a *m., f.* neighbor 12
veinte twenty 1
veinticinco twenty-five 1
veinticuatro twenty-four 1
veintidós twenty-two 1
veintinueve twenty-nine 1
veintiocho twenty-eight 1
veintiséis twenty-six 1
veintisiete twenty-seven 1
veintitrés twenty-three 1
veintiún, veintiuno/a *adj.* twenty-one 1
veintiuno twenty-one 1
vejez *f.* old age 9
velocidad *f.* speed 11
velocidad máxima *f.* speed limit 11
vencer *v.* to expire 14
vendedor(a) *m., f.* salesperson 6
vender *v.* to sell 6
venir *v.* to come 3
ventana *f.* window 2
ver *v.* to see 4
a ver *v.* let's see
ver películas *f., pl.* to see movies 4
verano *m.* summer 5
verbo *m.* verb
verdad *f.* truth 4
(no) es verdad it's (not) true 13
¿verdad? right? 1
verde *adj., m. f.* green 6
verduras *pl., f.* vegetables 8
vestido *m.* dress 6
vestirse (e:i) *v.* to get dressed 7
vez *f.* time 6
viajar *v.* to travel 2
viaje *m.* trip 5
viajero/a *m., f.* traveler 5

vida *f.* life 9
video *m.* video 1
videoconferencia *f.* videoconference
videojuego *m.* video game 4
vidrio *m.* glass 13
viejo/a *adj.* old 3
viento *m.* wind
viernes *m., sing.* Friday 2
vinagre *m.* vinegar 8
vino *m.* wine 8
  vino blanco *m.* white wine 8
  vino tinto *m.* red wine 8
violencia *f.* violence
visitar *v.* to visit 4
  visitar monumentos *m., pl.* to visit monuments 4
visto/a *p.p.* seen 14
vitamina *f.* vitamin 15
viudo/a *adj.* widower/widow 9
vivienda *f.* housing 12
vivir *v.* to live 3
vivo/a *adj.* clever; living
volante *m.* steering wheel 11
volcán *m.* volcano 13
vóleibol *m.* volleyball 4
volver (o:ue) *v.* to return 4
volver a ver(te, lo, la) *v.* to see (you, him, her) again
vos *pron.* you
vosotros/as *fam., pl.* you 1
votar *v.* to vote
vuelta *f.* return trip
vuelto/a *p.p.* returned 14
vuestro(s)/a(s) *poss. adj.* your 3; your, (of) yours *fam., pl.* 11

Y

y *conj.* and 1
  y cuarto quarter after (time) 1
  y media half-past (time) 1
  y quince quarter after (time) 1
  y treinta thirty (minutes past the hour) 1
  ¿Y tú? *fam.* And you? 1
  ¿Y usted? *form.* And you? 1
ya *adv.* already 6
yerno *m.* son-in-law 3
yo *sub. pron.* I 1
yogur *m.* yogurt 8

Z

zanahoria *f.* carrot 8
zapatería *f.* shoe store 14
zapatos de tenis *m., pl.* tennis shoes, sneakers 6

English-Spanish

A

a **un/a** *m., f., sing.; indef. art.* 1
@ (*symbol*) **arroba** *f.* 11
a.m. **de la mañana** *f.* 1
able: be able to **poder (o:ue)** *v.* 4
aboard **a bordo**
above all **sobre todo** 13
accident **accidente** *m.* 10
accompany **acompañar** *v.* 14
account **cuenta** *f.* 14
  on account of **por** *prep.* 11
accountant **contador(a)** *m., f.*
accounting **contabilidad** *f.* 2
ache **dolor** *m.* 10
acquainted: be acquainted with **conocer** *v.* 6
action (genre) **de acción** *f.*
active **activo/a** *adj.* 15
actor **actor** *m.*, **actriz** *f.*
addict (*drug*) **drogadicto/a** *m., f.* 15
additional **adicional** *adj.*
address **dirección** *f.* 14
adjective **adjetivo** *m.*
adolescence **adolescencia** *f.* 9
adventure (genre) **de aventuras** *f.*
advertise **anunciar** *v.*
advertisement **anuncio** *m.*
advice **consejo** *m.*
  give advice **dar consejos** 6
advise **aconsejar** *v.* 12
advisor **consejero/a** *m., f.*
aerobic **aeróbico/a** *adj.* 15
  aerobics class **clase de ejercicios aeróbicos** 15
  to do aerobics **hacer ejercicios aeróbicos** 15
affected **afectado/a** *adj.* 13
  be affected (by) **estar** *v.* **afectado/a (por)** 13
affirmative **afirmativo/a** *adj.*
afraid: be (very) afraid (of) **tener (mucho) miedo (de)** 3
  be afraid that **tener miedo (de) que**
after **después de** *prep.* 7; **después de que** *conj.* 13
afternoon **tarde** *f.* 1
afterward **después** *adv.* 7
again **otra vez**
age **edad** *f.* 9
agree **concordar** *v.*
agree **estar** *v.* **de acuerdo**
  I agree. **Estoy de acuerdo.**
  I don't agree. **No estoy de acuerdo.**
agreement **acuerdo** *m.*
AIDS **SIDA** *m.*
air **aire** *m.* 13
  air pollution **contaminación del aire** 13
airplane **avión** *m.* 5
airport **aeropuerto** *m.* 5
alarm clock **despertador** *m.* 7
alcohol **alcohol** *m.* 15
  to consume alcohol **consumir alcohol** 15
alcoholic **alcohólico/a** *adj.* 15
all **todo(s)/a(s)** *adj.*
  all of us **todos**
allergic **alérgico/a** *adj.* 10
  be allergic (to) **ser alérgico/a (a)** 10
alleviate **aliviar** *v.*
almost **casi** *adv.* 10
alone **solo/a** *adj.*
along **por** *prep.* 11
already **ya** *adv.* 6
also **también** *adv.* 2; 7
altar **altar** *m.* 9
aluminum **aluminio** *m.* 13
  (made) of aluminum **de aluminio** 13
always **siempre** *adv.* 7
American (*North*) **norteamericano/a** *adj.* 3
among **entre** *prep.* 2
amusement **diversión** *f.*
and **y** 1, **e** (*before words beginning with i or hi*)
  And you? **¿Y tú?** *fam.* 1; **¿Y usted?** *form.* 1
angel **ángel** *m.* 9
angry **enojado/a** *adj.* 5
  get angry (with) **enojarse** *v.* **(con)** 7
animal **animal** *m.* 13
ankle **tobillo** *m.* 10
anniversary **aniversario** *m.* 9
  (wedding) anniversary **aniversario** *m.* **(de bodas)** 9
announce **anunciar** *v.*
announcer (*TV/radio*) **locutor(a)** *m., f.*
annoy **molestar** *v.* 7
another **otro/a** *adj.* 6
answer **contestar** *v.* 2; **respuesta** *f.*
answering machine **contestadora** *f.*
antibiotic **antibiótico** *m.* 10
any **algún, alguno/a(s)** *adj.* 7
anyone **alguien** *pron.* 7
anything **algo** *pron.* 7
apartment **apartamento** *m.* 12
apartment building **edificio de apartamentos** 12
app **aplicación** *f.* 11
appear **parecer** *v.*
appetizers **entremeses** *m., pl.* 8
applaud **aplaudir** *v.*
apple **manzana** *f.* 8
appliance (electric) **electrodoméstico** *m.* 12
applicant **aspirante** *m., f.*
application **solicitud** *f.*
  job application **solicitud de trabajo**
apply (*for a job*) **solicitar** *v.*
  apply for a loan **pedir (e:i)** *v.* **un préstamo** 14
appointment **cita** *f.* 9
  have an appointment **tener** *v.* **una cita** 9
appreciate **apreciar** *v.*
April **abril** *m.* 5
archeologist **arqueólogo/a** *m., f.*
archeology **arqueología** *f.* 2
architect **arquitecto/a** *m., f.*
area **región** *f.*
Argentine **argentino/a** *adj.* 3
arm **brazo** *m.* 10
armchair **sillón** *m.* 12
army **ejército** *m.*
around **por** *prep.* 11
  around here **por aquí** 11
arrange **arreglar** *v.* 11
arrival **llegada** *f.* 5
arrive **llegar** *v.* 2
art **arte** *m.* 2
  (fine) arts **bellas artes** *f., pl.*
article **artículo** *m.*
artist **artista** *m., f.* 3
artistic **artístico/a** *adj.*
arts **artes** *f., pl.*
as **como** 8
  as a child **de niño/a** 10
  as... as **tan... como** 8
  as many... as **tantos/as... como** 8
  as much... as **tanto... como** 8
  as soon as **en cuanto** *conj.* 13; **tan pronto como** *conj.* 13
ask (*a question*) **preguntar** *v.* 2
  ask for **pedir (e:i)** *v.* 4
asparagus **espárragos** *m., pl.* 8
aspirin **aspirina** *f.* 10
at **a** *prep.* 1; **en** *prep.* 2
  at + *time* **a la(s)** + *time* 1
  at home **en casa**
  at least **por lo menos** 10
  at night **por la noche** 7
  At what time...? **¿A qué hora...?** 1
  At your service. **A sus órdenes.**
ATM **cajero automático** *m.* 14
attempt **intento** *m.* **11**
attend **asistir (a)** *v.* 3
attic **altillo** *m.* 12
audience **público** *m.*
August **agosto** *m.* 5
aunt **tía** *f.* 3
  aunts and uncles **tíos** *m., pl.* 3
automobile **automóvil** *m.* 5; **carro** *m.*; **coche** *m.* 11
autumn **otoño** *m.* 5
avenue **avenida** *f.*
avoid **evitar** *v.* 13
award **premio** *m.*

B

backpack **mochila** *f.* 2
bad **mal, malo/a** *adj.* 3
  It's bad that... **Es malo que...** 12
  It's not bad at all. **No está nada mal.** 5
bag **bolsa** *f.* 6
bakery **panadería** *f.* 14

balanced **equilibrado/a** *adj.* 15
to eat a balanced diet **comer una dieta equilibrada** 15
balcony **balcón** *m.* 12
ball **pelota** *f.* 4
banana **banana** *f.* 8
band **banda** *f.*
bank **banco** *m.* 14
bargain **ganga** *f.* 6; **regatear** *v.* 6
baseball (*game*) **béisbol** *m.* 4
basement **sótano** *m.* 12
basketball (*game*) **baloncesto** *m.* 4
bathe **bañarse** *v.* 7
bathing suit **traje** *m.* **de baño** 6
bathroom **baño** *m.* 7; **cuarto de baño** *m.* 7
be **ser** *v.* 1; **estar** *v.* 2
be... years old **tener... años** 3
be sick of... **estar harto/a de...**
beach **playa** *f.* 5
beans **frijoles** *m., pl.* 8
beautiful **hermoso/a** *adj.* 6
beauty **belleza** *f.* 14
beauty salon **peluquería** *f.* 14; **salón** *m.* **de belleza** 14
because **porque** *conj.* 2
because of **por** *prep.* 11
become (+ *adj.*) **ponerse (+** ***adj.*****)** 7; **convertirse** *v.*
bed **cama** *f.* 5
go to bed **acostarse (o:ue)** *v.* 7
bedroom **alcoba** *f.*, **recámara** *f.*; **dormitorio** *m.* 12
beef **carne de res** *f.* 8
beer **cerveza** *f.* 8
before **antes** *adv.* 7; **antes de** *prep.* 7; **antes (de) que** *conj.* 13
beg **rogar (o:ue)** *v.* 12
begin **comenzar (e:ie)** *v.* 4; **empezar (e:ie)** *v.* 4
behalf: on behalf of **de parte de** 11
behind **detrás de** *prep.* 2
believe (in) **creer** *v.* **(en)** 3; **creer** *v.* 13
not to believe **no creer** 13
believed **creído/a** *p.p.* 14
bellhop **botones** *m., f. sing.* 5
below **debajo de** *prep.* 2
belt **cinturón** *m.* 6
benefit **beneficio** *m.*
beside **al lado de** *prep.* 2
besides **además (de)** *adv.* 10
best **mejor** *adj.*
the best **el/la mejor** *m., f.* 8 **lo mejor** *neuter*
better **mejor** *adj.* 8
It's better that... **Es mejor que...** 12
between **entre** *prep.* 2
beverage **bebida** *f.* 8
alcoholic beverage **bebida alcohólica** *f.* 15
bicycle **bicicleta** *f.* 4
big **grande** *adj.* 3
bill **cuenta** *f.* 8
billion **mil millones**
biology **biología** *f.* 2
bird **ave** *f.* 13; **pájaro** *m.* 13
birth **nacimiento** *m.* 9
birthday **cumpleaños** *m., sing.* 9
have a birthday **cumplir** *v.* **años**
black **negro/a** *adj.* 6
blackboard **pizarra** *f.* 2
blanket **manta** *f.* 12
block (city) **cuadra** *f.* 14
blog **blog** *m.* 11
blond(e) **rubio/a** *adj.* 3
blouse **blusa** *f.* 6
blue **azul** *adj. m., f.* 6
boarding house **pensión** *f.*
boat **barco** *m.* 5
body **cuerpo** *m.* 10
bone **hueso** *m.* 10
book **libro** *m.* 2
bookcase **estante** *m.* 12
bookshelves **estante** *m.* 12
bookstore **librería** *f.* 2
boot **bota** *f.* 6
bore **aburrir** *v.* 7
bored **aburrido/a** *adj.* 5
be bored **estar** *v.* **aburrido/a** 5
get bored **aburrirse** *v.*
boring **aburrido/a** *adj.* 5
born: be born **nacer** *v.* 9
borrow **pedir (e:i)** *v.* **prestado** 14
borrowed **prestado/a** *adj.*
boss **jefe** *m.*, **jefa** *f.*
bother **molestar** *v.* 7
bottle **botella** *f.* 9
bottle of wine **botella de vino** 9
bottom **fondo** *m.*
boulevard **bulevar** *m.*
boy **chico** *m.* 1; **muchacho** *m.* 3
boyfriend **novio** *m.* 3
brakes **frenos** *m., pl.*
bread **pan** *m.* 8
break **romper** *v.* 10
break (one's leg) **romperse (la pierna)** 10
break down **dañar** *v.* 10
break up (with) **romper** *v.* **(con)** 9
breakfast **desayuno** *m.* 8
have breakfast **desayunar** *v.* 2
breathe **respirar** *v.* 13
bring **traer** *v.* 4
broadcast **transmitir** *v.*; **emitir** *v.*
brochure **folleto** *m.*
broken **roto/a** *adj.* 14
be broken **estar roto/a**
brother **hermano** *m.* 3
brother-in-law **cuñado** *m.* 3
brothers and sisters **hermanos** *m., pl.* 3
brought **traído/a** *p.p.* 14
brown **café** *adj.* 6; **marrón** *adj.* 6
browser **buscador** *m.* 11
brunet(te) **moreno/a** *adj.* 3
brush **cepillar(se)** *v.* 7
brush one's hair **cepillarse el pelo** 7
brush one's teeth **cepillarse los dientes** 7
bucket **balde** *m.* 5
build **construir** *v.*
building **edificio** *m.* 12
bump into (*something accidentally*) **darse con** 10; (*someone*) **encontrarse** *v.* 11
burn (a CD/DVD) **quemar** *v.* **(un CD/DVD)**
bus **autobús** *m.* 1
bus station **estación** *f.* **de autobuses** 5
business **negocios** *m. pl.*
business administration **administración** *f.* **de empresas** 2
business-related **comercial** *adj.*
businessperson **hombre** *m.* **/ mujer** *f.* **de negocios**
busy **ocupado/a** *adj.* 5
but **pero** *conj.* 2; (rather) **sino** *conj.* (*in negative sentences*) 7
butcher shop **carnicería** *f.* 14
butter **mantequilla** *f.* 8
buy **comprar** *v.* 2
by **por** *prep.* 11; **para** *prep.* 11
by means of **por** *prep.* 11
by phone **por teléfono**
by plane **en avión** 5
by way of **por** *prep.* 11
bye **chau** *interj. fam.* 1

C

cable television **televisión** *f.* **por cable** *m.*
café **café** *m.* 4
cafeteria **cafetería** *f.* 2
caffeine **cafeína** *f.* 15
cake **pastel** *m.* 9
chocolate cake **pastel de chocolate** *m.* 9
calculator **calculadora** *f.* 2
call **llamar** *v.* 11
be called **llamarse** *v.* 7
call on the phone **llamar por teléfono**
calm **tranquilo/a** *adj.* 15
calorie **caloría** *f.* 15
camera **cámara** *f.* 11
camp **acampar** *v.* 5
can (*tin*) **lata** *f.* 13
can **poder (o:ue)** *v.* 4
Could I ask you something? **¿Podría pedirte algo?**
Canadian **canadiense** *adj.* 3

candidate **aspirante** *m., f.*; **candidato/a** *m., f.*
candy **dulces** *m., pl.* 9
capital city **capital** *f.*
car **coche** *m.* 11; **carro** *m.* 11; **auto(móvil)** *m.* 5
caramel **caramelo** *m.* 9
card **tarjeta** *f.*; (*playing*) **carta** *f.* 5
care **cuidado** *m.*
  take care of **cuidar** *v.* 13
career **carrera** *f.*
careful: be (very) careful **tener** *v.* **(mucho) cuidado** 3
caretaker **ama** *m., f.* **de casa** 12
carpenter **carpintero/a** *m., f.*
carpet **alfombra** *f.* 12
carrot **zanahoria** *f.* 8
carry **llevar** *v.* 2
cartoons **dibujos** *m, pl.* **animados**
case: in case (that) **en caso (de) que** 13
cash (a check) **cobrar** *v.* 14;
  cash **(en) efectivo** 6
  cash register **caja** *f.* 6
  pay in cash **pagar** *v.* **al contado** 14; **pagar en efectivo** 14
cashier **cajero/a** *m., f.*
cat **gato** *m.* 13
CD **disco compacto** *m.* 11
CD player **reproductor de CD** *m.* 11
CD-ROM **cederrón** *m.*
celebrate **celebrar** *v.* 9
celebration **celebración** *f.*
cellar **sótano** *m.* 12
(cell) phone **(teléfono) celular** *m.* 11
cemetery **cementerio** *m.* 9
cereal **cereales** *m., pl.* 8
certain **cierto/a** *adj.*; **seguro/a** *adj.* 13
  it's (not) certain **(no) es cierto/seguro** 13
chalk **tiza** *f.* 2
champagne **champán** *m.* 9
change **cambiar** *v.* **(de)** 9
change: in change **de cambio** 2
channel (*TV*) **canal** *m.* 11
character (*fictional*) **personaje** *m.*
  (main) character *m.* **personaje (principal)**
charger **cargador** *m.* 11
chat **conversar** *v.* 2; **chatear** *v.* 11
cheap **barato/a** *adj.* 6
check **comprobar (o:ue)** *v.*; **revisar** *v.* 11; (*bank*) **cheque** *m.* 14
  check the oil **revisar el aceite** 11
checking account **cuenta** *f.* **corriente** 14
cheese **queso** *m.* 8
chef **cocinero/a** *m., f.*
chemistry **química** *f.* 2
chest of drawers **cómoda** *f.* 12
chicken **pollo** *m.* 8
child **niño/a** *m., f.* 3
childhood **niñez** *f.* 9
children **hijos** *m., pl.* 3
Chinese **chino/a** *adj.* 3
chocolate **chocolate** *m.* 9
  chocolate cake **pastel** *m.* **de chocolate** 9
cholesterol **colesterol** *m.* 15
choose **escoger** *v.* 8
chop (*food*) **chuleta** *f.* 8
Christmas **Navidad** *f.* 9
church **iglesia** *f.* 4
cinnamon **canela** *f.* 10
citizen **ciudadano/a** *m., f.*
city **ciudad** *f.*
class **clase** *f.* 2
  take classes **tomar clases** 2
classical **clásico/a** *adj.*
classmate **compañero/a** *m., f.* **de clase** 2
clean **limpio/a** *adj.* 5; **limpiar** *v.* 12
  clean the house *v.* **limpiar la casa** 12
clear (*weather*) **despejado/a** *adj.*
  clear the table **quitar la mesa** 12
  It's (very) clear. (*weather*) **Está (muy) despejado.**
clerk **dependiente/a** *m., f.* 6
climate change **cambio climático** *m.* 13
climb **escalar** *v.* 4
  climb mountains **escalar montañas** 4
clinic **clínica** *f.* 10
clock **reloj** *m.* 2
close **cerrar (e:ie)** *v.* 4
closed **cerrado/a** *adj.* 5
closet **armario** *m.* 12
clothes **ropa** *f.* 6
  clothes dryer **secadora** *f.* 12
clothing **ropa** *f.* 6
cloud **nube** *f.* 13
cloudy **nublado/a** *adj.* 5
  It's (very) cloudy. **Está (muy) nublado.** 5
coat **abrigo** *m.* 6
coffee **café** *m.* 8
  coffee maker **cafetera** *f.* 12
cold **frío** *m.* 5;
  (*illness*) **resfriado** *m.* 10
  be (*feel*) (very) cold **tener (mucho) frío** 3
  It's (very) cold. (*weather*) **Hace (mucho) frío.** 5
college **universidad** *f.* 2
collision **choque** *m.*
color **color** *m.* 6
comb one's hair **peinarse** *v.* 7
come **venir** *v.* 3
come on **ándale** *interj.* 14
comedy **comedia** *f.*
comfortable **cómodo/a** *adj.* 5
commerce **negocios** *m., pl.*
commercial **comercial** *adj.*
communicate (with) **comunicarse** *v.* **(con)**
communication **comunicación** *f.*
  means of communication **medios** *m. pl.* **de comunicación**
community **comunidad** *f.* 1
company **compañía** *f.*; **empresa** *f.*
comparison **comparación** *f.*
composer **compositor(a)** *m., f.*
computer **computadora** *f.* 1
  computer disc **disco** *m.*
  computer monitor **monitor** *m.* 11
  computer programmer **programador(a)** *m., f.* 3
  computer science **computación** *f.* 2
concert **concierto** *m.*
conductor (*musical*) **director(a)** *m., f.*
confident **seguro/a** *adj.* 5
confirm **confirmar** *v.* 5
  confirm a reservation **confirmar una reservación** 5
confused **confundido/a** *adj.* 5
congested **congestionado/a** *adj.* 10
Congratulations! **¡Felicidades!**; **¡Felicitaciones!** *f., pl.* 9
conservation **conservación** *f.* 13
conserve **conservar** *v.* 13
considering **para** *prep.* 11
consume **consumir** *v.* 15
container **envase** *m.* 13
contamination **contaminación** *f.*
content **contento/a** *adj.* 5
contest **concurso** *m.*
continue **seguir (e:i)** *v.* 4
control **control** *m.*; **controlar** *v.* 13
conversation **conversación** *f.* 1
converse **conversar** *v.* 2
cook **cocinar** *v.* 12; **cocinero/a** *m., f.*
cookie **galleta** *f.* 9
cool **fresco/a** *adj.* 5
  It's cool. (*weather*) **Hace fresco.** 5
corn **maíz** *m.* 8
corner **esquina** *f.* 14
cost **costar (o:ue)** *v.* 6
Costa Rican **costarricense** *adj.* 3
costume **disfraz** *m.* 9
cotton **algodón** *f.* 6
  (made of) cotton **de algodón** 6
couch **sofá** *m.* 12
couch potato **teleadicto/a** *m., f.* 15
cough **tos** *f.* 10; **toser** *v.* 10
counselor **consejero/a** *m., f.*
count **contar (o:ue)** *v.* 4
country (*nation*) **país** *m.* 1
countryside **campo** *m.* 5
(married) couple **pareja** *f.* 9
course **curso** *m.* 2; **materia** *f.* 2
courtesy **cortesía** *f.*
cousin **primo/a** *m., f.* 3

cover **cubrir** *v.*
covered **cubierto/a** *p.p.*
cow **vaca** *f.* 13
crafts **artesanía** *f.*
craftsmanship **artesanía** *f.*
crater **cráter** *m.* 13
crazy **loco/a** *adj.* 6
create **crear** *v.*
credit **crédito** *m.* 6
  credit card **tarjeta** *f.* **de crédito** 6
crime **crimen** *m.*
cross **cruzar** *v.* 14
cry **llorar** *v.* 15
Cuban **cubano/a** *adj.* 3
culture **cultura** *f.* 2
cup **taza** *f.* 12
currency exchange **cambio** *m.* **de moneda**
current events **actualidades** *f., pl.*
curtains **cortinas** *f., pl.* 12
custard (*baked*) **flan** *m.* 9
custom **costumbre** *f.*
customer **cliente/a** *m., f.* 6
customs **aduana** *f.*
  customs inspector **inspector(a)** *m., f.* **de aduanas** 5
cybercafé **cibercafé** *m.* 11
cycling **ciclismo** *m.* 4

D

dad **papá** *m.*
daily **diario/a** *adj.* 7
  daily routine **rutina** *f.* **diaria** 7
damage **dañar** *v.* 10
dance **bailar** *v.* 2; **danza** *f.*; **baile** *m.*
dancer **bailarín/bailarina** *m., f.*
danger **peligro** *m.* 13
dangerous **peligroso/a** *adj.*
date (*appointment*) **cita** *f.* 9; (*calendar*) **fecha** *f.* 5; (*someone*) **salir** *v.* **con (alguien)** 9
  have a date **tener una cita** 9
daughter **hija** *f.* 3
daughter-in-law **nuera** *f.* 3
day **día** *m.* 1
  day before yesterday **anteayer** *adv.* 6
death **muerte** *f.* 9
decaffeinated **descafeinado/a** *adj.* 15
December **diciembre** *m.* 5
decide **decidir** *v.* **(+ *inf.*)** 3
declare **declarar** *v.*
deforestation **deforestación** *f.* 13
delicious **delicioso/a** *adj.* 8; **rico/a** *adj.* 8; **sabroso/a** *adj.* 8
delighted **encantado/a** *adj.* 1
dentist **dentista** *m., f.* 10
deny **negar (e:ie)** *v.* 13
  not to deny **no negar** 13
department store **almacén** *m.* 6
departure **salida** *f.* 5
deposit **depositar** *v.* 14
describe **describir** *v.* 3
described **descrito/a** *p.p.* 14
desert **desierto** *m.* 13
design **diseño** *m.*
designer **diseñador(a)** *m., f.*
desire **desear** *v.* 2
desk **escritorio** *m.* 2
dessert **postre** *m.* 9
destroy **destruir** *v.* 13
develop **desarrollar** *v.* 13
diary **diario** *m.* 1
dictatorship **dictadura** *f.*
dictionary **diccionario** *m.* 1
die **morir (o:ue)** *v.* 8
died **muerto/a** *p.p.* 14
diet **dieta** *f.* 15; **alimentación**
  balanced diet **dieta equilibrada** 15
  be on a diet **estar a dieta** 15
difficult **difícil** *adj. m., f.* 3
digital camera **cámara** *f.* **digital** 11
dining room **comedor** *m.* 12
dinner **cena** *f.* 8
  have dinner **cenar** *v.* 2
direct **dirigir** *v.*
director **director(a)** *m., f.*
dirty **ensuciar** *v.*; **sucio/a** *adj.* 5
  get (something) dirty **ensuciar** *v.* 12
disagree **no estar de acuerdo**
disaster **desastre** *m.*
discover **descubrir** *v.* 13
discovered **descubierto/a** *p.p.* 14
discrimination **discriminación** *f.*
dish **plato** *m.* 8, 12
  main dish *m.* **plato principal** 8
dishwasher **lavaplatos** *m., sing.* 12
disk **disco** *m.*
disorderly **desordenado/a** *adj.* 5
divorce **divorcio** *m.* 9
divorced **divorciado/a** *adj.* 9
  get divorced (from) **divorciarse** *v.* **(de)** 9
dizzy **mareado/a** *adj.* 10
do **hacer** *v.* 4
  do aerobics **hacer ejercicios aeróbicos** 15
  do household chores **hacer quehaceres domésticos** 12
  do stretching exercises **hacer ejercicios de estiramiento** 15
  (I) don't want to. **No quiero.** 4
doctor **doctor(a)** *m., f.* 3; 10; **médico/a** *m., f.* 3
documentary (*film*) **documental** *m.*
dog **perro** *m.* 13
domestic **doméstico/a** *adj.*
  domestic appliance **electrodoméstico** *m.*
done **hecho/a** *p.p.* 14
door **puerta** *f.* 2
doorman/doorwoman **portero/a** *m., f.* 1
dormitory **residencia** *f.* **estudiantil** 2
double **doble** *adj.* 5
  double room **habitación** *f.* **doble** 5
doubt **duda** *f.* 13; **dudar** *v.* 13
  not to doubt **no dudar** 13
  there is no doubt that **no cabe duda de** 13; **no hay duda de** 13
download **descargar** *v.* 11
downtown **centro** *m.* 4
drama **drama** *m.*
dramatic **dramático/a** *adj.*
draw **dibujar** *v.* 2
drawing **dibujo** *m.*
dress **vestido** *m.* 6
  get dressed **vestirse (e:i)** *v.* 7
drink **beber** *v.* 3; **bebida** *f.* 8; **tomar** *v.* 2
drive **conducir** *v.* 6; **manejar** *v.* 11
driver **conductor(a)** *m., f.* 1
drug **droga** *f.* 15
  drug addict **drogadicto/a** *m., f.* 15
dry (oneself) **secarse** *v.* 7
during **durante** *prep.* 7; **por** *prep.* 11
dust **sacudir** *v.* 12; **quitar** *v.* **el polvo** 12
dust the furniture **sacudir los muebles** 12
duster **plumero** *m.* 12
DVD player **reproductor** *m.* **de DVD** 11

E

each **cada** *adj.* 6
ear (outer) **oreja** *f.* 10
early **temprano** *adv.* 7
earn **ganar** *v.*
earring **arete** *m.* 6
earthquake **terremoto** *m.*
ease **aliviar** *v.*
east **este** *m.* 14
  to the east **al este** 14
easy **fácil** *adj. m., f.* 3
eat **comer** *v.* 3
ecological **ecológico/a** *adj.* 13
ecologist **ecologista** *m., f.* 13
ecology **ecología** *f.* 13
economics **economía** *f.* 2
ecotourism **ecoturismo** *m.* 13
Ecuadorian **ecuatoriano/a** *adj.* 3
effective **eficaz** *adj. m., f.*
egg **huevo** *m.* 8
eight **ocho** 1
eight hundred **ochocientos/as** 2
eighteen **dieciocho** 1
eighth **octavo/a** 5
eighty **ochenta** 2
either... or **o... o** *conj.* 7
elect **elegir (e:i)** *v.*
election **elecciones** *f. pl.*

electric appliance **electrodoméstico** *m.* 12
electrician **electricista** *m., f.*
electricity **luz** *f.* 12
elegant **elegante** *adj. m., f.* 6
elevator **ascensor** *m.* 5
eleven **once** 1
e-mail **correo** *m.* **electrónico** 4
e-mail address **dirección** *f.* **electrónica** 11
e-mail message **mensaje** *m.* **electrónico** 4
read e-mail **leer** *v.* **el correo electrónico** 4
embarrassed **avergonzado/a** *adj.* 5
embrace (each other) **abrazar(se)** *v.* 11
emergency **emergencia** *f.* 10
emergency room **sala** *f.* **de emergencia(s)** 10
employee **empleado/a** *m., f.* 5
employment **empleo** *m.*
end **fin** *m.* 4; **terminar** *v.* 2
end table **mesita** *f.* 12
endure **aguantar** *v.* 14
energy **energía** *f.* 13
engaged: get engaged (to) **comprometerse** *v.* **(con)** 9
engineer **ingeniero/a** *m., f.* 3
English (*language*) **inglés** *m.* 2; **inglés, inglesa** *adj.* 3
enjoy **disfrutar** *v.* **(de)** 15
enough **bastante** *adv.* 10
entertainment **diversión** *f.* 4
entrance **entrada** *f.* 12
envelope **sobre** *m.* 14
environment **medio ambiente** *m.* 13
environmental science **ciencias ambientales** 2
equality **igualdad** *f.*
erase **borrar** *v.* 11
eraser **borrador** *m.* 2
errand **diligencia** *f.* 14
essay **ensayo** *m.* 3
establish **establecer** *v.*
evening **tarde** *f.* 1
event **acontecimiento** *m.*
every day **todos los días** 10
everything **todo** *m.* 5
exactly **en punto** 1
exam **examen** *m.* 2
excellent **excelente** *adj.* 5
excess **exceso** *m.* 15
in excess **en exceso** 15
exchange **intercambiar** *v.*
in exchange for **por** 11
exciting **emocionante** *adj. m., f.*
excursion **excursión** *f.*
excuse **disculpar** *v.*
Excuse me. (*May I?*) **Con permiso.** 1; (*I beg your pardon.*) **Perdón.** 1
exercise **ejercicio** *m.* 15; **hacer** *v.* **ejercicio** 15; (a degree/profession) **ejercer** *v.*
exit **salida** *f.* 5
expensive **caro/a** *adj.* 6
experience **experiencia** *f.*
expire **vencer** *v.* 14
explain **explicar** *v.* 2
explore **explorar** *v.*
expression **expresión** *f.*
extinction **extinción** *f.* 13
eye **ojo** *m.* 10

F

fabulous **fabuloso/a** *adj.* 5
face **cara** *f.* 7
facing **enfrente de** *prep.* 14
fact: in fact **de hecho**
factory **fábrica** *f.* 13
fall (down) **caerse** *v.* 10
fall asleep **dormirse (o:ue)** *v.* 7
fall in love (with) **enamorarse** *v.* **(de)** 9
fall (season) **otoño** *m.* 5
fallen **caído/a** *p.p.* 14
family **familia** *f.* 3
famous **famoso/a** *adj.*
fan **aficionado/a** *m., f.* 4
be a fan (of) **ser aficionado/a (a)**
far from **lejos de** *prep.* 2
farewell **despedida** *f.*
fascinate **fascinar** *v.* 7
fashion **moda** *f.* 6
be in fashion **estar de moda** 6
fast **rápido/a** *adj.*
fat **gordo/a** *adj.* 3; **grasa** *f.* 15
father **padre** *m.* 3
father-in-law **suegro** *m.* 3
favorite **favorito/a** *adj.* 4
fax (machine) ***fax*** *m.*
fear **miedo** *m.*; **temer** *v.* 13
February **febrero** *m.* 5
feel **sentir(se) (e:ie)** *v.* 7
feel like (*doing something*) **tener ganas de (+ *inf.*)** 3
festival **festival** *m.*
fever **fiebre** *f.* 10
have a fever **tener** *v.* **fiebre** 10
few **pocos/as** *adj. pl.*
fewer than **menos de** (+ *number*) 8
field: major field of study **especialización** *f.*
fifteen **quince** 1
fifteen-year-old girl celebrating her birthday **quinceañera** *f.*
fifth **quinto/a** 5
fifty **cincuenta** 2
fight (for/against) **luchar** *v.* **(por/contra)**
figure (*number*) **cifra** *f.*
file **archivo** *m.* 11
fill **llenar** *v.* 11
fill out (a form) **llenar (un formulario)** 14
fill the tank **llenar el tanque** 11
finally **finalmente** *adv.*; **por último** 7; **por fin** 11
find **encontrar (o:ue)** *v.* 4
find (each other) **encontrar(se)**
find out **enterarse** *v.*
fine **multa** *f.*
That's fine. **Está bien.**
(fine) arts **bellas artes** *f., pl.*
finger **dedo** *m.* 10
finish **terminar** *v.* 2
finish (*doing something*) **terminar** *v.* **de (+ *inf.*)**
fire **incendio** *m.*; **despedir (e:i)** *v.*
firefighter **bombero/a** *m., f.*
firm **compañía** *f.*, **empresa** *f.*
first **primer, primero/a** 2, 5
fish (*food*) **pescado** *m.* 8; **pescar** *v.* 5; (*live*) **pez** *m., sing.* (**peces** *pl.*) 13
fish market **pescadería** *f.* 14
fishing **pesca** *f.*
fit (*clothing*) **quedar** *v.* 7
five **cinco** 1
five hundred **quinientos/as** 2
fix (*put in working order*) **arreglar** *v.* 11; (*clothes, hair, etc. to go out*) **arreglarse** *v.* 7
fixed **fijo/a** *adj.* 6
flag **bandera** *f.*
flexible **flexible** *adj.* 15
flood **inundación** *f.*
floor (*of a building*) **piso** *m.* 5; **suelo** *m.* 12
ground floor **planta baja** *f.* 5
top floor **planta** *f.* **alta**
flower **flor** *f.* 13
flu **gripe** *f.* 10
fog **niebla** *f.*
folk **folclórico/a** *adj.*
follow **seguir (e:i)** *v.* 4
food **comida** *f.* 4, 8
foolish **tonto/a** *adj.* 3
foot **pie** *m.* 10
football **fútbol** *m.* **americano** 4
for **para** *prep.* 11; **por** *prep.* 11
for example **por ejemplo** 11
for me **para mí** 8
forbid **prohibir** *v.*
foreign **extranjero/a** *adj.*
foreign languages **lenguas** *f., pl.* **extranjeras** 2
forest **bosque** *m.* 13
forget **olvidar** *v.* 10
fork **tenedor** *m.* 12
form **formulario** *m.* 14
forty **cuarenta** 2
four **cuatro** 1
four hundred **cuatrocientos/as** 2
fourteen **catorce** 1
fourth **cuarto/a** *m., f.* 5

free **libre** *adj. m., f.* 4
  be free (of charge) **ser gratis** 14
  free time **tiempo libre**; spare (free) time **ratos libres** 4
freedom **libertad** *f.*
freezer **congelador** *m.* 12
French **francés, francesa** *adj.* 3
  French fries **papas** *f., pl.* **fritas** 8; **patatas** *f., pl.* **fritas** 8
frequently **frecuentemente** *adv.*; **con frecuencia** *adv.* 10
Friday **viernes** *m., sing.* 2
fried **frito/a** *adj.* 8
  fried potatoes **papas** *f., pl.* **fritas** 8; **patatas** *f., pl.* **fritas** 8
friend **amigo/a** *m., f.* 3
friendly **amable** *adj. m., f.* 5
friendship **amistad** *f.* 9
from **de** *prep.* 1; **desde** *prep.* 6
  from the United States **estadounidense** *m., f. adj.* 3
  from time to time **de vez en cuando** 10
  I'm from... **Soy de...** 1
front: (cold) front **frente (frío)** *m.* 5
fruit **fruta** *f.* 8
  fruit juice **jugo** *m.* **de fruta** 8
  fruit store **frutería** *f.* 14
full **lleno/a** *adj.* 11
fun **divertido/a** *adj.*
  fun activity **diversión** *f.* 4
  have fun **divertirse (e:ie)** *v.* 9
function **funcionar** *v.*
furniture **muebles** *m., pl.* 12
furthermore **además (de)** *adv.* 10
future **porvenir** *m.*
  for/to the future **por el porvenir**
  in the future **en el futuro**

G

gain weight **aumentar** *v.* **de peso** 15; **engordar** *v.* 15
game **juego** *m.*; (*match*) **partido** *m.* 4
  game show **concurso** *m.*
garage (*in a house*) **garaje** *m.* 12; **garaje** *m.* 11; **taller (mecánico)** 11
garden **jardín** *m.* 12
garlic **ajo** *m.* 8
gas station **gasolinera** *f.* 11
gasoline **gasolina** *f.* 11
gentleman **caballero** *m.* 8
geography **geografía** *f.* 2
German **alemán, alemana** *adj.* 3
get **conseguir (e:i)** *v.* 4; **obtener** *v.*
  get along well/badly (with) **llevarse bien/mal (con)** 9
  get bigger **aumentar** *v.* 13
  get bored **aburrirse** *v.*
  get good grades **sacar buenas notas** 2
  get into trouble **meterse en problemas** *v.* 13
  get off of (a vehicle) **bajar(se)** *v.* **de** 11
  get on/into (a vehicle) **subir(se)** *v.* **a** 11
  get out of (a vehicle) **bajar(se)** *v.* **de** 11
  get ready **arreglarse** *v.* 7
  get up **levantarse** *v.* 7
gift **regalo** *m.* 6
ginger **jengibre** *m.* 10
girl **chica** *f.* 1; **muchacha** *f.* 3
girlfriend **novia** *f.* 3
give **dar** *v.* 6; (*as a gift*) **regalar** 9
  give directions **indicar cómo llegar** 14
glass (*drinking*) **vaso** *m.* 12; **vidrio** *m.* 13
  (made) of glass **de vidrio** 13
glasses **gafas** *f., pl.* 6
  sunglasses **gafas** *f., pl.* **de sol** 6
global warming **calentamiento global** *m.* 13
gloves **guantes** *m., pl.* 6
go **ir** *v.* 4
  go away **irse** 7
  go by boat **ir en barco** 5
  go by bus **ir en autobús** 5
  go by car **ir en auto(móvil)** 5
  go by motorcycle **ir en moto(cicleta)** 5
  go by plane **ir en avión** 5
  go by taxi **ir en taxi** 5
  go down **bajar(se)** *v.*
  go on a hike **ir de excursión** 4
  go out (with) **salir** *v.* **(con)** 9
  go up **subir** *v.*
  Let's go. **Vamos.** 4
goblet **copa** *f.* 12
going to: be going to (*do something*) **ir a (+ *inf.*)** 4
golf **golf** *m.* 4
good **buen, bueno/a** *adj.* 3, 6
  Good afternoon. **Buenas tardes.** 1
  Good evening. **Buenas noches.** 1
  Good morning. **Buenos días.** 1
  Good night. **Buenas noches.** 1
  It's good that... **Es bueno que...** 12
goodbye **adiós** *m.* 1
  say goodbye (to) **despedirse** *v.* **(de) (e:i)**
good-looking **guapo/a** *adj.* 3
government **gobierno** *m.* 13
GPS **navegador GPS** *m.* 11
graduate (from/in) **graduarse** *v.* **(de/en)** 9
grains **cereales** *m., pl.* 8
granddaughter **nieta** *f.* 3
grandfather **abuelo** *m.* 3
grandmother **abuela** *f.* 3
grandparents **abuelos** *m., pl.* 3
grandson **nieto** *m.* 3
grape **uva** *f.* 8
grass **hierba** *f.* 13
grave **grave** *adj.* 10
gray **gris** *adj. m., f.* 6
great **fenomenal** *adj. m., f.* 5; **genial** *adj.*
great-grandfather **bisabuelo** *m.* 3
great-grandmother **bisabuela** *f.* 3
green **verde** *adj. m., f.* 6
greet (each other) **saludar(se)** *v.* 11
greeting **saludo** *m.* 1
  Greetings to... **Saludos a...** 1
grilled **a la plancha** 8
ground floor **planta baja** *f.* 5
grow **aumentar** *v.* 13
guest (*at a house/hotel*) **huésped** *m., f.* 5 (*invited to a function*) **invitado/a** *m., f.* 9
guide **guía** *m., f.*
gymnasium **gimnasio** *m.* 4

H

hair **pelo** *m.* 7
hairdresser **peluquero/a** *m., f.*
half **medio/a** *adj.* 3
  half-brother **medio hermano** *m.* 3
  half-past... (*time*) **...y media** 1
  half-sister **media hermana** *f.* 3
hallway **pasillo** *m.* 12
ham **jamón** *m.* 8
hamburger **hamburguesa** *f.* 8
hand **mano** *f.* 1
hand in **entregar** *v.* 11
handsome **guapo/a** *adj.* 3
happen **ocurrir** *v.*
happiness **alegría** *v.* 9
Happy birthday! **¡Feliz cumpleaños!** 9
happy **alegre** *adj.* 5; **contento/a** *adj.* 5; **feliz** *adj. m., f.* 5
  be happy **alegrarse** *v.* **(de)** 13
hard **difícil** *adj. m., f.* 3
hard-working **trabajador(a)** *adj.* 3
hardly **apenas** *adv.* 10
hat **sombrero** *m.* 6

hate **odiar** *v.* 9
have **tener** *v.* 3
have time **tener tiempo** 14
have to (*do something*) **tener que (+ *inf.*)** 3
have a tooth removed **sacar(se) un diente** 10
he **él** 1
head **cabeza** *f.* 10
headache **dolor** *m.* **de cabeza** 10
health **salud** *f.* 10
healthy **saludable** *adj. m., f.* 10; **sano/a** *adj.* 10
lead a healthy lifestyle **llevar** *v.* **una vida sana** 15
hear **oír** *v.* 4
heard **oído/a** *p.p.* 14
hearing: sense of hearing **oído** *m.* 10
heart **corazón** *m.* 10
heat **calor** *m.*
Hello. **Hola.** 1; (*on the telephone*) **Aló.** 11; **Bueno.** 11; **Diga.** 11
help **ayudar** *v.*; **servir (e:i)** *v.* 5
help each other **ayudarse** *v.* 11
her **su(s)** *poss. adj.* 3; (of) hers **suyo(s)/a(s)** *poss.* 11
her **la** *f., sing., d.o. pron.* 5
to/for her **le** *f., sing., i.o. pron.* 6
here **aquí** *adv.* 1
Here is/are... **Aquí está(n)...** 5
Hi. **Hola.** 1
highway **autopista** *f.* 11; **carretera** *f.* 11
hike **excursión** *f.* 4
go on a hike **ir de excursión** 4
hiker **excursionista** *m., f.*
hiking **de excursión** 4
him *m., sing., d.o. pron.* **lo** 5; to/for him **le** *m., sing., i.o. pron.* 6
hire **contratar** *v.*
his **su(s)** *poss. adj.* 3; (of) his **suyo(s)/a(s)** *poss. pron.* 11
history **historia** *f.* 2
hobby **pasatiempo** *m.* 4
hockey **hockey** *m.* 4
hold up **aguantar** *v.* 14
hole **hueco** *m.* 4
holiday **día** *m.* **de fiesta** 9
home **casa** *f.* 2
home page **página** *f.* **principal** 11
homework **tarea** *f.* 2
honey **miel** *f.* 10
hood **capó** *m.* 11; **cofre** *m.* 11
hope **esperar** *v.* **(+ *inf.*)** 2; **esperar** *v.* 13
I hope (that) **ojalá (que)** 13
horror (genre) **de horror** *m.*
hors d'oeuvres **entremeses** *m., pl.* 8
horse **caballo** *m.* 5
hospital **hospital** *m.* 10
hot: be (*feel*) (very) hot **tener (mucho) calor** 3
It's (very) hot. **Hace (mucho) calor.** 5
hotel **hotel** *m.* 5
hour **hora** *f.* 1
house **casa** *f.* 2
household chores **quehaceres** *m. pl.* **domésticos** 12
housekeeper **ama** *m., f.* **de casa** 12
housing **vivienda** *f.* 12
How...! **¡Qué...!**
how **¿cómo?** *adv.* 1, 2
How are you? **¿Qué tal?** 1
How are you?**¿Cómo estás?** *fam.* 1
How are you?**¿Cómo está usted?** *form.* 1
How can I help you? **¿En qué puedo servirles?** 5
How is it going? **¿Qué tal?** 1
How is the weather? **¿Qué tiempo hace?** 5
How much/many? **¿Cuánto(s)/a(s)?** 1
How much does... cost? **¿Cuánto cuesta...?** 6
How old are you? **¿Cuántos años tienes?** *fam.*
however **sin embargo**
hug (each other) **abrazar(se)** *v.* 11
humanities **humanidades** *f., pl.* 2
hundred **cien, ciento** 2
hunger **hambre** *f.*
hungry: be (very) hungry **tener** *v.* **(mucha) hambre** 3
hunt **cazar** *v.* 13
hurricane **huracán** *m.*
hurry **apurarse** *v.* 15; **darse prisa** *v.* 15
be in a (big) hurry **tener** *v.* **(mucha) prisa** 3
hurt **doler (o:ue)** *v.* 10
husband **esposo** *m.* 3

I

I **yo** 1
I hope (that) **Ojalá (que)** *interj.* 13
I wish (that) **Ojalá (que)** *interj.* 13
ice cream **helado** *m.* 9
ice cream shop **heladería** *f.* 14
iced **helado/a** *adj.* 8
iced tea **té** *m.* **helado** 8
idea **idea** *f.*
if **si** *conj.* 4
illness **enfermedad** *f.* 10
important **importante** *adj.* 3
be important to **importar** *v.* 7
It's important that... **Es importante que...** 12
impossible **imposible** *adj.* 13
it's impossible **es imposible** 13
improbable **improbable** *adj.* 13
it's improbable **es improbable** 13
improve **mejorar** *v.* 13
in **en** *prep.* 2; **por** *prep.* 11
in the afternoon **de la tarde** 1; **por la tarde** 7
in a bad mood **de mal humor** 5
in the direction of **para** *prep.* 11
in the early evening **de la tarde** 1
in the evening **de la noche** 1; **por la tarde** 7
in a good mood **de buen humor** 5
in the morning **de la mañana** 1; **por la mañana** 7
in love (with) **enamorado/a (de)** 5
in search of **por** *prep.* 11
in front of **delante de** *prep.* 2
increase **aumento** *m.*
incredible **increíble** *adj.* 5
inequality **desigualdad** *f.*
infection **infección** *f.* 10
inform **informar** *v.*
injection **inyección** *f.* 10
give an injection *v.* **poner una inyección** 10
injure (oneself) **lastimarse** 10
injure (one's foot) **lastimarse** *v.* **(el pie)** 10
inner ear **oído** *m.* 10
inside **dentro** *adv.*
insist (on) **insistir** *v.* **(en)** 12
installments: pay in installments **pagar** *v.* **a plazos** 14
intelligent **inteligente** *adj.* 3
intend to **pensar** *v.* **(+ *inf.*)** 4
interest **interesar** *v.* 7
interesting **interesante** *adj.* 3
be interesting to **interesar** *v.* 7
international **internacional** *adj. m., f.*
Internet **Internet** 11
interview **entrevista** *f.*; interview **entrevistar** *v.*
interviewer **entrevistador(a)** *m., f.*
introduction **presentación** *f.*
I would like to introduce you to (name). **Le presento a...** *form.* 1; **Te presento a...** *fam.* 1
invest **invertir (e:ie)** *v.*
invite **invitar** *v.* 9
iron (clothes) **planchar** *v.* **la ropa** 12

it **lo/la** *sing., d.o., pron.* 5
Italian **italiano/a** *adj.* 3
its **su(s)** *poss. adj.* 3; **suyo(s)/a(s)** *poss. pron.* 11
it's the same **es igual** 5

J

jacket **chaqueta** *f.* 6
January **enero** *m.* 5
Japanese **japonés, japonesa** *adj.* 3
jeans **(blue)jeans** *m., pl.* 6
jewelry store **joyería** *f.* 14
job **empleo** *m.;* **puesto** *m.;* **trabajo** *m.*
job application **solicitud** *f.* **de trabajo**
jog **correr** *v.*
journalism **periodismo** *m.* 2
journalist **periodista** *m., f.* 3
joy **alegría** *f.* 9
juice **jugo** *m.* 8
July **julio** *m.* 5
June **junio** *m.* 5
jungle **selva, jungla** *f.* 13
just **apenas** *adv.*
have just done something **acabar de (+** *inf.***)** 6

K

key **llave** *f.* 5
keyboard **teclado** *m.* 11
kilometer **kilómetro** *m.* 11
kiss **beso** *m.* 9
kiss each other **besarse** *v.* 11
kitchen **cocina** *f.* 9, 12
knee **rodilla** *f.* 10
knife **cuchillo** *m.* 12
know **saber** *v.* 6; **conocer** *v.* 6
know how **saber** *v.* 6

L

laboratory **laboratorio** *m.* 2
lack **faltar** *v.* 7
lake **lago** *m.* 13
lamp **lámpara** *f.* 12
land **tierra** *f.* 13
landscape **paisaje** *m.* 5
language **lengua** *f.* 2
laptop (computer) **computadora** *f.* **portátil** 11
large **grande** *adj.* 3
large (*clothing size*) **talla grande**
last **durar** *v.;* **pasado/a** *adj.* 6; **último/a** *adj.* 7
last name **apellido** *m.* 3
last night **anoche** *adv.* 6
last week **semana** *f.* **pasada** 6
last year **año** *m.* **pasado** 6
the last time **la última vez** 7
late **tarde** *adv.* 7
later (on) **más tarde** 7
See you later. **Hasta la vista.** 1; **Hasta luego.** 1
laugh **reírse (e:i)** *v.* 9
laughed **reído** *p.p.* 14
laundromat **lavandería** *f.* 14
law **ley** *f.* 13
lawyer **abogado/a** *m., f.*
lazy **perezoso/a** *adj.*
learn **aprender** *v.* **(a +** *inf.***)** 3
least, at **por lo menos** *adv.* 10
leave **salir** *v.* 4; **irse** *v.* 7
leave a tip **dejar una propina**
leave behind **dejar** *v.*
leave for (*a place*) **salir para**
leave from **salir de**
left **izquierda** *f.* 2
be left over **quedar** *v.* 7
to the left of **a la izquierda de** 2
leg **pierna** *f.* 10
lemon **limón** *m.* 8
lend **prestar** *v.* 6
less **menos** *adv.* 10
less... than **menos... que** 8
less than **menos de** (+ *number*)
lesson **lección** *f.* 1
let **dejar** *v.*
let's see **a ver**
letter **carta** *f.* 4, 14
lettuce **lechuga** *f.* 8
liberty **libertad** *f.*
library **biblioteca** *f.* 2
license (*driver's*) **licencia** *f.* **de conducir** 11
lie **mentira** *f.* 4
life **vida** *f.* 9
lifestyle: lead a healthy lifestyle **llevar una vida sana** 15
lift **levantar** *v.* 15
lift weights **levantar pesas** 15
light **luz** *f.* 12
like **como** *prep.* 8; **gustar** *v.* 2
I like... **Me gusta(n)...** 2
like this **así** *adv.* 10
like very much **encantar** *v.;* **fascinar** *v.* 7
Do you like...? **¿Te gusta(n)...?** 2
likeable **simpático/a** *adj.* 3
likewise **igualmente** *adv.* 1
line **línea** *f.* 4; **cola** (*queue*) *f.* 14
listen (to) **escuchar** *v.* 2
listen to music **escuchar música** 2
listen to the radio **escuchar la radio** 2
literature **literatura** *f.* 2
little (*quantity*) **poco** *adv.* 10
live **vivir** *v.* 3; **en vivo** *adj.* 7
living room **sala** *f.* 12
loan **préstamo** *m.* 14; **prestar** *v.* 6, 14
lobster **langosta** *f.* 8
located **situado/a** *adj.*
be located **quedar** *v.* 14
long **largo/a** *adj.* 6
look (at) **mirar** *v.* 2
look for **buscar** *v.* 2
lose **perder (e:ie)** *v.* 4
lose weight **adelgazar** *v.* 15
lost **perdido/a** *adj.* 13, 14
be lost **estar perdido/a** 14
lot, a **muchas veces** *adv.* 10
lot of, a **mucho/a** *adj.* 3; **un montón de** 4
love (*another person*) **querer (e:ie)** *v.* 4; (*inanimate objects*) **encantar** *v.* 7; **amor** *m.* 9
in love **enamorado/a** *adj.* 5
love at first sight **amor a primera vista** 9
luck **suerte** *f.*
lucky: be (very) lucky **tener (mucha) suerte** 3
luggage **equipaje** *m.* 5
lunch **almuerzo** *m.* 4, 8
have lunch **almorzar (o:ue)** *v.* 4

M

ma'am **señora (Sra.); doña** *f.* 1
mad **enojado/a** *adj.* 5
magazine **revista** *f.* 4
magnificent **magnífico/a** *adj.* 5
mail **correo** *m.* 14; **enviar** *v.*, **mandar** *v.* 14; **echar (una carta) al buzón** 14
mail carrier **cartero** *m.* 14
mailbox **buzón** *m.* 14
main **principal** *adj. m., f.* 8
maintain **mantener** *v.* 15
major **especialización** *f.* 2
make **hacer** *v.* 4
make a decision **tomar una decisión** 15
make the bed **hacer la cama** 12
makeup **maquillaje** *m.* 7
put on makeup **maquillarse** *v.* 7
man **hombre** *m.* 1
manager **gerente** *m., f.* 8
many **mucho/a** *adj.* 3
many times **muchas veces** 10
map **mapa** *m.* 1, 2
March **marzo** *m.* 5
margarine **margarina** *f.* 8
marinated fish **ceviche** *m.* 8
lemon-marinated shrimp **ceviche** *m.* **de camarón** 8
marital status **estado** *m.* **civil** 9
market **mercado** *m.* 6
open-air market **mercado al aire libre** 6
marriage **matrimonio** *m.* 9
married **casado/a** *adj.* 9
get married (to) **casarse** *v.* **(con)** 9
I'll marry you! **¡Acepto casarme contigo!**

marvelous **maravilloso/a** *adj.* 5
massage **masaje** *m.* 15
masterpiece **obra maestra** *f.*
match (*sports*) **partido** *m.* 4
match (with) **hacer** *v.* **juego (con)** 6
mathematics **matemáticas** *f., pl.* 2
matter **importar** *v.* 7
maturity **madurez** *f.* 9
maximum **máximo/a** *adj.* 11
May **mayo** *m.* 5
May I leave a message? **¿Puedo dejar un recado?** 11
maybe **tal vez** 5; **quizás** 5
mayonnaise **mayonesa** *f.* 8
me **me** *sing., d.o. pron.* 5
  to/for me **me** *sing., i.o. pron.* 6
meal **comida** *f.* 8
means of communication **medios** *m., pl.* **de comunicación**
meat **carne** *f.* 8
mechanic **mecánico/a** *m., f.* 11
  mechanic's repair shop **taller mecánico** 11
media **medios** *m., pl.* **de comunicación**
medical **médico/a** *adj.* 10
medication **medicamento** *m.* 10
medicine **medicina** *f.* 10
medium **mediano/a** *adj.*
meet (each other) **encontrar(se)** *v.* 11; **conocer(se)** *v.* 8
  meet up with **encontrarse con** 7
meeting **reunión** *f.*
menu **menú** *m.* 8
message **mensaje** *m.*
Mexican **mexicano/a** *adj.* 3
microwave **microonda** *f.* 12
  microwave oven **horno** *m.* **de microondas** 12
middle age **madurez** *f.* 9
midnight **medianoche** *f.* 1
mile **milla** *f.*
milk **leche** *f.* 8
million **millón** *m.* 2
  million of **millón de** 2
mine **mío(s)/a(s)** *poss.* 11
mineral **mineral** *m.* 15
  mineral water **agua** *f.* **mineral** 8
minute **minuto** *m.*
mirror **espejo** *m.* 7
Miss **señorita (Srta.)** *f.* 1
miss **perder (e:ie)** *v.* 4; **extrañar** *v.*
mistaken **equivocado/a** *adj.*
modern **moderno/a** *adj.*
mom **mamá** *f.*
Monday **lunes** *m., sing.* 2
money **dinero** *m.* 6
monitor **monitor** *m.* 11
monkey **mono** *m.* 13
month **mes** *m.* 5
monument **monumento** *m.* 4
moon **luna** *f.* 13
more **más** 2
  more... than **más... que** 8
  more than **más de (+ *number*)** 8
morning **mañana** *f.* 1
mother **madre** *f.* 3
mother-in-law **suegra** *f.* 3
motor **motor** *m.*
motorcycle **moto(cicleta)** *f.* 5
mountain **montaña** *f.* 4
mouse **ratón** *m.* 11
mouth **boca** *f.* 10
move (*from one house to another*) **mudarse** *v.* 12
movie **película** *f.* 4
  movie star **estrella** *f.* **de cine**
  movie theater **cine** *m.* 4
MP3 player **reproductor** *m.* **de MP3** 11
Mr. **señor (Sr.)**; **don** *m.* 1
Mrs. **señora (Sra.)**; **doña** *f.* 1
much **mucho/a** *adj.* 3
mud **lodo** *m.*
murder **crimen** *m.*
muscle **músculo** *m.* 15
museum **museo** *m.* 4
mushroom **champiñón** *m.* 8
music **música** *f.* 2
musical **musical** *adj., m., f.*
musician **músico/a** *m., f.*
must **deber** *v.* **(+ *inf.*)** 3
my **mi(s)** *poss. adj.* 3; **mío(s)/a(s)** *poss. pron.* 11

N

name **nombre** *m.* 1
  be named **llamarse** *v.* 7
  in the name of **a nombre de** 5
  last name **apellido** *m.* 3
  My name is... **Me llamo...** 1
  name someone/something **ponerle el nombre** 9
napkin **servilleta** *f.* 12
national **nacional** *adj. m., f.*
nationality **nacionalidad** *f.* 1
natural **natural** *adj. m., f.* 13
  natural disaster **desastre** *m.* **natural**
  natural resource **recurso** *m.* **natural** 13
nature **naturaleza** *f.* 13
nauseated **mareado/a** *adj.* 10
near **cerca de** *prep.* 2
neaten **arreglar** *v.* 12
necessary **necesario/a** *adj.* 12
  It is necessary that... **Es necesario que...** 12
neck **cuello** *m.* 10
need **faltar** *v.* 7; **necesitar** *v.* **(+ *inf.*)** 2
neighbor **vecino/a** *m., f.* 12
neighborhood **barrio** *m.* 12
neither **tampoco** *adv.* 7
neither... nor **ni... ni** *conj.* 7
nephew **sobrino** *m.* 3
nervous **nervioso/a** *adj.* 5
network **red** *f.* 11
never **nunca** *adj.* 7; **jamás** 7
new **nuevo/a** *adj.* 6
newlywed **recién casado/a** *m., f.* 9
news **noticias** *f., pl.*; **actualidades** *f., pl.*; **noticia** *f.* 11
newscast **noticiero** *m.*
newspaper **periódico** 4; **diario** *m.*
next **próximo/a** *adj.* 3
  next to **al lado de** *prep.* 2
nice **simpático/a** *adj.* 3; **amable** *adj.* 5
niece **sobrina** *f.* 3
night **noche** *f.* 1
  night stand **mesita** *f.* **de noche** 12
nine **nueve** 1
nine hundred **novecientos/as** 2
nineteen **diecinueve** 1
ninety **noventa** 2
ninth **noveno/a** 5
no **no** 1; **ningún, ninguno/a(s)** *adj.* 7
  no one **nadie** *pron.* 7
nobody **nadie** 7
none **ningún, ninguno/a(s)** *adj.* 7
noon **mediodía** *m.* 1
nor **ni** *conj.* 7
north **norte** *m.* 14
  to the north **al norte** 14
nose **nariz** *f.* 10
not **no** 1
  not any **ningún, ninguno/a(s)** *adj.* 7
  not anyone **nadie** *pron.* 7
  not anything **nada** *pron.* 7
  not bad at all **nada mal** 5
  not either **tampoco** *adv.* 7
  not ever **nunca** *adv.* 7; **jamás** *adv.* 7
  not very well **no muy bien** 1
  not working **descompuesto/a** *adj.* 11
notebook **cuaderno** *m.* 1
nothing **nada** 1; 7
noun **sustantivo** *m.*
November **noviembre** *m.* 5
now **ahora** *adv.* 2
nowadays **hoy día** *adv.*
nuclear **nuclear** *adj. m., f.* 13
  nuclear energy **energía nuclear** 13
number **número** *m.* 1
nurse **enfermero/a** *m., f.* 10
nutrition **nutrición** *f.* 15
nutritionist **nutricionista** *m., f.* 15

O

o'clock: It's... o'clock **Son las...** 1
It's one o'clock. **Es la una.** 1
obey **obedecer** *v.*
obligation **deber** *m.*
obtain **conseguir (e:i)** *v.* 4; **obtener** *v.*
obvious **obvio/a** *adj.* 13
it's obvious **es obvio** 13
occupation **ocupación** *f.*
occur **ocurrir** *v.*
October **octubre** *m.* 5
of **de** *prep.* 1
Of course. **Claro que sí.; Por supuesto.**
offer **oferta** *f.*; **ofrecer (c:zc)** *v.* 6
office **oficina** *f.* 12
doctor's office **consultorio** *m.* 10
often **a menudo** *adv.* 10
Oh! **¡Ay!**
oil **aceite** *m.* 8
OK **regular** *adj.* 1
It's okay. **Está bien.**
old **viejo/a** *adj.* 3
old age **vejez** *f.* 9
older **mayor** *adj. m., f.* 3
older brother, sister **hermano/a mayor** *m., f.* 3
oldest **el/la mayor** 8
on **en** *prep.* 2; **sobre** *prep.* 2
on behalf of **por** *prep.* 11
on the dot **en punto** 1
on time **a tiempo** 10
on top of **encima de** 2
once **una vez** 6
one **uno** 1
one hundred **cien(to)** 2
one million **un millón** *m.* 2
one more time **una vez más**
one thousand **mil** 2
one time **una vez** 6
onion **cebolla** *f.* 8
only **sólo** *adv.* 6; **único/a** *adj.* 3
only child **hijo/a único/a** *m., f.* 3
open **abierto/a** *adj.* 5, 14; **abrir** *v.* 3
open-air **al aire libre** 6
opera **ópera** *f.*
operation **operación** *f.* 10
opposite **enfrente de** *prep.* 14
or **o** *conj.* 7
orange **anaranjado/a** *adj.* 6; **naranja** *f.* 8
orchestra **orquesta** *f.*
order **mandar** 12; (*food*) **pedir (e:i)** *v.* 8
in order to **para** *prep.* 11
orderly **ordenado/a** *adj.* 5
ordinal (*numbers*) **ordinal** *adj.*
organize oneself **organizarse** *v.* 12
other **otro/a** *adj.* 6
ought to **deber** *v.* **(+ *inf.*)** *adj.* 3
our **nuestro(s)/a(s)** *poss. adj.* 3; *poss. pron.* 11
out of order **descompuesto/a** *adj.* 11
outside **afuera** *adv.* 5
outskirts **afueras** *f., pl.* 12
oven **horno** *m.* 12
over **sobre** *prep.* 2
(over)population **(sobre)población** *f.* 13
over there **allá** *adv.* 2
own **propio/a** *adj.*
owner **dueño/a** *m., f.* 8

P

p.m. **de la tarde, de la noche** *f.* 1
pack (one's suitcases) **hacer** *v.* **las maletas** 5
package **paquete** *m.* 14
page **página** *f.* 11
pain **dolor** *m.* 10
have pain **tener** *v.* **dolor** 10
paint **pintar** *v.*
painter **pintor(a)** *m., f.*
painting **pintura** *f.* 12
pair **par** *m.* 6
pair of shoes **par** *m.* **de zapatos** 6
pale **pálido/a** *adj.* 14
pants **pantalones** *m., pl.* 6
pantyhose **medias** *f., pl.* 6
paper **papel** *m.* 2; (*report*) **informe** *m.*
Pardon me. (*May I?*) **Con permiso.** 1; (*Excuse me.*) Pardon me. **Perdón.** 1
parents **padres** *m., pl.* 3; **papás** *m., pl.*
park **estacionar** *v.* 11; **parque** *m.* 4
parking lot **estacionamiento** *m.* 14
partner (*one of a married couple*) **pareja** *f.* 9
party **fiesta** *f.* 9
passed **pasado/a** *p.p.*
passenger **pasajero/a** *m., f.* 1
passport **pasaporte** *m.* 5
past **pasado/a** *adj.* 6
pastime **pasatiempo** *m.* 4
pastry shop **pastelería** *f.* 14
path **sendero** *m.* 13
patient **paciente** *m., f.* 10
patio **patio** *m.* 12
pay **pagar** *v.* 6
pay in cash **pagar** *v.* **al contado; pagar en efectivo** 14
pay in installments **pagar** *v.* **a plazos** 14
pay the bill **pagar la cuenta**
pea **arveja** *m.* 8
peace **paz** *f.*
peach **melocotón** *m.* 8
peak **cima** *f.* 15
pear **pera** *f.* 8
pen **pluma** *f.* 2
pencil **lápiz** *m.* 1
penicillin **penicilina** *f.*
people **gente** *f.* 3
pepper (*black*) **pimienta** *f.* 8
per **por** *prep.* 11
perfect **perfecto/a** *adj.* 5
period of time **temporada** *f.* 5
person **persona** *f.* 3
pharmacy **farmacia** *f.* 10
phenomenal **fenomenal** *adj.* 5
photograph **foto(grafía)** *f.* 1
physical (exam) **examen** *m.* **médico** 10
physician **doctor(a), médico/a** *m., f.* 3
physics **física** *f. sing.* 2
pick up **recoger** *v.* 13
picture **cuadro** *m.* 12; **pintura** *f.* 12
pie **pastel** *m.* 9
pill (tablet) **pastilla** *f.* 10
pillow **almohada** *f.* 12
pineapple **piña** *f.*
pink **rosado/a** *adj.* 6
place **lugar** *m.* 2, 4; **sitio** *m.* 3; **poner** *v.* 4
plaid **de cuadros** 6
plans **planes** *m., pl.*
have plans **tener planes**
plant **planta** *f.* 13
plastic **plástico** *m.* 13
(made) of plastic **de plástico** 13
plate **plato** *m.* 12
play **drama** *m.*; **comedia** *f.* **jugar (u:ue)** *v.* 4; (*a musical instrument*) **tocar** *v.*; (*a role*) **hacer el papel de;** (*cards*) **jugar a (las cartas)** 5; (*sports*) **practicar deportes** 4
player **jugador(a)** *m., f.* 4
playwright **dramaturgo/a** *m., f.*
plead **rogar (o:ue)** *v.* 12
pleasant **agradable** *adj.*
please **por favor** 1
Pleased to meet you. **Mucho gusto.** 1; **Encantado/a.** *adj.* 1
pleasing: be pleasing to **gustar** *v.* 7
pleasure **gusto** *m.* 1; **placer** *m.*
The pleasure is mine. **El gusto es mío.** 1
poem **poema** *m.*
poet **poeta** *m., f.*
poetry **poesía** *f.*
police (force) **policía** *f.* 11
political **político/a** *adj.*
politician **político/a** *m., f.*
politics **política** *f.*
polka-dotted **de lunares** 6
poll **encuesta** *f.*
pollute **contaminar** *v.* 13

polluted **contaminado/a** *m., f.* 13
be polluted **estar contaminado/a** 13
pollution **contaminación** *f.* 13
pool **piscina** *f.* 4
poor **pobre** *adj., m., f.* 6
poor thing **pobrecito/a** *adj.* 3
popsicle **paleta helada** *f.* 4
population **población** *f.* 13
pork **cerdo** *m.* 8
pork chop **chuleta** *f.* **de cerdo** 8
portable **portátil** *adj.* 11
portable computer **computadora** *f.* **portátil** 11
position **puesto** *m.*
possessive **posesivo/a** *adj.*
possible **posible** *adj.* 13
it's (not) possible **(no) es posible** 13
post office **correo** *m.* 14
postcard **postal** *f.*
poster **cartel** *m.* 12
potato **papa** *f.* 8; **patata** *f.* 8
pottery **cerámica** *f.*
practice **entrenarse** *v.* 15; **practicar** *v.* 2; (a degree/profession) **ejercer** *v.*
prefer **preferir (e:ie)** *v.* 4
pregnant **embarazada** *adj. f.* 10
prepare **preparar** *v.* 2
preposition **preposición** *f.*
prescribe (*medicine*) **recetar** *v.* 10
prescription **receta** *f.* 10
present **regalo** *m.*; **presentar** *v.*
press **prensa** *f.*
pressure **presión** *f.*
be under a lot of pressure **sufrir muchas presiones** 15
pretty **bonito/a** *adj.* 3
price **precio** *m.* 6
(fixed, set) price **precio** *m.* **fijo** 6
print **imprimir** *v.* 11
printer **impresora** *f.* 11
prize **premio** *m.*
probable **probable** *adj.* 13
it's (not) probable **(no) es probable** 13
problem **problema** *m.* 1
profession **profesión** *f.* 3
professor **profesor(a)** *m., f.*
program **programa** *m.* 1
programmer **programador(a)** *m., f.* 3
prohibit **prohibir** *v.* 10
project **proyecto** *m.* 11
promotion (*career*) **ascenso** *m.*
pronoun **pronombre** *m.*
protect **proteger** *v.* 13
protein **proteína** *f.* 15
provided (that) **con tal (de) que** *conj.* 13
psychologist **psicólogo/a** *m., f.*
psychology **psicología** *f.* 2
publish **publicar** *v.*
Puerto Rican **puertorriqueño/a** *adj.* 3
purchases **compras** *f., pl.*
pure **puro/a** *adj.* 13
purple **morado/a** *adj.* 6
purse **bolsa** *f.* 6
put **poner** *v.* 4; **puesto/a** *p.p.* 14
put (a letter) in the mailbox **echar (una carta) al buzón** 14
put on (*a performance*) **presentar** *v.*
put on (*clothing*) **ponerse** *v.* 7
put on makeup **maquillarse** *v.* 7

Q

quality **calidad** *f.* 6
quarter (*academic*) **trimestre** *m.* 2
quarter after (*time*) **y cuarto** 1; **y quince** 1
quarter to (*time*) **menos cuarto** 1; **menos quince** 1
question **pregunta** *f.*
quickly **rápido** *adv.* 10
quiet **tranquilo/a** *adj.* 15
quit **dejar** *v.*
quiz **prueba** *f.* 2

R

racism **racismo** *m.*
radio (*medium*) **radio** *f.* 2
radio (set) **radio** *m.* 11
rain **llover (o:ue)** *v.* 5; **lluvia** *f.*
It's raining. **Llueve.** 5; **Está lloviendo.** 5
raincoat **impermeable** *m.* 6
rain forest **bosque** *m.* **tropical** 13
raise (*salary*) **aumento de sueldo**
rather **bastante** *adv.* 10
read **leer** *v.* 3; **leído/a** *p.p.* 14
read e-mail **leer el correo electrónico** 4
read a magazine **leer una revista** 4
read a newspaper **leer un periódico** 4
ready **listo/a** *adj.* 5
reality show **programa de realidad** *m.*
reap the benefits (of) *v.* **disfrutar** *v.* **(de)** 15
receive **recibir** *v.* 3
recommend **recomendar (e:ie)** *v.* 8; 12
record **grabar** *v.* 11
recover **recuperar** *v.* 11
recreation **diversión** *f.* 4
recycle **reciclar** *v.* 13
recycling **reciclaje** *m.* 13
red **rojo/a** *adj.* 6
red-haired **pelirrojo/a** *adj.* 3
reduce **reducir** *v.* 13; **disminuir** *v.*
reduce stress/tension **aliviar el estrés/la tensión** 15
refrigerator **refrigerador** *m.* 12
region **región** *f.*
regret **sentir (e:ie)** *v.* 13
relatives **parientes** *m., pl.* 3
relax **relajarse** *v.* 9
Relax. **Tranquilo/a.** 7
Relax, sweetie. **Tranquilo/a, cariño.** 11
remain **quedarse** *v.* 7
remember **acordarse (o:ue)** *v.* **(de)** 7; **recordar (o:ue)** *v.* 4
remote control **control remoto** *m.* 11
renewable **renovable** *adj.* 13
rent **alquilar** *v.* 12; (payment) **alquiler** *m.* 12
repeat **repetir (e:i)** *v.* 4
report **informe** *m.*; **reportaje** *m.*
reporter **reportero/a** *m., f.*
representative **representante** *m., f.*
request **pedir (e:i)** *v.* 4
reservation **reservación** *f.* 5
resign (from) **renunciar (a)** *v.*
resolve **resolver (o:ue)** *v.* 13
resolved **resuelto/a** *p.p.* 14
resource **recurso** *m.* 13
responsibility **deber** *m.*; **responsabilidad** *f.*
responsible **responsable** *adj.* 8
rest **descansar** *v.* 2
restaurant **restaurante** *m.* 4
résumé **currículum** *m.*
retire (from work) **jubilarse** *v.* 9
return **regresar** *v.* 2; **volver (o:ue)** *v.* 4
returned **vuelto/a** *p.p.* 14
rice **arroz** *m.* 8
rich **rico/a** *adj.* 6
ride a bicycle **pasear** *v.* **en bicicleta** 4
ride a horse **montar** *v.* **a caballo** 5
ridiculous **ridículo/a** *adj.* 13
it's ridiculous **es ridículo** 13
right **derecha** *f.* 2
be right **tener razón** 3
right? (*question tag*) **¿no?** 1; **¿verdad?** 1
right away **enseguida** *adv.*
right now **ahora mismo** 5
to the right of **a la derecha de** 2
rights **derechos** *m.*
ring **anillo** *m.*

ring (*a doorbell*) **sonar (o:ue)** *v.* 11
river **río** *m.* 13
road **carretera** f. 11; **camino** *m.*
roast **asado/a** *adj.* 8
roast chicken **pollo** *m.* **asado** 8
rollerblade **patinar en línea** *v.*
romantic **romántico/a** *adj.*
room **habitación** *f.* 5; **cuarto** *m.* 2; 7
 living room **sala** *f.* 12
roommate **compañero/a** *m., f.* **de cuarto** 2
roundtrip **de ida y vuelta** 5
 roundtrip ticket **pasaje** *m.* **de ida y vuelta** 5
routine **rutina** *f.* 7
rug **alfombra** *f.* 12
run **correr** *v.* 3
 run errands **hacer diligencias** 14
 run into (*have an accident*) **chocar (con)** *v.*; (*meet accidentally*) **encontrar(se) (o:ue)** *v.* 11; (*run into something*) **darse (con)** 10
 run into (each other) **encontrar(se) (o:ue)** *v.* 11
rush **apurarse, darse prisa** *v.* 15
Russian **ruso/a** *adj.* 3

S

sad **triste** *adj.* 5; 13
 it's sad **es triste** 13
safe **seguro/a** *adj.* 5
said **dicho/a** *p.p.* 14
sailboard **tabla de windsurf** *f.* 5
salad **ensalada** *f.* 8
salary **salario** *m.*; **sueldo** *m.*
sale **rebaja** *f.* 6
salesperson **vendedor(a)** *m., f.* 6
salmon **salmón** *m.* 8
salt **sal** *f.* 8
same **mismo/a** *adj.* 3
sandal **sandalia** *f.* 6
sandwich **sándwich** *m.* 8
Saturday **sábado** *m.* 2
sausage **salchicha** *f.* 8
save (*on a computer*) **guardar** *v.* **11**; save (money) **ahorrar** *v.* 14
savings **ahorros** *m.* 14
 savings account **cuenta** *f.* **de ahorros** 14
say **decir** *v.* 4; **declarar** *v.*
say (that) **decir (que)** *v.* 4
 say the answer **decir la respuesta** 4
scan **escanear** *v.* 11
scarcely **apenas** *adv.* 10
scared: be (very) scared (of) **tener (mucho) miedo (de)** 3
schedule **horario** *m.* 2
school **escuela** *f.* 1
sciences *f., pl.* **ciencias** 2
science fiction (genre) **de ciencia ficción** *f.*
scientist **científico/a** *m., f.*
scream **grito** *m.* 5; **gritar** *v.*
screen **pantalla** *f.* 11
scuba dive **bucear** *v.* 4
sculpt **esculpir** *v.*
sculptor **escultor(a)** *m., f.*
sculpture **escultura** *f.*
sea **mar** *m.* 5
 (sea) turtle **tortuga (marina)** *f.* 13
season **estación** *f.* 5
seat **silla** *f.* 2
second **segundo/a** 5
secretary **secretario/a** *m., f.*
sedentary **sedentario/a** *adj.* 15
see **ver** *v.* 4
 see (you, him, her) again **volver a ver(te, lo, la)**
 see movies **ver películas** 4
 See you. **Nos vemos.** 1
 See you later. **Hasta la vista.** 1; **Hasta luego.** 1
 See you soon. **Hasta pronto.** 1
 See you tomorrow. **Hasta mañana.** 1
seem **parecer** *v.* 6
seen **visto/a** *p.p.* 14
sell **vender** *v.* 6
semester **semestre** *m.* 2
send **enviar; mandar** *v.* 14
separate (from) **separarse** *v.* **(de)** 9
separated **separado/a** *adj.* 9
September **septiembre** *m.* 5
sequence **secuencia** *f.*
serious **grave** *adj.* 10
serve **servir (e:i)** *v.* 8
service **servicio** *m.* 15
set (*fixed*) **fijo/a** *adj.* 6
 set the table **poner la mesa** 12
seven **siete** 1
seven hundred **setecientos/as** 2
seventeen **diecisiete** 1
seventh **séptimo/a** 5
seventy **setenta** 2
several **varios/as** *adj. pl.*
sexism **sexismo** *m.*
shame **lástima** *f.* 13
 it's a shame **es una lástima** 13
shampoo **champú** *m.* 7
shape **forma** *f.* 15
 be in good shape **estar en buena forma** 15
 stay in shape **mantenerse en forma** 15
share **compartir** *v.* 3
sharp (*time*) **en punto** 1
shave **afeitarse** *v.* 7
shaving cream **crema** *f.* **de afeitar** 5, 7
she **ella** 1
shellfish **mariscos** *m., pl.* 8
ship **barco** *m.*
shirt **camisa** *f.* 6
shoe **zapato** *m.* 6
 shoe size **número** *m.* 6
 shoe store **zapatería** *f.* 14
 tennis shoes **zapatos** *m., pl.* **de tenis** 6
shop **tienda** *f.* 6
shopping, to go **ir de compras** 5
 shopping mall **centro comercial** *m.* 6
short (*in height*) **bajo/a** *adj.* 3; (*in length*) **corto/a** *adj.* 6
short story **cuento** *m.*
shorts **pantalones cortos** *m., pl.* 6
should (*do something*) **deber** *v.* **(+ *inf.*)** 3
shout **gritar** *v.*
show **espectáculo** *m.*; **mostrar (o:ue)** *v.* 4
 game show **concurso** *m.*
shower **ducha** *f.* 7; **ducharse** *v.* 7
shrimp **camarón** *m.* 8
siblings **hermanos/as** *pl.* 3
sick **enfermo/a** *adj.* 10
 be sick **estar enfermo/a** 10
 get sick **enfermarse** *v.* 10
sign **firmar** *v.* 14; **letrero** *m.* 14
silk **seda** *f.* 6
 (made of) silk **de seda** 6
since **desde** *prep.*
sing **cantar** *v.* 2
singer **cantante** *m., f.*
single **soltero/a** *adj.* 9
 single room **habitación** *f.* **individual** 5
sink **lavabo** *m.* 7
sir **señor (Sr.), don** *m.* 1; **caballero** *m.* 8
sister **hermana** *f.* 3
sister-in-law **cuñada** *f.* 3
sit down **sentarse (e:ie)** *v.* 7
six **seis** 1
six hundred **seiscientos/as** 2
sixteen **dieciséis** 1
sixth **sexto/a** 5
sixty **sesenta** 2
size **talla** *f.* 6
 shoe size *m.* **número** 6
(in-line) skate **patinar (en línea)** 4
skateboard **andar en patineta** *v.* 4
ski **esquiar** *v.* 4
skiing **esquí** *m.* 4
 water-skiing **esquí** *m.* **acuático** 4
skirt **falda** *f.* 6
skull made out of sugar **calavera de azúcar** *f.* 9
sky **cielo** *m.* 13
sleep **dormir (o:ue)** *v.* 4; **sueño** *m.*
 go to sleep **dormirse (o:ue)** *v.* 7
sleepy: be (very) sleepy **tener (mucho) sueño** 3
slender **delgado/a** *adj.* 3
slim down **adelgazar** *v.* 15
slippers **pantuflas** *f.* 7
slow **lento/a** *adj.* 11
slowly **despacio** *adv.* 10
small **pequeño/a** *adj.* 3
smart **listo/a** *adj.* 5
smile **sonreír (e:i)** *v.* 9
smiled **sonreído** *p.p.* 14

smoggy: It's (very) smoggy. **Hay (mucha) contaminación.**
smoke **fumar** *v.* 15
  (not) to smoke **(no) fumar** 15
smoking section **sección** *f.* **de fumar** 8
  (non) smoking section *f.* **sección de (no) fumar** 8
snack **merendar (e:ie)** *v.* 8
  afternoon snack **merienda** *f.* 15
  have a snack **merendar** *v.* 8
sneakers **los zapatos de tenis** 6
sneeze **estornudar** *v.* 10
snow **nevar (e:ie)** *v.* 5; **nieve** *f.*
snowing: It's snowing. **Nieva.** 5; **Está nevando.** 5
so (*in such a way*) **así** *adv.* 10; **tan** *adv.* 5
  so much **tanto** *adv.*
  so-so **regular** 1
  so that **para que** *conj.* 13
soap **jabón** *m.* 7
soap opera **telenovela** *f.*
soccer **fútbol** *m.* 4
sociology **sociología** *f.* 2
sock(s) **calcetín (calcetines)** *m.* 6
sofa **sofá** *m.* 12
soft drink **refresco** *m.* 8
software **programa** *m.* **de computación** 11
soil **tierra** *f.* 13
solar **solar** *adj., m., f.* 13
  solar energy **energía solar** 13
soldier **soldado** *m., f.*
solution **solución** *f.* 13
solve **resolver (o:ue)** *v.* 13
some **algún, alguno/a(s)** *adj.* 7; **unos/as** *indef. art.* 1
somebody **alguien** *pron.* 7
someone **alguien** *pron.* 7
something **algo** *pron.* 7
sometimes **a veces** *adv.* 10
son **hijo** *m.* 3
song **canción** *f.*
son-in-law **yerno** *m.* 3
soon **pronto** *adv.* 10
  See you soon. **Hasta pronto.** 1
sorry: be sorry **sentir (e:ie)** *v.* 13
  I'm sorry. **Lo siento.** 1
soul **alma** *f.* 9
soup **sopa** *f.* 8
south **sur** *m.* 14
  to the south **al sur** 14
Spain **España** *f.*
Spanish (*language*) **español** *m.* 2; **español(a)** *adj.* 3
spare (free) time **ratos libres** 4
speak **hablar** *v.* 2
  Speaking. (*on the telephone*) **Con él/ella habla.** 11
special: today's specials **las especialidades del día** 8
spectacular **espectacular** *adj. m., f.*
speech **discurso** *m.*
speed **velocidad** *f.* 11
  speed limit **velocidad** *f.* **máxima** 11
spelling **ortografía** *f.*, **ortográfico/a** *adj.*
spend (*money*) **gastar** *v.* 6
spoon (*table or large*) **cuchara** *f.* 12
sport **deporte** *m.* 4
  sports-related **deportivo/a** *adj.* 4
spouse **esposo/a** *m., f.* 3
sprain (one's ankle) **torcerse (o:ue)** *v.* **(el tobillo)** 10
spring **primavera** *f.* 5
(city or town) square **plaza** *f.* 4
stadium **estadio** *m.* 2
stage **etapa** *f.* 9
stairs **escalera** *f.* 12
stairway **escalera** *f.* 12
stamp **estampilla** *f.* 14; **sello** *m.* 14
stand in line **hacer** *v.* **cola** 14
star **estrella** *f.* 13
start (*a vehicle*) **arrancar** *v.* 11
station **estación** *f.* 5
statue **estatua** *f.*
status: marital status **estado** *m.* **civil** 9
stay **quedarse** *v.* 7
  stay in shape **mantenerse en forma** 15
steak **bistec** *m.* 8
steering wheel **volante** *m.* 11
step **escalón** *m.* 15
stepbrother **hermanastro** *m.* 3
stepdaughter **hijastra** *f.* 3
stepfather **padrastro** *m.* 3
stepmother **madrastra** *f.* 3
stepsister **hermanastra** *f.* 3
stepson **hijastro** *m.* 3
stereo **estéreo** *m.* 11
still **todavía** *adv.* 5
stockbroker **corredor(a)** *m., f.* **de bolsa**
stockings **medias** *f., pl.* 6
stomach **estómago** *m.* 10
stone **piedra** *f.* 13
stop **parar** *v.* 11
  stop (*doing something*) **dejar de (+ *inf.*)** 13
store **tienda** *f.* 6
storm **tormenta** *f.*
story **cuento** *m.*; **historia** *f.*
stove **cocina, estufa** *f.* 12
straight **derecho** *adv.* 14
  straight (ahead) **derecho** 14
straighten up **arreglar** *v.* 12
strange **extraño/a** *adj.* 13
  it's strange **es extraño** 13
street **calle** *f.* 11
stress **estrés** *m.* 15
stretching **estiramiento** *m.* 15
    do stretching exercises **hacer ejercicios** *m. pl.* **de estiramiento** 15
strike (*labor*) **huelga** *f.*
striped **de rayas** 6
stroll **pasear** *v.* 4
strong **fuerte** *adj. m., f.* 15
struggle (for/against) **luchar** *v.* **(por/contra)**
student **estudiante** *m., f.* 1; 2; **estudiantil** *adj.* 2
study **estudiar** *v.* 2
stupendous **estupendo/a** *adj.* 5
style **estilo** *m.*
suburbs **afueras** *f., pl.* 12
subway **metro** *m.* 5
  subway station **estación** *f.* **del metro** 5
success **éxito** *m.*
successful: be successful **tener éxito**
such as **tales como**
suddenly **de repente** *adv.* 6
suffer **sufrir** *v.* 10
  suffer an illness **sufrir una enfermedad** 10
sugar **azúcar** *m.* 8
suggest **sugerir (e:ie)** *v.* 12
suit **traje** *m.* 6
suitcase **maleta** *f.* 1
summer **verano** *m.* 5
sun **sol** *m.* 13
sunbathe **tomar** *v.* **el sol** 4
Sunday **domingo** *m.* 2
(sun)glasses **gafas** *f., pl.* **(de sol)** 6
sunny: It's (very) sunny. **Hace (mucho) sol.** 5
supermarket **supermercado** *m.* 14
suppose **suponer** *v.* 4
sure **seguro/a** *adj.* 5
  be sure **estar seguro/a** 5
surf **hacer** *v.* **surf** 5; (*the Internet*) **navegar** *v.* **(en Internet)** 11
surfboard **tabla de surf** *f.* 5
surprise **sorprender** *v.* 9; **sorpresa** *f.* 9
survey **encuesta** *f.*
sweat **sudar** *v.* 15
sweater **suéter** *m.* 6
sweep the floor **barrer el suelo** 12
sweets **dulces** *m., pl.* 9
swim **nadar** *v.* 4
swimming **natación** *f.* 4
  swimming pool **piscina** *f.* 4
symptom **síntoma** *m.* 10

T

table **mesa** *f.* 2
tablespoon **cuchara** *f.* 12
tablet (*pill*) **pastilla** *f.* 10
take **tomar** *v.* 2; **llevar** *v.* 6
  take care of **cuidar** *v.* 13
  take someone's temperature **tomar** *v.* **la temperatura** 10
  take (*wear*) a shoe size **calzar** *v.* 6
  take a bath **bañarse** *v.* 7
  take a shower **ducharse** *v.* 7
  take off **quitarse** *v.* 7

take out the trash *v.* **sacar la basura** 12
take photos **tomar** *v.* **fotos** 5; **sacar** *v.* **fotos** 5
talented **talentoso/a** *adj.*
talk **hablar** *v.* 2
talk show **programa** *m.* **de entrevistas**
tall **alto/a** *adj.* 3
tank **tanque** *m.* 11
taste **probar (o:ue)** *v.* 8
taste like **saber a** 8
tasty **rico/a** *adj.* 8; **sabroso/a** *adj.* 8
tax **impuesto** *m.*
taxi **taxi** *m.* 5
tea **té** *m.* 8
teach **enseñar** *v.* 2
teacher **profesor(a)** *m., f.* 1, 2; **maestro/a** *m., f.*
team **equipo** *m.* 4
technician **técnico/a** *m., f.*
telecommuting **teletrabajo** *m.*
telephone **teléfono** 11
television **televisión** *f.* 2
television set **televisor** *m.* 11
tell **contar** *v.* 4; **decir** *v.* 4
tell (that) **decir** *v.* **(que)** 4
tell lies **decir mentiras** 4
tell the truth **decir la verdad** 4
temperature **temperatura** *f.* 10
ten **diez** 1
tennis **tenis** *m.* 4
tennis shoes **zapatos** *m., pl.* **de tenis** 6
tension **tensión** *f.* 15
tent **tienda** *f.* **de campaña**
tenth **décimo/a** 5
terrible **terrible** *adj. m., f.* 13
it's terrible **es terrible** 13
terrific **chévere** *adj.*
test **prueba** *f.* 2; **examen** *m.* 2
text message **mensaje** *m.* **de texto** 11
Thank you. **Gracias.** *f., pl.* 1
Thank you (very much). **(Muchas) gracias.** 1
Thanks (a lot). **(Muchas) gracias.** 1
Thanks for inviting me. **Gracias por invitarme.** 9
that **que, quien(es)** *pron.* 12
that (one) **ése, ésa, eso** *pron.* 6; **ese, esa,** *adj.* 6
that (*over there*) **aquél, aquélla, aquello** *pron.* 6; **aquel, aquella** *adj.* 6
that which **lo que** 12
that's why **por eso** 11
the **el** *m.*, **la** *f. sing.*, **los** *m.*, **las** *f., pl.* 1
theater **teatro** *m.*
their **su(s)** *poss. adj.* 3; **suyo(s)/a(s)** *poss. pron.* 11
them **los/las** *pl., d.o. pron.* 5
to/for them **les** *pl., i.o. pron.* 6
then (*afterward*) **después** *adv.* 7; (*as a result*) **entonces** *adv.* 5, 7; (*next*) **luego** *adv.* 7
there **allí** *adv.* 2
There is/are... **Hay...** 1
There is/are not... **No hay...** 1
therefore **por eso** 11
these **éstos, éstas** *pron.* 6; **estos, estas** *adj.* 6
they **ellos** *m.*, **ellas** *f. pron.* 1
They all told me to ask you to excuse them/forgive them. **Todos me dijeron que te pidiera una disculpa de su parte.**
thin **delgado/a** *adj.* 3
thing **cosa** *f.* 1
think **pensar (e:ie)** *v.* 4; (believe) **creer** *v.*
think about **pensar en** *v.* 4
third **tercero/a** 5
thirst **sed** *f.*
thirsty: be (very) thirsty **tener (mucha) sed** 3
thirteen **trece** 1
thirty **treinta** 1; thirty (*minutes past the hour*) **y treinta; y media** 1
this **este, esta** *adj.*; **éste, ésta, esto** *pron.* 6
those **ésos, ésas** *pron.* 6; **esos, esas** *adj.* 6
those (over there) **aquéllos, aquéllas** *pron.* 6; **aquellos, aquellas** *adj.* 6
thousand **mil** *m.* 2
three **tres** 1
three hundred **trescientos/as** 2
throat **garganta** *f.* 10
through **por** *prep.* 11
Thursday **jueves** *m., sing.* 2
thus (*in such a way*) **así** *adv.*
ticket **boleto** *m.* 2; **pasaje** *m.* 5
tie **corbata** *f.* 6
time **vez** *f.* 6; **tiempo** *m.* 14
have a good/bad time **pasarlo bien/mal** 9
I've had a fantastic time. **Lo he pasado de película.**
What time is it? **¿Qué hora es?** 1
(At) What time...? **¿A qué hora...?** 1
times **veces** *f., pl.* 6
many times **muchas veces** 10
two times **dos veces** 6
tip **propina** *f.* 8
tire **llanta** *f.* 11
tired **cansado/a** *adj.* 5
be tired **estar cansado/a** 5
title **título** *m.*
to **a** *prep.* 1
toast (*drink*) **brindar** *v.* 9
toast **pan** *m.* **tostado** 8
toasted **tostado/a** *adj.* 8
toasted bread **pan tostado** *m.* 8
toaster **tostadora** *f.* 12
today **hoy** *adv.* 2
Today is... **Hoy es...** 2
toe **dedo** *m.* **del pie** 10
together **juntos/as** *adj.* 9
toilet **inodoro** *m.* 7
tomato **tomate** *m.* 8
tomorrow **mañana** *f.* 1
See you tomorrow. **Hasta mañana.** 1
tonight **esta noche** *adv.*
too **también** *adv.* 2; 7
too much **demasiado** *adv.* 6; **en exceso** 15
tooth **diente** *m.* 7
toothpaste **pasta** *f.* **de dientes** 7
top **cima** *f.* 15
tornado **tornado** *m.*
touch **tocar** *v.*
touch screen **pantalla táctil** *f.*
tour **excursión** *f.* 4; **recorrido** *m.* 13
tour an area **recorrer** *v.*
tourism **turismo** *m.*
tourist **turista** *m., f.* 1; **turístico/a** *adj.*
toward **hacia** *prep.* 14; **para** *prep.* 11
towel **toalla** *f.* 7
town **pueblo** *m.*
trade **oficio** *m.*
traffic **circulación** *f.* 11; **tráfico** *m.* 11
traffic light **semáforo** *m.* 14
tragedy **tragedia** *f.*
trail **sendero** *m.* 13
train **entrenarse** *v.* 15; **tren** *m.* 5
train station **estación** *f.* **de tren** *m.* 5
trainer **entrenador(a)** *m., f.* 15
translate **traducir** *v.* 6
trash **basura** *f.* 12
travel **viajar** *v.* 2
travel agency **agencia** f. **de viajes** 5
travel agent **agente** *m., f.* **de viajes** 5
traveler **viajero/a** *m., f.* 5
(traveler's) check **cheque (de viajero)** 14
treadmill **cinta caminadora** *f.* 15
tree **árbol** *m.* 13
trillion **billón** *m.*
trimester **trimestre** *m.* 2
trip **viaje** *m.* 5
take a trip **hacer un viaje** 5
tropical forest **bosque** *m.* **tropical** 13
true: it's (not) true **(no) es verdad** 13
trunk **baúl** *m.* 11
truth **verdad** *f.* 4
try **intentar** *v.*; **probar (o:ue)** *v.* 8
try (*to do something*) **tratar de (+ *inf.*)** 15
try on **probarse (o:ue)** *v.* 7
t-shirt **camiseta** *f.* 6
Tuesday **martes** *m., sing.* 2
tuna **atún** *m.* 8
turkey **pavo** *m.* 8
turn **doblar** *v.* 14
turn off (*electricity/appliance*) **apagar** *v.* 11
turn on (*electricity/appliance*) **poner** *v.* 11; **prender** *v.* 11

twelve **doce** 1
twenty **veinte** 1
twenty-eight **veintiocho** 1
twenty-five **veinticinco** 1
twenty-four **veinticuatro** 1
twenty-nine **veintinueve** 1
twenty-one **veintiuno** 1; **veintiún, veintiuno/a** *adj.* 1
twenty-seven **veintisiete** 1
twenty-six **veintiséis** 1
twenty-three **veintitrés** 1
twenty-two **veintidós** 1
twice **dos veces** 6
twin **gemelo/a** *m., f.* 3
two **dos** 1
  two hundred **doscientos/as** 2
  two times **dos veces** 6

U

ugly **feo/a** *adj.* 3
uncle **tío** *m.* 3
under **debajo de** *prep.* 2
understand **comprender** *v.* 3; **entender (e:ie)** *v.* 4
underwear **ropa interior** 6
unemployment **desempleo** *m.*
unique **único/a** *adj.* 9
United States **Estados Unidos (EE.UU.)** *m. pl.*
university **universidad** *f.* 2
unless **a menos que** *conj.* 13
unmarried **soltero/a** *adj.* 9
unpleasant **antipático/a** *adj.* 3
until **hasta** *prep.* 6; **hasta que** *conj.* 13
urgent **urgente** *adj.* 12
  It's urgent that... **Es urgente que...** 12
us **nos** *pl., d.o. pron.* 5
  to/for us **nos** *pl., i.o. pron.* 6
use **usar** *v.* 6
used for **para** *prep.* 11
useful **útil** *adj. m., f.*

V

vacation **vacaciones** *f., pl.* 5
  be on vacation **estar de vacaciones** 5
  go on vacation **ir de vacaciones** 5
vacuum **pasar** *v.* **la aspiradora** 12
  vacuum cleaner **aspiradora** *f.* 12
valley **valle** *m.* 13
various **varios/as** *adj. m., f. pl.*
vegetables **verduras** *pl., f.* 8
verb **verbo** *m.*
very **muy** *adv.* 1
  (Very) well, thank you. **(Muy) bien, gracias.** 1
video **video** *m.* 1
  video camera **cámara** *f.* **de video** 11
  video game **videojuego** *m.* 4
videoconference **videoconferencia** *f.*
vinegar **vinagre** *m.* 8
violence **violencia** *f.*
visit **visitar** *v.* 4
  visit monuments **visitar monumentos** 4
vitamin **vitamina** *f.* 15
voice mail **correo de voz** *m.* 11
volcano **volcán** *m.* 13
volleyball **vóleibol** *m.* 4
vote **votar** *v.*

W

wait (for) **esperar** *v.* **(+ *inf.*)** 2
waiter/waitress **camarero/a** *m., f.* 8
wake up **despertarse (e:ie)** *v.* 7
walk **caminar** *v.* 2
  take a walk **pasear** *v.* 4
  walk around **pasear por** 4
wall **pared** *f.* 12; **muro** *m.* 15
wallet **cartera** *f.* 4, 6
want **querer (e:ie)** *v.* 4
war **guerra** *f.*
warm up **calentarse (e:ie)** *v.* 15
wash **lavar** *v.* 12
  wash one's face/hands **lavarse la cara/las manos** 7
  wash (the floor, the dishes) **lavar (el suelo, los platos)** 12
  wash oneself **lavarse** *v.* 7
washing machine **lavadora** *f.* 12
wastebasket **papelera** *f.* 2
watch **mirar** *v.* 2; **reloj** *m.* 2
  watch television **mirar (la) televisión** 2
water **agua** *f.* 8
  water pollution **contaminación del agua** 13
  water-skiing **esquí** *m.* **acuático** 4
way **manera** *f.*
we **nosotros(as)** *m., f.* 1
weak **débil** *adj. m., f.* 15
wear **llevar** *v.* 6; **usar** *v.* 6
weather **tiempo** *m.*
  The weather is bad. **Hace mal tiempo.** 5
  The weather is good. **Hace buen tiempo.** 5
weaving **tejido** *m.*
Web **red** *f.* 11
website **sitio** *m.* **web** 11
wedding **boda** *f.* 9
Wednesday **miércoles** *m., sing.* 2
week **semana** *f.* 2
weekend **fin** *m.* **de semana** 4
weight **peso** *m.* 15
  lift weights **levantar** *v.* **pesas** *f., pl.* 15
welcome **bienvenido(s)/a(s)** *adj.* 1
well: (Very) well, thanks. **(Muy) bien, gracias.** 1
well-being **bienestar** *m.* 15
well organized **ordenado/a** *adj.* 5
west **oeste** *m.* 14
  to the west **al oeste** 14
western (*genre*) **de vaqueros**
whale **ballena** *f.* 13
what **lo que** *pron.* 12
what? **¿qué?** 1
  At what time...? **¿A qué hora...?** 1
  What a pleasure to...! **¡Qué gusto (+ *inf.*)...!**
  What day is it? **¿Qué día es hoy?** 2
  What do you guys think? **¿Qué les parece?**
  What happened? **¿Qué pasó?**
  What is today's date? **¿Cuál es la fecha de hoy?** 5
  What nice clothes! **¡Qué ropa más bonita!** 6
  What size do you wear? **¿Qué talla lleva (usa)?** 6
  What time is it? **¿Qué hora es?** 1
  What's going on? **¿Qué pasa?** 1
  What's happening? **¿Qué pasa?** 1
  What's... like? **¿Cómo es...?**
  What's new? **¿Qué hay de nuevo?** 1
  What's the weather like? **¿Qué tiempo hace?** 5
  What's up? **¿Qué onda?** 14
  What's wrong? **¿Qué pasó?**
  What's your name? **¿Cómo se llama usted?** *form.* 1; **¿Cómo te llamas (tú)?** *fam.* 1
when **cuando** *conj.* 7; 13
When? **¿Cuándo?** 2
where **donde**
where (to)? (*destination*) **¿adónde?** 2; (*location*) **¿dónde?** 1, 2
  Where are you from? **¿De dónde eres (tú)?** (*fam.*) 1; **¿De dónde es (usted)?** (*form.*) 1
  Where is...? **¿Dónde está...?** 2
which **que** *pron.*, **lo que** *pron.* 12
which? **¿cuál?** 2; **¿qué?** 2
  In which...? **¿En qué...?**
  which one(s)? **¿cuál(es)?** 2
while **mientras** *conj.* 10
white **blanco/a** *adj.* 6
  white wine **vino blanco** 8
who **que** *pron.* 12; **quien(es)** *pron.* 12
who? **¿quién(es)?** 1, 2
Who is...? **¿Quién es...?** 1
  Who is speaking/calling? (*on telephone*) **¿De parte de quién?** 11
  Who is speaking? (*on telephone*) **¿Quién habla?** 11
whole **todo/a** *adj.*

whom **quien(es)** *pron.* 12
whose? **¿de quién(es)?** 1
why? **¿por qué?** 2
widower/widow **viudo/a** *adj.* 9
wife **esposa** *f.* 3
win **ganar** *v.* 4
wind **viento** *m.*
window **ventana** *f.* 2
windshield **parabrisas** *m., sing.* 11
windsurf **hacer** *v.* **windsurf** 5
windy: It's (very) windy. **Hace (mucho) viento.** 5
wine **vino** *m.* 8
  red wine **vino tinto** 8
  white wine **vino blanco** 8
wineglass **copa** *f.* 12
winter **invierno** *m.* 5
wireless connection **conexión inalámbrica** *f.* 11
wish **desear** *v.* 2; **esperar** *v.* 13
  I wish (that) **ojalá (que)** 13
with **con** *prep.* 2
  with me **conmigo** 4; 9
  with you **contigo** *fam.* 5, 9
within (ten years) **dentro de (diez años)** *prep.*
without **sin** *prep.* 2; **sin que** *conj.* 13
woman **mujer** *f.* 1
wool **lana** *f.* 6
  (made of) wool **de lana** 6
word **palabra** *f.* 1
work **trabajar** *v.* 2; **funcionar** *v.* 11; **trabajo** *m.*
  work (*of art, literature, music, etc.*) **obra** *f.*
  work out **hacer gimnasia** 15
world **mundo** *m.* 8
worldwide **mundial** *adj. m., f.*
worried (about) **preocupado/a (por)** *adj.* 5
worry (about) **preocuparse** *v.* **(por)** 7
  Don't worry. **No te preocupes.** *fam.* 7
worse **peor** *adj. m., f.* 8
worst **el/la peor** 8
Would you like to...? **¿Te gustaría...?** *fam.*
Would you do me the honor of marrying me? **¿Me harías el honor de casarte conmigo?**
wow **híjole** *interj.* 6
wrench **llave** *f.* 11
write **escribir** *v.* 3
  write a letter/an e-mail **escribir una carta/un mensaje electrónico** 4
writer **escritor(a)** *m., f*
written **escrito/a** *p.p.* 14
wrong **equivocado/a** *adj.* 5
  be wrong **no tener razón** 3

X

X-ray **radiografía** *f.* 10

Y

yard **jardín** *m.* 12; **patio** *m.* 12
year **año** *m.* 5
  be... years old **tener... años** 3
yellow **amarillo/a** *adj.* 6
yes **sí** *interj.* 1
yesterday **ayer** *adv.* 6
yet **todavía** *adv.* 5
yogurt **yogur** *m.* 8
you **tú** *fam.* **usted (Ud.)** *form. sing.* **vosotros/as** *m., f. fam. pl.* **ustedes (Uds.)** *pl.* 1; (to, for) you *fam. sing.* **te** *pl.* **os** 6; *form. sing.* **le** *pl.* **les** 6
  you **te** *fam., sing.,* **lo/la** *form., sing.,* **os** *fam., pl.,* **los/las** *pl, d.o. pron.* 5
You don't say! **¡No me digas!** *fam.;* **¡No me diga!** *form.*
You're welcome. **De nada.** 1; **No hay de qué.** 1
young **joven** *adj., sing.* (**jóvenes** *pl.*) 3
  young person **joven** *m., f., sing.* (**jóvenes** *pl.*) 1
  young woman **señorita (Srta.)** *f.*
younger **menor** *adj. m., f.* 3
younger: younger brother, sister *m., f.* **hermano/a menor** 3
youngest **el/la menor** *m., f.* 8
your **su(s)** *poss. adj. form.* 3; **tu(s)** *poss. adj. fam. sing.* 3; **vuestro/a(s)** *poss. adj. fam. pl.* 3
your(s) *form.* **suyo(s)/a(s)** *poss. pron. form.* 11; **tuyo(s)/a(s)** *poss. fam. sing.* 11; **vuestro(s) /a(s)** *poss. fam.* 11
youth *f.* **juventud** 9

Z

zero **cero** *m.* 1

Text Credits

297 Reproduced from: "Elegía nocturna" by Carlos Pellicer. Fondo de Cultura Economica.
474–475 Reproduced from: Denevi, Marco, Cartas peligrosa y otros cuentos. Obras Completas, Tomo 5, Buenos Aires, Corregidor, 1999, pages 192-193.
504–505 Gabriel García Márquez, "Una día de éstos", Los funerales de la mamá grande. © 1962 Gabriel García Márquez y Herederos de Gabriel García Márquez.

Comic Credits

31 © Joaquín Salvador Lavado (QUINO) Toda Mafalda - Ediciones de La Flor, 1993.
368–369 © TUTE

Film Credits

103 Courtesy of IMCINE.
205 © Susan Béjar.
303 Courtesy of IMCINE.
409 © Esteban Roel & Juanfer Andrés.
509 © Manuela Moreno.

Television Credits

102 Courtesy of Cencosud Supermercados.
204 Courtesy of Comercial Mexicana.
302 © Javier Ugarte, Chilevisión Network. Santiago, Chile.
408 Courtesy of Centros Comerciales Carrefour S.A.
508 © Getty Better Creative Studio.

Photography Credits

Frontmatter: 3: Andres Rodriguez/Shutterstock.

Lesson 1: 1: Paula Díez; **2:** John Henley/Corbis; **3:** Martín Bernetti; **4:** Martín Bernetti; **10:** (l) Rachel Distler; (r) Ali Burafi; **11:** (l) Matt Sayles/AP/Corbis; (m) Paola Ríos-Schaaf; (r) Hans Georg Roth/Corbis; **12:** (l) Janet Dracksdorf; (r) Tom Grill/Corbis; **16:** (l) Jose Girarte/iStockphoto; (r) Blend Images/Alamy; **19:** (t) Dario Eusse Tobon; (m) Anne Loubet; (r) Digital Vision/Getty Images; **28:** (tl) VHL; (tr) VHL; (bl) Martín Bernetti; (br) VHL; **31:** (ml) Ana Cabezas Martín; (mml) Martín Bernetti; (mmr) Shvadchak Vasyl/123RF; (mr) Vanessa Bertozzi; (bl) Corey Hochachka/Design Pics/Corbis; (bm) VHL; (br) Ramiro Isaza/Fotocolombia; **32:** (t) Robert Holmes/Corbis; (m) Photogal/Shutterstock; (b) Andresr/Shutterstock; **33:** (tl) PhotoLink/Getty Images; (tr) Tony Arruza/Corbis; (bl) Stocksnapper/123RF; (br) RMNOA357/Shutterstock.

Lesson 2: 35: Radius Images/MaXx Images; **38:** Martín Bernetti; **44:** (l) William Perugini/Shutterstock; (r) Pablo Corral V/Corbis; **45:** (t) Teerawat Sumrantin/123RF; (b) Paul Almasy/Corbis; **53:** Stephen Coburn/Shutterstock; **55:** (l) Paola Ríos-Schaaf; (r) Image Source/Corbis; **63:** (tl) Rick Gómez/Corbis; (tr) LWA/Larry Williams/Media Bakery; (b) VHL; **64:** José Blanco; **65:** PNC/Media Bakery; **66:** (tl) Jose Blanco; (tr) José Blanco; (m) Elke Stolzenberg/Corbis; (b) Reuters/Corbis; **67:** (tl) The Washington Post/Getty Images; (tr) José Blanco; (ml) Erich Lessing/Art Resource, NY; (mr) VHL; (b) Iconotec/Fotosearch.

Lesson 3: 69: Paul Bradbury/AGE Fotostock; **71:** Martín Bernetti; **72:** (tl) Anne Loubet; (tr) Blend Images/Alamy; (tml) Ana Cabezas Martín; (tmr) Elena Kouptsova-Vasic/Shutterstock; (ml) Martín Bernetti; (mr) Martín Bernetti; (bl) Bikerider London/Shutterstock; (br) AGE Fotostock; **78:** (tl) David Cantor/AP Images; (tr) Rafael Pérez/Reuters/Corbis; (b) Martial Trezzini/EPA/Corbis; **79:** (t) Dani Cardona/Reuters/Corbis; (b) Lote/Splash News/Corbis; **82:** (l) Martín Bernetti; (r) José Blanco; **84:** Andrés Rodríguez/Alamy; **89:** (l) Tyler Olsen/Fotolia; (r) Martín Bernetti; **90:** Martín Bernetti; **98:** (all) Martín Bernetti; **99:** (t) Nora y Susana/Fotocolombia; (m) Chuck Savage/Corbis; (b) Martín Bernetti; **100:** Tom & Dee Ann McCarthy/Corbis; **101:** Martín Bernetti; **104:** (tr) Martín Bernetti; (tl) Martín Bernetti; (ml) Iván Mejía; (mr) Lauren Krolick; (b) Martín Bernetti; **105:** (tl) Martín Bernetti; (tr) Pablo Corral V/Corbis; (ml) Martín Bernetti; (mr) Fotos593/Shutterstock; (b) Martín Bernetti.

Lesson 4: 107: Digital Vision/Getty Images; **109:** George Shelley/Corbis; **111:** Nora y Susana/Fotocolombia; **116:** (l) Javier Soriano/AFP/Getty Images; (r) Fernando Bustamante/AP Images; **117:** (l) PhotoWorks/Shutterstock; (r) Zuma Press/Alamy; **127:** Warner Bros/The Kobal Collection/Art Resource; **131:** Anne Loubet; **133:** Nagy Vincze-Adam/Shutterstock; **134:** Martín Bernetti; **135:** Fernando Llano/AP Images; **136:** (tl) Randy Miramontez/Shutterstock; (tr) Albright-Knox Art Gallery/Corbis; (ml) Ruben Varela; (mr) Carolina Zapata; (b) Henry Romero/Reuters/Corbis; **137:** (tl) Radius Images/Alamy; (tr) Bettmann/Corbis; (m) Corel/Corbis; (b) David R. Frazier Photolibrary/Alamy.

Lesson 5: 139: Gavin Hellier/Getty Images; **150:** Gary Cook/Alamy; **151:** (t) AFP/Getty Images; (b) Pierre-Yves Babelon/123RF; **155:** Ronnie Kaufman/Corbis; **168:** Janet Dracksdorf; **169:** (tl) Corel/Corbis; (tr) Dudarev Mikhail/Shutterstock; (m) Epic Stock Media/123RF; (b) Volodymyr Goinyk/Shutterstock; **170:** (tl) Eddie Toro/123RF; (tr) José Blanco; (ml) Israel Pabon/Shutterstock; (mr) Capricornis Photographic/Shutterstock; (b) Dave G. Houser/Corbis; **171:** (tl) Jose Blanco; (tr) Lawrence Manning/Corbis; (m) Stocktrek/Getty Images; (b) Danny Alvarez/123RF.

Lesson 6: 173: Hero Images/Media Bakery; **182:** (t) Jose Caballero/Digital Press Photos/Newscom; (b) Janet Dracksdorf; **183:** (t) Carlos Alvarez/Getty Images; (bl) Guiseppe Cacace/Getty Images; (br) Mark Mainz/Getty Images; **185:** Jack Hollingsworth/Corbis; **188:** Pascal Pernix; **193:** Martín Bernetti; **194:** Paula Diez; **195:** Paula Diez; **200-201:** Paula Díez and Shutterstock; **202:** Noam Armonn/Shutterstock; **203:** Martín Bernetti; **206:** (t) Pascal Pernix; (tml) Pascal Pernix; (tmr) Pascal Pernix; (m) Pascal Pernix; (b) PhotoLink/Getty Images; **207:** (tl) Don Emmert/AFP/Getty Images; (tr) Pascal Pernix; (bl) Pascal Pernix; (br) Road Movie Prods/The Kobal Collection.

Lesson 7: 209: Media Bakery RF; **218:** Stewart Cohen/Blend Images/Corbis; **219:** (t) Ali Burafi; (b) Janet Dracksdorf; **221:** (l) Martín Bernetti; (r) Martín Bernetti; **223:** (l) Martín Bernetti; (r) Igor Mojzes/123RF; **226:** José Blanco; **227:** Martín Bernetti; **236-237:** Didem Hizar/Fotolia; **238:** (t) Martín Bernetti; (mtl) Daniel Ferreia-Leites/123RF; (mtr) Martín Bernetti; (bml) Richard Franck Smith/Sygma/Corbis; (bmr) Charles & Josette Lenars/Corbis; (b) Yann Arthus-Bertrand/Corbis; **239:** (tl) Elzbieta Sekowska/Shutterstock; (tr) Mick Roessler/Corbis; (bl) Jeremy Horner/Corbis; Marshall Bruce/iStockphoto.

Lesson 8: 241: Terry Vine/Media Bakery; **247:** (l) Monkey Business Images/Shutterstock; (r) Anne Loubet; **252:** (t) Rachel Distler; (b) Media Bakery; **253:** (t) Carlos Cazalis/Corbis; (m) Carlos Cazalis/Corbis; (b) Rafael Rios; **256:** Paula Diez; **258:** (l) Pixtal/Age Fotostock; (r) José Blanco; **262:** (l) Andresr/Shutterstock; (r) José Blanco; **263:** (l) José Blanco; (r) Monkey Business Images/Shutterstock; **272:** (t) Henryk Sadura/Shutterstock; (ml) Dave G. Houser/Corbis; (mb) Henryk Sadura/Shutterstock; (b) Dave G. Houser/Corbis; **273:** (tl) Jenkedco/Shutterstock; (tr) Michael & Patricia Fogden/Corbis; (bl) Vladimir Korostyshevskiy/Shutterstock; (br) Paul W. Liebhardt/Corbis.

Lesson 9: 275: Susana/Fotocolombia; **279**: Cathy Yeulet/123RF; **284**: (l) Jose Manuel Espigares Garcia/123RF; (r) PictureNet/Corbis; **285**: (t) Simon Cruz/AP Images; (b) Rune Hellestad/Corbis; **298**: (t) Katrina Brown/123RF; (b) Esteban Corbo; **299**: Armando Brito; **300**: Blend Images/Alamy; **304**: (tl) Lauren Krolick; (tr) Lauren Krolick; (tml) Kathryn Alena Korf; (tmr) Lauren Krolick; (bml) Bettmann/Corbis; (bmr) Macarena Minguell/AFP/Getty Images; (b) Bruce R. Korf; **305**: (tl) Lars Rosen Gunnilstam; (tr) Lauren Krolick; (bl) Nikolay Starchenko/Shutterstock; (br) Lauren Krolick.

Lesson 10: 307: Custom Medical Stock Photo/Alamy; **316**: (t) Jose Blanco; (r) Ricardo Figueroa/AP Images; **317**: (t) Gianni Dagli Orti/The Art Archive at Art Resource, NY; (m) Photolicensors International AG/Alamy; (b) AFP/Getty Images; **321**: ISO K° Photography/Fotolia; **325**: Oscar Artavia Solano; **326**: (l) Lisa Fletcher/iStockphoto; **331**: Martín Bernetti; **334**: Corel/Corbis; **335**: Danita Delimont/Newscom; **336**: (tl) Oscar Artavia Solano; (tr) Oscar Artavia Solano; (ml) Bill Gentile/Corbis; (mm) Oscar Artavia Solano; (mr) Oscar Artavia Solano; (b) Bob Winsett/Corbis; **337**: (t) Frank Burek/Corbis; (tm) Martin Rogers/Corbis; (bm) Janet Dracksdorf; (b) Oscar Artavia Solano; **338**: (tl) Endless Traveller/Shutterstock; (tr) RJ Lerich/Shutterstock; (tm) Tobe_DW/Shutterstock; (bm) Bill Gentile/Corbis; (b) Scott B. Rosen/Alamy; **339**: (t) Grigory Kubatyan/Shutterstock; (m) Claudia Daut/Reuters/Corbis; (b) Holdeneye/Shutterstock.

Lesson 11: 341: Ann Summa/Corbis; **350**: (l) GM Visuals/AGE Fotostock; (r) Quka/Shutterstock; **351**: (t) StockLite/Shutterstock; (b) M. Timothy O'Keefe/Alamy; **355**: LDF/iStockphoto; **359**: Katie Wade; **360**: (l) Paula Diez; (r) Paula Diez; **364**: (t) Greg Nicholas/iStockphoto; (ml) Konstantin Shevtsov/Shutterstock; (mm) Dmitry Kutlayev/iStockphoto; (mr) Liliana Bobadilla; (bl) LDF/iStockphoto; (bm) Martín Bernetti; (br) Liliana Bobadilla; **370**: (t) Ali Burafi; (ml) María Eugenia Corbo; (mm) Galen Rowell/Corbis; (mr) Lauren Krolick; (b) Ali Burafi; **371**: (t) María Eugenia Corbo; (mt) Ali Burafi; (mb) Ali Burafi; (b) Ali Burafi; **372**: (t) Reuters/Corbis; (tm) Bettmann/Corbis; (bm) María Eugenia Corbo; (b) María Eugenia Corbo; **373**: (t) Janet Dracksdorf; (tm) Jonathan Larsen/Diadem Images/Alamy; (bm) Andres Stapff/Reuters/Corbis; (b) Wolfgang Kaehler/Corbis.

Lesson 12: 375: Rolf Bruderer/Corbis; **379**: (t) Terry J Alcorn/iStockphoto; (b) Harry Neave/Fotolia; **384**: (l) Dusko Despotovic/Corbis; (r) Martín Bernetti; **385**: (l) Fran Fernandez/Snapwire; (r) Rafal Cichawa/123RF; **387**: (l) Paula Diez; (r) Anne Loubet; **388**: Blend Images/Alamy; **404**: Danny Lehman/Corbis; **406**: Dragon Images/Shutterstock; **407**: Jolanda van den Oudenalder/123RF; **410**: (tl) Kevin Schafer/Corbis; (tr) Danny Lehman/Corbis; (b) Hernan H. Hernandez A./Shutterstock; **411**: (tl) Danny Lehman/Corbis; (tr) Danny Lehman/Corbis; (m) Courtesy of www.Tahiti-Tourisme.com; (b) Claudio Lovo/Shutterstock; **412**: (tl) José F. Poblete/Corbis; (tr) L. Kragt Bakker/Shutterstock; (ml) Leif Skoogfors/Corbis; (mr) Andre Nantel/Shutterstock; (b) Corbis RF; **413**: (t) Courtesy of www.Tahiti-Tourisme.com; (m) Corbis RF; (b) Romeo A. Escobar, La Sala de La Miniatura, San Salvador. www.ilobasco.net.

Lesson 13: 415: Blend Images/Alamy; **417**: (tl) Gaccworship/Big Stock Photo; (tr) Goodshoot/Alamy; (bl) National Geographic Singles 65/Inmagine; (br) Les Cunliffe/123RF; **424**: (t) Lauren Krolick; (b) Jeremy Woodhouse/Getty Images; **425**: (t) Cédric Hunt; (m) David South/Alamy; (b) Paul Zahl/National Geographic; **428**: Andrey Shchekalev/123RF; **433**: (t) Courtesy of Mary Axtmann; (b) Media Bakery; **444**: (tl) Andrey Gontarev/Shutterstock; (tr) Cédric Hunt; (ml) Jose Blanco; (mr) Santiago Saldarriaga GDA/Newscom; (b) Adam Woolfitt/Corbis; **445**: (t) Javarman/Shutterstock; (mt) Reuters/Corbis; (mb) Jess Kraft/Shutterstock; (b) Jeremy Horner/Corbis; **446**: (tl) Stuart Westmorland/Corbis; (tr) Alfredo Maiquez/Getty Images; (ml) Sandra A. Dunlap/Shutterstock; (mr) Robert Harding World Imagery/Alamy; (b) Martín Bernetti; **447**: (t) Holger Mette/Shutterstock; (m) Elmer Martinez/AFP/Getty Images; (b) José Antonio Velasquez (Honduran, b.**1906**, d.**1983**) View of San Antonio de Oriente,**1957** oil on canvas, **26** x **37**" Art Museum of the Americas Organization of American States, Washington, D.C.

Lesson 14: 415: Blend Images/Alamy; **417**: (tl) Gaccworship/Big Stock Photo; (tr) Goodshoot/Alamy; (bl) National Geographic Singles **65**/Inmagine; (br) Les Cunliffe/123RF; **424**: (t) Lauren Krolick; (b) Jeremy Woodhouse/Getty Images; **425**: (t) Cédric Hunt; (m) David South/Alamy; (b) Paul Zahl/National Geographic; **428**: Andrey Shchekalev/123RF; **433**: (t) Courtesy of Mary Axtmann; (b) Media Bakery; **444**: (tl) Andrey Gontarev/Shutterstock; (tr) Cédric Hunt; (ml) Jose Blanco; (mr) Santiago Saldarriaga GDA/Newscom; (b) Adam Woolfitt/Corbis; **445**: (t) Javarman/Shutterstock; (mt) Reuters/Corbis; (mb) Jess Kraft/Shutterstock; (b) Jeremy Horner/Corbis; **446**: (tl) Stuart Westmorland/Corbis; (tr) Alfredo Maiquez/Getty Images; (ml) Sandra A. Dunlap/Shutterstock; (mr) Robert Harding World Imagery/Alamy; (b) Martín Bernetti; **447**: (t) Holger Mette/Shutterstock; (m) Elmer Martinez/AFP/Getty Images; (b) José Antonio Velasquez (Honduran, b.**1906**, d.**1983**) View of San Antonio de Oriente,**1957** oil on canvas, **26** x **37**" Art Museum of the Americas Organization of American States, Washington, D.C.

Lesson 15: 481: Thinkstock Images/Getty Images; **485**: Javier Larrea/Age Fotostock; **490**: (l) Krysztof Dydynski/Getty Images; (r) Oscar Artavia Solano; **491**: (t) David Mercado/Reuters/Newscom; (b) Stockcreations/Shutterstock; **501**: Diego Cervo/iStockphoto; **504-505**: Tom Grill/Corbis; **506**: Martín Bernetti; **507**: Javier Larrea/AGE Fotostock; **509**: Katie Wade; **510**: (tl) Elzbieta Sekowska/Shutterstock; (tr) SIME SRL/eStock Photo; (m) Interfoto/Alamy; (b) Jess Kraft/Shutterstock; **511**: (t) Daniel Wiedemann/Shutterstock; (m) Anders Ryman/Alamy; (r) Martín Bernetti; **512**: (t) Peter Guttman/Corbis; (ml) Paul Almasy/Corbis; (mr) Choups/Alamy; (b) Carlos Carrión/Sygma/Corbis; **513**: (t) JTB Media Creation/Alamy; (m) Joel Creed/Ecoscene/Corbis; (b) Hugh Percival/Fotolia.

About the Authors

José A. Blanco founded Vista Higher Learning in 1998. A native of Barranquilla, Colombia, Mr. Blanco holds a B.A. in Literature from the University of California, Santa Cruz, and a M.A. in Hispanic Studies from Brown University. He has worked as a writer, editor, and translator for Houghton Mifflin and D.C. Heath and Company and has taught Spanish at the secondary and university levels. Mr. Blanco is also the co-author of several other Vista Higher Learning programs: **Vistas, Aventuras,** and **¡Viva!** at the introductory level, **Ventanas, Facetas, Enfoques, Imagina,** and **Sueña** at the intermediate level, and **Revista** at the advanced conversation level.

Philip Redwine Donley received his M.A. in Hispanic Literature from the University of Texas at Austin in 1986 and his Ph.D. in Foreign Language Education from the University of Texas at Austin in 1997. Dr. Donley taught Spanish at Austin Community College, Southwestern University, and the University of Texas at Austin. He published articles and conducted workshops about language anxiety management, and the development of critical thinking skills, and was involved in research about teaching languages to the visually impaired. Dr. Donley was also the co-author of **Vistas** and **Panorama**, two other introductory college Spanish textbook programs published by Vista Higher Learning.

About the Illustrators

Yayo, an internationally acclaimed illustrator, was born in Colombia. He has illustrated children's books, newspapers, and magazines, and has been exhibited around the world. He currently lives in Montreal, Canada.

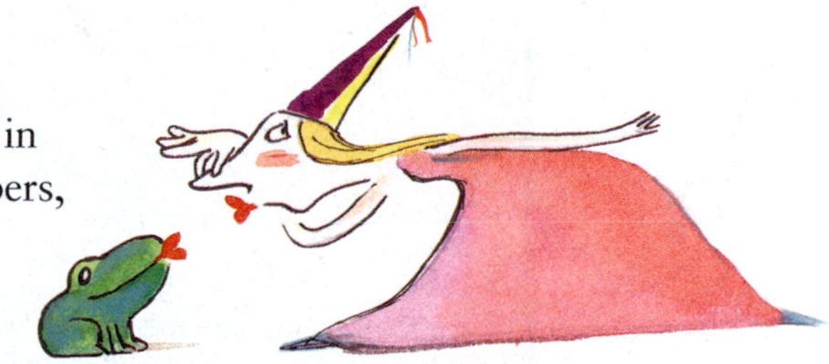

Pere Virgili lives and works in Barcelona, Spain. His illustrations have appeared in textbooks, newspapers, and magazines throughout Spain and Europe.

Born in Caracas, Venezuela, **Hermann Mejía** studied illustration at the *Instituto de Diseño de Caracas*. Hermann currently lives and works in the United States.

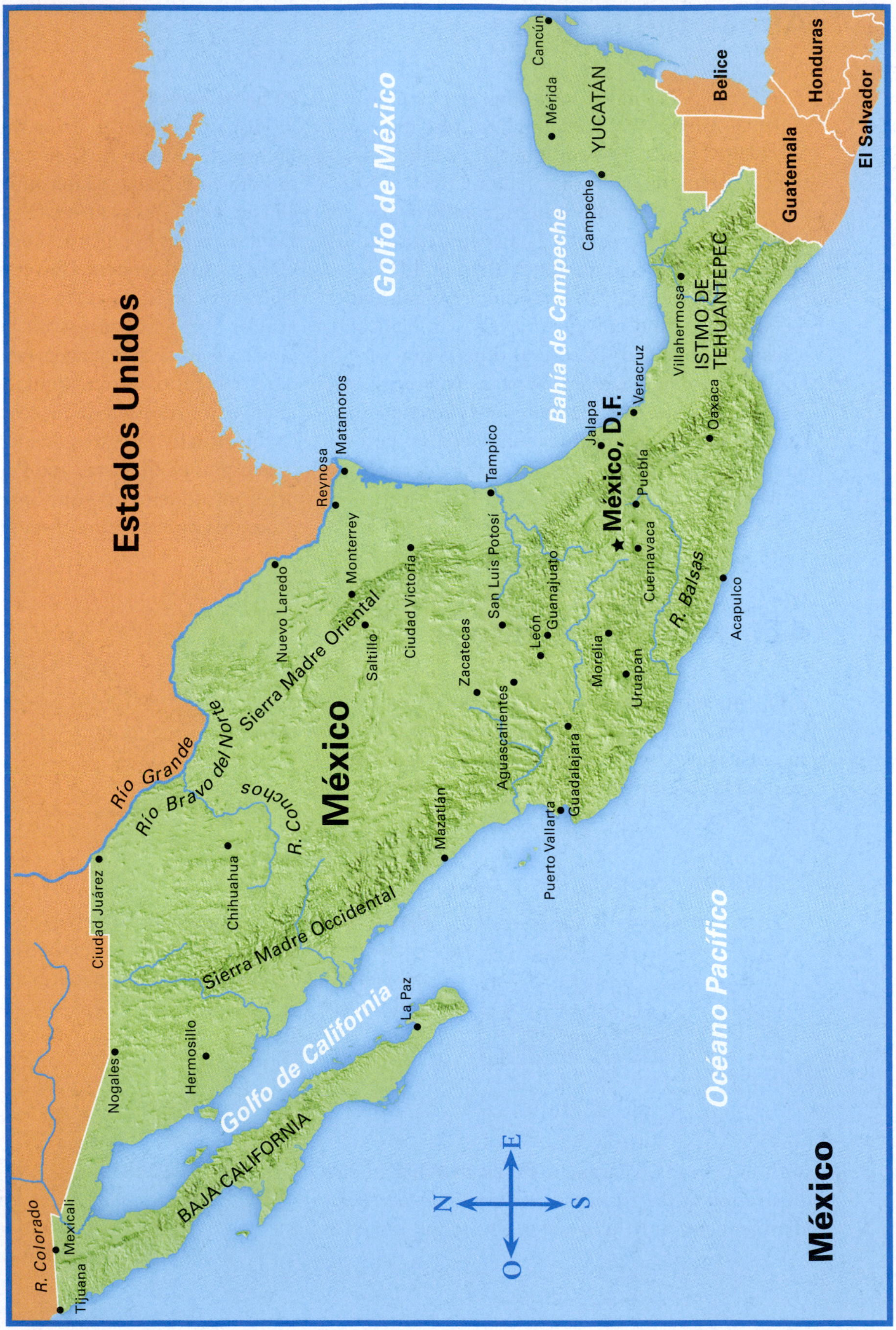
México
Estados Unidos
México
Golfo de México
Bahía de Campeche
Océano Pacífico
Golfo de California
BAJA CALIFORNIA
YUCATÁN
ISTMO DE TEHUANTEPEC
Sierra Madre Oriental
Sierra Madre Occidental
Río Grande
Río Bravo del Norte
R. Conchos
R. Colorado
R. Balsas
Belice
Guatemala
Honduras
El Salvador
México, D.F.
Tijuana
Mexicali
Nogales
Hermosillo
La Paz
Ciudad Juárez
Chihuahua
Mazatlán
Nuevo Laredo
Reynosa
Matamoros
Monterrey
Saltillo
Ciudad Victoria
Tampico
Zacatecas
San Luis Potosí
Aguascalientes
León
Guanajuato
Guadalajara
Puerto Vallarta
Morelia
Uruapan
Cuernavaca
Puebla
Jalapa
Veracruz
Oaxaca
Acapulco
Villahermosa
Campeche
Mérida
Cancún
N
S
E
O

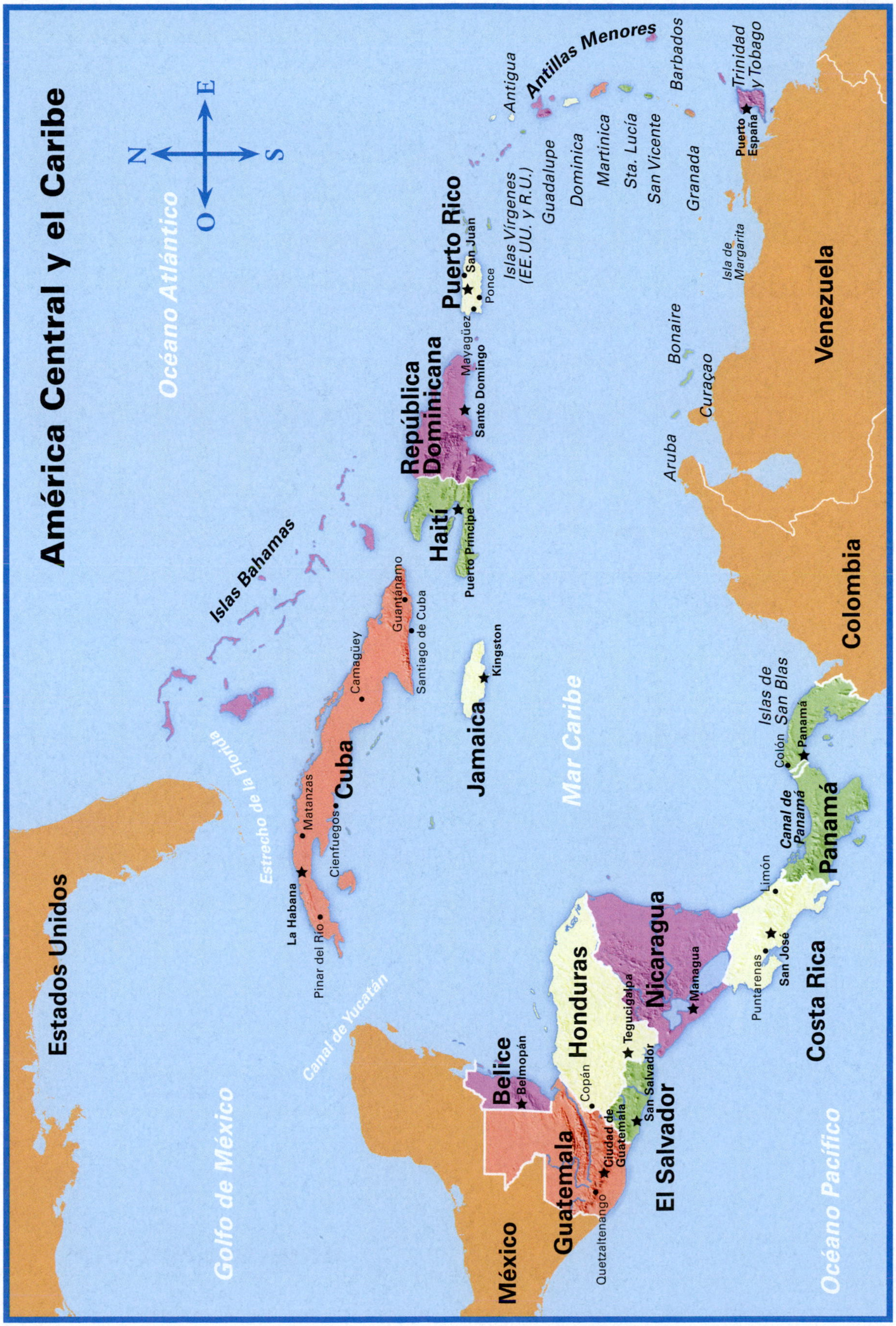
América Central y el Caribe
N
S
E
O
Océano Atlántico
Estados Unidos
Golfo de México
Estrecho de la Florida
Canal de Yucatán
Islas Bahamas
Cuba
La Habana
Pinar del Río
Matanzas
Cienfuegos
Camagüey
Santiago de Cuba
Guantánamo
Jamaica
Kingston
Haití
Puerto Príncipe
República Dominicana
Santo Domingo
Puerto Rico
San Juan
Mayagüez
Ponce
Islas Vírgenes (EE.UU. y R.U.)
Antillas Menores
Antigua
Guadalupe
Dominica
Martinica
Sta. Lucía
San Vicente
Barbados
Granada
Trinidad y Tobago
Puerto España
Isla de Margarita
Bonaire
Curaçao
Aruba
Mar Caribe
Venezuela
Colombia
México
Belice
Belmopán
Guatemala
Ciudad de Guatemala
Quetzaltenango
Copán
Honduras
Tegucigalpa
El Salvador
San Salvador
Nicaragua
Managua
Costa Rica
San José
Puntarenas
Limón
Panamá
Canal de Panamá
Colón
Islas de San Blas
Océano Pacífico

Mar Caribe
Barranquilla
Maracaibo
Caracas
Puerto España
Trinidad y Tobago
Venezuela
R. Orinoco
Georgetown
Guyana
Paramaribo
Surinam
Cayena
Guayana Francesa
Colombia
Medellín
Bogotá
Cali
Pasto
Quito
Ecuador
Guayaquil
Iquitos
Perú
Cordillera de los Andes
Lima
Cuzco
Lago Titicaca
Arequipa
R. Negro
R. Amazonas
Manaus
Belém
R. Madeira
Recife
Salvador
Brasil
Brasilia
La Paz
Bolivia
Sucre
Arica
Iquique
Océano Pacífico
R. Paraguay
R. Paraná
Belo Horizonte
São Paulo
Río de Janeiro
Santos
Antofagasta
Paraguay
Salta
Asunción
Chile
R. Uruguay
Córdoba
Porto Alegre
Valparaíso
Mendoza
Santiago
Rosario
Buenos Aires
Uruguay
Montevideo
Concepción
Argentina
Bahía Blanca
Océano Atlántico
Puerto Montt
N
O
E
S
Estrecho de Magallanes
Islas Malvinas
Punta Arenas
Tierra del Fuego
América del Sur
Islas Galápagos
Océano Pacífico
Isla Pinta
Isla Marchena
Isla Genovesa
Isla Isabela
Línea Ecuatorial
ECUADOR
Volcán Darwin
Isla Santiago
(San Salvador)
Isla Fernandina
Puerto Ayora
Isla San Cristóbal
Isla Santa Cruz
Santo Tomás
Puerto Barquerizo Moreno
Isla Santa María
Isla Española

Mar Cantábrico
Océano Atlántico
Mar Mediterráneo
Andorra
Pirineos
España
Portugal
Marruecos
Islas Baleares
Menorca
Mallorca
Palma
Ibiza
Formentera
Islas Canarias
La Palma
Santa Cruz de la Palma
Tenerife
Santa Cruz de Tenerife
Gomera
Hierro
Lanzarote
Arrecife
Fuerteventura
Puerto del Rosario
Gran Canaria
Las Palmas
Marruecos
Océano Atlántico
GALICIA
ASTURIAS
CANTABRIA
PAÍS VASCO
NAVARRA
LA RIOJA
ARAGÓN
CATALUÑA
CASTILLA-LEÓN
CASTILLA-LA MANCHA
COMUNIDAD VALENCIANA
EXTREMADURA
ANDALUCÍA
Sierra Morena
Sierra Nevada
Serra da Estrela
Madrid
Lisboa
La Coruña
Pontevedra
Vigo
Avilés
Gijón
Oviedo
Santander
Bilbao
San Sebastián
Pamplona
Burgos
Palencia
Valladolid
Zamora
Salamanca
Ávila
Segovia
Toledo
Zaragoza
Lérida
Barcelona
Tarragona
Gerona
Valencia
Albacete
Alicante
Murcia
Cartagena
Almería
Granada
Jaén
Córdoba
Málaga
Sevilla
Huelva
Cádiz
Algeciras
Gibraltar (R.U.)
Ceuta (Esp.)
Melilla (Esp.)
Estrecho de Gibraltar
Cáceres
Mérida
Badajoz
Braga
Oporto
Coimbra
Setúbal
N
S
E
O